Stephanie J. Cacioppo is an Assistant Professor of Psychiatry and Behavioral Neuroscience in the University of Chicago Pritzker School of Medicine and serves as the director of the school's Brain Dynamics Laboratory. Named a "Rising Star" by the Association for Psychological Science (APS) for her innovative and "outstanding contributions to the science of psychology in the areas of research, teaching, and/or application," Dr. Steph Cacioppo is considered a world authority on emotion-driven brain dynamics and well-being. Her work focuses on the dynamics of emotions and social connections and their impact on brain health and human performance. She has a demonstrated history of working in woman's health, motivation, and neuropsychology, and with elite and everyday athletes in emotional fitness, high-performance brain dynamics, and human potential. Dr. Steph Cacioppo is also the first female president of the Society for Social Neuroscience. She has authored more than 120 scientific publications and has been interviewed by prestigious outlets like the *New York Times*, *Scientific American*, *Washington Post*, *Discover Magazine*, and *National Geographic*.

Stephanie Cacioppo

Brief Contents

1 The Science of Mind THE DISCIPLINE OF PSYCHOLOGY 3

2 The Measure of Mind THE SCIENTIFIC METHODS OF PSYCHOLOGY 35

3 The Evolving Mind NATURE AND NURTURE INTERTWINED 71

4 The Biological Mind THE PHYSICAL BASIS OF BEHAVIOR 105

5 The Perceiving Mind SENSATION AND PERCEPTION 149

6 The Aware Mind ELEMENTS OF CONSCIOUSNESS 193

7 The Feeling Mind EMOTION AND MOTIVATION 231

8 The Adaptive Mind LEARNING 277

9 The Knowing Mind MEMORY 317

10 The Thinking Mind THINKING, LANGUAGE, AND INTELLIGENCE 361

11 The Developing Mind LIFE SPAN DEVELOPMENT 407

12 The Individual Mind PERSONALITY AND THE SELF 459

13 The Connected Mind SOCIAL PSYCHOLOGY 499

14 The Troubled Mind PSYCHOLOGICAL DISORDERS 549

15 Healing the Troubled Mind THERAPY 597

16 The Healthy Mind STRESS AND COPING, HEALTH PSYCHOLOGY, AND POSITIVE PSYCHOLOGY 639

References R-1

Name Index N-1

Subject Index/Glossary S-1

Contents

1 The Science of Mind
THE DISCIPLINE OF PSYCHOLOGY

What Is Psychology? 5

Psychology as a Hub Science Why Is Psychology a Hub Science? 5

Why Do We Study Psychology? 6

Where Did Psychology Originate? 7

What Are Psychology's Philosophical Roots? 8

What Are Psychology's Natural Sciences Roots? 8

The Two Disciplines Merge to Create a New Science 9

SUMMARY 1.1 10

How Did the Science of Psychology Begin? 10

Wilhelm Wundt and Structuralism 10

Connecting to Research The First Official Psychology Experiment 11

Gestalt Psychology 12

William James and Functionalism 12

Clinical Roots: Freud and the Humanistic Psychologists 13

Sigmund Freud 13

Humanistic Psychology 14

Experiencing Psychology Testing Reaction Time 14

The Behaviorists and the Cognitive Revolution 15

SUMMARY 1.2 20

What Are Psychological Perspectives? 22

What Are the Five Perspectives of Psychology? 22

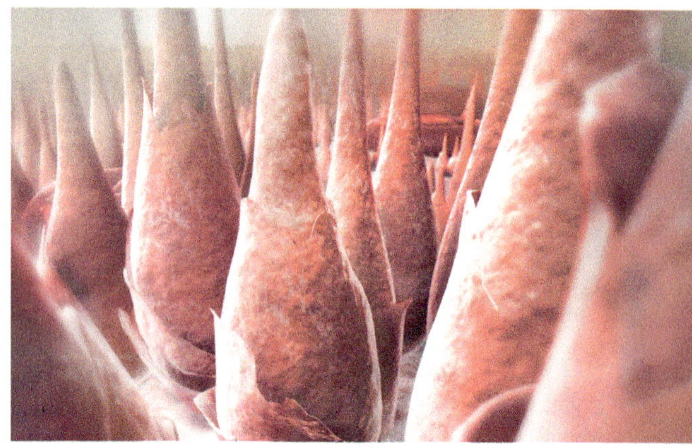

Argosy Publishing, Inc.

A New Connectivity: Integrating Psychology's Five Perspectives 26

Diverse Voices in Psychology Culture and Diversity as "Cross-cutting Themes" in Psychology 27

Thinking Scientifically Can the Use of a Single Perspective Be Misleading? 28

What Does It Mean to Be a Psychologist? 28

Interpersonal Relationships How Can We Use Relationships to Illustrate Psychological Perspectives? 30

Psychology Takes on Real-World Problems Tackling the Problem of a Pandemic 31

SUMMARY 1.3 32

Key Terms: The Language of Psychological Science 32

2 The Measure of Mind

THE SCIENTIFIC METHODS OF PSYCHOLOGY

What Is Science? 36

How Do We Develop a Scientific Mindset? 36

The Importance of Critical Thinking 37

Experiencing Psychology Using Critical Thinking to Evaluate Popular Press Reports 38

The Scientific Enterprise 40

Scientific Theories 40

Generating Good Hypotheses 41

Communicating Science 42

Thinking Scientifically Does Psychology Have a Replication Problem? 43

SUMMARY 2.1 44

How Do Psychologists Conduct Research? 44

Descriptive Methods 44

The Case Study 44

Naturalistic Observation 46

The Survey 46

Diverse Voices in Psychology How Do We Recruit Diverse Research Participants? 47

Correlational Methods 48

Experimental Methods 51

Meta-analyses 53

The Importance of Multiple Perspectives 54

How Do We Study the Effects of Time? 54

SUMMARY 2.2 55

How Do We Draw Conclusions from Data? 56

The Importance of Valid and Reliable Measures 56

Descriptive Statistics 57

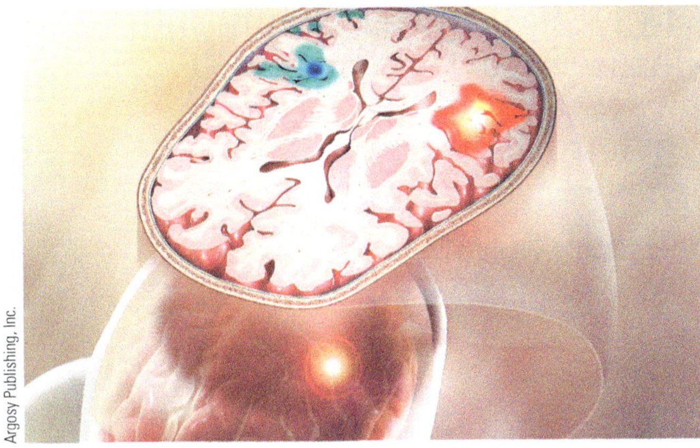
Argosy Publishing, Inc.

Central Tendency 58

Variance 59

The Normal Curve 59

Descriptive Statistics with Two Variables 60

Connecting to Research Do You Believe in ESP? 61

Inferential Statistics 62

Psychology as a Hub Science The Invention of Factor Analysis 64

How Can We Conduct Ethical Research? 64

Human Participants 65

Animal Subjects 66

Interpersonal Relationships The Methodological Perspective 67

Psychology Takes on Real-World Problems Research Methods for Studying a Pandemic 68

SUMMARY 2.3 69

Key Terms: The Language of Psychological Science 69

3 The Evolving Mind

NATURE AND NURTURE INTERTWINED

Why Do We Say That Nature and Nurture Are Intertwined? 72

What Are the Building Blocks of Behavior? 73

Experiencing Psychology The Genetics of Cats 75

Genetic Variation 76

Relatedness 76

Sex Chromosomes 76

Which Fields of Genetics Are Relevant to Psychology? 77

Behavioral Genetics and Heritability 78

Diverse Voices in Psychology Avoiding Social Prejudice in Genetic Research 80

The Search for Candidate Genes 82

Epigenetics 83

Thinking Scientifically The "Warrior Gene" and Criminals 84

Psychology as a Hub Science Understanding the Epigenetic Influences of Nutrition 86

Connecting to Research Can Transgenerational Epigenetic Change Occur? 87

SUMMARY 3.1 88

How Does Evolution Occur? 89

Mechanisms of Evolution 89

Adaptation 91

Evolution of the Human Brain 92

The Contemporary Human Brain 93

Argosy Publishing, Inc.

SUMMARY 3.2 94

How Does Evolution Influence Behavior? 95

The Evolutionary Psychology Perspective 95

Origins of Social Behavior 95

Sexual Selection 98

Parental Investment 98

Traits Possibly Influenced by Sexual Selection 99

Culture 99

Interpersonal Relationships The Evolutionary Perspective 101

Psychology Takes On Real World Problem Can Genetics Explain Differing Responses to COVID-19 Social Distancing? 102

SUMMARY 3.3 103

Key Terms: The Language of Psychological Science 103

4 The Biological Mind
THE PHYSICAL BASIS OF BEHAVIOR

What Is Biological Psychology? 106

Diverse Voices in Psychology What Is Cultural Neuroscience? 107

Early Attempts to Understand Biological Psychology 108

Contemporary Approaches in Biological Psychology 109

How Is the Nervous System Organized? 110

What Are the Structures and Functions of the Central Nervous System? 111

The Spinal Cord, Brainstem, and Cerebellum 113

Subcortical Structures 116

- The Thalamus 116
- The Basal Ganglia 116
- The Hypothalamus 117
- The Hippocampus 117
- The Cingulate Cortex 117
- The Amygdala 117
- The Nucleus Accumbens 118

The Cerebral Cortex 118

Thinking Scientifically Why Does Moving Your Eyes Reduce Negative Emotions? 119

- Localization of Functions in the Cerebral Cortex 119
- The Frontal Lobe 121
- The Occipital Lobe 122
- The Temporal Lobe 122
- The Parietal Lobe 123

Psychology as a Hub Science Law, Responsibility, and the Brain 123

- Mirror Neurons 124
- Right Brain and Left Brain 124

Connecting to Research Mirror Systems and Predicting Tennis Serves 125

- Right–Left Brain Myths 126
- The Function of Lateralization 126

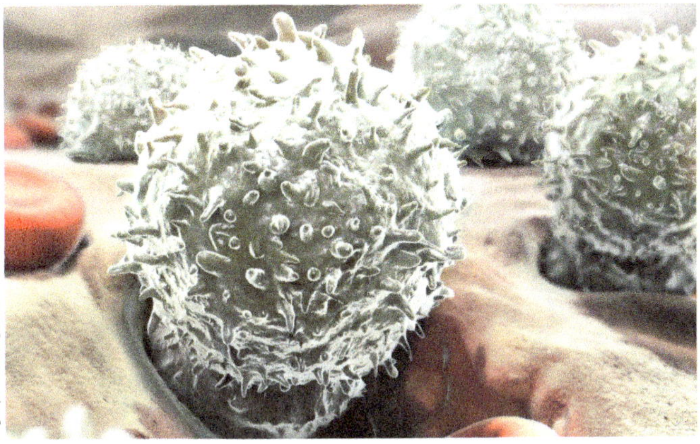

Argosy Publishing, Inc.

Experiencing Psychology Handedness 127

SUMMARY 4.1 128

The Peripheral Nervous System (PNS) and the Endocrine System 129

The Somatic Nervous System 129

The Autonomic Nervous System 129

The Endocrine System 132

SUMMARY 4.2 133

How Do Neurons Communicate? 134

Neurons and Glia 134

Neural Signaling 137

- Electrical Signaling 137
- Chemical Signaling 141

Types of Neurotransmitters 143

Interpersonal Relationships The Biological Perspective 144

Psychology Takes on Real-World Problems Social Distancing, Loneliness, and the Nervous System 145

SUMMARY 4.3 146

Key Terms: The Language of Psychological Science 147

5 The Perceiving Mind
SENSATION AND PERCEPTION

How Does Sensation Lead to Perception? 150

Sensory Information Travels to the Brain 150
The Brain Constructs Perceptions From Sensory Information 151
  Measuring Perception 153
  Signal Detection 153
SUMMARY 5.1 156

How Do We See? 156

The Visual Stimulus 156
The Biology of Vision 157
  Photoreceptors 158
  Visual Pathways 159
Visual Perception and Cognition 160
  Color Vision 160
Psychology as a Hub Science Color and Accessible Web Design 161
  Recognizing Objects 162
  Gestalt Psychology 163
  Recognizing Depth 164
Developmental and Individual Differences in Vision 166
Connecting to Research Do Children with Autism See the World Differently? 168
Diverse Voices in Psychology Culture Shapes Eye Movements 169
Thinking Scientifically The Roger Shepard Parallelogram Illusion: "Turning the Tables" 170
SUMMARY 5.2 171

How Do We Hear? 172

The Auditory Stimulus 172
The Biology of Audition 172
Auditory Perception and Cognition 175
  Pitch Perception 175
  Perceiving Loudness 175
  Localization of Sound 176
  Auditory Groupings 176

Developmental and Individual Differences in Audition 177
Sociocultural Influences on Auditory Perception 177

How Do We Feel Body Position, Touch, Temperature, and Pain? 178

Body Position 179
Touch 179
Pain 181

How Do We Process Smells and Tastes? 183

Olfaction 183
Gustation 184
Perception and Cognition in the Chemical Senses 185
Developmental and Individual Differences in the Chemical Senses 186
Experiencing Psychology Are You a Supertaster? 186
Sociocultural Influences on the Chemical Senses 187
Interpersonal Relationships Sensation and Perception Perspectives 188
Psychology Takes on Real-World Problems Social Distancing, Loneliness and the Perception of Social Threat 189
SUMMARY 5.3 190
Key Terms: The Language of Psychological Science 191

6 The Aware Mind
ELEMENTS OF CONSCIOUSNESS

What Does It Mean to Be Conscious? 194
The Evolution of Consciousness 195
Consciousness as Variations in Alertness 195
Consciousness as an Awareness of Ongoing Sensations 195
Consciousness as Self-Awareness 195
Psychology as a Hub Science Can Machines Become Conscious? 196
Searching for Consciousness in the Brain 197
SUMMARY 6.1 199

What Happens to Consciousness During Waking and Sleep? 199
Circadian Rhythms 199
Modern Living and Circadian Rhythms 200
Individual Variations in Circadian Rhythms 201
Waking 202
Sleep 203
Stages of Sleep 203
Experiencing Psychology The Epworth Sleepiness Scale 204
The Benefits of Sleep 206
The Special Benefits of REM Sleep 207
Dreams 208
Sleep Disorders 208
Nightmares and Sleep Terrors 208
Insomnia 209
Narcolepsy and Cataplexy 209
Breathing-Related Sleep Disorders 209
Sudden Infant Death Syndrome (SIDS) 210
Restless Legs Syndrome (RLS) 210
SUMMARY 6.2 211

How Is Consciousness Affected by Brain Damage? 211
Specific Areas of Brain Damage and Consciousness 211
Coma, Vegetative State, Brain Death, and Near-Death 212

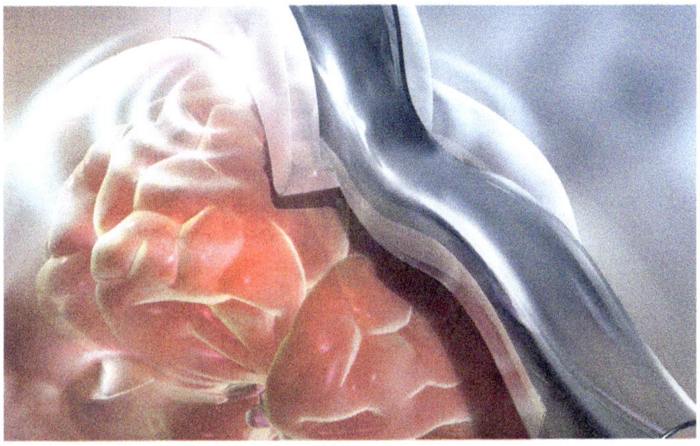
Argosy Publishing, Inc.

Coma 212
Vegetative State (VS) 212
Brain Death 212
Near-Death Experiences 213
Seizures 213

How Do People Intentionally Alter Their States of Consciousness? 214
General Features of Psychoactive Drugs 215
Tolerance and Withdrawal 215
Addiction 215
Commonly Used Psychoactive Drugs 216
Marijuana 216
Thinking Scientifically Do Hallucinogens Have Therapeutic Potential? 217
LSD 218
Caffeine 218
Connecting to Research Psychedelics and Consciousness 218
Diverse Voices in Psychology Entheogens Across Cultures 219
Nicotine 220
Cocaine and Amphetamines 221
Methylphenidate (Ritalin) 222
MDMA (Ecstasy) 222
Alcohol 222
Opioids 223

Nondrug Methods for Altering Consciousness 224
Hypnosis 224
Meditation 225
Other Methods for Altering Consciousness 225
Interpersonal Relationships The Consciousness Perspective *How Does Imitation Influence Liking?* 227
Psychology Takes on Real-World Problems Sleep During a Pandemic 228
SUMMARY 6.3 228
Key Terms: The Language of Psychological Science 229

7 The Feeling Mind
EMOTION AND MOTIVATION

Argosy Publishing, Inc.

How Are Emotion and Motivation Related? 232

Why Are We Emotional? 233
Theories of Emotion 233
The James–Lange Theory of Emotion 233
The Cannon–Bard Theory of Emotion 235
The Schachter–Singer Two-Factor Theory 236
Connecting to Research Botox and the Ability to Read the Emotions of Others 236
Contemporary Approaches to Emotion 238
The Evolution of Emotion 239
The Biology of Emotion 241
The Autonomic Nervous System 241
The Hypothalamus 242
The Amygdala 242
The Insula 243
The Cingulate Cortex 243
The Basal Ganglia 244
The Cerebral Cortex and Emotion 244
Expressing Emotion 245
Interpreting Emotion 248
Experiencing Psychology Emotional Regulation 248
Diverse Voices in Psychology Emotional Expressivity, Smiling, and a History of Immigration 249
Psychology as a Hub Science Lie Detection and the Law 250
SUMMARY 7.1 252

What Does It Mean to Be Motivated? 252
Hunger and Eating 253
The Sensation of Hunger 254
The Sensation of Satiety 256
Obesity 257
Anorexia Nervosa, Bulimia Nervosa, and Binge-Eating Disorder 260
Sexual Motivation 262
Biology and Sexual Motivation 262
Sexual and Emotional Satisfaction 264
Sexual Orientation 264
Cognitive and Social Motives 267
The Motivation to Affiliate 267
Achievement Motivation 268
Thinking Scientifically Do Participation Trophies Affect Entitlement and Competitiveness? 270
Motivational Priorities 271
Approach and Avoidance 271
Motivational Theories 271
Interpersonal Relationships The Emotional Perspective 273
Psychology Takes on Real-World Problems Prioritizing Motives During a Pandemic 274
SUMMARY 7.2 274
Key Terms: The Language of Psychological Science 275

8 The Adaptive Mind
LEARNING

How Do Animals Respond to Their Environment? 278

What Are the Three Main Types of Learning? 280

SUMMARY 8.1 281

What Is Classical Conditioning? 281

Classical Conditioning Terminology 282

Classical Conditioning Phenomena 283

Acquisition 283

Extinction and Spontaneous Recovery 284

Inhibition 285

Generalization and Discrimination 285

Higher-Order Conditioning 286

Latent Inhibition 286

Cognitive and Biological Influences on Classical Conditioning 286

The Element of Surprise 287

Taste Aversion 288

Applying Classical Conditioning 289

Overcoming Fear 289

Addiction 290

Attitudes and Prejudice 290

Creativity and Schizophrenia 291

Connecting to Research Classical Conditioning and Opioid Overdose 292

Psychology as a Hub Science Classical Conditioning Informs Wildlife Conservation 293

SUMMARY 8.2 294

What Is Operant Conditioning? 295

Types of Consequences 296

Positive Reinforcement 296

Thinking Scientifically Is Too Much Praise Bad for Children? 297

Negative Reinforcement 298

Punishment 299

Diverse Voices in Psychology Does Physical Punishment Have Different Effects in Different Cultural Contexts? 300

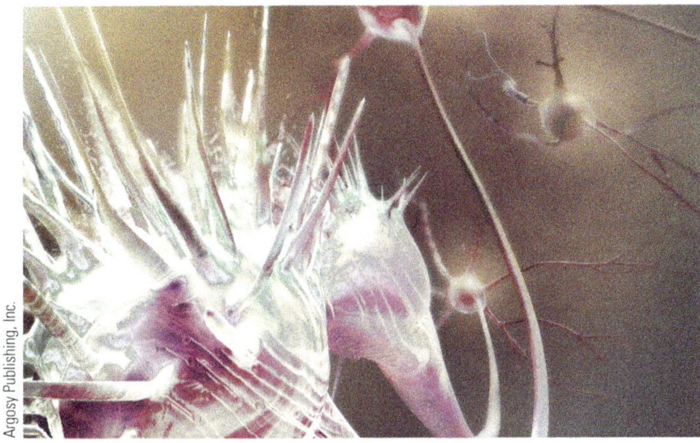

Argosy Publishing, Inc.

Schedules of Reinforcement 300

Fixed Ratio Schedules 301

Variable Ratio Schedules 302

Fixed Interval Schedules 302

Variable Interval Schedules 302

Partial Reinforcement Effect in Extinction 303

Comparing Schedules 303

The Method of Successive Approximations (Shaping) 304

Cognitive, Biological, and Social Influences on Operant Conditioning 305

Cognitive Influences on Operant Conditioning 305

Biological Influences on Operant Conditioning 306

Social Influences on Operant Conditioning 307

Applying Operant Conditioning 307

Token Economies 308

Behavior Therapies 308

Experiencing Psychology How Do I Break a Bad Habit? 309

SUMMARY 8.3 310

What Is Observational Learning? 310

Albert Bandura and Aggression 311

Cultural Transmission of Learning 312

Interpersonal Relationships The Learning Perspective 313

Psychology Takes on Real-World Problem Can People Learn to be Less Lonely? 314

SUMMARY 8.4 315

Key Terms: The Language of Psychological Science 315

9 The Knowing Mind
MEMORY

What Is Memory? 318

Memory and the Continuum of Information Processing 318
Memory Provides an Adaptive Advantage 319

How Are Memories Processed? 319

Sensory Memory 320
Short-Term Memory 321
Long-Term Memory 325
  Moving Information into Long-Term Memory 325
  Differences Between Working and Long-Term Memory 326

What Are the Different Types of Long-Term Memory? 328

Declarative Memories 329
Nondeclarative Memories 330
  Procedural Memories 330
  Priming 331

SUMMARY 9.1 332

How Is Long-Term Memory Organized? 333

Connectionist Theories 333
Inferences: Using Schemas 334

Experiencing Psychology Schemas and False Memories 334

How Do We Retrieve Memories? 335

Retrieval From Short-Term Memory 335
Retrieval from Long-Term Memory 336
  The Role of Cues 336

Diverse Voices in Psychology What Is the "Own-Race Bias" in Memory for Faces? 336

  Tip of the Tongue 337
  Reconstruction During Retrieval 338
  Retrieval of Emotional Events 340

Psychology as a Hub Science How Reliable Are Eyewitnesses? 341

SUMMARY 9.2 342

Why Do We Forget? 342

Decay 343

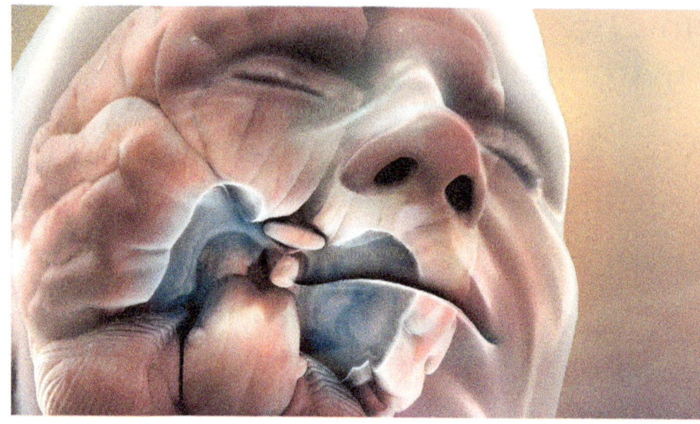
Argosy Publishing, Inc.

Interference 343
Motivated Forgetting 344

What Is the Biology of Memory? 345

Memory at the Level of the Synapse 345
Working Memory and the Brain 347
Long-Term Memories and the Brain 347
  Declarative Memories and the Hippocampus 347
  Declarative Memories and the Cerebral Cortex 347
  Procedural Memories and the Basal Ganglia 348
Biochemistry and Memory 349

How Can We Improve Memory? 350

Distribute Practice over Time 350

Thinking Scientifically Does Using a Laptop or Longhand to Take Notes Make a Difference? 351

Take Tests 352
Interleaving 352

Connecting to Research How Can We Protect Memory Retrieval from Stress? 353

Exercise 354
Sleep 354
Recite 354
Use Mnemonics 355

Interpersonal Relationships The Memory Perspective 356

Psychology Takes on Real-World Problems Compliance with Social Distancing and Working Memory 357

SUMMARY 9.3 358

Key Terms: The Language of Psychological Science 358

10 The Thinking Mind

THINKING, LANGUAGE, AND INTELLIGENCE

What Do We Think About? 362

Thoughts as Images 363
Thoughts as Concepts 363
Prototypes and Exemplars 365
Concepts as Theories 366
Concepts and Schemas 367
Concepts and the Brain 367

How Do We Solve Problems? 368

Understand the Problem 370
Make a Plan 370
Generating Solutions 370
Decide on a Solution 374
Carry Out the Plan 376
Look Back 377
Computer Models of Decision Making 377
The Biological Psychology of Decision Making 377

Experiencing Psychology What Is Your Decision Style? 380

SUMMARY 10.1 382

How Does Language Influence Behavior? 382

The Origins of Human Language 383
The Basic Building Blocks of Language 384
The Biological Psychology of Language 384
Lessons From Language Disorders 385
Are Nonhuman Animals Capable of Real Language? 386
How Do We Learn Language? 387

Diverse Voices in Psychology Is the "Language Gap" Real? 388

Variations in Language Processing 389
Dyslexia 389
Multilingualism 390
Signed Languages 391

SUMMARY 10.2 391

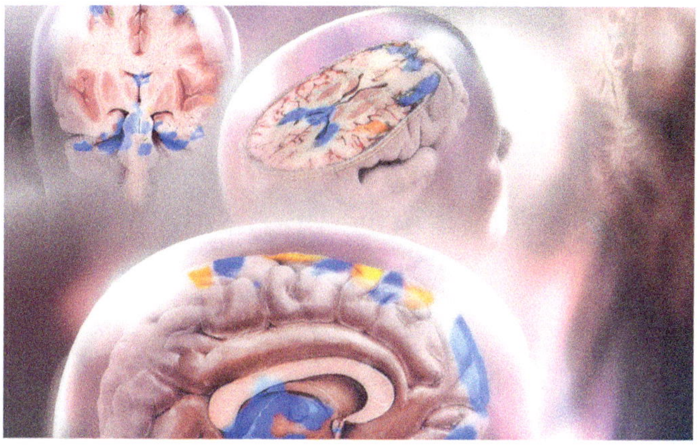

Argosy Publishing, Inc.

What Is Intelligence? 392

Assessing Intelligence 392
General and Specific Abilities 392
Emotional and Social Intelligence 394
Biological Influences on Intelligence 395
Brain Structure, Brain Activity, and Intelligence 395

Psychology as a Hub Science How Beliefs About Intelligence Impact Education 396

Genetics and Intelligence 397

Connecting to Research What Is Collective Intelligence? 398

Extremes of Intelligence 399
Intellectual Disability 400
Giftedness and Genius 401

Thinking Scientifically Can Children's IQ Scores Be Increased with Special Baby Videos? 402

Interpersonal Relationships The Cognitive Perspective 403

Psychology Takes on Real-World Problems COVID-19 and the Availability Heuristic 404

SUMMARY 10.3 404

Key Terms: The Language of Psychological Science 405

11 The Developing Mind

LIFE SPAN DEVELOPMENT

What Does It Mean to Develop? 408

Nature and Nurture Intertwined 409

Continuity or Discontinuity 409

Universal or Ecological Development 410

How Do We Change Prenatally? 411

Genetic Risks to Development 412

Environmental Risks to Development 413

What Can Newborns Do? 416

The Newborn's Reflexes 416

The Newborn's Activity 416

The Newborn's Sex and Gender Development 417

The Newborn's Senses 418

SUMMARY 11.1 419

What Physical Changes Occur in Infancy and Childhood? 420

Nervous System Development 421

Motor Development 421

Gender Development in Childhood 423

Diverse Voices in Psychology What Are the Implications of Gender Assignment? 425

How Does Cognition Change During Infancy and Childhood? 425

Jean Piaget's Theory of Cognitive Development 426

The Sensorimotor Stage 427

The Preoperational Stage 427

The Concrete Operational Stage 428

The Formal Operational Stage 428

Criticisms of Jean Piaget's Theory 428

Alternative Approaches to Cognitive Development 429

Lev Vygotsky 429

Information Processing 429

Naïve Theories 430

Theory of Mind 430

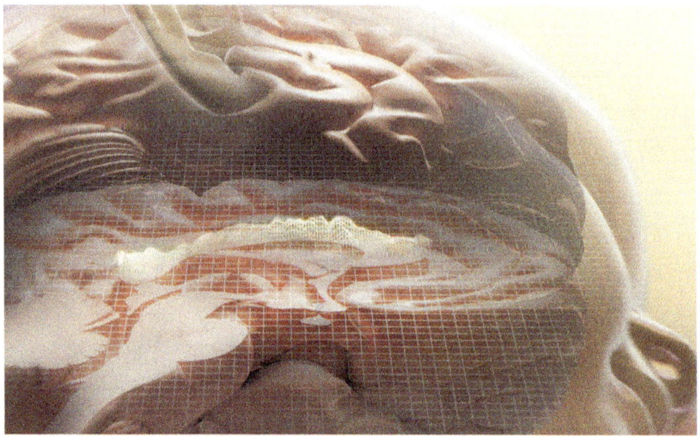

How Do Social and Emotional Behaviors Change During Infancy and Childhood? 432

Temperament 432

Attachment 433

Connecting to Research The Evolution of Attachment Behavior 433

Parenting Styles 436

SUMMARY 11.2 438

What Does It Mean to Be an Adolescent? 438

Physical Changes in Adolescence 439

Sex, Gender, and the Adolescent 439

The Adolescent Brain 439

Experiencing Psychology How Risky Are You? 440

Cognitive and Moral Development in Adolescence 442

Adolescent Cognition 442

Moral Reasoning 442

Social and Emotional Development in Adolescence 443

Identity Formation in Adolescence 443

The Benefits of Ethnic Identity 444

Family and Peer Influences 444

What Is It Like to Be an Emerging or Young Adult? 446

Physical Status in Emerging and Young Adulthood 446

Cognition in Emerging and Young Adulthood: Postformal Thought 446
Thinking Scientifically Are Younger Generations More Narcissistic Than Previous Generations? 447
Relationships in Emerging and Young Adulthood 448

What Happens During Midlife? 448
Physical and Cognitive Aspects of Midlife 449
Social Changes in Midlife 449

What Is Late Adulthood Like? 450
Physical Changes in Late Adulthood 450
Cognition in Late Adulthood 450
Social and Emotional Aspects of Late Adulthood 451
Psychology as a Hub Science Psychology and the Well-being of Older Americans 452
Interpersonal Relationships The Developmental Perspective 454
Psychology Takes on Real-World Problems Pandemic Anxiety Across the Lifespan 455
SUMMARY 11.3 456
Key Terms: The Language of Psychological Science 456

12 The Individual Mind
PERSONALITY AND THE SELF

What Is Personality? 461

Historical Approaches to Personality 462
How Do Psychodynamic Theories View Personality? 462
The Id, Ego, and Superego 462
Freudian Defense Mechanisms 463
Psychosexual Stages of Development 463
Contemporary Assessments of Sigmund Freud's Approach 464
The Neo-Freudians 464
Classic Behaviorist Approaches to Personality 465
How Do Humanistic Psychologists Approach Personality? 466

How Do Trait Theories Explain Personality? 467
Early Trait Theories 468
The Big Five Theory 468

How Do Situations Affect Personality? 470
Experiencing Psychology A Short Version of the Big Five Inventory 470
Locus of Control 472
Reciprocal Determinism and Self-Efficacy 472
If–Then Relationships 473

Argosy Publishing, Inc.

What Are the Biological Bases of Personality? 473
Temperament and Personality 473
Connecting to Research Temperament Traits Can Be Contagious 474
Genetics and Personality 475
Personality, Brain Structure, and Brain Function 476
The Evolution of Personality 477

How Do We Assess Personality? 478
Personality Inventories 478
Thinking Scientifically Evaluating the Validity and Reliability of Personality Tests 480
Projective Tests 481
The Ethics of Personality Testing 482

Diverse Voices in Psychology Diversity and Personality Assessments 482
SUMMARY 12.1 483
What Does It Mean to Have a Self? 483
Self-Concept 484
Self-Awareness 485
Self-Esteem 486
Sources of Self-Esteem 486
Gender, Race, and Culture and Self-Esteem 487
Using Self-Enhancement to Protect Self-Esteem 488
The Advantages of Self-Esteem 489
Psychology as a Hub Science Self-Esteem, Academic Performance, and Aggression 490
Self-Regulation 491
The Brain and the Self 491
The Social Self 493
The Interpersonal Self 493
Cultural Influences on the Self 493
Interpersonal Relationships The Personality Perspective 494
Psychology Takes on Real-World Problem Personality and Responses to a Pandemic 496
SUMMARY 12.2 497
Key Terms: The Language of Psychological Science 497

13 The Connected Mind

SOCIAL PSYCHOLOGY

Why Are Humans So Social? 500
How Accurate Are First Impressions? 501
Experiencing Psychology The UCLA Loneliness Scale 502
Why Did That Just Happen? 505
The Correspondence Bias and the Fundamental Attribution Error 505
Defensive Attributions 506
Connecting to Research Farming, Collectivism, and Individualism 507
Cultural Influences on Attribution 508
How Are Our Attitudes Influenced by Others? 509
Attitude Formation 510
Cognitive Dissonance 510
Why Does Persuasion Happen? 512
The Elaboration Likelihood Model 512
Routes to Persuasion 512
Psychology as a Hub Science Social Media, Persuasion, and Fake News 514

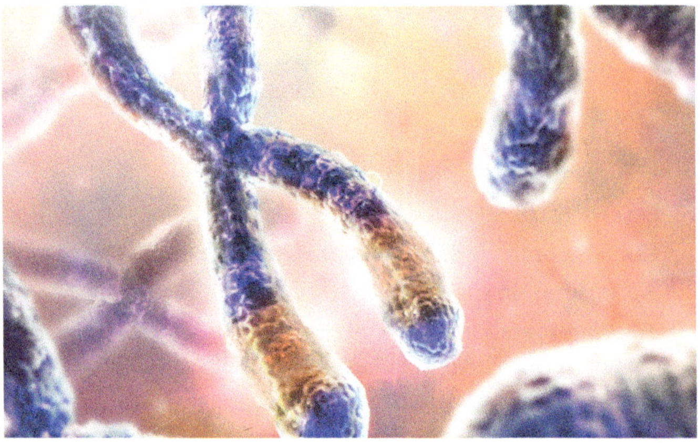

The Neuroscience of Persuasion 515
SUMMARY 13.1 516
Why Are We Prejudiced? 516
Sources of Prejudice and Stereotyping 516
Outcomes of Prejudice 518
Reducing Prejudice 519
Diverse Voices in Psychology The Shooter Bias 520
Why Do We Go Along with the Group? 522
Conformity 523

Compliance 524
Obedience 524
The Power of One 527

How Do Groups Work Together? 527

Social Facilitation 527
Social Loafing 528
Deindividuation 528
Group Polarization 528
Groupthink 529

SUMMARY 13.2 530

How Well Do We Get Along with Others? 531

Attraction and Liking 531
Building Relationships 533
Maintaining Relationships 533
Ending Relationships 534

SUMMARY 13.3 534

Why Do We Cooperate in Some Situations and Compete in Others? 535

Competition and Cooperation in Animals 535
Individual Differences in Cooperation and Competition 536
The Influence of Culture on Competition and Cooperation 536
Choosing Between Cooperation and Competition 536
Altruism and Helping 537

Why Are We Aggressive? 539

The Biological Psychology of Aggression 539
Learning and Aggression 541
Preventing Aggression 541
Thinking Scientifically Brain Damage and Criminal Behavior 542
Interpersonal Relationships The Social Perspective 544
Psychology Takes on Real-World Problems Persuasion During a Pandemic 545

SUMMARY 13.4 546
Key Terms: The Language of Psychological Science 546

14 The Troubled Mind
PSYCHOLOGICAL DISORDERS

What Does It Mean to Have a Psychological Disorder? 550

How Are Psychological Disorders Diagnosed? 553

What Do the Psychological Perspectives Tell Us About Disorders? 554

Which Disorders Emerge in Childhood? 555

Autism Spectrum Disorder (ASD) 555
Diagnosing ASD 555
Causes of ASD 556
Attention Deficit Hyperactivity Disorder (ADHD) 558

Argosy Publishing, Inc.

Diagnosing ADHD 558
Causes of ADHD 560

SUMMARY 14.1 561

What Is Schizophrenia? 561

Symptoms of Schizophrenia 562

Causes of Schizophrenia 562
Biological Factors in Schizophrenia 562
Environmental Factors in Schizophrenia 565
Thinking Scientifically Does Cannabis Use Increase Risk of Schizophrenia? 566

What Is Bipolar Disorder? 567

What Is Major Depressive Disorder (MDD)? 568

Prevalence of MDD 568
Causes of MDD 569
Learning Explanations for MDD 569
Cognitive Explanations for MDD 570
Social Explanations for MDD 571
Biological Explanations for MDD 571
Connecting to Research Recognition of Facial Expression by People with Depression 572
Stress and MDD 573
Diverse Voices in Psychology Race, Ethnicity, Gender, Sexual Orientation, and Prevalence of Suicidality 574
SUMMARY 14.2 575

What Is an Anxiety Disorder? 576

Specific Phobias 576
Social Anxiety Disorder 577
Panic Disorder 578
Biological Explanations for Panic Disorder 578
Cognitive Explanations for Panic Disorder 578
Social Explanations for Panic Disorder 579
Integrating the Perspectives 579
Agoraphobia 579
Generalized Anxiety Disorder 580
Biological Explanations for GAD 580
Cognitive Explanations for GAD 580
Social Explanations for GAD 580
Integrating the Perspectives 580

OCD and Related Disorders 581

Obsessive-Compulsive Disorder (OCD) 581
Biological Explanations for OCD 581
Learning Explanations for OCD 581
Social Explanations for OCD 582
Body Dysmorphic Disorder 582

What Is Posttraumatic Stress Disorder? 582

Biological Explanations for PTSD 583
Learning Explanations for PTSD 584
Social and Cultural Explanations for PTSD 584

What Are Dissociative Disorders? 584

What Are Somatic Symptom Disorder and Related Disorders? 585

What Are Personality Disorders? 586

Antisocial Personality Disorder (ASPD) 586
Borderline Personality Disorder (BPD) 587
Narcissistic Personality Disorder (NPD) 587
Psychology as a Hub Science The "Dark Side" of Leadership 588
Experiencing Psychology Assessing Narcissism 590
Interpersonal Relationships The Clinical Perspective 592
Psychology Takes on Real-World Problems Is COVID-19 Making Cases of OCD Worse? 593
SUMMARY 14.3 594
Key Terms: The Language of Psychological Science 595

15 Healing the Troubled Mind
THERAPY

How Do Psychologists Provide Therapy? 598
Approaches to Treatment 599
Biological Approaches 599
Psychological Approaches 600
Evidence-Based Practice 601
Clinical Assessment 602
The Therapists 602
Delivering Psychotherapy 605
Variations in Length of Treatment 605
Alternatives to Individual Therapy 605
Innovative Delivery Systems 606
Diverse Voices in Psychology Psychotherapy with Native Americans 607
Contemporary Challenges in Treatment 608
SUMMARY 15.1 608

Historical Approaches to Psychotherapy 609
Psychoanalysis 609
Humanistic Therapies 610

Contemporary Approaches to Psychotherapy 612
Behavioral Therapies 612
Cognitive Therapies 613
Biopsychosocial Approaches 614

What Are Biological Therapies? 614
Medication 615
Electroconvulsive Therapy 615
Psychosurgery 615
Brain Stimulation 616
Neurofeedback 617
SUMMARY 15.2 618

How Are Specific Disorders Treated? 618
Treating Neurodevelopmental Disorders 618
Treating ASD 618

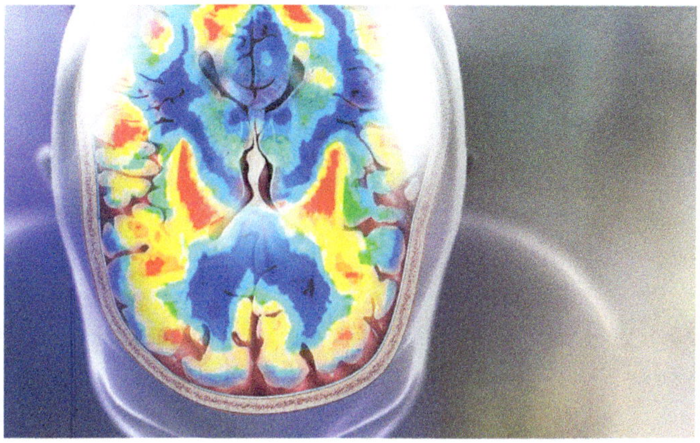
Argosy Publishing, Inc.

Thinking Scientifically Should Autism Spectrum Disorder (ASD) Be Treated? 619
Treating ADHD 620
Treating Schizophrenia 623
Treating Bipolar Disorder 624
Treating Major Depressive Disorder (MDD) 624
Connecting to Research Mindfulness and the Prevention of Relapse in Major Depressive Disorder (MDD) 627
Treating Anxiety Disorders 628
Treating OCD 629
Experiencing Psychology Progressive Relaxation 629
Treating Body Dysmorphic Disorder 630
Treating PTSD 630
Psychology as a Hub Science Using Virtual Reality (VR) to Treat Anxiety and PTSD 630
Treating Dissociative Identity Disorder 631
Treating Somatic Symptom Disorders 632
Treating ASPD 632
Treating Borderline Personality Disorder 632
Treating NPD 632
Integration of Specific Treatments 633
Interpersonal Relationships The Treatment Perspective 634
Psychology Takes on Real-World Problems Online Therapy During the COVID-19 Pandemic 635
SUMMARY 15.3 636
Key Terms: The Language of Psychological Science 637

16 The Healthy Mind

STRESS AND COPING, HEALTH PSYCHOLOGY, AND POSITIVE PSYCHOLOGY

What Is Stress? 640

The Stress Response 640

Experiencing Psychology What Is Your Stress Mindset? 641

Sources of Stress 643

What Are the Biological and Social Correlates of Stress? 645

Stress and the Amygdala 645

Stress, the Sympathetic Adrenal–Medullary System, and the Hypothalamic–Pituitary–Adrenal Axis 647

The Epigenetics of Stress 648

Gender Differences in the Stress Response 649

Socioeconomic Status and Stress 649

How Does Stress Affect Our Health? 650

Stress and the Immune System 650

Stress and Heart Disease 651

Connecting to Research Social Challenges Early in Life Affect the Developing Immune System 652

Stress, Mood, Sleep, and Obesity 652

An Integrated View of Stress and Health 654

Psychology as a Hub Science Belongingness, Stress, Achievement, and Health 655

How Can We Cope Effectively With Stress? 656

Managing Stress 656

Three Types of Coping 658

Resilience: Individual Differences in Response to Stress 659

SUMMARY 16.1 660

What Is the Relationship Between Psychology and Health? 660

Behavior and Health 662

- Tobacco Use 663
- Nutrition 665
- Alcohol 666
- Exercise 668
- Loneliness and Health 669

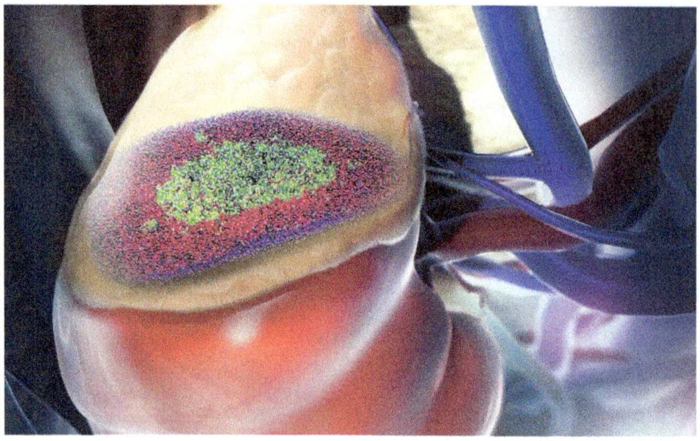

Argosy Publishing, Inc.

Culture and Health 670

An Integrated Understanding of Health Behaviors 671

SUMMARY 16.2 672

What Is Positive Psychology? 672

Positive Emotions 673

- What Is Happiness? 674

Diverse Voices in Psychology Optimism Across Race and Ethnicity 674

- Happiness and Marriage 675
- Happiness and Wealth 675

Thinking Scientifically Does Parenting Increase Happiness? 676

- Can We Increase Happiness? 678

Positive Traits 680

Positive Institutions 681

Positive Psychology and the Future 682

Interpersonal Relationships The Health Psychology Perspective 682

Psychology Takes on Real-World Problems Resilience in the Face of a Pandemic 683

SUMMARY 16.3 684

Key Terms: The Language of Psychological Science 684

References R-1

Name Index N-1

Subject Index/Glossary S-1

Preface

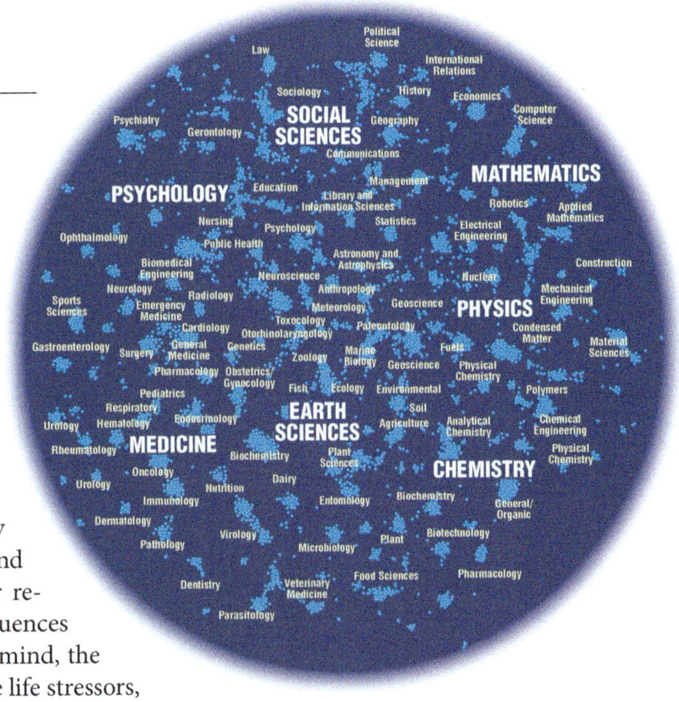

These unprecedented times call for an even better understanding of the mind than ever before. In 2020, our minds have been challenged, stressed, calmed, and stressed again. There is a need, as a society, to better comprehend the healing and connecting power of the mind to keep transforming adversity into an opportunity to grow stronger and healthier together. Over the past months, we learned that we can be physically distant yet remain emotionally connected with our friends and family—we also realized that the same situation can feel extremely friendly or extremely ostracizing—just with the power of our mind and our inner dialogue. The way we interpret a situation may drive our response to it—and in turn, our response to a situation may have consequences for our mental health and well-being. The more we understand the mind, the more we can adapt and reframe our perspectives on current and future life stressors, develop evidence-based coping mechanisms, and improve our mental well-being. This textbook offers a rare opportunity to further discover the powerful psychological science of the mind.

In line with our first edition, this fourth edition of *Discovering Psychology: The Science of Mind* is a textbook that reflects Dr. John Cacioppo's visionary mission to write a textbook as a bridge to the future. *Discovering Psychology: The Science of Mind* describes the psychological science of mind as a hub science—a discipline whose work provides foundational material for many other scientific fields and a wide range of applications from eating habits to real-world problem solving. Psychological science is also inherently interdisciplinary, and we wanted to write a textbook that presents psychology not as a series of isolated areas of inquiry, but as an integrated, holistic science of mind. Contemporary psychological science is also a global affair, and we sought to produce a textbook that draws on evidence from diverse samples of healthy participants and patients, as well as studies of animals. These goals and our implementation of them resonated with all of us: both instructors and students using our previous editions. In honor of John, we have stayed true to his mission and have attempted to expand its implementation in this, our fourth edition.

The science of psychology developed in the 20th century as a collection of loosely organized, independent subspecialties. Now, in the second decade of the 21st century, the discipline is moving rapidly toward maturity as an integrative, multidisciplinary science. Not only are psychologists forming rich collaborations with scholars in other fields, from medicine to business to education to law, but we are returning to original conceptions of psychology put forward by thinkers such as William James, who sought a complete understanding of the human mind and was not content to view psychology from narrow, isolated perspectives. We share a mutual excitement about this evolution of psychological science, and we marvel at the speed at which new developments are emerging in the theory, methods, and applications of psychological science. This fourth edition is designed to capture some of the most important developments that have emerged in recent years and to reflect the power of psychological science to help us manage the types of challenges that emerged in 2020.

For many years, the introductory psychology course has served primarily as a jumping-off point for advanced courses in the field, and the textbooks prepared to support the course have reflected this goal. Each chapter in these conventional textbooks provided a capsule of stand-alone information designed to acquaint students with the terminology and hypotheses of a single psychological perspective. Human behavior is influenced by factors across multiple perspectives, however. We see our introductory textbook as providing a unique opportunity to discuss *all* of psychology, in one place and at one time. This approach allows us to reflect on the intersections among various perspectives as they inform the whole of our understanding of the human mind. Given that most students

We see the introductory course as providing a unique opportunity to discuss all of psychology in one place and at one time.

in our introductory classes will take only this one course in the field, we have a responsibility to provide a comprehensive structure that will support their lifelong learning and understanding of human behavior.

Our goal is to engage our students in the fascinating, integrated discipline of psychological science as it exists in the 21st century, and we view the fourth edition of *Discovering Psychology: The Science of Mind* as another plank in the bridge toward this goal. The structure of the bridge is a traditional chapter organization. The piers on which the bridge rests are the foundational theories of the discipline developed in the late 19th, 20th, and early 21st centuries. The steel beams of which the bridge is composed consist of the theories and research painstakingly developed throughout the 20th century until today, and the rivets, trusses, and tie rods that hold the bridge together are integrative themes that have been reinvented in the past decade or so. Finally, the smooth roadbed that transports students across the bridge is a clear, inviting, warm, and lively writing style and visual narrative.

As active instructors in the introductory psychology classroom, we recognize the balance that busy faculty members must find between their preparation for class and their many other duties, especially while navigating an online delivery system. Our intent is to make the transition to a 21st-century textbook as seamless and effortless as possible for faculty and students alike. Our discussions of complex and emerging issues, such as epigenetics, include sufficient information and explanation to provide a sense of mastery. Clear writing, frequent examples, visual narratives, and engaging pedagogy energize students and provide the support needed for success. After completing the course, students will be able to appreciate the distinction between how laypeople and psychologists think about human behavior.

As citizens of the so-called COVID era, community leaders, influencers, and college graduates will need a firm foundation in the understanding of human behavior and critical thinking to cope with stressors and confront successfully the myriad issues of social isolation, health, privacy, free will, human dignity, public policy, and well-being that might face them again in the future. This fourth edition of *Discovering Psychology: The Science of Mind* is designed to provide that foundation.

Our Integrative and Functionalist Approach

Early writings about psychology were integrated and inclusive. Diverse elements of behavior were combined into the whole. William James (1890) cautions us about the risks of missing the big picture by breaking the phenomenon of mind into little pieces. Mental life for James was not an entity that can be "chopped up in bits" (p. 233). Despite the long-lived popularity of his dominant psychology textbook, James did not prevail. Psychology soon split into camps of scholars who viewed behavior and mental life through their own single, narrow perspectives, rarely speaking with those who held different views and producing curricula and textbooks that emphasized the parts rather than the whole. There are good reasons for specialization in science, but introductory psychology provides an opportunity to put these pieces back together. Doing so shows students how much our notions have changed regarding how the mind and behavior work, and how much this understanding can improve their lives.

As psychological science became increasingly siloed in the 20th century, its origins in the late 19th century as a unified whole were forgotten. In 20th-century introductory psychology textbooks, the writings and experiments of Wilhelm Wundt, Edward Titchener, and James are described as the discipline's prehensile tail, long ago lost and interesting only from a historical perspective. The organization of the study of mind into separate, disconnected chapters not only transformed the topics of psychology into islands without bridges, but actually built barriers to students' understanding of the connectedness among them. A memory cannot be fully understood from one isolated point of view; only when the social and personality, cognitive, biological and evolutionary, developmental, and clinical perspectives are combined can it be thoroughly grasped. James (1890, vol. 1, p. 1) warns us that when mental phenomena are "superficially considered, their variety and complexity is such as to leave a chaotic impression on the observer." This confusion, unfortunately, is the legacy for many of our students exposed only to outdated textbooks in psychology.

Breaking from the approach of other textbooks, we reflect throughout our text on the integrative influences of the founders in our functionalist approach to the material. We seek not only to describe behavior, but also to answer questions about why a particular behavior occurs. Viewed through this lens, behavior is neither random nor unexplainable, and it shifts into focus when we consider its goals and functions. For example, people do not just experience feelings of loneliness; instead, loneliness acts as a warning signal to remind us of the importance of social connectedness.

Our book is subtitled *The Science of Mind*, and unlike other contemporary texts with their occasional references to *mind*, the word appears in each of the chapter titles, highlighting the scientific study of the nature and behavior of the theoretical construct of the mind. Throughout the book, we emphasize the relationship between rigorous scientific methods and observations, as well as the implications of these observations for competing theories about the structure and operations of the human mind.

Integration in this textbook extends in two directions, both within psychology and between psychology and other disciplines. We hope to highlight for students the many connections within the discipline of psychology, as well as its connections with other disciplines.

Implementing the Goals of Integration

Many introductory psychology textbooks are marketed as "integrated," but saying that you are integrated and actually implementing integration are two different things. We have spent a great amount of time and effort discussing ways to provide a truly integrated presentation of the science of mind.

Integration in this textbook extends in two directions, both within psychology and between psychology and other disciplines. We hope to highlight for students the many connections within the discipline of psychology, as well as its connections with other disciplines. Many introductory psychology textbooks share our goal of providing integration, but we would like to make our methods of achieving this goal explicit:

1. Within the body of each chapter, we make frequent connections to material in other chapters, forming bridges that connect subtopics. In the electronic version of the textbook, these connections will be hyperlinked for the convenience of the reader. For example, in a discussion of the causes of anxiety disorders in our chapter on psychological disorders (Chapter 14), we say:

   > A reasonable place to start looking for correlates of anxiety in brain structure and function is the fear circuit involving the amygdala, which is discussed in Chapters 4 and 7. The amygdala is particularly rich in receptors for GABA, a neurotransmitter that inhibits brain activity. As discussed in Chapter 6, drugs such as alcohol and the benzodiazepine tranquilizers (e.g., Valium) have their main anxiety-reducing effects at these GABA receptors.

2. We use frequent examples from other parts of the discipline to illustrate principles within a chapter. For example, when we discuss latent inhibition in our chapter on learning (Chapter 8), we illustrate that principle by linking to clinical research about latent inhibition, creativity, and schizophrenia and to social psychology research on prejudice.
3. We specifically identify and explore five integrative perspectives that weave the standard topics more closely together: social and personality psychology, cognition, biology and evolution, development, and clinical psychology. The need to consider major perspectives in psychology was reinforced in a report titled "Strengthening the Common Core of the Introductory Psychology Course," published in 2014 by the American Psychological Association (APA Board of Educational Affairs Working Group, 2014) and expanded upon by the APA's Introductory Psychology Initiative. In keeping with the standard organization of introductory psychology textbooks, the fundamentals of these perspectives are covered in distinct chapters, but the threads of each perspective are woven into all the chapters. These perspectives are explained in greater detail in the following section.

4. Each chapter includes eight features, which are described in more detail in a later section: Chapter Opener, Psychology as a Hub Science, Experiencing Psychology, Thinking Scientifically, Connecting to Research, Perspectives on Interpersonal Relationships, Diverse Voices in Psychology, and Psychology Takes on Real-World Problems. These features are designed to promote active learning and to increase student interest. Four of these in particular (Chapter Opener, Perspectives on Interpersonal Relationships, Psychology Takes on Real-World Problems, and Psychology as a Hub Science) also contribute to our integrative approach. In the chapter openers, we show how multiple psychological perspectives address a phenomenon by zooming in to see the biological approach and then zooming out again to gain insight from the developmental, cognitive, individual difference, social, and clinical perspectives. Each Perspectives on Interpersonal Relationships feature shows how a particular perspective colors questions about successful relationships, so by the end of the textbook, the student can see how integrating 16 approaches to a single issue enriches our understanding of a psychological phenomenon. Psychology Takes on Real-World Problems tackles the issue of the COVID-19 pandemic, highlighting research relevant to each chapter that can be applied to understanding behavior during a pandemic and developing thoughtful policy. The Psychology as a Hub Science features address the larger integration picture of where psychology stands in the context of the scientific community.

Integrative Features in Detail

Extensive literature supports the idea that an engaged and cognitively active student is more likely to master content. Although students are accustomed to textbooks, their approaches to learning have been affected by technologies that transfer information at an ever-increasing pace, with a strong emphasis on rapidly presented visual images. Consequently, it becomes all too easy to go through the motions of reading a text without really thinking about what they have read. We have incorporated the following eight features, designed to model good textbook-reading practices in students while maintaining a high level of interest and understanding.

Chapter Opener To introduce and engage interest in upcoming chapter material, many textbooks use a vignette or case study, accompanied by either a fine art piece or a photo that is not discussed further. We begin each chapter with a combination of two images—one gives the big picture, and the other gives the microview of the same topic. The chapter opener guides the student through the significance of the images. We use the terms *zoom in* and *zoom out* to emphasize the need to understand the underpinnings of a psychological phenomenon without losing the impact of its larger context. For example, in the biological psychology chapter (Chapter 4), the opening images show a woman accompanying two friends (zoom out) and a beautiful image of a white blood cell exiting bone marrow (zoom in). Does the woman feel like part of a group of friends, or does she feel left out? Depending on how she perceives her social situation, biological cascades are set in motion that prepare her immune system for fighting either the viruses found in close social contact or the bacteria that might be more of a risk when a person is solitary. The reader is drawn into the reciprocal relationships that exist between biology and behavior.

The integrative hub feature broadens the discussion of a psychological topic to include ways in which it is engaged in cooperative science with other disciplines, from medicine to the social sciences.

Psychology as a Hub Science This integrative feature broadens the discussion of a psychological topic to include ways in which psychology engages in cooperative science with other disciplines, from medicine to the social sciences. It is accompanied by a graphic adapted from a citation analysis by Boyack, Klavans, and Börner (2005) that shows psychology citations as nodes with connections to other related disciplines. Tailored to each of the 16 features, this graphic highlights the connections between psychology and the relevant disciplines of psychiatry, nursing, public health, emergency medicine, pharmacology, computer science, law, education, management, and the other social sciences. Given these connections, psychology has a central role to play in our efforts to deal with economic collapses, the spread of pandemics, energy conservation, the spread of terrorism, rising health care costs, and our crumbling educational system. For example, cardiovascular disease is surely a medical condition, but contemporary scientists recognize that a full understanding of this killer requires consideration of psychological domains, including stress appraisal, reactivity to stressors, individual resilience, and a person's social context. Seeing the impact of psychology on many disciplines makes the introductory course relevant for students of all majors, as well as rekindling some "psych pride" in those of us in the field.

Experiencing Psychology This interactive feature provides ways for students to connect the course material to their own lives and interests. Some hands-on examples are the Epworth Sleepiness Scale in the consciousness chapter (Chapter 6), Coren's handedness scale in the biological psychology chapter (Chapter 4), the BFI-10 personality test in the chapter on personality and the self (Chapter 12), and the Hypersensitive Narcissism Scale in the chapter on psychological disorders (Chapter 14). In other cases, this feature provides longer-term opportunities for students to apply their learning, such as working to reduce the frequency of a bad habit (Chapter 8).

Thinking Scientifically This interactive feature models critical thinking skills for students by providing them with opportunities to critique the progress of science. For example, in the chapter on research methods (Chapter 2), students review the current controversies about replication in psychology. In the chapter on psychological treatments (Chapter 15), students are asked to evaluate whether autism spectrum disorder (ASD) is simply a difference or something requiring treatment.

Connecting to Research To emphasize psychology as a science, this feature explores either a classic or a contemporary study relevant to the chapter's material and comments on its significance to the field. Sections on the question, methods, ethics, results, and conclusions provide a guided introduction for the student to the essentials of the peer-reviewed literature. From Wundt's classic studies of reaction time, to the discovery of mirror neurons, to distinctions between romantic love and lust in the brain, students are given insight into what psychological scientists do.

Perspectives on Interpersonal Relationships In keeping with the integrative mission of this textbook, the goal of this feature is to demonstrate how the information in a particular chapter can be applied to a single topic—building and maintaining important relationships. This issue is personally meaningful to college students, especially first-year students, and it applies across the board—regardless of gender, race, age, ethnicity, sociocultural background, sexual orientation, or level of academic preparation. The feature has two main purposes: (1) to engage and maintain student interest throughout the text and (2) to stitch together into an integrative, thematic quilt the patchwork of traditional introductory psychology topic areas.

Diverse Voices in Psychology The American Psychological Association (APA) report on best practices for introductory psychology (Gurung et al., 2016) emphasized the inclusion of culture and diversity as a "cross-cutting theme" (p. 112). Although we concur with Trimble, Stevenson, and Worell (2003; see later discussion in this forward) regarding the need to integrate diversity across topics in an organic way, which guided all four editions of this textbook, we thought additional in-depth discussions would be useful. This feature explores timely topics such as the shooter bias (Chapter 13) and culturally competent counseling and psychotherapy with Native Americans (Chapter 15).

Psychology Takes on Real-World Problems Introductory psychology courses provide a unique opportunity to not only prepare students for continued study in psychology, but also to provide tools to majors and nonmajors alike that can be used to tackle significant human problems. Once again taking a cue from the APA's introductory psychology report, we have incorporated aspects of the "Big Problems" activity described in the report's appendix into this feature. For this fourth edition, we selected the topic of the COVID-19 pandemic, which is not only top-of-mind for today's students, but also provides opportunities to apply multiple aspects of psychological science. We provide a template for policy development, emphasizing the utility of psychological science to real-world problems. Each chapter highlights ways in which its material can be used to address the causes of and solutions to problems related to the pandemic, emphasizing the practical significance of psychological science and encouraging students to apply their learning to policy evaluation and change.

Integrative Perspectives in Detail

The separate perspectives taken by psychologists are reviewed for students in the context of the historical discussion in Chapter 1. In each subsequent chapter, we pay especially close attention to the contributions of each of the following perspectives to the topic at hand.

Social and Personality English writer and poet John Donne was correct in stating that "no man is an island." The cultural differences that are increasingly apparent as we become a more global world are a testament to how strongly social structures and processes affect the operation of factors from other perspectives. We are a social species, and much of our behavior can be understood in terms of how it maintains our social relatedness with one another. The consequences of failing to maintain connectedness are severe. For example, chronic feelings of social isolation are associated with poor mental and physical health and premature mortality, and longitudinal studies in humans and experimental studies in animals indicate that perceived isolation contributes to these outcomes. In short, feeling left out can be toxic. Behavioral systems are particularly prone to variation, and we illustrate how such variation can be regarded as a source of important data in its own right. In addition to exploring individual differences within the context of personality, we integrate this facet with other perspectives. For example, we discuss how individual differences in responses to stress are best understood by considering epigenetics, learning, and social factors.

Cognitive The human is above all else a thinking organism, and the way that we process information affects our behavior. Whether we are considering the development of behavior, learned behavior, or the aberrations of behavior that accompany psychological disorders, an understanding of how we think provides considerable insight. For example, we understand that an effective way to improve depressed people's moods is to help them restructure the way that they process information. Instead of students' thinking that flunking an exam means they are not good enough to attend college, we can encourage them to think that although flunking an exam isn't fun, it's not the end of the world either, and they can make some changes that will lead to better performance next time.

Biological and Evolutionary We believe that all introductory psychology students, even those who will never take another psychology course, will gain a better understanding of contemporary psychology in the context of the relationships between biological processes and behavior. For example, when we discuss attraction and close relationships, we mention data showing that viewing a photograph of somebody we love, as opposed to somebody we like, activates the brain's reward circuits and decreases activity in areas associated with social judgment. Not only is love somewhat socially blind, but it really does feel good. Throughout the textbook, we stress the role of evolutionary pressures in shaping both the structures and the functions of the mind. We devote a complete chapter to providing students with a foundation for understanding the interactions between genes and environment, including a basic primer on epigenetics. The importance of gene–environment interactions is woven throughout our discussion of development, but it is also highlighted in other contexts, including discussions of children's responses to being bullied.

Developmental The structures and processes of behavior, as well as behavior itself, change over time. Knowing that most children achieve a theory of mind by the age of 4 years not only is relevant to our understanding of children and their behavior, but also informs discussions of the development of language and social skills and the deficits found in individuals with autism spectrum disorder (ASD). The importance of the developmental perspective does not end in childhood either. January 1, 2011, marked the date at which the oldest of the baby boomers turned 65. From that date, about 10,000 people will turn 65 every day for the next 19 years. As a result of these demographic changes, the percentage of the U.S. population whose social role is retiree is projected to increase dramatically in the coming decades. Understanding developmental changes across the life span is therefore increasingly important.

Clinical We can understand behavior by observing what works, but it is also highly useful to see what happens when things go wrong. Just as the neuroscientist learns about normal brain function by observing changes following the damage caused by a stroke, we can learn much about behavior by observing how it changes because of a psychological disorder. For example, we consider the effects of schizophrenia on classical conditioning in the chapter on learning (Chapter 8).

Delivering Complex Content to Contemporary Learners

We were delighted to see that our first three editions were embraced by faculty working with students representing a wide range of preparation, from community colleges to elite, private universities, as well as by international faculty teaching students with first languages other than English. Our teaching philosophy rejects the common construct of a textbook "level." Instead, we believe that all students can master complex content if it is presented in the right way.

As this text goes to press, we are unsure about the direction institutions will take regarding virtual versus face-to-face instruction. As active instructors of introductory psychology, we have shared the journey of many of our colleagues as we navigate the online teaching space. One of our authors (LF) has more than ten years of experience in a completely online environment (Argosy University Online), and we have attempted to keep the needs of online students and instructors top of mind as we revise this latest edition. Many students and faculty are using electronic text resources for the first time, and we are hearing concerns about screen fatigue and other perceived challenges of this medium. Developing an electronic version of a text is not about converting a print book to pdf files. Instead, proactive strategies such as breaking material into reasonable sections and providing sufficient illustrations work for both print and electronic versions alike.

Student-Friendly Writing and Pedagogy

Our goal in writing this textbook is to provide students with the best science possible, which means that we do not avoid complex topics or dumb down the material.

To make psychological science accessible to students with wide ranges of preparation, we rely on a student-friendly writing style with supportive pedagogy. We break chapters into meaningful chunks, and we use thumbnail images of chapter photos and figures in our summary tables as a mnemonic device that students can use to recall where they read about a topic. Margin definitions and carefully selected key terms help the students focus their learning.

One of our reviewers had this to say about the first chapter of our textbook, which can be one of the most difficult to write: "I am impressed with the History of Psychology chapter in Cacioppo/Freberg. The figures, timeline, interesting AND relevant pictures, and examples throughout the text are fantastic and engaging. It is one of the best history/intro chapters I've read." This reviewer also noticed another one of our goals—to use all photos and figures as teachable moments, not just repetitions of the narrative or pretty placeholders.

Implementation of Guidelines for "Inclusive Psychology"

Today's college and university students represent a wide range of diverse demographic variables, and these variables should be reflected thoughtfully in the textbooks that they read. As this textbook goes to press, issues of diversity and fairness are especially salient in our conversations and news reports. On behalf of the APA, Trimble, Stevenson, and Worell (2003) provided considerable guidance to textbook authors and publishers regarding opportunities for including diversity content in an introductory psychology textbook. They focus on the following types of diversity: age, culture, race/ethnicity, gender, disability, language, and sexual orientation. Gurung et al. (2016, p. 112), also writing on behalf of the APA, emphasized the need to present culture and diversity as "cross-cutting themes" throughout the introductory psychology course. We have used these papers as a blueprint for incorporating the dimension of diversity in our textbook.

We adamantly concur with Trimble et al. (2003, p. 2) when they state, "Culture, race/ethnicity, gender, disability, sexual orientation, language, and age can be integrated into the main text of every textbook chapter. Highlighting these issues only in special sections or boxes fosters the continued marginalization of members of nondominant groups." We incorporate diversity issues seamlessly throughout the narrative and in illustrations and examples. For example, while we note that Roland Fryer was the youngest African-American professor to obtain tenure at Harvard University, we do so in the context of how his childhood and youth shaped his approaches to educational incentives within a discussion of motivation. Although Trimble et al. (2003) appear to dislike feature boxes, we have found it useful to augment the discussion of culture and gender in the narrative by highlighting special topics in our *Diverse Voices in Psychology* feature. We believe that this combination represents the antithesis of the biggest concern raised by Trimble et al. (2003)—isolated, disconnected discussion of diversity in boxes alone.

Trimble et al. (2003) provide extensive, detailed suggestions for specific content, such as inclusion of stereotype threat and gender and cultural issues in eating disorders, that we have found useful. For interested faculty and students, we have a comprehensive, separate document with chapter and page references indicating how we have implemented these recommendations. Please feel free to email lfreberg@calpoly.edu to obtain a copy.

In addition, great care has been taken to adhere to APA standards on language. The illustrations feature individuals of diverse races, ethnicities, ages, abilities, and gender. When possible, they show people in a positive light (e.g., no sad older adults feeding pigeons) and avoid traditional depictions (e.g., male therapist helping female client). Large numbers of illustrations feature cross-cultural examples. Cross-cultural research is featured whenever possible, such as global studies of subjective well-being.

A Complete Course—Teaching and Learning Supplements

A rich array of supplements accompanies Cacioppo/Freberg/Cacioppo's *Discovering Psychology: The Science of Mind*, 4th edition, including several that make use of the latest technologies. These supplements are designed to make teaching and learning more effective. Many are available free to professors or students. Others can be packaged with this textbook at a discount. Contact your local sales representative for more information on any of the listed resources.

MindTap

MindTap for *Discovering Psychology: The Science of Mind* creates a unique learning path that fosters increased comprehension and efficiency. It engages students and empowers them to produce their best work—consistently. In MindTap, course material is seamlessly integrated with videos, activities, apps, and more.

For students:

- MindTap delivers real-world relevance with activities and assignments designed to help students build critical thinking and analytical skills that can be applied to other courses and to their professional lives.
- MindTap serves as a single destination for all course materials so that students can stay organized and efficient and have the necessary tools to master the content.
- MindTap shows students where they stand at all times—both individually and compared to the highest performers in the class. This information helps to motivate and empower performance.

In MindTap, instructors can do the following:

- **Control the content.** Instructors select what students see and when they see it.
- **Create a unique learning path.** In MindTap, the *Discovering Psychology: The Science of Mind* text is enhanced with multimedia and activities to encourage and motivate learning and retention, moving students up the learning taxonomy. Materials can be used as is or modified to match an instructor's syllabus.
- **Integrate their own content.** Instructors can modify the MindTap Reader using their own documents or pulling from sources like Rich Site Summary (RSS) feeds, YouTube videos, websites, Google Docs, and more.

- **Follow student progress.** Powerful analytics and reports provide a snapshot of class progress, time students spend logging into the course, and completion to help instructors assess level of engagement and identify problem areas.

The Instructor Companion Site

The Instructor Companion Site for this title includes an *Instructor's Resource Manual*, which provides a wealth of teaching tips and classroom resources; *Cengage Learning Testing Powered by Cognero* featuring questions correlated to learning objectives, Bloom's taxonomy level, and difficulty; and *PowerPoint slides* providing concept coverage with dynamic animations, photographs, and video.

Changes in the Fourth Edition

An obvious change in the fourth edition is the addition of Steph Cacioppo to our author team. Steph not only collaborated closely with John (they shared a desk), but she brings her own unique perspectives as a licensed clinician to the textbook.

Progress in psychological science continues to move forward at a blistering pace, and this fourth edition has been updated to include many new photos and figures and several hundred new references that reflect the advances in the field since the last edition went to press.

A sample of the content updates and revisions to each chapter include the following:

Chapter 1 The Science of Mind: The Discipline of Psychology

- Expands ties between the textbook and the pillars and cross-cutting themes recommended by the APA Introductory Psychology Initiative.
- Added new section explicitly outlining the advantages of studying psychology for contemporary students.
- Expanded discussion of perspectives to include APA divisions that are not typically covered in intro psychology textbooks.
- Includes a table of common myths in psychology.
- Refreshed the *Psychology Takes on Real-World Problems* feature (cyberbullying in 3e) to a discussion of pandemics. Includes specific information on policy development.

Chapter 2 The Measure of Mind: Methods of Psychology

- Updated discussion of confirmation bias.
- Added section on "truthiness" or how we can be fooled into thinking false information is true.
- Updated section on hypothesis testing and the null hypothesis.
- Expanded discussion of quasi-experiments.
- Expanded discussion of correlations and mistakes in interpretation.
- Updated discussion of descriptive statistics and central tendency with new examples.
- Updated and clarified discussion of statistical significance and effect sizes.
- Refreshed *Experiencing Psychology* feature to the use of critical thinking to evaluate popular press reports of scientific findings. The example used is a report about depression and social media use.
- Updated the *Hub Science* feature to discuss the development of factor analysis.
- The *Psychology Takes on Real-World Problems* feature discusses the application of the research methods covered in the chapter to a specific question with policy implications: Why do people wear masks in some situations and not others?

Chapter 3 The Evolving Mind: Nature and Nurture Intertwined

- Emphasized application of genetics to understanding of causes of psychological disorders and their potential treatments.
- Discussed rates of gene expression as differentiating between species, e.g. humans and other primates.
- Clarified discussion of heritability.
- Uses a study about blood type and risk of COVID-19 severity to illustrate genome-wide association studies (GWAS).
- Updated Flynn effect discussion.
- Refreshed *Experiencing Psychology* feature with an activity for identifying your cat's genome related to length of fur and fur coloring.
- Reformatted Warrior Gene *Thinking Scientifically* feature to include critical thinking questions discussed in Chapter 2.
- Refreshed *Real-World Problems* feature with a discussion of the impact of genetics on responses to social distancing recommendations.

Chapter 4 The Biological Mind: The Physical Basis of Behavior

- Refreshed *Thinking Scientifically* feature to discuss eye movement desensitization and reprocessing therapy (EMDR).
- Updated *Hub Science* feature to discuss the use of neuroscience in courts to assess "dangerousness" at parole hearings.
- Refreshed *Real-World Problems* feature to cover social distancing, loneliness, and the brain.

Chapter 5 The Perceiving Mind: Sensation and Perception

- Inclusion of ganglion cells related to circadian rhythms and sensitivity to brightness.
- Added discussion of perfect pitch and autism spectrum disorder.
- Inclusion of a "hermunculus," or an attempt to map parts of the body to the sensory cortex in females (instead of the traditional homunculus, or male version).
- Update of *Diverse Voices* feature to include new research on culture and vision.
- Perceptions of taste and culture—including crispy tarantulas!
- Refreshed *Real-World Problems* feature to look at social distancing and the perception of threat.

Chapter 6 The Aware Mind: Elements of Consciousness

- Expanded coverage of the default mode network (DMN) relative to conditions such as autism spectrum disorder.
- Update on "social jet lag."
- Update on sleep spindles, learning, and Alzheimer's disease.
- Update on screen time and insomnia.
- Update on brain death.
- Update on LSD's mode of action.
- Update on opioid epidemic.
- Refreshed *Connecting to Research* feature with discussion of the effects of psychedelics on consciousness.

- Refreshed *Thinking Scientifically* feature to discuss the potential for using hallucinogens in therapy.
- Refreshed *Real-World Problems* feature with discussion of sleep during a pandemic.

Chapter 7 The Feeling Mind: Emotion and Motivation

- Added discussion of "power posing" and its replication issues to the facial feedback section.
- Added discussion of somatic markers (without using that term, however).
- Updated section on female sexual interest.
- Updated section on genetics and sexual orientation with discussion of the important Ganna et al. (2019) GWAS study.
- Expanded discussion of achievement motivation.
- Added application of Maslow's hierarchy of needs to understanding behavior during COVID-19.
- Refreshed *Thinking Scientifically* feature with a discussion of participation trophies and motivation.
- Refreshed *Real-World Problems* feature with discussion of COVID-19 and motivational priorities.

Chapter 8 The Adaptive Mind: Learning

- Expanded discussion of operant conditioning applications to spanking practices and behavior in HOV lanes.
- Discussion of classical conditioning and opioid overdose.
- Expanded *Hub Science* feature on taste aversion and endangered species to include the marbled murrelet and the quoll in addition to the Mexican wolf.
- Refreshed *Thinking Scientifically* feature to discuss appropriate ways to praise children.
- Refreshed *Real-World Problems* feature to discuss whether people can learn to be less lonely during social distancing.

Chapter 9 The Knowing Mind: Memory

- Added discussion of reconsolidation following retrieval.
- Added discussion of caffeine and memory.
- Added discussion of interleaving to study skills recommendations.
- Refreshed *Thinking Scientifically* feature with a discussion of taking notes longhand or using a computer.
- Refreshed *Real-World Problems* feature with discussion on compliance with social distancing and working memory.

Chapter 10 The Thinking Mind: Thinking, Language, and Intelligence

- Updated discussion of neuromarketing.
- Expanded discussion of rumination in problem solving.
- Update and revision of section on heuristics.
- Added explicit best practices for decision making.
- Update and revision of section on dyslexia.
- Update and revision of section on bilingualism and multilingualism.
- Revision of section on emotional and social intelligence.
- Update and revision of section on brain structure and intelligence.

- Updated section on giftedness with discussion of acceleration effects.
- Updated *Thinking Scientifically* section on baby videos, e.g. Baby Einstein.
- Refreshed *Real-World Problems* section with a discussion of the availability heuristic and COVID-19.

Chapter 11 The Developing Mind: Life Span Development

- Update on teratogens, including acetaminophen (Tylenol/Anacin), and ADHD and autism spectrum disorder.
- Addition of research on COVID-19 effects on the fetus.
- Revision of discussion of sex chromosomes and intersex.
- Added discussion of research on infant's understanding of social power.
- Expanded discussion of attachment to include cross-cultural data and correlations with adult romantic attachments.
- Expanded discussion of indulgent parenting, which has become more common in recent years.
- Addition of other theories of moral reasoning following Kohlberg's.
- Addition of stage of emerging adulthood, with contrasts to adolescence and young adulthood.
- Update and revision of cognitive changes in later adulthood.
- Refreshed *Relationships* feature with a discussion of a "perfect" time to get married.
- Refreshed *Real-World Problems* feature with a discussion of pandemic anxiety across the lifespan.

Chapter 12 The Individual Mind: Personality and the Self

- Updated discussion of serotonin transporter gene and culture.
- Added discussion of ambiverts.
- Updated discussion of genetics, brain structure, and personality.
- Updated discussion of personality assessment to reflect changes in the most recent version of the MMPI.
- Updated discussion of gender, race/ethnicity, and self-esteem.
- Updated discussion of individualistic versus collectivistic cultures.
- Refreshed *Diverse Voices* feature with discussion of diversity and personality assessment.
- Refreshed *Real-World Problems* feature with discussion of personality and responses to a pandemic.

Chapter 13 The Connected Mind: Social Psychology

- Updated discussion of first impressions.
- Revised section on the neuroscience of cognitive dissonance.
- Added section on the neuroscience of persuasion.
- Expanded discussion of social identities.
- Expanded section on reducing prejudice.
- Updated and expanded *Hub Science* feature on social media and fake news, including explicit hints for avoiding belief in fake news stories.
- Refreshed *Thinking Scientifically* feature with a discussion of brain damage and criminal behavior.
- Refreshed *Real-World Problems* feature to discuss persuasion during a pandemic.

Chapter 14 The Troubled Mind: Psychological Disorders

- Included update on the 11th edition of ICD.
- Update of causal factors related to autism spectrum disorder.
- Expanded discussion of schizophrenia to include saccade differences.
- Added discussion of oxidative stress in bipolar disorder.
- Update of learned helplessness and major depressive disorder section to reflect Maier and Seligman's (2016) rethinking of the original experiments.
- Added discussion of genetics in height phobia.
- Update of discussion of culture in social anxiety.
- Update of biological correlates of OCD.
- Update on causal factors and PTSD.
- Update of biological correlates of antisocial personality disorder.
- Refreshed *Thinking Scientifically* feature with discussion of cannabis and psychosis.
- Refreshed *Diverse Voices* feature with discussion of culture, race, ethnicity, sexual orientation, and suicidality.
- Revised and updated *Hub Science* feature on leadership and psychopathy.
- Refreshed *Real-World Problems* feature with discussion of COVID-19 and OCD.

Chapter 15 Healing the Troubled Mind: Therapy

- Updated discussion of life coaching.
- Added discussion of transcranial direct electrical stimulation for the treatment of auditory hallucination.
- Update on research about the efficacy of antidepressant medications.
- Revised section on treatment of PTSD.
- Refreshed *Diverse Voices* feature with a discussion of psychotherapy with Native Americans.
- Refreshed *Thinking Scientifically* feature with a discussion of neurodiversity versus disorder/disability in autism spectrum disorder. This includes Simon Baron-Cohen's "4 D's": disorder, disability, difference, and disease.
- Refreshed *Real-World Problems* feature with a discussion of online therapy during COVID-19.

Chapter 16 The Healthy Mind: Stress and Coping, Health Psychology, and Positive Psychology

- Added discussion of stress and COVID-19.
- Added discussion of robotic pets as stress reducers for patients with Alzheimer's disease.
- Expanded discussion of vaping.
- Expanded discussion of loneliness interventions.
- Updated culture and health section with data regarding COVID-19.
- Expanded positive psychology section to include PERMA model.
- Revised happiness discussion with latest world happiness data.
- Expanded discussion of the "meaningful life" and happiness.
- Revised *Thinking Scientifically* feature on parenting and happiness.
- Refreshed *Real-World Problems* feature to discuss resilience during a pandemic.

Acknowledgments

We thank William James for bringing so many disparate threads of scholarship together to form the backbone of what continues to be the study of psychology.

Cengage Learning Team

We are grateful to our Cengage Learning team. Colin Grover shared our vision for this textbook from the outset and went many extra miles to make it a reality. Christy Frame, Nick Barrows, Deanna Ettinger, and Jessica Witzcak gave us their full support through each step of the process. We also thank Michelle Shiota of Arizona State University and instructional designer Jan Johnson.

Manuscript Reviewers

We could not produce this textbook without the meticulous and thoughtful input of our peers. We continue to stand in awe of the care that our colleagues put into their teaching and their desire for their students to succeed. Many thanks to the following reviewers of this book:

Judith Addelston, *Valencia College, East*
Anthony Ahrens, *American University*
John Allen, *University of Arizona*
Roxanna Andersen, *Palm Beach State College, Boca Raton*
Stacy Anderson, *Florida Gulf Coast University*
Ted Barker, *Northwest Florida State College*
Mark Basham, *Regis University*
Kyle Baumbauer, *Texas A&M University*
Kathy Becker-Blease, *Oregon State University*
Kristen T. Begosh, *University of Delaware*
Richard Bernstein, *Broward College, South Campus*
Melissa A. Berry, *University of Dayton*
Kathleen Bey, *Palm Beach State College, Lake Worth*
Rachel Blaser, *University of San Diego*
Sara Broaders, *Northwestern University*
Christina M. Brown, *Saint Louis University*
Eric Bruns, *Campbellsville University*
Kathryn Caldwell, *Ithaca College*
Aimee A. Callender, *Auburn University*
David Campbell, *Humboldt State University*
John Timothy Cannon, *University of Scranton*
Brian D. Carpenter, *Washington University, St. Louis*
Lawrence Cohen, *University of Delaware*
Kyle Evan Conlon, *Boise State University*
John Connor, *Daytona State College*
Brian Cowley, *Park University*
Verne Cox, *University of Texas, Arlington*
David Seth Crystal, *Georgetown University*
Natalie Dautovich, *University of Alabama*
Sarah D'Elia, *George Mason University and Northern Virginia Community College*
Matthew Draper, *Utah Valley University*
Patrick Drumm, *Ohio University, Lancaster*
Robert DuBois, *Waukesha County Technical College*
Kimberly Duff, *Cerritos College*
Megan Dunbar, *California State University San Marcos and Palomar College*
Darlene Earley, *Southern Union State Community College*

Dawn Eaton, *San Jacinto College-South*
Jennifer Engler, *York College of Pennsylvania*
Kathy Erickson, *Pima Community College*
Carlos Escoto, *Eastern Connecticut State University*
Kendall Eskine, *Loyola University New Orleans*
Melanie Evans, *Eastern Connecticut State University*
Bryan D. Fantie, *American University*
Stephen L. Forssell, *George Washington University*
Debra Lynn Frame, *University of Cincinnati*
Andrea Friedrich, *University of Kentucky*
Perry Fuchs, *University of Texas, Arlington*
Philip Gable, *University of Alabama*
Bridgett Galvin, *Framingham State College*
Deborah Garfin, *Georgia State University*
Jeanette Gassaway, *Ohio University*
Bryan Gibson, *Central Michigan University*
Allen Gorman, *Angelo State University*
Ruth Grahn, *Connecticut College*
Ruth M. Grant, *Sacred Heart University*
Alexis S. Green, *Hanover College*
Anthony Greene, *University of Wisconsin, Milwaukee*
Christina Grimes, *Duke University*
Scott Gustafson, *University of Mississippi*
Carrie E. Hall, *Miami University*
Erin E. Hardin, *Texas Tech University*
Gregory Harris, *Polk State College*
Jeffrey Henriques, *University of Wisconsin, Madison*
Robert J. Hines, *University of Arkansas, Little Rock*
Kelly Huffman, *University of California, Riverside*
Linda Jackson, *Michigan State University*
Jennifer Johnson, *Bloomsberg University*
Todd Joseph, *Hillsborough Community College, Dale Mabry*
Irene P. Kan, *Villanova University*
Kevin Keating, *Broward College, North*
Craig Kinsley, *University of Richmond*
Michelle (MiKi) Kitchen, *University of South Carolina*
Cheri Kittrell, *State College of Florida, Manatee-Sarasota*
Megan L. Knowles, *Franklin and Marshall College*
Jordan Labouff, *Baylor University*
Debra Laino, *Philadelphia University*
Carrie Lane, *Florida State University*
Jamison D. Law, *Utah Valley University*
Natalie Lawrence, *James Madison University*
Jennifer Lee, *Cabrillo College*
Angela M. Legg, *Pace University, Pleasantville*
Fabio Leite, *Ohio State University, Lima*
Robin Lightner, *University of Cincinnati*
Carrie A. Lloyd, *Huntington University*
Christine Lofgren, *University of California, Irvine*
Nicolette Lopez, *University of Texas, Arlington*
David Malcolm, *Fordham University*
Michael Mangan, *University of New Hampshire*
Abigail Marsh, *Georgetown University*
Daniel McConnell, *University of Central Florida*
Anna Medina, *Gonzaga University*
Sean P. Meegan, *University of Utah*
Antoinette Miller, *Clayton State University*

Robin K. Morgan, *Indiana University Southeast*
Ronald Morrison, *Daytona State College*
Michelle Niculescu, *Lebanon Valley College*
Charlotte Nolan-Reyes, *Cabrillo College*
Kevin O'Neil, *Florida Gulf Coast University*
Hajime Otani, *Central Michigan University*
Gwendolyn Parsons-Spurrier, *Hillsborough Community College, Ybor City Campus*
Lois Pasapane, *Palm Beach State College, Lake Worth*
Marion Perlmutter, *University of Michigan, Ann Arbor*
David J. Rademacher, *Carthage College*
Gabriel Radvansky, *University of Notre Dame*
Cynthia Reidi, *Morrisville State College*
Ann E. Renken, *University of Southern California*
Heather J. Rice, *Washington University, St. Louis*
Michael Roberts, *DePauw University*
Marylou Robins, *San Jacinto College-South*
Dario Rodriguez, *University of Dayton*
Ronnie Rothschild, *Broward College, Central Campus*
Sharleen Sakai, *Michigan State University*
Catherine Sanderson, *Amherst College*
Patrick Saxe, *State University of New York, New Paltz*
Luis Schettino, *Lafayette College*
David Schroeder, *University of Arkansas*
Dennis Shaffer, *Ohio State University, Mansfield*
Alex Sharpe, *Santa Fe College*
Donald Sharpe, *University of Regina*
Caroline Shelton-Toney, *Polk State College*
Cindy Sledge, *San Jacinto College-South*
Mikle Don South, *Brigham Young University*
William Suits, *Seminole State College of Florida*
Cyril Svoboda, *University of Maryland University College*
Lara Tedrow, *Tidewater Community College*
Brian Thomas, *Baldwin-Wallace College*
Lisa Thomassen, *Indiana University, Bloomington*
Clarissa Thompson, *University of Oklahoma*
Terry Trepper, *Purdue University Southwest*
Alexa Tullet, *University of Alabama*
Lindsey West, *Georgia Regents University*
Eliah White, *University of Cincinnati, Blue Ash College*
Katherine Urquhart, *Lake Sumter Community College*
Anre Venter, *University of Notre Dame*
Craig Vickio, *Bowling Green State University*
Mark Walter, *Salisbury University*
Shannon Welch, *University of Idaho*
Lona Whitmarsh, *Fairleigh Dickinson University*
John Wright, *Washington State University*
Erin Young, *Texas A&M University*

We also thank Suzanne Corkin (1937–2016) for reading and commenting on sections describing the amnesic patient H. M. (Henry Molaison) in our first edition.

Finally, we could not have done this without the patience and support of our families.

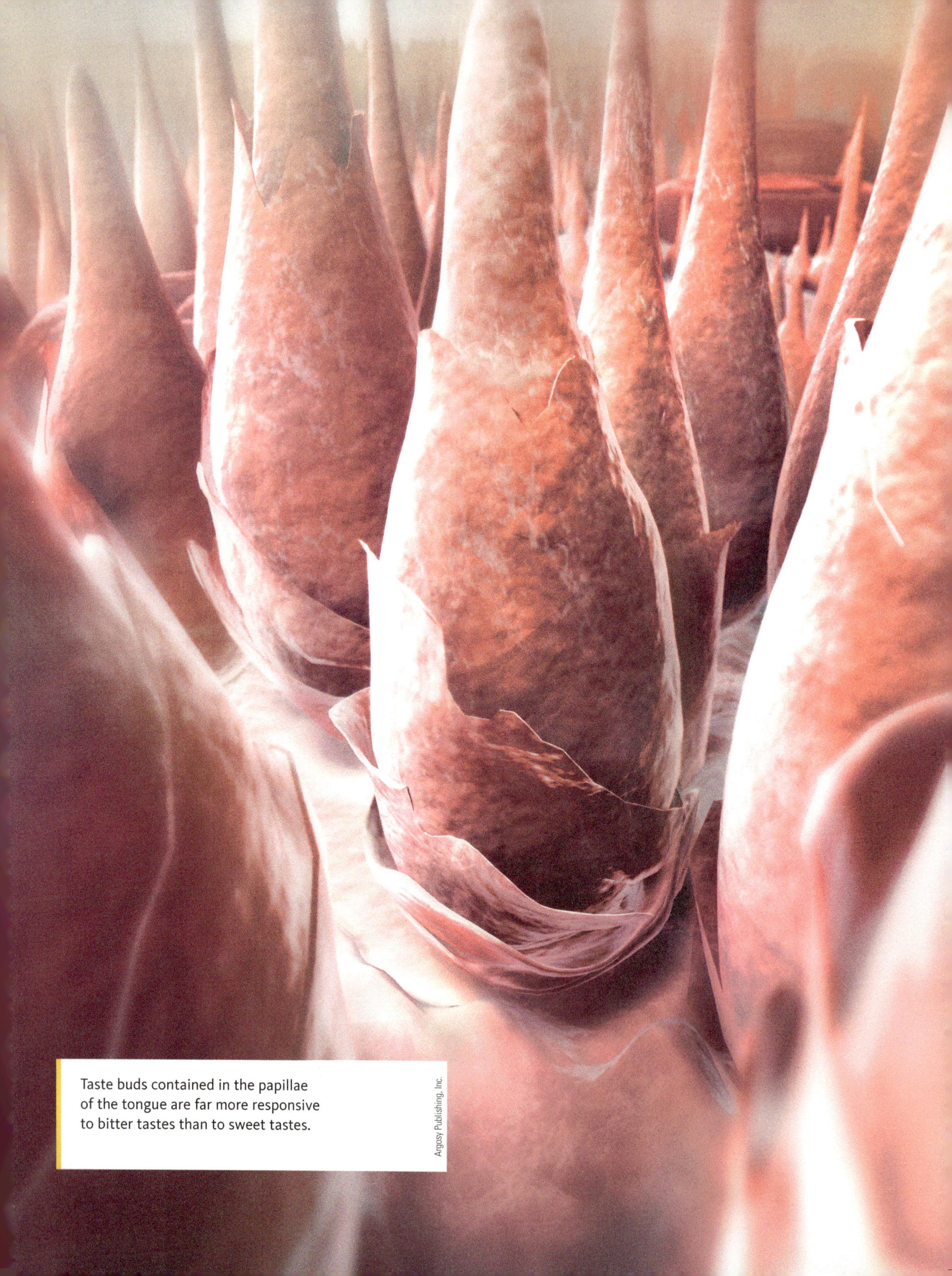

Taste buds contained in the papillae of the tongue are far more responsive to bitter tastes than to sweet tastes.

Argosy Publishing, Inc.

1

The Science of Mind

THE DISCIPLINE OF PSYCHOLOGY

LEARNING OBJECTIVES

1. Identify the five in-depth perspectives of psychology and explain how integrating these perspectives leads to a more comprehensive and accurate view of behavior and mental processes.
2. Explain why issues of diversity and ethics are important to explore across all topics in psychology.
3. Explain the contributions of philosophy and the natural sciences to our understanding of modern psychology.
4. Describe how early movements in psychology are significant for modern psychology.
5. Discuss the importance of the scientific method as a foundation for psychology.
6. Explain why psychology's role as a hub science supports applications in many academic fields, contributes to the solutions of critical contemporary problems, and informs the development of public policies.

STUDYING THE SCIENCE OF PSYCHOLOGY CAN lead you to see yourself and other people in completely new ways. Hundreds of years ago, people believed that the world was flat and the Sun and stars circled the Earth. Careful scientific research slowly dispelled these inaccurate notions. Nonetheless, we hold tightly to many equally false commonsense beliefs about the human mind and behavior. We all "know" that opposites attract, but we also "know" that birds of a feather flock together—so why do we need psychology to tell us what we already "know"? The problem is that both statements cannot be true at the same time, so the real state of affairs is neither obvious nor simple. Just as careful science was required to understand our planet's place in the universe, the same scientific techniques are providing us with a more accurate, complete view of the human mind.

Let's begin with a seemingly simple and familiar example: our ability to taste. We know a lot about taste—what we like or dislike, the different qualities of taste, and so on. Most of us can taste sweetness in a solution made of 1 part sugar and 200 parts water. As remarkable as this sensitivity appears to be, however, people can detect 1 part bitter substance (like quinine or the chemicals in broccoli) in 2 million parts water. This contrast in taste sensitivity between sweet and bitter does not reflect the actual difference between sweet and bitter substances—that is, bitter tastes are not 10,000 times stronger than sweet tastes—but rather how we experience them. Why would we have such a vast difference in sensitivity between these types of tastes?

Masterfile

Our personal experience of taste does not help us much in answering this question, but psychological science can. As it turns out, our greater sensitivity to bitter tastes is highly adaptive: Most poisons or toxins taste bitter, and if you want to stay alive, it is more important to avoid swallowing poison than to enjoy something sweet. Being far more sensitive to tastes that are

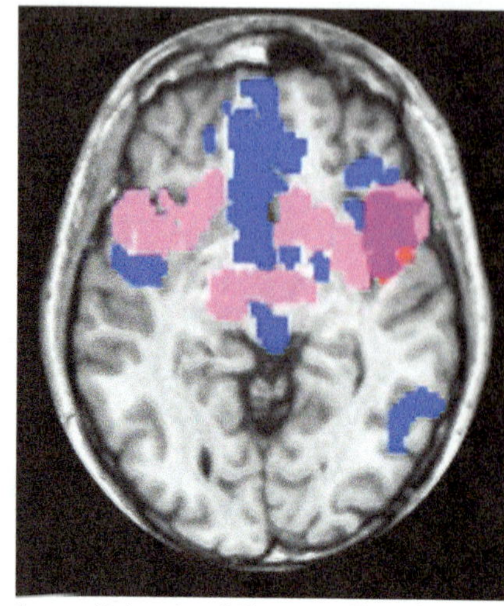

Can you tell whether you're experiencing lust or romantic love? *Introspection* is the personal observation of our own thoughts, feelings, and behaviors. Because we are not perfect observers of the operations of our own minds, psychologists developed other methods that provide scientific insight into the mind. In this functional magnetic resonance imaging (fMRI) scan, areas of the brain that were more active when participants were feeling lust are shown in blue and areas that were more active when people are experiencing feelings of romantic love are shown in pink. Through technology, researchers can better understand complex behaviors like love and lust.

From https://news.uchicago.edu/story/researchers-find-brains-sweet-spot-love-neurological-patient

Source: University of Chicago Office of Communications

bitter is a trait that has served our species well because it helps us avoid eating things that could kill us. Psychology helps us understand why we do the things we do by providing a context for understanding the mind and behavior.

To gain that understanding, psychology addresses questions from the multiple scientific perspectives discussed in this chapter. One can think of this like the zoom feature in Google Earth. In some parts of this textbook, we will zoom in on human behaviors, like looking at the highly magnified image of the papillae on the tongue (pictured on page 2), which allow us to taste, and trace the messages about taste sent from the tongue to the brain. At other times, we'll zoom out, to take in the larger picture and better understand why the boy on the previous page is giving his bitter-tasting broccoli a skeptical look.

To begin, we can look at the little boy's reaction to his broccoli from a developmental perspective, which tells us that children are more sensitive to taste than adults. Using a biological perspective, we can trace the neural mechanisms responsible for taste sensitivity. Or, using the social perspective, we can think about social influences like culture on food preferences. Cottage cheese, enjoyed by many Americans, is viewed with disgust in some other parts of the world. Meanwhile, deep-fried tarantulas, a delicacy in Cambodia, might not be a popular item in the United States.

Although single perspectives tell us a great deal about a phenomenon like our sensitivity to bitter tastes, no one perspective gives us a complete answer. The best view comes from putting multiple perspectives together. You can learn about your house by zooming in on it in Google Earth, but when you see how your home fits into the larger context of city, state, country, and planet, that viewpoint adds something special to your understanding.

iStock.com/NASA/kutay tanir

We'll start by learning more about psychology's main perspectives, along with a little background about their origins. Our approach to these perspectives is consistent with contemporary recommendations for teaching introductory psychology made by the American Psychological Association (e.g., Gurung et al., 2016). Once we understand these perspectives, we'll be in a better position to see how they come together to give us the big picture.

What Is Psychology?

Psychology is the scientific study of the **mind**, which includes thought, emotion, and behavior. A quick look at this textbook's table of contents will show you the variety of approaches to mind that you will encounter, such as the thinking mind (cognitive psychology) and the troubled mind (abnormal psychology).

The word *psychology* is a combination of two Greek words: *psyche* (or *psuche*), or "mind," and *logos*, meaning "the objective study of." Literally translated, therefore, **psychology** means "the objective study of the mind." Today, we define psychology as the scientific study of behavior, mental processes, and brain functions.

The phrase "behavior, mental processes, and brain functions" has undergone several changes over the history of psychology. *Behavior* refers to any action that we can observe. For many years, our definition stopped at this point. The more recent addition of *mental processes* and *brain functions* to our definition was made possible by the development of improved research methods. Early efforts to study mental processes were generally unsatisfactory because they relied on the use of **introspection**, or the personal observation of your own thoughts, feelings, and behaviors. Because it is difficult for others to confirm your introspections, this subjective approach does not lend itself well to the scientific method. If you say that you are in

mind The brain and its activities, including thought, emotion, and behavior.

psychology The scientific study of behavior, mental processes, and brain functions.

introspection A personal observation of your own thoughts, feelings, and behavior.

PSYCHOLOGY AS A HUB SCIENCE

Why Is Psychology a Hub Science?

MOST READERS OF THIS BOOK are not pursuing careers in psychology, so how will this material help you in your chosen career? Psychology is all about people, and nearly all occupations require an understanding of people and their behavior. An architect cannot design a functional space without considering how people respond to being crowded. An attorney cannot cross-examine a witness without an understanding of memory, motivation, emotion, and stress. A teacher cannot encourage students to reach their potential without an understanding of child development and learning. Business leaders and economists cannot predict the movements of markets without understanding the minds making the relevant decisions. The study of psychology, then, provides you with better insight into and understanding of many occupations and fields of study.

You probably have seen applications that allow you to map your friendship networks on social media, with shorter links indicating greater connectivity and larger bubbles indicating more overlapping friendships with another person. Kevin Boyack and his colleagues generated a similar map of the sciences (see Figure 1.1) but used reference lists in journal articles instead of friendship networks (Boyack et al., 2005). The resulting map shows the extent to which each of the sciences are influential and what other sciences they most influence. Boyack and colleagues referred to the most influential sciences as hub sciences. Their analysis shows that psychology is one of the seven major hub sciences, with strong connections to the medical sciences, the social sciences, and education. In the upcoming chapters of this book, we will highlight these connections with examples that are relevant to each particular chapter.

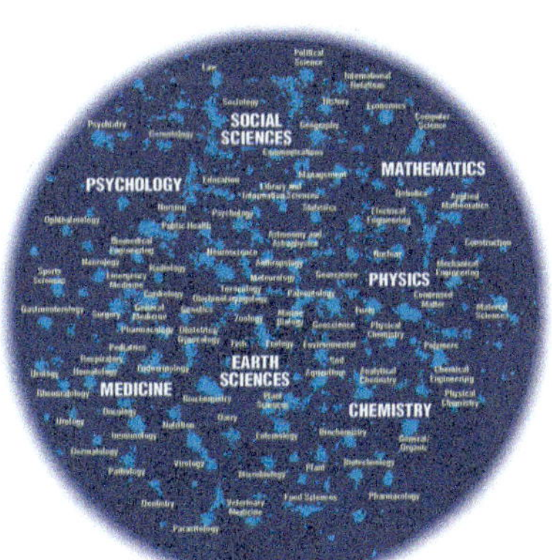

FIGURE **1.1**

Psychology as a Hub Science. This map of science was generated by comparing citations from more than 1 million papers published in more than 7,000 journals since 2000. Psychology appears among the seven major areas of science, indicated in the map by a different font. The other six major areas are social sciences, mathematics, physics, chemistry, earth sciences, and medicine.

Source: Adapted from K. W. Boyack, et al. (2005). "Mapping the Backbone of Science," *Scientometrics, 64*(3), 351–374. With kind permission from Springer Science1Business Media.

love, how can anyone else know whether your observation is accurate? In addition, your mind and behavior are governed by many processes of which you are unaware. Fortunately, innovations in the methods used to investigate brain activity and behavior, such as brain imaging technologies, have allowed psychologists to revisit the question of mental processes and brain functions with greater objectivity and success.

Why Do We Study Psychology?

The empiricist philosophers had a profound influence on the foundations of American political thought—that all of us are created equal. For generations, Europe had been ruled by people who were born into positions of power instead of earning the privilege of leading through hard work and education. If knowledge is not innate or inborn, any of us can learn enough to grow up to be president.

You have plenty of company while taking this course. Between 1.2 and 1.8 million undergraduates in the United States enroll in introductory psychology each year, not to mention the 30% of high school graduates who have already completed a psychology course (American Psychological Association [APA], 2019; Gurung et al., 2016). Increasing numbers of students outside the United States share your journey. Today, the United States is home to only 21 to 24% of the world's psychologists, down sharply from 80% in the 1980s (Takooshian et al., 2016).

What do all of these people hope to gain by studying psychological science? We recognize that introductory psychology is often a required course, but we hope that before too long, you will see many benefits more important than the ability to check a box:

- Among the many advantages of studying psychology is a deeper understanding of ourselves as individuals and of the people around us. One of the major themes of this textbook is the social nature of the human species and the importance of social connectivity to our health and well-being. We can all benefit from improved self-knowledge and social skills.
- Psychology provides many opportunities to improve your critical thinking skills, a necessity in an era of "fake news" and a highly prized skill among employers.
- As you will see in our chapter sections on real-world problems, psychology can make contributions to the understanding of and solutions to many pressing contemporary issues, from pandemics and social justice to poverty and climate change.
- Psychology can answer many questions that we ask out of simple curiosity. People behave in interesting ways, and we often find ourselves asking, "Why?" What questions do you have about human behavior?

Many students mistakenly believe that they don't "need" a course in psychology, because they already have a good understanding of human behavior. We are not saying that your understanding of others is poor, but by studying psychological science, all of us can improve our knowledge. See how many of the common myths listed in Table 1.1 you or others you know believe.

Air Images/Shutterstock.com

Have you ever wondered why people in elevators stand facing the doors and watching the numbers? Psychologists explain this behavior in terms of personal space, or the imaginary bubbles we keep around ourselves that strangers should not invade. When our personal space is violated by necessity, as in a crowded elevator, we cope by pretending nobody else is really there.

TABLE 1.1

Ten Common Myths about Human Behavior

1.	We only use 10% of our brains.
2.	Some people are left-brained while others are right-brained.
3.	Playing Mozart to infants makes them more intelligent.
4.	Hypnosis improves your memory.
5.	Students learn better when instruction matches their individual learning styles.
6.	Lie detector (polygraph) tests are accurate.
7.	Low self-esteem is a major source of personal and societal problems.
8.	The teen years are typically disruptive.
9.	Memory for traumatic events is usually poor.
10.	In romantic relationships, opposites attract.

Lilienfeld, S. O., Lynn, S. J., Ruscio, J., & Beyerstein, B. L. (2009). *50 great myths of popular psychology.* Hoboken, NJ: Wiley-Blackwell.

Where Did Psychology Originate?

Psychology is a relatively young discipline, dating only to the 1870s. However, topics that interest modern psychologists go back much farther in the history of human thought. People living as long ago as 6000 to 5000 BCE in Assyria described their dreams (Restak, 1988). Among these accounts are descriptions of being chased, which are still among the most common dreams that people experience (Nielsen et al., 2003). See Figure 1.2 for common dream themes.

The psychology family tree is a hybrid with two major roots: **philosophy** and the **natural sciences**. Psychologists answer questions traditionally posed by philosophers using scientific research methods of the natural sciences, described in more detail in Chapter 2.

philosophy The discipline that systematically examines basic concepts, including the source of knowledge.

natural sciences Sciences that study the physical and biological events that occur in nature.

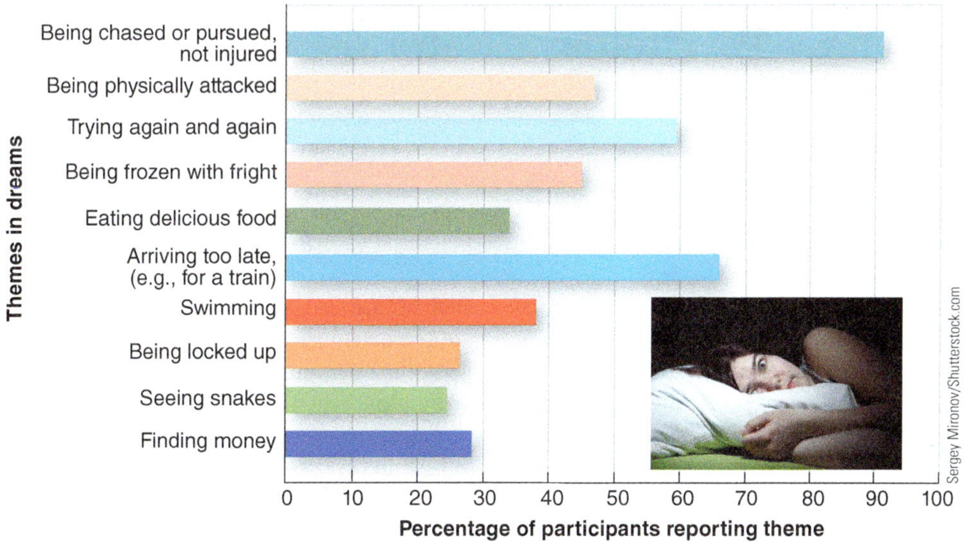

FIGURE 1.2

Many People Report Dreams with the Same Themes. Although we don't understand why we dream about certain things, many people report similar themes in their dreams.
Source: Adapted from T. A. Nielsen, et al. (2003). "The Typical Dreams of Canadian University Students," *Dreaming, 13*, 211–235. doi: 10.1023/B:DREM.0000003144.40929.0b

(a) www.BibleLandPictures.com/Alamy Stock Photo

(b) Georgios Kollidas/Shutterstock.com

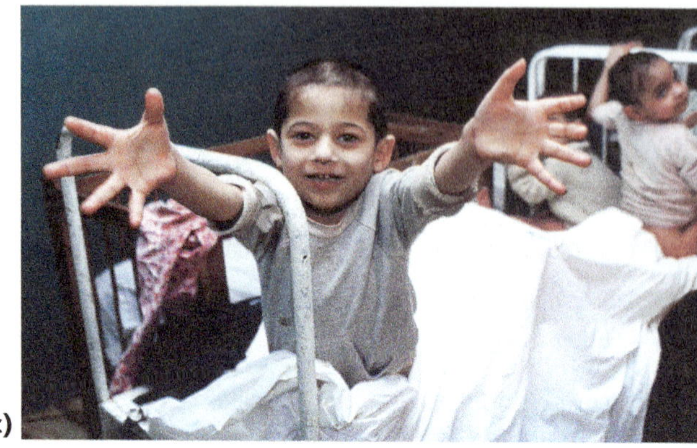

(c) Cynthia Johnson/Hulton Archive/Getty Images

One of the most significant questions shared by philosophy and psychology asks whether the mind is inborn or is formed through experience. (a) Philosophers beginning with Aristotle (384–322 BCE) believed that all knowledge is gained through sensory experience. (b) Beginning in the 17th century, this idea flourished in the British philosophical school of *empiricism*. Empiricists, like John Locke, viewed the mind as a "blank slate" at birth, which then was filled with ideas gained by observing the world. (c) Contemporary psychologists believe that experience interacts with inborn characteristics to shape the mind. Intelligence, for example, is influenced by both genetics and experience. During the 1970s, Romanian orphans adopted at young ages recovered from the effects of their seriously deprived social circumstances, but those who endured years of deprivation had more severe cognitive deficits (Ames, 1997).

New York Public Library/Science Source

Ancient people might have attempted to cure headaches, seizures, or psychological disorders by drilling holes in the skull. Bone growth around the hole indicates that some patients survived the procedure. Surprisingly, some people today engage in DIY trepanation, a practice that obviously concerns the medical community ("Doctors warn of the dangers of trepanning," 2000).

What Are Psychology's Philosophical Roots?

Philosophers and psychologists share an interest in questions regarding the nature of the self, the effects of early experience, the existence of free will, and the origin of knowledge. Both disciplines consider the relative balance of biological factors (nature) and environmental factors (nurture) in the resulting human behavior. Both attempt to determine the relationships between self-interest and community welfare, between body and mind, and between humans and other species with which we share the planet. Although we typically consider questions of the unconscious mind and abnormal behavior to be the realm of the psychologist, philosophers investigated these issues thousands of years before the first psychologist was born.

What Are Psychology's Natural Sciences Roots?

While philosophers tackled these difficult questions, physicians were laying the foundation of our knowledge of the brain and nervous system, discussed in detail in Chapter 4. During this pursuit, physicians helped develop the scientific methods that would become central to psychology and previewed the application of scientific knowledge to the improvement of individual well-being.

Beginning in the 17th and 18th centuries, scientists armed with new technologies, including the light microscope (see • Figure 1.3), made important discoveries that established the mind as physical rather than magical. For example, they demonstrated that a single sensory nerve carried one type of information instead of multiple types. You might have already duplicated this research yourself while rubbing your sleepy eyes—you see a flash of light. The nerves serving the retina of the eye do not know how to process information about touch or pressure. When stimulated, they are capable of only one type of message—light. Hermann von Helmholtz (1821–1894) asked his participants to push a button as soon as they felt a touch. When a thigh was touched, participants reacted faster than when a toe was touched. Because

FIGURE 1.3

Microscopes Changed the World of Science. This light microscope was used by Antonie van Leeuwenhoek to discover red blood cells in 1676. Microscopes opened a new world to scientists interested in living things.

A = Screw for adjusting the height of the object being examined

B = Metal plate serving as the body

C = Skewer to impale the object and rotate it

D = Lens, which was spherical

the toe is farther from the brain than the thigh, signals from the toe required more time to reach the brain. These types of discoveries convinced scientists that the mind was not supernatural and could be studied scientifically.

The Two Disciplines Merge to Create a New Science

Philosophers began to incorporate physiological and psychological concepts into their work, and natural scientists began to explore the questions asked by philosophers. The gradual merger of these approaches resulted in a series of experiments that looked increasingly like contemporary psychology. Gustav Fechner (1801–1889) was curious to know how soft a sound a person could hear. He randomly presented sounds of different intensities to which a participant would respond “yes” or “no.” When the “yes” responses passed 50%, or better than chance, Fechner concluded that the sound was within the range that the human ear could detect (see Chapter 5). Although Fechner’s research seems very similar to von Helmholtz’s, note the importance of “mental processes” in Fechner’s work, as opposed to the simple measurement of physiology in von Helmholtz’s experiment. The stage was set for a modern science of psychology.

The work of Hermann von Helmholtz (1821–1894) on reaction time helped establish the mind as something that could be studied scientifically.

SUMMARY 1.1 Highlights in the Philosophical and Scientific Roots of Psychology

	Person or group	Things to remember
	Ancient Greek philosophers	Observations can be accounted for by natural, not supernatural, explanations.
	British empiricists	Knowledge is the result of experience.
	Ancient physicians	The brain is the source of the mind.
	17th- and 18th-century natural scientists	Discoveries about sensation and movement showed that the mind was physical.
	Hermann von Helmholtz	Studies of reaction time reinforced the idea of the mind as physical.

Credits: Top row—www.BibleLandPictures.com/Alamy Stock Photo; Second row—Georgios Kollidas/Shutterstock.com; Third row—New York Public Library/Science Source; Fourth row—Mary Evans Picture Library/The Image Works; inset: World History/Topham/The Image Works; Bottom row—bilwissedition Ltd. & Co. KG/Alamy Stock Photo.

How Did the Science of Psychology Begin?

As psychology developed from the gradual merger of philosophical questions and scientific reasoning, the young discipline struggled to determine which questions and methods were best suited to its goals. Lively debates arose among psychologists who helped to shape the field.

Wilhelm Wundt and Structuralism

The credit for being the very first psychologist goes to Wilhelm Wundt (1832–1920), a former research assistant to von Helmholtz, who conducted the first documented psychological experiment in 1879. This landmark experiment was a simple test of reaction time: How quickly after hearing a ball drop onto a platform could a person respond by striking a telegraph key?

INTERFOTO/Alamy Stock Photo

Wilhelm Wundt (1832–1920), seated in this photo, is considered the first experimental psychologist.

structuralism An approach in which the mind is broken into the smallest elements of mental experience.

Gestalt psychology An approach that saw experience as being different from the sum of its elements.

functionalism An approach that saw behavior as purposeful and contributing to survival.

CONNECTING TO RESEARCH

The First Official Psychology Experiment

WE HAVE GIVEN CREDIT to Wilhelm Wundt for conducting the first experiments in psychology. What did those crucial first experiments look like?

Wundt's experiments reflected both his interests in consciousness and his training as a medical doctor. He was aware of methods that were used by researchers in physiology, such as the reaction-time measures pioneered by F. C. Donders in the Netherlands, and he sought to apply these methods to measure psychological processes such as attention and decision making (Danziger & Ballantyne, 1997).

The Questions: Is it possible to "time" mental processes? Are simple reaction times different from reaction times involving choices?

METHODS

Wundt's methods involved two sets of apparatus: one that would deliver a stimulus precisely to a participant, and a second that would measure and record the participant's responses. His imposing-looking brass instruments used to carry out these tasks were displayed to an admiring public at the 1893 Chicago World's Fair.

The first experiments carried out by Wundt involved the presentation of stimuli, such as the sound of a ball dropped onto a platform, and measurements of reaction time, as indicated by the participant pressing a telegraph key. In addition to these simple reaction-time experiments, Wundt asked participants to make decisions: When you see this light, press the button on the left, but if you see that light, press the button on the right.

ETHICS

As you continue reading your textbook, you will review a number of experiments like this one. Many will highlight important ethical considerations regarding the treatment of participants. These ethical concerns will be reviewed in more detail in Chapter 2, but in the meantime, Wundt's experiment appears to have posed little risk to his participants. After you consider the criteria for conducting ethical research outlined in Chapter 2, however, you might want to return to this description and see if you agree with our assessment or not.

RESULTS

Wundt viewed reaction time as "mental chronometry" (Hergenhahn & Henley, 2013, p. 255). In other words, he believed that reaction time provided a measure of the amount of mental processing required to carry out a task. As his tasks became more complex, reaction time increased accordingly.

CONCLUSIONS

As mentioned earlier in this chapter, Wundt's mentor, Hermann von Helmholtz, had performed a number of experiments similar to those performed by Wundt. Von Helmholtz touched the participant on the thigh and toe and discovered that the participant pushed a button faster in response to the thigh touch than the toe touch. What makes von Helmholtz's demonstration a physiological experiment and Wundt's a psychology experiment?

Part of the answer is the interpretation that each scientist made of his results. For von Helmholtz, differences in reaction time in these two instances represented the effects of the speed of conduction of neural signaling. Because the toe is farther from the brain than the thigh is, messages from the toe take more time to reach the brain. Wundt's simple reaction-time experiments were not that different, but his experiments on choice were more clearly psychological. As decisions became more complex, reaction time increased. ■

Bettmann/Contributor/Getty Images

Max Wertheimer (1880–1943) was one of the founders of Gestalt psychology. Please note that there is no connection between the Gestalt psychology of Wertheimer, Köhler, and Koffka, and the later similarly named Gestalt approach to therapy.

Wundt saw mental experience as a hierarchy. The mind constructs an overall perception (the food I'm eating tastes good) out of building blocks made up of separate sensations, such as taste and vision, and emotional responses. One of Wundt's students, Edward Titchener (1867–1923), expanded on Wundt's views to establish a theory of **structuralism**, in which the mind could be broken down into the smallest elements of mental experience. Titchener's approach to psychology paralleled the general trends in the physical sciences of his day, such as efforts in chemistry to break molecules into elements and attempts by physicists to describe matter at the level of the atom.

Gestalt Psychology

The structuralists' effort to break behavior into its essential elements was rejected by a group of early 20th-century German psychologists, including Kurt Koffka, Max Wertheimer, and Wolfgang Köhler, who founded **Gestalt psychology**. *Gestalt*, although difficult to translate into English, basically means "form" or "whole." The Gestalt psychologists believed that breaking a "whole" perception into its building blocks, as advocated by the structuralists, would result in the loss of important psychological information. ● Figure 1.4 demonstrates the importance of context to our interpretation of visual information. The structuralists would have a difficult time explaining why the same visual building blocks could lead to such different conclusions.

William James and Functionalism

While the structuralists and Gestalt psychologists continued their debate, a new type of psychology emerged, partly in response to the publication of Charles Darwin's *The Origin of Species* in 1859 and *The Descent of Man* in 1871. **Functionalism** viewed behavior as purposeful because it led to survival. Instead of restricting themselves to exploring the structure of the mind, functionalists were more interested in why behavior and mental processes worked in a particular way.

Functionalism's chief proponent was William James (1842–1910), whose textbook, *Principles of Psychology* (1890), dominated psychology for 50 years. There are few topics in psychology that James did not address in his book, and many of his ideas sound modern. For example, he

Mary Evans Picture Library/The Image Works

William James (1842–1910) proposed *functionalism*, an approach to the mind that viewed behavior as purposeful.

Courtesy of the Wellesley College Archives

Mary Whiton Calkins (1863–1930) was a student of William James at Harvard University, although she could not officially register because of her gender. She studied memory and the self and served as president of the American Psychological Association in 1905.

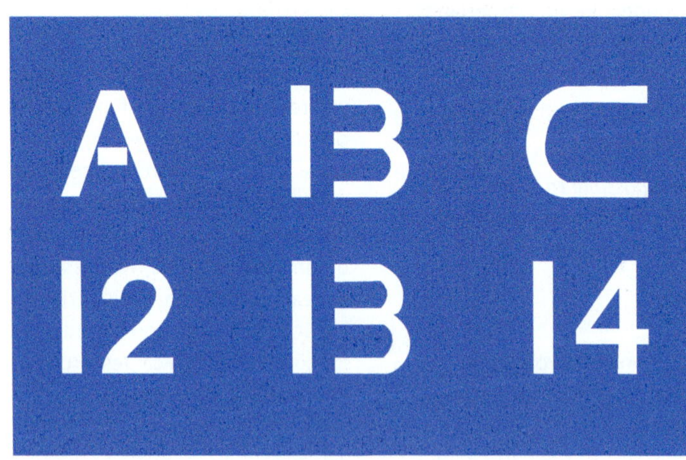

FIGURE **1.4**

Gestalt Psychologists Challenged Structuralism. Participants usually see the middle figure as a B when instructed to look at the first row, but see a 13 when instructed to read the second row, even though the images are exactly the same. Structuralists, who believed that experiences could be reduced to small building blocks, would have difficulty explaining these results. In contrast, Gestalt psychologists, who emphasized the role of context or the "whole" in perception, would have no problem.

coined the term *stream of consciousness* to describe the flow of ideas that people experience while awake. Throughout his discussions of mental processes and behavior, James emphasized the role of evolution. If we enjoy ice cream, it might be because eating sweet, high-fat foods enhanced survival for our ancestors, for whom famine was more of a problem than obesity.

It is difficult to overestimate the impact of James on psychology. Structuralism came and went, but all contemporary psychologists are functionalists at heart. As described by two psychology historians, "As a systematic point of view, functionalism was an overwhelming success, but largely because of this success it is no longer a distinct school of psychology. It was absorbed into the mainstream psychology. No happier fate could await any psychological point of view" (Chaplin & Krawiec, 1979, p. 53).

Clinical Roots: Freud and the Humanistic Psychologists

When a case of capital punishment is discussed, we often hear about the prisoner's terrible childhood from one side of the argument and the need to protect society from further misdeeds by this person from the other side. Where would the Freudians and humanistic psychologists line up in this debate?

The history of efforts to aid those with psychological disorders has not always been enlightened. With the exception of occasional bursts of insight from the ancient Egyptians and Greeks, the most common view of psychological disorders over the course of history has been the supernatural approach. According to this view, psychological disorders resulted from the actions of evil spirits or other external, magical forces, and associated "treatments" were often harsh. Between the 17th and the 19th centuries, supernatural explanations for psychological disorders began to give way to two scientific approaches: a medical model and a psychological model. The medical model of psychological disorders emphasized physical causes of abnormal behavior and medical treatments, such as medication. The psychological model suggested that abnormal behavior can result from traumatic life experiences, leading to fear, anxiety, and other counterproductive emotional responses. Psychological treatments take many forms, from offering support to applying cognitive and behavioral methods to help people think and problem-solve in new ways. As Chapters 14 and 15 will explain, contemporary psychologists typically combine medical and psychological approaches to understand disorders and develop effective treatments. For example, we know that feeling depressed has both physical components (changes in the activity of chemical messengers in the brain) and experiential components (exposure to stressful situations). Treatment for depression often combines medication with efforts to change the way a person thinks about situations.

Everett Collection Inc/Alamy Stock Photo

Prior to advances in psychological science, people with psychological disorders were subjected to bizarre "treatments," such as this 18th-century spinning device intended to calm patients.

Sigmund Freud Sigmund Freud (1856–1939) built a bridge from his medical training as a physician to his belief in the impact of life experiences on behavior. His psychodynamic theory and its applications to the treatment of psychological disorders dominated much of psychological thinking for the first half of the 20th century. Freud's ideas about the existence of the unconscious mind, the development of sexuality, dream analysis, and psychological roots of abnormal behavior influenced not just psychology, but also culture. He nearly single-handedly founded the study of personality in psychology, a topic explored more fully in Chapter 12. He developed the techniques of psychoanalysis for treating mental disorders, which are discussed in Chapter 15. He popularized the use of psychological principles for explaining everyday behavior, and his theories are as likely to be covered in an English literature course as in a psychology course.

Our enthusiasm for Freud is tempered by a number of valid concerns. Freud's theories do not always lend themselves to experimentation, an essential requirement for any scientific theory as discussed further in Chapter 2. For example, how could you design an experiment to test whether dreaming

akg-images/Newscom

The work of Sigmund Freud (1856–1939) on consciousness, sexuality, abnormal behavior, and psychotherapy played a dominant role in psychology during the first half of the 20th century.

Courtesy of the Moorland-Spingarn Research Center, Howard University Archives

In 1920, Francis Cecil Sumner (1895–1954) became the first African American to receive a doctorate in psychology for his work on psychoanalysis. Sumner's later work focused on religion and racism.

humanistic psychology An approach that saw people as inherently good and motivated to learn and improve.

about a house really means that you're thinking about yourself (Freud, 1913)? Although psychoanalysis is still used as a therapy technique, it is rarely conducted in the strict Freudian manner. Other techniques, discussed in Chapter 15, exceed psychoanalysis in effectiveness and popularity among contemporary therapists.

Humanistic Psychology By the 1960s, American psychology was dominated by behaviorism (discussed in a later section of this chapter) on one side and Freud's theories on the other. Structuralism had fallen into disfavor, and functionalism and Gestalt psychology were no longer distinct schools of thought. Just as other aspects of American culture at this time began to feature rebelliousness against current ways of thinking, some psychologists began to push against the restrictions of psychodynamic theory. Many of these disenchanted psychologists had been trained in psychoanalysis but were not seeing the results they desired. This dissatisfaction with prevailing views led these psychologists to propose new ways of thinking about the human mind through an approach known as **humanistic psychology**. Humanistic psychology was referred to as a "third force," separate from the prevailing behaviorist and psychodynamic theories.

One area of disagreement between the humanistic psychologists and Freud related to the question of basic human nature as good or evil. Like James, Freud was heavily influenced by Charles Darwin, whose work stimulated his decision to study medicine. Freud believed that human behavior was on a continuum with animal behavior, and that society had a civilizing function on the otherwise selfish and aggressive human. In contrast, the humanistic psychologists extended the philosophy of Jean-Jacques Rousseau and other 18th-century Romantic philosophers into a belief that people are innately good, are motivated to improve themselves, and behave badly only when corrupted by society.

This more positive view of human nature led the humanistic psychologists to ask novel questions. Abraham Maslow (1908–1970) was curious about what made a person "good." As Chapter

EXPERIENCING PSYCHOLOGY

Testing Reaction Time

YOU HAVE READ about a number of reaction-time experiments in this chapter, including those conducted by Hermann von Helmholtz and Wilhelm Wundt. It is possible to conduct similar experiments without the brass equipment used by these early researchers.

This exercise, developed by Dr. Erik Chudler of the University of Washington, is designed to measure your reaction time to a visual stimulus. All you need is a partner and a simple footlong ruler or yardstick. Hold the ruler vertically, with the highest numbers at the top, and ask your partner to place a hand at the bottom of the ruler without touching it. Tell your partner that you will drop the ruler sometime in the next 5 seconds and to grab the ruler as quickly as possible and hold it. Note the number at the top of the person's hand after the ruler is caught,

Number on ruler at top of person's hand	Reaction time
2 in. (about 5 cm)	0.10 s (100 ms)
4 in. (about 10 cm)	0.14 s (140 ms)
6 in. (about 15 cm)	0.17 s (170 ms)
8 in. (about 20 cm)	0.20 s (200 ms)
10 in. (about 25.5 cm)	0.23 s (230 ms)
12 in. (about 30.5 cm)	0.25 s (250 ms)
17 in. (about 43 cm)	0.30 s (300 ms)
24 in. (about 61 cm)	0.35 s (350 ms)
31 in. (about 79 cm)	0.40 s (400 ms)
39 in. (about 99 cm)	0.45 s (450 ms)
48 in. (about 123 cm)	0.50 s (500 ms)
69 in. (about 175 cm)	0.60 s (600 ms)

16 will show, Maslow's emphasis on what is good about people, as opposed to Freud's focus on what goes wrong with people, reemerged in the form of contemporary positive psychology.

Humanistic psychologists not only disagreed with Freud about the nature of human beings, but also rebelled against Freudian approaches to treatment. As described in more detail in Chapter 15, the humanistic therapist Carl Rogers (1902–1987) developed a new approach called *client-centered therapy*. In this type of therapy, the people receiving treatment are called *clients* rather than the more medical term, *patients*, reflecting their equal standing with the therapist and their active role in the therapy process. Humanistic approaches to therapy have also influenced best practices in communication, group process, parenting, and politics. The emphasis on active listening and the use of "I hear what you're saying" reflections have become nearly cliché in courses of leadership training and interpersonal communication. Advice to parents to provide unconditional love to their children is a direct application of humanistic beliefs, discussed in more detail in Chapter 11. Finally, humanistic psychology continues to flavor our political and social domains. When issues such as capital punishment arise, the humanistic contention that there are no bad people, just bad societies that fail people, typically appears as part of the debate.

Bettmann/Contributor/Getty Images

Abraham Maslow (1908–1970) contributed a theory of motivation and ideas about exceptional people to the growing humanistic psychology movement.

The Behaviorists and the Cognitive Revolution

Beginning at the dawn of the 20th century, the concepts of "mental processes" and "brain function" in our definition of psychology took a back seat to observable behavior for the better part of the next 50 years. Psychologists following the approach of **behaviorism** concentrated on observable, measurable behaviors instead. As part of their effort to measure behavior carefully, many behaviorists restricted their research to studies using animals. Armed with Darwin's evidence linking humans to animals, the behaviorists comfortably drew parallels between their observations of animals and their assumptions about human behavior. In particular, behaviorists were fascinated by learning, which is examined in depth in Chapter 8.

behaviorism An approach that features the study and careful measurement of observable behaviors.

and use this chart to convert your results to reaction time. In other words, if the number above the participant's hand is 8, record 0.20 seconds or 200 ms (a millisecond is one one-thousandth of a second).

Test your participant five times and average the response times. Wundt eventually discarded reaction time as a measure because he became so frustrated with the variability that he observed among participants and across tasks (Hergenhahn & Henley, 2013), but you can have some fun exploring these same sources of variability. Are you faster than your friends? Try testing people who are older than you. Are they faster or slower? Do your participants improve with practice? What happens to your reaction time if you dim the lights?

Roger Freberg

Measuring the spot where a person catches a falling ruler gives you a rough estimate of that individual's reaction time to a visual stimulus.

Humanistic therapists, like Carl Rogers (1902–1987), often rebelled against Freudian approaches to therapy. For example, Rogers (in the white shirt leading a group therapy session) referred to people as *clients* rather than *patients*, the term that Freud used.

Michael Rougier/Contributor/The LIFE Picture Collection/Getty Images

Ivan Petrovich Pavlov (1849–1936) had a particularly significant impact on behaviorism and psychology. While studying digestion in dogs, he realized that the dogs' salivation in response to the arrival of the handler or to being harnessed for an experiment, rather than just to the food itself, indicated that the dogs had associated, or linked, these signals with the arrival of food. The dogs' ability to use this learned association to anticipate important future events was a remarkable advantage in terms of survival. This type of learning is now called *classical conditioning* and will be covered in detail in Chapter 8.

Psychology textbooks would spend little time on Pavlov if his research applied only to salivating dogs. Although classical conditioning occurs in rather primitive organisms, including fruit flies, snails, and slugs, it also occurs quite frequently in humans. Many of our emotional responses associated with environmental cues are the result of this type of learning. If you feel especially anxious prior to taking an exam, you can thank classical conditioning. If you are repulsed by the idea of eating a food that you once consumed just before becoming ill, this is again a likely result of classical conditioning.

The Freudians and humanistic psychologists had conflicting views on human nature, with the Freudians believing that we are naturally selfish and aggressive and the humanistic psychologists believing that we are naturally good. These philosophical differences continue to color our discussions of topics: Is a criminal a "bad" person who was never properly socialized or a "good" person who was corrupted?

Bill Fritsch/Getty Images

John B. Watson (1878–1958) began experimenting with learning in rats and independently came to many of the same conclusions as Pavlov. Watson echoed the blank-slate approach of the British empiricist philosophers in his emphasis on the role of experience in forming human behavior. Later in his career, Watson applied his understanding of behavior to the budding American advertising industry. By 1930, he was earning $70,000 per year as an advertising executive—an astronomical salary for the time, much higher than the $3,000 per year he earned as a professor. After discovering that blindfolded participants couldn't tell the difference between brands of cigarettes, Watson

Sovfoto/Contributor/Universal Images Group/Getty Images

Mark Stivers

While studying digestion, Ivan Petrovich Pavlov (1849–1936) realized that his dogs could learn that certain signals meant food was on the way.

concluded that to be successful, a product must be associated with an appealing image. The advertising industry was never the same, and today's advertisers continue to apply Watson's principles.

Watson's legacy in psychology was enormous. He restricted psychology to the study of observable behavior. As we will see in Chapter 2 and throughout this text, even psychologists who are interested in internal events, like the visual recognition of an object, seek related observable behaviors, such as brain images or reaction time.

Like Pavlov, Watson approached psychology with a focus on the relationships between environmental cues and behavior. Other behaviorists were more interested in the effects of consequences on behavior, an idea that was derived from basic functionalism. Edward Thorndike (1874–1949) proposed the *law of effect*, which suggested that behaviors followed by pleasant or helpful outcomes would be more likely

AP Images/NOOR KHAN

Classical conditioning helps us understand the links that we make between environmental cues and our emotions. If a soldier associated the smell of diesel fuel with traumatic experiences, smelling diesel fuel at a gas station back home could trigger distress.

JHU Sheridan Libraries/Gado/Contributor/Archive Photos/Getty Images

Cover Images/Newscom

John B. Watson (left, 1878–1958) was a strong believer in the blank-slate approach of the earlier empiricist philosophers. After working as a psychology professor, he applied his knowledge of human behavior to advertising with great success. Watson believed that a product would sell better if it were paired with an appealing image. His ideas are still used by advertisers today. For instance, celebrity endorsements, like Ed Sheeran's for Heinz ketchup, continue to be a popular way to promote products.

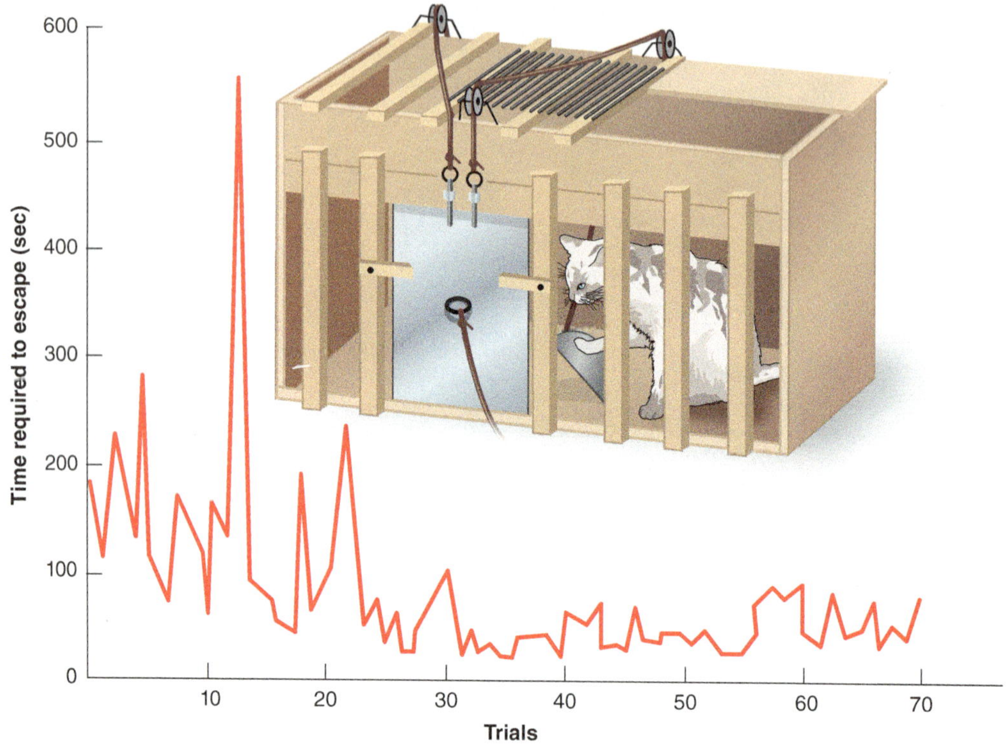

FIGURE **1.5**

Thorndike's Law of Effect Emerged from Observations of Cats. If you own a cat, you probably know that cats don't like to be enclosed in boxes. Edward Thorndike (1874–1949) studied the escape strategies of a cat to build his law of effect.

Nina Leen/The LIFE Picture Collection/Getty Images

B. F. Skinner (1904–1990), shown here with the apparatus that bears his name—the Skinner box—was interested in the effects of reward and punishment on future behavior.

to occur in the future, whereas behaviors followed by unpleasant or harmful outcomes would be less likely to occur. He based his law on observations of cats' behavior in a puzzle box he had constructed (see ● Figure 1.5). To escape the box, a cat was required to complete a sequence of behaviors. Through trial-and-error learning, the cat would escape faster and faster on successive trials. In other words, the cat repeated effective behaviors and abandoned ineffective ones.

Like Thorndike, B. F. Skinner (1904–1990) was interested in the effects of consequences on how frequently behaviors were performed. Skinner shared Watson's belief that psychology did not benefit from consideration of consciousness or internal mental states (see ● Figure 1.6). He believed that inner, private states such as thinking and feeling existed, but he viewed them as behaviors that followed the same rules as public behaviors, like driving a car (Jensen & Burgess, 1997). He not only reduced his study of behavior to the actions of rats and pigeons in adapted cages that came to be known as *Skinner boxes*, but he also was comfortable generalizing from the behavior of rats and pigeons to complex human behaviors. Despite its strong focus on a limited set of animals and situations, Skinner's behaviorism has provided a wealth of beneficial applications. Smokers attempting to quit, doctors and nurses engaging in self-paced continuing education courses, and children receiving treatment for autism spectrum disorder are all likely to be benefiting from Skinner's efforts.

By the 1950s, the behaviorists' lack of interest in mental states and activity was challenged by scientists from diverse fields, including linguistics and computer science, leading to a cognitive revolution. Cognition covers the private and internal mental processes that the behaviorists avoided studying—information processing, thinking, reasoning, and problem solving. Ulric Neisser (1928–2012) gave the new field its name in his 1967 book, *Cognitive Psychology*.

Breakthroughs in computer technology allowed these new cognitive psychologists to use mathematical and computer models to illuminate the mental processes leading

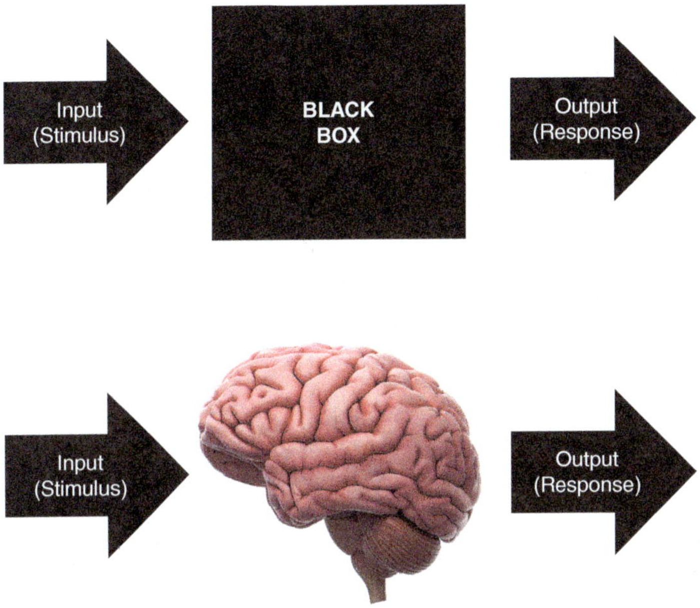

Eraxion/iStock/Getty Images

FIGURE **1.6**

Behaviorism Set the Stage for Behavioral Neuroscience. Strict behaviorists often referred to a "black box" model, in which stimuli enter and responses exit, but you don't need to know much about what the box is doing to the data. When psychologists began substituting what they learned about the brain for the inner workings of the black box, this led to the development of the biological psychology perspective, also known as *behavioral neuroscience*.

NARA/Science Source

Computers were named after the job title of the women who did most computation tasks before the machines were invented, and who continued to operate them. Although these early computers were less powerful than your cell phone (not to mention more expensive), their operation gave psychologists new ideas about how the mind might process information.

to observable behaviors. Alan Newell (1927–1992) and Herbert Simon (1916–2001) wrote groundbreaking artificial intelligence programs using human information processing as their model. By the 1980s, most university psychology departments were offering courses in cognition. By the 1990s, collaborations between cognitive and biological psychologists led to a new field of cognitive neuroscience, which seeks to identify brain structures and functions involved in processing information. Chapter 10 will explore the contributions of cognitive psychologists in more detail.

Courtesy of Cornell University

Ulric Neisser (1928–2012) contributed the term *cognition* to the emerging field that studied information processing, thinking, reasoning, and problem solving.

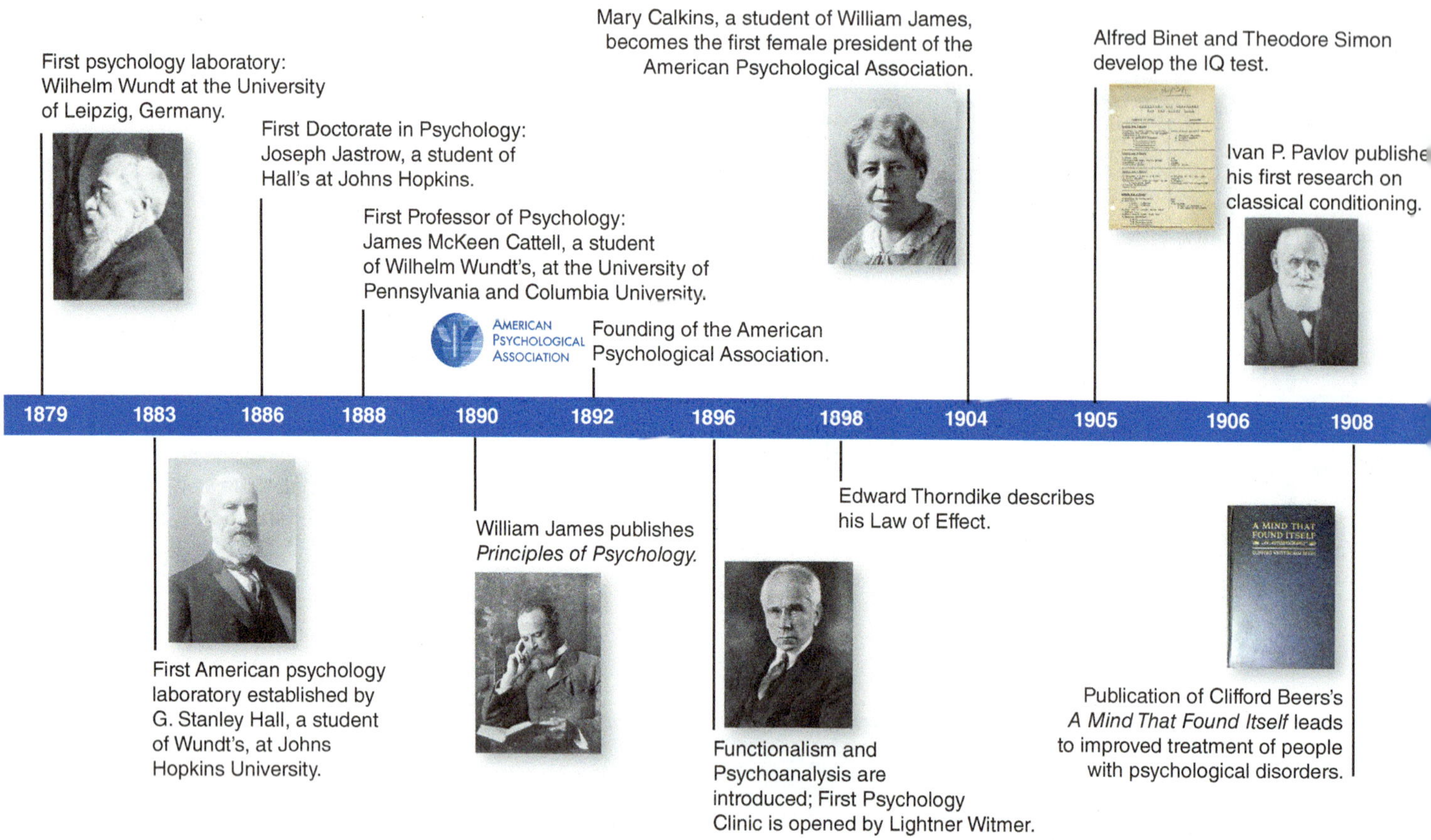

FIGURE 1.7

Milestones in the History of Psychology.

INTERFOTO/Personalities/Alamy; LOC/Science Source; The APA logo is a trademark of the American Psychological Association. Reproduced with permission. No further reproduction or distribution is permitted without written permission from the American Psychological Association; Mary Evans Picture Library/The Image Works; Elias Goldensky/From the Collections of the University of Pennsylvania Archives; U.S. National Library of Medicine; Courtesy of the Wellesley College Archives; INTERFOTO/Alamy Stock Photo, Courtesy Special Collections & Archives, Truman State University; Library of Congress Prints and Photographs Division [LC-USZ62-117329]; Reproduced with permission of Mental Health America.

SUMMARY 1.2 Pioneering Approaches to Psychology

	Foundation of psychology	Things to remember
Wilhelm Wundt (1832–1920) 	Structuralism	Behavior can be broken down into its components.
Max Wertheimer (1880–1943) 	Gestalt psychology	Breaking behavior into components loses meaning.

INTERFOTO/Alamy Stock Photo; Bettmann/Contributor/Getty Images

on publishes
s the Behaviorist

1920

First African-American Doctorate in Psychology: Francis Cecil Sumner, a student of G. Stanley Hall's, at Clark University.

1921

Gestalt journal is
hed in Germany.

1928

Jean Piaget publishes *Judgment and Reasoning in the Child.*

1929

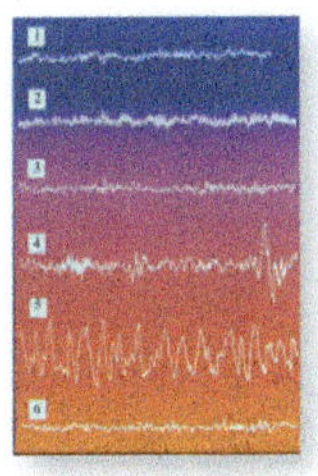

Hans Berger invents the electroencephalogram (EEG), still used today to study brain activity.

1938

B. F. Skinner's *The Behavior of Organisms* contributes to the dominance of behaviorism.

1942

Carl Rogers introduces Humanistic approaches to therapy.

1949

The Boulder Conference establishes the scientist-practioner model of clinical psychology.

1954

Gordon Allport, a social psychologist, publishes *The Nature of Prejudice.* Wilder Penfield publishes the results of his observations of patients undergoing surgery for epilepsy.

1956

George Miller's "The Magical Number Seven, Plus or Minus Two" stimulates work in Cognitive Psychology.

1959

Noam Chomsky's criticism of Skinner's *Verbal Behavior* also contributes to the cognitive revolution.

1976

Richard Dawkins's *The Selfish Gene* popularizes Evolutionary Psychology.

JHU Sheridan Libraries/Gado/Contributor/Archive Photos/Getty Images; Ferdinand Hamburger Archives, Sheridan Libraries, Johns Hopkins University; Courtesy of the Moorland-Spingarn Research Center, Howard University Archives; Farrell Grehan/Historical/Corbis; VEM/Science Source; Nina Leen/Getty Images; Michael Rougier/Getty Images; Jon Roemer LLC; from "The Magical Number Seven, Plus or Minus Two: Some Limits on Our Capacity for Processing Information," by G. A. Miller, *Psychological Review, 63*(2), 1956, 81–97. doi: 10.1037/h0043158; Dennis Van Tine/Retna Ltd./Corbis; Nina Leen/The LIFE Picture Collection/Getty Images; Jon Roemer Photography; Patrick Grehan/Contributor/Corbis Historical/Getty Images; Luis Gutierrez/NortePhoto.com/Alamy Stock Photo; Michael Rougier/Contributor/The LIFE Picture Collection/Getty Images

SUMMARY 1.2 *(Continued)*

	Foundation of psychology	Things to remember
William James (1842–1910) 	Functionalism	Behavior is purposeful and contributes to survival.
Sigmund Freud (1856–1939) 	Psychodynamic theory	Ideas about the unconscious mind, the role of experience in abnormal behavior, and new approaches to therapy laid a foundation for later study in personality and therapy.

SUMMARY 1.2 *(Continued)*

	Foundation of psychology	Things to remember
Abraham Maslow (1908–1970) 	Humanistic psychology	People are naturally good and are motivated to improve.
Ivan Petrovich Pavlov (1849–1936) 	Behaviorism	Experience is the primary source of behavior.
Ulric Neisser (1928–2012) 	Cognitive revolution	Private mental processing can be studied scientifically.

Credits: Top row—Mary Evans Picture Library/The Image Works; Second row—akg-images/Newscom; Third row—Courtesy of Cornell University; Fourth row—Sovfoto/Contributor/Universal Images Group/Getty Images; Fifth row—Bettmann/Contributor/Getty Images.

What Are Psychological Perspectives?

William James, the Freudians, and the behaviorists all tried to answer psychological questions with a comprehensive "big theory" approach. However, it is difficult to build a big theory without a large body of experimental data, and psychology was still a young science. To fill this gap, psychological scientists began to build a database by specializing in more specific points of view, or perspectives. By focusing on one part of the discipline, as opposed to trying to answer everything at once, psychologists began to gain an in-depth understanding of at least one aspect of mind at a time.

By the second half of the 20th century, most psychologists were examining psychological phenomena from one of a handful of perspectives. The use of different perspectives does not imply disagreement or conflict. In most cases, the use of each perspective depended on specialized expertise and methods, so different fields of psychology became characterized by their distinct theories and methods. For example, understanding how a child learns a new vocabulary word would be investigated using different theories and methods by the biological, developmental, cognitive, social, or behavioral psychologist.

biological psychology The psychological perspective that focuses on the relationships between mind and behavior, as well as their underlying biological processes, including genetics, biochemistry, anatomy, and physiology; also known as *behavioral neuroscience*.

evolutionary psychology A psychological perspective that investigates how physical structure and behavior have been shaped by their contributions to survival and reproduction.

Reflecting the traditional divisions of the field, it is common today for psychologists to refer to themselves as "social psychologists," "developmental psychologists," and so on, indicating their area of specialization and interest. Psychology departments of universities often continue this organization, and students applying to graduate school in psychology might specialize in one particular area, like choosing an undergraduate major.

What Are the Five Perspectives of Psychology?

The need to consider major perspectives in psychology was reinforced in a report titled "Strengthening the Common Core of the Introductory Psychology Course," published in 2014 by the American Psychological Association (Gurung et al., 2014). We have already seen how the various perspectives might address the question of why some children don't like broccoli. To further illustrate the distinctions among some of the main perspectives, outlined in Figure 1.8, we will consider how each might approach the question of human memory, discussed in detail in Chapter 9.

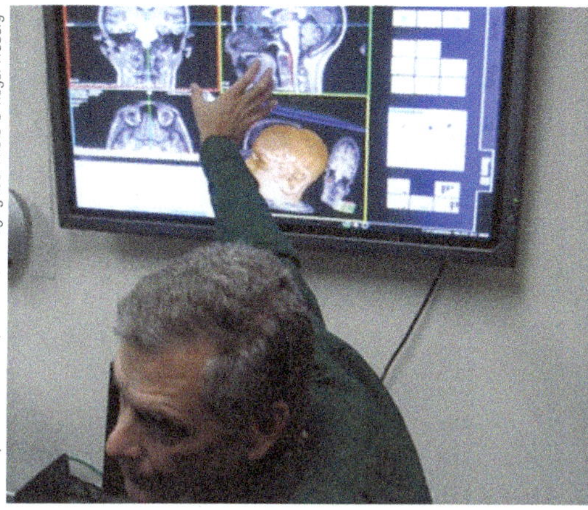

Courtesy of Scott Grafton, UCSB Brain Imaging Lab. Photo © Roger Freberg

Biological psychologists explore the relationships among mind, behavior, and their underlying biological processes. They often use technology such as functional magnetic resonance imaging (fMRI). Scott Grafton of the University of California, Santa Barbara, is pointing out the features of the brain of one of the authors of this book.

Biological psychology, also called *behavioral neuroscience*, focuses on the reciprocal relationships between mind and behavior and their underlying biological processes, including genetics, biochemistry, anatomy, and physiology. In other words, biological psychologists are interested in the physical mechanisms associated with behavior and mental processes. In addition to the basic behavioral genetics presented in Chapter 3 and the biological psychology presented in Chapter 4, this perspective is emphasized in Chapter 5 (sensation and perception), Chapter 6 (consciousness), and Chapter 7 (motivation and emotion). As Chapter 4 will show, technological advances beginning in the 1970s, especially new methods for observing brain activity, initiated an explosion of knowledge about the connections between brain and behavior. Using these new technologies, biological psychologists have approached the question of storage and retrieval of memories in many ways, ranging from observing changes in communication between nerve cells in slugs to investigating the effects of stress hormones on the ability to form memories.

A branch of the biological perspective, **evolutionary psychology**, attempts to answer the question of how our physical structure and behavior have been shaped by their contributions to our species' survival. This perspective should sound familiar—it is a modern extension of

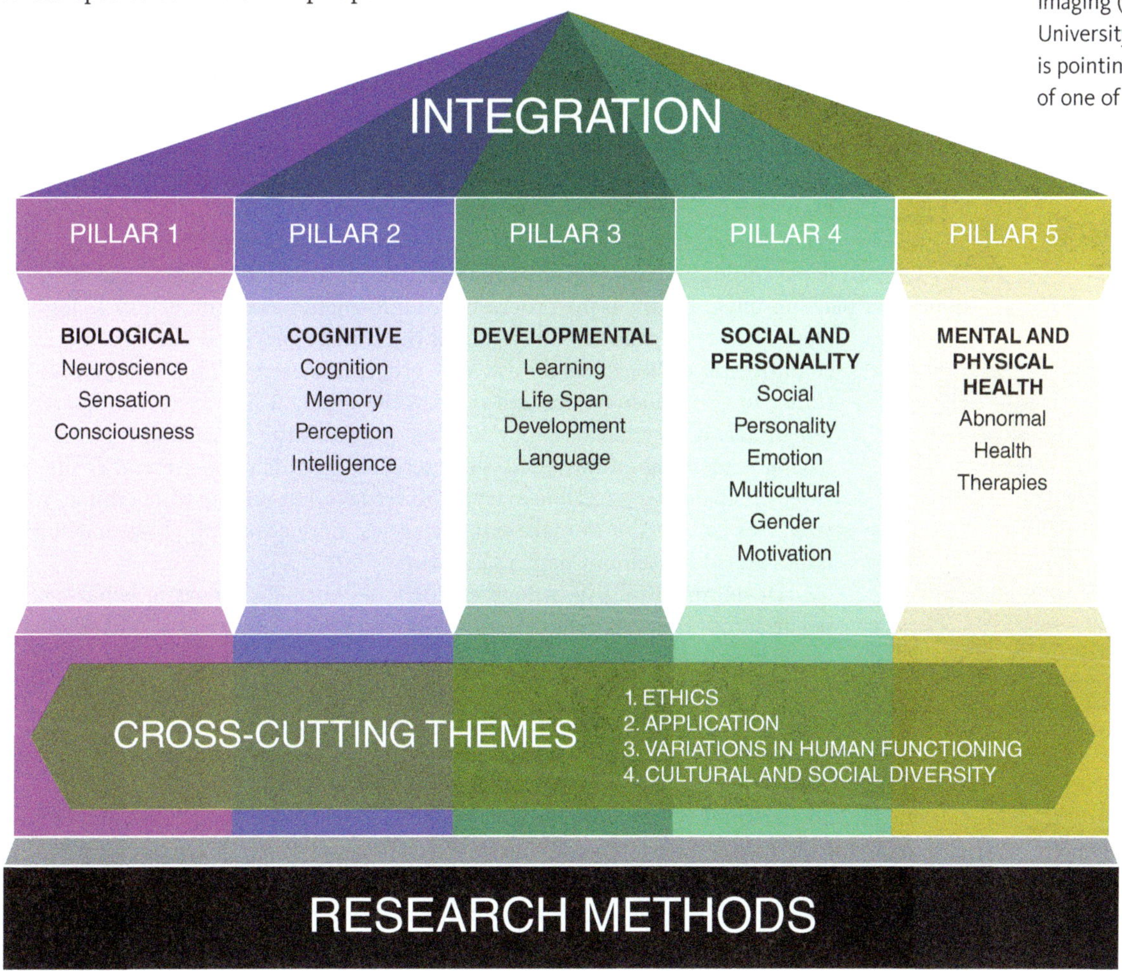

FIGURE **1.8**

Psychology Features Five Main Perspectives. Five major psychological perspectives feature unique theories and methods, yet share a foundation of scientific research methods and cross-cutting themes.

Source: Gurung, R., et al. (2016). "Teaching introductory psychology: Content, context, and resources." *American Psychologist 71*(2), 112–124.

Christian Jegou/Publiphoto/Science Source

EPA/Newscom

Evolutionary psychologists are interested in how our modern behaviors are shaped by our species' history.

James's functionalism, discussed previously in this chapter. Earlier, we also saw evolutionary psychology at work in the shaping of our sensitivity to bitter tastes. The basic principle of evolutionary psychology is that our current behavior exists in its present form because it provided some advantage in survival and reproduction to our ancestors. An evolutionary psychologist might be interested in our good memory for faces, and particularly for faces of people who have cheated us in the past (Barclay & Lalumiere, 2006). In the world of the hunter–gatherer, being cheated out of a fair share of the hunt was likely to lead to starvation for a family, and people who could not keep track of the cheaters were unlikely to survive and reproduce.

cognitive psychology A psychological perspective that investigates information processing, thinking, reasoning, and problem solving.

Cognitive psychology focuses on the processing of information. Because our ability to remember plays an integral part in the processing of information, a cognitive psychologist is likely to have a great deal to say about the storage and retrieval of memories. A cognitive psychologist might ask why processing seems different when we are trying to remember names and dates while taking a history test compared to remembering how to ride a bicycle. What produces the frustrating experience of having something on the "tip of your tongue," in which you remember the first letter or a part of a word you're trying to retrieve, but not the whole thing? What strategies can we use to make our memories more efficient? These and similar issues are addressed in Chapters 9 and 10.

Developmental psychology explores the normal changes in behavior that occur across the life span. Using the developmental perspective, a psychologist might look at how memory functions in people of different ages. Without further practice, 3-month-old babies can retain for about a month the memory that kicking moves a mobile suspended above their crib (Rovee-Collier, 1997). Teens and young adults are able to remember names faster than are older adults (Bashore et al., 1997). These and other age-related changes are explored in Chapter 11.

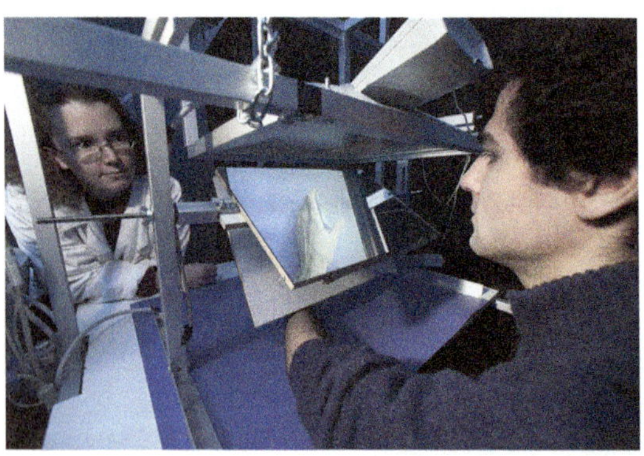

Pascal Goetgheluck/Science Source

Cognitive psychologists investigate the ways that the human mind processes information. This cognitive psychologist is studying the use of mirrored images to help individuals overcome phantom pain due to the loss of a limb. Seeing images of what appears to be a healthy limb in place of the missing limb changes the way the mind thinks about the missing limb, leading to a reduction in perceived pain.

Social and personality psychology describes the effects of the social environment, including social and **cultural diversity**, and individual differences on the behavior of individuals (see Figure 1.9). Social and personality psychologists recognize that we construct our own realities and that the social environment influences our thoughts, feelings, and behavior. Early psychologists were limited in their understanding of mind by their exclusive focus on their own sociocultural contexts. More recently, social psychologists have emphasized the need to explore the influences of diverse sociocultural contexts and biology on our behavior. Returning to our memory example, the social psychologist might ask how being in the presence of others influences the storage and retrieval of data. When we are sitting comfortably in our own homes, the answers to *Jeopardy!* questions come relatively easily. In front of millions of viewers, however, we might be lucky to remember our own names.

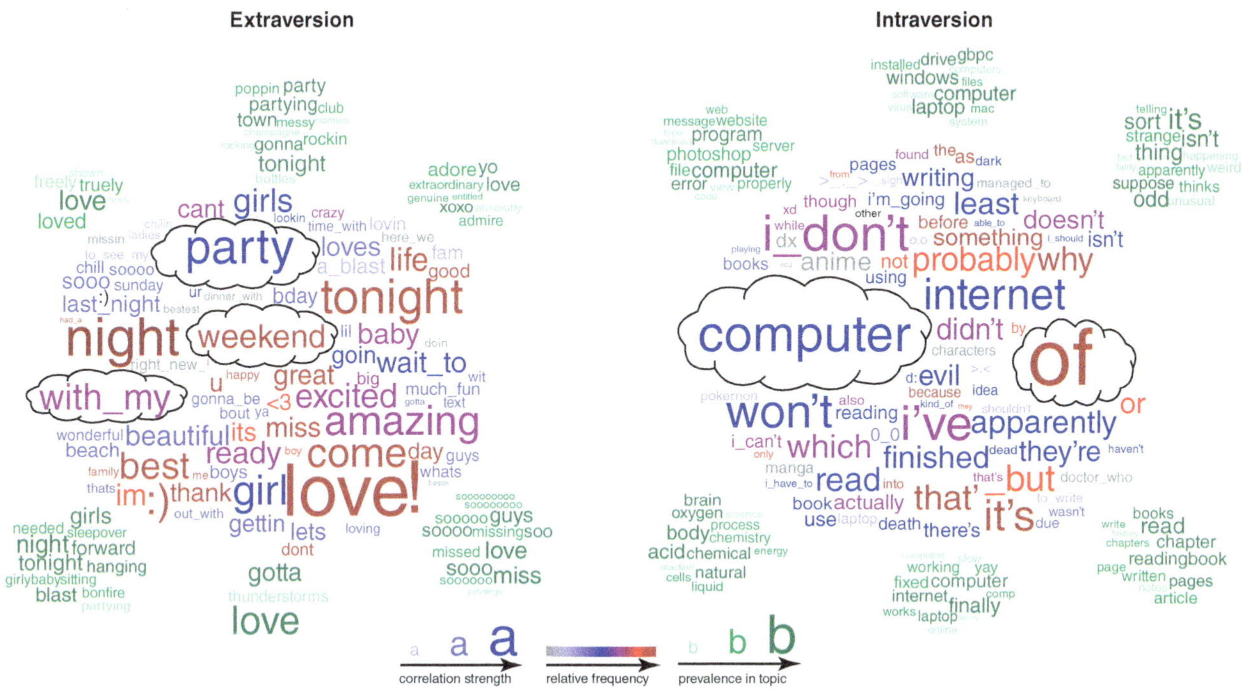

FIGURE **1.9**

Personality and Social Media. The emergence of social media has provided social and personality psychologists with new methods for examining the social mind and individual differences. What do your updates say about your personality? When the updates of more than 70,000 people who completed a Facebook personality test were examined, clear differences in their choices of words were observed.

Source: G. Park, et al. (2015). "Automatic Personality Assessment through Social Media Language," *Journal of Personality and Social Psychology, 108*(6), 934–952. doi:10.1037/pspp0000020

Although much of psychology explores how the average person thinks, feels, or acts, some people are not average. Behavior can vary dramatically from one individual to another as a function of personality factors and many aspects of diversity, including age, gender and gender identity, sexual orientation, race, ethnicity, disability status, and socioeconomic status. Using our example of memory, we can see how individual differences in "need for cognition" can predict memory for verbal material (Cacioppo et al., 1996). People who have a high need for cognition enjoy mental challenges, like solving difficult puzzles. As Chapter 13 will explore, individuals who are high in need for cognition also remember more of the messages to which they are exposed and respond differently to persuasive messages.

developmental psychology A psychological perspective that examines the normal changes in behavior that occur across the life span.

social psychology A psychological perspective that examines the effects of the social environment on the behavior of individuals.

personality An individual's characteristic way of thinking, feeling, and behaving.

cultural diversity Variations in the practices, values, and goals shared by groups of people.

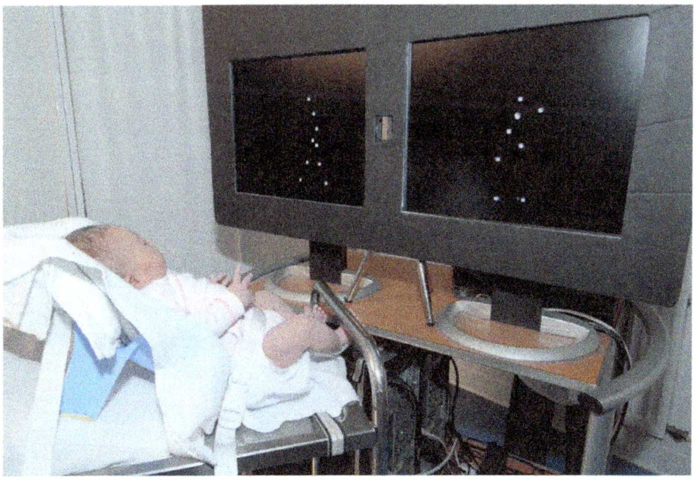

Thierry Berrod, Mona Lisa Production/Science Source

Developmental psychologists look at the behavior that is typical for people of certain ages, from infancy to old age. The amount of time this infant spends looking at moving stick figures helps us understand at what point in life we perceive biological motion.

iStock.com/Alina555

Clinical psychologists seek to understand and treat psychological disorders.

clinical psychology A psychological perspective that seeks to explain, define, and treat abnormal behaviors.

Finally, the **clinical psychology** perspective seeks to explain, define, and treat psychological disorders, as explained in detail in Chapters 14 and 15. More recently, the clinical perspective has expanded to include positive psychology, or the promotion of general well-being and health, described further in Chapter 16. Many types of psychological disorders affect memory. Freud believed that traumatizing experiences were more difficult to remember, a process that he labeled *repression* (discussed in Chapters 9 and 14). In other cases, war veterans and others who have experienced trauma might be troubled by memories that are too good, producing intrusive flashback memories of disturbing events.

These five main perspectives do not fully capture the range of specialization within psychology. The American Psychological Association (APA) recognizes 54 divisions for psychologists interested in topics such as military psychology, community psychology, hypnosis, religion and spirituality, and culture, ethnicity, and race. Some of the divisions represent the main perspectives, such as Division 7, Developmental Psychology, and Division 8, the Society for Personality and Social Psychology. Others include psychologists from a number of main perspectives who come together to explore shared questions. For example, psychologists participating in Division 35, the Society for the Psychology of Women, might also identify with any of the five major perspectives.

A New Connectivity: Integrating Psychology's Five Perspectives

Although the 20th-century perspective approach to psychology generated detailed understanding of aspects of behavior and mental processes, it has become apparent that single perspectives are insufficient for fully describing and explaining psychological phenomena. Armed with in-depth research results compiled from these various perspectives, many psychological scientists in the 21st century have returned to the more comprehensive view of the mind envisioned more than 100 years ago by James (Cacioppo, 2013). Their questions and methods are more likely to blur the lines of the perspectives outlined earlier, often with remarkable results.

For example, a full understanding of romantic relationships is more likely to emerge from combinations of perspectives than through the use of single perspectives. "Zooming out" to combine an understanding of cultural and social contexts, biological factors (such as the "bonding" hormone oxytocin), personality (individual traits), social experience (such as self-fulfilling prophesies), cognitions (such as automatic thought), and the effects of psychological disorders (as in borderline personality disorder) give us a more comprehensive view of the phenomenon (see ● Figure 1.10).

Valery Bareta/Alamy Stock Photo

FIGURE **1.10**

Using Multiple Perspectives Can Help Us Better Understand Complex Phenomena Like Attraction. What accounts for our romantic attraction to that special someone? Single perspectives provide considerable insight, but combining perspectives gives us a richer understanding of human behavior.

Diverse Voices in Psychology

Culture and Diversity as "Cross-cutting Themes" in Psychology

IN ADDITION TO THE FIVE PSYCHOLOGICAL PERSPECTIVES reviewed in this chapter, a more general perspective provided by culture and diversity is also essential to our understanding of behavior. The guidelines proposed for the introductory psychology course by Gurung et al. (2014, 2016) emphasize the need to use culture and diversity as a "cross-cutting theme." In accordance with this view, each of the editions of this textbook has been crafted following the guidance provided by Trimble et al. (2004) about integrating issues of diversity into all relevant discussions in an organic way.

In addition to incorporating diversity seamlessly throughout our topics, we also believe that it is useful to provide opportunities to highlight diversity issues in greater depth, which is the purpose of having this feature in each chapter. As suggested by Betancourt and López (1993, p. 636), "psychology as a discipline will benefit both from efforts to infuse culture in mainstream research and theory and from efforts to study culture and develop theory in cross-cultural and ethnic psychology."

This first chapter has reviewed psychology's historical timeline and explored some of the career paths that psychologists can follow. From a diversity perspective, we see that the history of psychology features a dramatic underrepresentation of ethnic and racial minorities. Stanley Sue (2009) noted that it wasn't until 1975 that the first African-American woman was licensed as a psychologist (Gail Wyatt) in the state of California. Sue himself was told that in 1971, he was the only Chinese-American with a regular faculty appointment in an American Psychological Association–accredited clinical psychology program in the entire nation. As Sue and others have pointed out, underrepresentation has negative consequences both for psychologists themselves and for the people they serve as teachers, researchers, or therapists.

Recognition of the problem has led to remedial efforts, but there is still a long way to go.

Psychology, of course, is not alone in facing this problem, but as students of the mind, we must include diverse viewpoints to ensure accuracy. In Chapter 5, you will read about how white Americans and Asians respond differently to objects (a tiger) and backgrounds (a jungle) in a photograph. If we studied only one of these groups, we would end up with faulty conclusions. ■

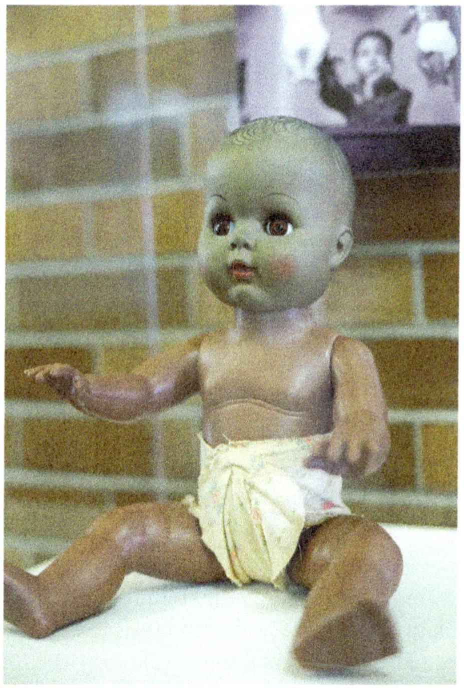

Jim West/Alamy Stock Photo

Kenneth and Mamie Clark conducted some of the most famous experiments in psychology in 1939–1940. Children in segregated schools were shown two dolls that were identical except for hair, eye, and skin color, and asked questions such as whether one doll was nicer, or if the child would prefer to play with one doll over the other. The majority of children, regardless of their own race, preferred the white doll. The Clarks not only made contributions to our understanding of the social context of child development, but their research was applied as evidence in hearings by the U.S. Supreme Court on the detrimental effects of segregated schools. In 2005, an 18-year-old high school student, Kiri Davis, repeated the Clark's doll study for her film *A Girl Like Me: The Gwen Araujo Story*. She found that 15 out of 21 African-American girls still preferred the white doll.

We don't have a crystal ball that will allow us to foresee psychology's future. However, we strongly believe that this future will involve combining and integrating new and existing perspectives. Many of these new ways of looking at the mind will take advantage of the revolution in techniques for studying the brain that began in the 1970s and continues. Already, today's cognitive neuroscientists investigate the brain as an information-processing system and search for the biological basis of topics such as attention, decision making, and memory. Social neuroscientists investigate the biological factors that vary with people's feelings and experiences of social inclusion, rejection, or loneliness. Behavioral neuroscientists pick up previous lines of research on learning, memory, motivation, and sleep, and search for connections between these processes and our biology. Clinical and counseling psychologists are likely to consider biological processes in their theories about the causes of psychological disorders. By merging the five perspectives of mind, we stand a better chance of tackling the remarkable problem of understanding the human mind.

THINKING SCIENTIFICALLY

Can the Use of a Single Perspective Be Misleading?

WE HAVE ARGUED that restricting our thinking about an aspect of mind to the information provided by one perspective can result in an incomplete picture, but can this single-perspective approach actually lead us in the wrong direction?

The answer to that question is a resounding "yes." Consider the following example. For many years, researchers were puzzled in their efforts to understand the relationships between child maltreatment and later antisocial behavior. Although maltreatment often seems to be linked to later criminal behavior, the majority of maltreated children do not become delinquents or adult criminals (Caspi et al., 2002).

To solve this dilemma, a clinical psychologist might focus on environmental factors, such as the presence of a trusted adult or delinquent peer group, or personal factors, like resilience. Working in parallel, biological psychologists know something about certain candidate genes and their relationships with aggressive behavior in animals. In particular, animals with a low-activity version of the *MAOA* gene seemed to be more aggressive than animals with a higher-activity version. However, links between variations in *MAOA* and human aggression are not clear.

Separately, neither group of psychologists is likely to do a very good job of explaining why some children exposed to maltreatment engage in antisocial behavior while others do not. The solution, however, becomes apparent when we combine the clinical psychologists' observations of environmental factors with the genetic information provided by the biological psychologists. It appears that a gene-environment interaction takes place, in which children with the low-activity version of the *MAOA* gene responded to maltreatment by becoming antisocial, while children with the higher-activity version do not (Fergusson et al., 2011; Caspi et al., 2002; Nilsson et al., 2018). Restricting ourselves to one perspective might cloud our understanding, but combining perspectives leads us to an accurate conclusion.

DNA Strand: Science Picture Co/Superstock; Teenager: Suzanne Tucker/Shutterstock.com

Experiencing childhood maltreatment does not reliably predict aggressiveness in youth, but combining genetics and exposure to maltreatment provides a clearer picture.

What Does It Mean to Be a Psychologist?

In 2016–2017, nearly 117,000 students in the United States received a bachelor's degree in psychology (APA, 2019). This amounts to approximately 6% of the 1.9 million bachelor's degrees awarded that year, making psychology the fourth-most-frequent bachelor's degree program (following business, the health professions, and combined social sciences and history). What are these psychology graduates likely to be doing in the workforce?

Psychology is unlike some other disciplines in which people with a bachelor's degree can refer to themselves as a practicing member of the relevant profession, such as a chemist or biologist. Calling oneself a psychologist is restricted to holders of graduate (usually doctorate) degrees. This does not mean that students who completed a bachelor's degree in psychology cannot be employed in relevant fields. Some undergraduate psychology graduates prefer employment in fields that are directly related to psychology, such as working in research facilities or rehabilitation centers for drug abuse or brain damage. Others are quite successful in a variety of people-oriented jobs, such as those found in management, sales, customer service, public affairs, education, human resources, probation, and journalism. This diversity of career pathways reflects the hub relationship of psychology with other fields, as described earlier in this chapter.

iStock.com/BirdofPrey

Forensic psychologists attempt to understand the criminal mind and to develop effective treatments for criminal behavior.

More than half of people holding graduate degrees in psychology work in health care, counseling, financial services, or legal services professions (Stamm, Lin, & Christidis, 2016). Graduates with a master's degree in psychology, usually requiring 1 to 2 years of additional study past the bachelor's degree, can teach at the community college (2-year) level and obtain licensing as therapists in most states, as discussed in Chapter 15. School psychologists with a master's degree typically work on elementary, middle school, or high school campuses. These psychologists participate in academic and career counseling, as well as the identification and remediation of problems that interfere with student success.

Many people working in psychology have earned doctoral degrees, which usually take 2 to 5 years of study beyond the master's level. As shown in ● Figure 1.11, about 34% of new doctoral-level psychologists do what your professor and the authors of this textbook do: teach, conduct research at colleges and universities, or both. About 45% of new doctoral-level psychologists work as therapists. Smaller numbers of new doctoral-level psychologists find employment in business and government settings, elementary and secondary schools, and other related fields.

REUTERS/Alamy Stock Photo

Sports psychologist Julie Elion gives Phil Mickelson some final tips during his preparation for an important PGA championship.

Psychologists entering doctoral programs traditionally identify with one of the major perspectives discussed earlier, such as social, cognitive, or biological. Choosing a graduate perspective is similar to choosing an undergraduate major. Although all psychology graduate students might take core courses in research methods and statistics, they typically pursue coursework and research in their particular area of specialization. However, training of psychologists in the 21st century is beginning to reflect the connections occurring in the field. Increasingly, students are being trained in combined specialties (e.g., cognitive neuroscience) as psychology becomes an increasingly integrated field of study.

The most rigid distinction occurs between graduate students who plan to specialize in clinical or counseling psychology and those who do not. The clinical or counseling track includes extensive internships and supervised training prior to government-regulated licensure that usually add at least 1 year to students' graduate studies. Do not assume that your psychology professors are all therapists; it is most likely they are not. It is important to distinguish

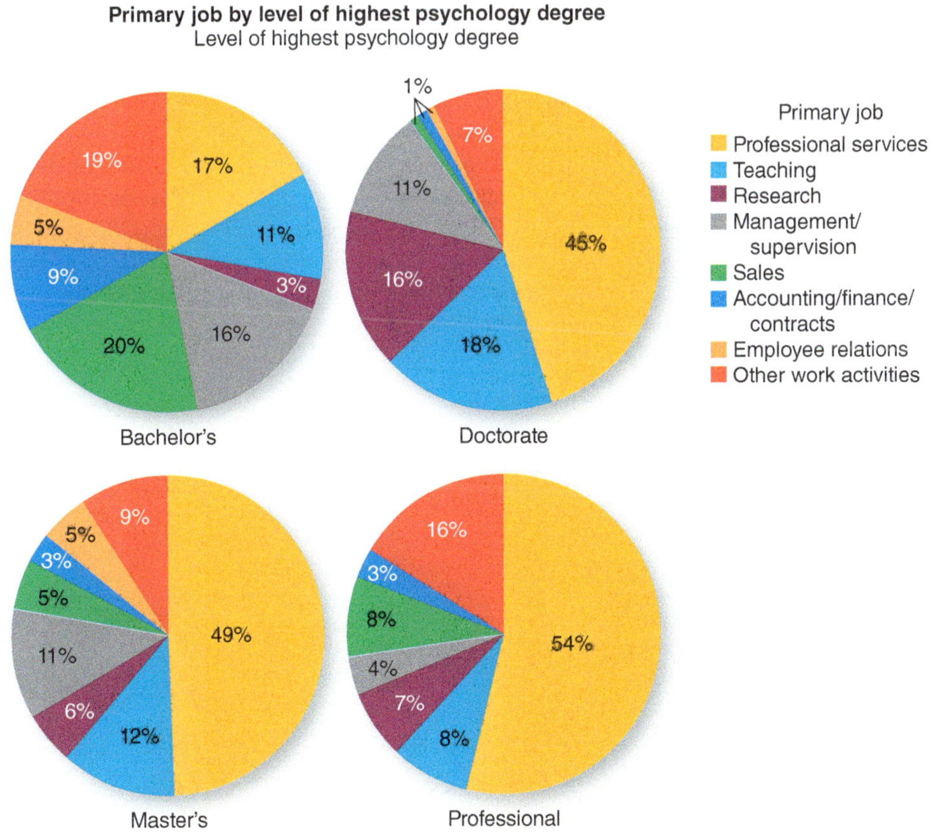

FIGURE **1.11**

Individuals earning psychology degrees work in a variety of settings. Most psychologists with graduate degrees are employed in clinical and higher-education settings, but opportunities for students of psychology also exist in schools, businesses, government, and other places in which an understanding of human behavior is helpful. *Source:* Data from Stamm et al. (2016).

between therapists with doctoral degrees in psychology (PhDs or PsyDs) and psychiatrists, who are medical doctors (MDs). The biggest difference between the two professions is that psychiatrists can prescribe medication, but psychologists usually cannot. In New Mexico, Louisiana, Illinois, Iowa, and Idaho however, specially trained psychologists can legally prescribe medications, and this trend might spread to other states. In Chapter 15, we will provide more detail about the types of therapists who treat adjustment problems and psychological disorders.

Interpersonal Relationships

How Can We Use Relationships to Illustrate Psychological Perspectives?

WE GAVE QUITE A LOT OF THOUGHT to how we might help you, the students reading our book, to see psychology more as an interconnected discipline than as a collection of separate perspectives. The introductory psychology course provides a unique opportunity to see all perspectives at one time, in contrast to upper-division courses, which typically focus on one specialty at a time (biological, developmental, social, cognitive, clinical, and so on). At the beginning of each chapter, we will take a question relevant to the chapter, such as "Why are we sensitive to bitter tastes?" and explore it using multiple perspectives. At the end of each chapter, we'll mirror this process by taking a single problem and seeing how the material in the chapter can be applied.

OlegD/Shutterstock.com

This feature of the textbook will have more of a perspective flavor than the beginnings of each chapter, but by the end of the textbook, you will have seen how each of the major perspectives in psychological science contributes to the whole picture. Because it is most helpful to know something about the perspectives before you see how they can be applied, we save this feature for the end of each chapter. Ideally, seeing the chapter material in action will make it more memorable for you.

The single problem we have chosen to consider this way is one that we know to be on the minds of many of our students: their relationships with others. We are a social species, and the quality of our relationships has a huge impact on our physical and psychological well-being (Cacioppo & Hawkley, 2009). We will see how each of the major perspectives views the question of relationship quality and how the perspectives work together to give us the best possible understanding of this important aspect of life. ■

Psychology Takes on Real-World Problems

Tackling the Problem of a Pandemic

AS YOU HAVE SEEN in this chapter, psychological science is the study of behavior, mental processes, and brain functions. As such, psychology has much to say about the causes and solutions of contemporary human problems. To illustrate psychology's power to contribute to the understanding and solution of these problems, each chapter will focus on a "big problem" from the point of view of the chapter content. While each chapter addresses only a part of the problem, by the time you reach the end of the textbook, you will have been exposed to many ways that psychology can contribute to solving some of the biggest challenges that human beings face today, such as pollution, climate change, education, poverty, terrorism, pandemics, food insecurity, crime, and social injustice.

Solving such big problems might seem overwhelming, but by breaking each problem into little steps, real progress can be made. We'd like to model this process for you by tackling a single problem, but we encourage you to expand on our model by applying what you've learned to other issues that you find important. You'll be reading more about good problem solving methods in Chapter 10.

The problem we'll model for you is a pandemic, and COVID-19 in particular. We will ask how human behavior contributes to the causes and course of the pandemic as well as how human behavior can lead to solutions. We might ask why some people hoard toilet paper while others think masks are unnecessary. Exploring these behaviors illustrates the power and applicability of psychological science outside the classroom.

In the upcoming chapters, we want you to think about how the different perspectives might view both the causes and solutions to our problem. What research results and other information do you need to understand the problem better? Do ethical concerns and issues of diversity influence the causes and solutions of the problem? How would our lives be affected if the problem continues to worsen or if solutions actually can be found? If you were tasked with writing a policy to influence pandemic responses at your school, how would you proceed? For example, what policies should a college or university implement for wearing masks? For maintaining social distancing? We'll be demonstrating how psychology can assist the formation of policy components, including:

- Rationale: Why isn't our current policy working well?
- Proposed Policy Options: Why isn't our current policy working well?
- Policy Recommendations: Which option should we try first? ■

Kevin McGovern/Shutterstock.com

SUMMARY 1.3 Five Psychological Perspectives

	Perspective	Things to remember
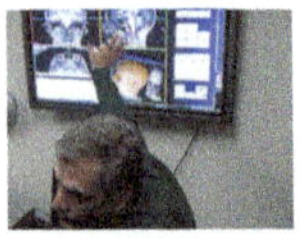 	Biological and evolutionary psychology	Investigates the connections among mind, behavior, and biological processes, and asks how our evolutionary past continues to shape our behavior
	Cognitive psychology	Investigates mental processes, including thinking, problem solving, and information processing
 	Social and personality psychology	Asks how our behavior is affected by the presence of others; Recognizes that behavior varies around averages and that individual differences often interact with environments
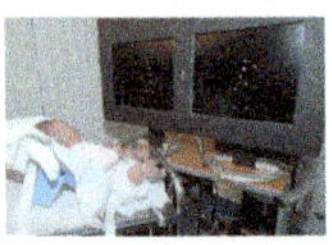	Developmental psychology	Investigates the normal changes in behavior that occur across the life span
	Clinical psychology	Explains, defines, and treats psychological disorders and promotes general well-being

Credits: Top row—Courtesy of Scott Grafton, UCSB Brain Imaging Lab. Photo © Roger Freberg; Christian Jegou/Publiphoto/Science Source; Second row—Pascal Goetgheluck/Science Source; Third row—Joel Gordon 2001; Fourth row—Thierry Berrod, Mona Lisa Production/Science Source.

KEY TERMS The Language of Psychological Science

Be sure that you can define these terms and use them correctly.

behaviorism, p.15
biological psychology, p.23
clinical psychology, p.26
cognitive psychology, p.24
cultural diversity, p.24
developmental psychology, p.24
evolutionary psychology, p.23
functionalism, p.12
gestalt psychology, p.12
humanistic psychology, p.14
introspection, p.5
mind, p.5
natural sciences, p.7
philosophy, p.7
psychology, p.5
social and personality psychology, p.24
structuralism, p.12

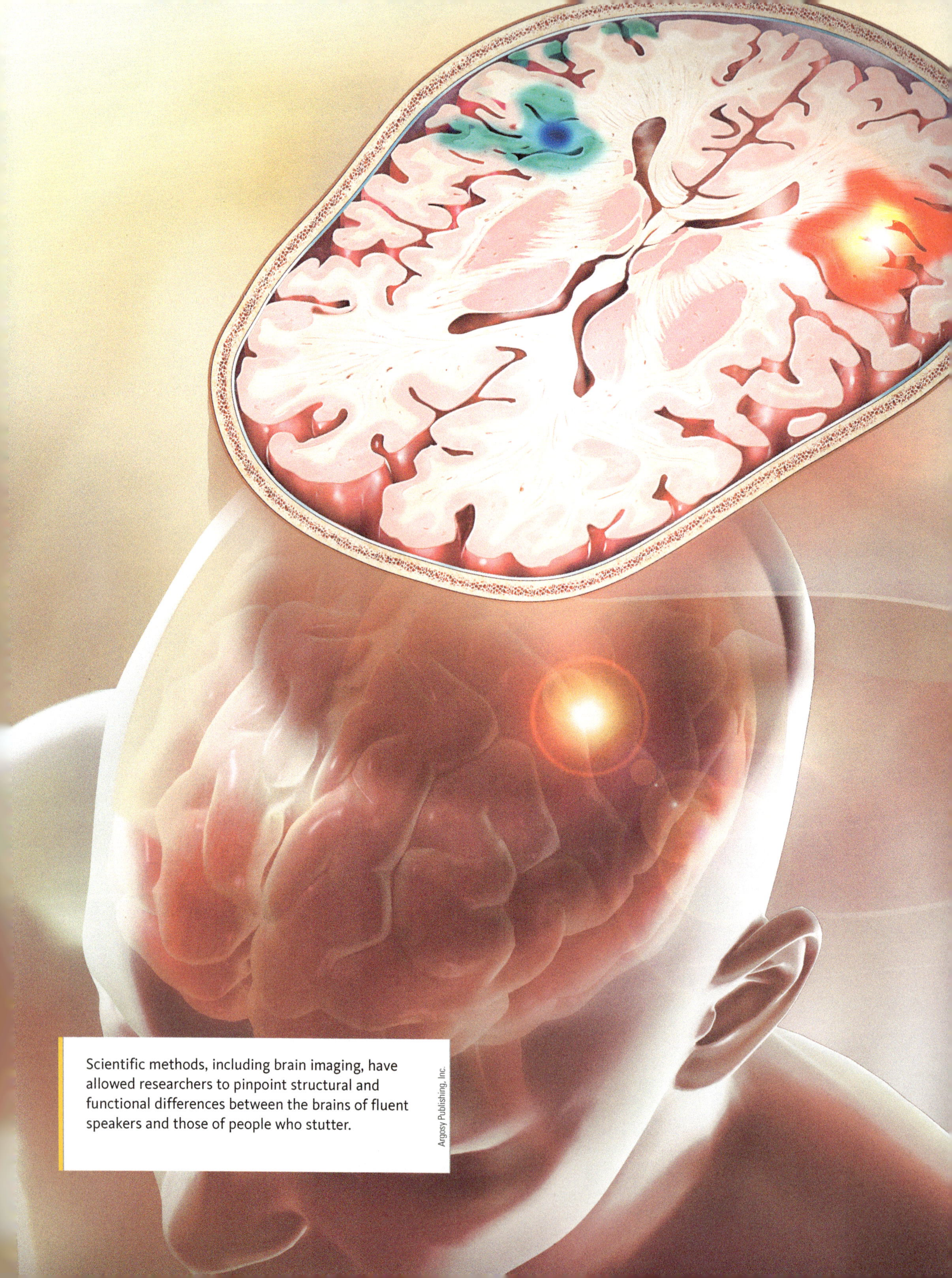

Scientific methods, including brain imaging, have allowed researchers to pinpoint structural and functional differences between the brains of fluent speakers and those of people who stutter.

Argosy Publishing, Inc.

2

The Measure of Mind

THE SCIENTIFIC METHODS OF PSYCHOLOGY

LEARNING OBJECTIVES

1. Distinguish between scientific reasoning and common sense.
2. Assess the value of case studies, naturalistic observations, and surveys to describe behavior.
3. Analyze the key features, strengths, and limitations of correlational and experimental methods.
4. Understand reliability and validity.
5. Differentiate descriptive and inferential statistics.
6. Critique the ethical guidelines for using human and animal participants in research.

AMONG THE MANY CELEBRITIES WHO STUTTER is action actor Samuel L. Jackson. At a gala for the American Institute for Stuttering, Jackson shared one of his strategies for avoiding stuttering—uttering a particular swear word under his breath.

iStock.com/EdStock

Stuttering involves disruptions in normal speech production, such as repeating the starting letter of a word (b-b-b-bird), holding a vowel sound for a long time (ah ah ah), or having difficulty initiating speech. About 5% of the population experience stuttering (Månsson, 2000), with males two to five times more likely to stutter than females (Craig & Tran, 2005).

Stuttering has been described since the days of the ancient Greeks and occurs across all cultures and ethnicities. Many interesting myths exist regarding its causes and remedies (Kuster, 2015). South African traditions suggest that stuttering results from leaving a baby out in the rain or tickling the infant too much. A Chinese folk remedy for stuttering was to hit the person in the face when the weather was cloudy. In Iceland, people believed that a pregnant woman who drank from a cracked cup was likely to produce a child who stuttered.

Many of us might ask, "How could anybody believe these things?" But how do we know these are merely myths and not facts? Instead of dismissing these efforts to explain and predict, think about what might have happened to lead people to these particular conclusions. What is missing from these conclusions is a system for reaching logical, objective results. Science provides us with this system.

What does science have to say about stuttering? Based on the careful evaluation of stuttering using the methods outlined in this chapter, scientists have concluded that there are multiple causes for stuttering (Kang et al., 2010). Many cases seem to have a basis in genetics, which is discussed in Chapter 3 (Han et al., 2019; Raza et al., 2015). Scientists have used brain-imaging technologies to zoom in on brain structures and functions that appear to differ between stutterers and fluent speakers, with stutterers showing more activation of the right hemisphere during speech (Gordon, 2002). As mentioned in the previous chapter, some of the most thorough explanations combine multiple psychological perspectives (Ward, 2013). A complete explanation of stuttering zooms back out to combine a predisposition for the problem resulting from genetics and biology with developmental, emotional, and social factors, like feeling embarrassed or anxious about speaking in front of peers.

steineranden/Shutterstock.com

Science has provided explanations for many natural phenomena, like lightning, that were probably quite frightening for our ancestors.

Although there is no "cure" for stuttering, carefully tested scientific explanations combining input from various perspectives are leading to more effective treatments. In this chapter, you will learn how science provides a system that allows us to construct increasingly realistic models of the world around us.

What Is Science?

Throughout human history, we have been motivated to understand, predict, and control the world around us. To meet these goals, we need methods for gaining knowledge.

We often take contemporary scientific knowledge for granted, but our ancestors did not enjoy the benefits of science while trying to explain and predict their world. Early in history, people attempted to understand natural phenomena by applying human characteristics to nature (Cornford, 1957). Skies could look "angry" or a lake could be "calm." Other explanations involved spirits inhabiting humans and all other objects. Earthquakes and illness were viewed as the actions of spirits, and people attempted to influence these spirits through magical rituals. Later on, people looked to authorities, such as religious leaders and philosophers, for explanations of natural phenomena.

science A method for learning about reality through systematic observation and experimentation.

objectivity The practice of basing conclusions on facts, without the influence of personal emotion and bias.

People often form strong beliefs about their world based on faith, which literally means "trust." *Faith* is belief that does not depend on proof or evidence. We might accept friends' excuses for being late based on our faith in their honesty, without knowing for certain whether they are telling the truth. In contrast to faith, science definitely requires proof and evidence. The word **science** comes from the Latin *Scientia*, which means "knowledge." Science doesn't refer to just any type of knowledge, but rather to a special way of learning about reality through systematic observation and experimentation. The methods described in this chapter are designed to supply that evidence.

Stefano Bianchetti/Contributor/Corbis Historical/Getty Images

Throughout history, people have often turned to authorities, such as religious leaders, instead of to science. The astronomer Galileo Galilei was interrogated as part of the Roman Inquisition for believing that the Earth was not the center of the universe.

How Do We Develop a Scientific Mindset?

Not all observations are scientific. How does science differ from everyday, common sense observations, like the belief that "opposites attract"? As you will learn in Chapter 13, "opposites" do not, in fact, find each other very attractive.

First, science relies on objectivity, rather than subjectivity. **Objectivity** means that conclusions are based on facts, without influence from personal emotions or biases. In contrast, *subjectivity* means that conclusions reflect personal points of view. In a study by Allport and Postman (1945), research participants described from memory what they had heard about some photos. One photo showed a White man threatening another person. Some participants switched the race of the man from White to Black, possibly to fit a biased, subjective worldview. Scientists strive to be objective, but any observation by a human is, by definition, subjective. Recognizing when we are being subjective can be difficult, so scientists cannot rely on their introspections to maintain objectivity. The scientific methods described in this chapter promote objectivity and help prevent biased, subjective observations from distorting a scientist's work.

The second important difference between science and everyday observations is the use of systematic as opposed to hit-or-miss observation. By "hit or miss," we mean making conclusions based only on whatever is happening around us. To make conclusions about the human mind, we cannot restrict our observations to our immediate circle of acquaintances, friends, and loved ones. Our observations of the people we see frequently are probably quite valid. It's just that the people we know represent a small slice of the greater population. For example, we might be surprised to learn that our favorite candidate lost an election because "everyone we know" voted for that candidate.

Based on observations of people they know, college students often believe that drinking alcohol, and even binge drinking (five drinks on one occasion for men, four drinks for women), is a nearly universal behavior for anyone over the age of 18 or so. We can see why a college student might believe this after making hit-or-miss observations (see Figure 2.1). Fifty-eight percent of college students aged 18 to 22 reported drinking alcohol in the last 30 days, compared to 48% of age peers who are not attending college. About 37% of college students report binge drinking during this period, compared to 32.6% of 18- to 22-year-olds not attending college and 26.9% among all adults (National Institute on Alcohol & Alcoholism, 2018).

From Allport, G. W., & Postman, L. J. (1945), "The Basic Psychology of Rumor," from Transactions of The New York Academy of Sciences, 8, 61–81

Science strives to be objective, making judgments that are free from personal emotion or bias. In contrast, people's subjectivity emerged in a classic experiment by Allport and Postman (1945). Some participants remembered hearing that this picture illustrated a Black man threatening another person rather than the objective fact—a White person is doing the threatening.

Finally, science relies on observable, repeatable evidence, whereas everyday observation often ignores or rejects evidence, especially when it runs counter to strongly held beliefs and expectations. Our tendency to notice and remember instances that support our beliefs more than instances that contradict them is termed **confirmation bias**. Confirmation bias tends to protect people's stereotypes, as they see only what they expect to see. For example, if people are convinced that women are worse drivers than men, they will notice only bad driving by women. Good driving by women and bad driving by men will be ignored, strengthening the stereotypical belief. However, as shown in Figure 2.2, males of all ages are much more likely than females to be killed in traffic accidents, in spite of their relatively equal proportions of the driving population.

confirmation bias The tendency to notice and remember instances that support your beliefs more than instances that contradict them.

Scientific knowledge is both stable and changing. It is a work in progress, not a finished product. The fact that we may learn something new tomorrow should not make you assume that today's knowledge is flawed. Most change occurs slowly on the cutting edges of science, not quickly or at the main core of its knowledge base. Unlike with many other fields, we expect science to improve over time. An important feature of scientific literacy is to learn to be comfortable with the idea that scientific knowledge is always open to improvement and will never be considered certain.

The Importance of Critical Thinking

Critical thinking, or the ability to think clearly, rationally, and independently, is one of the foundations of scientific reasoning. The skilled critical thinker can follow logical arguments, identify mistakes in reasoning, prioritize ideas according to their importance, and apply logic to personal attitudes, beliefs, and values.

critical thinking The ability to think clearly, rationally, and independently.

Critical thinking is not built in; rather, it is a skill that people need to learn. You can begin by using five critical thinking questions to evaluate new information you come across in your everyday life, starting with what you read in this textbook (Bernstein, 2011):

- What am I being asked to believe or accept?
- What evidence supports this position?
- Are there other ways that this evidence could be interpreted?

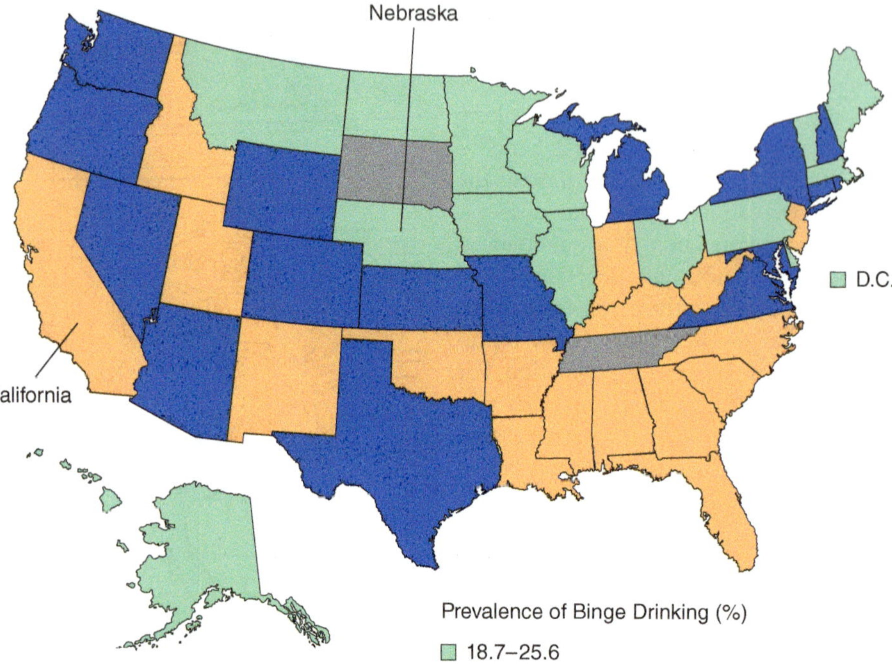

FIGURE **2.1**

Scientific Observations Are Systematic, Not Hit or Miss. Science provides ways to make systematic observations. Judgments that we make based on the people we know might not apply to larger groups of people. Based only on personal experience, college students living in Nebraska and California might disagree about the prevalence of binge drinking.

EXPERIENCING PSYCHOLOGY

Using Critical Thinking to Evaluate Popular Press Reports

POPULAR PRESS REPORTS OFTEN SUMMARIZE the results of scholarly papers published in peer-reviewed journals. It is very important to use your very best critical thinking in evaluating these reports, which often distort the results and conclusions of the papers they describe. *U.S. News & World Report* (2019) featured a headline that read "Millennials' Odds for Depression Rise with Social Media Use." Using the steps to good critical thinking outlined in this chapter, let's see how this headline holds up.

1. What Am I Being Asked to Believe or Accept?

We are being asked to believe that there is a positive correlation between depression and social media use within the Millennial age cohort (those born between 1980 and 2000).

2. What Evidence Supports This Position?

The news report references an article in a peer-reviewed publication entitled "Social comparisons, social media addiction, and social interaction: An examination of specific social media behaviors related to major depressive disorder in a millennial population" (Robinson et al., 2019). The study consisted of an online survey administered to 504 undergraduates attending Texas State, San Marcos. The participants completed standardized instruments assessing their social media use and depressive symptoms. Based on their responses, participants were divided into depressed and non-depressed groups for further analysis. In this chapter, we refer to this type of design as a quasi-experiment, because the participants

13_Phunkod/Shutterstock.com

U.S. News & World Report claimed that "Millennials' Odds for Depression Rise with Social Media Use." Evaluating claims like this requires our best critical thinking skills.

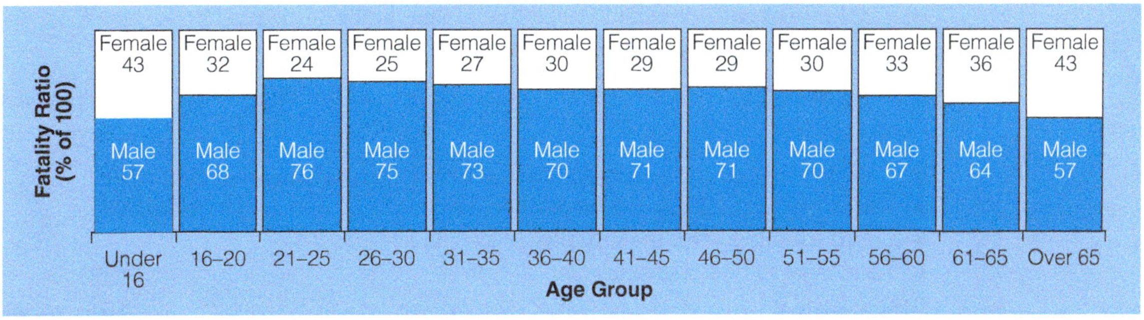

Alex Brylov/Shutterstock.com

FIGURE **2.2**

Confirmation Bias Supports Stereotypes.
Confirmation bias leads people to see what they expect to see, which is not necessarily the truth. People who believe a false stereotype about women being bad drivers are likely to notice instances of women driving badly while ignoring men driving badly or women driving well. Actual data show that males are much more likely to die in traffic accidents than females, in spite of their relatively equal proportions in the population.

Source: NHTSA's National Center for Statistics and Analysis 1200 New Jersey Avenue SE., Washington, DC 20590 DOT HS 810 853 July 2008

are not randomly assigned into these groups.

Participants meeting criteria for major depressive disorder on the basis of their survey responses (see Chapter 14) were more likely to engage in social comparisons with others on social media and to show signs of addiction to social media. Participants who were not depressed were more likely to use social media for social interaction. At no point did the original study argue that the quantity of social media use was correlated with depressive symptoms, in contrast to the headline.

3. Are There Other Ways That This Evidence Could Be Interpreted?

While it is possible that social media use affects our mood, it is also possible that being depressed makes us use social media differently. Confounding factors might also contribute to these results. Perhaps feelings of social exclusion lead to both depression and different use of social media.

4. What Other Evidence Do We Need?

First, we need a better sample. The study was conducted with a very limited sample of college students at a single university, who are likely to differ from "Millennials" in a number of ways. For example, Millennials born in 1980 are nearing mid-life and are probably quite different from young adult college students. Millennials who have not attended college or whose race and ethnicity differs from the sample might behave differently, too. We can't conclude that social media affects Millennials differently than it does other age groups unless we assess other age groups.

Second, to answer a question about the causal effects of social media exposure on depression requires an experiment, which presents practical and ethical challenges. It might be possible to assess depressive symptoms before and after exposing participants to social media stimuli, but this would be somewhat artificial and not necessarily ethical.

5. What Are the Most Reasonable Conclusions?

The original study appears to be making some valid points, although the sample is quite limited. The news report, however, generally overstates and misinterprets the findings of the original study, such as implying causality where none can be established from the data. Although reading the original source described in news reports is always the safest bet, we rarely have time to do this. What we can do is recognize that news reports might not be accurate reflections of an original study.

Now It's Your Turn

Using our model critical thinking questions, explore a popular press headline about psychology of your choice, and evaluate the item. Do you think you might have evaluated the claim differently before reading this chapter? Why or why not? ■

- What other evidence would I need to evaluate these alternatives?
- What are the most reasonable conclusions?

It is also helpful to recognize the signs that you are not thinking critically (excerpt taken from Lau, 2019):

- I prefer being given the correct answers rather than figuring them out myself.
- I don't like to think a lot about my decisions, as I rely only on gut feelings.
- I don't usually review the mistakes I have made.
- I don't like to be criticized.

Our abilities to think critically and accurately can also be undermined by a number of very normal cognitive processes (Marsh et al., 2016). If we understand our vulnerabilities, we might be better able to protect ourselves from making these mistakes:

- We are biased to believe that most information is true. It's easier in terms of time and effort to accept a false statement like "Omaha is the capital of Nebraska" than to question its truthfulness.
- Information that is easier to retrieve feels more like the truth. Information that is repeated is also easier to recall, making it more likely to be considered true.
- Compared to plain verbal statements, statements accompanied by pictures have more "truthiness" even though the picture does not provide additional evidence for the statement.
- We use inferences to bridge gaps between ideas (dolphins live in pods + dolphins use clicks and squeaks to communicate = pods communicate with clicks and squeaks). While this remarkable ability usually serves us well, it can also lead us in false directions.
- Prior knowledge can sometimes interfere with new learning. If you begin your course believing that we only use 10% of our brains or that vaccines cause autism, your professor's very best efforts to convince you that these statements are false may still fail.
- We often neglect important information. When asked where the authorities should bury the survivors of a plane crash at a border between two countries, many people fail to consider that we don't bury survivors at all.

theory A set of facts and relationships between facts that can explain and predict related phenomena.

Critical, accurate thinking not only is essential to good science, but also provides the underpinning of a free society. Our ability to think clearly, rationally, and independently gives us the skills to evaluate information and the confidence to question the actions of people in authority instead of engaging in blind obedience. We hope you will continue to practice good critical thinking skills long after you finish reading this textbook.

The Scientific Enterprise

Courtesy of John Cacioppo

Learning scientific facts is not the same as understanding how science works. Science, including psychological science, is more than a collection of facts—it is a process (see Figure 2.3).

Scientific Theories Science uses careful observations to understand how something works and develops **theories** based on those observations. Theories are sets of facts and relationships between facts that can be used to explain and predict phenomena (Cacioppo et al., 2004). In other words, scientists construct the best possible models of reality based on the facts known to date. Unfortunately, the English language can be the source of considerable confusion regarding the nature of scientific theories. In addition to its use in science, the word *theory* can be used in nonscientific ways to describe a guess, such as "I have a theory about why my professor seems unusually cheerful this morning," or a hypothetical situation, as in "That's the theory, but it may not work in practice." Confusion over the multiple meanings of the word *theory* have led people mistakenly to view truly scientific theories, like the theory

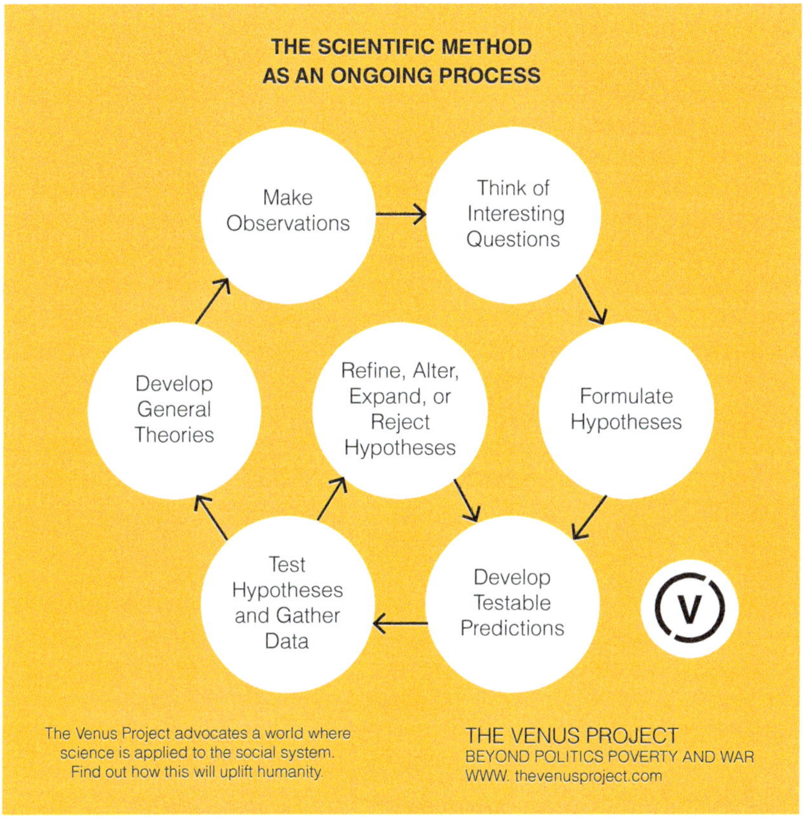

FIGURE **2.3**

Science Is a Process. Theory building begins with generating hypotheses that are then systematically tested. Hypotheses that are not rejected contribute to the theory and help generate new hypotheses.

of evolution, as nothing more than casual guesses or hunches, rather than the thoroughly investigated and massively supported principles that they are.

The best scientific theories not only explain and organize known facts, but also generate new predictions. The word *prediction* comes from the Latin words for "saying before." A scientific prediction is more than a guess or hunch. It is usually stated in a rigorous, mathematical form that allows the scientist to say that under a certain set of circumstances, a certain set of outcomes are likely to occur (if A, then B). In some cases, a theory's predictions can be surprising. For example, you might believe that it's impossible to be happy and sad at the same time. However, one model of emotion, discussed in Chapter 7, predicted that it is quite possible to feel happy and sad at the same time (Cacioppo et al., 2012). This prediction was reinforced by research showing that first-year college students reported feeling either happy or sad, but not both, on a normal day of school, but experiencing both emotions simultaneously on the day they moved out of campus housing to go home for the summer.

Before attempting to generate your own scientific questions, it pays to become familiar with relevant theories and previous discoveries. As Sir Isaac Newton noted, scholars stand on the shoulders of giants (Turnbull, 1959)—we build on the work of those who came before us. New lines of research can also originate in observation. Scientists are observers and thinkers not just in the laboratory, but also in everyday life. Scientific progress often takes a giant leap forward when a gifted observer recognizes a deeper meaningfulness in an everyday occurrence. As we discovered in Chapter 1, Ivan Petrovich Pavlov realized that when his dogs learned to salivate to signals predicting the arrival of food, something more significant than drooling dogs was happening. The learning that he observed explains why we can be conditioned to feel a certain way in certain situations, such as getting nervous before a big test.

Generating Good Hypotheses Once you understand the theoretical foundations of your area of interest, you are ready to generate a hypothesis. A **hypothesis** is a type of inference, or an educated guess, based on prior evidence and logical possibilities. A good hypothesis links concrete variables based on your theory and makes specific predictions. For example, based on prior research, scientists interested in obesity hypothesized that

hypothesis A proposed explanation for a situation, usually taking the form "If A happens, then B will be the result."

consuming coffee would increase brown fat activity (Velickovic et al., 2019). The concrete variables in this study are exposure to coffee and measures of brown fat activity. When formulating the hypothesis that coffee would have a significant effect on brown fat activity, the researchers also must consider the additional possibility that coffee would have no effect on brown fat activity.

Scientists can never "prove" that a hypothesis is true because some future experiment, possibly using new technology not currently available, might show the hypothesis to be false. All scientists can do is find additional evidence that *reinforces* that hypothesis. They can also show when a hypothesis is false. A false hypothesis must always be modified or discarded. This aspect of the scientific method explains why so many scientists are frustrated with popular arguments against vaccinating children. Extensive research has demonstrated that a hypothesis linking vaccinations with autism spectrum disorder is false, yet many people refuse to accept the need to modify or discard the hypothesis, as good science demands.

Once you have a hypothesis, you are ready to collect the data necessary to evaluate it. The existing scientific literature in your area of interest provides considerable guidance regarding your choice of methods, materials, types of data to collect, and ways to interpret your data.

peer review The process of having other experts examine research prior to its publication.

replication Repeating an experiment and producing the same results.

Communicating Science Science is a vastly collaborative enterprise. Not only do we stand on the shoulders of giants because we benefit from the work that has been done previously, but we depend on many others in the scientific community to help us improve our work and avoid mistakes. Normally, this evaluation is done by submitting research to conferences and for publication. During this process, research undergoes **peer review**, in which it is scrutinized by other scientists who are experts in the same area. Only if other experts conclude that new research is important, accurate, and explained thoroughly should it be added to the existing body of scientific knowledge. To demonstrate the importance of this peer review, contrast this process to what happens when a person simply decides to transmit a tweet or launch a personal website. The author is solely responsible for the content, and there are no checks on the accuracy of that content.

Published results should undergo **replication**, which means that other scientists independently attempt to reproduce the results of a study (Klein et al., 2014). If the data are replicated, they will be accepted quickly. If other scientists are unable to replicate the data, the results are rejected or remain in question pending further study. Although this process might slow the acceptance of some innovative findings, the result—more accuracy—is worth the effort.

A contemporary theory of emotion correctly predicted the circumstances for when we might experience mixed emotions of happiness and sadness. Graduation from college is an important accomplishment, but we might feel sad about leaving our friends.

The methods of psychological science can help us evaluate questions like the effects, if any, that playing violent video games has on physical aggression.

THINKING SCIENTIFICALLY

Does Psychology Have a Replication Problem?

ONE OF THE checks on science is the practice of replicating, or attempting to reproduce, scientific data. A scientist producing the original data might want to double-check his or her results, or other scientists might want to see if they can produce the same results (Simons, 2014). What happens if a study fails to replicate?

When a group of nearly 300 psychologists led by Brian Nosek, known as the Open Science Collaboration (OSC), set out to replicate 100 studies from three well-respected psychology journals, the results were not encouraging (Nosek, 2015). Only 36% of the replications produced significant results, meaning that the researchers were unable to duplicate the original findings of the studies the majority of the time. The average effect size, or the strength of a phenomenon, in the replications was only about half of that reported in the original studies. In other words, if a study found that 50% of the difference in physical aggressiveness was due to hot weather, the replication might show that only about 25% of the difference in aggressiveness was accounted for by the weather. Does this mean that we have to throw out these results?

While failure to replicate should give scientists a reason to reflect on their results, some psychologists are not particularly alarmed by the findings of Nosek and his colleagues (Gilbert et al., 2016). The methods used in the replication efforts were sometimes different from the original study. For example, a sample of Italians substituted for Americans in a study of attitudes toward African Americans and a study of college students being called on by a professor was replicated with people who had not attended college. These differences in sampling, rather than the validity of the original study, might have been the key reason for finding different outcomes.

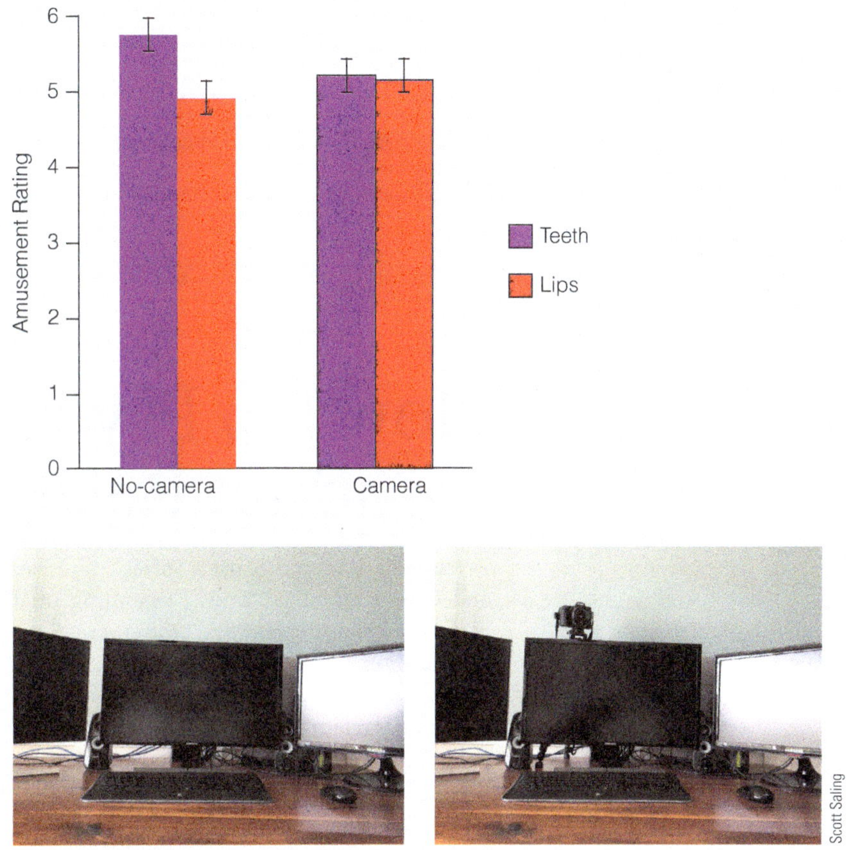

FIGURE **2.4**

Changes in Method Can Impact Replication. A classic study by Strack et al. (1988) concluded that participants would rate cartoons as more amusing if they were holding a pen in their teeth (mimicking smiling) than in their lips. The study failed to replicate (Wagenmakers et al., 2016). The replicating studies, however, added a camera (see photo on right) to the original method to ensure participants were holding their pens correctly. When the camera was removed, returning to the original method of Strack et al., 1988, the results did replicate (Noah et al., 2018). Now psychologists face the task of explaining why the presence of a camera, or the feeling of being observed, could change the results.

Scientific debates usually move us in the right direction. Regardless of how big a replication problem psychology might or might not have, psychologists are looking for new methods to make their results even more reliable. For example, submitting a public "registered report" of the methods and statistical analyses that a researcher plans to run *prior* to conducting a study discourages any after-the-fact efforts to tweak data and results to find something interesting when the main purpose of the study fails. Sharing data, detailed methods, and results in public places allows others to evaluate a researcher's findings. Addressing unrealistic pressure on academics to "publish or perish" and putting quality of research ahead of quantity should also contribute to a more robust scientific environment.

SUMMARY 2.1 Steps to Critical Thinking

Questions for Detecting Good Critical Thinking	Questions for Detecting Poor Critical Thinking (All answers should be no)
What am I being asked to believe or accept?	Do I prefer being given the correct answers rather than figuring them out myself?
What evidence supports this position?	Do I rely on gut feelings instead of thinking a lot about my decisions?
Are there other ways that this evidence could be interpreted?	Am I forgetting to review my conclusions to check for mistakes?
What other evidence would I need to evaluate these alternatives?	Am I oversensitive to criticism about my conclusions?
What are the most reasonable conclusions?	

How Do Psychologists Conduct Research?

Psychological scientists use a variety of research methods, including descriptive, correlational, and experimental methods, depending on the type of question being asked. Descriptive methods, including surveys, case studies, and naturalistic observations, provide a good starting place for a new research question. Correlational methods help psychologists see how two variables of interest, like the number of hours spent playing video games and level of physical aggression, relate to each other. Psychologists use experiments to test their hypotheses and to determine the causes of behavior.

In the next sections, we will describe the common research methods used in psychological science and then compare how they might be used to approach a particular question—whether exposure to video game violence increases aggression. Each method—descriptive, correlational, and experimental—provides a different view of the phenomenon in question, and each has a particular profile of strengths and weaknesses. Each requires different types of statistical analyses, which are described in more depth later in the chapter. Many psychological studies combine several of these methods. When similar outcomes are observed using multiple methods, we have even more confidence in our results.

Descriptive Methods

descriptive method Research methods designed for making careful, systematic observations.

Descriptive methods include case studies, naturalistic observations, and surveys. As we have seen, personal observations and common-sense ideas are especially vulnerable to bias, but descriptive methods allow a researcher to make careful, systematic, real-world observations. Descriptive methods can illuminate associations between variables and establish prevalence rates. Armed with these scientific observations, the researcher will be in a strong position to generate hypotheses.

case study An in-depth analysis of the behavior of one person or a small number of people.

The Case Study A **case study** provides an in-depth analysis of the behavior of one person or a small number of people. Many fields in addition to psychology, including medicine, law, and business, use the case study method. Psychologists often use case studies when large numbers of participants are not available or when a particular participant possesses unique characteristics, as in the case described in this section. Interviews, background records, observation, personality tests, cognitive tests, and brain imaging provide information necessary to evaluate the case. Case studies not only are a useful source of hypotheses, but also can be used to test hypotheses. A hypothesis stating that no life exists outside our solar system would be rejected if you did a case study on a planet outside our solar system and discovered life there.

One of the most productive case studies in psychology chronicled more than 50 years of examinations of Henry Molaison (1926–2008), known in the scientific literature as "the amnesiac patient H.M." In 1953, Molaison underwent brain surgery to control his frequent, severe seizures. Although the surgery may have saved his life, he was left with profound memory deficits, which are described in Chapter 9. Through painstaking testing and evaluation of Molaison, psychologists learned a great deal about the brain structures and processes that support the formation of memories (Corkin, 2002). Even after his death, Molaison continues to contribute to our knowledge. Researchers from the Massachusetts Institute of Technology (MIT), the Massachusetts General Hospital, and the University of California, San Diego (UCSD) are analyzing Molaison's preserved brain today.

s44/ZUMA Press/Newscom

One of the most famous case studies in psychology is that of Henry Molaison, who was known in the literature as "the amnesic patient H.M." until his death in 2008. For more than 50 years, Molaison allowed psychologists to evaluate his memory deficits resulting from brain surgery. After his death, scientists like Jacopo Annese of the University of California, San Diego, began a careful examination of Molaison's brain that continues today.

How could you use the case study method to learn about exposure to video game violence and aggression? You could conduct a case study of Michael Carneal, who was sentenced to life in prison after he began shooting students at his high school in West Paducah, Kentucky in 1997, killing three students and seriously wounding five others. He had never shot a real gun before, but he was fond of playing first-person-shooter games like *Doom*. To conduct your case study, you gather background facts about Carneal's case, possibly by interviewing others associated with the case, viewing legal and medical documents, and observing media accounts. You interview Carneal and possibly administer established personality and clinical tests like those discussed in Chapters 12 and 15. Licensed clinicians who examined Carneal with these methods concluded that he met the criteria for schizophrenia (see Chapter 14). We should be careful, however, to avoid making broad generalizations about relationships between mental illness and mass shootings based on any single case. The majority of people with mental illness do not commit violent crimes (Baumann & Teasdale, 2018), and not all violent offenders are mentally ill.

What are the advantages of using the case study method to learn about the effects of playing violent video games on aggression? Mass shooters are thankfully quite rare (when defined as four or more people killed at one time by a gunman, excluding criminal or gang activity), and the case study method is well suited to learning about unusual situations. A case study can contribute to science by testing hypotheses. If a hypothesis made a strong prediction that all mass shooters play violent video games, finding and documenting a case of a mass shooter who did not play violent video games would require rejection of the hypothesis. Based on the detailed data that you obtain from Carneal's case, you will be better prepared to generate and test additional hypotheses.

John Sommers II/Reuters

Michael Carneal is serving a life sentence in prison for shooting and killing fellow students at his high school in 1997, when he was 14.

Avalon/Bruce Coleman Inc/Alamy Stock Photo

Jane Goodall used naturalistic observation to illuminate the world of the chimpanzee.

Naturalistic Observation If you are interested in learning about larger groups of people than are possible with the case study method, you might pursue **naturalistic observation**, or an in-depth study of a phenomenon in its natural setting. Compared to the case study method, we are looking at a larger group of people, which will strengthen our ability to apply our results to the general population. We also have the advantage of observing individuals in their natural, everyday circumstances, as opposed to the more artificial setting of a laboratory.

A classic example of the method of naturalistic observation is the careful, long-term study of chimpanzees conducted in their habitat by Jane Goodall. In the summer of 1960, Goodall, then 26 years old, began her painstaking observations of chimpanzees living in Gombe National Park in Tanzania. Among her discoveries was that chimpanzees were not vegetarians, as previously assumed (Goodall, 1971, p. 34):

> I saw that one of them was holding a pink-looking object from which he was from time to time pulling pieces with his teeth. There was a female and a youngster and they were both reaching out toward the male, their hands actually touching his mouth. Presently the female picked up a piece of the pink thing and put it to her mouth: it was at this moment that I realized the chimps were eating meat.

As a result of Goodall's years spent following the chimpanzees, scientists have a rich, accurate knowledge of the behavior of these animals in the wild.

Impressed by Goodall's results, you plan to pursue further knowledge about violent video games and aggression by attending local area network (LAN) parties, where attendees bring their computers to a gathering place to play multiplayer, networked video games. You hope that by observing people playing violent video games and watching their subsequent behavior for signs of aggression, you might reach some conclusions about the relationships between video game violence and aggression. As in Goodall's case, this approach has the advantage of providing insight into natural, real-world behaviors with large numbers of participants.

Some naturalistic observations are conducted when people know that they are being observed, while in other cases, people are unaware of being observed. Both situations raise challenges. If we know we are being observed, we might act differently. Your LAN party participants know that aggression is not viewed positively in our culture, so they might act less aggressively when they know that they're being watched. Watching people who do not know that they're being watched raises ethical issues, which will be explored later in this chapter. How would you feel if you discovered that you had been an unwitting participant in a study?

The use of naturalistic observation illustrates the importance of choosing a method that is well suited to the research goals. Like the case study method, naturalistic observation can be helpful for developing hypotheses, but typically, other methods must be used to test them. Most hypotheses in psychology look at the relationships between two or more concepts, like the exposure to violent video games and aggression in this example. Testing a hypothesis would allow you to say whether a relationship between exposure to violent video games and aggression exists, how strong the relationship is, what direction it goes in, and so on. It might appear to you that the people you observe are more aggressive following their LAN parties, but you have no way to demonstrate your point. People engage in many different behaviors during LAN parties. Perhaps eating pizza or staying up all night at LAN parties enhances aggressive tendencies. With only your naturalistic observations to go on, you can't say for sure.

naturalistic observation An in-depth study of a phenomenon in its natural setting.

survey A descriptive method in which participants are asked the same questions.

sample A subset of a population being studied.

population The entire group from which a sample is taken.

The Survey **Surveys** allow us to ask large numbers of people questions about attitudes and behavior. Surveys provide a great deal of useful information quickly, at relatively little expense. Commercial online survey services make conducting surveys easier than in the past.

One of the primary requirements for a good survey is the use of an appropriate **sample**, or subset of a population being studied. The **population** consists of the entire group from which a sample is taken. Good results require large samples that are typical, or representative, of the population that we wish to describe. Major pollsters, like the Pew Research Center and Gallup, take great pains to recruit survey participants who mirror the characteristics of the public across factors such as gender, age, race or ethnicity, education, occupation, income, and geographical location.

Surveys use self-reporting, so results can be influenced by people's natural tendency to want to appear socially appropriate (Corbett, 1991). As we will discover in Chapter 13, people have strong tendencies to conform to the expectations of others. In some surveys, this factor is not a problem. If you ask people whether they prefer lattes or mochas, you will probably get a fairly honest answer. However, when people believe that their true attitudes and behaviors will not be viewed favorably by others, they are more likely to lie, even when their answers are confidential and anonymous.

kolvenbach/Alamy Stock Photo

To pursue the question of the effects of violent video games on aggression, you could do a naturalistic observation at a LAN party.

Let's see how scientists have used the survey method to explore video game violence. One survey asked 374 individuals about their motivations for playing violent video games (Kneer et al., 2018). Participants responded to 20 motives for playing video games on a 5-point scale, from strongly agree to strongly disagree. Although this survey, like all surveys, relied on self-report, the questions were stated in the third person ("People play violent video games because" rather than "I choose to play violent video games because") to minimize conformity with perceived social ideals. As shown in ● Figure 2.5, participants ranked the "fun/challenge" aspects of violent video games as being the most important reason for playing, whereas their attraction to the violence itself was lower.

Diverse Voices in Psychology

How Do We Recruit Diverse Research Participants?

IF WE WANT TO GENERALIZE our conclusions to "people," it is very important for us to sample from the population of "people" rather than depending on handy convenience samples of undergraduate students enrolled in psychology courses. Given limited resources (time and money), how do psychological scientists reach a diverse sample of participants?

You might think that using online recruitment, such as MTurk and Survey Monkey, could solve this problem, but that does not appear to be the case (Maner, 2016). These participants are probably not typical of the adult population in terms of their education and understanding of technology, and they have been exposed to the research methods used by behavioral scientists. Jon Maner (2016) makes a strong case for conducting studies in the field as a way of recruiting more diverse and representative samples. He describes a study of diet and exercise effects on diabetes conducted in 27 geographically diverse clinical centers. Not only were the researchers able to find a large sample (over 3,000 people participated), but 45% of the sample identified themselves as members of underrepresented minority groups. An additional advantage of these field studies, according to Maner, is their stronger likelihood of being replicable. In another section of this chapter, we explored the controversy over the replicability of psychological research.

Rawpixel/istock/Getty Images

Psychological scientists continue their search for methods that will provide more accurate results. Ensuring that a research sample is diverse, mirroring the population, is an important step in this direction. ■

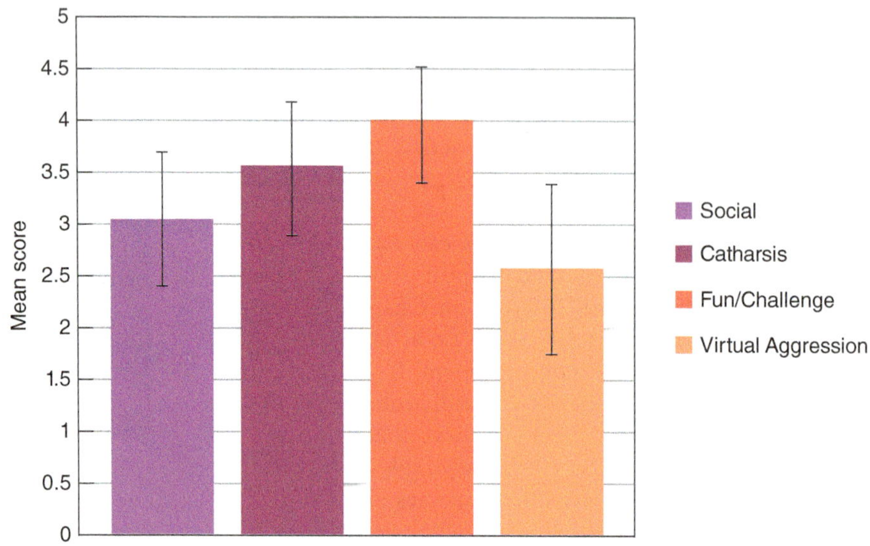

FIGURE 2.5

Results from a Real Survey on Motives for Playing Violent Video Games. A survey showed that participants who regularly play video games, including violent ones, ranked the experience of virtual aggression as a less important motivation for playing than fun/challenge, catharsis, and social motives. Asking about "people who play" rather than "you" might help improve the likelihood that participants will make honest answers rather than socially acceptable answers.

Source: Kneer, J., et al. (2018). "You could have just asked: The perception of motivations to play violent video games." *Studies in Media and Communication* 6(2), 1–11.

correlation A measure of the direction and strength of the relationship between two variables.

variable A factor that has a range of values.

measure A method for describing a variable's quantity.

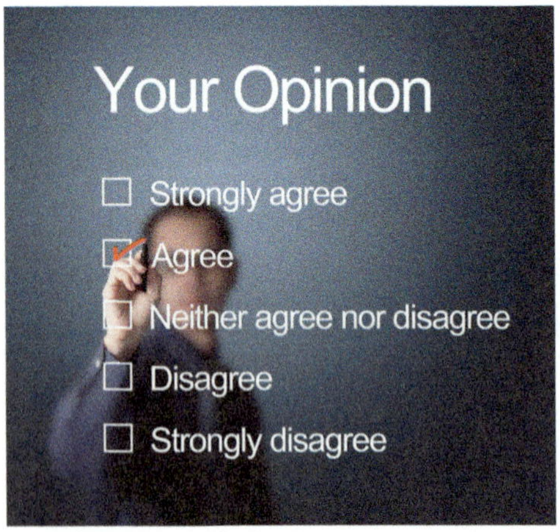

Dusit/Shutterstock.com

People taking surveys might be more interested in pleasing others or appearing "normal" than in answering honestly.

Correlational Methods

Correlations measure the direction and strength of the relationship between two **variables**, or factors that have values that can differ, like a person's height and weight. Correlations allow psychologists to explore whether hours of sleep are related to student grade point averages (Trockel et al., 2000) or whether the age of parents is related to the rate of autism spectrum disorder among their children (Parner et al., 2012). If you're curious about the results of these studies, the first showed that sleep and GPA were not related, and the second showed that the likelihood of producing a child diagnosed with autism spectrum disorder increased with parental age.

We begin our analysis of correlations by measuring our variables. A **measure** answers the simple question of "how much" of a variable we have observed. After we obtain measures of each variable, we compare the values of one variable to those of the other and conduct a statistical analysis of the results. Three possible outcomes from the comparison between our two variables can occur: positive, negative, or zero correlation. In a positive correlation, high levels of one variable are associated with high levels of the other. Height and weight usually show this type of relationship. In most cases, people who are taller weigh more than people who are shorter. Two variables also can show a negative correlation, in which high values of one variable are associated with low values of another. For example, high levels of alcohol consumption among college students are associated with low GPAs. The third possible outcome is a zero correlation, in which the two variables have no systematic relationship with each other. When variables have a zero correlation, knowing the value of one variable does not tell us anything about the value of the other (see Figure 2.6). For example, emergency room and law enforcement personnel are often convinced that they are busier with emergencies and crime on nights with a full moon. In contrast, numerous scientific studies of lunar cycles show zero correlation with emergency room admissions, traffic accidents, or other types of trauma (Stomp et al., 2010).

FIGURE 2.6

Correlations Describe the Direction and Strength of Relationships Between Two Variables. (a) In positive correlations, high levels of one variable are associated with high levels of the other variable. (b) In negative correlations, high values of one variable are associated with low levels of the other variable. (c) In zero correlations, the two variables do not have any relationship with each other.

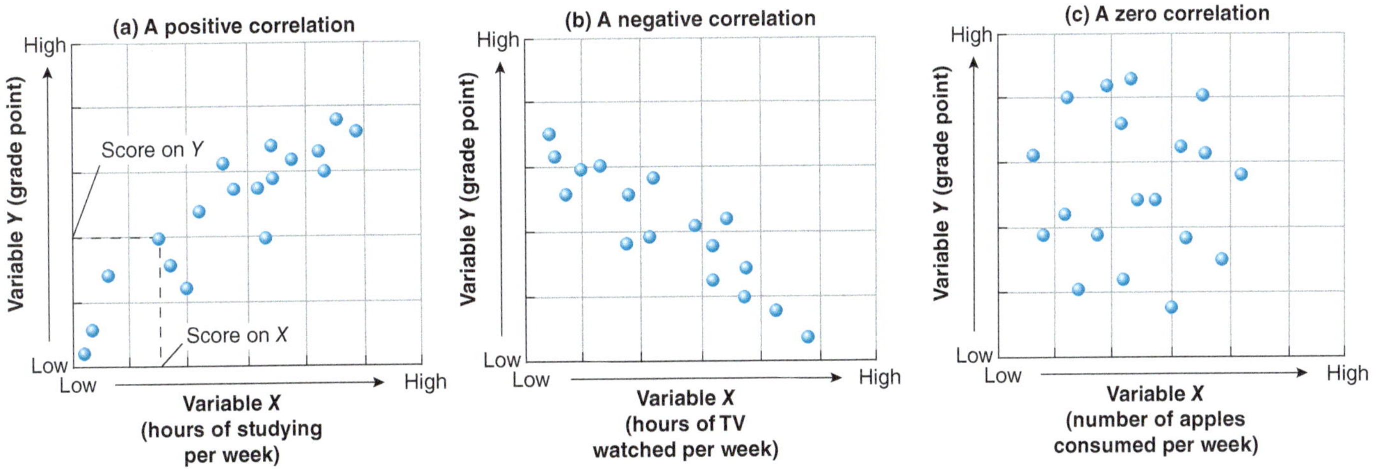

Correlational research results are frequently misunderstood (see Figure 2.7). Correlations permit us to discuss the relationships between two variables but tell us nothing about whether one variable causes any changes in the other. Let us say that we discover a positive correlation between violent video games and aggression: Youth who play the most hours of violent video games have the most reports of physical aggression at school. These results do not allow us to say that playing violent video games *causes* physical aggression at school. This conclusion may seem

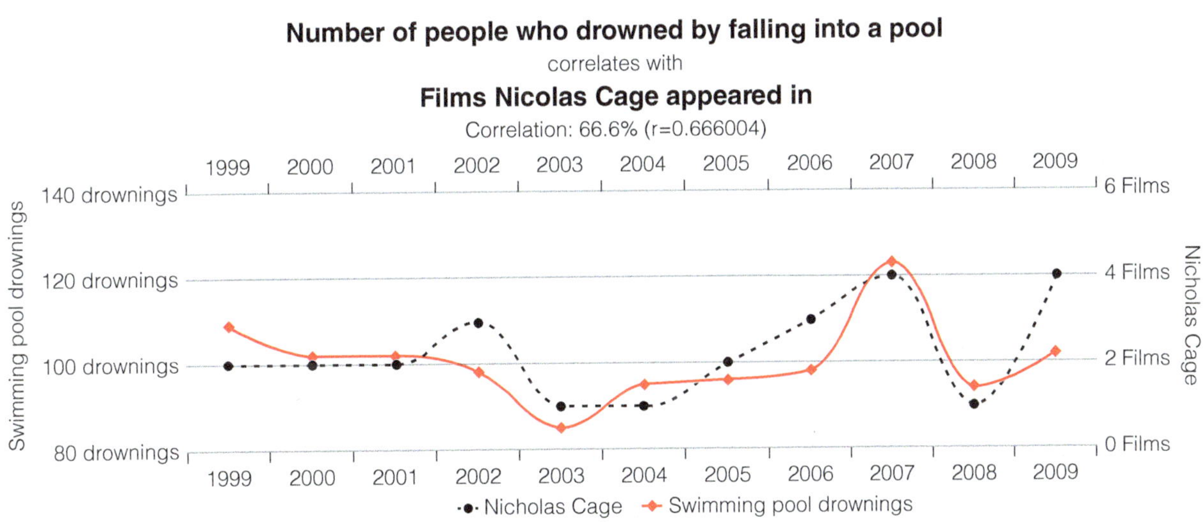

FIGURE 2.7

Correlations Do Not Tell Us About Causality. Tyler Vigen has collected an amusing series of correlations on his Spurious Correlations website to remind us that correlations cannot be used to make conclusions about causality. Few people are likely to conclude that watching Nicholas Cage films leads to higher risk of drowning in swimming pools. However, even experts are tempted to use correlational data to argue that violent video games *cause* aggressiveness, which is just as inaccurate.

reasonable and possibly true, so why must we abandon it? First, the two variables in a correlation can influence each other simultaneously. Although it may be true that playing violent video games leads to physical aggression at school, youth who are physically aggressive at school may be more attracted to violent video games. Second, a **third variable** might be responsible for the correlation between our two variables of interest. Consider the observation that school shootings are often perpetrated by people who had been bullied relentlessly by others. Perhaps the experience of having been bullied (the third variable in this case) predisposes both a choice of violent recreation and a tendency to engage in aggressive behavior at school.

third variable A variable that is responsible for a correlation observed between two other variables of interest.

If we cannot make conclusions about causality using correlations, why would we use them? In a number of circumstances, correlations are more appropriate than other research methods. For example, it would be unethical to ask pregnant women to consume different amounts of alcohol to assess the effects of prenatal alcohol on their infants. Instead, we can ask pregnant women to identify their alcohol intake in diaries, which can then be correlated with various measures of infant functioning. Although this method will not allow us to conclude that drinking during pregnancy causes damage to the fetus, we can correctly identify the strength and direction (positive, negative, or zero) of any correlation between drinks consumed and infants' outcome measures (see ● Figure 2.8). Using this approach, researchers have shown that heavy maternal alcohol consumption is correlated with abnormal amounts of thickening of the outer layer of the brain (the cortex, which is discussed in Chapter 4; Gautam et al., 2015).

To identify studies that are correlational, watch for the use of these and similar phrases: is related to, is linked to, is associated with. These typically refer to correlational research, not experimental results.

FIGURE **2.8**

Correlations Can Help Us Learn About Situations in Which Experiments Would Be Unethical. Even though we cannot make conclusions about causes based on correlations, we can obtain useful information. It would be unethical to assign pregnant women to drinking and nondrinking groups, but the negative correlation that we find between drinks consumed by pregnant women and measures of infant mental development can tell us that drinking during pregnancy is not a good idea. The more alcohol the women consumed, the lower their children scored on tests of infant mental development.

Source: Adapted from M. Testa, B. M. Quigley, & R. D. Eiden (2003). "The Effects of Prenatal Alcohol Exposure on Infant Mental Development: A Meta-analytical Review," *Alcohol and Alcoholism*, *38*(4), 295–304. doi:10.1093/alcalc/agg087

wavebreakmedia/Shutterstock.com

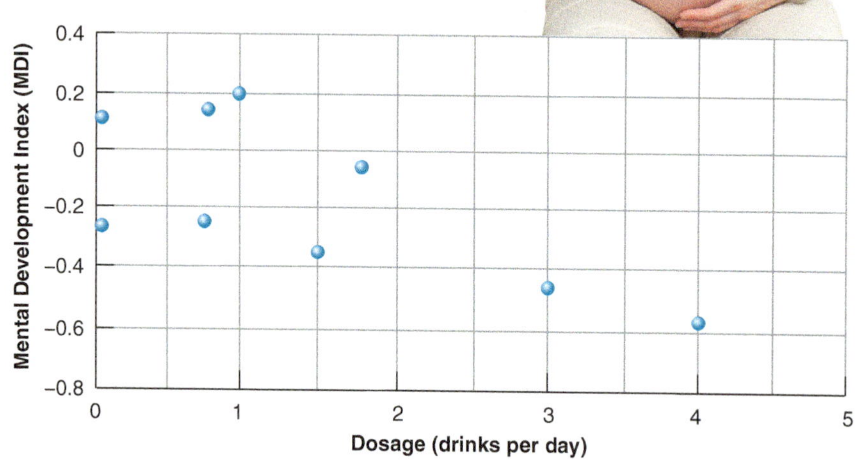

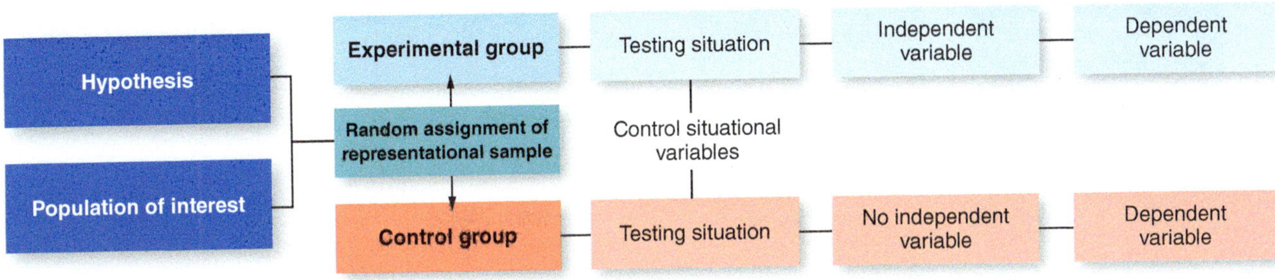

FIGURE 2.9

How to Design an Experiment. A good experimental design features random assignment of participants to groups, appropriate control groups, control of situational variables, and carefully selected independent and dependent variables.

Experimental Methods

The scientist's most powerful tool for drawing conclusions about research questions is the formal **experiment**. Unlike cases in which descriptive methods are used, the researcher conducting an experiment has a great deal of control over the situation. Unlike correlational methods, the use of the formal experiment allows us to talk about cause (see ● Figure 2.9).

A researcher begins designing an experiment with a *hypothesis*, which can be viewed as a highly educated guess based on systematic observations, a review of previous research, or a scientific theory. An experimental hypothesis takes this form: "If I do this, that will happen." To test the hypothesis, the researcher manipulates or modifies the value of one or more variables and observes changes in the values of others. The variable controlled and manipulated by an experimenter ("If I do this") is known as the **independent variable**. We need some way to evaluate the effects of this manipulation. We use a **dependent variable**, defined as a measure used to assess the effects of the manipulation of the independent variable, to tell us "what will happen" as a result of our manipulation of the independent variable. Like the independent variable, our choice of dependent variable is based on our original hypothesis.

"When you're reading or listening to the news, watch for the use of words like *link*, *association*, or *relationship* used to describe two variables, such as a headline that states "Lack of sleep linked to depression" or "Drinking red wine associated with lower rates of heart disease." These keywords usually mean that the data are correlational but are often mistaken for causal. Now you know how you should—and should not—interpret these reports.

After determining our independent and dependent variables, we still have quite a bit of work to do. In most experiments, we want to know how simply going through the procedures of being in an experiment influences our dependent variable. Perhaps the hassle of going to a laboratory and filling out paperwork changes our behavior. To evaluate these irrelevant effects and establish a baseline of behavior under the experimental conditions, we assign some of our participants to a **control group**. In many experiments, the control group will experience all experimental procedures except exposure to the independent variable. When a new treatment is being tested, the control group might experience the standard treatment for a condition. The experience of the control group should be as similar as possible to that of the **experimental groups**, who experience different values of the independent variable.

We want to ensure that our dependent variables reflect the outcomes of our independent variables instead of individual differences among the participants' personalities, abilities, motivations, and similar factors. To prevent these individual differences from masking or distorting the effects of our independent variable, we randomly assign participants to experimental or control groups. **Random assignment** means that each participant has an equal chance of being assigned to any group in an experiment. With random assignment, differences that we see between the behavior of one group and that of another are unlikely to be the result of the individual differences among the participants, which tend to cancel each other out.

Individual differences among participants are an example of **confounding variables**, or variables that are irrelevant to the hypothesis being tested that can alter or distort our conclusions. For example, a researcher might want to test the effects of aerobic exercise on blood pressure. If some participants competed in triathlons without the researcher's knowledge, their athletic experience would confound the interpretation of the results. Random assignment to groups typically controls for confounds because of these types of individual differences, but other sources of confounds exist. Situational confounds, such as time of day or noise levels in a laboratory, also could affect the interpretation of an experiment. Scientists attempt to run their experiments under the most constant circumstances possible to rule out situational confounding variables.

experiment A research method that tests hypotheses and allows researchers to make conclusions about causality.

independent variable An experimental variable controlled and manipulated by the experimenter; the "if A happens" part of a hypothesis.

dependent variable A measure that demonstrates the effects of an independent variable; the "result" part of a hypothesis.

control group A group that experiences all experimental procedures, with the exception of exposure to the independent variable.

experimental group A group of participants who are exposed to the independent variable.

random assignment The procedure in which each participant has an equal chance of being placed in any group in an experiment.

confounding variable Variables that are irrelevant to the hypothesis being tested but can alter a researcher's conclusions.

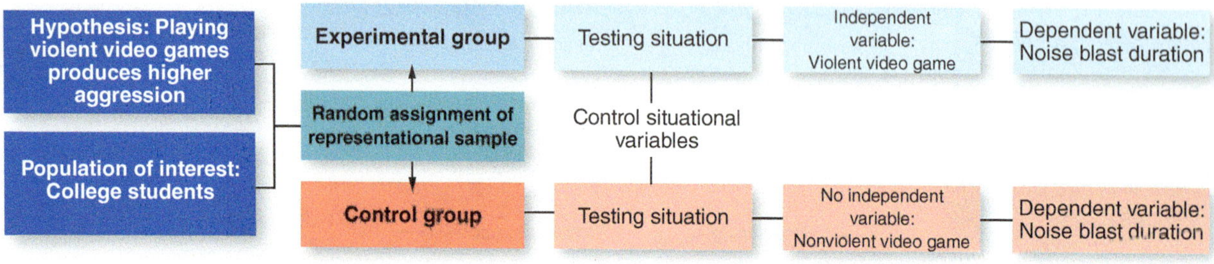

FIGURE **2.10**

Experimental Method in Action. Anderson and Dill (2000) randomly assigned participants to groups playing violent and nonviolent video games. After playing, each participant was asked to choose the strength and duration of a blast of noise to be administered to another person. Keeping conditions in the laboratory as constant as possible would help to reduce the impact of situational variables.

In some cases, we are unable to randomly assign participants to groups based on the independent variable, either for ethical or practical reasons. For example, we are often interested in gender as an independent variable, but we certainly do not assign participants to gender groups. In these cases, we conduct a quasi-experiment. "Quasi" means to resemble, so the quasi-experiment resembles the true experiment, but without random assignment to groups. The quasi-experiment does not do as good a job as the true experiment at controlling for individual differences. For example, we might be interested in how attending Head Start programs affects later school achievement. To participate in Head Start, children must qualify on the basis of their families' having income below a poverty threshold. These children are likely to be different from children who do not attend Head Start on a number of variables related to socioeconomic status which might cloud the impact of attending the program. Nonetheless, a quasi-experiment may be the best we can do in some situations.

Let's return to our question about violent video games and aggression and see how one real experiment addressed the issue (see ● Figure 2.10). The researchers tested a hypothesis stating that playing video games varying in violent content (the independent variable) would influence subsequent levels of aggression (the dependent variable; see Anderson & Dill, 2000).

Researchers attempt to reduce the impact of confounding variables on their results. In a test of the effects of aerobic exercise on blood pressure, situational confounding variables, such as (1) traffic outside the building, (2) a noisy treadmill, and (3) a neighbor breathing heavily, can be controlled by holding the environment as constant as possible for all participants. Individual differences, such as (4) an early morning after little sleep or (5) superior fitness, can be controlled by randomly assigning participants to groups.

Tetra Images/Alamy Stock Photo

The experimental group played a violent game (*Wolfenstein 3D*), while the control group played a nonviolent game (*Myst*). Participants were randomly assigned to groups. You can imagine how the results might be distorted if the experimental group consisted of rugby players and the control group consisted of members of the chess club. Following their game-playing, participants had an opportunity to choose the intensity and duration for a blast of noise to punish a remotely located loser (who didn't exist) in a competitive reaction time activity, and their choices served as the dependent variable. We're assuming that laboratory conditions were held constant to avoid situational confounds. For example, we know that people feel more aggressive in hot temperatures (Carlsmith & Anderson, 1979). What would happen to our experiment if the air conditioner in the laboratory broke while some participants played violent video games, but was fixed right before the next participants played nonviolent games? Results of this carefully controlled experiment confirmed the researchers' hypothesis: Playing the violent game led to the stated intent to administer longer noise blasts to another person.

Mary Kate Denny/PhotoEdit

To conduct an experiment, we must carefully operationalize, or define our variables in practical terms. One way to operationalize physical aggression is to measure how often a preschooler has a physical fight with others.

As powerful as it is, the experimental method, like the other methods discussed previously, has some limitations. Experiments can be somewhat artificial. Participants know that they are in a research study, and they may vary their behavior as a result. However, making a laboratory experiment more realistic can raise ethical challenges. In a study conducted in 1962, before current ethical guidelines for research had been adopted, military personnel were led to believe that their lives were in danger so that experimenters could realistically assess the effects of panic on performance (Berkun et al., 1962). Although the responses of these participants were probably quite representative of real life, few of us would want to be put in their position. This type of research could not be conducted under today's ethical standards, as explained later in this chapter.

Artificiality is also a problem with the Anderson and Dill (2000) video game study. Our real-world question relates to the likelihood that playing violent video games may elicit real physical violence in real situations. Is a person's willingness to inflict a loud sound on another person in a professor's laboratory truly representative of the type of violence involved in mass shootings like Carneal committed? It may or may not be; we need additional research to find out.

Another issue with the experimental method arises from differences in the choices of independent and dependent variables. Independent (controlled) and dependent (measured) variables have to be defined and implemented in some concrete fashion. The process of translating abstract independent and dependent variables into measurable forms is called **operationalization**. The first step in operationalization is to identify the concept to be measured clearly, such as the violence in a video game. Next, the quantitative measures of the concept must be determined. What measures do you need to tell a violent video game from a nonviolent one? You might develop a rating scale based on the number of times violent images, such as depictions of physical injury or blood, are presented in a particular game. Finally, a method for obtaining this measure must be developed. The Entertainment Software Rating Board (ESRB) uses a panel of trained raters to evaluate a DVD of representative game-play submitted by a manufacturer of a new game to establish an appropriate age group rating (Entertainment Software Rating Board [ESRB], 2019).

operationalization Defining variables in ways that allow them to be measured.

There are many ways to operationalize variables in practical terms. Anderson and Dill (2000) operationalized aggression in terms of how lengthy and loud a sound blast a person was willing to inflict on another person. One of the odder dependent variables used in video game aggression research is the hot sauce paradigm, in which the amounts of hot sauce that participants choose to be administered to another participant are used to measure aggression (Lieberman et al., 1999). Other researchers might choose different ways to operationalize aggression, such as frequency of physical fights among preschoolers. As a result, even though there is a large body of work regarding the impact of violent video games on aggression, the variables used are so different that few direct comparisons can be made among the many studies.

Ruslan Guzov/Shutterstock.com

Nearly all studies of video games and aggression use participants playing alone. If we add the social perspective by studying people playing together, we find that aggressive behavior actually decreases following play, regardless of whether the game was violent.

Meta-analyses The point of this discussion is not to convince you that scientists don't know what they're talking about, but rather to impress upon you the importance of reviewing research results using your best critical thinking skills. In seeking to understand something as complicated as the science of mind, it is unlikely that any single study could provide complete information about

meta-analysis A statistical analysis of many previous experiments on a single topic.

publication bias The possibility that published studies are not representative of all work done on a particular phenomenon.

a phenomenon. Instead, progress in our understanding results from the work of many scientists using diverse methods to answer the same question. Conducting a **meta-analysis**, or a statistical analysis of many previous experiments on the same topic, often provides a clearer picture than do single experiments observed in isolation.

Meta-analyses have their own share of challenges, however. A meta-analysis is only as good as the studies on which it is based. Published studies available to researchers conducting a meta-analysis might be subject to **publication bias**, or the possibility that they are not representative of all the work done on a particular problem. A "file drawer" problem also exists, in which journals are more likely to publish studies that demonstrate significant effects of an independent variable, such as video game violence, on a dependent variable, such as aggression, than studies that show no significant effects. If publication bias is present, the results of any meta-analysis might be misleading.

The Importance of Multiple Perspectives As we will see in so many examples in this textbook, even the best research designs might mislead us if they fail to take multiple perspectives into account. Most of the research discussed so far regarding video games and aggression has involved single participants playing alone. What happens when we "zoom out," using the social perspective to look at the effects of video games on groups of people playing together? Playing video games cooperatively is associated with less subsequent aggressive behavior, regardless of whether the game played was violent or not (Jerabeck & Ferguson, 2013).

The research discussed throughout the remainder of this textbook has been subjected to considerable skeptical review by other experts in the field. Most studies have survived the dual tests of peer review and replication by others. Converging evidence from descriptive, correlational, and experimental research provides us with confidence in our conclusions. Psychology, like any science, has followed its share of wrong turns and dead ends, but most knowledge presented here has been carefully crafted to present the most accurate view possible of behavior and mental processes.

How Do We Study the Effects of Time?

Modifications of the methods discussed previously might be necessary for answering specific questions. Psychological scientists frequently ask questions about normal behaviors related to age. As Chapter 11 will show, aggression in preschoolers means something different from aggression in a 16-year-old. Considering the impact of video game violence on aggression within the context of age-related change adds a new and useful dimension to our hypothesis, but it requires additional attention to the research methods to be used.

cross-sectional study An experimental design for assessing age-related changes in which data are obtained simultaneously from people of differing ages.

longitudinal study An experimental design for assessing age-related changes in which data are obtained from the same individuals at intervals over a long period of time.

Psychologists have three specific techniques for assessing the normal behaviors associated with age: cross-sectional, longitudinal, and mixed longitudinal designs. To do a **cross-sectional study**, we might gather groups of people of varying ages and assess both their exposure to violent video games and their levels of physical aggression. We might be able to plot a developmental course for age-related differences in both video game exposure and aggressive behavior. However, the cross-sectional method introduces what we refer to as *cohort effects*, or the generational effects of having been born at a particular point in history. Being 20 years old in 1960 was different from being 20 years old in 1990 or 2020 because of a variety of cultural influences. Today's 10-year-olds, who do not know of a time without the Internet, might respond differently to violent video games than today's 60-year-olds, for reasons that have nothing to do with age. Any such cohort effects could mask or distort our cross-sectional results.

Cross-sectional studies usually show that intelligence scores decrease with age. These results are most likely a cohort effect. Performance on IQ tests has fluctuated over the past 100 years for reasons that are not fully understood (Flynn, 1984).

A method that lessens this dilemma is the **longitudinal study**, in which a group of individuals is observed for a long period (see Figure 2.11). For example, the Fels Longitudinal Study began in 1929 to observe the effects of the Great Depression on children, and it now has enrolled great-grandchildren of the original participants. One longitudinal study found no evidence that exposure to violent video games led to antisocial behavior (Smith et al., 2018). The longitudinal approach has few logical drawbacks

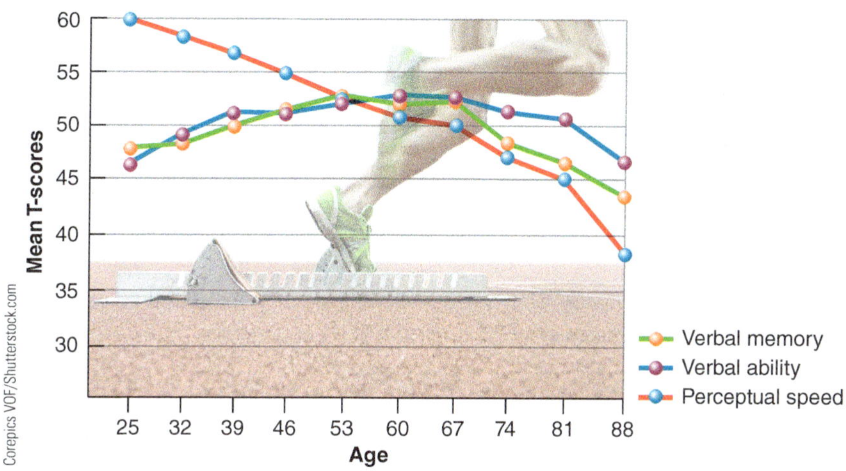

FIGURE **2.11**

Special Designs Let Us See Behaviors Associated with Age. Longitudinal designs control for the cohort effects that are often seen in cross-sectional designs. This longitudinal study shows that verbal ability and verbal memory are fairly stable over the lifetime, but that perceptual speed gradually worsens with age.

Source: Adapted from K. W. Schaie (1996). *Intellectual development in adulthood: The Seattle Longitudinal Study*, p. 271, Cambridge, UK: Cambridge University Press.

Corepics VOF/Shutterstock.com

but is expensive and time consuming. Participants might drop out of the study because they move or lack incentive. Researchers then must worry about whether those who remain in the study still comprise a representative sample.

The third approach, the **mixed longitudinal design**, combines the cross-sectional and longitudinal methods. Participants from a range of ages are observed for a limited time (usually about 5 years). This approach is faster and less expensive than the longitudinal method and avoids some of the cohort effects of the pure cross-sectional method.

mixed longitudinal design A method for assessing age-related changes that combines the cross-sectional and longitudinal approaches by observing a cross-section of participants over a shorter period than is used typically in longitudinal studies.

SUMMARY 2.2 Principles of Research Methods

Research Method	Strengths	Weaknesses
Descriptive methods		
Case study 	Can explore new and unusual phenomena; can provide the basis for rejecting a hypothesis	Has limited generalization or ability to be replicated
Naturalistic observation 	Provides insight into natural, real-world behaviors	Participants act differently when watched; the process has ethical issues
Survey 	Provides large amounts of data quickly and inexpensively	Requires a large representative sample; people wish to appear socially appropriate and may lie

(Continued)

Research Method	Strengths	Weaknesses
Correlations 	Allow us to predict behavior; stimulate development of hypotheses; address some difficult ethical situations	Cannot be used to discuss causality
Experiments 	Allow control of situations, strong hypothesis testing, and judgment of causality	Raise artificiality and ethical concerns; are time consuming
Assessing the effects of time: 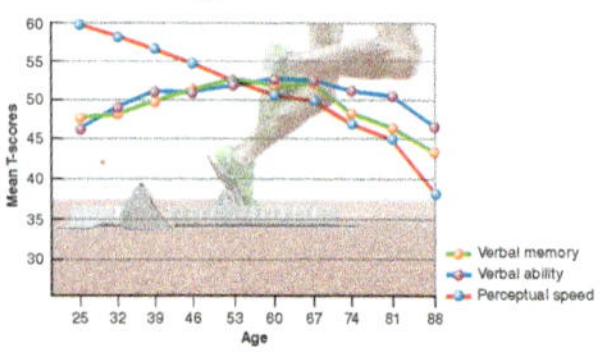		
• Cross-sectional study	Is quick and relatively inexpensive	Is subject to cohort effects
• Longitudinal study	Reduces the impact of cohort effects	Is expensive and time consuming; people drop out
• Mixed longitudinal study	Is less expensive and time consuming than longitudinal, with some control of cohort effects	Is still relatively expensive and time consuming; dropout problem remains

Credits: Top row—s44/ZUMA Press/Newscom; Second row—Avalon/Bruce Coleman Inc/Alamy Stock Photo; Third row—Dusit/Shutterstock.com; Fourth row—wavebreakmedia/Shutterstock.com; Fifth row—Mary Kate Denny/PhotoEdit; Bottom row—Corepics VOF/Shutterstock.com.

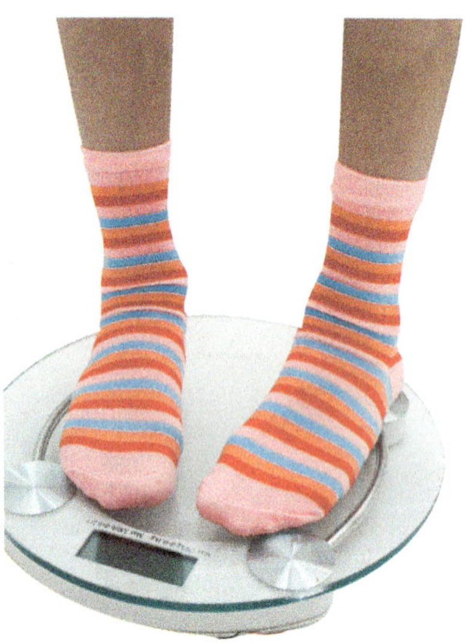

PhotoAlto/Alamy Stock Photo

A valid measure actually measures what it is supposed to measure. In this case, your bathroom scale is supposed to tell you how much you weigh.

How Do We Draw Conclusions from Data?

Asking the right questions and collecting good information are only the beginning of good science. Once we have collected our results, or data, we need to figure out what those data mean for our hypotheses and theories. The interpretation of data is not an arbitrary act—scientists follow specific rules when drawing their conclusions.

The Importance of Valid and Reliable Measures

Data are only as good as the measures used to obtain them. How would we know whether a measure is good or bad? Two standards that any measure must meet are reliability and validity.

Reliability refers to the consistency of a measure. There are several meanings of reliability in science, including test–retest, interrater, inter-method, and internal consistency. For example, test–retest reliability of the Scholastic Aptitude Test (SAT) is quite good, as you might have noticed if you took the test more than once. If you were ill for the first test, or you invested in a preparation course before taking it the second time, your score might change; otherwise, your scores are likely to be about the same. Good measures also show high interrater reliability, or consistency in the interpretation of a measure across different observers. You can imagine

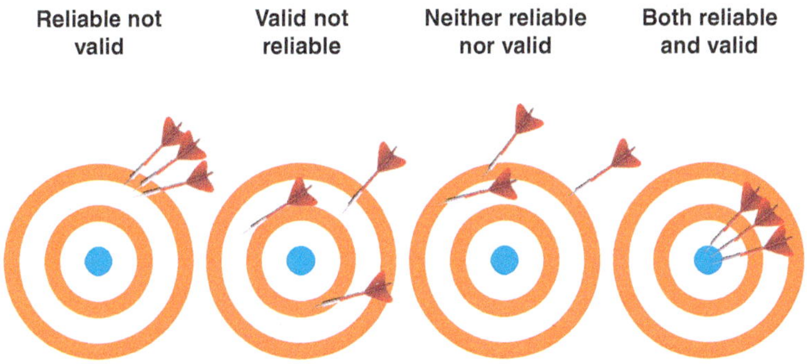

FIGURE **2.12**

Good Measures Are Both Reliable and Valid. Think of hitting the bullseye as having a measure that works perfectly (my scale tells me how much I weigh). If our arrows consistently miss the bullseye but in the same way, we have reliability but no validity (my scale repeatedly tells me I am ten pounds less than I really weigh). If our arrows hit around the bullseye, but not consistently, we have validity without reliability (my scale weighs me five pounds too heavy one day and five pounds too light the next—the average over time is likely to be close to my true weight). If the arrows end up away from the bullseye in a random pattern, we have neither reliability nor validity (who knows what the scale will tell me today). Finally, when the arrows consistently hit the bullseye, we have both validity and reliability (my scale weighs me accurately).

Source: https://socialresearchmethods.net/kb/relandval.php

how distressing it would be if, for example, one lab identified you as having a fatal disease on the basis of a blood test and another did not. Inter-method reliability describes the positive correlation of several approaches to measure a feature in an individual. Returning to the SAT example, it is likely that your SAT and high school grades are positively correlated, which supports the reliability of these measures. Finally, internal consistency results from measures within a single test that positively correlate with one another.

reliability The consistency of a measure, including test-retest, interrater, inter-method, and internal consistency.

validity A quality of a measure that leads to correct conclusions (i.e., the measure evaluates the concept that it was designed to do).

Validity means that a measure leads to correct conclusions or evaluates the concept that it is designed to do. For example, your bathroom scale is supposed to measure how much you weigh. The data obtained from your bathroom scale can lead you to a valid conclusion (this is how much I weigh) or an invalid conclusion (wow, I'm much lighter than the doctor's scale said I am).

How would we determine whether a measure leads to valid conclusions? One approach is to see whether a measure correlates with other existing, established measures of the same concept. Many universities use the SAT to help select the best candidates for admission. This test is supposed to measure a student's aptitude for success in college, but some universities have abandoned it in favor of other measures. We could ask which of the following measures—the SAT, SAT Subject Tests, or high school GPA—shows the highest positive correlation with first-year college grades. The results of this comparison indicate that the SAT Subject Tests show the highest positive correlation with first-year college grades compared to both the SAT and the high school GPA (Geiser & Studley, 2002). Thus, we can conclude that SAT Subject Tests are the most valid of the three measures for predicting first-year college grades.

Reliability and validity are not the same. You can obtain a consistent result (reliability) that lacks meaning (validity; see Figure 2.12). For example, if you weigh 200 pounds and your bathroom scale consistently reports that you weigh 150 pounds, whether you're looking at the number or your roommate reads it for you, the scale has reliability but not validity. If you get a wildly different number each time you step on the scale, you have neither reliability nor validity. The measure is not consistent (no reliability) and also fails to measure the construct—weight in this case—that it is designed to measure (no validity). Only when the scale repeatedly reports your correct weight of 200 pounds do you have both reliability and validity.

Descriptive Statistics

Just as we might explore a new research topic using the descriptive research methods outlined earlier, we can use descriptive statistics to explore the characteristics of the data obtained from our research. **Descriptive statistics** help us organize individual bits of data into meaningful patterns and summaries. However, descriptive analyses tell us only about the sample we have

descriptive statistics Statistical methods that organize data into meaningful patterns and summaries, such as finding the average value.

studied. To determine whether the results from our sample apply to larger populations requires additional statistical analysis, described in a subsequent section of this chapter.

To illustrate the use of descriptive statistics, let's look at some real data. The National Survey of Sexual Attitudes and Lifestyles (*Natsal-3*) uses a large sample of the British population between the ages of 16 and 74 years (Mitchell et al., 2019). Understanding these results would be overwhelming without some way of summarizing the individual data points in meaningful ways. We might approach this mass of data first by asking how numbers of lifetime sex partners are distributed. We could arrange the numbers from low to high and note how many participants reported each number. The result of our work would be a frequency distribution. We often illustrate frequency distributions with a bar chart, or histogram, like the one shown in ● Figure 2.13.

Central Tendency Frequency distributions are a useful starting place, but we might also be interested in identifying the "average" score on our measures, or the central tendency of our data set. Central tendency helps us understand what the "most typical" score in a data set might be. If you met only one person from the *Natsal-3* sample, what is their most likely number of lifetime sex partners?

There are three types of measures for central tendency, each having its own set of advantages: the mean, median, and mode. The **mean** is the numerical average of a set of scores, computed by adding all the scores together and dividing by the number of scores. Your professors are likely to tell you about the mean score of your class on an exam, to help you figure out how you're doing relative to your classmates. The *Natsal-3* reported means of 14 lifetime sex partners for men and 7 for women (Mitchell et al., 2019). Please note that in many self-report studies, males appear to overestimate their number of sex partners for a variety of interesting reasons.

The **median** represents a halfway mark in the data set, with half of the scores above it and half below. In many data sets, the median scores are quite close to the mean scores. Why, then, would you ever need to consider a median? In some cases, you might find some extreme scores that could affect the mean. In most studies of the number of lifetime sex partners people report, the median is substantially below the mean. This suggests the presence of outliers, or people who have many more lifetime sex partners than others (look back again at Figure 2.13).

The **mode** refers to the score that occurs most frequently, and it is easy to determine by looking at a histogram. In our *Natsal-3* data, the mode for both males and females is one lifetime sex partner. In particular, the mode can be an advantage over a mean or median when

mean The numerical average of a set of scores.

median The halfway mark in a set of data, with half of the scores above it and half below.

mode The most frequently occurring score in a set of data.

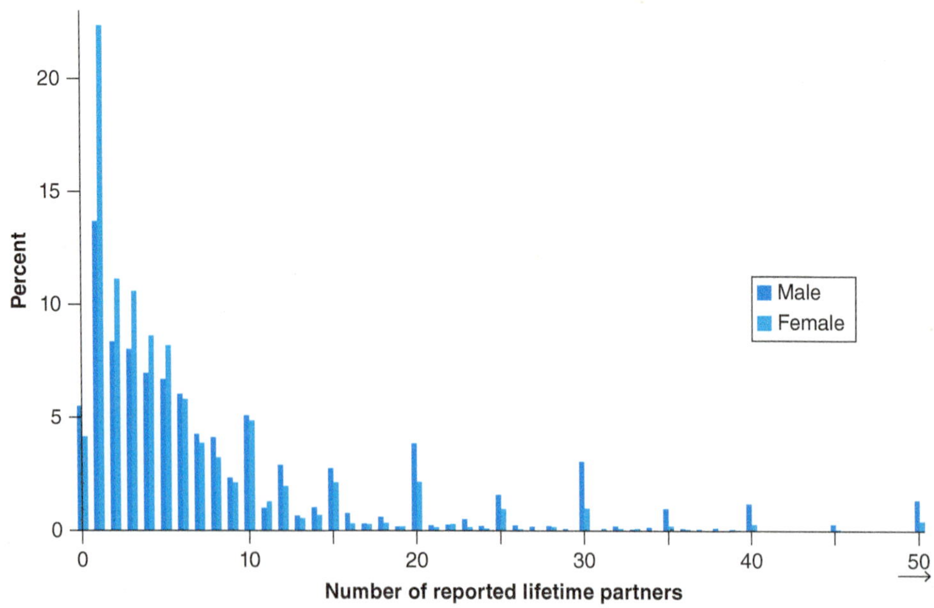

FIGURE **2.13**

Frequency Distributions.
Descriptive statistics, such as this frequency distribution of male and female numbers of lifetime opposite sex partners, allow us to see meaningful patterns and summaries in large sets of data.

Source: Mitchell, K. R., et al. (2019). "Why Do Men Report More Opposite-Sex Sexual Partners Than Women? Analysis of the Gender Discrepancy in a British National Probability Survey." *The Journal of Sex Research 56*(1), 1–8.

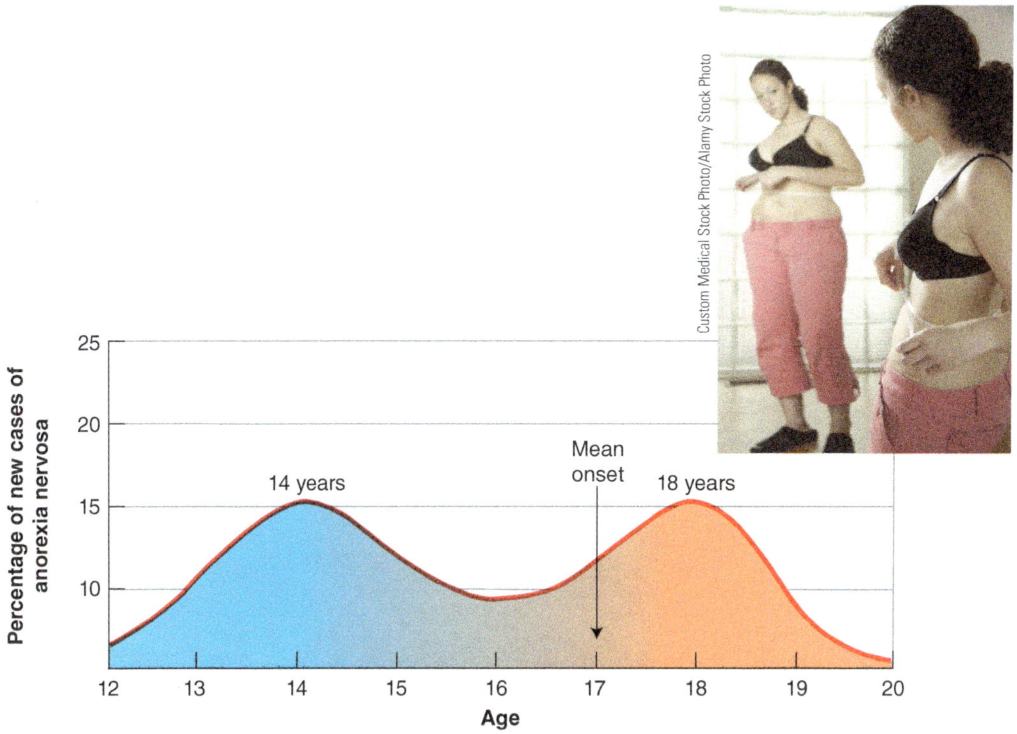

FIGURE **2.14**

What New Information Can We Learn from a Mode? The average age of onset for the anorexia nervosa is 17 years, but this measure masks the important fact that age of onset shows two modes—one at 14 years and a second at 18 years. For public health officials wishing to target vulnerable groups for preventive education, the modes provide better information than the mean.

Source: Adapted from K. A. Halmi, R. C. Casper, E. D. Eckert, S. C. Goldberg, and J. M. Davis (1979). "Unique Features Associated with Age of Onset of Anorexia Nervosa," *Psychiatry Research*, *1*(2), 209–215. doi: 10.1016/0165-1781(79)90063-5

there is more than one mode in a set of data. For example, the mean age of onset for anorexia nervosa, which is discussed in Chapter 7, is 17 years of age, but the distribution is bimodal, which means that it has two substantial modes. One peak occurs around the age of 14, when many teens struggle with their changing shapes due to puberty, and another occurs around the age of 18, when many teens leave home and make food choices without the watchful eyes of their parents (Halmi et al., 1979). An intervention program designed to coincide with the most likely ages of onset would probably be more effective than one timed to coincide with the mean age of onset (see ● Figure 2.14).

Variance In addition to being curious about central tendency, we might want to know how clustered our scores are (variance). The traditional way to look at the variance of scores is to use a measure known as the **standard deviation**, which tells us how tightly clustered around the mean a group of scores is. A smaller standard deviation suggests that most scores might be found near the mean, whereas a larger standard deviation means that the scores are spread out from the mean (see ● Figure 2.15).

standard deviation A measure of how tightly clustered around the mean a group of scores is.

The Normal Curve Many measures of interest to psychologists, such as scores on intelligence tests, which are discussed in Chapter 10, appear to form a **normal distribution**, illustrated in ● Figure 2.16. The ideal normal curve in this illustration has several important

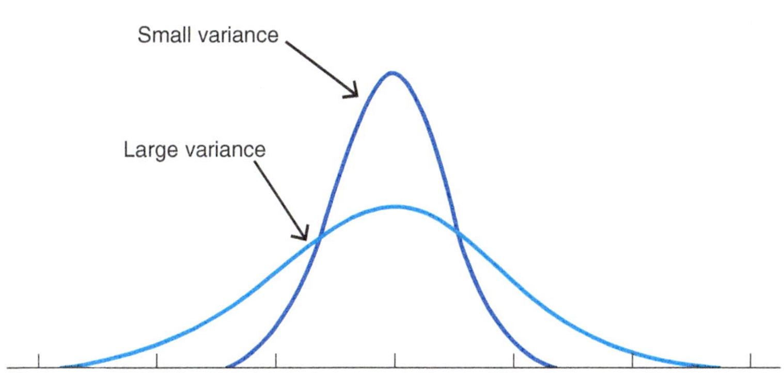

FIGURE **2.15**

Variance. Measures of variance tell us how tightly clustered our scores are around the mean. Small amounts of variance indicate that scores are tightly clustered and larger variance tells us that the scores are more spread out.

FIGURE 2.16

The Normal Curve. Many measures of interest to psychologists take the approximate form of a normal distribution. These graphs compare a standard normal curve, shown in (a), to the distribution of scores on a standardized test of intelligence, the Wechsler Adult Intelligence Scale, shown in (b).

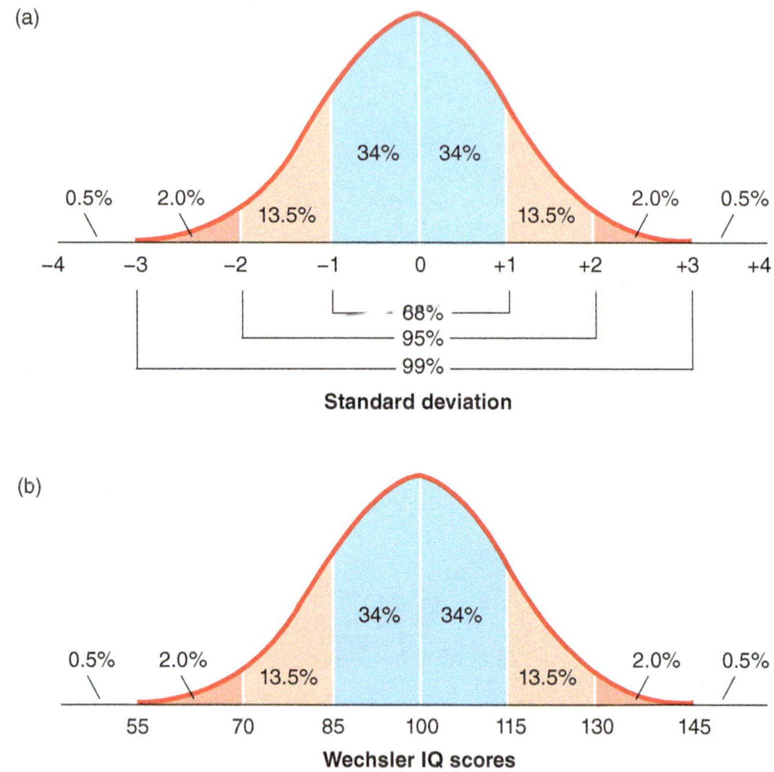

features. One, it is symmetrical. Equal numbers of scores should occur above and below the mean. Second, its shape indicates that most scores occur near the mean, which is where our measure of variance plays a role. In the standard normal curve, shown in Figure 2.16(a), 68% of the population falls within one standard deviation of the mean, 95% falls within two standard deviations, and 99% of the population falls within three standard deviations. Instruments for assessing intelligence, discussed in Chapter 10, frequently convert raw scores earned by many participants to fit a normal distribution with a mean of 100 and a standard deviation of 15. As a result, we would expect 68% of test takers to receive an IQ score between 85 and 115. Another 95% would most likely score between 70 and 130, leaving only 2.5% to score above 130 and another 2.5% to score below 70.

Descriptive Statistics with Two Variables In our discussion so far, we have been describing single variables, such as number of lifetime sex partners and IQ test scores. In psychological research, we often want to describe the relationships among multiple variables.

We can illustrate the relationship between two variables in a scatterplot like the one shown in Figure 2.17. Each dot represents the intersection between scores on two variables of interest. For example, we can compare the distributions of math SAT scores as a function of grade point average (GPA). From our scatterplot, it looks like math SAT scores and GPAs are systematically related to each other. As one increases, the other does as well, which you should recognize from the earlier discussion as a positive correlation.

Although this scatterplot gives a sense that GPAs and math SAT scores have a systematic relationship, we can compute the strength of that relationship using a correlation coefficient. Correlation coefficients can range from −1.00 to +1.00. A correlation of −1.00 and a correlation of +1.00 are equally strong but differ in the direction of the effect. Negative coefficients indicate a negative correlation and positive coefficients indicate a positive correlation. A zero correlation indicates that the two variables have no systematic relationship. The closer a correlation coefficient is to −1.00 or to +1.00, the stronger is the relationship between the two variables. When the score is −1.00 or +1.00, the correlation is perfect—all data points follow the pattern.

CONNECTING TO RESEARCH

Do You Believe in ESP?

ESP STANDS FOR *EXTRASENSORY PERCEPTION*, with *extra* in this case meaning "outside" the boundaries of the normal information that we obtain from our various senses, such as vision, hearing, and touch. The study of ESP is part of the larger field of *parapsychology*, or the study of psychic phenomena lying outside the typical boundaries of the field of psychology described in Chapter 1. Among the abilities grouped into the category of ESP are *telepathy* (the ability to communicate with other minds without using the usual methods of speaking or writing), *clairvoyance* (the ability to perceive objects that do not affect the known senses), *precognition* (knowledge of future events), and *premonition* (emotional anticipation of future events). In 2005, Gallup pollsters found that 41% of Americans said that they believed in ESP, with 25% not sure and 32% not believing (Gallup Poll News Service, 2005). Of the scientists who are members of the National Academy of Sciences, 96% said that they did not believe in ESP (McConnell & Clark, 1991).

A study of ESP (Bem, 2011) generated considerable discussion in the scientific community about everything from the statistics that we use to the effects of investigator bias. Evaluating this study provides a good opportunity to practice your critical thinking skills and to apply what you have learned about validity and reliability.

Syfy Channel/Courtesy Everett Collection

The popularity of television shows like *Ghost Hunters* might be related to the large number of Americans who report a belief in ESP (41%). In contrast, 96% of the members of the National Academy of Sciences say they do not believe in ESP.

The Question: Nine experiments involving more than 1,000 participants tested different types of precognition and premonition. We will focus our attention on the first experiment, which tested the following hypothesis: Participants should be able to anticipate the position (right side or left side of a computer screen) of an erotic photograph (see Figure 2.18). Is the following study of this hypothesis an example of good science?

METHODS

A total of 100 undergraduates (50 men and 50 women) participated. Stimuli (both erotic and nonerotic photographs) were selected from a standard set known as the International Affective Picture System. During each trial, participants saw two curtains on a computer screen and were asked to predict which curtain hid a picture. The sequencing of the erotic and nonerotic pictures and the left–right positions was determined by a random number generator after the participant made a selection. This timing was designed to test the precognition of future events (the participants selected a side of the screen before the random number generator selected a location for the picture).

Here is where Bem's methods get a bit murky. The first 40 participants saw 12 erotic pictures, 12 negative pictures (unpleasant images), and 12 neutral pictures. Then, for reasons not well explained in the paper, the method was changed for the remaining 60 participants, who were shown 18 erotic and 18 nonerotic photos, 8 of which were described as romantic but not erotic (couple at a wedding, etc.). It is quite unusual for researchers to change their methods in the middle of an experiment, and more troubling when there doesn't seem to be a good reason to do so.

ETHICS

The only potential ethical challenge in this study is the presentation of erotic photos. Potential participants should be warned of this aspect before they agree to continue with the study.

Anson0618/Shutterstock.com

FIGURE 2.17

Evidence of ESP? Participants in Bem's (2011) study were supposed to predict behind which of two curtains a picture would appear.

RESULTS

If we have two choices, we have a 50% chance of guessing correctly on each trial. Bem reported that the future position of the erotic images was chosen correctly on 53.1% of the trials, and the future position of the nonerotic images was chosen correctly on 49.8% of the trials. Bem reported that his results were statistically significant using the $p < .05$ standard discussed in this chapter.

CONCLUSIONS

Bem concluded that the choices made by his participants were better than chance, supporting his hypothesis that precognition could be demonstrated.

What do others think of Bem's results? James Alcock, writing for the *Skeptical Inquirer*, concluded that "just about everything that could be done wrong in an experiment occurred here" (Alcock, 2011, p. 31). Among Alcock's concerns were Bem's changing of his method midway through the experiment and his questionable use of statistical analyses.

As discussed earlier, replication provides an important check on possible researcher bias, and failure to replicate can indicate serious flaws in an experiment. So far, the three known replications of Bem's experiments have failed to produce significant results. Despite the flaws, however, Bem's experiments have contributed to science by stimulating a lively discussion of scientific and statistical methods.

FIGURE **2.18**

A Scatterplot. A scatterplot allows us to visualize the relationship between two variables, such as the math SAT score and the high school GPA for one small sample of college students. This relationship should look familiar to you—it is an example of a positive correlation.

Source: Adapted from F. Young (2011). "The Pearson Correlation Coefficient," retrieved from http://forrest.psych.unc.edu/research/vista-frames/help/lecturenotes/lecture11/pearson.html.

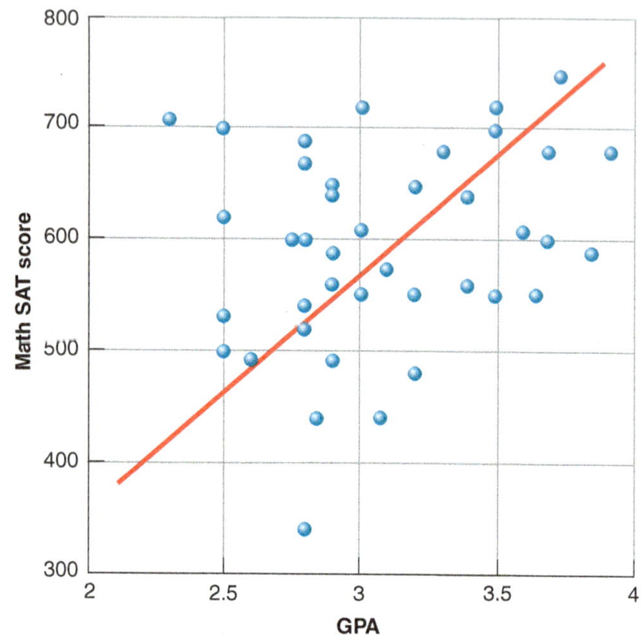

Inferential Statistics

Although we can learn a great deal from descriptive statistics, most research described in this textbook features the use of **inferential statistics**, so called because they permit us to draw inferences or conclusions from data. Descriptive statistics allow us to talk about our sample data but do not allow us to extend our results to larger groups. To reach conclusions about how our observations of a sample might fit the bigger picture of groups of people who didn't participate in our research, we use inferential statistics.

Although inferential statistics can be powerful, we must be cautious about making **generalizations** from our results to larger populations. To generalize means to extend your conclusions to people outside your research sample. Psychology over the years has been justifiably criticized as being the "psychology of the college sophomore." This criticism arises because researchers are usually college professors, and the students in their courses are a convenient source of willing study participants, especially when extra credit is available. Today's psychological scientists recognize that college students do not comprise a representative sample of people, and they go to great lengths to recruit samples of participants that are more diverse in age, race, ethnicity, socioeconomic background, and other demographic variables. Having a diverse sample supports more generalization than using a sample of college students.

To illustrate the use of inferential statistics, let's consider the 2009 SAT mathematics test. Men scored an average of 534 out of 800 and women scored an average of 499 out of 800 on this test. Does this mean that men perform better than women on this test? Or do men and women perform similarly, and this group is just an unusual sample of test takers? The default position, stating that there is no real difference between two measures (math scores produced by men and women in this example), is known as the **null hypothesis**. Recall that we cannot "prove" a hypothesis to be correct. We can either reinforce a hypothesis or demonstrate that it is false. Rejecting the null hypothesis suggests that alternative hypotheses (there might be a relationship between gender and math scores) should be explored and tested.

How do we know when a hypothesis should be rejected? Like most sciences, psychology has defined **statistical significance** as a probability or "p value" of .05 (5%) or less that a score at least as extreme as the observed result could occur if the null hypothesis is true. More recently, a large number of influential scientists have argued that the term "statistical significance" should be reserved for a p value of only .005 (.5%) or less for any new discoveries (Benjamin et al., 2018). Results meeting the old criterion of 5% but not the new criterion of .5% would be described as "suggestive." We can assess the likelihood of observing a result by repeating a study, like throwing dice multiple times. We could give the mathematics portion

normal distribution A symmetrical probability function.

inferential statistics Statistical methods that allow experimenters to extend conclusions from samples to larger populations.

generalize To extend conclusions to larger populations outside your research sample.

null hypothesis A hypothesis stating the default position that there is no real difference between two measures.

statistical significance A standard for deciding whether an observed result is likely in the event the null hypothesis is true.

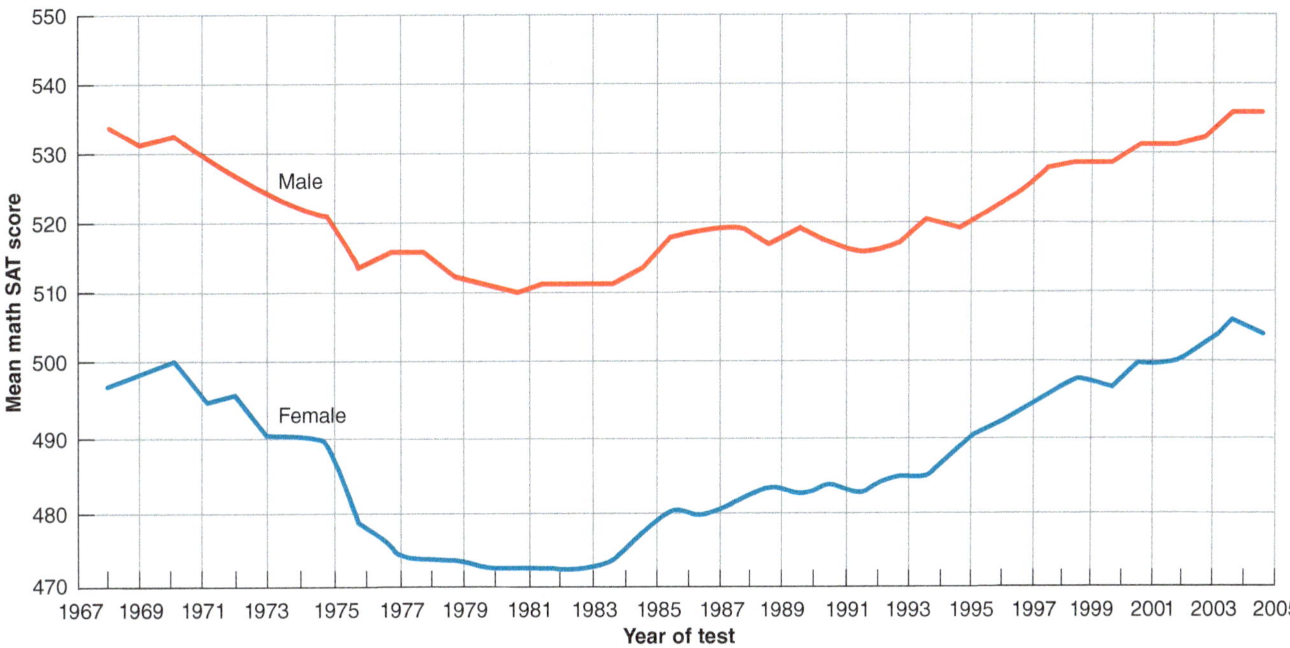

FIGURE **2.19**

Are Male and Female Scores on the Math SAT Different? Inferential statistics allow us to decide whether the observed differences between the performance of males and that of females on the math SAT represents a real gender difference.

Source: Adapted from The College Board (2009).

of the SAT to many randomly selected samples of male and female college-bound students. If men and women score about the same or women score higher than men in .5% or more of these samples, we would reject our "Men score higher than women" hypothesis as false. In reality, scientists rarely repeat their studies many times. Instead, statistical methods help us to evaluate statistical significance based on a single sample.

This type of careful analysis of the SAT data has confirmed that the differences on the mathematics portion of the test between male and female test takers are statistically significant (Halpern et al., 2007; see ● Figure 2.19). Does this result mean that we should consider this difference when deciding on a major or career? Probably not. Keep in mind that the goal of the SAT is to predict college grades. When the math SAT scores of men and women receiving the same letter grade in a mathematics course at the same university were compared, the women scored 33 points less than the men (Wainer & Steinberg, 1992). This is about the same difference that we observed between the mean scores of men and women on the SAT math test. It appears that the SAT might be underestimating women's ability to achieve in college mathematics courses.

Although psychology and most other sciences have relied heavily on testing the significance of the null hypothesis, this approach has its share of weaknesses (Cumming, 2013). Testing and rejecting a null hypothesis encourages us to view variables, like exposure to violent video games, as producing discrete either/or outcomes (aggression or no aggression) when that is unlikely to be the case in reality. Instead, we might think of people's aggression as existing along a continuum from high to low or none.

Significance testing lets us know if an effect exists, but we are also interested in how important our effect might be. A result can be statistically significant and still demonstrate a tiny effect size. For example, Facebook manipulated the sentiment (positive or negative) of the newsfeeds of nearly 700,000 users (the independent variable) and then observed the impact of this manipulation on people's use of positive and negative words in their own status updates (Kramer et al., 2014). Although some of the reported differences in the sentiment of updates were highly significant ($p < .001$), the largest effect size

PSYCHOLOGY AS A HUB SCIENCE

The Invention of Factor Analysis

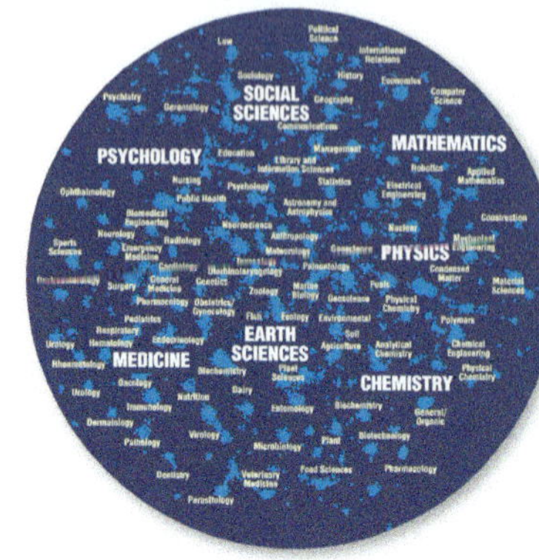

In Chapter 1, we mentioned that the field of psychology developed as scientists began combining questions asked previously by philosophers with methods developed by natural scientists. However, over the course of its short history, psychology has also contributed new methods that have been applied across many other disciplines.

Factor analysis is a statistical technique that has a long list of contemporary applications, from machine learning and data mining to marketing and finance to the physical and biological sciences. Factor analysis allows researchers to discover clusters within large data sets, such as smaller numbers of personality traits among long lists of words that describe personality (see Chapter 12). A marketing professional can use factor analysis to understand sources of customer satisfaction, and an environmental scientist can use factor analysis to identify sources of water pollutants.

The invention of factor analysis is usually attributed to British psychologist Charles Spearman (1863–1945), a student of Wilhelm Wundt, our very first psychologist whom we met in Chapter 1. Spearman developed factor analysis to study intelligence (Lovie & Lovie, 1993; see Chapter 10). He believed that scores on intelligence tests were composed of two factors—one general factor that did not change across the tests (g) and another that was specific to each particular test (see Chapter 10). Not only has Spearman's method served a wide number of fields very well, but it stimulated a mathematical approach to understanding the mind that continues to influence modern psychology.

reported was .02, which is considered to be tiny. In other words, manipulating the sentiment of people's news feeds had a significant, but trivial effect on their use of positive and negative words. In contrast, the differences between the performance of people with and without dementia on standard cognitive screening tests have very large effect sizes (more than 100 times larger than in the Facebook study; Larner, 2014). We would certainly hope that having dementia or not would have a big impact on how you score on diagnostic tests for dementia (Kramer et al., 2014; Larner, 2014).

How Can We Conduct Ethical Research?

We mentioned earlier that deceiving participants into thinking they were truly in danger raised ethical questions. On what basis do researchers decide what they can and cannot do to their research participants?

Although most studies published in psychological journals involve the use of human participants, psychology also has a rich heritage of animal research. Separate guidelines have been developed for each type of subject. Researchers working in universities and other agencies receiving federal funding seek the approval of institutional review boards (IRBs) for human participant research and institutional animal care and use committees (IACUCs) for animal research before conducting their studies. The IRBs and IACUCs are guided by federal regulations and research ethics endorsed by professional societies such as the American Psychological Association (APA), the Association for Psychological Science (APS), and the Society for

Neuroscience (SfN). IRBs and IACUCs must include at least one member of the community outside the university or agency, avoiding the possibility that inappropriate research might be conducted in secret. These procedures do not apply to institutions that do not have federal funding, such as private genetics research corporations or consumer product corporations (cosmetics, etc.), although efforts are being made to bring these organizations into compliance with federal standards.

As you review the ethical guidelines for both human and animal research participants, keep in mind that the guidelines look simpler when you read about their provisions than when you try to implement them in the context of real research. This is why the final approval decision lies with a committee, as opposed to an individual.

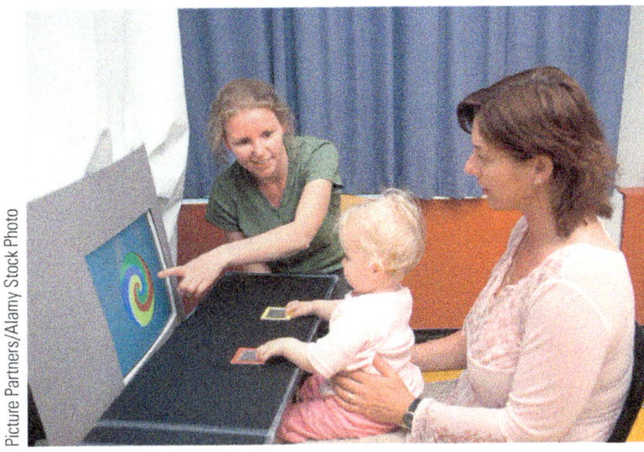

Picture Partners/Alamy Stock Photo

Many populations that are interesting to psychologists are unable to sign informed consent forms legally and require additional ethical protection. In the case of research with infants, parents are required to sign informed consent forms on their child's behalf.

Human Participants

At the core of ethical standards for human research is the idea that participation is voluntary. No participant should be coerced into participating. Although psychologists are well aware that people who volunteer to participate in research are probably quite different in important ways from those who don't volunteer, we have chosen to give research ethics a higher priority than our ability to generalize research results.

To ensure that a participant is a willing volunteer, researchers must make provisions for reasonable incentives. Incentives, such as pay or extra credit for participation, must not be so extreme that they become the primary motivation for prospective volunteers. To decide whether to volunteer for research, a person must have some knowledge of what the research will entail. Researchers must provide prospective participants with an **informed consent** form, which provides details about the purpose of the study and what types of procedures will occur. You might be curious about the Facebook study mentioned earlier. The study has raised many ethical concerns, because Facebook neither solicited informed consent nor mentioned the possibility of participating in research in its terms of service (Flick, 2015).

informed consent Permission obtained from a research participant after the risks and benefits of an experimental procedure have been thoroughly explained.

In psychological research, we have the added burden of occasionally dealing with participants who are limited in their abilities to provide informed consent because of the conditions that make them interesting to study. Developmental psychologists have an obvious interest in children, but a person cannot sign a legal informed consent form until age 18. Can you obtain informed consent from a patient with schizophrenia who suffers from hallucinations and irrational, delusional beliefs, or from a person in the later stages of Alzheimer's disease whose memory and reasoning have deteriorated because of the condition? In these cases, legal permission must be obtained from a qualified guardian. The university IRBs play an essential role in evaluating these ethical dilemmas case by case.

The Tuskegee syphilis experiment, conducted by the U.S. Public Health Service from 1932 to 1972, involved 400 African-American men who had contracted syphilis. The study's failure to treat or inform these participants about their health led to new regulations to prevent such unethical research from being repeated.
Source: Department of Health, Education, and Welfare. Public Health Service. Health Services and Mental Health Administration. Center for Disease Control. Venereal Disease Branch (1970–1973)/ National Archives

Research also should be conducted in a manner that does no irreversible harm to participants. In some cases, to avoid participants' desire to appear normal and their tendency to try to outguess the research, researchers might say that they are investigating one factor when they are interested in another. Most cases of deception are quite mild, such as when participants are told that a study is about memory when it is actually a study of some social behavior. When researchers must deceive their participants, the informed consent form must indicate that deception will occur, although the exact form of that deception does not need to be specified. Extra care must be taken to debrief participants about the deception and answer all their questions following the experiment.

Research using human participants should be rigorously private and confidential. *Privacy* refers to the participants' control over the sharing of their personal

While examining the papers of Dr. John Cutler, who led the Tuskegee syphilis study, Wellesley College historian Susan Reverby discovered that during the 1940s, U.S. and Guatemalan health officials had deliberately exposed prisoners, soldiers, and mental patients to syphilis and gonorrhea to test the effectiveness of penicillin.

Wellesley College/MCT/Newscom

information with others, and methods for ensuring privacy are usually stated in the informed consent paperwork. For example, some studies involve the use of medical records, which participants agree to share with the researchers for the purpose of the experiment. *Confidentiality* refers to the participants' right to have their data revealed to others only with their permission. Confidentiality is usually maintained by such practices as substituting codes for names and storing data in locked cabinets. Collecting data anonymously, so that even the researchers do not know the identity of participants, is the surest way to protect privacy and confidentiality.

Science learns from its past ethical lapses. One of the most egregious examples of unethical research was the Tuskegee syphilis experiment, which lasted from 1932 until 1972. Researchers from the U.S. Public Health Service recruited about 400 impoverished African-American men who had contracted syphilis to study the progression of the disease. None of the men were told they had syphilis, and none were treated, even after penicillin became the standard treatment for the disease in 1947. Many current federal regulations related to research ethics were developed in response to this experiment.

Animal Subjects

The topic of using animals in research is guaranteed to stimulate lively, and possibly heated, discussion. Some people are adamantly opposed to any animal research, whereas others accept the concept of using animals, so long as certain conditions are met. The United Kingdom has some of the most rigorous protections for animals in research, based on the "3 R's:" Reduce (the number of animals used), Replace (do not use animals if you can answer your research question a different way), and Refine (adjust your methods to be as humane as possible; Russell & Burch, 1959).

About 7% to 8% of published research in psychology journals involves the use of animals as subjects (American Psychological Association [APA], 2012). A total of 90% of the animals used are rodents and birds, with 5% or fewer animal studies involving monkeys and other primates. According to the APA, the use of dogs and cats in psychological research is rare.

Ethical guidelines for animal research require setting a clear purpose for the experiment, providing excellent care for the animals, and minimizing pain and suffering.

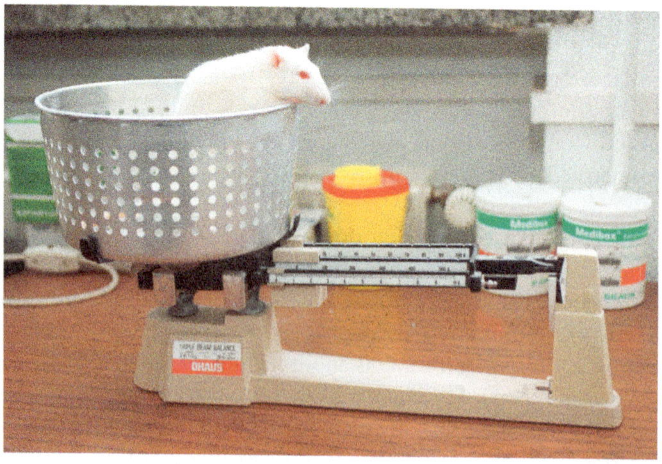

Agencja Fotograficzna Caro/Alamy Stock Photo

Research using animals must demonstrate a clear purpose, such as benefiting the health of humans or other animals. In addition to serving a clear purpose, animal research requires excellent housing, food, and veterinary care. The most controversial ethical standards relate to minimizing the pain and suffering experienced by animal research subjects. Federal regulations provide guidelines for the use of pain, surgery, stress, and deprivation with animal subjects, as well as the termination of an animal's life. The standards approximate the community standards that we would expect from local humane societies tasked with euthanizing animals that are not adopted.

Interpersonal Relationships
The Methodological Perspective

CAN WE DIFFERENTIATE "LIKE" FROM "LOVE"?

AT THE END OF CHAPTER 1, we noted that each chapter would feature a discussion of how the chapter's material could be used to talk about relationships. For this chapter on research methods, we ask whether psychological research methods can be used to differentiate between liking and loving another person.

Using the methods described in this chapter, you can probably think of many ways to approach this question. You could observe friends and compare their behavior to that of romantic partners. You could conduct a survey, asking people to rate certain characteristics of people they love versus those of people they like. Perhaps you could correlate physiological arousal measures, like pupil diameter or heart rate, with ratings of how much a participant likes or loves another person. Conducting an actual experiment might be a bit tricky, though, in terms of both methods and ethics. How could people be randomly assigned to love and like groups?

An example of research on the neuroscience of relationships was contributed by Bartels and Zeki (2000). These researchers chose to use correlational methods in the form of brain imaging, which we discuss further in Chapter 4. Brain imaging studies are typically correlational because we assume that brain activity in particular areas has a relationship with some ongoing behavior. It is important to recall that we cannot make conclusions about causality based on correlational data.

Bartels and Zeki's participants were instructed to supply photographs of people they like and people they love. The photographs were then presented to the participants while their brain activity was observed using functional magnetic resonance imaging (fMRI; see Chapter 4). Several differences in brain activity occurred when the participants viewed a lover as opposed to a friend. Not too surprisingly, areas of the brain associated with reward became more active when viewing lovers than when viewing friends. Areas of the brain associated with social judgment, negative emotions, and assessing the intentions and emotions of other people were less active when viewing lovers than when viewing friends. Love, according to these results, appears to be a combination of reward and less social judgment (see ● Figure 2.20).

The results of this scientific research might help us understand some of our everyday experiences with relationships. We feel rewarded in the presence of a loved one, and we have to admit that we may miss a flaw or two in someone we love. Friends and family members, whose social judgment has not been silenced, do not miss these flaws and often try in vain to alert us to them. ■

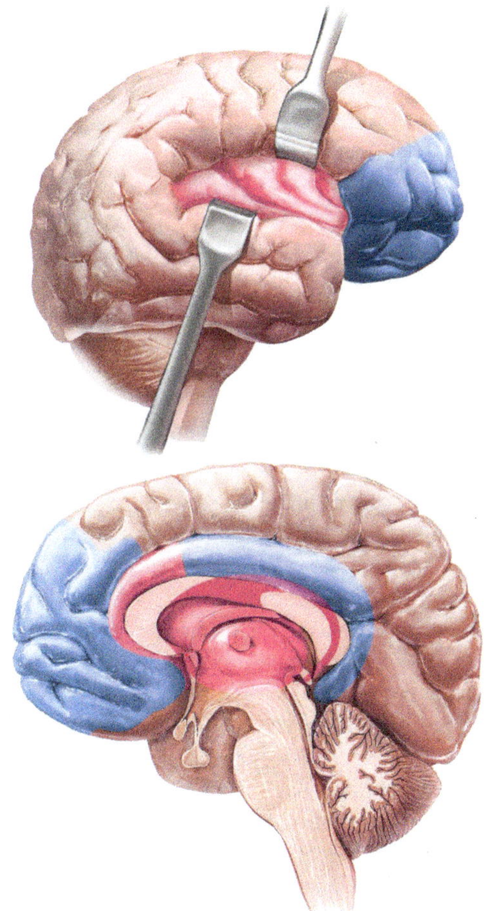

FIGURE **2.20**

Imaging Love. When people view a photo of a person they say they "love," brain imaging shows increased activation in reward areas of the brain and decreased activation in areas involved with social judgment.

Psychology Takes on Real-World Problems

Research Methods for Studying a Pandemic

IN CHAPTER 1, we suggested using the COVID-19 pandemic to illustrate the power of psychological science for understanding and solving real-world problems. Specifically, we can consider the policies your campus might put in place to ensure everyone's safety during the pandemic. As we mentioned in Chapter 1, our goals in policy development are to (1) figure out what we're doing that isn't working, (2) identify what else we could be doing, and (3) decide which option we should try first. Good research, described in the current chapter, forms an essential foundation for addressing these goals.

For the purposes of this exercise, we will assume that your campus is letting at least some classes meet face-to-face. You might have an existing policy that calls for everyone on campus to wear a mask. You have noticed that people are generally compliant with this policy in the classroom, but not necessarily in other campus venues, such as in out-of-doors spaces and at parties, club functions, and sporting events. To understand why members of the campus community are complying some, but not all the time, requires systematic research.

We might start with naturalistic observation. Is it actually true that people are less likely to wear masks outside the classroom? Carrying out these observations must be done ethically, as people might have a reasonable expectation of privacy even in public locations. If your observations confirm a problem exists, we can begin to ask why. It might be possible to conduct a campus-wide attitude survey like the one developed by Pew Research (Igielnik, 2020). The survey found that in June 2020, about 65% of American adults had worn masks in stores or other businesses all or most of the time in the past month. Pew Research investigated a number of variables in an attempt to clarify the motivation for wearing masks, such as race and ethnicity (Asians wore masks more often than other races and ethnicities), living in areas with high impact of the disease (mask wearing was more common in high impact areas), political affiliation (Democrats were more likely than Republicans to wear masks), education (college graduates were more likely to wear masks), and age (older adults were more likely to wear masks). To produce a good survey on your campus, you would need to consider these and other relevant variables carefully. What variables might be especially relevant to a college community that might not have been included by Pew Research in their more general survey?

Syda Productions/Shutterstock.com

Your results might provide insights into how your current mask policy is and is not working and why. If you gain some systematic understanding of the whys and why nots for mask wearing on your campus, you will then be in a position to modify your approach. If you keep your overall mask policy in place, you could possibly change your persuasive messaging, which we cover in Chapter 13. Or you might consider modifications of your mask policy, such as being more lenient out-of-doors or in situations that allow for appropriate social distancing.

Regardless of the policy you devise, more research will be needed to see if your policy is actually working. This, of course, raises significant ethical concerns. You can't randomly assign your classmates to mask and no mask groups and ask who is more likely to get sick! In these cases, scientists use so-called experiments of nature. For example, comparisons of COVID-19 growth rates before and after mask mandates showed a slowing of daily COVID-19 growth following the mask mandates (Lyu & Wehby, 2020). You could run a similar study to see if your policy approach was effective. If not, then it's time to try another approach. ■

SUMMARY 2.3 Principles of Ethical Research

Human Participants	Animal Subjects
	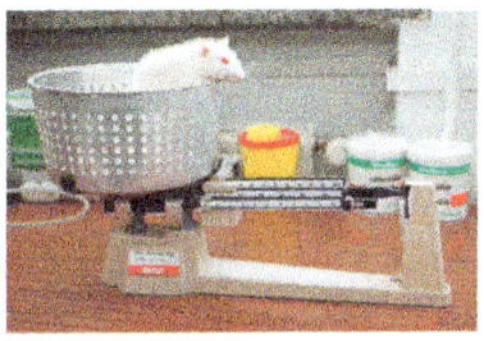
No coercion	Necessity
Informed consent	Excellent food, housing, and veterinary care
No harm	Minimal pain and suffering
Confidentiality and privacy	

Credits: Left—Department of Health, Education, and Welfare. Public Health Service. Health Services and Mental Health Administration. Center for Disease Control. Venereal Disease Branch (1970–1973)/National Archives; Right—Agencja Fotograficzna Caro/Alamy Stock Photo.

KEY TERMS The Language of Psychological Science

Be sure that you can define these terms and use them correctly.

case study, p. 44
confirmation bias, p. 37
confounding variable, p. 51
control group, p. 51
correlation, p. 48
critical thinking, p. 37
cross-sectional study, p. 54
dependent variable, p. 51
descriptive method, p. 44
descriptive statistics, p. 57
experiment, p. 51
experimental group, p. 51
generalize, p. 62
hypothesis, p. 41
independent variable, p. 51
inferential statistics, p. 62
informed consent, p. 65
longitudinal study, p. 54
mean, p. 58
measure, p. 48
median, p. 58
meta-analysis, p. 54
mixed longitudinal design, p. 55
mode, p. 58
naturalistic observation, p. 46
normal distribution, p. 62
null hypothesis, p. 62
objectivity, p. 36
operationalization, p. 53
peer review, p. 42
population, p. 46
publication bias, p. 54
random assignment, p. 51
reliability, p. 57
replication, p. 42
sample, p. 46
science, p. 36
standard deviation, p. 59
statistical significance, p. 62
survey, p. 46
theory, p. 40
third variable, p. 50
validity, p. 57
variable, p. 48

Environmental factors such as stress, diet, smoking, and exercise can influence whether a gene is turned on or off.

Argosy Publishing, Inc.

3

The Evolving Mind

NATURE AND NURTURE INTERTWINED

LEARNING OBJECTIVES

1. Analyze the role of genes as the building blocks of human nature.
2. Appraise the importance of heritability estimates, twin studies, adoption studies, and epigenetic analyses in the field of behavioral genetics.
3. Compare the roles played by mutation, natural selection, migration, and genetic drift as mechanisms of evolution.
4. Discuss how the human brain might represent an adaptation for coping with complex social behavior.
5. Explain the mechanisms by which intrasexual and intersexual selection might influence the evolution of human behavior.
6. Identify the cultural mechanisms by which nature and nurture can interact to influence human behavior.

WE ALL KNOW THAT IDENTICAL TWINS, LIKE THE little girls appearing in the photo, are, well, identical. Or are they?

For a long time, scientists were puzzled not by the similarities between identical twins, but by their differences. If two people share the same deoxyribonucleic acid (DNA), as identical twins do, why does one get cancer while the other stays healthy? Why does one become obese while the other remains fit?

When science began to unravel some mysteries about genes and how they work, answers to these questions emerged. You have the same DNA in each cell of your body, yet some cells develop into heart cells, others into brain cells, and so on. How does the same set of DNA know how to make these different types of cells? *Genes*, or segments of DNA that produce specific proteins, can be turned on and off. The genes that are not turned off are free to produce the proteins needed to build a particular kind of cell, whether that is a skin cell or a liver cell. Only about 10% to 20% of the genes in a particular type of cell, such as a skin cell or brain cell, are active.

Genes do not just turn on and off as they build a body during development. Your ongoing interactions with the environment can also turn genes on or off. What you eat, whether you smoke or drink, your stress levels, and other environmental factors can influence how your DNA works. Our understanding of these ongoing interactions between genes and the environment is the main reason psychologists no longer argue about the separate contributions of nature and nurture. In this chapter, we will explore these interactions in more detail.

iStock.com/LSOphoto

Courtesy Randy L. Jirtle, Ph.D.

When pregnant mice are fed a diet containing BPA, found in plastics and other consumer products, their offspring are more likely to have yellow fur and to be obese.

Let's zoom in to see what's happening when the environment interacts with DNA. In mice, a gene called *Agouti* produces yellow fur and obesity when it is turned on, but brown fur and normal weight when it is turned off (Dolinoy et al., 2007). Certain environmental factors can turn the gene on or off. When pregnant mother mice ate food containing bisphenol A (BPA), a chemical found in food and beverage containers, baby bottles, dental sealants, and food cans, their pups had yellow fur and were obese. The BPA turned on the *Agouti* gene.

How does studying the fur color of mice help us understand the differences between identical human twins? The young twins on the previous page have a great deal in common, but as they get older, they are more likely to eat different foods and have different experiences. These environmental influences can change the way their genes are turned on or off, just as the BPA affected the *Agouti* gene in the mice. These changes accumulate over time, so identical twins become less similar as they age.

In this chapter, we will explore how nature and nurture interact to build the mind across the life span, and how the interactions between nature and nurture have been shaping the human mind over millennia.

Why Do We Say That Nature and Nurture Are Intertwined?

nature The contributions of heredity to our physical structure and behaviors.

nurture The contributions of environmental factors and experience to our physical structure and behaviors.

genotype An individual's profile of alleles.

phenotype An observable characteristic.

gene A small segment of DNA located in a particular place on a chromosome that produces a protein.

Along with an understanding of the structures and processes of the brain, covered in Chapter 4, knowing how our biological history shapes our behavior is an important part of understanding the mind. Contemporary psychologists view the contributions of **nature** (our heredity or innate predispositions) and **nurture** (the results of our experience with the

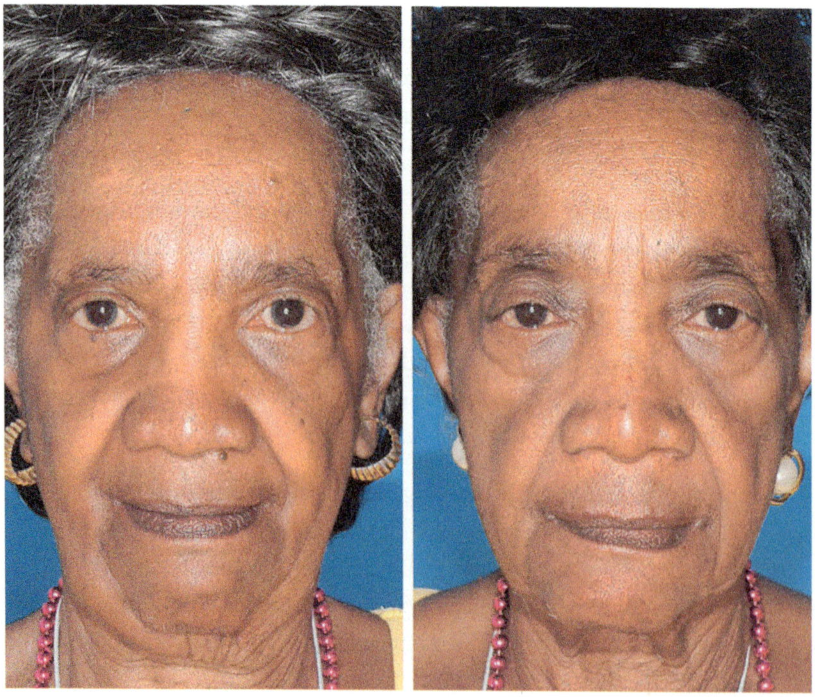

American Society of Plastic Surgeons/Shutterstock.com

These identical twins probably do not look as similar as they did as small children. The twin on the left is a nonsmoker, while her sister on the right smoked for 29 years.

environment) as being closely intertwined, as opposed to somehow competing for control over structure and behavior.

Scholars have not always thought about nature and nurture the way we do today. Instead of viewing the actions of nature and nurture as inseparable, earlier scholars talked in terms of nature *versus* nurture and debated the relative contributions of nature or nurture to a particular type of behavior. Credit for describing the contrast between heredity and environment as "nature versus nurture" usually goes to Francis Galton (1869), who was Charles Darwin's cousin. Galton believed that intelligence was largely the result of inheritance, a topic tackled in Chapter 10. Over the next 150 years or so, many thinkers engaged in a highly spirited debate on this question. As Chapter 10 will demonstrate, contemporary psychologists view intelligence as another example of an outcome shaped by both genetic inheritance and environment.

We can say with some certainty that the either/or approach to human behavior has produced some of the most contentious discussions in the history of psychology. Our motive for arguing in favor of the intertwined approach to nature and nurture is intended not to sidestep difficult questions, but rather to support good science. By zooming out to integrate a number of perspectives, both biological and experiential, we can achieve a more accurate understanding of these questions.

akg-images/Newscom

Francis Galton was the first to use the phrase "nature versus nurture."

What Are the Building Blocks of Behavior?

Before we explore the interactions between nature and nurture that contribute to psychological phenomena, let's look at the genetic mechanisms that help shape the mind.

Every nucleus in the approximately 37 trillion cells of your body, with the exception of your red blood cells and sperm or eggs, contains two complete copies of the human genome, a set of instructions for building a human. Your personal set of instructions is known as a **genotype**, which interacts with the environment to produce observable characteristics, known as a **phenotype**.

One half of your genotype was provided by your mother's egg, and the other half was provided by your father's sperm. Each parent contributes a set of 23 chromosomes, which in turn are composed of many molecules of DNA. A smaller segment of DNA located in a particular place on a chromosome is known as a **gene**. Each gene contains instructions for

Featureflash Photo Agency/Shutterstock.com

Some genes have a large number of alleles. Of the more than 500 alleles for the *BRCA1* (Breast Cancer 1) gene, a small number are associated with a higher risk for breast and other cancers. Actress Angelina Jolie, who possesses the high-risk alleles, chose to undergo a preventive mastectomy to reduce her chances of developing breast cancer.

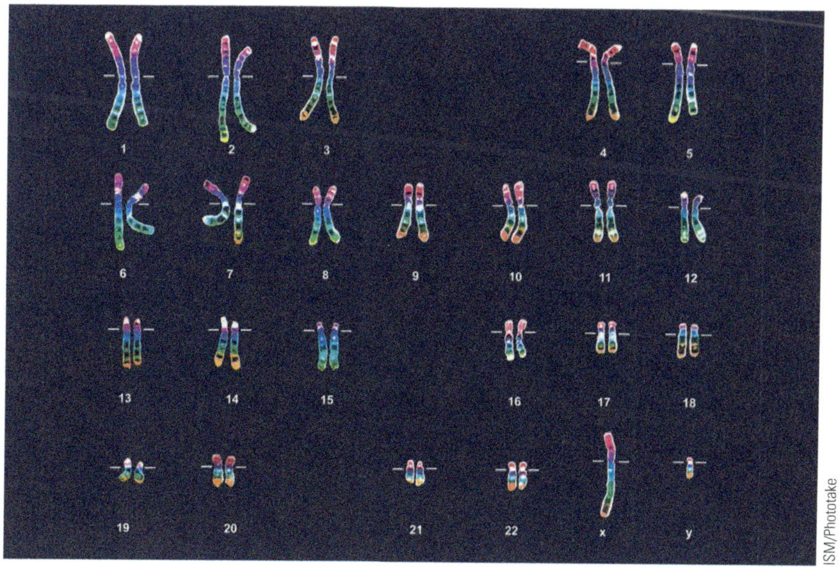

ISM/Phototake

Twenty-three pairs of chromosomes make up the human genome.

FIGURE 3.1

Genotypes and Phenotypes of Blood Type. The three possible blood type alleles—A, B, and O—can be combined to produce Type A, Type B, Type O, or Type AB blood.

	Father's allele		
Mother's allele	A	B	O
A	AA (Type A blood)	AB (Type AB blood)	AO (Type A blood)
B	AB (Type AB blood)	BB (Type B blood)	BO (Type B blood)
O	AO (Type A blood)	BO (Type B blood)	OO (Type O blood)

gene expression The process in which genetic instructions are converted into a feature of a living cell.

allele One of several versions of a gene, as in having an A, B, or O blood type allele.

homozygous Having two of the same alleles for a gene.

heterozygous Having two different alleles for a gene.

recessive A feature of an allele that produces a phenotype only in the homozygous condition.

dominant A feature of an allele that determines a phenotype in either the homozygous or the heterozygous condition.

making a particular type of protein. **Gene expression** occurs when these genetic instructions are read to produce a particular protein. Each cell contains the instructions for an entire human organism, but only a subset of instructions is expressed at any given time and location. Gene expression in a nerve cell is different from gene expression in a muscle cell or a skin cell.

Different versions of a gene, or **alleles**, can give rise to different phenotypical traits. Many alleles can occur in the population for a given gene, but an individual receives only two—one from each parent. For example, alleles for blood type include A, B, and O, but typically, nobody has all three. As shown in ● Figure 3.1, combinations of your two alleles make your blood Type A (AA or AO), Type B (BB or BO), Type AB (AB), or Type O (OO).

If both parents contribute the same type of allele, such as a version of the *MC1R* gene related to having freckles, the child would be considered **homozygous** for that gene (*homos* means "same" in Greek). If the parents contribute different alleles, such as one for freckles from one parent and one related to not having freckles from the other, the child is **heterozygous** for that gene (*hetero* means "different" in Greek). **Recessive** alleles determine a phenotype only when an individual is homozygous for a particular gene, whereas **dominant** alleles determine a phenotype in either the homozygous or the heterozygous condition. Because alleles for no freckles are recessive and alleles for freckles are dominant, the typical way that an individual has no freckles is if that person receives two copies of the no-freckle allele, one from each parent. Any individual receiving either two freckle alleles or one freckle allele and one no-freckle allele will have freckles (see ● Figure 3.2).

	Father's allele	
Mother's allele	Freckles (F)	No freckles (f)
Freckles (F)	FF (homozygous freckles)	Ff (heterozygous freckles)
No freckles (f)	Ff (heterozygous freckles)	ff (homozygous no freckles)

FIGURE 3.2

Effects of Dominant and Recessive Genes. Having freckles (F) is dominant, whereas having no freckles (f) is recessive. The only way that a child can have no freckles is to inherit two of the recessive "no freckle" alleles, one from each parent. In this example, both parents are heterozygous (Ff) with freckles.

Source: https://data.worldbank.org/indicator/sp.dyn.tfrt.in

EXPERIENCING PSYCHOLOGY

The Genetics of Cats

Most human traits simply do not fit the simple Mendelian principles of genetics taught in grade school. Did you know that two blue-eyed parents can in fact produce a child who does not have blue eyes? Traits like widow's peak, attached earlobes, tongue rolling, hand-clasping, and other commonly presented examples are either only somewhat genetic or are the result of multiple interacting genes. So where can we look for good examples of the basic principles outlined in this chapter? If you have a cat, that's a good place to start (Christensen, 2000). If you don't have a cat or want to compare different cats, take a look at the photos on petfinder.com. We can compare the following genetic traits in cats:

- Hair Length: Short hair in cats is dominant, so cats with LL or Ll genotypes will have short hair. Your long-haired kitty has a homozygous ll genotype.
- White Hair: Cats with one or two W alleles (WW or Ww) will be completely white, which is very rare (and often linked with deafness and eyes of two different colors, such as one blue and one green eye), while cats with two recessive (ww) alleles will have some other color. This feature will combine with the *spotted* trait we discuss next. This feature also reminds us that dominant alleles are not necessarily the most common in the population.
- Spotting: Cats with the dominant S (SS or Ss) will have some white fur, which can range from white toes to a mostly white body. Some observers believe that SS cats have white fur over more than 50% of their bodies while Ss cats have white fur on less than 50% of their bodies. Cats with an ss genotype have no white fur at all.
- Dense Color: A cat with a DD or Dd genotype will have vivid black, orange, or brown fur, whereas a dd cat will have cream, light brown, or gray fur.
- Orange Fur: This is a sex-linked trait (like hemophilia or red-green dichromacy in humans, discussed in Chapter 5), because the gene is located on the X chromosome. Orange females have an OO genotype and orange males have a single O. Black or gray results from an oo genotype in females and an o in males. Females with an Oo genotype will be calico (with some white fur) or tortoiseshell (no white fur). Males cannot be calico or tortoiseshell unless they have an XXY genotype, which can happen also in humans (Klinefelter syndrome) but is relatively rare.

Still other genes affect the striping of some cats, the "points" of color in Siamese cats, and hairlessness. Can you now identify the genotype of your cat? What pieces of information might be missing?

Courtesy of Laura Freberg

Coco is a long-haired (ll), non-white (ww and ss), low density (dd) tortoiseshell (Oo) kitty. Other genes determine the patterns of her striping and curliness of fur. How does your cat compare?

Whether you have freckles or not is a simple example of how dominant and recessive genes interact, but one allele does not always dominate another. In a study of gene–environment interactions involving the serotonin transporter gene (*SERT* or 5-HTTLPR) and a child's response to bullying, the authors note that with two types of alleles (S for short or L for long), individuals could have one of three genotypes: SS, SL, or LL (Sugden et al., 2010). Neither the S nor the L allele dominates the other. As you can see in Figure 3.3, the SL group had levels of emotional disturbance in response to frequent bullying that fell between the extremes of the SS and the LL groups (Sugden et al., 2010). If either the S or the L alleles were dominant, the SL group would behave like that dominant group instead.

FIGURE **3.3**

Some Alleles Do Not Show Dominance. Neither the S nor the L allele of the serotonin transporter gene dominates the other. Among children who have been bullied frequently, those with the SL genotype (shown in green) experience a level of emotional problems midway between the levels of those with the SS and LL genotypes. If either the S or the L allele was dominant, we would expect the SL group to behave the same way as the homozygous dominant group.

Source: Adapted from K. Sugden, et al. (2010). "Serotonin Transporter Gene Moderates the Development of Emotional Problems Among Children Following Bullying Victimization," *Journal of the American Academy of Child and Adolescent Psychiatry, 49*(8), 830–840. doi:10.1016/j.jaac.2010.01.024

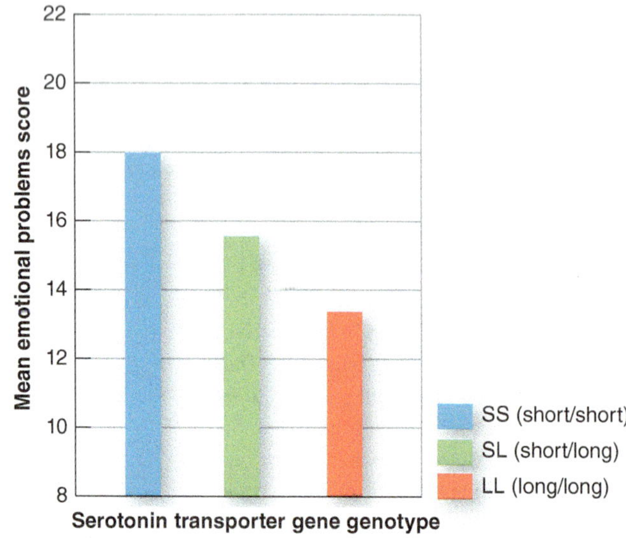

Genetic Variation

If you have siblings, you are aware that having the same biological parents does not guarantee similar appearance, personality, and behavior. The development of an egg or sperm cell is like shuffling a deck of cards. In both cases, a large number of possible outcomes may occur. When a parent's cell divides to make an egg or a sperm cell, each resulting cell contains 23 chromosomes, one chromosome from each of the parent's original 23 chromosome pairs. As a result, a single human can produce eggs or sperm with 2^{23} (8,388,608) combinations of chromosomes. Add this variability to the different possibilities provided by the other parent, and it may seem surprising that we resemble our relatives as much as we do.

Relatedness

relatedness The probability that two people share the same allele from a common ancestor.

Despite this potential variability, we remain similar to our genetic relatives. This important point will be revisited later in the chapter, when the evolution of social behavior is discussed. **Relatedness** is defined as the probability that two people share copies of the same allele from a common ancestor. If we go back in history far enough, we all share common ancestors. Relatedness, however, is usually computed within a limited number of generations.

The chance that you share an allele with one of your parents is one-half, as is the chance that you share an allele with a sibling. First cousins have a one-eighth likelihood of sharing an allele (see ● Figure 3.4). These types of calculations led geneticist J. B. S. Haldane to allegedly proclaim, "I would lay down my life for two brothers or eight cousins!" (Bynum & Porter, 2005, p. 261). Haldane was computing the likelihood that his genes would be passed down to future generations. As discussed later in the chapter, evolutionary psychologists suggest that sacrificing yourself for others is more likely when the others are genetically related relatives.

Relatedness represents probability. In some cases, similarities will be more or less than the predicted amount. Second cousins should share approximately 1/32 of their alleles (about 3%), but this particular pair might be mistaken for brothers.

Courtesy of Laura Freberg

Courtesy of Laura Freberg

Sex Chromosomes

Of the 23 pairs of human chromosomes from each parent, 22 pairs are perfectly matched. In other words, a gene appearing on one of a pair of chromosomes (perhaps a gene for blood type) has a corresponding gene on its partner. In contrast, the X and Y chromosomes do not carry the same genes. The much-larger X chromosome contains about 2,000 active genes, while the Y has fewer than 100. In most

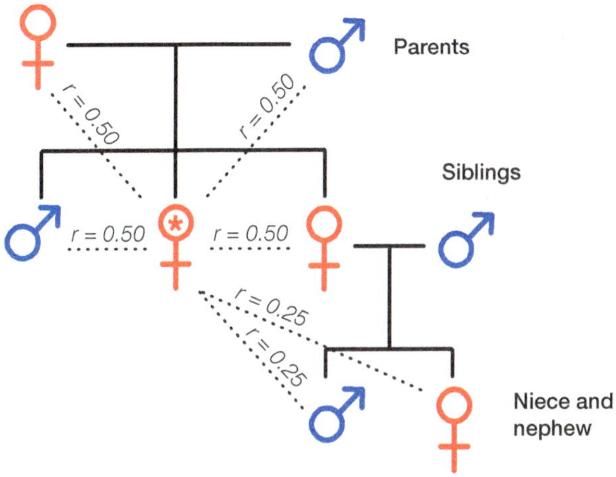

FIGURE 3.4

Relatedness. Relatedness refers to the probability that two people share a particular allele from a common ancestor. The chance that you share an allele with one of your parents or a brother or sister is 0.50, or one-half. The chance that you share an allele with a niece or nephew is 0.25, or one-quarter.

cases, females carry two copies of the X chromosome, whereas males carry one X and one Y chromosome.

The allele responsible for hemophilia, a disease characterized by the failure of blood to clot, is found only on the X chromosome. This allele is recessive, leading to different outcomes based on the sex of the child receiving the alleles. If a female receives a healthy allele on the X chromosome from one parent and a disease-causing allele on the X chromosome from her other parent, she will be a carrier for the condition but not experience it. In contrast, a male receiving a disease-causing allele on the X chromosome from his mother will have the condition. Because there is no equivalent allele on the Y chromosome to offset the disease-causing recessive allele, the disease-causing allele will be expressed. As a result, conditions such as hemophilia are more frequent among males and are called *sex-linked characteristics* (see ● Figure 3.5). As illustrated in ● Figure 3.6, the family of Queen Victoria of Great Britain (1819–1901) spread hemophilia to a number of European royal houses.

Even when genes are duplicated on the X and Y chromosomes, they can differ depending on their location. Forensic experts determine the sex of the source of a genetic sample by observing the amelogenin gene, which contributes to the development of tooth enamel (Akane, 1998). The size of the amelogenin gene on the X chromosome is different than on the Y chromosome.

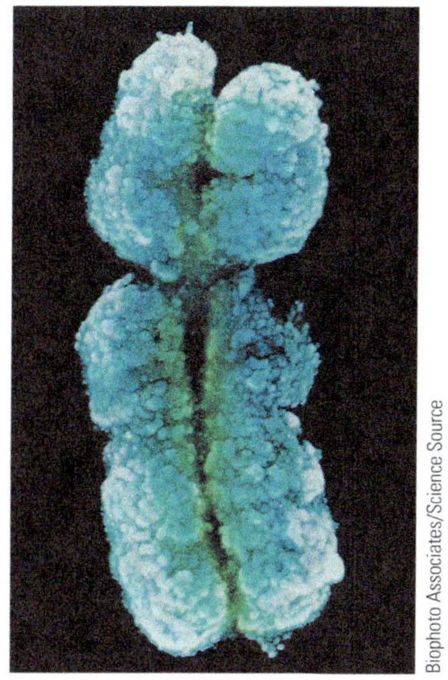

X chromosome

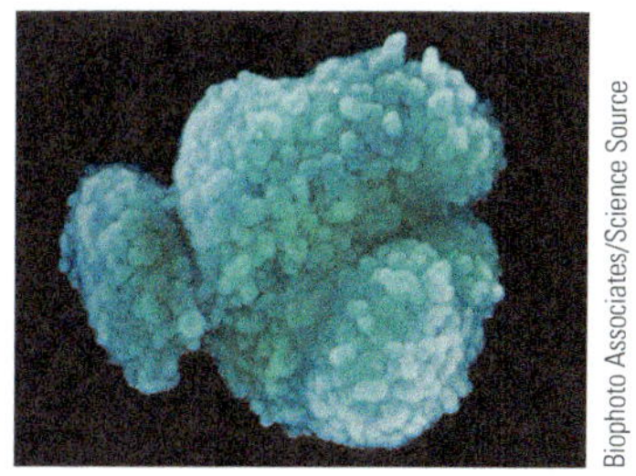

Y chromosome

Which Fields of Genetics Are Relevant to Psychology?

Our species shares quite a few genes with chimpanzees, mice, fruit flies, yeast, and even a weed known as *thale cress* (see ● Figure 3.7). At the same time, humans have genes that definitely set them apart from other animals (and plants). For example, research points to differences between humans and chimpanzees in a single gene, *FoxP2*, which appears to have had a significant effect on distinctly human behaviors, including spoken language (Konopka et al., 2009). Simply having different genes is only part of the story. Rates of expression of large numbers of shared genes are quite different in human brains compared to other primate brains (Cáceres et al., 2003).

Table 3.1 compares several subfields of genetics that are relevant to our understanding of behavior and mental processes. Behavioral geneticists attempt to discover the strength of genetic influences on a particular behavior. Molecular geneticists look for *candidate genes*, or genes that have a greater impact on a trait of interest than other genes. Functional geneticists study the entire genome, looking for whole patterns of genetic differences linked to a given trait. Finally, geneticists studying gene–environment interactions look for situations in which candidate genes appear to have different effects.

	X_HX Mother	
XY Father	X_HX	XX
	X_HY	XY

FIGURE 3.5

Hemophilia Is a Sex-Linked Trait. If a daughter inherits her mother's X chromosome containing the allele for hemophilia (X_H), she will be a carrier but will not have the disease. If a son inherits this X_H chromosome, he will have the disease. Unlike his sister, he does not have a healthy X chromosome to offset the disease allele.

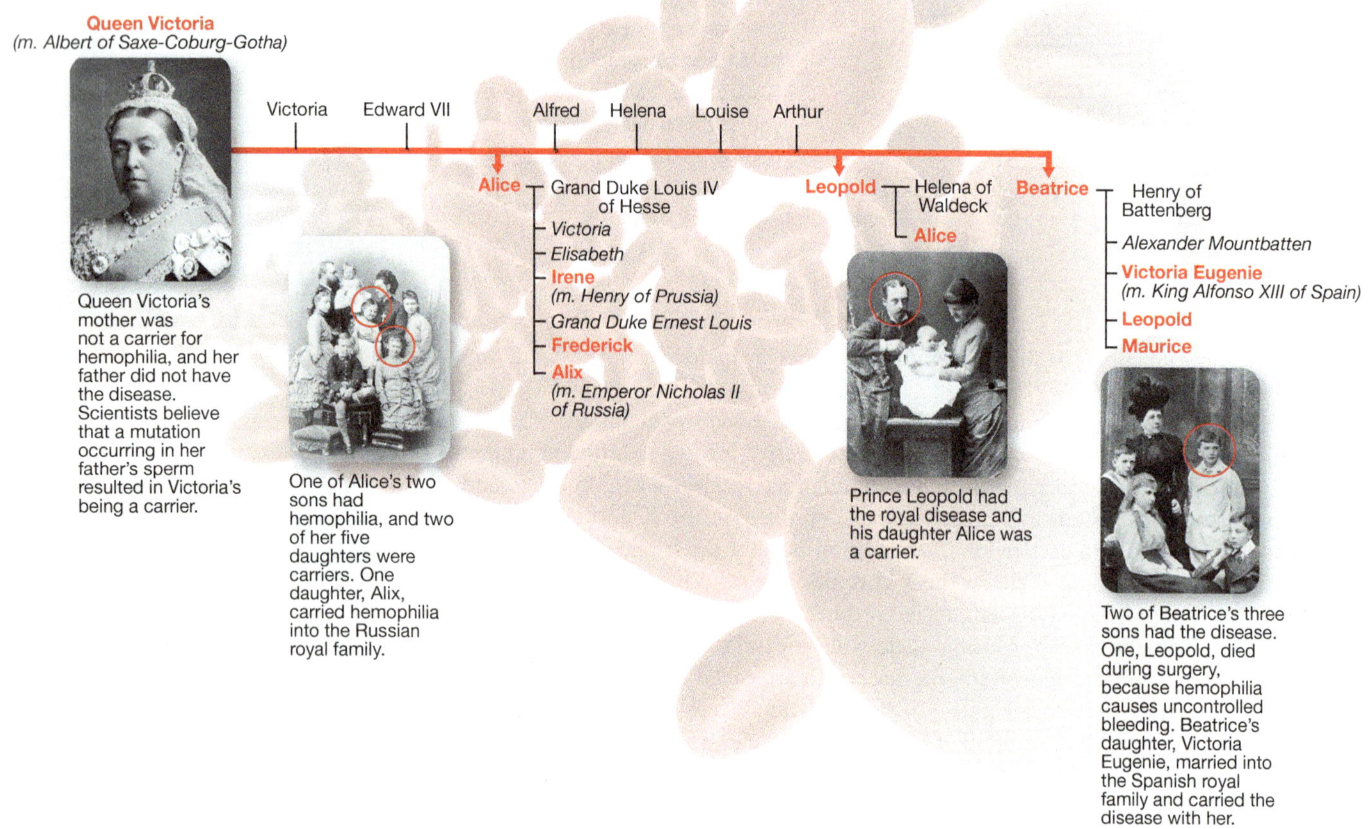

Photos, left to right: Pictorial Press Ltd/Alamy Stock Photo; Mary Evans Picture Library; Mary Evans Picture Library/CHARLOTTE ZEEPVAT; Mary Evans/The Image Works; Mary Evans Picture Library/

FIGURE **3.6**

Hemophilia and European Royalty. Queen Victoria of Great Britain (1819–1901) had nine children. One son (Prince Leopold, Duke of Albany) had hemophilia, and two daughters (Princess Alice and Princess Beatrice) were carriers for the condition. As a result of their marriages to other European royalty, the three children spread the hemophilia gene to the royal families of Germany, Russia, and Spain. Therefore, hemophilia was once popularly called "the royal disease."

Behavioral Genetics and Heritability

Behavioral genetics investigates the strength of genetic influences on a particular behavior. **Heritability** is the statistical likelihood that variations in a trait observed across individuals in a population are due to genetics. It is usually computed by comparing monozygotic (identical) and dizygotic (fraternal) twin pairs. As you can see in ● Figure 3.8 heritability is only one piece contributing to a trait, along with shared experience (both twins have Thanksgiving dinner with family every year) and non-shared experience (one twin plays soccer and the other plays basketball).

behavioral genetics The scientific field that attempts to identify and understand links between genetics and behavior.

heritability The statistical likelihood that variations observed in a population are because of genetics.

If genes play no part in producing phenotypical differences among individuals, heritability is zero. For example, genes are responsible for human hearts, but there is no individual variation in the population in terms of the presence of a heart—each of us has one. Consequently, the heritability of having a heart is zero. If genes are totally responsible for all phenotypical differences among individuals, heritability is 1.0. For example, all variation in the population in terms of having or not having a fatal neurological condition known as *Huntington's disease*

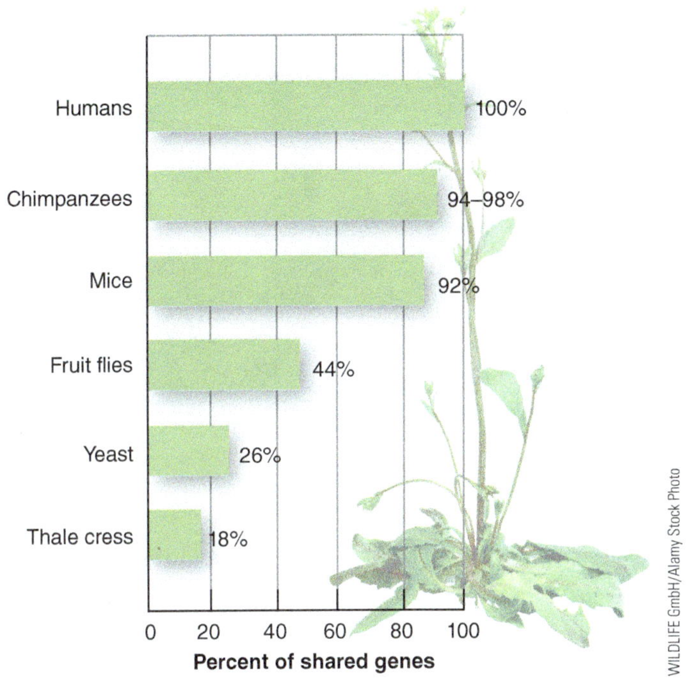

FIGURE **3.7**

Genes Shared with Other Species. Humans share quite a few genes with other species, such as the 18% of genes that we share with a weed known as *thale cress*. However, geneticists are most interested in the genes that differ from those of other species, such as the *FoxP2* gene, which appears to influence spoken language. Mutations of this gene cause severe speech and language disorders.

is entirely because of genetics. If you inherit a Huntington's gene from one parent, you will develop the condition. Heritability of most human traits is typically in the range of 0.30 to 0.60. ● Figure 3.9 shows the heritability of a number of important psychological conditions.

Heritability is a concept that is frequently misunderstood. It always refers to populations, never to individuals. Saying that a trait such as shyness is 40% heritable does not say that 40% of one individual's shyness is produced by genes and the other 60% by his or her environment. Instead, this suggests that the variations in shyness that we see across the population (some people are more shy than others) are the result of both genetic and environmental factors.

Heritability cannot be assessed without taking the environment into account, which is another source of potential confusion. If the environment is held constant (i.e., everybody is treated the same way), the heritability of a trait will appear to be high. For example, if you plant seeds in trays with identical nutrients, water, and sunlight, the height of the resulting plants will reflect their genetic differences. In variable environments, heritability is lower.

TABLE 3.1

Subfields of Genetics

Branch of Genetics	Topic	Example
Behavioral genetics	Amount of heritability	Variations in loneliness across the population appear to be strongly influenced by genetics.
Molecular genetics	Candidate genes	Certain genes seem to impact loneliness more than others.
Functional genomics	Links between the global genome and particular traits	Genes might be expressed differently in lonely and nonlonely individuals.
Gene–environment Interactions	Candidate genes have different effects in different situations	Candidate genes seem to have more impact on loneliness in some environments compared to others.

After L. Goossens et al. (2009), Loneliness and solitude in adolescence: A confirmatory factor analysis of alternative models. Personality and Individual Differences, 47(8), 890–894.

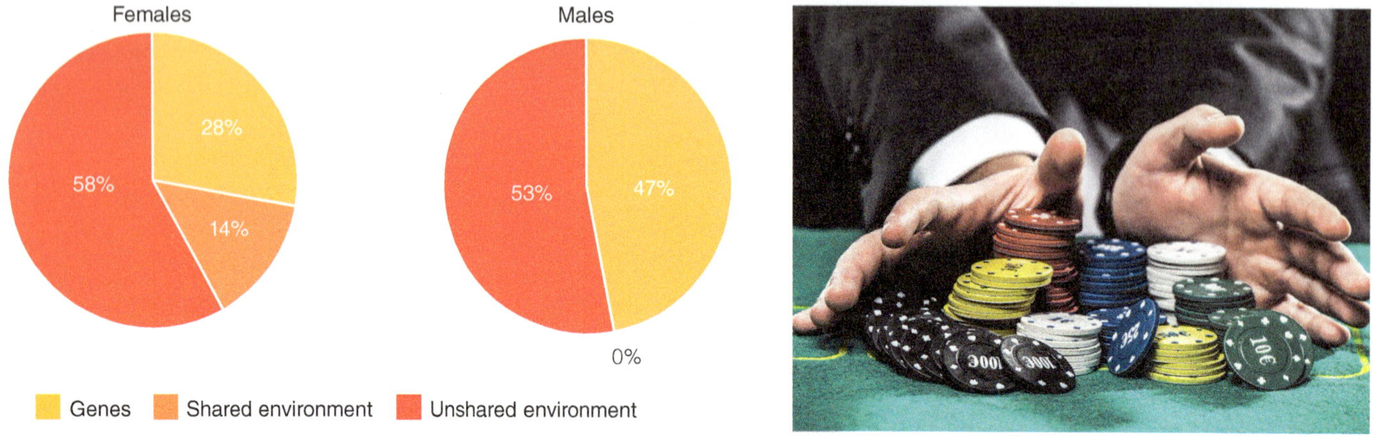

FB studio/Shutterstock.com

FIGURE **3.8**

Contributions to an Observed Trait. Behavioral geneticists, often using studies of identical and fraternal twins, attempt to quantify the contributions of genes, shared environments, and unshared environments. These contributions are not constant. Instead, they can vary over the lifespan and among genders. In this case, a large meta-analysis of twin studies reported that a shared environment influenced female but not male gambling behavior. For both males and females, genes play a significant role in predicting gambling behavior.

Source: Adapted from Y.-H. Xuan, et al. (2017). "Genetic and Environmental Influences on Gambling: A Meta-Analysis of Twin Studies," *Frontiers in Psychology*, *8*, 2121. doi: 10.3389/fpsyg.2017.02121

Diverse Voices in Psychology

Avoiding Social Prejudice in Genetic Research

GENETIC RESEARCH OFTEN PUSHES THE BOUNDARIES of research ethics, discussed in Chapter 2. Conclusions from genetic research can apply to entire groups of people, far beyond the individuals who agreed to participate. Even when individual participants are protected, the possibility that data could stigmatize an entire group should be considered and avoided.

For example, most anthropologists argue that the political concept of "race" is not clearly defined at the genetic level. Individuals of European and Asian backgrounds, but not individuals from sub-Saharan backgrounds, usually trace 1% to 4% of their DNA back to non–*Homo sapiens* ancestors, such as Neanderthals or Denisovans. This type of finding could be misinterpreted by the public as representing an important racial divide, an idea that has been soundly rejected by geneticists (Yudell et al., 2016).

Many indigenous groups have been reluctant to participate in genetics research. The possibility of promoting social prejudices due to stigmatization is a common source of concern, along with cultural values that are inconsistent with genetics methods. Many studies require storage of biological samples in biorepositories. This practice might be inconsistent with cultural values. For example, the Maori people of New Zealand view tissue samples, DNA, and any associated data as *taonga* ("precious") and *tapu* ("sacred"). To engage the Maori in genetics research, researchers developed a culturally sensitive plan that tailored informed consent, control over the procedures and data, and community engagement to existing Maori values (Beaton et al., 2016). Although the model was developed for use with Maori participants, it provides guidance for researchers setting up biorepositories with many types of communities. ■

davidf/E+/Getty Images

Using culturally sensitive procedures for handling biosamples collected for genetics research built trust between researchers and Maori communities in New Zealand.

If you plant seeds in trays receiving different amounts of nutrients, water, and sunlight, the height of the resulting plants will appear to be less influenced by genetics. If you studied the heritability of human intelligence in participants living in extremely wealthy or extremely poor circumstances, genetic influences would be exaggerated, just as they are when you hold the nutrients, water, and sunlight constant for your plants. Researchers assessing the heritability of human traits attempt to do so within a typical range of environments.

Because of the influence of environment on heritability, some researchers question the use of adoption studies for assessing the relative influences of genetics and environment on development. These studies compare adopted children to their biological and adoptive parents in an effort to assess the relative impact of heritability. Like plants with constant amounts of nutrients, water, and sunlight, adoptive families share many common features as a result of the screening process required before adopting. Consequently, adoptive parents rarely represent as much diversity as the group of biological parents whose children they adopt. If all adoptive families provide a consistent environment, this factor would inflate the apparent heritability of characteristics examined in their adopted children.

iStock.com/digitalskillet

The environments provided by adoptive parents are more similar to one another than to the environments provided by biological parents. This environmental similarity can exaggerate genetic influences—a result that must be taken into account when investigating heritability using adopted children.

Comparisons of twins are often used in behavioral genetics to evaluate relative contributions of genetics and environment. The differences between identical twins, who share identical DNA, and fraternal twins, whose DNA shows the same approximately 50% of overlap found in any two siblings, are particularly useful because both types of twins share similar environments. The Minnesota Study of Twins Reared Apart (Bouchard et al., 1990) not only compares identical to fraternal twins, but includes pairs of identical twins and fraternal twins adopted at birth and raised in separate homes (see Figure 3.10).

Twin studies are also useful in establishing **concordance rates**, which are statistical probabilities that a trait observed in one person will be seen in another. Concordance rates are especially useful to psychologists interested in psychological disorders because they provide estimates of the heritability of a condition. For example, concordance rates for autism spectrum disorder (see Chapter 14) are high in identical twins (95.2%) relative to fraternal twins (4.3%; Nordenbæk et al., 2014). Because both types of twins share a uterine environment and

concordance rates The statistical probability that a trait in one person will be shared by another; usually discussed in relation to identical and fraternal twins.

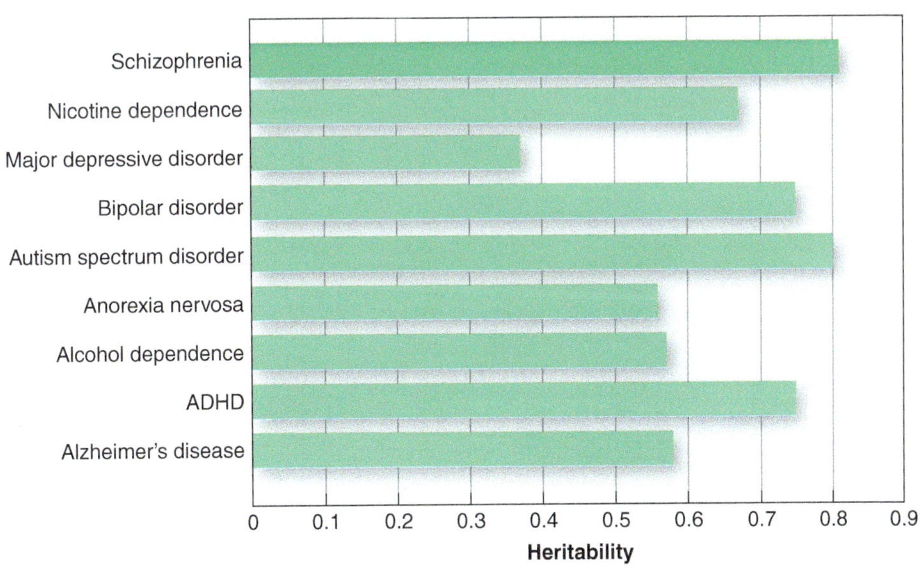

FIGURE **3.9**

Heritability of Some Human Conditions. Heritability rates, typically based on twin studies, tell us how much of the variability seen in a population can be due to genetics. Most human traits feature heritability between 0.30 and 0.60.

Source: Adapted from P. F. Sullivan, M. J. Daly, & M. O'Donovan (2012). "Genetic Architecture of Psychiatric Disorders. The Emerging Picture and Its Implications," *Nature Reviews Genetics*, *13*, 537–551. doi:10.1038/nrg3240 are exposed to similar parenting, this discrepancy makes a strong argument for the importance of genetic influences on autism spectrum disorder.

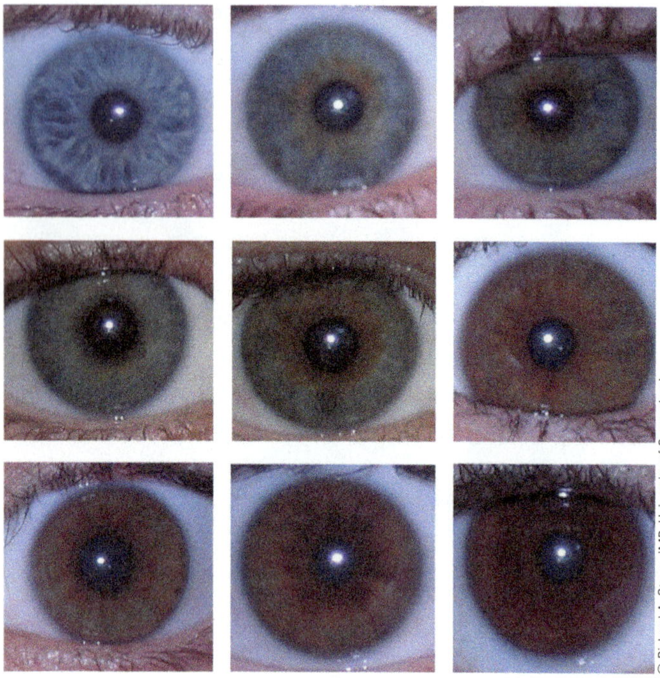

Our species shares genes for eye color, but combinations of alleles produce many possible shades.

The Search for Candidate Genes

Although we can say that all humans share 100% of their genes, we do not share 100% of our alleles, giving each of us a unique version of the genome. In other words, we all share genes that produce eye color of some sort, but our different combinations of alleles result in a variety of shades. There are at least 3 million DNA variations in the human genome—enough for us to differ from one another in nearly every gene (Plomin & Spinath, 2004).

A primary goal in psychology is the understanding and effective treatment of psychological disorders, many of which are described in Chapter 14. Genotypes related to psychological disorders can provide a starting point for this understanding, although as shown in • Figure 3.11, scientists must fill in the gaps between genes and observed symptoms. Comparing variations of DNA in individuals who do or do not have a particular trait of interest can help scientists pinpoint the causes of problems and suggest preventive strategies.

A common misunderstanding is the belief that we can identify "a gene for" a particular behavior. For example, a headline in *Time* magazine trumpeted, "The Genes for Pot Addiction Have Been Identified" (Szalavitz, 2016). It is important to remember that genes encode for proteins, not behaviors. Genes build proteins that construct brains, and brains might or might not become addicted to cannabis. Rather than viewing a gene as causing a complex behavior, it is more accurate to view genes as contributing, along with many other factors, to the development and functioning of the nervous system, which in turn generates observable behavior.

candidate gene A gene that has a greater impact on a trait of interest than other genes.

FIGURE **3.10**

Twins Raised Together or Apart Show Comparable Levels of Similarity Across Several Traits. Comparisons of identical twins raised together or in separate adoptive families show that some traits are more similar in twin pairs (fingerprint ridge count) than others (nonreligious social attitudes). However, regardless of the degree of similarity for a trait, living apart or together seems to have had relatively little impact on the degree of similarity within twin pairs. In other words, twins raised apart are just about as similar on each trait as twins raised together.

Source: Adapted from T. Bouchard, Jr. et al. (1990). "Sources of Human Psychological Differences: The Minnesota Study of Twins Reared Apart," *Science*, *250*, 223–228. doi: 10.1126/science.2218526

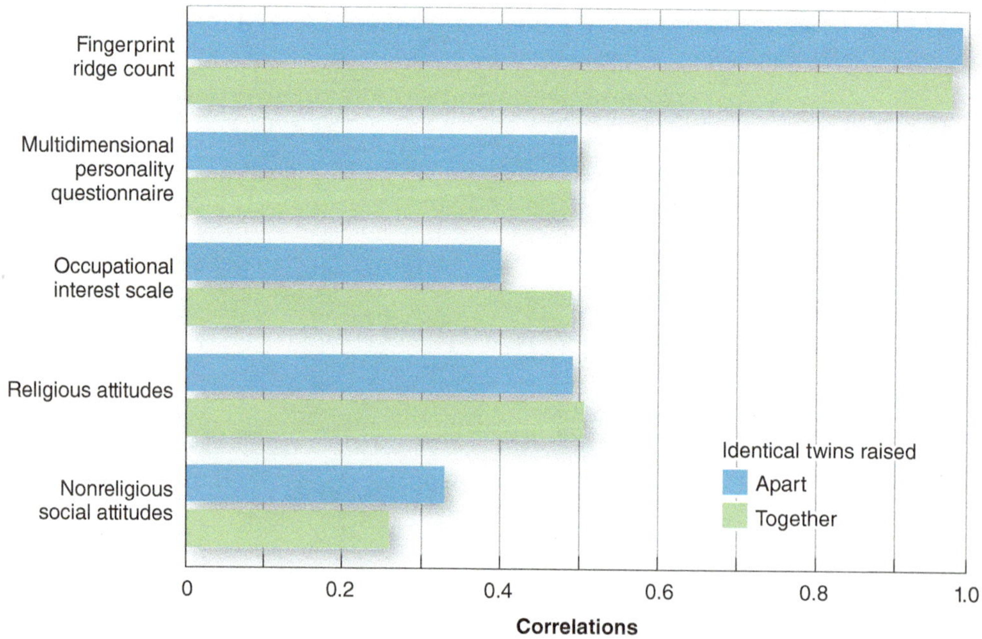

Prior to the development of databases made possible by the Human Genome Project and the International HapMap Project, investigating more than a few genes at a time was not feasible. Instead, **candidate gene** research studies were conducted, in which one gene or a small number of genes were compared between groups of people with and without a condition of interest. This search for candidate genes for a particular phenotype, such as schizophrenia, did not always result in accurate or complete findings (Farrell et al., 2015). Rather than testing single genes, contemporary functional geneticists often use **genomewide association studies (GWAS)** or whole-genome sequencing (WGS). Emerging technologies now allow researchers to scan complete sets of DNA from many participants, looking for variations associated with a particular phenotype, condition, or disease. A GWAS study identified a higher risk for severe COVID-19 with respiratory failure among people with Type A blood, while those with Type O blood experienced lower risk (Ellinghaus et al., 2020). As our methods for conducting genetic research improve, our answers become more complete and accurate (Prata et al., 2019).

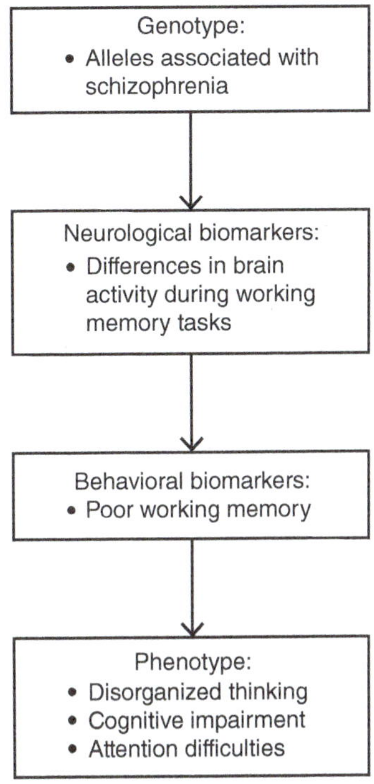

FIGURE **3.11**

From Genes to Behavior. In addition to our desire to view nature and nurture accurately, incorporating genetics in psychology helps us understand the development of psychological disorders, from genes to observed and clinical symptoms. Understanding this pathway should improve our ability to develop effective treatments.

Source: Author

genomewide association study (GWAS) A scan of complete sets of DNA from many participants, which is performed to look for variations associated with a particular phenotype, condition, or disease.

epigenetics The study of gene–environment interactions in the production of phenotypes.

Epigenetics

Having identical genotypes, as is the case with identical twins, does not guarantee identical phenotypes, or observed characteristics. As we explained in the example of the *Agouti* gene's effects on the fur color and weight of baby mice, different phenotypes can result from the same genotype due to interactions between the organism and its environment. When factors other than the genotype produce changes in a phenotype, we say that an **epigenetic** change has occurred. *Epi* is Greek for "over" or "above," so *epigenetics* refers to the reversible development of traits by factors "above" the genes themselves that determine how genes perform. The field of epigenetics explores these gene–environment interactions.

Epigenetic change influences gene expression, the process by which DNA builds proteins that contribute to features of living cells. Genes can be turned on or off by internal signals (hormones or neurochemicals) or by signals from external sources (diet or toxins). There is an obvious need for epigenetics in development, as the differences between a skin cell and a muscle cell result from turning on the right set of genes and turning off others. Thus, the magnitude of epigenetic change depends on an organism's age. The fetus experiences the highest rate of epigenetic change, followed by the child and finally, the adult. While epigenetic changes are reversible, many last entire lifetimes. For example, individuals who experienced traumatic life events prenatally or during childhood were found to have long-term epigenetic changes in brain structure, influencing lifetime vulnerability to mental health problems (Ambeskovic et al., 2019).

Among the factors known to produce epigenetic change are nutrition, disease-causing organisms, drugs, stress, and environmental toxins. In particular, malnutrition and stress experienced by pregnant women have the potential to influence the epigenetics of the fetus, leading to lifelong effects on physical and psychological well-being. In the discussion of psychological

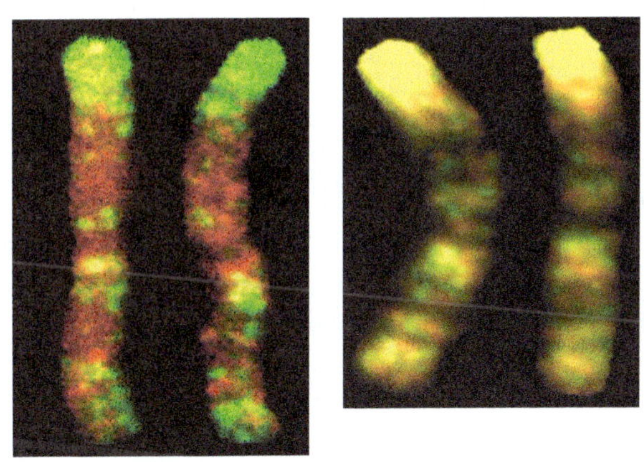

"Epigenetic differences arise during the lifetime of monozygotic twins," by Mario Fraga et al., in *Proceedings of the National Academy of Sciences* 2005 Jul 102 (30) 10407-8, Fig. 3. Copyright (2005) National Academy of Sciences, U.S.A.

Fraga et al. (2005) studied 160 identical twin pairs between the ages of 3 and 74. The two chromosomes on the right belong to a pair of 3-year-old twins, and those on the left belong to a pair of 50-year-old twins. Areas of red indicate differences between the two chromosomes in each pair related to differences in gene expression. As twins age, their gene expression becomes more different, as indicated by the greater amount of red in the chromosomes from the older twins. Twins who had spent the most time apart showed the greatest epigenetic differences.

THINKING SCIENTIFICALLY

The "Warrior Gene" and Criminals

ALTHOUGH WE HAVE CAUTIONED YOU against "a gene for" reasoning for complex human behaviors, the examination of candidate genes continues to be a viable approach to understanding the "nature" part of the nature–nurture interaction. In some cases, identification of candidate genes can have profound influences on public policy. One such candidate gene is the *MAOA* (monoamine oxidase A) gene, located on the X chromosome, which has been implicated in antisocial behavior. The protein produced by the *MAOA* gene is an enzyme that affects several important neurochemicals, including dopamine and serotonin, which are discussed further in Chapter 4. Variations in *MAOA* are classified as low or high activity. The low-activity allele has been linked to impulsive antisocial behavior, leading to its popular reputation as "the warrior gene." How valid is this point of view? To evaluate this concept, we will return to the critical thinking questions we outlined in Chapter 2.

What Am I Being Asked to Believe or Accept?

The "warrior gene" concept asks us to believe that variations in a single gene can predict antisocial behavior.

What Evidence Supports This Position?

An early case study (see Chapter 2) of a Dutch family characterized by an unusual zero-activity version of *MAOA* and a multi-generational history of extreme aggression encouraged further investigations of the "warrior gene" (Brunner et al., 1993).

Are There Other Ways That This Evidence Could Be Interpreted?

The original study is based on a rare and unusual situation. Studies of more typical *MAOA* alleles demonstrate very small effect sizes. As we discussed in Chapter 2, this means that only a small part of the variation in antisocial behavior across the population can be linked to people's *MAOA* alleles. Genes interact with environments, too. The *MAOA* alleles were more predictive of violent behavior in children with known histories of child maltreatment (Caspi et al., 2002; Fergusson et al., 2011).

What Other Evidence Would I Need to Evaluate These Alternatives?

Antisocial behavior is very complex (see Chapters 13 and 14). Using multiple perspectives to evaluate antisocial behavior should provide a clearer picture of the issue.

What Are the Most Reasonable Conclusions?

Although *MAOA* alleles might play a part in antisocial behavior, single genes rarely determine simple human traits like eye color, let alone complex behaviors.

This has not, however, stopped the legal system from considering *MAOA* status in criminal cases. Not only has *MAOA* status been admitted as evidence in courts in the European Union and in the United States, but this information has been used to support the idea that defendants had reduced responsibility for aggressive actions because they "couldn't help" being violent. However, it is also possible that courts of law might administer more stringent punishments, such as longer prison terms, under the belief that the person is relatively untreatable (González-Tapia & Obsuth, 2015). Geneticists and psychologists have a responsibility to communicate the correct interpretation of findings to policymakers to avoid improper applications of research results.

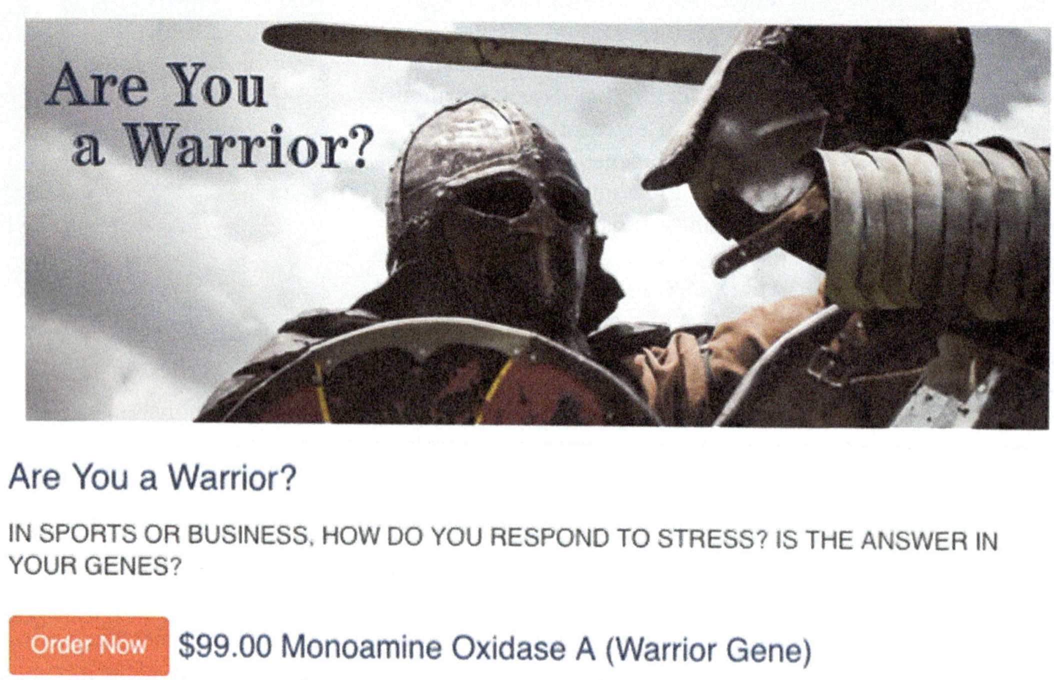

This advertisement for direct-to-consumer genetics tests suggests that a single gene, MAOA, is responsible for your being a "warrior" and how you respond to stress. It is very likely that this claim oversimplifies and exaggerates what we know about the MAOA gene.

Source: FamilyTreeDNA

disorders in Chapter 14, you will see that many disorders trace their roots to a combination of genetic vulnerability and disruptions experienced by the pregnant woman, such as illness or malnourishment.

Geneticists have identified four processes that produce lasting but reversible changes in gene expression: ribonucleic acid (RNA) interference, RNA editing, histone modification, and DNA methylation (see ● Figure 3.12). For the purposes of this overview, we will focus on histone modification and DNA methylation. *Histones* are protein structures around which your DNA is wound. If the DNA in a single cell were not wound up in this fashion, it would be over 6 feet long (Annunziato, 2008). When either the core or the tail of a histone interacts with regulatory proteins, the expression of nearby segments of DNA can become more or less likely. *DNA methylation* occurs when a methyl group (one carbon atom bonded to three hydrogen atoms) is added to the DNA molecule. This usually has the result of turning genes off. You can think about DNA methylation as being similar to stapling some pages in a book together. Because of the staples, you can't read the pages.

Although many epigenetic studies examine physical features like fur color, more complex features of interest to psychologists are also subject to epigenetic influences. For example, rats that were licked frequently during infancy by their mothers (the rat equivalent of getting a hug from mom) were calmer when faced with stress later in life than rats licked infrequently (Champagneet al., 2003). By licking their pups, these mothers influenced the expression of genes that determined responses to a stress hormone. The nurture provided by the mother had a lifelong impact on the offspring's ability to cope with stress.

A human being has about 100 trillion meters of DNA. To put this in perspective, this means that our DNA could go to the Sun and back more than 300 times.

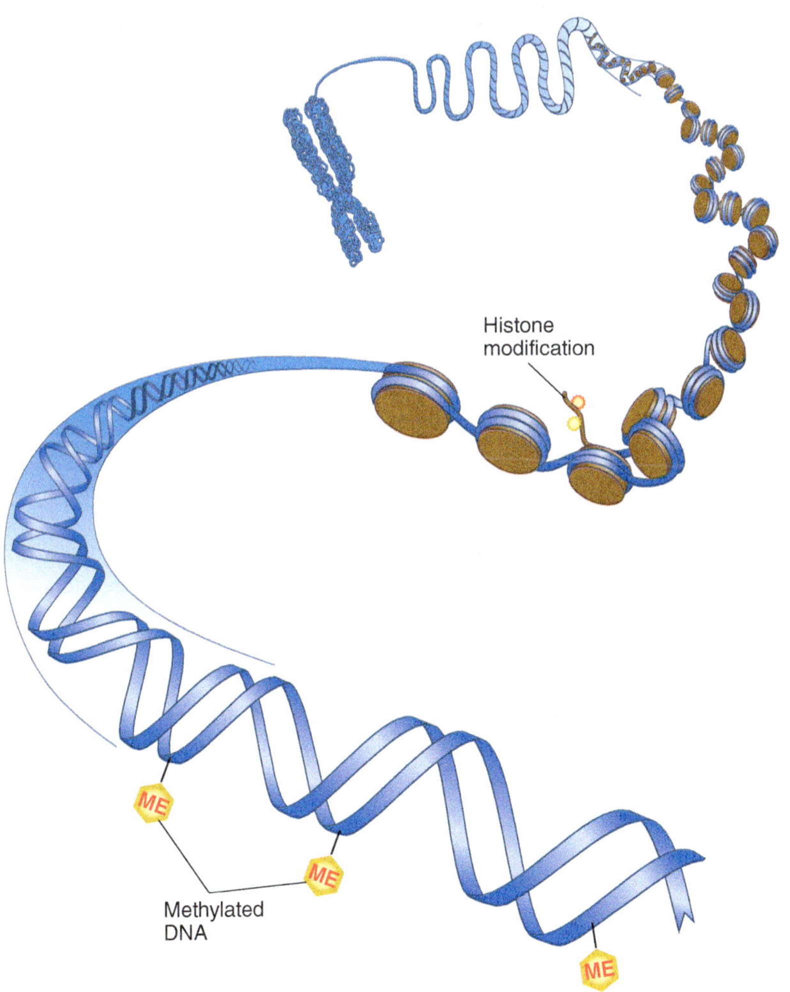

FIGURE **3.12**

Mechanisms of Epigenetic Change. Two important processes for producing epigenetic change are histone modification and DNA methylation. Histone modification occurs when certain chemicals interact with the tail or core of a histone. DNA methylation occurs when a methyl group (one carbon atom bonded to three hydrogen atoms) attaches to the DNA molecule. These modifications affect the likelihood that particular genes will be expressed or silenced.

PSYCHOLOGY AS A HUB SCIENCE

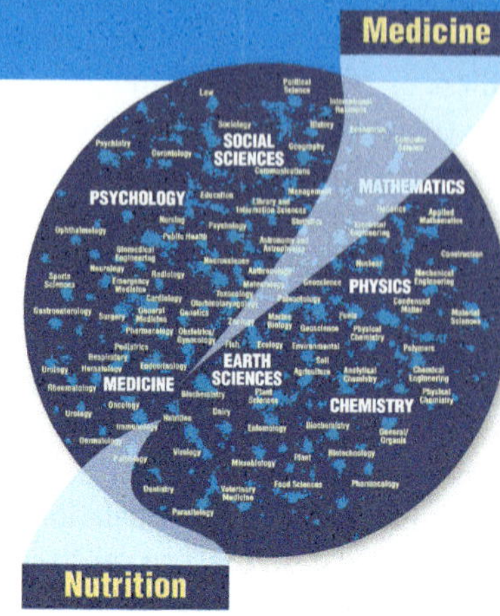

Understanding the Epigenetic Influences of Nutrition

WE TYPICALLY THINK OF NUTRITIONISTS as providing good advice about what to eat, especially for pregnant women, children buying school lunches, and people facing health challenges. But we also understand that the food we eat is one of the key environmental factors that produce epigenetic change. A new field known as *nutrigenomics* has emerged to explore the epigenetic influences of diet. In the not-too-distant future, you might be given an individualized diet plan by a nutritionist based on your personal methylation pattern. Although this might initially help us with certain cancers and other disease states, we know that some psychological disorders are also influenced by epigenetics. Following a healthier diet is linked with lower risk for depression (Molendijk et al., 2018; Berk & Jacka, 2019), and epigenetic factors might play a role in these findings. It is possible that in addition to more conventional treatments, individuals with psychological disorders might benefit from diets tailored to their epigenetic histories.

Many common foods have known epigenetic effects. Intake of garlic, broccoli, and dietary fiber can turn on anticancer and other protective genes. We saw earlier in this chapter how mother mice exposed to BPA gave birth to offspring that had yellow fur and were obese due to reduced methylation of the *Agouti* gene. However, if the mother exposed to BPA was also given a diet rich in the nutrients choline, betaine, and vitamin B12, all of which contribute to increased methylation, the offspring had normal weight and brown fur. We might not be able to control the environmental toxins to which we are exposed, but a greater understanding of epigenetics might help balance our exposure with appropriate nutrition. ■

gephoto/Shutterstock.com

Children exposed to child abuse have been found to have similar long-lasting changes in the expression of genes related to stress hormones (Neigh et al., 2009), as well as a number of genes associated with later medical problems and psychological disorders (Yang et al., 2013). Happily, these changes appear to be reversible in children who experience consistent and responsive caregiving by foster parents (Fisher et al., 2011).

Epigenetics has the potential to illuminate the causes of many psychological disorders, as discussed in Chapter 14. Hundreds of separate genes appear to be linked to disorders like schizophrenia, autism spectrum disorder, and bipolar disorder, yet no single gene produces more than a tiny effect on a person's risk of developing these disorders. In contrast, patterns of DNA methylation and unusual histone modifications are strongly associated with risk for these conditions. For example, epigenetic differences help to distinguish between identical twin pairs in which one twin has schizophrenia or bipolar disorder while the other remains healthy (Abdolmaleky et al., 2015).

CONNECTING TO RESEARCH

Can Transgenerational Epigenetic Change Occur?

WE HAVE SEEN IN THIS CHAPTER that individual experience can influence gene expression, but scientists also are considering the possibility that epigenetic changes can be passed along to subsequent generations. How might this happen?

Brian Dias and Kerry Ressler (2013) investigated transgenerational epigenetics using fear conditioning in mice. As explained in Chapter 8, animals (including humans) can learn to associate a signal with an important event through the process of classical conditioning. If a mouse learned to fear an odor associated with shock prior to becoming a parent, could this experience affect the offsprings' reaction to the odor?

The Question: Can a learned fear response to an odor be passed from one generation to the next?

METHODS

Dias and Ressler began by training mice to fear the smell of a chemical called *acetophenone*, which to us smells like almonds and cherries (see ● Figure 3.13). After the odor was infused into the mouse's cage, the mouse experienced electric shock through the grid floor. After sufficient training, the mice showed fear in the presence of the odor, even when they didn't get shocked. The researchers conditioned fear to another odor in one control group and included another control group that had no fear conditioning at all.

All of the mice were mated following conditioning, and their offspring were tested for their reaction to acetophenone.

ETHICS

As you learned in Chapter 2, all animal research in psychology is regulated by a set of strict ethical guidelines. The use of electric shock in this experiment must conform to federal regulations regarding pain.

RESULTS

Offspring of the father mice receiving the acetophenone–shock pairings showed fear to the acetophenone, even though they had never experienced it. Even more surprisingly, the grandchildren of the original conditioned mice also showed fear of acetophenone, as did mice conceived using in vitro fertilization with sperm from the original trained mice.

CONCLUSIONS

What could possibly produce this response to an odor that a parent learned to fear? The original trained mice responded to their fear training by increasing the production of a protein related to detecting acetophenone. The researchers suggested that DNA methylation had changed on the genes responsible for producing the receptor protein. Because the next two generations showed similar changes, the researchers argued that the epigenetic changes were passed along through the sperm by mechanisms that are not fully understood. Sperm contain RNA, proteins, and metabolites in addition to DNA, and some or all of these molecules might influence offspring (Perez & Lehner, 2019).

While some scientists support the conclusions put forward by Dias and Ressler, others are more skeptical. Successful replications and further research on mechanisms of transgenerational epigenetics might clarify the processes responsible for these observations. ■

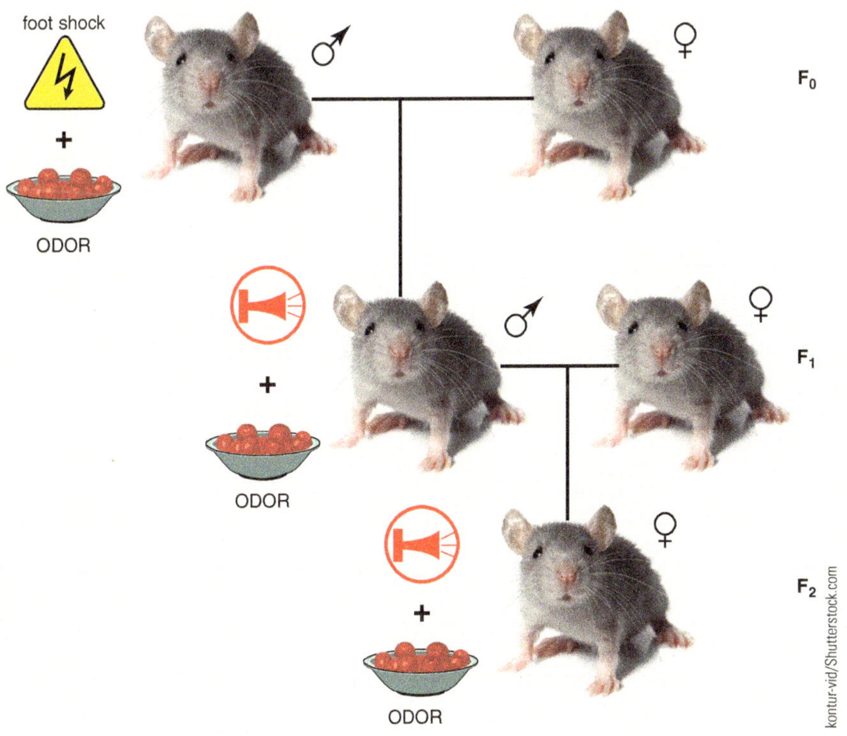

FIGURE **3.13**

Can Epigenetic Changes Affect Future Generations? According to Dias and Ressler (2013), a changed response to a distinctive odor can be passed to a mouse's children and grandchildren. A male mouse (F_0) is exposed to an odor similar to cherries and almonds that is paired with foot shock. The male offspring of this mouse (F_1) is tested with a combination of odor and a blast of noise (a standard way of measuring startle). The grandchild of the original mouse (F_2) is tested the same way. Compared to mice whose fathers and grandfathers did not receive a pairing of odor and foot shock, these F_1 and F_2 mice demonstrated an enhanced startle effect to the odor plus noise, suggesting that a greater sensitivity to the odor might have been passed along due to epigenetic change.

SUMMARY 3.1 Major Concepts in Genetics

Concept	Definition	Example
Genotype 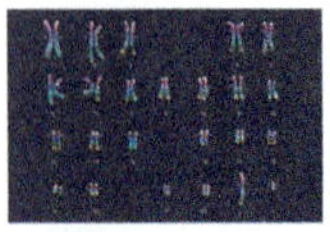	An individual's genetic makeup.	A person might have an allele for freckles and an allele for no freckles.
Phenotype 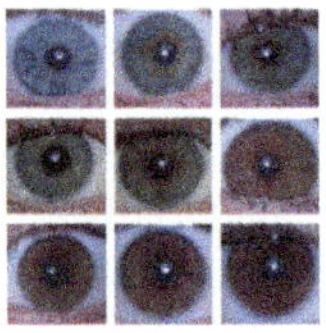	An individual's observable trait.	A person has green eyes.
Gene 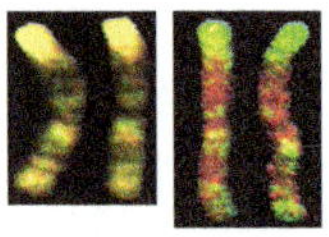	A sequence of DNA in a specific location on a chromosome that contains the instructions for making a protein.	The serotonin transporter gene is located on chromosome 17.
Gene expression 	Information from a gene is used to produce a protein.	Maternal diet in mice can affect the expression of the *Agouti* gene.
Allele 	One of two or more possible variations of a gene.	A small number of *BRCA1* alleles are associated with cancer risk.
Homozygous 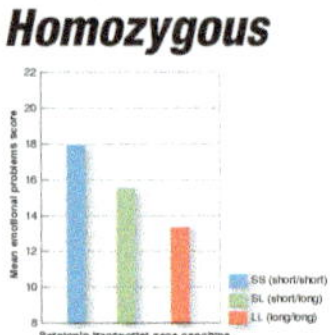	Having two of the same alleles.	A person has the SS or the LL form of the serotonin transporter gene.
Heterozygous	Having two different alleles.	A person has the SL form of the serotonin transporter gene.
Dominant 	An allele that is expressed regardless of whether it is homozygous or heterozygous.	The allele for freckles is dominant.
Recessive	An allele that is expressed only when it is homozygous.	The allele for no freckles is recessive.

Credits: Top row—ISM/Phototake; Second row—©Richard A. Sturm, IMB, University of Queensland; Third row—"Epigenetic differences arise during the lifetime of monozygotic twins," by Mario Fraga et al., in *Proceedings of the National Academy of Sciences* 2005 Jul 102 (30) 10407-8, Fig. 3. Copyright (2005) National Academy of Sciences, U.S.A.; Fourth row—Courtesy Randy L. Jirtle, Ph.D.; Fifth row—Featureflash Photo Agency/Shutterstock.com; Bottom row—Strauss/Curtis/Corbis/Getty Images.

How Does Evolution Occur?

The human genome is the product of millions of years of **evolution**, defined by biologists as descent with modification from a common ancestor. The study of evolution allows us to trace the family tree of living things.

In his book *The Origin of Species*, Charles Darwin proposed that species evolve or change from one form to the next in an orderly manner (Darwin, 1859). Darwin was well aware of the procedures used by farmers to develop animals and plants with desirable traits by mating particular individuals. A farmer's goal to raise the strongest oxen for pulling a plow might be accomplished by breeding the strongest available oxen to each other. In these cases, the farmer is using *artificial selection* to determine which individuals have the opportunity to produce offspring. Darwin suggested that instead of a farmer making these decisions, the pressures of survival and reproduction in the wild would make the choice, a process that he called **natural selection**. Organisms that survive long enough to reproduce would pass their traits to the next generation. Organisms that did not reproduce would not have the opportunity to pass their traits to future generations. As geneticists often remind us, we have no infertile ancestors.

In the more than 150 years since *The Origin of Species* was first published, our understanding of genetics and the fossil record has expanded exponentially, lending substantial further support for Darwin's views. Surprisingly, Darwin was able to derive his theory without the benefit of a basic understanding of genetics. He was unable to account for the variations he observed in a particular trait. That understanding was provided by Gregor Mendel (1822–1884), who discovered ways to predict the inheritance of particular traits, like the color of flowers, in his research on pea plants (Mendel, 1866). Mendel, in turn, was working without our modern understanding of genes. Combining current understanding of genetics with the natural selection processes proposed by Darwin provides scientists with powerful hypotheses about the progression of species over time.

DEA/C. BEVILACQUA/Contributor/De Agostini/Getty Images

Charles Darwin's theory of evolution described how species change in an orderly manner.

Mechanisms of Evolution

In addition to the process of natural selection described by Darwin, evolution can result from mutation, migration, and genetic drift. A **mutation** is an error that occurs when DNA is replicated. The average human baby is born with about 130 new mutations, but most have no effect (Zimmer, 2009). Mutant alleles providing some advantage spread through the population, but most mutant alleles that result in a disadvantage disappear from future generations. **Migration** occurs when organisms move from one geographical location to the next. Moving to a new location can affect the survival of individuals and the frequency of certain alleles in the population. Phenotypical traits that are advantageous in one environment might be less so in another. **Genetic drift** produces change from one generation to the next through chance or accident. Type B blood is virtually absent in contemporary populations of Native Americans, most likely due to chance (Halverson & Bolnick, 2008). The group of ancestors who first made their way to the Western hemisphere and survived to reproduce did not include anyone with the Type B allele. If the ancestors' blood type alleles had been more representative of the entire human population, more of their descendants would have Type B blood.

We can explore the effects of evolutionary processes—mutation, migration, genetic drift, and natural selection—on the history of one allele: the recessive allele for blond hair. Although as many as eight genes might participate in hair color, a tiny difference in *KITLG* is significantly linked to blond hair

evolution Descent with modification from a common ancestor.

natural selection The process by which survival and reproduction pressures act to change the frequency of alleles in subsequent generations.

mutation An error that occurs when DNA is replicated.

migration Movement to a new location.

genetic drift Change in a population's genes from one generation to the next because of chance or accident.

TIMOTHY CLARY/AFP/Getty Images/Newscom

Darwin understood that breeders could influence the traits of offspring by mating particular individuals. He believed that natural selection operated according to the same principles. The pressures of survival and reproduction in the wild would take the role of the breeder—determining which traits are passed to the next generation.

/AKG Images

Gregor Mendel (1822–1884) made important discoveries about inheritance at about the same time that Darwin was working on his theory of evolution, but neither scientist knew about genes and chromosomes. Modern geneticists combine this knowledge to form powerful hypotheses about the nature of living things.

in humans (Guenther et al., 2014). The original appearance of the allele for blond hair was probably the result of a random mutation occurring in northern Europe some 10,000 years ago (Frost, 2006). Migration, or rather the lack of it, might account for the relatively restricted area in northern Europe populated by blondes until fairly recently. Genetic drift undoubtedly reduced the global frequency of the blond allele between 1300 and 1700, as waves of bubonic plague decimated the European population. If by chance every person carrying the blond allele had died from the plague before reproducing, the allele would have disappeared from the human genome (see ● Figure 3.14).

Has natural selection influenced the blond gene? Some scientists believe it has. When people have a choice of mates of equal value, they will select the one that stands out from the crowd (Bem, 2001; Frost, 2006). Therefore, individuals with relatively rare blond hair might have enjoyed more reproductive success than those with more common, darker hair colors (Field et al., 2016). In Germany, with its high percentage of blondes, the trait of blondness is viewed differently than in countries where blondes are relatively rare. German men report that they view blondes as good homemakers, but they find women with dark hair more sexually attractive.

Any consideration of evolution must include the question of what natural selection selects. Natural selection favors the organism with the highest degree of **fitness**, defined as the ability of one genotype to reproduce relative to other genotypes. The concept of fitness includes survival to adulthood, ability to find a mate, and reproduction. Fitness is not some static characteristic, such as being strongest or fastest. Instead, *fitness* describes the interaction between characteristics and the environment in which they exist. A genotype that succeeds during the Ice Age may be at a significant disadvantage during periods of warmer temperatures. Animals in cold climates have short legs and stocky bodies, which help retain heat, whereas animals in warm climates have long legs and slim bodies, which release heat. Again, we see the need to consider nature within the context of nurture.

fitness The ability of one genotype to reproduce more successfully relative to other genotypes.

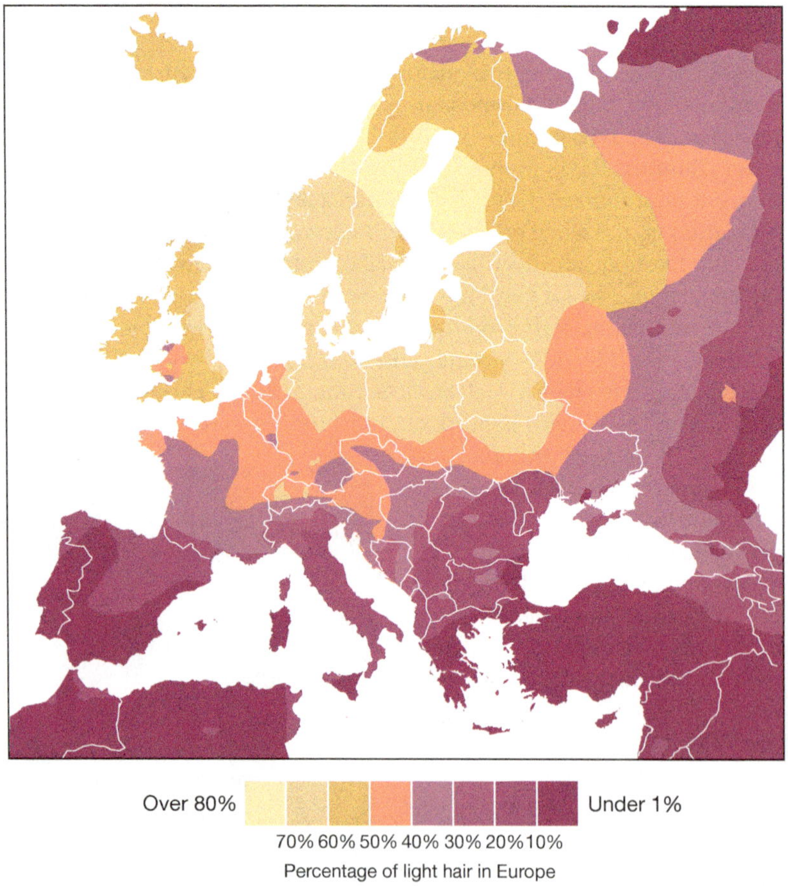

FIGURE **3.14**

Spread of the Blond Allele. After the first appearance of the blond hair allele about 10,000 years ago as a result of a chance mutation, its frequency might have been affected by migration, genetic drift, and natural selection.

Adaptation

Adaptation refers to either the process or the result of change because of natural selection. In other words, a species can respond to an environmental change by adapting, and features of the new phenotype may be called adaptations. Adaptations can take many forms. They can be behaviors, such as jumping higher to better avoid a predator, or anatomical features, such as eyes that can see color. Adaptations do not necessarily produce perfection. Any adaptation that is good enough to contribute to the fitness of an organism will carry forward into future generations.

A classic example of rapid adaptation is the case of the English peppered moth (*Biston betularia*). Before the Industrial Revolution, most peppered moths found in Britain were light gray, which allowed them to hide against the similar colors of tree bark. Darker moths occasionally appeared beginning around 1848, but because they were less capable of hiding from predators, they made up only about 1% of the population. With increasing industrialization, tree bark became frequently coated in soot. The once-camouflaged light gray moths became an easy target for predators against the darker background of the sooty trees. The darker moths rapidly became the norm, reaching frequencies of about 98%. As pollution came under better control, tree bark returned to its original light gray, and the lighter moths again became the norm. The peppered moth population successfully adapted to changing environmental circumstances, with color playing the role of an adaptation. The moths did not "decide" to change color. Natural selection, in the form of greater rates of reproductive success on the part of moths with a particular color, changed the frequencies of color alleles within the population.

Adaptations often appear to be compromises between costs and benefits. Adult human males have about 10 times as much testosterone as adult human females. Testosterone conveys a reproductive advantage because men with higher testosterone report having more sex partners and earlier age at intercourse (Lassek & Gaulin, 2009). On the negative side, however, high testosterone levels lead to lower immune system functioning, making the high testosterone males more vulnerable to disease (Muehlenbein & Bribiescas, 2005).

Adaptation is only one source of evolutionary change. Random events, such as the collision of meteors with the Earth and resulting climate changes, are believed to have destroyed some types of life and provided broad opportunities for others. We are also limited in our ability to use adaptation to predict the future. The study of evolution is similar to the study of history. Although we gain insight into wars by studying the causes of World War II, we cannot use our knowledge to predict future wars with precision. We can be fairly certain that

20TH CENTURY FOX/Album/Newscom

Marilyn Monroe and Jane Russell starred in the 1953 film *Gentlemen Prefer Blondes*. In some parts of the world, the sentiment in this title appears to be true.

adaptation A change because of natural selection.

Corbis

Jeff Vanuga/Spirit/Corbis

Peter Burian/Spirit/Corbis

Fitness varies across environments. Characteristics like long ears and long legs work in hot, desert climates, but short ears and legs conserve heat in colder climates.

Michael Willmer Forbes Tweedie/Science Source

Perennou Nuridsany/Science Source

The dark and light coloring of the peppered moth population in Great Britain changed in response to pollution from soot that collected on trees and changed again when pollution controls reduced the soot.

antibiotic-resistant bacteria, climate change, pollution, and reproductive technologies are probably changing the face of the human population as this text goes to press, but where all these changes will lead us remains unknown.

Evolution of the Human Brain

Our interest as psychologists is in the mind, and the mind and the behavior that it produces originate in the structures and processes of the brain and nervous system. Nervous systems are fairly recent innovations that separate animals from plants (see Figure 3.15). We can place the origin of the Earth at 4.5 billion years ago and the first single-celled life forms 1 billion years later, but the first neural nets appeared only 700 million years ago. In these primitive animals, the nerves in the abdomen were as likely to be important to behavior as the ones in the head. True brains residing in heads did not appear until animals formed skeletons, around 500 million years ago. The first decidedly human brain made its appearance only 7 million years ago, a small blip in the timeline of evolution (Calvin, 2004). The current model of the human brain has only been available for the last 100,000–200,000 years.

Anthropologists use the term *hominin* to describe species that walked on two feet, had large brains, and are assumed to be related to modern humans. Over the 7 million years of hominin evolution, brains grew rapidly, suggesting that improved intelligence was quickly translated into substantial advantages in survival. Early tool-using hominins, the australopithecines, had brains that were a bit larger than contemporary newborns and about the same size as those of modern chimpanzees, or about 400 cm^3. *Homo erectus*, a hominin living about 1.5 million years

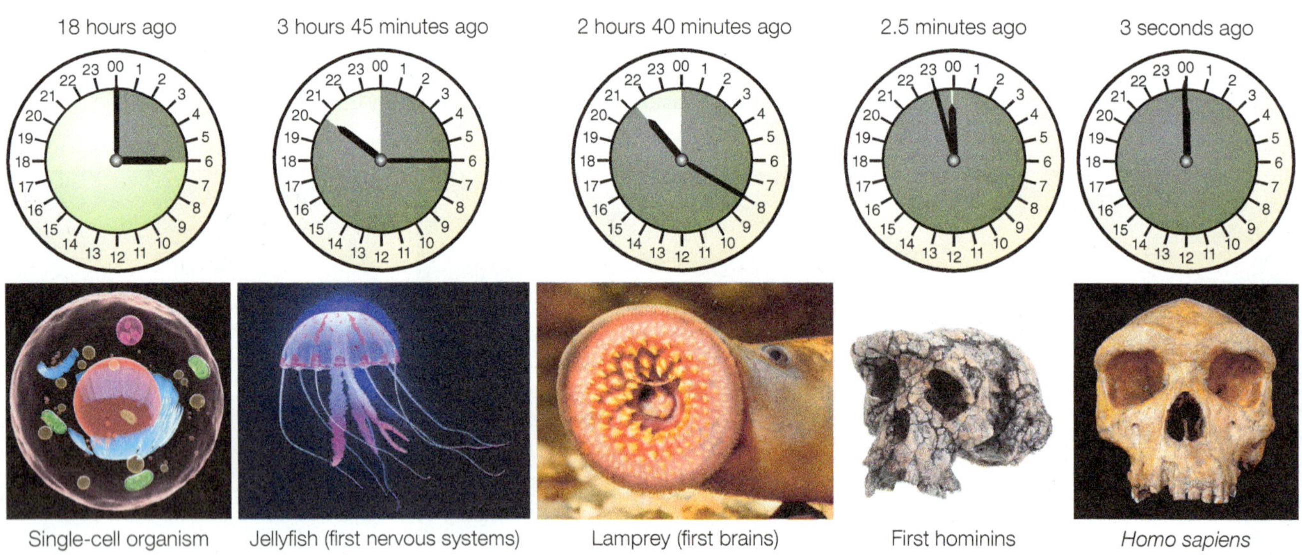

FIGURE 3.15

Timeline of Brain Evolution. If the 4.5-billion-year history of the Earth were expressed as a 24-hour day:

- The first single-celled organisms would have emerged 18 hours ago.
- The first nervous systems would have emerged about 3 hours and 45 minutes ago.
- The first true brain would have emerged about 2 hours and 40 minutes ago.
- The first hominin brain would have emerged less than 2.5 minutes ago.
- The current version of the human brain would have emerged less than 3 seconds ago.

ago, had a brain of about 700 cm^3, and the brains of modern humans, or *Homo sapiens*, are about 1,400 cm^3.

Hominins were not the only creatures who evolved large brains and considerable intelligence. The other primates, elephants, and whales are not lacking in these areas. Although the challenges of finding food, avoiding predators, and navigating through territories require considerable intelligence, these ecological challenges are no match for the complexity of social life faced by the hominins. The major factor distinguishing human intelligence from intelligence of other species is the richness and complexity of the social behavior supported by the human brain. Managing the abilities to distinguish friend and foe, imitate the behavior of others, use language to communicate, recognize and anticipate the emotions, thoughts, and behavior of others, maintain relationships, and cooperate required the evolution of a special brain (Cacioppo et al., 2002; Hrdy, 2005; Roth & Dicke, 2005). Comparisons of the challenges faced by different species support a stronger role for social complexity than for ecological complexity in building bigger brains (Dunbar & Schultz, 2007). Cacioppo & Decety, 2011a).

John Barrett/ZUMA Press/New York/New York/U.S./Newscom

Males with high testosterone report more chances to reproduce, but testosterone also might lower the response of the immune system. Extremely high levels of testosterone, because of the use of performance-enhancing drugs, might be contributing to the early deaths of some professional wrestlers, like Curt Hennig (1958–2003).

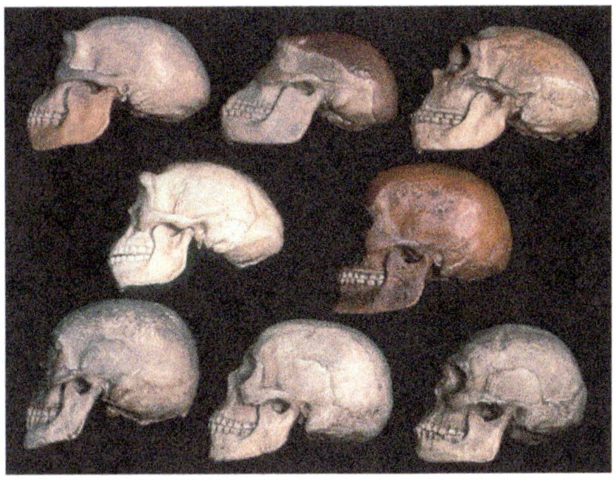
E. R. Degginger/Science Source

Over the course of hominin evolution, the size of the brain increased dramatically. It is possible that the ability of bigger brains to manage social relationships could have driven this rapid change.

The Contemporary Human Brain

You surf the Internet, complete your calculus homework, and read this textbook with a brain that is essentially the same size as that of your early *Homo sapiens* ancestors.

Although we can understand the advantages to survival of big, intelligent brains, we do not know why advances such as agriculture, literacy, and urbanization have not been accompanied by additional increases in brain size. It is possible that we have reached equilibrium between our needs for intelligence and the costs of a big brain. Brains are expensive to run in terms of nutrients. Although the brain comprises only about 2% of the body's weight, it requires about 20% of the body's resources (Raichle & Gusnard, 2002). In addition, brain size may be limited by the dimensions of the birth canal. Further change may not occur unless we experience a drop in the costs of big brains, a change in nutrients, or additional pressures for greater intelligence.

Although brain size has changed little during *Homo sapiens's* time on the Earth, the evolution of the human brain has not ended, and average intelligence has not remained the same. Modern genetic techniques allow researchers to date changes in a particular gene. Genes involved with brain development appear to have changed as recently as 6,000 years ago (Evans et al., 2004; Evans et al., 2005). As discussed in Chapter 10, IQ test scores first increased about 100 points worldwide during the 20th century (Flynn, 1999) and then began to drop again in those born after 1975 (Bratsberg & Rogeberg, 2018). If brain size has not changed for 100,000 years, let alone during the last 100 years or so, how can we account for the observed changes in intellectual performance? It is likely that environmental factors, including health, nutrition, education, and environmental toxins might explain the ups and downs.

Archive Image/Alamy Stock Photo

It is somewhat surprising that humans figured out how to go to the Moon and back with brains that were the same size as those of *Homo sapiens* living 100,000 years ago.

SUMMARY 3.2 Principles of Evolution

Concept	Definition	Example
Natural selection 	A trait's frequency in a population is determined by the survival and reproductive success of the organisms with the trait.	Faster rabbits are more likely to survive and reproduce than slow rabbits, leading to more fast rabbits in subsequent generations.
Mutation 	Genetic changes that occur spontaneously or because of external factors like radiation.	A mutation about 10,000 years ago led to the appearance of blond hair.
Migration 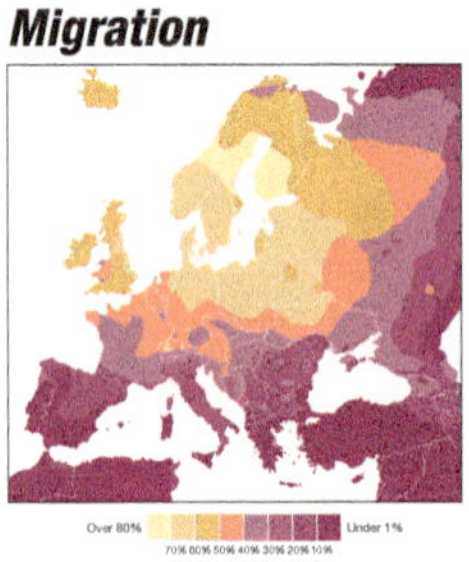	Populations move from one area to another.	Moving from a cold to a warm climate might change the natural selection of traits in a species.
Genetic drift	Chance events influence the frequency of alleles.	Huntington's disease is more common than usual among the Afrikaner population of South Africa because a carrier of the disease was among the small number of Dutch immigrants who survived to reproduce.
Fitness 	The ability of one genotype to reproduce relative to other genotypes in a particular environment.	The recessive sickle-cell trait has low fitness in general because it can produce disease, but because the trait protects the individual from malaria, it has higher fitness in populations living where malaria is common.
Adaptation 	Evolutionary changes whereby a population becomes better suited to its environment.	The moth population changed from primarily light to dark colors when the trees they inhabited became darker because of pollution.

Credits: Top row—TIMOTHY CLARY/AFP/Getty Images/Newscom; Second row—20TH CENTURY FOX/Album/Newscom; Fifth row—Corbis, Jeff Vanuga/Spirit/Corbis, Peter Burian/Spirit/Corbis; Bottom row—Michael Willmer Forbes Tweedie/Science Source, Perennou Nuridsany/Science Source.

How Does Evolution Influence Behavior?

Mitsuaki Iwago/Minden Pictures/Getty Images

Physical features, like the coloring of an animal that allows it to hide, are well-understood types of adaptations. Evolutionary psychologists attempt to explain how behaviors can be adaptive too.

We mentioned in an earlier section that behavior can be adaptive. If an animal that is good at hiding in the bushes is more successful than others of its species in escaping predators, it is likely that the ability to hide will spread through subsequent generations of the population.

Behavior like hiding, however, is unlike the other adaptations discussed so far, such as the color of a moth or blond hair. Color is a physical characteristic, and it is a fairly simple matter to identify the genes associated with these phenotypes. Behavior as a phenotype is considerably more complex. It is not an anatomical structure like a wing or an eye. Can we assume that behavior is shaped by the same evolutionary forces that affect physical traits? Darwin thought so. In *The Descent of Man and Selection in Relation to Sex,* he writes:

> The difference in mind between man and the higher animals, great as it is, certainly is one of degree and not of kind. We have seen that the senses and intuitions, the various emotions and faculties, such as love, memory, attention, curiosity, imitation, reason, etc., of which man boasts, may be found in an incipient, or even sometimes in a well-developed condition in lower animals. (Darwin, 1871, p. 126)

The Evolutionary Psychology Perspective

Among the psychological specialties discussed in Chapter 1, evolutionary psychology, a subspecialty within biological psychology, is the most relevant to our current discussion of the evolution of behavior. This approach to the mind assumes that our current behavior exists in its present form because it provided some advantage in survival and reproduction to our ancestors (Cosmides & Tooby, 1997).

The evolutionary psychology approach not only owes an obvious debt to Darwin, but also is a direct descendant of the functionalism supported by William James. As the term functionalism implies, behavior is seen as promoting survival, as opposed to being random and pointless. The goal of evolutionary psychology is to explain how the patterns of behavior that we share with other humans have been shaped by evolution.

MAURICIO HANDLER/National Geographic Image Collection

Predator fish typically hunt on the perimeter of a fish ball, where it is easier to isolate and capture prey. Humans who are on the social perimeter also may be at risk from predation, but usually from their own kind.

Origins of Social Behavior

Reconstructing the evolution of the nervous system is difficult, and tracing the origins of individual behavior is even more challenging, but identifying the roots of social behavior might be the most difficult task of all. Occasionally, physical evidence has allowed scientists to determine whether dinosaur parents stayed around to look after their young, but such accounts leave much detail unexplored and unexplained.

Individuals belonging to social species congregate in a number of ways, from pairs to families to whole societies. Belonging to a social group provides the benefits of mutual protection and assistance. Predatory fish are most likely to hunt in the perimeter of a school of

TABLE 3.2

Outcomes of Social Interactions

The first organism:	And the second organism: Wins	Loses
Wins	Cooperation	Selfishness
Loses	Altruism	Spite

Kim Hill/Arizona State University

Although no cultures today exist exactly like the hunters–gatherers of the past, the Ache of Paraguay are often used as a model of how that life might have been. Here, the Ache cooperate with one another to fish. Social behaviors like cooperation might have allowed humans, who are not particularly strong individuals, to survive.

fish because it's easier to isolate prey there than in the middle of the school (Ioannou et al., 2012). Being on the social perimeter is risky for our species as well. This simple fact of survival might be one of the reasons that we react so emotionally when we believe that we are being socially excluded. Being social carries costs as well as benefits. Social animals face injury in competition for food and mates and are exposed to contagious illnesses (Alexander, 1974), but the benefits of being social have clearly outweighed the costs for many species.

In typical environments, individual animals experience a variety of possible interactions when they come into contact with others of their kind. In each case shown in Table 3.2, individuals either benefit or do not benefit from the interaction, ultimately affecting their survival and reproductive success. Both parties benefit equally if they cooperate. For example, two hunters can work together to bring down an animal that neither could successfully hunt alone. Sharing the resulting meat with the families of both hunters would contribute to their survival and reproductive success. Much social behavior probably originated in these types of situations, in which the benefits of cooperation for an individual's survival and reproduction outweighed the disadvantages of cooperating, such as having less food or sharing with someone who later does not reciprocate.

Gherasim Rares/Shutterstock.com

Altruism, or the sacrifice of yourself for others, is more common among related individuals, but it also occurs when we are in close social contact with others. Honeybees sting to defend their hive, but in doing so, they end their own lives.

Cooperation, however, is not the only way that two individuals can interact. In selfish interactions, one person could steal food from another, allowing the thief's family to survive while the victim's family starves to death. In spiteful interactions, both participants lose. In some divorce proceedings, the partners are so determined to keep each other from maintaining resources that everything goes to the attorneys. Finally, in **altruism**, one individual's self-sacrifice is designed to benefit another individual.

Altruism is widespread in the animal kingdom. Most of us have experienced a honeybee sting, which is suicidal behavior on the part of the bee in an effort to protect its hive (Wilson, 1975). Altruism can extend to entire social organizations, regardless of the degree of relatedness (Chicago Social Brain Network, 2011). Among emperor penguins (*Aptenodytes forsteri*), survival of the chicks in the hostile Antarctic cold depends not only on an individual parent, but on the larger huddle formed by other parents.

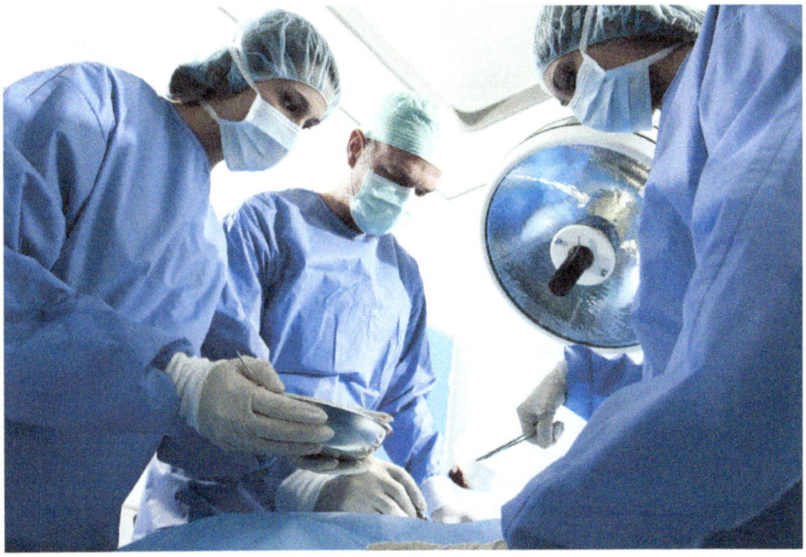

stefanolunardi/Shutterstock.com

Cooperation allows humans to carry out complex behaviors that would be impossible for a single individual to perform successfully.

As discussed in greater detail in Chapter 13, altruism is one of the most challenging social behaviors to explain in evolutionary terms. Darwin himself was puzzled by the apparent sacrifice of some individuals that led to the survival of the group. If altruism results in the destruction of the individual with altruistic genes, why doesn't this behavior disappear from the population? To explain this phenomenon, we return to the concept of relatedness presented earlier in the chapter. Sacrificing your life to save a close blood relative might increase the likelihood that your alleles would be passed along to subsequent generations. Self-sacrifice in this case does not need to be a conscious decision. Any behavior that results in a greater frequency of the relevant genes in subsequent generations will become more common.

You might be thinking that you often behave altruistically toward people who are not related to you. You might have comforted a friend who experienced a death in the family instead of studying for an upcoming midterm. This type of behavior, known as **reciprocal altruism**, occurs when we help another individual who is likely to return the favor at some future date (Trivers & Burt, 1999).

altruism Behavior on behalf of another that fails to benefit or harms the individual performing it.

reciprocal altruism Help that you provide for another person when you expect the person to return the favor in the future.

3/NaturePL/Superstock

Survival of emperor penguin chicks in the hostile cold of the Antarctic depends not just on the individual parent, but also on the larger huddle formed by the other parents.

Sexual Selection

sexual selection The development of traits that help an individual compete for mates.

Sexual selection was Darwin's term for the development of traits that help an individual compete for mates (Darwin, 1871). To what extent is human behavior influenced by sexual selection?

Parental Investment Sexual selection is influenced by the different investments in parenting made by males and females (Emlen & Oring, 1977). In many species, including our own, the female bears most costs of reproduction, from the carrying of the developing organism until birth to the nurturance of the young until adulthood. As a result, human females face sharper limitations than human males on the number of children that they can produce in a lifetime. If the goal is to pass your genes to subsequent generations and you are going to produce only one or two children, each child had better be as healthy and well nurtured as possible. The average number of children per woman worldwide dropped dramatically from 4.98 in 1960 to 2.45 in 2014 (The World Bank, 2017; see ● Figure 3.16).

Because males have a lower investment of time and resources in reproduction compared to females, it might seem that the best reproductive strategy for males would be promiscuity, but this is not always the case. In species such as our own, with lengthy and complex development leading to adulthood, a male who abandons his offspring puts their survival at risk (Gibson, 2008). Even if a man fathers many children, his genes are less likely to make it into the next generation if most or all perish from lack of care or protection.

Genghis Khan may have been the most prolific human male in history. His distinctive Y chromosome has been identified in 16 million living men, or 0.5% of the world's current total (Zerjal et al., 2003).

The mother can maximize her children's chances of survival by choosing a father who will not only pass along healthy genes, but also participate in the raising of children. Women have the ability to make accurate predictions of a man's interest in children simply by looking at a photograph of his face (Roney et al., 2006). Men with facial features correlated with high testosterone (strong brow ridge, square chin) are viewed as less likely to participate in childrearing than are men with facial features correlated with lower testosterone. These results suggest that women would be able to determine a man's potential as a father before reproductive investment occurs.

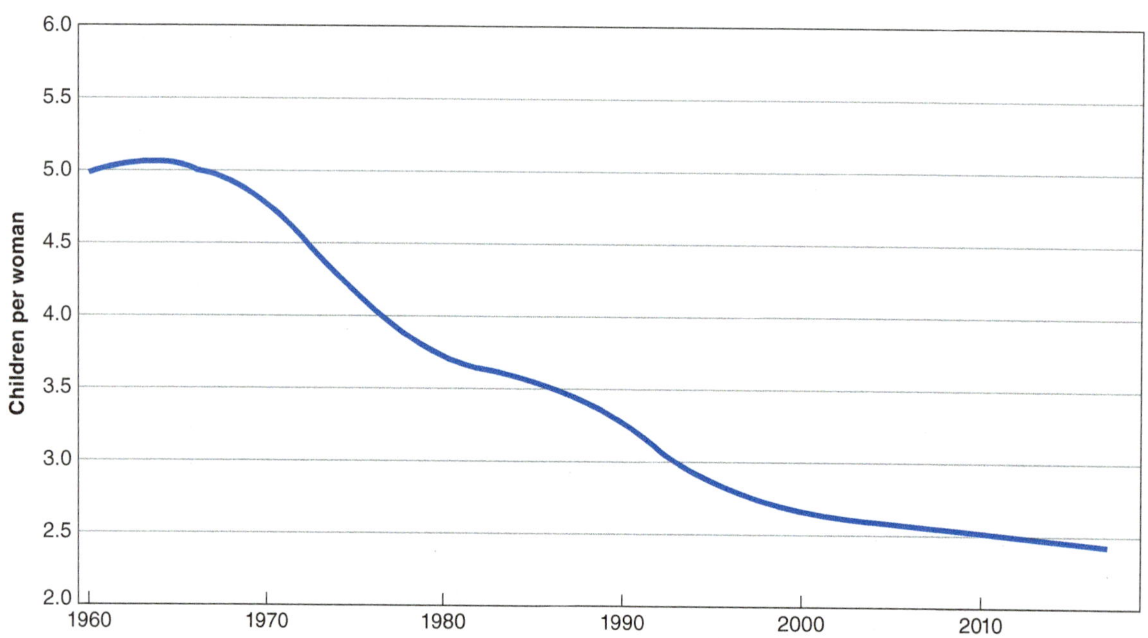

FIGURE 3.16

The Human Birth Rate Is Dropping Rapidly. The average number of children per woman worldwide dropped dramatically between 1960 and 2017.

Source: Adapted from the World Bank (https://data.worldbank.org/indicator/sp.dyn.tfrt.in).

Traits Possibly Influenced by Sexual Selection Earlier in this chapter, we discussed how blond hair might have provided a reproductive advantage because its relative novelty made it an attractive feature. What other types of human traits appear to fit Darwin's ideas about sexual selection?

Sexual selection might occur in two ways. In intrasexual selection (*intra* means "within"), members of one sex compete with one another for access to the other sex. In some species, such as deer, males engage in fights that determine which males are allowed to mate and which are not. Features like large antlers, which assist in winning a fight, could become sexually selected. In intersexual selection (*inter* means "between"), characteristics of one sex that attract the other might become sexually selected. The male peacock's luxurious tail appears to have developed for the sole purpose of attracting mates.

Evolutionary psychologists have argued that a number of human traits might have been subjected to sexual selection, including humor and vocabulary. According to this argument, human males use humor (Cherkas et al., 2000) and their vocabularies (Rosenberg & Tunney, 2008) to impress females with their intelligence because of intersexual selection. In romantic situations, males use more uncommon words than they do in other situations. We can also tell you about one behavior that does not successfully attract females—taking unnecessary risks like driving recklessly (Wilke et al., 2006). However, risky activities might have indirect positive outcomes for males. Dominant, successful males are likely to attract more females, and dominance among males is often decided on the basis of intrasexual competition in risky endeavors.

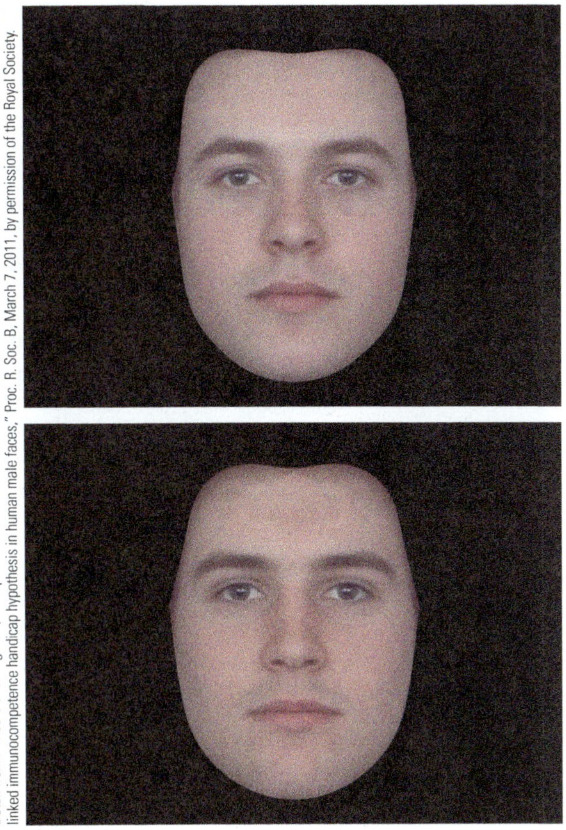

Detail from F. Moore et al. Figure 1, "Composite male faces constructed to differ in levels of T and C," from the article "Evidence for the stress-linked immunocompetence handicap hypothesis in human male faces," Proc. R. Soc. B, March 7, 2011, by permission of the Royal Society

Women show the ability to predict a man's score on the Infant Interest Questionnaire, which might indicate how involved a father he would be, by detecting the influence of testosterone on his facial features. These facial stimuli are constructed by combining photographs of many people. The face at the top has been manipulated to illustrate the impact of higher testosterone, while the one at the bottom reflects the impact of lower testosterone.

Culture

You might be surprised to find a section on culture in a chapter on genetics. However, genetics and evolution have shaped the human brain, which universally forms cultures. Cultures, which arise from socially transmitted knowledge, provide practices, values, and goals that can be shared by groups of people. Languages, morality, arts, laws, and customs make up a diverse and vibrant part of human social interactions.

Experiences shaped by culture, like other types of experiences, interact with survival and reproductive pressures. How might cultural differences have affected our ancestors' survival? We can gain insight into our species' cultural history by observing contemporary preagricultural societies, such as the Waorani and Yanomamö of the Amazon Basin. These groups are remarkably combative, resulting in high death rates among male warriors. Anthropologists have engaged in robust debates over the effects of the groups' violence on the warriors' reproductive success. Chagnon (1988) reported that aggressive men among the Yanomamö had larger numbers of children, although his data have been criticized due to methodological concerns. Beckerman et al. (2009) found the opposite to be true among the Waorani. Assuming these observations are correct, how can we reconcile the difference? Alès (2008) suggested that the Yanomamö cultural norm of "time outs" between raids, which is not a practice shared by the Waorani, could allow the more aggressive warriors more opportunities to recover and reproduce.

Our social minds were shaped by the cultures of hunter–gatherer groups until the development of agriculture approximately 10,000 years ago. With improved control of the food supply, less geographical mobility, and larger communities, humans entered a new era of social interaction. Although we believe that many features found in modern human behavior, such as reciprocal altruism, originated in the hunter–gatherer society, further social adjustments were required as groups became larger and more complex.

Agriculture, with its emphasis on land ownership, might have been the origin of patriarchal systems, in which men maintain control of resources, and inheritances follow the male line. Unlike hunter–gatherer societies, which are relatively egalitarian so far as the rights of males and females go, agricultural societies tilted the control of food and important resources

Francois ANCELLET/Contributor/Gamma-Rapho/Getty Images

Wave Royalty Free/Design Pics Inc/Alamy Stock Photo

Culture and Genetics Interact The Waorani (left) and Yanomamö (right) of the Amazon Basin share high rates of aggression, but the groups might differ in the effects of aggression on reproductive success. Some anthropologists report that aggression is related to greater numbers of children for aggressive Yanomamö warriors, but fewer children for aggressive Waorani warriors. This discrepancy is possibly the result of the Yanomamö cultural practice, not shared by the Waorani, of standing down between raids. This time out would give aggressive Yanomamö men chances to rest, heal, and reproduce that are not available to aggressive Waorani men.

in favor of men. Early industrialization merely built upon agricultural systems and, if possible, accentuated the power differential between males and females. Contemporary trends are again moving in a more egalitarian direction, with females in developed countries enjoying considerable financial independence and reproductive choice. These changes will no doubt have further effects on our social environment.

As societies became larger, humans took advantage of their large brains to devise new cultural systems to maintain group cohesion. Emerging societies shared many of the same types of internal conflict, so we typically find similar moral, religious, and legal systems across diverse cultures that attempt to control marriage, "character" issues such as honesty, and the transfer of precious resources.

With all the flaws of our groups, whether we're looking at families, communities, or nations, we retain a strong need to belong. As we will see on many occasions in this textbook, humans do not thrive in isolation. Our dependence on kinship, friendship, and group membership, honed over the course of 100,000 years or more of social living, continues to influence our behavior today.

Chuck Liddy/Raleigh News & Observer/Contributor/Tribune News Service/Getty Images

Humans have developed a strong need to belong and often adopt traditions that enhance a sense of group membership.

Samo Trebizan/Shutterstock.com

The development of agriculture 10,000 years ago changed the shape of human cultures.

Interpersonal Relationships
The Evolutionary Perspective

CAN WE USE GENETICS TO SELECT A MATE?

A CLUSTER OF GENES known as the *major histocompatibility complex (MHC)* appears to be subject to intersexual selection (Wedekind & Füri, 1997). As described in this chapter, this type of sexual selection operates on traits in one sex that influence the choices by the other. A child with a heterozygous set of MHC genes is better prepared to battle infections than is a child who receives two sets of MHC genes that are similar to one another. As a result, our children are more likely to survive if we select a mate that has a different set of MHC genes than we do.

There is some evidence that too much MHC similarity affects not just our children, but also our relationships. Garver-Apgar et al. (2006) reported that among romantic couples, increases in the number of MHC alleles shared by a couple reduced the woman's sexual responsivity to her partner and increased her number of extrapair sexual partners and her attraction to men other than her partner.

In a world before genetic testing, it appears that we were able to select partners with compatible MHC profiles on the basis of odor. Different configurations of the MHC genes produce distinctive body odors. When participants were asked to rate the pleasantness of the odors of T-shirts that had been worn by other people, they preferred smells associated with MHC genotypes that were different from their own (Wedekind & Füri, 1997).

Instead of relying on smell, some people are taking advantage of relatively affordable genetic testing to assess their relationships. Instant Chemistry provides clients and their partners with information about genes related to immune function, serotonin transport, oxytocin receptors, and dopamine function. It is too soon to tell whether such endeavors will improve relationships. We hope that you will use the critical thinking skills discussed in Chapter 2 to evaluate Instant Chemistry's claim that they "can help give you insights into how your relationship ticks and where strengths and weaknesses may lie" (Instant Chemistry, 2019). ■

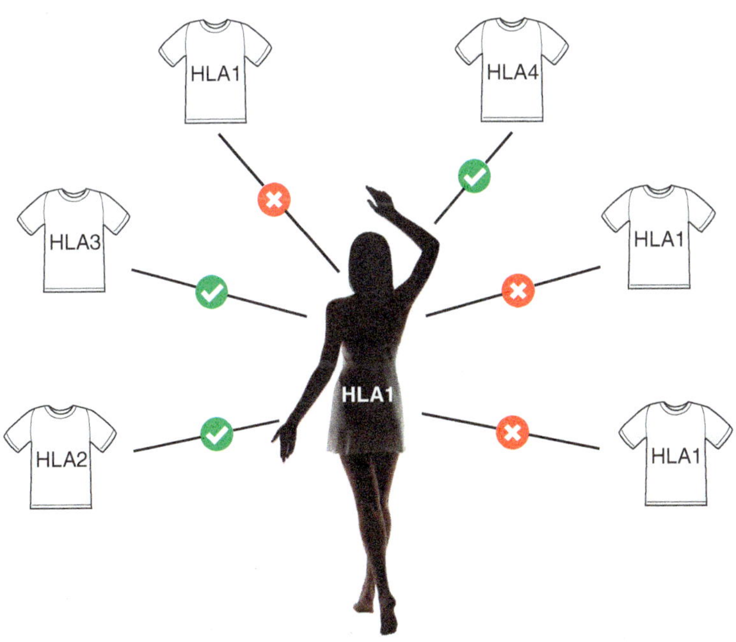

Boris Ryaposov/Shutterstock.com

Participants in a study preferred the smell of T-shirts worn by people who have MHC genotypes different from their own. Historically, these smell preferences might have helped people select partners with whom they are most likely to have healthy children.

Psychology Takes On Real-World Problems

Can Genetics Explain Differing Responses to COVID-19 Social Distancing?

WHAT CAN WE LEARN about human behavior during a pandemic by incorporating concepts and research related to genetics and evolution?

News reports are filled with stories of people flaunting expert recommendations for social distancing while others carefully avoid large social gatherings. While psychological science can provide a substantial list of factors that probably contribute to this behavior, our focus in this chapter is on genetics and evolution. As you've seen in this chapter, our human mind has been shaped over time to be highly social. Interruptions to social connectivity, such as solitary confinement, are among the most stressful experiences a human can experience. When we do not experience the social connectivity we desire, the result is loneliness (Cacioppo & Cacioppo, 2018). The quarantines and social distancing associated with COVID-19 certainly have the potential to make individuals feel more lonely.

You might not think of your capacity for loneliness as being a trait that is influenced by your genotype, but there is substantial evidence that it is. Numerous studies have identified loneliness as being approximately 48% heritable (Boomsma et al., 2005; Cacioppo et al., 2014). Recall that heritability refers to the amount of variability explained by genes in populations, not individuals.

When attempting to establish an evolutionary influence on a trait, we often look to other species to see if they respond similarly to humans. If you own a dog, you're probably already anticipating the answer—many species, from fruit flies to pigs, respond adversely to social isolation, but social species like our own have the worst responses (Cacioppo et al., 2014).

Most of us would agree that feelings of loneliness are distinctly unpleasant. Why would evolution favor those who had the capacity for this aversive experience? An Evolutionary Theory of Loneliness (ETL; Cacioppo & Cacioppo, 2018) suggests that feelings of loneliness could be adaptive by serving as a warning signal that stimulates efforts to repair social connectivity. Unfortunately, loneliness can also elicit a number of other subconscious behaviors that might work to support survival in the short term but also interfere with connectivity. For example, loneliness can lead to selfishness and self-preservation. While these behaviors might promote survival in people who are socially isolated, they rarely endear us to others (Cacioppo & Cacioppo, 2018).

If a trait is somewhat genetic, does this mean we have no control over it? Absolutely not. A trait can be 100% heritable, like the condition phenylketonuria, and still be completely treatable. Phenylketonuria interferes with the digestion of a particular amino acid and used to be a major cause of intellectual disability. Today, following an appropriate diet prevents adverse effects of the condition. So even if a person has a tendency toward feeling lonely, many steps can be taken to remedy the situation. This should encourage us in our efforts to design policies for reducing loneliness during a pandemic. Even if a condition features considerable heritability, we can still improve the situation. ■

FIGURE **3.17**

Perceived Loneliness Is Heritable. Scores on a measure of perceived loneliness were more similar in identical (monozygotic) twins than in fraternal (dizygotic) twins. It is likely that genetic influences contribute to a person's "set point" for feeling socially connected or not.

Source: Boomsma, D. I., Willemsen, G., Dolan, C. V., Hawkley, L. C., & Cacioppo, J. T. (2005). Genetic and Environmental Contributions to Loneliness in Adults: The Netherlands Twin Register Study. Behavior Genetics, 35(6), 745-752. doi: 10.1007/s10519-005-6040-8

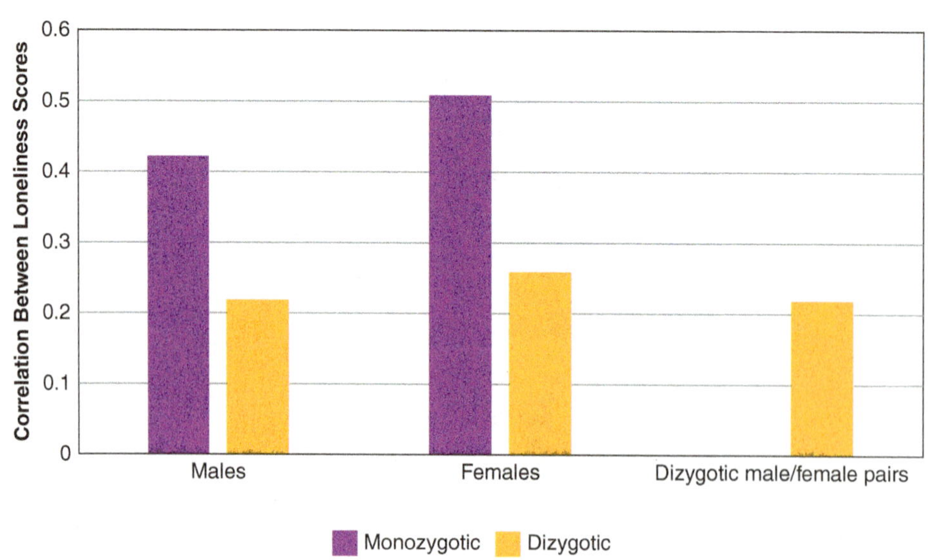

SUMMARY 3.3 Evolutionary Influences on Behavior

Concept	Definition	Example
Cooperation 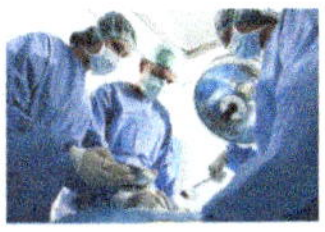	Working together to benefit all parties involved.	Hunters work together to kill an animal that an individual could not kill alone.
Altruism 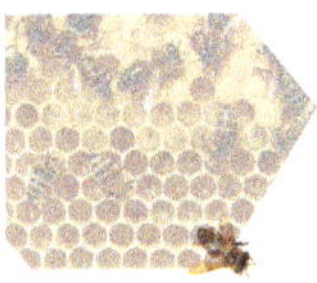	Sacrificing your personal interests to benefit another.	A young mother threw herself over her infant during a parking lot shootout. She died, but the infant survived.
Reciprocal altruism 	Sacrificing when you expect the recipient might do the same for you at some future time.	You share food with a hungry person, thinking that someone might share with you later.
Sexual selection 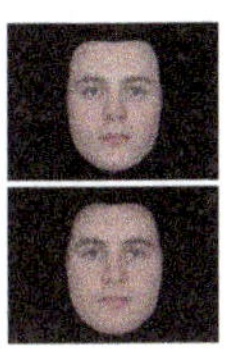	The evolutionary pressure on traits that help individuals find mates.	A woman may choose a man whose facial appearance is correlated with being a good father.

Credits: Top row—stefanolunardi/Shutterstock.com; Second row—Gherasim Rares/Shutterstock.com; Third row—3/NaturePL/Superstock; Bottom row—Detail from F. Moore et al. Figure 1, "Composite male faces constructed to differ in levels of T and C, from the article "Evidence for the stress-linked immunocompetence handicap hypothesis in human male faces," Proc. R. Soc. B, March 7, 2011, by permission of the Royal Society.

KEY TERMS The Language of Psychological Science

Be sure that you can define these terms and use them correctly.

adaptation, p. 91
allele, p. 74
altruism, p. 97
behavioral genetics, p. 78
candidate gene, p. 83
concordance rates, p. 81
dominant, p. 74
epigenetics, p. 83
evolution, p. 89
fitness, p. 90
gene, p. 73
gene expression, p. 74
genetic drift, p. 89
genomewide association study (GWAS), p. 83
genotype, p. 73
heritability, p. 78
heterozygous, p. 74
homozygous, p. 74
migration, p. 89
mutation, p. 89
natural selection, p. 89
nature, p. 72
nurture, p. 72
phenotype, p. 73
recessive, p. 74
reciprocal altruism, p. 97
relatedness, p. 76
sexual selection, p. 98

Perceived social isolation or connectedness can produce changes in the cells of our immune system.

Argosy Publishing, Inc.

4

The Biological Mind

THE PHYSICAL BASIS OF BEHAVIOR

LEARNING OBJECTIVES

1. Identify the brain structures and processes relevant to our understanding of mind and behavior.
2. Differentiate the major branches of the nervous system, explaining the core functions of each branch.
3. Associate key structures in, and regions of, the brain and peripheral nervous system with important aspects of physical and psychological functioning.
4. Explain the process by which hormones influence psychological experience and behavior.
5. Describe the process by which neurons communicate with one another, allowing the nervous system to integrate complex information.
6. Differentiate the roles played by major neurotransmitters in supporting physical functioning and psychological experience.

THROUGHOUT HISTORY, HUMAN SURVIVAL HAS been threatened by the various bacteria and viruses that try to make us their home. The bacteria-driven Black Death decimated Europe between 1346 and 1400, killing an estimated 30 to 60% of the population (Austin Alchon, 2003). Smallpox, measles, and influenza carried by Europeans to the Western Hemisphere killed as many as 90% of native populations (Public Broadcasting Service [PBS], 2005). The Spanish flu of 1918, which is related to contemporary bird flu strains, killed between 50 million and 100 million people worldwide in about a year (Patterson & Pyle, 1991). The full extent of deaths caused by COVID-19 remains to be seen as the pandemic runs its course.

Although you might think surviving a pandemic is more a question of biology and medicine, behavior and mental processes have a considerable amount of influence on our abilities to fight bacteria and viruses (Cacioppo & Berntson, 2011). Again, zooming out to the human social environment and then zooming back in to a smaller scale gives us a complete and interesting picture.

SHipskyy/iStock/Getty Images

Humans, who lack impressive teeth or claws, formed groups to enhance the odds of their survival. Anyone who was socially excluded from these groups experienced a more hostile environment. Social exclusion not only separated a person from the help of others in life-threatening situations, perhaps in fending off a predator, but worse, could lead to outright conflict with others, including combat. Under such hostile circumstances, socially excluded people faced a greater risk from bacterial infections than from viruses. Bacteria enter the body through cuts and scratches, whereas viruses are transmitted through body fluids (e.g., sneezing), so you are most likely to be exposed to them when you are in close contact with other people.

With that background in mind, look at the group of people in the image on the previous page. Do you think the woman on the right is feeling included or excluded? Surprisingly, whether we typically feel socially isolated or socially connected can have serious implications for our health (Cole et al., 2015; Cacioppo & Cacioppo, 2018a, 2018b). If this woman feels isolated and often left to fend for herself, she will, like her excluded ancestors, face a greater threat from bacteria than from viruses. Her brain will respond to her subjective feelings of isolation by generating hormonal signals that will tell her immune system (shown in the larger image at the beginning of the chapter) to gear up to protect her against bacteria.

In contrast, if she usually feels socially connected to others, her brain will initiate a cascade of hormonal signals that tell her immune cells to prepare to protect her against viruses instead of bacteria. This is just one example of how the mind's perceptions of the social environment—whether it is friendly or not, for instance—can affect biological processes that are important to health and survival. This finding is especially relevant to the COVID-19 pandemic. The perception of isolation during a lockdown could reduce a person's ability to combat viruses just when that ability is needed the most. As we will see in our later section on real-world problems, psychological science can make important contributions to public policies by providing this type of important background research.

Human brains such as this one, carefully held by one of your authors, weigh about 3 pounds and contain approximately 86 billion neurons. That's about the same number as the stars in our galaxy, the Milky Way.

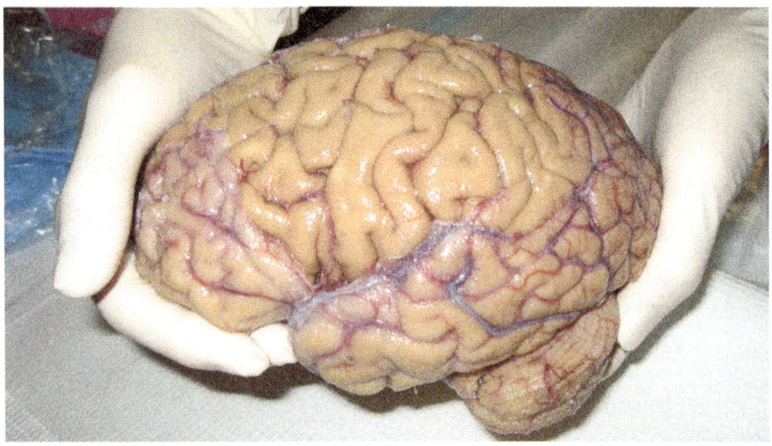

Courtesy of Dr. Skirmantas Janusonis/University of California, Santa Barbara. Photo © Roger Freberg

In Chapter 3, we learned how the challenges of surviving and reproducing in particular physical and social environments could shape a species' biology and behavior. In turn, the resulting biological structures and processes of the mind exert profound influences on our physical and social environments. In this chapter, we will provide a foundation for understanding the biological bases of behavior and mental processes by exploring the structures of the nervous system and the ways that they function.

Why do we think this information, which is often challenging for students to master, is so important to include in a textbook on introductory psychology? Isn't this something better left to biology courses? While our biology courses do an excellent job of outlining the structures and processes of the nervous system, psychological science is in a unique position to build bridges from that understanding to a deeper appreciation of the biological correlates of both healthy and unhealthy behaviors and their treatments. This will not be the only place where you will engage with these concepts. We will build a foundation in this chapter that is used to support our understanding of the many aspects of mind explored in the upcoming chapters.

What Is Biological Psychology?

Many of us find the concept that our minds are somehow a result of the activity of nerve cells a bit unsettling. How could our feelings, thoughts, and memories be caused by a bunch of cells? Shouldn't there be more to who we are than something so physical? Such ideas led thinkers like Renaissance philosopher René Descartes to propose a philosophy of dualism, which suggests that our mind is somehow different and separate from our physical being. If you are more comfortable with thinking about the mind this way, go ahead, as long as you recognize that the field of biological psychology, and the neurosciences in general, embrace the competing philosophy of monism. According to the monistic approach, the mind is what the brain does.

Diverse Voices in Psychology

What Is Cultural Neuroscience?

CONSISTENT WITH OUR ARGUMENT that multiple perspectives considered together produce a richer and more accurate analysis of the mind, we would like to introduce you to a combination of two seemingly distant fields—culture and neuroscience—to form cultural neuroscience. Cultural neuroscience has been defined as "an interdisciplinary field that examines how cultural and biological mechanisms mutually shape human behavior across phylogenetic, developmental, and situational timescales" (Chiao, 2015, p. 283). In other words, cultural neuroscientists explore how genetics, brain structures, and cultures interact to shape behavior (see Figure 4.1).

Cultural neuroscience asks two main questions. First, how do cultural phenomena such as beliefs and values influence genetics and brain structures? We saw an example of this question in our discussion of the Waorani and Yanomamö tribes in Chapter 3. The Yanomamö cultural value of standing down between raids, not shared by the Waorani, led to changed reproductive success on the part of the most aggressive Yanomamö warriors. A common way to categorize cultures is to designate them as collectivistic or individualistic (see Chapter 13). People from collectivistic cultures, such as many in East Asia, focus on context and relationships. In contrast, people from individualistic Western cultures focus on objects and favor highly arousing, positive emotional states. Han and Ma (2015, p. 671) suggest that "culturally patterned brain activity" allows the individual to voluntarily take actions that fit with their cultural context. Recent immigrants from a different type of culture probably work harder to conform to the demands of their new culture.

The second question asks how genetics and brain structure shape cultural phenomena. At a minimum, we might argue that forming cultures is something the human brain always seems to do. In addition, the brain produces the behaviors that shape cultures, such as the invention of social media technologies that change communication patterns radically. ■

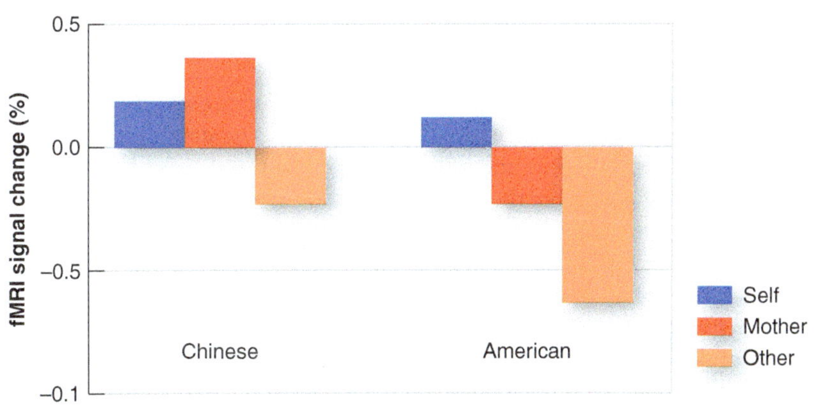

FIGURE 4.1

Culture and the Brain. Scientists working in the new discipline of cultural neuroscience argue that brain activity can be different when people of different cultures complete the same task. Here participants undergoing brain imaging were asked to think about their own traits (self), their mother's traits (mother), and a famous person's traits (other). Both American and Chinese participants showed more activation in relevant areas of the brain in response to thinking about themselves versus thinking about the other famous person, but their responses to their mothers differed. The Chinese did not show different patterns of activity when thinking about themselves and their mothers, but the Americans did.

Data from Y. Zhu, L. Zhang, J. Fan, & S. Han (2007), "Neural Basis of Cultural Influence on Self-Representation," *NeuroImage, 34*(3), 1310–1316. doi: http://dx.doi.org/10.1016/j.neuroimage.2006.08.047

Biological psychology, also known as *behavioral neuroscience*, is the scientific study of the reciprocal connections between the structure and activity of the nervous system and behavior and mental processes. Biological changes often influence behavior and cognition. For example, when your stomach is empty, a gut hormone called ghrelin is released. When ghrelin reaches the brain, you respond by feeling hungry. After you eat, ghrelin release is suppressed and you feel satisfied, so biology (amount of ghrelin released) initiates behavior and cognitions (feeling hungry and beginning to eat, or feeling full and stopping eating). However, your behavior and cognitions can also have substantial effects on your biology. When participants were told that

Gibbs Graphics

Gibbs Graphics

Not only can our biology affect our behavior, but our behavior and cognitions can have significant effects on our biology as well. Alia Crum and her colleagues gave participants the same 380-calorie milkshakes, but made some participants think they were drinking an indulgent milkshake and others a sensible milkshake. Their subsequent levels of the hormone ghrelin varied with feelings of satisfaction in spite of their having consumed the same number of calories.

Source: A. Crum et al. (2011), "Mind Over Milkshakes: Mindsets, Not Just Nutrients, Determine Ghrelin Response." *Health Psychology, 30*(4), 424–429. doi: 10.1037/a0023467

a 380-calorie milkshake that they consumed was a "sensible" 140-calorie shake, their ghrelin levels barely changed, whereas consuming the same 380-calorie milkshake was followed by a steep decrease in ghrelin when they were told it was a 620-calorie "indulgent" shake (Crum et al., 2011). In other words, the way people thought about the shake (cognitions) had remarkable effects on their biology (amount of ghrelin released). We can't guarantee that praising your healthy salad for its "indulgent" qualities will make it easier to stick to your diet, but the milkshake experiment reinforces the power of thought to influence biology.

Early Attempts to Understand Biological Psychology

Advances in the methods and technology we use to observe the structure and function of the nervous system have driven the history of biological psychology. The development of contemporary methods, such as the recording and imaging of brain activity, opened new areas of inquiry to biological psychologists. Before these methods were available, however, most of our knowledge of the nervous system resulted from clinical observations of injured or mentally ill individuals or from autopsy, the examination of bodies after death. When used with other contemporary methods, clinical observation and autopsy are quite accurate, but early thinkers lacking contemporary methods often struggled in their attempts to understand the physical basis of mind. They understood many things correctly while making some notable errors. Aristotle (384–322 BCE) mistakenly believed that the heart, not the brain, was the source of mental activity.

An interesting historical mistake was phrenology. Toward the end of the 18th century, phrenologists proposed that the pattern of bumps on an individual's skull correlated with that person's personality traits and abilities (Simpson, 2005). The brain supposedly worked like a muscle, getting larger through use, which led frequently used areas of the brain to grow so much that the skull above these areas would bulge. Phrenologists "read" a person's character by locating the bumps on a person's head and identifying the personality traits below each bump according to a map. None of these ideas were close to being accurate. Although the phrenologists were wrong about the significance of bumps on the skull and the effects of activity on the structure of the brain, they did reach one correct conclusion: Their notion that some behavioral functions are localized to certain areas of the brain is one we share today.

Contemporary Approaches in Biological Psychology

More modern perspectives of the nervous system emerged from the work of scientists such as Nobel Prize–winning anatomist Santiago Ramón y Cajal (1852–1934) and neurologist John Hughlings Jackson (1835–1911).

Ramón y Cajal's work helped us understand the microscopic level of the nervous system. Surprisingly, it took scientists a long time to accept the idea that the nervous system was made up of separate cells just like other tissues in the body. Even in the late 19th century, scientists such as Camillo Golgi still argued that the nervous system was a single continuous network. Ironically, Ramón y Cajal used a microscopic stain invented by Golgi to prove him wrong. Using Golgi's stain, Ramón y Cajal demonstrated conclusively that the nervous system was made up of separate cells, an idea that became known as the Neuron Doctrine. Consequently, both men shared the 1906 Nobel Prize in Physiology or Medicine.

Jackson's conclusions illuminated the relationships among the larger structures of the brain. Based on observations of his patients with seizure disorders, Jackson proposed that the nervous system is organized as a hierarchy, with progressively more complicated behaviors being managed by more recently evolved and complex structures (Jackson, 1884). We can see Jackson's hierarchy at work when we observe people drinking alcohol. Alcohol specifically decreases the activity of parts of the brain involved with decision making. When a person has had too much to drink, the more complex social controls normally provided by higher level areas of the brain are diminished. Without the influence of these controls, people start doing things that they would not do while sober. This change in behavior reflects the now-unrestrained influence of the more primitive parts of the brain involved with behaviors such as aggression and sexuality. Under the influence of alcohol, you might, for example, pick a fight with someone when you normally think fighting is wrong. The aggression and sexuality were there all along, but the activity of the higher levels of the nervous system usually restricted their expression to more appropriate circumstances (Siever, 2008).

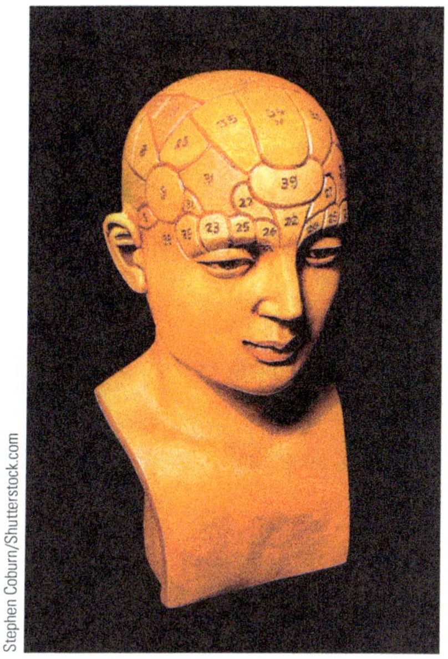

Stephen Coburn/Shutterstock.com

Phrenologists believed that "reading" the bumps on a person's head, using a bust like this as a reference, could tell them about a person's character.

Over the last 100 years, our understanding of the correlations between brain and behavior leaped forward with continuing improvements in research methods, including many of those found in ● Table 4.1. In particular, methods that allow scientists to observe the activity of the living brain, including positron emission tomography (PET) and functional magnetic resonance imaging (fMRI), began to answer questions that were impossible to study previously. While these imaging technologies are still far away from "mind reading," researchers have been able to use imaging data to identify the gender of perceived faces and even faces that are just imagined (VanRullen & Reddy, 2019).

Moving into the 21st century, the ranks of neuroscientists continue to grow, from 500 members of the Society for Neuroscience in 1969 to nearly 40,000 members today (Society for Neuroscience, 2019). Many university departments of psychology have added phrases such as "and neuroscience," "and behavioral neuroscience," or "and brain sciences" to their names. In 1986, only seven universities in the United States offered undergraduate degrees specifically in neuroscience (Ramos et al., 2011). That number tripled by 1996 and more than tripled again by 2006. It is very likely that your college or university psychology department offers a number of courses in neuroscience, and your campus might have a separate major or minor as well. As more scientists are trained in the neurosciences, we can look forward to continued innovations in both technology and our knowledge about the biological basis of mind.

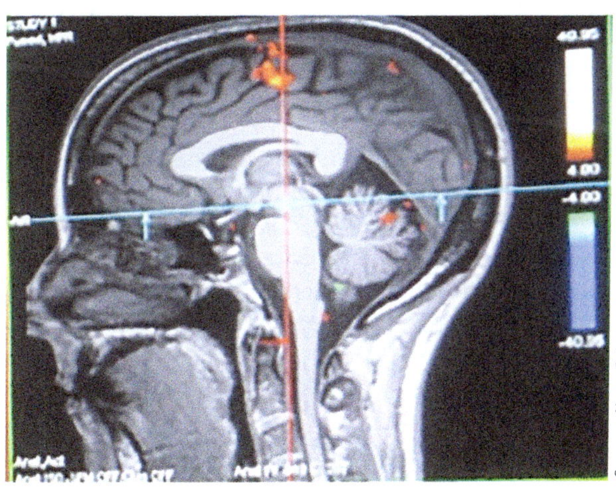

Courtesy of Laura Freberg

This functional magnetic resonance image (fMRI) was taken while one of your authors engaged in a finger-tap exercise, touching each digit of her right hand one by one with her thumb for 20 seconds followed by holding very still for 20 seconds. The red and yellow areas indicate parts of her brain that were selectively more active during the finger-tapping task than when she tried to stay very still.

TABLE 4.1

Research Methods in Biological Psychology

Research method	Description	What questions can we answer?
Histology	Microscopic examination of the nervous system.	How does the structure of nervous system cells correlate with behavior?
Skin conductance response (formerly galvanic skin response)	Measurement of electricity passed between two surface electrodes placed on the skin of the hand or finger.	What is a person's state of arousal?
Electroencephalogram (EEG)	Measurement of the brain's electrical activity using electrodes placed on the scalp.	What is a person's state of arousal?
Event-related potential (ERP)	Measurement formed by averaging EEG responses to a stimulus, such as a light or tone.	Did the person perceive the stimulus?
Single cell recording	Measurement of a single neuron's activity obtained through a surgically implanted electrode.	What types of stimulation make this neuron respond?
Magnetoencephalography	Recording of the tiny amounts of magnetic output of the brain.	What parts of the brain react to this stimulus?
Positron emission tomography (PET)	Measurement that uses the accumulation of radioactively tagged glucose or oxygen to identify activity levels in parts of the brain.	What parts of the brain are active during a particular task?
Functional magnetic resonance imaging (fMRI)	Identification of active parts of the brain using magnetism to track the flow of oxygen.	What parts of the brain are active during a particular task?
Electrical stimulation	Application of small amounts of electricity through a surgically implanted electrode.	What behaviors occur if we stimulate this part of the brain?
Optogenetics	Genetically inserted light-sensitive proteins allow cells in the brain to be turned on with light.	Which types of cells are active during particular behaviors?
Transcranial magnetic stimulation	Application of magnetic fields to the brain through an instrument held near the scalp.	What behavioral changes occur when magnetism is applied to the brain?
Lesions	Naturally occurring or deliberate damage to the brain.	What behavioral changes are correlated with brain damage?

How Is the Nervous System Organized?

To examine the relationships between nervous system and behavior, we will first zoom out to examine the larger view of the structures making up the nervous system, and then we'll zoom in later in the chapter to look at the microscopic world of the nerve cells, or neurons. Talking about the connections between structures of the nervous system and behavior requires a quick word of caution. As mentioned in Chapter 3, saying that we have a "gene for" a behavior is overly simplistic. Saying we have a "center for" a behavior in the brain is equally misleading. Although we can identify structures that participate in certain behaviors, the biology of mind involves intricate and overlapping patterns of activity involving networks made up of richly connected structures.

central nervous system (CNS) The brain and spinal cord.

The nervous system can be divided into two major components: the central and the peripheral nervous systems (see ● Figure 4.2). The **central nervous system (CNS)** consists

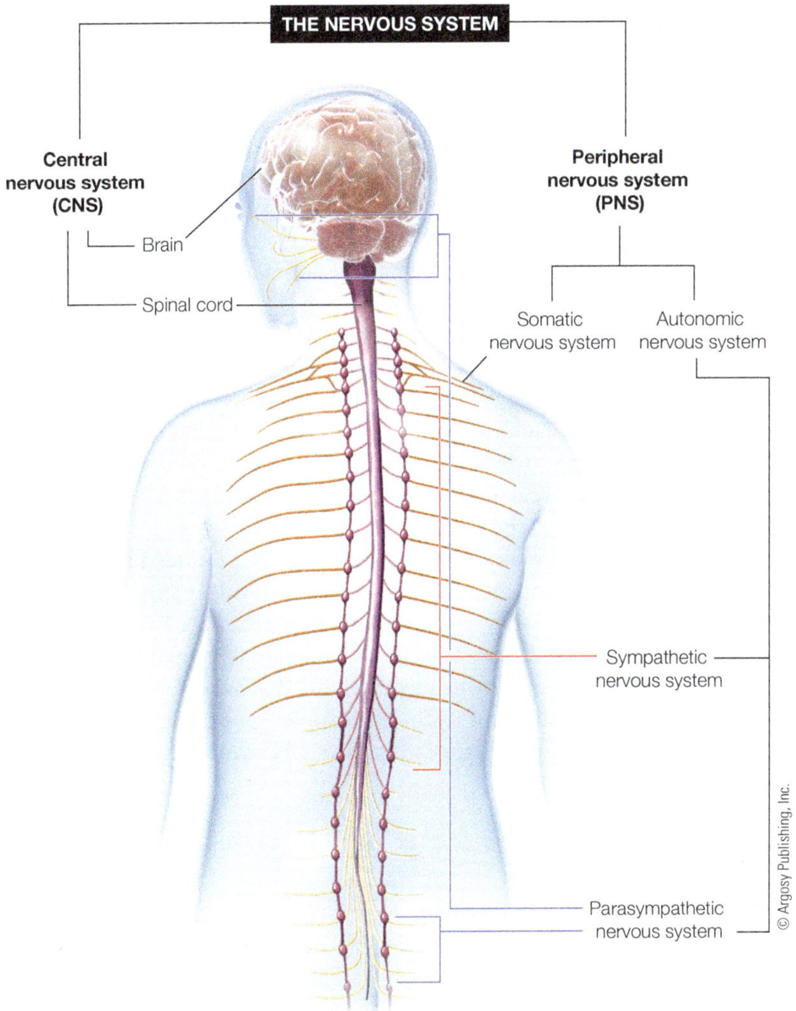

FIGURE **4.2**

The Organization of the Nervous System. The nervous system has two major divisions: the CNS, containing the brain and the spinal cord, and the PNS, containing all nerves that exit the brain and the spinal cord. The CNS is protected by bone, but the PNS is not.

of the brain and the **spinal cord**, which extends from the brain down the back of the body. Although we often see the brain and the spinal cord referred to as separate structures, they form one continuous unit of tissue. You might think of the brain as having a tail known as the spinal cord. Nerves branch outward from the CNS to all areas of the body—the lungs, heart, and other organs; the eyes and ears; and the arms, legs, fingers, and toes. As soon as a nerve branches outward from the CNS, it is considered part of the **peripheral nervous system (PNS)**. Another way to know you have left the CNS for the PNS is to look for the protection of bone. Nerves of the CNS are encased in bone, but those of the PNS are not.

What Are the Structures and Functions of the Central Nervous System?

The appearance of the human brain is not particularly impressive. It is covered in wrinkles, measures about 5½ inches (14 centimeters) wide, 6½ inches (17 centimeters) long, and 3⅔ inches (9 centimeters) high, and weighs about 3 pounds (1.5 kilograms). The brain contains about 86 billion nerve cells, which make trillions of connections. The spinal cord contains about 1 billion nerve cells, reaches a length of about 18 inches (45 centimeters), and

spinal cord A long cylinder of neural tissue extending from the medulla of the brain down to the middle of the back; part of the CNS.

peripheral nervous system (PNS) The nerves exiting the CNS that carry sensory and motor information to and from the rest of the body.

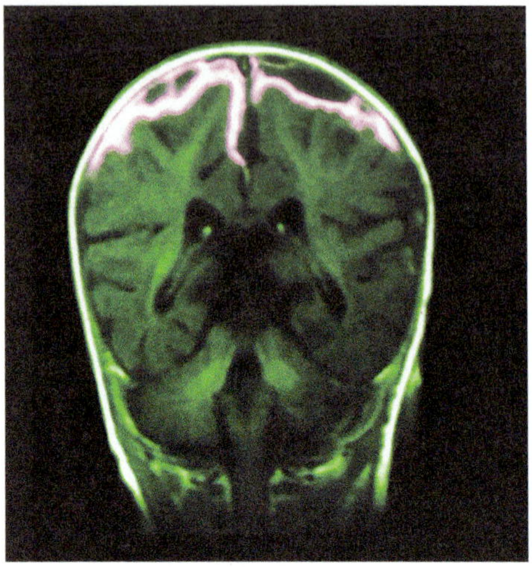

Meningitis is the inflammation of the membranes ("meninges") covering the brain and the spinal cord. This condition can result from infection with bacteria, viruses, or fungi, with the bacterial infections being the most dangerous. Fortunately, most cases of bacterial meningitis can be prevented by vaccination. This image shows the distortion of the membranes caused by infection.

weighs about 1.2 ounces (35 grams). Its diameter ranges from about 0.4 inches (1 centimeter) to 0.6 inches (1.5 centimeters). The adult spinal cord is shorter than your spine. Your bony spinal column continues to grow into adulthood, but the spinal cord itself stops growing in length at about four years of age.

The brain and the spinal cord are among the best protected parts of your body, which is not surprising given their importance for your survival. Surrounding the brain and the spinal cord are the heavy bones of the skull and spinal vertebrae. Under these bones, membranes known as meninges provide further protection. Infections of these membranes result in potentially life-threatening cases of meningitis, for which you were possibly vaccinated before beginning your college studies.

The brain and the spinal cord are further protected by a clear, plasma-like fluid known as cerebrospinal fluid (CSF). CSF seeps out of the lining of hollow spaces in the brain known as the ventricles (see ● Figure 4.3). Near the base of the skull, openings enable CSF to flow from the ventricles into a space within the meninges, allowing the fluid to flow around the outer surfaces of the brain and spinal cord. CSF is constantly produced, so blockages in its circulation cause the fluid to build up. The result is hydrocephalus, which means "water on the head."

The cushioning provided by the CSF limits the damage produced by a blow to the head. As a result, single minor concussions are unlikely to produce long-term problems, but multiple concussions are possibly more serious (Mannix et al., 2016). The CSF also "floats" the brain within the skull, preventing false signals that might result from the weight of some neurons pressing down on others. To diagnose some medical conditions, it is helpful to obtain a sample of CSF. This is done through a spinal tap, in which a physician removes some of the CSF circulating through the meninges surrounding the spinal cord.

FIGURE **4.3**

The Ventricles of the Brain. The ventricles of the brain are filled with circulating cerebrospinal fluid (CSF), which floats and cushions the brain.

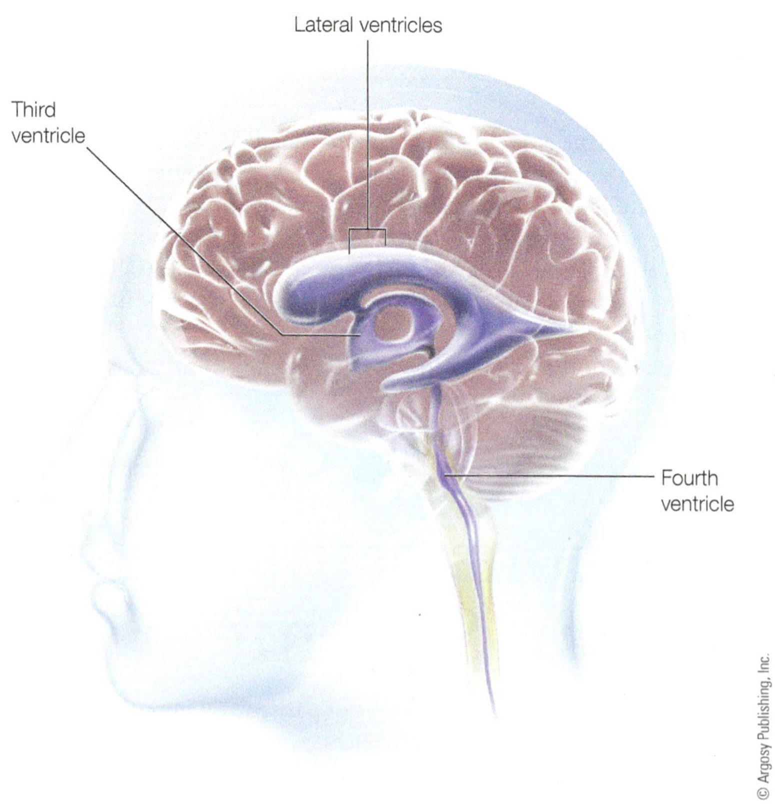

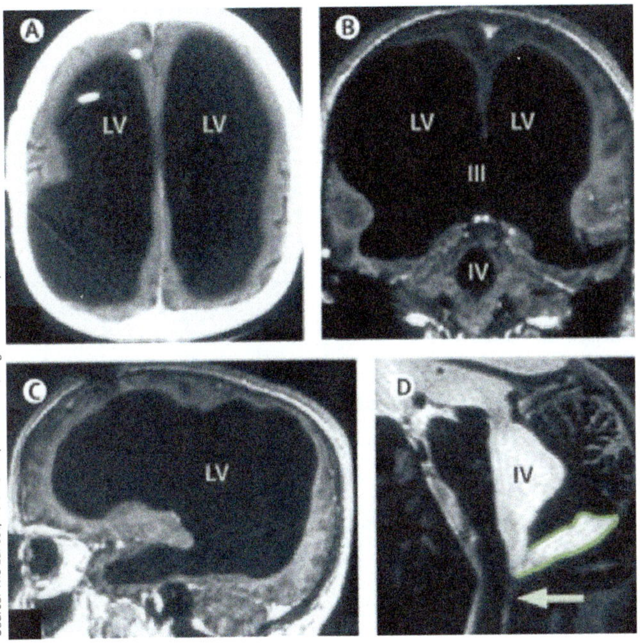

French neurologists were shocked when they saw brain images taken of a middle-aged man who sought treatment for some minor weakness in one leg. His lateral ventricles (LV) take up most of the volume in his skull, and the brain appears as a thin layer on the outside. The patient reported that he had been treated for hydrocephalus from infancy until the age of 14. The patient was a married father of two who worked as a civil servant with a low but still normal IQ of 75.

The Spinal Cord, Brainstem, and Cerebellum

The spinal cord extends from the lowest part of the brain down into the middle of your back (see Figure 4.4). If you feel the back of your skull where it curves to meet your spine, your fingers will be just below the junction of the spinal cord and the lowest structure of the brain. Although the spinal cord is only 2% of the weight of the CNS, its functions are vital, as evidenced by the challenges faced by people with spinal damage. The spinal cord serves as a major conduit for information flowing to and from the brain along large bundles of nerve fibers, carrying sensory information from the body and delivering commands to muscles. A total of 31 pairs of spinal nerves exit the spinal cord between segments of the bony vertebrae in your spine to serve the body.

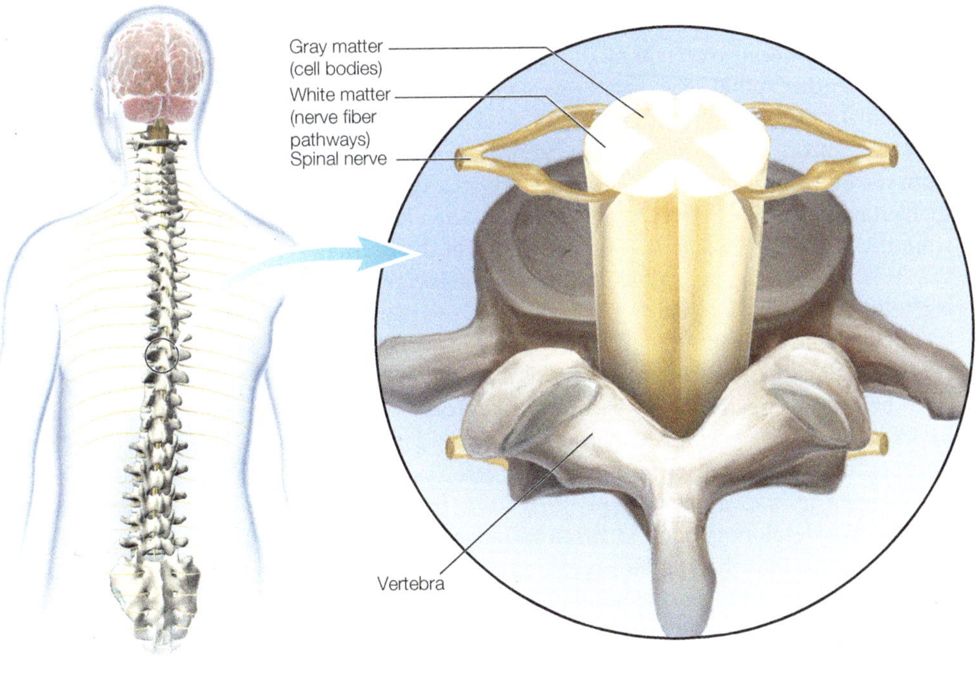

FIGURE **4.4**

The Spinal Cord and the Spinal Nerves. Thirty-one pairs of spinal nerves exit between the bones of the vertebrae to bring sensory information back to the CNS and carry motor commands to muscles.

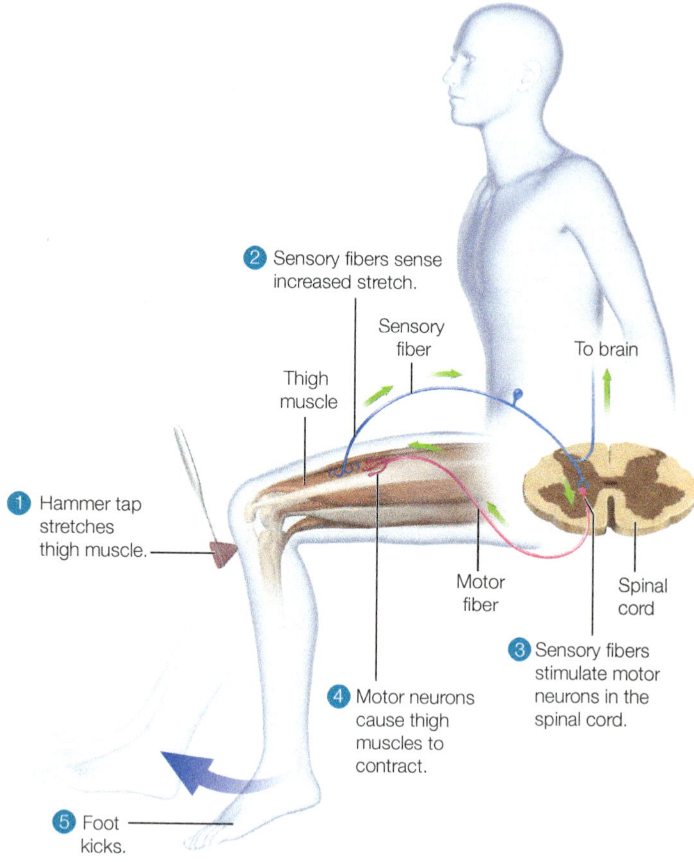

FIGURE **4.5**

Checking Spinal Reflexes. When your physician taps on your knee, your thigh muscle stretches. Information about the stretch is carried to the spinal cord by a sensory nerve. The spinal cord sends a command to the muscle to contract to counteract the stretch, and your foot kicks out. The spinal cord manages this reflex alone. No higher level of processing in the nervous system is necessary for this reflex to occur.

Many important reflexes are initiated by the spinal cord without any assistance from the brain. One type of spinal reflex makes you pull your body away from a source of pain. It doesn't take long for your hand to fly up when you've touched something hot on the stove. When tapping your knee with a hammer during a routine physical, your doctor is checking another type of spinal reflex, the knee-jerk reflex (see ● Figure 4.5). This reflex is interesting to your doctor because certain medical conditions, such as diabetes, affect the strength of the reflex. Still other spinal reflexes help us stand and walk.

Spinal reflexes give us an opportunity to look at the functions of three types of nerve cells, or neurons. Sensory neurons carry information from the external environment or from the body back to the CNS. In the knee-jerk reflex, sensory neurons tell the spinal cord that a muscle has been stretched by the tap of the hammer. Motor neurons carry commands from the CNS back to the muscles and glands of the body. In response to information about the stretched muscle, the spinal cord sends a message through motor neurons back to your leg, telling the muscle to contract to counteract the stretch. You know what happens next—your foot kicks as the muscles contract. Neurons that have neither sensory nor motor functions are called interneurons. *Inter* in this case means "between," because many interneurons form bridges between sensory and motor neurons. The knee-jerk reflex forms a simple arc between a sensory neuron and a motor neuron and does not require interneurons. However, interneurons play important roles in other reflexes and throughout the nervous system.

brainstem The part of the brain containing the midbrain, pons, and medulla.

Moving up from the spinal cord brings us to the brainstem. In the fourth gestational week, the embryo's developing brain forms three bulges. The most forward of these bulges, the forebrain, develops into the two large cerebral hemispheres, which we discuss in a later section. The remaining two bulges, the hindbrain and midbrain, form the **brainstem**. If you examine ● Figure 4.6, you can see that the brainstem looks like the stem of a flower, supporting the larger blossom of the cerebral hemispheres. Directly branching from the brainstem are the cranial nerves, which perform the same functions for the head and neck areas that the spinal

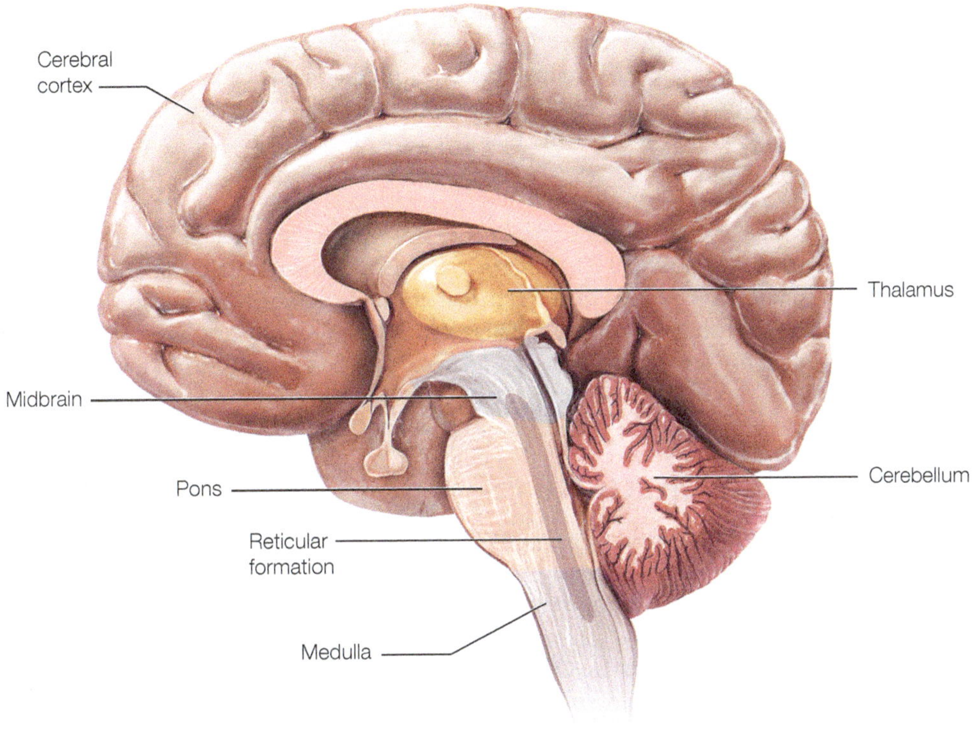

© Argosy Publishing, Inc.

FIGURE **4.6**

Structures of the Brainstem. The brainstem contains structures responsible for reflexive behaviors, heart rate, breathing, arousal, sleep, preliminary sensory analysis, balance, and movement.

nerves manage for the remainder of the body. We will discuss the cranial nerves in more depth in a later section on the PNS.

The hindbrain consists of the medulla, pons, and cerebellum. The **medulla** is located just above the spinal cord. Like the spinal cord, the medulla contains large bundles of nerve fibers traveling to and from higher levels of the brain. The medulla manages many functions essential to life, such as heart rate, breathing, and blood pressure.

Just above the medulla is the **pons**, which contains structures involved with the management of sleep, arousal, and facial expressions. *Pons* means "bridge" in Latin. The pons not only serves as a bridge between the higher and lower portions of the brain, but it also connects the **cerebellum** to the rest of the brain. Essential for maintaining balance and motor coordination, the cerebellum is one of the first structures in the brain to be affected by alcohol. As a result, alcohol consumption impairs balance (walking a straight line) and motor coordination (touching your finger to the tip of your nose with your eyes closed). Most sobriety tests are the same tests a neurologist would use to assess the function of the cerebellum.

Surprisingly, the cerebellum contains more nerve cells than the rest of the brain combined. Not only does the cerebellum contain huge numbers of neurons, but it is also richly connected with the rest of the CNS. Because of the cerebellum's position on the brainstem, which is relatively ancient in terms of evolution compared to the cerebral hemispheres, neuroscientists initially underestimated its importance to human behavior. They believed that the cerebellum's activities were restricted to managing the timing and strength of movements. While we still do not know exactly what the cerebellum does, today's neuroscientists believe that it has a broader role in making mental and motor skills more automatic. Damage to the human cerebellum produces subtle deficits in language, cognition, and perception. In autism spectrum disorder, a condition that affects language, sensory, and social behaviors, abnormalities in the cerebellum are common (Courchesne, 1997; Fatemi et al., 2012).

The **midbrain** sits above the pons and contains a number of structures involved in sensory reflexes, movement, and pain. For example, the periaqueductal gray of the midbrain plays an important role in the body's management of pain because it contains receptors for endorphins, our natural opioids,

medulla The brainstem structure that lies just above the spinal cord.

pons A part of the brainstem located between the medulla and the midbrain.

cerebellum A structure attached to the brainstem that participates in skilled movement and, in humans, complex cognitive processing.

midbrain The part of the brainstem that lies between the pons and the cerebral hemispheres. Opiate painkillers such as morphine and OxyContin produce some of their analgesic effects by interacting with opioid receptors in the periaqueductal gray.

Zuma Press, Inc./Alamy Stock Photo

Most sobriety tests assess the function of the cerebellum, which helps us maintain balance and muscle coordination. The individual in this photo passed.

discussed later in this chapter and in Chapter 6. When endorphins are present in the periaqueductal gray, they reduce the perception of pain by decreasing the strength of pain messages traveling to higher levels of the brain. Activity in the periaqueductal gray is also associated with maternal (Bartels & Zeki, 2004) and unconditional love (Cacioppo et al., 2012). Nearby are other cell clusters that serve as the major sources of two important chemical messengers in the brain, serotonin and norepinephrine. These structures participate in states of arousal, mood, appetite, and aggression.

Running the length of the brainstem's core from the upper medulla into the midbrain is the **reticular formation**, which participates in the management of levels of arousal, discussed further in Chapter 6. The cells in the reticular formation have two settings—fast and slow. When the cells are firing quickly, we usually show other signs of being awake. When the cells are firing slowly (or are damaged due to a stroke or other injury), an individual will enter either deep sleep or unconsciousness.

reticular formation A collection of structures located along the midline of the brainstem that participate in mood, arousal, and sleep.

thalamus A subcortical structure involved with the processing of sensory information, states of arousal, and learning and memory.

basal ganglia A collection of subcortical structures that participate in reward and the control of movement.

Subcortical Structures

Embedded within the vast tracts of nerve fibers or white matter that make up the bulk of the cerebral hemispheres are a number of subcortical structures that participate in self-awareness, learning, emotion, movement, communication, the inhibition of impulses, and the regulation of body states. We call them *subcortical* because they lie *sub*, which means "below," the cerebral cortex, which comprises the wrinkled outermost covering of the cerebral hemispheres.

Early anatomists collected some of these subcortical structures into a limbic system (*limbic* means "border," and these structures form a gentle curve below the cerebral cortex), but this term is losing popularity with contemporary anatomists (Rolls, 2015). You might also have heard the limbic system called "your emotional brain." As you will see in the next sections, some of these structures do participate in our emotional life, but they perform many other functions as well. We usually discuss subcortical structures in the singular, as in *thalamus* or *hippocampus*, but they actually are paired sets of structures, one on either side of the brain.

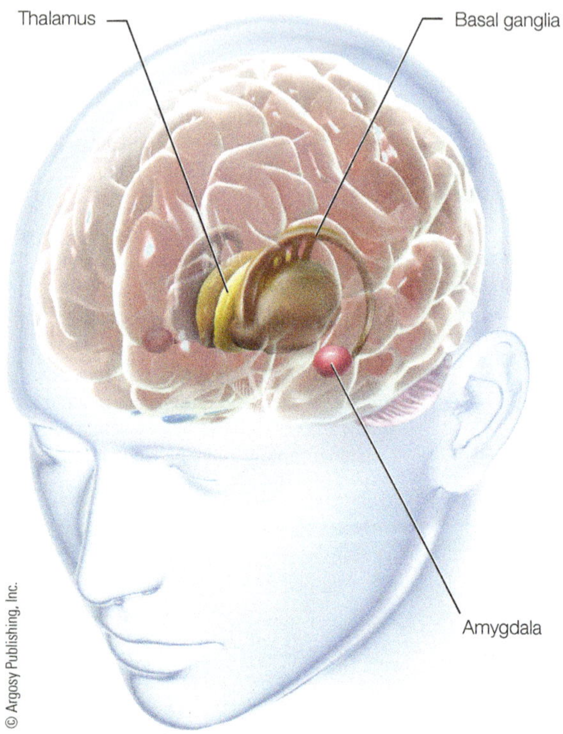

FIGURE **4.7**

The Thalamus and the Basal Ganglia. Near the center of the brain, the thalamus receives input from most of our sensory systems and relays the information to the cerebral cortex. Curving around the thalamus are the basal ganglia, which form an important part of our voluntary movement systems.

The Thalamus

Almost at the center of the brain lies the **thalamus**. The thalamus is often called the gateway to the cortex, because input from most of our sensory systems (vision, hearing, touch, and taste) travels first to the thalamus, which then forwards the information to the cerebral cortex. The cortex, in turn, forms large numbers of connections with the thalamus. In addition to its role in sensation, the thalamus is involved with memory and states of consciousness. Some lesions in the thalamus are associated with profound memory loss (Cipolotti et al., 2008). As you will learn in Chapter 6, during our deepest stages of sleep, the thalamus coordinates the activity of cortical neurons, "tuning out" the outside world, making it difficult to awaken. Disturbances in the circuits linking the thalamus and the cortex accompany some seizures.

The Basal Ganglia

The **basal ganglia** consist of several large structures that help us select movements that bring us closer to our goals (Aron et al., 2005). These structures curve around to cup the thalamus (see ● Figure 4.6 and ● Figure 4.7) and form complex circuits with motor structures located in the brainstem, the thalamus, and the cerebral cortex.

Degeneration of the basal ganglia occurs in Parkinson's disease, a condition that makes the initiation of voluntary movement extremely difficult. The basal ganglia also contribute to several psychological disorders described in Chapter 14, including obsessive-compulsive disorder (OCD), autism spectrum disorder (ASD), and attention deficit hyperactivity disorder (ADHD). These disorders are characterized by inadequate control of voluntary movement. In the case of OCD, patients may endlessly repeat a behavior, such as hand washing, while in ADHD, voluntary movements can be unusually frequent, rapid, and impulsive. Individuals with ASD often experience repetitive thoughts and movements.

The Hypothalamus The **hypothalamus** is involved with motivation and homeostasis (see Chapter 7), or the regulation of body functions such as temperature, thirst, hunger, biological rhythms, and sexual activities (see Figure 4.8). The hypothalamus is often described as contributing to the "4F" behaviors: feeding, fleeing, fighting, and, well, sex (fornication). The hypothalamus carries out its motivational and homeostatic tasks by directing the autonomic nervous system and the endocrine system and its hormones, which we discuss in detail later in this chapter.

The Hippocampus The **hippocampus**, named for its shape after the Greek word for seahorse, is essential to the formation of long-term memories, which we discuss in more detail in Chapter 9. Memories are not stored permanently in the hippocampus, but it is likely that the hippocampus is involved in the storage and retrieval of memories located elsewhere in the brain. Damage to the hippocampus results in profound impairments in the ability to form new memories, but intelligence, personality, and most memories of events that occurred before hippocampal damage remain intact.

The hippocampus also plays a role in our management of stress (see Chapter 16). It contains receptors for some stress hormones, allowing it to "put on the brakes" if levels get too high. This function of the hippocampus can be less effective in cases of major depressive disorder (see Chapter 14).

The Cingulate Cortex The **cingulate cortex** forms a fold of tissue on the inner surface of each cerebral hemisphere. The forward two thirds of this structure, known as the anterior cingulate cortex (ACC), participate, along with the hypothalamus, in the control of the autonomic nervous system, which we discuss later in this chapter. The ACC also plays significant roles in decision making, emotion, anticipation of reward, and empathy. The rear third, or posterior cingulate cortex (PCC), participates in memory and visual processing.

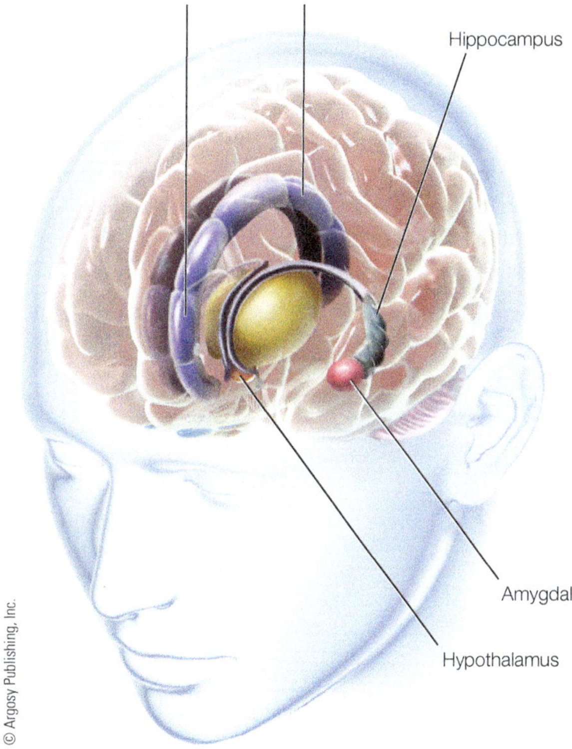

FIGURE 4.8

Other Important Subcortical Structures. Subcortical structures located under the cerebral cortex participate in attention, decision making, learning, memory, and emotion.

The Amygdala The **amygdala** gets its name from the Greek word for "almond" because of its shape. One amygdala is deeply embedded in the temporal lobe, the wing of cortex that curves around the side of the brain, in each hemisphere. The amygdala receives sensory information (vision, hearing, and smell) from the thalamus and produces emotional and motivational output that is sent to the cerebral cortex.

Historically, the amygdala has been associated with the perception of threat and fear, but contemporary research indicates that its role is much broader (Adolphs, 2008, 2018). Activation of the amygdala is associated with salient or relevant stimuli regardless of whether they are positive or negative. The amygdala plays important roles in social behavior, emotion, and learning about reward.

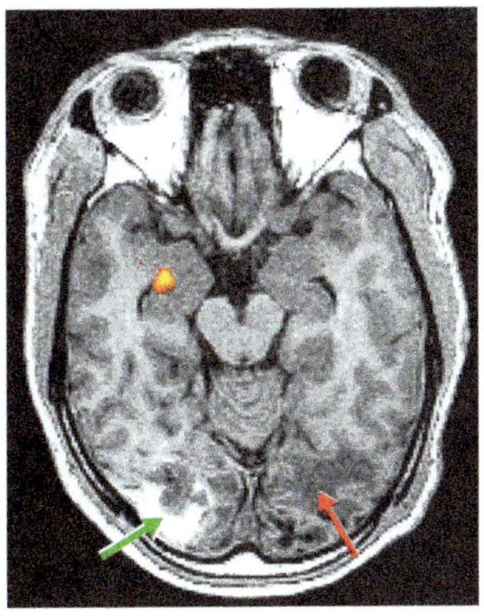

This image is taken from a man who is blind because of damage caused by a stroke to his visual areas, indicated by the red and green arrows. The orange area indicates activation of his amygdala when he is shown a photo of an angry face. This man couldn't tell you whether he is looking at a tree, a building, or a face, let alone a happy or angry one, but his amygdala knows and reacts appropriately.

hypothalamus A subcortical structure that participates in the regulation of thirst, temperature, hunger, sexual behavior, and aggression.

hippocampus A subcortical structure that participates in memory and stress.

cingulate cortex A subcortical structure above the corpus callosum. Its anterior (forward) segment participates in decision making and emotion, and its posterior (rear) segment participates in memory and visual processing.

amygdala A subcortical structure located in the temporal lobe believed to participate in emotional processing.

FIGURE **4.9**

Results of Damage to the Amygdala. In addition to her difficulties in responding to fear stimuli, Patient S.M. shows other behavioral deficits related to her damaged amygdalae. Personal space, although variable across cultures, is consistent within cultures. Healthy control participants in the United States stand about 0.64 meter (about 2 feet) or arm's length away from people they don't know. In contrast, Patient S.M. prefers to stand nearly twice as close to others, or 0.34 meter (about 1 foot). Standing closer to strangers than is normal for your culture is likely to send inappropriate social messages of either threat or intimacy.

Source: D. P. Kennedy, J. Gläscher, J. M. Tyszka, & R. Adolphs (2009). "Personal Space Regulation by the Human Amygdala," *Nature Neuroscience, 12,* 1226–1227. doi: 10.1038/nn.2381

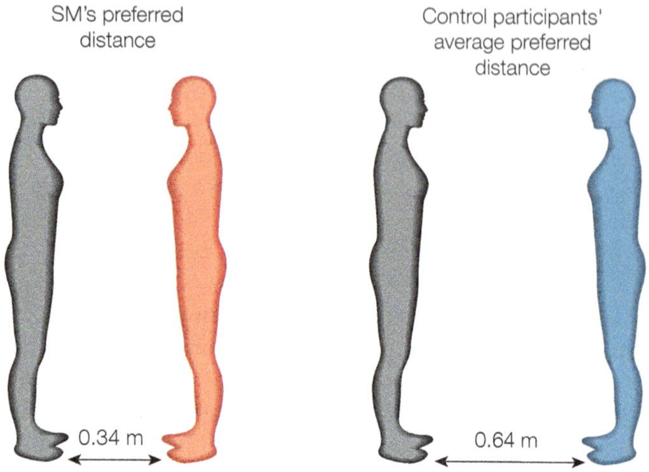

Several behavioral deficits have been identified in a patient, known as Patient S.M., who experienced a rare medical condition that damaged her amygdalae in both hemispheres (Adolphs et al., 1998; see Figure 4.9). Although the patient can identify facial expressions of happiness, sadness, and disgust in photographs, she has a specific difficulty identifying expressions of fear. When researchers exposed Patient S.M. to snakes, spiders, and scary movies, she showed no signs of fear (Feinstein et al., 2011). Observations of Patient S.M. have contributed to our understanding of autism spectrum disorder, which also features abnormalities of the amygdala (Blair et al., 2002; Marsh & Blair, 2008; Adolphs, 2018).

The Nucleus Accumbens The **nucleus accumbens** is an important part of the brain's reward and pleasure circuitry. Whether you are eating, having sex, using addictive drugs, gambling, or simply enjoying a beautiful sunset, this circuitry comes into play (Comings & Blum, 2000). One important part of this circuitry originates in cell bodies located in the midbrain that form connections with many subcortical structures and with the nucleus accumbens in particular.

The activity of the nucleus accumbens is related to a person's sense of social inclusion. When people who have strong connections to friends and family view a happy social scene, their nucleus accumbens becomes active. In contrast, when people with weaker social connections view the same happy scenes, their nucleus accumbens shows less activity than those of the socially connected people (Cacioppo et al., 2009).

The Cerebral Cortex

Above the brainstem, we find the two large cerebral hemispheres, which are connected by a large bundle of nerve fibers known as the **corpus callosum**. The thin layer of cells covering the outer surface of the cerebral hemispheres is the **cerebral cortex** (see Figure 4.10). The *cortex*, which means "bark" in Latin, covers the cerebral hemispheres like the bark of a tree. Most of the remaining bulk of the hemispheres is made up of white matter, or nerve fiber pathways, that connects the cortex with other parts of the nervous system. The average 20-year-old human brain has around 100,000 miles (162,500 kilometers) of white matter (Marner et al., 2003). The subcortical structures discussed earlier are distributed within this white matter.

If stretched out flat, the human cerebral cortex would cover an area of about 2.5 square feet (about 0.23 square meters). To fit within the confines of the skull, the cortex is convoluted or wrinkled. The degree of cortical convolution positively correlates with the general intellectual capacities of a species. For instance, human brains are more convoluted than sheep brains, which in turn are more convoluted than rat brains (see Figure 4.11).

Each hemisphere of the cerebral cortex can be divided into four lobes, named after the bones of the skull that cover them (see Figure 4.12). Toward the front of the brain, we find the **frontal lobe**, and directly behind the frontal lobe lies the **parietal lobe**. At the back of the brain is the **occipital lobe**. Curving around the side of each hemisphere, we find the **temporal lobe**. Because we have two hemispheres, it follows that we have pairs of each type of lobe, usually denoted right or left (e.g., right frontal lobe and left frontal lobe).

nucleus accumbens A subcortical structure that participates in reward and addiction.

corpus callosum A wide band of nerve fibers connecting the right and left cerebral hemispheres.

cerebral cortex The thin layer of neurons covering the outer surface of the cerebral hemispheres.

frontal lobe The most forward of the four lobes of the cerebral cortex; location of the primary motor cortex and areas responsible for some of the most complex cognitive processes.

parietal lobe The lobe of the cerebral cortex that lies at the top of the brain between the frontal and the occipital lobes; location of the primary somatosensory cortex.

occipital lobe The lobe of the cerebral cortex located at the back of the brain; location of the primary visual cortex.

temporal lobe The lobe of the cerebral cortex that curves around the side of each hemisphere; location of the primary auditory cortex.

THINKING SCIENTIFICALLY

Why Does Moving Your Eyes Reduce Negative Emotions?

EYE MOVEMENT DESENSITIZATION AND Reprocessing (EMDR) is a psychotherapy technique with a somewhat controversial history. In the 1980s, Francine Shapiro began experimenting with EMDR after noticing that her eyes moved rapidly while she recalled something disturbing, while consciously controlling her eye movements reduced her distress. The therapy she developed consists of asking the client to recall disturbing images followed by side-to-side eye movements (or in other cases another activity such as hand-tapping).

Outcome studies have been surprisingly positive, although research in this area suffers from low quality, such as small numbers of participants and possible researcher bias (Bisson et al., 2013). Nonetheless, EMDR is considered an "evidence-based" treatment (see Chapter 15) by many professional and government organizations.

You might be wondering why something like this would ever work. What do eye movements have to do with recovering from traumatic experiences? One group of researchers suggests that the eye movements have the ability to reduce activation of the amygdala (de Voogd et al., 2018). As you are learning in this chapter, the amygdala receives visual input and plays an important role in emotional processing.

Voisin/Phanie/Superstock

What Am I Being Asked to Believe or Accept?

We are being asked to believe that moving our eyes consciously will reduce anxiety and fear related to traumatic memories by suppressing activity in the amygdala.

What Evidence Supports This Position?

De Voogd and her colleagues (2018) used functional MRI (fMRI) to observe brain activity during the EMDR process. They compared brain activity during EMDR to activity during a working memory task (remembering if a digit had been presented previously; see Chapter 9). They reported that both the working memory task and the eye movements reduced amygdala activity. So although the eye movements are probably an effective way to reduce emotion, other tasks that engage conscious cognitive control are probably equally effective. The researchers suggest that given the limited resources of the brain, functions might compete. Activating cognitive control suppresses the amygdala and activating the amygdala suppresses cognitive control.

Are There Other Ways That This Evidence Could Be Interpreted?

Advocates of EMDR therapy propose different reasons for the efficacy of the eye movements, including unlearning and relearning with "appropriate emotions" (EMDR Institute, 2019). Unfortunately, results reported by de Voogd and her colleagues (2018) directly challenge the idea of EMDR's ability to produce unlearning.

What Other Evidence Would I Need to Evaluate These Alternatives?

Criticisms raised by meta-analyses mentioned previously, such as small sample sizes and researcher bias, must be addressed in future studies.

What Are the Most Reasonable Conclusions?

Other research confirms the fact that tasks that engage our working memory reduce the emotionality of other memories. It is unlikely, then, that there is anything special about moving your eyes other than this task's ability to engage conscious cognitive control. The technique does seem to have merit, so if a person benefits from it, then there is no reason to discontinue. ■

Localization of Functions in the Cerebral Cortex As we mentioned earlier in this chapter, the phrenologists were wrong in assuming that behavioral characteristics were reflected in bumps of the skull, but they were correct in suggesting that some functions were localized in particular parts of the brain.

The functions performed by different areas of the cerebral cortex within the lobes fall into three categories: sensory, motor, and association. The sensory cortex processes incoming information from the sensory systems, such as vision or hearing, which we describe in Chapter 5. The primary visual cortex is in the occipital lobe, and the primary auditory cortex is in the temporal lobe. The primary somatosensory cortex (*soma* refers to "body") is in the parietal lobe and processes information about touch, pain, body position, and skin temperature. The primary motor cortex is in the

Early scientists discovered that nerves carry only one type of information. When you take a blow to the back of the head, where your primary visual cortex is found, your occipital lobe does not know how to say, "ouch." Instead, it responds to the blow as if you saw a flash of light (not necessarily the tweeting birds or stars indicated in cartoons).

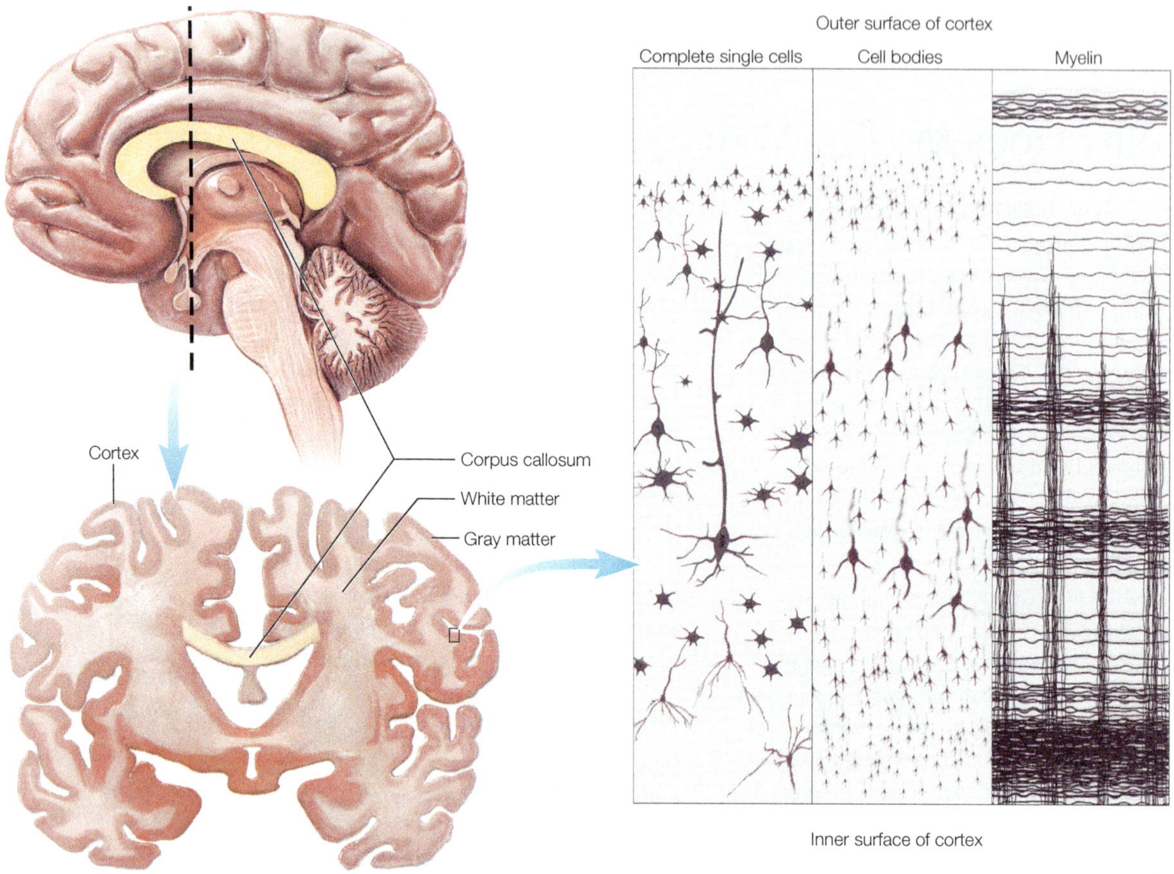

FIGURE 4.10

The Cerebral Cortex. The cerebral cortex (cortex means "bark") is a thin layer of cells on the outer surface of the brain. The close-up shows different views of the cortex, including the distribution of complete single cells, cell bodies, and myelin, the insulating material that covers most nerve fibers.

rearmost portion of the frontal lobe and provides the highest level of voluntary control over movement. Areas of the cortex that do not have specific sensory or motor functions are known as association cortex. *Association* means "connection" in this case, and association cortex helps us form bridges between sensation and action, language, and abstract thought. Association areas are distributed throughout the cortex.

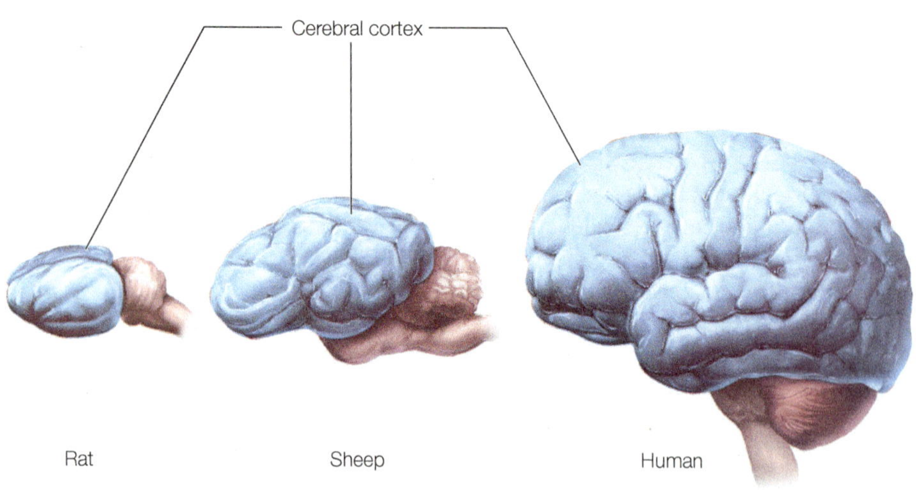

FIGURE 4.11

Degree of the Convolution of the Cortex Predicts Intellect. As species' behavior becomes more complex, we see a corresponding increase in the degree of convolution (wrinkling) of the cerebral cortex. This wrinkling of the brain permits more brain tissue to fit within the skull. As a result, cortical size has increased more quickly over the course of evolution than skull size—an important adaptation given that large skulls are difficult to get through the birth canal.

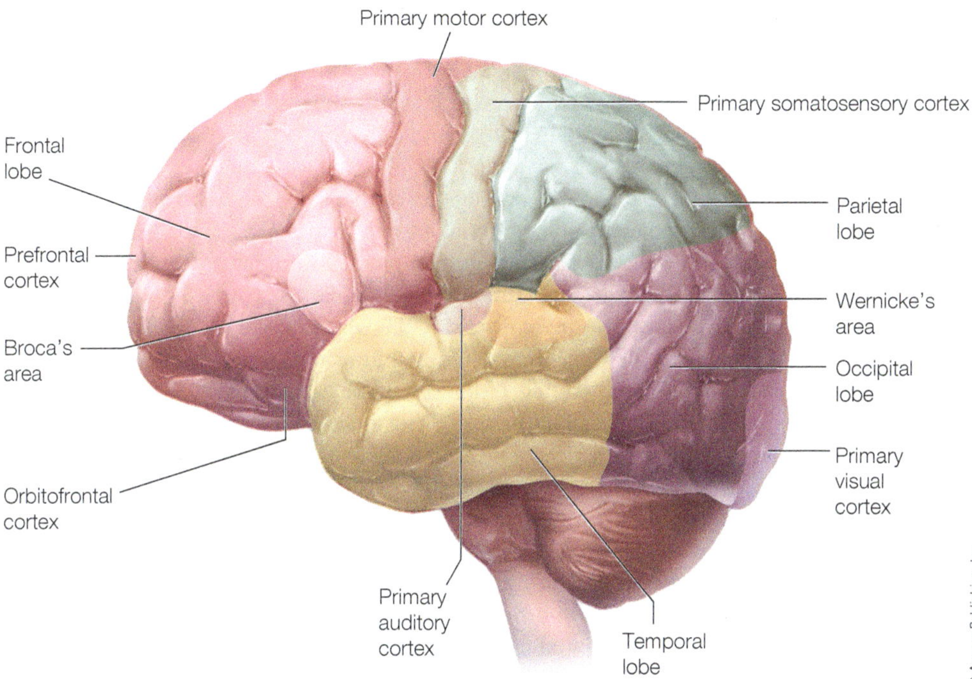

© Argosy Publishing, Inc.

FIGURE **4.12**

Lobes of the Cerebral Cortex. The cerebral cortex is traditionally divided into four lobes: frontal, parietal, occipital, and temporal.

The Frontal Lobe In addition to being the home of the primary motor cortex, the frontal lobe has a number of important, sophisticated cognitive functions. Adjacent to the primary motor cortex is Broca's area, named after Paul Broca, who helped identify its functions in the 1860s. Broca's area participates in the production of speech. Consequently, damage to Broca's area caused by a stroke or a tumor produces considerable difficulty in speaking, although comprehension of speech remains good (see Chapter 10). The most forward portion of each frontal lobe, known as the **prefrontal cortex** (*pre* means "before"), is involved with the planning of behavior, attention, and judgment. Abnormalities of frontal lobe activity may account for characteristics of some psychological disorders, including schizophrenia and ADHD, which we will discuss in detail in Chapter 14.

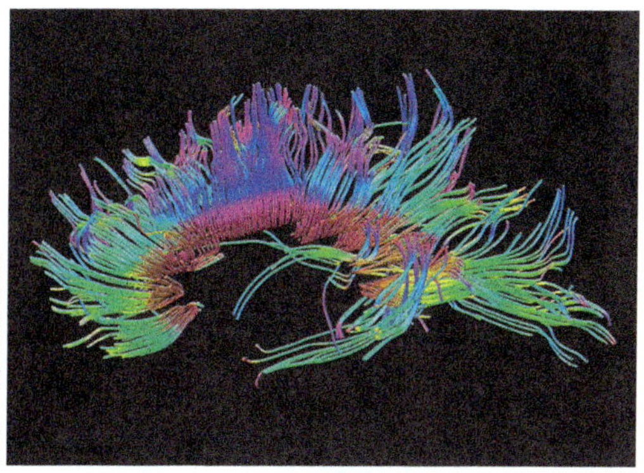

Simon Fraser/Science Source

Diffusion tensor imaging highlights the rich arrays formed by the white matter in the brain.

The role of the frontal lobes in the planning of behavior is illustrated by a bizarre condition known as alien hand syndrome, which occurs when connections between the prefrontal cortex and the lower areas of the brain involved in movement are damaged (Kikkert et al., 2006). This condition has no effect on sensory feedback from the limb, such as touch and position. However, patients with this condition do not seem to have control over their affected limbs and often remain unaware of the limbs' activities until they are pointed out by another person. For instance, a hand might undo a button or remove clothing without the patient's awareness of the activity. Patients do not recognize the rogue limb as their own and may use the other hand to wrestle with it in an attempt to control it forcibly or punish it for its activities.

The importance of the frontal lobes is also illustrated by the results of a terrible accident that befell a young railroad worker named Phineas Gage in 1848. While Gage was preparing to blast through some granite, a freak accident sent an iron tamping rod through his head before it landed about 30 feet (about 9 meters) away. The rod entered his head under his left cheekbone, passed behind his left eye, and exited out the middle of his forehead. Remarkably, Gage survived, but he was not the same person as before his accident. Although outwardly normal in his intelligence, speech, and movement, Gage became prone to angry outbursts and unreliability, which made it difficult for him to find and keep employment. As his doctor noted, "His contractors, who regarded him as the most efficient and capable foreman in their employ previous to his injury, considered the change in his mind so marked that they could not give him his place again" (Fleischman, 2002, p. 20).

prefrontal cortex The most forward part of the frontal lobe of the cerebral cortex.

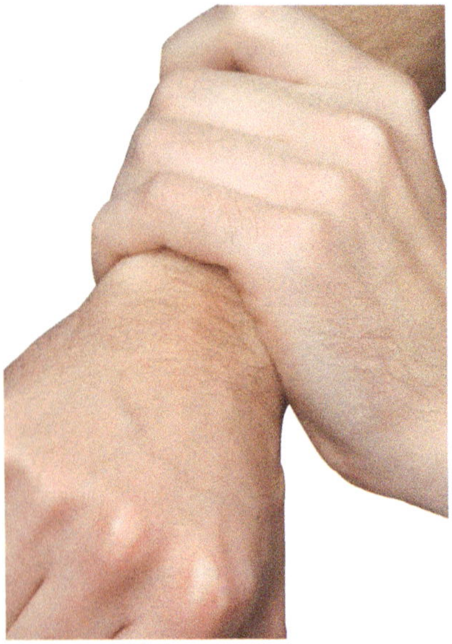

ImageShop/Cardinal/Corbis

Gage suffered his accident when modern imaging technologies were nowhere to be seen on the scientific horizon. Today, we know more about why Gage behaved the way he did because of his accident. Scientists initially recreated the pathway that Gage's tamping rod must have traveled (Damasio et al., 1994). More recent analyses show that the rod did more damage to the fiber pathways (11% were damaged) than to the cells (4% were damaged) of Gage's cerebral cortex (Van Horn et al., 2012).

The rod missed areas involved in speech, voluntary movement, and the senses of touch, body position, and pain. Thus, Gage had no difficulty speaking or performing complex movements, such as driving a stagecoach, following his accident. Modern patients with damage in this area exhibit many of the same social deficits that Gage demonstrated (Damasio & Anderson, 1993). They are often impulsive, emotionally unstable, unpredictable, and unable to make reasonable decisions.

Knowing the outcome of the Gage case, you might be astonished to learn that physicians in the 1940s and 1950s deliberately damaged the frontal lobes of nearly 50,000 American patients in a procedure known as a frontal lobotomy. The intent of the procedure was to reduce fear and anxiety in patients with serious psychological disorders, which it accomplished in many cases but at great expense to the patient. As you might suspect from reading about Gage, many patients who underwent the procedure were unable to work or live normal lives because of their impulsive, antisocial behavior.

The **orbitofrontal cortex**, a part of the prefrontal cortex located just behind the bony orbits protecting the eyes, plays an important role in our emotional lives (see Figure 4.13). People with damage to the orbitofrontal cortex demonstrate dramatic deficits in their social behavior and experience of emotion, despite retaining their intelligence, language skills, and abilities to pay attention, learn, and remember (Bechara et al., 2000).

orbitofrontal cortex A part of the prefrontal cortex located right behind the eyes that participates in impulse control.

Patient E.V.R. experienced orbitofrontal damage during surgery for a tumor (Eslinger & Damasio, 1985). Before his surgery, E.V.R. was considered a role model and a respected member of his community. Following his surgery, E.V.R. lost his job, went bankrupt, and divorced his wife to marry a prostitute, whom he divorced 2 years later. Although he had no difficulties talking about moral dilemmas, he experienced enormous problems when trying to make everyday decisions, such as buying toothpaste or choosing a restaurant.

Bio-feedback training helps people gain conscious control over some autonomic processes that normally run in the background. People who suffer from migraine headaches can be trained to reduce blood flow to the brain.

Researchers have made other connections between abnormalities in the orbitofrontal cortex and antisocial behavior. In a sample of 21 individuals diagnosed with antisocial personality disorder, a condition characterized by disregard for others that we discuss in Chapter 14, the volume of the prefrontal cortex, which includes the orbitofrontal cortex, was about 11% less than in control participants who did not have the condition (Raine et al., 2000). Individuals with antisocial personality disorder or orbitofrontal damage not only fail to anticipate the emotional consequences of situations but also are unable to delay gratification (Raine, 2019). They typically choose immediate rewards over long-term benefits, such as stealing something despite knowing the long-term benefits of staying out of jail.

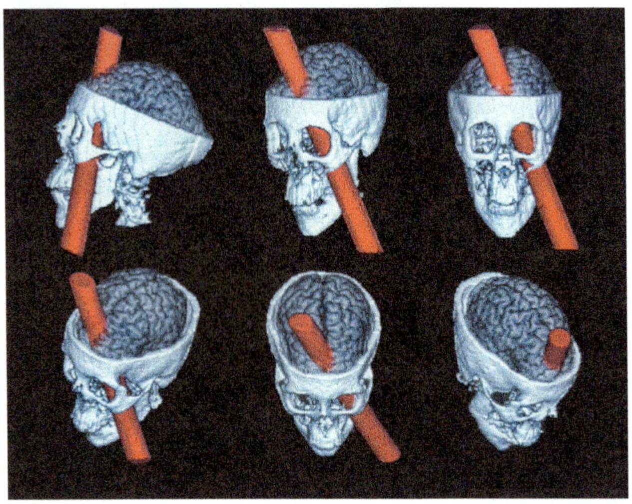

SPL/Science Source

Phineas Gage suffered a terrible injury to his frontal lobes. Modern imaging techniques allowed scientists to recreate the pathway of Gage's tamping iron through his brain. Remarkably, Gage survived, although his friends described him as a "changed man."

Source: H. Damasio et al. (1994). "The Return of Phineas Gage: Clues About the Brain from the Skull of a Famous Patient." *Science, 264,* 1102–1105. doi: 10.1126/science.81781688

The Occipital Lobe

The occipital lobe, located at the back of the brain, is home to the primary visual cortex. The primary visual cortex begins the process of interpreting input from the eyes by responding to basic information about an image, such as its borders, shading, color, and movement. This amount of processing by itself does not allow you to read this page or recognize your professor in the library. Two important pathways link the occipital lobe with the rest of the brain. A pathway connecting the occipital lobe with the temporal lobe allows you to recognize objects you see. A second pathway connects the occipital lobe with the parietal lobe and allows you to process the movement of objects. We discuss these processes further in the next sections.

The Temporal Lobe

The temporal lobe has several areas that are specialized for particular functions. The temporal lobe is home to the primary auditory cortex, which allows us to process incoming sounds. As mentioned earlier, the temporal lobe processes some higher visual system tasks, including the recognition of objects and the faces of familiar people. Patients with damage to the temporal lobe are often unable to recognize their loved ones by sight. They must wait until the person speaks. We discuss this processing of vision and hearing by the temporal lobe in more detail in Chapter 5.

We saw earlier how damage to Broca's area in the frontal lobe produced difficulty in speaking. Damage to another language area located in the temporal lobe, Wernicke's area, produces different results (see Figure 4.12). As we discuss in Chapter 10, patients with damage to their Wernicke's area speak fluently but make no sense. They cannot comprehend speech, but they seem blissfully unaware of their deficits.

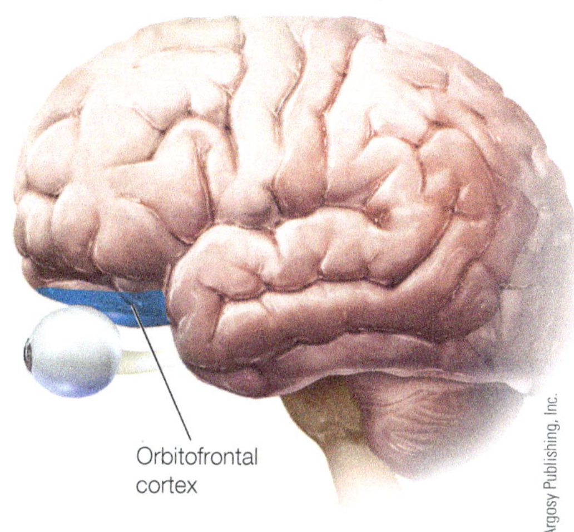

FIGURE **4.13**

The Orbitofrontal Cortex. People with damage to their orbitofrontal cortex have difficulty controlling impulses and anticipating the negative outcomes of poor decisions. This part of the brain is one of the last areas to mature.

The Parietal Lobe

The parietal lobe is home to the primary somatosensory cortex, which helps us localize touch, pain, skin temperature, and body position. The parietal lobe helps us better understand where our body (or even our self) is in time and space. Damage to the parietal lobe can produce neglect syndrome. Patients with this condition have difficulty paying attention to the space opposite the side of their brain damage (see ● Figure 4.14).

The parietal lobe processes input about taste and, like the temporal lobe, it engages in some complex processing of vision. Whereas the temporal lobe participates in visual recognition, the parietal lobe helps us coordinate vision and movement. People with parietal lobe damage would experience great difficulty while trying to insert a credit card into a card reader. We discuss these functions of the parietal lobe in depth in Chapter 5.

PSYCHOLOGY AS A HUB SCIENCE

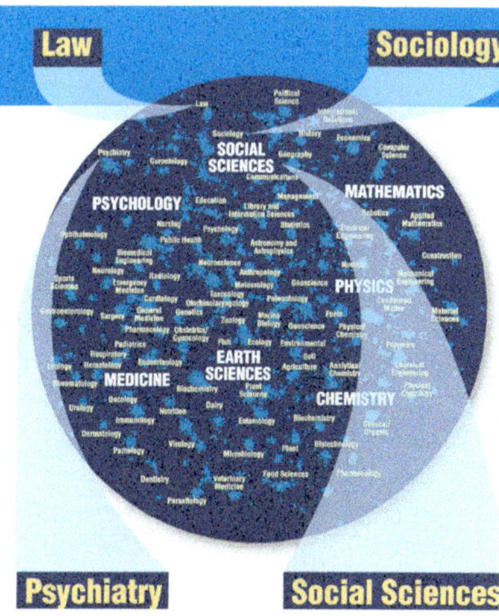

Law, Responsibility, and the Brain

PSYCHOLOGY, AND BIOLOGICAL PSYCHOLOGY IN PARTICULAR, have a great deal to say to the criminal justice system. In particular, neuroscience is entering the courtroom to evaluate "dangerousness," or the likelihood that a person will commit additional crimes (Aharoni et al., 2013; Kiehl et al., 2018). This trend is consistent with an overall paradigm shift in forensics from punishing perpetrators to protecting society from future crimes.

Assessing dangerousness is not new. Courts have used the opinions of forensic psychiatrists and psychologists for years, often bolstered with standardized instruments that test psychopathy (see Chapter 14). What is somewhat new is the use of brain imaging to link differences in structure and function with future criminal behavior. For example, Aharoni et al. (2013) argued that offenders with low activity in the anterior cingulate cortex (ACC) had twice the risk of re-offending as offenders with higher activity in this structure. Analyses of brain structure outperformed traditional models featuring psychopathic traits, drug and alcohol use, and tasks requiring behavioral inhibition in predicting future offenses (Kiehl et al., 2018).

While the goal to use neuroscience to improve forensics is worthy, ethical concerns must be fully explored. Research data tell us what "most people" do, but not whether a particular individual will fall within the "most people" group. Given the stakes of a person's freedom and the safety of society, neuroscientific evaluations of dangerousness merit the best scientific assessments possible. ■

ZUMA Press, Inc./Alamy Stock Photo

The U.S. criminal justice system continues to struggle with issues of maturity, mental illness, and responsibility for one's actions. In 2005, 13-year-old Roberto Holguin murdered 87-year-old Army veteran Gerald O'Malley by hitting him in the head with a skateboard. In 2014, while still incarcerated, Holguin sent California Governor Jerry Brown an email that said, "I will shoot you with a real gun." Brown subsequently overturned a parole board decision for early release for Holguin, but by law, Holguin could not be held longer than his 25th birthday in 2017.

FIGURE **4.14**

Damage to the Parietal Lobe Causes Neglect. Patients with certain types of brain damage in the parietal lobe experience "hemispatial neglect," or the inability to pay attention to stimuli located in space on the opposite side relative to their damage. They seem unaware that there is anything wrong with their perceptions. The patient whose drawings are featured in this figure experienced damage to the right hemisphere, resulting in neglect for anything to the left in space. Neglect does not affect vision alone but can also affect the sense of body location. One patient was unable to recognize his own leg and suspected the hospital staff of putting a cadaver leg into his bed.

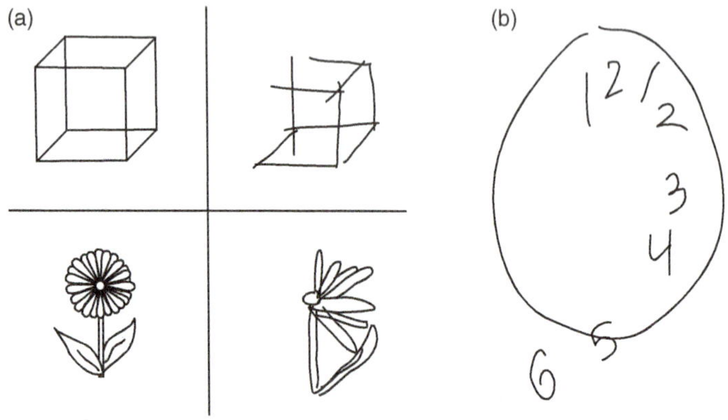

Mirror Neurons In the early 1990s, Giacomo Rizzolatti and a team of Italian scientists were busy studying the brain correlates of movement when they noticed something odd (di Pellegrino et al., 1992). They had observed that certain neurons in a part of a monkey's brain became especially active when the monkey performed certain actions, like reaching for a piece of banana or a peanut. What surprised them was that the same neurons fired when the monkey observed the experimenter pick up a piece of food to place it within his mouth and eat. Suspecting something important was behind these observations, the researchers began to study these "mirror neurons" more carefully. The scientists believed that mirror neurons provided a mechanism for understanding the actions and the intentions of others (Rizzolatti & Craighero, 2004; Rizzolatti & Sinigaglia, 2016).

Do human beings, as well as monkeys, possess mirror neurons? Research on humans typically involves brain imaging, such as functional magnetic resonance imaging (fMRI), so we see the activity of larger areas of the brain (mirror "systems") rather than single neurons, as recorded through surgically implanted electrodes in monkeys. It does appear, though, that human beings possess mirror systems that help us understand not just the actions and emotions of others, but their intentions as well (Grafton, 1996; Ortigue et al., 2010).

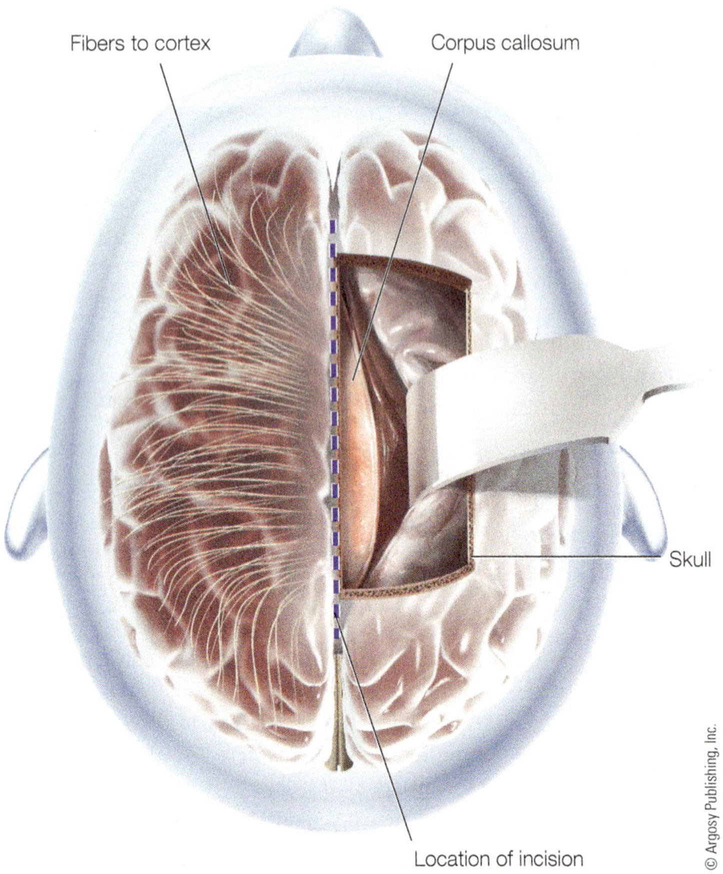

FIGURE **4.15**

The Split-Brain Operation. To save patients from life-threatening seizures, physicians cut the corpus callosum, a large band of nerve fibers connecting the right and left hemispheres.

Right Brain and Left Brain A special type of localization of function in the cerebral cortex is known as lateralization, or the localization of a function in either the right or the left cerebral hemisphere. A basic type of lateralization occurs in the somatosensory and voluntary motor systems in the brain. Movement and sensation on the right side of the body are processed by the left hemisphere, and movement and sensation on the left side of the body by the right hemisphere. If you observe a person who is paralyzed on the right side of the body, you can be fairly certain that this paralysis is a result of motor cortex damage in the left hemisphere. In a similar manner, the visual cortex of the left hemisphere processes all data from the right half of the visual field, while the right hemisphere processes all data from the left half of the visual field. In other words, when you look straight ahead, holding your eyes and head still, everything to the right or left of center is processed by the opposite hemisphere (see Chapter 5 for more detail).

Early knowledge of lateralization of the human brain resulted from the careful analysis of a surgical procedure known as a split-brain operation (see Figure 4.15). To treat rare

CONNECTING TO RESEARCH

Mirror Systems and Predicting Tennis Serves

ATHLETIC SUCCESS OFTEN DEPENDS upon the athlete's ability to predict an opponent's intentions quickly enough to react appropriately. In tennis, the reading of an opponent's serve is especially important, as the time required to plan and implement a response is longer than the flight time of the ball (Cacioppo et al., 2014).

The Question: How do expert tennis players predict their opponents' serve quickly enough to respond well?

METHODS

Twenty-five male tennis players were observed using fMRI as they viewed films of players serving the ball in one of two conditions: (1) the player serving the ball knew where he wanted to place the serve (initially intended) or (2) the player was told by an experimenter where he should place the serve *after* he had already tossed the ball (noninitially intended). The players viewing the films were asked to indicate where they thought the ball would go.

ETHICS

Because fMRI is a safe procedure, this study raises few ethical concerns. Nonetheless, the participants must freely volunteer and provide informed consent. Their confidentiality should be strictly protected.

RESULTS

The more expert the tennis player being scanned, the more successful he was at predicting where the serve would land, but only when the server in the film knew where the ball was supposed to go *before* he tossed the ball in the air. When the server didn't know until the last minute where the ball was supposed to go, all viewers performed no better than chance. Accurate predictions of the location of the serve were correlated with activation of mirror neuron systems and subcortical structures involved with motor memory.

CONCLUSIONS

The scientists demonstrated that "reading" the intentions of others is a remarkably complex process involving the mirror neuron system. This system is more likely to be activated when we observe a person whose actions are relevant to our goals, such as our opponent in a tennis match, than if a person's actions are irrelevant, such as an usher in the grandstand. Correctly reading your opponent's intentions, but not the usher's, is critical to your success. ■

iStock.com/nycshooter

cases of life-threatening seizures, surgeons in the 1960s cut the patients' corpus callosum and other pathways connecting the right and left cerebral hemispheres (Bogen et al., 1988). The procedure not only succeeded in reducing or eliminating seizures, but it also produced no changes in personality, intelligence, or speech. Only when patients were studied in the laboratory were the consequences of their surgery evident. A typical experiment demonstrating the differences in processing by the right and left hemispheres (Gazzaniga, 1967) is illustrated in ● Figure 4.16.

Subsequent research indicated that language, for most people, is lateralized to the left hemisphere, although a minority of individuals process language either in the right hemisphere or in both hemispheres (Rasmussen & Milner, 1977). The lateralization of language is correlated, although not completely, with a person's handedness. As shown in a later section, nearly all right-handed people lateralize language to the left hemisphere, as do about 70% of people who are left-handed. The remaining individuals process language either in the right hemisphere or in both hemispheres.

Language is not the only cognitive process to show evidence of lateralization. Other suspected lateralized processes include mathematical computation and logical reasoning (left hemisphere) and some music functions, spatial information, intuition, and the visual arts (right hemisphere). Emotional behavior also appears to be lateralized. Neurological patients with right hemisphere damage show greater impairments than patients with left hemisphere damage in the comprehension and expression of emotion (Gainotti, 2019).

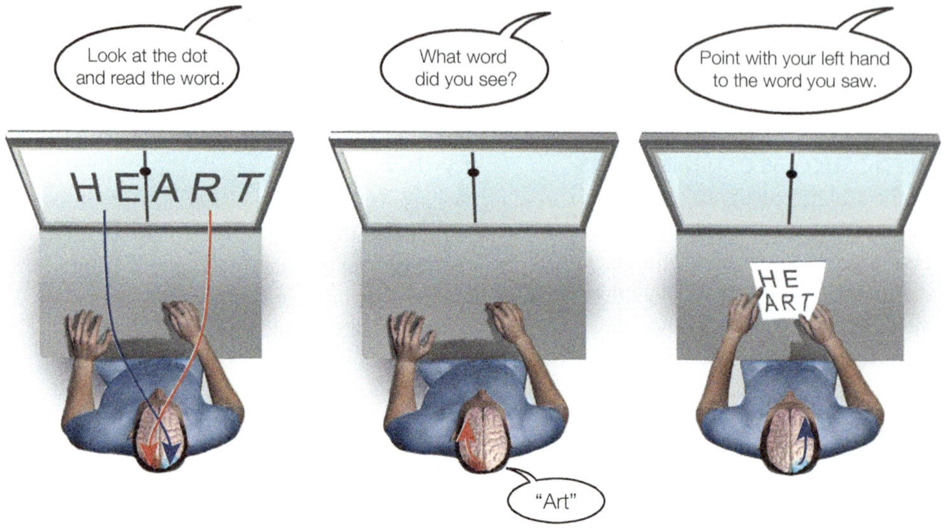

© Argosy Publishing, Inc.

FIGURE **4.16**

The Hemispheres Have Different Capacities for Language Functions. If participants who have experienced a split-brain surgery fixate on a dot in the middle of the screen, information to the left of the dot is processed by the right hemisphere, and information to the right of the dot is processed by the left hemisphere. When asked verbally what word was seen, participants answered "art," which was seen by the verbal left hemisphere. When asked to point with the left hand, which is controlled by the right hemisphere, to the word that was seen, the participants pointed to "he," which is the word seen by the right hemisphere.

Humans are not the only animals to have a preferred hand. However, the fact that over 90% of humans are right-handed sets the species apart. While other primates, such as this chimpanzee using a stone to open nuts, are also more likely to be right- than left-handed, only about 65–70% of chimpanzees are right-handed (Hopkins, 2006).

Martin Harvey/Alamy Stock Photo

Right–Left Brain Myths A word of caution is in order here. As noted by Roger Sperry, who won the 1981 Nobel Prize for his investigations of lateralization in the human brain, "The left–right dichotomy in cognitive mode is an idea with which it is very easy to run wild" (Sperry, 1982, p. 1225). Most of us have not undergone a split-brain procedure. Our intact corpus callosum and other connections between the two cerebral hemispheres allow information to pass rapidly from one hemisphere to the other. Suggestions that you can improve your artistic or athletic talent or reduce inattention by "learning to access your right brain" have gained considerable attention in the popular press, but they do not hold up to scrutiny in the laboratory. One of the most popular myths about lateralization is the idea that individual differences in artistic talent or logical thinking correlate with a person's dominant hemisphere. Hemisphere dominance, as measured by the relative size of the hemispheres and the localization of language and handedness, does not predict occupational choice or artistic talent (Springer & Deutsch, 1998).

The Function of Lateralization What are the advantages of lateralization? Most species of animals show a preference for one hand or the other, such as when a cat reaches for its prey (Cole, 1955; Holder, 1999).

Lateralization might provide organisms with the ability to multitask (Rogers, 2000). Chicks raised in the dark fail to lateralize normally and are at a disadvantage compared to normal chicks when feeding and watching for predators simultaneously. Success in this type of multitasking has obvious survival advantages.

Human lateralization of brain structures might have made language possible (Berlim et al., 2003). This development could have a big price tag, however, because lateralization might account for our species' vulnerabilities for schizophrenia and autism spectrum disorder, as discussed in Chapter 14. People with schizophrenia show abnormal hemisphere lateralization and are more likely to be left-handed or to have ambiguous handedness (Berlim et al., 2003). Autism spectrum disorder is also associated with extensive differences in lateralization (Paquet et al., 2017).

EXPERIENCING PSYCHOLOGY

Handedness

AS SHOWN IN ● TABLE 4.2, LATERALIZATION OF LANGUAGE is correlated with handedness (Milner, 1974). Handedness represents a continuum, with some people being nearly ambidextrous and others having strong preferences for using one hand or the other. Although most of us would have no trouble answering a question asking whether we are right- or left-handed, researchers like Milner must apply systems for determining a person's handedness. One of the frequently used instruments follows.

Simply read each of the questions in ● Table 4.3. Decide which hand you use for each activity, and then circle the answer that describes you the best. If you are unsure of any answer, try to act out the action. To find your score, count the number of circled "right" answers and subtract the number of circled "left" answers. Ignore "either" answers. Ambidextrous people will score around 0, very right-handed people will score near +12, and very left-handed people will score near −12

Although this test can't tell you which hemisphere you use for language, your odds of using your left hemisphere for language if you're very right-handed are quite high. ■

TABLE 4.2

Relationships Between Handedness and Language Localization

Handedness	Language left	Language right	Mixed dominance
Right-handed (90%)	96%	4%	0%
Left-handed (10%)	70%	15%	15%

TABLE 4.3

The Lateral Preference Inventory

1. With which hand do you draw?	Left	Right	Either
2. Which hand would you use to throw a ball to hit a target?	Left	Right	Either
3. In which hand would you use an eraser on paper?	Left	Right	Either
4. Which hand removes the top card when you are dealing from a deck?	Left	Right	Either
5. With which hand do you normally write?	Left	Right	Either
6. In which hand do you use your racquet for tennis, squash, etc.?	Left	Right	Either
7. With which hand do you use your toothbrush?	Left	Right	Either
8. Which hand holds a knife when you are cutting things?	Left	Right	Either
9. Which hand holds the hammer when you are driving a nail?	Left	Right	Either
10. In which hand would you hold a match to strike it?	Left	Right	Either
11. Which hand holds the thread when you are threading a needle?	Left	Right	Either
12. In which hand would you use a fly swatter?	Left	Right	Either

Source: Adapted from S. Coren (1993). "The Lateral Preference Inventory for Measurement of Handedness, Footedness, Eyedness, and Earedness: Norms for Young Adults," *Bulletin of the Psychonomic Society*, *31*(1), 1–3. doi: 10.3758/BF03334122

Although efforts to connect brain lateralization, which is highly correlated with handedness, with occupational choice or artistic talent have not been successful, being in the left-handed minority might provide advantages in sports and in combat. Right-handed pitchers, such as Tim Lincecum, are often challenged by left-handed hitters such as Adrian Gonzalez. Some of the most famous hitters of all time were lefties, including Barry Bonds, Ty Cobb, Lou Gherig, Stan Musial, Babe Ruth, and Ted Williams.

Mike Powell/Sports Illustrated Classic/Getty Images

Michael Zagaris/Contributor/Getty Images Sports/

SUMMARY 4.1 Structures of the Central Nervous System

	Structure	What to Remember
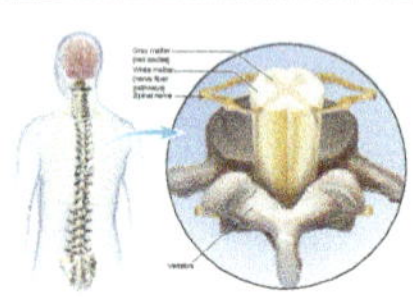	Spinal Cord	• Continuous with brainstem • Large white matter pathways • Reflexes
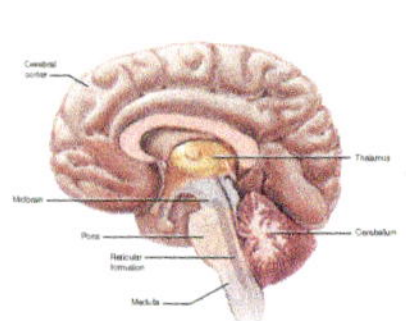	Brainstem and Cerebellum	• Large white matter pathways, arousal, reflexes, and body functions (heart rate, etc.) • Midbrain • Pons • Cerebellum • Medulla • Reticular formation
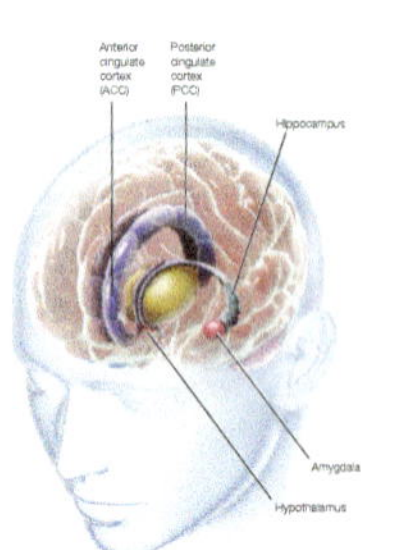	Subcortical Structures	• Embedded in the white matter of the cerebral hemispheres • Thalamus • Basal ganglia • Hypothalamus • Hippocampus • Cingulate cortex • Amygdala • Nucleus Accumbens
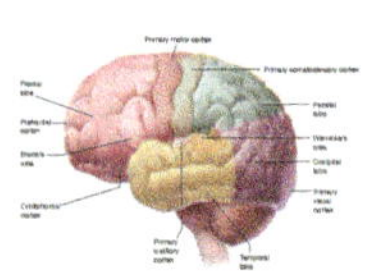	Cerebral Cortex	• Thin layer of gray matter enveloping the hemispheres • Divided into four lobes • Areas with sensory, motor, or association functions • Some localized and lateralized functions

Credits: Top row—© Argosy Publishing, Inc.; Second row—© Argosy Publishing, Inc.; Bottom row—© Argosy Publishing, Inc.

The Peripheral Nervous System (PNS) and the Endocrine System

The brain and spinal cord are spectacular processing units, but without input or ability to implement commands, they would be no different from your computer's central processing unit (CPU) without its mouse, keyboard, monitor, printer, and Internet connection. The lights may be on, but not much is going to happen.

In this section, we will explore the structures of the PNS that provide these essential input and output functions in the body. The PNS can be separated into two divisions: the somatic nervous system and the autonomic nervous system. The somatic nervous system includes the peripheral portions of the sensory and voluntary movement systems. The autonomic nervous system is responsible for the actions of many glands and organs. Additional output is provided by the endocrine system, through which the CNS can communicate with the body by releasing chemical messengers into the bloodstream. These systems coordinate their efforts to produce consistent patterns of movement, hormone release, and arousal.

somatic nervous system The part of the peripheral nervous system that brings sensory information to the central nervous system and transmits commands to the muscles.

autonomic nervous system The division of the peripheral nervous system that directs the activity of glands, organs, and smooth muscles.

sympathetic nervous system The division of the autonomic nervous system that coordinates arousal.

The Somatic Nervous System

The **somatic nervous system** is the part of the PNS that transmits commands for voluntary movement from the CNS to the muscles and brings sensory input back to the CNS for further processing. These functions are carried out by the 31 pairs of spinal nerves serving the torso and limbs and the 12 pairs of cranial nerves serving the head, neck, and some internal organs (see ● Figure 4.17).

The Autonomic Nervous System

The function of the **autonomic nervous system** is the control of tissues other than the skeletal muscle (Langley, 1921)—in other words, our glands and organs. The term *autonomic* has the same root as the word *autonomy*, or independence. You might think of this system as the cruise control of the body because it ensures that your heart keeps beating and your lungs continue to inhale and exhale without your conscious direction. The autonomic nervous system contains three subdivisions: the sympathetic, the parasympathetic, and the enteric.

The sympathetic and parasympathetic divisions are active under different circumstances. The **sympathetic nervous system** prepares the body for situations requiring the expenditure of energy, while the

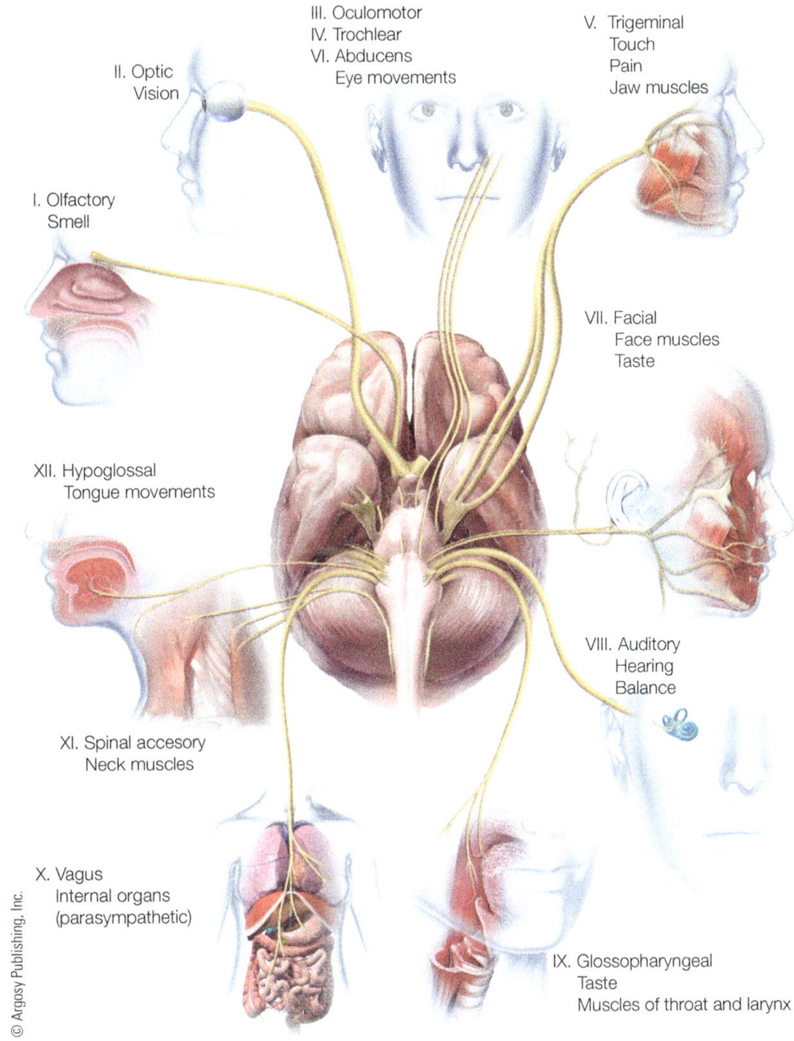

FIGURE 4.17

The Cranial Nerves. Twelve pairs of cranial nerves carry sensory and motor information from the brain to the head, the neck, and some internal organs.

Stress activates the sympathetic nervous system, preparing the body for fight or flight or, in this case, fast paddling. We're told, however, that this is a porpoise, not a shark.

Kurt Jones

parasympathetic nervous system directs the storage of energy. You have probably experienced intense sympathetic arousal, perhaps because of a close call on the highway. In the aroused state produced by the sympathetic nervous system, our hearts race, we breathe rapidly, our faces become pale, and our palms sweat. All these activities are designed to provide the muscles with the resources they need for a fight-or-flight reaction. The sympathetic nervous system is important to our understanding of stress, described further in Chapter 16. In contrast, the parasympathetic nervous system controls the glands and organs at times of relative calm. Instead of using up energy like the sympathetic nervous system does, the parasympathetic nervous system allows you to store nutrients, repair your body, and return the activities of internal organs to baseline levels.

The responses of the internal organs to environmental stimuli reflect a sophisticated combination of inputs from both the sympathetic and the parasympathetic nervous systems (Berntson et al., 1991). These systems usually have antagonistic effects on the organs they serve and are designed to alternate their activities (see ● Figure 4.18). We cannot be simultaneously relaxed and aroused. The sympathetic nervous system dilates the pupils of the eye, whereas the parasympathetic nervous system constricts the pupils. The heart responds to sympathetic commands by beating faster but responds to parasympathetic commands by slowing down. The two divisions do manage, however, to cooperate during sexual activity.

The **enteric nervous system**, shown in ● Figure 4.19, consists of nerve cells embedded in the lining of the gastrointestinal system. This system is often called a "second brain" because it contains as many nerve cells as are found in the spinal cord. The enteric nervous system communicates with the endocrine system, described later in this chapter, to ensure the release of chemicals essential to digestion. Enteric cells also communicate directly with the vagus nerve, one of the cranial nerves, forming a gut-brain axis (Breit et al., 2018). This communication channel also transmits information about the gut's microbiome, or bacteria population, to the brain. Some functions of the enteric nervous system result in conscious perceptions, such as gastrointestinal pain, hunger, and satiety (fullness), while others operate below the threshold of conscious awareness. The latter give rise to our references to having a "gut feeling." Disturbances of the enteric environment might contribute to the development of autism spectrum disorder (Slattery et al., 2016). The enteric nervous system is the source of 95% of the body's serotonin, a neurochemical discussed later in this chapter. Individuals with autism spectrum disorder (see Chapter 14) show higher than normal levels of serotonin in their blood (Janusonis, 2008) and often experience gastric distress (Holingue et al., 2018).

parasympathetic nervous system The division of the autonomic nervous system associated with rest, repair, and energy storage.

enteric nervous system A division of the autonomic nervous system consisting of nerve cells embedded in the lining of the gastrointestinal system.

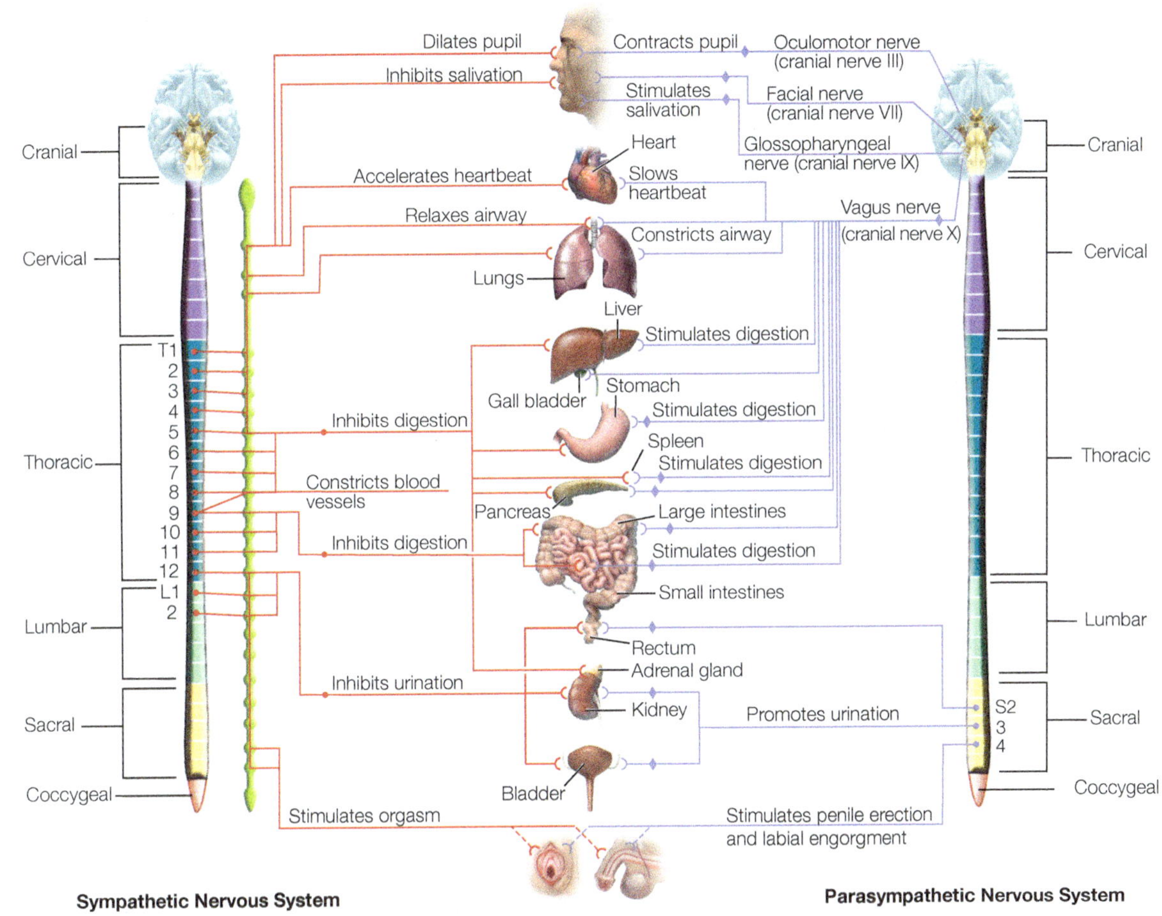

FIGURE **4.18**

The Autonomic Nervous System. The sympathetic nervous system (left) usually has the opposite effect on an organ compared with the parasympathetic nervous system (right). For example, sympathetic input tells the heart to beat faster, while parasympathetic input tells the heart to slow down. However, both systems cooperate during sex.

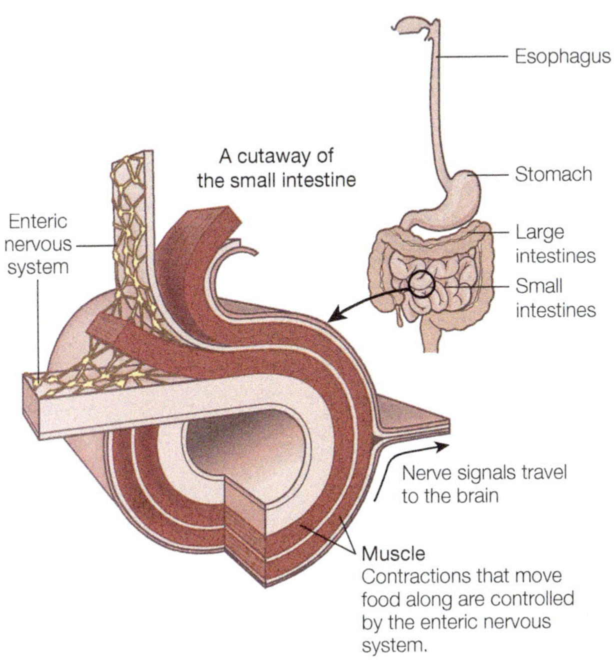

FIGURE **4.19**

The Enteric Nervous System. The enteric nervous system is often called a second brain. It has about the same number of neurons as the spinal cord, or about as many found in the entire brain of an adult cat.

Human growth hormone, released normally by the pituitary gland, has become a popular substance among actors and athletes. Sylvester Stallone (b. 1946), star of *Rocky* and *Rambo*, is one of the few Hollywood stars to discuss his use of the hormone publicly.

Tsuni/USA/Alamy Stock Photo

The Endocrine System

The nervous system communicates by passing messages along nerves. In contrast, the **endocrine system** is made up of glands that release chemical messengers known as hormones into the blood (see ● Figure 4.20). These chemicals are often identical to those used by one nerve cell to communicate with another, but their actions affect more distant cells in a coordinated fashion. Ultimately, the endocrine system responds to input from the nervous system and from the hypothalamus in particular. The endocrine system is especially involved with arousal, metabolism, growth, and sex. Among the important glands of the endocrine system are the pineal gland, the pituitary gland, the thyroid gland, the adrenal glands, the islets of Langerhans, and the ovaries in females and testes in males.

endocrine system A system responsible for the release of hormones into the bloodstream.

The pineal gland, and its release of the chemical messenger melatonin, is important in the maintenance of our sleep–wake cycles, which we discuss in Chapter 6. Although not an officially approved and tested medication, melatonin is used by some travelers to offset the unpleasant effects of jet lag. Melatonin is normally released in the early evening, and it breaks down in the presence of light. Thus, exposure to artificial light at night can have negative implications for our health. However, research attempting to link night shift work to higher risk of cancer remains inconclusive (Jones et al., 2019).

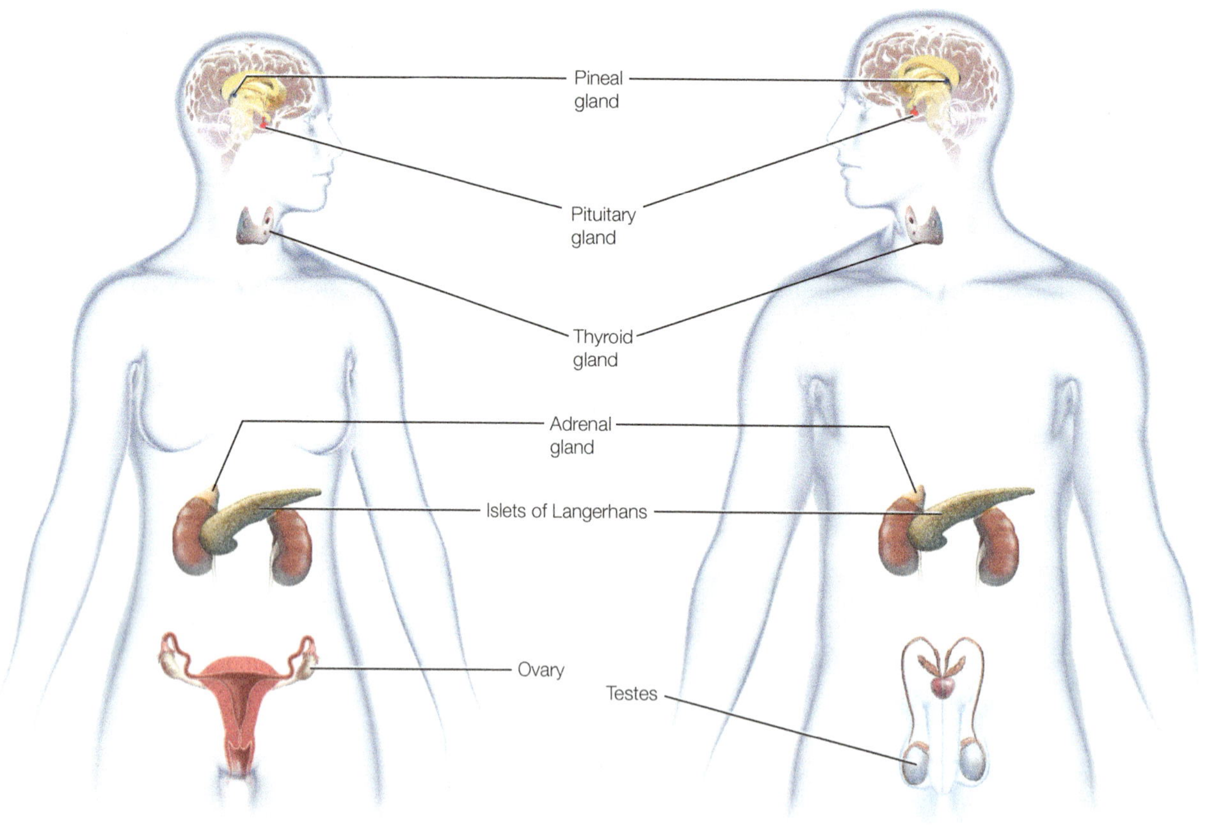

© Argosy Publishing, Inc.

FIGURE **4.20**

Glands of the Endocrine System. The endocrine system communicates with other body tissues by releasing hormones from glands into the bloodstream.

The pituitary gland, located just above the roof of your mouth, is often called the body's master gland, because many of the hormones it releases activate other glands. The pituitary in turn is regulated by the hypothalamus, which lies directly above it. One type of pituitary hormones, including oxytocin, vasopressin, and human growth hormone, is released directly from the pituitary. Oxytocin and vasopressin participate in several important physical functions, such as breastfeeding and maintenance of fluid levels, respectively. However, these hormones are also implicated in cooperation and trust, memory for social information, recognition of emotions, and resilience during stress (Meyer-Lindenberg et al., 2011). Growth hormone stimulates growth and regeneration, making it a popular performance-enhancing substance used illegally by some elite athletes.

A second type of pituitary hormone influences the release of hormones by other glands. For example, pituitary hormones control the production and release of sex hormones by the ovaries and the testes, initiating puberty and maintaining fertility. In response to pituitary hormones, the thyroid gland—located just below your larynx, or voice box, in your throat—raises or lowers your rate of metabolism, or the chemical processes your body needs to sustain life. Low levels of thyroid can mimic the symptoms of depression, described further in Chapter 14. At times of stress, pituitary hormones activate the adrenal glands, which are located just above the kidneys in the lower back. In response, the adrenal glands release other hormones, including cortisol, that travel throughout the body and the brain to provide a general wake-up message.

The islets of Langerhans, located in the pancreas, produce hormones essential to digestion, including insulin.

Gino Santa Maria/Shutterstock.com

Oxytocin released by the pituitary gland is correlated with human bonding between parent and child and between romantic partners.

SUMMARY 4.2 Peripheral Nervous and Endocrine Systems

	Structure	What to remember
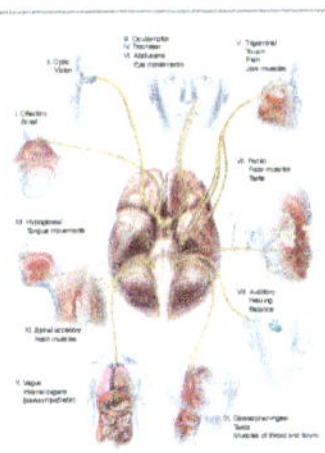	Somatic nervous system	• Sensation and movement • 12 pairs of cranial nerves • 31 pairs of spinal nerves
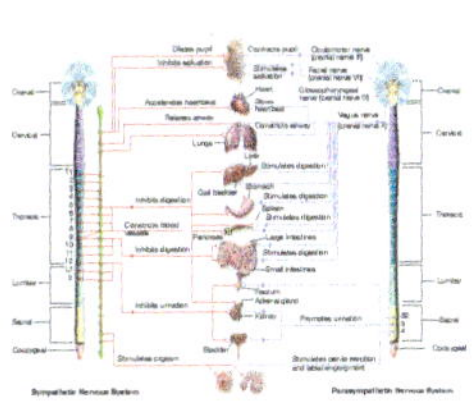	Autonomic nervous system	• Sympathetic nervous system: arousal and fight or flight • Parasympathetic nervous system: rest and repair • Enteric nervous system: control of the gastrointestinal system
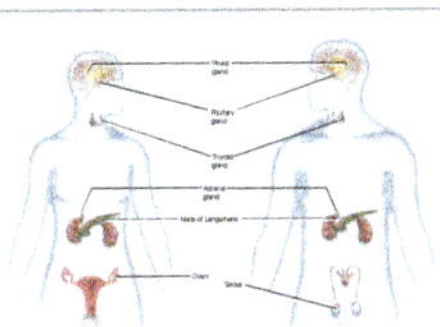	Endocrine system	• Metabolism, arousal, growth, sex • Glands • Hormones

Credits: Top row—© Argosy Publishing, Inc.; Second row—© Argosy Publishing, Inc.; Third row—© Argosy Publishing, Inc.; Bottom row—© Argosy Publishing, Inc.

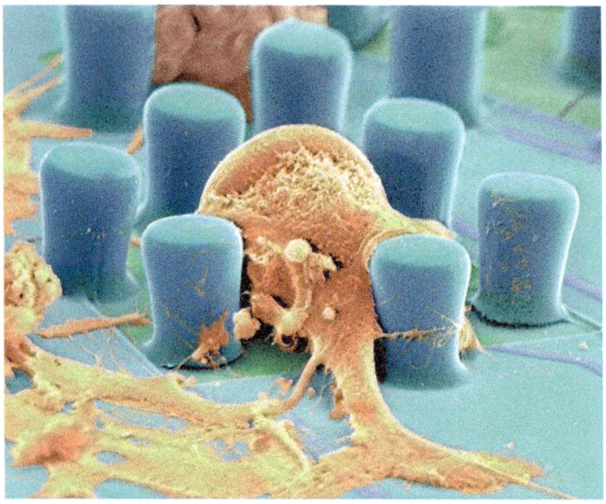

Although it sounds like a script from a science fiction film, researchers are capable of growing neurons, such as these from the retina of the eye, on silicon chips. The chip electrically stimulates the growing neurons. Future uses of this type of technology might include brain-like computer networks and better prostheses for people who have lost a limb.

How Do Neurons Communicate?

We now zoom in to explore the microscopic building blocks of the nervous system, which are the nerve cells, or **neurons**. Human brains have about 86 billion neurons. To put this number into perspective, consider the following: If each neuron represented a second, ticking off the neurons in your body alone would take more than 3,000 years. With each neuron forming an average of several thousand connections with other neurons, the connections in the human brain number in the hundreds of trillions. In addition to these large numbers of neurons, the nervous system contains many supporting cells, known as **glia**.

Once you are familiar with the structure of neurons and glia, we will explore the ways neurons communicate with one another. Neural communication is a two-step process. The first step takes place within a single neuron and involves the generation of an electrical signal. The second step takes place between two neurons and involves the release of a chemical messenger from one neuron that affects the activity of the second.

Neurons and Glia

Neurons share many characteristics with other cells found in the body. Like other cells, a neuron has a large central mass or **cell body**, and within the cell body, it has a nucleus (see ● Figure 4.21). Most housekeeping tasks of the cell, such as the translation of genetic codes into the manufacture of proteins, take place in the cell body. Like other cells, neurons feature an outer membrane, which surrounds the neuron and forms a barrier between the fluid outside the cell (the extracellular fluid) and the fluid inside the cell (the intracellular fluid). The neural membrane is composed of fatty materials that do not dissolve in water, so even though it is only two molecules thick, it is able to hold apart the water-based fluids on either side. Pores within the membrane act as channels that allow chemicals to move into or out of the cell.

Unlike other types of body cells, neurons have two types of branches that extend from the cell body to allow the neuron to perform its information-processing and communication functions. The branches known as **axons** are responsible for carrying information to other neurons, while the branches known as **dendrites** receive input from other neurons. Although neurons may have many dendrites, each neuron typically has only one axon.

Many axons communicate with immediately adjacent cells and are, therefore, only small fractions of a millimeter in length, but other axons are much longer. When you stub your big toe on a rock, the neurons that process this information have cell bodies in your lower back and axons that extend all the way down to your sore toe, a distance of around 3 feet (about 0.9 meters), depending on your height. At its farthest point from the cell body, an axon bulges to form a terminal. If you look inside an axon terminal with an electron microscope, you can see round, hollow spheres known as synaptic vesicles, which contain molecules of chemical messengers.

We have been using the term *white matter* to describe pathways formed by nerve fibers or axons. You have probably heard the term *gray matter* as well. Now that you understand the structure of neurons, these terms will make more sense. When we prepare neural tissue for study using microscopes, the chemicals used to preserve the tissue are absorbed by cell bodies. This gives cell bodies a pink-gray coloring. In contrast, these chemicals are repelled by the insulating material covering most axons because the insulation has a fatty composition that doesn't mix well with the watery preservatives (we discuss the nature of this insulation shortly). As a result, axons look white, like the fat in a steak. When we examine images of the brain, areas that look gray have a high density of cell bodies, whereas areas that look white consist of large bundles of axons.

neuron A cell of the nervous system that is specialized to send and receive neural messages.

glia Nervous system cells that perform a variety of support functions, including formation of the blood–brain barrier and myelin.

cell body The large, central mass of a neuron, containing the nucleus.

axon The branch of a neuron that is usually responsible for transmitting information to other neurons.

dendrite A branch from the neural cell body that usually receives input from other neurons.

The blood–brain barrier might offer too much protection to the brain in some cases. Many chemotherapy agents used to treat cancer in other parts of the body cannot penetrate the blood–brain barrier, which complicates the treatment of tumors in the brain.

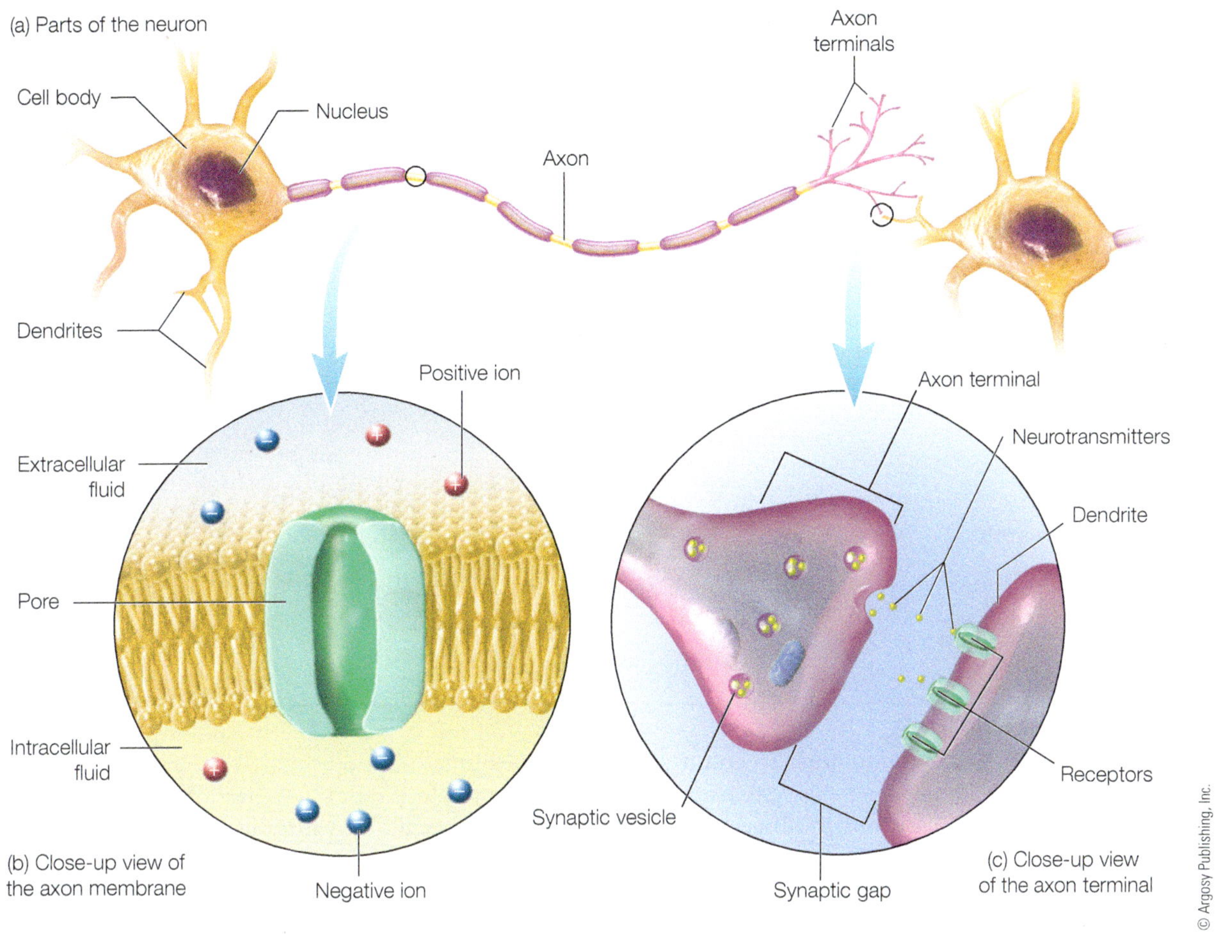

FIGURE 4.21

The Neuron. Neurons share many features with other living cells but are specialized for the processing of information. **(a) Parts of the neuron.** Like other types of animal cells, the neuron features a nucleus in its cell body and a fatty membrane that separates intracellular and extracellular fluids. Unlike most other cells, the neuron has specialized branches, the axon and the dendrites, that pass information to and receive information from other cells. **(b) A closeup view of the axon membrane.** A thin, oily membrane separates the intracellular fluid inside the neuron from the extracellular fluid outside the neuron. Pores spanning the membrane act as channels that allow ions to move into and out of the neuron. **(c) A closeup view of the axon terminal.** Within the axon terminal are synaptic vesicles, which contain chemical messengers called neurotransmitters that transmit signals between neurons. Later in the chapter, we'll see how these neurotransmitters communicate with receptors on the dendrites of other neurons.

If neurons are the stars of the nervous system team, glia are the trainers, coaches, and scorekeepers. They make it possible for neurons to do their job effectively. Some glia (from the Greek word for "glue") provide a structural matrix for neurons, ensuring that the neurons stay in place (see ● Figure 4.22). Other glia are mobile, allowing them to move to a location where neurons have been damaged to clean up debris. Glia form tight connections with the blood vessels serving the nervous system. This forms a blood–brain barrier that prevents many toxins circulating in the blood from exiting into brain tissue where neurons could be harmed. Psychoactive drugs, by definition, are substances capable of penetrating the blood–brain barrier with ease. We discuss psychoactive drugs and the ways in which they act on the nervous system in Chapter 6.

In vertebrates such as humans, glia wrap around some axons like sausages on strings at a delicatessen, forming an important layer of insulation called **myelin**. Myelin makes neural signaling fast and energy efficient. We will discuss how myelin accomplishes this in a later section on neural signaling. By speeding up the transmission of neural signals and contributing to quicker recovery between signals, myelin increases the amount of information a neuron

myelin The insulating material covering some axons.

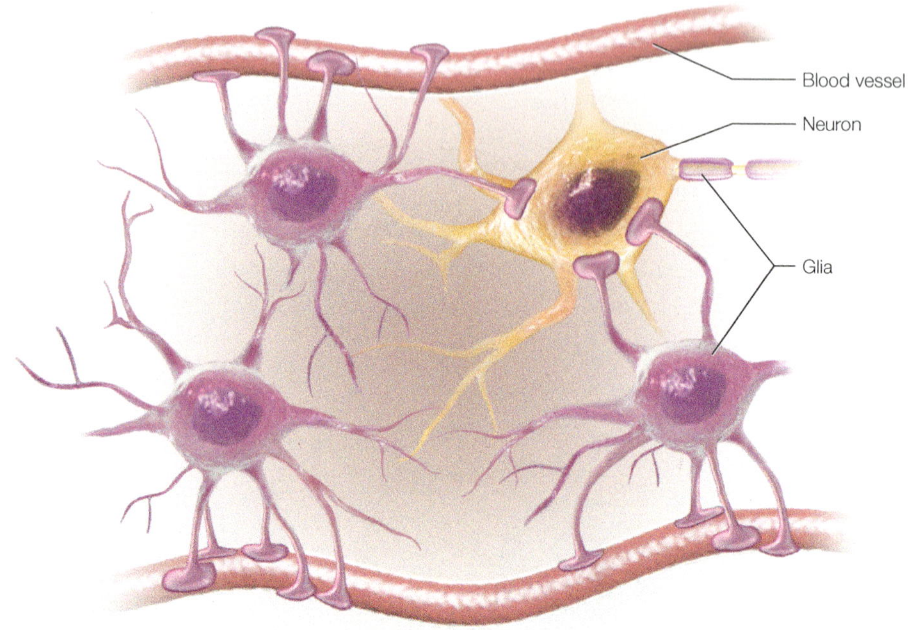

FIGURE **4.22**

The Blood–Brain Barrier. Glia form tight connections with the blood vessels in the nervous system, preventing many toxins from entering the brain. Glia also help hold neurons in place and form the myelin on some axons.

can transmit per second by a factor of 3,000 times (Giedd et al., 2015). Not all axons in the human nervous system are myelinated. When you hurt yourself, the fast, sharp "ouch" message is carried to the brain by myelinated axons, but the dull, achy message that lasts a lot longer is carried by unmyelinated axons.

One type of glia forms the myelin in the brain and the spinal cord, and a second type forms the myelin in the remainder of the nervous system (see ● Figure 4.23). These two types

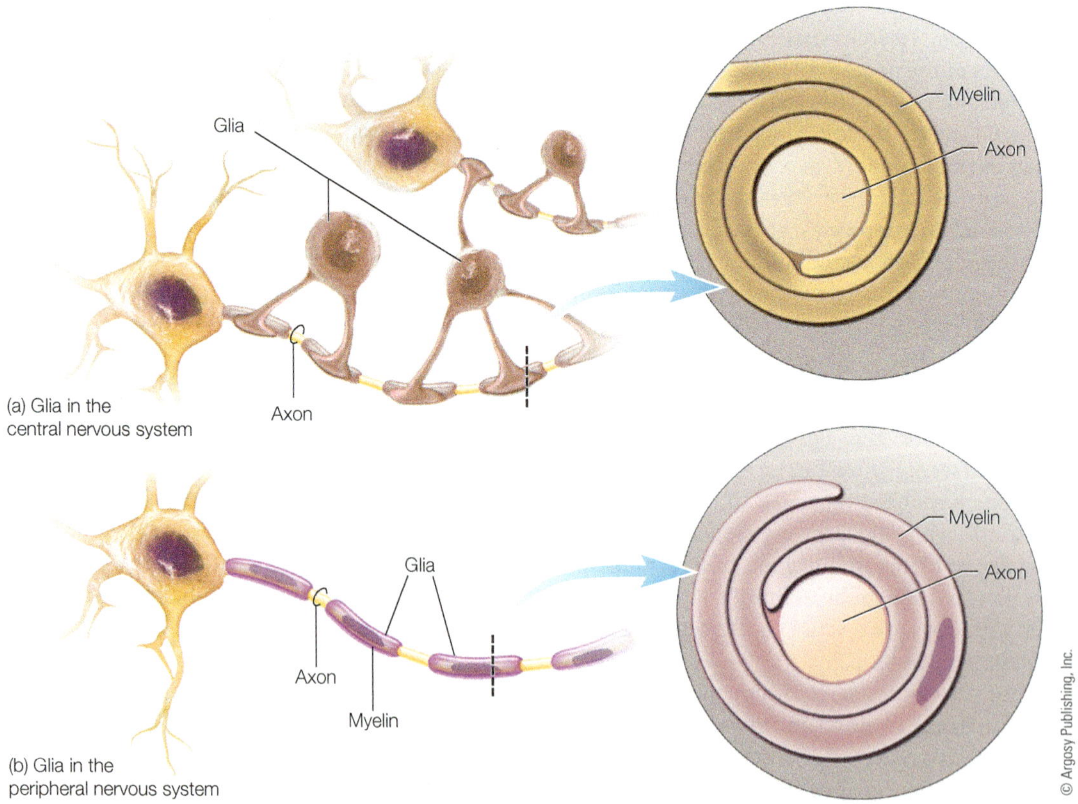

FIGURE **4.23**

Glia Form Myelin. One type of glia forms myelin in the CNS, and a second type forms myelin in the PNS. These types of glia respond differently to nerve damage, making nerve damage outside the brain and spinal cord easier to repair.

of glia behave quite differently from each other when they are damaged. Glia in the brain and the spinal cord form scar tissue, inhibiting repair to the damaged nerves. Because of this feature, we consider damage in the CNS to be permanent. Considerable research is under way to figure out how to repair such damage, including work using stem cells to grow bridges across the damaged areas. In contrast, damaged glia in the PNS do not form scar tissue and instead help the damaged axons regrow. As a result, nerve damage in these areas can heal. If this were not so, operations to reattach limbs would be doomed to failure. Today, not only are digits and even limbs that were lost in accidents routinely reattached to their rightful owners, but a number of patients whose own hands or faces were damaged beyond repair have undergone successful transplants from cadavers (Dubernard et al., 2001; Clarke & Butler, 2009).

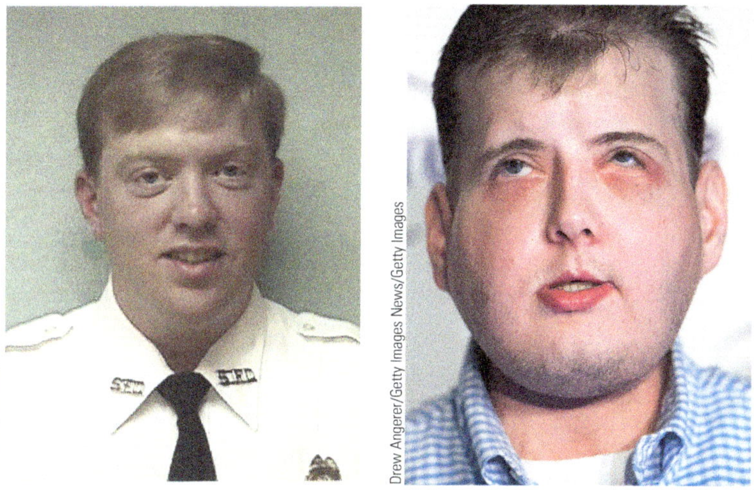

CORTESIA/Notimex/Newscom

Drew Angerer/Getty Images News/Getty Images

While on duty as a volunteer fireman in 2001, Patrick Hardison experienced catastrophic burn damage to his face. His original appearance before the accident is shown on the left. In 2015, a team of over 100 medical professionals transplanted a donor face onto Hardison. His current appearance is shown on the right. This type of operation would be useless unless the nerves in the face were able to establish new connections. Hardison expressed joy in an interview about his ability to feel his children's touch on his face again.

Neural Signaling

Now that we have a working knowledge of the structure of neurons, we are ready to talk about how they function. A neuron is a sophisticated communication and information-processing system that receives input, evaluates it, and decides whether to transmit information to neurons downstream. Its actions are similar to your own when you receive great news from a friend and then decide whether to tell somebody else. Understanding this process is important for anyone using psychoactive substances, whether recreational or therapeutic, as psychoactive drugs typically produce their effects (and side effects) by interacting with neural signaling.

As we mentioned earlier, neural communication is a two-step process. In the first step, which takes place in the signaling neuron's axon, the neuron generates an electrical signal known as an **action potential**. This signal travels the length of the axon from its junction with the cell body to its terminal. In the second step, which takes place between two neurons, the arrival of an action potential at the axon terminal of the first neuron signals the release of chemical messengers, which float across the extracellular fluid separating the two neurons. These chemicals influence the likelihood that the second neuron will respond with its own action potential, sending the message along.

action potential The electrical signal arising in a neuron's axon.

Electrical Signaling The production of action potentials can be demonstrated using axons dissected from a squid and placed in a tub of seawater, which has a chemical composition

Source: Tau, G. Z., & Peterson, B. S. (2010). "Normal development of brain circuits". *Neuropsychopharmacology Reviews, 35*, 147–168. doi: 10.1038/npp.2009.115

Myelination of the human nervous system takes more than 20 years to complete.

FIGURE **4.24**

Recording From the Axons of Squid Some squid axons are large enough to be seen with the naked eye and remain active in a bath of seawater for hours. These features make studying neural activity in a squid axon relatively simple.

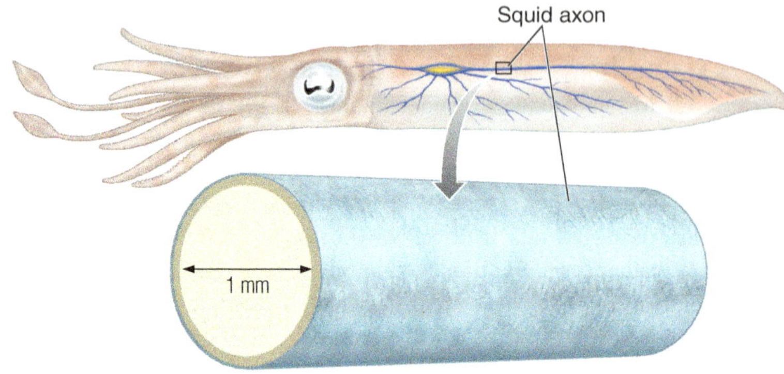

similar to the fluid surrounding our body cells (Hodgkin & Huxley, 1952). Of all the possible sources of axons on the Earth, why choose squid? Certain axons from a squid can be as much as 1 millimeter in diameter, large enough to see with the naked eye. The squid axon is also large enough that you can insert a recording electrode into its interior without disrupting its function. The readings from inside the axon can then be compared with readings from a recording electrode placed in the seawater.

When a neuron is not processing information, we say that it is at rest. When a cell is at rest, the difference between the readings from the interior of the axon and the external fluid is known as the **resting potential**. Our recording will show that the interior of the neuron is negatively charged relative to its exterior due to the different chemical composition of the intracellular and extracellular fluids. This is similar to the minus sign (the cell's interior) and the plus sign (the cell's exterior) on a battery.

Let's assume that our resting neuron now begins to receive chemical messages from another neuron, a process we discuss in more detail shortly. Neurons can respond to incoming chemical signals by becoming either depolarized or hyperpolarized. The word *polarized* means "far apart," such as when political factions disagree. Being depolarized means we have moved closer together, and being hyperpolarized means we have moved even farther apart than before. In the case of neurons, depolarization means that the difference between the electrical charges of the extracellular and the intracellular recordings is decreasing. Hyperpolarization means that the difference is increasing.

When a neuron is depolarized by sufficient input, it reaches a threshold for producing an action potential. A threshold is the point at which an effect, the action potential in this case, is initiated. Once this threshold is reached, the generation of an action potential is inevitable. Approaching the threshold for initiating an action potential is similar to pulling the trigger of a gun. As you squeeze the trigger, nothing happens until you reach a critical point. Once that critical point is reached, the gun fires, and there is nothing you can do to stop it.

Reaching threshold initiates a sequence of events that reliably produces an action potential (see ● Figure 4.25). These events involve the opening and the closing of pores or channels in the neural membrane, which in turn allow certain chemicals to move into and out of the cell. These chemicals are in the form of ions or electrically charged particles dissolved in water. When threshold is reached, channels open, allowing one type of ion, sodium, to rush into the neuron. Because sodium ions carry a positive electrical charge, we can see their movement reflected in a steep rise in our recording of the difference between the internal and the external electrodes. At the peak of the action potential, our recording has reversed itself from the resting state. Now the interior of the cell is more positively charged than the outside.

Near the peak of the action potential, channels open that allow another type of ion, positively charged potassium, to move across the membrane. Potassium begins to leave the cell. As the interior loses these positively charged potassium ions, our recording heads in the negative direction again. Following the production of the action potential, the neuron requires a time-out or refractory period, during which it returns to its resting state. During this refractory period, the cell is unable or unlikely to respond to further input by producing another action potential.

The size and shape of action potentials are always the same, whether we're recording them in a squid or in a human. You won't see recordings of short, fat action potentials or tall,

resting potential The measure of the electrical charge across a neural membrane when the neuron is not processing information.

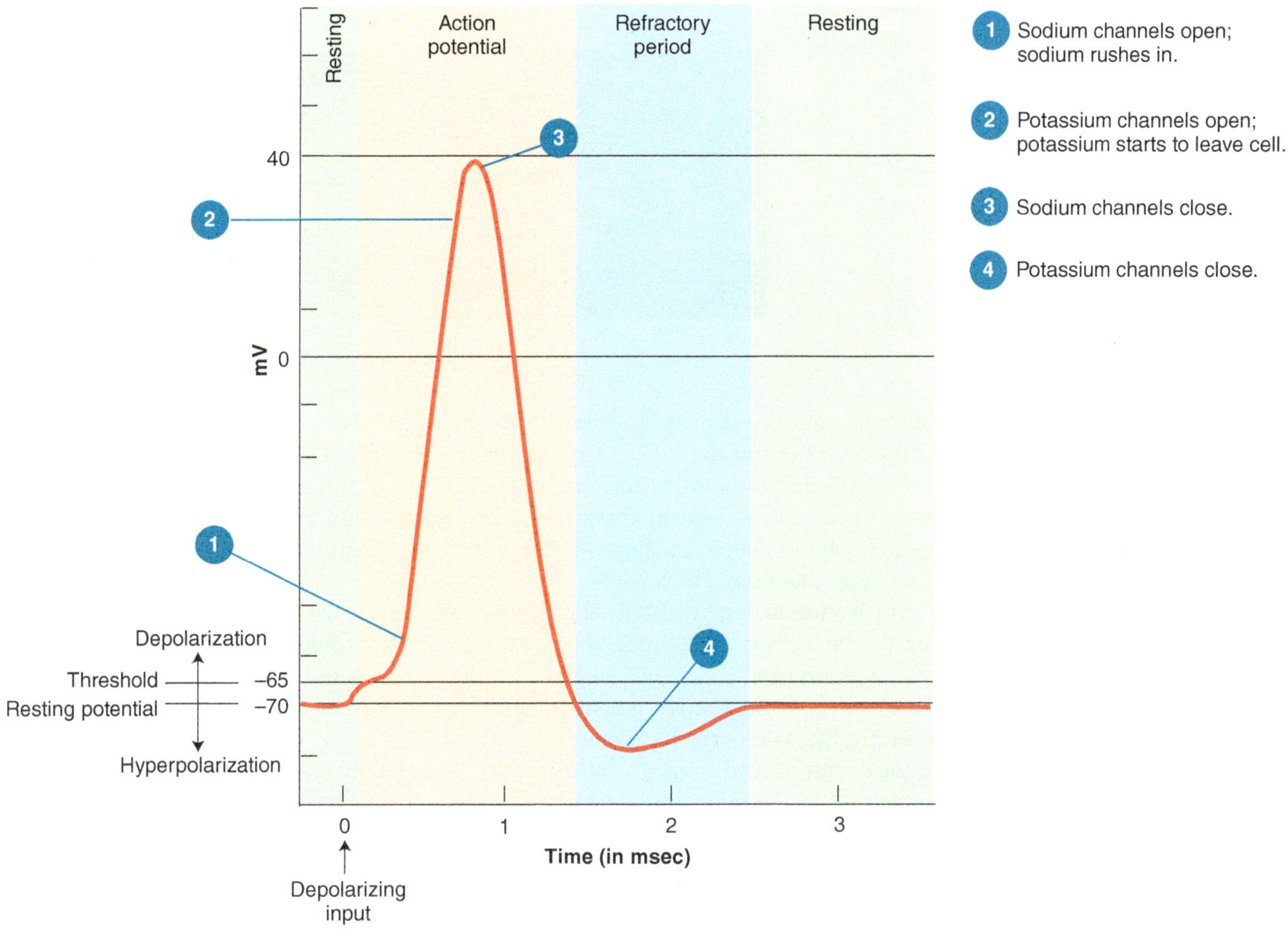

FIGURE **4.25**

The Action Potential. Once threshold is reached, an action potential is triggered. The movement of sodium and potassium ions across the axon membrane is reflected in the rise and fall of our recording, respectively. A refractory period follows each action potential, and triggering another action potential during this time is more difficult.

skinny ones. Either an action potential occurs, or the cell remains at rest—there is no middle ground. Because of this consistency, we say that action potentials are all or none.

Action potentials do not affect the entire axon all at once. The process we just described takes place first in a small segment of the axon where the axon connects to the cell body. The next step is propagation, or the duplication of the electrical signal down the length of the axon to the axon terminal, where it initiates the release of chemical messengers.

We mentioned earlier that myelinated neurons enjoyed some advantages in efficiency and speed, and we are now ready to discuss why that is the case. Propagation takes place differently in myelinated and unmyelinated axons. In an unmyelinated axon, action potentials occur step by step, from one small section of the axon to the next adjacent section, down

JOE SCHERSCHEL/National Geographic Image Collection

Sushi made from puffer fish, known as *fugu*, is a delicacy, but when prepared poorly, it can result in sickness or death. Chefs who prepare *fugu* undergo extensive training and licensing in Japan. The puffer fish toxin blocks the movement of sodium into cells, making electrical signaling impossible. As a result, diners who eat poorly prepared fugu can become paralyzed and suffocate to death.

A node of Ranvier, located between two adjacent segments of myelin, is rich in sodium channels, which makes the formation of action potentials at the node possible.

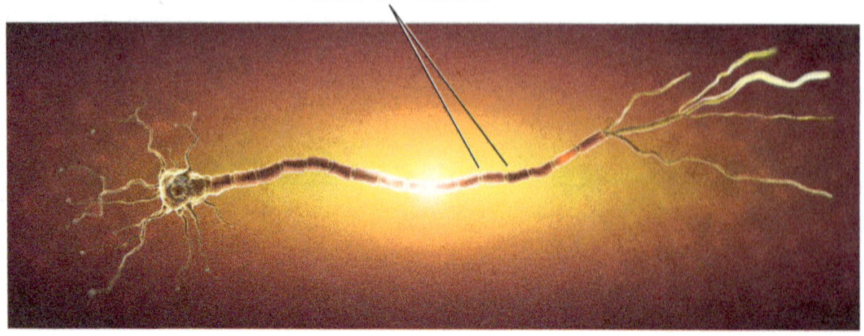

the entire length of the axon. In contrast, action potentials in myelinated axons are formed only at the sections of the axon membrane between adjacent segments of myelin, known as nodes of Ranvier. In other words, propagation in myelinated axons can "skip" the sections covered by myelin. You might think about propagation in unmyelinated versus myelinated axons as being similar to shuffling your feet versus taking long strides. Which covers the most ground faster and more efficiently?

Propagation in unmyelinated axons works well, as evidenced by the wealth of invertebrate life on the Earth, from the snails in your garden to the giant squid of the oceans. These animals survive with no myelin, but their neural communication is not fast or energy efficient compared to ours. Forming action potentials at each section down the length of the axon is time consuming, like taking the local bus that stops at every block. In addition, cleaning up after all these action potentials uses a lot of energy (Swaminathan et al., 1982). The more action potentials it takes to move a signal down the length of the axon, the more energy is expended returning the cell to its resting state.

synapse A point of communication between two neurons.

neurotransmitter A chemical messenger that communicates across a synapse.

Propagation in myelinated axons is fast and efficient (see Figure 4.26). After an initial action potential is generated near the cell body, the current flows beneath a segment of myelin until it reaches a node of Ranvier, where another action potential occurs. Like the express bus, the action potentials skip the myelinated sections of the axon, reaching their destination, the

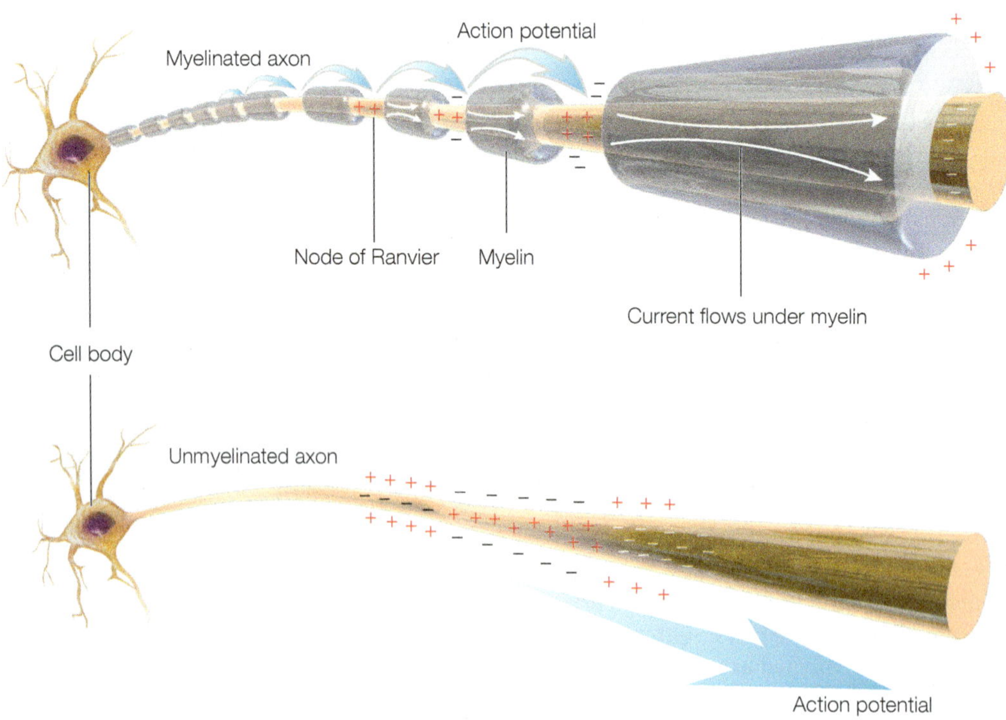

FIGURE **4.26**

Propagation of the Action Potential. Action potentials move down the length of the myelinated axon more quickly than they move down an unmyelinated axon.

axon terminal, about 20 times faster than if the axon were unmyelinated. By covering the same distance with fewer action potentials, the myelinated axon uses less energy returning to the resting potential than an unmyelinated axon would need.

Once the action potential reaches the axon terminal, the neural communication system switches from an electrical signaling system to a chemical signaling one.

Chemical Signaling The point of communication between two neurons is known as a **synapse**. At the synapse, neurons do not touch one another physically. Instead, they are separated by tiny gaps filled with extracellular fluid. Because electrical signals are unable to jump this gap, neurons send chemical messengers instead. These chemical messengers are called **neurotransmitters** (see ● Table 4.4).

● Figure 4.27 illustrates the sequence of events triggered by the arrival of an action potential at an axon terminal. The neurotransmitters in the axon terminal are contained in synaptic vesicles. The arrival of an action potential releases the vesicles from their protein anchors, much like boats leaving a dock, and the vesicles migrate rapidly to the cell membrane. Because the vesicles are made of the same thin, oily material as the membrane, they easily fuse with the membrane and spill their contents into the synaptic gap, similar to popping soap bubbles in a bathtub. Following release, the vesicles are pinched off the membrane and refilled.

The neurotransmitters released across the synaptic gap come into contact with special channels on the receiving neuron, known as receptors. **Receptors** work with the neurotransmitters like locks and keys. Only a neurotransmitter with the right shape (the key) can attach itself or bind to a particular receptor (the lock). Neurotransmitters do not stay bound to receptors long. Once they pop out of the receptor binding site, neurotransmitter molecules drift away from the gap, are broken down by enzymes, or return to the axon terminal from which they were released in a process called reuptake. In **reuptake**, special channels in the axon terminal membrane known as transporters allow the neurotransmitters to move back into the releasing neuron where they are repackaged for later use. Many important drugs, including the antidepressant drug fluoxetine (Prozac), cocaine, and amphetamines, interfere with or inhibit this reuptake process.

The interaction between neurotransmitters and their receptors can have one of two effects on the receiving neuron: excitation or inhibition. When a neurotransmitter has an excitatory effect, it slightly depolarizes the receiving neuron, increasing the likelihood that the neuron will reach threshold and initiate an action potential. Recall that depolarization reduces the difference between the electrical environments inside and outside the neuron. When a neurotransmitter has an inhibitory effect, it slightly hyperpolarizes the receiving neuron, moving the cell farther from threshold and reducing the likelihood that it will initiate an action potential. Recall that hyperpolarization increases the difference between the electrical environments inside and outside the neuron.

Excitatory messages seem logical. One neuron is telling another to "pass the message along." Inhibitory messages, however, seem somewhat strange at first glance. Why would our nervous systems need a message that says, "Don't pass the message along"? Tetanus, for which you probably have been vaccinated, provides a dramatic example of what can happen when inhibition doesn't work properly. The toxin produced by the bacteria responsible for tetanus selectively damages inhibitory neurons in the parts of the nervous system that control muscle contraction. Normally, excitatory inputs that contract muscles coordinate their activity with inhibitory inputs that tell muscles to relax, allowing the steady hands we need to put in a contact lens, for example. Without the input of the inhibitory neurons, the system is left with excitation only, and the result is the extreme muscle contraction that gives tetanus its other name—lockjaw (see ● Figure 4.28).

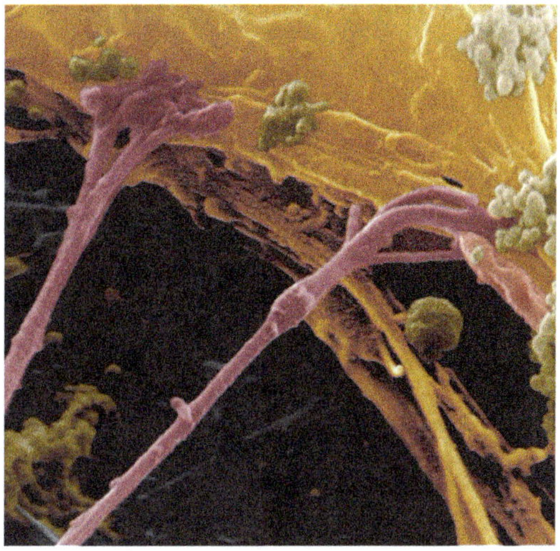

Eye of Science/Science Source

Two axons (in purple) are forming synapses or junctions where communication will occur with a neuron's cell body (in yellow).

receptor A special channel in the membrane of a neuron that interacts with neurotransmitters released by other neurons.

reuptake A process in which molecules of neurotransmitter in the synaptic gap are returned to the axon terminal from which they were released.

TABLE 4.4

Important Neurotransmitters

Neurotransmitter	Behaviors influenced by the neurotransmitter
Acetylcholine (ACh)	• Movement • Memory • Autonomic nervous system function
Epinephrine (adrenalin)	• Arousal
Norepinephrine (noradrenalin)	• Arousal • Vigilance
Dopamine	• Movement • Planning • Reward
Serotonin	• Mood • Appetite • Sleep • Dominance/Aggression
Glutamate	• Excitation of brain activity
GABA	• Inhibition of brain activity
Endorphins	• Pain management

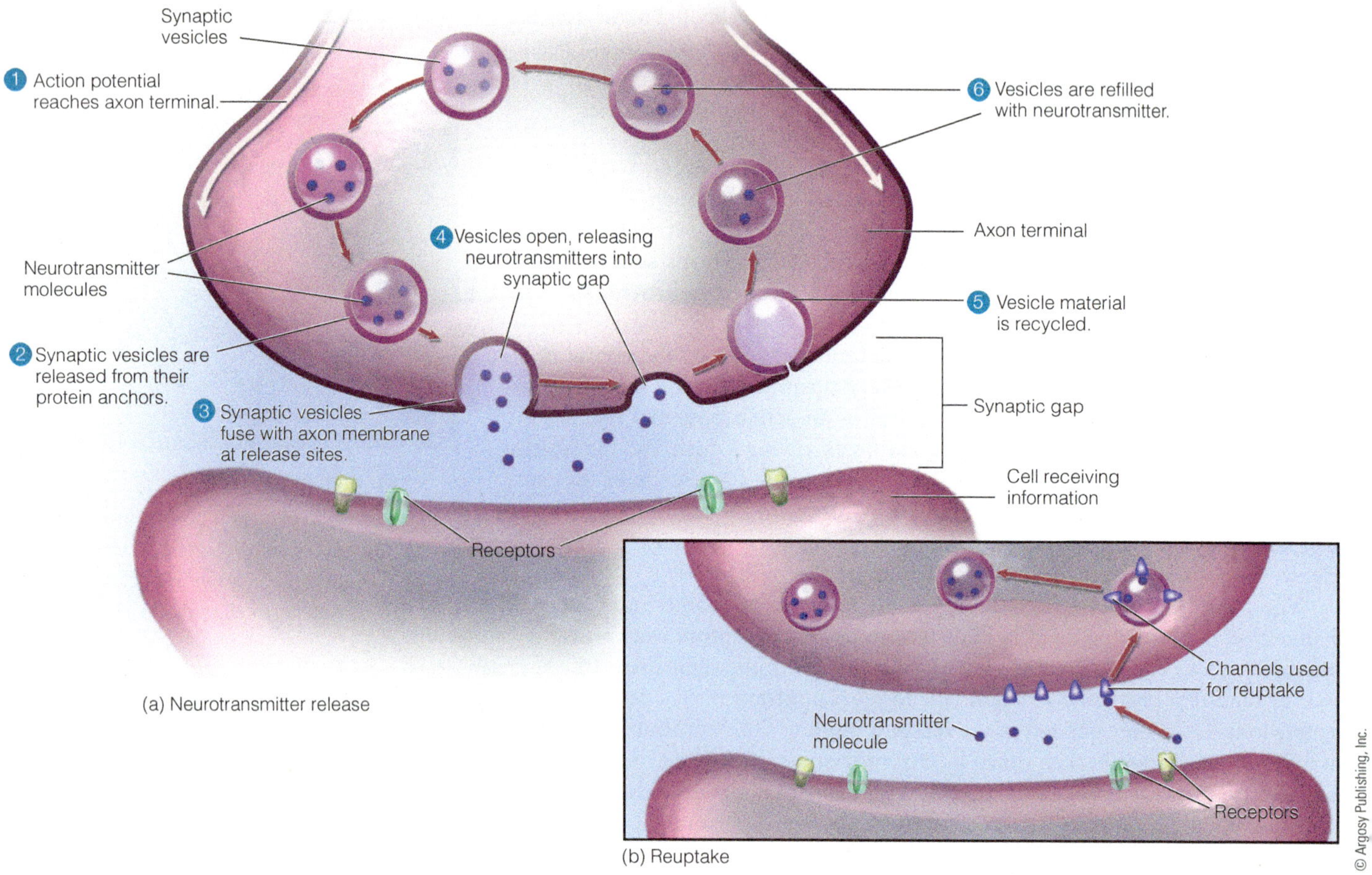

FIGURE **4.27**

Chemical Signaling. Because most neurons are separated from one another by extracellular fluid, the action potential cannot jump from one neuron to the next. To cross the gap between neurons, chemical signals are used instead. **(a) Neurotransmitter release**. The arrival of an action potential at the axon terminal triggers a sequence of events that results in the release of neurotransmitter molecules, which float across the synaptic gap to interact with receptors on the receiving neuron. **(b) Reuptake**. After interacting with receptors, neurotransmitter molecules are often recaptured by the neuron that released them to be recycled and used again later.

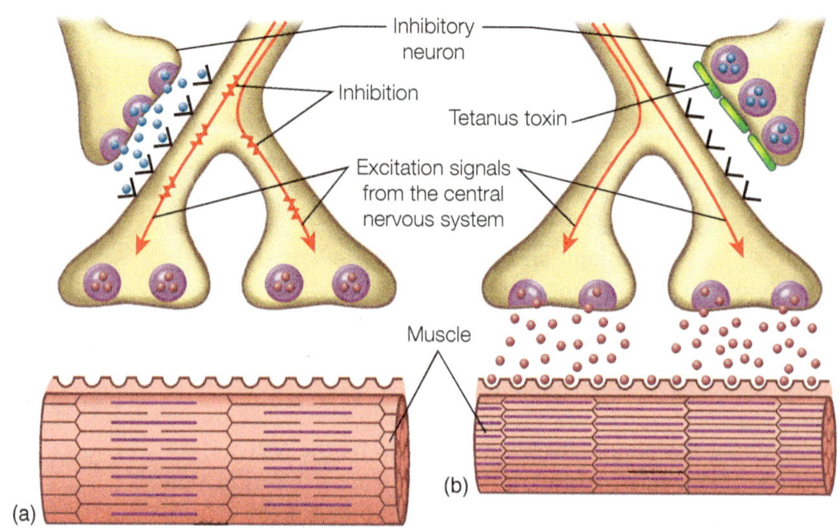

FIGURE **4.28**

Tetanus Blocks Motor Inhibition. The severe muscle contraction that gives tetanus its nickname of lockjaw results from the toxin's blocking the release of inhibitory neurotransmitters in the motor systems of the brain and spinal cord. (a) Normally, inhibitory input balances contraction to maintain smooth movements. (b) Without the counterbalance of inhibition, too much muscle contraction occurs.

Synapses usually occur in many locations on the dendrites or cell body of the receiving neuron, and the depolarizing or hyperpolarizing current that results from neurotransmitter activity at these synapses drifts to the junction of the cell body and axon. If there is sufficient depolarization to reach threshold at this junction, the neuron generates an action potential. If not, it remains at rest. The neuron's "decision" to generate an action potential or not is called summation; the neuron is adding up all incoming messages and making a decision based on that information. The neuron's task is not unlike the situation we face when we ask friends and family for advice. We will receive some excitatory advice (Go for it!), along with some inhibitory advice (Don't even think about it!). Our job, like the neuron's, is to sum our input and make a decision. Unlike us, however, the neuron cannot disregard the advice it receives.

The SSRI label for some antidepressant medications, including Prozac, stands for selective serotonin reuptake inhibitor. People who are depressed often have lower-than-normal serotonin activity at the synapse. If you inhibit reuptake of serotonin, more molecules remain in the synaptic gap longer where they can continue to interact with receptors. Serotonin activity increases, relieving depression, because we get more "bang for the buck" each time serotonin is released.

Types of Neurotransmitters

Researchers have identified more than 50 chemicals that serve as neurotransmitters. Table 4.4 lists some of the neurotransmitters that are particularly interesting to psychologists, and we will highlight a few of these in this section. In Chapter 6, we explore examples of psychoactive drugs, both therapeutic and recreational, that interact with the normal biochemistry of the nervous system.

Acetylcholine (ACh) is a neurotransmitter found in many systems important to behavior. ACh is found at the neuromuscular junction, the synapse at which the nervous system commands muscles. Interference with the action of ACh at the muscles can result in paralysis and death, making drugs that act on ACh popular for use as pesticides and as bioweapons. ACh also serves as a key neurotransmitter in the autonomic nervous system, discussed previously, which carries commands from the brain to the glands and organs. ACh is also intimately involved in the brain circuits related to learning and memory. These brain circuits are among the first to deteriorate in Alzheimer's disease. Not surprisingly, memory deficits are among the earliest symptoms of Alzheimer's disease to appear. Among the many drugs that act on ACh systems is the nicotine found in tobacco.

Jack Fields/Science Source

A Yagua hunter in Peru loads a dart tipped with curare into the mouthpiece of his blowgun. Curare is derived from native plants and causes paralysis by blocking receptors for acetylcholine (ACh) at synapses between the nervous system and the muscle fibers.

Norepinephrine activity in the brain leads to arousal and vigilance. Consistent with this role in arousal, norepinephrine is also released by the sympathetic nervous system. As we observed previously, the sympathetic nervous system prepares us to react to emergencies by providing necessary resources, such as the extra oxygen that is needed to run or throw a punch. Abnormalities in norepinephrine activity have been implicated in several psychological conditions that feature disturbances in arousal and vigilance, including bipolar disorder and posttraumatic stress disorder (PTSD), discussed in Chapter 14.

Dopamine is involved with systems that govern movement, planning, and reward. Parkinson's disease, which makes normal movement difficult, results when dopamine-releasing neurons in the brain's movement circuits begin to die. In addition, dopamine participates in the brain's reward and pleasure circuits by becoming active whenever we engage in behaviors that promote survival and successful reproduction, such as eating a great meal or having sex. Most drugs that produce addiction, including cocaine and methamphetamine, stimulate increased activity in dopamine circuits. In Chapter 14, we will see how disruptions to dopamine circuits have been implicated in schizophrenia and ADHD.

Serotonin is involved with systems regulating sleep, appetite, mood, and aggression. Consequently, these behaviors are tightly linked. As we will see in Chapter 14, people who experience depressed mood also show abnormalities in appetite and sleep.

Botox, which is used to treat muscle spasms or reduce wrinkles, is made from an inactive form of the toxin responsible for botulism, which is produced by bacteria that spoil food. Botox interacts with ACh by preventing its release from the axon terminal. Without the activity of ACh telling a muscle to contract, the muscle remains paralyzed.

This image highlights areas of the human brain that are rich in receptors for endorphins, our natural opioids. The red areas have the most endorphin receptors, followed by the yellow areas. Opioid drugs, such as heroin or morphine, affect our behavior by interacting with these receptors.

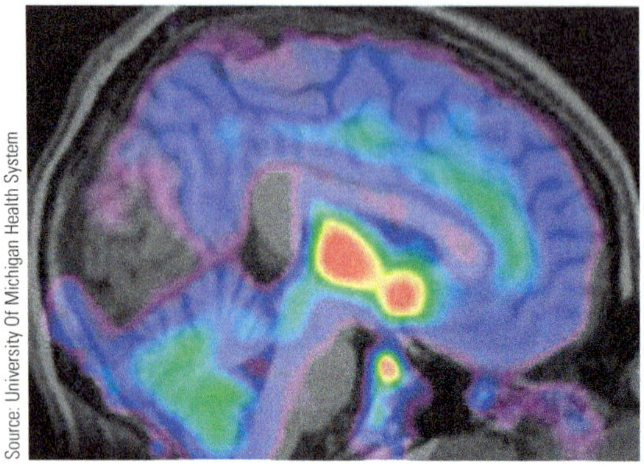

Endorphins, short for endogenous morphine or morphine produced by the body, modify our natural response to pain. In evolutionary terms, it makes sense to have a system that reduces your chances of being disabled by pain during an emergency. All too frequently, however, we underestimate the extent of our injuries until we wake up the next morning feeling sore. "Runner's high," in which people who regularly engage in endurance sports experience a sense of well-being and reduced sensation

Interpersonal Relationships

The Biological Perspective

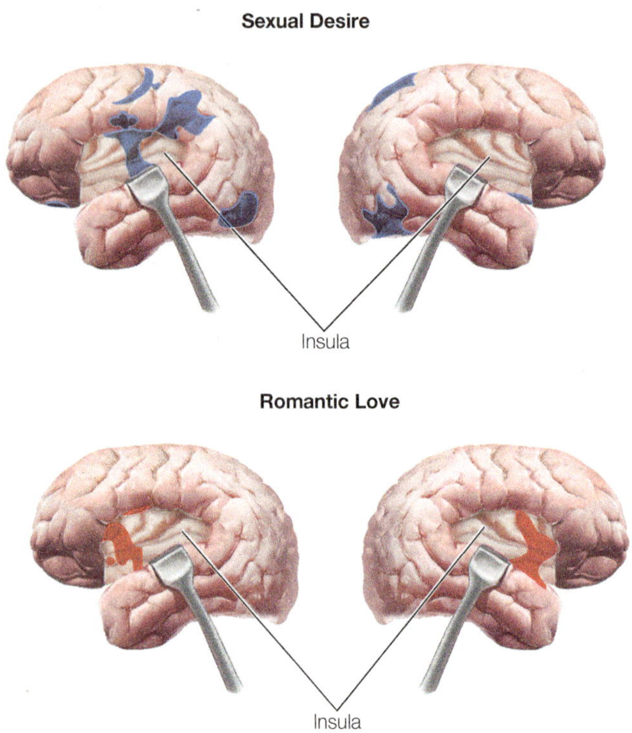

FIGURE **4.29**

Brain Areas Associated with Sexual Desire and Romantic Love. Areas shown in blue are uniquely active during sexual desire, while areas shown in red are uniquely active during romantic love. One of the areas where activity reliably varies between the states of sexual desire and romantic love is the insula. Activity in the posterior insula (toward the back of the brain) is associated with sexual desire, while activity in the anterior insula (toward the front of the brain) is associated with romantic love.

FOR MANY PEOPLE, love and lust seem close together. Using the biological perspective, however, these two states look related yet distinct.

On a neurochemical level, sexual desire or lust is driven primarily by levels of testosterone for males and levels of estrogens for females (Cappelletti & Wallen, 2016), while the bonding we associate with romantic love is largely associated with oxytocin (Diamond, 2004). This suggests that, at least on a hormonal level, it is possible to differentiate the two states.

Further understanding of the relationship between lust and love comes from brain imaging research. Of particular interest is the insula, an area of cortex lining the lateral sulcus, which separates the temporal lobes from the frontal and parietal lobes. Pulling the temporal lobe away from the rest of the brain reveals the insula within the sulcus. As shown in Figure 4.28, researchers found that activation of the posterior (back) part of the insula is more closely associated with lust (Cacioppo et al., 2012). In contrast, these same researchers found that activation of the anterior or forward part of the insula is more associated with romantic feelings. They conclude that passionate/romantic "love grows out of and is a more abstract representation of the pleasant sensorimotor experiences that characterize desire" (Cacioppo et al., 2012, p. 1048).

Additional support for the role of the anterior insula in love comes from a unique case study (Cacioppo et al., 2013). A male patient who had experienced damage to his anterior insula was asked to indicate whether a series of attractive individuals could be the object of his lust or his love. Compared to healthy control participants, the patient showed a selective deficit in his decisions about love yet performed normally on decisions about lust. The patient was similar to the controls in the number of people he categorized as objects of love or lust, and his response time to objects of lust appeared normal. However, his response time for categorizing objects of love was slower than that of the healthy controls.

Should we conclude that the anterior insula is a "love center" of the brain? It would be better to conclude, as Cacioppo et al. (2013) do, that the anterior insula participates in a larger network that helps us figure out internal states, which includes feelings of romantic love. ■

Psychology Takes on Real-World Problems

Social Distancing, Loneliness, and the Nervous System

FEELINGS OF SOCIAL ISOLATION are common among people practicing social distancing during a pandemic. These feelings initiate quite a few physical responses, including the changes in immune functioning described at the beginning of the chapter. These phenomena provide additional examples of how the way we think can influence our biology. Among the other responses to social isolation relevant to this chapter are changes in sympathetic nervous system activity and the activity of several brain areas and networks.

Being socially isolated for our ancestors also meant being more vulnerable to threats of many kinds. In this chapter, we have noted that the sympathetic nervous system participates in making our bodies ready for fight or flight in response to threat. As we'll see in Chapter 16, some of the long-term, negative consequences of stress result from too much activation in this system. Loneliness, however, produces a somewhat different response in the sympathetic nervous system (Cacioppo & Cacioppo, 2018a). Instead of a fight or flight reaction, loneliness is associated with a type of watchful anticipation of threat. While not as dramatic, this activity nonetheless might be associated with high blood pressure and other physical problems.

What happens in the lonely brain? In this chapter, we described the reward pathways of the brain, which support feelings of pleasure for everything from eating a delicious meal to having sex to gambling and drug addiction. As shown in Figure 4.29, when lonely and non-lonely individuals are exposed to pleasant pictures of people and objects, activity in their reward pathways differed (Cacioppo et al., 2014). Lonely people showed greater activity when viewing objects than people, whereas non-lonely people showed greater activity when viewing people than objects.

As we stated in Chapter 1, the goal of this section of each chapter is to think about real-world problems in ways that inform policy. An understanding of this important reciprocal relationship between nervous system activity and the perception of loneliness can help us emphasize to policy makers the importance of solving problems related to social isolation, not just for people's emotional well-being but for their health. ■

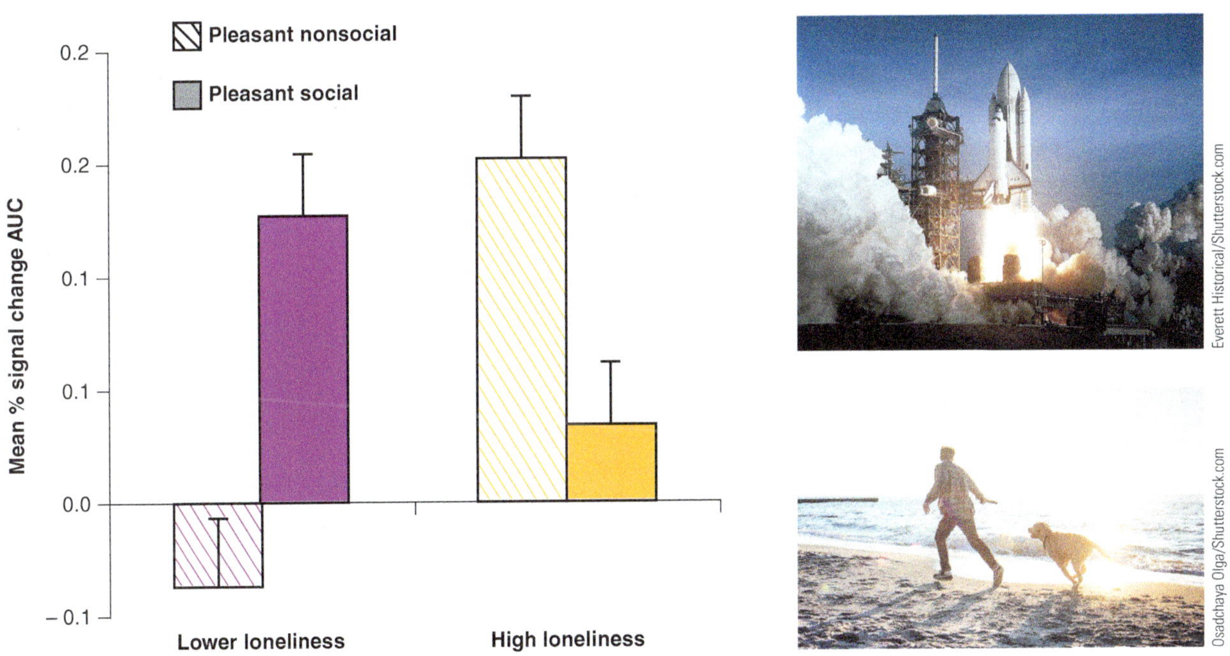

FIGURE **4.30**

Loneliness Changes Brain Responses to Pleasant Photos. When lonely and non-lonely individuals are exposed to pleasant pictures of people (e.g., man playing with dog) and objects (e.g., rocket launch), activity in their reward pathways differed. (AUC means "area under curve" and provides a measure of change in the brain's activity as shown in functional MRI).

of pain, results from the release of endorphins initiated by high levels of activity. Opioid drugs such as morphine, heroin, and oxycodone (OxyContin) produce their pain-relieving effects by mimicking the action of endorphins at the synapse. In other words, the opioid drugs are so similar in chemical structure to our natural endorphins that the receptors cannot tell them apart and treat the opioids as if they were natural endorphins.

SUMMARY 4.3 Neural Communication

	Structure	What to remember
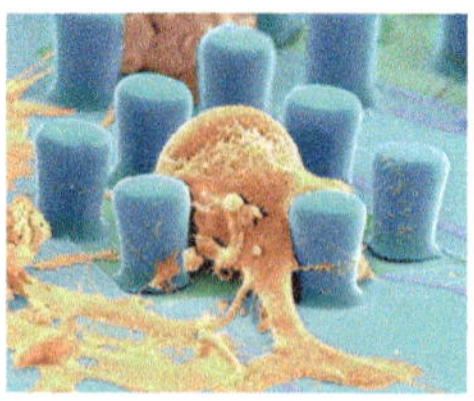	Neuron	• Cell body: contains the nucleus and carries out most housekeeping functions • Axon: Used to send information • Dendrite: Used to receive information
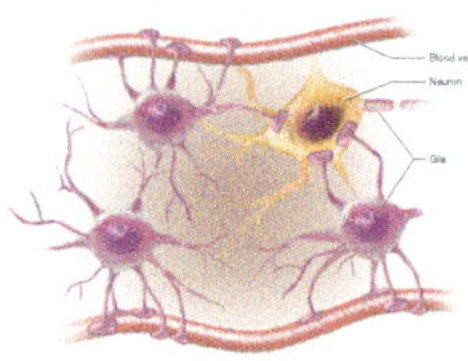	Glia	• Hold neurons in place • Clean up debris • Form myelin • Blood–brain barrier
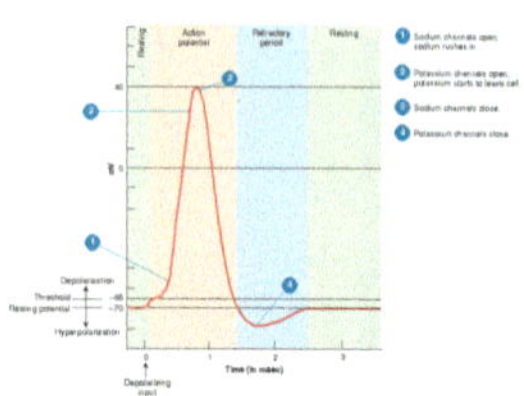	Action potentials	• Propagated down the axon to the terminal • Resting potential: No incoming signals • Action potential: Occurs when cell reaches threshold • Refractory period: Follows action potential
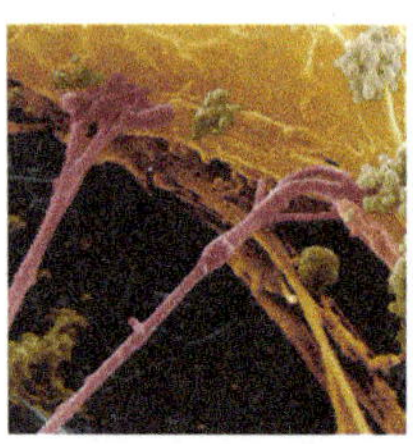	Synapse	• Point of communication between two neurons
	Neurotransmitters	• Released when an action potential arrives at a terminal • Interact with receptors in the receiving neuron's membrane • Deactivated if they remain in the synaptic gap • ACh • Norepinephrine • Dopamine • Serotonin • Endorphins

KEY TERMS The Language of Psychological Science

Be sure you can define these terms and use them correctly.

action potential, p. 137
amygdala, p. 117
autonomic nervous system, p. 129
axon, p. 134
basal ganglia, p. 116
brainstem, p. 114
cell body, p. 134
central nervous system (CNS), p. 110
cerebellum, p. 115
cerebral cortex, p. 118
cingulate cortex, p. 117
corpus callosum, p. 118
dendrite, p. 134
endocrine system, p. 132
enteric nervous system, p. 130
frontal lobe, p. 118
glia, p. 134
hippocampus, p. 117
hypothalamus, p. 117
medulla, p. 115
midbrain, p. 115
myelin, p. 135
neuron, p. 134
neurotransmitter, p. 141
nucleus accumbens, p. 118
occipital lobe, p. 119
orbitofrontal cortex, p. 122
parasympathetic nervous system, p. 130
parietal lobe, p. 118
peripheral nervous system (PNS), p. 111
pons, p. 115
prefrontal cortex, p. 121
receptor, p. 141
resting potential, p. 138
reticular formation, p. 116
reuptake, p. 141
somatic nervous system, p. 129
spinal cord, p. 111
sympathetic nervous system, p. 129
synapse, p. 141
temporal lobe, p. 119
thalamus, p. 116

The rods and cones in the retina begin the process of interpreting the light energy that enters the eye.

Argosy Publishing, Inc.

5

The Perceiving Mind

SENSATION AND PERCEPTION

LEARNING OBJECTIVES

1. Explain the basic concepts of sensation and perception, including transduction of stimuli into neural signals, distinctions between bottom-up and top-down perceptual processing, thresholds, and measurement.
2. Identify the process by which the physical structures of the eye transduce light waves into neural signals, producing the sense of vision.
3. Summarize the processes responsible for color vision, object recognition, and depth perception.
4. Describe the process by which physical structures of the ear transduce sound waves into neural signals, producing perception of pitch, loudness, and spatial location in hearing.
5. Explain the mechanisms by which the somatosensory and chemical sense systems produce perception of body position, touch, skin temperature, pain, smell, and taste.
6. Analyze the causes of various individual differences in perception, including development and culture, in terms of biology, experience, and their interaction.

WE LIKE TO THINK WE UNDERSTAND REALITY. After all, we can see, hear, touch, smell, and taste it. We don't live in some science fiction universe where things are not how they appear. Or do we?

The human eye can see many different colors, but what does it mean to "see" a color? Is color something that is a fixed quality of an object? Is the sky really blue? Is an apple really red? Or does the human mind construct these colors from the light reflected from these objects into the eye? Consider the image of the blue/black or white/gold dress that became an Internet sensation in February 2015. A friend of a Scottish bride posted the dress worn by the bride's mother on her Tumblr blog, leading to a discussion that engaged everyone from Justin Bieber to esteemed neuroscientists. Why do people see this photo so differently?

Neuroscientists disagree about why the dress produced such different responses. The *Journal of Vision* prepared an entire issue ("A Dress Rehearsal for Vision Science") devoted to explaining the dress phenomenon. A survey of 1,400 people found that 57% described the dress as blue/black (which is correct), 30% as white/gold, 11% as blue/brown, and 2% as something else (Lafer-Sousa et al., 2015). Older individuals and women were more likely to choose white/gold. These researchers believe that people choose dress colors based on their expectations regarding the lighting. If you think the dress is seen in daylight, you make different conclusions than if you think the dress is seen under artificial light.

Other scientists believe there is something special about the color blue due to our considerable experience with natural lighting (Winkler et al., 2015). Because indirect lighting and shadows are usually

Laura Freberg

"The Dress" became an Internet phenomenon as people debated its true colors. Do you see it as black and blue? White and gold? Something else?

Original Image

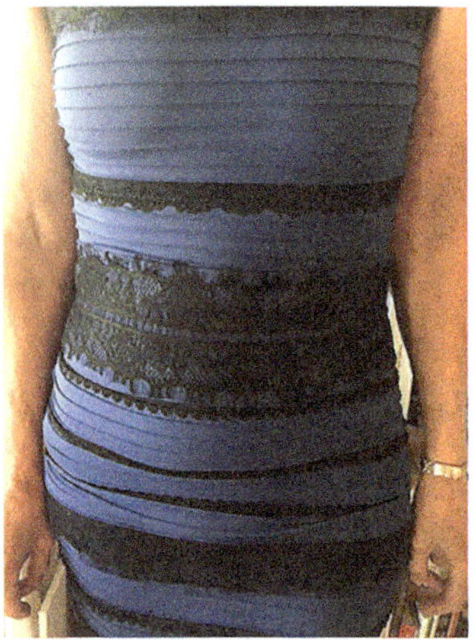

Tritanope Simulation

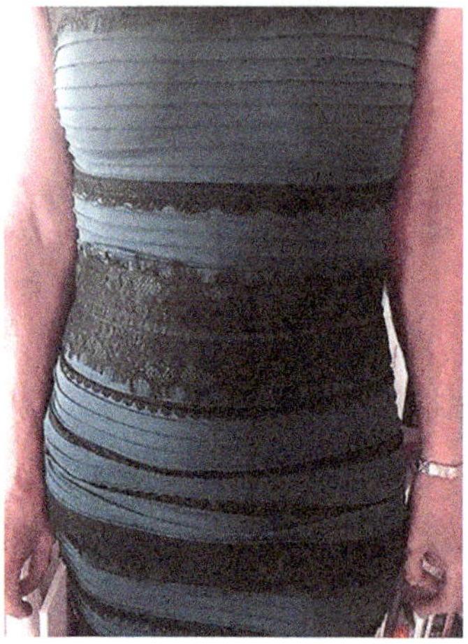

Laura Freberg

"Tritanopes" have a rare type of blue-yellow color vision deficiency. We can simulate how the mysterious dress would look to a tritanope. The differences are surprisingly subtle, which explains why we use the term "color vision deficiency" rather than "colorblindness." This example also reminds us that a single reality (the dress) can be sensed and perceived very differently by individual minds.

blue, participants are more likely to confuse blue objects with blue lighting. If you assume the light falling on the dress is somewhat blue, you will probably see it as white.

Would having a color vision deficiency change the way a person sees the dress? See for yourself. We can reconstruct how the image would look to a person with a rare type of blue-yellow color vision deficiency. Surprisingly, this has little effect, although the blue looks somewhat gray. Is the reality seen by a person with a color vision deficiency different from your reality? We're going to argue that it is not reality that changes but rather the way the brain views that reality.

As you'll see in this chapter, we construct models of reality from the information obtained through our senses. We like to think that we are aware of the world around us, and it is unsettling to realize that the world might be different from the representations of reality formed by the human mind. You will learn how the models built by the human mind have promoted our survival over many generations. Our models of reality are distinct from those built by the minds of other animals, whose survival depends on obtaining different types of information from their environments.

How Does Sensation Lead to Perception?

Our bodies are bombarded with information during wakefulness and sleep. This information takes many forms, from the electromagnetic energy of the sun to vibrations in the air to molecules dissolved in saliva on our tongues. The process of **sensation** brings information to the brain that arises in the reality outside our bodies, like a beautiful sunset, or originates from within, like an upset stomach.

Sensory systems have been shaped by natural selection, described in Chapter 3, to provide information that enhances survival within a particular niche. We sense a uniquely human reality, and one that is not shared by other animals. Your dog howls seconds before you hear the siren from an approaching ambulance because the dog's hearing is better than yours for high-pitched sounds. Horses bolt at the slightest provocation, but they may be reacting to the vibration of an approaching car or an animal that they sense through their front hooves, a source of information that is not available to the rider. Some animals sense light energy outside the human visible spectrum. Insects can see ultraviolet light, and some snakes use infrared energy to detect their prey.

Differences in sensation do occur from person to person, such as the need to wear corrective glasses or not, but they are relatively subtle. However, once we move from the process of sensation to that of **perception**, or the interpretation of sensory input, individual differences become more evident. For example, friends voting for different presidential candidates will come to different conclusions about who won a debate. Everyone watching the exchange sensed similar information, but each person's perceptions are unique.

sensation The process of detecting environmental stimuli or stimuli arising from the body.

perception The process of interpreting sensory information.

Sensory Information Travels to the Brain

Sensation begins with the interaction between a physical stimulus and our biological sensory systems. A stimulus is anything that elicits a reaction from our sensory systems. For example, we react to light energy that falls within our visual range, as we will see later in this chapter, but we cannot see light energy that falls outside that range, such as the microwaves that cook our dinner or the ultraviolet waves that harm our skin (see ● Figure 5.1).

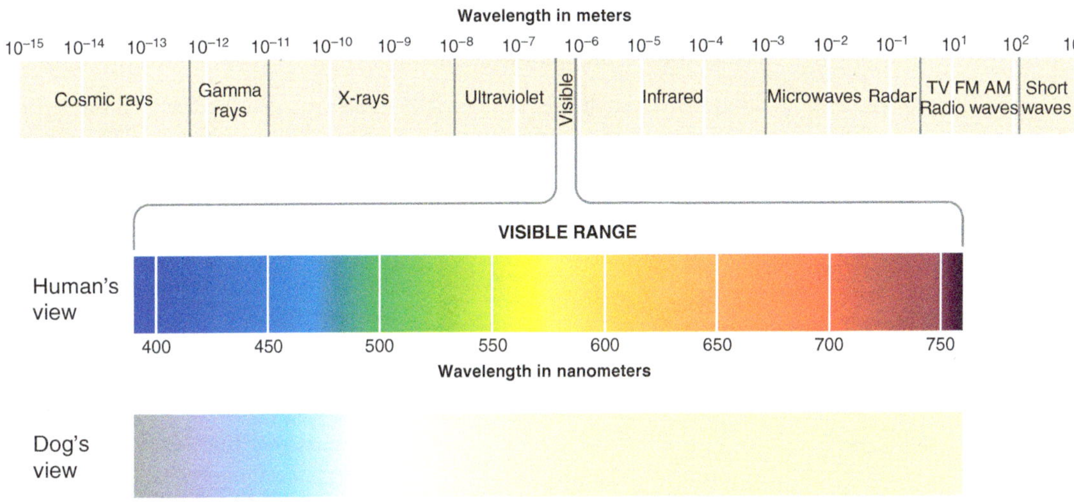

FIGURE **5.1**

All Species Experience an Adaptive Reality. Humans see only a small part of the electromagnetic energy emitted from the Sun. Some animals see even less. Dogs apparently do fine seeing blues, yellows, and grays, whereas humans have evolved to see a more colorful world. The dog's view of the world is simulated in the photo on the right.

Before you can use information from your senses, it must be translated into a form the nervous system can understand. This process of translation from stimulus to neural signal is known as **transduction**. You might think of sensory transduction as being similar to the processing of information by your computer. Modern computers transduce a variety of inputs, including voice, photos, keyboard, mouse clicks, and touch, into a programming language for further processing.

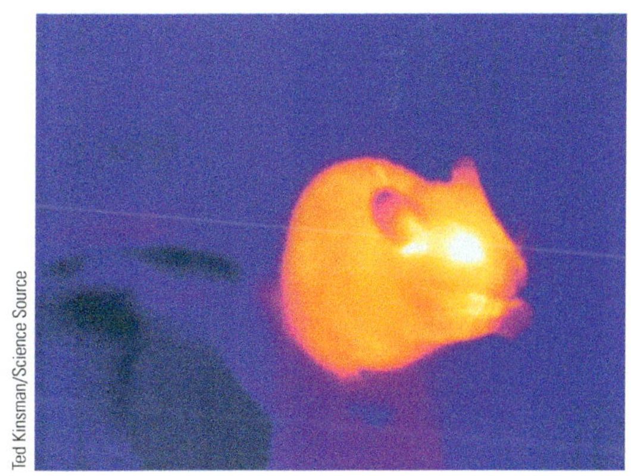

Some types of snakes (vipers, boas, and pythons) can locate prey by sensing infrared energy.

The Brain Constructs Perceptions From Sensory Information

Once information from the sensory systems has been transduced into neural signals and sent to the brain, the process of perception, or the interpretation of the sensory information, begins. Perception allows us to organize, recognize, and use the information provided by the senses.

An important gateway to perception is the process of attention, defined as a narrow focus of consciousness. As we discuss in Chapters 6, 9, and 10, attention often determines which features of the environment influence our subsequent thoughts and behaviors. Which stimuli are likely to grab our attention? Unfamiliar, changing, or high-intensity stimuli often affect our survival and have a high priority for our attention. Unfamiliar stimuli in our ancestors' environment might have meant a new source of danger (an unknown predator) or a new source of food (an unfamiliar fruit) that warranted additional investigation. Our sensory systems are particularly sensitive to change in the environment. Notice how you pay attention to the sound of your heating system

transduction The translation of incoming sensory information into neural signals.

sensory adaptation The tendency to pay less attention to a nonchanging source of stimulation.

bottom-up processing Perception based on building simple input into more complex perceptions.

top-down processing A perceptual process in which memory and other cognitive processes are required for interpreting incoming sensory information.

cycling on or off but pay little attention to the noise it makes while running. This reduced response to an unchanging stimulus is known as **sensory adaptation**. High-intensity stimuli, such as bright lights and loud noises, draw our attention because the situations that produce these stimuli, such as a nearby explosion, can have obvious consequences for our safety.

We rarely have the luxury of paying attention to any single stimulus. In most cases, we experience divided attention, in which we attempt to process multiple sources of sensory information. Students walk to class without getting run over by a car while texting. These divided attention abilities are limited. We simply cannot process all the information converging simultaneously on our sensory systems. To prioritize input, we use selective attention, or the ability to focus on a subset of available information and exclude the rest. These abilities may be disrupted in cases of attention deficit hyperactivity disorder (ADHD; Wimmer et al., 2015; also see Chapter 14).

If you think about the most memorable advertisements you have seen lately on television or online, it is likely that they share the features of attention-getting stimuli: novelty (we don't see talking geckos every day), change (rapid movement, use of changing colors, and the dreaded pop-up), and intensity (the sound is often louder than the program you're watching).

We refer to the brain's use of incoming signals to construct perceptions as **bottom-up processing**. For example, we construct our visual reality from information about light that is sent from the eye to the brain. However, the brain also imposes a structure on the incoming information, a type of processing known as top-down. In **top-down processing**, we use knowledge gained from prior experience with stimuli to perceive them. For example, a skilled reader has no trouble reading the following sentences, even though the words are jumbled:

All you hvae to do to mkae a snetnece raedalbe is to mkae srue taht the fisrt and lsat letrtes of ecah wrod saty the smae. Wtih prcatcie, tihs porcses becoems mcuh fsater and esaeir.

AP Images/Roberto Pfeil

We have all had the experience of watching events with others (sensation) and then being shocked by the different interpretations we hear of what just happened (perception).

How can we explain our ability to read these sentences? First, we require bottom-up processing to bring the sensations of the letter shapes to our brain. From there, however, we use knowledge and experience to recognize individual words. Many students have learned the hard way that term papers must be proofread carefully. As in our example, if the brain expects to see a particular word, you are likely to see that word, even if it is misspelled, a

metamorworks/Shutterstock.com

Divided attention abilities are limited. Some people believe that heads-up displays for cars assist drivers with divided attention, while others believe the displays are too distracting.

mistake that is unlikely to be made by the literal, bottom-up processing of a computer spell-checker.

Can we predict when the mind will use bottom-up or top-down processing? There are no hard and fast rules. Obviously, we always use bottom-up processing, or the information would not be perceived. It is possible that bottom-up processing alone allows us to respond appropriately to simple stimuli, like indicating whether you saw a flash of light, or stimuli that are unfamiliar to us. As stimuli become more complicated or familiar, like reading a sentence or recognizing a friend in a crowd, we are more likely to engage in top-down processing in addition to bottom-up processing.

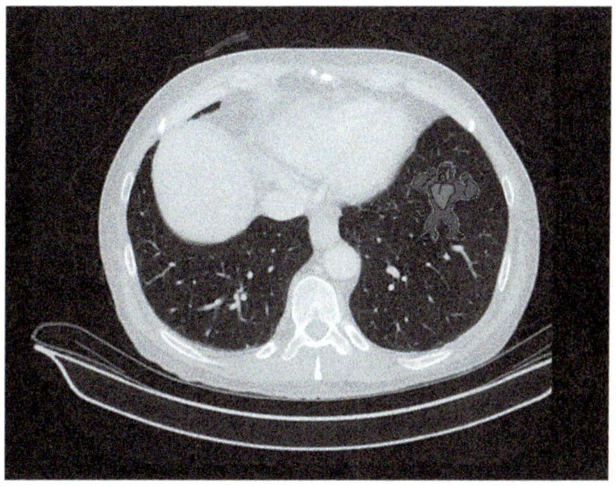

skyhawk x/Shutterstock.com

Selective attention, or our focus on a subset of input, prioritizes incoming information. However, we can sometimes be so focused that we miss important information. An astonishing 20 out of 24 expert radiologists completely missed the image of a gorilla superimposed on scans of lungs while scanning for signs of cancer. *Source*: T. Drew et al. (2013). "The Invisible Gorilla Strikes Again: Sustained Inattentional Blindness in Expert Observers," *Psychological Science*, *24*(9), 1848–1853, doi: 10.1177/0956797613479386

Measuring Perception Gustav Fechner (1801–1887) developed methods, which he called **psychophysics**, for studying the relationships between stimuli (the physics part) and perception of those stimuli (the psyche or mind part) (see Figure 5.2). Fechner's careful methods not only contributed to the establishment of psychology as a true science but are still used in research today.

The methods of psychophysics allow us to establish the limits of awareness, or thresholds, for each of our sensory systems. The smallest possible stimulus that can be detected at least 50% of the time is known as the **absolute threshold**. Under ideal circumstances, our senses are surprisingly sensitive (see Figure 5.3). For example, you can see the equivalent of a candle flame 30 miles (about 48 kilometers) away on a moonless night. We can also establish a **difference threshold**, or the smallest difference between two stimuli that can be detected at least 50% of the time. The amount of difference that can be detected depends on the size of the stimuli being compared. As stimuli get larger, differences must also become larger to be detected by an observer.

psychophysics The study of relationships between the physical qualities of stimuli and the subjective responses they produce.

absolute threshold The smallest amount of stimulus that can be detected.

difference threshold The smallest detectable difference between two stimuli.

Signal Detection Many perceptions involve some uncertainty. Perhaps you think you recognize the person coming toward you on the sidewalk. Do you wave right away? Or do you wait until the person is close enough that you know for sure it's your friend? How do your personal feelings about making mistakes affect your decision? How embarrassed would you be if you waved at a stranger?

This type of decision making can have serious implications, such as in the case of decisions made by radiologists examining the results of mammograms for signs of cancer or by intelligence officers assessing the possibility of an attack. Is there reason for concern or not?

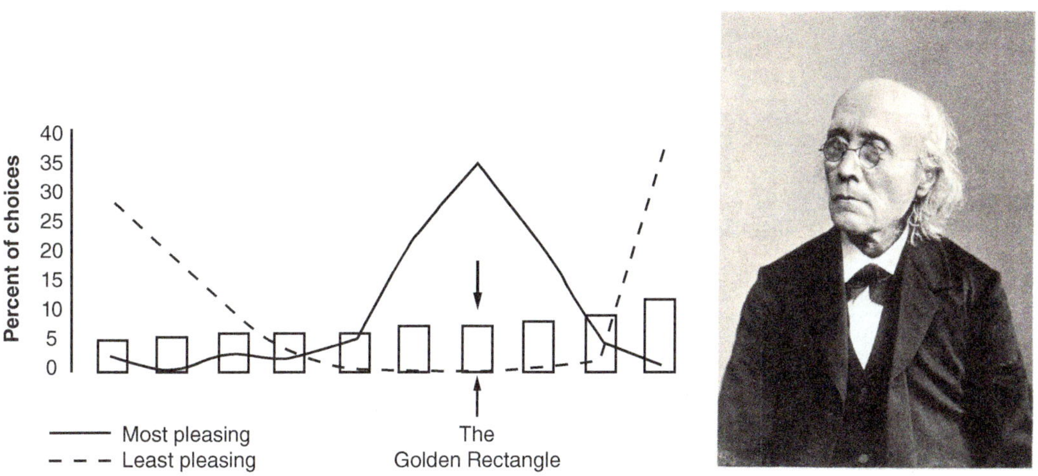

Photo Researchers, Inc/Alamy Stock Photo

FIGURE **5.2**

Connecting the Physical World and the Mind. "Golden" rectangles, named for their proportions rather than color, appear in art and architecture dating back to ancient Greece, but why are they attractive? Gustav Fechner (1801–1887) made many attempts to link physical realities with human psychological responses. He asked people to choose which rectangles are most pleasing or least pleasing. His results indicated that the most pleasing rectangle was fourth from the right. This rectangle is the closest to having golden proportions (1:1.618). Its sides have a ratio of 13:21.

FIGURE 5.3

Absolute Sensory Thresholds. An absolute threshold is the smallest amount of sensation that can be processed by our sensory systems under ideal conditions. Moving from left to right in this image, we see that the absolute threshold for touch is the equivalent of feeling the wing of a fly fall on your cheek from a distance of 0.4 inches (about 1 centimeter), the absolute threshold for olfaction is a drop of perfume in the air filling a six-room apartment, the absolute threshold for sweetness is the equivalent of one teaspoon (about 5 grams) of sugar in two gallons (about 7.5 liters) of water (the absolute threshold for bitter tastes is even more sensitive), the absolute threshold for hearing is the equivalent of the sound of a mosquito 10 feet (about 3 meters) away, and the absolute threshold for vision is seeing a candle flame 30 miles (about 48 kilometers) away on a dark, clear night.

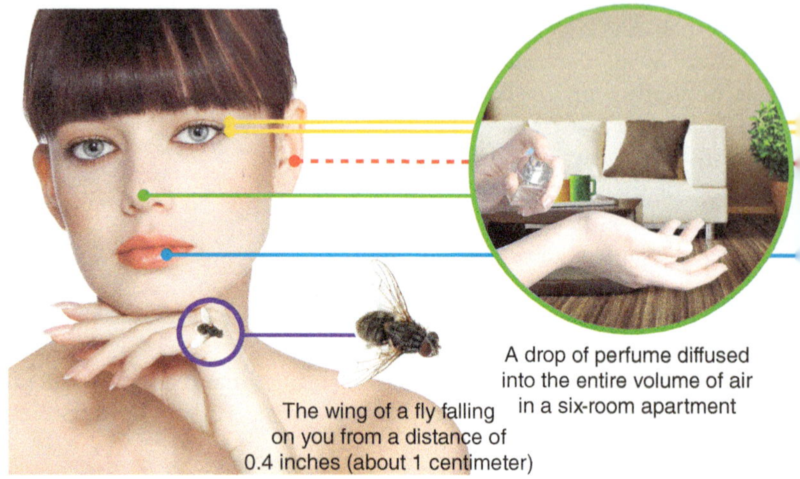

Photos, left to right: Gladskikh Tatiana/Shutterstock.com; Kuttelvaserova Stuchelova/Shutterstock.com; Christopher Elwell/Shutterstock.com; AlexRoz/Shutterstock.com.

signal detection The analysis of sensory and decision-making processes in the detection of faint, uncertain stimuli.

This situation is different from the thresholds described earlier because it adds the cognitive process of decision making to the process of sensation. In other words, **signal detection** is a two-step process involving (a) the actual intensity of the stimulus, which influences the observer's belief that the stimulus did occur, and (b) the individual observer's criteria for deciding whether the stimulus occurred.

Another example of signal detection is a jury's decision about whether a person is guilty. Based on frequently uncertain and conflicting evidence, jurors must weigh their concerns about convicting an innocent person (false alarm) or letting a real criminal go (miss).

Experiments on signal detection provide insight into this type of decision making. In these experiments, trials with a single, faint stimulus and trials with no stimulus are presented randomly. The participant states whether a stimulus was present on each trial. The possible outcomes of this experiment are shown in Table 5.1. In the case of reading mammograms, we can use such experiments to help us understand why two people might respond differently, even if they were sensing the same information. Ideally, a radiologist would identify 100% of all tumors without any false alarms, but mammograms are not that easy to evaluate. A radiologist afraid of missing a tumor might identify anything that looks remotely like a tumor as the basis for more testing. Few cases of cancer would be missed (high hit rate), but many healthy patients would go through unnecessary procedures (high false alarm rate). In contrast, another radiologist might need a higher level of certainty about the presence of a tumor before asking for further tests. This would reduce the number of false alarms, but it would also run a higher risk of overlooking tumors (high miss rate).

YURI CORTEZ/AFP/Getty Images/Newscom

According to Fechner's work on the difference threshold, British Olympian Zoe Smith would be more likely to notice the difference between 1 and 2 kilogram (about 2- and 4-pound) dumbbells than the difference between her new record of 121 kilograms (266.76 pounds) in the clean and jerk event and the former record of 120 kilograms (264.56 pounds).

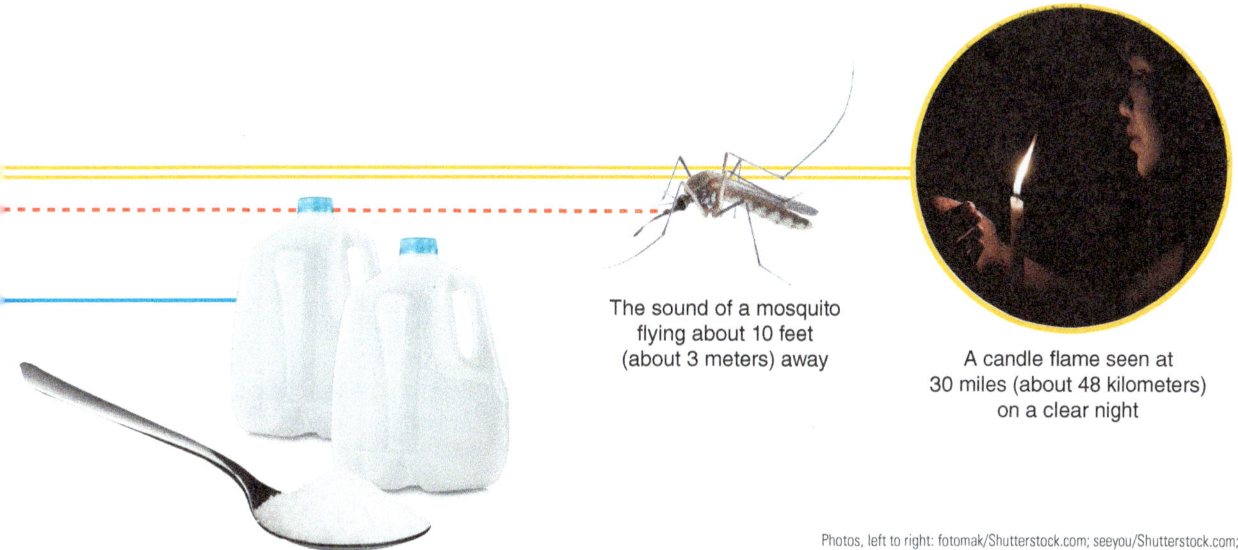

The sound of a mosquito flying about 10 feet (about 3 meters) away

A candle flame seen at 30 miles (about 48 kilometers) on a clear night

A teaspoon of sugar (about 5 grams) in two gallons (about 7.5 liters) of water

Photos, left to right: fotomak/Shutterstock.com; seeyou/Shutterstock.com; taedong/Shutterstock.com; Karen H. Ilagan/Shutterstock.com.

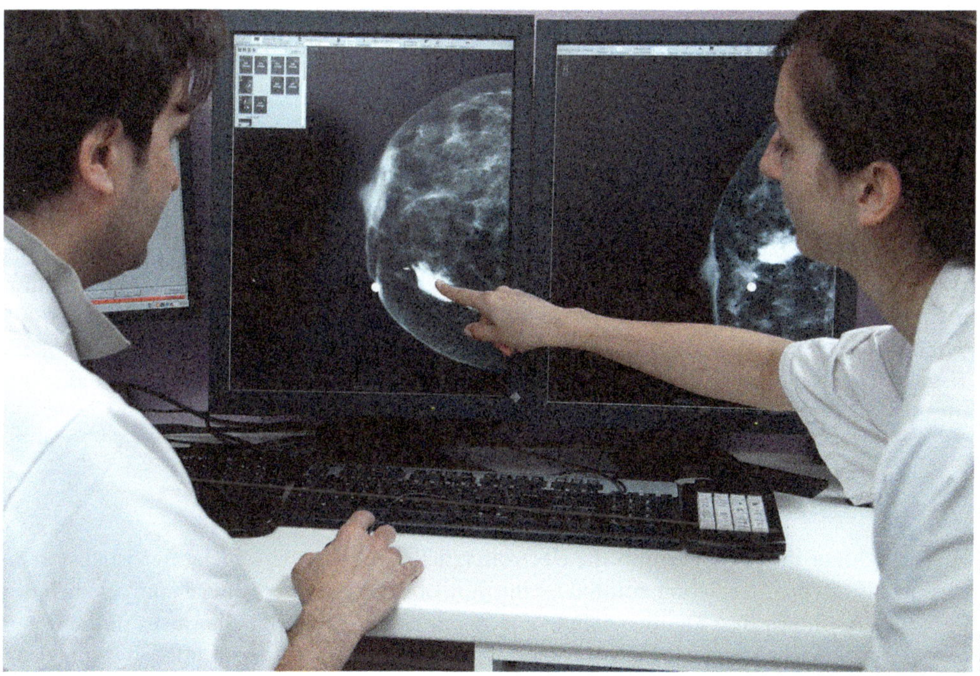

BSIP/Contributor/Universal Images Group/Getty Images

Does this mammogram indicate the woman has cancer or not? Many decisions we make are based on ambiguous stimuli. Signal detection theory helps us understand how an individual doctor balances the risks of missing a cancer and those of alarming a healthy patient.

TABLE 5.1

Possible Outcomes in Signal Detection

Participant Response	Stimulus Present	Stimulus Absent
Yes	Hit	False alarm
No	Miss	Correct rejection

SUMMARY 5.1 Assessing Perception

Concept	Definition	Example
Absolute threshold 	The smallest amount of stimulation that is detectable.	Seeing light from a candle flame 30 miles away on a dark night.
Difference threshold 	The smallest difference between two stimuli that can be detected.	Being able to detect the difference between two different weights.
Signal detection 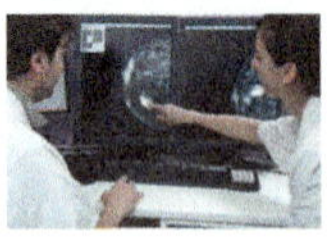	Correctly identifying when a faint stimulus is or is not present.	A radiologist correctly detecting cancer from a mammogram.

Credits: Top row—Karen H. Ilagan/Shutterstock.com; Second row—YURI CORTEZ/AFP/Getty Images/Newscom; Bottom row—BSIP/Contributor/Universal Images Group/Getty Images.

vision The sense that allows us to process reflected light.

How Do We See?

Vision, the processing of light reflected from objects, is one of the most important sensory systems in humans. Approximately 50% of our cerebral cortex processes visual information, in comparison to only 3% for hearing and 11% for touch and pain (Kandel & Wurtz, 2000; Sereno & Tootell, 2005). We will begin our exploration of vision with a description of the visual stimulus, and then we will follow the processing of that stimulus by the mind into a meaningful perception.

The Visual Stimulus

Visible light, or the energy within the electromagnetic spectrum to which our visual systems respond, is a type of radiation emitted by the Sun, other stars, and artificial sources such as a lightbulb. As shown in ● Figure 5.4, light energy moves in waves, like the waves in the ocean. Wavelength, or the distance between successive peaks of waves, is decoded by our visual system as color or shades of gray. The height, or amplitude, of the waves is translated by the visual system into brightness. Large-amplitude waves appear bright, and low-amplitude waves appear dim.

The human visual world involves only a small part of this light spectrum (review Figure 5.1). Gamma rays, x-rays, ultraviolet rays, infrared rays, microwaves, and radio waves lie outside the capacities of the human eye.

FIGURE **5.4**

Light Travels in Waves. The distance between two peaks in a light wave (wavelength) is decoded by the visual system as color and the height, or amplitude, of the wave as brightness.

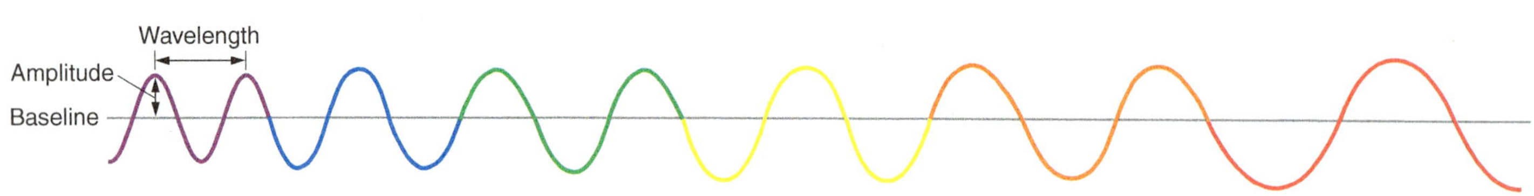

The Biology of Vision

Human vision begins with the eye. The eye is roughly sphere shaped and about the size of a ping-pong ball. Its hard outer covering helps the fluid-filled eyeball retain its shape. Toward the front of the eye, the outer covering becomes clear and forms the **cornea**. The cornea begins the process of bending light to form an image on the back of the eye. Traveling light next enters the **pupil**, which is actually an opening formed by the muscles of the **iris** (see ● Figure 5.5). The iris, which means "rainbow" in Greek, adjusts the opening of the pupil in response to the amount of light present in the environment and to signals from the autonomic nervous system, described in Chapter 4. Arousal is associated with dilated pupils, while relaxation is associated with more constricted pupils.

Directly behind the pupil and iris is the main optical instrument of the eye, the **lens**. Muscles attached to the lens can change its shape, allowing us to accommodate, or adjust our focus to see near or distant objects. Behind the lens is the main chamber of the eye, and located on the rear surface of this chamber is the **retina**, a thin but complex network of neurons specialized for the processing of light.

Located in the deepest layer of the retina are specialized receptors, the rods and cones, that transduce the light information. However, before light reaches these receptors, it must pass through layers of blood vessels and neurons. We normally do not see the blood vessels and neural layers because of sensory adaptation. As we mentioned previously in this chapter, adaptation occurs when sensory systems tune out stimuli that never change. Because the blood vessels and neural layers are always in the same place, we see them only under unusual circumstances, such as during certain ophthalmology (eye) tests.

cornea The clear surface at the front of the eye that begins the process of directing light to the retina.

pupil An opening formed by the iris.

iris The brightly colored circular muscle surrounding the pupil of the eye.

lens The clear structure behind the pupil that bends light toward the retina.

retina Layers of visual processing cells in the back of the eye.

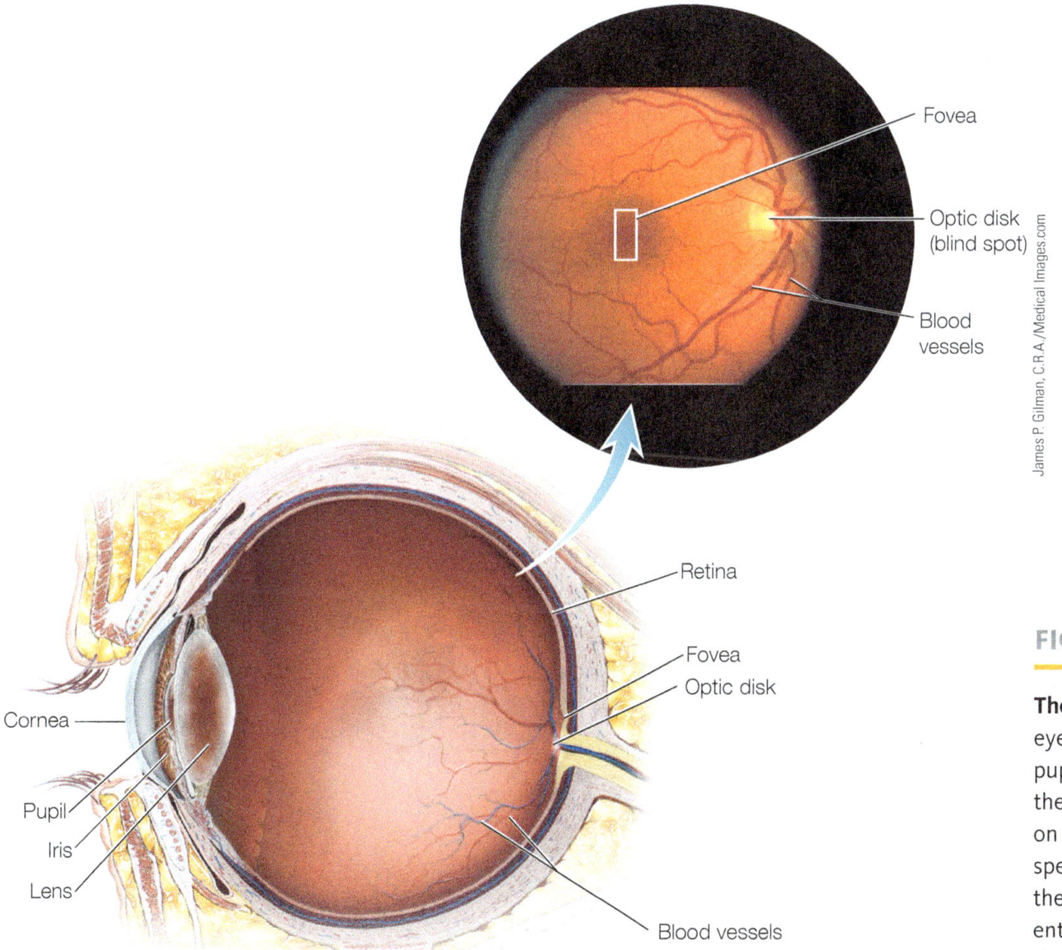

FIGURE 5.5

The Human Eye. Light entering the eye travels through the cornea, the pupil, and the lens before reaching the retina. Among the landmarks on the retina are the fovea, which is specialized for seeing fine detail, and the optic disk, where blood vessels enter the eye and the optic nerve exits the eye.

Source: Argosy Publishing, Inc.

FIGURE 5.6

Now You See It—Now You Don't. There are no photoreceptors in the optic disk, producing a blind spot in each eye. We do not see our blind spots with both eyes open because our brain fills in the hole. You can demonstrate your blind spot by holding your textbook at arm's length, closing one eye, focusing your other eye on the dot, and moving the book toward you until the stack of money disappears.

We can identify several landmarks on the surface of the retina. The blood vessels serving the eye and the axons that leave the retina to form the optic nerve exit at the optic disk. Because there are no rods and cones in the optic disk, each eye has a blind spot. Normally, we are unaware of our blind spots because perception fills in the missing details. However, if you follow the directions in ● Figure 5.6, you should be able to experience your own blind spot. Toward the middle of the retina is the **fovea**, which is specialized for seeing fine detail. When we stare directly at an object, the image of that object is projected onto the fovea. The fovea is responsible for central vision, as opposed to peripheral vision, which is the ability to see objects off to the side while looking straight ahead.

The image projected on the retina is upside down and reversed relative to the actual orientation of the object being viewed (see ● Figure 5.7). You can duplicate this process by looking at both sides of a shiny spoon. In the convex (or outwardly curving) side, you see your image normally. In the concave (or inwardly curving) side, you see your image as your retina sees it. Fortunately, the visual system easily decodes this image and provides realistic perceptions of the actual orientations of objects.

FIGURE 5.7

What the Retina "Sees." The image projected on the retina is upside down and reversed, but the brain is able to interpret the image to perceive the correct orientation of an object.
Source: Argosy Publishing, Inc.

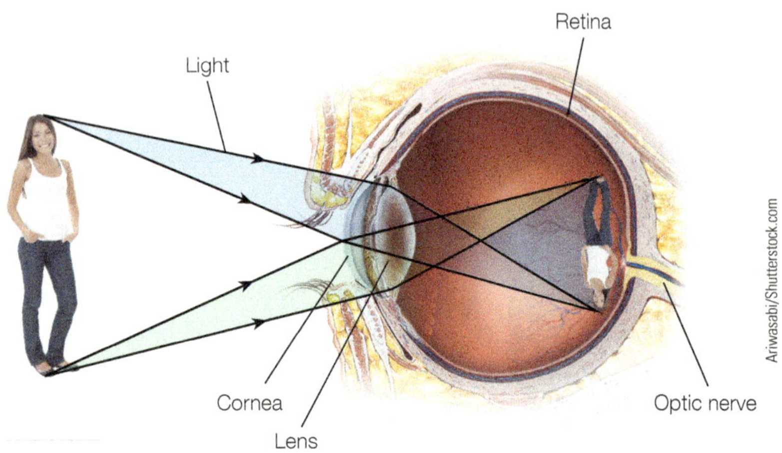

fovea An area of the retina that is specialized for highly detailed vision.

rod A photoreceptor specialized to detect dim light.

cone A photoreceptor in the retina that processes color and fine detail.

Photoreceptors

The human retina contains three types of photoreceptors: rods, cones, and a group of specialized ganglion cells that respond to brightness. **Rods** and **cones** are named after their shapes. Each human eye contains over 110 million rods and about 6 million cones. There are only about 50,000 of the specialized ganglion cells.

These photoreceptors are responsible for different aspects of vision. Rods are more sensitive to light than cones, and they excel at seeing dim light. As we observed previously, under ideal circumstances, the absolute threshold for human vision is the equivalent of a single candle flame from a distance of 30 miles (about 48 kilometers; see Hecht et al., 1942). Rods become more common as we move from the fovea to the periphery of the retina, so your peripheral vision does a better job of viewing dim light than your central vision does (see ● Figure 5.8). Before the development of night goggles, soldiers patrolling in the dark were trained to look to the side of a suspected enemy position rather than directly at their target.

FIGURE 5.8

Distribution of Rods and Cones Across the Retina. In humans, cones, indicated by red, blue, and green dots, become less frequent as you move from the fovea to the periphery of the retina. The colors of the dots representing cones indicate the colors to which each shows a maximum response (see Figure 5.11). Rods (light brown dots) and cones are named according to their shapes.
Source: Argosy Publishing, Inc.

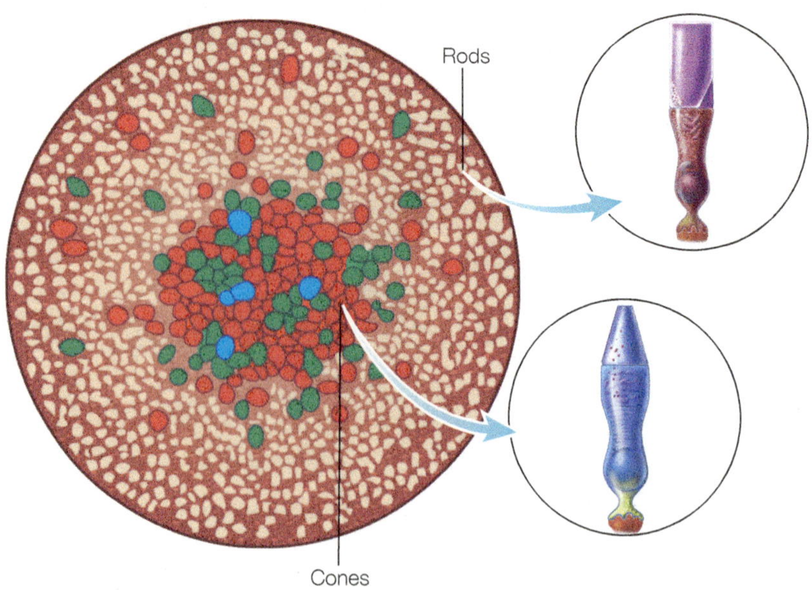

This extraordinary sensitivity of rods has costs. Rods do not provide information about color, nor do they provide clear, sharp images. Under starlight, normal human vision is 20/200 rather than the normal daylight 20/20. In other words, an object seen at night from a distance of 20 feet would have the same clarity as an object seen in bright sunlight from a distance of 200 feet. Cones function best under bright light and provide the ability to see both sharp images and color.

The observation that animals lacking rods and cones still showed some visual responses led to the search for additional photoreceptors in the retina. A special class of ganglion cells in the retina turned out to be important for setting our biological clocks (see Chapter 6), maintaining pupil reflexes, and assessing the brightness of a visual stimulus (Yamakawa et al., 2019).

Visual Pathways When rods and cones absorb light, they trigger responses in four additional layers of neurons within the retina. Axons from the final layer of cells, the ganglion cells, leave the back of the eye to form the **optic nerve**. The optic nerves cross the midline at the optic chiasm (named after its X shape, or the Greek letter *chi*). At the optic chiasm, the axons closest to the nose cross over to the other hemisphere, while the axons to the outside proceed to the same hemisphere. This partial crossing means that if you focus straight ahead, everything to the left of center in the visual field is processed by the right hemisphere, while everything to the right of center is processed by the left hemisphere. This organization provides us with significant advantages when sensing depth, which we discuss later in the chapter.

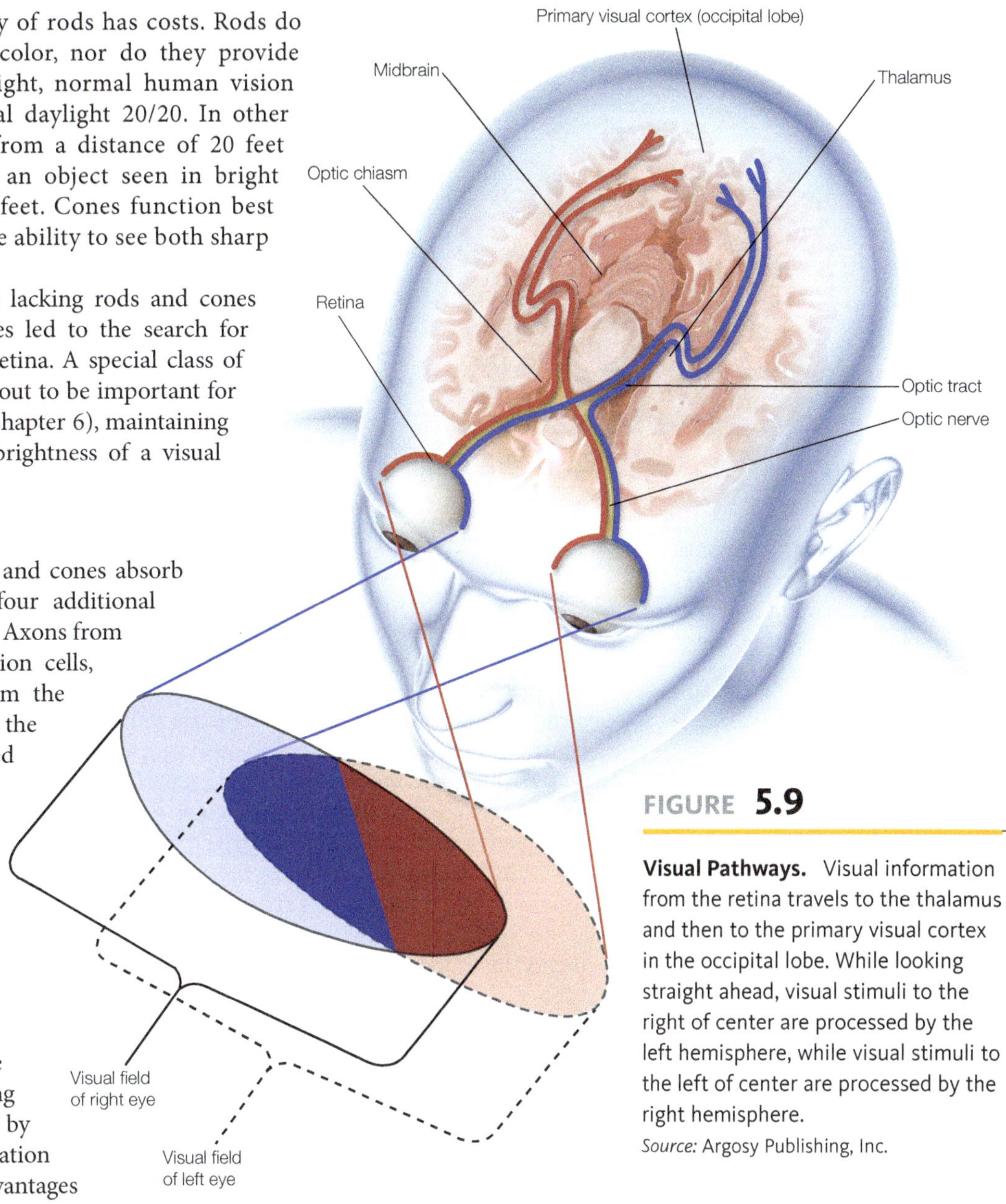

FIGURE **5.9**

Visual Pathways. Visual information from the retina travels to the thalamus and then to the primary visual cortex in the occipital lobe. While looking straight ahead, visual stimuli to the right of center are processed by the left hemisphere, while visual stimuli to the left of center are processed by the right hemisphere.

Source: Argosy Publishing, Inc.

Beyond the optic chiasm, the visual pathways are known as **optic tracts** (see Figure 5.9). About 90% of the axons in the optic tracts synapse in the thalamus. The thalamus sends information about vision to the amygdala and the primary visual cortex in the occipital lobe. The amygdala uses visual information to make quick emotional judgments, especially about potentially harmful stimuli. The remaining optic tract fibers connect with the hypothalamus, where their input provides information about light needed to regulate sleep-wake cycles, discussed in Chapter 6, or with the superior colliculi of the midbrain, which manage a number of visually guided reflexes, such as changing the size of the pupil in response to light conditions.

The primary visual cortex begins, but by no means finishes, the processing of visual input. The primary visual cortex responds to object shape, location, movement, and color (Hubel & Wiesel, 1959; Livingstone & Hubel, 1984; Hubel & Livingstone, 1987). Two major pathways radiating from the occipital cortex into the adjacent temporal and parietal lobes continue the analysis of visual input. The parietal pathway helps us process movement in the visual environment. The temporal pathway responds to shape and color and contributes to our ability to recognize objects and faces.

optic nerve The nerve exiting the retina of the eye.

optic tracts Nerve pathways traveling from the optic chiasm to the thalamus, hypothalamus, and midbrain.

FIGURE **5.10**

Mixing Colored Lights. The primary colors of paint might be red, yellow, and blue, but in the world of light, the primary colors are red, green, and blue. Mixed together, they produce white.

Visual Perception and Cognition

To see something requires the brain to interpret the information gathered by the eyes. How do you know your sweater is red or green, based on the information sent from the retina to the brain? How do you recognize your grandmother at your front door?

Color Vision Most of us think about colors in terms of the paints and crayons we used in elementary school. Any kindergartner can tell you that mixtures of red and yellow make orange, red and blue make purple, and yellow and blue make green. Mixing them all together produces a lovely muddy brown. Colored lights, however, work somewhat differently (see ● Figure 5.10). The primary colors of light are red, green, and blue, and mixing them together produces white light, like sunlight. If you have ever adjusted the color on your computer monitor or television, you know that these devices also use red, green, and blue as primary colors. Observations supporting the existence of three primary colors of light gave rise to a **trichromatic theory** of color vision.

Trichromatic theory is consistent with the existence of three types of cones in the retina that respond best to short (blue), medium (green), or long (red) wavelengths. Our ultimate experience of color comes not from the response of one type of cone but from comparisons among the responses of all three types of cones (see ● Figure 5.11).

Color vision deficiency occurs when a person has fewer than the typical three types of cones. We no longer use the term *colorblind*, as this is not accurate. Most people with color vision deficiencies see color differently than someone with all three cone types. Very rarely, individuals have either one type of cone or none. To these people, the world appears to be black, white, and gray.

Trichromatic theory does a good job of explaining color vision deficiency, but it is less successful in accounting for other color vision phenomena, such as color afterimages. For example, if you stare at the yellow, green, and black flag in ● Figure 5.12 and then focus on the dot within the white rectangle to the right, you will see an afterimage of the American flag in its more traditional colors of red, white, and blue.

An **opponent process theory** of color vision does a better job than the trichromatic theory in explaining these color afterimages. This theory proposes the existence of color

trichromatic theory A theory of color vision based on the existence of different types of cones for the detection of short, medium, and long wavelengths.

opponent process theory A theory of color vision that suggests we have a red–green color channel and a blue–yellow color channel in which activation of one color in each pair inhibits the other color.

FIGURE **5.11**

Responses by Cones to Colored Light. Our perception of color results from a comparison of the responses of the red, green, and blue cones to light. A 580-nanometer light is perceived as yellow and produces a strong response in green cones, a moderate response in red cones, and little response in blue cones.

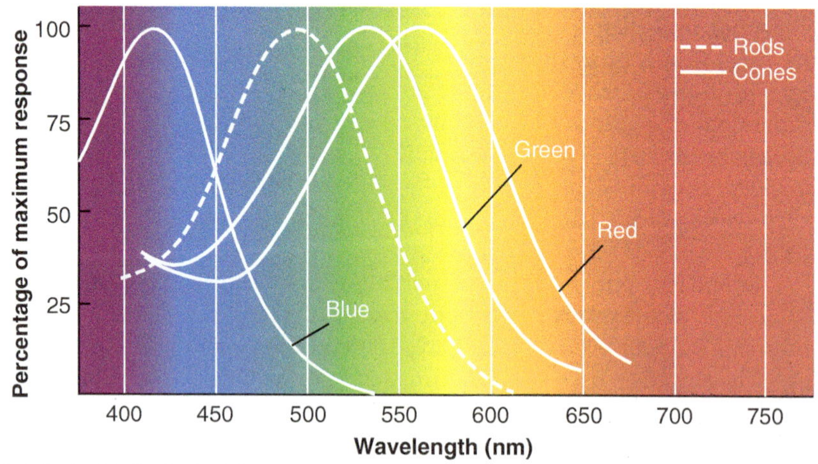

FIGURE **5.12**

Afterimages Demonstrate Opponent Process Theory. If you stare at the dot in the center of the yellow, green, and black flag for a minute and then shift your gaze to the dot in the white space on the right, you should see the flag in its traditional red, white, and blue.

channels: a red–green channel and a blue–yellow channel. We cannot see a color like reddish green or bluish yellow because the two colors share the same channel. The channels are "opponent" or competing. Activity in one color group in a channel inhibits activity in the other color group.

Returning to our green, yellow, and black flag, how can we use opponent process theory to explain our experience of the red, white, and blue afterimage? By staring at the flag, you fatigue some of your visual neurons. Because the color channels compete, reducing activity in one color group in a channel, such as green, increases activity in the other group, which is red. Fatiguing green, black, and yellow causes a rebound effect in each color channel, and your afterimage looks red, white, and blue. (Black and white also share a channel.) If you stare at an image of a real red, white, and blue flag and then look at a white piece of paper, your afterimage looks like our green, black, and yellow illustration.

Which of these two theories of color vision, trichromatic theory or opponent process theory, is correct? The trichromatic theory provides a helpful framework for the functioning of the three types of cones in the retina. However, as we move from the retina to higher levels of visual analysis, the opponent process theory seems to fit observed phenomena neatly. Both theories help us understand color vision but at different levels of the visual system.

Dan Tuffs/Contributor/Getty Images Entertainment/Getty Images

Monty Roberts, known as the Horse Whisperer, attributes his abilities to observe horse behavior to his complete lack of color vision. This condition is quite rare, occurring in only 1 person out of every 30,000.

PSYCHOLOGY AS A HUB SCIENCE

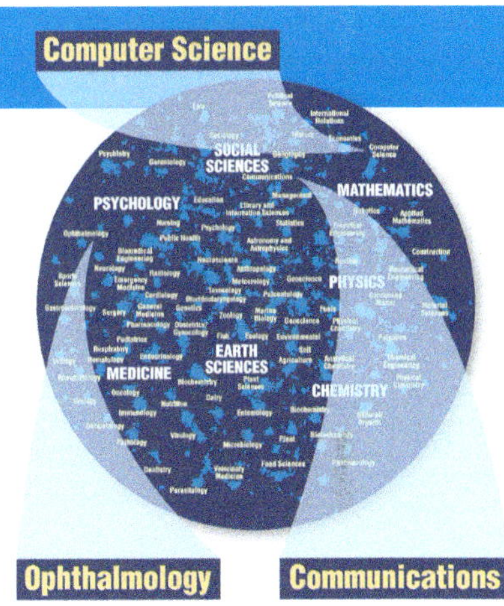

Color and Accessible Web Design

NOW THAT YOU HAVE AN UNDERSTANDING of color perception, we can consider one of the practical problems associated with individual differences in color vision. Between 7% and 10% of males and about 0.4% of females have a form of red–green color vision deficiency (see ● Figure 5.13). Males are more affected than females because the genes for the pigments used by red and green cones are located on the X chromosome, making red–green color deficiency a sex-linked condition (see Chapter 3). Smaller numbers of people lack blue cones (0.0011%) or cones altogether (0.00001%). Given the frequency of color vision deficiency, making visual materials accessible to people with all types of color vision is a serious concern.

Color can be an effective tool for designing exciting and engaging websites, but many graphic web designers, who typically have excellent vision, fail to consider how the site might look to a person with a color vision deficiency. One clue for designing an accessible site can be found in other systems based on color, such as traffic lights. Although most of us rely on the color information from the red, yellow, or green lights, the lights also vary in location. In other words, color should never be the only basis for extracting meaning. A second major concern is contrast, which we discuss in the next section. The strong contrast between black letters on the white pages makes text easy to read for most people. Colored text against a colored background might add interest, but it runs the risk of being harder to read, especially when reds and greens are used. As shown in ● Figure 5.14, online resources simulate how a web page looks to a person with color vision deficiency, which helps designers maximize accessibility. ■

PRISMA ARCHIVO/Alamy Stock Photo

FIGURE **5.13**

Detecting Color Vision Deficiency. The Ishihara Color Test, designed by Shinobu Ishihara in 1917, is a standard method for detecting color vision deficiency. The test is printed on special paper, so the recreated image here would not be considered a valid basis for diagnosing color deficiency.

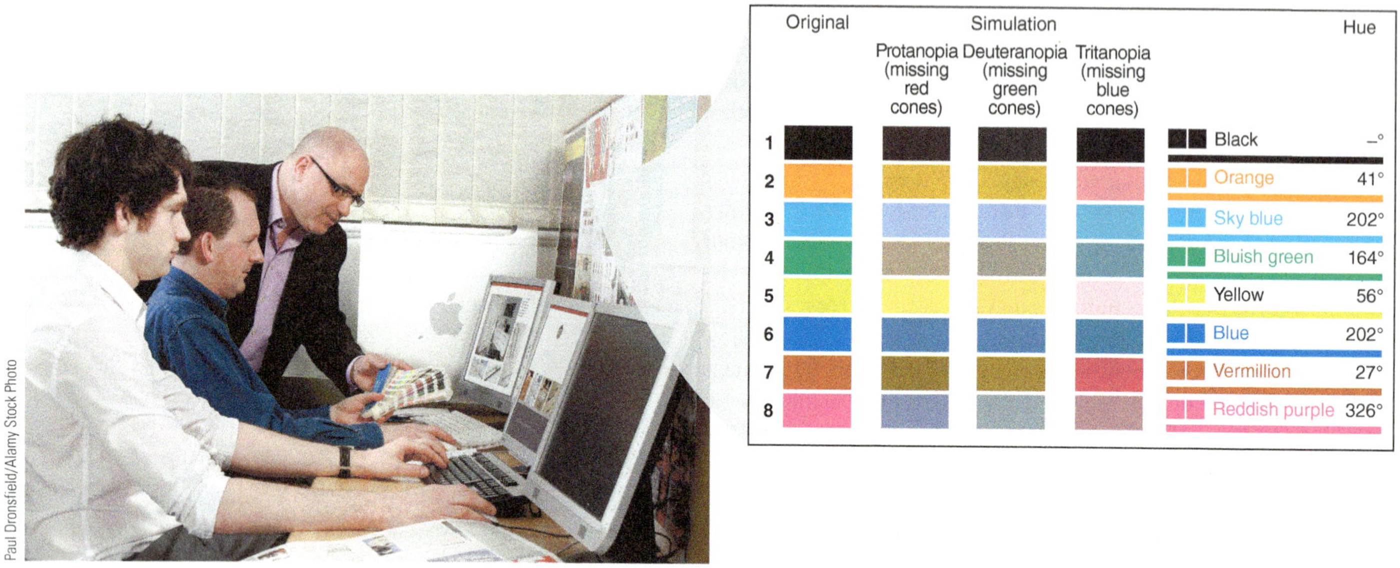

FIGURE **5.14**

Making Websites Accessible. Web designers have found colors that work for people with typical color vision and people who have color vision deficiency. This set of colors shows how different shades would be seen by people with typical vision and by people with three of the most common forms of color vision deficiency. Even though these colors are seen differently by the three groups, nobody mistakes one shade for another.

Recognizing Objects We asked earlier how your brain uses incoming visual signals to recognize your grandmother. A bottom-up approach assumes that as information moves from the retina to higher levels of visual processing, more complicated responses are built from simpler input. In this hierarchical model, the result would be a hypothetical "grandmother cell," or a single cell that could combine all previous input and processing to tell you that your grandmother is at the door.

Although the hierarchical model is attractive in many ways, it does not fit perfectly with what we know about the visual system. First, we would need a large number of single neurons to respond to all the objects and the events that we can recognize visually. In addition, the hierarchical model is unable to account for top-down processing. ● Figure 5.15a may appear to be a random pattern of black dots on a white background. ● Figure 5.15b may not appear to be a recognizable object at all. The sensations produced by these stimuli lead to no meaningful perceptions. However, once we tell you that the first image is a Dalmatian dog and the second image is a cow, you can instantly pick out their shapes. Now that you know what the images are, you will probably never see them again the way you did initially. Recognizing these objects requires knowledge and memory of what Dalmatians and cows look like. It is unlikely that a single cortical cell acting as a Dalmatian or cow detector could incorporate such complex inputs from memory.

If we don't use single cells to recognize objects, how can we accomplish this task? The visual system might perform a mathematical analysis of the visual field (De Valois & De Valois, 1980). While the hierarchical model implies a reality built out of individual bars and edges, the mathematical approach suggests that we analyze patterns of lines. The simplest

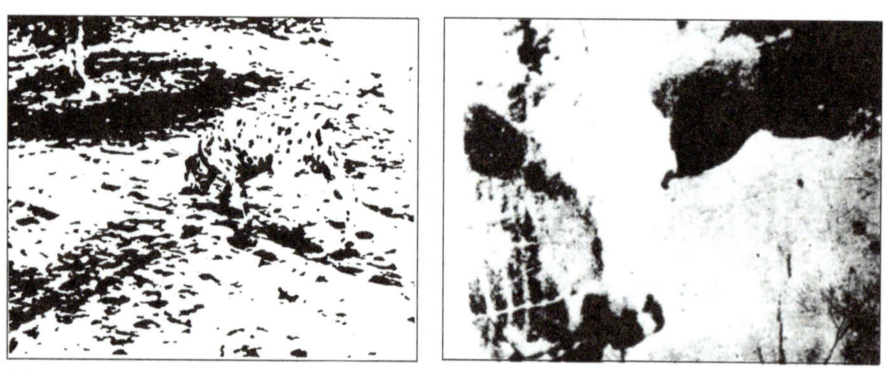

(a) (b)

FIGURE **5.15**

Can You Figure Out What These Images Are? (a) This might look like a splattering of black dots on a white page until you learn that it represents a Dalmatian dog. (b) Top-down processing ensures that once you know this is a photo of a cow, you can pick out its features easily.

From Richard L. Gregory (2005). "The Medawar Lecture 2001 Knowledge for Vision: Vision for Knowledge," *Philosophical Transactions of the Royal Society B, 360,* 1231–1251, by permission of the Royal Society. doi: 10.1098/rstb.2005.1662

From *American Journal of Psychology.* Copyright © 1951 by the Board of Trustees of the University of Illinois. Used with permission of the University of Illinois Press. K. M. Dallenbach (1951). "A Puzzle-Picture with a New Principle of Concealment," *64*(3) (July 1951), 431–433. doi: 10.2307/1419008 patterns of lines are gratings, as shown in ● Figure 5.16. Gratings can vary along two dimensions: frequency and contrast. High-frequency gratings have many bars in a given distance and provide fine detail, while low-frequency gratings have relatively few bars. High-contrast gratings have large differences in intensity between adjacent bars, like black next to white. The print you are reading in is an example of high contrast because the black letters are quite different from the white background. Low-contrast gratings have subtler differences in intensity between bars, such as dark gray next to black.

Observing responses to gratings gives us a window into the visual capacities of other species. At a certain point of contrast and frequency, gratings look plain gray. Animals can be trained to make a distinction between gratings and gray circles. For example, if a bird is rewarded with food for pecking at a disk with a grating but not for pecking a uniform gray disk, any performance that is better than 50-50, or chance, indicates that the bird can see the difference between the grating and the gray. We can graph the range of gratings that are visible to the observer as a function of their contrast and frequency. ● Figure 5.17 illustrates the visible ranges for human adults and cats. Compared to human adults, cats see less detail. However, cats see large (low-frequency), low-contrast objects better than humans do. Large, low-contrast shadows on the wall may get kitty's attention but not yours. You will think kitty is chasing ghosts again.

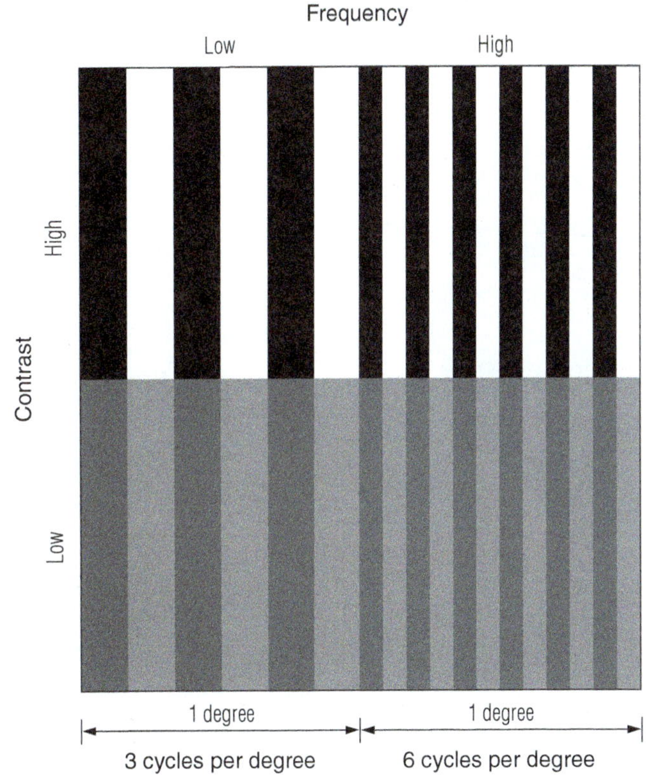

FIGURE 5.16

Features of Gratings. An alternative to the hierarchical model suggests that the visual system analyzes the visual environment as a collection of patterns, like these gratings. Gratings vary in frequency (number of bars in a given distance) and contrast (the difference in light intensity from one bar to the next).

Gestalt Psychology As we observed in Chapter 1, a group of German researchers known as the Gestalt psychologists tackled visual perception with a number of ingenious observations. These psychologists objected to efforts by Wilhelm Wundt and the structuralists to reduce human experience to its building blocks, or elements. Instead, the Gestalt psychologists argued that some experiences lose information and value when divided into parts. The main thesis of the Gestalt psychologists, as stated by Kurt Koffka, maintains, "It is more correct to say that the whole is something else than the sum of its parts" (Koffka, 1935, p. 176).

According to the Gestalt psychologists, we are born with built-in tendencies to organize incoming sensory information in certain ways. This natural ability to organize simplifies the problem of recognizing objects (Biederman, 1987). One organizing principle suggests that we spontaneously divide a scene into a main figure and ground. We frequently assume that the figure stands in front of most of the ground, and it seems to have more substance and shape. It is possible to construct ambiguous images, like the vase on the next page, in which the parts of the image seem to switch roles as figure or ground.

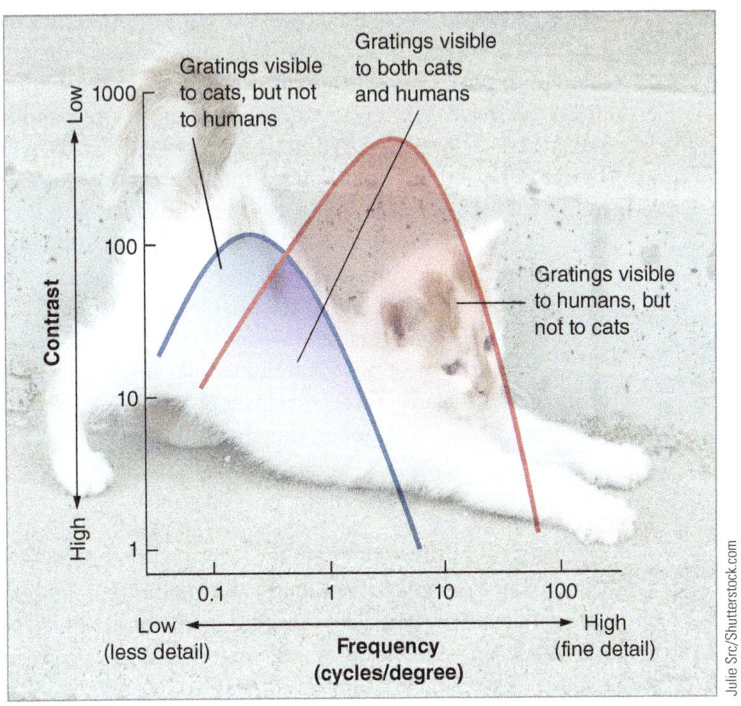

FIGURE 5.17

What Do Cats See? Using gratings, we get a window into the visual world of the cat. By comparing gratings to a uniform gray disk, we can learn when a grating with a certain contrast and frequency simply looks gray to humans or cats. We can see better detail than kitty, but she sees large shadows that we don't even notice.

SSPL/Science Museum / Art Resource, NY

The Gestalt psychologists believe we naturally see the difference between objects and their background, but this figure is designed to make us switch back and forth from the vase to the background faces. This vase was designed to commemorate an anniversary of Queen Elizabeth II of England (face on the right) and her husband, Prince Philip (face on the left).

A second Gestalt principle is proximity (see ● Figure 5.18). Objects that are close together tend to be grouped together. The dots that make up our Dalmatian in Figure 5.15a are close together, suggesting they belong to the same object. The principle of similarity states that similar stimuli are grouped together. On a close examination of the dog image, the dots that make up the dog are similar to one another and slightly different (more rounded perhaps) than the dots making up the remainder of the image.

The principle of continuity suggests that we assume that points that form smooth lines when connected probably belong together (see ● Figure 5.19). In our dog picture, continuity helps us see the border of the curb or sidewalk and the ring of shadow around the base of the tree. Continuity is perhaps a little less useful in identifying the dog, although we can pick out the lines forming the legs.

Closure occurs when people see a complete, unbroken image even when there are gaps in the lines forming the image (see ● Figure 5.20). We use this approach in viewing the dog in Figure 5.15a when we "fill in the blanks" formed by the white parts of its body.

Finally, the Gestalt psychologists believed in the principle of simplicity, which suggests that we will use the simplest solution to a perceptual problem. This principle may help explain the fun in pictures like that of our Dalmatian dog. It is simpler to assume that this is a random splash of black dots on white background. Finding a hidden picture within the dots is not the simplest solution, which may account for our surprise.

Recognizing Depth

An image projected onto the retina is two dimensional, as flat as the sheet of paper or screen on which these words appear. Somehow, the brain manages to construct a three-dimensional (3D) image from these data. Adelbert Ames constructed a room that was named in his honor, the Ames Room, which illustrated vulnerabilities in our **depth perception** (Ittleson, 1952). When viewed directly from the front, the room appears to be a rectangle. People within the room, shown in ● Figure 5.21, seem to be larger or smaller than normal. This distortion of perceived size results from the room's ability to confuse our judgment of distance.

To construct a 3D image, we use both **monocular cues** (one eye) and **binocular cues** (two eyes). Many monocular cues are found in paintings because the artists attempt to provide an illusion of depth in their two-dimensional pieces. The use of linear perspective, or the apparent convergence of parallel lines at the horizon, by Italian artists during the 15th century provided a realism unknown in earlier works. Linear perspective revolutionized the video game and movie industries, beginning humbly with Sega's *Zaxxon* in 1982 and advancing to the ever more realistic environments of *Halo*, Pixar's animated films, and the 2009 film *Avatar*. Other monocular cues include texture gradients and shading. We can see more texture in objects that are close to us, while the texture of distant objects is relatively blurry. Shading and the use of highlights can be used to suggest curved surfaces.

Among the most powerful monocular depth cues is occlusion, or the blocking of images of distant objects by closer objects. We also use relative size to judge the distance of objects, although this method requires you to be familiar with the real

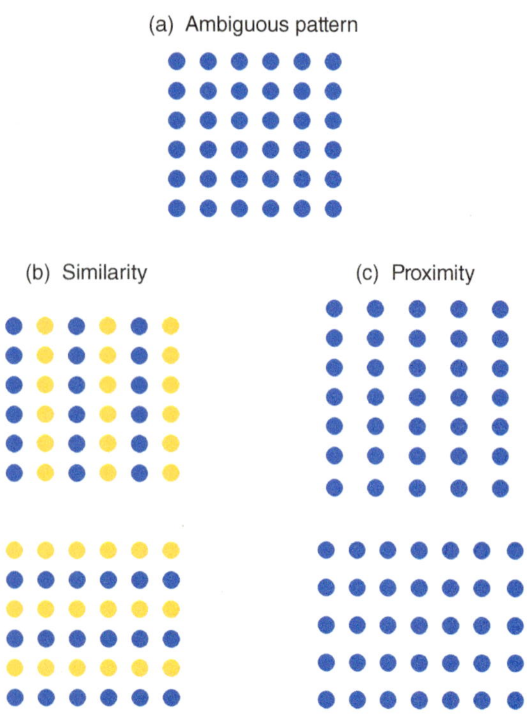

FIGURE **5.18**

The Gestalt Principles of Proximity and Similarity. The set of dots in (a) do not appear to have any particular relationship with one another, but when we color rows in (b), we suddenly see the dots in columns or rows. Moving two columns or rows slightly closer to each other in (c) makes us see the array differently too.

FIGURE **5.19**

The Gestalt Principle of Continuity. The Gestalt principle of continuity says that we perceive points forming a smooth line as belonging to the same object. If you follow this knot, you can see that it is formed by two objects, but our initial perception is of a single form.

size of an object. We know how big people are. When the retinal image of a person is small, we infer that the person is farther from us than when the retinal image of a person is larger.

Several illusions result from our use of monocular cues to judge depth. Relative size helps to explain the moon illusion. You may have noticed that the moon appears to be larger when it is just above the hills on the horizon than when it is straight overhead. The moon maintains a steady orbit 239,000 miles (385,000 km) above the Earth. How can we account for the discrepancy in its apparent size? When viewed overhead, the moon is seen without intervening objects, such as trees and hills, that might provide cues about its size and distance. However, when viewed near the horizon, we see the moon against a backdrop of familiar objects whose sizes we know well. We expect trees and hills to be smaller at the horizon than when they are close to us, and if we group the moon with those objects, we adjust its apparent size as well. The next time you are viewing the full moon as it rises over the hills, form a peephole with your hand, and you will see the moon in its normal small size. Although some researchers argue that atmospheric differences between the two viewpoints may contribute to the illusion, viewing the moon through your hand should demonstrate that most of the effect arises from your use of other objects to judge distance.

In the Müller–Lyer illusion, shown in Figure 5.22, we see the line with outward-pointing arrowheads as being farther from our position, even though the main lines project images of equal length on the retina. The Ponzo illusion, shown in Figure 5.23, confounds size and distance judgments in a similar fashion. The parallel lines signal depth, leading us to believe that the upper horizontal line is farther away than the lower line. If both lines project the same image on the retina, the more distant line must be longer.

So far, we have discussed monocular cues that involve a person and a scene that is not moving. The introduction of motion can heighten the impression of depth. As you ride in a car, focus your gaze at a distant point. The objects you pass will appear to be moving in the opposite direction of your car, with closer objects appearing to move faster than distant objects.

FIGURE **5.20**

The Gestalt Principle of Closure. Because of the principle of closure, we "fill in the blanks" to see a single object, the World Wildlife Fund logo, although it is made up of several objects.
Source: © 1986 Panda Symbol
WWF - World Wide Fund For Nature

depth perception The ability to use the two-dimensional image projected on the retina to perceive three dimensions.

monocular cue A depth cue that requires the use of only one eye.

binocular cue A depth cue that requires the use of both eyes.

FIGURE **5.21**

The Ames Room Tricks Our Depth Perception. Many distance cues, such as the apparently rectangular windows, conspire to make us believe that one person is much bigger than the other. The person on the right is actually much closer to us than the person on the left. The diagram shows the actual layout of the Ames Room.

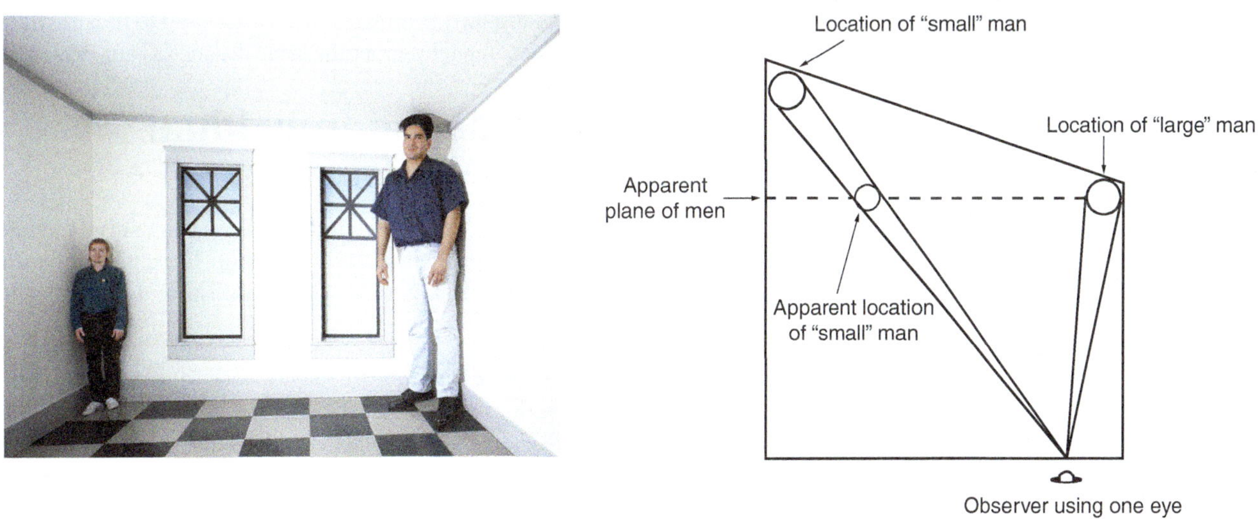

Field Museum Library/Contributor/PermiumArchive/Getty Images

FIGURE **5.22**

The Müller-Lyer Illusion. You might find it hard to believe that the two red vertical lines are actually the same length.

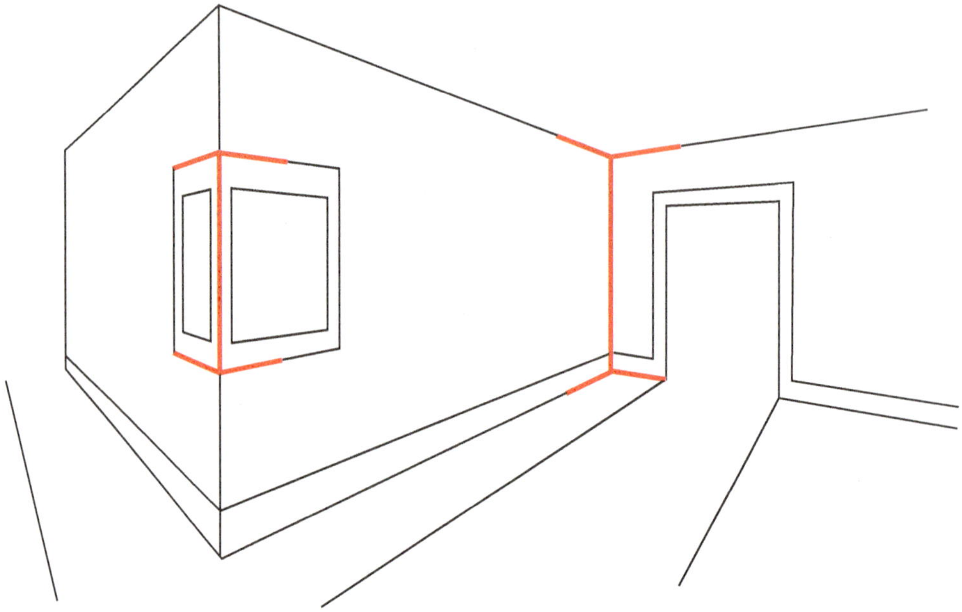

retinal disparity The difference between the images projected onto each eye.

FIGURE **5.23**

The Ponzo Illusion. We perceive depth because of linear perspective, which in turn make us see the upper horizontal bar as more distant than the lower bar. Even though they are the same length, the bar perceived as more distant looks longer.

Next, focus on a point about midway between you and the horizon. Now, the closer objects will continue to move in the opposite direction, but more distant objects appear to be traveling with you. This motion parallax has been used to enhance the 3D feeling in video games.

One of our most effective depth cues is **retinal disparity**. Because this cue requires the use of both eyes, we refer to retinal disparity as a binocular cue. Predator species, including ourselves, have eyes placed in the front of the head facing forward. As a result of this configuration, the visual scenes observed by the two eyes are different and overlapping, as shown in ● Figure 5.24. The differences between the images projected onto each eye are called disparities. These disparities do not tell us how far away an object is. Instead, they provide information about the relative distance between two objects in the visual field. As the distance between the objects increases, disparity increases. To illustrate the sensitivity of this system, you can identify an object as being 1 millimeter (about 0.04 inch) closer than another at a distance of 1 meter (about 3.3 feet) from your body, or a difference of 0.1% (Blake & Sekuler, 2006).

Why would this binocular depth system be an advantage to predators? Most prey species do an excellent job of hiding, often aided by an appearance that blends into the nearby environment. However, retinal disparity allows us to spot tiny variations in the depths of objects in the visual field. This might make an animal stand out against its background, even though it is well camouflaged. Retinal disparity has been used to identify camouflaged military equipment and counterfeit currency. Retinal disparity is imitated by cameras used to film 3D movies, which have two lenses separated by about the same distance as our two eyes.

Developmental and Individual Differences in Vision

Although human infants can't report what they see, we can take advantage of their longer gazing at patterns than at uniform stimuli, like a patch of a single color. This allows us to construct graphs of the contrasts and the frequencies

veryan dale/Alamy Stock Photo

Video games, such as Minecraft, incorporate many monocular cues to provide an experience of depth. The standard-sized blocks used to build structures in the game are separated by lines, which when placed in a row provide linear perspective. Texture gradients, shading, and relative size (players understand the size of the blocks well) also contribute to perceived depth.

YOSHIKAZU TSUNO/AFP/Getty Images/Newscom

The two lenses of 3D cameras are separated by about 2 inches (about 50 millimeters), mimicking the distance between two human eyes that makes retinal disparity possible.

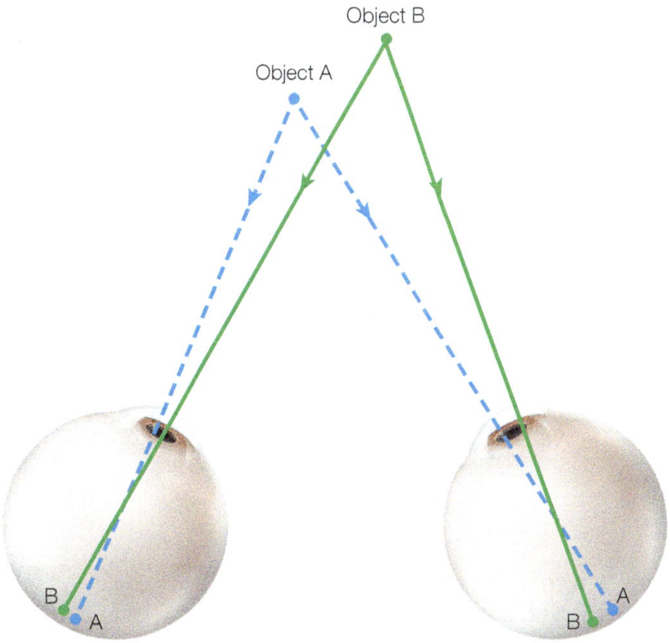

FIGURE **5.24**

Retinal Disparity. The right and left eyes see slightly overlapping versions of the visual scene in front of us. We can use the retinal disparity, or the discrepancy between the locations of where the two objects A and B are processed on the two retinas, as a sensitive depth cue that tells us which object is closer to us.

Source: Argosy Publishing, Inc.

to which children respond, similar to those we saw previously for cats. Based on these analyses, we know that human infants see everything human adults see but with less detail. To see well, the infant also needs more contrast than the adult. These findings help explain children's preferences for large, high-contrast objects.

The photographs shown below provide insight into the visual world of the infant. Frequencies that cannot be seen by the infant have been removed from each photograph. Other research shows that infants as young as 4 months not only show binocular disparity, but also show normal adult responses to color (Bornstein et al., 1976). Other depth cues discussed previously develop early too. Infants as young as 2 months understand occlusion (Johnson & Aslin, 1995), and the use of the relative size of objects to judge depth appears between the ages of 5 and 7 months (Granrud et al., 1985). Infants' abilities to perceive faces also develop quite rapidly, as 2-day-old newborns spend more time gazing at their mothers' faces than at a stranger's face (Bushnell, 2001; also see Chapter 11).

Predictable changes occur in other aspects of human vision as we grow older. Accommodation of the lens, which allows us to change focus from near to far objects, becomes slower beginning in middle adulthood. Older adults respond more slowly to changes in brightness, such as leaving a dark theater into the sunlight. The muscles of the iris lose their elasticity, so pupils remain smaller, further reducing vision by limiting the amount of light that enters the eye. The lens of the eye begins to yellow, which protects the eye from ultraviolet radiation but affects the perception of color.

At any age, individual differences shape what people see. In addition to the color vision deficiencies discussed previously, people differ in their abilities to see near and far objects.

We can filter out the frequencies and contrast that a baby cannot see to simulate what the world looks like to an infant.

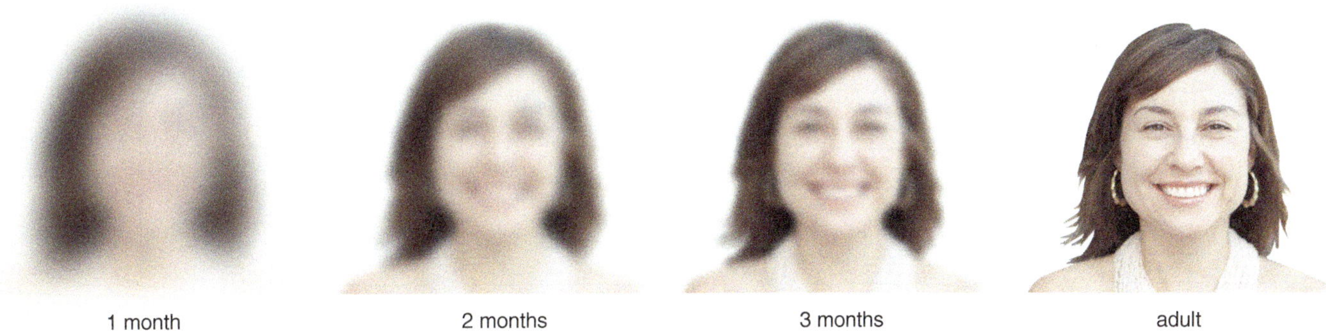

Felix Mizioznikov/Shutterstock.com

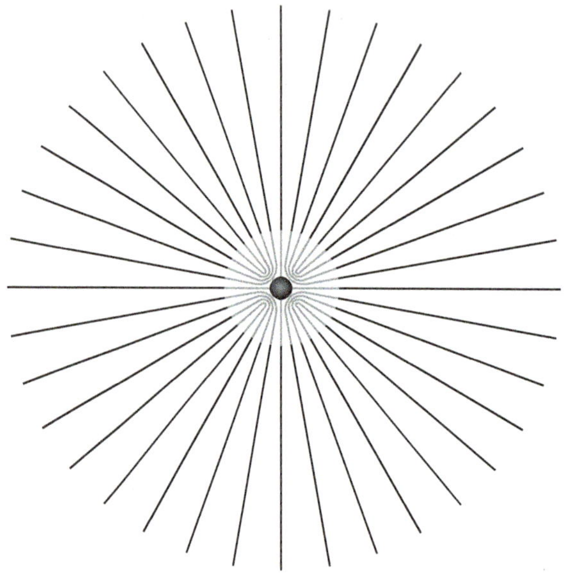

FIGURE **5.25**

Astigmatism. If you have astigmatism, which results from an uneven surface of your corneas, some spokes of this figure will appear darker than others.

Those who deviate from the average often wear corrective lenses or undergo laser surgery to reshape the cornea. The most common visual problems result from eyeball length, with elongated eyeballs interfering with a person's vision for distant objects (nearsightedness) and shortened eyeballs interfering with vision for close-up objects (farsightedness), as in reading. Vision is also affected by astigmatism, which means that the surface of the cornea is uneven. You can test yourself for astigmatism by looking at ● Figure 5.25.

CONNECTING TO RESEARCH

Do Children with Autism See the World Differently?

IN ADDITION TO DEFICITS in social skills and language (see Chapter 14), individuals with autism spectrum disorder (ASD) often demonstrate unusual responses to stimuli. In some cases, children seem to barely notice things, but in others, children seem to be hypersensitive to stimulation. Psychologists agree that diagnosing autism as early as possible leads to the best treatment outcomes. Identifying differences in sensation and perception at early ages might lead to better diagnoses (Gliga et al., 2015).

The Question: Do superior visual search skills predict autism?

METHODS

Eighty-two infants with older siblings diagnosed with ASD (high-risk) and 27 control infants with no relatives with ASD took part in a visual search task and measures of ASD risk (response to name, eye contact, social reciprocity, and imitation). Eye-tracking was used to measure the child's attending to the "odd" character within a visual array (● Figure 5.26). Children were assessed at 9 months, 15 months, and 2 years of age.

ETHICS

Children enjoy extra protection when they serve as research participants. Researchers must present parents with a thorough informed consent form, and great care must be taken to avoid coercion through rewards for participation. Procedures must be suited to the young participants to avoid fatigue. Parents whose children show evidence of risk for ASD should be referred to services.

RESULTS

Superior performance on the visual search task at 9 months was correlated with indicators of ASD symptoms at 15 months and 2 years of age.

CONCLUSIONS

Assessments of visual search might prove useful in identifying infants who may be diagnosed with autism spectrum disorder. The results also emphasize the role of attention and perception in the development of ASD. Previously, much research about ASD has focused on social deficits, but these might in fact emerge from more basic differences in information processing. ■

FIGURE **5.26**

Superior Visual Search in Autism. Eye-tracking showed that 9-month-old infants at risk for autism spectrum disorder (ASD) were able to find the "odd" character within each display faster than children at low risk for ASD. Performance on this visual search task predicted the severity of autism symptoms at the ages of 15 months and 2 years.

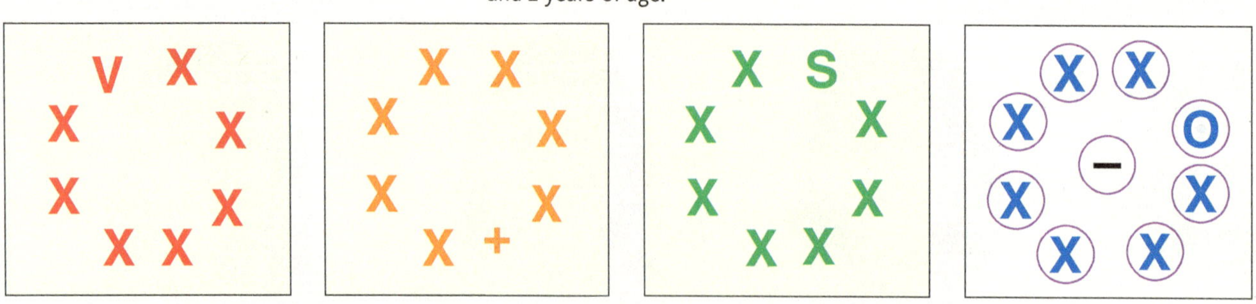

DIVERSE VOICES IN PSYCHOLOGY

Culture Shapes Eye Movements

PSYCHOLOGISTS HAVE DISCOVERED a number of differences in the ways that East Asians (e.g., people from China, Korea, and Japan) and European/North Americans process information. In general, people in Eastern cultures process information holistically, which means processing is based on context and relationships. In contrast, people in Western cultures process information analytically, focusing on salient objects and forming categories. To illustrate this difference, consider the following images (Chiu, 1972). Of the three images in each box, think about which go together, and ask yourself why you think this is correct. Children from East Asian cultures were most likely to group the woman shape with the baby shape and the cow with the grass, whereas children from Western cultures grouped the man and woman shape and the cow and chicken shape. The East Asian children reported grouping the woman and the baby together because the mother takes care of the baby (relationship), whereas the Western children grouped the man and woman together because they shared a category as adults. East Asian children grouped the cow and grass together (context: the cow eats grass), whereas the Western children grouped the chicken and cow together (both are animals). Further research demonstrated that all children begin by using holistic reasoning regardless of culture, but Western children begin to ignore context and focus more on objects beginning around the age of 5 years.

What possible aspects of culture might shape thinking in this way? It is possible that child-rearing practices, such as the emphasis on appropriate social behavior in East Asian cultures versus the emphasis on labeling objects in Western culture, could lead to a divergent emphasis on context or object.

The stimuli used by Chiu (1972) are complex, and the connections among them are even more so. What happens when we simplify the stimuli down to something like the length of a line? When participants are asked to find a long line among short and vice versa, North Americans found the first task easier while Japanese participants performed equally well in both cases (Ueda et al., 2018). It is difficult to explain these types of cultural differences using the analytic/holistic distinction. Instead, cultures can have influence over the way visual features are perceived very early in the visual process, possibly due to exposure to environmental factors such as written alphabets. These results do not rule out an analytic/holistic distinction in the processing of more complex stimuli. Instead, they suggest that culture can have multiple, complex influences on visual perception. ■

FIGURE **5.27a and b**

(a) Which Ones Go Together? Western children group the man and woman shapes and the cow and chicken shapes using categorical reasoning. East Asian children group the woman and baby shapes and the cow and grass together based on relationships and context.
(b) **Perception of Simple Stimuli.** American participants found the task on the left (finding the longer line) easier than the task on the right (finding the shorter line), but Japanese participants performed equally on the two tasks. This suggests that cultural differences in perception might begin at a very early stage of perceptual processing.
Source: from Ueda, Y., Chen, L., Kopecky, J., Cramer, E. S., Rensink, R. A., Meyer, D. E., . . . Saiki, J. (2018). "Cultural Differences in Visual Search for Geometric Figures." *Cognitive Science, 42*(1), 286-310. doi: 10.1111/cogs.12490

THINKING SCIENTIFICALLY

The Roger Shepard Parallelogram Illusion: "Turning the Tables"

ANYONE CAN TELL, simply by looking, whether two tabletops are the same shape, right? For instance, most people would agree that the shapes and sizes of the two tabletops depicted in Figure 5.28 are different. One tabletop appears to be rectangular, while the other appears to be more square. As much as our perceptions may tell us otherwise, these tabletops are identical.

What Am I Being Asked to Believe or Accept?

We are being asked to believe that two very different looking objects are not, in fact, different, and that our visual system is playing a trick on us.

What Evidence Supports This Position?

To verify that the tabletops are the same, use a ruler to measure the sides of each table.

Are There Other Ways This Evidence Could Be Interpreted?

Objective measurement confirms that the two tables are in fact identical, but in the absence of the ability to measure, we would probably judge them to be quite different.

What Other Evidence Would I Need to Evaluate These Alternatives?

It might be helpful to identify other instances in which we make similarly inaccurate judgments.

What Are the Most Reasonable Conclusions?

Roger Shepard combined a profound scientific curiosity with a love of mischief. Shepard developed a number of creative visual illusions, including "Turning the Tables," which he illustrated himself (Shepard, 1990). The visual illusion produced in this illustration results from our use of a visual system designed to cope with the three dimensions of the physical world on stimuli that have only two dimensions.

In Roger Shepard's words:

The drawings ... achieve their effects by means of various visual tricks. But to call them tricks is not to imply that they are without psychological significance. The tricks work by taking advantage of fundamental perceptual principles that have been shaped by natural selection in a three-dimensional world. Our ability to make pictures, which emerged only recently on an evolutionary time scale, enables us to present the eyes with visual patterns that systematically depart from the patterns that we and our ancestors experienced in nature. In considering the ways pictures can trick the eye, we can gain insight into the nature and ultimate source of the principles of visual perception. (Shepard, 1990, p. 121)

More generally, examples like this underscore the importance of relying on scientific investigation and evidence to unveil how sensation and perception work. ■

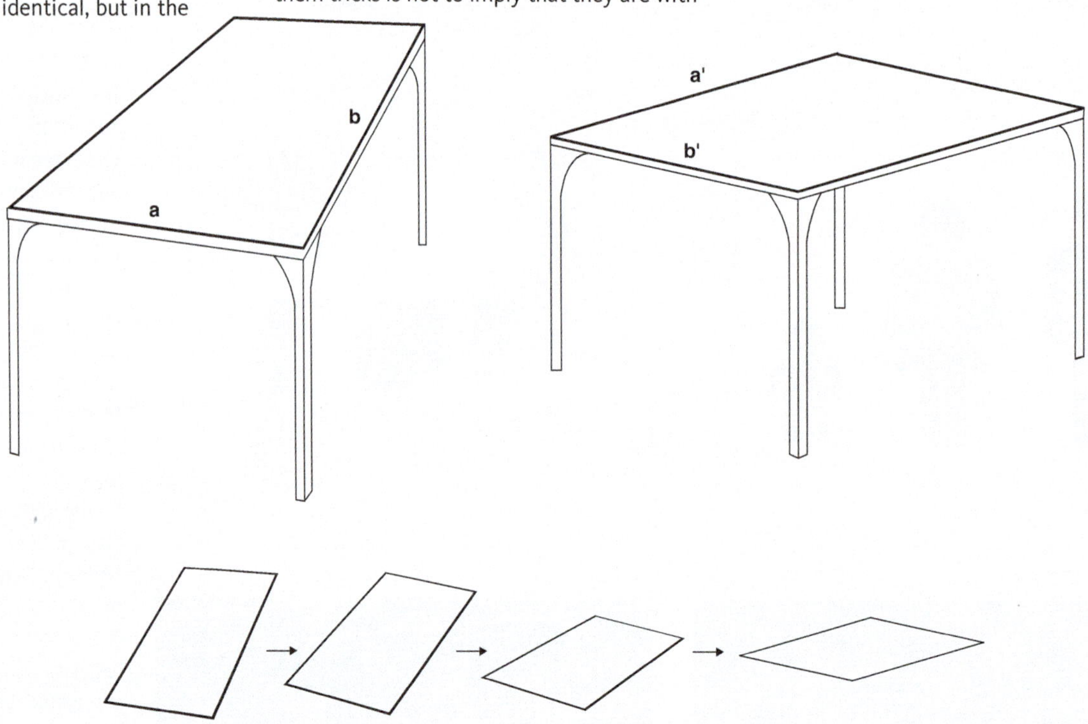

FIGURE 5.28

Are These Tables the Same or Different? You will probably want to use a ruler to prove to yourself that the lines marked "a" are the same and that the lines marked "b" are the same.

SUMMARY 5.2 Important Features of the Visual System

Feature	Significance
Cornea 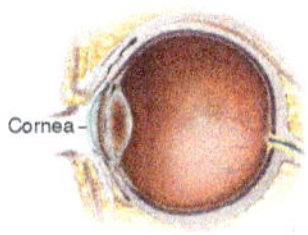	Bends light toward the retina.
Pupil 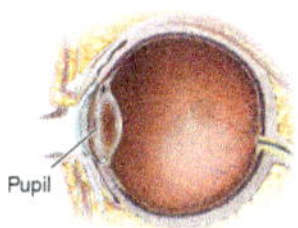	Forms an opening in the iris.
Lens 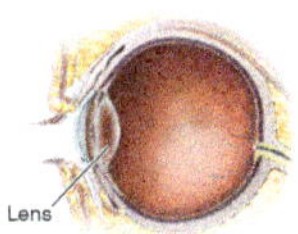	Focuses light onto the retina.
Retina 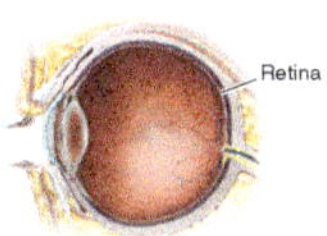	Contains rods, cones, and other visual neurons in its layers of cells.
Fovea (area of the retina) 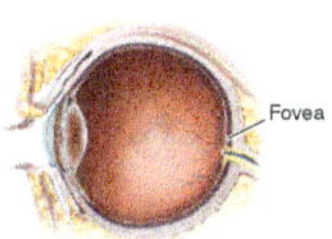	Processes detailed vision.
Thalamus 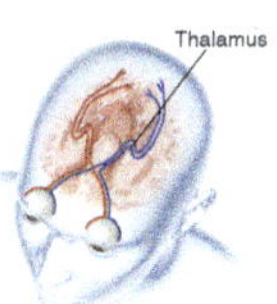	Acts as the target for most axons forming the optic tracts.
Primary visual cortex (area in the occipital lobe) 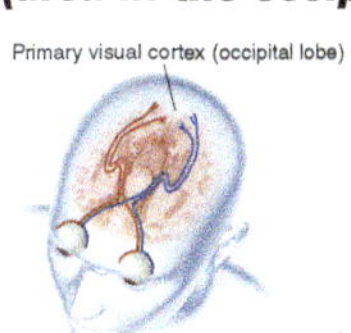	Receives visual input from the thalamus and performs initial analysis of input.

Credits: Top row—Argosy Publishing, Inc.; Second row—Argosy Publishing, Inc.; Third row—Argosy Publishing, Inc.; Fourth row—Argosy Publishing, Inc.; Fifth row—Argosy Publishing, Inc.; Sixth row—Argosy Publishing, Inc.; Bottom row—Argosy Publishing, Inc.

How Do We Hear?

audition The sense of hearing.

We have spent a considerable amount of time on the sense of vision, which might be considered a dominant source of information for humans. However, when Helen Keller, who was both blind and deaf, was asked which disability affected her the most, she replied that blindness separated her from things, while deafness separated her from people (Keller, 1933). **Audition**, our sense of hearing, not only allows us to identify objects in the distance but also plays an especially important role in our ability to communicate with others through language.

The Auditory Stimulus

Sound begins with the movement of an object, setting off waves of vibration in the form of miniature collisions between adjacent molecules in air, liquid, or solids. Because sound waves require this jostling of molecules, sound cannot occur in the vacuum of space, which contains no matter. Those explosions we enjoy in *Star Wars* films are great entertainment but not good science.

Earlier in this chapter, we described light energy as waves with different amplitudes and frequencies. Sound waves possess the same dimensions. However, in the case of sound, the height or amplitude of the wave is encoded as loudness or intensity and the frequency of the wave is encoded as pitch. High-amplitude waves are perceived as loud, and low-amplitude waves are perceived as soft. High-frequency waves (many cycles per unit of time) are perceived as high pitched, whereas low-frequency sounds are low pitched. In sound, amplitude is measured in units called decibels (dB), and frequency is measured in cycles per second, or hertz (Hz; see ● Figure 5.29).

In addition to dizziness and nausea, being exposed to infrasound makes people report feelings of chills down the spine, fear, and revulsion, even though they cannot consciously detect the sound. Some scientists believe that infrasound produced in certain places leads people to conclude the places are haunted.

As we observed in the case of the light spectrum, parts of the auditory spectrum are outside the range of human hearing. Ultrasound stimuli occur at frequencies above the range of human hearing, beginning around 20,000 Hz (see ● Figure 5.30). Ultrasound can be used to clean jewelry or your teeth or to produce noninvasive medical images. Infrasound refers to frequencies below the range of human hearing, or less than 20 Hz. Many animals, including elephants and marine mammals, use infrasound for communication. Infrasound is particularly effective in water because it allows sound to travel long distances.

The Biology of Audition

Human audition begins with an ear located on either side of the head. The components that make up the ear are divided into three parts: the outer ear, the middle ear, and the inner ear (see ● Figure 5.31).

The outer ear consists of the structures that are visible outside the body. The pinna, the outer visible structure of the ear, collects and focuses sounds, like a funnel. In addition, the pinna helps us localize sounds as being above or below the head. Sounds collected by the pinna are channeled through the auditory canal, which ends at the tympanic membrane, or eardrum, at the boundary between the outer and the middle ear. The boundary between the

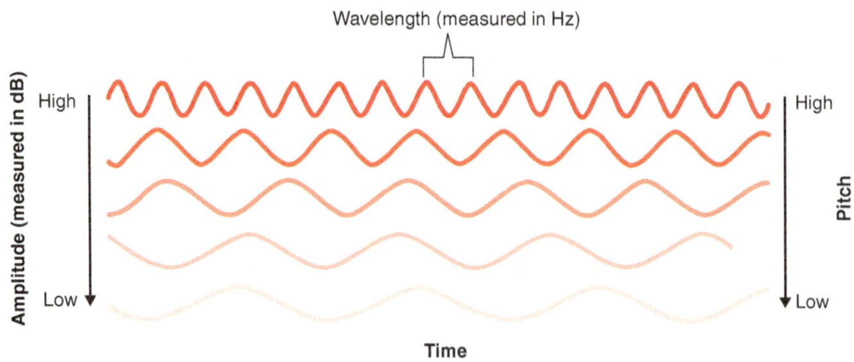

FIGURE **5.29**

Features of Sound. Like the light energy we see, sound waves are characterized by frequency and amplitude. We perceive frequency as the pitch of the sound (high or low), measured in hertz (Hz), and we perceive amplitude as the loudness of the sound, measured in decibels (dB).

FIGURE **5.35**

The McGurk Effect The McGurk effect is an auditory illusion that occurs when we combine vision and hearing. In this demonstration, hearing "ba-ba" at the same time you see a person's lips making "ga-ga" results in your perceiving "da-da."

Developmental and Individual Differences in Audition

Hearing in the human fetus is functional at 24 weeks of gestation, and the fetus shows evidence of recognizing the mother's voice (Moon, 2017). Newborns as young as 2 days respond preferentially to their native language (Moon et al., 1993). Infants younger than 3 months show strong startle reactions to noise. By the age of 6 months, infants turn their heads in the direction of a loud or interesting sound. It is likely that their thresholds for sounds are nearly at adult levels by this age (Olsho et al., 1987). By the age of 1 year, children should reliably turn around when their name is called (Nadig et al., 2007).

An important developmental change in audition is age-related hearing loss. Hearing loss occurs first at higher frequencies. After the age of 30, most people cannot hear sounds above 15,000 Hz. After the age of 50, most people cannot hear above 12,000 Hz, and people older than 70 years have difficulty with sounds above 6,000 Hz. Because speech normally ranges up to 8,000 to 10,000 Hz, older adults might begin to have difficulty understanding the speech of others.

Among individual differences in hearing is having absolute pitch, which means that you can name a musical tone that you hear. The brains of individuals with absolute pitch are structurally different from those of people who do not have this ability. Areas of the left hemisphere are larger in musicians with absolute pitch (Schlaug et al., 1995). Large-scale genetics studies have identified genes associated with absolute pitch (Theusch et al., 2009). Musicians who do have absolute pitch show a higher level of autistic traits (see Chapter 14), and relatively high numbers of people with autism spectrum disorder have absolute pitch (Wenhart et al., 2019). Brain activity in both populations shows weaker network connectivity compared to typical individuals.

Sociocultural Influences on Auditory Perception

Human culture and social life often provide a framework for the interpretation of stimuli. A dramatic example of this type of influence is our reaction to sine wave speech. To produce this stimulus, scientists artificially alter recordings of speech to resemble regular, repeating sine waves, as shown in ● Figure 5.36 (Davis, 2007). When people hear these artificial sounds without further instructions, they describe them as tweeting birds or other nonlanguage stimuli. However, if people are told the sounds represent speech, they suddenly "hear" language elements (Remez et al., 1981).

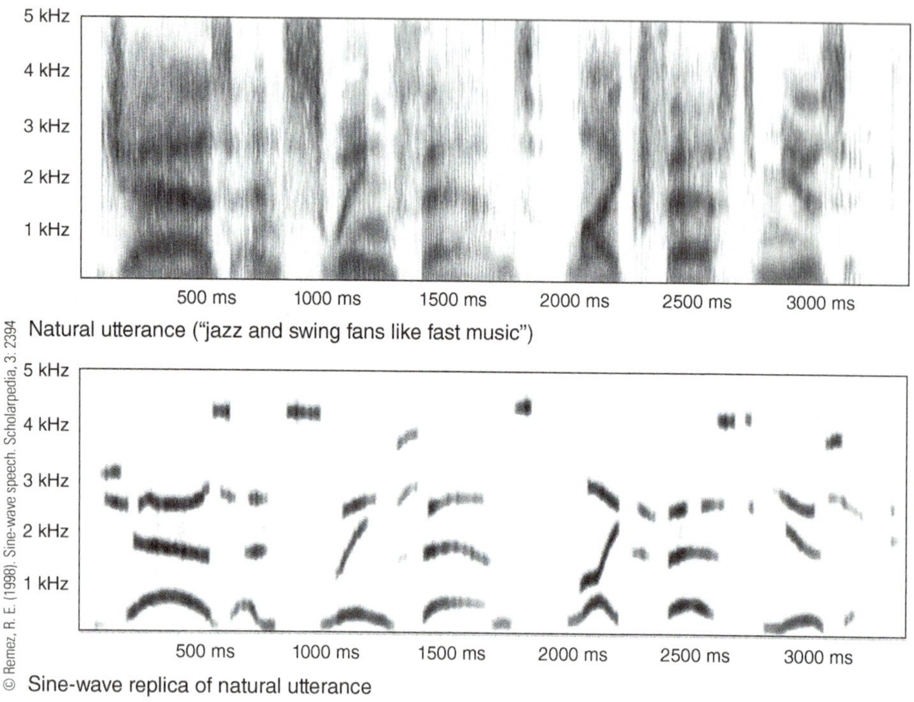

FIGURE 5.36

Expectations Influence the Interpretation of Sine Waves. Sine waves are regular and repetitive waveforms, such as the ones we included earlier to show how the height and frequency of light and sound waves are interpreted by the mind. Researchers can record speech sounds and transform the recordings into artificial sine waves, such as those in this image. If the sounds are played without information about their source, most people interpret the sounds as tweeting birds. However, if people are told that the recordings are language, they report "hearing" language, another example of top-down cognitive influences on perception.

Sine wave speech shows us how culture in the form of experience with language can shape perception, but in other instances, perception can shape culture. For many people with hearing loss and for their families and friends, being deaf means something other than having a disability. Instead, deafness is viewed as a culture, complete with its own set of attitudes, language, and norms. American Sign Language (ASL) is viewed as being quite distinct from signed English and is difficult for signing people in Great Britain and Australia to understand (Mindess, 2006).

How Do We Feel Body Position, Touch, Temperature, and Pain?

Somatosensation (*soma* comes from the Greek word for "body") provides us with many types of information about the position and movement of our bodies, touch, skin temperature, and pain. Like many other organisms, human beings even have the ability to sense magnetic fields impacting the body (Wang et al., 2019). Although these senses may not seem as glamorous as vision and hearing, we are severely disabled by their loss. You might think it would be a blessing to be born without a sense of pain, but people who have impaired pain reception often die prematurely because of their inability to respond to injury. Although unpleasant, pain tells us to stop and assess our circumstances, which might have promoted the survival of our ancestors.

Unlike the visual and auditory stimuli we have discussed so far in this chapter, somatosensory stimuli arise from within the body or make contact with its surface. As a result, these stimuli provide an organism little time to react. We can deal with a predator seen or heard from a distance using strategies different from those we use for one that is touching us. Nonetheless, the somatosenses provide essential feedback needed for movement, speech, and safety.

somatosensation The body senses, including body position, touch, skin temperature, and pain.

Body Position

The vestibular system helps us maintain a steady view of the world, even when riding the most extreme roller coaster.

To begin our exploration of the somatosensory systems, we return to the inner ear. Adjacent to the structures responsible for encoding sound, we find the structures of the **vestibular system**, which provide us with information about body position and movement (review Figure 5.32). The proximity of these structures to the middle ear, which can become congested because of a head cold, is often responsible for those rather unpleasant feelings of dizziness that accompany an illness. The receptors of the vestibular system provide information about the position of the head relative to the ground, linear acceleration, and rotational movements of the head. We sense linear acceleration when our rate of movement changes, such as when our airplane takes off.

Like the cochlea, the vestibular receptors contain sensitive hair cells that are bent back and forth within their surrounding fluid when the head moves. When extensive movement stops suddenly, perhaps at the end of an amusement park ride, these fluids reverse course. You may have the odd sensation that your head is now moving in the opposite direction, even though you are sitting or standing still. The movement of these hair cells results in the production of signals in the auditory nerve, the same nerve that carries information about sound. These axons form connections in the medulla and in the cerebellum. You may recall from Chapter 4 that the cerebellum participates in balance and motor coordination, functions that depend on feedback about movement. In turn, the medulla receives input from the visual system, the cerebellum, and other somatosenses. This arrangement provides an opportunity to coordinate input from the vestibular system with other relevant information. The medulla forms connections directly with the spinal cord, allowing us to adjust our posture to keep our balance. Vestibular information travels from the medulla to the thalamus, the primary somatosensory cortex of the parietal lobe, and then the primary motor cortex in the frontal lobe. This pathway allows vestibular information to guide voluntary movement.

vestibular system The system in the inner ear that provides information about body position and movement.

In humans particularly, information from the vestibular system is tightly integrated with visual processing. As we move, it is essential that we maintain a stable view of our surroundings. To accomplish this task, rotation of the head results in a reflexive movement of the eyes in the opposite direction. This action should allow you to maintain a steady view of the world, even on the most extreme roller coaster.

Touch

Touch provides a wealth of information about the objects around us. By simply exploring an object with touch, we can determine features such as size, shape, texture, and consistency. These judgments confirm and expand the information we obtain about objects through visual exploration. Touch is not only a means of exploring the environment. Particularly in humans, touch plays a significant role in social communication. Infants who are touched regularly sleep better, remain more alert while awake, and reach cognitive milestones at earlier ages (Cascio et al., 2019). We hug our friends and loved ones to provide comfort, pat others on the back for a job well done, and shake hands to greet a colleague or conclude a deal. The contributions of the sense of touch to human sexuality are obvious.

Our sense of touch begins with skin, the largest and heaviest organ in the human body. Embedded within the skin are several types of specialized neurons that produce action potentials whenever they are physically bent or stretched. Different types of receptors respond to certain features of a touch stimulus, such as pressure, vibration, or stretch (see Figure 5.37). In addition to their locations in the skin, receptors are located in blood vessels, joints, and internal organs. Unpleasant sensations from a headache or a too-full stomach or bladder originate from some of these receptors. Some receptor fibers wrap around hair follicles and respond whenever a hair is pulled or bent. Others, as we will see later in this section, participate in our senses of pain and skin temperature.

Information about touch travels from the skin to the spinal cord. Once inside the spinal cord, touch pathways proceed to the thalamus, along with input from the cranial nerves originating in the touch receptors in the skin of the face, the mouth, and the tongue. The thalamus transmits touch information to the primary somatosensory cortex, located in the parietal lobe.

A classic map of the body's representation in the primary somatosensory cortex is called a sensory *homunculus* ("little man") (Penfield & Boldrey, 1937). This odd figure illustrates how areas of the body are represented based on their sensitivity rather than their size (see Figure 5.38). Different species show different patterns of cortical organization for touch. Humans need sensitive feedback from the lips and the hands to speak and make skilled hand movements for tool use and other tasks. Rats devote a great deal of cortical real estate to whiskers, whereas lips have a high priority in squirrels and rabbits.

A notable area that is missing from the homunculus is the brain, which has neither touch receptors nor pain receptors. We can only assume that for much of evolutionary history, intrusion into the brain was likely to be fatal. Consequently, there would be no advantage to "feeling" your brain. Because of the lack of somatosensation in the brain, neurosurgeons can work with an alert patient using local anesthesia for the skull and tissues overlying the brain. The surgery produces no sensations of pressure or pain.

The representation of touch in the primary sensory cortex is plastic, which means that it changes in response to increases or decreases in input from a body part. Many individuals who lose a body part experience a phenomenon known as phantom limb, a term first used by a Civil War physician to describe his patients' experience of pain from a missing limb. Phantom sensations can result from the reorganization of the somatosensory cortex following the loss of a body part (Borsook et al., 1998). In one case study, touching different parts of a patient's face produced "feeling" from the patient's missing hand (Ramachandran & Rogers-Ramachandran, 2000). When his cheek was touched, he reported feeling his missing thumb, along with the expected cheek, while touching his lip elicited feeling from the missing index finger, along with the normal lip sensations. In an even more bizarre example, a patient was embarrassed to report that he experienced a sensation of orgasm in his missing foot.

Increased input also changes the organization of the somatosensory cortex. When monkeys were trained to use specific fingers to discriminate among surface textures to obtain food rewards, the areas of the cortex responding to the trained fingertips expanded (Merzenich & Jenkins, 1993). A similar reorganization occurs when blind individuals learn to read Braille

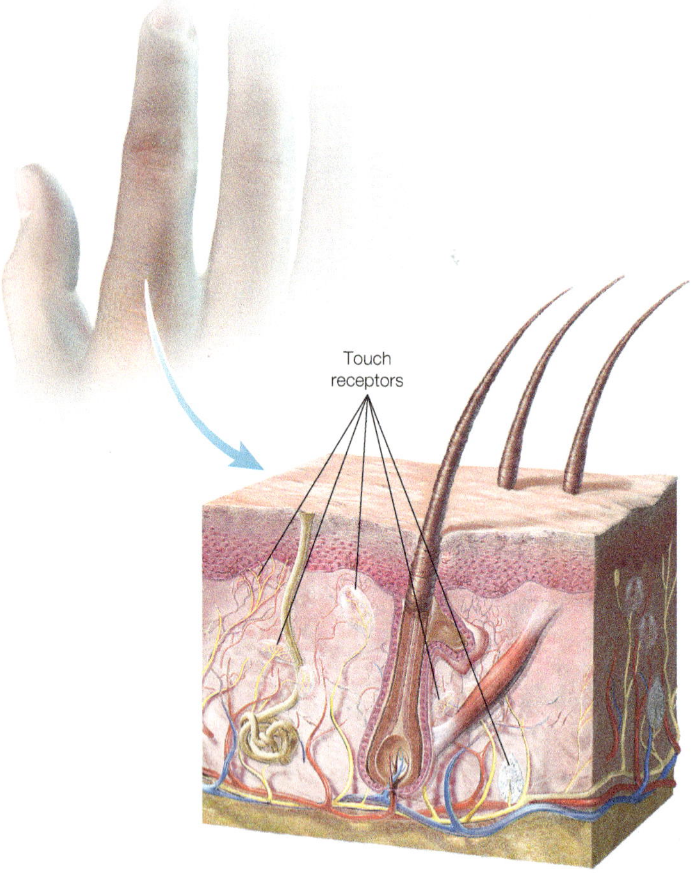

FIGURE **5.37**

Touch Receptors. Different receptors in the skin help us sense pressure, vibration, stretch, or pain. *Source:* Argosy Publishing, Inc.

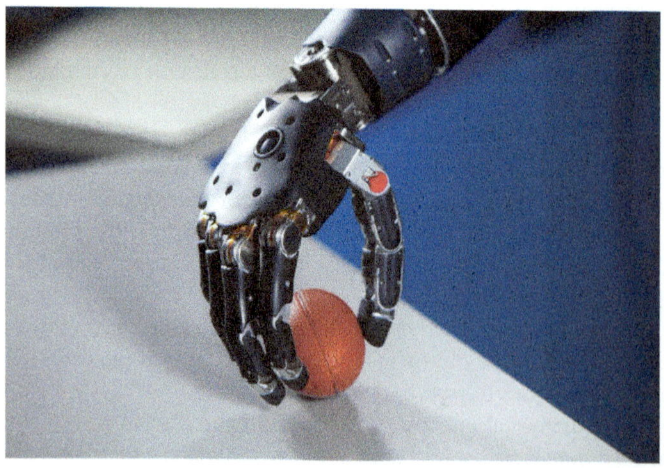

H.S. Photos/Alamy Stock Photo

Advances in robotics combined with better understanding of how touch is processed in the brain are leading to the development of prosthetics that can feel. Using fMRI, researchers were able to map areas of the sensory cortex that reacted when a participant imagined something touching different parts of the hand. With electrodes implanted in the relevant areas, the participant could then respond accurately to touch applied to the prosthetic hand, even when blindfolded. With this more natural feedback, the prosthetic hand should be able to manage delicate tasks, like picking up an egg.

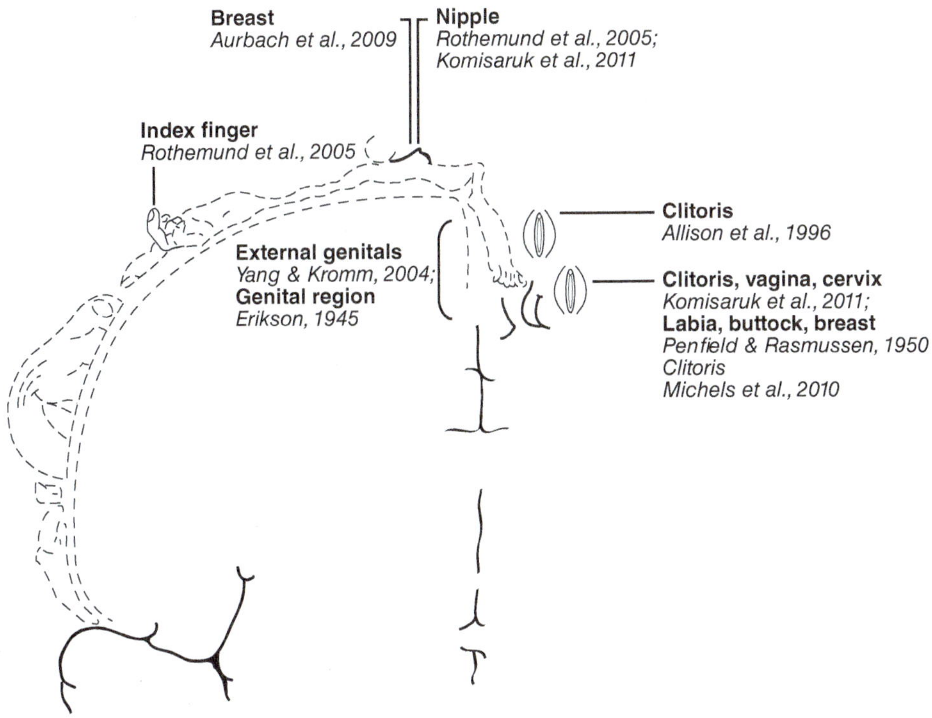

FIGURE 5.38

Sensory Homunculus. For over 70 years, textbooks have featured versions of the original homunculus published by Penfield and Boldrey (1937), which depicts a male. Only recently have scientists attempted to map the female somatosensory cortex in a similar manner. One attempt, shown here, outlines the female "hermunculus" against the grayed out background of the original male image by Penfield and Boldrey. Much work still needs to be done on the female version (Di Noto et al., 2012).

Source: Di Noto, P. M., Newman, L., Wall, S., & Einstein, G. (2012). The Hermunculus: What Is Known about the Representation of the Female Body in the Brain? *Cerebral Cortex, 23*(5), 1005-1013. doi: 10.1093/cercor/bhs005

(Pascual-Leone & Torres, 1993) or when people train extensively on stringed musical instruments (Elbert et al., 1995). Using your thumbs for text messaging will probably result in adaptations in cortical representation not seen in older generations (Ghosh, 2017).

Individuals with autism spectrum disorder (ASD) experience a very different sensory world (see Chapter 14). Many individuals with ASD are oversensitive to touch, leading to rejection of hugs and cuddling. In addition, brain responses to touch of self or others differ between individuals with ASD and healthy controls (Deschrijver et al., 2017). The extent of the differences correlated with the individuals' reports of sensory and social difficulties.

wavebreakmedia/Shutterstock.com

The representation of body parts in the primary sensory cortex changes in response to the amount of input from a body part. Children who study stringed instruments show more space in the sensory cortex devoted to fingers.

Pain

Given the anguish experienced by patients with chronic pain, it is tempting to think that not having a sense of pain would be wonderful. However, as mentioned earlier, we need pain to remind us to stop when we are injured, to assess the situation before proceeding, and to allow the body time to heal.

Free nerve endings and networks of glial cells (see Chapter 4) that respond to pain are triggered by a number of stimuli associated with tissue damage (Abdo et al., 2019). Some pain receptors respond to mechanical damage, such as that caused by a sharp object, while others respond to temperature or chemicals. Among the chemicals that stimulate pain receptors is capsaicin, an ingredient found in hot peppers (Caterina et al., 1997). Information about pain is carried centrally to the brain by two types of fibers. Fast, myelinated axons are responsible for that sharp "ouch" sensation that often accompanies an injury. Slower, unmyelinated axons are responsible for dull, aching sensations.

Pain fibers from the body form synapses with cells in the spinal cord, which in turn sends pain messages to the thalamus. This information takes a relatively direct route, with only

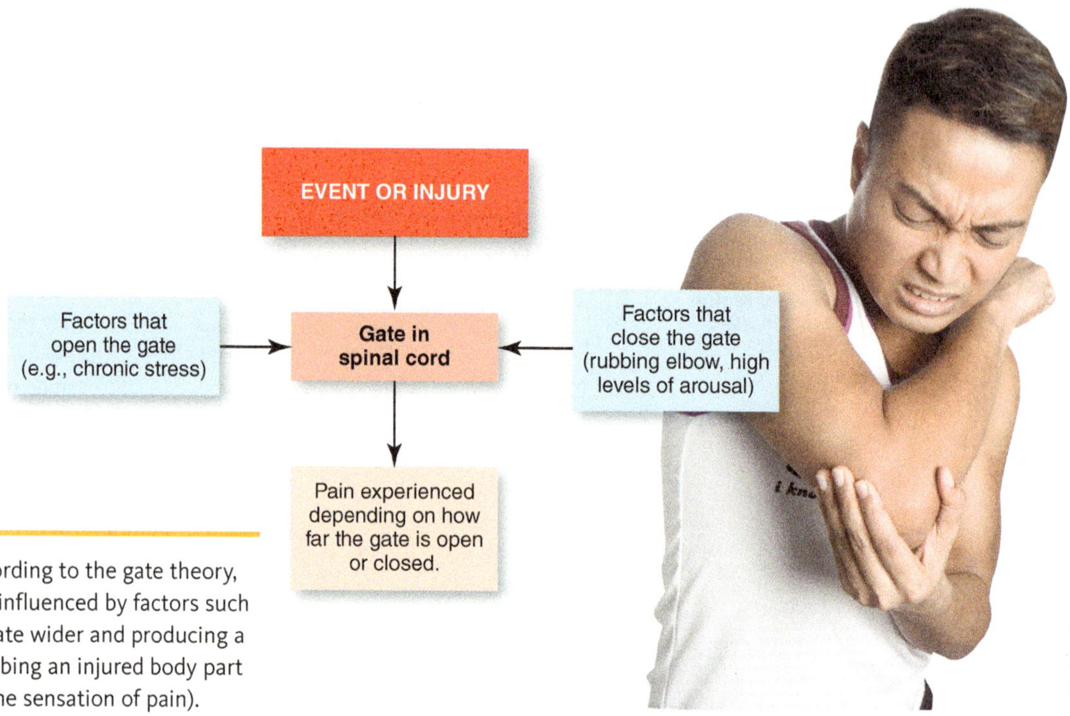

Juriah Mosin/Shutterstock.com

FIGURE 5.39

The Gate Theory of Pain. According to the gate theory, incoming pain messages can be influenced by factors such as chronic stress (opening the gate wider and producing a greater sensation of pain) or rubbing an injured body part (closing the gate and reducing the sensation of pain).

AP Images/Stephen Morton

Ashlyn Blocker was born with a rare condition preventing her from feeling pain. Without complaint, she went several days with a broken ankle after falling off her bicycle.

gate theory The theory that suggests that input from touch fibers competes with input from pain receptors, possibly preventing pain messages from reaching the brain.

In one of the most dramatic examples of how stress can interfere with the perception of pain, Guy Gertsch unknowingly ran the final 19 miles (about 30 km) of the 1982 Boston Marathon on a broken leg. Gertsch finished the race with a highly respectable time of 2 hours and 47 minutes.

one synapse in the spinal cord separating the periphery of the body and the thalamus in the forebrain. This arrangement ensures that pain messages are received by the brain with great speed. From the thalamus, pain information is sent to the anterior cingulate cortex, the insula, and the amygdala, which manage the emotional qualities of pain, and to the somatosensory cortex in the parietal lobe, which manages information about the location and intensity of pain (Wiech, 2016; Corder et al., 2019).

Pain messages traveling to the brain may be modified by competing incoming sensory signals. Many of us spontaneously rub our elbow after bumping it painfully. The **gate theory** of pain accounts for this phenomenon (Melzack & Wall, 1965). According to this model, input from touch fibers (reacting to rubbing your elbow) competes with input from pain receptors for activation of cells in the spinal cord (see ● Figure 5.39). Activation of the touch fibers effectively dilutes the amount of pain information reaching the brain.

The perception of pain is affected by the descending influence of higher brain centers. Many forebrain structures form connections with the periaqueductal gray of the midbrain. As we observed in Chapter 4, this area is rich in receptors for our natural opioids, the endorphins. The periaqueductal gray is a major target for opioid painkillers, such as morphine. Electrical stimulation of the periaqueductal gray produces a significant reduction in the experience of pain (Hosobuchi et al., 1977).

Pain is an actively constructed experience that involves our expectations and past experiences (Wiech, 2016). The power of expectation can be seen in placebo effects, which occur when people experience pain reduction, even though they have been exposed to an ineffective substance or treatment, such as a sugar pill instead of an aspirin tablet. Traditionally, scientists thought placebo effects were due to the ability of people's belief that they are being treated for pain to initiate a real decrease in pain sensation. However, even when people are told they are receiving a placebo, pain relief can occur as long as they are also told that placebo effects can be powerful (Carvalho et al., 2016).

No other sensory modality is as dramatically affected by culture, context, and experience as our sense of pain. The connection between culture and experience of pain is vividly illustrated by the hook-swinging ritual practiced in India (Melzack & Wall, 1983). This ritual, designed to promote the health of children and crops, involves hanging a male volunteer from steel hooks embedded into the skin and muscles of his back. Instead of suffering excruciating pain, as Westerners might expect, the volunteers appear to be in a state of exaltation.

Women who have participated in prepared childbirth classes report less pain than women who are uninformed regarding the birth process. Although athletes and nonathletes share similar pain thresholds, these groups are quite different in their tolerance of pain (Scott & Gijsbers, 1981). Compared to nonathletes, athletes in contact sports such as boxing, rugby, and football tolerate higher levels of pain before identifying a stimulus as painful. Patients who are allowed to self-administer morphine for pain require less medication than patients who receive injections from hospital staff (Bennett et al., 1982). The sense of control may reduce anxiety and the need for pain medication.

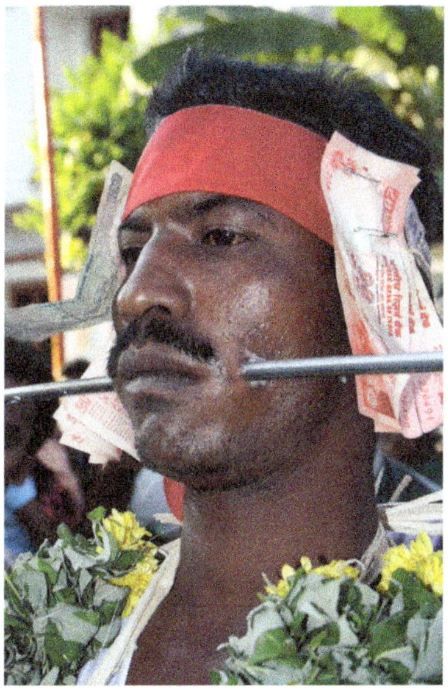
Louise Batalla Duran/Alamy Stock Photo

Culture, context, and experience can shape our perception of pain. During a festival dedicated to penance and atonement, Tamil Hindus walked through the streets carrying devices called kavadis that hold hooks that are pierced through the skin. Without this cultural context, it is likely that most people would find this experience excruciatingly painful.

How Do We Process Smells and Tastes?

The famous philosopher Immanuel Kant (Kant, 1798/1978, p. 46) considered **olfaction**, or our sense of smell, to be the "most dispensable" sense. Other species rely more heavily on olfaction and **gustation**, or the sense of taste, than humans do. Nonetheless, our chemical senses provide warning of danger, such as smelling smoke from a fire or tasting spoiled food. The chemical senses also contribute a richness to our emotional and social experiences. The smell of perfume or the taste of chocolate may be accompanied by strong emotional reactions. Contrary to Kant's view, people who have lost their sense of smell because of head injury often experience profound depression (Zuscho, 1983). Sharing a meal has a strong effect on bonding for humans and other primates (Brosnan, 2010; Wobber et al., 2010).

Our chemical senses begin with molecules suspended in the air in the case of olfaction and dissolved in saliva in the case of gustation. Olfaction provides more information from a distance, like vision and audition, whereas gustation, like the somatosenses, involves information from contact with the body.

Like the somatosenses, the chemical senses are quite ancient in terms of evolution and have undergone little change over time. However, our sense of smell has been influenced by walking on two feet instead of four. Most olfactory stimuli are relatively heavy and tend to fall to the ground. Consider how your dog puts its nose to the ground when tracking something interesting.

Olfaction

Air containing olfactory stimuli is taken in through the nostrils and circulated within the nasal cavities connected to the nostrils, where it interacts with olfactory receptors (see Figure 5.40). The receptors are located in a thin layer of cells within the nasal cavity. Unlike most neurons, the olfactory receptors regularly die and are replaced by new receptor cells in cycles lasting 4 to 6 weeks. Cells at the base of the receptors are responsible for producing the mucus surrounding the receptors. One branch of each receptor interacts with molecules dissolved in the mucus. The other branch carries information back to the central nervous system as part of the **olfactory nerve**. The olfactory nerve fibers synapse in one of the two **olfactory bulbs**, located just below the mass of the frontal lobes. Although we often hear that human olfaction is not as good as olfaction in other species, human olfactory bulbs have about the same number of neurons as in 24 other mammalian species (McGann, 2017).

Unlike most other sensory input to the brain, olfactory pathways do not make direct connections with the thalamus before the information reaches the cerebral cortex. Instead, fibers from the olfactory bulbs proceed to the olfactory cortex, located in the lower portions of the frontal lobe extending into the temporal lobe, and to the amygdala. Because of the role these areas of the brain play in emotion, which we described in Chapter 4, these pathways may account for the significant emotional reactions we experience (disgust or pleasure) in

olfaction The sense of smell.

gustation The sense of taste.

olfactory nerve A nerve carrying olfactory information from the olfactory receptors to the olfactory bulbs.

olfactory bulb One of two structures below the frontal lobes of the brain that receive input from the olfactory receptors in the nose.

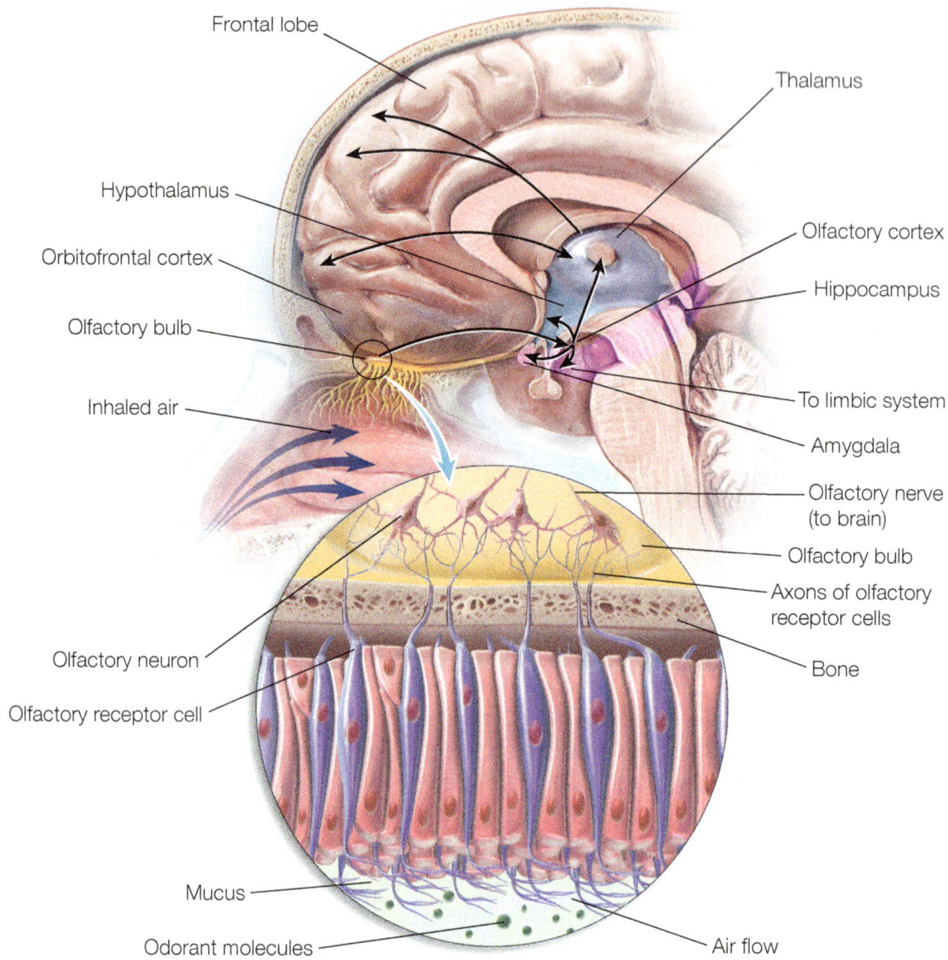

FIGURE 5.40

Olfactory Receptors. Receptors in the nose interact with airborne chemicals to begin the sensing of odor.
Source: Argosy Publishing, Inc.

response to odor. The olfactory cortex makes connections with the thalamus, which in turn sends information to the orbitofrontal cortex. It is likely that this pathway contributes to the conscious awareness of odors.

Gustation

The most likely original purpose of our sense of gustation, or taste, was to protect us from eating poisonous or spoiled food and to attract us to foods that boost our chances of survival. Although we seem biased toward detecting negative stimuli (Cacioppo & Gardner, 1999), our attraction to certain tastes also reflects our historical past. Because most of our ancestors were constantly facing the threat of famine, we find fatty and sugary foods to be especially tasty. Unfortunately, given the current availability of safe and palatable foods, our sense of taste may drive us to eat more than we need.

Most of us are familiar with four major categories of taste: sweet, sour, salty, and bitter. A fifth type of taste has been proposed, known by the Japanese term *umami*, which roughly translated means "savory" or "meaty" (Chaudhari et al., 2000). In addition, the tongue and the mouth contain receptors for carbohydrates (Turner et al., 2014) and capsaicin, an active ingredient in hot peppers. Mice lacking capsaicin receptors happily consumed water containing capsaicin at levels that were rejected by normal mice (Caterina et al., 2000).

Taste receptors are located on the tongue and in other parts of the mouth (see Figure 5.41). Contrary to a popular myth (usually accompanied by an equally mythological map of "taste centers" on the tongue), receptors sensitive to all types of taste are equally distributed across the tongue. You are probably aware of the bumpy texture of your tongue, which results from the presence of **papillae**. Most papillae contain somewhere between 1 and 100 **taste buds**. Each taste bud contains between 50 and 150 receptor cells, which extend tiny hairlike cilia into the saliva that interact with dissolved taste stimuli and transduce the resulting information into neural signals. Like olfactory receptors, taste buds have a limited life before they are replaced. If you burn your tongue by drinking hot liquid, your taste is affected for a day or two. However, when the taste buds are replaced, taste should be back to normal.

Information about taste travels from the mouth and the tongue to the medulla. The medulla in turn communicates with the thalamus, which sends taste information to the insula, lower somatosensory cortex of the parietal lobe, and to the orbitofrontal cortex, where the emotional pleasantness or unpleasantness of particular stimuli is processed (Kobayakawa et al., 2005). As we will see in Chapters 7 and 8, taste information interacts with motivation and learning.

Perception and Cognition in the Chemical Senses

Olfaction and gustation share three interesting perceptual themes: (a) We can easily identify a number of complex stimuli combining many types of molecules, such as the aroma of coffee; (b) we can detect small differences among similar smells and tastes; and (c) our experience often shapes our perception of an olfactory or gustatory stimulus (Goldstein, 2010). Humans can distinguish among at least 1 trillion odors (Bushdid et al., 2014). An example of the impact of experience and top-down processing on olfaction is the effect of labeling an odor on people's rating of its pleasantness. If participants smell an onion stimulus labeled "pizza," they rate the odor as more pleasant than if the identical stimulus is labeled "body odor" (Herz, 2003).

The chemical senses interact to provide the perception of flavor. You have probably noticed that food doesn't taste good when your sense of smell is decreased by a bad cold. If you close your eyes and hold your nose, you are unable to distinguish between a slice of apple and a slice of raw potato. The orbitofrontal cortex plays an important role in the perception of flavor because the pathways serving olfaction and gustation converge in this part of the brain (Rolls, 2000).

papillae Small bumps on the tongue that contain taste buds.

taste bud A structure found in papillae that contains taste receptor cells.

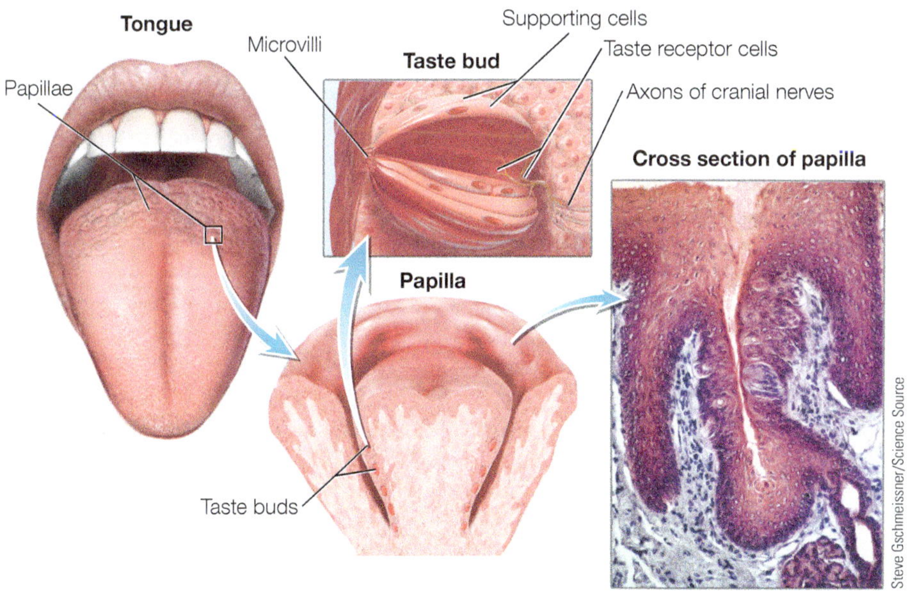

FIGURE 5.41

Taste Receptors. Taste buds are located in the bumps, or papillae, located on the tongue.
Source: Source: Argosy Publishing, Inc.

Developmental and Individual Differences in the Chemical Senses

Young children are notorious for putting things in their mouths that adults would quickly reject based on taste, including poisonous substances such as drain cleaner. However, this propensity does not mean that children lack a sense of taste. Using facial expressions, researchers have demonstrated that newborns differentiate among sweet, bitter, and sour tastes but seem relatively oblivious to salty tastes (Rosenstein & Oster, 1988). As we get older, the overall number of taste buds decreases, reducing the intensity of many tastes and providing a possible explanation for why some strong flavors, such as that of broccoli, are enjoyed more by adults than by children. As we age, our sensitivity to smell also decreases (Cain & Gent, 1991). Because olfaction and taste interact to form the flavor of foods, decreased sensitivity in both senses might affect overall appetite as we age.

Like the other sensory modalities discussed in this chapter, the chemical senses vary from person to person. Females are generally more sensitive to smell than are males (Doty et al., 1984). The average person has approximately 6,000 taste buds, but this number may vary widely. Supertasters have unusually high numbers of papillae and, therefore, have more taste buds (Bartoshuk, 2000).

Disturbances in the chemical senses are correlated with several psychological disorders. Olfaction and the experience of posttraumatic stress disorder (PTSD; see Chapter 14) appear to interact in combat veterans. PTSD is often characterized by intrusive, disturbing flashbacks in which the patient essentially relives the traumatic experience. Given the close association

EXPERIENCING PSYCHOLOGY

Are You a Supertaster?

ABOUT 25% OF THE POPULATION are supertasters, or people who are extrasensitive to taste; 25% are nontasters, or people who are relatively insensitive to taste; and the remaining 50% fall between these two extremes. You can use the following exercises to determine your taste category.

1. How Does Mint Taste to You?

Place a mint Life Saver on your tongue, and allow it to dissolve (no chewing please). Rate the following qualities of the Life Saver on a scale of 1 to 5, with 1 being "very intense" and 5 being "not intense":

Sweetness	1	2	3	4	5
Smell	1	2	3	4	5
Coolness	1	2	3	4	5
"Rush"	1	2	3	4	5

How to interpret your results: Mint tasters fall into four groups:

Group 1: Mint is mild, no rush.
Group 2: Mint is moderate, no rush.
Group 3: Mint is moderate, rush.
Group 4: Mint is intense, rush.

● Table 5.3 shows further characteristics of these taste groups.

TABLE 5.3

Interpreting Your Supertaster Results

Mildly Sensitive Tasters (Group 1)	Moderately Sensitive Tasters (Groups 2 and 3)	Supertasters (Group 4)
Weak to undetectable sensation from mint.	Moderate to strong sensation from mint.	Very strong sensation from mint.
Flavor of food is not that important.	Flavor of food is important.	Flavor of food is important.
Many foods liked, few foods disliked, and not passionate about food.	Many foods liked, few foods disliked, and often passionate about food.	Great variation in the number of foods liked and often passionate about food.

2. Count Your Papillae

You need a gummed reinforcer (sticky white ring for notebooks), a swab, blue food coloring, and a mirror.

Place one reinforcer on the front of your tongue just to the side of midline. Use a swab to apply blue food coloring to the part of your tongue that shows through the center of the reinforcer. The blue food coloring should make your papillae (bumps) more obvious. Count the number of papillae you see in the ring. More than 25 papillae within the reinforcer ring means you're a super-between olfaction and memory, researchers hypothesized that some PTSD flashbacks could be initiated by relevant smells. When compared to combat veterans who did not have PTSD, combat veterans with the disorder experienced marked anxiety when exposed to the smell of diesel, accompanied by changes in the activity of the amygdala (Vermetten et al., 2007).

Sociocultural Influences on the Chemical Senses

The sense of smell might seem to play a secondary role to vision and audition in humans, but people have manipulated scent for religious, medicinal, and personal purposes since ancient times. We can speculate that once people learned to control fire, a recognition that some burning things smelled better than others could not have been far behind, possibly leading to the use of incense in religious rituals. Use of natural materials for medicine and self-adornment provides the historical roots for large, contemporary industries that manufacture scent for a host of consumer products, including perfume, air fresheners, "new car smell" products, and detergents.

Although olfaction often seems to run in the background of our other cognitive processes, it is not immune to the effects of culture and experience. Americans spend millions on products that remove or mask body odor, whereas other cultures do not find such odors offensive. One study compared the categorization of odors by French, American, and Vietnamese participants (Chrea et al., 2004). Although the participants sorted odors similarly into broad categories of floral, sweet, bad, and natural, they differed along subtler dimensions. The French and American participants quickly sorted odors into fruit or flower categories, but this separation had little relevance to the Vietnamese participants. French and French-Canadian

taster. The number of papillae of mildly or moderately sensitive tasters will be less than 25, but these two groups cannot be distinguished based on this factor.

Supertasters tend to dislike bitter foods; they have many low numbers. Supertasters also tend to be picky eaters as children and are better at detecting differences in fats in foods. ■

3. Other Eating Habits

Rate the tastes of the following foods and drinks using a 1-to-5 scale, with 1 being "dislike strongly" and 5 being "like a great deal":

Broccoli	1	2	3	4	5
Grapefruit	1	2	3	4	5
Coffee (black)	1	2	3	4	5
Dark chocolate	1	2	3	4	5

As a child, were you ever described by a parent, teacher, or other adult as a "picky eater"? (circle one)

- YES
- NO

Can you easily tell the difference between the fat content of milk, for example, between whole and 2% milk or between 1% and 2% milk? (circle one)

- YES
- NO

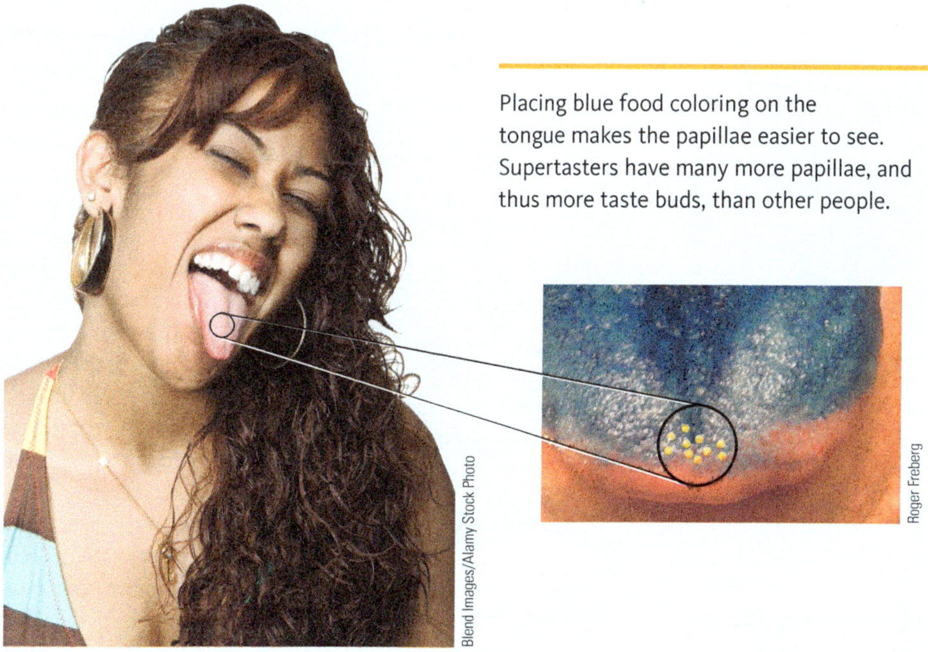

Placing blue food coloring on the tongue makes the papillae easier to see. Supertasters have many more papillae, and thus more taste buds, than other people.

Different cultures can prefer different foods. It is unlikely that you will find crispy tarantulas, a popular snack in Cambodia, in many American restaurants.

Jamie Stamey/iStock/Getty Images

participants rated the pleasantness of wintergreen quite differently (Ferdenzi et al., 2016). Wintergreen is used in candy in Canada, but in medicine in France.

Experience clearly plays a role in developing an individual's taste preferences. The effects of experience on taste begin in the prenatal environment. Infants whose mothers consumed carrot juice during pregnancy showed stronger preferences for carrot flavor (Mennella & Beauchamp, 1996; Mennella et al., 2001). In terms of survival, this result makes perfect sense. Infants are born with a predisposition to like the safe foods available in their environment. Because the food supply historically has varied widely from place to place, delicacies such as crispy fried tarantulas are appreciated in Cambodia but not necessarily in the United States.

Interpersonal Relationships

Sensation and Perception Perspectives

CAN RELATIONSHIPS BUFFER THE EXPERIENCE OF PAIN?

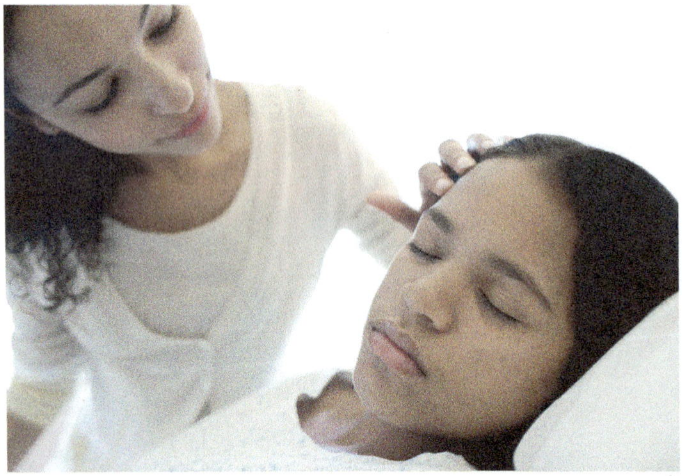

Science Photo Library/Alamy Stock Photo

Research shows that physical contact with loved ones reduces the sensation of pain.

WE MENTIONED EARLIER that of the senses we discussed in this chapter, pain was particularly influenced by cognition and context. Can being in a close relationship affect the way you feel pain?

The answer appears to be "yes." Physical contact with a loved one can affect how the brain processes pain. Women who were expecting an electric shock showed reduced activity in parts of the brain associated with the emotional and arousing aspects of pain when they held their husbands' hands (Coan et al., 2006). In addition, the amount of reduction of activity in these pain areas of the brain correlated with the quality of the marriage—happily married women experienced greater decreases in activity associated with pain than less happily married women.

Perhaps this buffering effect is why you may reach for your partner when frightened during a scary movie. Knowing that such intimacy could reduce a loved one's pain might compel you to accompany your partner to a doctor's appointment or visit a friend in the hospital. Our understanding of pain in connection with our interpersonal relationships can help us in tangible ways to create and maintain stronger, healthier relationships. ■

Psychology Takes on Real-World Problems

Social Distancing, Loneliness and the Perception of Social Threat

AS WE HAVE SEEN IN THIS CHAPTER, different people watching the same event can reach different conclusions about what just happened. If we are to develop effective policies for solving real-world problems, we must have methods for identifying perceptions of the experience from the perspectives of those involved.

While we understand the benefits of lockdowns and social distancing in a pandemic, we also understand that these preventive measures can increase loneliness. In a matter of just a few weeks of lockdown, the number of UK adults who reported feelings of loneliness more than doubled. Young people between the ages of 18 and 24 were the most likely to be lonely as a result of the lockdown, with nearly half reporting feeling lonely (Mental Health Foundation, 2020).

Perception is key to our understanding of loneliness. Feelings of loneliness are not initiated until an individual perceives insufficient or unsatisfactory social connection (Cacioppo & Cacioppo, 2014). In other words, one person might be unhappy in spite of having many close friends while another might be perfectly happy with one or two friends. It is the perception of one's social life falling short of expectations that initiates feelings of loneliness.

Once loneliness has taken hold, further changes in perception take hold. People who are lonely become more sensitive to social threats, such as images of social rejection, compared to non-social threats, such as images of snakes (Cacioppo et al., 2016). These differences in reactions to social and non-social threat happen so quickly that they are likely to result from implicit, or unconscious processing as opposed to explicit, conscious reasoning.

What might be the implications of this heightened sensitivity to social threats? At the same time lonely people should be working to repair weak social connections, their heightened sensitivity to social threats might instead initiate self-preservation, or putting their own needs ahead of the needs of others. Self-preservation behavior is not exactly endearing, so behaving in this way can perpetuate feelings of loneliness (Cacioppo, Chen, & Cacioppo, 2017). ■

gpointstudio/Shutterstock.com

Joel Sartore/National Geographic Image Collection

Lonely people become more sensitive to social threats, such as social rejection, but not to non-social threats, such as snakes.

SUMMARY 5.3 Important Structures in the Non-visual Senses

Structure	Function
Ear 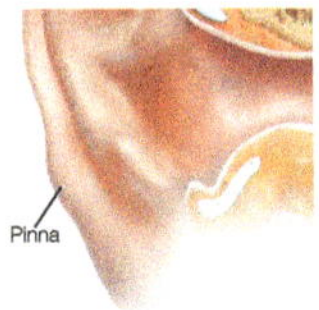	Transduces sound waves to neural signals. Includes pinna, tympanic membrane, and cochlea.
Vestibular system 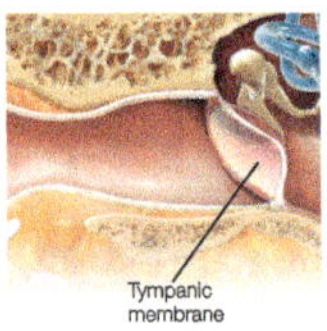	Provides information about body movement and position.
Touch receptors 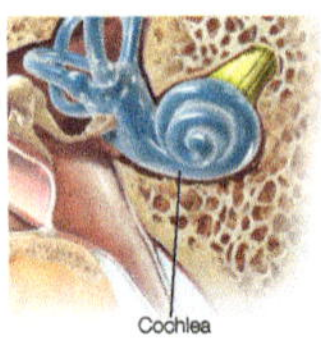	Receptors embedded in the skin report about pressure, vibration, stretch, and pain.
Olfactory receptors 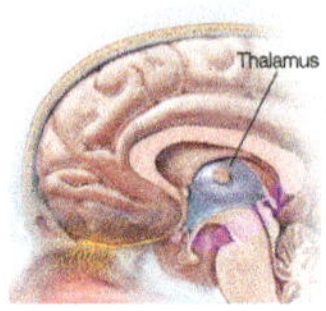	Airborne chemicals interacting with olfactory receptors in the nose begin the process of sensing odors.
Taste receptors 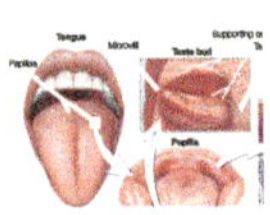	Taste receptors located in the mouth and in the bumpy papillae of the tongue interact with chemicals dissolved in saliva to provide information about taste.

Credits: Top row—Argosy Publishing, Inc.; Second row—Argosy Publishing, Inc.; Third row—Argosy Publishing, Inc.; Fourth row—Argosy Publishing, Inc.; Bottom row—Argosy Publishing, Inc.

6

The Aware Mind

ELEMENTS OF CONSCIOUSNESS

LEARNING OBJECTIVES

1. Compare and contrast the different meanings of consciousness.
2. Describe the effects of different stages of waking and sleep on consciousness, electroencephalogram (EEG) patterns, autonomic nervous system function, and muscle activity.
3. Differentiate several sleep-wake disorders in terms of their symptoms and the type of sleep disturbed.
4. Explain disorders of consciousness in terms of damage or dysfunction of the brain.
5. Categorize the neurochemical mechanisms and effects on consciousness of major types of psychoactive drugs.
6. Describe the use of hypnosis, meditation, and other nondrug methods for altering consciousness.

WHAT DOES IT MEAN TO HAVE "FREE WILL"? THIS MIGHT sound more like a philosophy question than a psychology question, but advances in biological and cognitive psychology have allowed psychologists to tackle it.

Usually, we think of free will as the ability to consciously control our actions and decisions. In the children's game of "rock, paper, scissors," we feel like we are making a conscious decision to choose one of the three options, but how would such a decision be made? What types of processes in the brain correspond to choosing scissors over the other two possibilities?

Controversial research into voluntary movements, such as forming your hand into scissors, has shown that the brain makes a commitment to a choice before we become aware of the decision (Libet et al., 1993; Soon et al., 2008). (See Figure 6.1.) Other research shows that the brain can be manipulated to make an unusual choice without disrupting the individual's sense of free will. Right-handed people normally use their right hand 60% of the time or more when forced to choose to use one hand over the other, but when researchers exposed right-handed subjects' right hemispheres to transcranial magnetic stimulation (TMS), illustrated in the large image on the previous page, they chose to use their left hand 80% of the time (Ammon & Gandevia, 1990). Despite making the uncharacteristic choice to use "the wrong hand," the participants in this experiment reported feeling in control of their hand movements. If the brain has already committed to a movement, what purpose does a conscious sense of having decided to move serve?

Insight into this question emerged from the study of split-brain patients described in Chapter 4. These patients have undergone surgery that severs the connections between their right and their

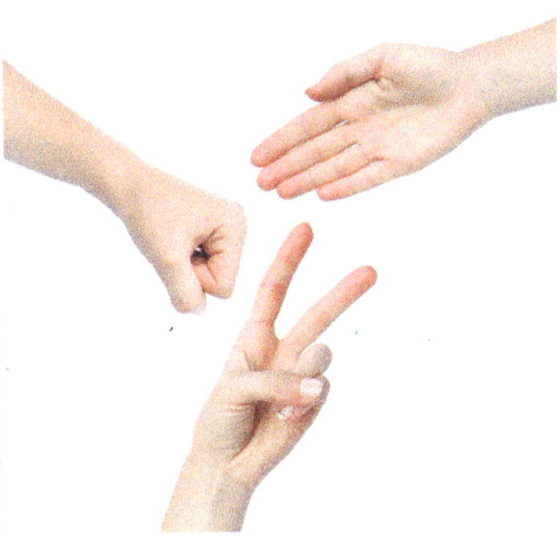
LeventeGyori/Shutterstock.com

FIGURE **6.1**

The Intention to Move Precedes Conscious Awareness. Benjamin Libet demonstrated that a "readiness potential," or a change in the participant's EEG activity, could be seen about 350 msec (1 msec is one one-thousandth of a second, so about ⅓ second) prior to the participant's conscious intent to flex a finger. Libet's results initiated a lively discussion among psychologists and philosophers about the nature of human free will.

Source: https://www.world-of-luciddreaming.com/is-free-will-an-illusion.html

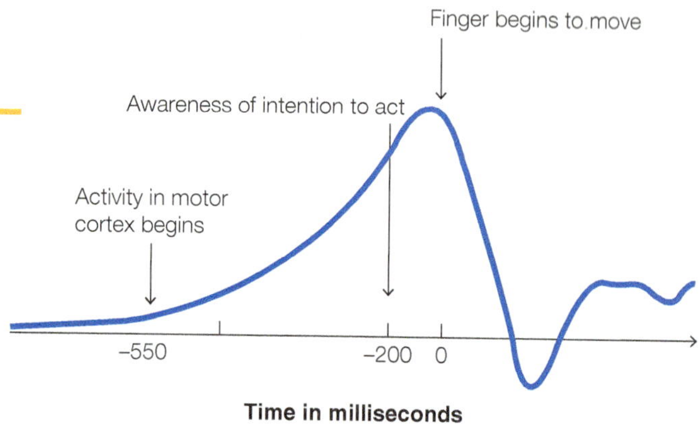

Maximilian Weinzierl/Alamy Stock Photo

Social context plays a role in sleep, even for the fruit fly. Fruit flies living with other fruit flies rather than alone need more sleep, suggesting that one of the functions of sleep is to process learning about social experiences. The larger the group of flies, the longer each fly needed to sleep.

From I. Ganguly-Fitzgerald, J. Donlea, & P. J. Shaw (2006). "Waking Experience Affects Sleep Need in Drosophila," *Science, 313*(5794), 1775–1781. doi:10.1126/science.1130408

left hemispheres, making it possible to expose one hemisphere at a time to a stimulus. For example, you can show the relatively nonverbal right hemisphere the word *stand*, and the patient usually stands up. However, because of the limitations of the right hemisphere in processing language, the patient is consciously unaware of having read the word. When asked why they stood up, patients responded by saying they felt the need to stretch. In other words, the mind is building a theory about the behavior that was just performed (Gazzaniga, 2011). This type of observation leads to a view of consciousness as an interpreter, making sense out of our actions and the world within and around us. This view helps us understand the observed delay between the brain's commitment to an action and our conscious awareness of that decision—the interpreter needs time to analyze the situation.

In this chapter, we will explore many situations that affect the performance of the interpreter, from the variations found in stages of sleep and waking to the alterations produced by psychoactive drugs and damage to the brain. This journey will require us to zoom in to observe underlying processes in the brain and then zoom out again to understand the influences of the social context on the phenomenon of conscious awareness.

What Does It Mean to Be Conscious?

Our English word *conscious* is derived from the Latin *conscientia*, which means "to know." **Consciousness** refers to knowing or being aware of ongoing experiences occurring both internally and in the world around us. We understand that to be unconscious, perhaps because of a blow to the head, means that we are unaware of what is happening within and around us. However, the term *consciousness* has multiple meanings. Consciousness can refer to a state of awareness (alert versus drowsy, for example) or the current content of awareness (while reading this page, you hear your neighbor's music). A special type of consciousness, **self-awareness**, occurs when we focus on ourselves as individuals.

Consciousness has been a favorite topic among psychologists for many years. William James coined the term "stream of consciousness" to capture the moving, seemingly

consciousness A state of awareness.
self-awareness The special understanding of the self as distinct from other stimuli.

unbroken flow of conscious awareness (1899, p. 15). Sigmund Freud used the term *consciousness* to refer to aspects of the mind that could be retrieved voluntarily, in contrast to the unconscious parts of the mind that remain hidden to voluntary searches for information. Cognitive psychologists debate why some information becomes conscious while other information does not (Baars, 1988).

The Evolution of Consciousness

Most of us would agree that bacteria do not possess consciousness, but people do. This implies that consciousness emerged at some point in the course of evolution. The exact location of that point remains highly debatable. James (1890, p. 141) maintained that "consciousness grows the more complex and intense the higher we rise in the animal kingdom. That of a man must exceed that of an oyster." If consciousness evolved as suggested by James, what advantages might account for this development?

The question of the emergence of consciousness in animals is complicated by the multiple meanings of *consciousness* described previously. Most animals show variations in states of awareness. Even the humble fruit fly takes periods of rest, which are believed to be the fruit fly equivalent of sleep (Shaw et al., 2000). Consciousness defined as an awareness of ongoing sensations is probably less common in the animal kingdom. Many animals would survive quite well by simply responding automatically to the world around them ("food" or "predator") without necessarily thinking "I smell food" or "I see a predator." The self-awareness aspect of consciousness—as exemplified in "I" statements—might be the rarest of all among living things, as we will see later.

Consciousness as Variations in Alertness Varying states of awareness might allow animals to repair their bodies and conserve energy. Food requirements would be higher if we stayed awake for 24 hours, as you may have noticed while studying for final exams. Another possible benefit of varying states of awareness is maximizing safety. Most animals are specialized for activity in either the light or the dark. Sleeping during the cycle for which an animal is poorly equipped for activity might contribute to its survival. However, being inactive is not a safe thing to do unless you have a safe place to hide (Allison & Cicchetti, 1976). Horses and rabbits are both frequently preyed upon, but horses sleep in the open, while rabbits sleep in burrows. Consequently, wild horses sleep as little as 1 or 2 hours per day, while wild rabbits sleep at least 8 hours.

ARCO/W Dolder/AGE Fotostock

Sleeping habits of different species reflect how likely they are to be preyed upon by other animals and whether they have shelter. The lion has few predators and is likely to fall asleep wherever it is convenient.

Consciousness as an Awareness of Ongoing Sensations One possible advantage of being consciously aware of ongoing sensations is the ability to choose responses rather than to respond instinctively (Gazzaniga, 2011). If suddenly faced with a predator, any animal could respond automatically using reflex and instinct, which we discuss in Chapter 8. Horses are notorious for running whenever the slightest stimulus bothers them. It is unlikely that the horse in these cases is thinking, "I hear a mountain lion—I should run." Conscious awareness of sensations provides more options. If a conscious animal hears a sound in the distance that might indicate the presence of a predator, it could choose to continue on, flee, or pause while obtaining further information. This flexibility would be likely to increase the animal's chances of survival.

Consciousness as Self-Awareness The self-awareness aspect of consciousness could heighten an animal's drive to survive. Recognition and understanding of being alive is correlated with heightened meaningfulness of self-preservation.

Developmental psychologists have provided a technique for demonstrating self-awareness that can be used with many species. Recognizing one's self in the mirror is believed to be a major developmental milestone in achieving self-awareness. In the so-called rouge test, a dot of rouge or other odorless dye is placed on a child's forehead, and the child is allowed to look in a mirror (Lewis & Brooks-Gunn, 1979). Before the age of about 18 months, children do not seem to understand the image in the mirror is their own. At about that age, they rub at the spot

Ghislain & Marie David de Lossy/The Image Bank/Getty Images

Diana Reiss, Ph.D.

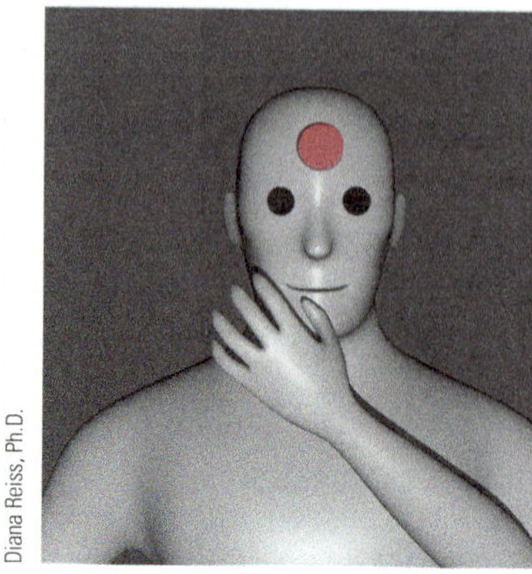

Rensselaer Artificial Intelligence and Reasoning Lab

Babies 18 months and older are able to recognize themselves in a mirror, which psychologists believe indicates a sense of self-awareness. Happy the elephant, a resident of the Bronx Zoo, repeatedly used her trunk to touch a mark that researchers placed above her eye, suggesting that she too can recognize her image in the mirror. Researchers have suggested that even robots might be able to pass the mirror test.

Organisms like the army ant stretch our definitions of what it means to be conscious. Individual army ants (*Eciton*) are not impressive, but colonies of army ants show signs of collective intelligence and sophisticated problem solving, such as using their bodies to build nests of up to 700,000 individuals (Franks, 1989).

Dr Morley Read/Shutterstock.com

of rouge or turn their bodies to get a better look, thus demonstrating self-awareness.

Chimpanzees "pass" the rouge test by demonstrating behavior similar to that of 18-month-old children (Gallup, 1970). In addition to chimpanzees, orangutans, gorillas raised by humans, bottle-nosed dolphins, Asian elephants, magpies, and parrots have demonstrated self-awareness in this type of experiment (Patterson, 1984; Gallup & Suarez, 1986; Povinelli, 1993; Patterson & Cohn, 1994; Plotnik et al., 2006; Prior et al., 2008).

Other researchers restrict the possibility of self-aware consciousness to species that exhibit complex social behavior. Of what use would self-awareness be if one did not frequently interact with others of the same kind? Social animals must be able to recognize other individuals and respond to them accordingly. Dolphins appear to have special whistles that they use for particular individuals, like names (Janik et al., 2006). Some social animals, including chimpanzees and elephants, show an awareness of death and appear to grieve at the loss of family members. Elephants in particular have been known to remain in the area of a relative's bones for lengthy periods (McComb et al., 2006).

PSYCHOLOGY AS A HUB SCIENCE

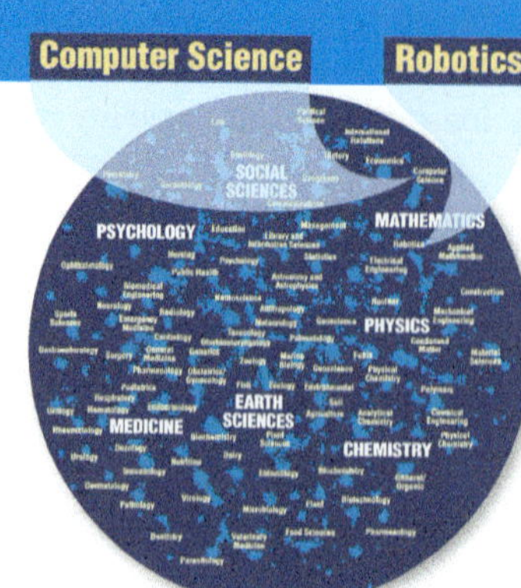

Can Machines Become Conscious?

EXTENDING THE QUESTION OF WHAT CREATURES ARE CONSCIOUS A STEP FURTHER, we can ask whether it is possible to construct an artificial consciousness. From the *Terminator* to *Her*'s Samantha, Hollywood loves to tell the story of the machine that develops consciousness. Stephen Hawking, Bill Gates, and Elon Musk have warned us that self-aware robots are likely to jeopardize the continuity of the human race.

What does it mean for a machine to be conscious? John Searle (1980) distinguishes between "strong" and "weak" artificial intelligence (AI). Weak AI, which all current robots possess, refers to the ability to demonstrate intelligent behavior but without the ability to experience conscious states or subjective awareness. Strong AI refers to machines possessing the full range of human cognition.

How would we judge whether a machine has achieved consciousness? In 1950, Alan Turing devised a test of a machine's ability to think. According to the Turing test, if a human had a conversation with two other beings, one human and one machine, without being able to distinguish between them, then the machine would have passed the test. The 2014 Eugene Goostman program, which impersonated a 13-year-old from the Ukraine, managed to convince 10 out of 30 judges that "he" was human. The ability to meet Turing's criteria may be within reach.

Daily Mail

One Nao robot appears to have the answer to the dilemma posed to the group, which researchers claim is evidence for self-awareness.

One type of consciousness discussed in this chapter is self-awareness. Selmer Bringsjord and his colleagues (2015) claim that their robots have demonstrated evidence of self-awareness in the mirror test described in this chapter. In another demonstration, the researchers told three Nao robots that two were given "dumbing" pills to prevent them from speaking, while one was given a placebo. In actuality, mute buttons were pressed on two of the robots. When asked who had been given the active pills, all three tried to answer, but of course only one was able to say, "I don't know." The robot paused, then stood up and said, "Sorry, I know now. I was able to prove that I was not given a dumbing pill."

Daniel Dennett (1991) argues that it might be more interesting to set aside the question of consciousness and simply build the most human robot possible. Robots are becoming more natural both in looks and behavior, and robotics experts hope to make them indistinguishable from humans. Hanson Robotics' Sophia has cameras in her eyes that allow her to make eye contact and recognize people. She uses Google Chrome voice recognition to process speech, chat with people, and learn. Hiroshi Ishiguro has plans to make his robots suitable for jobs such as a hotel receptionist, a museum tour guide, and a language tutor. Already, 80% of Ishiguro's participants greeted his robots by saying "hello," as they mistakenly believed the robots to be human.

Where will this technology lead us? That remains unknown, but the effort to construct artificial consciousness might yield new insights into our own human consciousness. ■

Searching for Consciousness in the Brain

Is it possible to find consciousness in the brain? Consciousness, the mind, and the brain are like a set of nested Russian dolls. The brain, the outside doll, houses the mind but has other functions as well, such as maintaining breathing and body temperature. The mind, the middle doll, houses consciousness, the innermost doll, but also manages unconscious functions such as long-term memory, discussed in Chapter 9.

In this chapter, we will examine a number of natural, artificial, and pathological circumstances that correlate with variations in consciousness. As a result of these investigations, we can begin to view consciousness as requiring complex interactions between areas of the cerebral cortex and the thalamus, discussed in detail in Chapter 4. In particular, lesions of the thalamus result in the type of profound unconsciousness typically associated with brain death (Bogen, 1995). We discuss the concept of brain death more fully in a later section of this chapter.

Certain structures in the brain, such as the thalamus, might be necessary, but not sufficient, for consciousness. For example, observing that your television screen no longer produces a picture after you remove a component does not necessarily imply that the sole source of the picture is that particular component; it's likely that other components need to be attached simultaneously and contribute to the creation of the visual image. Likewise, additional brain structures, such as the reticular formation of the brainstem, play an active role in raising or lowering the thresholds of conscious awareness (see ● Figure 6.2). Because of these variations, you are far more likely to hear and respond to a sound while awake than while deeply asleep. Structures such as the thalamus and reticular formation have been described as "enabling" consciousness, but they do not produce its content (Crick & Koch, 2003).

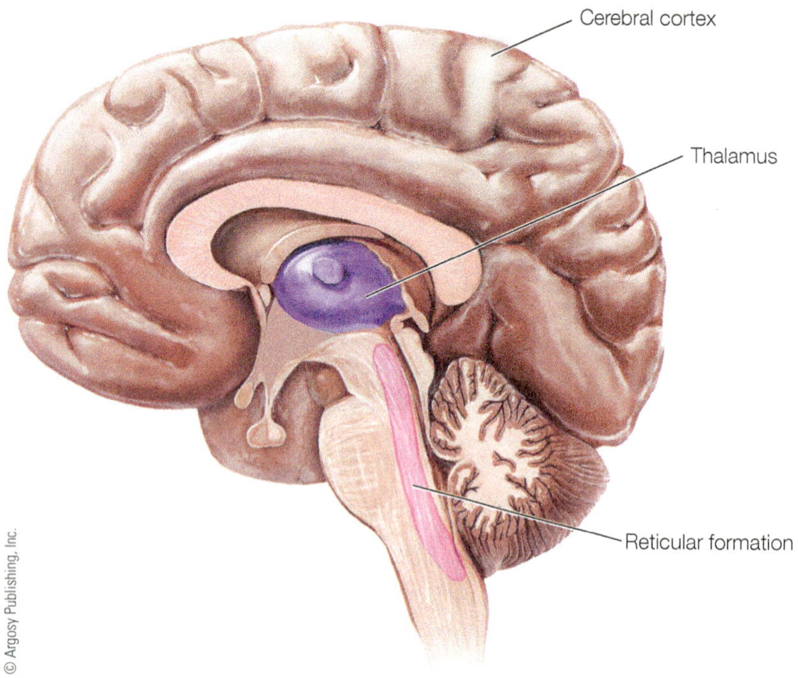

FIGURE 6.2

Brain Structures Associated With Consciousness. Among the brain structures that are believed to participate in consciousness are the cerebral cortex, thalamus, and reticular formation, as well as the complex pathways connecting these parts of the brain. These structures make consciousness possible, which we know because damage to these circuits results in unconsciousness, but they do not determine the content of consciousness.

Instead of looking for consciousness as resulting from the activity of particular structures, it is more useful to consider consciousness as resulting from activity changes in brain networks. Neuroscientists initially believed that when your thought is unfocused during a state known as *mind wandering*, the brain would be quiet, but as you focus on a specific task, the brain would "light up." This does not seem to be the case. The brain uses only about 5% more energy when people are focused compared to when they are unfocused (Raichle & Snyder, 2011; Raichle, 2015). These observations have led to the identification of a default mode network (DMN), which maintains a high level of unconscious, background activity as it helps prepare the brain for conscious thought (see ● Figure 6.3). Activity in the DMN actually decreases a bit when the person engages in a conscious task requiring attention. Activity in the DMN is correlated with thinking about the self, others, and a person's past and future.

Functional connectivity in the DMN in healthy individuals is stronger in adulthood than in childhood and older adulthood (Mak et al., 2017). Functional connectivity of the DMN, in turn, is associated with cognitive function. Abnormal connectivity of the DMN has been observed in individuals with autism spectrum disorder (Cherkassky et al., 2006) and Alzheimer's disease (Greicius et al., 2004). It is possible that other psychological disorders might have correlating disturbances in DMN function.

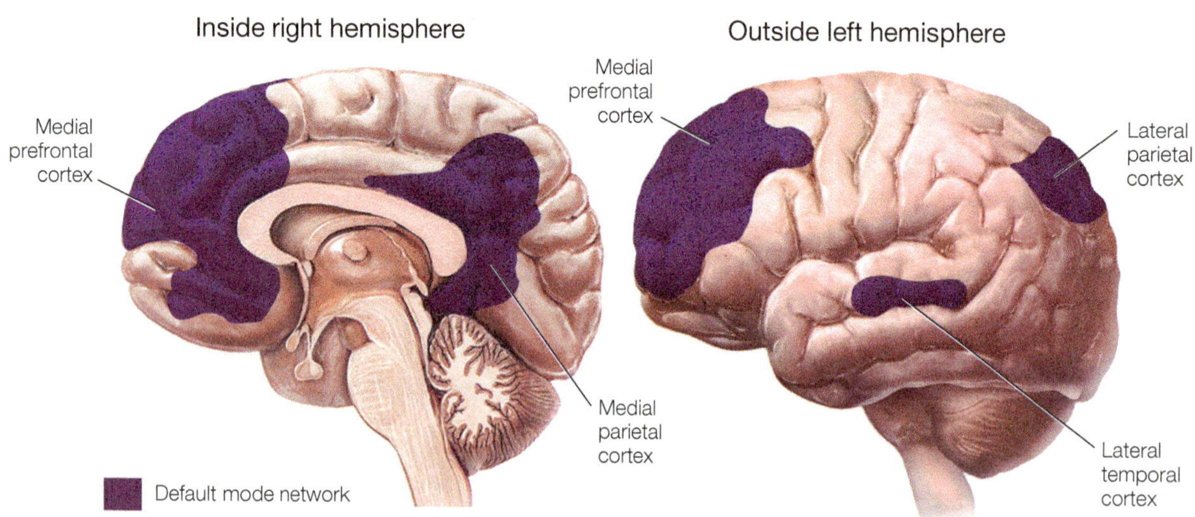

FIGURE 6.3

The Default Mode Network (DMN) of the Brain. Activity of the DMN corresponds to mind wandering, thinking about the self, and preparing for conscious thought.

Source: Adapted from M. E. Raichle (2010). "The Brain's Dark Energy," *Scientific American*, *314*(5803), 44–49. doi: 10.1126/science. 1134405

SUMMARY 6.1 Definitions of Consciousness

Aspect of consciousness	Definition	Example
State of awareness 	The level of conscious awareness of internal states or surroundings, which can be high or low and realistic or distorted.	• Asleep or awake. • Perceiving realistically or hallucinating. • Hypnotized or not. • Meditating or not.
Content of awareness 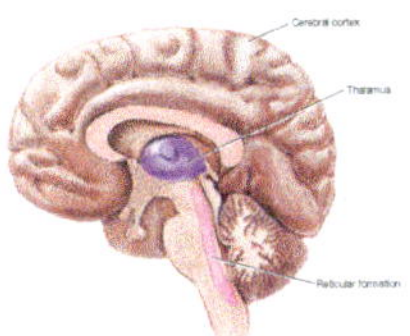	The ongoing catalog of internal and external stimuli that are the focus of current attention.	• Hearing a neighbor's music. • Thinking that you're hungry and it's time to eat. • Considering the implications of a news report.
Self-awareness  	The special understanding of the self as distinct from other stimuli.	• Knowing that you are looking at yourself in the mirror. • Knowing that you are sleeping and dreaming.

Credits: Top row—ARCO/W Dolder/AGE Fotostock; Second row—Argosy Publishing Inc.; Bottom row—Ghislain & Marie David de Lossy/The Image Bank/Getty Images / Diana Reiss, Ph.D.

What Happens to Consciousness During Waking and Sleep?

Our first meaning of consciousness involves variations in an animal's state of awareness. Awareness changes dramatically across cycles of **sleep** and **waking**. These cycles follow **circadian rhythms**, or daily rhythms. The term *circadian* comes from the Latin words for "about a day."

Circadian rhythms are only one example of a number of important biorhythms. Animals have birth seasons and migration patterns. Human females experience menstrual cycles. Within a single day, we also see regular fluctuations in arousal, with peaks occurring every 90 to 120 minutes.

Circadian Rhythms

Circadian rhythms respond to a combination of internal and external factors. Internal **biological clocks**, controlled by the hypothalamus, provide an approximate schedule for various physical processes, including sleep and waking, body temperature, and hunger. These internal biological clocks interact with external stimuli, known as *zeitgebers* (*zeit* means "time" and *geber* means "to give" in German; hence, these stimuli are "time givers").

Light is one of the most important zeitgebers for humans. Exposure to the rising sun each day helps to reset the internal biological clocks to the correct time. In the absence of light, our internal clocks run a few minutes longer than a 24-hour cycle. Over time, the distortion adds

sleep A normal state of consciousness characterized by reduced awareness of external stimuli.

waking A normal state of consciousness characterized by alertness and awareness of external stimuli.

circadian rhythm A daily biological rhythm.

biological clock An internal mechanism that provides an approximate schedule for various physical processes.

up, and behavior is only occasionally synchronized with normal cycles of day and night. Totally blind people and sailors on submarines experience longer than normal circadian cycles because of their lack of exposure to natural light (Kelly et al., 1999; Skene et al., 1999).

Eating patterns are also significant zeitgebers, as many midnight snackers know. Mice normally sleep during the day and feed at night. However, when mice are fed only during the day, they begin sleeping at night and exploring more during the day (Mieda et al., 2006).

Modern Living and Circadian Rhythms Our human ancestors remained awake during daylight and slept throughout the dark of night, although some historians argue they did so in two shifts rather than continuously (Ekirch, 2001). They lacked the technology needed to travel rapidly across time zones.

Modern sleep and waking patterns are substantially different from those of our ancestors, often resulting in challenges to health. Technology, particularly the invention of artificial light, has shaped our contemporary sleep–wake patterns by making it easy to be awake at night (see • Figure 6.4). Artificial lighting, including that produced by tablets and phones, affects sleep by breaking down melatonin, a hormone released in the evening that regulates sleep cycles. Changes in melatonin release have been implicated in a long list of human diseases, including cancer, diabetes, and heart disease, which might be more common among people who work night shifts (Touitou et al., 2017). "Social jet lag," or the disrupted sleep resulting from modern inconsistencies in weekday and weekend sleep times, has been associated with overweight, obesity, and metabolic syndrome (Espitia-Bautista et al., 2017).

Some occupations, such as hospital and public safety jobs, involve work around the clock, which in turn is correlated with physical and psychological problems (Kecklund & Axelsson, 2016). Between 40% and 80% of workers on graveyard shifts (11:00 p.m. to 7:30 a.m.) experience shift maladaptation syndrome, characterized by health, personality, mood, and interpersonal problems (Wagner, 1996). Accident rates in the industrial swing shift (3:00 p.m. to 11:30 p.m.) are higher than in the traditional day shift, and the graveyard shift is the most dangerous work period (Caruso, 2014). Not only do shift workers experience more accidents, but they also make more errors. Hospital workers are more likely to make significant errors during evening shifts than during day shifts (Chang et al., 2011).

Our modern ability to cross time zones leads to the experience of jet lag, which produces fatigue, irritability, and sleepiness. The travel is not to blame because north–south travel of equal distance does not produce the symptoms of jet lag (Herxheimer & Waterhouse, 2003). Chronic jet lag has even more serious consequences. Flight attendants with 4 or more years of experience in which time zones were crossed at least once a week had reduced reaction times and made 9% more mistakes on memory tasks than local crews (Cho et al., 2000).

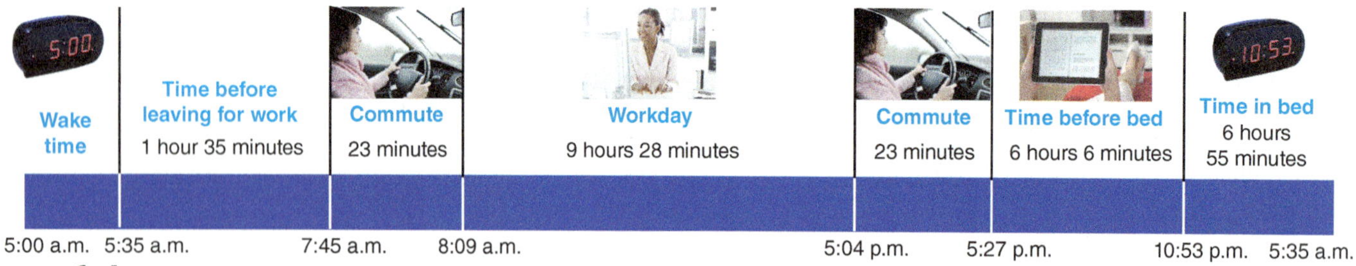

FIGURE **6.4**

A Day in the Life of a Typical American Worker. Americans are believed to be somewhat sleep deprived because the average adult spends only 6 hours and 55 minutes in bed, which includes time needed to initiate sleep. Although people try to make up for lost sleep on weekends by sleeping longer, this solution is not very effective.

Source: Data from National Sleep Foundation (2008). "2008 Sleep in America Poll," retrieved from http://www.sleepfoundation.org/sites/default / files/2008%20POLL%20SOF.PDF

Illustration: photos, left to right: Hurst Photo/Shutterstock.com; Martin Novak/Shutterstock.com; StockLite/Shutterstock.com; Martin Novak/Shutterstock.com; iStock.com/hocus-focus; iStock.com/funkypoodle

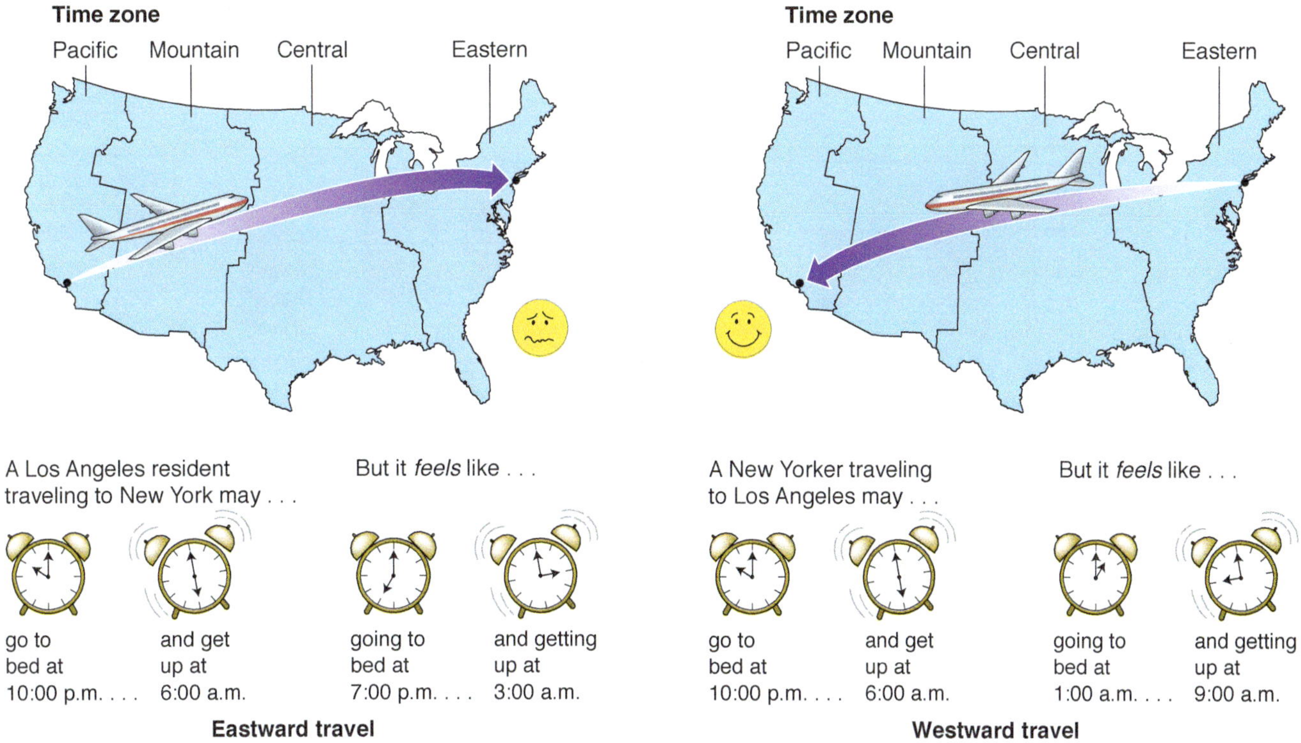

FIGURE **6.5**

Jet Lag Is Worse When Traveling East. Traveling eastward is more disruptive to circadian rhythms than traveling westward. Los Angeles residents visiting New York feel like they are going to bed 3 hours earlier than usual (7:00 p.m. Los Angeles time) and waking up in the middle of the night (3:00 a.m. Los Angeles time). New Yorkers traveling to Los Angeles have to stay up a little later (1:00 a.m. New York time) but then can sleep later to compensate (9:00 a.m. New York time). Most people find the latter scenario easier.

Some challenges to our circadian rhythms are easier to manage than others. It is easier to adjust when we set the clock to a later point than to an earlier point. The experiences of two people, one traveling from Los Angeles to New York City (setting the clock forward) and the other traveling from New York City to Los Angeles (setting the clock back), are compared in ● Figure 6.5. Let's assume that both travelers usually go to bed at 10:00 p.m. and get up at 6:00 a.m. To stay on the same sleep schedule, the LA–NYC traveler must now go to sleep at 7:00 p.m. and wake up at 3:00 a.m., which is difficult, whereas the NYC–LA traveler must stay up until 1:00 a.m. but can sleep until 9:00 a.m., which is easier.

Daylight saving time offers another opportunity to observe our responses to abrupt changes in our daily schedules (see ● Figure 6.6). This energy-saving relic from World War I requires the setting of clocks forward 1 hour in the spring and back 1 hour in the fall. When Canadian traffic accident data were correlated with the two annual daylight saving shifts, the shift back in the fall resulted in a 7% decrease in traffic accidents on the following Monday compared to other fall Mondays. In the spring setting of the clock forward, a comparable 7% increase in traffic accidents occurred (Coren, 1996).

When less light is available for setting the body's internal clocks, approximately 4 to 6% of the population experience **major depressive disorder with seasonal pattern**, formerly known as *seasonal affective disorder* (Jepson et al., 1998; APA, 2013). During the winter months at higher latitudes, the reduction in daylight hours interferes with circadian rhythms. This disruption may lead to symptoms of depression, discussed in more detail in Chapter 14, that lift once the days become longer again. A relatively small group of individuals experience symptoms in the spring and summer instead. Rates of seasonal depression vary from 1.4% in Florida to 9.7% in New Hampshire (Jepson et al., 1998). Seasonal depression is typically treated by exposure to bright light, with or without melatonin supplements or antidepressant medications (Wirz-Justice, 2018). The lights used in this therapy are stronger than what is normally experienced indoors but not as strong as the light at the beach on an August afternoon.

major depressive disorder with seasonal pattern A mood disorder in which depression occurs regularly at the same time each year, usually during the winter months; formerly known as seasonal affective disorder (SAD).

Individual Variations in Circadian Rhythms You might believe that the day should start around 2:00 p.m., whereas your roommate pops out of bed smiling at an alarming 6:30 in the morning. What accounts for these individual differences in sleep patterns?

Some individual differences become evident in infancy and remain consistent over the life span. "Morning" people have been called larks, and "night" people have been called owls

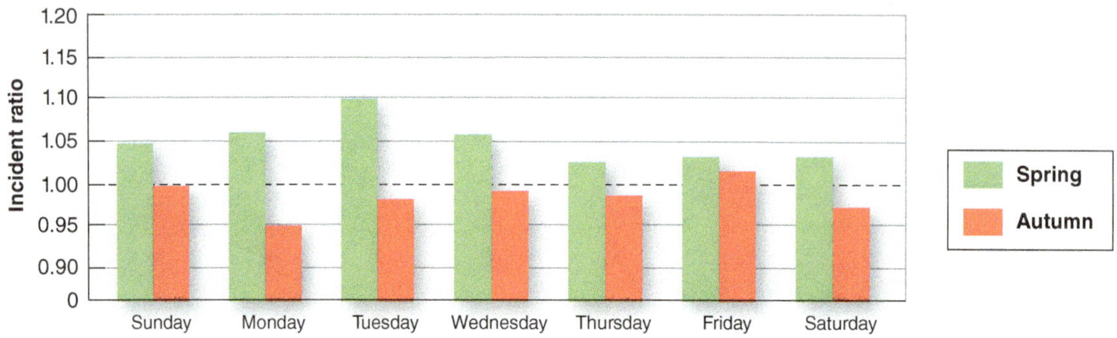

FIGURE **6.6**

Daylight Saving Time Affects the Number of Heart Attacks. Fifteen years of data show that rates of heart attack increase significantly in the days following the spring shift in daylight saving time and decrease following the fall shift. The incidence ratio is computed by comparing the number of heart attacks on the specified day following the shift to the mean number of heart attacks for the same day 2 weeks before and 2 weeks after the shift. The likely reason for the increase is sleep deprivation; it increases sympathetic nervous system activation and inflammation, which can be dangerous to people with existing health problems.

Source: I. Janszky & R. Ljung (2008). "Shifts to and from Daylight Saving Time and Incidence of Myocardial Infarction," *New England Journal of Medicine*, *359*(18), 1966–1968. doi: 10.1056/NEJMc0807104.

(Åkerstedt & Fröberg, 1976). Many people fall somewhere between these two extremes and are at their best in the middle of the day. Research on the genetic basis of circadian rhythms suggests that the different patterns result from different versions of the genes responsible for the activity of our internal clocks (Katzenberg et al., 1998).

Other differences appear to be more age related. Nearly everyone acts like an owl during adolescence and young adulthood (Carskadon et al., 1998). In their mid to late 20s, many temporary owls revert to their previous lark or medium state. The exact cause for such a shift during and after adolescence and young adulthood is unclear, but researchers suspect that the shift correlates with a burst of brain development that is initiated at puberty. Some researchers view the return to a previous sleep pattern in young adulthood as a reliable indicator that the brain is fully mature (Roenneberg et al., 2004).

Waking

Varying states of awareness can be described using electroencephalogram (EEG) recordings, which provide a general measure of overall brain activity. During waking, we alternate among three patterns of activity indicated by the recording of **beta waves**, **alpha waves**, and **gamma waves** in the EEG (see ● Figure 6.7). During beta activity, a person is actively

CrackerClips Stock Media/Shutterstock.com; Courtesy Earth Observatory/NASA

Modern artificial light breaks down the hormone melatonin, which is released only at night. Disruptions caused by the effects of light on melatonin might be responsible for higher rates of disease among employees who work at night.

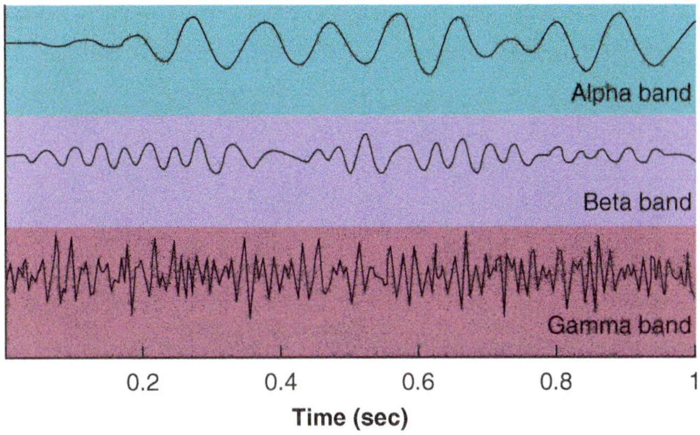

FIGURE 6.7

The EEG During Waking. EEG recordings during waking usually alternate between alpha waves and beta waves. Alpha waves are associated with a relaxed, possibly drowsy state, whereas beta waves are associated with alertness. Gamma waves are seen in response to sensory input.

thinking and alert. Beta activity is characterized by rapid (15 to 30 cycles per second), irregular, low-amplitude waves that indicate the cerebral cortex is processing large amounts of diverse data. A person showing alpha activity is awake but relaxed. Alpha waves are slightly slower, larger, and more regular than beta waves, with a frequency of 9 to 12 cycles per second. Improvements in EEG technology provided the means to record waking waveforms that are faster than 30 cycles per second, known as gamma waves (Miller, 2007). Gamma waves accompany the processing of sensory input, particularly visual stimuli.

Daydreaming, or mind wandering, "refers to spontaneous, subjective experiences in a no-task, no-stimulus, no-response situation" (Vaitl et al., 2005, p. 100). Daydreaming is correlated with activity in the DMN, as described earlier in the chapter. EEG studies show that activity in the DMN is most closely correlated with alpha waves (Knyazev et al., 2011). The function of daydreaming is unclear. We might daydream simply because we evolved the ability to divide our attention, as described in Chapter 5 (Mason et al., 2007). However, during activation of the DMN, we often think about our past experiences and plan our future (Kahn, 2013). This contradicts the commonly held view that daydreaming is a "waste of time."

JohnMeyers/Shutterstock.com

Regardless of whether they were larks or owls as children, most teens act like owls by naturally staying up late and sleeping in. Legislators in the United States have recently begun to take notice, and have mandated later start times for middle and high schools. Usually by the mid-20s, young adults go back to whichever sleeping pattern they showed before puberty, a change that may mark the final maturity of the brain.

Sleep

We spend one-third of our lives sleeping. Despite all that experience, few of us know what is going on during sleep. By carefully recording and observing the experience of volunteers sleeping in laboratories, psychologists have been able to unravel many mysteries of sleep.

Stages of Sleep On the basis of observations of sleeping volunteers, we divide sleep into two types: **rapid eye movement (REM) sleep** and **non-rapid eye movement (N-REM) sleep**. These types of sleep are differentiated by EEG recordings, muscle tone, autonomic activity, and mental activity (see ● Figure 6.8).

N-REM sleep is divided into four stages. Stage 1 usually occurs when we first go to sleep. Our examination of the participant's EEG shows patterns that are difficult to distinguish from those of the drowsy, waking volunteer. Some **theta waves** (4 to 7 cycles per second), which are larger and slower than alpha waves, are now observed. At this stage, people may not be aware that they are sleeping. Frequently, we awaken a friend or a family member who has fallen asleep in front of the television by turning off the program only to have the sleeping person deny being asleep.

beta wave A waveform of 15 to 30 cycles per second recorded by electroencephalogram that usually indicates alert waking.

alpha wave A waveform of 9 to 12 cycles per second recorded by electroencephalogram that usually indicates relaxed waking.

gamma wave A waveform of more than 30 cycles per second recorded by electroencephalogram that indicates attention to sensory input.

rapid eye movement (REM) sleep The component of sleep characterized by waveforms resembling waking, as measured by electroencephalogram, accompanied by rapid motion of the eyes, muscular paralysis, and sympathetic nervous system activation.

FIGURE 6.8

The EEG During Sleep. Sleep is divided into two components: rapid eye movement (REM) sleep and non-REM (N-REM) sleep. The EEG during REM sleep is similar to wakefulness. Stages 1 and 2 of N-REM sleep feature theta waves. Special waveforms known as sleep spindles and K complexes, which might represent the brain's attempts to tune out environmental stimuli, appear in stage 2. Stages 3 and 4 of N-REM sleep feature delta waves and represent the deepest stages of sleep.

Source: Adapted from J. Horne (1988). *Why We Sleep: The Functions of Sleep in Humans and Other Mammals*, New York, NY: Oxford University Press.

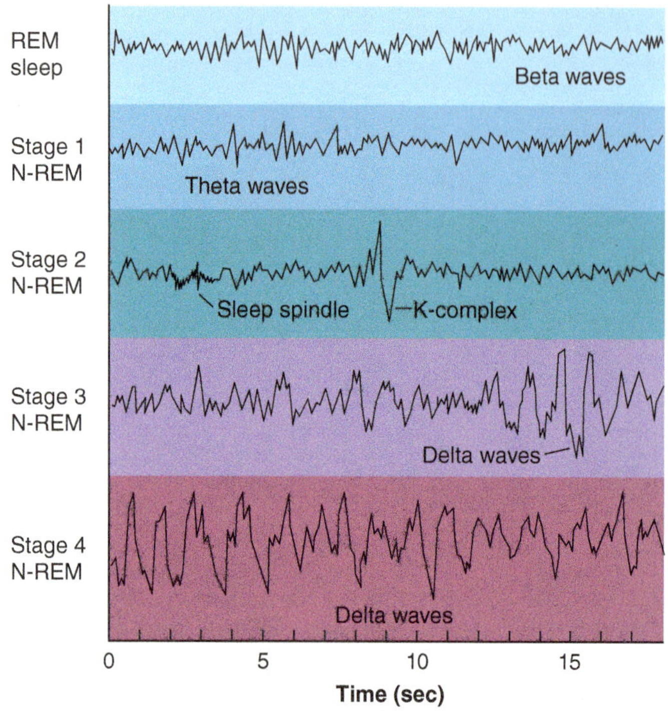

non–rapid eye movement (N-REM) sleep The components of sleep characterized by theta and delta wave activity, as recorded by electroencephalogram, and deep physical relaxation.

theta wave A waveform of 4 to 7 cycles per second recorded by electroencephalogram that is characteristic of lighter stages of non–rapid eye movement sleep.

delta wave A waveform of 1 to 4 cycles per second recorded by electroencephalogram that usually indicates deep non–rapid eye movement sleep.

After 10 to 15 minutes, stage 1 of N-REM sleep gives way to stage 2. Now there is no doubt that the person is asleep. Further reductions in heart rate and muscle tension occur, and the EEG begins to show special waveforms called K complexes and sleep spindles that occur only in N-REM sleep. Spindles reflect brain activity associated with the consolidation of memories, and their frequency increases after a period of pre-sleep learning (Jegou et al., 2019). Decreased spindle frequency is characteristic of Alzheimer's disease and reduced cognitive functioning (Gorgoni et al., 2016).

After about 15 minutes in stage 2, we enter stage 3 and then stage 4 N-REM sleep. Both of these stages show **delta wave** activity, which is the largest, slowest (1 to 4 cycles per second) EEG waveform. Stages 3 and 4 differ primarily in the amount of delta activity that occurs, with stage 4 having the most. We are deeply asleep in these stages. Awakening from stage 4 is

EXPERIENCING PSYCHOLOGY

The Epworth Sleepiness Scale

COLLEGE STUDENTS OFTEN neglect sleep time to study, work, and socialize. Sixty percent of students reported staying awake for an entire night at least once since coming to college (Thacher, 2008). Poor sleep habits lead to daytime sleepiness, which can affect how much you learn in your classes, how well you work, and your safety when driving and operating other machinery. How much sleepiness is too much?

Try using the Epworth Sleepiness Scale to see how sleepy you tend to be (Johns, 1991). In contrast to just feeling tired, how likely are you to doze off or fall asleep in the situations in the list? Even if you have not done some of these things recently, try to work out how they would have affected you. Use the scale to choose the most appropriate number for each situation. A score greater than 10 indicates excessive daytime sleepiness. If you scored at this level or above, it's time for some lifestyle changes. ■

difficult, and considerable disorientation may occur before a person becomes fully awake. You may have received a telephone call about an hour after you first go to sleep, when you are likely to be experiencing stage 4 N-REM sleep. If you hear the telephone, it may take several seconds to locate the phone and wake up enough to have a decent conversation.

The first episode of REM sleep occurs between 90 and 120 minutes after the onset of sleep. This stage is often called paradoxical sleep, reflecting a combination of brain activity resembling waking with the external appearance of deep sleep. During REM sleep, the EEG cycles between beta and theta rhythms (Vijayan et al., 2017). The eyes make the periodic movements back and forth that give this stage its name. The sympathetic nervous system becomes very active. Heart rate, blood pressure, and breathing become rapid or irregular. Males experience erections, while females experience increased blood flow in the vicinity of the vagina (Hirshkowitz & Moore, 1996). If awakened during this stage, most people report vivid, storylike dreams, which we discuss in more detail in a later section.

Major postural muscles are inactive during REM sleep, effectively paralyzing the sleeper, although smaller muscles in the fingers and the toes might twitch. You might have experienced dreams in which something terrible was coming, but you couldn't move. Your dream probably reflects recognition on the part of the brain that you are paralyzed. This paralysis provides a protective mechanism that prevents you from acting out your dreams. In cases of REM sleep behavior disorder, paralysis fails, and people injure themselves or their sleeping partners. When one patient dreamed of playing football, he knocked everything off his dresser, hit his head against the wall, and banged his knee on the dresser (Schenck et al., 2002).

Because the body is paralyzed during REM sleep, sleepwalking cannot happen in this stage. Instead, sleepwalking occurs when a person is in stage 3 or 4 of N-REM sleep. Sleep talking is most common during lighter stages of N-REM sleep, but it is also possible during REM sleep. These phenomena become progressively less common with age.

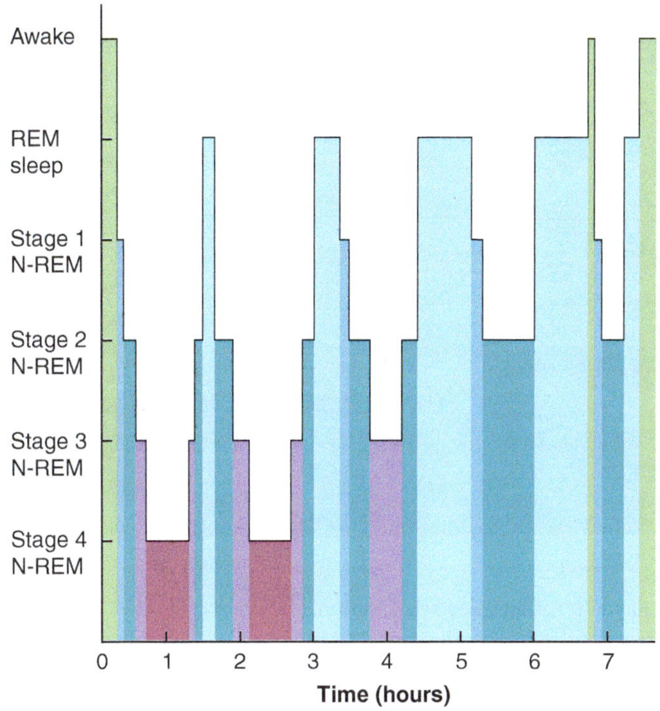

FIGURE **6.9**

Nightly Sleep Patterns. Sleep shows a typical progression over the night. The first 4 hours are dominated by N-REM sleep, and most stage 3 and 4 N-REM sleep occurs at this time. The second 4 hours feature large amounts of REM sleep.

Source: Adapted from R. D. Cartwright (1978). *A Primer on Sleep and Dreaming*, Reading, MA: Addison-Wesley.

The cycling between REM sleep and N-REM sleep in humans follows a characteristic pattern over a period of 8 hours of sleep (see Figure 6.9). The first half of a night's sleep is characterized by longer periods of N-REM sleep and brief periods of REM sleep. Stages 3 and 4 of N-REM sleep are especially dominant during these first 4 hours. The second half of

Situation	Chance of dozing
Sitting and reading	
Watching television	
Sitting inactive in a public place (e.g., a theater)	
Riding as a car passenger for an hour without a break	
Lying down to rest in the afternoon	
Sitting and talking to someone	
Sitting quietly after lunch without alcohol	
In a car, while stopping for a few minutes in traffic	
TOTAL SCORE	

0 = Would never doze
1 = Slight chance of dozing
2 = Moderate chance of dozing
3 = High chance of dozing

Human error, and sleep deprivation in particular, frequently contributes to major accidents and disasters. The 1979 nuclear meltdown at Three Mile Island changed the power industry in the United States. The 1986 explosion of the space shuttle Challenger rattled confidence in the U.S. space program. The 1989 oil spill caused by the running aground of the tanker Exxon Valdez, shown in this photo, energized concerns about environmental protection. More recently, the operator of a commuter train that ran off the tracks up an escalator at Chicago O'Hare International Airport admitted to "dozing off."

the night's sleep switches to a different pattern. REM sleep is now dominant, and N-REM sleep remains in the lighter stages. Stages 3 and 4 may be infrequent or absent during the last 4 hours of sleep. We usually spend the last half hour or so of the night's sleep in REM sleep and often wake up with the awareness that we have been dreaming.

The Benefits of Sleep

Although we still have many unanswered questions about why we spend one-third of our lives sleeping, we know that lack of sleep can have many negative effects. Excess sleepiness on the part of decision makers has contributed to many disasters, including the Three Mile Island nuclear meltdown, the Challenger space shuttle explosion, and the grounding of the oil tanker Exxon Valdez (Coren, 2012). In 2014, a commuter train at Chicago's O'Hare airport controlled by an operator who admitted to dozing off ran off the tracks and climbed an escalator. Staying awake for 17 to 19 straight hours produces worse reaction time than being legally drunk (Williamson & Feyer, 2000). Sleep deprivation can result in obesity and risk for type 2 diabetes (Benedict et al., 2016).

Sleep, and in particular stages 3 and 4 of N-REM sleep, plays an important role in repairing the body. Sleep deprivation slows the healing of injuries (Murphy et al., 2007), reduces the activity of the immune system (Zager et al., 2007), and results in the production of fewer new neurons in adult brains (Akers et al., 2018). Nearly all human growth hormone, which plays important roles in repairing the body, is released during stages 3 and 4 of N-REM sleep but rarely during other stages of sleep and waking (Savine & Sönksen, 2000) (see ● Figure 6.10). Another line of evidence supporting the restorative hypothesis of sleep is the behavior of people following daytime physical activity. Aerobic exercise increased the amount of N-REM sleep as well as subjective reports of "feeling rested" (Aritake-Okada et al., 2019).

It is possible to selectively deprive volunteers in a sleep laboratory of stage 3 and 4 N-REM sleep. After a night of such deprivation, volunteers typically complain of muscle and joint pain (Moldofsky & Scarisbrick, 1976). Because time spent in N-REM sleep decreases about 30 minutes per decade after the age of 50 (Van Cauter et al., 2000), it is possible that reduced N-REM sleep is the source of some of the muscle and joint aches and pains experienced by older adults.

Sleep plays a significant role in memory. Staying up all night results in poor memory performance, and two subsequent nights of normal sleep do not make up for the initial sleep deprivation effects (Stickgold & Walker, 2007). Sleep may serve as a special state for consolidating memories, in contrast to the acquisition and initial processing of new memories that occurs during waking (Rasch & Born, 2013). During N-REM sleep, memories are reactivated

FIGURE **6.10**

Human Growth Hormone Release. Human growth hormone stimulates growth and repair. Most human growth hormone release occurs during the first 4 hours of sleep each night, primarily during stages 3 and 4 of N-REM sleep. The drop in time spent in stages 3 and 4 among older adults might contribute to reduced abilities to heal compared to those of younger adults.

Source: Adapted from R. M. Coleman (1986). *Wide Awake at 3:00 a.m. by Choice or by Chance?* New York, NY: W. H. Freeman.

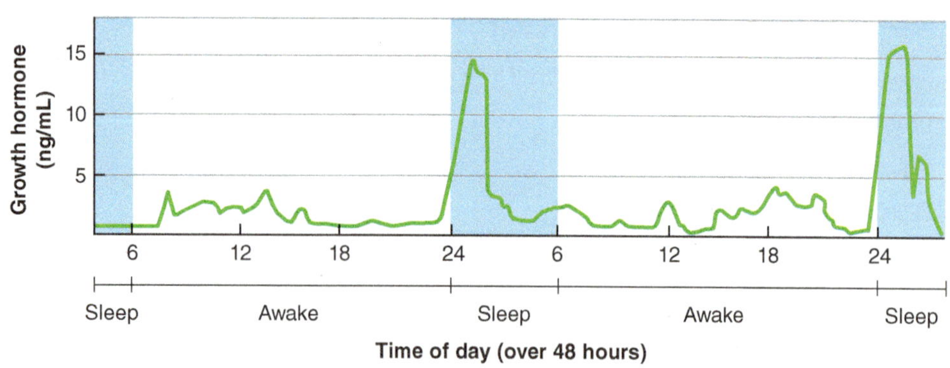

and transformed into versions that can be stored in long-term memory (see Chapter 9). REM sleep then stabilizes the newly transformed memories (Li et al., 2017). While students often view forgetting as a bad thing, the ability to forget unnecessary information is essential to maintaining an efficient memory, and much of this forgetting occurs during sleep (Hashmi et al., 2013). Overall, students who wish to retain the material they've studied and the ability to retrieve it easily would be well advised to get a good night's sleep (Mazza et al., 2016).

The Special Benefits of REM Sleep Birds and mammals are the only creatures to show clear evidence of REM sleep, suggesting that this sleep stage is a fairly recent development in the course of evolution. When volunteers are specifically deprived of REM sleep, they show many of the same symptoms as people who experience an overall lack of sleep, including irritability and difficulty concentrating. In addition, REM sleep-deprived individuals show a phenomenon known as REM rebound (Dement, 1960). When allowed to sleep normally, they spend an unusually large amount of their sleep time in REM sleep. You may have experienced REM rebound during a nap following a night with little sleep. You might be aware of having dreamed vividly during the nap, and you're unlikely to feel rested. These attempts to make up for lost REM sleep suggest that REM sleep is associated with necessary functions.

One clue to a possible function of REM sleep is the fact that the proportion of sleep spent in REM sleep is a function of a species' relative maturity at birth (Siegel, 2001). The human infant, born at an immature stage of brain development relative to other primate species, spends about half of its sleep time in REM sleep (see • Figure 6.11), compared to the 20% of sleep time spent in REM sleep by adolescents and adults (McCarley, 2007). Premature infants spend up to 80% of their sleep time in REM sleep. REM sleep may provide at least part of the stimulation necessary to correctly "wire" the immature brain (Grigg-Damberger, 2017; Marks et al., 1995).

REM sleep and mood are tightly interwoven, providing us with a further clue regarding the possible functions of REM sleep. As we will see in Chapter 14, individuals with depression experience disruptions in their normal sleep patterns. Without treatment, they enter REM sleep earlier in the night than typical participants do, and they spend a greater proportion of their sleeping time in REM sleep. One of the possible mechanisms by which antidepressant medications regulate mood is their suppression of REM sleep. Individuals with bipolar disorder, which can be characterized by moods that swing from euphoria to depression, experience an abnormally low need for sleep, including REM sleep.

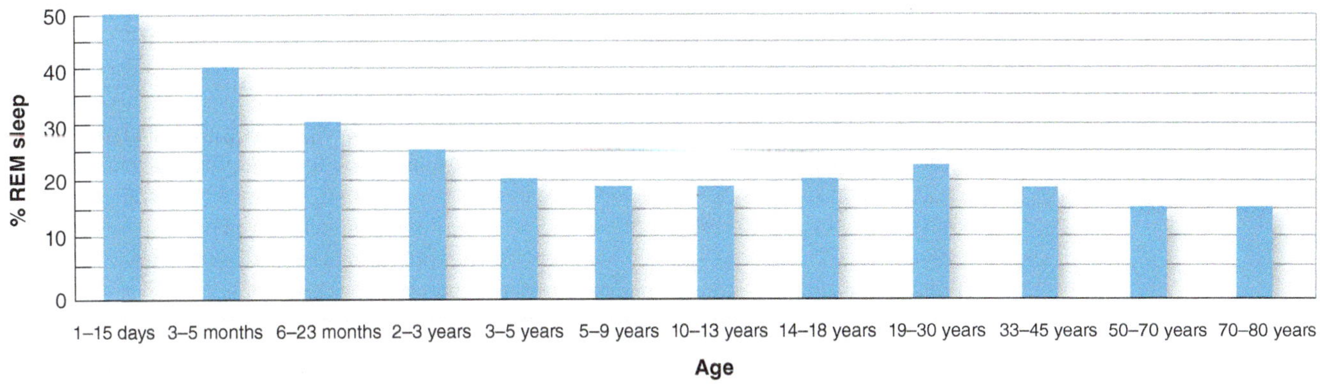

FIGURE **6.11**

REM Sleep Over the Life Span. Infants and young children spend greater percentages of their sleep time in REM sleep than do adolescents and adults, suggesting that brain activity during REM sleep might help wire the developing brain.

Source: Adapted from H. P. Roffwarg et al. (1966). "Ontogenetic Development of the Human Sleep-Dream Cycle," *Science, 152*, 604–619. doi: 10.1126/science.152.3722.604

These correlations between REM sleep and mood may represent a common underlying biochemical mechanism. Brainstem neurons that release serotonin and norepinephrine are especially quiet during REM sleep, although they are active during waking and somewhat active during N-REM sleep (Gottesman, 2002). These same neurotransmitters have also been implicated in the regulation of mood states, which helps explain links between REM sleep and mood.

Jose Luis Pelaez, Inc./Blend Images/Corbis

The activation-synthesis theory of dream content suggests that the content of dreams represents the mind's efforts to make sense out of real physical sensations. During REM sleep, the vestibular system of the inner ear is quite active. Because the vestibular system normally informs us about the position and movement of the head, vestibular activity during REM sleep might lead to the commonly experienced dreams of flying or falling.

Dreams From the earliest times in our history, people have searched for the significance and meaning of their dreams. In ancient Egypt, many people believed that dreams predicted the future. In his classic book *The Interpretation of Dreams*, Freud (1900/1953) argued that the unconscious mind expressed itself symbolically through our dreams. These are interesting ideas, but what does science have to say about **dreaming?**

The use of EEG technology to track a volunteer's sleep patterns allowed researchers to awaken volunteers and assess a dream experience scientifically for the first time (Aserinsky & Kleitman, 1953; Dement & Kleitman, 1957). Improved methods, including brain imaging, magnetic stimulation, and improved EEG, have produced further insights into dreaming (Cipolli et al., 2016). Rather than proposing sharp distinctions between dreaming during sleep and other types of thought, dream activity is seen as being on a continuum extending across focused thought and mind wandering during wakefulness to thought-like and dream-like behaviors during sleep.

An activation–synthesis theory of dreaming suggests that the content of dreams simply reflects ongoing neural activity. For example, dreams of being unable to move in a dangerous situation might accurately mirror the muscle paralysis present during the REM state (Hobson & McCarley, 1977). Common dreams of flying or falling may be caused by the unusual activation of the vestibular system during REM sleep (Hunt, 1989). In Chapter 5, we discussed the vestibular system's role in helping us maintain balance. Dreams with sexual content are consistent with the physical sexual arousal that occurs during REM sleep. Combining results of brain imaging experiments and cognitive psychology leads to yet another view of dreams. Dreaming behavior correlates with activity in circuits that overlap substantially with the DMN (Fox et al., 2013). According to this view, daydreaming and dreaming during sleep are on a continuum. Simultaneous changes in brainstem activity result in lower sensitivity to outside stimuli, and reduced overall frontal lobe activity might lead to less self-awareness and logical thought than occurs during daydreaming. Once the dream state is initiated, the brain draws on memories of general knowledge and personal experience to produce a story line (Foulkes, 1999).

About 55% of adults report having experienced at least one episode of **lucid dreaming**, in which dreamers become aware that they are dreaming and may use this awareness to control or direct the content of the dream (Saunders et al., 2016). Lucid dreaming occurs when frontal areas of the brain inexplicably "wake up" during a dream (Mota-Rolim & Araujo, 2013). Lucid dreaming is particularly associated with increased activity in the dorsolateral prefrontal cortex, an area of the brain believed to participate in higher-order executive functions, including people's sense of control and voluntary behavior (Dresler et al., 2013). People with narcolepsy, a sleep disorder described in the next section, are more likely than others to experience lucid dreaming (Dodet et al., 2015).

Sleep Disorders

Observing what goes wrong during sleep provides additional insights into the natural variations of consciousness we experience.

Nightmares and Sleep Terrors When the content of a REM dream is especially upsetting, we refer to the experience as a nightmare. If lucid dreamers become stuck in a nightmare, they may have the option of "changing channels" and exiting that line of content. Some researchers report that training in lucid dreaming may serve as an effective treatment for recurring, upsetting nightmares (Mota-Rolim & Araujo, 2013).

dreaming A mental state that usually occurs during sleep that features visual imagery.

lucid dreaming A conscious awareness of dreaming accompanied by the ability to control the content of the dream.

Nightmares are often mistaken for **sleep terrors**, but these are different phenomena. Nightmares are dreams that occur during REM sleep, while sleep terrors occur during N-REM sleep, particularly during the first 3 hours of sleep. In sleep terrors, the usually smooth transition from stage 4 N-REM sleep upward into REM sleep goes awry. The sleeper becomes acutely distressed despite remaining deeply asleep. If awakened, the person shows the disorientation and confusion typically demonstrated when a sleeper is disturbed during deep N-REM sleep. There is usually no memory of the sleep terror the next day. Twin studies suggest that there is a genetic predisposition to sleep terrors (Taheri & Mignot, 2002).

sleep terror A sleep disorder occurring in non-rapid eye movement sleep in which the sleeper wakes suddenly in great distress but without experiencing the imagery of a nightmare.

insomnia A sleep disorder characterized by an inability to either initiate or maintain normal sleep.

narcolepsy A sleep disorder characterized by the intrusion of rapid eye movement phenomena into waking.

sleep apnea A sleep disorder in which the person stops breathing while asleep.

Insomnia

After nightmares, the most common sleep problem is **insomnia**, in which a person has difficulty initiating or maintaining sleep. Although most people seem to need about 7 to 9 hours of sleep per night to function effectively, wider healthy variations exist. In one case of "healthy insomnia," an elderly woman slept only 1 hour per night without apparent detrimental effects (Meddis et al., 1973).

Insomnia occurs in one of two forms. In cases of onset insomnia, a person lies in bed for what seems to be a long period but is unable to go to sleep. Stress and anxiety are frequent causes of this type of insomnia. Maintenance insomnia occurs when sleep is frequently interrupted or early waking occurs. These cases typically result from stress, substance use, or psychological disorders. Insomnia medications, such as zolpidem (Ambien), have minor effects on sleep, producing sleep 15 minutes faster and lengthening it for about 30 minutes, which might not offset significant side effects, including dependence on the medication, driving or walking while asleep, memory loss, and loss of coordination (Buscemi et al., 2007).

Light, and especially the blue light that characterizes mobile technologies, can interfere with the sleep hormone melatonin. As a result, the use of tablets and smartphones right before bed can interfere with sleep quality (Grønli et al., 2016). Individuals with insomnia might benefit from wearing amber glasses, which block the blue light emitted from mobile devices, prior to bedtime (Shechter et al., 2018).

Narcolepsy and Cataplexy

Probably the most dramatic sleep disorder is **narcolepsy**. Narcolepsy consists of "sleep attacks," in which REM sleep occurs during wakefulness (Dahl et al., 1994). In addition to sleep attacks, other aspects of REM sleep may intrude into the wakefulness of patients with narcolepsy. Cataplexy occurs when the muscle paralysis normally associated with REM sleep occurs during wakefulness without loss of consciousness. Many patients with narcolepsy also experience sleep paralysis or muscle paralysis that either precedes actual sleep or lingers once the person has awakened. Although upsetting, this paralysis is easy to resolve. Simply touching the person is enough to end the paralysis.

Cells in the hypothalamus that normally secrete neurochemicals known as orexins are missing or damaged in the brains of patients with narcolepsy (Thannickal et al., 2000). Orexins help regulate sleep, arousal, and appetite. Although researchers have been able to selectively breed for narcolepsy in dogs (Foutz et al., 1978), the contribution of genetics to human narcolepsy is more complex. Narcolepsy results from a combination of genetic vulnerability and autoimmune processes that attack the cells in the brain that produce orexins (Taheri & Mignot, 2002). This interaction helps to explain an increase in narcolepsy cases in response to certain vaccines for the 2009-2010 H1N1 virus (Bomfim et al., 2017). In genetically vulnerable individuals, the vaccine appeared to have triggered an autoimmune process that resulted in narcolepsy.

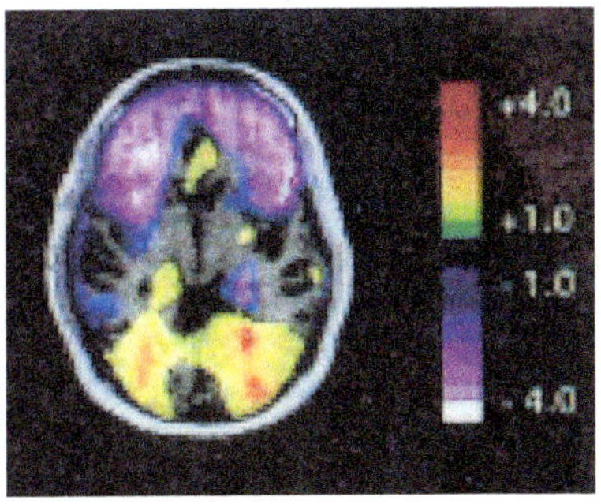

Courtesy A. R. Braun, National Institute of Deafness, NIH, Bethesda

Brain imaging can be used to compare activity during waking with activity during sleep. In this image, areas that are blue or purple are less active during REM sleep than during waking, and areas that are red or yellow are more active during REM sleep than during waking. The bizarre content of dreams occurring during REM sleep might be the result of the lower activity in the frontal lobes (purple) at the top of the image. The visual vividness of dreams might be accounted for by the higher amount of activity in the visual areas of the occipital lobes toward the bottom of the image (yellow and red).

Breathing-Related Sleep Disorders

We take it for granted that automatic functions such as breathing continue uninterrupted during sleep, but this is not the case in **sleep apnea**. In a person with sleep apnea, breathing can stop for a minute or two, and the sleeper awakens abruptly gasping for air. Not only does this lack of air disrupt the sleep quality of the person with sleep apnea, but it can increase the risk for heart disease (Kendzerska et al., 2014). Because many cases of sleep apnea occur in people who are obese and who snore, losing weight and surgical correction of airway blockages are common treatments. Other cases occur when brainstem neurons responsible for maintaining breathing during sleep malfunction. In these cases, the use of a machine that regulates airflow during sleep is an inconvenient but effective solution.

Despite her suspected narcolepsy, Harriet Tubman (1820–1913) helped hundreds of slaves escape through the Underground Railroad during the Civil War era. Tubman appears on the left in this photo with some of the former slaves whom she helped. Unfortunately, narcoleptic attacks are often brought on by stress. Tubman had a number of close escapes when she experienced sleep attacks while being pursued by Confederate troops and irate slave owners.

Bettmann/Contributor/Getty Images

Dr. Mignot

Sleep researcher Emmanuel Mignot is holding Bear, one of his dogs with narcolepsy. Research with dogs like Bear showed that narcolepsy is a genetic disorder often triggered by exposure to flu viruses. Sadly, Bear passed away in 2014.

Sudden Infant Death Syndrome (SIDS) **Sudden infant death syndrome (SIDS)** occurs when a healthy infant simply dies while asleep. Approximately 3,500 infants die from SIDS in the United States each year (Moon & Task Force on Sudden Infant Death Syndrome, 2016). Rates prior to the 1990s were even higher. Between 1992 and 2003, rates of SIDS in the United States were cut in half when the American Academy of Pediatrics (AAP) began telling parents to put their infants to sleep on their backs instead of on their stomachs (National Institute of Child Health and Human Development [NICHHD], 2003). As we will see in Chapter 11, young infants cannot turn over easily for the first few months of life, making suffocation on blankets and stuffed animals a greater risk.

Despite these improvements, SIDS remains the most common cause of death in the first 6 months of life in industrialized nations, even as the cause of these cases remains elusive (Krous, 2014). A Triple Risk Model of SIDS suggests that a combination of individual vulnerabilities, developmental period, and stressors such as infection result in death. Current recommendations for preventing SIDS from the American Academy of Pediatrics include putting infants to sleep on their backs; using a firm sleep surface; room-sharing without bed-sharing; avoidance of soft bedding and overheating; avoidance of exposure to smoke, alcohol, and illicit drugs; breastfeeding; routine immunization; use of pacifiers; and skin-to-skin care for newborns (Moon & Task Force on Sudden Infant Death Syndrome, 2016).

Findings that new narcolepsy cases resulted from either infection with or vaccination for the H1N1 flu virus support the idea that narcolepsy is linked to activity in the immune system. American vaccines provoking weaker immune responses were less likely to result in narcolepsy than stronger European vaccines and the disease itself (Dauvilliers et al., 2010; Dauvilliers et al., 2013).

Restless Legs Syndrome (RLS) **Restless legs syndrome (RLS)** occurs when one of a person's limbs, usually a leg, experiences a tingling feeling and moves at regular intervals. RLS appears to be quite common, with 15% of a large sample of adults in the United States reporting these symptoms (National Sleep Foundation, 2009). Of special interest to psychologists is the high frequency of RLS among children and adults with attention deficit hyperactivity disorder (ADHD) and the potential links between these two conditions (Schimmelmann et al., 2009). As we will see in Chapter 14, ADHD is correlated with differences in dopamine functioning, a characteristic shared by RLS (Taheri & Mignot, 2002).

sudden infant death syndrome (SIDS) A sleep disorder in which an otherwise healthy infant dies while asleep.

restless legs syndrome (RLS) A disorder characterized by the involuntary movement of an extremity, usually one leg.

The number of deaths from SIDS dropped dramatically when the American Academy of Pediatrics began telling parents to put their babies to sleep on their backs instead of on their stomachs. SIDS still occurs, however, so sleeping position is only one of many risk factors, including exposure to cigarette smoke in the home.

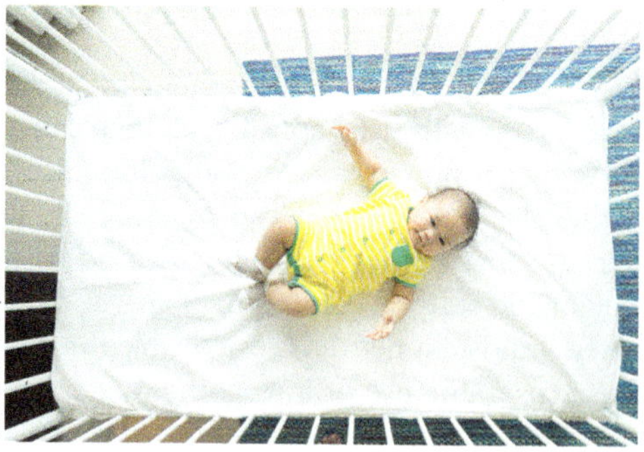
iStock.com/alice-photo

SUMMARY 6.2 Features of Waking and Sleep

Stage of waking or sleep		Brain activity recorded by EEG	Observations
Waking 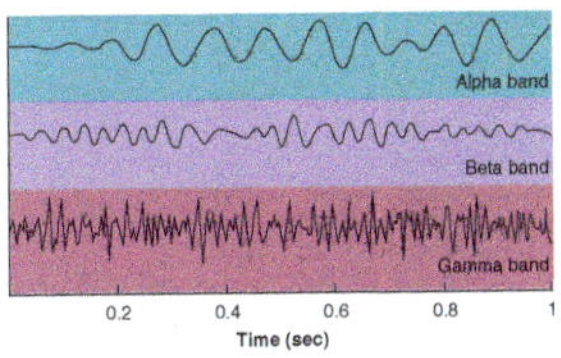		Alpha, beta, gamma	• Alternating periods of alertness and relaxation. • Logical thought. • Voluntary movement. • Responsive to stimuli.
N-REM sleep 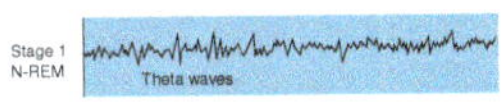	Stage 1	Some theta	• Logical thought. • Reduced heart rate and muscle tension. • Some responsiveness to stimuli.
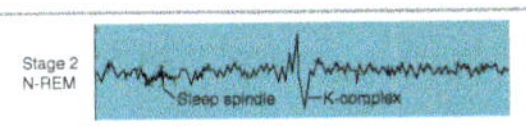	Stage 2	Larger amounts of theta	• Less responsiveness to stimuli. • Further reductions in heart rate and muscle tension.
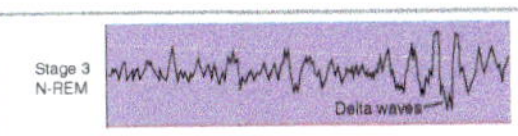	Stage 3	Some delta	• Further reductions in heart rate and muscle tension.
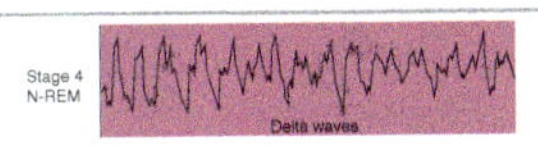	Stage 4	Larger amounts of delta	• Profound reductions in heart rate and muscle tension. • Very low responsiveness to stimuli.
REM sleep 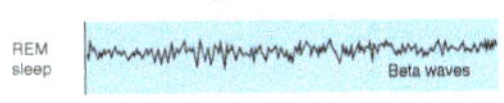		Similar to waking	• Rapid motion of the eyes. • Muscle paralysis. • Irregular autonomic activity. • Vivid dreams.

How Is Consciousness Affected by Brain Damage?

If consciousness is a function of the brain, we should be able to identify aspects of consciousness that change reliably when the brain is damaged.

Specific Areas of Brain Damage and Consciousness

Lessons about consciousness have emerged from the clinical study of patients with damage to specific parts of the nervous system.

The effects of brain damage on face recognition illustrate how the brain integrates sensory information, memory, and emotion to form a conscious experience. Prosopagnosia is a condition that affects a person's ability to recognize faces (Bauer, 1984). One patient was unable to identify familiar faces but was still able to show differing autonomic responses to familiar versus unfamiliar faces. Separate pathways process the features of faces, emotional responses to faces, and recognition of faces.

In a situation that is reminiscent of many horror film classics, patients with Capgras syndrome are convinced that imposters have taken the place of familiar people. In certain

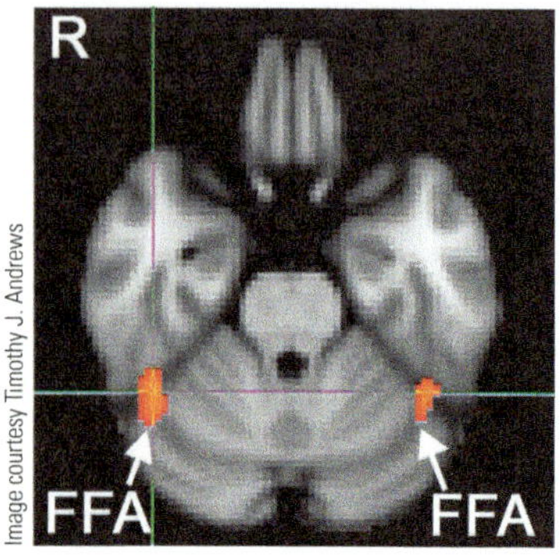

Prosopagnosia results from damage to a part of the temporal lobes on the bottom of the brain known as the fusiform face area (FFA). In this scan using functional magnetic resonance imaging (fMRI), the FFA activity indicates that the person is looking at the image of a face as opposed to a landscape or building.

Source: From Timothy J. Andrews et al. (2010). "Internal and External Features of the Face Are Represented Holistically in Face-Selective Regions of Visual Cortex," *The Journal of Neuroscience*, *30*(9), 3544–3552, doi:10.1523/JNEUROSCI.4863-09.2010.

tragic instances, patients with Capgras even try to harm the "imposters." Capgras syndrome and prosopagnosia produce opposite effects. In Capgras syndrome, the ability to recognize faces remains intact, but the sense of emotion and familiarity is distorted. Capgras syndrome appears to result from damage to general brain circuits that process familiarity and violations of expectations (Darby et al., 2016).

Coma, Vegetative State, Brain Death, and Near-Death

Consciousness is altered not only by damage in particular areas of the brain but by the severity of damage as well.

Coma Our word coma comes from the Greek word for "deep sleep." **Coma** produces a profound state of unconsciousness in which the person does not have sleep–wake cycles, cannot be awakened, does not respond to pain or light, and is incapable of voluntary behavior. Coma usually results from disruptions in the functions of the reticular formation or both cerebral hemispheres (Liversedge & Hirsch, 2010). A stroke affecting a single hemisphere typically does not lead to coma. Comas last anywhere from a few days to several weeks. After a period of 2 to 4 weeks, most patients recover, move into a vegetative state (described later in this section), or die. Among those who recover, improvement is usually slow and gradual.

EEG recordings of comatose patients vary depending on the problem that initially led to coma. Following resuscitation from cardiac arrest, many patients show a distinctive pattern of alpha rhythms, especially in the frontal lobes, known as *alpha coma* (Chatrian, 1990). These alpha patterns do not change when the patient is exposed to various types of stimulation. Other patterns feature a low level of overall activity occasionally interrupted by spikes. None of these patterns are found in the typical, healthy EEG described previously in our section on sleep and waking (see ● Figure 6.12).

coma A state of deep unconsciousness resulting from brain damage or illness.

vegetative state (VS) An abnormal state following brain injury featuring wakefulness without consciousness.

Vegetative State (VS) Coma can be distinguished from similar conditions, such as **vegetative state (VS)** and brain death. VS often follows a period of coma. VS is characterized by waking without consciousness. In contrast to the patient with coma, patients with VS look rather normal. Their eyes open periodically; they demonstrate sleep and waking cycles; they grind their teeth, scream, smile, and cry. Some are responsive to pain. The discovery that about 20% of patients diagnosed as being in a vegetative state are actually conscious yet unable to respond physically has changed the evaluation, treatment, and legal standing of unresponsive patients (Owen, 2019; see ● Figure 6.13).

Brain Death With the advent of technologies that can artificially maintain bodily functions, including respiration and blood circulation, we have been placed in the odd position of requiring a new definition of death. Brain death is defined as an irreversible loss of all functions of the brain including the brainstem (Russell et al., 2019). Although professional

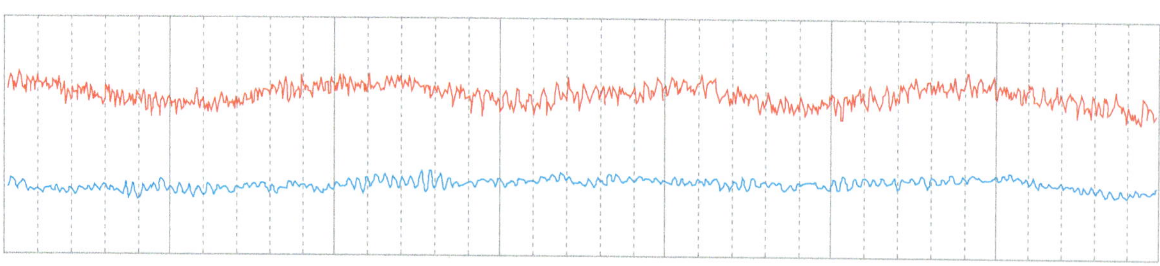

FIGURE 6.12

Normal Versus Comatose EEGs. Even though the patient with the normal EEG recording is drowsy, which should produce a dominant pattern of alpha waves, the normal recording is quite different from the more uniform alpha activity recorded from a patient in a coma.

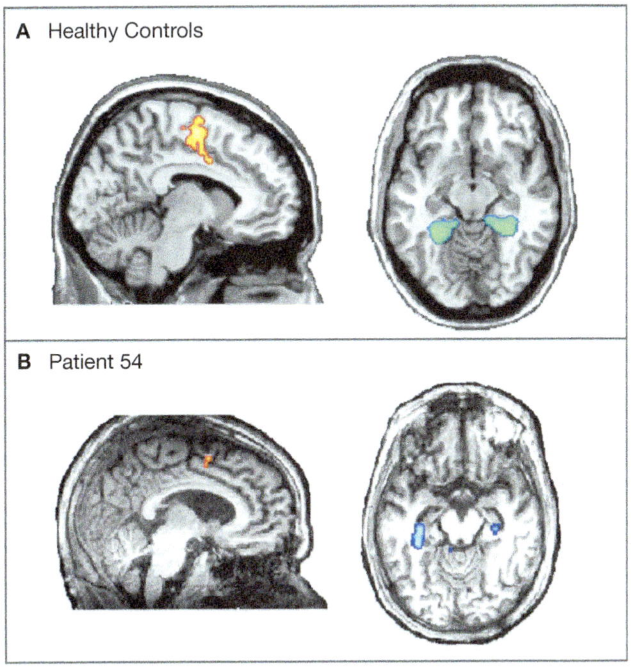

FIGURE **6.13**

Is Consciousness Possible in VS Patients? Using functional magnetic resonance imaging (fMRI), a small number of patients diagnosed as being in a vegetative state (VS) showed brain activation to specific tasks that closely resembled the activation of healthy control participants. The yellow-red areas were active when thinking about movement, and the bluish areas were active when thinking about a spatial task. This research emphasizes the need to develop new ways of assessing the cognitive correlates of brain injuries so that patients can receive the best care possible.

Source: From Martin M. Monti et al. (2010). "Willful Modulation of Brain Activity in Disorders of Consciousness," *New England Journal of Medicine*, *362*(7), 579–589, doi: 10.1056/NEJMoa0905370

associations have provided guidance regarding the determination of brain death, actual practices and policies vary widely within the United States and abroad (Greer et al., 2016). Although medical experts claim that no patients appropriately diagnosed with brain death have ever recovered, sensational media accounts of individuals who recover after hearing their organ donation process discussed by hospital staff emphasize the need to have complete compliance with the best standards possible (Nguyen, 2016).

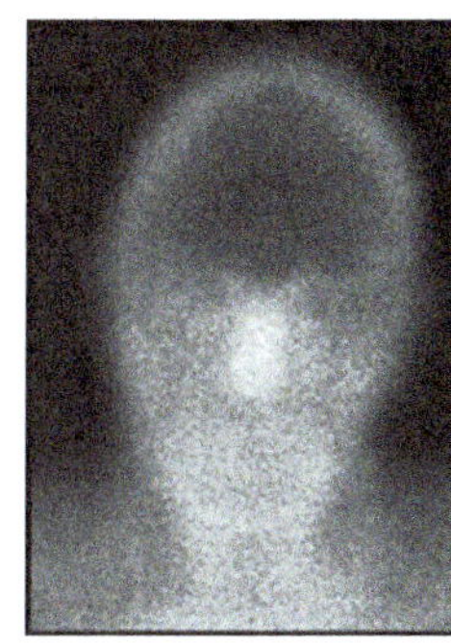

Brain death is often determined by a study of blood circulation. In this image, blood can be seen flowing into the neck, scalp, and face (particularly the nose, which leads to the phrase "hot nose sign"). However, no blood flow is seen in the brain itself, which remains dark. A careful determination of brain death is required because of the common practice of organ donation following death.

Source: Reprinted by permission of the Society of Nuclear Medicine from: A. MacDonald, & S. Burrell (2009). "Infrequently Performed Studies in Nuclear Medicine: Part 2," *Journal of Nuclear Medicine Technology*, *37*(1), 1–13. Figure 5. doi: 10.2967/jnmt.108.057851

Near-Death Experiences Because of improvements in technology that literally bring people "back to life," as many as one out of ten people has reported a **near-death experience**. Patients who recover following a cardiac arrest or some other life-threatening condition often report similar experiences. These experiences typically feature an out-of-body experience in which people feel they are viewing their body from a floating position above it. In addition, many people report a "light at the end of the tunnel" visual experience, which may include images of deceased friends, relatives, or deities. These visual sensations are accompanied by a peaceful, calm emotional state and followed by a reluctant return to the body.

The similarities among documented cases of near-death experiences suggest that the dying-revival experience produces consistent responses in the human brain similar to the intrusion of REM sleep into waking. In animal models of cardiac arrest, a surge of brain activity occurs near death, suggesting a state of heightened consciousness (Borjigin et al., 2013). Strong out-of-body sensations and other near-death phenomena occur in volunteers using ketamine (Martial et al., 2019). A damaged brain may release its own chemicals, similar to ketamine, in an effort to minimize cell loss.

Seizures

Seizures are uncontrolled electrical disturbances in the brain that often produce changes in consciousness, providing further evidence that cortical activity is correlated with consciousness. People with recurring seizures are diagnosed with epilepsy. Seizures occur as a result of brain injury or infection but can also appear without an obvious cause. Disturbances in the activity of the inhibitory neurotransmitter GABA might account for many seizures. Drugs that inhibit GABA reliably produce seizures, while drugs that enhance GABA activity, such as barbiturates, prevent or control seizures.

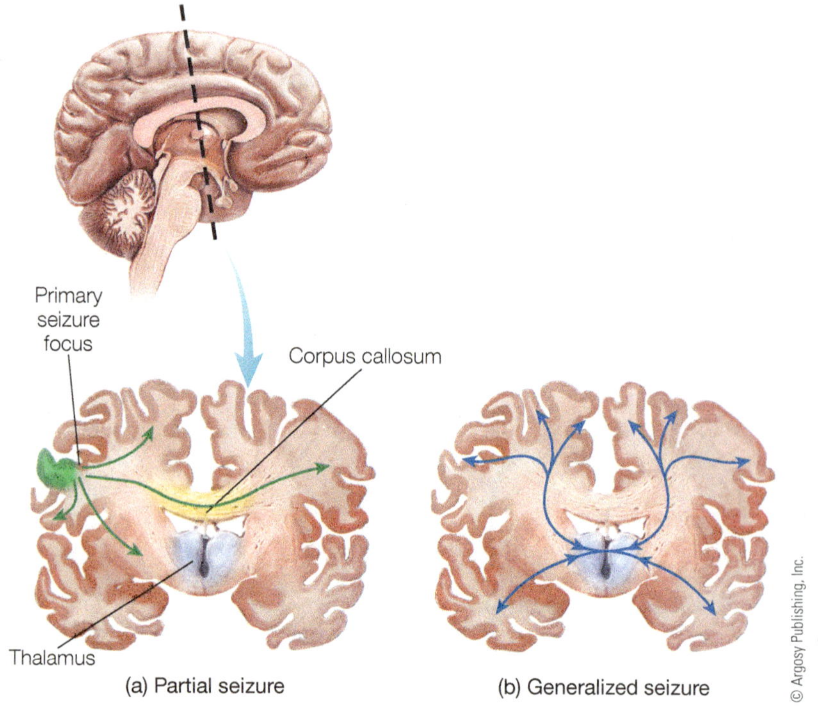

FIGURE 6.14

Pathways for the Spread of Partial and Generalized Seizures. (a) Partial seizures originate in a focal area and spread to cortical and subcortical structures. (b) Generalized seizures do not originate in a focal area. Once they begin, generalized seizures spread through the brain symmetrically via connections between the thalamus and the cortex.

Seizures are classified as partial or generalized. Partial seizures originate in a particular part of the brain known as the focal area and are often accompanied by an aura or a premonition that a seizure is about to occur. Generalized seizures do not arise from a focal area. Instead, these seizures are characterized by the abnormal activation of circuits connecting the cortex and the thalamus. Generalized seizures are typically not accompanied by an aura (see ● Figure 6.14).

Partial seizures originating in the temporal lobe often produce distortions of consciousness, leading to the experience of *déjà vu* (French for "already seen"), a feeling that one is reliving the past, or *jamais vu* (French for "never seen"), a sense that one's familiar circumstances are suddenly foreign or strange. Consciousness is lost completely in generalized seizures. The two major categories of generalized seizure are tonic-clonic and absence seizures. Tonic-clonic seizures begin with a loss of consciousness, cessation of breathing, and intense muscular contraction. This phase usually gives way to violent, rhythmic contractions that may result in broken bones or other physical injuries. These phases are followed by a period of coma, lasting about 5 minutes. In an absence seizure, the person loses consciousness and awareness of surroundings, and motor movements are limited to blinking, head turns, and eye movements.

How Do People Intentionally Alter Their States of Consciousness?

near-death experience An altered state of consciousness reported by people who were close to death because of cardiac or other medical problems that features out-of-body experiences, light-at-the-end-of-a-tunnel perceptions, and a state of calmness.

seizure An abnormal level of brain activation with a sudden onset.

Humans have intentionally altered consciousness in religious, recreational, and healing contexts. Methods may vary dramatically, but we will see that some common themes of these efforts emerge. Individuals who deliberately alter their state of consciousness may be seeking insight, positive emotion (bliss or ecstasy), or a sense of unity or "oneness." The universality of such efforts, which often underlie religious behavior, strongly suggests that these states confer some advantages, although what those advantages may be remains unknown.

General Features of Psychoactive Drugs

Historically, humans have gone to great lengths to obtain **psychoactive drugs**, or substances that alter consciousness. Humans may be unique among animals in their willingness to voluntarily seek alterations in consciousness through the deliberate use of psychoactive substances. Most psychoactive substances are quite poisonous (livestock eating tobacco leaves in the field will die) and usually have the bitter taste associated with most poisons. On the rare occasions when nonhuman animals consume psychoactive substances (cats and catnip or elephants and alcohol), we have no way of knowing whether this consumption is motivated by a desire to alter consciousness.

Before exploring commonly used drugs, we will outline several general principles related to their use, including tolerance, withdrawal, and addiction.

AP Images/Per Johansson

Most animals avoid psychoactive substances, but this Swedish moose managed to get stuck in a tree after eating fermented apples that had fallen on the ground. We have no way of knowing whether the moose was motivated by a desire to experience an altered state of consciousness or it simply liked the taste of the fruit.

psychoactive drug Any drug with the capability of altering a person's state of consciousness.

tolerance The need to administer greater quantities of a drug to achieve the same subjective effect.

withdrawal Physical responses to the removal of some habitually administered drugs.

addiction A compulsive physical or psychological dependence on a substance or activity that continues in spite of negative consequences.

Tolerance and Withdrawal

Tolerance occurs when a person must take larger quantities of a drug to produce the desired effects. The nervous system seeks to maintain homeostasis, a steady internal balance or equilibrium discussed further in Chapter 7. When a person takes a drug repeatedly, the nervous system attempts to compensate for the drug's effects. These compensations are both biological and learned (via mechanisms described in more detail in Chapter 8). The user must take more of a drug to overcome these compensations.

When some habitually used drugs are no longer available, the user might experience **withdrawal**, a set of effects that are the opposite of those produced by the drug. Withdrawing from alcohol, which slows down the nervous system, produces a rebound effect characterized by so much excess brain activity that life-threatening seizures might occur. Withdrawing from stimulants such as caffeine can make the user sluggish and lethargic. Not all drugs that are abused produce significant withdrawal. For example, heroin and nicotine produce powerful withdrawal effects, but cocaine usually does not (Coffey et al., 2000).

Addiction

Addiction is a compulsive physical or psychological dependence on a substance or activity that continues in spite of negative consequences. Addiction overwhelms normal control of behavior, distorts typical systems of reward, and interferes with the recognition of problems.

In addiction, people make choices on the basis of short-term outcomes (getting high) instead of on the basis of long-term outcomes (family, finances, job, and staying out of jail). This disruption in normal, logical decision making can occur because of distortions in one or more of three related neural systems: an impulsive system involving dopamine pathways connecting the midbrain and the basal ganglia, a reflective system in the frontal lobes that weighs the pros and the cons of a decision and controls impulses, and a craving system involving the insula (Noël et al., 2013; see ● Figure 6.15). Activity in the insula is correlated with participants' craving for their drug of choice, and strokes that damage the insula eliminate the urge to use some addictive drugs (Verdejo-Garcia et al., 2012). Excess activity in the impulsive system, inadequate activity in the reflective system, and increased desire appear to set the stage for maintaining compulsive addictive behaviors.

Zalmai/Contributor/Reportage Archive/Getty Images

Should we be concerned about military veterans returning from service in Afghanistan with opioid addictions? If the experiences of returning Vietnam veterans are repeated, the answer will be "no." Even though heroin was readily available in Vietnam and large numbers of soldiers used heroin while serving, nearly all quit using upon their return to the United States. These observations remind us that addiction is a complex phenomenon with multiple causes.

hallucinogen A drug that stimulates the experience of false perceptions.

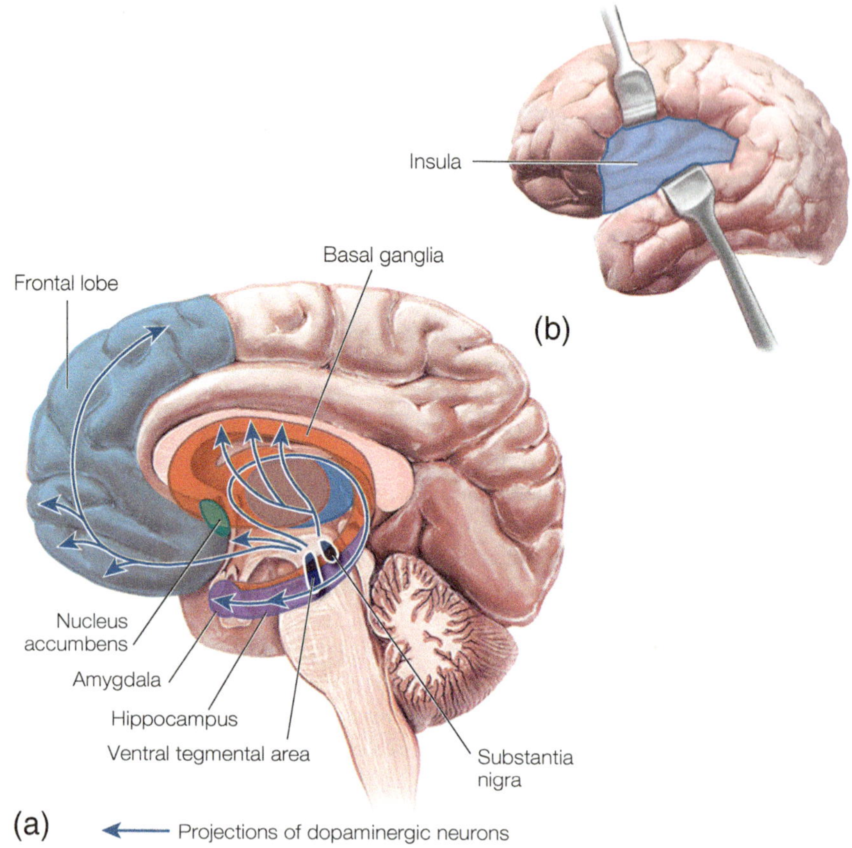

FIGURE 6.15

Addiction Involves Multiple Brain Networks. Addiction is correlated with activity in a number of brain circuits. (a) An impulsive, reward-seeking system that uses the neurochemical dopamine connects the midbrain (ventral tegmental area and substantia nigra) with the basal ganglia, including the nucleus accumbens. A reflective system involving the frontal lobes controls impulses and makes decisions. (b) A craving system involves the insula.

Commonly Used Psychoactive Drugs

Marijuana Cannabis, from the *Cannabis sativa* plant, has a long human history. It was included in the pharmacy written by Chinese emperor Shen Neng nearly 5,000 years ago. Marijuana, the smoked form of cannabis, remains the most commonly used federally illegal substance in the United States today. The behavioral effects of cannabis are often so subtle that people may report no changes in response to its use. Most individuals experience some excitation, vivid imagery, and mild euphoria. Others respond with depression and social withdrawal. Cannabis distorts perception of time and space and produces hallucinations in some users, leading to its formal classification as a **hallucinogen**.

Cannabis contains more than 50 psychoactive compounds, known as cannabinoids. The most important of these is tetrahydrocannabinol (THC). THC produces some of its behavioral effects by interacting with receptors for endogenous cannabinoids, natural substances that are similar to THC in chemical composition. One type of cannabinoid receptor is located in parts of the brain involved with pain, appetite, learning, reasoning, and movement (see Figure 6.16). Another type is found elsewhere in the body, particularly in structures associated with the immune system.

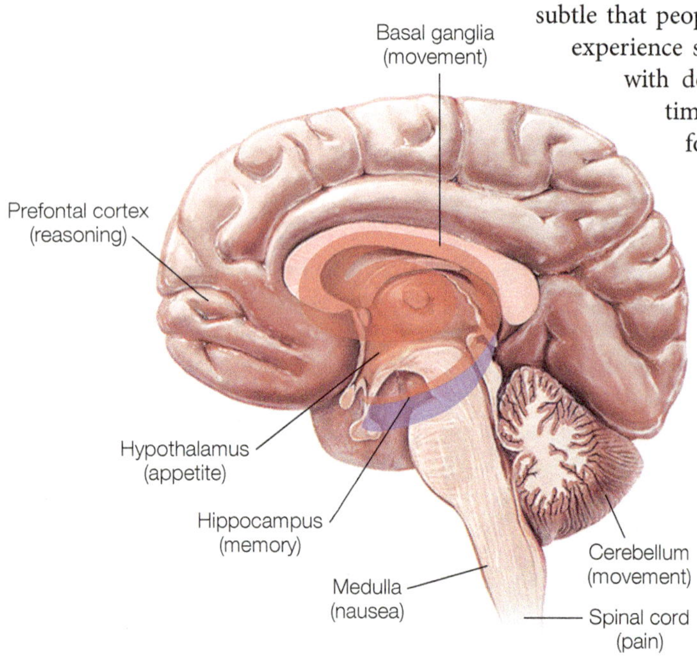

FIGURE 6.16

Locations of Cannabinoid Receptors in the Brain. Cannabinoids, such as THC, interact with receptors located in many parts of the brain. In particular, cannabinoid receptors are numerous in the hippocampus and the prefrontal cortex.

THINKING SCIENTIFICALLY

Do Hallucinogens Have Therapeutic Potential?

Elsewhere in this chapter, you will read about the use of ayahuasca, which contains DMT, and MDMA (Ecstasy) to achieve positive altered states of consciousness. The active chemicals in these substances have something in common with each other and with most hallucinogens—they interact with serotonin systems in the brain. Psychologists are interested in the potential of using LSD, ketamine, and psilocybin (from hallucinogenic mushrooms), along with DMT (the active ingredient in ayahuasca) and MDMA, to treat patients with a variety of disorders, including major depressive disorder (MDD), anxiety, posttraumatic stress disorder (PTSD), and substance abuse disorders.

WHAT AM I BEING ASKED TO BELIEVE OR ACCEPT?

We are being asked to believe that hallucinogens can be useful in treating conditions such as depression, anxiety, and substance abuse.

WHAT EVIDENCE SUPPORTS THIS POSITION?

Since the 1950s, studies evaluating the safety and efficacy of hallucinogens for the treatment of a number of psychological disorders have produced promising results. This line of research was complicated by the recreational use of hallucinogens in the 1960s and 1970s, which led to government restrictions of their availability and use in research. Research on the therapeutic potential of hallucinogens resumed in the 1990s and continues to expand (dos Santos & Hallack, 2020). Hallucinogens appear particularly effective in treating cases of MDD, anxiety, and substance abuse. In published research, adverse reactions have been very infrequent or completely absent. Results have been promising enough to gain support of the U.S. Food and Drug Administration for further research with larger sample sizes.

ARE THERE OTHER WAYS THIS EVIDENCE COULD BE INTERPRETED?

The sample size in many of these studies has been quite small, on the order of a dozen individuals. It is virtually impossible to run "gold standard" double-blind, placebo-controlled studies, in which neither participant nor experimenter knows whether the participant is receiving the active drug or a placebo until the study is concluded, due to the lack of a believable placebo. An additional challenge is the fact that hallucinogens can provoke psychosis (see Chapter 14) in individuals at risk for schizophrenia or other psychotic conditions (De Gregorio et al., 2016).

WHAT OTHER EVIDENCE WOULD I NEED TO EVALUATE THESE ALTERNATIVES?

As dos Santos and Hallack (2020) have recommended, studies with larger sample sizes would be helpful. Although the double-blind, placebo-controlled design is preferred, alternatives do exist. For example, patients with MDD could experience standard care (see Chapter 15) or standard care plus hallucinogens to see if the hallucinogens produced a superior outcome. This design provides an ethical advantage in that none of the participants would be treated with placebo only. Individuals could be screened for a family history and symptoms of psychosis before being accepted as participants.

WHAT ARE THE MOST REASONABLE CONCLUSIONS?

Preliminary results seem to support further research in this area, assuming the safety of the participants is managed carefully. ■

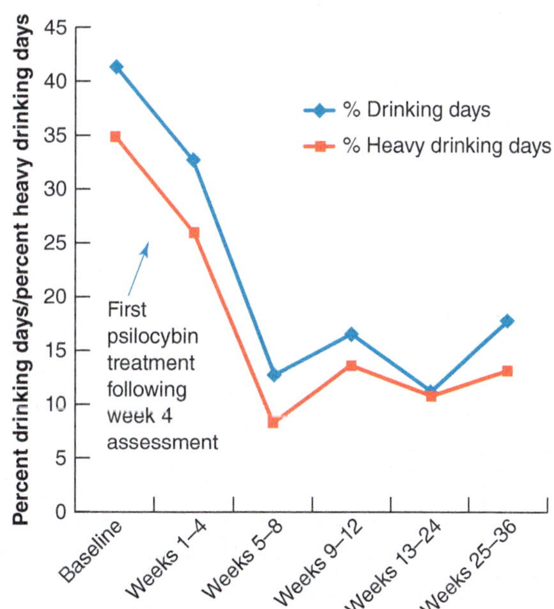

FIGURE **6.17**

Participants in treatment for alcohol dependence received psychotherapy during weeks 1 through 4, followed by two treatments with psilocybin at week 4 and again at week 8. Both drinking days and heavy drinking days were reduced significantly and persistently following treatment.

Source: M. P. Bogenschutz et al. (2015). "Psilocybin-assisted Treatment for Alcohol Dependence: A Proof-of-concept Study." *Journal of Psychopharmacology, 29*(3), 289–299. doi: 10.1177/0269881114565144

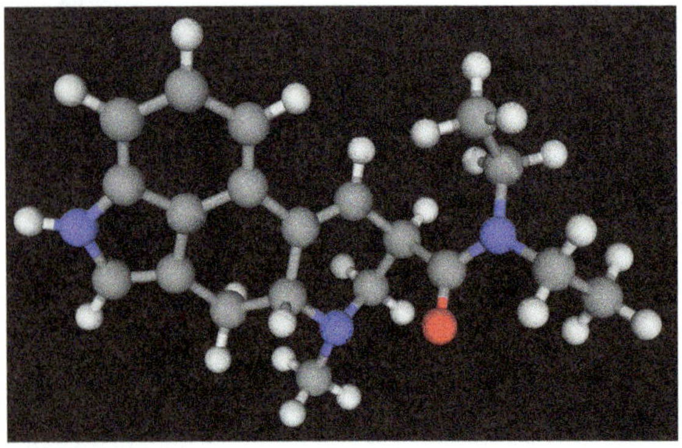

Laguna Design/Science Photo Library/Corbis

Lysergic acid, a metabolite of LSD, is similar in chemical structure to naturally occurring serotonin. Although the exact mechanism responsible for producing hallucinations is poorly understood, we do know that lysergic acid interacts with serotonin receptors.

stimulant Any drug that increases the activity of the nervous system.

Our main endogenous cannabinoid, anandamide, removes unnecessary memories and slows movement, leading to relaxation. Unlike THC, though, anandamide's effects last only briefly. Anandamide increases dopamine activity, and substances that increase dopamine activity are often addictive for many people. Because THC shares anandamide's ability to stimulate dopamine activity, cannabis has the potential to produce dependency (Weinstein & Gorelick, 2011).

LSD In 1938, researcher Albert Hoffman reported some unusual sensations after working with lysergic acid diethylamide (LSD). Hoffman then deliberately ingested some of the chemical and reported vivid, colorful visual hallucinations.

LSD is chemically similar to serotonin, and it interacts with serotonin receptors (Carhart-Harris et al., 2016). LSD use is correlated with increased activity in the visual cortex, changes in alpha activity recorded using EEG, and decreased connectivity in the default mode network (Carhart-Harris et al., 2016). These findings are consistent with participants' reports of their hallucination experiences. One of the interesting cognitive outcomes of LSD use is the experience of flashbacks, intrusive and involuntary hallucinations, even after the drug has been discontinued (Halpern & Pope, 2003). Further research is necessary to identify the mechanisms for this experience.

Caffeine Caffeine, used by 85% of adults in the United States, is a **stimulant** found in a range of sources, including coffee, tea, cola, energy drinks, and many over-the-counter pain relievers (Temple et al., 2017; see Figure 6.18). Caffeine interferes with the inhibition

CONNECTING TO RESEARCH

Psychedelics and Consciousness

Psychedelic drugs, including LSD, psilocybin, and ketamine, produce profound changes in perception and ongoing awareness without a loss of consciousness like that occurring during sleep or anesthesia. As such, they provide interesting insights into our definitions of conscious experience. Researchers investigated the effects of these three psychedelics on a measure of consciousness (Schartner et al., 2017).

The Question: What do psychedelics do to consciousness?

METHODS

Forty-eight healthy adults underwent magnetoencephalography, a method for recording the tiny amounts of magnetic output from the brain, after having been administered a placebo and again after the administration of one of the following drugs: LSD, psilocybin, or ketamine.

ETHICS

While the doses used in this experiment were within safe boundaries, the researchers took care to exclude participants who were pregnant, who reported any one of a number of health conditions, or who reported a history of substance abuse or mental health issues. It is interesting to note that all participants had used psychedelics before, although the authors did not provide further information about their recruiting methods. The study was cleared by the appropriate institutional review board (see Chapter 2).

RESULTS

Compared to placebo, all three drugs increased measures of "signal diversity." High levels of signal diversity imply that the brain is busy doing multiple, complex things, whereas low levels imply a more quiet, less complex mental state.

CONCLUSIONS

The authors argued that the psychedelic state provides an even more active state of consciousness than that which occurs during focused wakefulness and REM sleep. They suggested using similar analyses to assess the levels of signal diversity that might characterize typical variations in sleep and waking but also less typical states such as mania (see Chapter 16). ■

Adam Hart-Davis/Science Source

Psilocybin extracted from hallucinogenic mushrooms, along with ketamine and LSD, produced a higher level of brain activity than that which is usually seen in conscious waking.

FIGURE **6.18**

Sources of Caffeine. Although most people think immediately of coffee when they hear the word *caffeine*, caffeine can be found in many beverages, foods, and over-the-counter medications.

Source: Adapted from C. O. Byer & L. W. Shainberg (1995). *Living Well: Health in Your Hands* (2nd ed.), New York, NY: HarperCollins. The Starbucks Jolt and Red Bull data are from L. P. Somogyi (2010). *Caffeine Intake by the U.S. Population,* retrieved from http://www.fda.gov/downloads/AboutFDA/CentersOffices/OfficeofFoods/CFSAN/CFSANFOIAElectronicReadingRoom/UCM333191.pdf

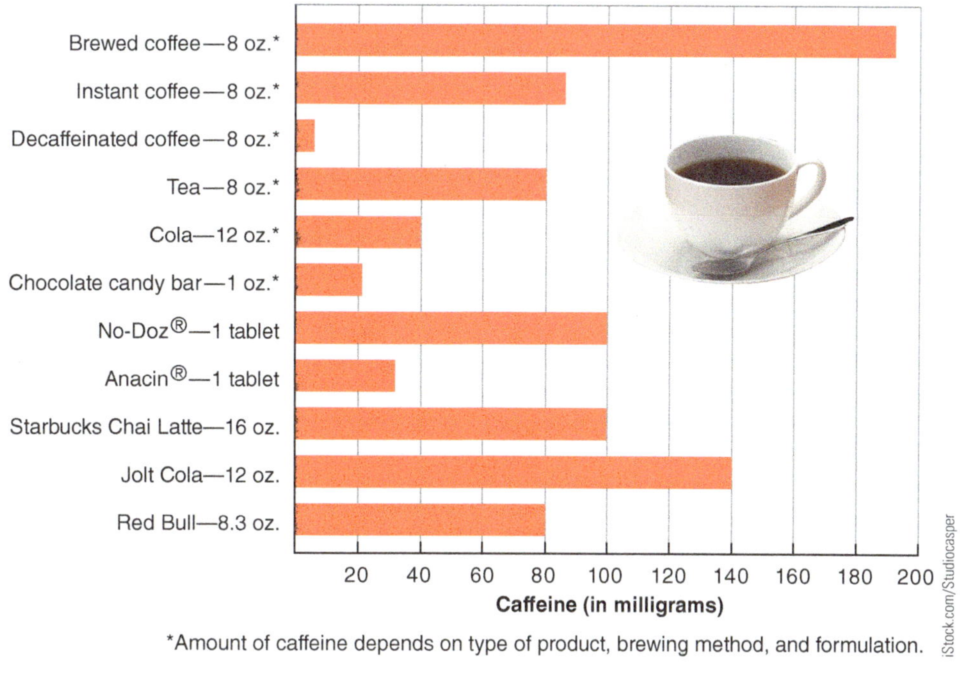

DIVERSE VOICES IN PSYCHOLOGY

Entheogens Across Cultures

AS WE MENTION in this chapter, many historical efforts to achieve altered states of consciousness emerged in religious contexts. These methods for producing altered states frequently move out of their original contexts, such as the migration of drum circles from Native American culture into contemporary men's gatherings.

Use of drugs, and hallucinogens in particular, have a long history in religious rituals. When used in religious contexts, hallucinogens are often referred to as entheogens, loosely translated as "generating the divine within." In South America, people were using a brew known as ayahuasca centuries ago as part of their religious rituals, but the practice has since spread globally. Ayahuasca contains the hallucinogen N, N-dimethyltryptamine (DMT), which like most hallucinogens is chemically very similar to serotonin. DMT, which occurs naturally in small amounts in the brain, produces vivid visual hallucinations and euphoria but also intense vomiting. In contrast to the acceptance of ayahuasca in South America, DMT use is illegal in most countries. However, legal exceptions have been made for use of ayahuasca in religious settings. In 2006, the U.S. Supreme Court decided to allow ayahuasca churches to continue to use tea during their ceremonies.

A popular interest in ayahuasca has led to the development of ayahuasca retreats in Peru, Colombia, and Brazil. This commercialization of the practice brings money to poor regions but threatens the original context of the ritual. "Pseudo-shamans" are quite ready to make money from gullible tourists. The death of several ayahuasca tourists has raised concerns about the safety of the ayahuasca retreats.

Outside the religious context, scientists continue to be interested in possible applications of the main ingredients of ayahuasca for treating depression and other psychological disorders (Sessa & Johnson, 2015; Domínguez-Clavé et al., 2016).

Many hallucinogens have their historical roots in religious practice. In South America, a hallucinogenic tea known as ayahuasca has been used for centuries. Interest on the part of tourists has led to the establishment of ayahuasca retreats, but opinions about the commercialization of historical religious practices are mixed.

normally produced by adenosine in the brain. If you keep an inhibitory substance such as adenosine from doing its job, the result is increased excitation and alertness.

Caffeine produces a withdrawal syndrome characterized by headaches and fatigue. Some people experience problems with heart rhythms related to caffeine use. Caffeine crosses the placenta easily and also enters breast milk, leading to reduced rates of growth and other complications in the fetus and breastfed infant of a mother using the drug (Temple et al., 2017). On the positive side, caffeine use is correlated with a lower risk of Parkinson's disease, which causes difficulty moving (Ross & Petrovitch, 2001), as well as Alzheimer's disease and other forms of dementia (Eskelinen & Kivipelto, 2010). Because these are correlations, we don't know whether the apparent protection against these conditions is because of some specific action of caffeine in the brain or is simply the result of the characteristics of people who enjoy large amounts of caffeine.

Nicotine After caffeine, the most commonly used stimulant in the United States is nicotine, usually in the form of smoked or chewed tobacco (see ● Figure 6.19). Although rates of smoked tobacco use have dropped dramatically, use of e-cigarettes is growing, fueled by an inaccurate belief in the relative "safety" of smokeless nicotine (Perikleous et al., 2018). Nicotine mimics the action of the neurotransmitter acetylcholine, increasing heart rate and blood pressure, reducing fatigue, and improving cognitive performance while at the same time producing muscular relaxation. Normally, our bodies feel somewhat tense when we are mentally alert, so nicotine's combination of relaxation with alertness is unique.

Despite repeated warnings of the dangers of using nicotine, it continues to be a widely used substance (see Chapter 16). Nicotine use typically begins in adolescence, and adolescents become more rapidly dependent on the substance than do adults (Dani & Harris, 2005). People with anxiety, depression, and substance abuse disorders are more likely to use nicotine than others (Stanton et al., 2016). Use of tobacco is very common

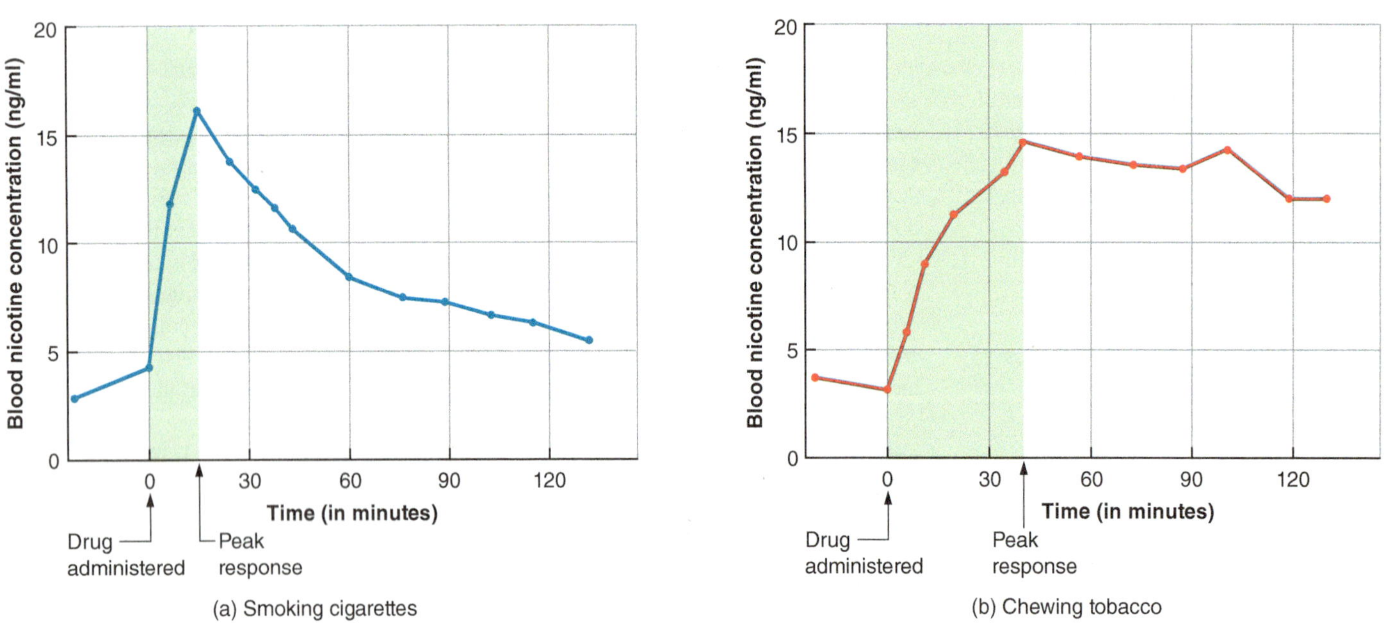

FIGURE **6.19**

Concentration of a Drug in the Blood Supply Depends on the Method of Administration. Drug effects depend on the concentration of the drug in the blood supply, and some methods of administration produce effective concentrations faster than others. In the case of nicotine, smoking a cigarette (a) produces a faster increase in blood nicotine concentration than produced by chewing an equivalent dose of tobacco (b). However, chewing tobacco produces higher sustained concentrations of nicotine than smoking does.

Source: Adapted from W. Bennett (1983). "The Nicotine Fix," *Rhode Island Medical Journal*, *66*, 455–458.

among people with schizophrenia, and adolescent use of nicotine doubles a person's risk of developing schizophrenia (Scott et al., 2018). Again, because these are correlations, we do not know whether nicotine has any causal role in the development of psychological disorders or whether people vulnerable to disorders are simply more likely to enjoy the effects of nicotine.

Cocaine and Amphetamines The behavioral effects of cocaine and amphetamines are quite similar. At moderate doses, cocaine and amphetamines produce alertness, elevated mood, confidence, and a sense of well-being. At higher doses, these drugs can produce symptoms that are quite similar to schizophrenia (see Chapter 14). Users experience hallucinations, such as a feeling of bugs running on the skin, and delusional fears that others are trying to harm them. Some users experience repetitive motor behaviors, such as chewing movements or grinding the teeth. Methamphetamine, the current commonly abused form of amphetamines, is particularly likely to lead to symptoms of psychosis (Lecomte et al., 2018; see ● Figure 6.20).

Although they produce similar types of behavior, cocaine and amphetamines act somewhat differently at the synapse. Both drugs distort the action of dopamine transporters, gates that move previously released dopamine back into the presynaptic cell (see Chapter 4), but they do so differently. Methamphetamine mimics dopamine, leading it to be moved out of the synaptic

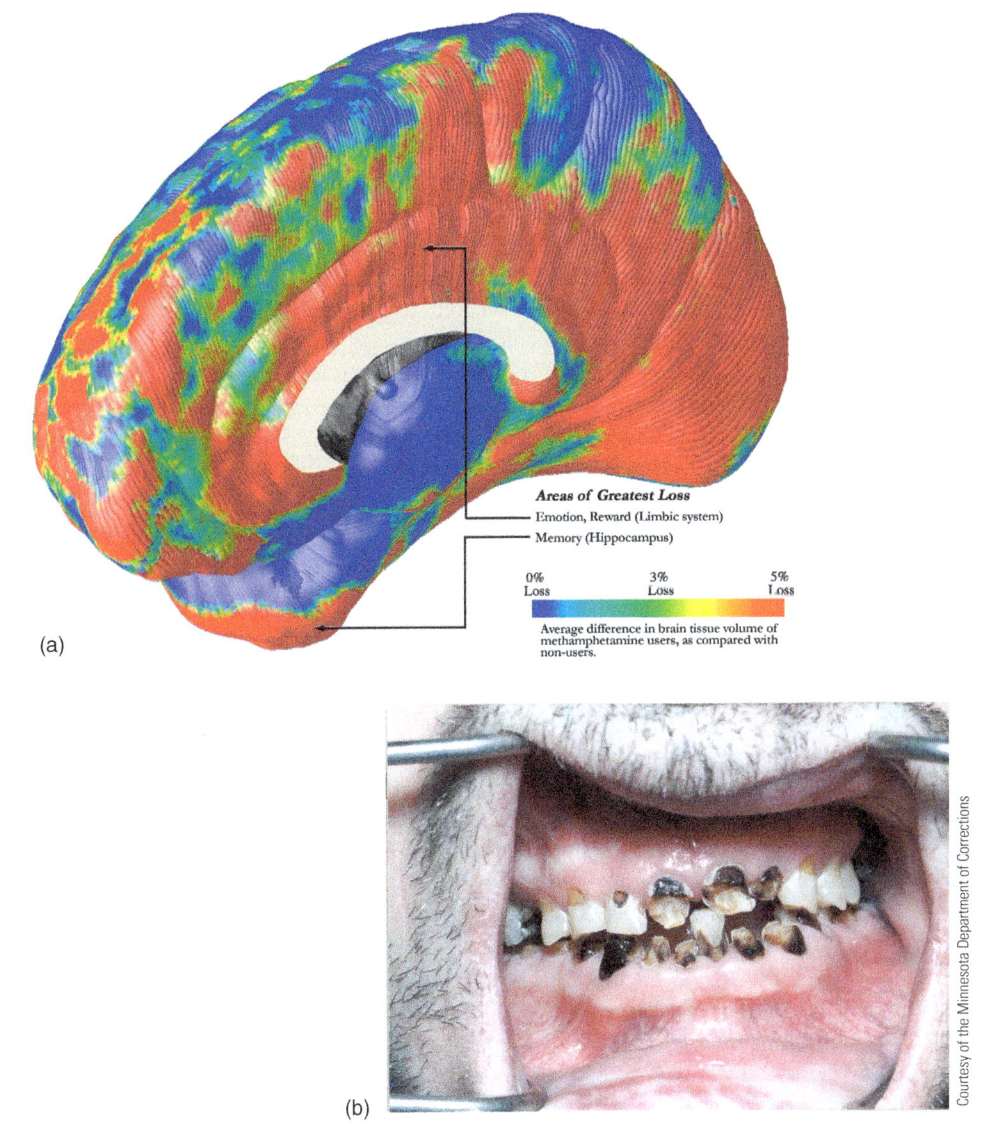

FIGURE **6.20**

Methamphetamine Produces Serious Health Consequences. (a) Methamphetamine users are likely to experience psychotic symptoms, probably because of substantial loss of brain volume in areas related to memory, emotion, and reward. (b) Methamphetamine also stimulates clenching and grinding of teeth, leading to a pattern of dental decay known as "meth mouth."

Source: Adapted from S. Berman et al. (2008). Abuse of amphetamines and structural abnormalities in the brain. *Annals of the New York Academy of Sciences, 1141*, 195–220. doi: 10.1196/annals.1441.031

gap into neurons by dopamine transporters. Once inside the neuron, methamphetamine enters synaptic vesicles, pushing the dopamine molecules out into the intracellular fluid of the axon terminal. The presence of large amounts of dopamine outside of vesicles makes the transporters begin to work in reverse, pushing dopamine out of the cell. With the transporters working in reverse and unable to retrieve the released dopamine, the molecules of dopamine become trapped in the synaptic gap, stimulating receptors continuously. Cocaine's action on the dopamine transporters is simpler. Cocaine simply blocks the transporters, keeping all previously released dopamine active in the synaptic gap. Because of their direct actions on the dopamine reward systems in the brain, these drugs are among the most addictive available substances.

Bettmann/Contributor/Getty Images

Before World War I, many commercial products contained cocaine. Freud originally believed that cocaine was an effective antidepressant. The ability of cocaine to produce rapid addiction eventually changed people's minds about the safety of the drug.

Methylphenidate (Ritalin) As we will see in Chapter 15, many children diagnosed with ADHD are treated with stimulant medications. The two most common choices are methylphenidate or a combination of amphetamine salts (Adderall). Both of these drugs boost the activity of dopamine and norepinephrine, which in turn increases users' ability to stay alert and concentrate. At clinical doses, these drugs do not seem to produce dependence, although they affect sleep and appetite. It is a common misconception that only people diagnosed with ADHD respond to these drugs with increased concentration. In fact, everybody reacts to these drugs in similar ways (Agay et al., 2010), which has led to an increase in their nonprescribed use by college students and others wishing to get a competitive edge in intellectual work.

MDMA (Ecstasy) 3,4-methylenedioxymethamphetamine (MDMA, or Ecstasy) is a relative of amphetamines and the hallucinogen mescaline that increases heart rate, blood pressure, and body temperature. MDMA increases sociability by stimulating the activity of serotonin and oxytocin (Thompson et al., 2007). MDMA mimics serotonin and is actually taken up more readily than serotonin itself by serotonin transporters. Once inside the cell, MDMA interferes with the storage of serotonin in vesicles and causes the transporters to begin acting in reverse, resulting in the release of large amounts of serotonin. Serotonin becomes trapped in the synaptic gap by the malfunctioning transporters, allowing it to continue to interact with receptors. Any excess serotonin activity resulting from MDMA use, overdose of antidepressants, or combinations of certain drugs can produce serotonin syndrome. Symptoms include dehydration, exhaustion, hyperthermia (high core body temperature), convulsions, and death (Pilgrim et al., 2011). MDMA has a smaller effect on dopamine than on serotonin, but the drug can still produce some dependency.

Use of MDMA is controversial, with some scientists expressing concern about its apparent detrimental effects on neurons that release serotonin (Capela et al., 2007; Biezonski & Meyer, 2011). On the other hand, MDMA has been used experimentally to treat alcohol use disorder and the anxiety related to autism spectrum disorder (Sessa et al., 2019). Use of MDMA for the treatment of post-traumatic stress disorder (PTSD) is awaiting approval by the U.S. Food and Drug Administration (FDA; Sessa et al., 2019).

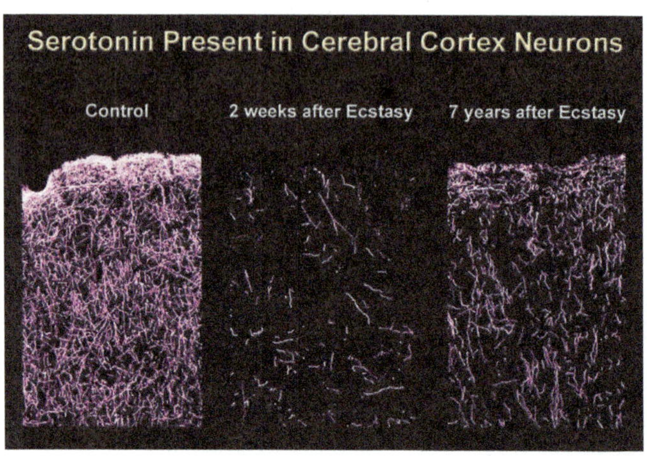

National Institute on Drug Abuse

MDMA (Ecstasy) appears to have long-term detrimental effects on neurons that release serotonin, associated with mood, appetite, sleep, and aggression.

Alcohol Alcohol is one of the earliest psychoactive drugs used by humans, dating back into our prehistory. In addition to seeking the relaxation produced by alcohol, early humans might have turned to fermented beverages as a safety precaution against contaminated water supplies because alcohol has natural antiseptic qualities.

At low doses, alcohol dilates blood vessels, giving people a warm, flushed feeling. It reduces anxiety, which makes relatively shy people more outgoing at a party. At higher doses, alcohol's inhibition of the higher levels of the brain leads to aggression, risky behaviors, and poor motor coordination. At very high doses, alcohol can produce coma and death, either from suppression of breathing or aspiration of vomit.

Alcohol produces its main behavioral effects by boosting the effects of GABA, the main inhibitory neurochemical in the brain. By boosting an inhibitor, alcohol depresses the activity of the brain, particularly that of the cerebral cortex. At the same time, alcohol blocks receptors for the brain's major excitatory neurotransmitter, glutamate. Finally, alcohol also stimulates reward pathways that release dopamine, which probably accounts for its addictive potential. Further information on the detrimental effects of alcohol on the developing fetus will be discussed in Chapter 11. Alcohol's impact on health in general is discussed in Chapter 16.

Opioids Natural or synthetic substances that interact with endorphin receptors are known as opioids. Opioids that are derived from the opium poppy are known as opiates. The opium poppy is the source of several psychoactive opiates, including morphine and codeine. Heroin can be synthesized through further processing of morphine. These substances are effective because they imitate the action of endorphins (short for endogenous morphine). Neurons possessing endorphin receptors are located in parts of the brain involved with pain, stress, and attachment. The activity of both natural endorphins and opioids results in the release of large amounts of dopamine, leading to feelings of well-being and reduction of pain.

Opioids have legitimate medical purposes, including pain control, cough suppression, and control of diarrhea. At low doses typical in medical practice, opioids produce a sense of euphoria, pain relief, reduced anxiety, muscle relaxation, and sleep. The higher doses characteristic of opioid abuse affect consciousness by producing a strong, rapid onset feeling of euphoria, or a "rush." With even higher doses, opioids exert a strong depression on breathing, occasionally leading to death.

Beginning in the 1990s, the United States has experienced an "opioid epidemic." Between 1999 and 2017, 700,000 people died from opioid overdose, or a current rate of about 130 per day (Centers for Disease & Prevention, 2019). The epidemic struck in three waves: a period of abuse of prescription opioids, abuse of heroin, and most recently, abuse of synthetic opioids such as fentanyl (see ● Figure 6.21). Law enforcement and health care entities are scrambling to intervene through awareness and education efforts.

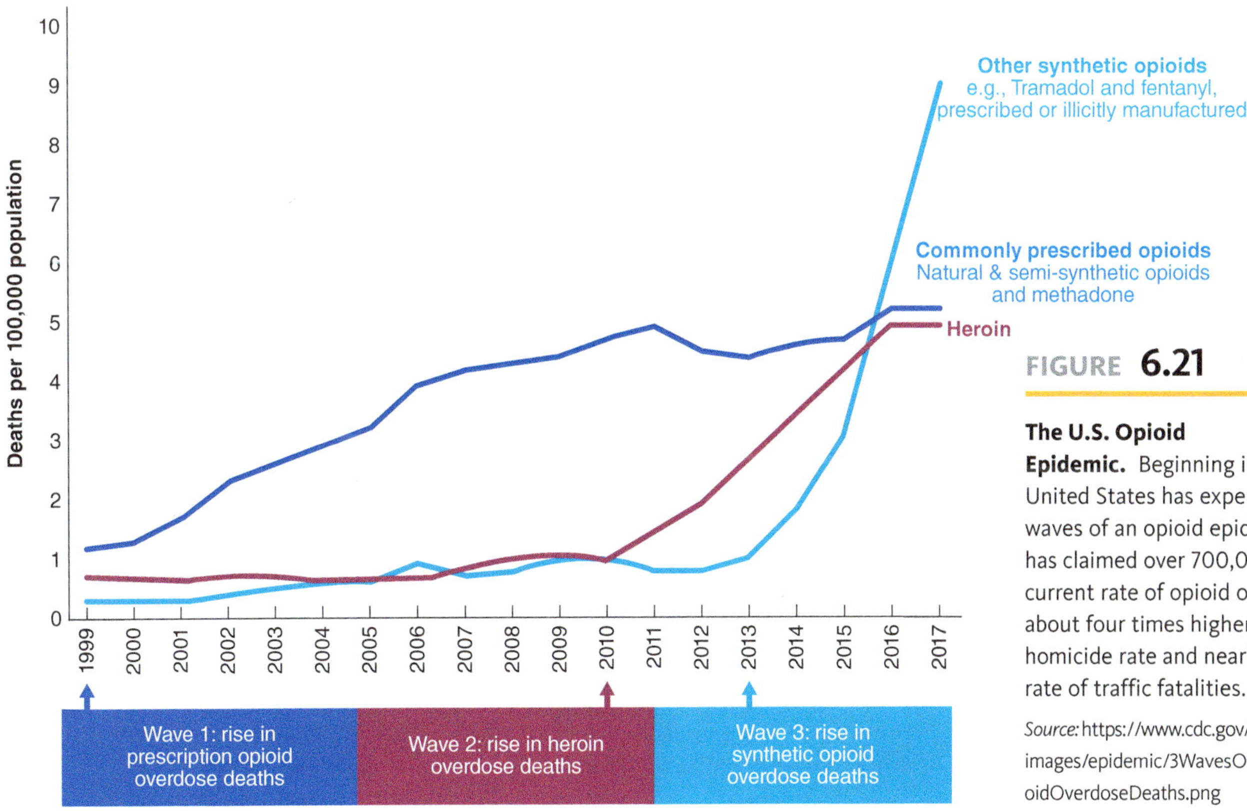

FIGURE **6.21**

The U.S. Opioid Epidemic. Beginning in 1999, the United States has experienced three waves of an opioid epidemic that has claimed over 700,000 lives. The current rate of opioid overdose is about four times higher than the homicide rate and nearly double the rate of traffic fatalities.

Source: https://www.cdc.gov/drugoverdose/images/epidemic/3WavesOfTheRiseInOpioidOverdoseDeaths.png

Nondrug Methods for Altering Consciousness

Hypnosis

Hypnosis is "a state of consciousness involving focused attention and reduced peripheral awareness characterized by an enhanced capacity for response to suggestion" (Elkinset al., 2015, p. 6).

Misunderstandings about what hypnosis can and cannot do are common. Early research suggested that hypnotized people were more likely to comply with requests to do dangerous things, such as pick up a poisonous snake or throw a beaker of what they believed to be acid into an experimenter's face (Rowland, 1939; Young, 1952). However, later experiments showed that equal compliance could be obtained with participants who were not hypnotized (Orne & Evans, 1965). In these situations, the participants' strong belief that the experimenters would be unwilling to harm them overrode any measurable influence of hypnosis. Contrary to popular belief (and a number of television crime shows), hypnosis does not sharpen memory and is instead likely to make it worse (Register & Kihlstrom, 1987). Hypnosis does have legitimate uses in therapy, however, including habit change (quitting smoking, etc.; Barnes et al., 2019), relieving symptoms of irritable bowel syndrome (Slomski, 2019), and pain relief (Taylor & Genkov, 2019).

One study that illustrates both the power and the limitations of hypnosis used a task known as the Stroop test (Stroop, 1935; Raz et al., 2006). In the Stroop test, participants are asked to respond to the color of the letters they are shown (see Figure 6.22). When the ink color and the word are congruent (e.g., the word *red* appears in red ink), reaction time is significantly faster (100–200 milliseconds faster) than when the ink color and the word are incongruent (e.g., the word *red* appears in green ink). Nearly everyone who can read shows a robust Stroop effect, and extensive training does not make the effect go away. This effect is typically explained in terms of a well-practiced skill (reading) taking precedence over a less practiced skill (naming the colors of letters). When instructed to ignore the practiced skill, attention is compromised, and reaction time becomes slower.

hypnosis An altered state of consciousness characterized by relaxation and increased suggestibility.

Using a posthypnotic suggestion, Raz et al. (2006) told their participants to respond to a cue by viewing the stimuli as gibberish instead of real words. Participants were assessed for their individual differences in suggestibility, or the ease with which someone can be

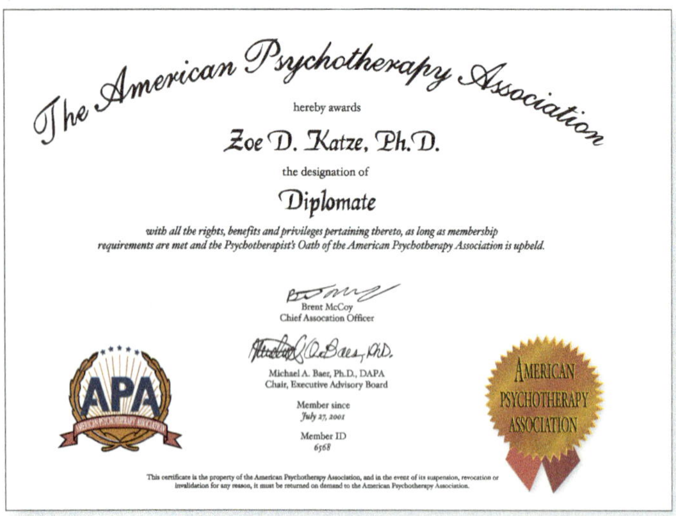

Sergey Peterman/Shutterstock.com

Frustrated licensed psychotherapist Steve Eichel demonstrated the lack of regulation of hypnotherapists by acquiring a number of impressive-looking credentials for Zoe D. Katze, who happens to be Eichel's cat. Zoe's name is a wordplay on the German *die Katze*, which literally means "the cat." Only three states in the United States have mandatory licensing and registration for hypnotherapists. Six others do not have mandatory licensing but regulate the practice somewhat. Many licensed psychotherapists like Eichel use hypnosis in their practices.

hypnotized. Participants who were rated as having low suggestibility performed in a typical manner on the Stroop test. In contrast, participants rated as having high suggestibility demonstrated little difference between the amount of time needed to identify the ink colors in the congruent and the incongruent conditions. The ability of posthypnotic suggestion to minimize the Stroop effect is remarkable because other efforts to modulate the effect have all failed. Clearly, hypnotic suggestion has the ability to reorganize cognitive processes, at least in highly suggestible individuals.

(a)	(b)
Red	Blue
Yellow	Green
Blue	Yellow
Green	Red
Green	Green
Yellow	Blue
Blue	Red

FIGURE **6.22**

Hypnosis and the Stroop Test. Under normal circumstances, results of the Stroop test show that participants identify ink colors faster when (a) the color of the letters matches the word being read (the word *red* appears in a red font) than when (b) it doesn't match (the word *red* appears in a yellow or green font). Highly suggestible hypnotized participants who were told that they were reading nonsense words instead of real words did not show this typical difference. Their reaction time for naming the ink color was the same whether it matched the color name or not.

Meditation

Meditation techniques vary widely and may occur in either religious or nonreligious contexts. When experienced practitioners are asked to describe the subjective experience produced by meditation, they describe a conscious state without thought, accompanied by a blissful emotional state (Travis, 2001). A variation on meditation known as mindfulness meditation has been used more frequently over recent years to treat substance abuse and a variety of psychological disorders (Wielgosz et al., 2019). Mindfulness refers to "nonjudgmental awareness of experiences in the present moment" (Hölzel et al., 2011, p. 537). Meditation incorporating mindfulness also appears to produce benefits in immune function, blood pressure, stress hormone levels, and cognitive functioning.

Brain activity correlates of meditation are challenging to discover, due to the effects of experience with meditation on the outcomes (Falcone & Jerram, 2018). However, EEG recordings during meditation typically feature increased proportions of alpha waves, which we described earlier as being characteristic of an awake but relaxed state. Recordings are slightly different depending on whether the participant is engaged in focused or mindfulness types of meditation (Travis, 2019).

Studies using functional magnetic resonance imaging (fMRI) suggest that meditation represents a voluntary regulation of attention and autonomic functions (Lazar et al., 2000). Brain imaging studies have discovered that experienced meditators showed less activity in the brain's DMN, which was described earlier in this chapter (Brewer et al., 2011). Activity in the DMN is usually correlated not only with mind wandering and thinking about the self but also with unhappiness. Relative inhibition of the activity of the DMN through meditation might be responsible for the feelings of bliss associated with this practice (see ● Figure 6.23).

Meditation appears to result in physical changes in the brain (Fox et al., 2014). It has been correlated with increased cortical thickness (Lazar et al., 2005), improved connectivity involving the anterior cingulate cortex (Posner, 2018), and increased gray matter in the brainstem (Vestergaard-Poulsen et al., 2009). The increased cortical thickness was more noticeable in older participants, suggesting that meditation might offset typical age-related changes in the brain.

meditation A voluntary alteration of consciousness characterized by positive emotion and absence of thought.

Other Methods for Altering Consciousness

A variety of environmental conditions initiate altered states of consciousness, including exposure to high altitudes during mountain climbing, underwater conditions in scuba diving, starvation, sleep deprivation, sensory deprivation, twirling, and rhythm-induced trance. These conditions may lead to hallucination and other consistent changes in cognition and emotion, possibly due to their ability to reduce activation in the prefrontal cortex (Dietrich & Al-Shawaf, 2018).

Several of these environmental factors characterize vision quests, which typically take place within religious contexts. In the traditional Native American vision quest, preparation typically involved 3 to 4 days of starvation and sleep loss. The individual would travel to an isolated location where no shelter could be built. The seeker would then be instructed to concentrate and watch for the appearance of a "guardian." This combination of events reliably led seekers to experience the following phenomena: a distorted sense of time, a sensation of "oneness," the appearance of light, the emotion of ecstasy or bliss, and a sense of improved insight (Steiger, 2000).

We have all observed young children experiment with their bodies by spinning. Although we do not know the precise reason for such spinning behavior, other than that it is fun, spinning probably represents the child's efforts to alter sensory and cognitive states.

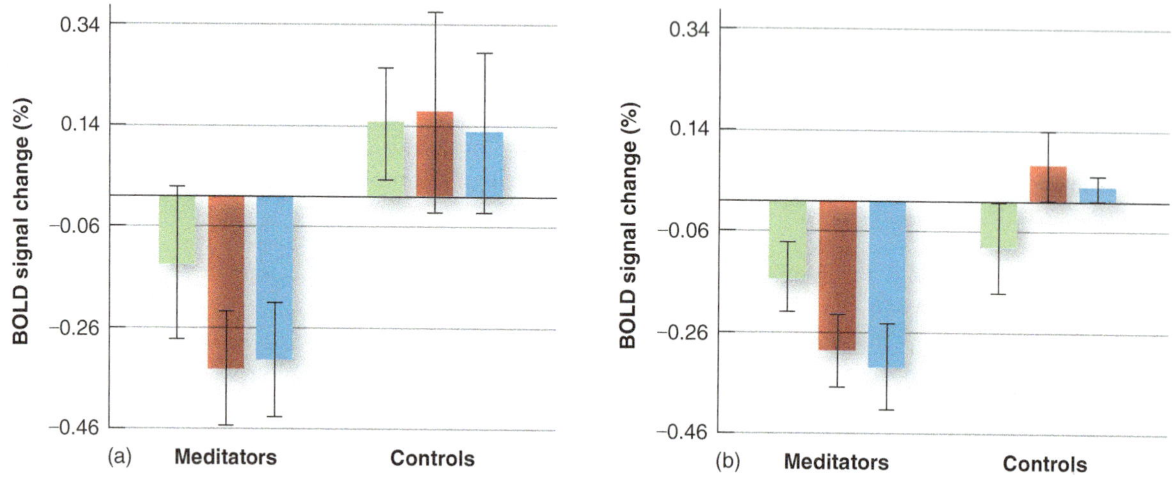

FIGURE **6.23**

Meditation Is Correlated With Decreased Activation of the Brain's Default Mode Network (DMN). Meditation is associated with a decrease in activation in the prefrontal cortex and posterior cingulate gyrus, which are important parts of the DMN, of experienced meditators compared to control participants who were introduced to the meditation methods right before being scanned. The amount of decrease in signal strength is shown (a) in the prefrontal cortex and (b) in the posterior cingulate cortex. The colored bars represent three methods of mindfulness meditation: choiceless awareness is shown in green, loving kindness is shown in red, and concentration is shown in blue.

Source: J. A. Brewer et al. (2011). Meditation experience is associated with differences in default mode network activity and connectivity. *Proceedings of the National Academy of Sciences, 108*(50), 20254–20259. doi: 10.1073/pnas.1112029108

Spinning is also used as a meditation-inducing method by the Sufis, a mystic Muslim sect. Sufis may whirl for an hour or more before falling to the ground, where they seek a feeling of oneness with the Earth.

It is likely that dancing has been a part of human cultures for thousands of years, both for recreational and for religious purposes. Accompanied by the equally ancient practice of drumming, dance is capable of initiating trancelike states in the participants (Vaitl et al., 2005). A trance state typically refers to an induced state of consciousness in which a person is less responsive to external stimuli (Hove & Stelzer, 2018). The altered states induced by drumming and dancing include distortion of time, vivid imagery, and strong positive emotions such as ecstasy and bliss (Vaitl et al., 2005). Participants listening to rhythmic drumming showed more theta wave activity in their EEGs, normally associated with light N-REM sleep, than did participants listening to unstructured beat sequences (Winkelman, 2003).

iStock.com/ansonmiao

Both dancing and psychoactive drugs have the potential to alter consciousness and are often combined in raves. Common themes of unity, or oneness, and positive emotion are primary goals reported by the rave participants.

Modern youth are fond of combining dance and psychoactive drugs to alter consciousness, particularly in the context of raves, which are large parties featuring electronic music, darkness, and the use of hallucinogens or MDMA (Redfield & Thouin-Savard, 2017). The raves feature some themes common to the contexts we have described previously. Unity, or oneness, and positive emotion are again primary goals reported by the participants.

Interpersonal Relationships

The Consciousness Perspective *How Does Imitation Influence Liking?*

WE ENGAGE IN A VARIETY OF UNCONSCIOUS BEHAVIORS, and not just when we're asleep. Among the unconscious behaviors that have been identified by psychologists is one that is particularly relevant to relationships—the effect of mimicry on liking and feeling close to others (Lakin et al., 2008). A substantial body of research supports the idea that we unconsciously copy the behavior of others and that when we do copy another person's behavior, that person likes us better without necessarily knowing why.

Under what circumstances are we most likely to copy the behavior of other people? One possible answer is that we mimic others to avoid or repair social exclusion. Jessica Lakin and her colleagues (2008) made their participants feel socially excluded (temporarily) and then observed that these excluded participants were more likely to mimic another person than were participants who had not been socially excluded. This process extends to group membership as well. Participants excluded by an in-group were subsequently more likely to mimic an in-group member than an out-group member. These results suggest that mimicry developed as an automatic behavior that we could use to respond to threats to our social connectivity, which as we have stated many times previously, could have been a matter of life or death to our hunter–gatherer ancestors.

Because this mimicry is quite automatic and unconscious, we are usually not aware that we are behaving this way. Knowing now that this is an adaptive behavior, look more closely at how you behave when encountering situations in which you feel excluded. It could be a social situation, such as at a party or an organizational event, where you are trying to mingle or initiate a dialogue with others. Or perhaps you observe mimicry when you are around someone you like romantically. Do you feign interest in things you wouldn't necessarily be interested in otherwise? Are you more apt to align yourself with the personality of the person you find interesting? Do you see this kind of behavior in friends or family? ■

Jose Luis Pelaez/Iconica/Getty Images

We often imitate the behavior of others without being consciously aware that we're doing so. Imitation seems to enhance liking and social inclusion.

Psychology Takes on Real-World Problems

Sleep During a Pandemic

Sleep disruptions in response to natural disasters, war, and other highly stressful events are common. Compared to a pandemic, however, the sleep disruption associated with such events tends to be somewhat localized in time and in geography. In contrast, the COVID-19 pandemic is associated with widespread and lasting changes in sleep habits (Morin & Carrier, 2020). In particular, lasting problems with insomnia are likely outcomes of a pandemic. Lin et al. (2020) reported a 37% increase in clinically significant insomnia between the pre-COVID and peak COVID period in China.

Not only does the stress and anxiety related to the pandemic itself have the ability to disrupt sleep, but many other factors are in play. Many people experience additional stress due to social isolation, financial concerns, employment conditions, and the need to combine family and work obligations. These sources of stress might rob people of the restorative actions of sleep so desperately needed during a pandemic for maintaining a strong immune response and good general health.

Sergii Sobolevskyi/Shutterstock.com

In addition to the normal worry about health in a pandemic, sleep can also be disrupted by stress related to juggling work and family obligations and disruptions to normal daily routines.

Potentially even more harmful is the disruption to the daily routines that help us maintain good circadian function. Working people typically are quite regular in the times they rise, eat, leave for work, and schedule social and leisure activities during the day. Without these habits, maintaining regularity in sleep-waking cycles might be more difficult. Government limits on outdoor activities might prevent people from obtaining the daylight exposure they need for good circadian function.

Policy responses to the problem of pandemic-induced insomnia might take the form of educating the public about good sleep hygiene, which is a benefit regardless of whether a pandemic is occurring. Simple rules such as keeping to a regular sleep schedule, monitoring the use of caffeine and other stimulants, obtaining a daily dose of sunlight, limiting screen time right before sleep, and getting regular exercise can go a long way toward preventing problems with sleep quantity and quality. ■

SUMMARY 6.3 Commonly Used Psychoactive Drugs and Their Methods of Action

Drug class	Acts on
LSD 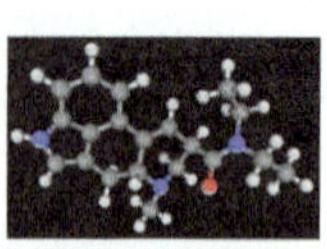	Serotonin
Marijuana 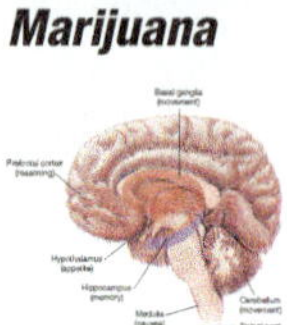	Endogenous cannabinoids
Caffeine 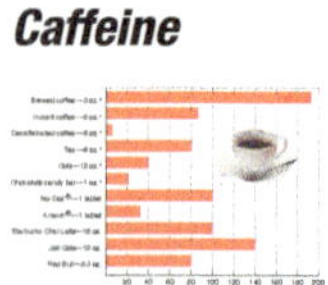	Adenosine

Drug class	Acts on
Nicotine 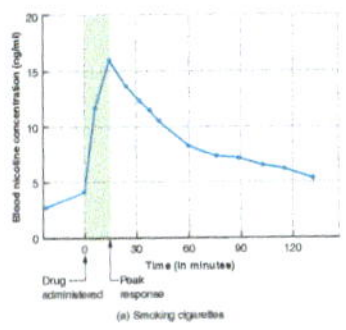	Acetylcholine
Cocaine, amphetamines, and methamphetamine 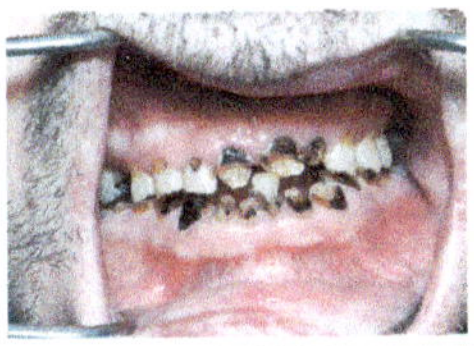	Dopamine
Methylphenidate	Dopamine
MDMA (Ecstasy) 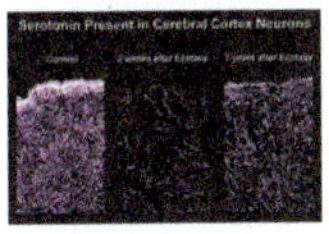	Serotonin, oxytocin
Alcohol	GABA, dopamine
Opioids 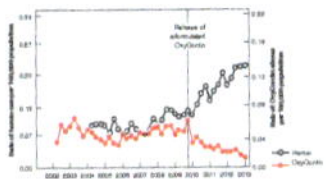	Endogenous endorphins

Credits: Top row—Laguna Design/Science Photo Library/Corbis; Third row—iStock.com/Studiocasper; Fifth row—Courtesy of the Minnesota Department of Corrections. Sixth row—National Institute on Drug Abuse.

KEY TERMS The Language of Psychological Science

Be sure that you can define these terms and use them correctly.

addiction, p. 215
alpha wave, p. 202
beta wave, p. 202
biological clock, p. 199
circadian rhythm, p. 199
coma, p. 212
consciousness, p. 194
delta wave, p. 204
dreaming, p. 208
gamma wave, p. 202
hallucinogen, p. 216
hypnosis, p. 224
insomnia, p. 209
lucid dreaming, p. 208
major depressive disorder with seasonal pattern, p. 201
meditation, p. 225
narcolepsy, p. 209
near-death experience, p. 213
non–rapid eye movement (N-REM) sleep, p. 203
psychoactive drug, p. 215
rapid eye movement (REM) sleep, p. 203
restless legs syndrome (RLS), p. 210
seizure, p. 213
self-awareness, p. 194
sleep, p. 199
sleep apnea, p. 209
sleep terror, p. 209
stimulant, p. 219
sudden infant death syndrome (SIDS), p. 210
theta wave, p. 203
tolerance, p. 215
vegetative state (VS), p. 212
waking, p. 199
withdrawal, p. 215

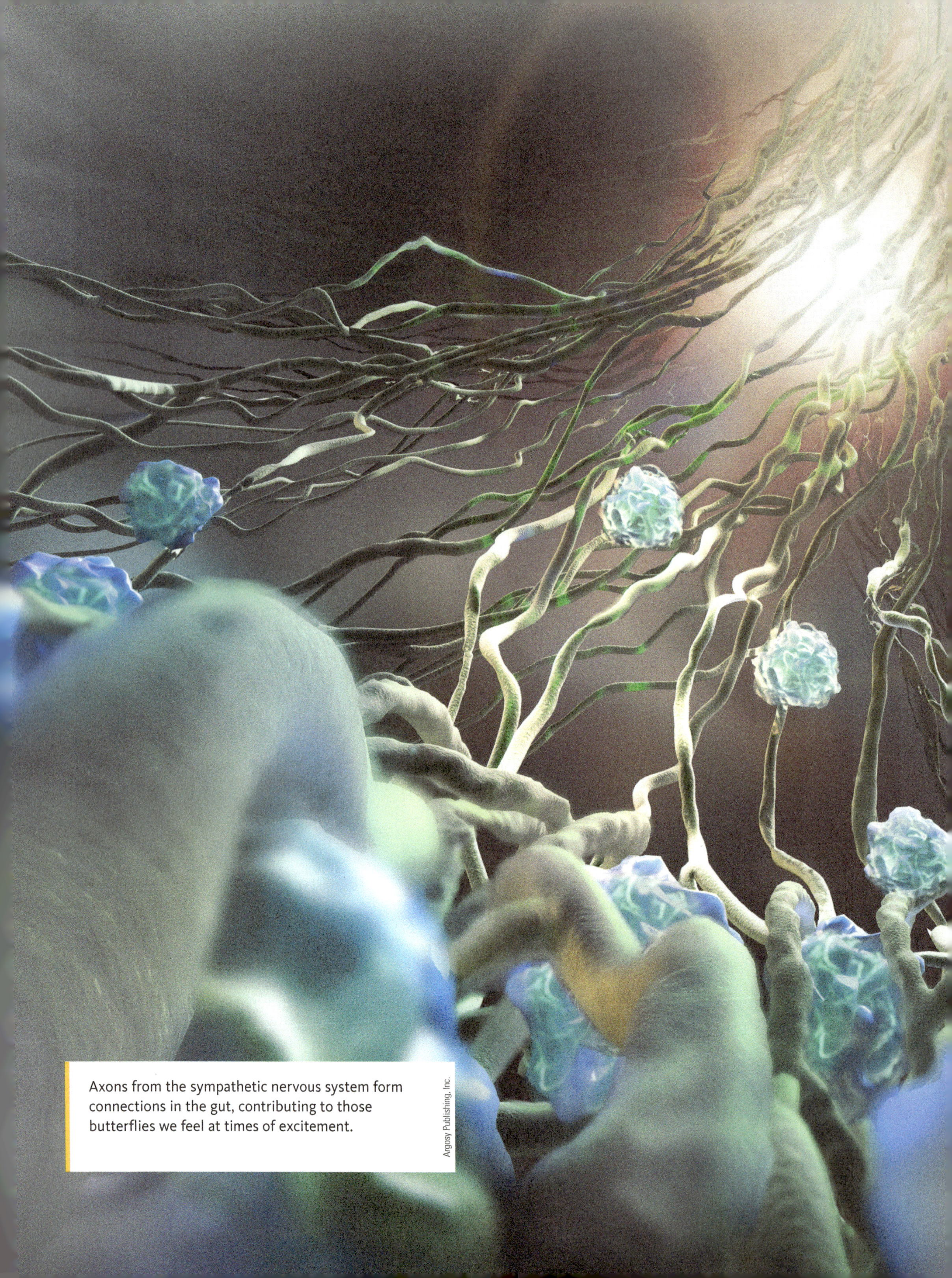

Axons from the sympathetic nervous system form connections in the gut, contributing to those butterflies we feel at times of excitement.

Argosy Publishing, Inc.

7

The Feeling Mind

EMOTION AND MOTIVATION

LEARNING OBJECTIVES

1. Distinguish between emotion, mood, and motivation.
2. Differentiate the features and predictions of major theories of emotion.
3. Explain the biological, social, and cognitive correlates of emotional expression and assessment.
4. Explain the key attributes of homeostasis, drive, and incentive.
5. Analyze the physiological and environmental factors that influence hunger and sexual behavior.
6. Describe motivations of affiliation and achievement in light of systems explaining the prioritization of motives.

EMOTION AND MOTIVATION, THE TOPICS OF THIS CHAPTER, involve neural circuits that often operate below the level of our conscious awareness. We can zoom in to look at these neural circuits, like these sympathetic axons (in blue in the large image on the previous page) forming connections with the gut. We have all had the feeling of butterflies in our stomach when we are excited, and these neural pathways are responsible for such feelings.

Michael Steele/Staff/Getty Images Sport/Getty Images

Zooming out, we can examine emotion and motivation in the larger context of the individual using the example of elite athletes at the Olympic Games. The 2016 Rio Games featured 11,544 athletes from 205 countries, a tiny fraction of the millions of people who compete in athletics worldwide. To stand out among these elites takes extreme motivation, not to mention talent and hard work. Many athletes competing at this level have focused on their sport to the exclusion of most other activities since they were in elementary school, yet of the more than 11,000 participants, only 972 (or 8%) went home with a medal.

Given the odds of obtaining a medal, you would think that any athlete winning one would be ecstatic, but that is not always the case. As you can see in the photograph of Olympic swimmers on the medal stand, the athletes are showing a range of emotions. Look for a moment at the way the three athletes are holding their flower bouquets. The gold and bronze medalists are holding their bouquets straight up, but the silver medalist is close to dropping his bouquet. His entire demeanor says dejection and disappointment.

Alan Williams/Axiom Photographic Agency/Getty Images

Why would a silver medalist be disappointed with such an exceptional achievement? To answer this question, we must zoom out even farther from the individual to consider the social context. Psychologists have found that the reactions of these swimmers are quite typical (Medvec et al., 1995 McGraw et al., 2005). Silver medalists are more likely to compare themselves to gold medalists, which leads to disappointment,

Emotions are spontaneous, automatic responses to our ongoing perceptions and thoughts.

while bronze medalists compare themselves to the fourth-place finishers who do not get a medal, which leads to joy.

In this chapter, we will explore the mechanisms responsible for our emotions and motivations, beginning with the underlying physical mechanisms and zooming out to look at individual and, ultimately, social influences on these behaviors.

How Are Emotion and Motivation Related?

emotion A combination of arousal, physical sensations, and subjective feelings that occurs spontaneously in response to environmental stimuli.

Emotion and motivation share the experience of subjective feelings and engage similar processes and structures in the brain. However, psychologists find it useful to distinguish between these two concepts.

If we are thirsty following a tough workout, we are motivated to seek a drink of water. It is unlikely that a thirsty person would be motivated to find a hamburger instead.

An **emotion** is a brief combination of physical sensations, such as a rapid heartbeat, and conscious, subjective feelings, like feeling afraid, that prepares an individual for action. Emotions are spontaneous, automatic responses to our ongoing perceptions and thoughts. We communicate our emotions to others through behaviors such as facial expression, body language, gestures, and tone of voice.

Psychologists have debated whether emotions should be viewed as discrete stand-alone states or points on a continuum. The discrete approach views emotional states such as happy, sad, or angry as being like primary colors of red, yellow, or blue, while the continuous view sees emotions like a rainbow, with particular emotions being located closer to some than others and even blending together (Russell, 1980; see Figure 7.1). Like many of the either/or discussions that we encounter in psychology, a compromise might be the best strategy. If we think instead of emotions as being stars, we can imagine a constellation containing clusters of positive emotions such as happiness and pride and another constellation containing clusters of negative emotions such as anger and sadness.

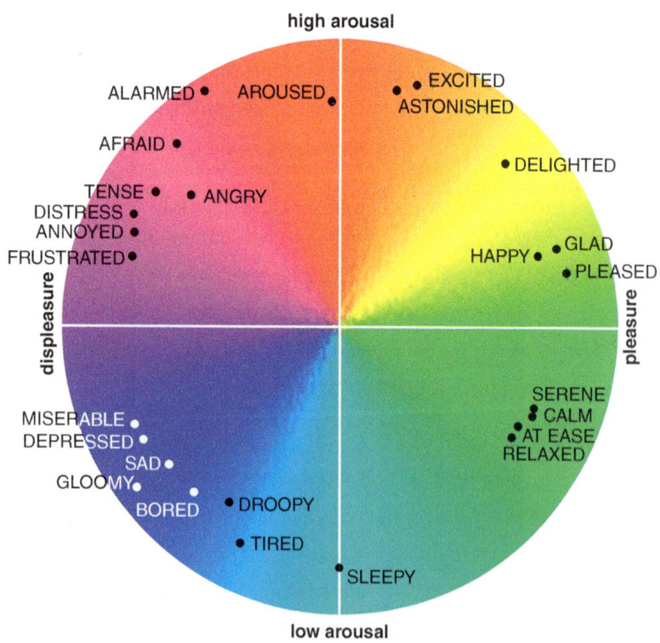

FIGURE 7.1

Continuous Versus Discrete Views of Emotion. Russell (1980) suggested that emotions could be viewed along dimensions of pleasant/unpleasant and high arousal to low arousal instead of as isolated states. This approach to emotion suggests that some emotions are closer together than others.

Emotions can be distinguished from moods. A mood is a more general state than an emotion. You can be in a good mood while feeling a variety of specific emotions, such as happiness, pride, or relief. A mood generally lasts longer than a single emotion. For example, when we discuss psychological disorders in Chapter 14, we will see that criteria for depression specify that depressed mood should characterize at least half a day every day for 2 weeks (American Psychiatric Association [APA], 2013). Because emotions are responses to the ongoing and ever-changing flow of environmental information, it is unlikely that any single emotion would last this long.

Motivation is defined as a process that arouses, maintains, and guides behavior toward a goal. For example, we are motivated to seek a drink of water in response to thirst. The process of motivation is accompanied by distinct emotional states. Thirst is generally quite distressing, and taking a drink of water can produce positive emotions like relief and happiness.

Emotion and motivation share the ability to arouse an organism and stimulate behavior, but motivation does so more directly and precisely than emotions do. People who feel motivated by thirst are likely to do one thing: seek something to drink. In contrast, experiencing the emotion of sadness stimulates behavior, but that behavior can take many forms. Some people respond to sadness by crying in a room by themselves, while others seek the company of friends.

carballo/Shutterstock.com

Many animals are motivated to explore their surroundings even when they have no immediate needs because being familiar with your neighborhood saves time when a need does arise, whether that is food, water, shelter from a storm, or a gas station. Today, many people rely on technology to help them navigate in unfamiliar locations.

motivation A process that arouses, maintains, and guides behavior toward a goal.

James–Lange theory A theory of emotion that proposes that physical sensations lead to subjective feelings.

Why Are We Emotional?

Whether we're experiencing happiness or sadness, anger or disgust, an emotion combines a physical sensation, such as a rapid heartbeat, and a conscious, subjective feeling, like joy or sadness. Psychologists have asked questions about how the physical sensations and subjective feelings might relate to one another.

Theories of Emotion

Several major theories of emotion describe the relationship between the physical responses and subjective feelings experienced during an emotion. In other words, what are the connections between those butterflies in your stomach and the knowledge that you're feeling afraid? These theories of emotion are similar in many ways to efforts to explain perception in Chapter 5. Some attempt to work from the bottom up (from physical sensation to cognitive appraisal), while others work from the top down (from appraisal to physical sensation).

The James–Lange Theory of Emotion Working independently, William James and Danish physiologist Carl Lange developed similar descriptions of the relationship between physical sensations and subjective feelings in emotion (James, 1890; Lange, 1885/1912). Consequently, the **James–Lange theory** bears the names of both men (see Figure 7.2).

James believed that emotions could arise from several sources, including the recall from memory of events that were emotional.

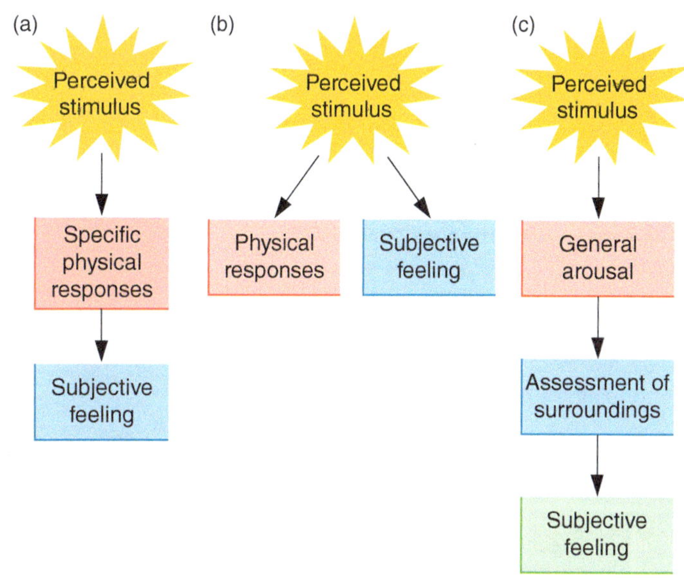

FIGURE **7.2**

Three Classic Theories of Emotion. Each of these theories of emotion—(a) the James–Lange theory, (b) the Cannon–Bard theory, and (c) the Schachter–Singer two-factor theory—attempts to explain the relationships between the physical responses and subjective feelings that occur when we experience an emotion.

However, his greatest interest was in emotions "that have a distinct bodily expression" (James, 1884/1969, p. 189). At the core of the James–Lange theory is the idea that this type of emotion is the result of a sequence of events. Once the individual perceives a stimulus, such as a grizzly bear, that person experiences a physiological response. This physiological response is subsequently interpreted by the individual, giving rise to a conscious awareness of a subjective feeling. This theory reversed the ordering of events in the prevailing view of James's time that we get sweaty palms and butterflies *because* we are scared. The James–Lange theory assumes that physical states related to each type of feeling (sadness and happiness, for instance) are distinct from one another. The theory also assumes that we are capable of correctly labeling these distinct physical states as separate feelings. As James wrote, "We feel sorry because we cry, angry because we strike, afraid because we tremble" (1890, p. 1006).

James's statement may seem counterintuitive to you. Shouldn't a good cry make us feel less sad, not more? Many people also believe that holding anger inside instead of expressing it somehow makes feelings of anger build up and become worse. These common sense notions support the concept of **catharsis**. In catharsis, emotions are viewed as filling an emotional reservoir. When the reservoir fills up, the emotion will spill over in an uncontrolled manner. For example, we talk about a "buildup of hostility or anger" that somehow overflows, producing a more extreme response than is warranted by the situation. Catharsis theorists recommend that we avoid this buildup by regularly expressing our emotions. In other words, it might be better to express some anger regularly than to repress your anger and "explode."

catharsis A theory of emotion that views emotion as a reservoir that fills up and spills over; it predicts that expressing an emotion will reduce arousal.

Catharsis and the implications of the James–Lange theory are contradictory. One suggests that expressing an emotion reduces that feeling, while the other argues that expressing an emotion leads to the subjective feeling. Which is correct? If we are feeling sad, does having a good cry make us feel better or more aware of our sadness?

The catharsis approach is challenged by the phenomenon of "psyching up." Traditional Maori warriors of New Zealand prepared for battle by performing a *haka*, featuring ritual grimaces, vocalizations, and battle moves. A contemporary rugby team, the New Zealand All Blacks, uses the traditional *haka* of the players' homeland to prepare for games. Not only do these performances contribute to the athletes' physical and emotional preparation for participation in a rather violent sport, but they no doubt intimidate the opposing team as well.

Consistent with the James–Lange theory, psyching up represents an ability to influence our subjective feelings by changing our physical sensations. By appearing to be happy, we might begin to feel happier. Further support comes from an experiment in which participants were directed to make specific movements of the face (Levenson et al., 1990). For example, they might be instructed to raise their eyebrows and form their mouth into the shape of an O. They were not informed that they were to make any particular facial expression, nor were they allowed to view their face in a mirror. They did, however, report "feeling" the emotion they had portrayed; you might have experienced a feeling of surprise if you followed the same directions.

Consistent with the James–Lange theory of emotion, the physical expression of an emotion might lead to subjective feelings. Traditional Maori warriors prepared for battle by performing a *haka*. The New Zealand All Blacks rugby team also uses the *haka* before a game. The James–Lange theory would predict that these men would feel more aggressive after performing the *haka*.

Roger Fletcher/Alamy Stock Photo

AP Images/Paul Thomas, File

However, there are apparent limits to this type of feedback loop. Although an initial study suggested that assuming a "power pose" would lead to higher testosterone and willingness to take risks (Carney et al., 2010), these results failed to replicate (Ranehill et al., 2015). It does appear, however, that assuming a power pose makes people report feeling more powerful (Cuddy et al., 2018), a more modest conclusion that is more in line with the predictions of the James–Lange theory. Whether feeling more powerful leads to acting in more powerful ways remains an open question.

Astrid Stawiarz/Getty Images Entertainment/Getty Images

Although the original reports claiming that power posing could change hormone levels and risk-taking failed to replicate, it does appear that assuming a power pose makes people feel more powerful. This outcome is consistent with implications of the James–Lange theory of emotion—physical sensations inform feelings.

Cannon–Bard theory A theory of emotion featuring the simultaneous and independent occurrence of physical sensations and subjective feelings during an emotional experience.

We might not be as good at reading our physical states as the James–Lange theory requires us to be. One experiment that challenged our ability to distinguish correctly among the physical states of different emotions was carried out in Capilano Canyon, located in British Columbia (Dutton & Aron, 1974). Capilano Canyon may be crossed at one of two locations. The first crossing involves a 450-foot-long bridge with low handrails, suspended about 230 feet above rocks and rapids. Farther upstream, the canyon may be crossed on a solid wooden bridge that is less frightening. In the study, an attractive female experimenter approached single men crossing one of the two bridges. After completing a short interview, the experimenter gave each man her telephone number, in case he had further questions about the experiment. Not only did the men on the frightening bridge include more sexual content in their interviews, but they were about four times as likely to telephone the female researcher later.

Although the study is flawed by a failure to randomly assign men to bridges (bolder men might be both more likely to choose the scary bridge and to telephone a stranger), it stimulated further thinking about the James–Lange theory. The results of this study suggest that its participants were not very good at discriminating the physical sensations associated with fear and sexual arousal. We can assume that the attractiveness of the female would be constant, suggesting that the setting in which she was seen largely accounted for the differences in sexual content in interviews and the likelihood of seeking further contact with her. One might speculate that similar mistakes underlie the popularity of horror films and amusement parks with impossibly high roller coasters as dating activities. Scare your dates to death, and they may interpret feelings of fear as love. These results suggest that in some circumstances, we might not be as good at interpreting our physical sensations as predicted by the James–Lange theory.

AP Images/Matt Dunham

John Stibbard, son of the owner of the Capilano Suspension Bridge, poses on the bridge with the Olympic torch after completing his leg of the torch run in preparation for the 2010 Winter Olympics in Vancouver, Canada.

The Cannon–Bard Theory of Emotion

Walter Cannon disagreed with the James–Lange theory and proposed his own theory, which was later modified by Philip Bard, resulting in the **Cannon–Bard theory** (Bard, 1934; Cannon, 1927, 1932; Bard, 1934). The James–Lange theory proposes a sequence of events, from physical sensations to subjective feeling, but the Cannon–Bard theory proposes that both factors occur simultaneously and independently.

How are these theories different? Let's assume that you are innocently reading your textbook in your room when a bear walks in the door. According to the James–Lange theory, the sight of the bear would immediately set off physical sensations that you would then cognitively interpret as fear. According to the Cannon-Bard theory, the sight of the bear would immediately and simultaneously trigger a subjective feeling of fear ("whoa, there's a bear in my room") and physical sensations (probably the autonomic nervous system's fight-or-flight response in this example). Unlike the James–Lange theory, the Cannon–Bard theory does not assume that the experience of a subjective feeling depends on physical sensations.

The Cannon–Bard theory fares somewhat better in explaining the Capilano Canyon results. Cannon and Bard would be comfortable with the notion that fear and sexual arousal would produce similar physical sensations and that study participants may simply have erred in their cognitive assessment of the situation. Instead of saying, "I'm really scared because I'm on this bridge," the participants would say, "I think this interviewer is very attractive." According to this model, a person's cognitive assessments of an emotional situation work independently of any physical sensations that might occur.

The Schachter–Singer Two-Factor Theory Stanley Schachter and Jerome Singer (1962) proposed a two-factor theory of emotion that adds an intermediate step between physical sensations and subjective feelings. Emotional arousal signals us to make a conscious, cognitive appraisal of our circumstances, which then allows us to identify the emotion we're experiencing. The same physical sensations may lead to several interpretations, based on the way an individual assesses a situation.

Schachter–Singer two-factor theory A theory of emotion in which general arousal leads to assessment, which in turn leads to subjective feelings.

Returning to our example of the bear entering your room, we can see how the **Schachter–Singer two-factor theory** would explain your reaction. For Schachter and Singer, the sight of the bear would initiate a general state of arousal. To identify the source of your arousal, you would assess your situation, attribute your arousal to the presence of a bear in your room, and identify your feelings as fear (with considerable accuracy, we would assume). Like the James–Lange theory yet unlike the Cannon Bard theory, physical sensations remain important for

CONNECTING TO RESEARCH

Botox and the Ability to Read the Emotions of Others

BOTOX, A DEACTIVATED FORM of the same toxin that causes botulism poisoning from spoiled food, helps people with migraine headaches and neurological disorders of movement, but it is also used for cosmetic purposes. Botox reduces wrinkling by paralyzing the small muscles used in facial expressions. The ability of Botox to prevent facial movement provides an interesting test for the James–Lange theory (Neal & Chartrand, 2011). Without feedback from our facial expressions, can we identify our own emotions? Without the ability to imitate the facial expressions of others, can we still identify how they're feeling?

The Question: How would increasing and decreasing the ability to move facial muscles affect participants' judgments of the emotions of others?

METHODS

In a first experiment, 31 female participants were recruited from cosmetic surgery clinics. Of those participants, 16 had been treated with Botox, and the other 15 had been treated with a dermal filler material, which does not restrict the movement of facial muscles. Participants viewed photographs of eyes and the surrounding area and were asked to choose which of four emotional adjectives (happy, sad, and so on) best fit the expression they saw (see Figure 7.3). In a second experiment, a gel that forced participants to put more effort into their facial movements was placed on the faces of half of a group of 95 participants and on the arms of the other half as a control. Participants completed the same test of identification of emotion as before, along with two control tests: identifying emotion in voices, which is unlikely to be affected by facial expression, and a set of arithmetic questions.

ETHICS

Because the participants were voluntarily seeking the Botox or dermal filler treatments, their participation in the experiment did not increase their risk. Their confidentiality must be strictly maintained, and a debriefing about the findings should be available.

Featureflash Photo Agency/Shutterstock.com

Actress Rachel Weisz, star of *The Mummy*, *The Bourne Legacy*, and *Black Widow*, is not a fan of Botox. She told an interviewer, "Acting is all about expression; why would you want to iron out a frown?"

identifying emotion in the two-factor theory. Unlike the James–Lange theory, physical sensations are more general rather than specific to individual emotional states, thus requiring an intermediate assessment stage.

Schachter and Singer (1962) directly tested this approach by injecting volunteers with epinephrine (adrenalin), which causes a high level of arousal. The participants had been told that they were getting an injection of a vitamin and that their vision would be tested as soon as another volunteer arrived to participate in the experiment. The second volunteer was actually an actor employed by the researchers. In half of the trials, the actor behaved in a happy, silly manner; in the other half, he acted angry and stomped out of the room. The results supported a role for cognitive appraisal of the environment in the identification of emotion. Participants who were exposed to the happy actor rated themselves as feeling happy, while participants exposed to the angry actor felt more negative. Importantly, when the participants were accurately informed that they were getting a drug that produced arousal instead of a vitamin, the behavior of the actor did not influence their assessment of the situation. Instead, they attributed their feelings to the drug.

A later attempt to replicate Schachter and Singer's study did not succeed (Marshall & Zimbardo, 1979). As we discussed in Chapter 2, a failure to replicate a study casts serious doubts on the results. Nonetheless, the two-factor theory has provided considerable insight into how we identify our subjective feelings. The two-factor theory explains the Capilano Canyon bridge study easily. Once aroused by being on the scary bridge, the male subjects

RESULTS

In Experiment 1, the Botox group performed significantly more poorly on the identification of emotions task than the control group. In Experiment 2, participants with the facial gel performed better than those with the gel on their arms.

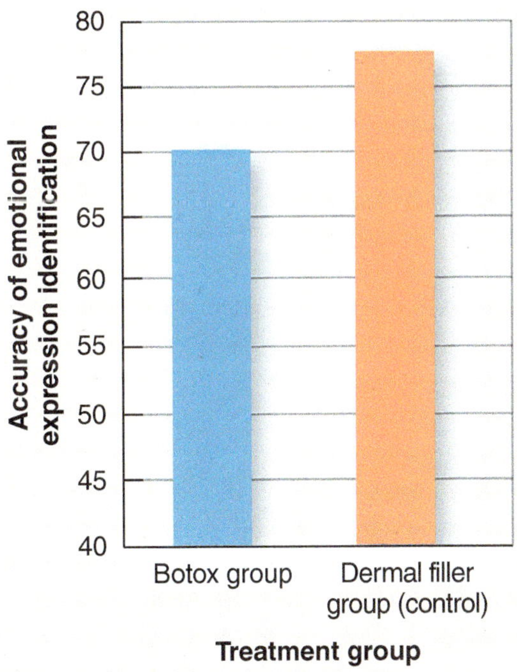

CONCLUSIONS

Both experiments support the idea that feedback from facial expressions of emotion influences the ability to identify emotional states in other people. The participants in the first experiment who used Botox had less facial mobility than the participants who used the dermal filler. The lack of facial mobility caused by Botox interfered with the participants' ability to accurately assess another person's facial expression of emotion. In the second experiment, making the muscles work harder to imitate a facial expression by applying a restrictive gel actually improved the participants' ability to identify the facial expressions of others. These results are quite consistent with the James–Lange theory's emphasis on feedback from the body as important to the subjective identification of emotion, not just in ourselves but also in other people. These results suggest that an important side effect of Botox might be a reduction in social competence and empathy because of an inability to read the emotions of other people correctly. ■

FIGURE **7.3**

Botox Reduces the Ability to Identify Facial Expressions in Others. Following treatment for wrinkles with either Botox or an injected dermal filler (Restylane), study participants were asked to identify the emotional expression of faces presented on a computer screen. The dermal filler group was significantly better than the Botox group at correctly identifying the emotions. This result suggests that by reducing the ability to imitate another person's facial expressions, Botox limits a person's perception of the emotions of other people.

Source: Adapted from D. T. Neal & T. L. Chartrand (2011). "Embodied Emotion Perception: Amplifying and Dampening Facial Feedback Modulates Emotion Perception Accuracy," *Social Psychological and Personality Science, 2*(6), 673–678, doi:10.1177/1948550611406138

assessed their circumstances and attributed their feelings to sexual attraction. Additional support is provided by research that demonstrates that arousal produced by one emotion can transfer to and intensify a second emotion. People who have just exercised (producing physiological arousal) are more likely to become angry or sexually aroused when exposed to relevant stimuli (Reisenzein, 1983).

Contemporary Approaches to Emotion Each of these classic theories offers important insights into our experience of emotion, yet none definitively resolves our original question regarding the relationship between physical sensations and subjective feelings. The same patterns of physical activity occur during a variety of emotions, and a single emotion may be associated with a variety of physical states. That mistakes can and do happen is certain. Nonetheless, we seem to manage quite well at interpreting our emotions in most situations.

somatovisceral afference model of emotion (SAME) A model of emotion in which a range of physical sensations from precise to general requires varying degrees of cognitive processing prior to subjective feelings.

A more contemporary model reconciles the debate regarding the impact of physical sensations on subjective feelings (Cacioppo et al., 1992). The **somatovisceral afference model of emotion (SAME)** begins with a recognition that physical responses to a stimulus can range from quite specific to quite general. For example, the physical sensations associated with disgust can be more precise than the physical sensations associated with pride.

The initial degree of specificity of the physical response leads to different cognitive processing. A highly specific physical response leads to unambiguous recognition of a subjective feeling. This is the situation that appeared most interesting to James. A bear walks in, you react physically, and you know you're scared. At the other extreme, instead of specific physical responses, a situation might produce general arousal, which requires significant cognitive processing and evaluation. For example, a valedictorian giving a graduation speech might not understand her arousal until she sees her parents and other members of the audience clapping and realizes the emotion she is feeling is pride. This scenario is closest to that proposed by Schachter and Singer (1962).

SAME provides middle ground between the James–Lange and the Schachter and Singer theories. If a physical response is only partially specific, an ambiguous message is sent forward that is clarified by the presence of additional cues or information. The model correctly predicts that emotional responses range from immediate to delayed based on the amount of cognitive processing that is required. Emotions that are associated with a precise set of physical responses, such as fear, occur quickly, but emotions that are associated with more general arousal, such as pride, occur relatively slowly.

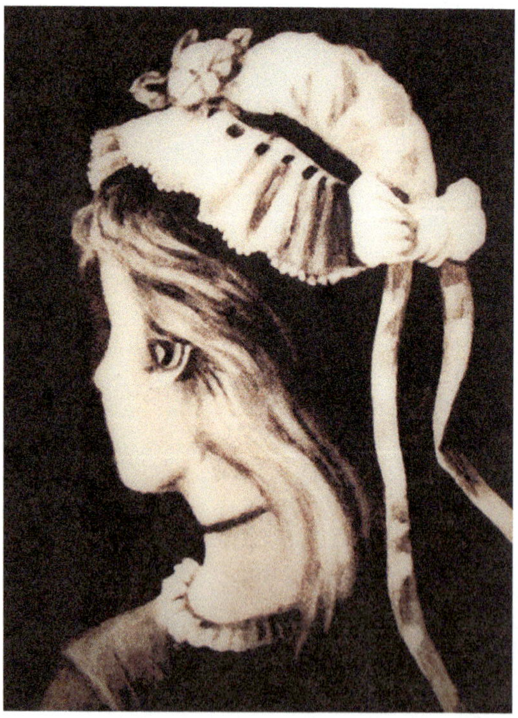

Ian Paterson/Alamy Stock Photo

This ambiguous image (you should find yourself alternating between seeing a young woman and seeing an old woman) can serve as a model for how the mind processes a range of emotional situations, from simple to complex. According to the somatovisceral afference model of emotion (SAME), if we look at a simple image, we need little cognitive assessment to respond appropriately. As images become more complex, we require increasing amounts of cognitive assessment before we respond. Processing the simple emotion of fear is similar to processing an unambiguous image. Processing more complex, ambiguous emotions, like pride, requires more cognitive assessment, just like viewing this ambiguous image does.

Asier Romero/Shutterstock.com

Monkey Business Images/Shutterstock.com

According to appraisal theory, a person who values wealth and a person who values family might experience different emotions in response to the same event.

Affective neuroscience, or the neuroscience of emotion, supports the sequential models featured in the James–Lange, two-factor, and SAME theories. Neuroscientists suggest that the physical sensations of emotion represent an evolved ability to respond to recurring environmental stimuli, such as recoiling at the sight of a snake or spider (Adolphs, 2016). What we know as feelings then emerge from the experience of our physical states. Finally, the experience of an emotion builds our concept of the emotion, or what it "feels like" to be happy, sad, or fearful (see Chapter 10), which we can then use to identify emotional states in others.

Contemporary cognitive approaches to emotion place little emphasis on the physical correlates that are featured so prominently in the classic and neuroscience theories. Instead, these approaches emphasize the role of **appraisals**, or the detection and assessment of stimuli with relevance for well-being, in eliciting emotion (Moors et al., 2013). For example, Ellsworth (1994, p. 223) expresses some frustration with the approach taken by James when she says, "Bears do not automatically cause us to run or tremble." Instead, the interpretation of the stimulus, the bear in this case, forms the critical starting point for the emotional cascade. Appraisal theory further assumes that interpretation is a continuous process rather than a single decision about a stimulus (Moors et al., 2013). For example, attention may be aroused by some change in the environment. A recognizable emotion has not yet occurred, and if the appraisal of the stimulus determines it to be of no significance, arousal returns to baseline. However, if the stimulus is found to have positive or negative value to the individual making the appraisal (a source of food or a predator, for instance), feelings and physiological responses change yet again.

appraisal The detection and assessment of stimuli that are relevant to personal well-being.

An emphasis on appraisal as a starting point for emotion may help us account for the vast range of emotional reactions that individuals might have to the same event (Moors et al., 2013). One person may view material wealth as essential to happiness, whereas another may view successful relationships with others as a primary goal. These different cognitive patterns should produce different emotional responses to the same event. A letter to an advice columnist described a situation in which a man's wife had wrecked his expensive antique automobile in a serious accident (Dear Abby, January 14, 2006). Our first person, who values money, is likely to respond with dismay at the loss of the expensive car. Our second person, who values relationships, is likely to be happy that his beloved wife survived the accident in one piece.

The Evolution of Emotion

Emotional behavior is not unique to humans. Charles Darwin (1872) made a careful study of the facial expressions produced by humans and other primates. He concluded that all primates form facial expressions using the same muscles, which in turn led him to state that emotional facial expression must have evolved. Although we are frequently cautioned about anthropomorphism, or the attributing of human qualities to other animals, it is easy

Darwin discovered that humans and other primates use the same facial muscles to produce emotional expressions, leading him to hypothesize that emotions evolved. Can you figure out what emotion is being expressed by both the chimpanzee and the man? Try imitating the expression and think about how you feel. Still no luck? The emotion being expressed is disappointment.

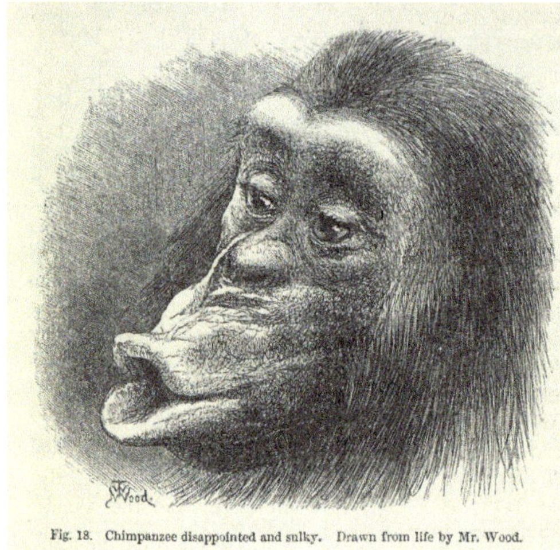

Fig. 18. Chimpanzee disappointed and sulky. Drawn from life by Mr. Wood.

Album/Alamy Stock Photo

Sergey Lavrentyev/123RF

Yerkes-Dodson law A description of the relationships among task complexity, arousal, and performance.

to identify with the anger of a mother bear defending her cubs or the fear of a gazelle trying to outrun a cheetah.

To say a behavior evolves implies that it makes survival more likely. How might the experience of emotion benefit an animal? According to Adolphs (2018), emotions allow animals to respond to the environment with more flexibility than reflexes provide (see Chapter 8) yet without requiring the expenditure of resources required by conscious, planned behavior. In particular, emotions have the ability to produce arousal, which in turn stimulates potentially life-saving actions. The word *emotion* is derived from the Latin word meaning "to move."

According to the classic **Yerkes–Dodson law**, the ideal amount of arousal interacts with the complexity of a task (Yerkes & Dodson, 1908). For simple tasks, such as outrunning a predator, greater arousal leads to greater performance. For more complex tasks, such as taking a difficult exam, arousal levels that are too high can begin to interfere with performance (see Figure 7.4). We have all had the experience of "choking," or performing badly because of too much arousal. In addition to providing general arousal, each emotion is associated with a positive or negative quality or valence, which "moves" us in the correct direction of either approach or avoidance (Russell & Mehrabian, 1978). The negative emotion of disgust tells us to avoid rotting food, and positive feelings of happiness cement our social bonds.

Emotions might also enhance survival by providing an important means of communication. Nonverbal forms of communication such as facial expression, calls, and body language were used to provide information to others long before humans began using spoken words (see Figure 7.5). If one person assumes a body posture indicating fear, the emotion ripples through a crowd to its edges in a short amount of time (de Gelder et al., 2004). Human infants communicate a range of needs to their parents before developing the ability to speak. Without hearing the words, you have no difficulty interpreting the facial expressions, body language, and gestures of a driver behind you who doesn't approve of your lane-change technique.

An additional and welcome benefit of having emotions is our ability to enjoy the arts. Evidence for a coordinated development of language and emotional communication remains in

FIGURE 7.4

The Effects of Arousal on Performance. The Yerkes–Dodson law predicts that the complexity of a task interacts with an organism's arousal level to determine the quality of performance. For simple tasks, such as running to escape a predator, greater arousal leads to a relatively steady improvement in performance. For difficult tasks, such as completing an exam, moderate amounts of arousal lead to the best performance, and high arousal can lead to weaker performance. Adapted from R. M. Yerkes & J. D. Dodson (1908). "The Relation of Strength of Stimulus to Rapidity of Habit-Formation," *Journal of Comparative Neurology and Psychology*, *18*(5), 459–482. doi: 10.1002/cne.920180503

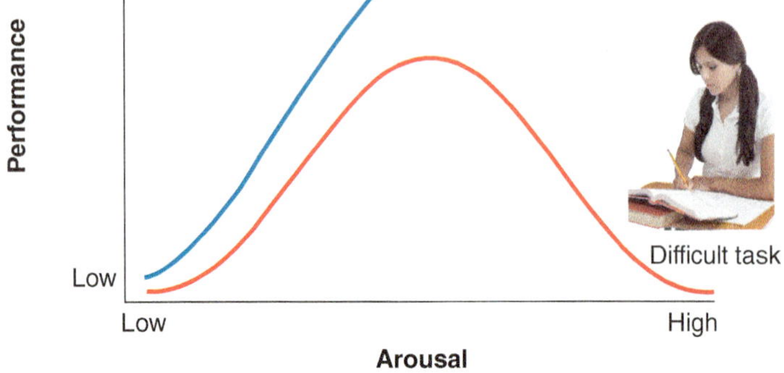

Tetra Images/Alamy Stock Photo; Design Pics Inc/Alamy Stock Photo; iStock.com/mocker_bat

FIGURE **7.5**

Body Language. One of the advantages of emotions is the ability to communicate nonverbally. Even with these simple stick figures, it is easy to interpret how each character feels.

our contemporary brain, which uses the same pathways for language and for the perception and appreciation of music (Schön et al., 2010). Without the capacity to feel, we would find it difficult to appreciate a Picasso or the moving strains of "Yesterday" by the Beatles. We wouldn't enjoy a good cry at the end of *Pride and Prejudice* or be glued to the edge of our seats while watching *Jaws*. The universal nature of human responses to many poems, pieces of music, and other artistic accomplishments points to shared underlying mechanisms, shaped through our evolutionary past. Similar neural activity is observed across performers and audiences during a musical performance (Hou et al., 2020). Shared enjoyment of the arts contributes greatly to social bonding in human societies. When we dance together, sing together, or watch plays and other visual displays of art, shared emotional responses contribute to feelings of community and closeness.

We can identify further advantages of emotion by studying people whose emotional lives have been affected by brain damage. In Chapter 4, we reviewed the case of Phineas Gage, whose frontal lobe damage changed him from a responsible, well-liked member of the community to an impulsive, indecisive, and emotionally volatile individual who had difficulty keeping a job. Antonio Damasio (1994) described the case of a young man named Eliot, who had frontal lobe surgery to remove a tumor. Like Gage, Eliot maintained his intelligence and other skills after his surgery but was unable to establish priorities. Damasio hypothesized that emotions provide a bridge to past experiences that can be used to set priorities such as approach and avoidance. In the absence of normal feedback from the body that can be used to identify emotional states ("my heart is beating fast, so I must be scared"), Eliot can no longer use these past experiences to guide his current decisions.

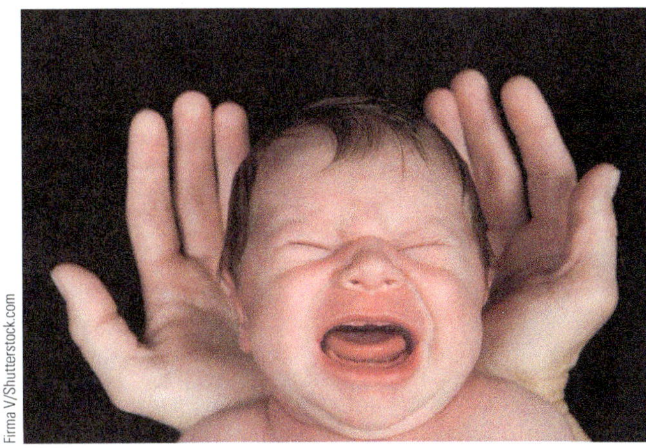

Firma V/Shutterstock.com

Long before infants learn to speak, they can communicate with adults by using facial expressions.

The Biology of Emotion

In Chapter 4, we identified several nervous system structures that participate in our emotional lives. Emotional responses combine bottom-up processing, in which lower parts of the nervous system send "alerts" to the cerebral cortex, with top-down processing, in which cortical executive functions such as attention and appraisal modify the activity of the lower structures.

The mind's priority for processing negative events has been described in earlier chapters. For example, in Chapters 1 and 5, we discussed how we are far more sensitive to bitter tastes because these are often associated with poisons than we are to sweet tastes, which are rarely life threatening.

The Autonomic Nervous System

The autonomic nervous system, which controls many activities of our glands and organs, participates in the general arousal associated with emotional states (Norman et al., 2014). In particular, activity of the sympathetic division of the autonomic nervous system is correlated with our fight-or-flight response to perceived danger. The autonomic nervous system is under the immediate control of the hypothalamus, a structure that also plays an important role in most motivated behavior.

Researchers have asked whether specific patterns of autonomic activity occur during particular emotional states. In a large meta-analysis, autonomic measures did not reliably predict particular emotional states, such as happiness or sadness (Cacioppo et al., 2000). However, the analysis indicated that the autonomic responses associated with negative emotions are stronger than those associated with positive emotions. Fear, with its rapid heartbeat and sweaty palms, provokes a more dramatic set of physical reactions than feelings of happiness.

The Hypothalamus In its direct management role over the autonomic nervous system, the hypothalamus participates in any of the emotional states that also engage that system. Is that the only role for the hypothalamus in emotion? It is clear that electrical stimulation of the hypothalamus in animals can elicit many behaviors, including sexual behaviors, eating, drinking, and aggression, but it is unclear whether these artificially induced behaviors are accompanied by the "feeling" part of an emotion.

Renewed interest in the hypothalamus and its role in emotion has resulted from experiments using deep brain stimulation, delivered through surgically implanted electrodes, to relieve various conditions from obesity to depression. During stimulation of the hypothalamus, one patient experienced both the physical and subjective feelings normally associated with a panic attack (see Chapter 14; Wilent et al., 2010). The physical responses, such as shortness of breath and rapid heartbeat, were not surprising given our knowledge of hypothalamic functions, but the patient's subjective feelings of overwhelming anxiety were unexpected. Subsequently, researchers have linked activity of the hypothalamus specifically to fear of predation (Silva et al., 2013; Silva et al., 2016).

The Amygdala The amygdala identifies emotional stimuli, both positive and negative, and initiates responses to the perception of these stimuli. The amygdala's role in the identification and classification of emotional stimuli is carried out through its participation in a circuit that includes the frontal lobes of the cortex, the cingulate cortex, and the insula.

The amygdala not only detects emotional stimuli, but it also forms a bridge between these stimuli and appropriate responses. The amygdala initiates responses through its tight connections with the hypothalamus, which in turn affects autonomic, hormonal, and behavioral processes. For example, when the amygdala perceives danger from environmental stimuli, it initiates a hormonal cascade involving the pituitary gland and the adrenal glands that produces an increased release of neurochemicals in the brain, leading to an increase in overall arousal. We will discuss this process in greater detail in Chapter 16.

One of the first clues to the importance of the amygdala to emotion resulted from an experiment conducted in 1939 in which researchers removed both temporal lobes, which include the amygdalae, from rhesus monkeys (Klüver & Bucy, 1939). After recovery, the normally hard-to-handle adult rhesus monkeys became tamer, and their emotions were less intense. They allowed themselves to be picked up and stroked, and they appeared to be relatively oblivious to stimuli that normally elicit intense fear, such as snakes. They made fewer fear-related grimaces and vocalizations.

We now understand that whenever the amygdala is damaged, animals respond inappropriately to danger. Rats with damaged amygdalae fail to learn to fear a tone or other stimulus that reliably predicts the onset of electric shock (LeDoux et al., 1990). Rhesus monkeys with lesioned amygdalae show less fear of rubber snakes and less restraint around unfamiliar monkeys, a potentially dangerous way of behaving in a species that enforces strict social hierarchies (Emery et al., 2001; Mason et al., 2006).

Insight into the role of the amygdala in humans has been provided by case studies in which disease has damaged this structure. Patient S.M. experienced damage to both amygdalae because of a rare disease (Adolphs et al., 1994). Although Patient S.M. can recognize the emotions of happiness, sadness, and disgust portrayed in photographs, she has selective difficulty identifying fear correctly. As shown in ● Figure 7.6, Patient S.M. has particular difficulty using information from the eye region of the face in judging emotion, although when she was instructed to pay attention to eyes, her performance improved (Adolphs et

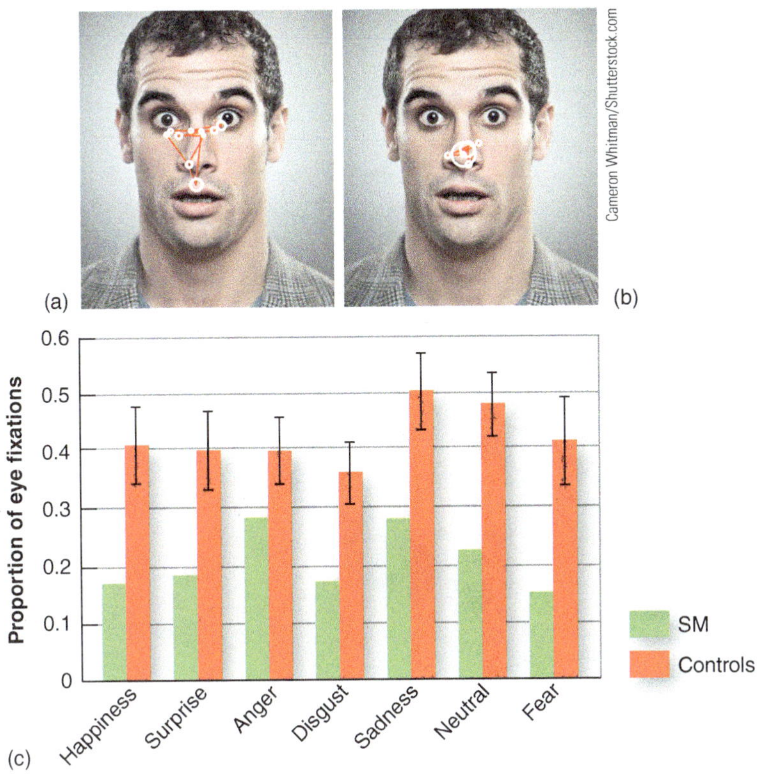

FIGURE 7.6

Amygdala Damage and the Perception of Emotion. People with amygdala damage, like Patient S.M., do not always use information about people's eyes to judge their emotions. Eye tracking shows (a) how a healthy control participant scans an emotional image and (b) how a person with amygdala damage might scan the same face. (c) For all emotions studied, Patient S.M. showed fewer eye fixations than normal controls (NC).
Source: R. Adolphs et al. (2005). "A Mechanism for Impaired Fear Recognition after Amygdala Damage," *Nature, 433*, 68–72. doi:10.1038/nature03086

al., 2005). Individuals with autism spectrum disorder, discussed in Chapter 14, share Patient S.M.'s reluctance to make eye contact and difficulty identifying other people's emotions, especially fear. One of the most consistent biological correlates of autism spectrum disorder is abnormal development of the amygdala (Amaral et al., 2008). These findings suggest that the amygdala participates in both the active exploration of the social environment and the interpretation of the results of that exploration (Adolphs, 2007).

insula Regions of cortex located at the junction of the frontal and temporal lobes.

The Insula

The **insula**, found in the fold between the junction of the temporal lobes with the frontal and parietal lobes, plays an important role in our subjective experiences, or feelings (Damasio, 2003; Wager & Barrett, 2017; see ● Figure 7.7).

Activity toward the back of the insula is associated with many internal sensations, including pain and itch, that can be localized as originating from particular parts of the body. This area is also associated with many of the physical sensations we associate with emotional feelings, including changes in blood pressure, breathlessness, and feelings of butterflies in the stomach. In contrast, activity in the forward areas of the insula is associated with more global feelings, including a particularly strong reaction to disgust (Gasquoine, 2014; Papagno et al., 2016).

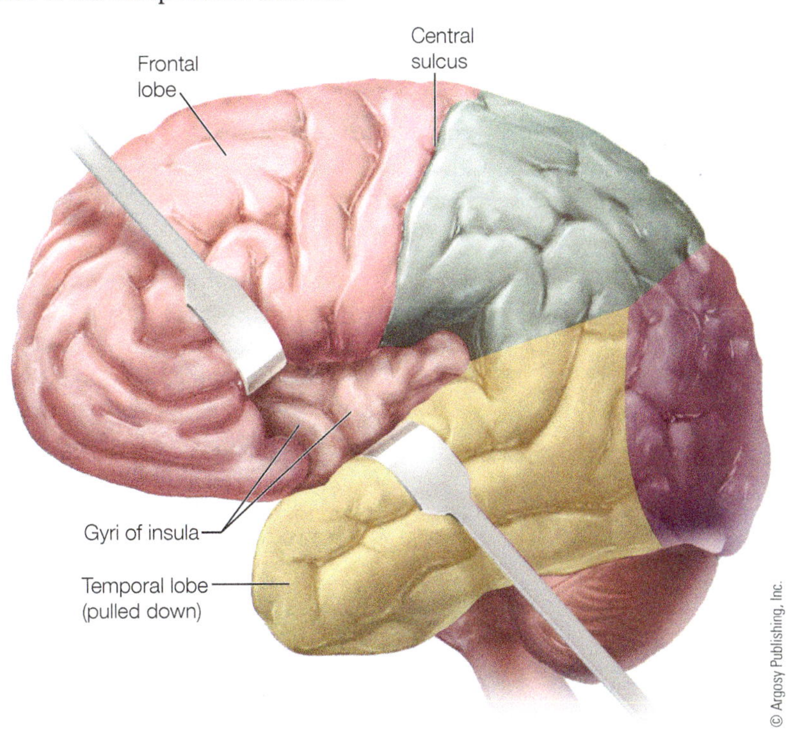

FIGURE 7.7

The Insula.

The Cingulate Cortex

The cingulate cortex, shown in ● Figure 7.8, serves as a major gateway between the amygdala and other subcortical structures and the frontal areas of the cortex. In particular, the cingulate cortex participates in processing the emotional quality of physical pain.

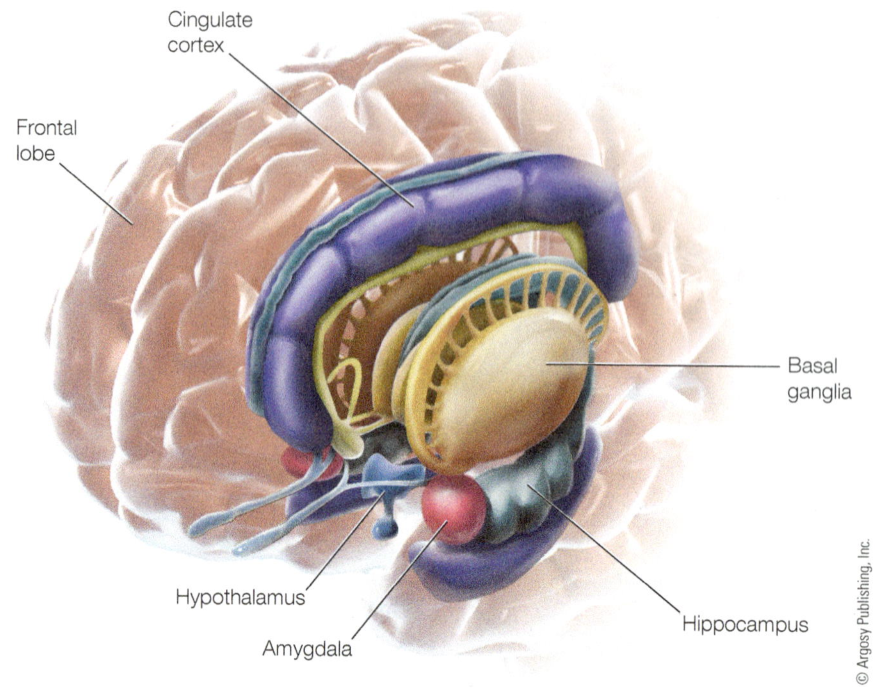

FIGURE 7.8

The Cingulate Cortex and Basal Ganglia. The cingulate cortex forms circuits with the frontal cortex, the amygdala, and other subcortical structures involved with emotional processing. The basal ganglia are part of the brain's voluntary movement systems and help coordinate movement in response to assessments of emotion. The basal ganglia show particularly strong activation that correlates with the emotion of disgust.

We often dislike our own photographs even when other people seem to think they look fine. Part of the problem is that we rarely see ourselves the way others do—we usually see ourselves in a mirror, which reverses our emotional expressions. Because our facial expressions are not symmetrical, due to the stronger role of the right hemisphere in emotion, that crooked smile looks wrong when we see it on the opposite side of our face.

The anterior cingulate cortex, along with the dorsomedial prefrontal cortex, contributes to the more conscious appraisal of threat compared to the less conscious signals arising from the amygdala (Kalisch & Gerlicher, 2014). As we will see in Chapter 14, some individuals are unusually anxious. Worrying and catastrophizing (focusing on the worst possible outcomes) by anxious people involves exaggerated appraisals of threat. Unusually high levels of activation in the anterior cingulate cortex have been observed during episodes of catastrophizing and worry.

The Basal Ganglia

As we discussed in Chapter 4, the basal ganglia are large, subcortical structures that participate in the generation of voluntary movement. These structures coordinate movements in response to emotional stimuli. Strokes that damage the basal ganglia result in an overall reduction in the experience of emotional intensity (Paradiso et al., 2013).

Along with the insula, the basal ganglia participate in the experience of disgust (Phan et al., 2002; Holtmann et al., 2020). This finding is consistent with clinical observations of people with diseases that damage the basal ganglia, such as Huntington's disease. These people have particular difficulty recognizing facial expressions of disgust, although their recognition of other major emotional facial expressions appears intact (Hennenlotter et al., 2004).

The nucleus accumbens, which is part of the basal ganglia, is particularly associated with pleasure and reward, and is implicated in addiction. This structure performs key functions related to positive emotional responses (Salgado & Kaplitt, 2015).

The Cerebral Cortex and Emotion

As we observed in Chapter 4, damage to the frontal lobes produces changes in emotional behavior. People with frontal lobe damage often experience a reduction in fear and anxiety, which may contribute to their engagement in impulsive, risky behaviors. They seem unable to experience "gut feelings" that serve as warnings in threatening situations (Damasio, 1994). Without such warnings, these individuals forge ahead impulsively where others would pause.

We do not appear to have "happy centers" or "sad centers" in the cerebral cortex. Instead, the experience of different emotions produces different patterns of cortical activation. When people are asked to recall a specific event from their past associated with the emotions of anger, sadness, fear, and happiness, brain imaging scans identify distinct patterns of activity for each emotion (Damasio et al., 2000; Saarimäki et al., 2015). However, the same brain regions usually participate in more than one of these states.

Expressing Emotion

Humans express emotion with their entire bodies. People who are feeling threatened or scared generally cross their arms and hunch forward. Angry, aggressive people typically lean forward, rise onto the balls of their feet, and raise their shoulders to appear larger and more intimidating. However, humans rely most heavily on the face for expressing emotion.

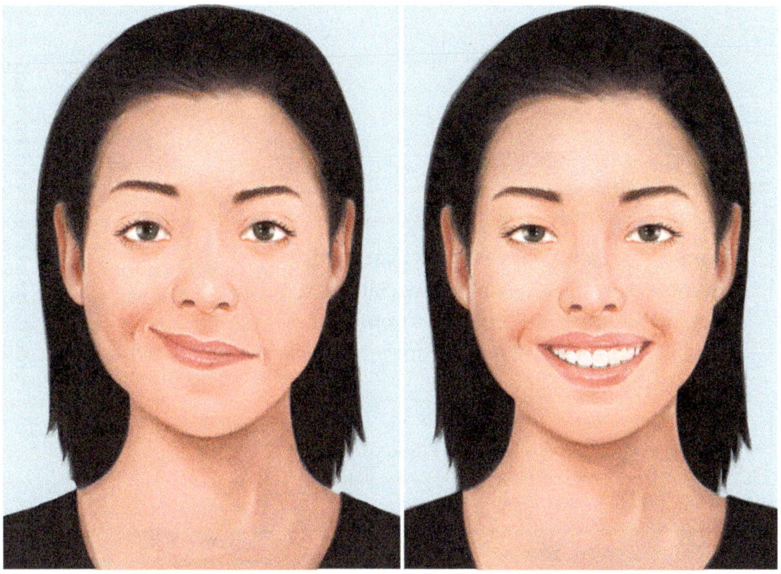

Having a tumor in the right primary motor cortex prevents patients from smiling on the left side of the face when asked to do so, as shown on the left. In contrast, these patients can smile spontaneously and naturally in response to a genuine, involuntary emotion, as shown on the right. These observations support the hypothesis that voluntary and spontaneous emotional expressions are managed by different areas of the brain.

The smiles, frowns, and other facial expressions we make are influenced by the way the brain controls the tiny muscles of our faces. These muscles receive input from the motor areas of the cerebral cortex, which control voluntary movement, as well as from subcortical areas, including the basal ganglia. The cortical input allows us to voluntarily "smile" for the camera. The subcortical input is responsible for more spontaneous expressions of emotion, such as laughing at a funny joke. It is possible to lose one type of input without affecting the other. The young woman shown in the drawing on this page has a tumor that affects the right motor cortex. When asked to smile voluntarily, the smile appears quite crooked because of the importance of the cortex in voluntary expression. When the patient smiles spontaneously to a joke, the smile appears more natural because the subcortical areas can still react normally. People with Parkinson's disease, which damages the subcortical emotional pathways, show the opposite pattern. They may be unable to smile spontaneously in response to a joke, but they can smile voluntarily when asked to do so.

Do we learn how to express emotions, or are these behaviors built in? Darwin (1872) believed that human emotional expression had been shaped through evolution. If he is correct, we would expect humans in all parts of the world to share common means of expression. Some major emotional expressions appear to be universal across cultures (Keltner & Ekman, 2000), although not all researchers agree (Gendron et al., 2014). The "primary colors" of emotional expression, including anger, sadness, happiness, fear, disgust, surprise, contempt, and embarrassment, are identified correctly by most people, regardless of the culture in which they live.

Further support for a view of emotional expression as being innate comes from the predictable developmental course shown by young children. Infants' social smiles (as opposed to smiles resulting from gas, etc.) emerge near the same age (around 3 months), regardless of whether an infant can see faces or is born blind (Freedman, 1964). Monozygotic (identical) twins are more similar than dizygotic (fraternal) twins in the ages at which they first show fear of strangers. As shown in Figure 7.9, children raised in diverse cultures (African bush, urban Guatemala, rural Guatemala, and Israeli kibbutz) showed similar age-related distress at being separated from their mothers (Kagan et al., 1978).

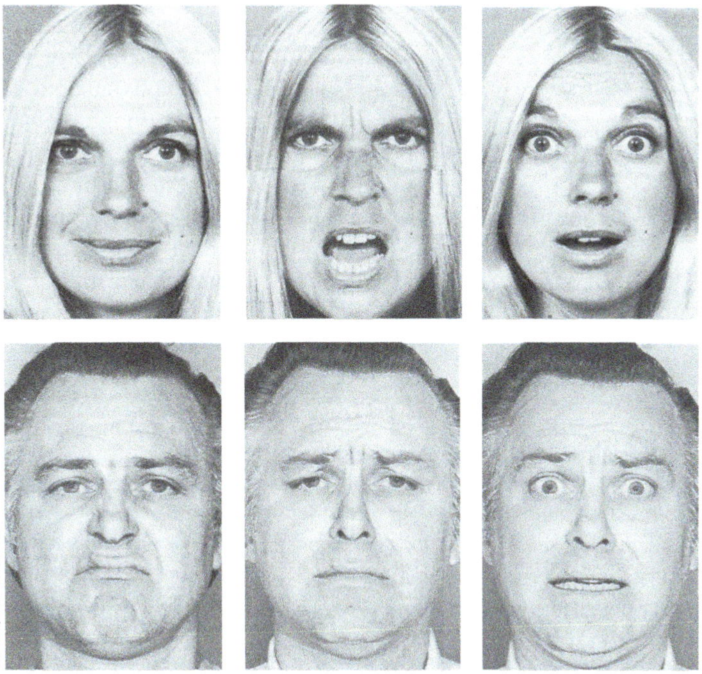

Courtesy Dr. Paul Ekman

These photos represent the possibly universal expressions of happiness, anger, surprise, disgust, sadness, and fear.

FIGURE 7.9

Infants' Separation Protests Occur at the Same Point in Development. Children in diverse cultures show the strongest emotional reactions to separation from their mothers around the same stage in development, suggesting that this emotional behavior has a biological origin.

Source: J. Kagan et al. (1978). *Infancy: Its place in human development.* Cambridge, MA: Harvard University Press.

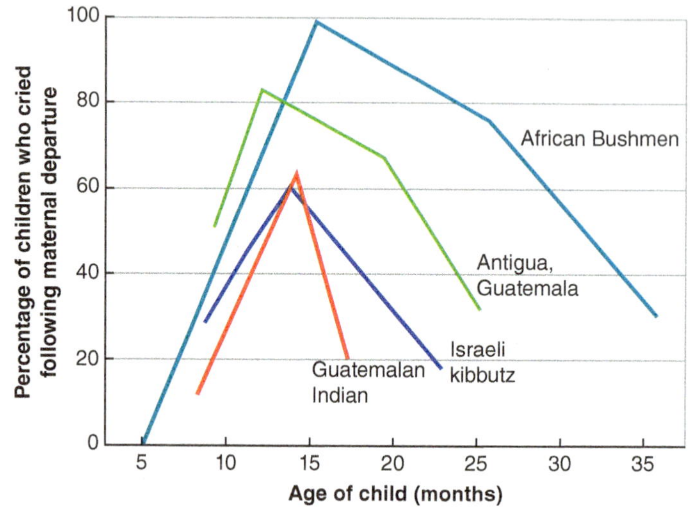

Developmental timelines for emotional behavior are also characteristic of nonhuman primate species. Rhesus monkeys raised in isolation performed typical fear responses when shown pictures of other monkeys engaging in threatening behaviors. The isolated monkeys demonstrated these fear responses at the same stage in development as monkeys raised in normal social conditions (Sackett, 1966).

Other researchers point to the universality of words for different emotional states as evidence of emotion's common biological source. Words for emotions have been found to be quite similar in a sample of 60 of the world's languages (Hupka et al., 1999). The exceptions, however, are also intriguing. The Japanese term *ijirashi* refers to a feeling that occurs when we see another person overcoming an obstacle. No equivalent term exists in English.

Despite the possibility of a shared biological basis for emotion, we can observe significant individual differences in emotional expressiveness. When young children are exposed to strong, novel stimuli, such as the odor of alcohol on a swab, some react strongly to the stimuli, while others appear to ignore them. Still others show a moderate response to the stimuli (Kagan, 1997). As we will see in Chapters 11 and 12, children who are highly responsive often develop into cautious, anxious adults. In contrast, children who are relatively oblivious to stimulation may develop into bold, fearless risk takers. If their insensitivity extends to social signals produced by others, this lack of sensitivity to stimuli may lead to antisocial behavior. Psychopaths incarcerated for murder show significantly reduced reactions to slides of pleasant, neutral, and unpleasant situations when compared to typical control participants (Herpertz et al., 2001).

Individuals also differ in their ability to regulate emotions (Gross, 1998). Two major strategies are used in emotion regulation: suppression, or inhibiting expression, and cognitive reappraisal, or modifying the meaningfulness of an event (English & John, 2013). Reappraisal as a strategy

David Matsumoto carefully compared thousands of photographs from the 2004 Olympic and Paralympic Games and found that all competitors, sighted or blind, displayed the same expressions in response to winning or losing. These results suggest that, as Darwin suggested, some emotional expressions are innate to the human species.

Source: D. Matsumoto & B. Willingham (2009). "Spontaneous Facial Expressions of Emotion of Congenitally and Noncongenitally Blind Individuals," *Journal of Personality and Social Psychology*, *96*(1), 1–10. https://doi.org/10.1037/a0014037

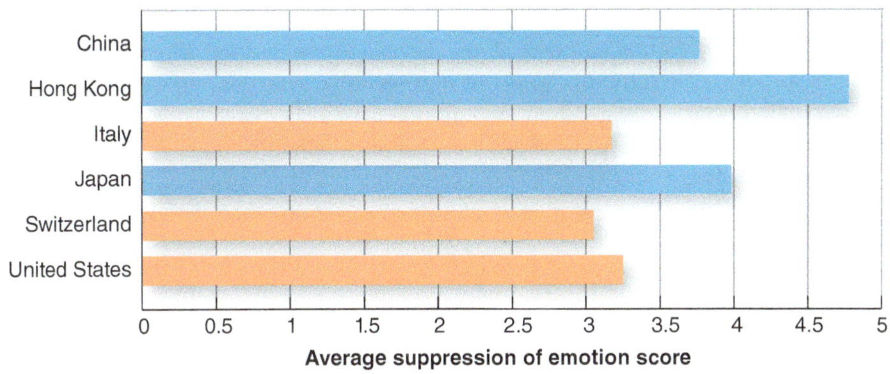

FIGURE **7.10**

Cultures Vary in Suppression of Emotional Expression. Although cultures worldwide are fairly similar in their emotional expressiveness, variations occur. Switzerland, with a suppression score of 3.05, shows emotion most freely of all these countries, and Hong Kong, with a suppression score of 4.72, shows the least emotion.

Source: Adapted from D. Matsumoto et al. (2008). "Culture, Emotion Regulation, and Adjustment," *Journal of Personality and Social Psychology, 94*(6), 925–937. doi: 10.1037/0022-3514.94.6.925

for regulating emotion involves thinking differently about the stimulus that elicits an emotional response rather than attempting to hold in a response. For example, we might be angry when another driver behaves aggressively, perhaps putting us in danger. To manage our anger through suppression, we might simply use willpower to avoid acting in angry ways ourselves. To manage our anger using reappraisal, we focus instead on the fact that the other driver might be having a tough day and that nobody was actually hurt. People who use the reappraisal strategy more than the suppression strategy experience less depression and higher life satisfaction (Gross, 2013).

The ability to suppress emotional expression can be learned. For example, medical personnel undergo training that affects their expression of disgust. Most patients would not appreciate a physician or nurse who said "oh, gross" during an examination. Military personnel learn to maintain their composure when a superior is yelling at them face to face, a skill that may be important when a soldier is captured by enemy forces.

Many cultures have **display rules**, or norms that specify when, where, and how a person should suppress emotion (see • Figure 7.10). The reactions of Japanese and American university students were recorded as they watched emotional movies either alone or with a

display rule A cultural norm that specifies when, where, and how a person should express an emotion.

Courtesy Staff Sergeant J. L. Wright, Jr./U.S. Marine Corps

Despite the strong evolutionary and biological heritage we have for spontaneous emotional expression, we can learn to control our emotional expressions to fit a situation. This Marine recruit is expected to remain calm while his drill instructor applies a "correction." This skill is believed to help military personnel maintain composure in highly emotional situations.

group of students they did not know (Ekman et al., 1972). The Japanese students showed more emotion when alone than when in the group of strangers. In contrast, the American students were about as emotional in either case. If anything, Americans tend to show more emotion when in a group than when alone. Americans made more intense expressions of disgust in response to an odor when in a group than when they were alone (Jancke & Kaufmann, 1994).

Ludmila P. Sundikova/Shutterstock.com

Psychologist Jerome Kagan described individual differences in emotionality based on children's responsiveness to the environment, ranging from the cautious child to the bold.

Suzanne Tucker/Shutterstock.com

Interpreting Emotion

Human adults are quite accurate in their ability to read emotions. When research participants watched only 10 seconds of a videotaped interaction between a teacher and an off-camera student, they were able to judge whether the teacher liked the student with considerable accuracy (Babad et al., 1991). We might think we do a good job of hiding our feelings, but the subtleties of emotional expression often give us away. At the same time, our ability to distinguish between genuine and fake expressions, while good, is far from perfect (Ekman et al., 1990; Frank & Ekman, 1993).

Individual differences in the ability to perceive the emotions of ourselves and others do occur. Twin studies demonstrate that individual differences in the ability to read emotional expression are heavily influenced by genetics (Anokhin et al., 2010). These differences form one of the key aspects of emotional intelligence (Salovey & Mayer, 1990). Emotional intelligence refers to our abilities to perceive, use, understand, and manage emotions. Individual differences in emotional intelligence predict the success of both work and personal relationships.

In addition to providing display rules, cultures influence interpretations of emotional expressions. Japanese and American study participants were asked to correctly identify emotional

EXPERIENCING PSYCHOLOGY

Emotional Regulation

THIS SHORT QUESTIONNAIRE (Gross & John, 2003) will assess how much you use suppression and reappraisal strategies to regulate emotion. For each item, select a number on a scale of 1 (strongly disagree) to 5 (strongly agree).

___ 1. I control my emotions by changing the way I think about the situation I'm in.
___ 2. When I want to feel less negative emotion, I change the way I'm thinking about the situation.
___ 3. When I want to feel more positive emotion, I change the way I'm thinking about the situation.
___ 4. When I want to feel more positive emotion (such as joy or amusement), I change what I'm thinking about.
___ 5. When I want to feel less negative emotion (such as sadness or anger), I change what I'm thinking about.
___ 6. When I'm faced with a stressful situation, I make myself think about it in a way that helps me stay calm.
___ 7. I control my emotions by not expressing them.
___ 8. When I am feeling negative emotions, I make sure not to express them.
___ 9. I keep my emotions to myself.
___ 10. When I am feeling positive emotions, I am careful not to express them.

Items 1 through 6 indicate your use of reappraisal, and items 7 through 10 indicate your use of suppression. It might surprise you to learn that these scales are independent. In other words, a person who uses the suppression strategy quite a bit is no more or less likely to use reappraisal strategies than a person who rarely uses suppression (Gross & John, 2003). Gross and John (2003) reported that men are more likely than women and non-European-Americans are more likely than European-Americans to use suppression. You might see evidence for these general findings (or not!) among your classmates. Keep in mind that college students are not a representative sample of the adult public. ■

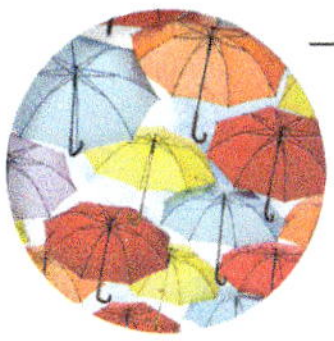

Diverse Voices in Psychology

Emotional Expressivity, Smiling, and a History of Immigration

THIS CHAPTER ASKS whether emotional expression is universal for the human species or more influenced by culture and learning. Some aspects of emotional expression do seem to be species-wide, while others are clearly influenced by environmental factors.

What types of processes might account for cultural differences in emotional suppression? We noted that Western cultures are more expressive than some Asian cultures, perhaps due to the contrast between individualism and collectivism. However, another factor that might explain variations in display rules is a culture's history of immigration. In countries such as the United States, which has a long history of people immigrating from many different places, emotional expressivity appears to be higher than in countries with less immigration from fewer sources (Rychlowska et al., 2015). In a relatively unpredictable social situation lacking shared language and norms, somewhat exaggerated emotional expression might help avoid misunderstandings.

Rychlowska et al. (2015) also found that cultural heterogeneity was predictive of how people interpreted smiling (see Figure 7.11). Smiling can be interpreted as a means of social bonding or friendliness, or as a sign of dominance. People from cultures with high levels of historical immigration from many places were more likely to endorse the bonding interpretation of smiling, while people from relatively homogeneous cultures rated dominance as the most likely reason to smile.

These results emphasize the importance of considering not just present cultural environments, but also historical influences on culture, when attempting to explain cultural differences in behavior. ■

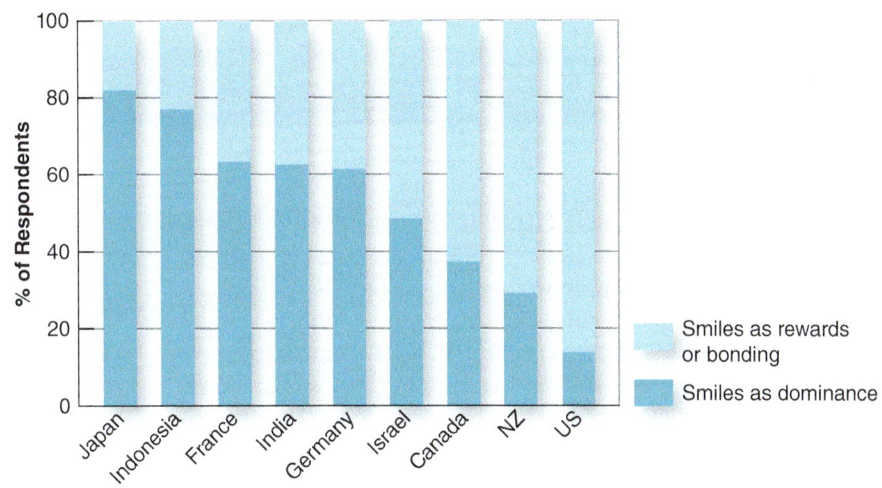

FIGURE **7.11**

Emotional Expressivity and a History of Immigration. Psychologists have usually interpreted cultural differences in emotional suppression as being the result of a culture's degree of individualism or collectivism. This explanation might be too simple. The amount of immigration experienced by a culture is related to the proportion of the population that interprets smiling as an attempt to reward or bond as opposed to an attempt to dominate.

Adapted from M. Rychlowska et al. (2015). "Heterogeneity of Long History-Migration Explains Cultural Differences in Reports of Emotional Expressivity and the Functions of Smiles," *Proceedings of the National Academy of Sciences, 112*(19), E2429–E2436. doi: 10.1073/pnas.1413661112

expressions with varying levels of intensity (Matsumoto, 2002). Individuals from both cultures identified the emotion being expressed with considerable accuracy, even at low levels of intensity. However, intensity was interpreted quite differently by the Japanese and the Americans. When emotional expression occurred at low intensities, Japanese participants assumed that people were feeling more than they were willing to express. In contrast, when emotional expression was highly intense, the American participants assumed that people were exaggerating their feelings.

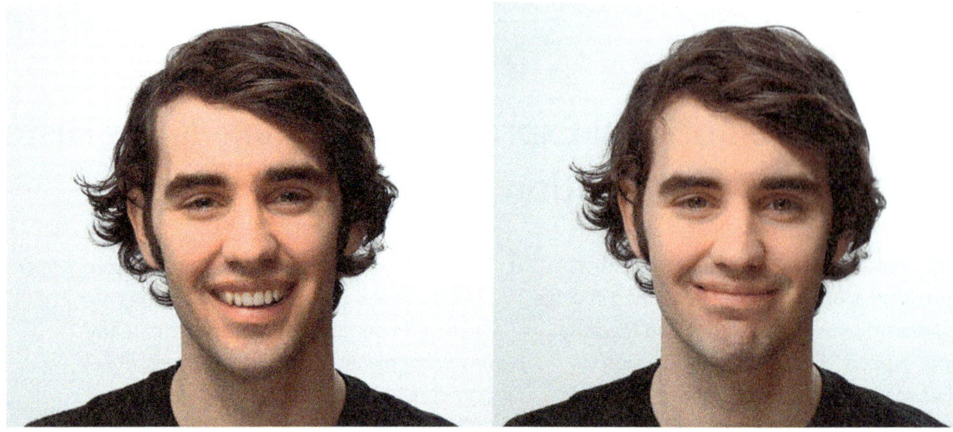

Photo Researchers/Science Source

Although fake and genuine smiles look similar, we usually do a good job of distinguishing between them. Which of these smiles do you think is real? Which is fake?

A person's ability to read others' emotional expressions can be reduced by certain psychological disorders (see Chapter 14). Individuals with schizophrenia and bipolar disorder have normal abilities to process facial features but perform worse than typical controls on tasks requiring them to distinguish among facial expressions (Kohler et al., 2009). People diagnosed with autism spectrum disorder and those with antisocial personality disorder have specific difficulties recognizing expressions of fear (Marsh & Blair, 2008).

PSYCHOLOGY AS A HUB SCIENCE

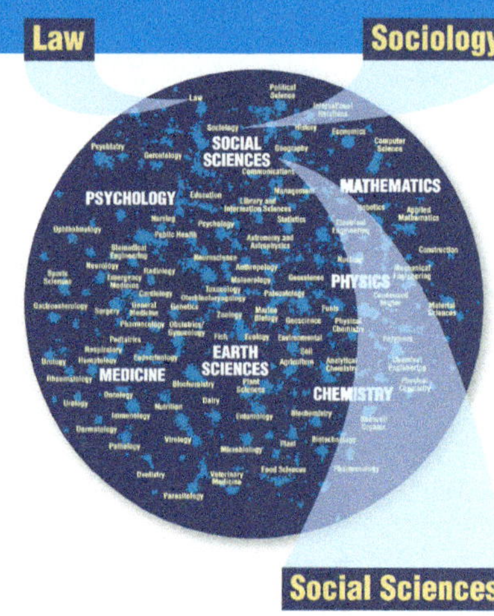

Lie Detection and the Law

EVEN THOUGH EMOTIONAL EXPRESSION is a major means of communication, our abilities to read emotions are not perfect (Sternglanz et al., 2019). Juries are made up of human beings, who detect deception in face-to-face encounters only slightly better than chance (Ekman & O'Sullivan, 1991). Polygraph methods are rejected for use in court because of their poor record of accuracy (Kleinmuntz & Szucko, 1984). Functional magnetic resonance imaging (fMRI) eventually might improve our ability to detect honesty, and fMRI results are beginning to be admitted to U.S. courts of law (see Figure 7.12) (Langleben & Moriarty, 2013). Some researchers consider fMRI to have potential for detecting deception (Langleben et al., 2016), while others are less convinced (La Tona et al., 2020). Until better technologies are available, what do psychologists know about lying that can help the legal system identify deception?

Lying is difficult, especially in high-stakes situations featuring high arousal. While aroused, people betray their lying in predictable ways (Ekman, 1996). Inappropriate smiling and nervous laughter might reflect the person's high arousal. A deceptive person stiffens the upper body, nods the head less frequently, and uses fewer hand gestures than normal. In contrast to the reduced mobility of the upper body, the feet swing. An unwillingness to make eye contact might indicate dishonesty. However, in many cultures, making eye contact is considered impolite, and failure to make eye contact should be interpreted cautiously.

Liars experience more cognitive demand than truthful people as they must multitask while assembling their deception (Vrij, 2015). The liar may stumble verbally, adding "um" and "uh" while seeking to construct a plausible lie. Liars must manage how credible they appear to others. They may be distracted by their goals for lying, such as preventing embarrassment, avoiding criminal charges, or making money. They must actively suppress the truth to avoid slips. If the interviewer can add to the liar's cognitive load by requesting continued eye contact and asking unanticipated questions, the liar is more likely to slip.

An excellent signal that someone is lying is the use of "scripted" stories, which are lacking in detail. People telling the truth add 20 to 30% more detail to a story compared to liars (Colwell et al., 2007). Another reliable way to identify lying is to ask people to tell their story backward in time (Fisher & Geiselman, 2010). A person telling the truth can simply move from one event to the next, but constructing a false story backward quickly overwhelms a person's memory for details. ■

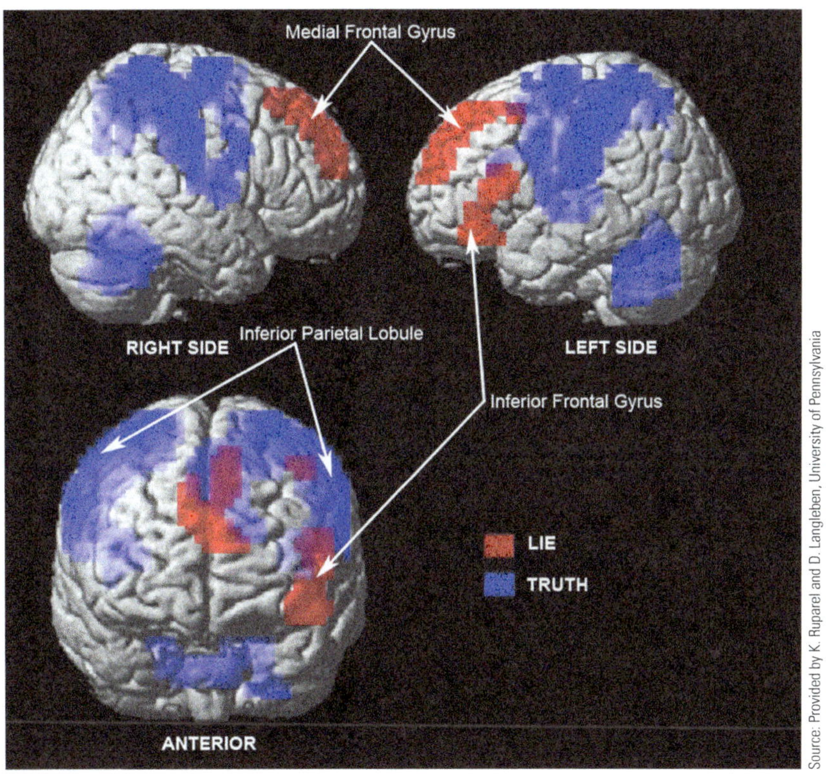

FIGURE **7.12**

Will fMRI Be Used to Detect Lies? During a standardized task known as the modified Guilty Knowledge Test, which is used to assess deception, participants' brains showed significantly different activation when lying compared to when they told the truth. Red areas represent brain regions that are more active when the participant is lying, and blue areas represent brain regions that are more active when the participant is telling the truth. So far, laboratory studies have used small numbers of law-abiding participants rather than real criminals and concrete tasks such as reporting which playing card is being held (e.g., ace of spades). It is unknown whether this technology will advance to the point where results will be admitted in a court of law on a regular basis.

Source: D. D. Langleben et al. (2002). "Brain Activity During Simulated Deception: An Event-related Functional Magnetic Resonance Imaging Study," *NeuroImage*, *15*(3), 727–732. https://doi.org/10.1006/nimg.2001.1003.

SUMMARY 7.1 Theories of Emotion

Name of theory	Major features
James–Lange theory 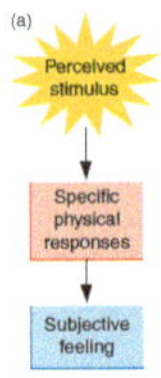	Specific physical sensations lead to an identification of the subjective feeling.
Cannon–Bard theory 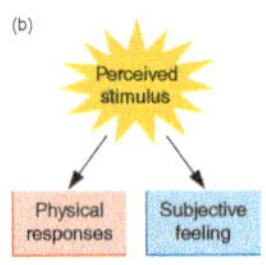	Physical sensations and subjective feelings occur simultaneously and independently.
Schachter–Singer two-factor theory 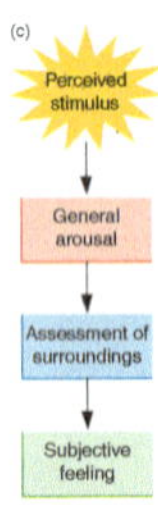	General arousal, not specific physical states, leads to an appraisal of our surroundings, which allows us to identify our subjective feelings.
SAME 	Different emotional states produce physical responses ranging from specific to ambiguous. Ambiguous responses require more appraisal than specific responses before a subjective feeling is identified.
Appraisal theory  	Emotions begin with the detection and assessment of stimuli that are relevant to personal well-being.

Credits: Fourth row—Ian Paterson/Alamy Stock Photo; Fifth row—Asier Romero/Shutterstock.com, Monkey Business Images/Shutterstock.com

What Does It Mean to Be Motivated?

Animals, including humans, have limited time and resources, and a state of arousal is expensive in terms of the energy it requires. Motivational systems allow an animal to be aroused only when necessary, such as when it needs food, and then reduce arousal following the solution of a problem, such as after a meal. Preventing the waste of precious energy resources provides a significant survival advantage. Motivation also provides the benefit of helping an animal prepare to meet future needs. Most animals are motivated to explore their environments because familiarity with an environment allows them to act more effectively when a need arises.

We can think of motivation as a process that maintains **homeostasis**, a term introduced by psychologist Walter Cannon (1932) to describe a steady internal balance or equilibrium. To achieve homeostasis, we carefully regulate such variables as core body temperature, fluid levels, and body weight around **set points**. Deviations from these set points stimulate behavior by the organism that is designed to reestablish the original values. You might think about this process as analogous to your home's thermostat. If your home's temperature drops below its set point, the furnace is activated until the set point is again established. If your home's temperature rises above the set point, the air-conditioning system is activated until the set point is regained. Similarly, if your core body temperature drops below 98.6 °F (37 °C), your body initiates several processes designed to increase its temperature, such as producing heat by the muscle contractions we know as shivering. If your core body temperature rises above its set point, cooling mechanisms are activated. You sweat, and the evaporating moisture cools your skin. Blood is diverted to the outer parts of the body, leading to a flushed appearance.

Motivation begins with a stimulus, arising from either the internal or the external environment of the organism, that serves as a cue for motivated behavior. Stimuli that are important to survival, such as the presence of a predator or a deficit in body fluids, generate arousal and tension, a state frequently called **drive** (Hull, 1943). Being in a drive state propels the organism into some sort of action related to the stimulus, whether that means running from the predator to safety or pulling a bottle of water from a backpack to quench thirst. If actions are successful in regaining equilibrium, we experience **drive reduction**, accompanied by a rewarding feeling of relief.

Drive theories of motivation are often described as push theories because drive is seen as pushing an organism toward a goal. However, not all psychologists agree that motivation requires the push of drive. Instead, they suggest that rewards or **incentives** have the capacity to pull an organism in a particular direction. According to this view, animals are viewed as naturally inclined to act on their environment rather than wait passively for a need to arise (Deci & Ryan, 2000). In incentive theories, no reference to unpleasant internal drive states is required to explain motivated behavior.

Incentives or rewards may be intrinsic or extrinsic. **Intrinsic rewards** arise internally, such as feelings of accomplishment when a goal is met. **Extrinsic rewards** come from outside sources, such as grades in school, money for completing work, or praise from a supervisor. These different types of reward can interact in complex ways (see ● Figure 7.13). In some cases, extrinsic rewards can have negative effects on intrinsic motivation. For example, if a child who enjoys reading suddenly gets paid for each book completed, the child's enjoyment of reading might decrease because the motivation shifts from intrinsic, the love of reading, to extrinsic, the love of reward money (DeCharms, 1968).

Psychologists have studied a range of motives, from the mostly physical motives of temperature control and thirst to the more cognitive and social motives to affiliate with others and to achieve. We will explore this range by discussing some specific motives in detail, including hunger, sexuality, affiliation, and achievement. After discussing these examples, we will examine the ways humans set priorities when faced with competing motives.

homeostasis A steady internal balance, or equilibrium.

set point A value that is defended to maintain homeostasis.

drive A state of tension and arousal triggered by cues important for survival.

drive reduction The state of relief and reward produced by removing the tension and arousal of the drive state.

incentive A reward that pulls an organism's behavior in a particular direction.

intrinsic reward A reward that arises internally.

extrinsic reward A reward from an outside source.

Hunger and Eating

Hunger is a complex motive. In comparison to the regulation of body temperature through processes such as sweating or shivering, the reduction of hunger through eating is more heavily influenced by emotion, learning, and culture. Humans take in a remarkable variety of nutrients. The traditional diet of the Inuit people living in Arctic regions contains little plant material, whereas vegans adhere to a diet that contains no animal material.

Humans consume a range of diets, from the nearly all-meat diet of the traditional Inuit cultures to the vegan diet.

Yvette Cardozo/Alamy Stock Photo

iStock.com/Elenathewise

Sonia Moskowitz-Globe Photos, Inc./Newscom

FIGURE **7.13**

Economist Roland Fryer Asks Whether Incentives Work. Harvard University economist Roland Fryer overcame a tough childhood in Daytona, Florida, to become the youngest tenured African American professor in the history of the university. Drawing on his personal experiences, Fryer experimented with different incentives for a variety of school-related behaviors. His results suggest that the relationships among intrinsic rewards, extrinsic rewards, and behavior can be quite complex. Although previous research has shown that extrinsic rewards can undermine intrinsic motivation, it is important to remember that this result occurs only when behavior is intrinsically motivated in the first place. If children do not intrinsically enjoy reading, Fryer suggests paying them to read might work. Unfortunately, Fryer has been the target of death threats for suggesting this simple solution to illiteracy.

Location	DALLAS	CHICAGO	WASHINGTON	NEW YORK CITY
What students were paid for	Reading	Grades	Various†	Test scores
Grade level participating	Second-graders	Ninth-graders	Sixth-, seventh-, and eighth-graders	Fourth- and seventh-graders
How much	$2 per book	$50 for A's $35 for B's $20 for C's	Up to $100 every two weeks	$25 (fourth-graders) to $50 (seventh-graders) per test
Average student earned	$13.81	$695.61	$532.85	$139.43 (fourth-graders) $231.55 (seventh-graders)
Study size*	1,780 from 22 schools	4,396 from 20 schools	3,495 from 17 schools	8,320 from 63 schools
Results	**Very Positive** Paying children to read dramatically boosted reading-comprehension scores.	**Mixed** Children cut fewer classes and got slightly better grades. Standardized test scores did not change.	**Positive** Rewarding five different actions, including attendance and behavior, seemed to improve reading skills.	**No Effect** Paying children for higher test scores did not lead to more learning or better grades—or any measureable changes.

*Not including control groups

† A combination of metrics that varied from school to school but always included attendance and behavior

The Sensation of Hunger We respond to combinations of external and internal cues that make us feel hungry. External cues for hunger include time of day, the sights and smells of favorite foods, admonitions that we should "clean our plates," or the social settings in which food is presented. These external cues may encourage us to eat when our bodies do not need nutrients or to eat more food than we require. Individuals who are very responsive to external cues might find maintaining a healthy weight to be somewhat challenging.

Internal cues for hunger are generated when our bodies are genuinely short on nutrients. "Short on nutrients" applies to the maintenance of current, not necessarily ideal, weight. A morbidly obese person is likely to feel as hungry as a thin person when sufficient nutrients are not available to maintain the status quo.

Walter Cannon believed that stomach contractions were an important component in the detection of hunger, and to prove his point, he persuaded his colleague A. L. Washburn to

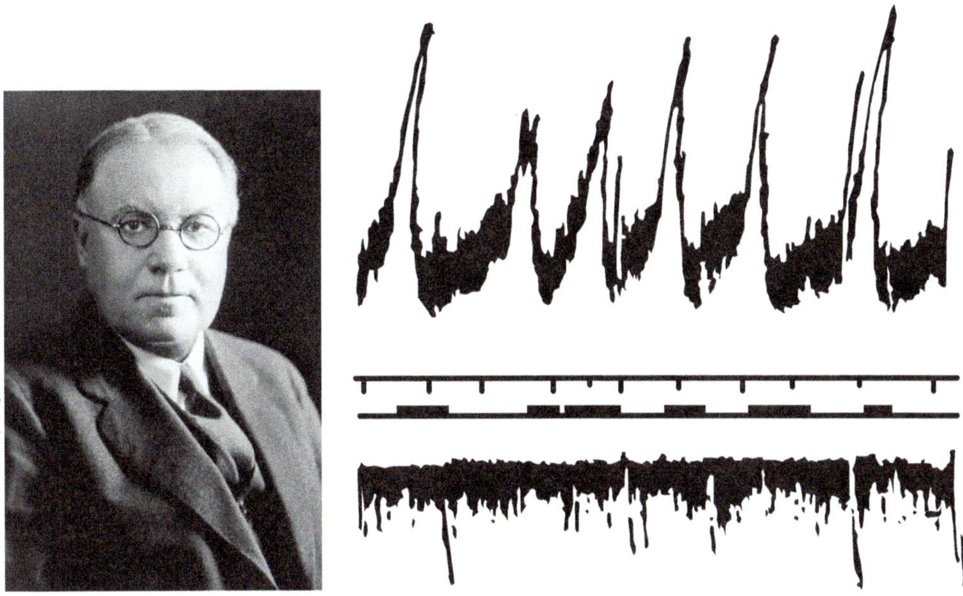

Bettmann/Contributor/Getty Images

FIGURE **7.14**

Stomach Contractions and Hunger. Walter Cannon (1871–1945) and his assistant, A. L. Washburn, performed one of the earliest experiments on the relationship between stomach contractions and feelings of hunger. The large waves at the top were Cannon's recordings of Washburn's stomach contractions, and the smaller waves at the bottom represent Washburn's key taps indicating hunger. Although these two events are correlated, there is more to hunger than a growling stomach.

swallow a balloon attached to an air pump (Cannon & Washburn, 1912). The balloon allowed Washburn's stomach contractions to be monitored while Washburn indicated feelings of hunger by pushing a telegraph key (because he couldn't talk with a tube down his throat). Although Washburn's key presses correlated with his stomach contractions, these signals do not tell the whole story. People who have had their stomachs surgically removed still experience a sense of hunger in the general region where the stomach used to be. Most of us start eating long before our stomachs begin to growl, indicating that additional types of signaling must be at work (see ● Figure 7.14).

glucose A type of sugar that plays an important role in hunger levels.

An important hunger cue is a low level of circulating sugars, particularly **glucose**. Glucose concentrations in the blood are highest just following a meal. As glucose levels drop over time, a person begins to feel hungry again. Glucose levels are intimately connected with levels of the hormone insulin. Insulin, released by the pancreas, moves circulating glucose from the blood into cells awaiting nutrients. Typically, glucose and insulin levels are positively correlated. Right after a meal, both are high. Glucose levels rise as glucose is extracted from the food that has been consumed, and insulin is high because its release is triggered by the anticipation and consumption of food. As time goes by without more food, glucose moves from the blood into other tissues, and insulin is no longer released, leading to lower levels of both substances in the blood. These lower levels of glucose and insulin should signal the need for more food (see ● Figure 7.15).

This is an overly simplistic conclusion, however. High glucose levels occur in poorly managed diabetes because of either a lack of insulin production (type 1 diabetes) or the body's resistance to insulin (type 2 diabetes). Without sufficient insulin activity, circulating glucose is unable to move out of the blood into the cells that need nutrients. If hunger results from low levels of circulating glucose, we would expect people with untreated diabetes to not feel very hungry, but this is not the case. Most people with diabetes who have high blood sugar report

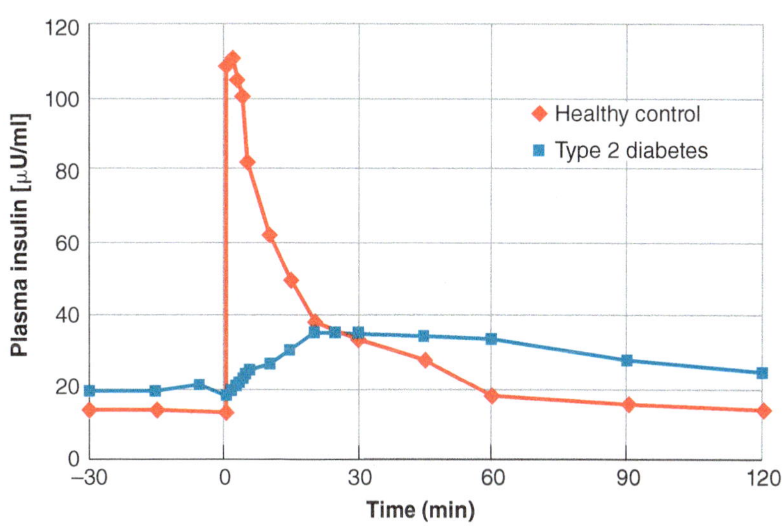

FIGURE **7.15**

Insulin Release Is Reduced in Type 2 Diabetes. Following a meal (time 0), a healthy person experiences a large spike in insulin levels. In contrast, a person with type 2 diabetes has a slower and less dramatic release of insulin. The person with diabetes will not be able to move glucose out of the blood into cells requiring nutrients. The appetite-suppressing action of insulin will be less effective, and the person with diabetes will remain hungry.

Source: M. A. Pfeifer et al. (1982). "Insulin Responses to Nonglucose Stimuli in Non-Insulin-Dependent Diabetes Mellitus during a Tolbutamide Infusion," *Diabetes*, *31*(2), 154–159, doi: 10.2337/diab.31.2.154

When glucose availability, fat stores, and leptin levels are low and ghrelin and orexins are active:

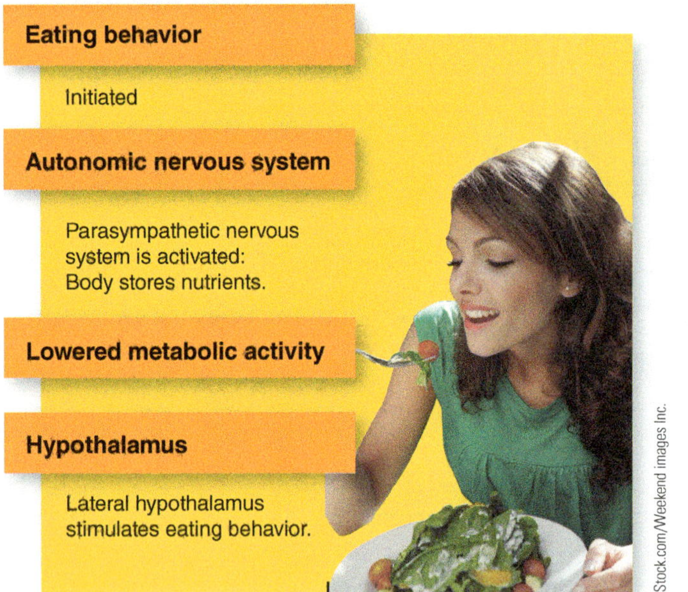

Result: Stored fat levels increase and feeding stops.

FIGURE 7.16

Mechanisms of Hunger.

leptin A hormone secreted by fat cells that helps the body maintain an appropriate level of stored fat.

satiety A sense of feeling full and not requiring further food.

feeling hungry all the time. This makes sense when you consider that their cells are starving because of their inability to obtain glucose from the blood. It is more accurate to say that the amount of glucose that is available to cells is an indicator of hunger (Mayer, 1955; Abraham, 1974). Hunger results whenever cells are unable to obtain the glucose they require.

Hunger also occurs in response to low levels of stored fats (Kennedy, 1953). If you maintain a healthy weight, you are carrying sufficient body fat to survive 5 to 6 weeks of total starvation. The heavier the person, the longer that individual can survive without food. One person survived a medically supervised fast of 382 days, during which time his weight dropped from 455.4 pounds (207 kilograms) to 179.5 pounds (81.6 kilograms) (Stewart & Fleming, 1973).

The body monitors fat stores by assessing levels of the hormone **leptin**. Leptin, from the Greek word *leptos*, or "thin," is produced and secreted by fat cells (Zhang et al., 1994). Because fat stores and leptin levels are positively correlated, leptin levels provide a measure for the amount of fat that has been stored. As shown in ● Figure 7.16, leptin levels and their associated fat stores initiate a cascade of events that influence eating behavior.

When available glucose, fat stores, and leptin levels are low, brain areas that include the lateral hypothalamus (LH) initiate feeding. When the LH is lesioned, rats fail to eat and die of starvation unless force-fed (Anand & Brobeck, 1951). Stimulation of the LH typically initiates immediate eating. Low glucose availability, fat stores, and leptin levels also activate the parasympathetic division of the autonomic nervous system, enhancing the body's ability to digest and store nutrients. Metabolism, or the chemical reactions required by life, slows down, allowing nutrients to be stored rather than used up right away. Activation of the parasympathetic nervous system, initiation of feeding behavior, and reduction in metabolic rate allow the animal to find, eat, and store nutrients.

As glucose, insulin, and leptin levels increase and fat stores return to normal, the feeding cycle tapers off. Unfortunately for the person trying to lose weight, this system does a good job of defending a set point. As the dieter successfully decreases body fat levels, the associated low levels of leptin initiate a feeding cycle. The dieter feels constantly hungry, making the maintenance of weight loss often more difficult than the initial loss.

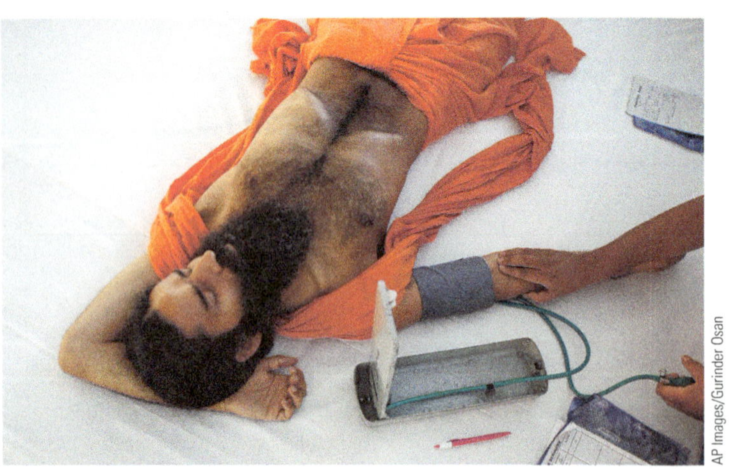

People of normal weight carry enough fat to survive 5 to 6 weeks of total starvation, although this is obviously not a good thing to do for one's health. Baba Ramdev, a yoga guru, was hospitalized after losing 12 pounds by the seventh day of a hunger strike against corruption. It is likely that Ramdev was already quite thin at the beginning of his fast.

Feeding is stimulated by two additional hormones: ghrelin, which is released by the pancreas and the lining of the stomach (Howard et al., 1996), and orexins, produced in the LH (de Lecea et al., 1998; Sakurai et al., 1998). Ghrelin release increases with time since the last meal and appears to contribute to the rewarding aspects of feeding. Orexin activity contributes to feeding because it is negatively correlated with blood glucose levels (Cai et al., 1999). Orexins also participate in sleep (see Chapter 6), suggesting that they might link feeding, activity levels, and sleep.

The Sensation of Satiety We reach the point of **satiety** or fullness long before the nutrients we have eaten can make their way to waiting cells.

Just as stomach contractions serve as signals for hunger, an obvious sign of satiety is a feeling of stomach fullness. In extreme cases of obesity, some people choose to have a portion of the stomach stapled or banded to produce this feeling of fullness after less food has been eaten.

In the brain, the ventromedial hypothalamus (VMH) participates in sensing satiety. As shown in ● Figure 7.17, lesions of the VMH produce a syndrome of large weight gains

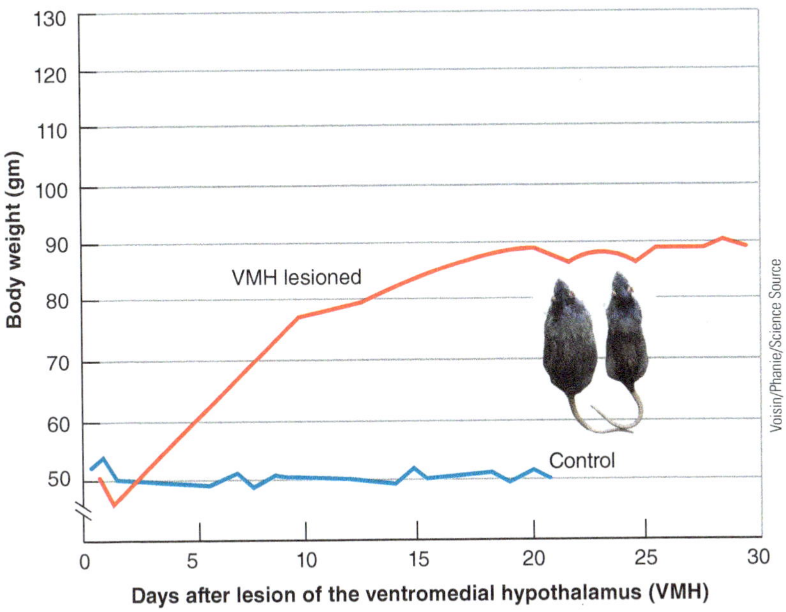

FIGURE **7.17**

Lesions of the Ventromedial Hypothalamus (VMH) Lead to Obesity. Following lesioning of the VMH, rats nearly tripled their normal weight, suggesting that the VMH plays a significant role in satiety. However, satiety is too complex to be explained as the function of a single part of the brain.

Source: Adapted from R. G. Kurtz, P. Rozin, P. and Teitelbaum, (1972). "Ventromedial Hypothalamic Hyperphagia in the Hypophysectomized Weanling Rat," *Journal of Comparative and Physiological Psychology, 80*(1), 19–25. doi: 10.1037/h0032820

(Hoebel & Teitelbaum, 1966). Although the VMH plays a significant role in satiety, it is overly simplistic to assume that it works alone and directly. Among the many indirect effects of VMH lesions are boosts in insulin production, which in turn produce low blood glucose levels and hunger.

Satiety also results from the release of the gut hormone cholecystokinin (CCK) by the digestive system in response to the arrival of food, especially fatty foods. CCK not only acts in the digestive tract but also serves as a chemical messenger in the brain. CCK limits meals by activating pathways that connect the hindbrain to the digestive system (Blevins et al., 2009). Drugs that inhibit CCK's action in the brain increase eating behavior, further supporting the hypothesis that CCK normally acts to inhibit further eating (Cooper & Dourish, 1990).

Earlier we observed the cascade of events initiated by low levels of available glucose, stored fat and leptin that led to feeding and the storage of nutrients. What happens when glucose, fat, and leptin levels rise again? Increased glucose, insulin, stored fat, and leptin levels initiate a sequence of events that inhibit feeding (see ● Figure 7.18). The sympathetic division of the autonomic nervous system is activated, leading to the expenditure of energy, metabolic rate increases, and inhibition of feeding. As time without food progresses, glucose, fat, and leptin levels drop and the feeding sequence is reinitiated.

FIGURE **7.18**

Mechanisms of Satiety.

Because of leptin's role in satiety, scientists initially believed it might be helpful as a dieting aid. Mice genetically engineered to lack genes that produce leptin become obese. Injections of leptin allow them to lose weight (Halaas et al., 1995). Unfortunately, people do not respond like mice; obese humans have very high circulating leptin levels but appear to become resistant to the satiety messages this state should produce (Friedman & Halaas, 1998). Adding further leptin is unlikely to lead to weight loss.

Our ancestors were much more likely to starve than to be troubled by having too much food. Those who lived and reproduced exhibited characteristics best suited for surviving famine. As we will see in the next sections, the same motivational mechanisms that evolved to prevent starvation among hunter-gatherers might not work well in a society featuring cultural influences on body image and an ample and calorie-rich food supply.

Obesity What do we mean by obesity? One medical approach to body weight is the **body mass index (BMI)**, shown in ● Figure 7.19. The BMI is a simple height-to-weight ratio computed

body mass index (BMI) A height-to-weight ratio used to identify healthy weight, underweight, overweight, and obesity.

Height (inches)	80	90	100	110	120	130	140	150	160	170	180	190	200	210	220	230	240	250
80	9	10	11	12	13	14	15	17	18	19	20	21	22	23	24	25	26	28
78	9	10	12	13	14	15	16	17	19	20	21	22	23	24	25	27	28	29
76	10	11	12	13	15	16	17	18	20	21	22	23	24	26	27	28	29	30
74	10	12	12	14	15	17	18	19	21	22	23	24	26	27	28	30	31	32
72	11	12	14	15	16	18	19	20	22	23	24	26	27	28	30	31	33	34
70	12	13	14	16	17	19	20	22	23	24	26	27	29	30	32	33	35	36
68	12	14	15	17	18	20	21	23	24	26	27	29	30	32	34	35	37	38
66	13	15	16	18	19	21	23	24	26	27	29	31	32	34	36	37	39	40
64	14	15	17	19	21	22	24	26	28	29	31	33	34	36	38	40	41	43
62	15	17	18	20	22	24	26	27	29	31	33	35	37	38	40	42	44	46
60	16	17	20	22	23	25	27	25	31	33	35	37	39	41	43	45	47	49
58	17	19	21	23	25	27	29	31	34	36	38	40	42	44	46	48	50	52
56	18	21	22	25	27	29	31	34	36	38	40	43	45	47	49	52	54	56
54	19	22	24	27	29	31	34	36	39	41	43	46	48	51	53	56	58	60
52	21	23	26	29	31	34	36	39	40	44	47	49	52	55	57	60	62	65
50	23	25	28	31	34	37	39	42	45	48	51	53	56	59	62	65	68	70
48	24	28	31	34	37	40	42	46	49	52	55	58	61	64	67	70	73	76

Weight (pounds)

- BMI under 18.5: Underweight
- BMI between 18.5 and 24: Healthy weight
- BMI between 25 and 29: Overweight
- BMI between 30 and 39: Obese
- BMI over 40: Severely/morbidly obese

FIGURE 7.19

Body Mass Index (BMI).

by dividing weight in kilograms by the square of height in meters. We have converted Figure 7.19 to inches and pounds for convenience. A BMI score between 18.5 and 24.9 is considered healthy. A BMI score between 25 and 30 is considered overweight, and a BMI score above 30 is considered obese. This system works well for most people, but it does not account for those who have unusually heavy skeletons or musculature. Many elite athletes would score in the overweight or even obese range despite being quite fit.

Using a BMI score of 30 or above as a criterion, rates of obesity in the United States tripled from 12% of the adult population in 1991 to 37% in 2014 (Ogden, 2015). In 1990, no state reported that more than 15% of its adult population was obese, but by 2018, no state reported fewer than 20% of its adult population was obese, and nine states reported that over 35% of their adult population was obese (see ● Figure 7.20). How can we account for this rapid

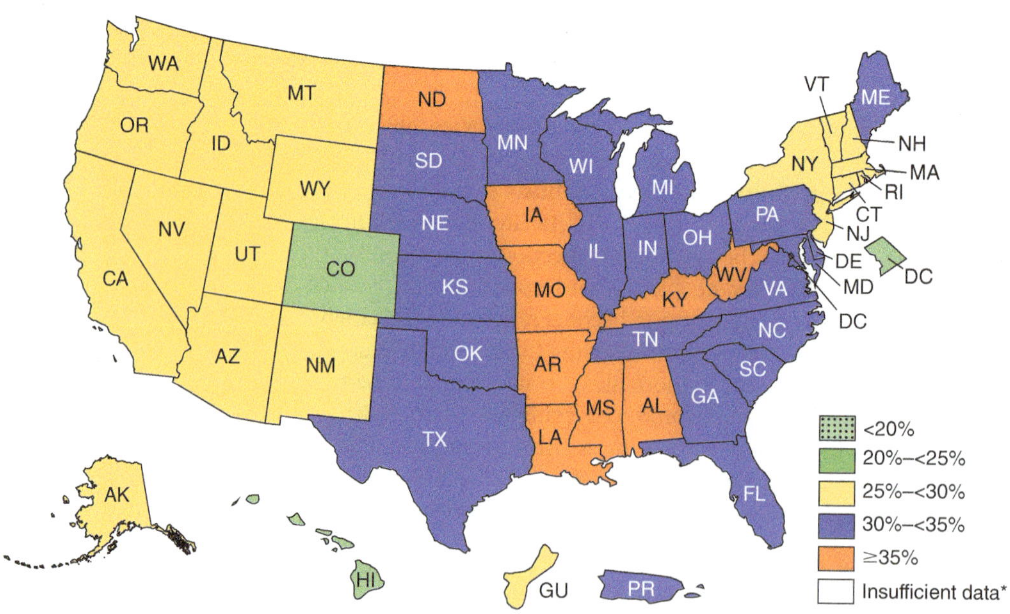

FIGURE 7.20

U.S. Obesity Rates Have Risen Dramatically. In 1990, no state reported that more than 15% of its population was obese, and the overall national rate of obesity was 12%. By 2018, no state reported that less than 20% of its adult population was obese, and nine states reported that more than 35% of their adult population was obese. *Source:* Behavioral Risk Factor Surveillance System, CDC.

increase in obesity over the last two and a half decades? It is unlikely that current obesity levels are the result of a single cause. Genetic predispositions, lifestyle issues, and social comparisons all make significant contributions to obesity.

Genes can influence factors such as set point and rate of metabolism, and twin studies indicate that some people are more likely than others to become obese (Livshits et al., 2007). Although genes are unlikely to have changed dramatically over a few decades, complex interactions between genes and environmental factors, such as the bisphenol A in plastic products discussed in Chapter 3, could affect current rates of obesity (Dolinoy et al., 2007). Genes might also interact with the bacteria populations in the gut, which differ considerably between obese and lean humans (Million et al., 2013). Manipulations of bacteria through antibiotics and probiotics have been used to promote weight gain in livestock for decades. Transplantation of gut bacteria from obese to lean animals led to obesity (Turnbaugh et al., 2006). The bacteria found in the obese animals appears to be more efficient at harvesting energy from the animal's diet.

A cultural contribution to obesity is our contemporary, sedentary lifestyle, with many people spending hours sitting in front of televisions or computers. Humans use energy efficiently. At rest, we use only 12 kilocalories (usually described simply as calories) per pound per day. This means that the average 150-pound couch potato needs only about 1,800 calories of food per day. Even the most demanding activities require a remarkably small investment in resources. Cyclists competing in the challenging Tour de France use an average of 5,900 calories per day (Armstrong & Jenkins, 2000). Meals at many chain restaurants contain more than 2,500 calories, the total daily requirement for a person who weighs 208 pounds and has a typical level of activity.

To avoid starvation, our ancestors developed strong preferences for calorie-rich foods containing sugars and fats. When food supplies are limited, these preferences ensured that humans would spend the greatest amounts of time and energy seeking these rich sources of calories. Unfortunately, we retain these preferences today and continue to gravitate to sugary, fatty foods.

Beginning in the 1800s, in an effort to prevent starvation, initiatives leading to increased cheap sources of high-calorie foods were adopted worldwide. Currently, global agriculture produces 2,600 calories per person per day, which is expected to rise to 3,000 calories per person per day by 2030 (Caballero, 2007). With such a plentiful food supply, we can see why obesity is becoming a global problem even as starvation remains a serious concern in many parts of the world.

Zooming out from individual factors to the larger social context, we see that social factors also contribute to obesity. We apparently "keep track" of how we are doing by comparing our size to that of those in our social circles. Having an obese spouse raises your risk of obesity by 37%, and having obese friends raises your risk by 57% (Christakis & Fowler, 2007).

The path to a healthy weight can be difficult. Unfortunately, weight loss for our ancestors usually meant they were one step closer to death by starvation, and we are well prepared to prevent that occurrence. Once a person is obese, a new set point is established and subsequently staunchly defended. Even the surgical removal of fat, or liposuction, does not result in permanent weight loss because the fat removed by the process is replaced or redistributed to other parts of the body within one year (Hernandez et al., 2011).

Calorie-reducing and low-carb diets work, but dietary changes cannot be viewed as something to do until a goal weight is reached. If the dieter returns to previous eating habits, the lost weight is quickly regained. Successful diets should be viewed as lifestyle changes that are sustainable for an individual. For example, removing one sugared soft drink per day should result in about a 10-pound weight loss over the next year. It is essential for the dieter to avoid triggering mechanisms designed to prevent starvation, such as lowering metabolic rates. By keeping activity levels up and restricting weight loss to a pound or two per week at most, it is possible to slide weight loss under the radar of our vigilant weight maintenance systems.

Mark Avery/ZUMA Press/Irvine/California/USA/Newscom

The average adult weighing 150 pounds needs only 1,800 calories per day. When a single dessert item such as cheesecake provides about 70% of that daily requirement, it becomes easy to see how people eating out frequently could become overweight or obese. It is also likely that before eating the cheesecake a diner might have an appetizer, salad, entrée, and beverage. This doesn't include meals and snacks consumed at other times throughout the day.

Drew D. Saur

Contrary to popular opinion, many people lose weight by dieting and are successful in maintaining their weight loss for years. The National Weight Control Registry tracks more than 5,000 case studies of successful maintainers, including Drew Saur. Saur lost more than 150 pounds and has maintained his loss since 2005. He began by counting the calories he was consuming and was astonished to find that he was eating about 5,000 calories per day, not surprising given his starting weight of 325 pounds. By gradually reducing calories and waiting to eat until he felt hungry, Saur lost about 2 to 3 pounds per week. He began walking, and when his weight loss permitted more activity, he switched to running. Successful dieters and maintainers such as Saur do not view dieting as something drastic to do before a wedding or class reunion but as a gradual lifestyle change that is livable.

Efforts to use chemicals to control weight have been discouraging. During the 1950s and 1960s, it was not uncommon for American doctors to prescribe amphetamines for weight loss. Although amphetamines suppress appetite, their psychoactive and addictive properties make this approach less than desirable. More recently, several new medications have been approved for the treatment of obesity. One, orlistat (Xenical), reduces the absorption of fats by the digestive tract. The remaining approved medications target appetite mechanisms in the hypothalamus or prevent reabsorption of glucose by the kidneys. Medications do not "work on their own" but instead make it somewhat easier for obese individuals to maintain lifestyles that are more consistent with a healthy weight (Apovian et al., 2015).

Some individuals who become discouraged with diets and medication turn instead to surgical interventions, including stomach stapling and gastric bypass procedures, which literally reduce the amount of nutrients that can be consumed or processed. While the resulting weight loss can be dramatic (the average gastric bypass patient loses 90 pounds within 3 months of surgery) (Maggard et al., 2005), these procedures represent major surgery and often result in complications.

Although it is feasible that current research into brain mechanisms for hunger and satiety may eventually lead to better treatments for obesity, lifestyle changes leading to healthier eating and exercise habits remain the most reliable approach.

Anorexia Nervosa, Bulimia Nervosa, and Binge-Eating Disorder

Coexisting with our ongoing obesity epidemic are eating disorders characterized by unusual patterns of eating and distortions of a person's body image. Normally, we have an accurate view of what we look like. People with distorted body image can be convinced they are obese when they are in danger of starvation.

Traditionally, eating disorders have been viewed as a problem for females and as less typical for males. However, increasing numbers of males are experiencing eating disorders and body dissatisfaction. The lifetime incidence of eating disorders in males is approximately 0.17%, compared to about 3% in females (Pedersen et al., 2014). Rates of eating disorders are about six times higher among homosexual and bisexual males compared to heterosexual males, although sexual orientation does not seem to be associated with additional risks for eating disorders among females (Matthews-Ewald, Zullig, & Ward, 2014).

Anorexia nervosa is characterized by the maintenance of unusually low body weight, an intense fear of gaining weight, and a distorted view of the body as obese (APA, 2013). *Anorexia* literally means "loss of appetite." People with anorexia can show two patterns of behavior (APA, 2013). In the restricting type, people simply eat little food. In the bingeing-purging type, people combine restricted eating most of the time with behaviors associated with bulimia nervosa, which we discuss later.

Anorexia nervosa is dramatic but rare, affecting about 0.4% of females and perhaps 0.04% of males (APA, 2013). Anorexia nervosa is one of the few psychological disorders that can kill, with up to 5% of people with the disorder dying per decade from causes related to the condition, which includes an elevated risk for suicide (APA, 2013). Other symptoms include interruption of normal menstruation in females, very dry and yellow skin, fine downy hair (lanugo) on the face and other parts of the body, increased sensitivity to cold, and cardiovascular and gastrointestinal problems.

Bulimia nervosa is characterized by cycles of binge eating, in which unusually large amounts of food are consumed, and purging through the use of vomiting or laxatives. Bingeing is often followed by feelings of depression, disgust, and a sense of lost control. Bulimia is more common than anorexia, affecting 1.5% of females and between 0.15% and 0.5% of males (APA, 2013; Hudson et al., 2007).

anorexia nervosa An eating disorder characterized by the maintenance of unusually low body weight and a distorted body image.

bulimia nervosa An eating disorder characterized by bingeing, purging, and having feelings of depression, disgust, and lost control.

Binge-eating disorder is similar to bulimia nervosa in regard to eating abnormally large amounts of food at one sitting and feeling that eating is out of control, but it does not include compensatory behaviors such as induced vomiting or the use of laxatives (APA, 2013). People with binge-eating disorder eat rapidly, eat until they are uncomfortably full, eat when they are not hungry, and often eat alone because of embarrassment about the quantities they consume. Compared to other eating disorders, differences between males and females with binge-eating disorder are smaller. Approximately 1.6% of adult females and 0.8% of adult males meet the criteria for this disorder (APA, 2013).

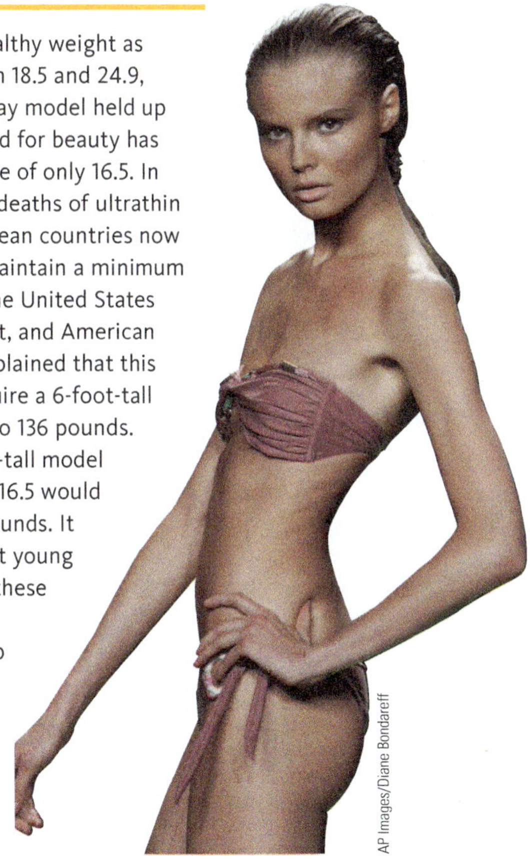

We have defined healthy weight as a BMI score between 18.5 and 24.9, yet the typical runway model held up as a cultural standard for beauty has an average BMI score of only 16.5. In response to several deaths of ultrathin models, some European countries now require models to maintain a minimum BMI score of 18.5. The United States has not followed suit, and American designers have complained that this standard would require a 6-foot-tall model to "balloon" to 136 pounds. In contrast, a 6-foot-tall model with a BMI score of 16.5 would weigh a scant 121 pounds. It is not surprising that young women exposed to these standards of beauty occasionally develop distorted images of their own bodies.

AP Images/Diane Bondareff

Environmental factors, especially cultural attitudes toward beauty, can play a significant role in the development of eating disorders. Anne Becker and her colleagues were observing eating patterns in the Fiji Islands when American television became available in 1995 (Becker et al., 2002). Prior to this time, Becker reported that dieting was unknown in this culture, which valued a "robust, well-muscled body" for both men and women. The Fijian language has a term for "going thin" that is used to express concern about someone who may be losing weight because of health problems. In the United States, people may say, "Have you lost weight? You look great!" In Fiji, a person is more likely to say, "Are you okay? You look like you're going thin."

These cultural norms underwent nearly overnight change with the introduction of American television, with its frequent images of glamorous, ultrathin actresses. Suddenly, 74% of the adolescent girls in Becker et al.'s study reported themselves as being "too big or too fat." Teens began to report dieting with the same frequency as their American counterparts, a radical shift from the researchers' observations since 1988. Because Becker et al.'s data are correlational, we cannot conclude that watching television produced disordered eating in Fiji. However, the results are suggestive of strong cultural influences on patterns of disordered eating.

binge-eating disorder An eating disorder characterized by eating abnormally large amounts of food at one sitting and feeling that eating is out of control, without compensatory behaviors such as induced vomiting or the use of laxatives.

It is likely that general personality characteristics that increase a person's risk for eating disorders may be heritable, not the disorders themselves (Farstad et al., 2016). Evidence from twin studies has been mixed, with some authors reporting heritability of 48% to 88% for eating disorders and others finding no evidence of genetic influences (Hinney & Volckmar, 2013). People might have a genetic vulnerability to disordered eating in general but not toward a specific type of eating disorder (Bulik et al., 2016). Genetic studies have focused primarily on anorexia nervosa, and further work on the other types of eating disorders is needed (Hübel et al., 2018).

Once an eating disorder is established, biological factors contribute to maintaining abnormal patterns of eating. Even after people with anorexia nervosa regain normal weight, some still show evidence of elevated levels of hormones that typically raise metabolism and inhibit feeding (Stanley et al., 2003). Bingeing has been discussed within a framework of food addiction, which is similar to an addiction to psychoactive drugs (Leslie et al., 2018; Mestre-Bach et al., 2019). A questionnaire known as the Yale Food Addiction Scale 2.0 shows that nearly all individuals with bulimia act as though they have a food addiction (Vries & Meule, 2016).

Treating anorexia nervosa can be challenging because the therapist is facing a person who is terrified of gaining weight. The first priority is keeping the person alive, and this effort typically involves hospitalization and careful monitoring of food intake. Cognitive behavioral therapy may be used to address distortions of body image (see Chapter 15), but no known medications are effective in treating anorexia (Dold et al., 2015). About 50% of people with anorexia make a full recovery, but nearly 20% fail to respond. Treating bulimia and binge-eating disorder is somewhat more encouraging. Antidepressant medications, particularly selective serotonin reuptake inhibitors (SSRIs), are usually quite effective, especially when combined with cognitive behavioral treatment (Kass et al., 2013).

Michael DeFreitas/Photoshot

Before the introduction of American television programming to the islands of Fiji in 1995, the cultural ideal for both men and women was a "robust, well-muscled body," as evidenced by this traditional dancer. Dieting and eating disorders were unknown. A short time after American television was available, however, Fijian rates of dieting and eating disorders grew to match American rates and ideal beauties became slimmer.

Sexual Motivation

Unlike eating, sexual behavior is not essential to the survival of an individual organism. However, individuals' sexual behavior appears to be maintained by processes similar to the life-sustaining motivations we have already discussed.

Sexuality is an extremely complex aspect of human behavior. In this chapter, we will focus on the more physical aspects of sexual motivation. In Chapter 11, we will explore sexuality across the life span, and in Chapter 13, we will discuss phenomena related to attraction and maintaining relationships. Most of our discussion relies on research with individuals who identify as heterosexual, simply due to the relatively sparse amount of research to date about sexual minorities (Mark et al., 2018). Hopefully, more scientists will step up to fill this gap soon.

Biology and Sexual Motivation The females of most mammalian species undergo estrus, a period of hours or days during which the female is receptive or willing to have sex. In these species, hormone levels and sexual behavior are tightly linked. In humans and Old World primates, menstrual cycles replace periods of estrus. The sexual behavior of estrus and nonestrus species is quite different (Rushton et al., 2001).

Human females show receptivity throughout the menstrual cycle. However, females who are not using chemical contraception report feeling more interest in sex around the time of ovulation (Cappelletti & Wallen, 2016). This situation has obvious advantages for the reproduction of the species because this is when sexual behavior is most likely to lead to pregnancy.

Female sexual interest forms complex correlations with hormones. Female sexual interest has a negative relationship with progesterone levels and weaker positive associations with levels of **estradiol**, the major female sex hormone (Jones et al., 2018). For decades, female sexual interest was viewed as a function of **testosterone** levels, and testosterone has been administered to women reporting low sexual interest. However, more contemporary research has thrown some doubt on this conclusion (Cappelletti & Wallen, 2016).

Testosterone is clearly correlated with sexual interest in males. However, as long as a man's testosterone falls within a normal range, it does not provide a strong predictor of an individual's sexual frequency (Mazur & Booth, 1998; Gray et al.,). Below-normal levels of testosterone, as in castration, are usually accompanied by very low sexual desire and activity.

Male testosterone levels fluctuate over the course of a day and are influenced not only by a man's biology but also by several environmental factors, notably situations perceived as competitive. Male collegiate athletes experience increases in testosterone in anticipation of upcoming competitive events. Following a competition, testosterone continues to rise among the winners and temporarily decreases among the losers (Booth et al., 1989). Simply observing a competition may influence testosterone levels. Men cheering for the successful Brazilian soccer team at the 1994 World Cup experienced increased testosterone levels, whereas men supporting the losing Italian team experienced a decrease (Bernhardt et al., 1998). These fluctuations are more dramatic when taking the location of the venue into account. Losing at home produces a more dramatic decrease in testosterone than losing a game as the visiting team. This response to losing a competition at home may represent a remnant of our ancestors' need to defend their territory. We can assume that losing a battle is catastrophic in any circumstance, but losing near your family and home makes them especially vulnerable to destruction.

Male testosterone levels are also influenced by relationship status. Men in stable, long-term relationships have lower testosterone levels than single men or men who are within a few years of divorce (Mazur & Michalek, 1998). Men's testosterone levels also drop significantly after the birth of a child (Gettler et al., 2011). These changes might reflect a feedback loop in which reproductive success signals a decrease in testosterone (Puts et al., 2015). High testosterone levels not only interfere with pair-bonding and parental care by stimulating continued competition for mates, but also reduce immune system functioning. It makes sense that the achievement of reproductive goals would lead to a reduction in the competitive behaviors and physical costs associated with high testosterone levels (see Figure 7.21).

estradiol An important type of estrogen, or female sex hormone.

testosterone A male hormone.

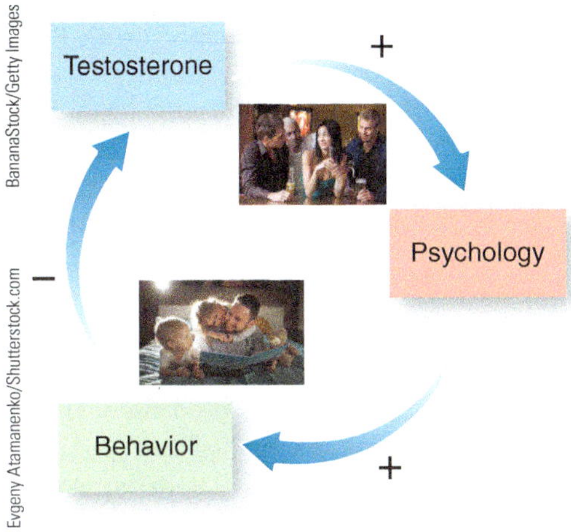

FIGURE **7.21**

A Negative Feedback Loop of Male Testosterone and Sexual Behavior. In males, higher testosterone levels are associated with psychological factors including increased competitiveness and sexual desire, which then lead to increased sexual behavior. As reproductive goals (e.g., mating and producing children) are achieved, male testosterone levels drop again. High testosterone levels are not compatible with pair-bonding and parenting and have detrimental effects on the immune system, so this decrease represents an effective adaptation.

Source: Adapted from D. A. Puts et al. (2015). "Fulfilling Desire: Evidence for Negative Feedback Between Men's Testosterone, Sociosexual Psychology, and Sexual Partner Number," *Hormones and Behavior*, *70*, 14–21, doi: 10.1016/j.yhbeh.2015.01.006

We have seen how sexual desire is correlated with testosterone for males and estradiol and low progesterone for females, but romantic love is associated with two other hormones, oxytocin and vasopressin (see ● Figure 7.22). In humans, both hormones are active in the brain, but vasopressin is expressed more by males, and oxytocin is expressed more by females (van Londen et al., 1997; Ishunina & Swaab, 1999). In all cases, oxytocin enhances bonding. Females release oxytocin during breastfeeding and even respond to a brief hug from their partners with a spike in oxytocin release (Light et al., 2005). Oxytocin is released at orgasm. However, because of the greater overall expression of oxytocin in the brains of females, along with the 10 times higher testosterone levels in males than in females, females are more likely than males to equate sexual desire with feelings of romantic love (Diamond, 2004). We do not mean to imply that males do not bond, but high testosterone levels are likely to make sexual activity highly salient for young men, with or without the bonding associated with oxytocin release.

Although cultural values often link sexual desire and romantic love, these two functions represent distinct biological and emotional states. Romantic love promotes the establishment of long-term relationships, whereas sexual desire promotes mating (Cacioppo, 2016). Both romantic love and sexual desire involve the insula. Sexual desire is correlated with activity toward the rear of the insula, consistent with other observations that the back of the brain is more involved with current and short-term sensory experiences. In contrast, romantic love is associated with activity toward the front of the insula, consistent with

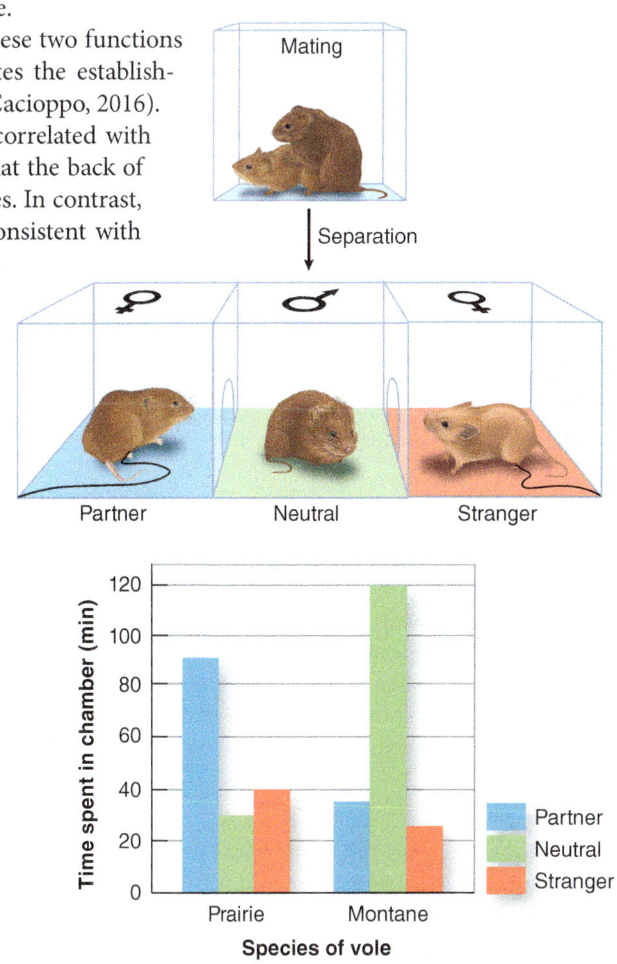

FIGURE **7.22**

Oxytocin, Vasopressin, and Two Species of Voles. The discovery of the importance of oxytocin and vasopressin to bonding originated in the study of two types of rodents: the prairie vole and the montane vole. Although similar in many ways, the two types of vole differed in both their bonding to a partner and their parenting behaviors. Prairie voles are monogamous for life, but montane voles are not. Prairie voles share parenting duties, but montane voles do not. Differences between the two types of vole in oxytocin and vasopressin were closely associated with the behavioral differences, with the prairie voles showing higher levels of both hormones than the montane voles. In one type of study, voles are allowed to mate, and then they are placed in a test box. On either side of the male, who can move freely, are two females—a stranger and the partner—who are tethered in their boxes and can't move. The chart shows how much time the average male prairie vole and montane vole spend with the partner, with the stranger, or alone. As you can see, the prairie voles prefer to be with their partners, but the montane voles prefer to be alone.

Source: H. P. Nair & L. J. Young (2006). "Vasopressin and Pair Bond Formation: Genes to Brain to Behavior," *Journal of Physiology*, *21*(2), 146–152. doi: 10.1152/physiol.00049.2005

future-thinking about more abstract concepts (Cacioppo & Cacioppo, 2013). Romantic love and sexual desire often occur along a time continuum, with the pleasant sensorimotor experiences associated with sexual desire leading to the more cognitive feelings of romantic love (Cacioppo et al., 2012). A study of a rare patient with a lesion in the insula suggests that activity in the insula does not simply correlate with romantic love and sexual desire but actually contributes to differences between these processes (Cacioppo et al., 2013).

Sexual and Emotional Satisfaction Humans show wide variations in sexual and emotional satisfaction within relationships (see ● Figure 7.23). Cross-cultural studies show that subjective sexual satisfaction depends on a number of factors, including relative equality between men and women, mental and physical health, and the importance of sexual behavior for an individual (Laumann et al., 2006). In the United States, more committed relationships produce the highest levels of both sexual and emotional satisfaction (Mark et al., 2015). Individuals who expect to continue a relationship are more attentive to their partners, both emotionally and sexually. In contrast, one-night stands receive the lowest sexual and emotional satisfaction scores from participants and promote the strongest feelings of regret (Fisher et al., 2012).

Historically, research on sexual satisfaction has focused on heterosexual couples. Relatively few studies have considered sexual satisfaction across sexual orientations. Mark and her colleagues (2015) found no differences in sexual and emotional satisfaction among heterosexual, bisexual, and homosexual individuals in committed relationships but did observe differences in casual sexual contexts. Individuals of all sexual orientations reported more emotional and sexual satisfaction from committed relationships than from casual sex situations. However, gay and bisexual men reported experiencing higher amounts of sexual and emotional satisfaction from casual sex contexts than heterosexual individuals, while lesbian women reported less, although the size of these differences was relatively small. Across a similarly sexually diverse sample, attachment style (see Chapter 11) was predictive of both relationship and sexual satisfaction (Mark et al., 2018).

sexual orientation A stable pattern of attraction to members of a particular sex.

Sexual Orientation Individual differences in human sexuality are substantial and normal. One of the ways individuals vary is in their **sexual orientation**, which refers to a stable pattern of attraction to members of a particular sex. A person's sexual orientation can incorporate behavior, attraction, and identity (Ward et al., 2014). These three components are often congruent, but not necessarily so. Many people engage in same-sex behavior and fantasy

FIGURE **7.23**

A Cross-Cultural Comparison of Relational and Sexual Satisfaction. A survey of nearly 30,000 people in 29 countries showed wide variations in sexual satisfaction. In most countries, there was a strong correlation between relational satisfaction (defined as a combination of physical pleasure with a partner and emotional satisfaction with a partner) and sexual satisfaction. Gender differences in satisfaction with sexual function were the smallest in Cluster 1 countries.

Source: Adapted from E. O. Laumann et al. (2006). "A Cross-National Study of Subjective Sexual Well-Being Among Older Women and Men: Findings from the Global Study of Sexual Attitudes and Behaviors," *Archives of Sexual Behavior, 35*(2), 145–161. doi: 10.1007/s10508-005-9005-3

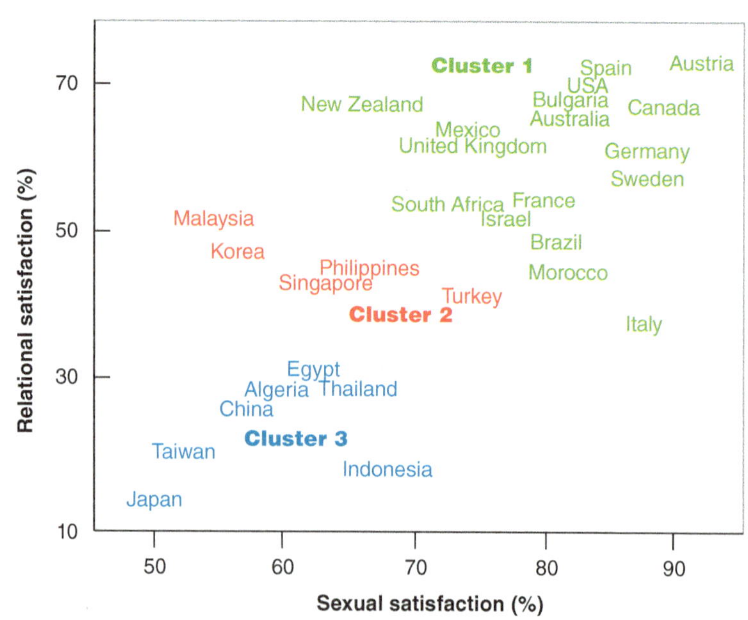

while maintaining a strong heterosexual orientation. In the Sambia tribal culture of New Guinea, all adolescent males are expected to engage in same-sex behavior before marrying women (Stoller & Herdt, 1985). The adult sexual orientation of these men remained overwhelmingly heterosexual.

The U.S. National Health Interview Survey incorporated carefully crafted questions about sexual orientation beginning with "Which of the following best represents how you think about yourself?" Choices for males included gay, straight (that is, not gay), bisexual, something else, and I don't know the answer. Choices for females included lesbian or gay, straight (that is, not lesbian or gay), bisexual, something else, and I don't know the answer. Individuals who chose something else or I don't know the answer were asked follow-up questions but were not included in the overall report of the data. Results showed that 97.7% of females and 97.8% of males identified themselves as straight, 1.5% of females and 1.8% of males identified themselves as homosexual, and 0.9% of females and 0.4% of males identified themselves as bisexual (Ward et al., 2014). As shown in ● Figure 7.24, people's self-reported sexual orientation tends to fall along a continuum (Savin-Williams & Vrangalova, 2013).

It is likely that male and female sexual orientations emerge along different pathways (Diamond, 2012). Sexual orientation in males tends to be stable, acting like a compass, whereas females experience more fluidity in their sexual attractions over time. Females are more likely than males to experience physical arousal and desire for both sexes and to report changes in their degree of same-sex or other-sex attraction over time (Diamond, 2012). More females endorse a bisexual than homosexual orientation, but the opposite is true of males (Bailey et al., 2016).

Hemis/Alamy Stock Photo

Sexual orientation is carefully defined as a stable pattern of attraction to people based on gender. Homosexual behavior can occur with or without a homosexual orientation. Among the Sambian people of New Guinea, young males are separated from their mothers and expected to engage in homosexual behavior with older males. The Sambian people believe that obtaining semen in this manner transforms them into powerful warriors (Herdt, 1987). After marriage, the now-adult man is no longer expected to engage in homosexual behavior.

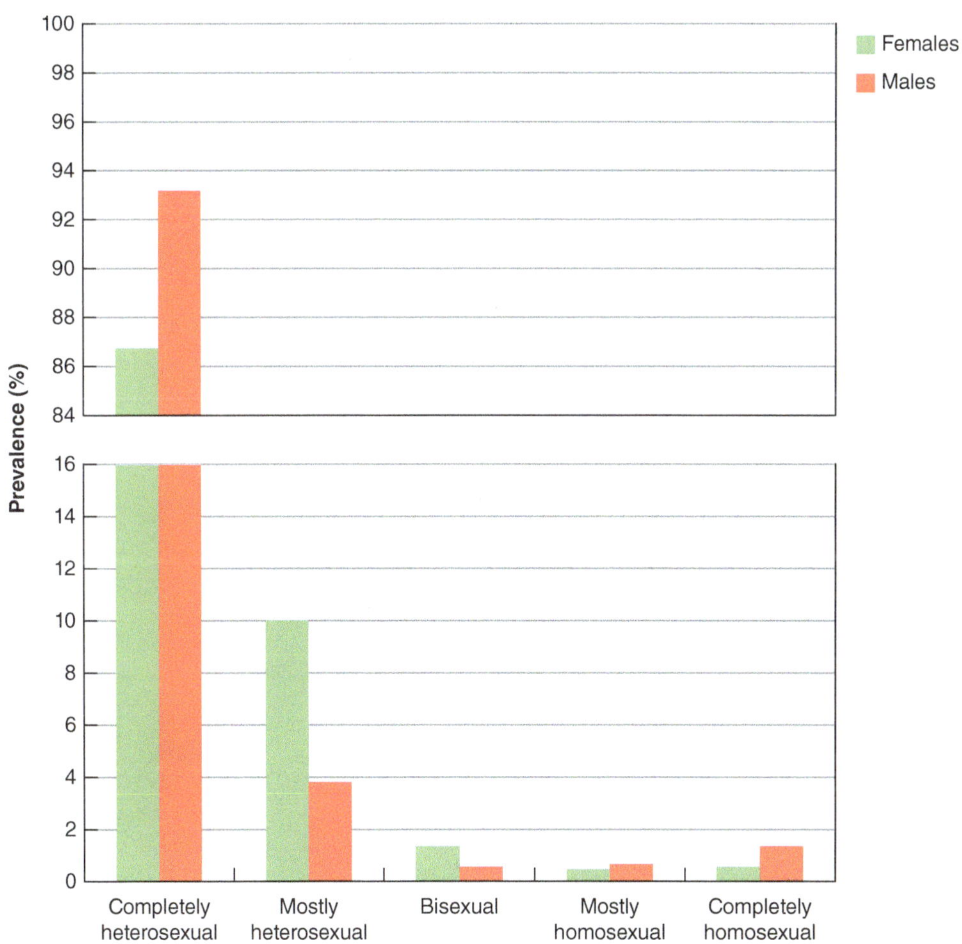

FIGURE **7.24**

Sexual Orientation Falls Along a Continuum. Self-report is considered one of the more reliable measures of sexual orientation. When asked to identify their sexual orientation, people's responses demonstrated more of a continuum than discrete categories.

Source: Data from R. C. Savin-Williams & Z. Vrangalova (2013). "Mostly Heterosexual as a Distinct Sexual Orientation Group: A Systematic Review of the Empirical Evidence," *Developmental Review, 33*(1), 58–88. doi: 10.1016/j.dr.2013.01.001. Figure based on Savin-Williams data in J. M. Bailey et al. (2016). "Sexual Orientation, Controversy, and Science," *Psychological Science in the Public Interest, 17*(2), 45–101. doi: 10.1177/1529100616637616

Genes appear to influence sexual orientation, although the exact mechanisms with which they do so are not well understood and are likely to be quite complex. Like most human behaviors, sexual orientation is probably the result of an interaction between genetic factors and other aspects of the individual's experience, which can include prenatal factors. To assess the genetic contribution to sexual orientation, researchers have compared rates of homosexuality in twins. If one identical male twin is homosexual, his twin has about a 50% chance of also being homosexual (Kirk et al., 2000). Analyses of twin reports of the number of lifetime same-sex partners showed that sexual orientation is somewhat heritable for both males (0.34–0.39) and females (0.18–0.19) (Långström et al., 2010). Genome-wide association studies (GWAS) compare complete sets of DNA for individuals that differ in a trait. A GWAS study of nearly 500,000 people found that genetics explained about one-third of the variation in same-sex behavior, but it was not possible to predict a person's sexual orientation on the basis of DNA (Ganna et al., 2019). As genetic methods continue to improve, it is likely that we will have a better understanding of the role of genes in sexual orientation in the future.

Among the other possible biological variables affecting sexual orientation are levels of prenatal, but not adult, sex hormones. Prenatal hormones have the ability to "organize" not just reproductive structures, but also the brain (Bailey et al., 2016). Females with a condition known as congenital adrenal hyperplasia (CAH) experience high prenatal levels of male hormones. Consequently, they are often born with masculinized external genitalia, are more likely to describe themselves as "tomboys," show greater interest in "male" toys and activities, and are more likely to engage in lesbian or bisexual behavior (Meyer-Bahlburg et al., 2008). However, most women with CAH are heterosexual, just as most lesbian and bisexual women do not have a history of CAH or similar conditions.

An interesting clue to the origin of sexual orientation arises from the observation that birth order influences the odds that a male is homosexual. Males who have older brothers from the same mother are more likely to be gay than males who have no siblings, younger siblings only, or older sisters (Blanchard, 1997; Balthazart, 2011). Theoretically, carrying a male fetus could provoke a mother's immune response, which would become stronger with each successive male fetus she carries. Her immune response could influence the development of her fetus by altering significant hormonal processes.

Several structures in the brain are known to be different in males and females and also seem to differ between homosexual and heterosexual males. Among these is a small cluster of neurons located in the hypothalamus known as the interstitial nucleus of the anterior hypothalamus (INAH; see Figure 7.25). There are four separate nuclei in INAH. Two of these, INAH-2 and INAH-3, are notably larger in males than in females (Allen et al., 1989). The exact function of these nuclei in humans is unknown, although animal research suggests that they participate in sexual behavior. Building on this research about differences between the brains

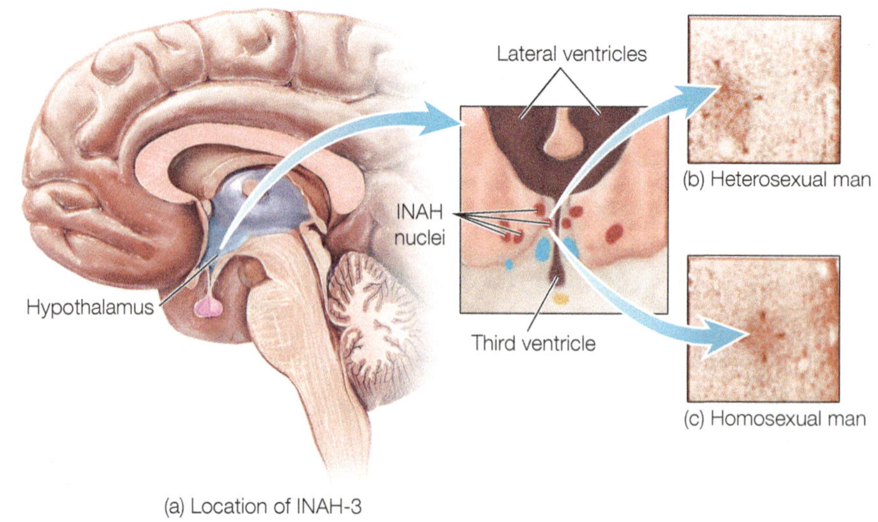

FIGURE 7.25

Some Brain Differences May Correlate With Sexual Orientation. Simon LeVay reported that an area of the hypothalamus known as INAH-3 differs between heterosexual and homosexual men. If you compare the samples in (b) and (c), you can see that INAH-3, indicated by the four dark arrows, appears to be larger in the heterosexual male sample than in the homosexual male sample. The impact of this size difference on adult sexual behavior or sexual orientation remains unknown, however, because these are correlational data. *Source:* Adapted from S. LeVay (1991). "A Difference in Hypothalamic Structure Between Heterosexual and Homosexual Men," *Science*, *253*, 1034–1037. doi: 10.1126/science.1887219 of males and females, Simon LeVay asked whether INAH-3 might be different in heterosexual and homosexual males. After examining the brains of more than 40 individuals, LeVay (1991) concluded that INAH-3 in homosexual males was about two to three times smaller than in heterosexual males, or about the same size as typically found in females.

LeVay was quite cautious in his interpretation of his results. The homosexual individuals in his sample had all died from HIV/AIDS. Otherwise, there would be little reason to note sexual orientation on a person's medical records. Although it is unlikely that HIV/AIDS would produce this type of change in the brain, LeVay could not rule out that possibility based on his data. LeVay also raised the possibility that engaging in homosexual behavior might influence INAH-3, even in the adult, although he gave little credence to that possibility. Nonetheless, LeVay's research had a profound effect on the way psychologists and the public looked at sexual orientation. Before the 1990s, the medical and psychological research literatures used the term *sexual preference* instead of today's *sexual orientation*.

Because of the difficulties arising from this type of research in humans, others have investigated the correlations between brain structure and sexual behavior in animals. Among domestic sheep, 6% to 8% of rams (males) mate exclusively with other males. The sheep equivalent of INAH-3 is about the same size in ewes (females) as in the rams that mated with other rams. This structure is larger in rams that mated with ewes (Roselli et al., 2004).

Cognitive and Social Motives

So far, our discussion has focused on motivational behavior that is central to maintaining life. In addition, humans experience a range of complex cognitive and social motives. A lengthy list of these types of complex motives published in 1938 included achievement, affiliation, autonomy, nurturance, dominance, play, and order (Murray, 1938). More recent work focuses on needs for competence and relatedness (Deci & Ryan, 2000). Although some psychologists retain strong distinctions between biological and psychological motives, the dividing line is surely blurred. When an individual's need for affiliation is not met, the consequences of the resulting loneliness include biological factors, such as increased rates of illness and death (Cacioppo et al., 2015).

The Motivation to Affiliate

Humans are a social species. Our need to belong might not seem to be in the same category to you as our need for nutrients and sexual behavior, but the results of many studies show that affiliation works similarly to the other motivations we have discussed so far (Baumeister & Leary, 1995). When people are asked to identify which pleasures are most important to their happiness, the overwhelming majority rate love, intimacy, and social **affiliation** above wealth, fame, and even physical health (Cacioppo & Patrick, 2008).

affiliation Being associated with other people.

Not only do people value affiliation, but a perceived lack of connection with others can have devastating effects. Solitary confinement is viewed as one of the worst punishments humans inflict on one another. The effects of social isolation can be as detrimental to good health as high blood pressure, lack of exercise, obesity, or smoking (House et al., 1988). Not all behaviors associated with feeling isolated are self-destructive. In some cases, feeling isolated can result in outwardly hostile behavior (see Figure 7.26). Students told in an experiment that a personality test had shown that they were "the type likely to end up alone later in life" showed less empathy and more aggression toward other students than did students told that they would enjoy "rewarding relationships throughout life" (Twenge et al., 2001). It is probably not an accident that most individuals responsible for mass shootings are described as outcasts or loners.

The experience of loneliness appears to serve as an aversive signal that, like hunger, thirst, and pain, evolved to warn humans that they are facing a threat to their survival and that their social connections are in need of repair (Cacioppo & Cacioppo, 2018). Social connections are especially important to the survival of humans. Compared to other species, humans require the greatest amount of parenting to survive to adulthood and reproduce. In addition, as we discuss in Chapter 13, humans are not well equipped to survive in isolation. Our ancestors formed hunter-gatherer groups because the cooperative sharing of responsibilities enhanced the survival of all group members.

FIGURE **7.26**

Effects of Social Exclusion on Helping Behaviors. People who were told that a personality test indicated they were likely to spend their future alone without significant relationships were far less helpful across different types of tasks than participants who were told that they were likely to have a future featuring acceptance and belongingness.

Source: Adapted from J. M. Twenge et al. (2007). "If You Can't Join Them, Beat Them: Effects of Social Exclusion on Aggressive Behavior," *Journal of Personality and Social Psychology, 81*, 1058–1069. doi: 10.1037/0022-3514.81.6.1058

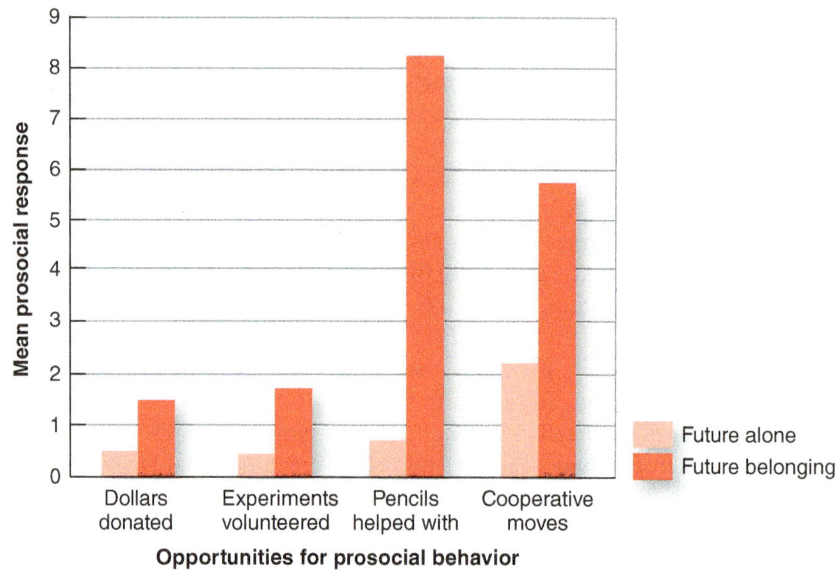

Individuals differ in the amount of social connection they desire. Early work on affiliation by Henry Murray (1938) and David McClelland (1985) viewed the need for others as similar to a personality trait, as we discuss further in Chapter 12. Some people are relatively happy working in a cubicle for hours on end, while this lack of social contact would be intolerable for others. Still others might feel lonely even when surrounded by large numbers of caring friends and family members. We appear to have a set point for social activity that operates similarly to the set points we mentioned in our discussion of hunger. When we sense a gap between our actual social connectivity and what we desire, we experience the unpleasant state of loneliness, which in turn motivates us to seek more social experiences. Twin studies show that this set point, like the others we have discussed, is influenced by our genetics (Boomsma et al., 2005). Knowing one identical twin's need for affiliation helps predict the other twin's need.

Individual predispositions interact with people's situations to predict desire for affiliation. We frequently join others to share good events, whether that means a birthday, a wedding, a promotion, or simply the end of another round of final exams. We have all enjoyed the camaraderie of staying in the stands long after our team has won an important game, celebrating with nearby fans and exchanging high fives.

Affiliation is not just for good times, however. People often find that the company of others helps to reduce stress. The social isolation resulting from pandemic quarantines and lockdowns contributes to high stress levels by removing a major source of comfort. In a classic series of experiments, Stanley Schachter (1959) showed that people expecting to be given a painful electric shock were more likely to seek the company of other study participants than to wait for their shock alone. Not all stressful situations are equally likely to produce affiliation, however. In one study, participants were told that they would be performing embarrassing behaviors, such as sucking on large pacifiers (Sarnoff & Zimbardo, 1961). These participants made different choices than the participants expecting shock in the previous study: They preferred to be alone.

Exactly what does the company of other people contribute to reducing stress? It appears that we appreciate the company of others when we expect them to reduce our stress. In many cases, other people can reduce our stress by providing information. Hospital patients awaiting dangerous surgeries preferred roommates who had already been through the procedure to those who had not yet had surgery (Kulik et al., 1996).

achievement motivation A desire to excel or outperform others.

Achievement Motivation **Achievement motivation** is the desire to excel or outperform others on tasks at which a person could objectively succeed or fail (Wigfield et al., 2015), and has been a topic of interest to psychologists beginning with William James (1890).

WPA Pool/Pool/Getty Images Entertainment/Getty Images

Justin Sullivan/Staff/Getty Images News/Getty Images

People affiliate not only to share happy occasions, such as the introduction of a royal baby, but also to reduce stress in sad times, such as when family members of victims of the September 11, 2001, terrorist attacks gathered to throw flowers in the memorial pools at Ground Zero.

Using measures of individual achievement motivation, people who are high in achievement motivation have been shown to seek and typically succeed in competitive, entrepreneurial occupations (McClelland, 1985). The role of individual achievement motivation in predicting performance has been of great interest in the fields of education, management, and athletics.

Many psychologists have recognized that individual differences in achievement motivation seem similar to personality traits, which we discuss in Chapter 12 (Elliot & Murayama, 2008). A trait is a stable characteristic that shows relatively little variation over time. However, traits also typically interact with situations. An introverted person might seem more introverted at a big party than when out to dinner with one friend. According to this more complex view, a person's trait achievement motivation interacts with the opportunities present in the environment (Hart & Albarracin, 2009). For example, achieving excellence might be viewed as an alternative to having fun or enjoying leisure time. High-achieving people do not dislike fun but are prepared to avoid or postpone some fun to meet their achievement goals. Low-achieving people may be perfectly capable of success but, for a variety of reasons, have simply prioritized fun alternatives and inhibited the achievement alternatives.

Carol Dweck (2012) argues that achievement motivation is influenced by people's beliefs about their own abilities. Individuals with a growth mindset, or a belief that capacities can be developed, outperform individuals with a fixed mindset, or a belief that capacities do not change. In other words, a person with a fixed mindset might say "I'm not good at math," while a person with a growth mindset might say "math is hard, but I'm getting better at it." Individuals with a fixed mindset avoid challenges, become defensive when criticized, and feel envious when they see someone performing better. In contrast, individuals with a growth mindset focus on the processes that lead to success, such as hard work and trying out new strategies. Instead of catastrophes, mistakes are viewed as important sources of information eventually leading to a solution.

The development of achievement motivation is complex. According to Wigfield et al. (2015), expectancies, or what people anticipate, and values, or the weight people put on outcomes,

A person's trait level of achievement motivation interacts with the opportunities to achieve available in the environment.

CHEN WS/Shutterstock.com

THINKING SCIENTIFICALLY

Do Participation Trophies Affect Entitlement and Competitiveness?

In 2015, Pittsburgh Steeler James Harrison posted a large photo of two participation trophies his young sons had received and which he had returned. He stated that he didn't want his boys to think that they deserved something because they tried hard, because "sometimes your best is not enough" (Dator, 2015). Research comparing the weight that should be put on effort in grades and pay for employment showed that college students believed that effort should count for much more in both situations than professors or employers believed it should (Altman et al., 2019).

The so-called trophy culture is a fairly recent phenomenon, leading some to believe that it has influenced young adults more than other age groups (Twenge, 2014). Has the participation trophy phenomenon had an impact on people's attitudes toward performance and achievement? In one study, endorsement of trophy culture was positively associated with higher feelings of entitlement and negatively correlated with competitiveness (Dickhaus et al., 2019).

WHAT AM I BEING ASKED TO BELIEVE OR ACCEPT?

The main hypothesis of Dickhaus et al. (2019) is that endorsement of trophy culture will have an impact on feelings of entitlement and levels of competitiveness.

WHAT EVIDENCE SUPPORTS THIS POSITION?

The researchers conducted a survey of 193 college students attending institutions located in the U.S. Southeast or Midwest. Participants were asked to note the extent of their agreement with statements such as "A kid that places 10th or 12th in a competition should get a reward just like a kid that places 1st or 2nd in that same competition" (Dickhaus et al., 2019, p. 49). They found that students who had participated in middle school or high school athletics had less positive attitudes toward participation trophies. The level of acceptance of participation trophies predicted entitlement both generally and in academic settings as well as lower levels of competitiveness. However, acceptance of participation trophies was not related to narcissism (see Chapter 14).

ARE THERE OTHER WAYS THIS EVIDENCE COULD BE INTERPRETED?

This study involved quite a bit of self-selection (e.g., to participate or not in middle school or high school athletics) and correlational data, which do not allow us to make conclusions about phenomena possibly "caused" by trophy culture. In other words, we do not know if James Harrison was right about the effects of participation trophies on his sons.

WHAT OTHER EVIDENCE WOULD I NEED TO EVALUATE THESE ALTERNATIVES?

This was a very small study involving self-report. To truly identify the causal outcomes of participation trophies, one might design a longitudinal study in which children are randomly assigned to groups exposed to participation trophies or not followed by measures of their entitlement and competitiveness.

WHAT ARE THE MOST REASONABLE CONCLUSIONS?

Participation trophies are one small factor out of many unique social and historical influences on young adults. People engage in youth sports for a variety of reasons, only one of which is to prepare for more elite competition in college and beyond. It is likely that the effects of participation trophies would be different for different people. ■

Sergey Nivens/Shutterstock.com

Messages in the popular culture regarding achievement might shape expectations and values.

influence how they choose tasks, persist in finding a solution, and perform. A person who expects to win a tennis match and thinks winning the match is important is likely to play tennis often and be very motivated to win. These expectancies and values are in turn influenced by both personal and social beliefs. Personal beliefs, such as perceptions of confidence and the difficulty of a task, interact with social factors, such as culture and the expectations and values of significant other people. Our tennis player's motivation might reflect her high levels of confidence, her respect for a difficult opponent, her concerns about disappointing a parent if she loses, and her culture's esteem for excellent athletes.

Motivational Priorities

We have discussed several different motivations, from hunger to sex to affiliation to achievement. If faced simultaneously with many drives and demands, how do we decide which motivations to follow first?

Approach and Avoidance As we observed in the case of achievement motivation, situations often present us with multiple, overlapping opportunities and goals (Elliot, 1999). Approach and avoidance differ in valence or natural attractiveness, with approach involving positive and desirable outcomes and avoidance involving negative and undesirable outcomes. A particular situation might stimulate us to engage in a behavior to approach an outcome, avoid one, or possibly do both simultaneously. When you think about your motivation for studying this textbook right now, you might think you are working to get a good grade in the course (approach), avoid getting a poor grade (avoidance), or do some combination of the two. In any case, you are motivated to study.

This example is only one of several forms conflicts among motives can take. In the example mentioned previously of the student facing a choice between doing well in school and enjoying fun and leisure time, the conflict occurs between two positive choices, or approach-approach. The individual must decide which goal has priority. In still other cases, choices occur between two unpleasant alternatives (avoidance-avoidance). If you don't stay late at work, your boss will think you're a lazy employee, but if you do stay late at work, your partner will be angry. In most real-world situations, choices typically have multiple, overlapping approach-avoidance aspects, making the prioritization of goals essential.

Motivational Theories An early effort to provide a model for prioritizing motives was contributed by Abraham Maslow (1943). Maslow viewed motivation as a hierarchy of needs, in which lower levels must be satisfied before the individual can pursue higher-level needs. As shown in Figure 7.27, Maslow's model is typically illustrated as a pyramid.

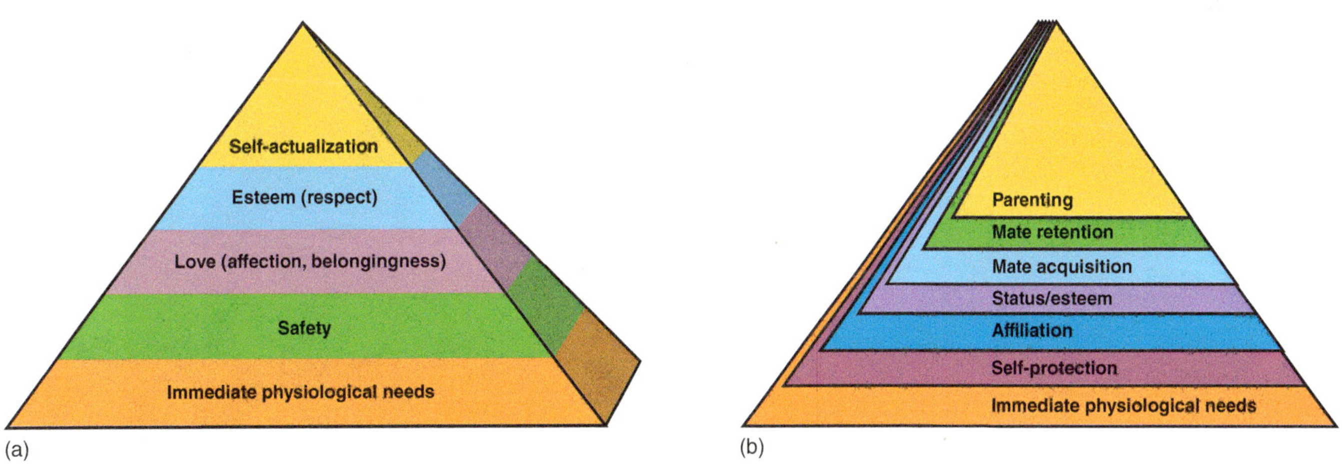

FIGURE 7.27

Classic and Contemporary Hierarchies of Needs. Maslow's classic pyramid depicting his hierarchy of needs is shown in (a). Kenrick et al. (2010) have proposed an updated version of the pyramid (b) that incorporates developmental and evolutionary perspectives.
Source: Adapted from D. T. Kenrick et al. (2010). "Renovating the Pyramid of Needs: Contemporary Extensions Built Upon Ancient Foundations," *Perspectives on Psychological Science*, 5(3), 292–314, doi:10.1177/1745691610369469

Miller (1944) shocked rats while they were eating a food reward they had earned by running down a maze alley, setting up a conflict between approach and avoidance toward the food box. Subsequently, the rat would run down the alley but stop without entering the food box. Miller could adjust where the rats stopped (a point of equilibrium between approach and avoidance) by changing either the rats' hunger levels or the intensity of the shock.

Vladimir Prusakov/Shutterstock.com

Schoolteachers often face students who come to school hungry or sick because of poverty or neglect. According to Maslow, it is difficult for teachers to interest these children, whose basic needs are unmet, in learning about long division and other subjects.

At the lowest level of the pyramid, we find physiological needs, including food, water, and shelter. These basic needs must be met daily; otherwise, life will be threatened. Consequently, if meeting these needs is a challenge for a person, Maslow predicted that the person will not pursue needs at higher levels of the hierarchy. In one classic study, young healthy men were given approximately 1,500 calories per day for 6 months, which resulted in a loss of about 25% of their normal body weight (Keys et al., 1950). Not only did the men become obsessed with food, but their interest in sex declined dramatically.

Abraham Maslow did not believe that everyone achieves self-actualization. Among the select few he believed had reached this pinnacle of motivation were Abraham Lincoln and Mahatma Gandhi—as well as U.S. First Lady Eleanor Roosevelt, shown in this photograph with Madame Chiang Kai-shek. Maslow's self-actualized people shared common attributes, including independence and a good sense of humor. Who would you add to this list of self-actualized people?

AP Images

Once physiological needs are met, Maslow suggests that we turn our attention to safety and then to belongingness, represented by the love and affection of others. We might question the ordering of these needs. During the COVID-19 pandemic, it is not unusual to see people placing a higher priority on belongingness (socializing) than on safety (practicing social distancing). For Maslow, the three lower categories (physiological, safety, and belongingness needs) are essential to human life.

Freed from the challenges of meeting basic needs, we begin to seek esteem, or the respect we receive from other members of the community. At the pinnacle of human striving, however, is the goal of **self-actualization**. People seeking self-actualization desire to fully meet their potential, as suggested by the 1980 U.S. Army slogan "Be all you can be." Cultures differ dramatically in their emphasis on self-actualization, with individualistic nations like the United States embracing this value more than collectivist nations in Asia, where harmony and belongingness are highly valued (Hofstede, 1984).

self-actualization A state of having fulfilled your potential.

Maslow's classic theory received an update that retained the overall hierarchical organization but added three new perspectives: the evolutionary functions of motives, the development of motives over the life span, and the cognitive priorities assigned to motives in response to environmental stimuli (Kenrick et al., 2010). This modified pyramid, illustrated in Figure 7.28, replaces self-actualization with mate acquisition, mate retention, and parenting. The authors of the revision noted that self-actualization was interesting, but they could not find an evolutionary explanation for why we would seek to reach this level. Many of the activities described by Maslow as helping people to reach self-actualization, such as art and poetry, might be better explained as efforts to gain status, which in turn would attract mates.

Interpersonal Relationships

The Emotional Perspective

WHAT IS THE IMPACT OF POSITIVE AND NEGATIVE INTERACTIONS ON RELATIONSHIPS?

THE IDEA THAT GOOD RELATIONSHIPS are characterized by positive emotions and that bad relationships feature many negative emotions sounds obvious. However, it is unrealistic to think that happy couples never experience conflict. They do, but the way they fight can have a big influence on the likelihood that they will stay together.

John Gottman uses a combination of heart rate, facial expression, and analysis of the way people talk about their relationships to each other and to others to make accurate predictions about whether a relationship will last (Gottman, 2011). A key observation is the ratio of positive to negative comments in a couple's discussion of a problem. Happy couples make five times more positive comments about each other and their relationship during these discussions (e.g., we laugh a lot versus we never have fun).

Research by John Gottman shows that happy couples do experience negative emotions with each other. However, for every negative incident, they tend to experience five times as many positive emotional interactions.

image100/Alamy Stock Photo

In several places in this textbook, we have emphasized how the human mind is skewed toward the negative, such as noticing bitter tastes over sweet. This slant suggests that it is easy to focus on your partner's negative qualities, leading to negative emotions and conflict. If we put our relationships on evolutionary cruise control, the ratio of positive-to-negative comments might drop to a point where the relationship is in danger. Maintaining a positive outlook on your partner requires attention and work.

Try observing how people talk about their partners, or watch your own behavior, if you're brave enough. Are you achieving Gottman's 5:1 ratio of positive to negative comments? ■

Psychology Takes On Real-World Problems

Prioritizing Motives During a Pandemic

During a pandemic, people experience a number of competing motives, including the need to work to obtain food, concerns about safety, and the need for social affiliation. How well does psychological science help us understand the choices people make?

Both Maslow's classic model of motivational priorities and the newer model by Kenrick et al. (2010) agree that attention to immediate physiological needs is a higher priority than safety. This appears to be consistent with the behavior of people who do and do not have the ability to perform their work during lockdown. Small business owners and their employees, such as barbers, restaurant owners, and nail salon and gym personnel, undergo immediate hardship when their source of income is cut off by governments wishing to avoid the spread of illness. In contrast, professionals who can work safely at home are much less likely to experience financial disruption during a pandemic. According to motivational models, these two groups can be expected to view safety and the risk of illness very differently. The small business owners and their employees are probably much more comfortable risking illness than the professionals working at home because their more immediate need to feed themselves and their families is so strong.

Things get a bit more complicated when we look at the relationship between safety and affiliation in the priority models. Both assume that safety needs will be prioritized ahead of affiliation. In this regard, the models might be doing a worse job of predicting actual behavior during a pandemic. Many people have expressed outrage when they are unable to attend funerals, graduations, weddings, and religious services. These ritualistic sources of social comfort are probably even more salient at times of extreme stress. In spite of government policies and to the dismay of many older adults, young adults continue to gather at parties and bars, often without masks or social distancing. It is safe to assume that these choices represent a higher value for affiliation than for safety.

Having observed these contradictions with motivational priority models, we might suggest that the models need to be revisited, accompanied by research testing people's choices of safety versus affiliation. It is likely that such choices are in turn influenced by a number of variables, including age. In terms of informing policy, it is important for policy makers to understand the power of the affiliation motive relative to the safety motive. Simple appeals to safety might not be sufficient to gain compliance with restrictions that require people to forego social contact. ■

Space_Cat/Shutterstock.com

Models attempting to explain how we prioritize motives usually put safety ahead of affiliation. However, during a pandemic, it appears that many people value affiliation even more than usual, possibly due to the ability of social contact to reduce stress.

SUMMARY 7.2 Important Concepts in Motivation

Term	Meaning	Example
Motivation 	A process that arouses, maintains, and guides behavior to a goal.	Being thirsty leads you to seek a drinking fountain and get a drink of water.
Homeostasis 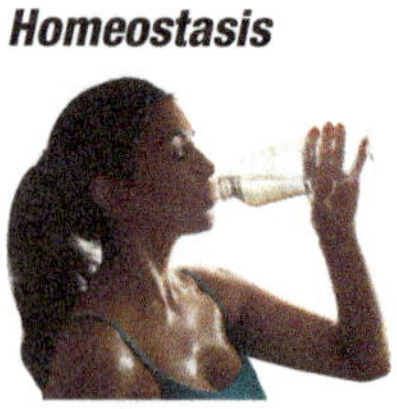	A steady internal balance or equilibrium.	We are motivated to maintain a constant internal temperature. If we feel cold, we shiver and put on more clothing.

Term	Meaning	Example
Set point 	A value actively defended to maintain homeostasis.	It is hard to lose weight because we actively defend our previous weight by slowing our metabolism when fewer calories are consumed.
Drive 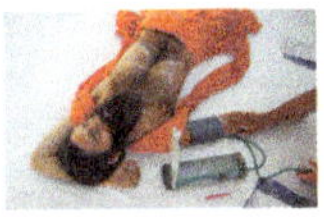	A state of arousal or tension resulting from stimuli that are important to survival.	Being hungry is unpleasant.
Drive reduction 	The feelings of relief and reward following a return to equilibrium.	Quenching your thirst on a hot day is rewarding.
Incentives 	Rewards that motivate behavior without the experience of any unpleasant drive state.	You enjoy throwing a great surprise party for a friend's birthday.

Credits: First row—Michael Steele/Staff/Getty Images Sport/Getty Images; Second row—Steve Cole/Photodisc/Getty Images; Third row—Drew D. Saur; Fourth row—AP Images/Gurinder Osan; Fifth row—Yvette Cardozo/Alamy Stock Photo, iStock.com/Elenathewise; Sixth row—Sonia Moskowitz-Globe Photos, Inc./Newscom.

KEY TERMS The Language of Psychological Science

Be sure that you can define these terms and use them correctly.

achievement motivation, p. 268
affiliation, p. 267
anorexia nervosa, p. 260
appraisal, p. 239
binge-eating disorder, p. 261
body mass index (BMI), p. 257
bulimia nervosa, p. 260
Cannon–Bard theory, p. 235
catharsis, p. 234
display rule, p. 247
drive, p. 253
drive reduction, p. 253
emotion, p. 232
estradiol, p. 262
extrinsic reward, p. 253
glucose, p. 255
homeostasis, p. 253
incentive, p. 253
insula, p. 243
intrinsic reward, p. 253
James–Lange theory, p. 233
leptin, p. 256
motivation, p. 233
satiety, p. 256
Schachter–Singer two-factor theory, p. 236
self-actualization, p. 273
set point, p. 253
sexual orientation, p. 264
somatovisceral afference model of emotion (SAME), p. 238
testosterone, p. 262
Yerkes-Dodson law, p. 240

Learning something new produces structural changes in neurons.

8

The Adaptive Mind

LEARNING

LEARNING OBJECTIVES

1. Compare and contrast reflexes, instincts, and learned behaviors.
2. Identify the components of a classical conditioning experiment and discuss major phenomena and applications related to classical conditioning.
3. Describe the major components of operant conditioning and distinguish operant conditioning from classical conditioning.
4. Analyze the processes that result in observational learning.
5. Discuss the interactions between learned processes and animals' preparation to learn in species-specific ways.
6. Apply learning principles and terminology to everyday situations and problems.

ALTHOUGH YOU MAY NOT HAVE HAD AN opportunity to learn to surf, we're assuming that in your role as a student, you are familiar with the process of learning. But knowing how to learn is different from understanding how and why learning occurs. What is going on in the minds of the people in the photo of surfers as they learn to do something new?

A behavior like learning to surf is complicated, so scientists interested in learning often begin their examinations using animals that are simpler than humans, observing as they learn to do behaviors simpler than surfing. Scientists have zoomed in to observe changes that happen in single neurons, like the large image at the beginning of this section, found in simple animals like the *Aplysia californica* sea slug. The sea slug is capable of learning to anticipate an electric shock that happens every time it is touched, and it demonstrates this knowledge by protectively withdrawing its body in response to touch before the shock is administered. Because the slug has such a simple nervous system compared to ours, scientists have been able to identify which neurons are involved in this learning and to describe the changes in a neuron's functioning that make new behaviors—like withdrawing prior to shock—possible.

Matt Cardy/Stringer/Getty Images News/Getty Images

Is it possible that human learning has anything in common with learning in slugs? The answer to this question is "yes and no." Zooming out, we will see that some types of learning are common across animals with vastly different evolutionary histories and complexities, like humans and sea slugs. In other cases, we see interactions between nature and nurture. Experience, or nurture, frequently interacts with the nature of the organism exposed to the experience. You can talk to your kitten and to an infant, but only the infant will respond to this experience by learning to understand what you're saying and how to reply. Each species brings unique and innate building blocks of learning, accumulated over many generations, to any given situation.

Zooming out still more, we will see how learning in groups can often be different from learning as an individual. Even the lowly sea slug learns differently when alone than when in a group of fellow slugs. Isolated slugs can't seem to stop trying to eat food that is too tough to swallow (Schwarz & Susswein, 1992), but they learn this task easily when in the presence of other slugs (Susswein et al.,1986). Apparently, slugs can communicate with one another using pheromones, and the presence or absence of these chemicals has a powerful effect on their ability to learn (Susswein et al., 1986). The surfers, who are learning to surf in a group, might have had a different experience if they were taking lessons individually. Students working independently at home during a pandemic might very well have a different learning experience than when they're in a face-to-face learning environment. A further understanding of the processes underlying learning should help us optimize these experiences.

Jane Burton/Darling Kindersley/Getty Images

Animals respond to the environment with reflexes, instinctive behaviors, and learned behaviors. Animals, like this "ferocious" kitten, use a reflex called *piloerection* to make themselves look bigger. The evolutionary purpose of this behavior is to appear so menacing that they can avoid conflict.

How Do Animals Respond to Their Environment?

Animals, including ourselves, behave in response to their environments. Behavior can take the form of either externally observable actions or internal processes, such as emotions, thoughts, and physiological responses. These behaviors fall into three broad categories: reflexes, instincts, and learned behaviors. Each type of behavior plays a role in helping us survive, but each differs dramatically in its ability to adapt to a changing world.

Reflexes are inevitable, involuntary responses to stimuli. In casual conversation, we sometimes attribute a baseball player's high batting average or our ability to step on the brake in time to avoid an automobile accident to great reflexes, but in fact, these examples involve learned behaviors that have become fast and automatic as a result of lots of practice. Nobody is born knowing how to hit baseballs or use the brakes of a car, so these behaviors do not meet this definition of a reflex.

In humans, most reflexes are controlled by nervous system circuits located in the spinal cord and brainstem, as described in Chapter 4. Your physician checks one of these reflexes by tapping your knee with a hammer. The tap stretches your leg muscles, and the stretch is sensed by neurons in the spinal cord. Motor neurons in the spinal cord tell your thigh muscle to contract to compensate for the stretching, and your foot kicks out. No experience with knee-tapping is necessary to produce this behavior, nor can you voluntarily prevent it. By the time your brain realizes your knee was

reflex An inevitable, involuntary response to stimuli.

instinct An inborn pattern of behavior elicited by environmental stimuli; also known as a *fixed action pattern*.

learning A relatively permanent change in behavior or the capacity for behavior due to experience.

David Trood/DigitalVision/Getty Images

Tyler Olson/Shutterstock.com

Goosebumps are what is left of piloerection in humans. These signals of arousal are remnants of a time when we had enough hair to make this an easily noticeable response.

tapped, you have already reacted. Other reflexes pull our bodies away from painful stimuli—such as when we step on a piece of glass or touch a hot stove—turn our heads in the direction of loud sounds, and help us stand upright and walk.

Reflexes have the advantage of producing fast, reliable responses that promote your welfare, but they also have the disadvantage of being inflexible. For example, we respond to stress or cold by forming goosebumps (bumps on the skin). This reflex appears to be left over from when our species had more body hair. Goosebumps raise each strand of hair, which in times of stress makes an individual look larger, scaring off predators or competitors, and, in response to cold, traps more insulating air near the skin. As humans lost most of their body hair over time, the advantages of this reflex decreased, but we still retain the behavior.

Instincts, also called *fixed action patterns*, are inborn patterns of behavior elicited or "released" by specific environmental stimuli. Once they begin, instinctive behaviors run until completion. Instincts share reflexes' reliability and lack of dependence on experience, but the resulting behaviors are more complex, requiring many more neurons than the number involved in a reflexive kick of your foot. Instinctive behaviors occur in the mating and parenting behaviors of many species (Tinbergen, 1951). For example, a male peacock displays its magnificent tail as soon as an appropriate female is noticed. An example of a human instinct is yawning. Once a yawn is initiated, it is difficult to stop.

iStock.com/CWLawrence

Although some scientists disagree, contagious yawning might represent an instinct for a number of species, including our own. In one study, puppies over the age of 7 months were susceptible to contagious yawning in response to seeing humans yawn.

Psychologists define **learning** as a relatively permanent change in behavior (or in the capacity for behavior) due to experience. The core of this definition is the phrase *change in behavior*. After learning, we can do something new that we couldn't do before, providing us with enormous advantages in surviving a changing world. Not all changes in behavior take place because of learning, however. Our behavior changes as we mature from infancy through adulthood, as we will see in Chapter 11. Behavior can be changed by brain damage or by having a psychological disorder. So our definition of learning limits the changes we consider to be learned to those that result from experience. The other qualification in this definition, "relatively permanent," prevents the labeling of brief or unstable changes—such as when we experience different moods or suffer from an illness—as learning. The extent to which learning is really permanent will be discussed in Chapter 9.

Mark Bridger/Shutterstock.com

Imprinting, in which a young organism bonds with adults, provides an example of how experience has different effects at different times in the life span. These baby swans are following their parents because the parents were the first things they saw when they hatched. After a delay of a day or two, exposure to the parents would not lead to following. If the baby swans saw a human experimenter instead of their parents upon hatching, they would follow the human instead.

Elena Rooraid/PhotoEdit

Organisms usually show imprinting by the time they are mobile, which for swans means the first day of life, but for human children means closer to 1 year. Because these children have imprinted on their primary caregivers instead of their preschool teacher, the teacher needs a bit of technological help to encourage his charges to follow him on a walk.

associative learning The formation of associations, or connections, among stimuli and behaviors.

classical conditioning A type of learning in which associations are formed between two stimuli that occur sequentially in time.

operant conditioning A type of learning in which associations are formed between behaviors and their outcomes.

nonassociative learning Learning that involves changes in the magnitude of responses to stimuli.

habituation A simple form of learning in which reactions to repeated stimuli that are unchanging and harmless decrease.

sensitization An increased reaction to many stimuli following exposure to one strong stimulus.

observational learning Learning that occurs when one organism watches the actions of another organism; also known as *social learning* or *modeling*.

What Are the Three Main Types of Learning?

Learning can be divided into three categories: associative, nonassociative, and observational. More than one type of learning can operate simultaneously in the same situation.

Associative learning occurs when we form associations, or connections, among stimuli, behaviors, or both. In other words, we learn that if A happens, then B is likely to follow. This type of learning helps us to predict the future based on past experience. The ability to anticipate the future provides enormous survival advantages because through it, animals gain time to prepare. Two important types of associative learning are classical conditioning and operant conditioning. In **classical conditioning**, we associate pairs of stimuli that occur sequentially in time. If a child sees a bee for the first time and then gets stung, the child forms a connection between seeing bees and the pain of being stung. The next time a bee flies by, the child is likely to feel quite frightened. In **operant conditioning**, we associate behaviors and their consequences. If you study hard, you will get good grades. We will discuss these forms of associative learning in more detail in later sections of this chapter.

Nonassociative learning involves changes in the magnitude of responses to a single stimulus rather than the formation of connections between stimuli. Two important types of nonassociative learning are habituation and sensitization. **Habituation** reduces our reactions to repeated experiences that have already been evaluated and found to be unchanging and harmless. For example, you might sleep better the second night than the first in the same hotel because you have adjusted to the unfamiliar noises in that environment. Sometimes we habituate to things that we should, ideally, still be noticing. A major concern about exposing children to violent media is the possibility that their emotional responses to violent images will habituate, leading to higher tolerance for violent behavior (Grizzard et al., 2015).

In contrast to habituation, **sensitization** increases our reactions to a range of stimuli following exposure to one strong stimulus. Following an earthquake, people experience exaggerated responses to movement, light, or noise. If you are awakened by a loud crash, even if you figure out it's just your roommate coming home late at night, it might be harder to get back to sleep because every little sound now seems magnified.

Why would we show habituation to some stimuli and sensitization to others? In general, habituation occurs in response to milder stimuli, whereas sensitization occurs in response to stronger stimuli. Habituation ensures that we do not waste precious resources monitoring low-priority stimuli. On the other hand, sensitization is useful in dangerous situations. After detecting one harmful stimulus, raising our overall level of responsiveness should improve reaction time should other dangers arise.

Observational learning, also known as *social learning* or *modeling*, occurs when one organism learns by watching the actions of another organism. If your knowledge of table manners does not extend to the many forks, knives, and spoons at a fancy dinner, you might want to watch what others do before diving into your food. Observational learning provides the advantage of transmitting information across generations within families and cultures.

treasure dragon/Shutterstock.com

It is likely that the first time this dog's owner attempted to dress it up, the dog was a bit upset. After repeated experiences of being dressed up, however, the dog probably has habituated, which means that it has learned that no harm results from the process. Now it remains calm.

Many universities offer special programs for students who are the first in their extended families to attend college in recognition of the need to level the playing field with students who enter college having already learned a great deal about college life from observing their college-educated family members.

Vitalij Lang/Shutterstock.com

Following an earthquake, this little boy is likely to be extra jumpy for a while in response to other stimuli, like loud noises, because of sensitization.

Blend Images/Alamy Stock Photo

Watching others is an efficient way to learn new skills, like dancing. Imagine for a moment how difficult it would be to write a description of how this dance should be performed. Watching others is also a useful way to learn what is harmful to do.

SUMMARY 8.1 Types of Learning

Associative learning 	Classical conditioning • Signal → Important event • Snakes → Snakebite Operant conditioning • Behavior → Consequences • Practice → Successfully riding a wave in surfing
Nonassociative learning 	Habituation • Responses to repeated, unchanging, irrelevant stimuli • Reduced response to neighbor's loud television every evening Sensitization • Responses to many stimuli • "Jumpiness" in response to many stimuli following an earthquake
Observational learning 	Watch → Imitate • Copy new dance moves from your favorite music video Watch → Avoid imitating • Watch friend get sick from alcohol—don't drink as much

Credits: Top row—Matt Cardy/Stringer/Getty Images News/Getty Images; Second row—Vitalij Lang/Shutterstock.com; Bottom row—Blend Images/Alamy Stock Photo

What Is Classical Conditioning?

Ivan Petrovich Pavlov (1849–1936) is so tightly connected to the study of classical conditioning that the phenomenon is frequently called *Pavlovian conditioning*. Pavlov switched his interests from the study of digestion to the study of learning after noticing that his dogs had

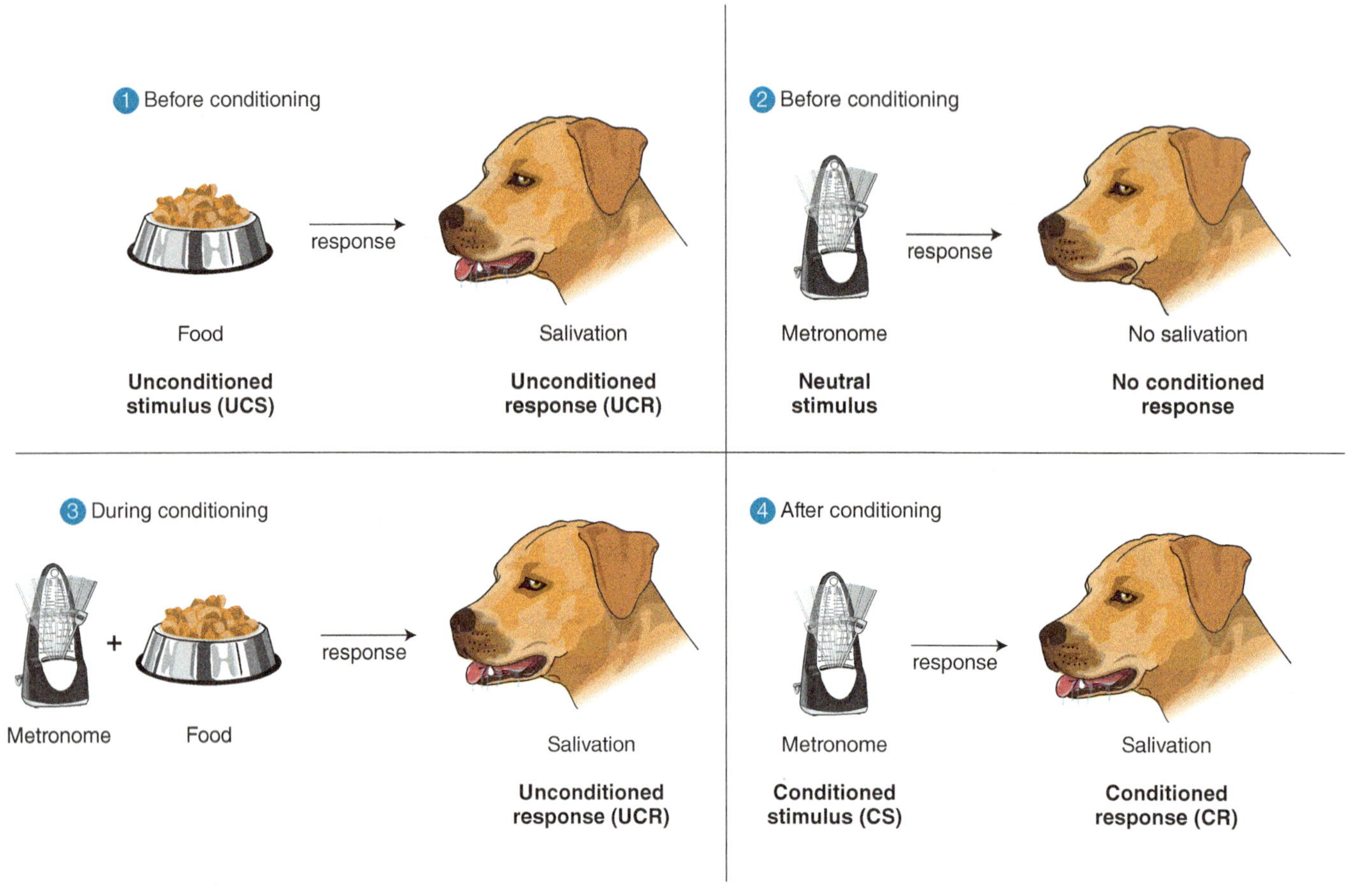

FIGURE **8.1**

Classical Conditioning Terminology. (1) and (2) Before conditioning, food (unconditioned stimulus, or UCS) reliably produces salivation (unconditioned response, or UCR), and the sound of the metronome produces no reliable responding. (3) During conditioning, the sound of the metronome is followed by the food (UCS), which again produces salivation (UCR). (4) After conditioning, the sound of the metronome (conditioned stimulus, or CS) by itself is sufficient to produce salivation (conditioned response, or CR). Learning has occurred.

learned to anticipate the arrival of food. Instead of salivating when presented with food, his dogs began to salivate as soon as the lab assistant retrieved them from the kennel or strapped them into their experimental harnesses in the laboratory. Most people would probably not have noticed the differences in the dogs' behavior. Pavlov not only noticed but realized the importance of his observations: the dogs had formed an association between the stimuli preceding the food and the arrival of the food. In other words, the dogs had learned that certain stimuli served as signals for the eventual appearance of food (see Figure 8.1).

If you are like most people reading about classical conditioning for the first time, you are probably wondering why psychologists spend so much time and effort discussing salivating dogs. If classical conditioning were that limited in its scope, it probably wouldn't warrant more than a small footnote in the history of psychology. Instead, classical conditioning explains many of our learned emotional responses to our environment. It forms the basis for many practical applications, from prepared childbirth methods to the treatment of drug addiction and unrealistic fears.

Classical Conditioning Terminology

In describing the process of classical conditioning, Pavlov distinguished between conditioned and unconditioned stimuli and responses. *Conditioned* refers to something that must be learned, while *unconditioned* refers to factors that are reflexive or that occur without learning.

Therefore, a **conditioned stimulus (CS)** refers to an environmental event whose significance is learned, while an **unconditioned stimulus (UCS)** has innate meaning to the organism. In a typical experiment by Pavlov, dogs heard the sound of a ticking metronome (Pavlov never used bells, contrary to popular mythology) just before food appeared through a small door. Dogs do not have an innate response to the sound of ticking metronomes, but they generally are born knowing what to do with food. By turning on the metronome before delivering food, Pavlov established the ticking sound as the CS, while the food was the UCS. A UCS may be pleasant, like food, but it may also be unpleasant, like an electric shock. The important features of a UCS are its innate biological significance and its reliable ability to elicit a response without prior exposure. Just as dogs don't require training to salivate in response to meat powder, few of us need experience with electric shock before we respond with fear and other negative emotions.

Conditioned responses (CRs) are learned reactions, while **unconditioned responses (UCRs)** don't need to be learned; they appear without prior experience with a stimulus. Salivating when food is put in your mouth is a UCR because we do this reflexively, without prior experience, but salivating to ticking metronomes occurs only as a result of experience. Our definition of learning requires behavior to change, so the appearance of a CR tells us that learning has occurred. Once learning has taken place, the organism now responds to CSs that reliably predict the arrival of the UCS.

As this section will show, understanding classical conditioning illuminates a range of behaviors that you might have seen in yourself or others—from the avoidance of foods that you associate with feeling sick, to the butterflies you feel in your stomach before a big performance, to the development of social prejudices.

conditioned stimulus (CS) An environmental event whose significance is learned through classical conditioning.

unconditioned stimulus (UCS) A stimulus that elicits a response without prior experience.

conditioned response (CR) A response learned through classical conditioning.

unconditioned response (UCR) A response to an unconditioned stimulus that requires no previous experience.

acquisition The development of a learned response.

Classical Conditioning Phenomena

Pavlov and those following in his footsteps have extended the usefulness of classical conditioning by exploring its features and development in more detail.

Acquisition

Acquisition refers to the development of a CR. Pavlov argued that acquisition requires contiguity, or proximity in time between the CS and the UCS. If the CS occurs long before the UCS, the organism may not view the two stimuli as related. A CS that occurs simultaneously with a UCS or, worse yet, following a UCS, is not a useful signal. A dinner bell sounded after food has been served is not helpful, and we're unlikely to learn about it (see Figure 8.2).

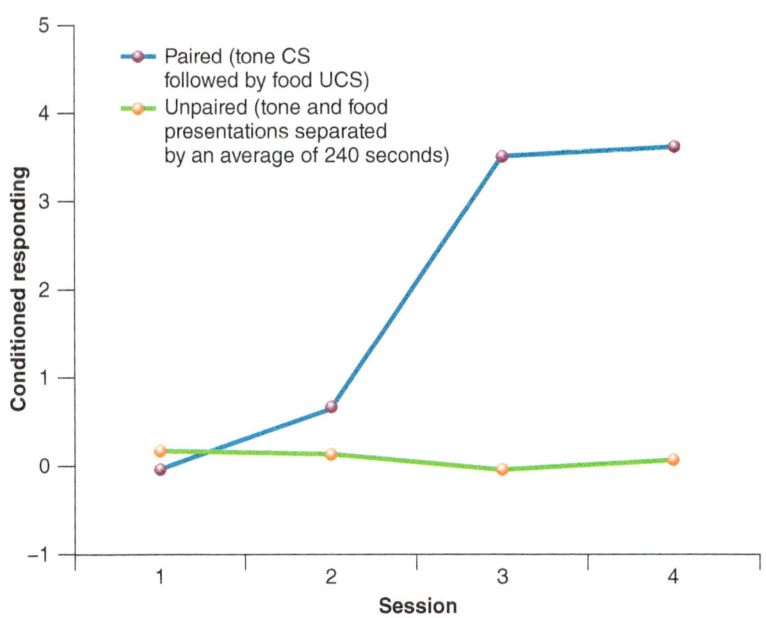

FIGURE **8.2**

Acquisition of Conditioned Responses (CRs). With each pairing of the conditioned stimulus and unconditioned stimulus, conditioned responses become more likely.

Acquisition also requires contingency, or a correlation between the CS and the UCS. Learning about a reliable signal is easier than learning about a signal that occurs only sometimes. To demonstrate the contingency factor, Robert Rescorla (1968) exposed rats to sound followed by a mild electric shock, which quickly produced fear of the sound. For some rats, a shock was administered only after a sound, while for other rats, shocks were administered following the sound on some occasions and without any sound on others. All the rats had the same number of contiguous sound–shock pairings. They differed in the correlation between sound and shock. Learning was faster for rats experiencing signaled shocks 100% of the time. As the percentage of signaled shocks decreased, learning about the signal slowed. If your migraine headaches are always preceded by exposure to bright light, you are more likely to fear bright lights in the future than if your headaches follow exposure to bright lights only once in a while (see Figure 8.3).

extinction The reduction of a learned response. In classical conditioning, extinction occurs when the unconditioned stimulus (UCS) no longer follows the conditioned stimulus (CS). In operant conditioning, extinction occurs when the consequence no longer follows the learned behavior.

spontaneous recovery During extinction training, the reappearance of conditioned responses (CRs) after periods of rest.

Extinction and Spontaneous Recovery CRs disappear, or undergo **extinction**, if the association between the CS and the UCS is broken. When Pavlov continued to expose his dogs to the ticking of the metronome without providing food, the dogs eventually stopped salivating in response to the sound of the metronome.

Pavlov believed that extinction is not the same thing as forgetting; rather, it is actually new learning that overrides old learning. As evidence for this belief, Pavlov pointed to the occurrence of **spontaneous recovery**, or the reappearance of CRs following periods of rest between sessions of extinction training. Even if a dog has stopped salivating to the sound of the metronome by the end of an extinction session, conditioned salivation reappears at the beginning of the next session. In other words, the CR decreases during a session of extinction training not because the dog is forgetting the relationship between ticking and food, but because the dog is now learning that ticking no longer predicts food, and it may take several sessions for this new learning to replace the old (see Figure 8.4).

Without the ability to extinguish CRs, adjusting to further changes in the environment would be difficult, if not impossible. We would not be able to learn to enjoy dogs again after being bitten by one. An addict whose associations between needles and the effects of using heroin never extinguished would have an even harder time overcoming addiction.

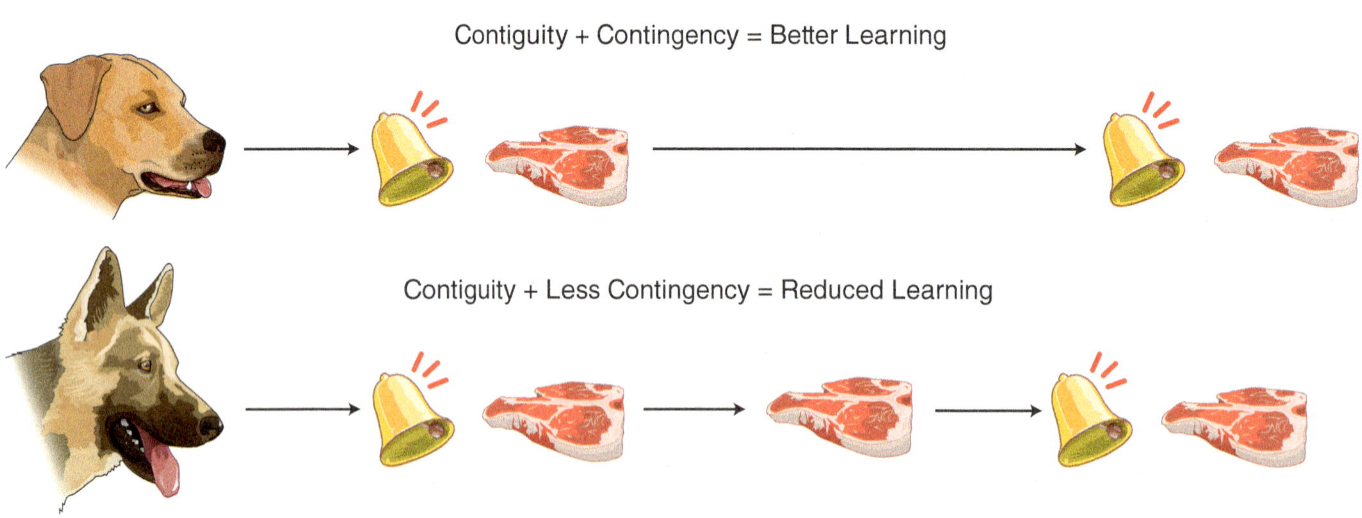

FIGURE **8.3**

Contingency Predicts Conditioning. Imagine the experience of the two dogs in this experiment. Food (unconditioned stimulus) always follows hearing the bell (conditioned stimulus) for both dogs, which demonstrates contiguity. However, the first dog receives food only after the bell, while the food is not always signaled by the bell for the second dog. The dog in the first case would learn the association between bell and food faster than the dog in the second one, because the first dog's bell is a more reliable signal for food (better contingency).

Inhibition So far, we have been discussing examples of *excitatory* classical conditioning, in which the organism learns that a CS predicts the occurrence of a UCS. Pavlov was also quite interested in the classical conditioning of **inhibition**, in which a CS predicts the nonoccurrence of a UCS (Pavlov, 1927). To demonstrate inhibition, we can begin by establishing excitatory conditioning by pairing a signal—a light—with shock. After some experience with this pairing, a rat learns to fear the light. Now we continue to present light–shock pairings, but we add other training trials that include an inhibitory CS—a sound—by presenting the light and sound together, followed by no shock. Even though the light is present, the rat learns that it is not going to be shocked in the presence of the sound, and it shows no fear.

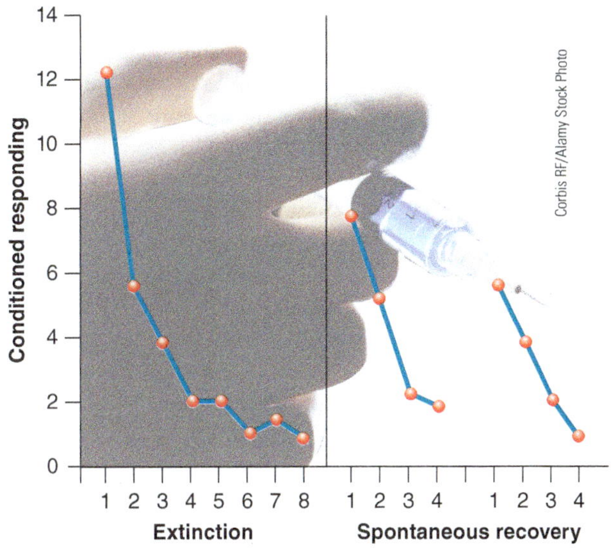

FIGURE **8.4**

Extinction and Spontaneous Recovery. Addiction often involves the association of conditioned stimuli (CSs), such as the syringe, with the unconditioned stimulus (UCS) of a drug. Recovering addicts can be exposed to extinction—viewing the syringe (CS) without receiving the drug (UCS). This process reduces conditioned responses (CRs) that might be contributing to cravings for the drug. However, extinction typically requires multiple sessions. When the recovering addict returns for the next extinction training session after a period of rest, that person is likely to show CRs again. Eventually, with enough training, extinction is complete, and no further spontaneous recovery is observed.

For a vulnerable animal in the wild, it is important to know not only that a predator at a water hole is in hunting mode (the sight of a prowling predator is an excitatory CS eliciting fear), but also that a predator relaxing after a recent kill is unlikely to kill again soon (the sight of a predator calmly drinking water is an inhibitory CS that tells the animal that the predator is unlikely to attack soon and therefore it is safe). For drug addicts, establishing inhibitory CSs associated with the lack of an expected drug effect might provide a powerful method for rehabilitation (Kearns et al., 2005). If an addict learns that drugs are never available in the presence of a certain signal, turning the signal on whenever the addict's resolve is weak might help prevent a relapse.

inhibition A feature of classical conditioning in which a conditioned stimulus (CS) predicts the nonoccurrence of an unconditioned stimulus (UCS).

generalization The tendency to respond to stimuli that are similar to an original conditioned stimulus (CS).

discrimination A learned ability to distinguish between stimuli.

Generalization and Discrimination Once a CR is successfully acquired, organisms often show a tendency to respond to stimuli that are similar to the CS. For example, the child who learned to be afraid of bees after being stung might also begin to fear wasps and yellow jackets, a process that Pavlov called **generalization**.

Generalization has obvious survival value. If our ancestors had one bad experience with a lion, it would make sense to avoid all lions, as well as other animals with lionlike characteristics. Unfortunately, our tendency to generalize can also have negative outcomes. For example, a soldier traumatized in combat might react with unnecessary fear to sounds that are similar to gunfire on the battlefield, such as the backfiring of a car back at home.

Counteracting our tendency to generalize is another learning process known as **discrimination**, which allows us to make fine distinctions between the implications of stimuli. In the laboratory, if you present food following a high tone but never following a low tone, a dog initially salivates following both tones because of

FRIEDRICHSMEIER/Alamy Stock Photo

Inhibition learning helps organisms behave adaptively when they've learned that something important will not occur. These zebras may have learned that when lions act a certain way, they are already full and unlikely to hunt again. These inhibitory signals tell the zebras that they can drink in safety—at least for a little while.

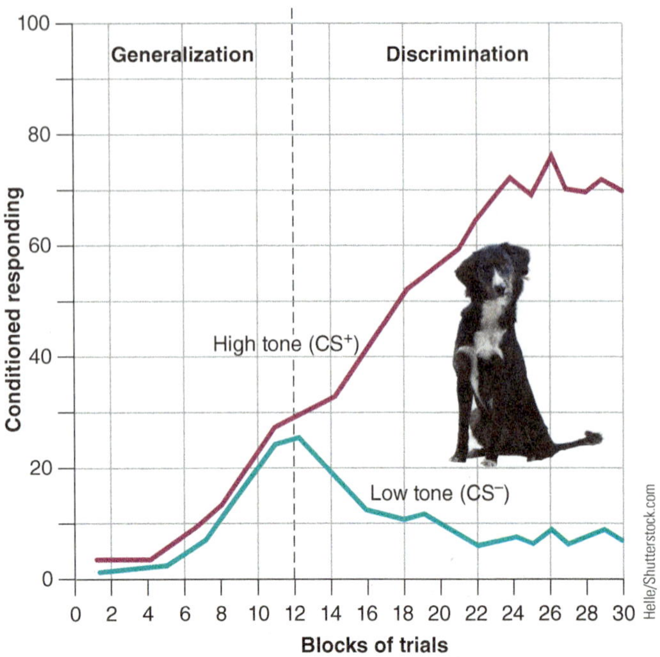

FIGURE 8.5

Generalization and Discrimination. The dog is receiving food after the high tone, but nothing after the low tone. Early in training, the dog salivates after both tones because of generalization. Further along in training, however, the dog learns to discriminate between the abilities of the two tones to signal food and salivates only after the high tone.

generalization. As learning progresses, the dog eventually learns to discriminate, or differentiate, between the abilities of the two stimuli to predict food. As a result, salivation to the high tone continues, but salivation to the low tone stops (see Figure 8.5). If generalization had led the soldier to react with fear to the sound of a backfiring car, further experience with the sound would help distinguish it from real gunfire in combat. Because the sound of a backfiring car is not followed by any fear-producing UCSs, it eventually loses its ability to elicit fear.

Higher-Order Conditioning We have seen how CRs spread to similar stimuli through generalization. In addition, CRs can occur in response to stimuli that predict the CS, a process known as **higher-order conditioning**.

Higher-order conditioning allows us to make even more distant predictions about the occurrence of significant events. A person who was bitten by a dog might show fear the next time the dog is seen because the sight of the dog (CS) is now associated with the pain of the bite (UCS). Subsequently, the sight of the dog (CS) might begin to act more like a UCS, producing fear in response to other stimuli (seeing the dog's yard or doghouse or hearing the dog bark) that might signal the appearance of the dog.

Latent Inhibition Pavlov's dogs had probably never heard a metronome before participating in his experiments. What happens when you are already familiar with a CS? The answer is that you will take a longer amount of time learning to respond to it. It takes more time to learn about a familiar CS than about an unfamiliar CS, a phenomenon known as **latent inhibition** (Lubow & Moore, 1959). The phenomenon is latent in the sense that its effects are not seen right away (when the stimuli are first presented), but emerge later when the rate of learning is examined. The inhibition part of the term refers to the relatively poor learning that occurs in response to familiar stimuli.

If you have eaten lots of pizzas over time (familiar CS) but get sick after eating one, you are unlikely to associate the pizza with feeling ill. In contrast, if you get sick the first time you eat chocolate-covered ants (assuming these are an unfamiliar CS), you'll quickly associate eating ants with feeling ill.

higher-order conditioning Learning in which stimuli associated with a conditioned stimulus (CS) also elicit conditioned responses (CRs).

latent inhibition The slower learning that occurs when a conditioned stimulus (CS) is already familiar compared to when the CS is unfamiliar.

Cognitive and Biological Influences on Classical Conditioning

Early behaviorists concentrated their study of learning on external behaviors that they could observe directly. As new technologies became available, such as brain imaging methods and more powerful computers used to model thinking and reasoning, psychologists interested in learning began to explore internal processes, leading to revolutionary advances in our understanding of cognition and biology.

Early behaviorists also limited most of their studies to simple animals rather than humans. This restriction resulted from strong beliefs that behavior followed the same rules in all organisms, which meant that it was safe to apply experimental results from studies using rats to the behavior of humans and that having more control over your experimental subjects (food, housing, etc.) led to better science. Although the latter may be true, psychologists discovered that treating the learning animal as some kind of interchangeable black box was overly simplistic. Some learning processes have clearly been conserved over the course of evolution. We can make conclusions relevant to humans about the changes at a synapse that accompany classical conditioning in the *Aplysia californica* sea slug (Carew & Kandel, 1973). In other cases, species bring their unique biology into the learning situation, as we will see in a later section on taste aversion learning. Psychologists have learned to be cautious about generalizing their conclusions across species.

The Element of Surprise In our earlier discussion of the acquisition of classical CRs, we talked about the contributions of contiguity (closeness in time) and contingency (the correlation between the CS and the UCS). It should be easy to learn about a signal that both precedes and is predictive of an important event. The bell on your microwave both precedes and predicts the availability of food, and we would not be surprised if your mouth starts watering a bit whenever you hear it.

What happens, however, if you already possess one good signal but add another one that also precedes and predicts a UCS? Based on past experience, you have learned that if your computer monitor suddenly goes blue (CS), something terrible (UCS) has happened to your computer. Whenever you see a blue screen, you feel extremely stressed (CR). Let's assume that the next time a blue screen appears, the computer also emits a funny sound. Even though the sound both precedes and predicts a hard drive crash, it's unlikely that you will learn much about the sound and its relationship with hard drive crashes. We don't bother to learn much about new signals that provide no additional information, even if they meet our requirements for contiguity and contingency (Kamin, 1968, 1969).

How can we account for this failure to learn under circumstances that should produce strong learning? Rescorla and Wagner (1972) proposed a model of classical conditioning in which learning occurs as a function of how surprising the association between the CS and the UCS appears. Early in training, more learning takes place because the relationship between the CS and the UCS is relatively unexpected. Later in training, less learning takes place with each exposure to the now-familiar relationship between the CS and the UCS (see ● Figure 8.6). We fail to learn to associate the funny sound with a hard drive crash because the crash is not a surprise any more—the blue screen has already alerted us to the hard drive's inevitable demise.

We can't imagine early behaviorists using terms like *expect*, *surprise*, and *predict*, because these represent internal states they believed were impossible to investigate scientifically. But today, it seems reasonable to discuss some aspects of learning using this vocabulary.

Tom Feiler/Masterfile

Higher-order conditioning occurs when stimuli associated with a conditioned stimulus (CS) gain the ability to elicit conditioned responses (CRs) on their own. If a child has learned to fear dogs (CS) because of a previous bite (unconditioned stimulus, or UCS), anything that signals "dog" might now produce fear too, including the sight of a doghouse, a dog's feeding bowl, or a chew toy.

Steph and John Cacioppo

Because of latent inhibition, classical conditioning proceeds more slowly when a new conditioned stimulus is familiar than when it is unfamiliar. If you got sick after eating a familiar food (perhaps pizza), you are less likely to associate your illness with the food than if you got sick after eating an unfamiliar food, like this scorpion lollipop that one of your textbook authors is about to try.

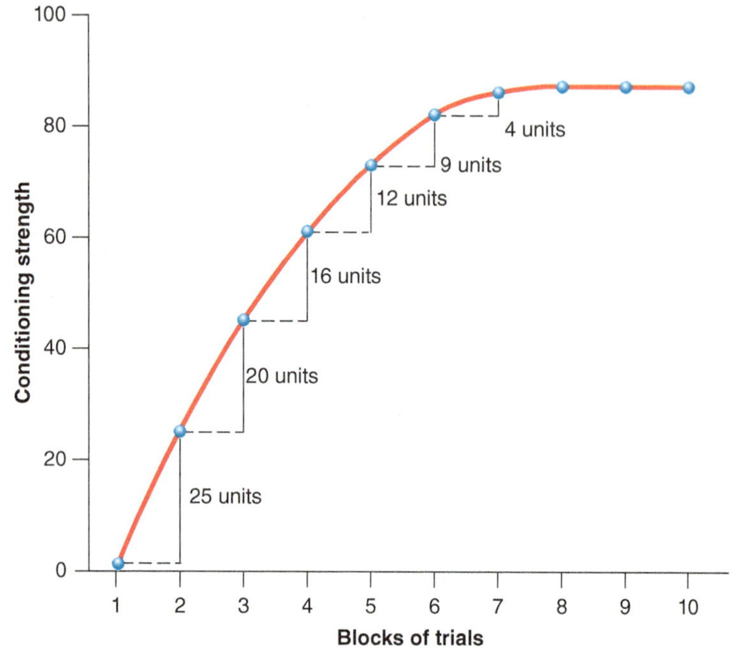

FIGURE 8.6

The Rescorla–Wagner Model. According to the Rescorla–Wagner model, the rate of learning about a conditioned stimulus (CS) depends on how new or surprising the association between the CS and the unconditioned stimulus (UCS) appears to be. Early in training, learning proceeds rapidly (25 units per block or set of trials) because the association is new and surprising. Later in training, gains in conditioning strength (measured by how often a conditioned response occurs) level off because the association between the CS and the UCS is now familiar and no longer surprising (4 units per block of trials).

Taste Aversion We have already used some examples of classical conditioning involving food that you dislike because you got sick after eating it. These classically conditioned taste aversions result when the sight, smell, or flavor of the food (CS) has been paired in the past with illness (UCS). Taste aversion, or dislike of the food, is the resulting CR.

Taste aversion isn't just another interesting example of classical conditioning. Its demonstration led to a substantial rethinking not only of classical conditioning, but of behaviorism in general. Pavlov believed that stimuli that met the CS or UCS criteria could be successfully paired to produce classical conditioning. He made no provisions in his theory for special interactions between particular types of stimuli. John Garcia, who had a background not only in psychology but also in biology, did not believe that stimuli were so interchangeable. In what became known as a classic taste aversion study, Garcia and Koelling (1966) demonstrated that the types of stimuli used as CSs and UCSs matter, and that some combinations are learned faster than others. As shown in ● Table 8.1, Garcia and Koelling presented groups of rats with either saccharin-flavored water ("tasty water") or plain water. When the rats consumed the plain water, their drinking triggered a light and a clicking sound, which the researchers called "bright-noisy water." After drinking either tasty or bright-noisy water, half the rats were given an injection of lithium chloride, which produces strong sensations of nausea, and the other half received an electric shock.

This type of experiment should look familiar to you by now as an example of classical conditioning. Tasty water or bright-noisy water served as CSs, while shock or lithium chloride served as UCSs. Garcia and Koelling subsequently presented tasty and bright-noisy water to see whether either would be avoided, with avoidance serving as an indication of the CR of disgust with or dislike of the water. Rats immediately learned associations between tasty water and subsequent illness but had difficulty learning to use the bright-noisy water as a signal for illness. Conversely, bright-noisy water, but not tasty water, became an effective signal for shock. After all, if you feel sick, you are more likely to decide that your illness was a result of eating mystery leftovers for breakfast rather than the flickering of the fluorescent lights in your classroom. However, if you receive an electric shock, you might be more suspicious of the flickering lights than of your breakfast.

This experiment had far-ranging implications. Not only did these findings challenge Pavlov's views of the relative interchangeability of stimuli, but they also prompted a renewed interest in the biological predispositions of organisms, or their

TABLE 8.1

Experimental Design Used by Garcia and Koelling (1966)

Unconditioned stimulus	**Conditioned stimulus**	
	Bright-noisy water	**Tasty water**
Lithium chloride (LiCl)	Weak learning	• Strong learning
Shock	Strong learning	• Weak learning

preparedness to learn certain things. Although rats readily formed associations between taste and illness, but not between visual stimuli and illness, birds easily formed associations between visual stimuli and illness, but not between taste and illness. Rats see poorly, so they usually depend on taste and smell for identifying food. Birds have excellent vision and typically identify food sources using visual cues, such as the markings of particular species of butterfly.

The willingness of behaviorists to treat organisms as interchangeable black boxes with irrelevant internal features was severely challenged by this work, paving the way to an abandonment of the rigid behaviorism that had dominated psychology for most of the 20th century. Many learning theorists closed down their rat and pigeon labs and turned their attention to emerging cognitive, biological, and evolutionary approaches.

James H. Robinson/Science Source

John Garcia and Robert Koelling's work on taste aversion explains why the monarch butterfly (on the top) is often rejected by birds as food. The milkweed on which the monarch caterpillar feeds contains cardiac glycosides, which are maintained in the mature insects' bodies. Ingested glycosides make the birds ill, so they avoid feeding on monarchs, as would be predicted by classical conditioning. Some scientists believe that by looking similar to the monarch, the viceroy butterfly (on the bottom) might escape being eaten too. Recall that visual stimuli ("bright—noisy" water) were not very effective signals for illness in rats, but apparently, they work just fine for birds. The natural capacities of a species prepare it to learn some things better than others.

Applying Classical Conditioning

Although strict behaviorism no longer dominates research in psychology, it still provides powerful explanations of human behavior and effective therapeutic tools for producing change. The pervasiveness of classical conditioning in everyday life is quite remarkable. When your palms get sweaty and you feel butterflies in your stomach before a big exam, awaken just before your alarm clock goes off, or feel more awake just because you smell coffee brewing, you can blame your responses on classical conditioning. If you are a clinician working with a traumatized combat veteran who is frightened by the smell of diesel fuel or a coach working with an athlete to overcome "choking" in big games, classical conditioning gives you the means to produce positive change.

Overcoming Fear In 1920, John B. Watson and Rosalie Raynor conducted an experiment with a 9-month-old infant named Albert (Watson & Rayner, 1920). By today's standards, this experiment hardly appears well designed or ethical, but the results of the experiment led to research that shed a great deal of light onto human fear. While Albert played with a tame, white laboratory rat (CS), Watson and Raynor made a loud noise (UCS) by hitting a steel bar with a hammer. Albert was quite frightened by this noise (UCR). A week later, Albert was again offered the rat, but this time, he was afraid (CR). His fear generalized to other white, furry objects, including a rabbit, a dog, a fur coat, and a Santa Claus mask. Watson and Raynor had successfully demonstrated that fears could result from classical conditioning.

Although Albert left Watson and Raynor's laboratory without treatment for his fear, one of Watson's students, Mary Cover Jones, demonstrated how classical conditioning procedures could be used to reduce learned fears. Her experiment featured a 3-year-old named Peter, who had a serious phobia, or intense, unrealistic fear, of rabbits (Jones, 1924). Could classical conditioning provide a way to reduce Peter's fears?

One possible approach would be to use extinction. As mentioned previously, CRs extinguish if the CS is presented alone, without the UCS. Treating phobias by exposing people to fear-producing stimuli in a manner that is safe until they no longer respond (i.e., extinction) is known as *exposure therapy*. Exposure therapy can be applied with a full-strength fear stimulus (flooding) or more gradually, beginning with versions of the fear stimulus that produce the least fear and then building up to more scary stimuli. Although exposure therapy works, it is potentially traumatic. Being exposed to a stimulus you find frightening until you are no longer afraid is not fun. Imagine forcing a person afraid of heights to bungee jump until the fear of heights has gone.

Instead of using simple exposure therapy, Jones treated Peter with counterconditioning, or the substitution of one CR for another, opposite response. Jones associated food, a new UCS, with the presence of a rabbit (CS). Eventually,

Psychologists have long been curious about what happened to Albert after he left Watson and Raynor's laboratory. One hypothesis suggests that Albert was Douglas Merritte, the child of one of the foster mothers living at the Harriet Lane home in 1920. Merritte died at age 6 of hydrocephalus. Another strong candidate is William Albert Barger, whose name and physical health appear to some to be a better match for the baby shown in Watson's films of his experiment. Barger died in 2007, at the age of 87. If Barger is indeed the famous Albert, we hope that his strong dislike of animals as an adult was not a remnant of Watson's experiment.

iStock.com/oleg66

Understanding classical conditioning provides insight into many situations where our emotional responses seem to be triggered by the environment, as in the case of performance anxiety.

Peter was able to stroke the rabbit while eating. While not particularly hygienic, this achievement represented a big improvement in Peter's life.

Counterconditioning has many useful applications. **Aversion therapy** can be used to replace inappropriate positive reactions to a stimulus with negative reactions. For example, a compound containing silver interacts with nicotine to make a tobacco cigarette taste terrible. Substituting a negative outcome for a positive outcome of smoking helps some smokers quit more easily (Rose et al., 2010).

A variation of counterconditioning used to treat fear is known as **systematic desensitization** (Wolpe, 1958). Associations between a phobic stimulus and fear are replaced by associations between the phobic stimulus and relaxation. The person undergoing treatment is first trained to achieve a state of physical and mental relaxation, usually by tensing and relaxing muscle groups from head to toe. If you would like to try this progressive relaxation technique yourself, we outline the procedure in Chapter 15. Once relaxation is achieved, the fear stimulus is gradually introduced, either in physical form, through guided imagery, in which the person is asked to imagine the stimulus, or by using virtual reality. If relaxation falters at any point, the person retreats to an earlier stage of exposure to the fear stimulus until he or she can relax again.

Addiction In addition to the influences on addiction discussed in Chapter 6, classical conditioning can contribute to dependence on a drug or behavior. Stimuli associated with drug use often become CSs for the effects of a drug. For example, peak caffeine levels occur about 45 minutes after drinking a cup of coffee (Liguori et al., 1997), yet most coffee drinkers report feeling more awake as soon as they take that first sip in the morning (or even smell the coffee brewing).

One of the challenges faced by people recovering from addiction to substances is that environmental cues (i.e., CSs) associated with the effects of substance use (i.e., UCSs) continue to elicit cravings (i.e., CRs) for the drug of choice. Most treatments for substance abuse involve simply abstaining from a drug, as opposed to extinction or counterconditioning. There is nothing about avoiding the use of a drug that substantially weakens the previously formed associations surrounding its use. Consequently, being exposed to established CSs, including the people with whom one did the drugs previously or the context in which one used the drugs, often leads to a former addict's relapse (Chaudhri et al., 2008). The sight, smell, or taste of a recovering alcoholic's favorite drink, or even a visit to a favorite bar, is often enough to undermine the person's abstinence from drinking. Reducing these associations through extinction can help the addict continue to abstain.

aversion therapy An application of counterconditioning in which a conditioned stimulus (CS) formerly paired with a pleasurable unconditioned stimulus (UCS) is instead paired with an unpleasant UCS.

systematic desensitization A type of counterconditioning in which people relax while being exposed to stimuli that elicit fear.

Attitudes and Prejudice Classical conditioning contributes to the formation and change of attitudes (Cacioppo & Berntson, 2001). After all, following the lead of behaviorist John Watson, advertisers have been using classical conditioning for years to influence consumer

Courtesy of Professor Benjamin Harris

John B. Watson and Rosalie Raynor observe Little Albert's generalization to a bunny mask worn by Watson. The mask is similar to the original conditioned stimulus in their experiment—a white laboratory rat—which stimulated Albert's conditioned fear.

attitudes about products. By forming associations between the products and other stimuli we value, like celebrities and influencers, advertisers hope that our opinions of their product will improve.

Prejudice, which is discussed further in Chapter 13, is a negative attitude about a group of people. Like other attitudes, it is influenced by classical conditioning, although it has many other roots as well. In particular, latent inhibition can contribute to the development of negative attitudes (Cacioppo et al., 1992). Because of latent inhibition, if children grow up with little exposure to people outside their own race, people of their own race are more familiar, and learning to associate their race with other attributes should be slow. In contrast, the children have had less preexposure to people of other races. Latent inhibition would predict that children exposed to news reports about crime would form stronger associations between people of unfamiliar races and crime than between people of their own race and crime.

Paul Vasarhelyi/Shutterstock.com

Creativity and Schizophrenia By reducing the amount of learning that occurs in response to familiar stimuli, latent inhibition helps us focus our energy on novelty and change in our environments.

Less latent inhibition is seen in creative people and in people diagnosed with schizophrenia than is seen in the general population (Baruch et al. 1988a, 1988b; Lubow et al., 1992). This difference means that creative people and people with schizophrenia form new associations with familiar stimuli faster than most people do. They make connections under circumstances in which most of us would not. Reduced latent inhibition might account for the creative person's ability to see familiar things in new ways, which is a positive outcome, but it also might lead to the tendency of a person with schizophrenia to make odd, inappropriate connections among ideas. Chapter 14 refers to this tendency as a "loosening of associations." For example, a person with schizophrenia might suggest that getting a job in a bakery will help him gain admission to medical school. This is not the type of association between stimuli that most people would make.

Archives of the History of American Psychology, The Center for the History of Psychology, The University of Akron.

While still a graduate student, Mary Cover Jones used classical conditioning principles to reduce a small child's fear of rabbits. As a result, she is often called the "Mother of Behavior Therapy."

AF archive/Alamy Stock Photo

Product placement in movies is expensive, but marketers hope that audiences will form associations between their products and the positive brand of a character. If the hero drives an Audi, maybe driving an Audi will make you feel heroic, too.

CONNECTING TO RESEARCH

Classical Conditioning and Opioid Overdose

OVER 70,000 AMERICANS lost their lives in drug overdoses in 2017, and deaths related to opioids account for about two-thirds of that number (Centers for Disease & Prevention, 2019). One of the curious findings, however, is that people who die from opioid overdoses do not seem to have unusual amounts of the drug in their bodies (Siegel, 2016). Instead, it is likely that the context in which an addict uses a drug has a very important influence on the outcome.

The context provides conditioned stimuli (CSs) that predict drug effects (UCSs), which in turn stimulate compensating actions on the part of the body that will offset the drug effects (CRs). As you learned in Chapter 7, our bodies do a good job of defending homeostasis. When an addict uses a drug in a novel context, however, the CSs that lead to compensating CRs might be absent. Without compensation, an addict could die from a conventional dose of a drug.

It is ethically impossible to conduct a study to test the classical conditioning of compensatory processes in humans, but a classic study using rodents has been conducted (Siegel et al., 1982).

The Question: Are addicts at greater risk of overdose when they use their drug in a novel location?

METHODS

Three groups of rats were exposed to a lethal dose of heroin on a test day. Prior to the test day, one group received a sub-lethal dose of heroin in the same environment in which they received the test dose, a second group received the same sub-lethal dose in a different environment, and a third group, the control group, received no heroin prior to the test.

ETHICS

Many of the rats in this experiment died from the heroin. By today's standards, researchers would be asked to justify the animals' suffering in light of the outcomes gained. A smaller, less dangerous dose that would still allow conclusions to be made might be recommended. Smaller numbers of animals (this experiment used 107) might be possible if appropriate statistical methods were used.

RESULTS

As shown in Figure 8.7, rats in the control group, which had no prior exposure to heroin, were the most likely to die than the animals in the two groups with prior exposure to a sub-lethal dose. However, animals that received the high dose in a familiar place were less likely to die than animals that received the high dose in a new place.

CONCLUSIONS

This study supported the role of classical conditioning in opioid overdose. Animals that could link compensatory behaviors to contextual cues were more likely to survive a later potentially lethal dose as long as it was administered in the same place. Understanding that using a drug in an unfamiliar place is a significant risk might save the lives of some addicts. ■

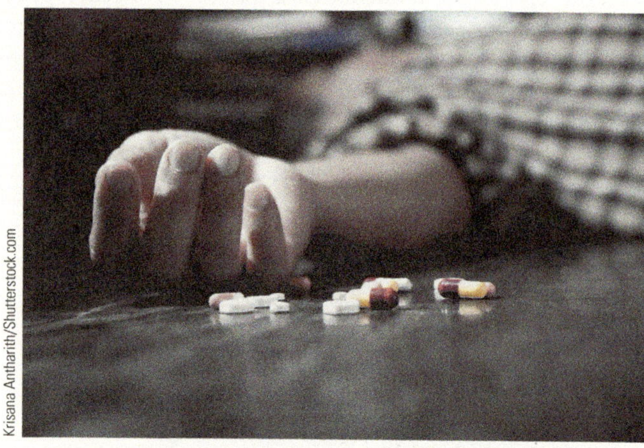

Krisana Antharith/Shutterstock.com

FIGURE 8.7

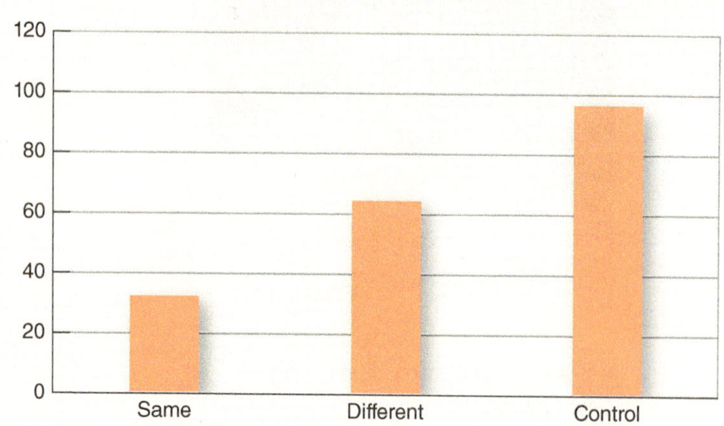

The Classical Conditioning of Opioid Overdose. Scientists were puzzled by the fact that opioid addicts were dying from relatively moderate doses. One clue to this puzzle was the observation that many of these cases involved people using drugs in unfamiliar places. Their customary locations provided powerful cues that allowed the body to compensate for the effects of the drug. Taking the drug in a new place that did not provide these cues and compensations caused problems. In this experiment (Siegel et al., 1982) control rats had not received any previous dose of heroin, and nearly all of them died when given a lethal test dose. Rats that had received a previous dose of heroin were much more likely to survive a lethal dose if both doses were administered in the same rather than a different location.

Source: S. Siegel (2016). "The Heroin Overdose Mystery." *Current Directions in Psychological Science, 25*(6), 375–379. doi:10.1177/0963721416664404

PSYCHOLOGY AS A HUB SCIENCE

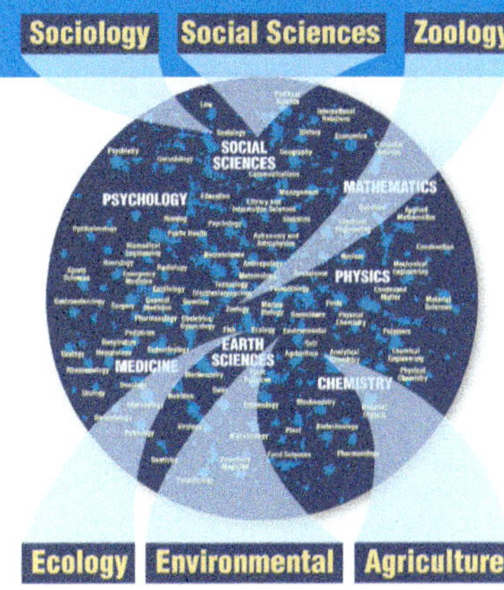

Classical Conditioning Informs Wildlife Conservation

WHILE READING ABOUT Ivan Petrovich Pavlov's experiments with salivating dogs, it might be difficult to grasp the full significance of Pavlov's results, but there were some good reasons that his laboratory continued to receive considerable resources during difficult times of war and revolution (Gantt, 1928).

As demonstrated in this chapter, the possible applications of classical conditioning range widely, from treating addictions and phobias to understanding prejudice and schizophrenia. One of the less typical applications was the result of work by John Garcia and one of his graduate students, Carl Gustavson (Gustavson et al., 1976). Gustavson was a child of the rural West, and he had grown up watching the ongoing battles among sheep ranchers, coyotes, and wolves. He asked whether the taste aversion work pioneered by Garcia might provide a useful solution.

With encouragement from Garcia, Gustavson set up an outdoor training facility with six coyotes and two wolves. The coyotes were fed rabbit meat laced with lithium chloride (LiCl), while the wolves were fed sheep meat with LiCl. He even experimented with a caged cougar that refused to eat deer meat after a single meal of venison laced with LiCl. Some of the researchers' observations of the captive animals were especially dramatic. When a lamb was tethered in the wolves' pen, the wolves approached in a normally threatening manner. The lamb froze, which is also species-typical behavior in this situation. Then, something interesting happened. The wolves sniffed at the lamb and then retreated, showing signs of defensive puppy play (crouching with ears and tail down). In response to these submissive displays, the lamb began to charge the wolves and even chased them around the pen.

Would these observations transfer to the real outdoors? The researchers distributed sheep-flavored bait and sheep carcasses laced with LiCl across a 3,000-acre sheep ranch in Washington State. A comparison of the ranch's loss records demonstrated a 30% to 60% reduction in sheep killed by coyotes following the treatment. A larger-scale test of 10 herds over a 3-year-period in Saskatchewan demonstrated a reduction in predator control costs of between 86% and 90% per year.

Gustavson's technique was used in an effort to save the endangered Mexican wolf. When released in the wild, the wolves, like Gustavson's coyotes, naturally run into conflict with ranchers and farmers. Professors Lowell Nicolaus and Dan Moriarty's initial results using conditioned taste aversion with captive gray wolves convinced U.S. government wildlife agencies to prepare to replicate the study with captive Mexican wolves (U.S. Fish and Wildlife Service, 2014). A total of 23 Mexican wolves were treated between 2011 and 2013. Two animals treated in 2011 were retested in 2012, and both still showed a conditioned aversion to cattle (U.S. Fish and Wildlife Service, 2014).

Taste aversion has also been used to boost populations of the endangered marbled murrelet (Gabriel, Halbert, & Golightly, 2014). Fake eggs designed to look like murrelet eggs were laced with carbachol and distributed in murrelet nesting areas in the Santa Cruz mountains of California. Subsequently, the number of eggs preyed upon by a key predator, Steller's jays, were reduced between 44% and 80%.

Australian quolls, small carnivorous marsupials, are another species whose survival can be enhanced through the use of taste aversion (O'Donnell et al., 2010). When quolls began feeding on an invasive species, the very toxic cane toad, they were literally wiped out in several of their habitats. Quolls who sampled treated cane toads were much more likely to survive in the wild. The authors advocated air drops of treated toads ahead of the invading species in an effort to save the quoll.

Hopefully, these promising results will encourage wildlife managers to apply taste aversion as an important tool for conservation. ■

Danita Delmont/Shutterstock.com

CraigRJD/iStock/Getty Images

Cynthia Kidwell/Shutterstock.com

Use of conditioned taste aversion to provide a nonlethal method of predator control is being explored in efforts to save a number of endangered species, including the marbled murrelet, the Australian quoll, and the Mexican wolf.

SUMMARY 8.2 Classical Conditioning Phenomena

Classical conditioning phenomenon	Description	Example
Acquisition 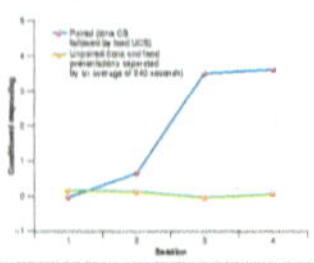	Gradual development of conditioned responses (CRs)	A dog salivates on a higher percentage of trials as training progresses.
Extinction 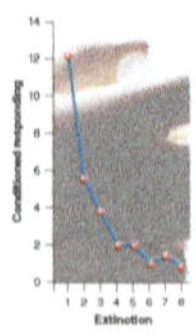	Reduction of CRs when a conditioned stimulus (CS) is presented without being followed by an unconditioned stimulus (UCS)	If the metronome is no longer followed by food, the dog stops salivating to the metronome.
Spontaneous recovery 	Reappearance of CRs following periods of rest between extinction training sessions	The dog shows no salivation at the end of the day's extinction training, but after a night of rest in the kennel, the dog salivates at the beginning of the next extinction session.
Inhibition 	A CS's prediction of the nonoccurrence of a UCS	So long as a gauge is "in the green," your equipment will not explode. You do not feel fear.
Generalization 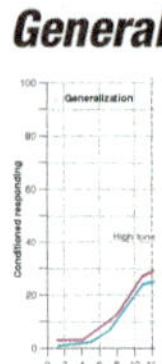	Responses to stimuli that resemble the CS	Albert's fear of white rats generalized to a Santa Claus beard.
Discrimination 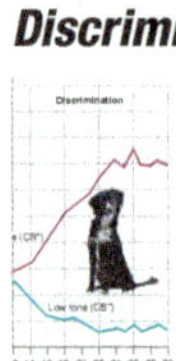	Responding to the CS, but not to similar stimuli that have not been paired with the UCS	A combat veteran learns to distinguish between the sound of gunfire and the backfire from a car.
Higher-order conditioning 	CRs to stimuli that predict the occurrence of a CS	A child who has been bitten by a dog begins to fear the street where the dog lives.
Latent inhibition 	Slower development of CRs to a familiar CS than to an unfamiliar CS	An American forms a taste aversion faster to scorpion lollipops than to hamburgers.

Credits: Second row—Corbis RF/Alamy Stock Photo; Third row—Corbis RF/Alamy Stock Photo; Fourth row—FRIEDRICHSMEIER/Alamy Stock Photo; Sixth row—Helle/Shutterstock.com; Seventh row—Tom Feiler/Masterfile; Bottom row—Steph and John Cacioppo.

What Is Operant Conditioning?

The discussion of behaviorism in Chapter 1 introduced you to Edward Thorndike and his law of effect. To recap, Thorndike had observed the learning that took place when a cat tried to escape one of his "puzzle boxes." According to Thorndike, the cats learned to escape by repeating actions that produced desirable outcomes and by eliminating behaviors that produced what he called "annoying" outcomes, or outcomes featuring either no useful effects or negative effects (1913, p. 50). Consequently, the law of effect states that a behavior will be "stamped into" an organism's repertoire depending on the consequences of the behavior (Thorndike, 1913, p. 129).

The association between a behavior and its consequences is called *operant* or *instrumental conditioning*. In this type of learning, organisms operate on their environment, and their behavior is often instrumental in producing an outcome. B. F. Skinner extended Thorndike's findings using an apparatus that bears his name—the Skinner box, a modified cage containing levers or buttons that can be pressed or pecked by animals (see ● Figure 8.8).

Operant conditioning differs from classical conditioning along several dimensions. By definition, classical conditioning is based on an association between two stimuli, whereas operant conditioning occurs when a behavior is associated with its consequences. Classical conditioning generally works best with relatively involuntary behaviors, such as fear or salivation, whereas operant conditioning involves voluntary behaviors, like walking to class or waving to a friend.

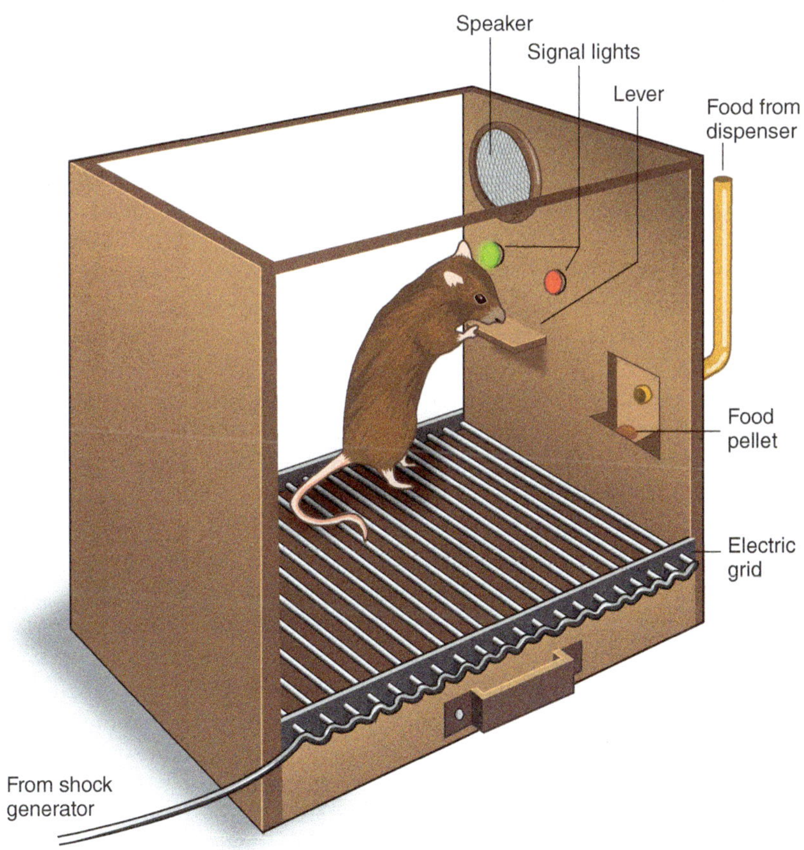

FIGURE 8.8

The Skinner Box. A specially adapted cage called a Skinner box, after behaviorist B. F. Skinner, allows researchers to investigate the results of reinforcement and punishment on the likelihood that the rat will press the bar.

TABLE 8.2

Types of Consequences

	Add stimulus to environment	Remove stimulus from environment
Increase behavior	Positive reinforcement	Negative reinforcement
Decrease behavior	Positive punishment	Negative punishment

Types of Consequences

As we all know from experience, some types of consequences increase the likelihood of behaviors, while others decrease the likelihood of behaviors. Skinner divided consequences into four classes: positive reinforcement, negative reinforcement, positive punishment, and negative punishment. Both types of reinforcement increase the frequency of their associated behaviors, whereas both types of punishment decrease the frequency of associated behaviors (see ● Table 8.2).

We all have unique sets of effective reinforcers and punishers. You might think that getting an A in a course is reinforcing, making all those extra hours spent studying worthwhile, but top grades may be less meaningful to the student sitting next to you, who came to college for the social life. A parent might spank a child, believing that spanking is an effective form of punishment, only to find that the child's unwanted behavior is becoming more rather than less frequent. For some children, the reward of getting the parent's attention overrides the discomfort of the spanking part of the interaction. In other words, the identity of a reinforcer or punisher is defined by its effects on behavior, not by some intrinsic quality of the consequence. The only accurate way to determine the impact of a consequence is to check your results. If you think you're reinforcing or punishing a behavior but the frequency of the behavior is not changing in the direction you expect, try something else.

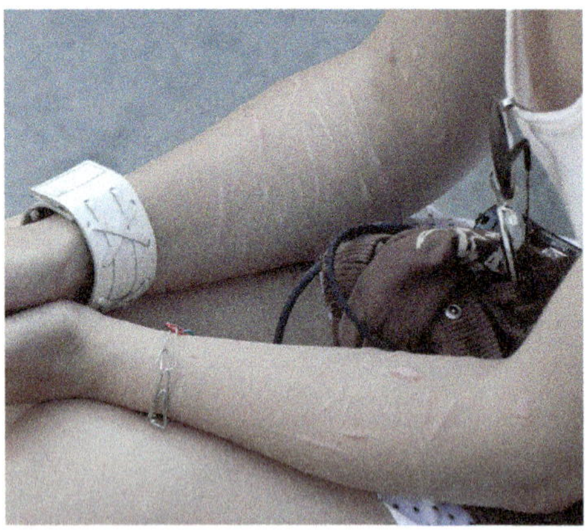

Rusig/Alamy Stock Photo

If the consequences of a behavior influence how likely a person is to repeat the behavior in the future, how can we explain the prevalence of self-injury? Why don't the painful consequences of the behavior make people stop? In situations like this, operant conditioning tells us that we need to look for possible reinforcers for the behavior that override the painful outcomes. In the case of self-injury, people report feeling calm and relief. To treat such behaviors effectively, psychologists need to understand what advantages they provide from the perspective of the person doing the behavior.

Positive Reinforcement By definition, a positive reinforcement increases the frequency of its associated behavior by adding a stimulus, a desired outcome, to the situation. Again, each person has a menu of effective reinforcements. In a common application of operant conditioning, children with autism spectrum disorder are taught language, with candy serving as the positive reinforcement. Benjamin Lahey tells of his experience trying to teach a child with autism spectrum disorder to say the syllable "ba" to obtain an M&M candy (Lahey, 1995). After 4 hours without progress, Lahey turned to the child's mother in frustration, asking her what she thought might be the problem. The mother calmly replied that her son didn't like M&Ms. Lahey switched to the child's preferred treat, chopped carrots, and the child quickly began saying "ba." Chopped carrots are probably not the first reinforcer you would try with a 4-year-old boy, but in this case, they made all the difference.

If everyone has a different set of effective reinforcers, how do we know which to use? A simple technique for predicting what a particular animal or person will find reinforcing is the Premack principle, which states that whatever behavior an organism spends the most time and energy doing is likely to be important to that organism (Premack, 1965). If Lahey had been able to observe his young client's eating habits before starting training, it is unlikely that he would have made the mistake of offering M&Ms as reinforcers. The opportunity to engage in a higher-priority activity is always capable of rewarding a lower-priority activity. Your grandmother may never have heard of Premack, but she knows that telling you to eat your broccoli to get an ice cream generally works.

Both Thorndike and Skinner agreed that positive reinforcement is a powerful tool for managing behavior. In our later discussion of punishment, we will argue that the effects of positive reinforcement are more powerful than the effects of punishment. Unfortunately, in Western culture, we tend to provide relatively little positive reinforcement. We are more likely to hear about our mistakes from our boss than all the things we've done correctly. It is possible that we feel entitled to good treatment from others, so we feel that we should not have to provide any reward for reasonably expected behaviors. The problem with this approach is that extinction occurs in operant, as well as in classical, conditioning. A behavior that is no longer reinforced drops in frequency. By ignoring other people's desirable behaviors instead of reinforcing them, perhaps with a simple thank-you, we risk reducing their frequency.

The Premack principle can help you maintain good time management. If you prefer socializing to studying, use the opportunity to socialize as a reward for meeting your evening's study goals.

THINKING SCIENTIFICALLY

Is Too Much Praise Bad for Children?

In this chapter, we mentioned that many people fail to provide positive reinforcement because they already feel entitled to good treatment. We encouraged you to consider ways to increase the amount of positive feedback you give to others to prevent putting desirable behaviors on extinction. But can we have too much of a good thing? Can too much praise produce negative outcomes? Is there a right way and a wrong way to provide positive feedback?

WHAT AM I BEING ASKED TO BELIEVE OR ACCEPT?

We're being asked to believe that positive reinforcement has the potential to produce negative outcomes under some circumstances.

WHAT EVIDENCE SUPPORTS THIS POSITION?

We often hear adults providing inflated praise to children, such as saying "that's the most beautiful drawing ever!" Unfortunately, for some children, inflated praise can reduce their willingness to take on challenging problems (Brummelman et al., 2014).

In another study, "overvaluation" of the child by the parents was associated with the child's having a higher narcissism score (Brummelman et al., 2015). Narcissism is characterized by feelings of superiority and of deserving of special treatment. When this characteristic is extreme, a person might be diagnosed with narcissistic personality disorder, described further in Chapter 14. "Overvaluation" by parents is evident in their beliefs that their child is more special and more entitled than others. This is distinct from parental warmth, which is characterized by affection and more modest appreciation for the child.

Andrew Twort/Alamy Stock Photo

ARE THERE OTHER WAYS THAT THIS EVIDENCE COULD BE INTERPRETED?

Praise is not the only feedback children receive from adults. Children are also on the receiving end of criticism, and often much of it. Studies on the effects of praise on children have not considered any background levels of criticism or negative feedback. What if the same parents who said "great job" more frequently were the same ones who were just as free with their critical comments when things go wrong?

WHAT OTHER EVIDENCE WOULD I NEED TO EVALUATE THESE ALTERNATIVES?

A more global view of all of the feedback received by a child, positive and negative, might provide us with a clearer picture of how praise affects children.

WHAT ARE THE MOST REASONABLE CONCLUSIONS?

Praise done well is likely to have positive outcomes, but how do we know how to praise well? As we mentioned frequently in this chapter, consequences must matter to the individual receiving them before they impact behavior. If children hear "good job" or "you're the best" all the time, especially when they realize that they didn't do such a good job or are the best one, the praise will have little reinforcing value. The best feedback is specific—"I like how you put all your toys away in the right places." Another important step is to evaluate your results. If your approach to praise is not producing more of the behavior you want, then try another approach. ■

Some reinforcers, known as *primary reinforcers*, are effective because of their natural roles in survival, such as food. Others must be learned. We are not born valuing money, grades, or gold medals. These are examples of **conditioned reinforcers**, also called *secondary reinforcers*, that gain their value and ability to influence behavior from being associated with other things we value. Here, we see an intersection between classical and operant conditioning. If you always say "good dog" before you provide your pet with a treat, saying "good dog" becomes a CS for food (the UCS) that can now be used to reinforce compliance with commands to come, sit, or heel (operant behaviors). Classical conditioning establishes the value of "good dog," and operant conditioning describes the use of "good dog" to reinforce the dog's voluntary behavior.

conditioned reinforcer A reinforcer that gains value from being associated with other things that are valued; also known as a *secondary reinforcer*.

Humans are capable of generating long chains of conditioned reinforcers extending far into the future. We might ask you why you are studying this textbook right now, at this moment. A psychologist might answer that you are studying now because studying will be reinforced by a good grade at the end of the term, which in turn will be reinforced by

Carolyn Jenkins/Alamy Stock Photo

Itani/Alamy Stock Photo

a diploma at the end of your college education, which in turn will be reinforced by a good job after graduation, which in turn will be reinforced by a good salary, which will allow you to live in a nice house, drive a nice car, wear nice clothes, eat good food, and provide the same for your family in the coming years.

According to the Premack principle, a preferred activity can be used to reinforce a less preferred activity. Most children prefer candy over carrots, so rewarding a child with candy for eating carrots often increases carrot consumption. One little boy with autism spectrum disorder, however, preferred carrots to M&Ms, and his training proceeded more smoothly when carrot rewards were substituted for candy rewards.

Negative Reinforcement **Negative reinforcement,** which sounds contradictory, involves the removal of a stimulus, an unpleasant consequence, from a situation to increase the frequency of an associated behavior. Negative reinforcement increases the frequency of behaviors that allow an organism to avoid, turn off, or postpone an unpleasant consequence; these are sometimes called *escape* and *avoidance behaviors*.

Let's look at a laboratory example of negative reinforcement before tackling real-world examples. If a hungry rat in a Skinner box learns that pressing a bar produces food, a positive consequence, we would expect the frequency of bar pressing to increase. This would be an instance of positive reinforcement. However, if pressing the bar turns off or delays the administration of an electric shock, we would still expect the frequency of bar pressing to increase. This would be an instance of negative reinforcement.

negative reinforcement A method for increasing behaviors that allow an organism to escape or avoid an unpleasant consequence.

Be careful to avoid confusing negative reinforcement with punishment, which is covered in the next section. By definition, a punishment decreases the frequency of the behaviors that it follows, whereas both positive and negative reinforcers increase the frequency of the behaviors that they follow. Returning to our Skinner box example, the rat's bar pressing increases following both positive reinforcement (food) and negative reinforcement (turning off a shock). If we shocked the rat every time it pressed the bar (punishment), it would stop pressing the bar quickly.

Many everyday behaviors are maintained by negative reinforcement. We buckle up in our cars to turn off annoying beeps or bells, open umbrellas to avoid getting wet, scratch an insect bite to relieve the itch, take an aspirin to escape a headache, apply sunscreen to avoid a sunburn or skin cancer, and apologize to avoid further misunderstandings with a friend.

In many real-world cases, positive and negative reinforcement act on behavior simultaneously. A heroin addict uses the drug to obtain a state of euphoria (positive reinforcer) but also to eliminate the unpleasant symptoms of withdrawal (negative reinforcer). You might study hard to achieve high grades (positive reinforcers) while also being motivated by the need to avoid low grades (negative reinforcers).

PA Images/Alamy Stock Photo

Serena Williams "loves" her Wimbledon trophy not for its intrinsic value (you can't eat it, etc.), but because trophies have become conditioned reinforcers.

Many superstitious behaviors, like wearing your "lucky socks," can be learned through operant conditioning. Operant conditioning does not require a behavior to cause a positive outcome to be strengthened. All that is required is that a behavior be followed by a positive outcome. Unless you suddenly have a string of bad performances while wearing the lucky socks, you are unlikely to have an opportunity to unlearn your superstition.

Punishment A **punishment** is any consequence that reduces the frequency of an associated behavior. **Positive punishment** refers to adding an aversive consequence to a situation that reduces the frequency of or eliminates a behavior. As described previously, we can demonstrate that a rat will quickly stop pressing a bar if each press results in an electric shock. **Negative punishment** involves the removal of something desirable from a situation to reduce the frequency of an associated behavior. In the Skinner box, we can change the rules for a rat that has learned previously to press a bar for food. Now, food is made available *unless* the rat presses the bar. Under these conditions, the rat will also quickly stop pressing the bar.

punishment A consequence that eliminates or reduces the frequency of a behavior.

positive punishment A consequence that eliminates or reduces the frequency of a behavior by applying an aversive stimulus.

negative punishment A method for reducing behavior by removing something desirable whenever the target behavior occurs.

Thorndike and Skinner were in agreement about the relative weakness of punishment compared to reinforcement as a means of controlling behavior. Three conditions must be met for punishment to have observable effects on behavior: significance, immediacy, and consistency (Schwartz, 1984). These same variables also influence reinforcement, but meeting these requirements while applying punishments in real-world settings can be more challenging. Many parents in the United States administer spankings to their young children, but there is no evidence that spankings reduce unwanted behavior. Instead, the evidence points toward increases in unwanted behaviors in children who are spanked (Gershoff et al., 2017).

As we observed in the case of the little boy willing to work for carrots but not for candy, reinforcers have to matter to the person or animal receiving them (i.e., significance). The same is true of punishments. If we use a punishment that is too mild for a particular individual, there is little incentive for that person to change behavior. Some students are willing to risk a ticket for parking illegally at their campus. How high would a parking fee have to be to gain complete compliance? What if you risked the death penalty for parking illegally? We can be fairly certain that most people would leave their cars at home rather than risk that particular consequence. The point is that punishment works if a sufficiently severe consequence is selected, but using the amount of force needed to produce results can be impractical and unethical. Free societies have long-standing social prohibitions against cruel and unusual punishments, and these conventions are incompatible with using the force that is needed to change the behavior of some individuals.

Greg McWilliams/Icon SMI 408/Greg McWilliams/Icon SMI/Newscom

Putting up an umbrella to avoid getting wet from the rain is an example of a negatively reinforced behavior.

Immediate rewards and punishments are more effective than delayed rewards and punishments (i.e., immediacy). For the rat in the Skinner box, delays of just 10 seconds can reduce the effectiveness of electric shock as a punisher. Humans are more capable than rats at bridging long intervals (Kamin, 1959). Nonetheless, the same principle holds true. Delayed punishment is less effective than immediate punishment. We should not be surprised that the months or years that are required to try and convict a serious criminal may greatly reduce the impact of imprisonment on that person's subsequent behavior.

Our final requirement for effective consequences is consistency. We can see the effects of inconsistent punishment in the behavior of people living in larger cities that feature high-occupancy vehicle (HOV) lanes. As many as 80% to 90% of the cars using the lanes have single occupants instead of the required two or more (Boston Globe, 2019). Some cities are investigating the use of cameras to enforce their HOV policies. Although cameras raise privacy concerns, the number of people misusing the lanes should decrease due to more consistent punishment.

Ernest R. Prim/Shutterstock.com

The degree of certainty of getting a ticket influences drivers' behavior. At an intersection with cameras, drivers are unlikely to run a red light, but at other intersections, behavior might be determined by whether a police officer is nearby.

Diverse Voices in Psychology

Does Physical Punishment Have Different Effects in Different Cultural Contexts?

PhotoAlto/Sandro Di Carlo Darsa/Brand X Pictures/Getty Images

Psychologists have wondered if spanking had different effects within different racial and ethnic contexts, but it does not. Spanking is associated with higher levels of child aggression, regardless of racial or ethnic context.

PSYCHOLOGISTS TYPICALLY RECOMMEND against the use of physical punishment with children, largely due to research showing a relationship between the use of physical punishment and increased aggressiveness on the part of a child. In addition, as you have seen in this chapter, there are many alternative ways to manage behavior successfully.

As is the case with many types of psychological research, however, the classic studies on physical punishment and child aggression were conducted with middle-class, white American families. How representative are these samples of families in general? Some researchers believe that they are not representative and that physical punishment effects depend very much on cultural context (Deater-Deckard & Dodge, 1997). These researchers believe that physical punishment in cultures in which it is considered "normal" has a much less detrimental effect than in cultures where it is considered less normal.

Racial and ethnic groups vary in the frequency with which they use physical punishment (Gershoff et al., 2012). In a sample of over 11,000 U.S. families with kindergarten-aged children, rates of spanking were generally high (about 80%) across all groups, with 89% of African Americans, 79% of whites, 80% of Hispanics, and 73% of Asians reporting having spanked their child. When asked if they had spanked their child in the previous week, 40% of African Americans, 28% of Hispanics, 24% of whites, and 23% of Asians reported that they had done so.

Does spanking have different effects on children's behavior across the racial and ethnic groups due to these different frequencies? Gershoff et al. (2012) concluded that it does not. Across all racial and ethnic groups, spanking was associated with higher levels of aggressive behaviors in the child, which in turn leads to more spanking in a "coercive cycle" of parenting. Expanding the diversity of participants even further, researchers have reported negative relationships between spanking and socioemotional development in children in 59 countries with no correlations in another five (Pace et al., 2019). In no country was spanking associated with improved socioemotional outcomes in children.

While many lines of research benefit from considerations of diversity, the message here is not modified by racial or ethnic identity—spanking children not only fails to decrease negative behaviors, but it actually appears to increase them. ■

If punishment is difficult to do correctly and ethically, how are we supposed to reduce unwanted behaviors? To solve this problem, Skinner (1953) recommended extinction as an alternative to punishment. In the discussion of classical conditioning earlier in this chapter, the term *extinction* was used to refer to the disappearance of CRs that occurs when the CS no longer signals the arrival of a UCS. Extinction in operant conditioning has a similar meaning. Learned behaviors stop when they are no longer followed by a reinforcing consequence. Attention is a powerful reinforcer for humans, and ignoring negative behavior should extinguish it. Parents and teachers cannot look the other way when one child is being physically aggressive toward another, but in many other instances, Skinner's approach is quite successful in reducing the frequency of unwanted behaviors (Brown & Elliot, 1965). Although ignoring a child's tantrums in a supermarket can be embarrassing for many parents, this can be an effective strategy for reducing their frequency.

Schedules of Reinforcement

Reinforcing a behavior every time it occurs is known as *continuous reinforcement*. Although it is highly desirable to use continuous reinforcement when a new behavior is being learned, it is inconvenient to do so forever. Dog owners want their dogs to walk with a loose leash, but once this skill is learned, the owners don't want to carry dog treats for reinforcement whenever they walk their dogs. Once we deviate from continuous reinforcement, however, the manner in which we do so may have a dramatic impact on the target behavior. To obtain the results we want, it is helpful to understand what happens when we use **partial reinforcement**, or the reinforcement of the desired behavior on some occasions, but not others.

partial reinforcement The reinforcement of a desired behavior on some occasions, but not others.

fixed ratio (FR) schedule A schedule of reinforcement in which reinforcement occurs following a set number of behaviors.

Psychologists have identified many ways to apply partial reinforcement, but we will concentrate on two variations: ratio schedules and interval schedules. In a ratio schedule of partial reinforcement, reinforcement depends on the number of times a behavior occurs. In an interval schedule of partial reinforcement, reinforcement depends on the passage of a certain amount of time. Either type of schedule, ratio or interval, can be fixed or variable. In fixed schedules, the requirements for reinforcement never vary. In variable schedules, the requirements for reinforcement are allowed to fluctuate from trial to trial, averaging a certain amount over the course of a learning session.

Fixed Ratio Schedules A **fixed ratio (FR) schedule** requires that a behavior occur a set number of times for each reinforcer. Continuous reinforcement, discussed earlier, is equivalent to an FR of 1. If we now raise our requirement to two behaviors per reinforcer, we have an FR schedule of 2, and so on. Using the Skinner box, we can investigate the influence of FR schedules on the rate at which a rat will press a bar for food. To do so, we track cumulative responses as a function of time. FR schedules produce a characteristic pattern of responding. In general, responses are fairly steady, with a significant pause following each reward. As the amount of work for each reward is increased, responding becomes slower (see Figure 8.9).

In early industrial settings, workers were often paid by the piece, a real-world example of the use of an FR schedule. In other words, workers would be paid every time they produced a fixed number of products or parts on an assembly line. Most workers find this system less than ideal. If the equipment malfunctions, the worker cannot earn money. Lunch breaks would also then be viewed as loss of income rather than a helpful time of rest. Some examples of piecework remain today, including the work of most physicians, who get paid by the procedure, and service workers like plumbers or hairstylists, who get paid for finishing a specific task.

SCPhotos/Alamy Stock Photo

Workers in the garment industry are often paid by the piece, or with a set amount of money for each finished garment. This compensation system is an example of a fixed ratio (FR) schedule. Because workers cannot make money when their equipment breaks down and they tend to view lunch and other breaks as costing them money, this schedule is not considered to be fair to workers.

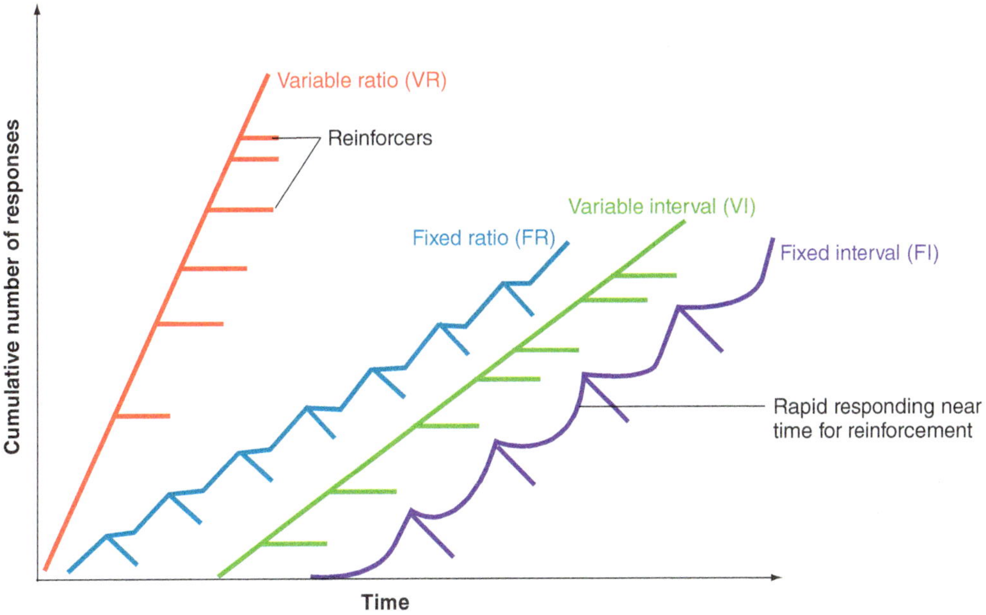

FIGURE **8.9**

Schedules of Reinforcement. The schedule used to deliver reinforcement has a big impact on the resulting behavior. In general, the variable schedules produce higher rates of responding than do their fixed counterparts. The fixed interval schedule produces a characteristic pattern of low rates of responding at the beginning of the interval and accelerated responding as the end of the interval approaches.

Tetra Images/Photoshot

Most casinos feature a large number of slot machines, which are essentially Skinner boxes for people. The slot machine is programmed on a variable ratio (VR) schedule, which means that the player cannot predict how many plays it will take to win. In response, players exhibit the same high, steady rate of responding that we observe in rats working on VR schedules in the laboratory.

Variable Ratio Schedules As in FR schedules, **variable ratio (VR) schedules** also involve counting the number of times that a behavior occurs. However, this time the required number of behaviors is allowed to fluctuate around some average amount.

In the Skinner box, we might set our VR schedule to 10 for a 1-hour session. This means that over the course of the session, the rat must press an average of 10 times to receive each food pellet. However, this schedule may mean that only 1 press delivers food on one trial, but 30 presses are required on the next trial. The rat is unable to predict when reinforcement is likely to occur, leading to a high, steady rate of responding in our cumulative record. We do not see the characteristic pausing observed following reinforcement in the FR schedule because the rat cannot predict when the next reward will occur.

variable ratio (VR) schedule A schedule of reinforcement in which reinforcement occurs following some variable number of behaviors.

fixed interval (FI) schedule A schedule of reinforcement in which the first response following a specified interval is reinforced.

variable interval (VI) schedule A schedule of reinforcement in which the first response following a varying period is reinforced.

One of the most dramatic real-world examples of the VR schedule is the programming of slot machines in casinos. Slot machines are human versions of Skinner boxes that use VR schedules. The casino sets the machine to pay off after some average number of plays, but the player doesn't know whether a payoff will occur after one coin or thousands are inserted. You don't have to observe the behavior of people playing slot machines long to see a demonstration of the high, steady responding that characterizes the VR schedule. The programming of slot machines can be sophisticated. Slot machines that are located in places where people are unlikely to return (airports and bus stations) pay off less frequently than those in places where people are more likely to play regularly.

Concerns about the effects of piecework on worker well-being contributed to the Fair Labor Standards Act of 1938, which included a provision for a minimum hourly wage.

Fixed Interval Schedules Unlike ratio schedules, reinforcement in interval schedules depends on the passage of time rather than the number of responses produced. In a **fixed interval (FI) schedule**, the time that must pass before reinforcement becomes available following a single response is set to a certain amount. In the Skinner box, a rat's first bar press starts a timer. Responses that occur before the timer counts down are not reinforced. As soon as the timer counts down to zero, the rat's next bar press is reinforced, and the timer starts counting down again. In the FI schedule, the interval is the same from trial to trial. Animals and people have a good general sense of the passage of time, leading to a characteristic pattern of responding in FI situations. Reinforcement is followed by a long pause. As the end of the interval is anticipated, responding increases sharply. A graph of the number of bills passed by the U.S. Congress as a function of time looks similar to the rat's performance on an FI schedule in the Skinner box (Weisberg & Waldrop, 1972). Few bills are passed at the beginning of a session, but many are passed at the end (see Figure 8.10).

Variable Interval Schedules As you already may have guessed, the **variable interval (VI) schedule** is characterized by an interval that is allowed to fluctuate around some average amount over the course of a session. This time, our bar-pressing rat experiences intervals that range around some average amount (say, 2 minutes). On one trial, the rat may obtain reinforcement after only 30 seconds, whereas the next trial may involve an interval of 5 minutes. Over the session, the average of all intervals is 2 minutes. As in the VR situation, we see a high, steady rate of responding.

You are probably quite familiar with VI schedules in the form of pop quizzes administered by your professors. Your professor might tell you that there will be five quizzes given during the term, but the timing of the quizzes remains a surprise. You might have the first two only 1 day apart, followed by a 2-week interval before the next quiz. Your best strategy, like the rat in the Skinner box on a VI schedule, is to emit a high, steady rate of behavior—studying, in this case.

FIGURE 8.10

Congress and Fixed Interval (FI) Behavior. As the end of a congressional session approaches, the U.S. Congress begins to pass more bills in patterns that look similar to the behavior of rats on FI schedules in Skinner boxes.

Source: T. S. Critchfield et al. (2003). "A Half Century of Scalloping In the Work Habits of the United States Congress," *Journal of Applied Behavior Analysis, 36*(4), 465–486. doi: 10.1901/jaba.2003.36-465

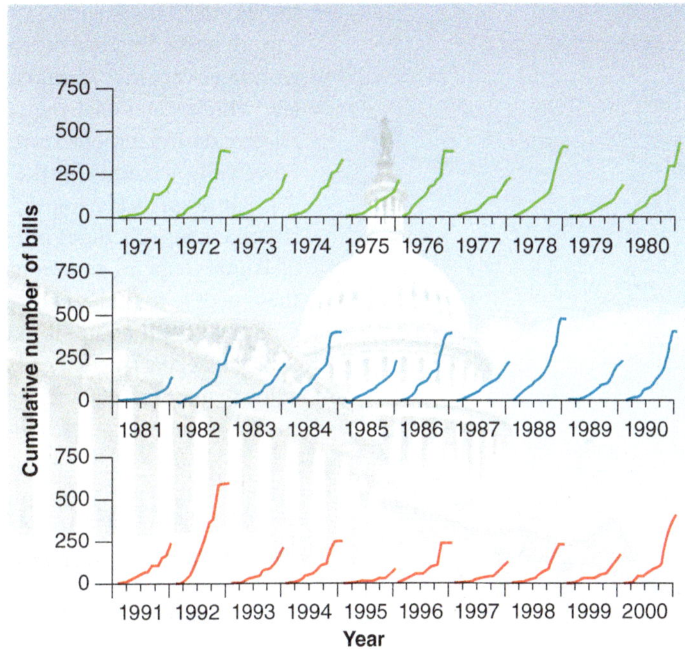

Library of Congress, Prints & Photographs Division, Reproduction number LC-DIG-highsm-12649 (digital file from original) LC-HS503-1388 (color film transparency)

Partial Reinforcement Effect in Extinction

Many parents have regretted the day that they unintentionally put an unwanted behavior on a partial reinforcement schedule by uttering the words, "OK, just this once." Perhaps a parent is strongly opposed to buying candy for a child at the supermarket checkout counter (where, because of John Watson and his applications of psychology to advertising, candy is displayed conveniently at child's-eye height). Then comes the fateful day when the parent is late coming home from work, the child is hungry because dinner is delayed, and unintentionally, the parent gives in "just this once," putting begging for candy behavior on a variable schedule. Subsequently, when the parent returns to the previous refusal to buy candy, a high, steady rate of begging behavior occurs before it finally extinguishes.

In the laboratory once more, we compare the behavior of two rats in separate Skinner boxes. One is working on a continuous (or FR 1) schedule of reinforcement. The other is working on a partial schedule of reinforcement (perhaps a VR 3 schedule). After several sessions of training, we stop reinforcement for both rats. It may surprise you to learn that the rat working on the continuous schedule will stop pressing long before the rat accustomed to the VR 3 schedule. In other words, extinction occurs more rapidly following continuous reinforcement than following partial schedules. This outcome is known as the **partial reinforcement effect in extinction**.

partial reinforcement effect in extinction The more rapid extinction observed following continuous reinforcement compared to that following partial reinforcement.

The partial reinforcement effect probably occurs because of one of two factors, or a combination of both. First, the transition from continuous reinforcement to extinction is more obvious than the transition from a partial schedule to extinction. If you are accustomed to being paid for a babysitting job every time you work, you will definitely notice any of your employer's failures to pay. In contrast, if your neighbor typically pays you about once a month for raking his yard each weekend, you might not notice right away that he hasn't paid you for a while. Second, partial schedules teach organisms to persist in the face of nonreinforcement. In a sense, partial schedules teach us to work through periods in which reinforcement does not occur. Consequently, we might view extinction as just another case where continuing to perform might eventually produce reinforcement. When positive behavior is occurring, such as working on your senior thesis regularly despite a much-delayed grade, persistence is an enormous advantage. However, as shown in our earlier example of begging for candy, placing an undesirable behavior on partial reinforcement makes it more difficult to extinguish.

Comparing Schedules

What happens if you are exposed to two or more schedules of reinforcement at the

Fishing works according to a variable interval (VI) schedule of reinforcement. Fish (the reinforcers) are caught after periods of waiting for fish to bite that vary in length. As in laboratory demonstrations of the VI schedule, fishing usually produces a steady rate of responding.

lunamarina/Shutterstock.com

same time? This scenario is realistic because we face these types of choices every day. Which is a more rewarding use of my time: studying for my midterm or making some extra money by working overtime? In making these types of choices, animals and people follow the matching law, which states that the relative frequency of responding to one alternative will match the relative reinforcement for responses on that alternative (Herrnstein & Heyman, 1979). The law powerfully accounts for the effects on behavior of frequency, magnitude, and delays in reward.

Time spent playing online video games provides an interesting example of the effects of simultaneous schedules of reinforcement. The millions of users of online games such as *World of Warcraft* spend an average of 22 hours per week on their games (Yee, 2006). What compels these people to make a choice favoring online interactions over face-to-face social experiences? One clue to this choice is that substantial numbers of players report that "the most rewarding or satisfying experience" they had over the last 7 or 30 days took place while gaming. We would assume that if the frequency and magnitude of rewards available in gaming were higher than those in face-to-face socializing, people would choose to spend their time accordingly.

The Method of Successive Approximations (Shaping)

So far, this discussion of operant conditioning has centered on increasing or decreasing the frequency of a particular behavior. What happens if you want to increase the frequency of a behavior that rarely or never occurs? Most parents would like to teach their children to use good table manners, but you could wait a long time for the opportunity to reward young children for using the correct utensil to eat their food.

method of successive approximations A method for increasing the frequency of behaviors that never or rarely occur; also known as *shaping*.

Fortunately, we have a method for increasing the frequency of behaviors that never or rarely occur. Using the **method of successive approximations**, or *shaping*, we begin by reinforcing spontaneous behaviors that are somewhat similar to the target behavior that we want to train. As training continues, we use gradually more stringent requirements for reinforcement until the exact behavior that we want occurs. You can think of shaping as a funnel. Using the table manners example, parents start out with generous criteria for reinforcement ("Thank you for picking up the spoon") and gradually narrow the criteria ("Thank you for putting the spoon in the food") until they are reinforcing only the target behavior ("Thank you for using the spoon to eat your applesauce"). One of the most positive features about the shaping process is that behavior doesn't have to be perfect to produce reinforcement.

The rats in Skinner boxes that have been described in this chapter do not spontaneously start pressing levers. We have to teach them to do so. We begin by making sure the hungry rat understands that food is available in the Skinner box. Using a remote control, we activate the food dispenser a few times. Quickly, the rat forms a classically conditioned association between the sound of the food dispenser (CS) and the arrival of food (UCS) in the cup. However, if we continue to feed the rat in this manner, it is unlikely that it will ever learn to press the bar. Indeed, there is no reason for it to do so because it already is obtaining the food it needs. So, we narrow our criteria for obtaining food from simply existing in the box to standing in the corner of the box that contains the bar. If we press our remote control every time the rat is in the correct corner, it will begin to stay there most of the time. Now we want the rat to rear on its back feet so that it is likely to hit the bar with its front feet on the way down. If we begin to reinforce the rat less frequently for staying in the corner, it will begin to explore. Eventually, the rat is likely to hit the bar with its front feet while exploring, pressing the bar. Now it will begin to press the bar on its own. In the hands of an experienced trainer, this process takes about half an hour.

Pictorial Press Ltd/Alamy Stock Photo

Whether training imaginary raptors in *Jurassic World* or real animals, using the method of successive approximations (shaping) can lead to the reliable performance of otherwise low-frequency behaviors. Like Chris Pratt's character, most trainers use a combination of classical conditioning (clicker sound leads to food) and operant conditioning (approximation of desired behavior leads to clicker sound).

Shaping involves a delicate tightrope walk between too much and too little reinforcement. If we reinforce too generously, learning stops because there is no incentive for change. If your piano teacher always tells you that your performances are perfect, you will stop trying to improve them. However, if we don't reinforce frequently enough, the learner becomes discouraged. Reinforcement provides important feedback to the learner, so insufficient reinforcement may slow or stop the learning process.

Teaching a complex behavior requires *chaining*, or breaking down the behavior into manageable steps. Chaining can be done in a forward direction, such as teaching the letters of the alphabet from A to Z, or in a backward direction, such as teaching the last step in a sequence, then the next to the last, and so on. Chaining can be useful when teaching new skills, such as working independently on academic projects, to children with special needs (Pelios et al., 2003). Backward chaining is used by most trainers of animals used in entertainment. For example, dogs have been taught to perform complex dances like the Macarena (Burch & Bailey, 1999). The trainer uses a verbal, gestural, or clicker cue while shaping the last step in the dance. When the dog performs this last step reliably, the trainer adds the next-to-last step, and so on until the entire complex sequence is mastered. You might have seen Internet memes featuring squirrels that perform a long sequence of tricks before reaching a bird feeder. It is likely that they learned this sequence through backward chaining, as new obstacles are added once the previous ones were mastered.

Cognitive, Biological, and Social Influences on Operant Conditioning

Even the most radical behaviorists, including Skinner, did not deny the existence of cognitive, social, or biological influences on learning (Jensen & Burgess, 1997). Instead, behaviorists believed that internal processes followed the same rules as externally observable behavior. As Skinner (1953) wrote, "We need not suppose that events which take place within an organism's skin have special properties. . . . A private event may be distinguished by its limited accessibility but not, so far as we know, by any special nature or structure" (p. 257). However, as we saw in the case of classical conditioning, the results of some operant conditioning experiments stimulated greater interest in the cognitive, social, and biological processes involved in learning.

Cognitive Influences on Operant Conditioning

One of the important principles of operant conditioning is that consequences are required in order for learning to occur. Edward Tolman (1948) challenged this notion by allowing his rats to explore mazes without food reinforcement. Subsequently, when food was placed in the goal boxes of the mazes, the previously unreinforced rats performed as well as the rats that had been reinforced all along. Tolman referred to the rats' ability to learn in the absence of reinforcement as **latent learning**. He argued that the rats had learned while just exploring, but that they did not demonstrate their learning until motivated by the food reward to do so. We usually judge whether learning has occurred by observing outward behavior. Tolman's rats remind us that there is a difference between what has been learned and what is performed. Students are all too familiar with the experience of performing poorly on exams despite having learned a great deal about the material.

latent learning Learning that occurs in the absence of reinforcement.

In addition to challenging the role of reinforcement in learning, Tolman disputed traditional behaviorist explanations of the nature of the learning that occurred in mazes. He believed that instead of learning a simple operant "turn right for food" association, rats learned "This is where I can find food" (Tolman, 1948, 1959). After training rats to follow a path in a maze to find food, Tolman blocked the path but allowed the rats to choose from a number of additional paths. If the rats had learned a simple turn left–get food response, they should have chosen the paths that were most similar to the training path. Instead, they showed evidence of choosing paths that required them to turn in a different direction from their previously trained path, but one that led them directly to the goal (Tolman et al., 1946; see Figure 8.11).

To account for his results, Tolman suggested that the rats had formed cognitive maps, or mental representations of the mazes. Map formation was viewed as a unique, nonassociative

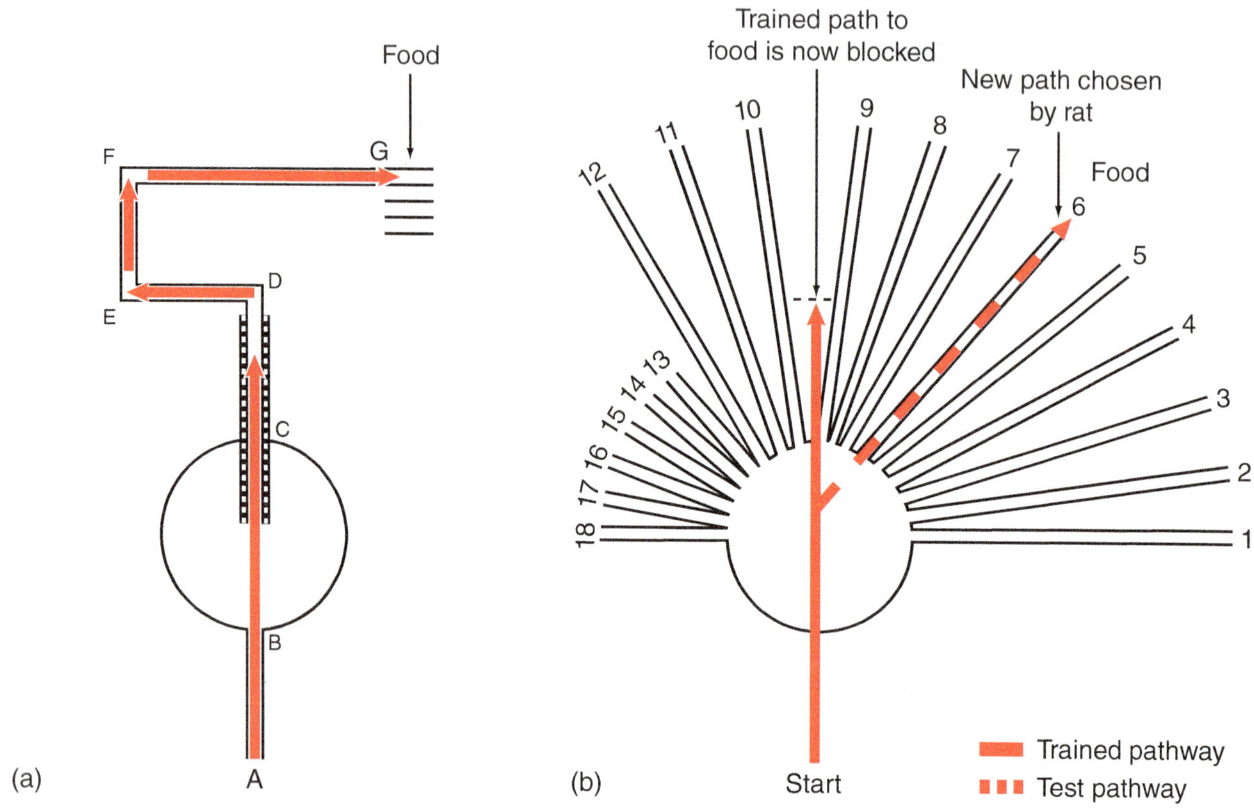

FIGURE 8.11

Tolman's Maze. Edward Tolman did not believe that rats wandering around a maze learned "turn left for food" in the way that early behaviorists believed that they did. Instead, Tolman believed that the rats were learning a more cognitive map of where they could find food. He provided evidence for his approach by blocking a learned pathway to food. If the behaviorists were right, the rats should choose the path most similar to the trained one (a). However, the rats did not do that. They showed evidence of having formed cognitive maps and were willing to turn in a different direction if that path led to food (b).

learning process that didn't follow the previously established rules of associative learning (O'Keefe & Nadel, 1978). For example, in contrast to the gradual acquisition of learning that usually occurs in classical and operant conditioning, cognitive maps are instantly updated when new information becomes available.

Chimpanzees show considerable ability to form cognitive maps (Menzel, 1978). After being carried around a circuitous route in their one-acre compound as nine vegetables and nine fruits were placed in 18 locations, chimpanzees were released in the center of the compound. They not only navigated to each food location using the shortest pathways, but, given their preference for fruit over vegetables, they visited the spots containing fruit first. They showed no indication that they were attempting to retrace the pathway over which they were carried as the food was put in place.

Biological Influences on Operant Conditioning Just as the work of Garcia and Koelling highlighted the need to consider biological limitations on classical conditioning, biological boundaries in operant conditioning were described by Keller and Marion Breland, two of Skinner's former students. In their 1961 article titled "The Misbehavior of Organisms" (a wordplay on Skinner's classic book, *The Behavior of Organisms*), the Brelands outlined some challenges they encountered while using operant conditioning to train animals for entertainment.

In one instance, the researchers described how they sought to train a pig to pick up large wooden coins and deposit the coins in a large, wooden "piggy bank." Initially, all went well. The pig would quickly learn to deposit four or five coins (an example of an FR schedule) for each food reward. Eventually, however, the pig began to work slower and slower, to the point where it couldn't obtain enough food for the day. Instead of taking the coins to the piggy bank, the pig would repeatedly toss them in the air and sniff around to find them. Raccoons trained with the coins ultimately tried to wash them instead of depositing them in the bank. The animals' natural approach to food (the rooting by the pigs and the washing by the raccoons) began to interfere with their handling of the coins. You may already have suspected that the coins had become the object of some higher-order classical conditioning because of their relationship with food. The Brelands concluded "that these animals are trapped by strong instinctive behaviors, and clearly we have here a demonstration of the prepotency of such behavior patterns over those which have been conditioned. We have termed this phenomenon 'instinctive drift'" (Breland & Breland, 1961, p. 683).

Social Influences on Operant Conditioning So far, our discussion of classical and operant conditioning has focused on the individual in isolation. Learning can take place when people or animals are alone, but it often occurs in the presence of others, especially in a species as social as ours. As we will see in a later section, people are particularly likely to learn by observing others. What do we know about the impact of others on our operant learning?

The presence of others may not just promote learning; it also may be necessary for learning. Human infants learn more about language when they are listening to another person face to face than when they are watching a person speak on television (Kuhl, 2007; Meltzoff et al., 2009). Although operant conditioning alone cannot account for language learning, as discussed in Chapters 10 and 11, these results emphasize the importance of social interaction in producing the arousal, focus, and motivation that contribute to effective learning. We are still in the process of evaluating the impact of moving school instruction from face-to-face to online formats.

Hulton Deutsch/Corbis Historical/Getty Images

Keller Breland observes the performance of one of the star pupils of the I.Q. Zoo attraction he developed with his wife, Marian. Unfortunately, the Brelands discovered that the animals' instinctive behaviors often interfered with their training. The Brelands referred to this phenomenon as "instinctive drift."

As mentioned previously in the discussion of cognitive maps, learning and the performance of learned behavior are not always identical. Our performance of learned behaviors varies depending on an interaction between the presence of others and the complexity of the learned task. For simple tasks, like pedaling a bicycle or reeling in a fishing line, the presence of others makes us perform faster, a phenomenon known as *social facilitation* (Triplett, 1898; also see Chapter 13). In complex tasks, such as taking a difficult college entrance exam, the presence of others can make our performance slower and poorer. Again, this effect is not restricted to complex organisms like ourselves; the same results can be observed in the lowly cockroach (Zajonc, 1965). In a straight maze leading to food, cockroaches with an audience of other cockroaches ran quickly. In a more complex maze involving several turns, the cockroaches responded to an audience by running more slowly.

Orlando Sentinel/Contributor/Tribune News Service/Getty Images

Experienced whale trainer Dawn Brancheau was killed by one of her favorite killer whales during a 2010 show at Sea World in Orlando, Florida. Animal experts believed that the whale did not intentionally kill Brancheau. Instead, the whale had simply reverted to normal whale behavior, similar to the instinctive drift observed by Keller and Marian Breland.

Applying Operant Conditioning

Important applications of operant conditioning may be found in contemporary approaches to psychotherapy, education, advertising, politics, and many other domains.

Possibly one of the oddest applications of operant conditioning was Skinner's secret World War II defense project, code-named Project Pigeon. Lagging well behind the Nazis in the area of guided missile technology, the United States invested $25,000 (worth nearly $500,000 in today's dollars) in Skinner's "organic homing device" (Capshew, 1993). Skinner, who had considerable experience training pigeons to peck at visual stimuli in his laboratory, now trained them to peck at a projected image of a missile's target. Riding in a chamber within the missile, the pigeon's pecks would be translated into updated commands for correcting the path of the bomb. Unfortunately for Skinner (but fortunately for his pigeons), Project Pigeon elicited laughter from military officers instead of approval (Skinner, 1960). Although never implemented, Project Pigeon stimulated Skinner and his intellectual descendants to look outside the laboratory for useful extensions of their work on learning.

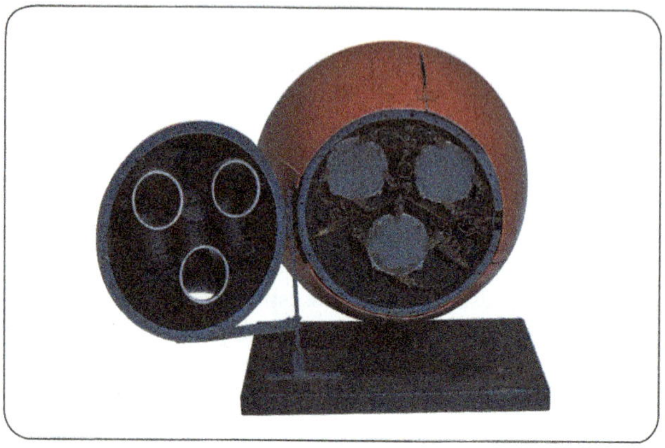

Source: Division of Political and Military History, National Museum of American History, Smithsonian Institution

B. F. Skinner's Project Pigeon was one of the more bizarre applications of operant conditioning research. Pigeons enclosed in this capsule were trained to peck at projected images of bomb targets. Even though Skinner's device was superior to other World War II missile guidance systems, it was never implemented.

token economy An application of operant conditioning in which tokens that can be exchanged for other reinforcers are used to increase the frequency of desirable behaviors.

Token Economies A widely used application of operant learning is the **token economy**. Money, in the form of coins, bills, cryptocurrency, or bank statements, is fairly useless. You can't eat it, wear it, or shelter in it. Nonetheless, people value it because it takes on secondary reinforcing qualities due to its history of association with other things that have intrinsic value. The use of money to buy things of personal value is an example of a token economy. You earn money for doing certain things, and then you have the opportunity to trade the money you earned for items of value to you. This system meets the best practices criteria that have been described in the context of positive reinforcement. Each person can obtain reinforcement that has unique personal value. One friend may spend discretionary money on going out to dinner, while another invests in the stock market. Both find money reinforcing for doing work.

An informed approach to compensating employees should include consideration of learning principles. "Menu" approaches to employee benefits provide an excellent example of this application. Historically, employers offered a set program of health, retirement, and other benefits to their entire workforce regardless of individual needs. We would expect this approach to be minimally reinforcing because it does not match reinforcers to worker priorities. Tailoring a benefits package to individual needs is more sensible. A young worker in good health might be more motivated by a benefits package that includes childcare, while a more mature worker may worry about long-term care in the event of a disability. By allowing workers to select their benefits from a menu, everybody can find something worth earning.

All of us respond positively to token economies, but they are especially useful in educational and institutional settings. Teachers provide frequent rewards in the form of checkmarks, stars, or tickets that can be exchanged later for popcorn parties or a night without homework. The key to an effective token economy is to offer ultimate rewards that are truly valuable to the people you wish to motivate. If students don't care about popcorn parties, offering them will have little effect. Token economies are equally useful in prison settings and in institutions serving people with an intellectual disability or mental illness.

Behavior Therapies As we will discuss in Chapter 15, learning theories have been applied successfully to the clinical setting in the form of behavior therapies, also called *applied behavior analysis (ABA)*. After all, our formal definition of learning states that it involves a change in behavior, and changing behavior is precisely what therapists usually seek to do. In addition to the extinction and counterconditioning applications of classical conditioning, behavior therapies use operant conditioning concepts such as extinction, reward, and on rare occasions, punishment.

OJO Images/Photoshot

Token economies can be effective ways of managing behavior. Tokens, including money, can be traded for a valued reinforcement of the worker's choice. This woman's purchase might motivate her work, but another worker might use the same paycheck to buy a motorcycle or go on vacation.

Coupled with cognitive methods designed to address the way that people think about their circumstances, these methods comprise the most popular and effective means for treating many types of disorder, from substance abuse to depression. One of the most dramatic applications of behavior therapy is the treatment for autism spectrum disorder pioneered by O. Ivar Lovaas (Lovaas et al., 1966; Lovaas, 1996). Autism spectrum disorder is characterized by language and social deficits. Although behavior therapy doesn't cure autism spectrum disorder, behavioral interventions, like the use of chaining described previously, typically improve an individual's level of functioning.

iStock.com/ktaylorg

An important application of operant conditioning principles is their use in behavior therapies for conditions like autism spectrum disorder. Operant conditioning can be used to increase the frequency of language use and socially appropriate behaviors, like eye contact.

EXPERIENCING PSYCHOLOGY

How Do I Break a Bad Habit?

WE ALL HAVE BEHAVIORS that could use some improvement. Maybe we eat poorly, drink too much, smoke, or lash out angrily at others. An understanding of the processes of learning provides us with powerful tools for changing behavior. Let's assume that your eating habits, like those of many students, do not meet the "My mom would approve" standard. Yet you are learning in your psychology course that good health habits are essential tools for managing stress (see Chapter 16). How do you bring about the necessary changes?

Before doing anything to produce change, you need to understand your current behavior. Many people have a poor understanding of what they actually eat during a day, so you could start by keeping a diary. What foods, and how much of them, do you eat? What else is going on when you eat well or poorly? What possible reinforcers or punishers are influencing your eating patterns? For example, let's say that you observe a tendency to eat high-calorie snacks late at night while studying, even when you are not hungry. Your goal, then, is to eliminate these late-night snacks. Your baseline shows that your snacking is a social behavior. You consume these extra foods only when studying with a group. The social camaraderie and good taste of the food serve as powerful reinforcers for the behavior.

Now that you have a better understanding of your problem behavior, you are in a good position to construct a plan. An important part of your plan is to choose appropriate consequences for your behavior. Again, it is essential that we design consequences that are meaningful to individuals. As we have argued in this chapter, positive reinforcement has many advantages over punishment. You might try placing the money you're saving on junk food in a designated jar to buy a special (nonfood) treat at the end of a successful week, or allow yourself an extra study break each night that you meet your goals. If you are convinced that the only way that you will change is through punishment, you could take an alternative approach. Although some people have successfully stopped smoking through the use of positive punishment, including electric shock (Law & Tang, 1995), this sounds quite unpleasant. Instead, a negative punishment, such as losing texting privileges for the day following a failure to meet one's goals, might work.

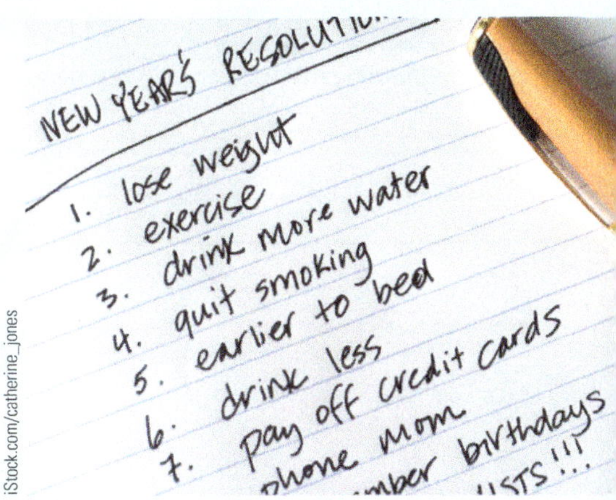

iStock.com/catherine_jones

As you implement your program, track your progress and make any modifications that seem necessary. In addition to the improvement of your target behavior, a beneficial side effect of applying learning methods to your behavior is the knowledge that given the right tools, you can control your behavior. ■

SUMMARY 8.3 Schedules of Reinforcement

Schedule	Features	In the lab	Everyday example
Fixed ratio 	Reinforcement occurs after a set number of responses.	A rat presses 3 times for each food pellet.	A garment worker is paid for finishing 10 shirts.
Variable ratio 	Reinforcement occurs after a variable number of responses, which average a set number for a session.	A rat is fed on average after three responses, but the number of responses required for obtaining food varies between 1 and 15.	People play slot machines and win, sometimes on the first play and other times after thousands of plays, on a schedule determined by the casino.
Fixed interval 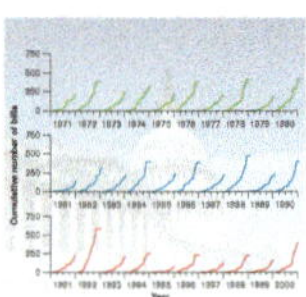	Each response begins an interval during which no reinforcement is available. The first response after the interval is reinforced.	A rat's first press after each 1-minute interval has timed out is reinforced.	Students study more hours right before finals than at the beginning of the term (although unlike in the rat's case, this behavior contributes to reinforcement).
Variable interval 	Each response begins an interval of varying length, with the average length for the session set by the experimenter.	A rat's first press after an interval is reinforced. The interval averages 1 minute over the session, but reinforcement could be obtained after intervals ranging between 10 seconds and 3 minutes.	A fisherman trails his line behind the boat, and at various time intervals, a fish is caught.

Credits: Top row—SCPhotos/Alamy Stock Photo; Second row—Tetra Images/Photoshot; Third row—Library of Congress, Prints & Photographs Division, Reproduction number LC-DIG-highsm-12649 (digital file from original) LC-HS503-1388 (color film transparency)—lunamarina/Shutterstock.com

What Is Observational Learning?

The ability to learn by watching others, known as *observational learning*, provides considerable advantages, especially in a social species like our own. Learning occurs without personally experiencing negative consequences. This ability to learn from observing others greatly expands our learning capacity, especially when we then generalize from these concrete examples (watching successful students) to produce effective rules (good time management is important to being a successful student). Observational learning also can have a dark side, as will be seen in our later discussion of the pioneering work by Albert Bandura and his colleagues (Bandura, Ross, & Ross, 1963; Bandura, 1965) on the modeling of aggression by children.

Not only do we learn by observing others, but it appears that observational learning can override other influences on behavior, possibly because we are such a social species. Parents learn (often the hard way) that children are more likely to pattern behavior after what they observe their parents doing than after what they hear their parents say.

Various behaviors, both positive and negative, appear to be influenced by observation, including aggression, achievement motivation, language development, phobias, cognitive development, moral judgment, and suicidal behavior. People benefit greatly from exposure to positive role models, especially those with whom they can identify. We worry about the

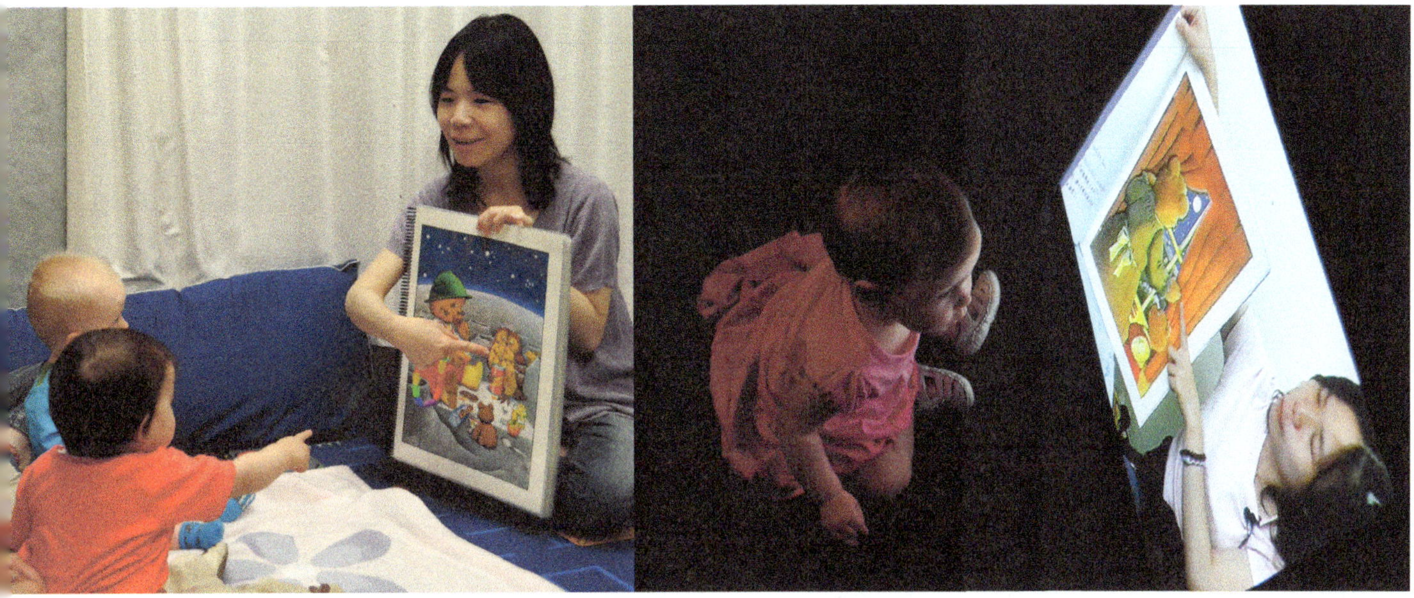

Both: From Patricia K. Kuhl, Brain Mechanisms in Early Language Acquisition, Neuron 67, September 9, 2010, (c) Elsevier Inc.

Babies learned more Chinese when listening to a person face to face than while watching the same person speak on a television monitor.

relatively small number of women in university math and science faculties, not only because of the possibility of discrimination, but also because seeing women in these positions might inspire young girls to follow in their footsteps. However, the use of performance-enhancing drugs by sports heroes might lead to role modeling of a different sort by young people.

It is easy to find examples of observational learning in our daily lives. Students "shadow" members of their chosen profession. We learn how to complete otherwise expensive household repairs by watching YouTube. Young athletes pore over films of superstars to perfect their technique. Popular cooking shows teach you to prepare a special meal. Cross-generational cycles of domestic violence persist as children continue the patterns of aggressive behavior they observe in their parents and grandparents. The goal of this section is to identify the circumstances in which this type of learning occurs and the variables that affect its outcomes.

imitation Copying behavior that is unlikely to occur naturally and spontaneously.

Albert Bandura and Aggression

Albert Bandura's work on the observational learning of aggression provides one of the strongest arguments against exposing children to violent media (Bandura et al., 1963; Bandura, 1965). Bandura was interested in **imitation**, which is defined as the copying of behavior that is unlikely to occur naturally and spontaneously (Thorpe, 1963).

Charlie Neuman/San Diego Union-Tribune/ZUMA Press/Newscom

Observational learning can provide a quick and easy way to learn without having to go through individual trial and error.

In a series of classic studies of the imitation of aggression in children, Bandura observed children's interactions with a Bobo doll, an inflatable toy clown with sand in the bottom, which allows it to rock back and forth when pushed. A number of 3- to 5-year-olds watched an adult model physically and verbally assault an unfortunate Bobo doll (Bandura et al., 1963). The adult yelled, "Pow, right in the nose!" when punching the doll in the face; "Sockeroo, stay down!" when hitting the doll with a mallet; "Fly away!" when kicking the doll around the room; and "Bang!" when throwing a ball at the doll. Subsequently, when the children were allowed an opportunity to play with a Bobo doll, they displayed a significant amount of aggression. In a later study, one group of children saw the adult being rewarded for aggression with candy and soda (Bandura, 1965). A second group of children saw the adult being verbally reprimanded, spanked, and threatened. The third group did not see any positive or negative consequences for the adult's actions. The group that witnessed the punishment of the adult model showed slightly less aggression than children in the other groups did.

After watching an adult model assault the Bobo doll, young children copied the adult's movements and verbalizations.

Albert Bandura/Stanford University

Bandura identified four necessary cognitive processes in the modeling of others' behavior: attention, retention, reproduction, and motivation. Models that get our *attention* are more likely to elicit imitation. A person must *retain* a memory of what the model did. We must be able to *reproduce* the behavior. Many of us enjoy watching elite athletes perform, but no matter how long and often we watch Serena Williams or LeBron James, few of us have the talent to duplicate their movements. If you happen to play tennis or basketball, however, you can learn to improve your game if you carefully observe these superstars. Finally, a person must have a *motivation* for imitating the behavior. Either past or anticipated reinforcement encourages us to model another person's behavior. In vicarious reinforcement, witnessing somebody else getting reinforced for a behavior raises the likelihood that we will imitate the behavior. At the same time, witnessing the other person getting punished for the behavior should reduce the likelihood that you will copy it.

Cultural Transmission of Learning

An individual's learning may serve that person well throughout a lifetime, but the invention of culture provides opportunities to pass the benefits of experience along for many generations. A society is a group of people living together. Culture, in contrast, consists of all the socially transmitted information used by the group of people, including ideas, concepts, and skills. Observational learning in particular provides a powerful tool for transmitting this information over time.

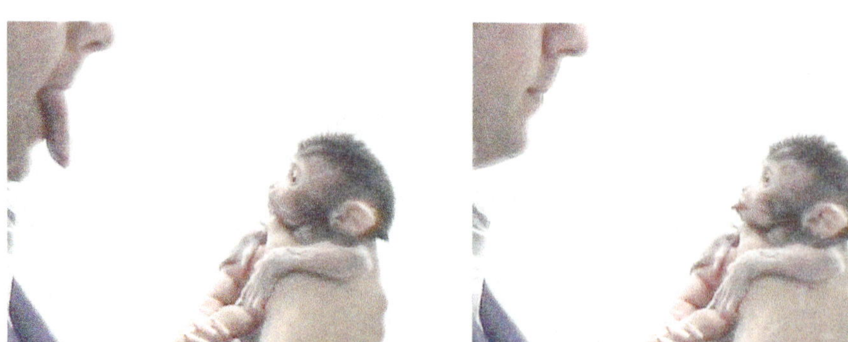

Humans are not the only species to show evidence of imitation.

Source: P. F. Ferrari et al. (2006). "Neonatal Imitation in Rhesus Macaques," *PLoS Biology*, *4*(9), e302. doi:10.1371/journal.pbio.0040302

© Pier Francesco Ferrari, University of Parma, from PLoS Biology, Sept. 2006, Vol. 4, Issue 9

Richard Dawkins (1976) envisioned a way to break culture down into observable parts. He referred to the basic unit of cultural transmission as a *meme*. Memes, he said, are transmitted by observational learning from one person to another and can take the form of ideas, symbols, or practices. Melodies, religious beliefs, catchphrases, and the technology for building arches are examples of memes. Dawkins viewed memes as the cultural equivalents of genes—they replicate from one person to the next and they respond to selection pressure. Memes that provide an advantage, such as knowledge of the use of fire, are likely to continue. Those that do not confer much advantage, such as some fads, are likely to die out quickly. Still others, such as pagers, are abandoned when more effective replacements (cell phones) emerge.

Josiah Kamau/BuzzFoto/Getty Images

Richard Dawkins defined *meme* as the basic unit of cultural transmission passed to others by observational learning. Internet memes are often unpredictable. "Chewbacca Mom" Candace Payne never imagined that her short video made for friends would become a viral sensation.

Among the most social of memes are Internet memes, which are "inside jokes" passed to others using technologies such as social networking sites and e-mail. Special websites that chronicle Internet memes allow viewers to provide updates of their favorite memes, which contributes to their popularity.

Interpersonal Relationships
The Learning Perspective

CAN WE INFLUENCE THE WAY OTHERS BEHAVE TOWARD US?

KNOWLEDGE OF THE WAY that people learn can improve your social life, and possibly even your love life. Operant conditioning can help you decrease unwanted behaviors and increase desired behaviors toward you by people with whom you interact. Your behavior influences the way that others behave toward you. If you regularly find that you are treated poorly in relationships, understanding the learning perspective provides powerful tools for change.

This chapter has recommended an emphasis on regularly noticing and rewarding desired behaviors. It is easy to fall into the trap of feeling entitled to good behavior from the people who are close to us, which can lead to these behaviors being taken for granted and ignored. Without positive reinforcement, these good behaviors might be extinguished. It takes little time and energy to thank people for the nice things they do for us, and this simple courtesy can increase the frequency of positive interactions in the future.

prodakszyn/Shutterstock.com

Ignoring annoying behavior can be difficult, but you don't want to reinforce it with attention.

When undesirable behaviors inevitably occur, many people turn to punishment. Skinner believed that part of the love affair that we have with punishment is because of the reinforcing properties of punishment to the punisher. Skinner (1971) stated, "We 'instinctively' attack anyone whose behavior displeases us—perhaps not in physical assault, but with criticism, disapproval, blame, or ridicule" (p. 190). Punishing a partner for bad behavior might make you feel better, but this comes at a significant cost. These punishing behaviors are not endearing, and frequent use of them is likely to end relationships.

If punishment is off the table, what then do we recommend you do when you experience negative behavior from a partner? If possible, try to ignore negative behaviors, putting them on extinction. Unfortunately, some people would rather have negative attention from you than no attention and prefer punishment from you to being ignored. This is particularly likely to be the case if you have forgotten to reinforce positive behaviors. If you combine positive reinforcement of good behavior and extinction of negative behavior, you should notice quite an improvement. Some behaviors like aggression cannot be ignored and require either a complete end to the relationship or professional counseling.

Thoughtfully observing the way that you treat other people and their reactions to your behavior, using the learning principles described in this chapter, should provide you with the understanding that you need to improve your relationships. ■

Psychology Takes On Real-World Problems

Can People Learn to be Less Lonely?

Many people experience loneliness and social isolation during the quarantines and lockdowns associated with a pandemic. Do we just have to suffer through this? Or can we use our new knowledge about learning to feel more connected to others? After all, we're defining learning as producing changes in behavior.

You might think that a person's loneliness is solely dependent on interactions with closely related people, such as family or friends. During a pandemic, these loved ones might be located far away. Our only social interactions might take place virtually or in brief encounters with staff at a grocery store. These latter interactions, handled well, might be more beneficial than you think. Dr. Gillian Sandstrom, of the University of Essex, conducts research on the benefits of talking to strangers to decrease loneliness (Sandstrom & Dunn, 2014). In one study, participants were told to enter a Starbucks and either conduct business as efficiently as possible (having payment ready and so on) or to start a short conversation with the barista. People in the latter group reported feeling more cheerful and connected to others.

A number of barriers exist to prevent our taking advantage of these small bits of socializing. Our social norms often prohibit us from connecting with strangers. We carefully avoid eye contact and certainly are reluctant to start up a conversation with a stranger. After all, our parents were very firm about "stranger danger." During a pandemic, extended interactions with others might also provoke fears of contagion.

Assuming that we do, in fact, need to interact with others for essential services, how can we overcome these barriers and use these simple interactions to boost our sense of social connectivity? Sandstrom describes a number of steps we could take to get started. Initially, she recommends starting small, perhaps with a smile and a "good morning." Granted, you can't see a smile through a mask, but as we learned in Chapter 7, emotions can be conveyed through the eyes, body language, and tone of voice. Express empathy for the circumstances your essential workers are experiencing by asking them how things are going. Being recognized as a human, rather than just a function, is important to workers, who then in turn appreciate you for asking.

How is this related to learning? Operant conditioning predicts that people who feel more cheerful and connected after conversing with a stranger are more likely to converse with strangers in the future. Having achieved this simple goal, Sandstrom shapes more extensive interactions by suggesting the goal of speaking with one new person each day. You might not be getting out of the house that much, but there are other options. While we all know the pitfalls of social media, it is possible to find supportive communities online where people sharing your interests gather. A question asked or answered might result in a new friend. ■

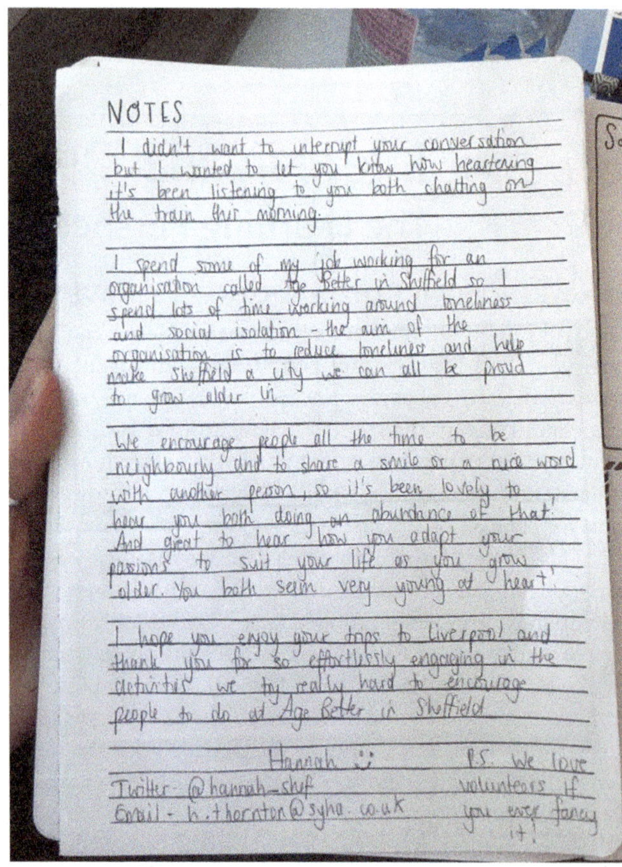

Hannah Thornton

Hannah Thornton left this note behind for two men who shared her table in a train compartment because she appreciated how they had interacted on the trip. She had no idea that the note and the follow-up email from one of the men would go viral. These small interactions among people who don't know one another make people feel more cheerful and connected to others.

SUMMARY 8.4 Features Promoting Observational Learning and Imitation

Feature	Description	Example
Attention 	We are more likely to model the behavior of people who get our attention.	Children wear the jerseys of the best players in the sport.
Memory 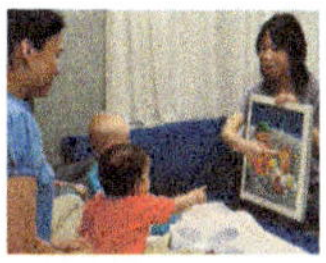	We must retain a memory of the behavior to be imitated.	A student re-creates from memory a math proof demonstrated earlier that day by a professor.
Reproduction 	We must have the ability to reproduce the behavior.	An athlete works on her technique after watching films of an elite athlete in her sport.
Motivation 	Past or anticipated reinforcement for a behavior motivates us to perform it too.	One student received extra credit for participating in an experiment, so his friends also signed up to participate.

KEY TERMS The Language of Psychological Science

Be sure that you can define these terms and use them correctly.

acquisition, p. 283
associative learning, p. 280
aversion therapy, p. 290
classical conditioning, p. 280
conditioned reinforcer, p. 297
conditioned response (CR), p. 283
conditioned stimulus (CS), p. 283
discrimination, p. 285
extinction, p. 284
fixed interval (FI) schedule, p. 302
fixed ratio (FR) schedule, p. 301
generalization, p. 285
habituation, p. 280
higher-order conditioning, p. 286
imitation, p. 311
inhibition, p. 285
instinct, p. 279
latent inhibition, p. 287
latent learning, p. 305
learning, p. 279
method of successive approximations, p. 304
negative punishment, p. 299
negative reinforcement, p. 298
nonassociative learning, p. 280
observational learning, p. 280
operant conditioning, p. 280
partial reinforcement effect in extinction, p. 303
partial reinforcement, p. 301
positive punishment, p. 299
punishment, p. 299
reflex, p. 278
sensitization, p. 280
spontaneous recovery, p. 284
systematic desensitization, p. 290
token economy, p. 308
unconditioned response (UCR), p. 283
unconditioned stimulus (UCS), p. 283
variable interval (VI) schedule, p. 302
variable ratio (VR) schedule, p. 302

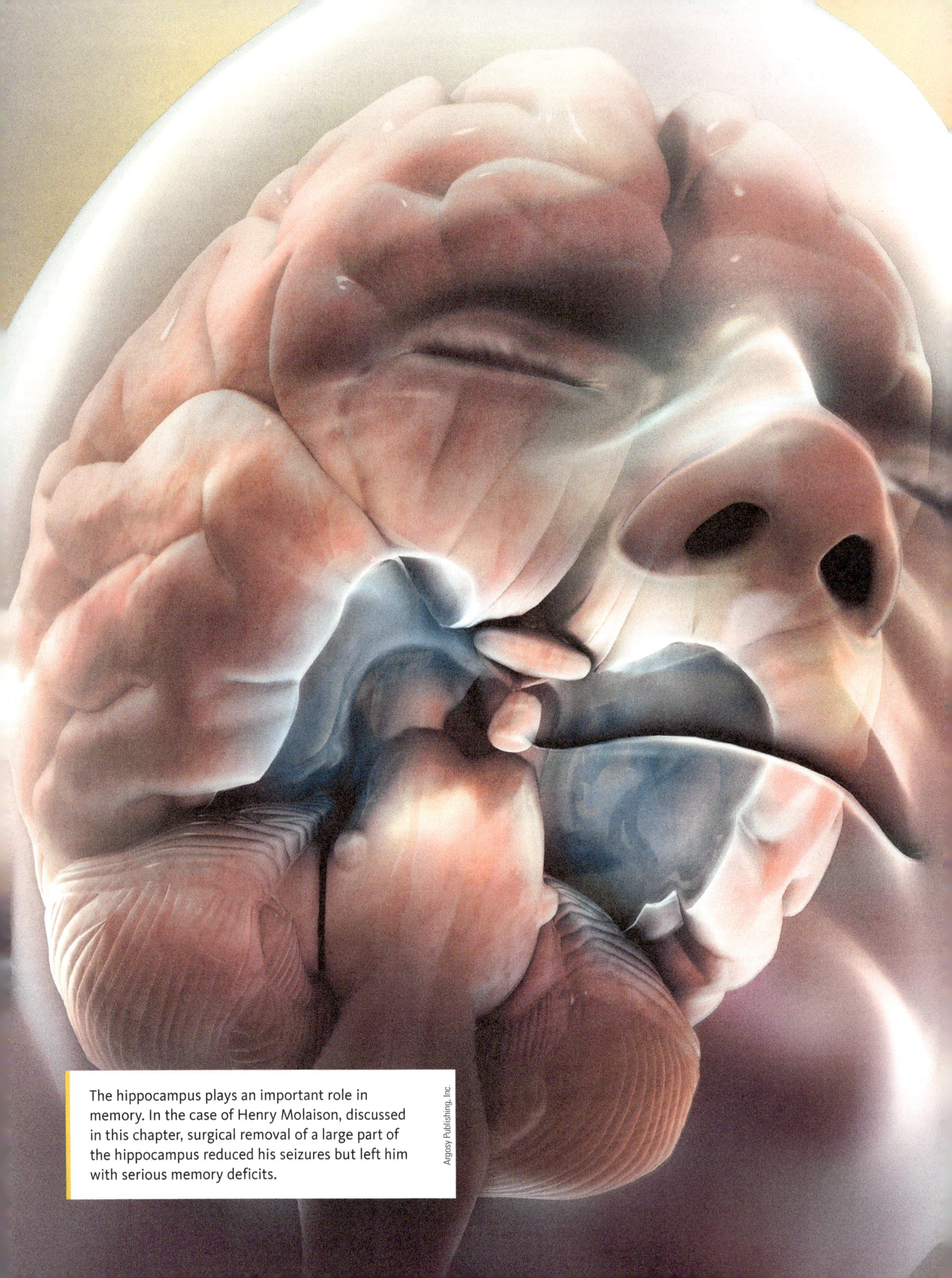

The hippocampus plays an important role in memory. In the case of Henry Molaison, discussed in this chapter, surgical removal of a large part of the hippocampus reduced his seizures but left him with serious memory deficits.

9

The Knowing Mind

MEMORY

LEARNING OBJECTIVES

1. Apply the concepts of encoding, storage, and retrieval of memory to relevant examples.
2. Differentiate among sensory memory, short-term or working memory, and long-term memory, as well as the subtypes of long-term memory.
3. Explain the models describing the organization of long-term memories.
4. Analyze the variables influencing retrieval from short- and long-term memory.
5. Explain forgetting, decay, interference, motivated forgetting, and confabulation.
6. Identify the biological correlates of memory.

IN CHAPTER 2, we introduced you to one of the most famous case studies in psychology—the case of Henry Molaison (1926–2008), who is known in the scientific literature as "the amnesic patient H.M." To reduce Molaison's severe seizures, possibly resulting from a minor head injury caused by a childhood accident, his neurosurgeons carried out an experimental procedure that would be considered radical today but was even more so in 1953. As shown in the large image to the left, they removed most of Molaison's hippocampus in both hemispheres, along with some of the surrounding neural tissue. As a result, Molaison's memory functions declined dramatically, although his personality and intellect remained intact.

Zooming in to consider the results of this type of surgery, we can ask what scientists learned from their study of Molaison. Brenda Milner, followed by her student Suzanne Corkin, studied Molaison for more than four decades. His case produced a string of surprises, which we discuss in more detail later in this chapter. For example, certain structures in the brain are important for memory, but more so for some types of memories than for others. We can perform some tasks automatically. In other words, we can remember how to do something without remembering that we know how to do it.

Zooming out to Molaison the individual, shown to the right, we can see that his story is more extensive than the study of his brain. According to people who knew him, he was a nice man who loved animals, watching trains, and doing crossword puzzles. Even though Molaison was the subject of decades of study, many questions about him remain. Why did he seem less

Henry Molaison, aged 60, at MIT in 1986. Photograph by Jenni Ogden, author of book Trouble in Mind: Stories from a Neuropsychologist's Casebook.

Henry Molaison.

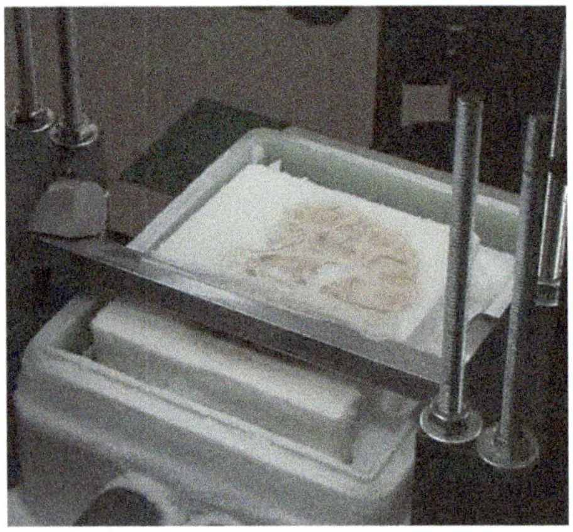

Dr. Jacopo Annese, The Brain Observatory

The careful slicing of Henry Molaison's preserved brain took more than 53 straight hours and was broadcast live on the Internet.

affected by pain than other people? Why was he accurately able to rate the intensity of an odor but unable to tell the difference between a rose and something rotten? Although his ability to learn new facts following his surgery was remarkably impaired, why did he know scattered facts from the following decade? Which of these observations shows the effects of his surgery? Of his accident? Of his seizures?

Zooming out still farther, we ask ourselves how our social interactions would be affected by being unable to remember new people we have met. Molaison remembered people, such as his surgeon, whom he had met before his surgery, but he never learned to recognize Milner, Corkin, or the other scientists who met him later, even though he saw them regularly for decades. He retained a genuine concern for other people and took great pride in the fact that he was helping science, but it is hard to imagine that his life was not somewhat lonely and socially isolated.

We often think of memory as something we need to succeed on exams, but in this chapter, you will learn that memory means much more to our human experience. Our memories allow us to form new connections with people, places, and things; to experience a new acquaintance, over time, becoming an old friend; and to experience the continuity of time rather than repeatedly living life as a single, isolated moment.

What Is Memory?

Memory is defined as the ability to retain knowledge. The problems encountered by Molaison provide us with a glimpse of how our lives would be altered without certain memory abilities, but what else do we know about how memory typically functions? Can we make more general conclusions about how memory helps animals adapt and survive?

Memory and the Continuum of Information Processing

Take a minute and write down the five most important things you need to remember today. How would your life be affected if you couldn't remember these things?

Cognitive psychologists see memory as part of a continuum of **information processing** that begins with attention, sensation, perception, and learning, which we explored in previous chapters, and progresses to the use of stored information in thinking, problem solving, language, and intelligent behavior, which we discuss in Chapter 10 (see Figure 9.1). Information flows in both directions along this continuum, leading to the bottom-up and top-down processing we observed in Chapter 5. Memories of the characteristics of Dalmatian dogs, for example, are gained by learning about Dalmatians through experience with them. These memories helped you identify the photograph of one in Chapter 5 and should help you interact with one appropriately (thinking and problem solving).

Memory can be divided into three steps: encoding, storage, and retrieval. **Encoding** refers to the process of acquiring information and transferring it into memory. In Chapter 5, we described how the sensory systems translate or transduce electromagnetic energy, sound waves, pressure, and chemical stimulation into action potentials that can be processed by the nervous system. These transduced signals can then be encoded in different forms in memory, such as visual codes, acoustic or sound codes, or semantic or meaningful codes. For example, when you meet your friend on the way to class, you encode her appearance visually, the sound of her voice acoustically, and how much you value her friendship semantically.

Encoded information needs to be retained, or stored. As we will see later in this chapter, **storage** of memories in the brain can last anywhere from fractions of a second (sensory memory) to several seconds (short-term and working memory) to indefinitely (long-term memory). Storage in the mind differs from storage of information in your computer in one important respect. Computers store encoded information in reliable and unvarying ways, like putting socks in a drawer or papers in a file. What you retrieve is identical to what was stored. In contrast, human memory does not generate exact records. Instead, bits of information are

memory The ability to retain knowledge.

information processing A continuum including attention, sensation, perception, learning, memory, and cognition.

encoding The transformation of information from one form to another.

storage The retention of information.

stored that are later reconstructed into usable memories. Although this process typically results in a useful memory, errors and distortions can occur.

The culmination of the memory process is the **retrieval** of stored information. As you have no doubt experienced, storing information is no guarantee that you can find the information again when you need it. Later in this chapter, we will discuss in detail ways that memory retrieval can fail. Two of the most common causes of retrieval failure are interference and stress. For example, we seem to know all the answers when watching a favorite game show in the safety of our homes, but when put on the spot, we might be lucky to remember our names. Fortunately, understanding the strengths and weaknesses of the brain's memory functions may be one of the more practical topics for students that we cover in psychology. Once you understand how memory works, you will have an easier time ensuring that your study habits maximize your performance in school.

FIGURE 9.1

The Information Processing Continuum. Memory is located on a continuum of information processing that flows both from the bottom up and from the top down. We use our memories of Dalmatian dogs to recognize one in an ambiguous photograph and interact with a new one we happen to meet.

Illustration: top to bottom: From Richard L. Gregory, "The Medawar Lecture 2001 Knowledge for vision: Vision for knowledge," Phil. Trans. R. Soc. B 2005 360, 1231–1251, by permission of the Royal Society; anetapics/Shutterstock.com; Steve Smith/The Image Bank/Getty Images

Memory Provides an Adaptive Advantage

Evolutionary psychologists view memory as "a component of a neural machine designed to use information acquired in the past to coordinate an organism's behavior in the present" (Klein, Cosmides, & Tooby, 2002, p. 308). The evolution of memory allowed animals to use information from the past to respond quickly to immediate challenges, a monumental advance in the ability to survive. Instead of reacting to each predator or source of food as a new experience, an animal with the ability to remember past encounters with similar situations would save precious reaction time.

As we discussed in Chapter 3, useful adaptations often come with a price, such as the unwieldy antlers of the male deer that require energy to build yet help the deer fight successfully for mates. The development of a memory system is no exception to this rule. Forming memories requires energy. For memory systems to flourish within the animal kingdom, the survival advantages needed to outweigh the energy costs. Given the 81 years or so of human life expectancy, it would be difficult to demonstrate the energy costs of memory in people, but we can observe the costs in a simpler organism, the fruit fly *(Drosophila)*, which has a life expectancy of only 10 to 18 days. Fruit flies are capable of learning classically conditioned associations between odors and electric shock (see Chapter 8). After experiencing pairings of odor and shock, the flies fly away from the odor 24 hours later (Mery & Kawecki, 2005). However, to form memories about odor and shock, the flies must use more energy than they use for activities that do not require memory. The flies that remembered how to avoid shock died about 4 hours earlier than flies that did not form memories. Nearly all animals have the capability of forming memories despite the high energy costs, which is a testament to memory's benefits to survival.

How Are Memories Processed?

Atkinson and Shiffrin (1968, 1971) proposed one of the most influential models of memory (Malmberg et al., 2019). According to this classic information processing model, data flow through a series of separate stages of memory (see ● Figure 9.2). Contemporary cognitive psychologists have continued to modify this original model while retaining the basic ideas that memories can be stored for different lengths of time and that executive control processes influence the system.

To illustrate the flow of information in this model, let's consider what happens when you use your memory to complete a specific task—remembering a phone number provided to you by a new acquaintance.

retrieval The recovery of stored information.

Gorodenkoff/Shutterstock.com

Encoding failure is one of the most common memory problems faced by students. If we don't encode information because we're not paying attention during a lecture, there will be no memory of the information to retrieve later.

Sensory Memory

While settling into your seat before class, you converse with a classmate about studying together for an upcoming exam. Your classmate gives you her cell phone number so that you can arrange a good time to meet. This incoming information, the auditory signals of your classmate's voice in this case, is processed in a first stage of the information processing model, the **sensory memory**. This stage holds enormous amounts of sensory data, possibly all information that affects the sensory receptors at one time. However, the data remain for brief periods, usually a second or less, that only last as long as the neural activity produced by a sensation continues. The information held in sensory memory has been compared to a rapidly fading "echo" of the real input. You can demonstrate the duration and "fade" of sensory memory information by rapidly flapping your hand back and forth in front of your eyes. When you do this, you can "see" where your fingers were at a previous point in time.

Sensory input is translated into several types of codes or representations. A representation of a memory refers to a mental model of a bit of information that exists even when the information is no longer available. Visual codes are used for the temporary storage of information about visual images (Baddeley et al., 2009). Haptic codes are used to process touch and other body senses. Acoustic codes represent sounds and words. Input from different sensory systems remains separate in sensory memory, and although these different sensory streams are processed similarly, there are also some differences. Acoustic codes, or echoic memories, last longer than visual codes, or iconic memories, possibly to meet our needs to hear entire words and phrases before we can understand spoken language.

JONATHAN NACKSTRAND/AFP/Getty Images

Both brains and computers feature the ability to store memories with one critical difference: The computer stores exact copies of data, but the brain does not. Instead, the brain stores bits of data that are reconstructed later for use. This photo shows the high-security computer memory storage at the Swedish Bahnhof, a facility located 100 feet underground in a concrete bunker. The facility manages servers for many secretive organizations, including WikiLeaks.

sensory memory The first stage of the Atkinson–Shiffrin model that holds large amounts of incoming data for brief amounts of time.

short-term memory (STM) The second stage of the Atkinson–Shiffrin model that holds a small amount of information for a limited time.

George Sperling demonstrated the duration of iconic memories by testing recall for matrices of 12 to 16 letters that were presented for as few as 15 milliseconds. Participants were usually able to identify four or five letters. However, the process of verbally instructing participants to do this task takes time, during which the sensory memory for the matrix fades rapidly. If different tones were used to signal a row of the matrix to be recalled instead of verbally asking for a response, participants demonstrated recall for as many as 12 of the original 16 items (Sperling, 1960; Averbach & Sperling, 1961; Sperling, 1960). If the tone was sounded less than a quarter of a second after the presentation of the matrix, participants could usually recall all four letters in a row. After a quarter of a second delay or more, recall fell to one letter (see ● Figure 9.3).

Why do we have a sensory memory? Only a small subset of this incoming data is processed by the next stage. It is likely that we need to collect incoming data until they make enough sense to process further. The first number in your classmate's phone number might be simple (2), but it still contains two speech sounds ("t" and "oo") that must be combined to make sense.

iStock.com/AlbanyPictures

Encoding and storing memories do not guarantee that they can be retrieved when you need them. Stress can make retrieving even the simplest of memories surprisingly difficult.

Short-Term Memory

A tiny amount of information in the sensory memory moves to the next stage of the information processing model, **short-term memory (STM)**, for further processing. If you focus on your new friend's phone number, the information moves from sensory memory to short-term memory. Consider all the other information that might be processed by your sensory memory at the same time. Perhaps your professor's first Microsoft PowerPoint slide has appeared on the screen, the heater in the classroom cycled on, and your stomach growled because you didn't have time for breakfast. None of these bits of information are processed in short-term memory unless you pay attention to them. If you are distracted by one of these, it is likely that you will need to ask your friend to repeat her number.

Short-term memory, like the sensory memory that precedes it, appears to have remarkable limitations in duration. Without additional processing, information in short-term memory lasts 30 seconds at most (Ellis & Hunt, 1983). In a classic experiment, participants were shown stimuli consisting of three consonants, such as RBP (Peterson & Peterson, 1959). After seeing one of these triplets, participants counted backward by 3s for periods of 0 to 18 seconds to prevent further processing of the consonant triplet. As shown in ● Figure 9.4, accuracy dropped rapidly. It is likely that the Petersons' task overestimates the length of time that

Stanislav Duben/Shutterstock.com

Even though processing memory requires energy, the benefits to survival far outweigh the costs. Without memory, this squirrel would be unable to retrieve the acorns stored weeks ago.

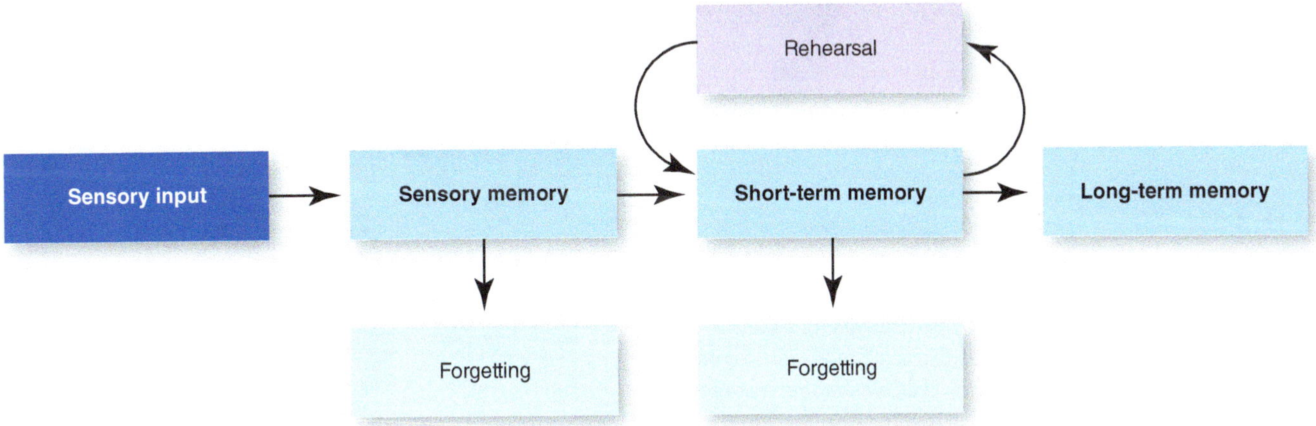

FIGURE **9.2**

The Atkinson–Shiffrin Model of Memory. According to this classic model of memory, information flows through a series of stages. If memory is not transferred to the next stage, it is permanently lost.

Source: Adapted from R. C. Atkinson, & R. M. Shiffrin (1971). "The Control of Short-Term Memory," *Scientific American*, *225*, 82–90. doi: 10.1038/scientificamerican0871-82

moomsabuy/Shutterstock.com

Our ability to "see" what we have written with a sparkler results from the remaining traces in our sensory memories. The actual light is long gone.

material is stored in short-term memory. The study's participants were aware in advance that they would be tested on the items, and despite the distraction of counting backward, they may have made deliberate efforts to retain the triplets in memory.

You are probably thinking right now that you know what to do to prevent this loss of information. If you repeat the information over and over, a process known as **rehearsal**, information stays in short-term memory indefinitely, so long as you don't think about anything else. While you are entering your classmate's number into your phone, you can rehearse the number in your short-term memory. However, if your attention is diverted from rehearsing the number when the professor calls on you, the phone number will be gone. The incoming information of the professor's question pushes the previous data out of the system. Data in short-term memory are easily displaced by new, incoming bits of data. If rehearsing the information has been insufficient for moving it into the next stage, long-term memory, the data will be lost.

In addition to limitations of duration, short-term memory is characterized by severe limitations in capacity. George Miller (1956) argued that we can process between five and nine items, or "bits" (such as digits, letters, or words), in short-term memory simultaneously, or in his words, "the magical number 7 plus or minus 2." More recently, psychologists have set the limit as about four items (Cowan, 2000). Memory capacities vary from individual to individual, and memory tasks appear prominently in standardized tests of intelligence, discussed in Chapter 10. People who enjoy larger than average short-term memory capacity excel at a number of cognitive tasks, including reading (Baddeley et al., 1985).

André Babiak/AGE Fotostock

Because our short-term memory holds limited amounts of information for only a short time, smartphone apps that keep track of things we need to remember to do are popular.

rehearsal Repetition of information.

You might be wondering how short-term memory could be useful, given these limitations. These limitations actually make short-term memory an ideal solution for the tasks that we ask it to complete. The brief duration of short-term memories ensures that room is freed regularly for incoming information. Most tasks for which we use short-term memory require us to search its contents to find the right information. If short-term memory were capable of holding dozens of pieces of information instead of nine or fewer, this search process would be lengthy and difficult. It is also convenient to have

FIGURE **9.3**

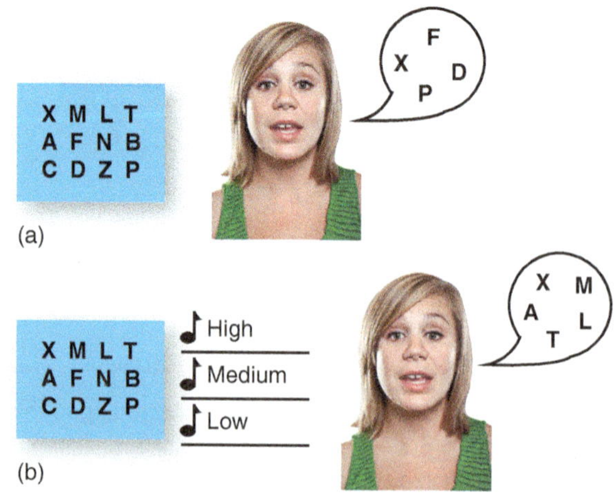

iStock.com/Camrocker

Sperling's Demonstration of the Duration of Sensory Memory. George Sperling presented a matrix of letters to study participants for as few as 15 milliseconds. When asked to recall the whole matrix (a), most participants could remember about four or five letters. However, when tones instead of verbal commands were used to signal which row to remember (b), participants were able to recall whole rows at a time, which implies they could remember more than four or five items. Sperling concluded that they could "see" the entire matrix in sensory memory briefly, which allowed them to respond correctly.

Source: Adapted from G. Sperling (1960). "The Information Available in Brief Visual Presentations," *Psychological Monographs*, *74*(11), 1–29. doi: 10.1037/h0093759

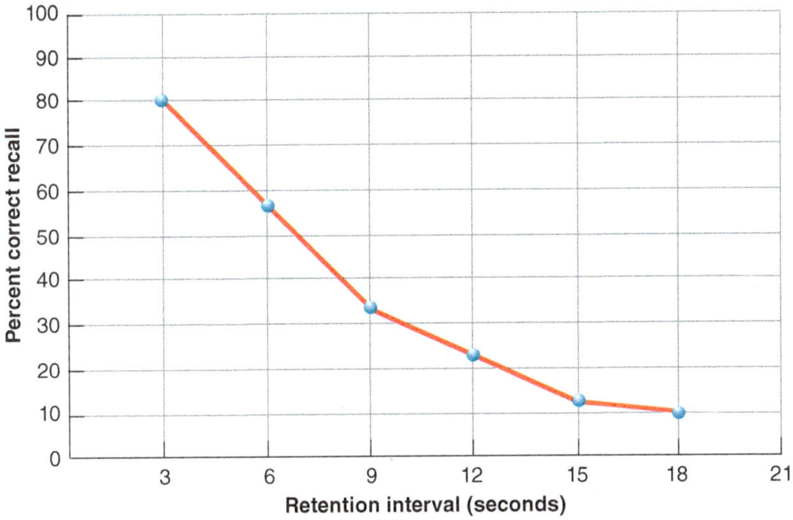

FIGURE **9.4**

The Duration of Short-Term Memory. In a classic study by Peterson and Peterson (1959), participants were given triplets of letters, such as XPJ or BTP, to recall. Their ability to remember the letters decreased as the time between presentation and recall increased. These results led the Petersons to propose that short-term memory might last up to 18 seconds, but more contemporary scientists using different methods think that it lasts as little as 2 seconds.
Source: Data from L. R. Peterson & M. J. Peterson (1959). "Short-Term Retention of Individual Verbal Items," *Journal of Experimental Psychology*, *58*, 193–198. doi: 10.1037/h0049234

Courtesy of the United States Federal Bureau of Investigation

Courtesy of the United States Internal Revenue Service

Courtesy of the United States Central Intelligence Agency

Courtesy of the United States Environmental Protection Agency

It is easier to remember FBI, IRS, CIA, and EPA in chunks than to remember FBIIRSCIAEPA

a mechanism that allows you to use information and then discard it. You may not wish to devote precious room in your memory to the telephone number of a plumber you need only once or twice. Short-term memory allows us to use information without overburdening our storage capacities.

Nonetheless, it is often desirable to expand our capacity for information in short-term memory. The best way to accomplish this is to redefine what a "bit" of data is by **chunking**, or grouping, similar or meaningful information together (Miller, 1956). If the last four digits of your friend's phone number are "one," "five," "seven," and "nine," she could reduce these four bits to two by saying "fifteen seventy-nine." Trying to remember the following sequence of letters—FBIIRSCIAEPA—appears to be an insurmountable task. After all, remembering 12 letters lies outside the capacity of short-term memory. The task is greatly simplified by chunking the letters into meaningful batches of common abbreviations—FBI IRS CIA EPA. Now you have only four meaningful bits to remember rather than 12, which is safely within the capacities of short-term memory. Failure to use chunking spontaneously as a strategy occurs frequently in people with verbal learning disabilities (Koeda et al., 2011). In the absence of chunking, each item is processed as a single, unrelated bit of information, which rapidly overwhelms the capacity of short-term memory.

The classic description of short-term memory viewed this stage as a place to store information for immediate use. As investigations into memory advanced, researchers proposed an adaptation of this model called **working memory**, shown in ● Figure 9.5 (Baddeley & Hitch, 1974). Short-term memory and working memory differed in two ways. First, short-term memory involves the passive storage of information, while working memory involves an active manipulation of information. Second, short-term memory was viewed as managing a single process at a time, whereas working memory was more complex, allowing multiple processes to occur simultaneously.

chunking The process of grouping similar or meaningful information together.

working memory An extension of the concept of short-term memory that includes the active manipulation of multiple types of information simultaneously.

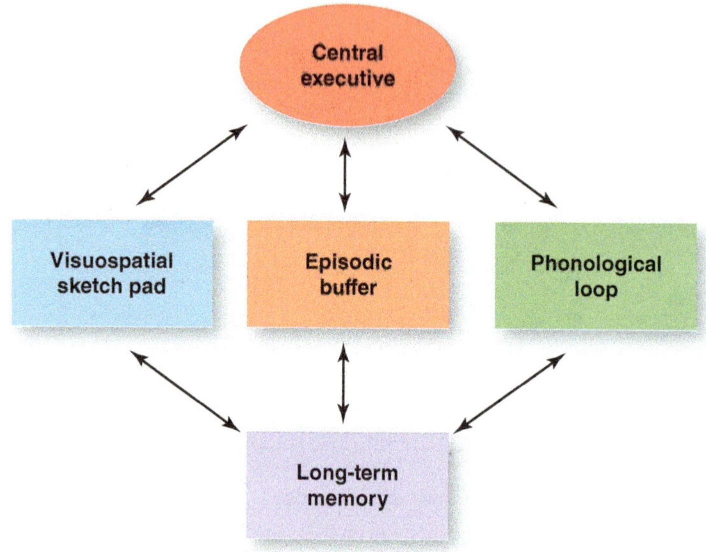

FIGURE **9.5**

Working Memory. Alan Baddeley's model of working memory differs from short-term memory in two important ways: (1) information in working memory can be actively manipulated, whereas short-term memory passively stores memory, and (2) working memory can manage multiple types of information simultaneously, whereas short-term memory cannot.

Source: A. D. Baddeley, & G. J. Hitch (1974). "Working Memory." In G. Bower (Ed.), *The Psychology of Learning and Motivation*, (Vol. 8, pp. 47–89). New York: Academic Press.

Observations that people could manage two short-term memory tasks at the same time led to modifications of this stage of memory (Baddeley & Hitch, 1974). For example, study participants could read a list of numbers and then read a paragraph. This task should quickly overwhelm the limited capacity of short-term memory because reading the paragraph should displace the earlier list of numbers. However, this outcome was not what the researchers observed. Participants had no difficulty remembering the numbers, suggesting that the numbers were stored separately from the words in the paragraph. After further exploration of the types of information that could be maintained separately in short-term memory, four components were proposed (Baddeley et al., 2009): a phonological loop, a visuospatial sketch pad, a central executive, and an episodic buffer.

The phonological loop is the working memory component responsible for verbal and auditory information. As you repeat your friend's phone number while reaching for your phone, you are using your phonological loop. The visuospatial sketch pad holds visual and spatial information. When you describe the route from your friend's dorm to your favorite coffee shop where you plan to hold your study session, you use your visuospatial sketch pad to describe the way. The central executive manages the work of the other components by directing attention to particular tasks (Baddeley, 1996). Divided attention, which we discussed in Chapter 5, requires the skills of the central executive. While discussing the route to the coffee shop with your friend (phonological loop), you visualize the route (visuospatial sketch pad), and your central executive parcels out the right amount of attention to allow you to do both tasks well.

The episodic buffer provides a mechanism for combining information stored in long-term memory, which we discuss in the next section, with the active processing taking place in working memory. This component helps explain why chunking the string of letters earlier (FBI IRS CIA EPA) is easier than remembering the letters as individual bits of information—FBIIRSCIAEPA. Without information from long-term memory about what FBI and the other abbreviations mean, making these chunks would not provide any advantage.

Long-Term Memory

The final stage of memory in the information processing model is **long-term memory**. Unlike sensory, short-term, and working memory, long-term memory has few limitations in capacity or duration. We do not run out of room in long-term memory for new data, and information can last a lifetime. The oldest person alive can still recall significant childhood memories and learn new things. Although old memories may become more difficult to retrieve, this process is different from losing them simply because of the passage of time.

Andre Jenny/Alamy Stock Photo

Chase and Simon (1973) presented images of chess pieces on chessboards for only 5 seconds to chess masters and people who didn't play chess. When the images were from real games, the chess masters recalled the placement of the pieces better than the nonplayers because they were able to use their knowledge of chess to chunk the images of the pieces' locations in short-term memory. When the pieces were placed randomly on the boards, however, the chess masters were unable to use chunking and performed no better than the nonplayers.

Moving Information into Long-Term Memory In most cases, information moves from short-term or working memory to long-term memory through rehearsal. After seeing your new friend's number several times as you text her, you memorize it without trying to do so. Rehearsal can be divided into maintenance rehearsal, which means simple repetition of the material, and elaborative rehearsal, which involves linking the new material to things you already know.

Of the two types of rehearsal, elaborative rehearsal is a more effective way to move information into more permanent storage. The benefits of elaborative rehearsal can be explained using the **levels of processing theory** (Craik & Lockhart, 1972). When we look at written words we want to remember, we can attend to many levels of detail: the visual appearance of the word (font, all caps, and number of letters), the sound of the word, the meaning of the word, and the personal relevance of the word. These characteristics can be placed along a continuum of depth of processing from shallow to deep, with the encoding of the appearance of a word requiring less processing and effort than the encoding of the sound of a word, which in turn requires less processing and effort than the encoding of the meaning or personal relevance of a word. According to the levels of processing theory, words encoded according to meaning would be easier to remember than words encoded according to their visual appearance because encoding meaningfulness produces a deeper level of attention and processing (Craik & Tulving, 1975).

In one study designed to test the levels of processing theory, participants recalled more words when their instructions elicited the encoding of word meanings than when they were instructed to determine more surface features of each word, such as whether it appeared in

long-term memory The final stage of the Atkinson–Shiffrin model that is the location of permanent memories.

levels of processing theory The depth (shallow to deep) of processing applied to information that predicts its ease of retrieval.

Suzy Bennett/Alamy Stock Photo

The accumulated knowledge of a long life, such as this Australian aborigine tribal elder's familiarity with his harsh surroundings, probably meant the difference between life and death for many of our ancestors. There is no evidence that older adults are unable to add new information to their long-term memories or necessarily lose information they have known a long time.

Our ATMs usually deliver our cash in $20 bills, but handling these regularly does not mean that we remember exactly what they look like. Which president is pictured on the bill? Whose signature as Secretary of the Treasury appears on the bill? Are the fonts used for all the 20s the same or different? Most people can't answer these questions from memory.

capital letters (see ● Figure 9.6) (Craik & Tulving, 1975). In another study, deeper levels of processing were accompanied by more subvocal speech (reminiscent of "talking to yourself"), indicated by measurements of tiny movements in the muscles of speech (Cacioppo & Petty, 1981). However, the levels of processing theory is not very specific about the meaning of deep or shallow processing. How would we apply this approach to evaluate participants' recall for music, touch, or visual images? Further work on this theory needs to identify what determines depth of processing during encoding.

Differences Between Working and Long-Term Memory In addition to not sharing the limitations of duration and capacity found with working memory, long-term memory appears to be unique in other ways.

Differences between working and long-term memories can be seen in classic experiments demonstrating the serial position effect. This phenomenon can be observed when people

FIGURE **9.6**

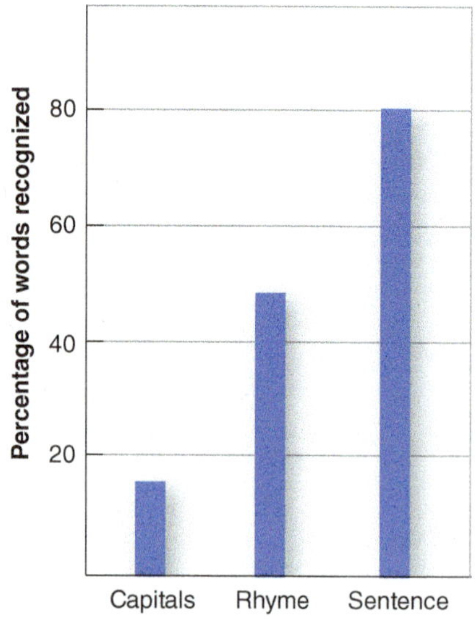

Levels of Processing Theory. Craik and Tulving (1975) tested the levels of processing theory by investigating their study participants' recognition of words they had seen only briefly (about one-fifth of a second) following one of three types of questions. The three types of questions focused the participants' attention on aspects of the word they were about to see. The questions pointed to surface features (Is the word in capital letters?), acoustic features (Does the word rhyme with another word?), or semantic features (Does the word make sense in this sentence?). Theoretically, deciding whether a word is in capital letters takes less processing than deciding whether it rhymes with another word, which in turn takes less processing than thinking about its meaning to answer the sentence question. The results supported the levels of processing theory. Recognition of words preceded by a semantic question was better than recognition of words preceded by a rhyme question, which were recognized better than words preceded by a font question.

Source: Adapted from F. I. M. Craik & E. Tulving (1975). "Depth of Processing and the Retention of Words in Episodic Memory," *Journal of Experimental Psychology: General*, *104*(3), 268–294. doi:10.1037/0096-3445.104.3.268

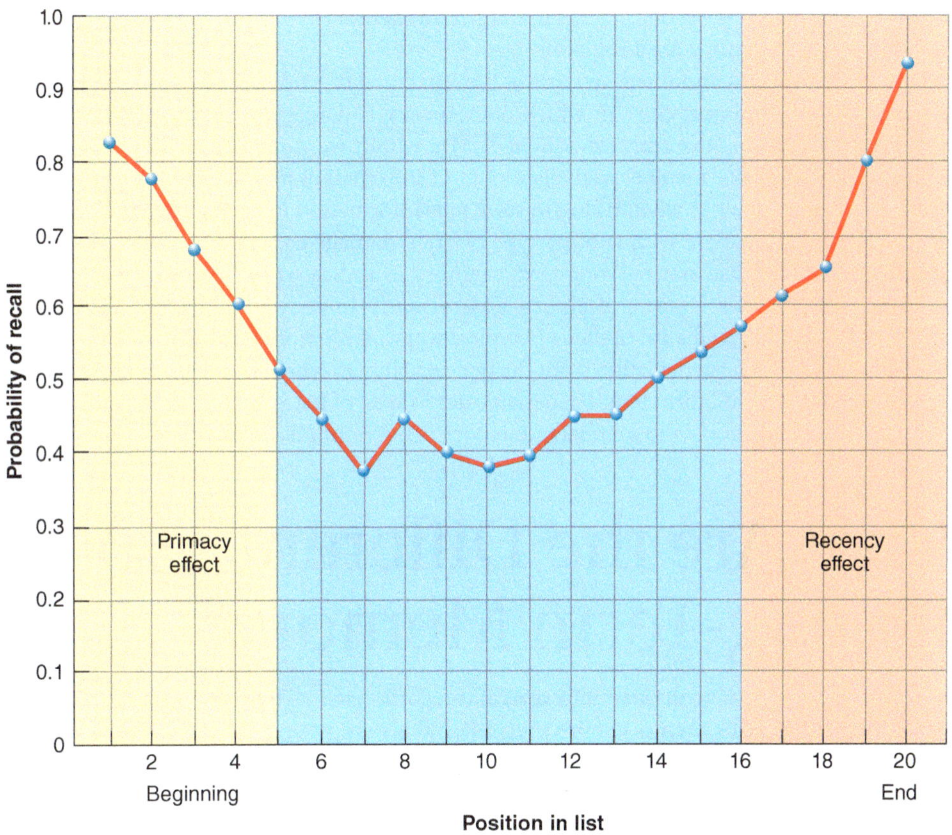

FIGURE 9.7

The Serial Position Effect. When people are given a list of words to remember and told they can recall the items in any order, the likelihood that a word on the list will be remembered depends on its position in the list. The primacy effect refers to the superior recall for the first words on the list, and the recency effect refers to the superior recall for the last words on the list. The primacy effect probably occurs because people have had more time to place these items in long-term memory. The recency effect probably occurs because these last words still remain in working memory at the time of retrieval. A delay in retrieval erases the recency effect but not the primacy effect.

are asked to learn a list of words and recall them in any order they choose. As shown in ● Figure 9.7, recall of items takes on a U-shaped appearance when retrieval is plotted as a function of an item's position in a list during presentation (Murdoch, 1962).

The superior recall for the first items on a list is known as the primacy effect, which results from the storage of these items in long-term memory. Using a list of 20 words, people would have the most rehearsal time for the first word, less for the second, and so on through the list. Because rehearsal moves information from working to long-term memory, the earlier words, with their greater share of rehearsal, would be more likely to be stored in long-term memory than the later words on the list, which probably were not rehearsed much.

The superior recall for the last words on the list is known as the *recency effect*, which occurs because these items remain in working memory at the time of recall. The recency effect, but not the primacy effect, disappears if recall is delayed by 30 seconds (Glanzer

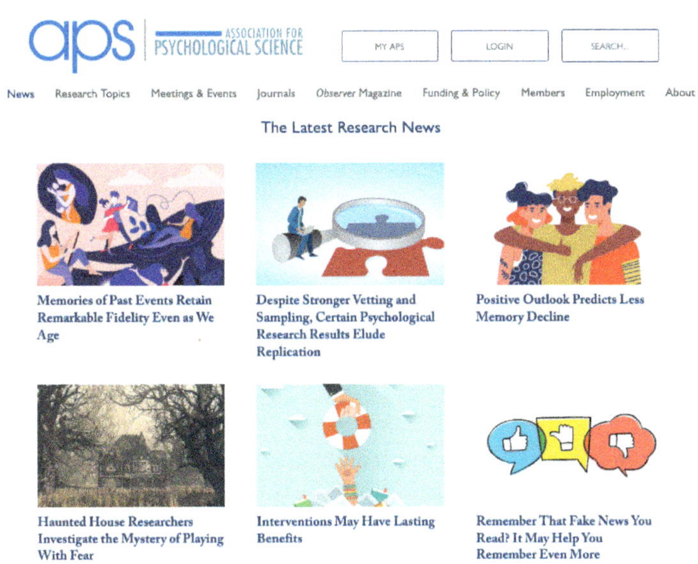

Source: Association for Psychological Science

According to research on primacy, recency, and website menus, we would predict that more people would click on the first and last news articles listed on the Association for Psychological Science's webpage. Which articles are least likely to get attention?

& Cunitz, 1966). After 30 seconds, items in long-term memory are still available for recall, but items in working memory are long gone.

One of the strongest arguments in favor of the separation of working and long-term memory is the occurrence of clinical cases in which one capacity is damaged while the other remains intact. Henry Molaison (the amnesic patient H.M.), whom we discussed at the beginning of this chapter, was able to remember a small amount of information for a few seconds but experienced enormous difficulties when trying to store new information in his long-term memory. In another case study, a patient with another type of brain damage appeared to have the opposite problem. Patient K. F. had normal long-term memory, as indicated by his ability to form new memories. However, his working memory was seriously impaired (Shallice & Warrington, 1970). When asked to recall a list of digits (a typical working memory task), he could remember only one or two digits, a big deviation from the typical ability to recall five to nine digits. The fact that Patient K.F. could still form long-term memories in spite of his STM deficits reminds us that the pathway between short- and long-term memory is not a simple, linear one.

What Are the Different Types of Long-Term Memory?

declarative memory A consciously retrieved memory that is easy to verbalize, including semantic, episodic, and autobiographical information; also known as explicit memory.

nondeclarative memory An unconsciously and effortlessly retrieved memory that is difficult to verbalize, such as a memory for classical conditioning, procedural learning, and priming; also known as implicit memory.

Long-term memory can be divided into several categories (see Figure 9.8). These categories not only help us describe memory more precisely, but also represent activity in different parts of the brain.

Long-term memory can be divided into declarative, or conscious, memories and nondeclarative, or unconscious, memories. **Declarative memories** are easy to "declare," or discuss verbally. Declarative memories are also called explicit memories because they are accessed in a conscious, direct, and effortful manner. In contrast to declarative memories, **nondeclarative memories** are difficult to discuss. For example, classical conditioning, which we examined in Chapter 8, produces nondeclarative memories. We might find it difficult to explain to another

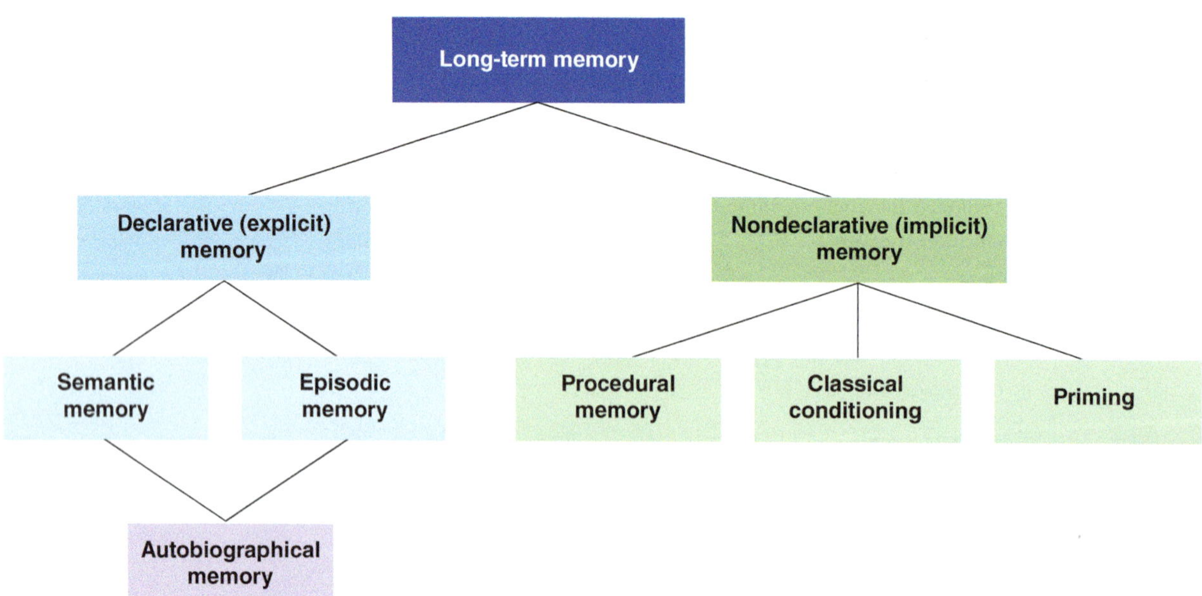

FIGURE 9.8

Types of Long-Term Memory. Long-term memory can be divided into several categories, beginning with a distinction between declarative (also known as explicit or conscious memories) and nondeclarative (also known as implicit or unconscious memories). Declarative memories are further divided into semantic and episodic memories, which are combined when we use autobiographical memories. Examples of nondeclarative memories are procedural memories, classical conditioning, and priming.

person why we get nervous right before an exam or dislike a food we ate once before becoming ill. Nondeclarative memories are also called implicit memories because they affect our behavior in subconscious, indirect, and effortless ways. We are aware of their outcomes ("I don't want to eat that food"), but we are usually unaware of the information processing that led to that outcome.

Declarative Memories

Declarative memories are further divided into semantic and episodic memories (Tulving, 1972, 1985, 1995). **Semantic memory** contains your store of general knowledge in the form of word meanings and facts. Using your semantic memory, you can answer questions such as "Which NFL team won last year's Super Bowl?" or "What is a churro?" **Episodic memory** is a more personal account of past experiences.

We can distinguish between semantic and episodic memories along four dimensions: the type of information processed, the organization of the information in memory, the source of the information, and the focus of the memory (Williams et al., 2008). Semantic memories contain general knowledge about the world, whereas episodic memories include more specific information about events, objects, and people. Semantic memory, as we will see later in this chapter, is organized according to categories. For example, we have a category for birds that contains our semantic knowledge of birds. Episodic memory, in contrast, is organized as a timeline. To answer a question from episodic memory, we often use time as a cue: "When I was in the eighth grade, my family took a vacation at the beach." Semantic knowledge originates from others, such as your professors, or from repeated experience: "The ocean is colder in California than in Florida because every time I've gone to the beach in either location, this is what I have observed." An episodic memory can result from a single, personal experience. Finally, the two types of memories serve different purposes. Semantic memory provides us with an objective understanding of our world, whereas episodic memory provides a reference point for our subjective experience of the self.

semantic memory A general knowledge memory.

episodic memory A memory for personal experience.

Karina Wallton/Shutterstock.com

You might have semantic memories that tell you about the characteristics of Labrador retrievers and episodic memories about the day you chose your first puppy. Your autobiographical memories combine these two elements to give you an account of your life. A semantic element of your autobiographical memory might be that your dog's parents were champions. The episodic elements of your autobiographical memory for the event might include memories of your puppy's warmth and the happy way you felt that day.

martin phelps/Alamy Stock Photo

Despite the differences just outlined, semantic and episodic memories often overlap. You could form an episodic memory of where you were when you stored a specific semantic memory. A colleague was introduced to a student's parents as follows: "Mom, Dad, this is Professor Jones. He's the one I told you about who taught us that rats can't barf." Not only did the student retain a semantic memory about rat behavior (which incidentally is true and is relevant to understanding the classical conditioning of taste aversion in rats), but the student correctly retained an episodic memory of when and where the fact was learned.

We can see that semantic and episodic memories interact dynamically to provide a complete picture of the past. Our semantic knowledge of the relative temperatures of the Pacific and Atlantic Oceans depends on the personal experiences of either hearing the fact in a geology classroom or vacationing on both coasts of the United States. At the same time, we use our semantic knowledge to interpret our episodic memories. Without semantic knowledge of the meanings of the words ocean, temperature, Atlantic, and Pacific, we would be unable to organize our experience into a coherent conclusion—the ocean is colder in California than in Florida.

This blending of semantic and episodic memories characterizes **autobiographical memories** (Williams et al., 2008). Autobiographical memories can contain factual, semantic aspects of personal experience without episodic aspects. You might know you were born in Pasadena, California, but you would not have any memory of being born. However, your autobiographical memories of Pasadena might also include episodic memories of attending the Rose Parade on New Year's Day as a child, complete with images of the sights, sounds, and emotions of that experience.

A small number of people have been identified as having a rare condition known as highly superior autobiographical memory (HSAM) (Parker et al., 2006; LePort et al., 2012; Ally et al., 2013). One individual with HSAM showed nearly perfect recollection of dates chosen at random from the time he was 11 years old. His recall was corroborated by entries in his grandmother's diary, interviews with family members, his medical records, and historical facts about his hometown. Individuals with HSAM show superior recall for public events, as well as personal experience, but otherwise perform about the same as typical controls on other tests of memory. HSAM is associated with physical differences in networks in the brain that are associated with autobiographical memory (LePort et al., 2012).

autobiographical memory Semantic or episodic memories that reference the self.

procedural memory A nondeclarative or implicit memory for how to carry out skilled movement.

priming A change in a response to a stimulus as a result of exposure to a previous stimulus.

Aurelien Hayman can recall detail from random dates in his past. When asked in 2012, Aurelien accurately recalled that October 1, 2006, was a cloudy day, he listened to "When You Were Young" by the Killers, asked a girl out and was turned down, wore a blue T-shirt, and experienced a power outage at his home. This rare type of memory, known as highly superior autobiographical memory (HSAM), has been the subject of only 20 published case studies.

Huw Evans/Shutterstock.com

Nondeclarative Memories

Earlier, we defined nondeclarative memories as unconscious or implicit memories that are difficult to verbalize (Smith & Grossman, 2008). In other words, nondeclarative memories influence our behavior without our conscious awareness of having used a memory. Using nondeclarative memories, you are able to do something, such as using rollerblades for the first time in years, without really knowing how you are doing it.

Three types of nondeclarative memories have been studied in detail: classical conditioning, discussed in Chapter 8, procedural memories, and priming. **Procedural memories** are also called skill memories because they contain information about how to carry out a skilled movement, such as driving a car. **Priming** occurs when exposure to a stimulus changes a response to a subsequent stimulus.

Procedural Memories Procedural memories tell us how to carry out motor skills and procedures and are especially difficult to describe in words. Consider the differences between showing somebody how to use scissors and writing an essay about how to use scissors. Which would be easier? Explaining in words how to use scissors, particularly for a person who had never seen a pair of scissors, would be quite a challenge. In contrast, few of us experience difficulties demonstrating procedures (Squire, 1987).

One great advantage of procedural memories is their ability to automate our performance. When a novice driver first learns to operate a car with a manual transmission, significant conscious effort is required to remember the correct sequence—clutch, gas, shift. Once the skill is well learned, the driver is far less aware of this sequence; the person "just drives." When procedures become automatic, we are free to direct our limited capacities for divided attention to other aspects of the task. A musician who has mastered the notes in a difficult piece can direct attention to the finer points of expression and phrasing. Unfortunately, if a procedure is learned incorrectly, such as a bad golf swing, considerable effort must be expended to fix the swing, which slows performance. The golfer must put in sufficient practice time to make the new, correct swing automatic.

age fotostock/Superstock

It might have been years since this grandfather last put on a pair of ice skates, but to help his granddaughter learn to skate, he's willing to get back out on the ice. He might be a little wobbly at first, but procedural memories for skilled movement are persistent. He'll quickly be skating as if he'd done it every day.

Priming Priming, or the change in our response to a stimulus because of pre-exposure to related stimuli, explains many everyday effects of familiarity. People rate advertisements they have seen previously, even if they can't consciously remember seeing them, more positively than those that they have not seen previously (Perfect & Askew, 1994). We agree that the unconscious way our attitudes can be manipulated is unsettling.

Priming is often studied using a lexical decision task (see Figure 9.9). In this task, a participant views two strings of letters and must decide whether the stimuli are both real words (such as *fork–roof*) or not (such as *mork–loof*). Reaction time, in the form of hitting one key for real words and another for nonwords, is the dependent variable. When the two stimuli are related words (e.g., *doctor–nurse*), reaction time for deciding that nurse is a real word is faster than when the stimuli are unrelated words (e.g., *butter–nurse)* (Meyer & Schvanevelt, 1971).

The distinction between nondeclarative procedural memories and declarative memories is one reason it is so challenging to be a computer help desk technician who must talk people through a repair procedure over the telephone. It would be easier to demonstrate how to fix the computer, which is why some software companies prefer to have the technician take over the computer remotely and apply the needed fixes as opposed to verbalizing procedures for the caller to undertake. It also explains why few star athletes go on to be good coaches. Performing a task is not the same as talking about it.

(a)

Stimuli	Marb Lork	Plame Doctor	Nurse Butter (unrelated)	Bread Butter (related)
Correct response	No	No	Yes	Yes

(b)

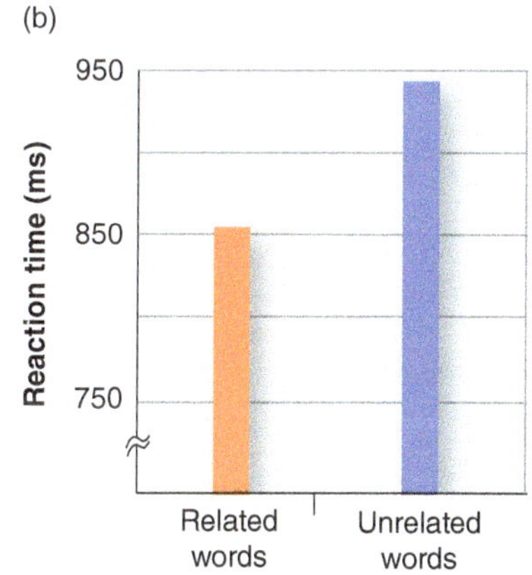

FIGURE **9.9**

Priming. Priming can be investigated within the lexical decision task, in which participants are asked to judge whether two words appearing together are both real words or not (a). Nonreal words are made by switching one letter from a real word, like *plame* from *flame* or *lork* from *fork*. Pairs of real words are either related to each other by meaning or not. The participants' reaction time in this task (b) demonstrates that participants respond faster to related word pairs (*bread–butter*) than to unrelated word pairs (*nurse–butter*). These results support the idea that we organize items in long-term memory based on their meaning.

Source: D. E. Meyer & R. W. Schvaneveldt (1971). "Facilitation in Recognizing Pairs of Words: Evidence of a Dependence Between Retrieval Operations," *Journal of Experimental Psychology*, *90*, 227–234. doi: 10.1037/h0031564

SUMMARY 9.1 Types of Memory

Type of memory	Major features
Sensory memory 	• Large capacity • Brief duration • Separate channels for different sensory types (acoustic, visual, etc.)
Short-term memory or working memory 	• Limited capacity (5–9 bits) • Limited duration (30 sec maximum) • Expansion of capacity through chunking • Expansion of duration through rehearsal • Central executive, visuospatial scratchpad, episodic buffer, phonological loop
Long-term memory 	• Very large capacity • Very long duration
Semantic memory 	• Declarative/explicit • General knowledge • Organized by category
Episodic memory 	• Declarative/explicit • Personal history • Organized chronologically
Autobiographical memory 	• Declarative/explicit • Combines semantic and episodic memories • References self
Procedural memory 	• Nondeclarative/implicit • Difficult to verbalize • Easy to demonstrate • Automated skills

Credits: Top row—moomsabuy/Shutterstock.com; Second row—André Babiak/AGE Fotostock; Third row—Suzy Bennett/Alamy Stock Photo; Fourth row—martin phelps/Alamy Stock Photo; Fifth row—Karina Wallton/Shutterstock.com; Sixth row—Huw Evans/Shutterstock.com; Bottom row—age fotostock/age fotostock/Superstock

How Is Long-Term Memory Organized?

Librarians use coding systems to group books on the shelf. Can we identify the systems that we use to organize our memories? Memories that share characteristics are more closely linked in long-term memory than memories that show little overlap among their various features.

Connectionist Theories

Connectionism views the mind as a network made up of simpler units or concepts. Connectionist models of memory suggest that thinking about one concept automatically leads to thinking about related concepts and their properties.

A **spreading activation model** (Collins & Loftus, 1975) recognizes that people form their own organizations in memory based on their personal experiences (see ● Figure 9.10). For example, if you ask people to report the first words that come to mind when they see the word *red,* you will get many different answers.

The spreading activation model also suggests that concepts differ in the strength of their connections. For example, even though avocados and oranges are both examples of the concept "fruit," most people have a closer link in their memories between "orange" and "fruit" than between "avocado" and "fruit." If asked whether an avocado or an orange is a fruit, reaction time to the second statement would be faster.

spreading activation model A connectionist theory proposing that people organize general knowledge based on their individual experiences.

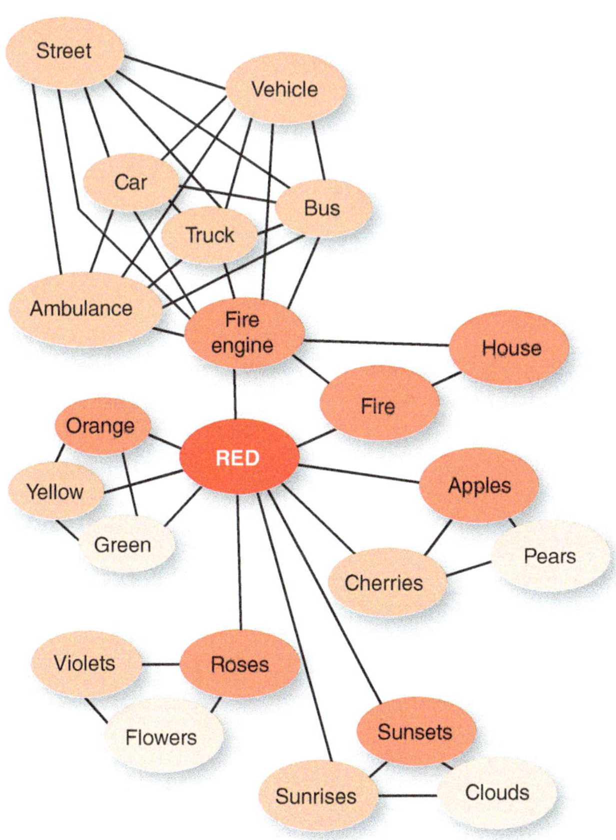

FIGURE **9.10**

Spreading Activation. According to the spreading activation theory, thinking about *red* will activate nearby concepts (*orange*, *green*, and *fire*) faster than more distant concepts (*sunsets* and *roses*). This network suggests that a person would answer the question "Is a bus a vehicle?" faster than the question "Is an ambulance a vehicle?"

Source: Adapted from A. M. Collins, & E. Loftus (1975). "A Spreading Activation Theory of Semantic Processing," *Psychological Review*, *82*, 407–428. doi: 10.1037/0033-295X.82.6.407

We are more likely to remember details that are consistent with our schemas than those that are not. We will remember books in the professor's office and brushes and canvases in the artist's studio.

The spreading activation model does an excellent job of accounting for the results of the lexical decision experiments described earlier. Using the spreading activation model, the first word activates a concept. This activation spreads to connected concepts and properties. For closely related concepts such as "doctor" and "nurse," activating the "doctor" concept would activate the "nurse" concept even before the person sees the word *nurse,* allowing a quick decision to be made as soon as the word appears. In contrast, with unrelated words like *butter* and *nurse,* the "nurse" concept would not be activated until the word actually appears, resulting in a relatively slower decision.

Inferences: Using Schemas

Frederic Bartlett (1932/1967) observed that memory does not work like a video recording of events. He read long, involved stories to study participants and then asked them to recall the stories 20 hours later. Not too surprisingly, the recalled stories were shorter and had less detail than the original story. Somewhat more surprisingly, participants added features to the recalled stories that had not appeared in the original. These additions were not random. In most cases, the details added by participants fit the theme or meaning of the story.

Bartlett concluded that memory storage does not occur in a vacuum. When we encounter new information, we attempt to fit the new information into an existing **schema**, or set of expectations about objects and situations. Details that are consistent with our schemas are more likely to be retained, whereas inconsistent details are more likely to be left out. Details may be added in memory if they make a story more consistent and coherent. For example, you are more likely to recall having seen books in a photograph of a professor's office than in a photograph of a farmer working in the fields. Even if no books appeared in the professor's office, you might recall seeing some, because most professors have offices filled with books. In Chapter 11, we will explore the development of schemas and the formation of concepts during childhood.

schema A set of expectations about objects and situations.

EXPERIENCING PSYCHOLOGY

Schemas and False Memories

FREDERIC BARTLETT OBSERVED that using schemas to frame our memories can lead us to add details that improve a memory's consistency and coherence. In other words, we can "remember" things that did not occur because they fit our schemas. We can demonstrate this "fill in the blank" tendency in memory by asking you to memorize some word lists.

1. Read through both lists of words in order, and try to remember as many words as you can.

   List 1 sheets, pillow, mattress, blanket, comfortable, room, dream, lay, chair, rest, tired, night, dark, time

   List 2 door, tree, eye, song, pillow, juice, orange, radio, rain, car, sleep, cat, dream, eat

2. Without looking back at the list, write down as many words as possible from List 1 in any order.

Analysis

Check your list of recalled words for any that did not appear in List 1. *Pillow* and *dream* appear in both lists, but *sleep* appears in List 2 only. Many people insert *sleep* into their List 1 responses (a false memory) because so many of the words on List 1 fit the sleep schema. It is unlikely that you will insert words into your recalled list that are not related to the schema of sleep. See whether you can construct some lists on your own that produce other false memories. We return to the issue of false memories and retrieval later in this chapter. ■

Schemas play important roles in memory storage, as demonstrated by a clever experiment in which participants were asked to read the following passage:

> The procedure is actually quite simple. First you arrange things into different groups depending on their makeup. Of course, one pile may be sufficient depending on how much there is to do. If you have to go somewhere else due to lack of facilities that is the next step, otherwise you are pretty well set. It is important not to overdo any particular endeavor. That is, it is better to do too few things at once than too many. In the short run this may not seem important, but complications from doing too many can easily arise. A mistake can be expensive as well. The manipulation of the appropriate mechanisms should be self-explanatory, and we need not dwell on it here. At first the whole procedure will seem complicated. Soon, however, it will become just another facet of life. It is difficult to foresee any end to the necessity for this task in the immediate future, but then one never can tell. (Bransford & Johnson, 1972, p. 722)

Alexander Image/Shutterstock.com

The self is one of the most important schemas we have for organizing our thinking. If you can think about how the material you study is reflected in your experience, it will be easier to remember.

At this point, you are probably scratching your head in confusion. Reading this passage is bad enough, and remembering much of it later seems impossible. However, what if we tell you that the passage is about doing your laundry? With the laundry schema in mind, try rereading the passage. It is likely to make a lot more sense than when you read it the first time, and you will remember more of what you read. Cartoonist Nathan Pyle delights in highlighting the importance of context and schemas as his aliens navigate our world. His character's statement "If I consume too much of this jitter liquid, it irritates my storage organ" make little sense unless you understand a schema related to drinking coffee.

How Do We Retrieve Memories?

Storing information does us little good unless we can locate the information when we need it. Without a system of retrieval, our stored memories would be no more useful to us than a library in which books were placed on shelves at random. You might get lucky and find what you are looking for, but in most cases, the search would take so long that the information would no longer be needed.

Retrieval From Short-Term Memory

Imagine that you were told to remember the following letters for a subsequent test:

c a f h k

During the test, you are shown a series of letters one at a time. If the letter you are shown matches one on your list, you pull the "yes" lever as quickly as possible. If the letter is not on your list, you pull the "no" lever. This procedure is used to investigate recall from short-term memory (Sternberg, 1966, 1967, 1969).

Because of the small number of items held in short-term memory, it is tempting to assume that we can retrieve them all simultaneously. However, this is not the way memory works. When the number of letters on the list was increased, a consistent 38 milliseconds of reaction time was added for each additional item. In other words, if you were asked to say whether "h" was on your list, you would first consider "c," then "a," then "f," and so on until you reached the target letter. These results suggest that we search through short-term memory one item at a time, rather than retrieving its contents all at once.

Tom Grill/Spirit/Corbis

Retrieval systems help us find the information we need, whether we are searching online, looking for a book, or trying to remember something important. Organized information is always easier to find than disorganized information.

The popularity of memory games, such as Trivial Pursuit, probably results from the rewarding feeling we get when we retrieve a sought-after memory.

Retrieval from Long-Term Memory

The popularity of games like *Trivial Pursuit*, crossword puzzles, and television game shows highlights an interesting aspect of memory retrieval. It feels good when you can remember something. At the same time, most students are all too familiar with the intense feelings of frustration that accompany the inability to retrieve information. You know the answer, but it isn't coming to mind.

The Role of Cues A **cue** is any stimulus that helps you access target information. Most students find recognition tasks such as true–false or matching exam items relatively easy. These tasks provide complete cues (the correct information is on the page in front of you). All you need to do is make a judgment about how well the presented information matches what is stored in memory. Compared to recognition tasks, recall tasks, such as essay exams, require an additional step. Information must be retrieved from memory and then recognized as correct, a process known as generate–recognize (Guynn et al., 2014). Recall tasks provide far fewer cues than recognition tasks and are typically more difficult as a result.

In addition to the amount of information provided, what makes a stimulus an effective cue? The most effective cues are those we generate ourselves, a finding that students might find particularly useful. In one experiment, one group of students wrote down 3 words of their choosing for each of the 600 words they were expected to learn, while another group studied the same 600 words accompanied by 3 words for each term selected by another person (Mäntylä & Nilsson, 1988). Although recall in the second group was an excellent 55%, the students who selected their own retrieval cues remembered a remarkable 90% of the words. In a later section on improving your memory, we will emphasize the benefits of incorporating your experience when forming new memories. If you are able to put concepts to be learned in your own words and associate them with personal experiences, they will be easier to remember.

Diverse Voices in Psychology

What Is the "Own-Race Bias" in Memory for Faces?

FOLLOWING THE MISIDENTIFICATION of five innocent African-American men by a white eyewitness in 1971, William Haythorn was inspired to ask whether cross-racial identifications were as accurate as same-race identifications (Meissner & Brigham, 2001). This led to decades of investigations into the own-race bias (ORB) in memory for human faces, also known as the cross-race effect or other-race effect.

Meta-analyses have supported significant ORB effects that are consistent across a number of racial and ethnic groups (Meissner & Brigham, 2001). Researchers still differ, however, in how they explain the effect. One school of thought suggests that the ORB results from perception (Rossion & Michel, 2011). Because people are more familiar with their own race than others, they might initiate different types of attention and perceptual processes when encoding information about faces representing different races (see Chapter 5). Other researchers focus on more social and cognitive factors, such as perceived in-group versus out-group membership (Hugenberg et al., 2010). According to this approach, a member of your in-group might seem more important to encode, leading to the use of different perceptual strategies.

Most of the ORB studies make use of an either-or approach to racial identity. What happens when the stimuli are more ambiguous? Given the large number of people with multiracial identities today, this seems like a logical and important question. When ambiguous racial group faces are used as stimuli, participants' memory for them depends on whether the ambiguous faces are viewed as in-group members or not (Pauker et al., 2009). When perceivers associated ambiguous faces with their in-group, memory was better, but when the ambiguous faces were not included in the in-group, memory was once again poor.

What happens if the perceiver is bicultural? Which faces would seem to fit the "own-race" category for these individuals? Latino-Americans were primed to focus on either their Latino or American cultural selves (Marsh et al., 2016). When primed to focus on their Latino cultural selves, the participants demonstrated better memory for Latino faces than for white faces. However, when primed to focus on their American cultural selves, memory for white faces was better than for Latino faces.

These results emphasize the importance of considering social and cognitive factors in addition to perceptual and learned aspects in efforts to understand the basis of the own-race bias. ■

Cues might work because of a process known as **encoding specificity** (Tulving, & Thomson, 1973; Flexser & Tulving, 1978; Tulving, 1983). Each time you form a long-term memory, target information is encoded along with other important bits present at the same time. As a result, each memory is processed in a unique and specific way because this exact combination of bits is unlikely to occur again. Any stimulus that was present and noticed during this encoding process could serve as a cue for retrieving the target memory.

Among the bits of information that get encoded along with target memories are features of the surrounding environment, leading to context-dependent memory. You have probably been advised to study in a well-lit, quiet, professional environment to perform your best on exams. Duplicating your testing situation when you study should provide the greatest number of retrieval cues. When study participants were asked to learn lists of words in one of two distinctive rooms while either standing or sitting, recall was best when participants were tested in the same room and position as when they learned the information (Greenspoon & Ranyard, 1957). As shown in ● Figure 9.11, scuba divers who learned words either on land or underwater retrieved the most words when their encoding and testing circumstances were the same (Godden & Baddeley, 1975). Although these effects are small, it is still a good idea to study in a quiet, classroom-like environment, which might explain why studying in the library has remained popular.

Mood and other internal states can serve as encoding cues. In one creative study, people with bipolar disorder (described in Chapter 14), whose moods can swing from mania to depression, learned words in one state (mania or depression) and tried to retrieve them in either the same state, mania–mania or depression–depression, or the opposite one, mania–depression or depression–mania (Weingartner et al., 1977). The participants were most successful when learning and retrieving occurred in the same state, whether that was mania or depression.

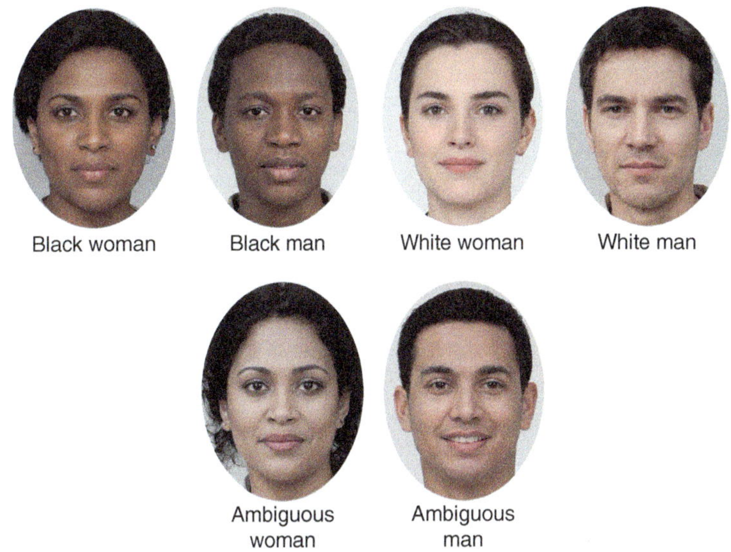

Participants typically show an improved memory for faces of people from their own race, a phenomenon known as the own-race bias (ORB). Researchers do not agree on the causes of the ORB, but some argue in favor of the importance of an in-group versus out-group hypothesis. When ambiguous faces are presented, participants' memories for the faces depend on whether they are primed to think of the ambiguous faces as members of their own in-group or not.

Generated.Photos

It may be tempting to blame context-dependent memory for the experience of alcohol-related blackouts, but these are more likely to result from alcohol's active interference with the formation of long-term memories (Lisman, 1974). There is no evidence that getting drunk again will make it easier to recall what happened the last time a person got drunk.

Tip of the Tongue Retrieval is not an all-or-none phenomenon. Instead, retrieval proceeds step by step, with each new step bringing you closer to the target. This gradual retrieval is best illustrated by the tip-of-the-tongue (TOT) phenomenon. TOT is probably a familiar experience for you. While trying to remember a word or name, you might retrieve the first letter of the item, but the complete item remains elusive.

cue A stimulus that aids retrieval.

encoding specificity A process in which memories incorporate unique combinations of information when encoded.

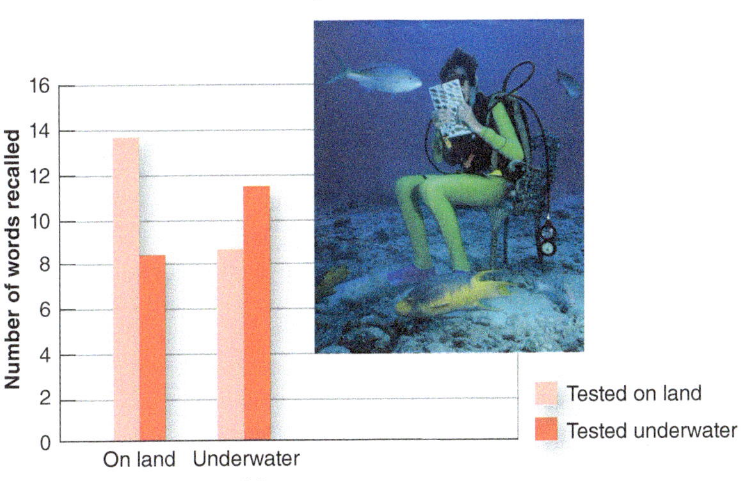

Ernest Manewal/Lonely Planet Images/Getty Images

FIGURE **9.11**

Our Surroundings Are Encoded in Context-Dependent Memories. Features of our environment get encoded along with target memories. Study participants learning lists of words either on land or while underwater recalled more words when tested in the same context compared to when they were tested in the opposite context. This diver might find it more difficult to retrieve information about types of fish if tested on dry land instead of underwater.

Source: Adapted from D. R. Godden, & A. D. Baddeley (1975). "Context-Dependent Memory in Two Natural Environments: On Land and Under Water," *British Journal of Psychology*, *66*, 325–331. doi: 10.1111/j.2044-8295.1975.tb01468.x

Drugs, including the caffeine in coffee, can produce strong context-dependent effects on memory. If you study while drinking coffee, taking a test without coffee is likely to make retrieval more difficult.

reconstruction Rebuilding a memory out of stored elements.

In a classic series of experiments, more than 200 TOT experiences were induced in research participants by presenting definitions of relatively rare English words (Brown & McNeill, 1966). For example, participants were asked to supply a word for "a navigational instrument used in measuring angular distances, especially the altitude of the sun, moon and the stars at sea" (Brown & McNeill, 1966, p. 333). You may be picturing the object right now, or thinking about a movie of an old salt using this instrument—it starts with an *s*—but most of you will have difficulty retrieving the word *sextant*.

Participants showed considerable evidence of partial recall during their TOT experiences. They were able to identify words that they recognized instantly, unlike words they did not know. Many were able to identify the first letter and the number of syllables in the target word. Incorrect words that were retrieved frequently sounded like the target, although their meanings were usually quite different. In some cases, retrieving the incorrect word blocked the retrieval of the correct item, but in other cases, the incorrect word was an additional cue.

Reconstruction During Retrieval When retrieved, information to be used flows from long-term memory back into working memory. The mind engages in **reconstruction**, or the building of a memory out of the stored bits by blending retrieved information with new content present in working memory (Bartlett, 1932/1967). When you retrieve the target information, you are reconstructing something sensible to fit the occasion, as opposed to simply reproducing some memory trace. Unfortunately, every time you retrieve a memory, it is weakened and then requires reconsolidation (Haubrich & Nader, 2016). If the memories are rather fresh, such as when you are describing an automobile accident to a police officer, this process might produce updates in the original memory that will then be reconsolidated into long-term memory. Changes you make in the original memory will be stored as the new "truth." However, if you are recalling a memory from a more remote time, less updating is likely to occur (Gräff et al., 2014).

Storytellers often discover that certain aspects of their stories provoke more of a reaction from the audience. These aspects are emphasized and perhaps exaggerated for even greater effect, and the new, more exciting story replaces the original version in long-term memory. Fish become larger, vacations become more exciting, and heroes become more heroic. When participants in a study were asked to repeat a complicated story on several occasions, they tended to simplify the story, highlight some aspects more than others, and adjust the story to fit their worldviews (Bartlett, 1932/1967). Such alterations probably form the basis of mythology. In the retelling of the adventures of Odysseus or King Arthur, accounts of the original true events are lost or hopelessly distorted.

Tip-of-the-tongue experiences were elicited in volunteers by describing rare words in English. One of the items was the name of the weird-looking instrument this naval cadet is learning to use. Study participants were often able to retrieve the first letter of the word (s) and the number of syllables (two) without necessarily retrieving the whole word (sextant), which demonstrates retrieval is not all or none.

Most of us believe that our memories, especially for important life events, are relatively accurate. Elizabeth Loftus set out to evaluate the reliability of eyewitness testimony in courtroom settings and discovered that memories are rather flexible. In one experiment, participants watched a video of an automobile accident and answered a number of questions about what they had seen (Loftus & Palmer, 1974). One group heard the question "How fast was the white sports car going while traveling along the country road?" while the other group heard the same question with a slight addition—"How fast was the white sports car going when it passed the barn while traveling along the country road?" There was no barn in the video, but when participants were asked one week later whether they had seen a barn, 20% of those who had heard the barn question answered "yes," while fewer than 5% of the other participants did so. One must assume that skilled attorneys are quite aware of this feature of memory and could use such leading questions to the advantage of their clients (see Figure 9.12).

If you began this psychology course believing, like many people do, that memory works like a video of life, it might

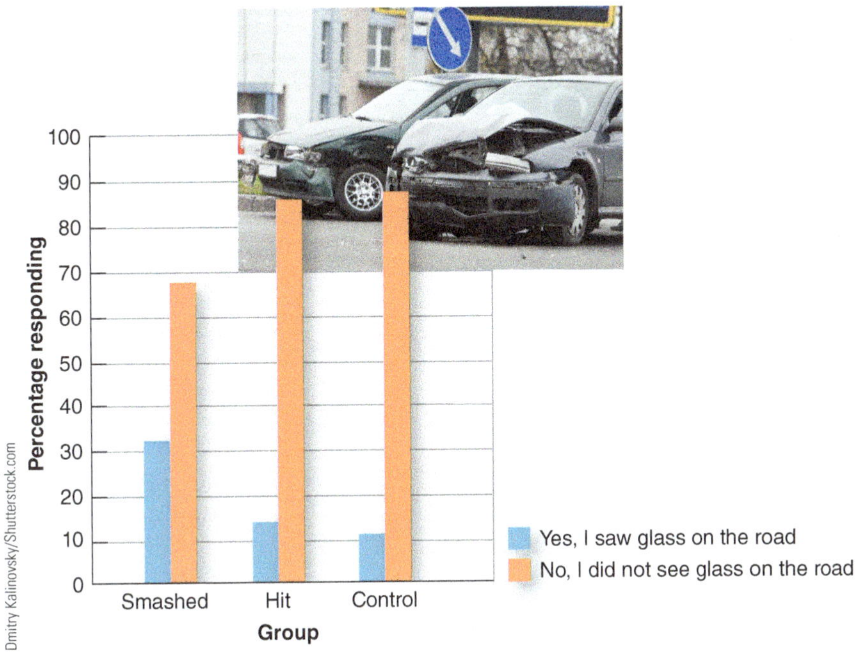

FIGURE 9.12

Memory Reconstruction. After study participants viewed a short video of an automobile accident, Loftus and Palmer (1974) asked one group, "About how fast were the cars going when they *hit* each other?" while a second group was asked, "About how fast were the cars going when they *smashed* each other?" One week later, both groups were asked if they recalled seeing glass on the road after the accident. There was no glass on the road in the video, so the correct answer was "no." Hearing the word *smashed* instead of *hit* increased the likelihood that a participant would "remember" glass on the road and answer "yes."
Source: Adapted from E. F. Loftus & J. C. Palmer (1974). "Reconstruction of Automobile Destruction: An Example of the Interaction Between Language and Memory," *Journal of Verbal Learning and Verbal Behavior*, *13*, 585–589. doi: 10.1016/S0022-5371(74)80011-3

surprise you to learn that this is not the case. It may be quite unsettling to realize that memories are open to change and revision and that those distinct and confident childhood memories we cherish may be somewhat inaccurate or even flat out wrong. However, it also doesn't make sense to think that we would evolve a system of memory that was usually wrong. Instead, fuzzy trace theory suggests that we use precious resources to form different types of memories based on our needs, ranging from verbatim, or exact accounts, to gist, which means we retain the general idea of events (Reyna, 2008). We use gist when a relatively vague level of information is sufficient because this is a more efficient use of resources. We use the more energy-intensive verbatim memories for situations that require detailed, accurate recall, such as remembering the periodic table of the elements in your chemistry class. This system works well for us most of the time, but later in this chapter, we will see how relying on gist instead of retrieving verbatim information can lead to false memories (see ● Figure 9.13).

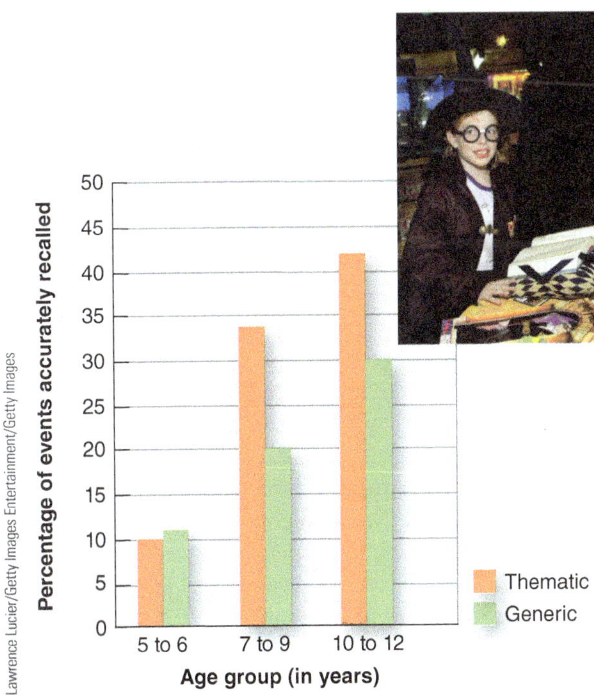

FIGURE 9.13

The Use of Gist Increases With Age. Older children, with their improved language skills, use gist more effectively than younger children (Odegard et al., 2009). When children attended birthday parties with a theme (e.g., Harry Potter or SpongeBob SquarePants), older children appeared to be able to use the theme of the party to provide gist, leading to their successful recall of more theme-related events, such as having magic potions at Hermione's party. Younger children, however, could not remember theme-related events better than generic birthday party events such as blowing out candles on a cake, suggesting that forming a theme gist was not helpful.
Source: Adapted from T. N. Odegard et al. (2009). "Children's Eyewitness Memory for Multiple RealLife Events," *Child Development*, *80*(6), 1877–1890. doi:10.1111/j.1467-8624.2009.01373.x

People often report especially vivid episodic memories about where they were and what they were doing when they first heard news that evoked a strong emotional response, such as the 9/11 terrorist attacks or the assassinations of President Kennedy and Dr. Martin Luther King. However, research evidence suggests that these memories are not always as accurate as we think they are.

SETH MCALLISTER/Stringer/AFP/Getty Images

A checkpoint for the accuracy of our memories results from source monitoring (Johnson, Hashtroudi, & Lindsay, 1993). Under normal circumstances, we do a good job of distinguishing between external and internal sources of information, as in "I said that" or "I thought about saying that." Again, this system works well for us most of the time, but it can produce false memories when we attribute a memory to the wrong source. For example, you might think you told your roommate you would be coming in late, but you may have only mentally reminded yourself to do so. You have mistaken an internal source of information ("I thought that") with an external source ("That happened").

Retrieval of Emotional Events Take a moment and write down the most important five events in your life last year. Do these events have anything in common with one another? We're willing to guess that each of the events on your list is associated with strong emotions. From an evolutionary perspective, this makes good sense. In Chapter 7, we argued that emotions provide quick guidance for approach-or-avoidance decisions. Many of our emotional experiences, while not life threatening, have significance for us, and forming strong memories of these events will help us respond effectively to similar situations in the future. Not too surprisingly, direct electrical stimulation of the amygdala produces stronger declarative memories (Inman et al., 2018). In Chapter 4, we identified the amygdala as being involved with a number of emotional responses, and fear in particular.

Emotions, particularly negative emotions, do not have a simple relationship with memory retrieval. In some cases, we have difficulty remembering negative events, which we discuss in a later section on motivated forgetting. For example, some individuals report that they can recall few or no details of having been sexually molested as children. In other cases, memories for negative events seem even more vivid and intrusive than other types of memories. Many adults in the United States formed a **flashbulb memory** of the terrorist attacks of September 11, 2001, or an especially vivid memory including details of where they were and what they were doing when they first heard the news. Individuals diagnosed with posttraumatic stress disorder (PTSD) often experience intrusive flashbacks of the events that originally traumatized them. How do we reconcile these differences in retrieval for emotional events?

As information moves through the stages described by the information processing model, it remains relatively fragile and subject to modification. Stress and strong negative emotions are accompanied by the release of hormones and by patterns of brain activity that can either enhance or impair memory processing, depending on the timing of the emotional response relative to target learning (Joëls, 2006). If stress and learning happen at the same time, an enhanced memory such as a flashbulb memory might be formed (Diamond et al., 2007). Stress occurring either before or after learning impairs memory formation (Joëls, 2006). Impairment of memory following an important life event might protect the fragile memories of that event from interference until they are fully consolidated.

flashbulb memory An especially vivid and detailed memory of an emotional event.

So far, we have been considering isolated events that elicit strong negative emotions and stress. As we will see in Chapter 16, chronic stress produces its own set of challenges for memory by producing a number of important changes in the parts of the brain associated with memory formation. For example, chronic stress is associated with a loss of volume in the hippocampus that is likely to have profound influences on the formation of new memories (Roozendaal et al., 2009).

PSYCHOLOGY AS A HUB SCIENCE

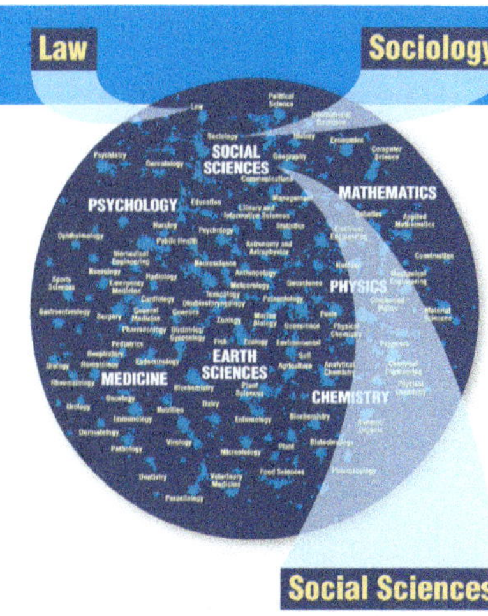

How Reliable Are Eyewitnesses?

OUR LEGAL SYSTEM RELIES HEAVILY on the testimony of eyewitnesses, especially those who have nothing to gain by telling a lie. Given the flexible nature of human memory as discussed in this chapter, is the trust we place in eyewitness accounts reasonable?

Carefully controlled research by Elizabeth Loftus into the use of eyewitness testimony (Loftus & Palmer, 1974; Loftus, 1979), along with the development of forensic deoxyribonucleic acid (DNA) testing in the 1990s, seriously compromised trust in eyewitness testimony. Out of all cases in which an innocent person has been cleared of a crime because of DNA evidence, about 75% involved mistaken identification of the perpetrator by an eyewitness (Wells et al., 2006).

Psychologists have used research on eyewitness behavior to make scientifically based recommendations to law enforcement officials. For example, the manner in which photograph lineups of possible suspects are shown to witnesses affects the likelihood of mistaken identification. In the typical procedure, witnesses view lineup photographs simultaneously, which allows them to compare all the people and choose the person who looks most similar to their memories of the perpetrator. Unfortunately, this procedure makes mistaken identification more likely if the real suspect does not appear in the lineup. The witness simply chooses the person who looks most like the remembered perpetrator. If a sequential procedure is used, in which the witness must respond "yes" or "no" to a picture before moving to the next one, mistaken identifications occur less frequently (Steblay et al., 2001).

Perhaps juries could evaluate eyewitness testimony more accurately if they took the witness's apparent confidence into account. In other words, a person who seems confident about identifying a suspect might be expected to be more accurate than a witness with less confidence. Unfortunately, witnesses testifying in court who express a 95% confidence in their judgment (expecting to be wrong only 5% of the time) are correct only 70% to 75% of the time (Brewer et al., 2002). However, witness confidence at the time of identification appears to be strongly related to accuracy (Wixted et al., 2015). If courts paid more attention to this early confidence rather than confidence in the courtroom months or even years later, fewer innocent people should be convicted.

Special consideration must be given to cases in which the eyewitness is a child. An understanding of children's memory development is critical for evaluating the child's ability to serve as a witness to a crime. Some data indicate that children's memories of significant events, such as a trip to an emergency room, are quite reliable as long as 4 to 5 years later (Peterson & Whalen, 2001). However, young children are accustomed to pleasing adults with their answers and are more suggestible than adolescents and adults. Fortunately, understanding the strengths and limitations of children's memory systems has allowed experts to develop methods for obtaining the most accurate reports possible from child witnesses (Bruck & Ceci, 2009).

Further improvements should accompany the development of new, more reliable measures of recognition, such as brain imaging, reaction time, rapid presentation of faces, and analyses of witness eye movements (Wells et al., 2006). ■

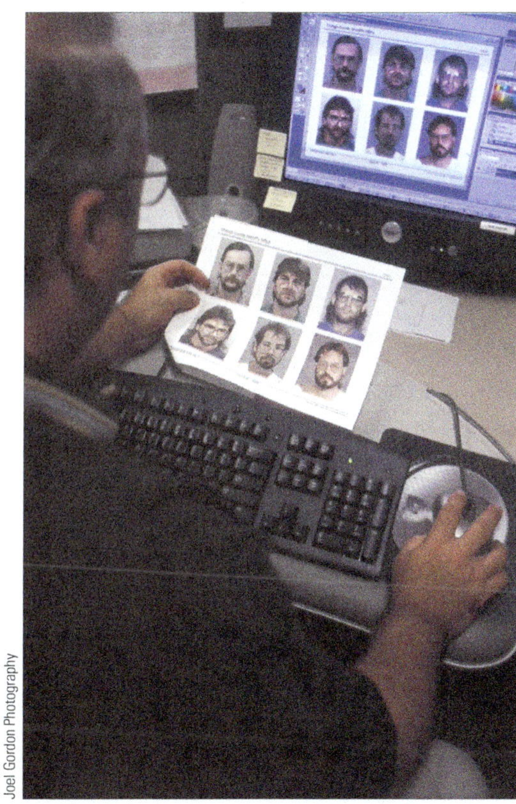

Joel Gordon Photography

The traditional lineup used in the criminal justice system is likely to produce a mistaken identification when the real perpetrator is not included. The witness simply picks the most similar person. Psychologists have shown that giving "yes" or "no" answers to one photo at a time reduces the risk of a mistaken identification.

SUMMARY 9.2 Retrieval from Long-Term Memory

Retrieval phenomenon	Major features
Cues 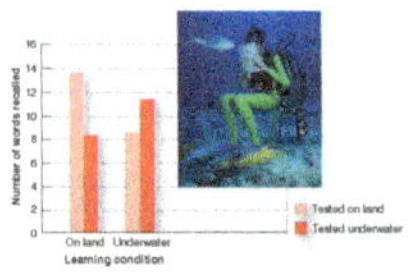	• Recognition versus recall • Self-generated cues • Encoding specificity • Context-dependent memory
Tip-of-the-Tongue 	• Retrieval is not all-or-none, but gradual • Incorrect retrievals can block correct retrievals or serve as cues
Reconstruction 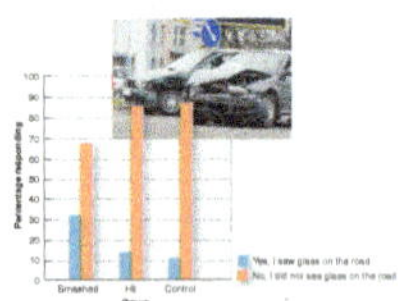	• Newer memories are more susceptible to reconstruction • Implications for eyewitness testimony • Fuzzy trace theory • Source monitoring
Effect of Emotions 	• Flashbulb memories • Importance of timing • Effects of chronic stress

Credits: First row: Ernest Manewal/Lonely Planet Images/Getty Images; Second row: andrey polivanov/Shutterstock.com; Third row: Dmitry Kalinovsky/Shutterstock.com; Fourth row: SETH MCALLISTER/Stringer/AFP/Getty Images

Why Do We Forget?

forgetting A decrease in the ability to remember a previously formed memory.

Now that we understand the processes involved with the formation, storage, and retrieval of memories, we can turn our attention to the troublesome topic of forgetting. For students, whose job description involves committing large amounts of information to memory, an understanding of forgetting is the source of practical advice for improving memory and avoiding memory failure.

Andy Reynolds/Getty Images

If this woman was never able to forget where she parked all the previous times she used this lot, finding her car today would be extremely difficult.

We define **forgetting** as a decrease in the ability to remember a previously formed memory. The key here is that to forget a memory, it has to have been formed in the first place. This definition excludes a number of instances that we have discussed previously. For example, many students maintain that they "forgot" information needed for an exam but instead were daydreaming during the lecture covering the material and never learned it. This example is better understood in terms of lack of attention and encoding failure than as an example of forgetting. When forgetting is the result of brain injury or disease, we usually refer to the loss of information as amnesia.

Understanding forgetting is complicated because we measure memory indirectly by looking at performance. As most students are all too aware, actual memory for a topic can be quite different from performance on an exam. It would be handy for both students and instructors if some sort of modern imaging technology would allow us to "see" whether introductory psychology had been adequately stored in the brain, but alas, this is not currently possible. Stress, illness, time pressure, and distractions can temporarily reduce our ability to recall information. When we discuss true forgetting, we are not considering the effects of these temporary difficulties.

Although forgetting can be frustrating, it also has its adaptive benefits. Forgetting provides a way to prioritize the things we should remember. For example, we are often asked to change our computer passwords to maintain security. At first, this can lead to annoying competition in memory between the old and the new passwords. Over time, however, the strength of an old password weakens. Functional magnetic resonance imaging (fMRI) studies have shown that prefrontal areas of the brain actively suppress memories that are used less frequently (Kuhl et al., 2007). By suppressing these lower priority memories, we can avoid confusion and reduce the amount of work we have to do to recall higher priority memories.

Decay

Decay occurs when our ability to retrieve information that we do not use fades over time. Imagine taking last term's final exams today. How would you do? You might think that the material you learned last term is gone forever, but just because you can't retrieve something doesn't mean that the memories are lost.

A classic method of measuring the retention of material in long-term memory over time is the method of savings. This method compares the rate of learning material the first time to the rate of learning the same material a second time. It might take you 50 practice trials to learn the periodic table of elements for your first chemistry class. In a subsequent course, you again need to memorize the table. This time, it only takes you 20 trials. The greater speed of learning the second time indicates that you retained or saved some prior memories of the table. Using this technique, we can demonstrate that people who studied high school Spanish but never used it later in life retained most of their memories for Spanish vocabulary words 50 years later (Bahrick, 1984). Instead of a large amount of forgetting because of the passage of time, most of the material we learn is retained nearly indefinitely.

Although the idea of decay fits our everyday experience of forgetting quite well, most contemporary psychologists believe that the simple passage of time does not do a good job of predicting memories that are easy or difficult to retrieve (Berman, 2009). It is likely that forgetting occurs because of a combination of factors, which may or may not include decay.

decay A reduction in ability to retrieve rarely used information over time.

interference Competition between newer and older information in memory.

Interference

Interference is the competition between newer and older information in the memory system. The brain requires a measurable amount of time to produce a physical representation of a memory. In the window of time in which memories are being processed but are not yet fully consolidated, they may be subject to distortion, loss, or replacement by interference from other bits of information.

How long is this window? The physical changes related to memory that occur at the level of the synapse might take minutes or hours. Memory loss usually occurs when this consolidation is interrupted. Individuals who experience unconsciousness as a result of a head injury rarely remember much about the immediate circumstances leading to the injury. Procedures such as general anesthesia or electroconvulsive therapy (ECT), described in Chapter 15,

People attending their 70th high school reunions might have forgotten the names of some of their classmates whom they hadn't seen in decades.

ZUMA Press Inc/Alamy Stock Photo

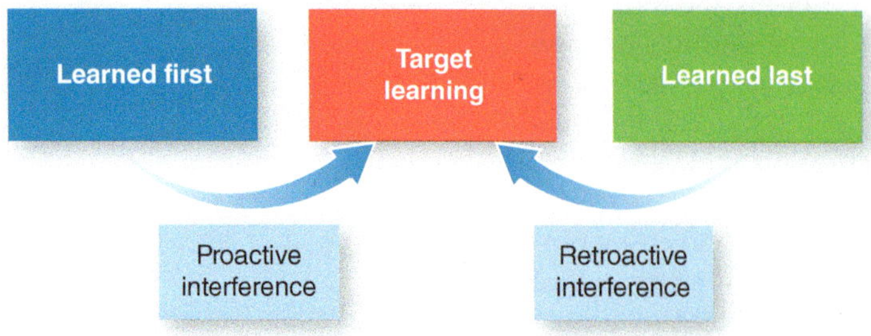

FIGURE **9.14**

Proactive and Retroactive Interference. If we measure recall of a target list of words, we find that it is worse both when preceded by learning another list (proactive interference) and when followed by learning another list (retroactive interference).

often produce slight memory deficits spanning a period of hours or possibly a day or two before and after treatment. In contrast, storage of memories in the cerebral cortex might take years, during which time information can be lost or distorted (Dudai, 2004).

Interference can be demonstrated by comparing performance in a list-learning task. The more lists someone must learn, the more difficult it becomes to remember words on the first list (Tulving & Psotka, 1971). In other words, learning new lists of words interfered with memory for the first list.

Does this mean that the first list is erased from memory by the incoming information? To test this hypothesis, researchers gave participants in one experiment a little help in the form of memory cues. The lists all contained categories of items, such as types of buildings (e.g., house, barn, garage, and hut). If the experimenters provided their participants with a cue in the form of the category (types of buildings), the effects of having learned additional lists were quite small. It appears that the words on the first list were maintained in memory, but learning additional lists made them hard to retrieve.

To make matters worse, interference can work in two directions (Underwood, 1957) (see ● Figure 9.14). Let's assume that your foreign language class is assigned one list of vocabulary words to study each night. You have procrastinated on your homework, and to catch up for a quiz the next day, you now have three lists of vocabulary words to study instead of the usual single list. Our interest will be in how well you can remember the second of the three lists. If we compare your memories for the second list to those of students who studied the first list when it was assigned, we find that your performance is relatively poor. In other words, learning the first list on the same night as the second list produces proactive interference for the second list. *Proactive interference* refers to reduced memory for target information as a result of earlier learning.

At the same time, we can compare your memories for the second list to the performance of your classmates who studied the third list the night after they studied the second list. Again, your performance is likely to be worse. Reduced memory for target information because of subsequent learning is known as *retroactive interference*. This type of interference was demonstrated in the multiple lists study we discussed previously, which you may recall unless too much retroactive interference has occurred.

motivated forgetting Failure to retrieve negative memories.

Motivated Forgetting

The Internal Revenue Service reports that far more people who owe money fail to sign their tax returns than do those who are due a refund. Assuming that the failure to sign the return is not a conscious act of defiance, how can we account for this lapse in memory? Theories of **motivated forgetting**, or the failure to remember or retrieve unpleasant or threatening information, suggest that the nonsigners are protecting themselves from further unpleasantness by "forgetting" to sign their tax forms.

Memory is a servant to our overarching goals. Retrieval, for better or worse, is often influenced by our motivations, and our motivations can distort the memories we retrieve. While not exactly forgetting in the sense of our earlier definition, motivated distortions of memory can be so extreme that the original information is essentially lost during the process.

In one example of the influence of motivation on recall, study participants were presented with a list of choices, such as between two internships, roommates, or cars for sale, with equal numbers of corresponding positive and negative features (high resale value or some rust

Elizabeth Loftus (2003) demonstrated that it was relatively easy to implant a false memory in study participants of having taken a hot air balloon ride during childhood.

pasphotography/Shutterstock.com

in the case of the cars). Subsequently, they remembered the positive features associated with their ultimate choices better than the negative features (Henkel & Mather, 2007). When they were deceived into thinking they had chosen the other option instead (because of a friendly "reminder" from the experimenter), they continued to remember the false choice more positively. In related research, participants conveniently demonstrated less recall for ethical rules after they had been given an opportunity to cheat (Shu et al., 2011). In Chapter 13, we will explore how these types of discrepancies between behavior and attitudes can change the attitudes, not just the memories for them.

Identifying the presence of motivated forgetting can have serious practical implications. Beginning in the 1970s, largely because of greater public recognition that incest was more common than previously believed, many adults began to report having been a victim of sexual abuse during childhood. These cases represented a range of possible motivated forgetting from suppression, in which the individual consciously remembered the incidents but had not reported them to parents or other authorities, to repression, in which the individual reported no conscious memory of the incidents until the memories were suddenly recovered during therapy or while reading a news report of a child molestation case.

A number of psychologists studying memory suspected that not all reports of recovered memories of child abuse were true, and some might represent confabulation or confusion between imagined and true memories. As we mentioned earlier in this chapter, our source monitoring abilities usually prevent us from mistaking false for true memories, but the system does not perform perfectly. Under the right set of circumstances, it is relatively easy for people to believe strongly in a memory that is simply not true.

We demonstrated in an earlier section on schemas that false recall for verbal stimuli can be produced by presenting words that are associated by meaningfulness (e.g., *bed*, *rest*, and *awake*). In this case, most study participants formed a false memory for the presentation of the word *sleep* (Deese, 1959). Perhaps you are thinking that memorizing strings of words in a laboratory has little relevance to the experience of traumatized victims of child abuse. Loftus, whom we met earlier in our discussion of memory reconstruction, addressed that concern by demonstrating that more complex false memories were rather easy to implant in study participants. Loftus (2003) described how imagining an event had happened or even reading the testimonials of witnesses could increase a person's confidence that a false event had occurred. Most persuasive is the use of photographs. When a real family photo was superimposed on a hot air balloon, 50% of participants "remembered" taking a ride, including details about how old they had been at the time and that the photo was taken by a particular person.

Until we understand more about the nature of confabulation, a cautious approach to repressed memories is probably the best course of action. We can neither prove nor disprove these memories without additional evidence, so any therapy should be aimed at relieving distressing symptoms without reference to their source (American Psychological Association [APA], 2014).

What Is the Biology of Memory?

Cognitive neuroscientists have made considerable progress in discovering the biological correlates of memory processing. In this section, we first zoom in for a look at how memory is managed at the cellular and biochemical levels. Next, we zoom out again to explore patterns of brain activation that are associated with certain types of memory processing.

Memory at the Level of the Synapse

Forming new memories requires changes in the connections neurons make with one another at the synapse, or synaptic consolidation. You might find it strange to think that such a process is going on in your brain as you read this chapter.

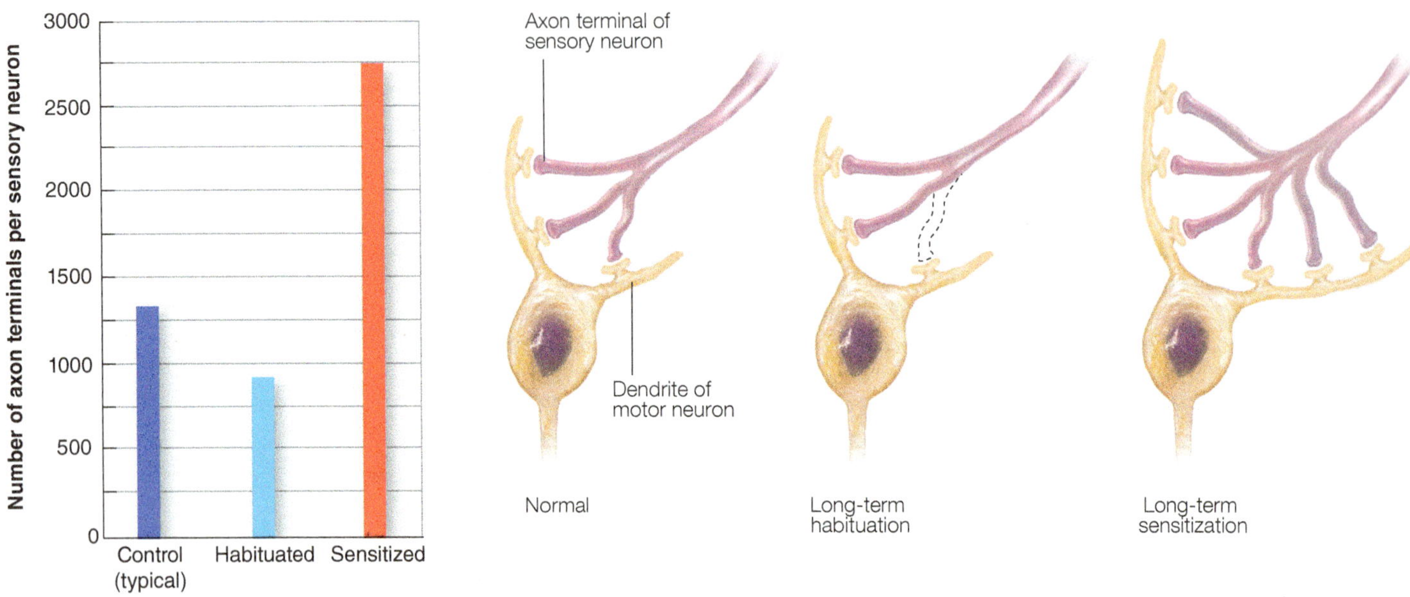

FIGURE **9.15**

Learning Changes Neural Structure. Neurons have smaller numbers of axon terminals following habituation but larger numbers following sensitization.

Source: C. H. Bailey & M. C. Chen (1983). "Morphological Basis of Long-Term Habituation and Sensitization in *Aplysia*," *Science*, *220*, 91–93. doi: 10.1126/science.6828885

long-term potentiation (LTP) The enhancement of communication between two neurons resulting from their synchronous activation.

Nobel Laureate Eric Kandel and his colleagues have demonstrated persistent changes in the strength of synapses responsible for several types of learning in the sea slug, including classical conditioning (Carew & Kandel, 1973; Brunelli et al., 1976; Antonov et al., 2003). In addition to changes in synaptic strength, it appears that learning stimulates a cascade of gene expression, which in turn produces the long-term structural changes in neurons that represent memories. The number of axon terminals increases following sensitization and decreases following habituation (Bailey & Chen, 1983; see Chapter 8). These observations are consistent with the behavior observed in each case—lower levels of responses to stimuli in habituation and higher levels of responses to stimuli in sensitization (see Figure 9.15).

One of the major processes responsible for change at the synaptic level during learning is **long-term potentiation (LTP)**, which enhances communication between two neurons. This phenomenon can be demonstrated experimentally by applying a rapid series of electric pulses to one area of the nervous system and observing the increased reactions of cells receiving input from that area (Bliss & Lømo, 1973; see Figure 9.16). Results from demonstrations of LTP suggest that the relatively simultaneous activation of a neuron sending information and the neuron receiving this information produces changes that make the synapse between them more efficient. LTP shares many features with memory, which makes it an attractive candidate for being one of the processes underlying memory phenomena. LTP lasts a long time, possibly

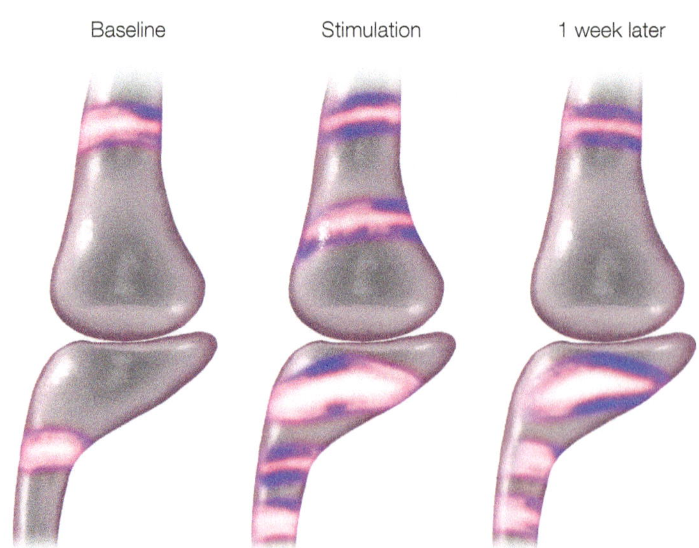

FIGURE **9.16**

Long-Term Potentiation (LTP). LTP can be demonstrated by applying a series of electrical pulses (center) and observing the increased reactions of cells receiving input (right) compared to their previous baseline (left). LTP shares many features with memory, such as being long-lasting and formed after a brief exposure to stimuli.

indefinitely, which is similar to our thinking about long-term memories. Second, both memories and LTP can be formed after only brief exposure to stimuli.

Working Memory and the Brain

Scientists have also made progress in their search for brain activity that correlates with working memory, although they continue to debate how the executive processes of working memory are organized (Nee et al., 2013). Studies of people with brain damage suggest that several executive functions are managed by different parts of the frontal lobes but that a single central executive probably does not exist (Stuss, 2011). Working memory does not occur in a separate, isolated part of the brain. Instead, the phonological loop and visuospatial sketch pad use the same posterior parts of the brain that are used in verbal and visual perception (Bledowski et al., 2010). Top-down influences originating in the prefrontal and parietal cortex provide the attention necessary to maintain stimulus information in working memory (Nee et al., 2013).

Long-Term Memories and the Brain

Through the careful observation of people with brain damage, along with brain imaging studies in healthy participants, scientists have discovered correlations between activity in parts of the brain and specific components of long-term memory. These discoveries support the distinctions made by cognitive psychologists between declarative and nondeclarative memories based on observations of behavior.

Declarative Memories and the Hippocampus In Chapter 4, we described the important role played by the hippocampus in memory. The hippocampus clearly participates in the consolidation of semantic and location information into long-term memory. The hippocampus might also be involved with the re-experiencing of episodic memories throughout the lifespan (Moscovitch et al., 2006).

Now that we are familiar with some distinctions between declarative and nondeclarative memories, we can examine the case study of Henry Molaison (the amnesic patient H.M.) in more detail. In follow-up observations of Molaison, Brenda Milner (1966, 2005) discovered that not all of his memories were equally affected by the surgery that damaged his hippocampus. Molaison retained most of his memory for events leading up to his surgery, but his ability to form new memories was profoundly reduced. The inability to form new memories is known as anterograde amnesia. Much to Milner's surprise, Molaison learned a new procedural task, mirror tracing, as well as typical control participants did. In one of these tasks, Molaison was asked to draw the shape of a star while looking at a sample star and his hand in a mirror. After 3 days, Molaison mastered the task. However, if asked, he would deny ever having performed the task. His procedural memories were intact, but his declarative memories for the details of the task were nonexistent (see • Figure 9.17).

Declarative Memories and the Cerebral Cortex Semantic memories appear to be widely distributed across the cerebral cortex (see • Figure 9.18). Using brain imaging, researchers can observe which parts of the cerebral cortex are active when a person is thinking about particular types of memories (Binder et al., 2009). Different areas are activated when a person is accessing knowledge of actions, items that can be manipulated, concrete concepts, and abstract concepts. For example, listing types of animals is associated with activity in the occipital lobes, suggesting that visualizing an animal's appearance might be helpful in this task (Martin et al., 1996). Listing types of tools activates areas of the frontal and parietal lobes normally associated with movements and action words. To name a hammer, for example, we might consider the hand movements associated with using hammers and words such as *pound* or *hit*.

In spite of the overlapping characteristics of semantic and episodic memory, they involve distinctive processing in the brain. Patients in the early stages of Alzheimer's disease showed much more dramatic episodic memory deficits than semantic memory deficits (Perry et al., 2000). The default mode network (DMN; see Chapter 6) is associated with thinking about the

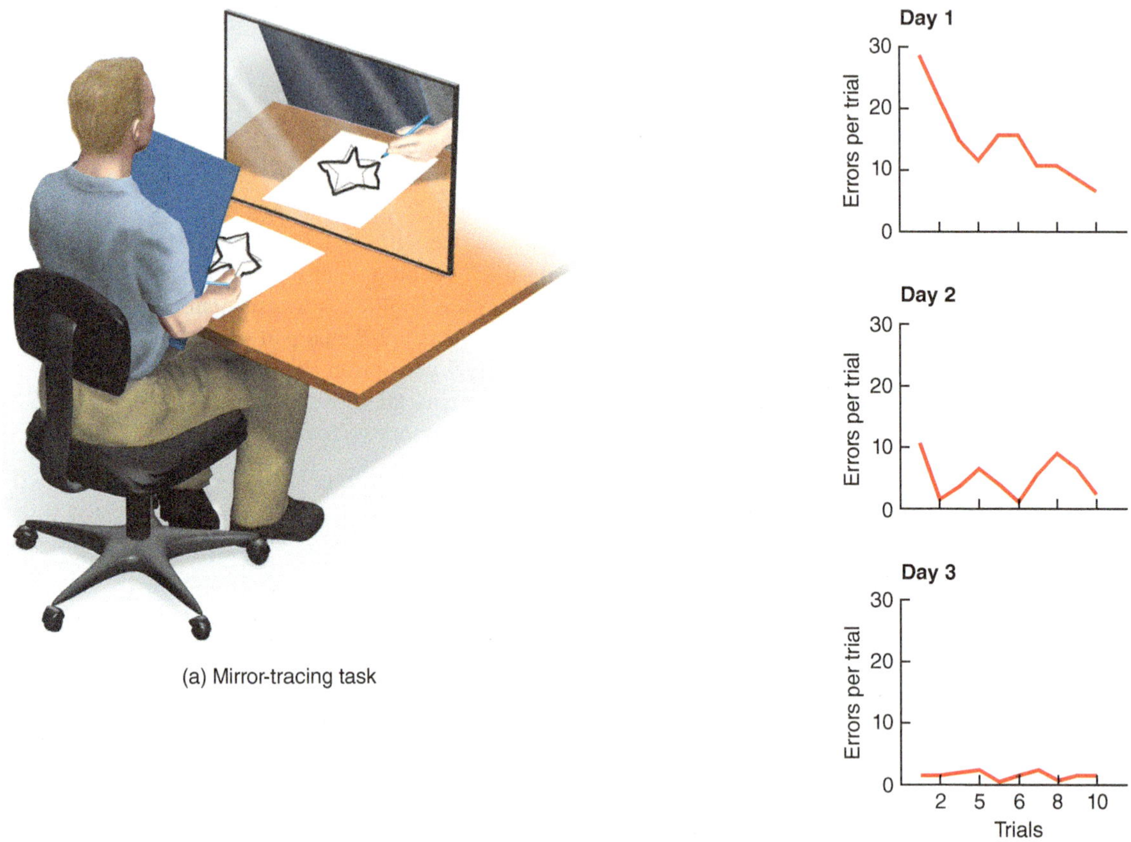

(a) Mirror-tracing task

(b) Performance of Henry Molaison

FIGURE **9.17**

Separating Declarative and Nondeclarative Memories. The mirror-tracing task requires a participant to trace a five-pointed star, which is mounted on a wooden board that blocks the participant's view of the star and his or her hand. The participant must view the star and his or her hand in a mirror. This task is especially challenging because the mirror reverses the image, so if you want the pencil to trace around the star away from your body, you have to move your pencil toward your body instead. Brenda Milner was surprised to observe that Henry Molaison learned the mirror-tracing task at a normal rate, even though he didn't remember the details of the task. This outcome suggested to Milner that nondeclarative, procedural memories such as the mirror-tracing task were not managed by the brain the same way as declarative memories.

Source: B. Milner (1965). "Memory Disturbance after Bilateral Hippocampal Lesions," in P. M. Milner & S. E. Glickman (Eds.), *Cognitive processes and the brain* (pp. 97–111). Princeton, NJ: Van Nostrand.

self, so it is not surprising to note that structures in this network are also implicated in episodic memory processing (Greicius et al., 2004). Areas of the temporal lobe and insula seem particularly important for remembering emotional personal experiences (Fink et al., 1996; Sheldon et al., 2016).

Episodic memories are also affected by damage to the prefrontal cortex. Damage in this area can produce a condition known as source amnesia. People with source amnesia maintain their semantic knowledge but do not recall how they acquired it. A man who experienced damage to his prefrontal cortex as the result of a traffic accident retained his semantic and procedural knowledge of the game of chess, but he could not remember how old he was when he learned or who taught him to play the game (Tulving, 1989).

Procedural Memories and the Basal Ganglia Procedural memories are correlated with activation of the basal ganglia, forebrain structures that are part of the brain's motor systems (see Chapter 4). People with Huntington's disease and Parkinson's disease, both of which

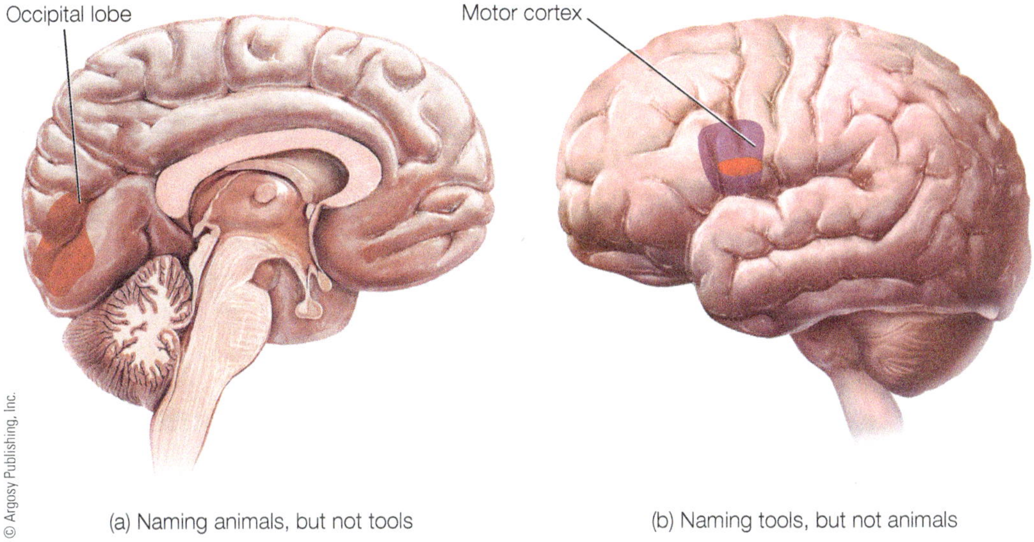

(a) Naming animals, but not tools

(b) Naming tools, but not animals

FIGURE 9.18

Semantic Memories Are Widely Distributed in the Brain. Different patterns of activity in the cerebral cortex are correlated with various types of semantic memories. Naming animals (a) is associated with activity in the visual cortex of the occipital lobe, suggesting that we think about what an animal looks like to name it. Naming tools (b) activates areas associated with hand movements, suggesting that we think about how we would use a hammer or saw to name one.
Source: Adapted from A. Martin et al. (1996). "Neural Correlates of Category-specific Knowledge." *Nature*, *379*, 649—652. doi:10.1038/379649a0

produce degeneration in the basal ganglia, typically have trouble learning new procedures (Knowlton et al., 1996; Krebs et al., 2001). In contrast, their declarative memories remain relatively intact. Recall that Henry Molaison experienced the opposite outcome. His procedural memory abilities were intact, but his declarative memory abilities were severely impaired.

Procedural memories quickly become automatic. When you learn to drive, you must attend to each step, but after learning the process, you "just drive."

Biochemistry and Memory

Throughout this chapter, we have emphasized that memory is not a single thing but rather a flexible, multistage process. It should not be surprising, therefore, that we do not have a simple biochemical account for memory.

Acetylcholine (ACh), discussed in Chapter 4, affects the encoding of new information (see ● Figure 9.19). Drugs that inhibit systems using ACh as a major neurotransmitter interfere with memory formation (Atri et al., 2004). People with Alzheimer's disease, which is characterized by severe memory deficits, show degeneration of neural circuits that use ACh. Medications prescribed to reduce the symptoms of Alzheimer's disease boost ACh activity (Holzgrabe et al., 2007). At the same time, high ACh levels might impair memory consolidation and retrieval (Micheau & Marighetto, 2011). Relatively low levels of ACh, characteristic of sleep, improve the transfer of information from temporary to more permanent storage (Diekelmann & Born, 2010).

Researchers are also interested in the role of the neurotransmitter glutamate in memory formation. One type of glutamate receptor, known as the *N*-methyl-d-aspartate (NMDA) receptor, is a prime candidate for learning-related changes such as those observed in LTP (Qiu & Knopfel, 2007). Not too surprisingly, chemicals that enhance the activity of glutamate receptors have been shown to boost memory formation in rats (Balschuna et al., 2006). Similar compounds are being tested for possible use in treating Alzheimer's disease.

Students are familiar with the use of caffeine to stay awake to study, but caffeine also has the ability to enhance memory directly through its ability to block adenosine, a by-product of the energy ATP molecule. Adenosine activity is implicated in the reduction of memory function in healthy aging and in Alzheimer's disease (Orr et al., 2015).

Individual differences in working memory capacity are correlated with activity in systems using GABA, the major inhibitory neurochemical in the brain, especially in a part of

Daniel Prudek/Shutterstock.com

FIGURE **9.19**

Acetylcholine (ACh), Caffeine, and Memory. Not only do drugs promoting ACh initiate changes in neural structure in honeybees (Weinberger, 2006), but so does caffeine. Bees rewarded with caffeine were 3 times as likely to remember a floral scent as bees rewarded with sucrose (Wright et al., 2013).

the frontal lobes known as the dorsolateral prefrontal cortex (Yoon et al., 2016). Individual differences in working memory play important roles in overall intelligence (see Chapter 10). At the same time, impairments in working memory are characteristic of conditions from schizophrenia to dementia.

How Can We Improve Memory?

Most college students by definition have good memory skills—this is an essential component of academic success, and those who lack these skills generally do not end up in higher education. However, we can always improve, and the observations made by psychologists studying memory provide many practical suggestions.

We have already discussed several lines of research that have practical implications for improved memory. The structure of long-term memory implies that organized material is easier to remember than disorganized material. Elaborative rehearsal, especially when you connect material to personal experience, anchors new material in your existing memory stores and makes it easier to retrieve. The effects of state, mood, and context on retrieval suggest that studying in circumstances that are most similar to those in which you will retrieve your memories will give you the best outcome. In addition to these basic suggestions, we would like to offer a few additional tips.

Distribute Practice over Time

Psychology professors will never give up trying to convince students that cramming is a terrible memory strategy. Persistent faith in cramming is surprising, given that we all know concert pianists and basketball players are better off practicing one hour a day each day for a week than practicing six hours straight the night before a performance. The mind works in similar ways whether it learns to play basketball or it learns the periodic table of elements, so the same learning strategies should work in either case.

THINKING SCIENTIFICALLY

Does Using a Laptop or Longhand to Take Notes Make a Difference?

FOR STUDENTS GROWING up surrounded by the wonders of technology, taking notes on a laptop or tablet seems natural. In comparison, writing notes by hand can seem slow, messy, and inconvenient. But is there a price to pay for using technology to take notes? Initial research on technology and notetaking focused on potential distractions. While working on a laptop or tablet, a student might be more tempted to wander away to look at social media. However, as shown in Figure 9.20, research has demonstrated that even when technology is used solely for notetaking, it produces worse memory outcomes than taking notes by longhand (Mueller & Oppenheimer, 2014).

WHAT AM I BEING ASKED TO BELIEVE OR ACCEPT?

We are being asked to believe that taking notes by longhand produces better memory than taking notes using a laptop.

WHAT EVIDENCE SUPPORTS THIS POSITION?

Mueller and Oppenheimer (2014) conducted three separate experiments comparing performance on factual and conceptual questions based on a lecture following notetaking using either a laptop or longhand. In each case, performance on factual questions did not differ according to notetaking method, but students taking notes using longhand performed better on conceptual questions than students taking notes using a laptop.

ARE THERE OTHER WAYS THIS EVIDENCE COULD BE INTERPRETED?

You might be thinking that other factors, such as typing skill or choice of notetaking method might account for these results. However, the researchers tested typing skill and found no effects. They also randomly assigned students to notetaking conditions, which would control for many individual factors that might otherwise influence the results, such as prior experience taking notes using technology.

WHAT OTHER EVIDENCE WOULD I NEED TO EVALUATE THESE ALTERNATIVES?

The study was published in 2014, and it is possible that familiarity with using technology has continued to increase in the intervening years. An update with a current cohort of students could be useful. In addition, technologies that allow you to write on a tablet using longhand would provide an interesting comparison.

WHAT ARE THE MOST REASONABLE CONCLUSIONS?

Mueller and Oppenheimer (2014) reported that notetaking behavior between their two groups was different. Students using laptops tended to write down as much of the lecture word-for-word as they could, while students using longhand were more likely to put the information in their own words. We know that putting information in your own words is an excellent memory strategy, so this aspect might account for much of the observed differences in performance. It is interesting that the two groups performed similarly on factual questions. It was only on the conceptual questions that notetaking method had strong effects. Students in the laptop condition were advised to NOT take word-for-word notes in one of the experiments, but they did anyway. It's possible, however, that with more practice, students using technology could nonetheless learn to take effective notes that promoted good conceptual performance. ■

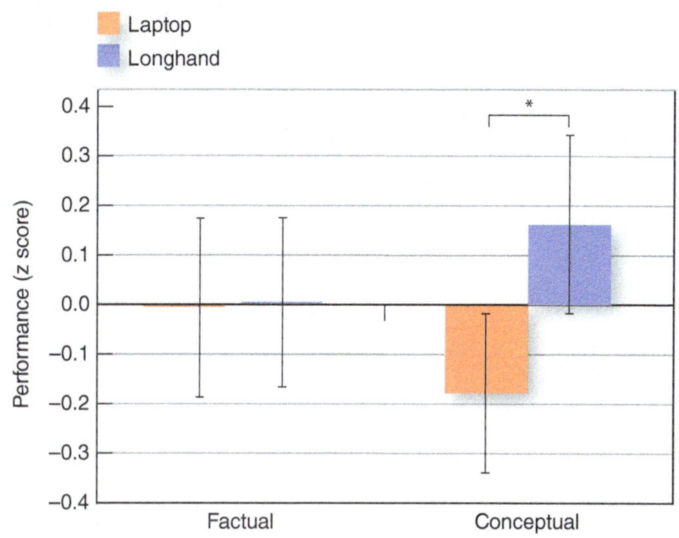

FIGURE 9.20

Taking Longhand Notes Is Superior to Typing Notes. Students taking notes on laptops performed as well as students taking longhand notes on factual questions, but performed relatively poorly on conceptual questions. Students taking notes on laptops tended to write down lectures word-for-word, whereas students taking longhand notes put the information into their own words.

Source: P. A. Mueller & D. M. Oppenheimer (2014). "The Pen Is Mightier Than the Keyboard: Advantages of Longhand Over Laptop Note Taking," *Psychological Science, 25*(6), 1159–1168. doi:10.1177/0956797614524581

Simon Winnall/The Image Bank/Getty Images

samuel wordley/Alamy Stock Photo

Most of us realize that the best way to improve our music or athletic skills is to practice every day (distributed practice). We would think it odd if an athlete or musician crammed practice in the night before a game or performance (massed practice). The same advantage of distributed over massed practice holds for academic work, but unfortunately, that fact does not deter some students from cramming for exams.

Nearly all forms of learning show evidence of an advantage of distributed practice (practice spread out over time) as opposed to massed practice (practice condensed to a short period; Russo & Mammarella, 2002). In other words, spacing the input of information to the brain over time produces better memory than cramming. Whether we are discussing the learning of classically conditioned responses by sea slugs or the learning of complex semantic information by college students, the advantage of distributing learning over time is a constant. By giving the brain more time to consolidate each memory, less is likely to be lost to interference.

Take Tests

We usually think about tests as measuring a student's ability to retrieve memories, but test taking is a powerful tool for forming memories, too (Roediger & Butler, 2011). Research demonstrates that taking a test produces superior long-term memory when compared with repeated studying of material. In addition, taking tests improved participants' ability to think about learned material with greater flexibility and to apply material to new situations. We are not advocating that you abandon reviewing your textbook and lecture notes, but we hope you will take advantage of the online testing opportunities that accompany this textbook.

Interleaving

Is it better to study different topics in blocks (AABBCC) or by interleaving (ABCABC)? Research indicates that interleaving, or mixing up your topics and skills, is a better strategy than blocking, or studying one thing at a time (Rohrer & Pashler, 2010).

Why would interleaving work better than blocking? One hypothesis suggests that interleaving improves our ability to discriminate between similar concepts. If you study one thing at a time, it's harder to see the contrasts. A second hypothesis suggests that interleaving has a direct effect on memory. Switching among topics requires more focus and attention, and these in turn promote better memory formation.

CONNECTING TO RESEARCH

How Can We Protect Memory Retrieval from Stress?

IT COMES AS NO SURPRISE to students to learn that stress impairs memory retrieval. All of us have had the experience of leaving a classroom after a test only to remember all the things we forgot as we make our way home. How can we avoid such frustrating experiences?

The way we study might have an effect on how well our memories hold up under stress. Many of us study by going over material multiple times, or "restudying." Research suggests that a more efficient method of studying includes "retrieval practice," or the taking of practice tests. These two methods were compared to each other in their ability to withstand stress (Smith et al., 2016).

The Question: Which study method (restudying versus retrieval practice) results in better retrieval during a stressful situation?

METHODS

Two groups of 60 participants were given the task of learning either 30 concrete nouns or 30 images of nouns, presented one at a time. Following this first presentation, the restudying group restudied the items, while the retrieval practice group recalled as many of the items as they could remember. No feedback was given to the retrieval practice group.

On the next day, half of each group was stressed by being asked to give an unprepared speech and solve math problems in front of judges and peers. While they were doing these activities, the other half was given a comparable but not stressful task. Five minutes into their respective tasks (stressful or not), and again 20 minutes later, the participants were asked to recall the items they studied the previous day.

ETHICS

The method of stressing participants used in this study has appeared in many other experiments without report of adverse effects. However, the possibility of being assigned to the stressful condition should be noted in the informed consent form, along with referrals to appropriate professionals who can help manage stress.

RESULTS

The groups showed no differences in recall during the first test, which occurred five minutes into their stress or no-stress control experience, but their performance was significantly different at the second, delayed test. For the restudying group, stress produced a significant decline in the items recalled. However, for the retrieval practice group, stress made no difference in the number of items recalled. Regardless of stress levels and time of testing, the retrieval practice groups outperformed the restudying groups (see Figure 9.21).

CONCLUSIONS

If you have been in the habit of relying on restudying as your major or only strategy for succeeding in your classes, you might want to rethink your methods in light of this experiment. Retrieval practice appears to buffer performance from stress effects much better than restudying. It is likely that retrieval practice accomplishes this feat by producing multiple routes for accessing a memory. Each time you attempt to retrieve information, you also think about associations and the context of the information in slightly different ways. This provides you with multiple pathways back to the information you seek. When you are stressed, physiological correlates of stress (see Chapter 16) might interfere with your use of some but not all of these pathways. The more pathways you have, the more likely you are to find the information in memory. ■

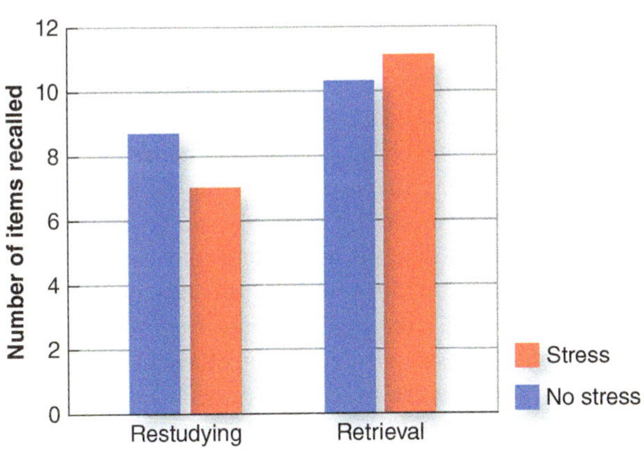

FIGURE 9.21

Retrieval Practice Protects Memory From Stress. A restudying group went over the material to be learned four times, while a retrieval group was asked to recall the items. The following day, half of both groups were stressed while the other half was given a nonstressful task to complete. When asked again to recall the items, stress had a significant, negative effect on the restudying participants. The retrieval group not only remembered more items than even the nonstressed restudying participants, but they were also unaffected by stress. Students prone to test anxiety might wish to incorporate the retrieval method of preparation into their study regimen.

Source: Data from A. M. Smith et al. (2016). "Retrieval Practice Protects Memory Against Acute Stress," *Science, 354*(6315), 1046–1048. doi: 10.1126/science.aah5067

Exercise

Physical exercise, especially vigorous exercise such as running, increases adult neurogenesis, or the birth of new neurons, in the hippocampus, at least in mice (Bolz et al., 2015; Moon et al., 2016). Not only did exercising mice experience more neurogenesis, but their memory performance improved compared to mice who did not exercise. We will not guarantee that taking up jogging will improve your grades, but it will certainly benefit your health and mood (Chen et al., 2017).

Sleep

Initially, many psychologists believed that the positive role of sleep in memory formation resulted from a lack of interference. If you learned something right before going to sleep, no further information would enter the system to cause interference. More sophisticated research, however, has demonstrated that sleep plays an active role in the consolidation of memories. During sleep, the hippocampus reactivates and shows activity that is similar to what it does during waking (Todorova & Zugaro, 2019). This reactivation of the hippocampus activates particular groups of cortical cells that make the changes necessary to stabilize a memory.

Most types of memories appear stronger after a period of sleep (Genzel et al., 2014; Boyce et al., 2016). We can also say with confidence that students who pull all-nighters are not doing their memory systems a favor (Havekes et al., 2016). In one experiment, staying up all night produced poor memory for a previous task, and two additional nights of adequate sleep did not compensate for the original deprivation (Stickgold et al., 2000).

Recite

Most students recognize that a certain number of rehearsals of reading and lecture notes are required for success on exams. However, we can mistake the ease with which we cover familiar material for actually knowing the material. Just because you can read something easily doesn't mean that you know it.

A somewhat more efficient method is recitation, or the verbalizing of the material to be learned in your own words. Recitation takes advantage of a general superiority for self-referential information. People who processed words in reference to themselves (e.g., "Does the word 'honest' describe you?") are more likely to remember the word *honest* than are people who processed the definition of the words (e.g., "Does 'honest' mean the same thing as 'trustworthy'?"; Rogers et al., 1977). This result has obvious relevance for students wishing to improve their memories. If you can think about the information you are trying to learn in self-referential ways ("This example of episodic memories in my textbook reminds me of something that happened to me the other day"), your memory for the information will be enhanced. By putting information in your own words, you make it more relevant to yourself.

Recitation is still used as a classroom technique in small classes, but you can duplicate this process on your own. After you have a reasonable grasp of the material, try talking about it. A significant benefit of recitation is that you quickly realize what you do not understand when you try to explain the material to someone else. You can think that you understand something, but when you try to explain it, it doesn't come out right. This is a signal that more work on the topic is needed.

Putting information you need to remember in your own words is an effective memory strategy. Recitation takes advantage of our tendency to remember things better when they're associated with the self. If they are your words, you will remember them.

Alexander Raths/Shutterstock.com

Use Mnemonics

The early Greeks devised a number of methods, known as **mnemonics**, for improving memory. Mnemonic devices expand memory capacity by linking the material to be remembered to information that is relatively effortless to retrieve. The first-letter approach takes advantage of chunking. You condense a large amount of information into an acronym. For example, in Chapter 12, we'll use the acronym OCEAN to help remember the five major personality traits: openness, conscientiousness, extraversion, agreeableness, and neuroticism.

One of the classic Greek techniques was the method of *loci*, or places. This technique is particularly handy when you are trying to memorize a list of items in order, such as the planets in our solar system or the cranial nerves. The method takes advantage of the fact that we form excellent representations of visual images in memory. You begin by imagining a familiar place, perhaps your childhood home. As you imagine yourself walking through your home, you visualize each item in a particular location. If you wish to remember your grocery list (although writing the items down is probably easier), you might imagine a carton of eggs on the little table in your entry, a loaf of bread on the sofa, a box of cereal on the television, and so on. To recall your list, all you need to do is to take another imaginary walk through your house, recalling the items you placed as you go. If all goes well, you should remember all your items in the correct order.

This technique may sound like a lot of work, but it can be effective. One of the authors of this textbook had a colleague in graduate school who performed so perfectly on her neuroanatomy exams that her professors accused her of cheating. She related to them how she had been taught the method of loci as a childhood game and had practiced the technique throughout her academic career. After they posed several difficult lists to her, all of which she recalled perfectly, they were convinced of her honesty.

mnemonics Memory aids that link new information to well-known information.

Blend Images/Shutterstock.com

The ancient Greek mnemonic device, the method of loci, takes advantage of our superior memory for visual images of familiar places. Although the method involves consciously imagining things in a particular place, we often use location as a memory aid less consciously. You are probably familiar with the layout of your favorite grocery store and use that mental image to guide your memories for the food you need to purchase. If the store reorganizes its layout between trips, you might forget something.

Interpersonal Relationships

The Memory Perspective

WHAT IS TRANSACTIVE MEMORY?

SHARED MEMORIES ARE a characteristic of close relationships. You may know people in close relationships who seem to know intuitively what the other is thinking, perhaps even finishing the partner's sentences. According to a theory of transactive memory, couples in long-term relationships also develop a division of labor in regard to memory, in which each partner knows certain things but also knows what information can be retrieved from the partner if needed (Wegner et al., 1985; Wegner, 1986). For example, one partner might not keep track of where candles are stored in the house but knows that the other partner knows where the candles are and can be called upon to provide that knowledge in the event of an emergency.

How do couples develop systems like this? Three major strategies have been identified (Wegner et al., 1991). First, one partner can explicitly agree to take on an area of expertise, such as managing the household finances. Second, as people get to know each other better through self-disclosure, they also learn about each other's relative areas of knowledge and expertise. One partner might have an interest in computer science, while the other thinks that computers work by magic. If something goes wrong with a household computer, the second person will turn to the first. Finally, couples learn about their partner's access to information. If you know that your partner discussed holiday plans with your families, you are likely to assume that your partner knows more about your holiday options than you do.

Bellurget Jean Louis/Getty Images

People in close relationships form transactive memories, or a division of labor for remembering certain things. This woman might remember how to do certain home repair tasks, and her partner might remember others. Together, they have access to far more information than either individual could manage separately.

From an evolutionary standpoint, what are the advantages of working out this division of memory labor? One major advantage of this type of transactive memory is that a couple working well together has access to far more knowledge than either individual could manage separately. The convenience of these systems, in contrast to managing knowledge individually, would contribute to further bonding. Transactive memory is negotiated over long periods between each couple in ways that are unique and not interchangeable with others.

The concept of transactive memory has been extended from intimate couples to larger groups (Peltokorpi, 2008; Peltokorpi & Hood, 2019). In the context of larger groups, transactive memory contributes to group cognition or information processing that differs from individual cognition. Transactive memory is critical to understanding the behavior of teams in organizations (Lee et al., 2014; Argote & Guo, 2016). As in the case of intimate couples, transactive memory contributes to the group's ability to manage more information than any individual could be expected to do in an efficient manner based on the relevant specialties of the individuals making up the group. Transactive memory contributes to the establishment, maintenance, and adaptation of organizational routines, or ways to solve familiar problems (Miller et al., 2014).

Whether transactive memory takes place at the couple or the organizational level, it takes time to develop. People beginning a new relationship can expect some miscommunications and misunderstandings (and overdue bills and lost candles) until their transactive memory system begins to take shape. ■

Psychology Takes On Real-World Problems

Compliance with Social Distancing and Working Memory

Have you felt overwhelmed by all of the information coming at you about COVID-19 from social media and other sources? Have you found it difficult under these circumstances to make logical, rational decisions? If so, you are probably not alone.

What mental processes give us this sense of overload? A clue to the answer rests in the relative capacities of the different components of memory. In particular, we learned in this chapter that short-term or working memory features severe limitations on capacity. When we are trying to juggle many different pieces of information during this stage of processing, it is very likely that some will get lost.

Working memory capacity varies from one person to the next. Do we have any evidence that individual differences in working memory capacity influence real-life decision making? A study by Xie et al. (2020) suggests that this is true. During the early stages of the COVID-19 pandemic, Xie et al. found that individual differences in working memory function predicted compliance with social distancing recommendations, possibly due to a better ability to weigh the benefits and costs of the practices.

Working memory, however, predicts academic achievement, even more so than IQ, which we discuss in Chapter 10 (Alloway & Alloway, 2010). If academic achievement predicts more education and higher socioeconomic status, isn't it likely that these factors are more likely than working memory capacity itself to explain compliance with social distancing recommendations? Xie et al. anticipated this concern, and found instead that working memory differences were important predictors of compliance even after they used statistics to control for differences in mood, personality, education, and income.

Our focus in each of these chapter features is on using psychological science to inform policy. We can't exactly wave a magic wand and give every person the working memory capacity they need to manage large volumes of information effectively. However, Xie et al. provide one additional cue. Working memory capacity also predicted performance on a computerized game that measured a person's sense of fair play. Perhaps we can't manipulate working memory capacity, but if we appeal to the public's sense of fair play, this might make the choices easier to comprehend. Please note that Xie et al. conducted their research at a time when social distancing was not mandated, but merely recommended. It is likely that many additional variables would play roles in determining compliance with authority, which we discuss in Chapter 13. ■

Travelerpix/Shutterstock.com

Why are some people more likely to voluntarily comply with social distancing recommendations during a pandemic? Researchers found that individual working memory capacity predicted both compliance with social distancing and fairness norms, even after other factors like mood, personality, education, and income were controlled.

SUMMARY 9.3 Types of Forgetting

Type of forgetting	Major feature	Assessment
Decay 	Reduced ability to retrieve infrequently used material over time.	Savings technique.
Interference 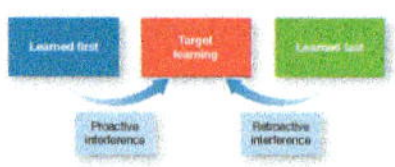	Competition between newer and older information in the memory system.	Comparison of performance in a list-learning task.
Motivated forgetting 	Failure to retrieve negative information.	Comparison of recall for memories associated with positive or negative emotions.

Credits: Top row—ZUMA Press Inc/Alamy Stock Photo; Bottom row— pasphotography/Shutterstock.com.

KEY TERMS The Language of Psychological Science

Be sure that you can define these terms and use them correctly.

autobiographical memory, p. 330
chunking, p. 323
cue, p. 336
decay, p. 343
declarative memory, p. 328
encoding, p. 318
encoding specificity, p. 337
episodic memory, p. 329
flashbulb memory, p. 340
forgetting, p. 342
information processing, p. 318
interference, p. 343
levels of processing theory, p. 325
long-term memory, p. 325
long-term potentiation (LTP), p. 346
memory, p. 318
mnemonics, p. 355
motivated forgetting, p. 344
nondeclarative memory, p. 328
priming, p. 330
procedural memory, p. 330
reconstruction, p. 338
rehearsal, p. 322
retrieval, p. 319
schema, p. 334
semantic memory, p. 329
sensory memory, p. 320
short-term memory (STM), p. 321
spreading activation model, p. 333
storage, p. 318
working memory, p. 323

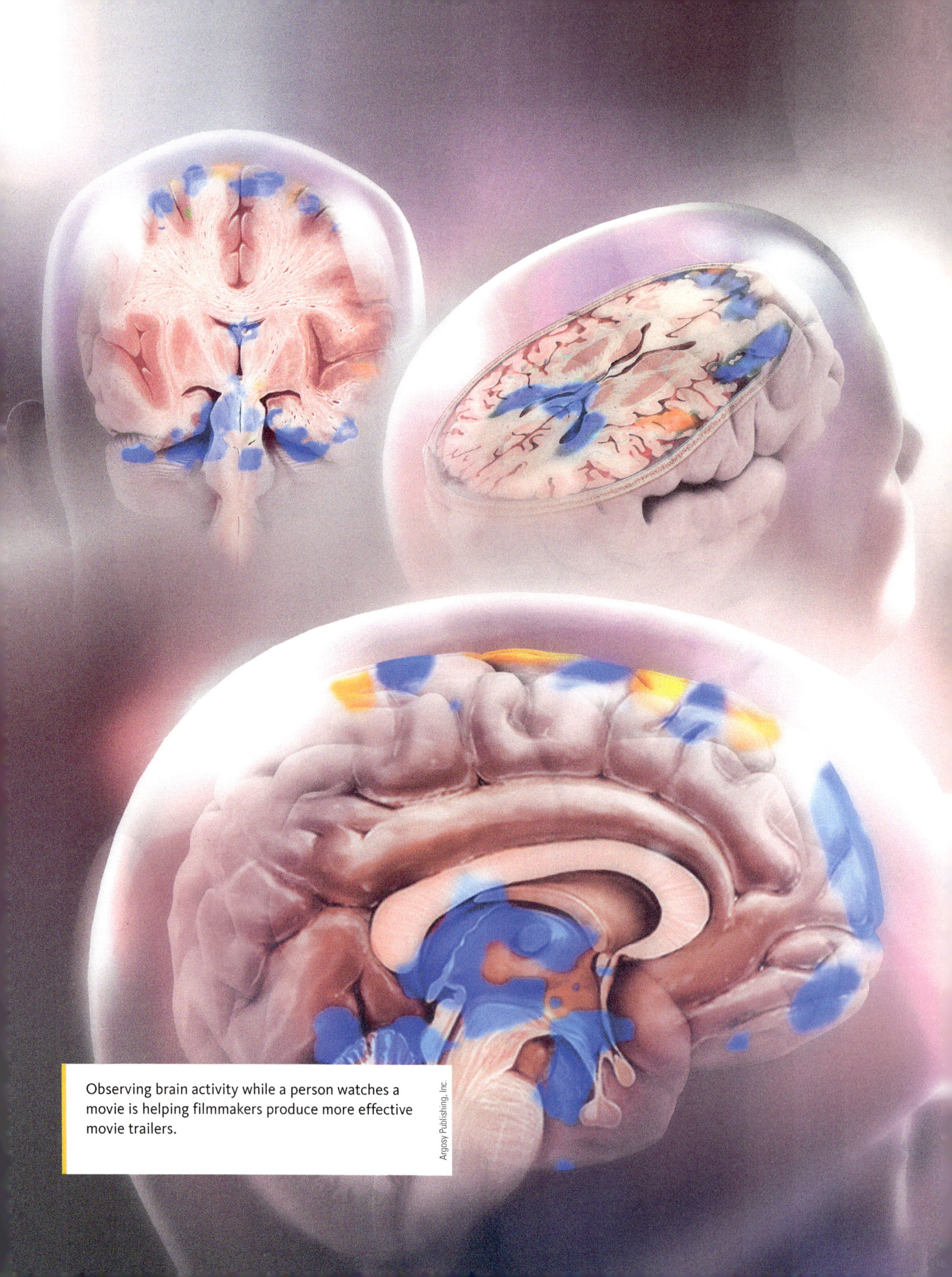

Observing brain activity while a person watches a movie is helping filmmakers produce more effective movie trailers.

Argosy Publishing, Inc.

10

The Thinking Mind

THINKING, LANGUAGE, AND INTELLIGENCE

LEARNING OBJECTIVES

1. Explain the role of mental representations in thinking, and compare and contrast models of concept formation.
2. Summarize the four steps of problem solving, incorporating existing research on how to approach each step successfully, and apply to a problem.
3. Analyze the building blocks and biological correlates of language.
4. Define general intelligence, and evaluate the evidence for multiple intelligence subtypes.
5. Analyze the interactions between nature and nurture in explaining individual differences in intelligence.

DAILY LIFE IS FULL OF DECISIONS—SOME BIG AND SOME SMALL. How does the mind reach a decision?

Psychologists have learned a great deal about the processes involved in reaching a decision and have identified many steps we can take to improve our decision making. Zooming in, we can use imaging technologies to observe how the brain reacts to a number of choices. For example, do you really want to see that movie based on its trailer?

Neurophysiological methods are being used to both craft movie trailers and predict audience responses to films. Film producers are using brain imaging when editing movie trailers to elicit the reactions they want from an audience (Randall, 2011; Boksem & Smidts, 2015). They have only a few seconds to convince the audience to see their film. Assuming that the film's ability to elicit emotion drives the decision to see it, filmmakers remove the parts of a trailer that produce neutral emotional responses and splice together the most dramatic parts. Using other neuroscience measures of responses to trailers, including EEG and eye-gaze activity, researchers were able to predict the popularity of films 23 times more accurately than more traditional methods, such as screenings, questionnaires, and focus groups (Christoforou et al., 2017).

These methods have been criticized appropriately by the scientific community as being overly simplistic applications of neuroscience, and very little peer-reviewed evidence to support their use is available. In spite of these concerns, commercial applications of neuromarketing are expanding rapidly. Nielsen, best known for their ratings of television shows, proudly proclaims "our foundation is in science," and offers an entire suite of "consumer neuroscience" tools, including EEG, biometrics like heart rate, coding of facial expressions of emotion, and eye tracking. Using EEG and eye tracking, Nielsen edited an ad for the Shelter Pet Project (Nielsen Neuroscience, 2017). The company claims that modifying the ad in response to their neuroscience findings boosted traffic to the non-profit's website. After exploring research

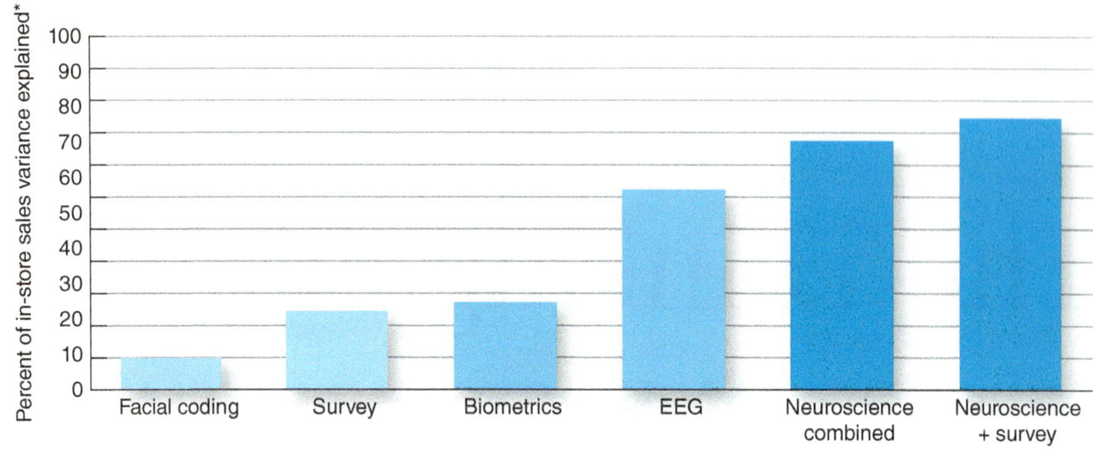

FIGURE **10.1**

Consumer research giant Nielsen claims that using "consumer neuroscience" tools, including EEG, heart rate, coding of facial expressions of emotion, and eye tracking, allow the firm to recommend improvements to clients' advertising, such as an ad for the Shelter Pet Project.
Source: https://www.nielsen.com/us/en/insights/case-study/2014/the-brains-behind-better-ads-optimizing-the-cute-and-cuddly-2/

methods in Chapter 2, you know that it would be important to compare the results of showing the unrevised ad versus the revised ad before making this claim about the benefits of their neuroscience approach.

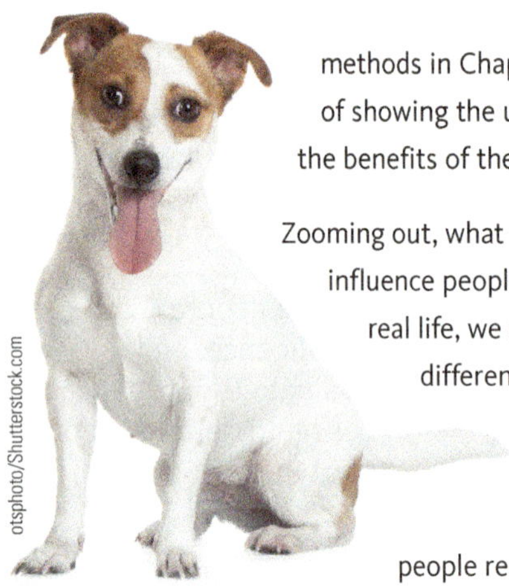
otsphoto/Shutterstock.com

Zooming out, what factors aside from seeing an emotional trailer or ad might influence people's decisions to see a particular film? With all of the trauma in real life, we might ask why people choose to see horror films? Individual differences play key roles in this decision. People who are low in fearfulness and empathy enjoy horror films more than people with higher empathy and fearfulness (Martin, 2019). Using the social perspective to zoom out still farther, we can see that people respond to horror films based on their beliefs about the expectations of others, particularly in regards to gender roles (Mundorf et al., 1989).

In this chapter, we will explore how we use the tools of language and intelligence to think, which in turn guides our behavior. Beginning with the parts of the brain that process information, we will zoom out to the individual differences of personality and experience and farther still to the social and larger cultural contexts that shape the way we think.

cognition Internal mental processes including information processing, thinking, reasoning, and problem solving.

What Do We Think About?

The word **cognition**, as in the term *cognitive psychology*, is derived from the Latin *cogito*, which literally means "to think." Thinking allows us to manipulate information internally to construct models of the world, plan our interactions with that world, and regulate ourselves to meet our goals. As you will see, cognitive psychology covers a broad area of topics. In addition to perception, learning, and memory, which we discussed in previous chapters, cognitive psychology addresses questions of thinking, language, and intelligence.

The mind uses symbols or mental representations to signify information, just as icons represent some of your favorite social networks, such as Facebook, Twitter, TikTok, Instagram, and Snapchat.

solomon7/Shutterstock.com
solomon7/Shutterstock.com
Michele Ursi/Alamy Stock Photo
Instagram
Brilliantist Studio/Shutterstock.com
tanuha2001/Shutterstock.com

We think about what we know. In the broadest sense of the word, knowledge is the entire body of information acquired through study, investigation, observation, and experience. To manage this large collection of knowledge, the mind uses symbols, or mental representations, to signify information. Using mental representations is similar to having an icon on your computer desktop that represents Microsoft Word and a profile photograph on Facebook that represents your best friend.

The most familiar uses of mental representations are found in language, both written and spoken. Depending on the language you choose, you could represent the animal coming toward you on the sidewalk as a *hund* (German), *chien* (French), *gau* (Chinese), *perro* (Spanish), or *dog* (English). Representations can be visual too. For example, you could snap a photo or sketch a picture of the dog. Despite the differences in these two visual representations, the dog that each portrays is the same. We can view the representation of the dog (the sound or the appearance of the word used, the patterns of light in your photo or drawing) as a vehicle for carrying information about the content of our knowledge of this dog (it seems to be a friendly, young golden retriever).

In this chapter, we explore the ability of minds to form mental representations and manipulate them to make sense of the world. What forms can representations take? What are the relationships between the representations and the content they symbolize?

Thoughts as Images

Temple Grandin, a college professor with autism spectrum disorder, describes her way of thinking as "thinking in pictures" (Grandin, 2010). Albert Einstein is also widely quoted as relying on mental visualization in the early stages of his thinking and only later putting his ideas into words (Einstein, 1945). To what extent do the rest of us think in mental images? By *mental image*, we are referring to a representation of any sensory experience that is stored in memory and can be retrieved for use later. For example, you can call up a visual image of your first car, picture the letters of your name, or silently hum the first bars of "Happy Birthday" to yourself quite easily.

People treat mental images much like they would a real object (Kosslyn, 1978, 1980). We can turn visual mental images around in our minds, zoom in or out, and identify their features (see ● Figure 10.2). If you were to think about a map of the United States (assuming you have a good grasp of geography), it would take you longer to mentally count the major cities between Los Angeles and New York than those between Chicago and New York, just as it would if you were looking at a real map.

Children are particularly likely to use visual images in their thinking. In one study, between 2% and 15% of elementary school children experienced long-lasting and detailed visual images of a complex picture they viewed for a short interval (Haber & Haber, 1964). The children described the scene using the present tense, suggesting that they were scanning a mental replica. Except for rare cases like Grandin, few adults can do this. It is possible that language becomes an increasingly important way to organize thinking during childhood and might begin to overwrite or interfere with the ability to directly access visual images.

Regardless of the exact form taken by mental representations, our knowledge would be useless unless we imposed some type of organization on all the bits we know. To supply this organization, we extract special, organizing ideas known as **concepts** from the specific instances and occurrences we experience.

concept An organizing principle derived from experience.

Kevin Mazur/WireImage/Getty Images

Temple Grandin, a college professor with autism spectrum disorder, is shown here with actress Claire Danes, who portrayed her in a 2010 made-for-television movie. Grandin has described her cognitive experience as "thinking in pictures." It is likely that young children depend on a similar approach to thinking, but learning language provides new dimension to our ability to think.

Thoughts as Concepts

Concept formation is not unique to humans. Nonhuman animals as diverse as pigeons and monkeys demonstrate concept formation (Herrnstein, 1979). In one study, pigeons learned to peck at projected images of water with fish to obtain food rewards but to withhold pecking at images of water without fish (Herrnstein & de Villiers, 1980). Subsequently, a new set of slides was presented. The pigeons successfully distinguished between the fish and the nonfish slides, even though they had not seen these particular images during their prior training. The

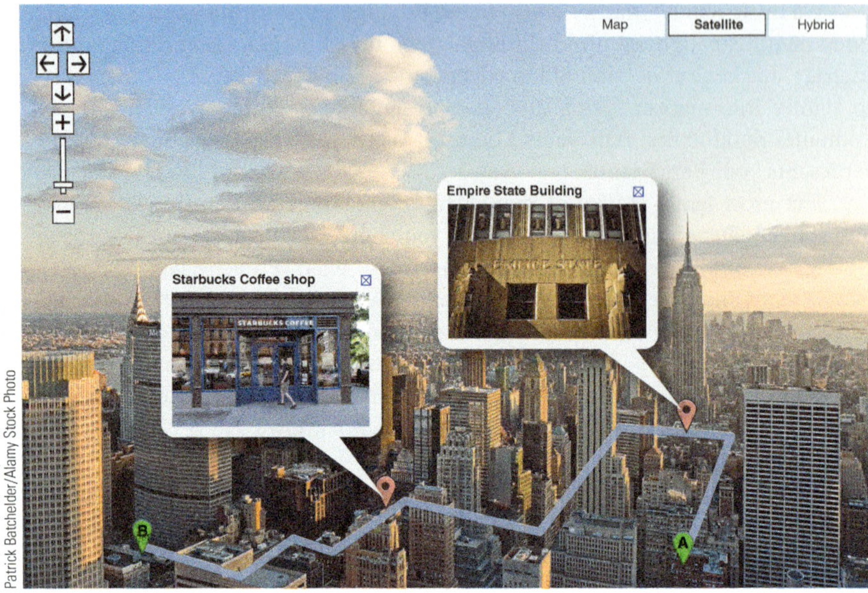

Martin Shields/Alamy Stock Photo; Justin Green/Alamy Stock Photo; Patrick Batchelder/Alamy Stock Photo

FIGURE **10.2**

Forming Mental Maps. A person familiar with New York City could follow a mental route among these buildings, zoom in or out, and identify important features like landmarks and a favorite place to have coffee.

Chip East (United States Society Entertainment)/Reuters

London-based artist Stephen Wiltshire, who like Temple Grandin has autism spectrum disorder, has been described as a "human camera." Wiltshire can fly over a major city such as New York in a helicopter for about 1 hour and then recreate highly accurate and detailed drawings of the city. His talent is an extreme and unusual form of the use of visual imagery.

pigeons appeared to have extracted a "fish" concept from their experience. What does it mean to have a "fish" or any other type of concept? How are we (and pigeons) able to construct a new concept?

Because of the memory processes discussed in Chapter 9, you already "know" what a dog is. If you were asked to feed your neighbor's dog while your neighbor goes on vacation, you could locate the correct animal, provide dog food instead of cat food, and exercise appropriate caution if your neighbor's dog is unfriendly. This activity sounds simple, but what if you recruited an alien from another planet to help you with your task? What information about dogs would the alien need to know to succeed? Essentially, what you must convey to your alien friend is the concept of "dog" (see ● Table 10.1).

You might start the discussion with a dictionary definition of *dog*. In the dictionary, you find that a dog is "a domesticated carnivorous mammal (*Canis familiaris*) related to the foxes and wolves and raised in a wide variety of breeds." This definition seems rather remote from what we know to be a dog. You don't need to know what dogs eat and who their nearest relatives are to identify one correctly.

Perhaps you could find some common features of dogs that would allow you to distinguish between dogs and nondogs. You could tell your alien friend that dogs are furry animals with four legs that bark and wag their tails. Unfortunately, this system has a logical flaw (Wittgenstein, 1953). No matter how careful your definition, even for the simplest concepts, somebody will think of an exception. Although we can agree that all dogs are animals, this feature alone is insufficient for distinguishing dogs from cats and raccoons. Having fur does not describe some chihuahuas, and basenjis don't bark. A dog that has lost a leg in an accident no longer has four legs. Most dogs we know wag their tails, but there may be an abused dog that keeps its tail perpetually between its legs, as well as dogs that have tails too stubby to wag.

To resolve this dilemma, you can make your definition more flexible. Instead of being rigidly defined by a checklist of features, a concept could describe a group of instances that share overlapping features. This approach is similar to a feature detection model (Smith et al., 1974). According to this type of model, people determine the truthfulness of statements like "a canary is a bird" by considering overlapping features (wings, beak, flies, and chirps). Using this approach, the alien could compare the features of an animal suspected of being a dog with a checklist of dog features. This approach has problems, too. Some categories are clear, such as triangles, but others do not have precise enough boundaries for the checklist approach to work. People in some cultures would list "tastes good" as a feature of dogs, but Americans probably would not. In addition, the feature checklist approach doesn't seem to

TABLE 10.1

Approaches to Concept Formation

Approach	Application to dog category	Disadvantages
Dictionary definition	Describe a dog as "a domesticated carnivorous mammal *(Canis familiaris)* related to the foxes and wolves and raised in a wide variety of breeds."	Gives more information than needed to classify a dog correctly.
Common features	Describe dogs as furry animals with four legs that bark and wag their tails.	Results in too many exceptions (e.g., Chihuahuas are not furry).
Overlapping features	Compare features of a suspected dog with features of the "dog" concept.	Lacks precise boundaries for most categories (e.g., "tastes good" might be a category feature for dogs in some cultures but not in others).
Prototype	Average all members of the dog category.	Does not provide a good way to think about a category's variability.
Exemplar	Use a specific instance of a category a model.	Excludes some category members that are too dissimilar to model.

Omikron/Science Source

Photo courtesy of Will Vaughan

Courtesy of Will Vaughan

Pigeons appear to be able to form concepts, such as "people" and "nonpeople." If their pecking is reinforced with food in the presence of an image containing people but not in the presence of images without people, they will learn to peck only when the people images are present. The experimenters used hundreds of images that showed people but varied in number, distance from the camera, age, ethnicity, and other features, but the pigeons still responded appropriately.

match personal experience with thinking. When you think about a dog, do you access a mental checklist of dog features?

Prototypes and Exemplars An alternate approach to thinking about concepts is to consider some type of "standard" dog, or a **prototype** that represents your entire category (Rosch, 1973, 1983). A prototype results from an averaging of all members of your category, and it may not even resemble a real instance (Posner & Keele, 1970). For example, the prototypical dog has an average size, an average tail, average ears, average coloring, and so on. When thinking about a category, you might also retrieve a specific instance of a concept or an **exemplar**. This could be the dog that you raised during your childhood or a dog featured in your favorite movie.

The processes in which prototypes and exemplars are used are quite similar. Whichever standard you choose, you compare new instances to it to get a sense of "fit." The more similar

prototype A representation of a category formed by averaging all members of the category.

exemplar A specific member of a category used to represent the category.

Although correct, this dictionary definition of a dog might not help you figure out whether an animal standing in front of you is a dog or not.

Dmitry Kalinovsky/Shutterstock.com

dog
[dawg, dog]
noun, *verb*, dogged, dog-ging.
-noun
A domesticated carnivorous mammal (*Canis familiaris*) related to the foxes and wolves and raised in a wide variety of breeds.

the new objects are to the standard, the more likely you are to include them in your concept. Both approaches are also able to account for the tendency of people to rate apples as more typical fruits than avocados or robins as more typical birds than penguins (Malt & Smith, 1984). Apples are not only closer to the "average" fruit than avocados are, but they are also more likely to be chosen as an exemplar fruit because of the extensive experience most people have with apples, at least in the United States.

Despite the similarities between the prototype and the exemplar approaches, exemplars have some advantages. Compared to prototypes, exemplars provide a better way of thinking about the variability of a category (Rips & Collins, 1993). Averages, which characterize prototypes, do not provide much information about the range of features found in a category. For example, imagine that you just met Joe Kovacs, who tells you that he is an athlete. Judging from Kovac's imposing physical appearance (he weighs 295 pounds), he seems more similar to your prototypical NFL football player than what he is—a star track-and-field athlete. In contrast, while your personal exemplar for a track-and-field athlete might be a sprinter or distance runner instead of a shot-putter like Kovacs, the individual instances that you know can help you comprehend the variability found within the concept.

Susan Schmitz/Shutterstock.com

Eric Isselee/Shutterstock.com

Using common features to identify dogs, such as "has hair" or "has four legs," would exclude these two: a dog with three legs and an American hairless terrier.

Just when you are feeling comfortable about using prototypes and exemplars to solve your alien's dog problem, you run into an additional dilemma. The use of prototypes and exemplars rests on similarity. Similar objects will be included in a concept, and dissimilar objects will be excluded. What if your new alien friend comes across a lifelike dog robot? In many ways, the robot looks and acts like your prototype and exemplar dogs, yet you know it is not a dog. What if you find an unfortunate dog that has been killed on the highway? It hardly retains much similarity to the prototype and exemplar dogs, yet nobody, except perhaps the alien, would question its identity as a dog. Clearly, you need more than prototypes and exemplars to solve your problem.

Concepts as Theories Concept formation can be a type of theory building. In Chapter 2, we defined theories as "sets of facts and relationships between facts that can be used to explain and predict phenomena." This definition can also apply to a concept. Like theories, concepts can guide our thinking and be continually tested for accuracy against new, incoming information. Also like theories, concepts do not exist in isolation. As we mentioned in Chapter 9, concepts can be viewed as part of a vast, interconnected network of memories.

Thinking about concepts as theories provides insight into the problem of judging category membership, such as deciding whether an avocado is a fruit. Prototypes and exemplars provide a useful starting place for judging category membership. We test our theory that the new item (avocado) fits the category by comparing it to the prototypes (average fruit) and exemplars (apple) of a concept (fruit). We might make the occasional mistake, such as including bats or excluding ostriches in a concept of "bird," but most of the time, we will be successful and fast.

This approach also has the advantage of being consistent with observations of how children acquire new concepts, which we explore in

Chapter 11. A child might start with a prototype or exemplar dog based on the family pet, possibly overapplying the concept to other four-legged animals at the zoo and failing to apply it to dogs of different breeds. With the help of feedback from others ("No, that's a tiger, not a dog" or "Yes, a Chihuahua is a dog"), the concept becomes more refined. Your alien friend is likely to need the same type of feedback from you when attempting to apply the newly learned concept of dog to a variety of animals.

Apples are more likely than avocados to be a person's exemplar fruit because of the extensive experience we have with apples in the United States.

Juice Team/Shutterstock.com

Concepts and Schemas Our "dog" concept is embedded in a rich, complex set of beliefs and expectations about dogs, animals, nature, and personal experience known as a schema, which we discussed in Chapter 9. This type of schema not only shapes memory storage and retrieval of information relevant to dogs but also allows us to predict new facts about them. If our schema includes "likes to play ball," we know that playing ball with a friend's new dog is likely to be successful.

Under what circumstances do people apply a schema to new information? Again, comparisons to typical members of a category appear to play a role. People who are told a new fact about a typical instance of a category are more willing to extend the new fact to all members of a category, whereas a new fact about an atypical category member is less likely to be widely applied (Rips, 1975). For example, if you learn about a new fruit disease found in apples (an exemplar fruit for many people), you are more likely to think other fruits are vulnerable than if you learn that the disease targets a less typical member of the fruit category, such as olives or avocados.

Concepts and the Brain Can we find brain activity that correlates with thinking about a particular concept? In Chapter 9, we described imaging studies that identified different patterns of brain activity when people thought about animals or tools (Martin et al., 1996). When asked to name animals, the participants showed activation in the visual cortex, suggesting that they would need to think about what a zebra looks like to name it correctly. Naming tools, in contrast, was accompanied by activation in frontal and parietal lobe areas associated with movement, implying that it is helpful to think about what to do with a screwdriver when attempting to name it correctly.

This specialization in the brain for processing different types of concepts is supported by observations of patients with brain damage. Some patients have specific difficulties naming pictures of animals, although they can successfully name other living things, such as fruits and vegetables, and nonliving things, such as tools and furniture (Mahon & Caramazza, 2009). Not only do these people have difficulty naming animals, but they also struggle to answer questions about animals, such as "Does a whale have legs?" Similar questions about nonliving things do not cause difficulty. Others demonstrate the opposite pattern. They are able to name living things but struggle to name nonliving things (Mahon & Caramazza, 2011; see • Figure 10.3). These observations suggest that our brains are predisposed to distinguish between living and nonliving things. If forming concepts helps to organize appropriate responses, our ancestors' ability to form some concepts quickly might have conferred a significant survival advantage.

Amyotrophic lateral sclerosis (ALS, or Lou Gehrig's disease) is primarily a movement disorder, but the condition also affects a person's ability to form new concepts. Performance by ALS patients on a concept formation task was correlated with the extent of gray matter loss they had experienced in the left prefrontal and parietal cortices (Libon et al., 2012). Although individual cases vary widely, current diagnostic criteria for ALS have been updated to incorporate features of frontotemporal dementia, a collection of symptoms associated with neural loss in the frontal and temporal lobes that includes deficits in cognition, language, and memory (Abramzon et al., 2020).

Harry How/Getty Images Sport/Getty Images

You might mistakenly put Olympic shot-putter Joe Kovacs in your category of NFL football player because of his appearance, which is closer to the prototypical football player than it is to the prototypical track-and-field athlete. Using exemplars instead of prototypes to guide the use of concepts helps us think about the variability of a category.

Even when a prototype is well understood, such as the signs and symptoms of a disease, evidence suggests that exemplars might work better. Physicians diagnosing cancer who had recently seen similar cases (exemplars) made more accurate diagnoses than those who had not (Brooks, 1990; Brooks, Norman, & Allen, 1991).

ton koene/Alamy Stock Photo

Prototypes and exemplars depend on similarity, which can result in similar items, such as this robotic dog, being included in our dog category.

It is unlikely that young children have vocabulary words for many of the animals seen for the first time, like this walrus. Theories of what kind of animal this is will be shaped with the help of the child's parents.

CBW/Alamy Stock Photo

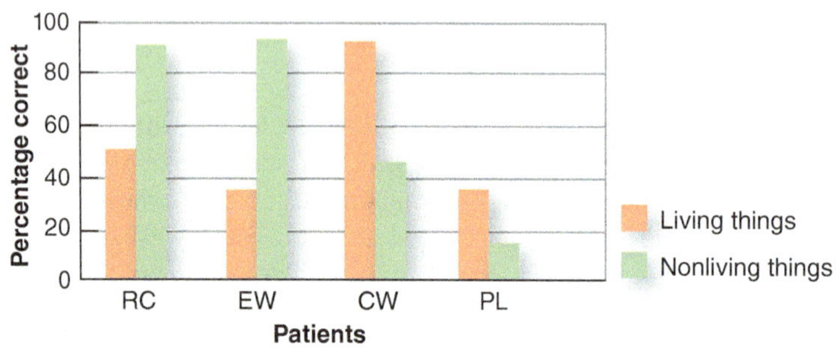

FIGURE **10.3**

Some Categories Might Be Hardwired in the Brain. Some individuals with brain damage have difficulty processing certain types of semantic information. The pattern of these deficits varies depending on the location of the damage. For example, patient CW can name living things better than nonliving things, while patient RC names nonliving things better than living things. However, the categories that are affected in this way are relatively few: animals, fruits and vegetables, nonliving things, and members of our own species. This suggests that our brains have been shaped through natural selection to form certain types of categories.

Source: Adapted from B. Z. Mahon & A. Caramazza (2011). "What Drives the Organization of Object Knowledge in the Brain?" *Trends in Cognitive Sciences, 15*(3), 97–103. doi:10.1016/j.tics.2011.01.004

How Do We Solve Problems?

problem A situation in which a current state is separated from an ideal state by obstacles.

Thinking helps us deal with the many types of problems we face daily. Whether you are figuring out how to manage a busy schedule, help a friend who is feeling blue, or complete your calculus homework, a **problem** exists whenever there is a difference between where you are and where you would like to be (Newell & Simon, 1972). For example, when you step on the bathroom scale after the holidays, the weight shown on the scale might be different from the ideal weight for your health and appearance; you now have a problem. In addition, referring to a situation as a *problem* implies that obstacles exist. Returning to your preholiday weight can be challenging.

Problems can be well defined or ill defined. Well-defined problems have a solution that can be verified as correct or incorrect, like an algebra problem, whereas ill-defined problems have solutions that are evaluated subjectively (Le et al., 2013). Our weight-loss problem is well defined because it is easy to verify whether you lose the newly gained weight or not, but many problems in everyday life are ill defined. Thinking that you need to improve your appearance would be an example of an ill-defined problem. People might not agree about what makes another person more attractive.

Problem solving is defined as the use of information to meet a specific goal (Lovett, 2002). As shown in ● Figure 10.4, problem solving begins with recognizing a problem exists (you now weigh too much) followed by the development and use of strategies that solve it (you go on a diet) and the evaluation of the success of those strategies (you have either lost the holiday weight or not). Ill-defined problems require additional thought about what constitutes an acceptable solution and how the solution should be justified. Reconfiguring an ill-defined problem into a set of well-defined problems can be helpful. If your ill-defined problem is to improve your appearance, you could divide this into well-defined problems like returning to your preholiday weight, eating five servings of fruits and vegetables per day, and exercising at least 30 minutes each day.

Because good problem-solving skills are important to psychological well-being, we will examine the process in detail using four steps (Polya, 1957):

1. Understand the problem.
2. Make a plan.
3. Carry out the plan.
4. Look back.

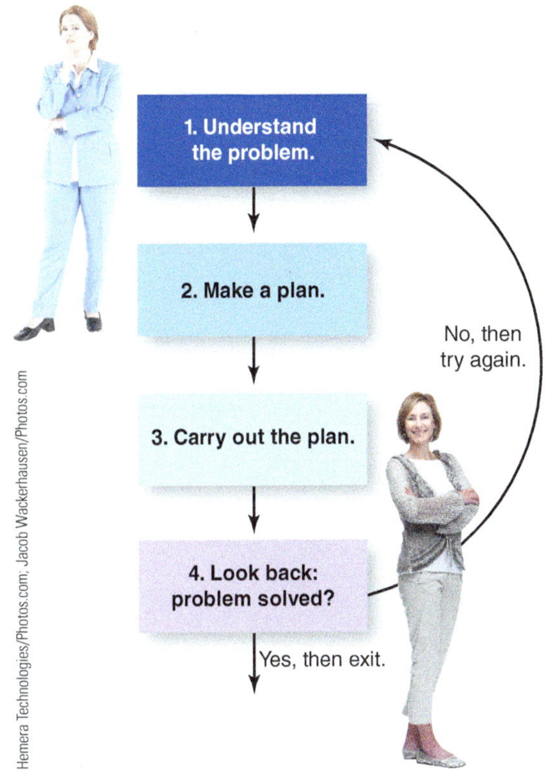

FIGURE **10.4**

Problem-Solving Flow Chart. Effective problem solving can be achieved by following a system proposed by Polya (1957). If you reach step 4 and the problem is solved, you can exit the system. If the problem is not solved, you return to step 1 and try again.

Given the close relationship between cognitive psychology and computer science that we described in Chapter 1, we should not be too surprised to see problem-solving as a type of looping computer program. If we reach step 4 and our solution has taken us to where we want to go, we stop. If we reach step 4 and our problem still exists, we return to earlier steps to try another solution or generate new solutions. This looping of steps, reminiscent of loops in computer programs, continues until the problem is resolved.

Problems that are more complex than our weight-loss example might require a systems engineer. Systems engineering is a Gestalt type of process for problem solving that considers the whole problem to be distinct from the parts (Ramo, 2005). Systems engineers use a looping program that differs from our four-step process in that evaluation takes place each step of the way (see ● Figure 10.5).

problem solving The use of information to meet a specific goal.

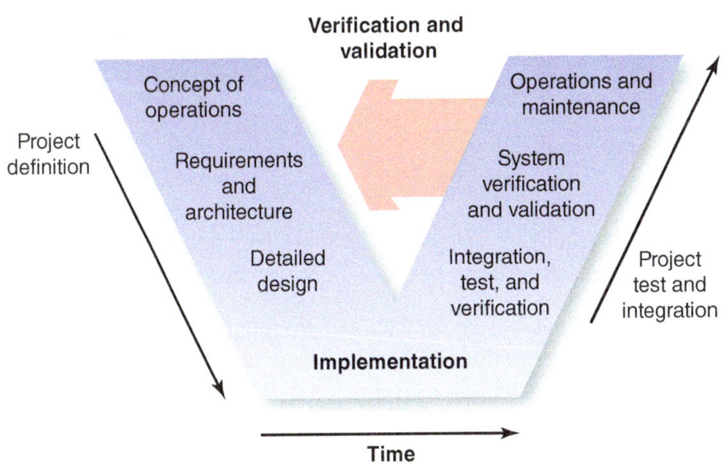

FIGURE **10.5**

Systems Engineering Process. Unlike our simple four-step problem-solving model, systems engineering evaluates progress along every step of the way, not just at the end of one attempted solution.

Source: https://upload.wikimedia.org/wikipedia/commons /2/22 /Systems_Engineering_Process_II.gif.

Understand the Problem

Although carefully formulating a problem takes time, this is generally time well spent. All relevant data should be collected, analyzed, and organized. What do we know? What information do we need that is missing? How does all this information fit together?

An important part of this step is to represent or frame the problem in a useful way (Lovett, 2002). Earlier in this chapter, we talked about forming mental representations of experiences that subsequently can be manipulated by the mind. In the case of problem solving, the mental representations we form relate to how we see the problem. For example, you might represent your weight problem as the result of your holiday splurge or as the result of a broken bathroom scale. These two representations clearly lead to different solutions, and in many cases, your representation will determine how successful you will be at solving the problem.

Psychologists have identified several helpful suggestions for making the most useful representations of problems and for avoiding some common mistakes that frequently lead to failure. For example, big, long-term problems are easier to solve if they are approached through components or intermediate goals. Your primary goal in college is to obtain a degree, but it is useful to consider how you plan to meet intermediate goals such as completing your general education courses, your major courses, and electives.

Personal biases can interfere with good problem solving. In our weight example, a reluctance to reduce treats might lead you to conclude that the bathroom scale is at fault instead of your behavior. Your amount of self-efficacy or belief in your abilities to succeed might also influence your approach to a problem (Bandura, 2001). You might believe that dieting doesn't work, so there is no point in even trying. By recognizing these biases, you can approach your problem and its potential solutions with a more open mind.

Like ill-defined problems, big complex problems, such as world hunger, can be tackled best by breaking the problem into smaller, intermediate problems.

Another barrier to forming useful representations of a problem is **functional fixedness**, or a person's tendency to think about a concept in its most typical form and no others. In an emergency, a belt or a computer cord can be used to tie a door shut, and a pot of hot coffee can be a weapon.

functional fixedness A possible barrier to successful problem solving in which a concept is considered only in its most typical form.

In keeping with our computer program analogy, it is important to know when you understand a problem sufficiently to move to the next step, planning a solution. It is possible to get "stuck" in the understanding step through a process known as rumination. Rumination is a repetitive focus on one's problems, and is a known correlate of depressed mood (Nolen-Hoeksema & Morrow, 1993). Rumination can be separated, however, into brooding and reflection (Treynor et al., 2003). Brooding, a judgmental process in which we compare our current situation with the ideal situation, not only predicts negative mood, but actually interferes with problem solving. While brooding, people tend to avoid addressing their problems. In contrast, reflection, in which we look inward while actively engaging in problem-solving, is weakly associated with depressed mood and can actually promote problem solving.

How do we know when our efforts to understand a problem are adaptive or maladaptive? When faced with your next negative experience, consciously attempt to observe whether you are focused on questions of "why?" (brooding—"Why oh why am I so overweight?) or "how?" (reflection—"How did I manage to gain these extra pounds?"). If you find yourself brooding, seek to distance yourself from the problem by trying to see the situation the way others might view it (Kross et al., 2012).

In an emergency, people need to use whatever they have in hand to solve problems. Functional fixedness might lead you to believe that a belt can only hold up your pants, but it can also make it harder for someone to come through a door.

Make a Plan

A plan to solve your problem involves generating possible solutions and then choosing the best one to implement.

Generating Solutions Generating possible solutions involves creativity, but most importantly, it requires time. People who spend the most time on a problem typically generate the most diverse solutions. Generating the most solutions raises your chances of finding one that will work.

Daxiao Productions/Shutterstock.com

When aggressive children are asked how to solve social problems, such as persuading another child to share a desirable toy, they generate fewer solutions than do more prosocial children. Eventually, most children will generate an aggressive solution (grab the doll and run), but perceiving additional options (trading a piece of candy for the toy or arguing that "sharing is nice") might make it less likely that the prosocial child will use the aggressive solution.

Several factors can interfere with finding appropriate solutions. You might be so upset about the numbers on the bathroom scale that you refuse to consider efforts to lose weight. Some people dislike risk so intensely that they fail to consider a full range of alternative solutions. To escape the chaos and the ambiguity involved with facing a problem, people can rush to find a solution, overlooking more appropriate courses of action. Judging and discarding solutions too early in the process also leads to failure. Generating impractical solutions requiring resources we don't have is not useful. An expensive stay at a weight reduction spa might work, but it probably doesn't fit a student budget. Understanding that we have these weaknesses in our approach to problem solving should help us avoid them in the future.

Some types of problems lend themselves to precise, step-by-step rules for reaching a particular solution, known as **algorithms**. Algorithms have the advantage of producing an accurate solution reliably. Let's assume you have a three-number combination lock on your bicycle, but you have forgotten the combination. You can start with using 001 for the first input, then 002, and so on, until you reach the correct solution for unlocking your bike. Algorithms are efficient when run by a computer, but their cost when used by the human brain can be high. You could be very late to your next class by the time you unlock your bike.

Because of the time needed to use algorithms, we often substitute rules of thumb, or shortcuts to problem solving, known as **heuristics**. Because heuristics do not go through the exhaustive evaluation of solutions required by algorithms, they are faster. Another advantage of heuristics is that they typically require far less information than algorithms do. However, unlike algorithms, heuristics do not guarantee a solution.

Heuristics allow us to make quick, effective, and efficient decisions, but these systems are not perfect. In Chapter 5, we explored the use of visual illusions to identify the limitations of our visual system. Similarly, seeing the flaws in our heuristics helps us understand how they work. Just as our visual system returns data that we need to survive, our minds have been shaped over the millennia to think in ways that usually result in good decisions (Haselton et al., 2009). However, heuristics that served our hunter-gatherer ancestors well might not always be up to the task of managing the massive amounts of complex information to which modern human minds are exposed. Heuristics are most likely to fail when a correct solution requires a sophisticated understanding of probability (Fenton & Neil, 2012).

The **recognition heuristic** (see ● Figure 10.6) predicts that people will place a higher value on the more easily recognized alternative (Gigerenzer, 2008). In one study, American college students were asked which of two cities was larger. In making size decisions about German cities, such as Hamburg and Munich, students tended to choose the city they recognized

algorithm A precise, step-by-step set of rules that will reliably generate a solution to a problem.

heuristic A shortcut to problem solving; also known as a rule of thumb.

recognition heuristic A rule of thumb in which a higher value is placed on the more easily recognized alternative.

Digital Vision/Getty Images

Gulcin Ragiboglu/Shutterstock.com

Recipes are examples of algorithms. If you follow the recipe step by step, you should be able to produce the cookies you want every time.

most (Goldstein & Gigerenzer, 2002). They were correct about 73% of the time (Hamburg has about 1.8 million residents compared to Munich's 1.3 million). People typically restrict the use of the recognition heuristic to situations in which recognition actually makes sense. For example, people are more likely to use recognition to decide which of two cities is larger than when deciding which of two cities is located closer to the center of a country (Pohl et al., 2017).

availability heuristic A rule of thumb in which the frequency of an event's occurrence is predicted by the ease with which the event is brought to mind.

Amos Tversky and Daniel Kahneman (1973, 1974) identified several heuristics that are more likely to produce faulty decisions. The first type, the **availability heuristic**, is used when people predict that events that are easy to think about will be more frequent. What makes an idea "easy to think about"? Why would it ever be adaptive to think this way? As we learned in Chapter 9, repetition influences memory. Events that are experienced more frequently come to mind more easily than rare events, and we often predict future frequency based on the past. People living in the middle parts of the United States known as "Tornado Alley" are more likely to expect a tornado in the near future than people living in California. The opposite might be true when considering major earthquakes.

Unfortunately, ideas that are "easy to think about" might be front of mind for reasons having nothing to do with their future likelihood. For example, sensational media reports of kidnapped children might be easy to think about because they elicit strong negative emotions

FIGURE **10.6**

The Recognition Heuristic. The recognition heuristic predicts that if you think the film *Avengers: Endgame* sounds more familiar than the film *Captive State*, you will correctly judge *Avengers: Endgame* as generating more international revenue for the producers than *Captive State*.

Source: boxofficemojo.com/year/world/2019/

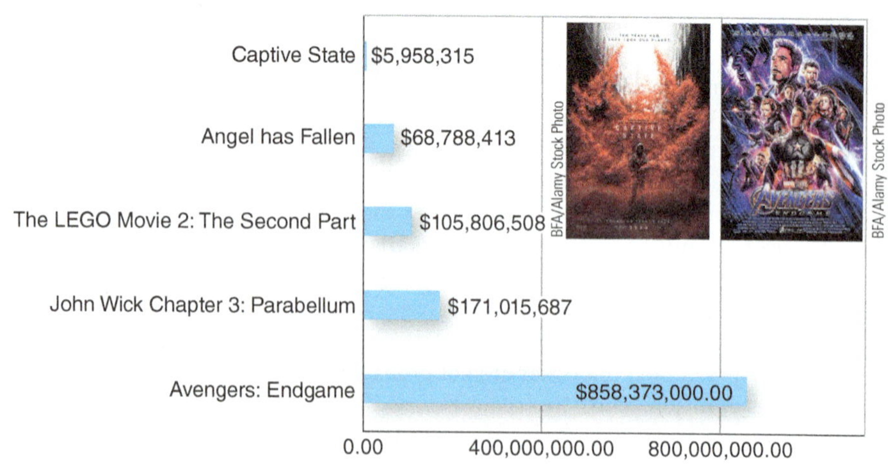

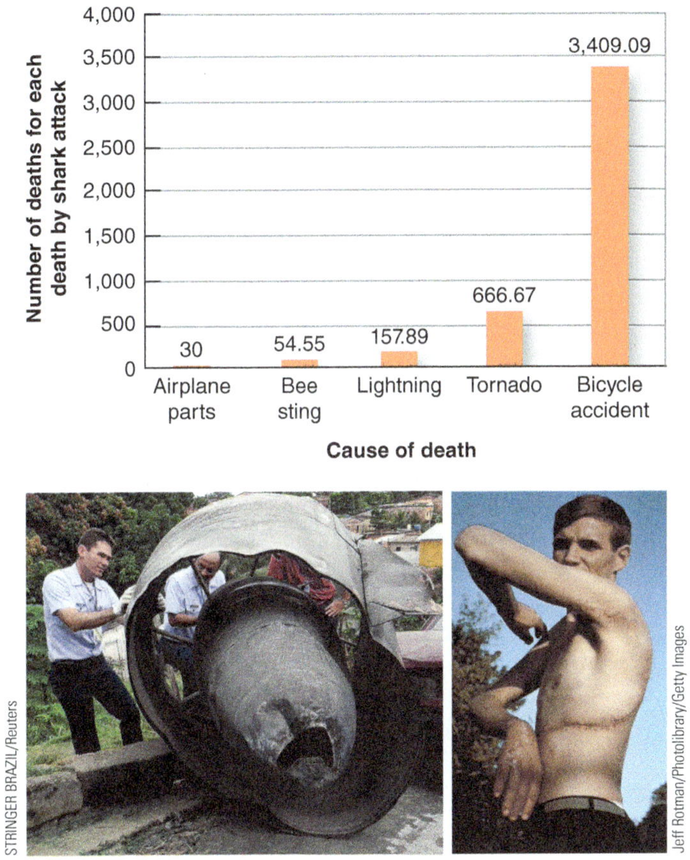

FIGURE **10.7**

The Availability Heuristic. Which is more likely? Being hit by an airplane part or being attacked by a shark? The availability heuristic leads us to believe that events that are easy to think about are more frequent. Because of the frequent media coverage of shark attacks, such as Rodney Fox's close call with a great white in Australia, people think shark attacks are common. You might be surprised to learn that you are 30 times more likely to be killed by falling airplane parts, like this turbine engine that fell from the sky onto a car in Brazil, than by a shark.

Source: Adapted from S. Plous (1993). *The psychology of judgment and decision making*. New York: McGraw-Hill.

like fear. Parents often respond with dire warnings to children about "stranger danger." In reality, abductions of children by strangers in the United States are fortunately quite rare, accounting each year for only about 100 out of the hundreds of thousands of missing children reported to law enforcement (Office of Juvenile Justice and Deliquency Prevention, 2016). The vast majority of missing children run away from home or are involved in a custody dispute, and nearly all are eventually returned to their homes. ● Figure 10.7 illustrates other mistakes due to the availability heuristic. Most people are surprised to learn that they are about 30 times more likely to be killed by falling airplane parts than by a shark (Plous, 1993). We are frequently exposed to news reports and movies featuring shark attacks, but when was the last time you heard about a person being killed by falling airplane parts?

As we mentioned earlier in this chapter, people often form prototypes or average examples when thinking about a category. These prototypes then represent the category when we are deciding which new examples might also fit the category. Recall that one of the weaknesses of using prototypes is their reduced ability to capture the full range of a category, such as a shot putter relative to the "average" track and field athlete. This weakness influences accuracy when using Tversky and Kahneman's second type of heuristic, the **representativeness heuristic**, which leads people to estimate that stimuli similar to a prototype are more likely to fit the category than are stimuli different from the prototype. If the instance you are considering is very "average" for its category, the strategy works. But when presented with an outlier, accuracy will suffer.

To illustrate the limitations of this heuristic, Tversky and Kahneman asked research participants whether Thomas, who is short, slim, and loves poetry, is more likely to be an Ivy League classics professor or a truck driver. Most people assumed that Thomas would be a classics professor because his description is closer to that of a prototypical professor than a prototypical truck driver. However, this conclusion is statistically quite unlikely. There are few Ivy League classics professors, and even if most fit Thomas's description, the numbers would still be quite low. In contrast, there are thousands of truck drivers in the United States. Even if a

representativeness heuristic A rule of thumb in which stimuli similar to a prototype are believed to be more likely than stimuli that are dissimilar to a prototype.

small proportion of them shared Thomas's characteristics, the numbers would be large. Consequently, the odds are that Thomas is a truck driver.

AP Images/Matt Dunham/Adrian Harlen

The representativeness heuristic makes us believe that stimuli similar to a prototype are more likely than stimuli that are dissimilar. Katrina Hodge, 2009 Miss England, may not fit your prototype of a Lance Corporal and Iraq War veteran. However, there are many more soldiers than beauty queens, so the likelihood that a beautiful woman is a soldier is higher than the likelihood that she is a beauty queen.

Decide on a Solution Once we have generated a set of solutions, we must decide which one to try first. How is this decision reached?

Just as we warned you in Chapter 2 about signs that you are not using good critical thinking skills, we can also share some signs that you are about to make a poorly considered decision:

- Thinking that a decision is "obviously right" or "obviously wrong" might result from confirmation bias, which we discussed in Chapter 2.
- Being influenced by what "everyone thinks" you should do is more about conformity than good decision making. "Everyone" might be wrong.
- Doing something "because we've always done it that way" can work, of course, but this shouldn't be the only reason to choose a solution.
- Choosing a simple solution instead of a more complex one because you understand it better is more about ease of processing than good decision making.

Psychologists have studied the conditions that promote good decision making. When participants' performance on skills related to decision making in the lab were compared with real-life decision making, such as buying new clothes or shoes they never wore, strong correlations were observed between their abilities on the identified decision making skills and the quality of their real-world decision making (Bruine de Bruin et al., 2007). Using your very best critical thinking skills is very important while making decisions, but there are other considerations as well:

- Understand probability. Yes, we know coursework about decks of cards and throwing dice might seem far removed from everyday decision making, but this basic skill provides an essential foundation for making the right choices. After all, a decision is essentially a bet on the future.
- Be mindful of relevant social norms and encourage dissenting opinions from others. Ask what concerns they see in the decisions you are contemplating. Others might bring up a concern that has escaped your notice.
- Make an accurate assessment of your own knowledge about the issues involved with your decision. Avoid both under- and overconfidence.
- Time is an important variable. Often we are called upon to make very fast decisions. However, if time permits, do not rush important decisions. Rest your mind by taking breaks to do less cognitively demanding tasks. Then return to your decision to see if it looks the same as before.

A good understanding of probability explains the vast majority of individual differences in decision making skills (Cokely et al., 2018). Surprisingly, many highly educated people are just not very good with numbers and probability. Nearly 50% of physicians were unable to answer the following correctly: If Patient A has a 1% risk of getting a disease in ten years and Patient B's risk is double that of A's, what is Patient B's risk? (No, this is not a trick. The answer is $2 \times .01 = .02$ or 2%.) Mistakes on problems like this are far less likely when the data are appropriately visualized (see ● Figure 10.8).

Although a good understanding of probability often distinguishes between high- and low-quality decision making, many people still make emotional, intuitive decisions rather than logical, rational decisions. The **affect heuristic** is particularly relevant to the way people make

affect heuristic A rule of thumb in which we choose between alternatives based on emotional or "gut" reactions to stimuli.

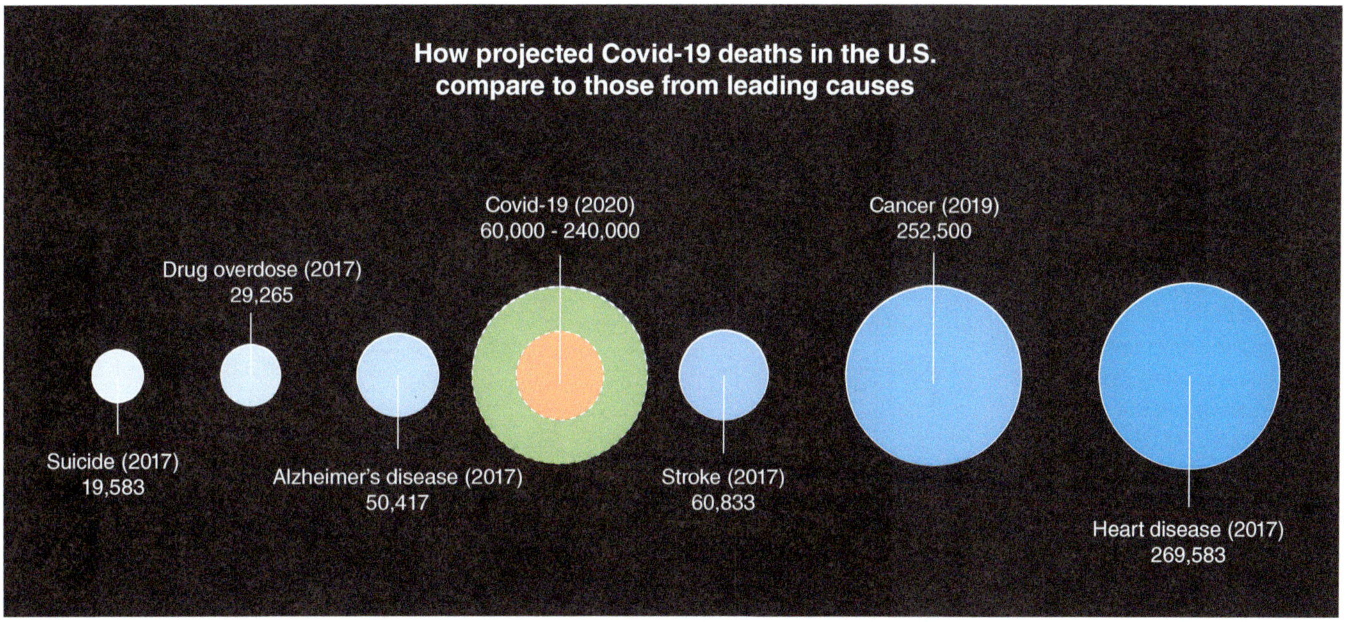

FIGURE **10.8**

Data Visualization. Even highly educated people benefit from properly visualized data. A discussion of potential deaths due to COVID-19 doesn't always make sense from looking at the numbers alone. This image, showing the lower and higher boundaries of 2020 estimates, enhances understanding of the risk of COVID-19 relative to other leading causes of death.

Source: https://www.statnews.com/2020/04/09/its-difficult-to-grasp-the-projected-deaths-from-covid-19-heres-how-they-compare-to-other-causes-of-death/.

important choices (Slovic et al., 2005). This heuristic uses emotional responses to guide our decisions. Through our past experiences with similar choices, we develop an implicit "gut" reaction to our options, pushing us toward alternatives we expect to produce desirable outcomes and away from alternatives we expect to produce undesirable outcomes. Our decision making is also affected by the need to avoid the emotion of regret (Connolly & Zeelenberg, 2002). By considering ways to justify the reasons for their decisions in advance, people can live more comfortably with the decisions they have made.

An alternate and less emotional approach to decision making, utility theory, suggests that we compute the expected outcomes of our choices and select the best one. Expected outcomes are computed by multiplying measures of the usefulness of the outcomes by their expected probability. For example, to choose an elective course for your next term, you might consider a course that provides positive outcomes, such as being interesting and satisfying a graduation requirement. At the same time, you wish to avoid negative outcomes, such as getting a poor grade or spending a lot of money on materials. If you multiply the assigned value of each outcome by its probability of occurrence and add up the results for each course, you can see which one is most likely to fit your needs.

You might find that applying utility theory is useful when faced with an important decision, such as whether to accept a job offer with modest pay in your hometown or one with higher pay in another state. It is clear, however, that we rarely make decisions by solving equations.

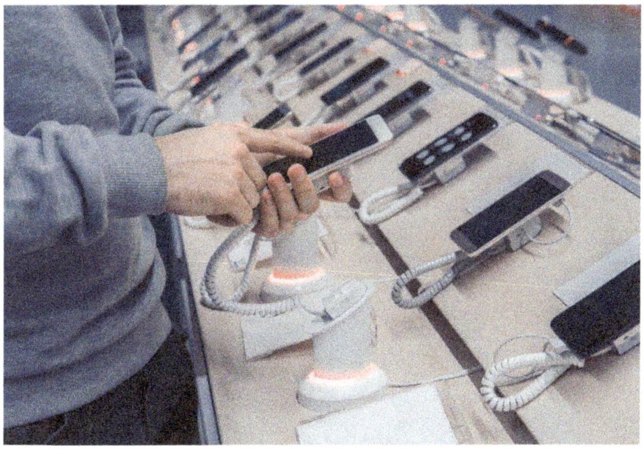

Igor Kardasov/Shutterstock.com

Even though we might carefully weigh the pros and cons of buying one cell phone over another, the affect heuristic suggests that we use our emotional or "gut" responses to make decisions, too.

FIGURE **10.9**

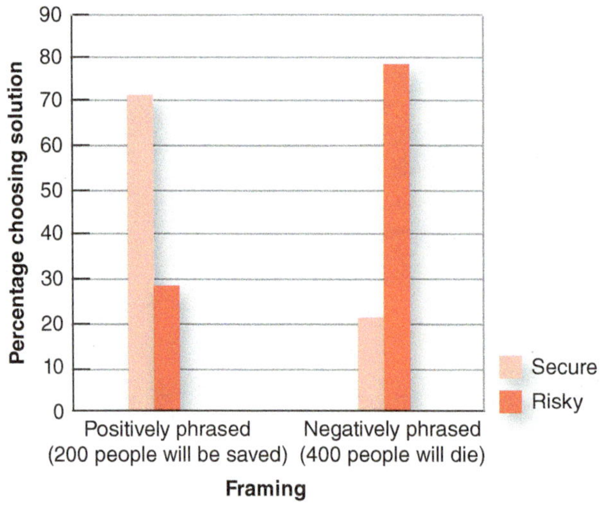

Framing Effects. Amos Tversky and Daniel Kahneman's classic 1987 Asian disease problem asks people to choose one of two solutions to the following problem: "If a disease was coming to the United States, and 600 people were expected to die, what should the president do?" Both solutions resulted in the deaths of the same number of people (400), but one was phrased positively (200 will be saved) and the other was phrased negatively (400 will die). When the question was framed negatively, people were more likely to choose the riskier alternative.

Source: A. Tversky & D. Kahneman (1987). "Rational Choice and the Framing of Decisions." In R. M. Hogarth & M. W. Reder (Eds.), *Rational choice: The contrast between economics and psychology* (pp. 67–94). Chicago: University of Chicago Press.

Even when utility is held constant, people show a preference for one solution or the other based on how the solutions are framed. People rate basketball players who are described as making 75% of their free throws higher than those who are described as missing 25% of the time, even though the math is identical in both cases. Medical treatments that are described as effective 80% of the time are viewed more positively than those that fail 20% of the time.

Tversky and Kahneman (1987) illustrated the importance of framing in decision making using an "Asian disease problem." Even though the outcome for each of two possible solutions is that 400 out of 600 people with the disease will die, 72% of respondents preferred a more secure solution when the problem was framed using the word *saved*. In contrast, when the problem was framed using the word *die*, the secure solution was preferred by only 22% (see Figure 10.9). As we mentioned earlier, the way a problem is represented or framed can have a large effect on whether it will be solved. Framing can affect the choice of a solution through its interaction with a person's tolerance for risk. When a problem is framed in terms of losses, as in the *will die* framing of the Asian disease problem, people are more comfortable choosing a risky solution. In contrast, when a problem is framed in terms of gains, as in the *saved* frame of the Asian disease problem, people generally become more cautious. If we have already "saved" 200 people, we don't want to risk saving fewer.

Carry Out the Plan

Your belief that you can implement a particular solution will determine whether you decide to pursue that solution or look for another solution. Once you have decided on a solution, it is time to try it out.

At this point, one of the most critical elements in successfully implementing your solution is planning. Solutions that might otherwise succeed can fail when people do not anticipate the time and the resources needed for implementation. It is one thing to decide that you

Measures of decision making skills, such as a person's understanding of probability, are negatively correlated with poor real-world decision making, such as the number of times you buy things you never use.

Corbis RF/Alamy Stock Photo

need to exercise more to lose your holiday weight, but without further planning, this solution might not work. How much exercise will you need? What activities should you do? When? Where? Is your solution practical? If you are a couch potato, thinking you will implement your exercise solution by training for next month's marathon might not be realistic. If time management is not your strongest skill, you might consider tools like an online calendar or a bullet journal.

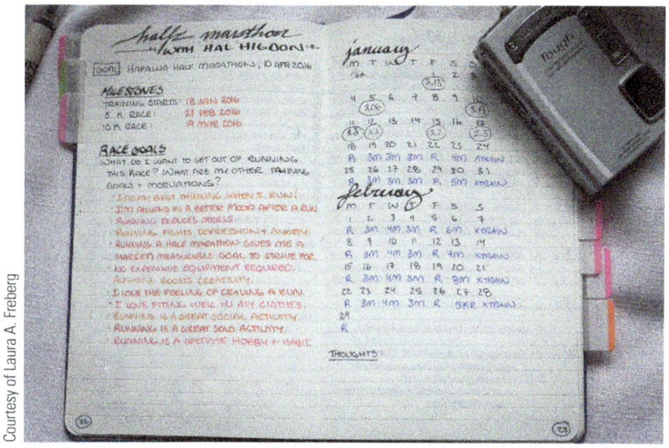

Courtesy of Laura A. Freberg

Many techniques for helping you manage your time are available, including online calendaring and bullet journals, such as the one shown in this image.

Look Back

As you implement your solution, you need to know whether it is bringing you closer to your goal, which usually means that you need some measurement of success. In the example of holiday weight gain, the logical way to assess progress is to get back on the scale at regular intervals. At the same time, solutions usually require time to work, and a failure to make immediate progress should not be the basis for discarding a promising solution.

Evaluation is an ongoing process, but it is especially important once a solution has been fully implemented. You might have predicted that 6 months of exercise should return you to your goal weight. At the 6-month point, we return to the original problem. Does it still exist? If not, the problem has been solved, and you can move on to other issues, although keeping up your exercise program is always a good idea. If the problem still exists, you return to the make-a-plan step and try again. Maybe this time you need to combine exercise with counting calories.

People have a reasonably effective commonsense approach to making decisions, but again, careful psychological research can point out where we are vulnerable to poor decision making. If you find yourself unhappy with outcomes of some of your previous decisions, following the steps in this section on future occasions might help you find better solutions.

Computer Models of Decision Making

An epic battle between world chess champion Garry Kasparov and IBM's Deep Blue ended in defeat for Kasparov in 1997. More recently, AlphaGo defeated several champion Go players (Silver et al., 2016). What makes this a remarkable achievement for AlphaGo's programmers is the 10^{360} possible moves in the typical game of Go, dwarfing the already huge number of options (10^{123}) in the typical game of chess.

This remarkable achievement parallels the four problem-solving steps we reviewed in this section. The programmers began by helping their AlphaGo neural network to (1) understand the problem by training it on 30 million board positions taken from real-life games on a Go database. The neural network (2) made plans by estimating the likelihood that a particular move will lead to a win. In the next step, these plans were (3) carried out repeatedly. Most importantly, the program contained a (4) "look back" strategy the programmers refer to as "deep reinforcement learning" while playing itself (see • Figure 10.10). Now, instead of evaluating moves from the real-life games, AlphaGo generates its own moves and estimates the likelihood that each move will lead to a win, leading to an ongoing tsunami of improvement in the program's capability.

Does this mean that our brains are destined to be outmatched by the machines? Not quite yet. Recall that even AlphaGo needed input from real-life games played by real-life people to get started.

The Biological Psychology of Decision Making

What processes can we observe in the brain during decision making? As we have seen on previous occasions in this textbook, observing the effects of brain damage on a behavior can illuminate the contributions of particular parts of the brain to that behavior. Damage to the

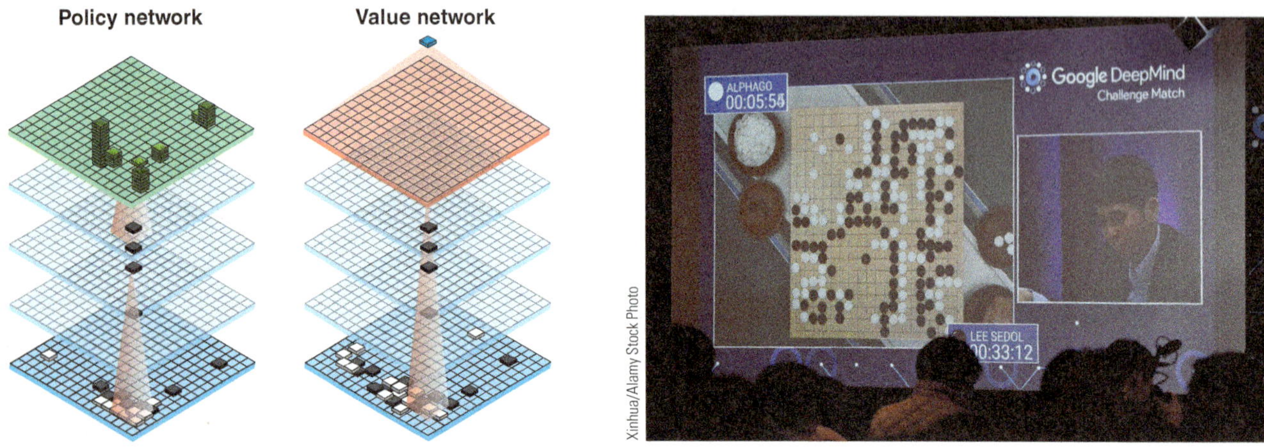

FIGURE **10.10**

AlphaGo Versus the Go Masters. The AlphaGo program recently beat one of the world's best human Go players, a feat considered nearly impossible with current technology due to the number of possible moves that characterize the game. The neural network program combined "policies," or the selection of moves, with "values," which predict whether a move will produce a win.

Source: D. Silver et al. (2016). "Mastering the Game of Go with Deep Neural Networks and Tree Search," *Nature*, *529*(7587), 484–489. doi:10.1038/nature16961

Making simple decisions about what to keep and what to throw away can be difficult for some individuals. Hoarding behavior is correlated with unusual levels of activity in the anterior cingulate cortex and insula (Stevens et al., 2020).

frontal lobes of the brain, as in the case of the unfortunate Phineas Gage described in Chapter 4, reliably produces impulsivity and poor judgment. Patients with this type of damage often begin to gamble obsessively, turn their personal lives upside down, and become unemployable.

Sometimes we need to make fast decisions, perhaps at the expense of accuracy. Different levels of activity in the subthalamic nucleus, part of the basal ganglia (see Chapter 4), are associated with fast and more cautious decision making (Herz et al., 2017). At other times, you might feel like you are "of two minds" when faced with a decision, and this is not so far from the truth. In reality, three major brain circuits interact during decision making (Goschke, 2014). One circuit assigns value to situations along the lines of pleasure or pain and involves the ventromedial prefrontal cortex, the orbitofrontal cortex, the nucleus accumbens, and the amygdala. A second circuit is an impulse control network that controls unwanted responses and includes the lateral prefrontal cortex and the parietal cortex. Finally, an attentional circuit monitors significant stimuli and involves the insula, the anterior cingulate cortex, and the amygdala. This circuit also seems to be involved with more complex social decision making, such as deciding whom to trust (Rilling & Sanfey, 2011).

The value circuit, which is impulsive, gradually comes under the control of the impulse control circuit as we mature and are exposed to the social rules of our community (Bechara, 2005). As college students, you are a prime example of this maturity. Spending long hours studying and writing papers produces immediate "pain" but also promises the future pleasure of obtaining an interesting job and making enough money to support yourself and perhaps a family.

Drug addiction provides an interesting example of what happens when these normal decision making circuits are disrupted. In many ways, drug addicts behave similarly to people who have brain damage in circuits related to decision making. Through their experience with drugs and possibly because of some biochemical consequences of addictive substances, the impulsive value system gains control over the impulse control system. The immediate pleasure promised by the drug experience overwhelms the impact of negative future events such as lost jobs, disrupted family life, and even prison. Addicts begin to experience exaggerated responses to the potential reward of drug cues while becoming less responsive to other types of reward (Bechara, 2005). Hyperactivity in this impulsive reward system seems to progressively weaken impulse control.

As you will see in Chapter 11, the prefrontal cortex is one of the last parts of the brain to mature (development continues into the early 20s), which might account for some of the impulsive, risky decisions made by adolescents (Blakemore & Robbins, 2012). At the same time that their impulse control system is relatively weak, adolescents might be hypersensitive to reward. Developmental changes in brain structure and function also account for the effects of peers on adolescent risk taking. Teens and young adults make about the same number of risky decisions while alone, but teens are more likely than young adults to make risky decisions in the presence of their peers. As shown in ● Figure 10.11, parts of the reward circuit were especially active in adolescents making a risky decision in the presence of peers.

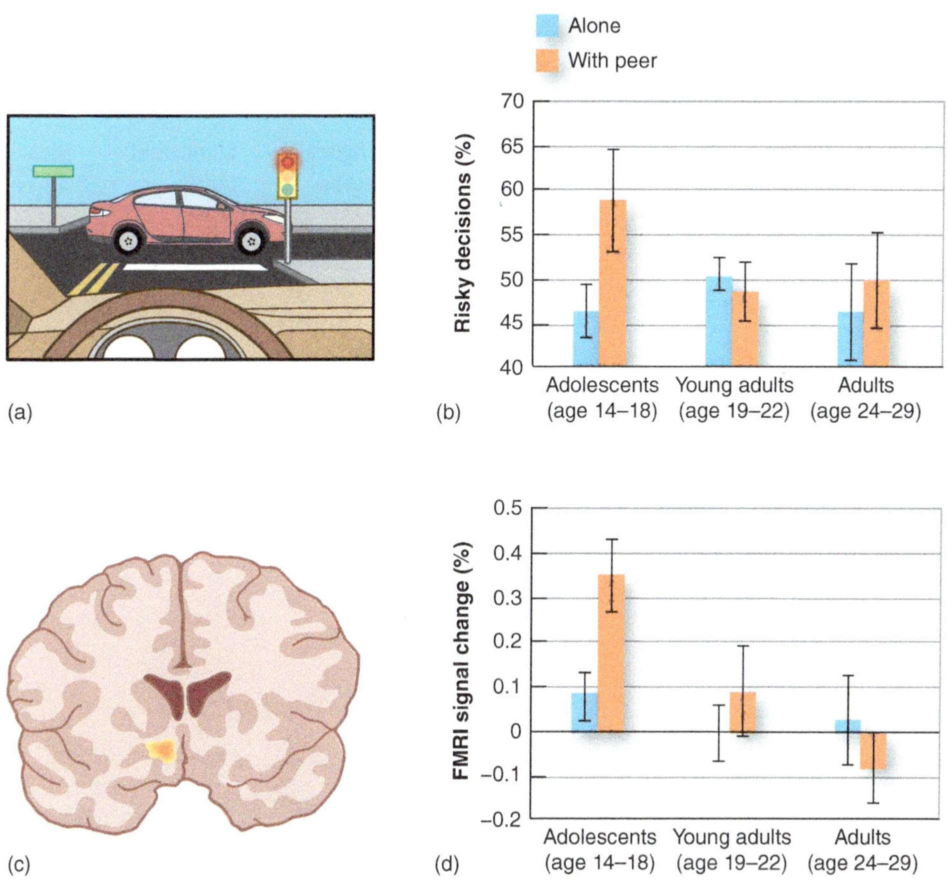

FIGURE 10.11

Adolescents Make Risky Decisions in the Presence of Peers. (a) The stoplight driving game is a simulation in which participants are told to reach the end of a track as quickly as possible. (b) Adolescents driving alone do not make more risky decisions than young adults or older adults, but they make many more risky decisions in the presence of a peer. (c) The ventral striatum, in orange, is part of the brain's reward pathways. It is also crucial to addiction. (d) This graph shows the amount of change in the ventral striatum for the three age groups in the alone and peer-present conditions.
Source: S. -J. Blakemore & T. W. Robbins (2012). "Decision-making In the Adolescent Brain." *Nature Neuroscience*, *15*, 1184–1191. doi:10.1038/nn.3177

EXPERIENCING PSYCHOLOGY

What Is Your Decision Style?

MANY VARIABLES INFLUENCE an individual's approach to decision making. The instrument in Table 10.2 was designed to identify which type of style you use (Scott & Bruce, 1995).

For each item, you will choose a score between 1 (strongly disagree) and 5 (strongly agree). When you're done, add up your scores for the following groupings:

Group R: 1, 6, 11, 16, 21
Group I: 2, 7, 12, 17, 22
Group D: 3, 8, 13, 18, 23
Group A: 4, 9, 14, 19, 24
Group S: 5, 10, 15, 20, 25

The question groups are relevant to the decision styles in this order: Rational, intuitive, dependent, avoidant, and spontaneous.

While you may have a dominant style, these scores are not mutually exclusive. People use multiple styles depending on the amount of information they have at hand

TABLE 10.2

Decision Styles Questionnaire

Listed below are statements describing how individuals go about making important decisions. Please indicate whether you agree or disagree with each statement.

	Strongly Disagree	Somewhat Disagree	Neither Agree nor Disagree	Somewhat Agree	Strongly Agree
1. I double-check my information sources to be sure I have the right facts before making a decision.	1	2	3	4	5
2. When making a decision, I rely upon my instincts.	1	2	3	4	5
3. I often need the assistance of other people when making important decisions.	1	2	3	4	5
4. I avoid making important decisions until the pressure is on.	1	2	3	4	5
5. I generally make snap decisions.	1	2	3	4	5
6. I make decisions in a logical and systematic way.	1	2	3	4	5
7. When I make decisions, I tend to rely on my intuition.	1	2	3	4	5
8. I rarely make important decisions without consulting other people.	1	2	3	4	5
9. I postpone decision making whenever possible.	1	2	3	4	5
10. I often make decisions on the spur of the moment.	1	2	3	4	5
11. My decision making requires careful thought.	1	2	3	4	5
12. I generally make decisions that feel right to me.	1	2	3	4	5
13. If I have the support of others, it is easier for me to make important decisions.	1	2	3	4	5

and the timing of the decision. Rational decision-makers use reasoning and logic to arrive at solutions, while intuitive decision-makers rely on emotion and feelings. Dependent decision-makers rely on other people to point them in the right direction. Avoidant decision-makers postpone making any decision while hoping a situation will resolve without any actions on their part. Finally, spontaneous decision-makers focus on the immediate needs of a situation.

Do your results fit with your experience? Are you generally satisfied with the decisions you make? In this chapter, we argue that decision-making ability is something you can learn to improve, so if you are not pleased with many of your past decisions, it is possible to change.

Elizaveta Smirnova/Alamy Stock Photo

	Strongly Disagree	Somewhat Disagree	Neither Agree nor Disagree	Somewhat Agree	Strongly Agree
14. I often procrastinate when it comes to making important decisions.	1	2	3	4	5
15. I make quick decisions.	1	2	3	4	5
16. When making a decision, I consider various options in terms of a specific goal.	1	2	3	4	5
17. When I make a decision, it is more important for me to feel the decision is right than to have a rational reason for it.	1	2	3	4	5
18. I use the advice of other people in making my important decisions.	1	2	3	4	5
19. I generally make important decisions at the last minute.	1	2	3	4	5
20. I often make impulsive decisions.	1	2	3	4	5
21. I explore all my options before making a decision.	1	2	3	4	5
22. When I make a decision, I trust my inner feelings and reactions.	1	2	3	4	5
23. I like to have someone to steer me in the right direction when I am faced with important decisions.	1	2	3	4	5
24. I put off making many decisions because thinking about them makes me uneasy.	1	2	3	4	5
25. When making decisions, I do what seems natural at the moment.	1	2	3	4	5

SUMMARY 10.1 Heuristics

Type of heuristic	Definition	Example
Recognition 	A more recognizable stimulus has a higher value.	Wine from California is rated higher than wine from North Dakota.
Availability 	Events that are easy to think about are more likely.	Despite news and missing child reports that make kidnappings appear to be common, fewer than 100 children per year are abducted by strangers in the United States.
Representativeness 	Stimuli that are similar to a prototype are more likely to fit a category than stimuli that are different from the prototype.	A big, muscular student at Ohio State University is probably a football player rather than an engineering student (even though fewer than 100 of Ohio State's 60,000-plus students are on the football team but there are about 8,000 undergraduate engineering majors).
Affect 	We use an emotional response ("gut" feeling) to choose one alternative over another.	Preferring Pepsi over Coca Cola when most people think they taste pretty much the same (McClure et al., 2004).

Credits: Top row—BFA/Alamy Stock Photo; Second row—Jeff Rotman/Photolibrary/Getty Images; Third row—AP Images/Matt Dunham/Adrian Harlen; Bottom row—Igor Kardasov/Shutterstock.com.

How Does Language Influence Behavior?

Language is a system for communicating thoughts and feelings using arbitrary signals, such as voice sounds, gestures, or written symbols. As we discussed previously, language provides us with powerful tools for organizing and manipulating our thinking, problem solving, and decision making. Although thoughts can be represented visually as well as verbally, language extends our thinking abilities to abstract concepts such as truth and beauty that would be difficult to visualize. Above all, language connects us with others. Not only can we communicate with people in our immediate vicinity, but language spans time and distance, allowing us to share the thoughts of people living long ago and in distant places. Because of language, the thoughts we record today might reach into the future to influence the thinking of people not yet born.

Language both reflects and shapes thought. Benjamin Lee Whorf's hypothesis of linguistic relativity examines the effect of having a rich vocabulary on a person's ability to think about a topic (Whorf, 1956). According to Whorf, a skier who can name and identify powder, slush, and other variations of snow thinks differently about snow than does a person born and raised in a tropical climate. Whorf's theory correctly predicted that the use of gender-free words such as *server* instead of *waiter* or *waitress* or *flight attendant* instead of *stewardess* would reduce gender stereotyping and discrimination (Sczesny et al., 2016). Further efforts to address the

language A system for communicating thoughts and feelings using arbitrary signals.

Electron and Confocal Microscopy Laboratory, Agricultural Research Service, USDA/Science Source; iofoto/Shutterstock.com

According to Benjamin Lee Whorf, a skier who knows what *early sintering* means is able to think differently about snow than a person who is unfamiliar with the term. Sintering occurs when snow crystals break down and fuse into larger crystals.

binary nature of English personal pronouns (he or she) to better reflect a continuum of gender identity have led to the use of completely gender-neutral pronouns (Lindqvist et al., 2019).

The Origins of Human Language

To fix the emergence of human languages in time, we can assume that certain complex social behaviors would be difficult to conduct without the ability to speak. Elaborate tool use and cooperation would be easier to accomplish using language. Because our version of the human species, *Homo sapiens*, appeared between 100,000 and 200,000 years ago, most anthropologists are convinced that human language existed at that time, if not earlier. A critical gene mutation in the *FOXP-2* gene occurring around 100,000 years ago possibly marked the start of modern language (Corballis, 2004). Regardless of timing, the enormous advantages of language to human culture and cooperation would ensure its continuity.

Much evidence points to Africa as the source of the first human languages. Some anthropologists suggest that it would be difficult for early humans to migrate successfully to other continents without the cooperation provided by language. Taking a different approach, an analysis of more than 500 contemporary languages has demonstrated that the number of speech sounds in a language decreases systematically with the culture's distance from Africa along migration routes (Atkinson, 2011). Many African languages feature more than 100 speech sounds, compared to 45 in English and 13 in Hawaiian (see ● Figure 10.12).

Languages are living entities, under constant pressure to change. Nearly half the world's spoken languages may soon be lost. Following assimilation into larger cultures, speakers stop using their native languages or fail to transmit them to their children. With each language lost goes an opportunity for scientists to understand the unique local knowledge of a culture, along with the historical and cognitive implications of the language (Roche, 2020).

Language is intimately connected to cultural values. For example, the English language contains many words that signify the passage of time. In contrast, the Hopi Native American tribes have only two words relevant to time, loosely translated as "sooner" and "later" (Le Lionnais, 1960). What does this difference tell you about the two cultures?

FIGURE **10.12**

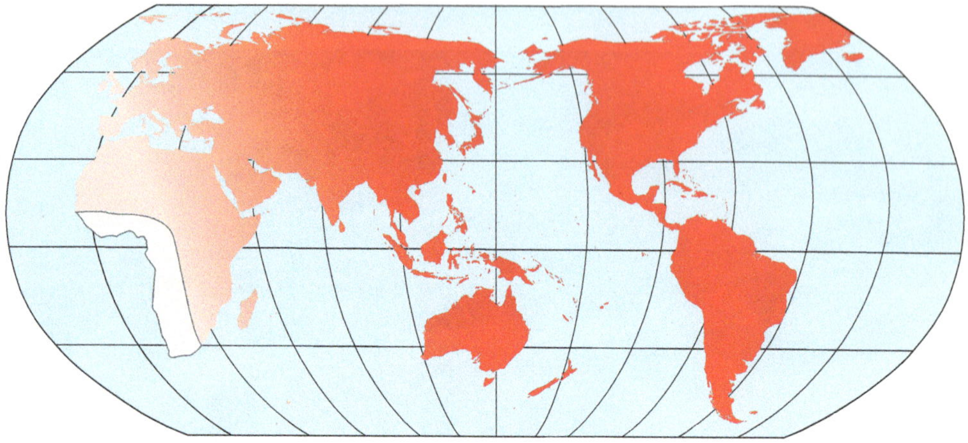

Phoneme Diversity Shows the Path of Language. The number of phonemes or speech sounds per language decreases with the distance of the culture using the language (indicated by shades of red) along migration routes from the western coast of Africa. Many African languages feature more than 100 speech sounds, compared to 45 in English and 13 in Hawaiian.
Source: Adapted from Q. D. Atkinson (2011). "Phonemic Diversity Supports a Serial Founder Effect Model of Language Expansion from Africa," *Science, 332*(6027), 346–349. doi: 10.1126/science.1199295

phoneme A speech sound.

morpheme The smallest component of speech that carries meaning.

The Basic Building Blocks of Language

Language works like a set of building blocks, beginning with basic speech sounds (phonemes), which are combined into meaningful units (morphemes) and then combined in meaningful strings according to the rules of grammar.

Humans produce more than 500 **phonemes** or speech sounds, such as the *c* in *cat*. The number and types of phonemes are limited only by the physical features of the human vocal apparatus. Not all phonemes appear in all languages. Individual world languages vary from as few as 11 phonemes to more than 140 (Holt et al., 1998). English features about 45 phonemes, which we represent visually using the 26 letters of the alphabet either singly (*s*) or in combination (*sh*). Most written languages attempt to match visual symbols to phonemes, although many new readers of English struggle with the different pronunciations represented by the same letters, as in the *ough* in *through, rough, trough, slough*, or *thought*.

Phonemes are combined into **morphemes**, which are the smallest components of speech that carry meaning. Most morphemes are words, but word prefixes (as in *pre*school and *sub*urban) and word endings (as in dog*s* and walk*ed*) also qualify as morphemes because they change the meaning of the root word. English contains approximately 100,000 morphemes, which can be used to produce more than a million words. The average 20-year-old native English speaker knows about 42,000 words, in addition to thousands of proper nouns (names) and other versions of the main words (Brysbaert et al., 2016). Education and age increase this number to a high of nearly 60,000 words (see Figure 10.13).

Morphemes are combined into phrases and sentences according to rules of grammar. For example, different languages have their own rules about the meaningful ordering of nouns and adjectives. In English, you say "the brown dog" but not "the dog brown," while the reverse is true in Spanish. This type of natural grammar is usually learned early in childhood by interacting with other speakers, in contrast to the formal grammar instruction featured in schools.

Boyd E. Norton/Science Source

Click languages include sounds made by clicking the tongue and are still used by groups in southern Africa like the Hazda of Tanzania. These might be among the earliest forms of language used by humans.

The Biological Psychology of Language

As we discussed in Chapter 4, language is typically managed by the left hemisphere of the brain. Further insights into the localization of language processing result from investigations of brain damage and efforts to teach language to nonhuman animals.

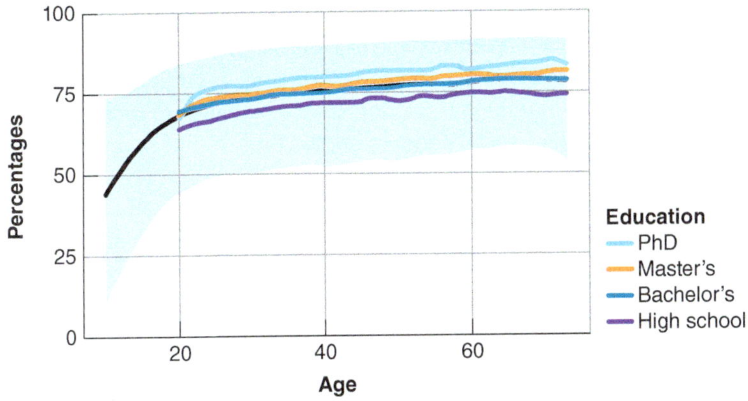

FIGURE **10.13**

Age and Education Correlate with Vocabulary. Two trends characterize the growth of vocabulary: age and education. A gradual increase in vocabulary takes place over the adult lifespan. People's level of education is also predictive of the number of words they know.

Source: M. Brysbaert et al. (2016). "How Many Words Do We Know? Practical Estimates of Vocabulary Size Dependent on Word Definition, the Degree of Language Input, and the Participant's Age," *Frontiers in Psychology*, 7(1116). doi: 10.3389/fpsyg.2016.01116

Lessons From Language Disorders We can learn about the biology of language by surveying problems that arise because of brain damage resulting from head injury or stroke. **Aphasia** is the loss of the ability to speak or understand language. The closely related processes of reading and writing are often, but not always affected by aphasia.

In 1861, Paul Broca conducted a case study of a 51-year-old man named Louis Leborgne, who had been institutionalized for more than 20 years (Domanski, 2013). Leborgne came to be called "Tan," because when questioned, "tan" was one of a few syllables he could produce. Leborgne entered the hospital after several months of being unable to speak. He apparently understood much of what was said to him and retained his ability to answer numerical questions by raising an appropriate number of fingers on his left hand (Herrnstein & Boring, 1965). After Leborgne died, Broca performed an autopsy on his patient's brain and found significant damage to the patient's left frontal lobe, possibly because of Leborgne's long history of epilepsy. The damaged area is now called Broca's area in honor of Broca's discovery (see ● Figure 10.14).

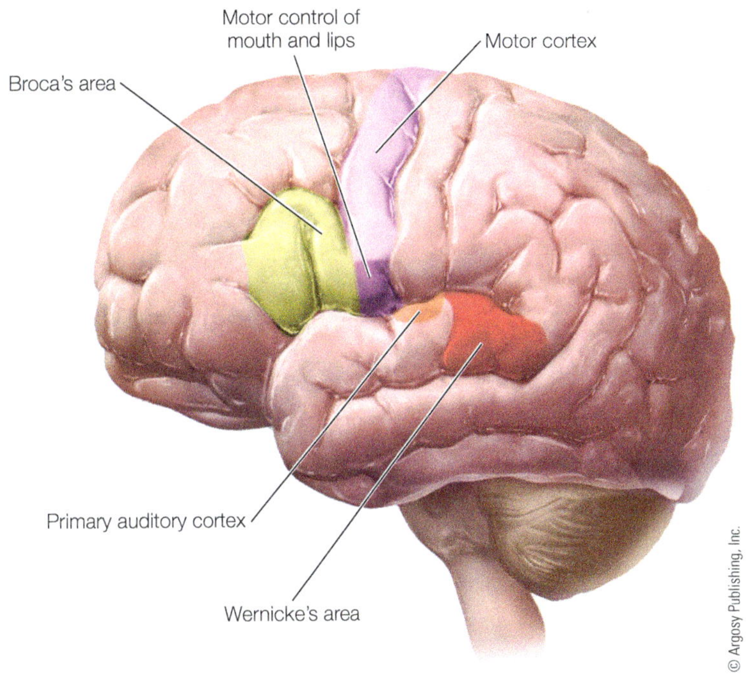

FIGURE **10.14**

The Major Brain Structures Participating in Language.

Today, Leborgne would be diagnosed with Broca's aphasia. This condition is characterized by difficulty producing speech. The speech that the patient manages to produce is slow and effortful, but it generally makes sense. In some cases, patients retain the ability to curse, as in one of Broca's other patient's "Sacre nom de Dieu!" ("In the name of God!"), which he uttered in frustration when unable to make himself understood with gestures. A contemporary patient with Broca's aphasia described his condition by saying, "Speech . . . can't say . . . talk, you see" (Gardner, 1976, p. 61).

About 13 years after Broca presented his revolutionary work on Leborgne, Carl Wernicke (1874) published his observations on another type of language deficit. In honor of his contributions, this syndrome is now called Wernicke's aphasia, and the affected area of the brain is known as Wernicke's area. Wernicke's area is located in the temporal lobe near the primary auditory cortex.

The symptoms of Wernicke's aphasia could hardly be more different from those of Broca's aphasia. Where Broca's aphasia affects the production of speech, Wernicke's aphasia affects its comprehension. In Broca's aphasia, speech is slow and laborious but generally meaningful. In Wernicke's aphasia, the opposite is true. Speech is rapid and fluent but virtually meaningless. A contemporary patient with Wernicke's aphasia said,

> Oh sure, go ahead, any old think you want. If I could I would. Oh, I'm taking the word the wrong way to say, all of the barbers here whenever they stop you it's going around and around, if you known what I mean, that is typing and tying for repucer, repuceration, well we were trying the best that we could while another time it was with the beds over the same thing. (Gardner, 1976, p. 68)

aphasia The loss of the ability to speak or understand language.

Pictorial Press Ltd/Alamy Stock Photo

The soundtracks of horror films, adventure films, dramas, and war films use sound features that characterize animal distress calls to heighten viewer arousal. It is likely that these sounds add to the fear produced by the visual images (Blumstein et al., 2010).

If you don't pay attention to the meaning, the speech of patients with Wernicke's aphasia sounds normal, if slightly fast. Grammar is generally correct. On further examination, we find that meaningfulness is lacking. These patients are locked into a world without social connection, yet they do not seem aware of their circumstances or in apparent distress.

It is simplistic to assume that the brain has only two main language "centers:" Broca's and Wernicke's areas. Instead, contemporary research has identified complex networks for processing language that connect cortical and subcortical areas related to language and cognition (Dronkers et al., 2017).

Are Nonhuman Animals Capable of Real Language?

Later in this chapter, we discuss several approaches to learning language. The evolutionary approach suggests that language results from some innate capacity shaped by natural selection. Animals and human infants demonstrate similar perceptual grouping, or the linking together of sounds with certain characteristics like the "tick-tock" of a clock (Toro, 2016). This evolutionary view implies that we should find precursors of human language in the behavior of other animals.

Many animals communicate with each other, often in complex ways. All forms of communication, however, do not involve the flexibility and the creativity of language. We can identify three major patterns of animal communication (Dronkers et al., 2000). One is an inflexible group of calls for signaling danger and identifying territories. A second contains signals that communicate magnitude, as in the case of bee dances. Finally, animals communicate through sequences of behavior, as in the case of birdsong. We don't know to what extent these animal forms of communication may have served as precursors for human language.

The most logical place to look for precursors to human language is the great apes. Chimpanzees, bonobos, and gorillas have a part of the brain analogous to the human Broca's area. In both humans and apes, this area shows a difference in size between the right and the left hemispheres that might be correlated with language ability (Cantalupo & Hopkins, 2001).

Many researchers have attempted to teach human languages to apes. In 1931, Winthrop N. and Luella Kellogg "adopted" a baby chimpanzee, Gua. Because of the limitations of the chimpanzee vocal apparatus, efforts to teach Gua to talk were doomed to failure (Kellogg & Kellogg, 1933). Allen and Beatrice Gardner (1969) taught sign language to a chimp named Washoe. After 4 years of work, Washoe had mastered 132 signs. The Gardners' efforts were followed by Francine Patterson (1978), who trained a gorilla named Koko to use signs. Sue Savage-Rumbaugh and her colleagues (1998) have successfully taught a bonobo chimpanzee named Kanzi to associate geometric symbols with words. Even before his training began, Kanzi learned 10 symbols simply by observing his mother's training sessions, although his mother never quite mastered the task. Kanzi also seems to be able to understand some human speech. When given 660 verbal requests, such as "Put the collar in the water," Kanzi behaved correctly 72% of the time.

In addition to investigations of language behavior in apes and monkeys, Irene Pepperberg (2014) makes a strong case for her African grey parrots. While we use the phrase "to parrot" to indicate mindless mimicry, Pepperberg argues that her parrots demonstrate complex cognitions related to language. Others have proposed that dolphins, whales, dogs, and prairie dogs possess language capabilities (Caldwell & Caldwell, 1976; Bloom, 2004; Janik et al., 2006; Slobodchikoff et al., 2009).

Whether animals demonstrate real language abilities is the subject of ongoing debate. Although children build vocabularies spontaneously, critics point out that ape language must be taught laboriously (Terrace, 1979). Word order does not seem to matter to apes, although it has an essential role in human language. Trainers of the apes might be making biased observations. When Washoe signed "waterbird" while observing a swan, the Gardners concluded that she was making a new, creative observation, but Washoe may simply have noticed a "bird" sitting on the "water." Human infants use cognitive strategies for language learning that are not found in other animals (Toro, 2016). For example, infants pay more attention to consonants than to vowels by the end of their first year. Consonants are often more important sources of information for identifying words than vowels, as you probably already know from the ease with which you interpret "txt mssgs."

Whether we believe that animals have true language or not, we retain an enormous respect for both the complexity and the intelligence of animal behavior and the remarkable sophistication of human language.

Efforts to teach sign language to chimpanzees have been more successful than efforts to teach them to speak. Here, the human instructor is teaching the chimpanzee to sign "eye."

How Do We Learn Language?

Learning language occurs differently than many types of learning. No specific instruction is needed, as it is for the related skills of reading and writing. A typical child exposed to language will learn language.

Language learning begins very early. Korean children adopted by Dutch parents showed evidence of having retained information about the Korean language from prenatal exposure (Choi et al., 2017). Early in life, between 6 and 12 months of age, children make an important perceptual shift that impacts their subsequent language learning. They become less successful in perceiving the differences between sounds that are not characteristic of their native language while becoming more successful at perceiving differences between sounds that do occur regularly in their native language (Kuhl, 2011). Underlying this transition is a type of computational or statistical learning, in which the infant pays attention to the frequencies of each type of sound they hear (see Figure 10.15).

Not just any type of exposure to language will engage the infant's computational learning. Social interaction is an essential component of this process, and two-way interaction in the form of conversation produces maximum results. Because language evolved to allow communication with others, social interaction may serve as a "gate" for initiating the infant's computational learning system (Kuhl, 2011). Conversing with children produces greater language competence than reading to them (Zimmerman et al., 2009). Even when exposure is one-way, such as when a child is listening to a speaker, more language learning occurs when

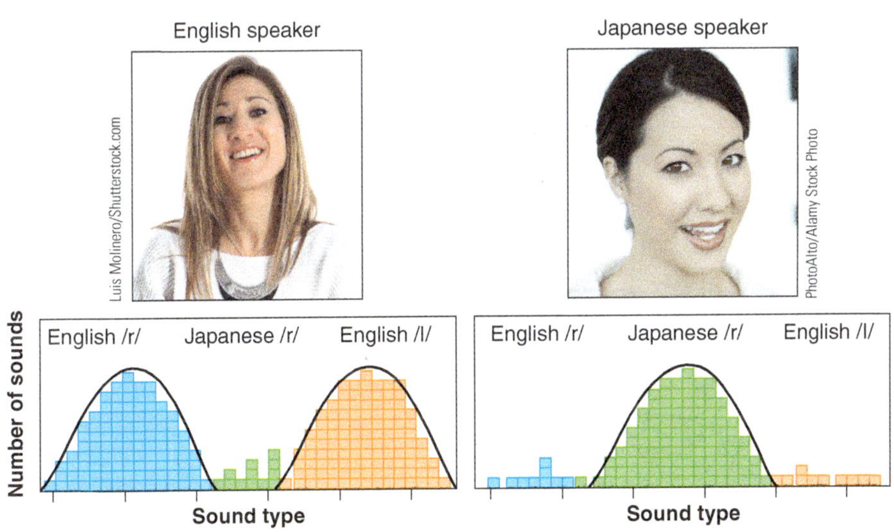

FIGURE 10.15

Infants Make Computational Assessments of Language. In the second half of their first year, infants use social interaction as a "gate" for conducting computational evaluations of how often they hear certain speech sounds. As a result, they become less sensitive to sounds that are not in their native languages and more sensitive to those that are. These graphs show an idealized distribution of the frequencies of the /r/ and /l/ sounds in English and the Japanese /r/.

Source: P. K. Kuhl (2011). "Early Language Learning and Literacy: Neuroscience Implications for Education," *Mind, Brain, and Education*, *5*(3), 128–142. doi: 10.1111/j.1751-228X.2011.01121.x

Irene Pepperberg's African grey parrots have demonstrated sophisticated languagelike behaviors. For example, when shown an object, Alex could correctly state its color, shape, and material. After only six repetitions, he correctly referred to himself as "gray" when asked his color.

Flashon Studio/Shutterstock.com

Two-way interaction in the form of conversation produces the fastest language learning, reinforcing the social nature of this behavior.

a real person is speaking with the child face to face than when a child is listening to the same speaker on television (Kuhl & Meltzoff, 1982; Kuhl, 2007). This finding implies that passive screen time is unlikely to improve a child's language learning.

Observations of the speed and ease with which very young infants can learn complicated language tasks have led to the assumption by many, including linguists Noam Chomsky (1957) and Steven Pinker (1994), that humans have an inborn capacity for learning language. No human culture on Earth exists without language. Language acquisition follows a common course regardless of the native language being learned. Whether a child is exposed to English or Cantonese, similar language structures appear around the same point in development. For example, children all over the world go through a stage in which they overapply language rules, as in the case of a child saying "goed" instead of "went." Eventually, the child switches to the correct forms, long before formal instruction. In addition, human brain structure is correlated with language. As we discussed in Chapter 4, most people process language in the left hemisphere of the brain. Damage to these left hemisphere language areas because of a stroke or other brain injury produces specific types of language deficits.

It is not necessary to assume, however, that we have a unique "language module" in the brain to account for the development of human language. Many linguists believe that spoken language was built on existing structures that allow primates to produce gestures (Corballis, 2020). Simultaneous vocalizations and gestures (pointing and saying "look") could have been followed by a greater reliance on vocalizations, which is the same progression we see in children. Vocalization requires less energy than gesturing, as any sign language interpreter can tell you. It also allows communication to occur at night or when hidden, and it frees the hands for tool use and hand-to-hand combat.

Assuming an inborn capacity for learning language further implies that language has a genetic basis. Several genetic conditions selectively affect individuals' language-learning abilities. A family known as the KE family has members who have severe difficulties with the production of language accompanied by a mutation in the *FOXP2* gene (Lai et al., 2001). This is the same gene suspected of mutating about 100,000 years ago, making modern human language possible. The *FOXP-2* gene appears to be critical for learning to produce vocalizations (Kohn et al., 2019).

Diverse Voices in Psychology

Is the "Language Gap" Real?

SOCIOECONOMIC DIFFERENCES impact language acquisition. By the age of 2 years, English-learning children from low-socioeconomic status Caucasian families were already 6 months behind children from wealthier homes in both vocabulary and language understanding (Fernald & Weisleder, 2015). Hart and Risley (1995) proposed a "language gap," characterized by the exposure to as many as 30 million more words to children in wealthier families than in poor families by the age of 3 years. This report, widely cited in the popular press, was consistent with a cultural deficit model, in which the poor performance of children from disadvantaged families resulted from low levels of cognitive stimulation. The cultural deficit model has been widely criticized as blaming parents for their children's poor school performance and being insensitive to cultural differences in the ways parents interact with children.

Quantity and quality of speech directed at young children are highly correlated, and Hart and Risley noted that quantity of words was just one indicator of possible quality of language exposure. However, the importance of the quantity of exposure remains hotly debated (Baugh, 2017). Many researchers argue that specific aspects related to the quality of the language input to the child, more so than its quantity, predicts later language skills (Ramírez-Esparza et al., 2014). For example, using "parentese," or language deliberately simplified for use in communicating with children, was associated with better child language outcomes. The use of rich vocabulary, complex ideas, and back-and-forth conversation promotes language growth in children (Fernald & Weisleder, 2015). Efforts to build parents' skills in nourishing their children's language development can bring benefits to all, regardless of socioeconomic status. ■

In most cases, individuals with intellectual disability experience difficulties with language, but individuals with Williams syndrome are fluent speakers with large vocabularies. Williams syndrome and another genetic disorder, Down syndrome, produce a similar level of intellectual disability, but language use in these two groups is quite different (Bellugi et al., 1994). When asked to name all the animals he knew, a child with Down syndrome replied, "Horsie, dog, ice cream." A child with Williams syndrome of the same age and with the same IQ score answered, "Weasel, newt, salamander, ibex, yak."

At the same time, it is not unusual for a person of normal to high intelligence to have significant difficulties learning language (Tallal et al., 1989). Accomplished people who have been diagnosed with verbal learning disabilities or are suspected of having learning disabilities include such notables as Einstein, Sir Winston Churchill, Leonardo da Vinci, Thomas Edison, and psychology's own William James.

Variations in Language Processing

Language learning and use can vary widely, and these variations provide us with a richer understanding of how humans communicate. We examine three variations of particular interest here. Why do some children have such a hard time learning to read? What happens when people learn more than one language? How does American Sign Language (ASL), which uses movement instead of sound, compare with more conventional spoken languages?

Dyslexia Individuals with dyslexia experience difficulties in learning to read despite typical intelligence and exposure to adequate teaching methods (Shaywitz et al., 1998). The first description of a dyslexic patient, Percy F., was published by W. Pringle Morgan in 1896 (Shaywitz, 1996). Percy F. was described by Morgan as "quick at games, and in no way inferior to others of his age. His great difficulty has been—and is now—his inability to learn to read" (Shaywitz, 1996, p. 98).

Relying on Broca's area while reading, as people with dyslexia do, is like reading out loud to yourself, which slows reading speed. If you have ever read a bedtime story to a child, you are aware of how much slower reading out loud is compared to reading silently.

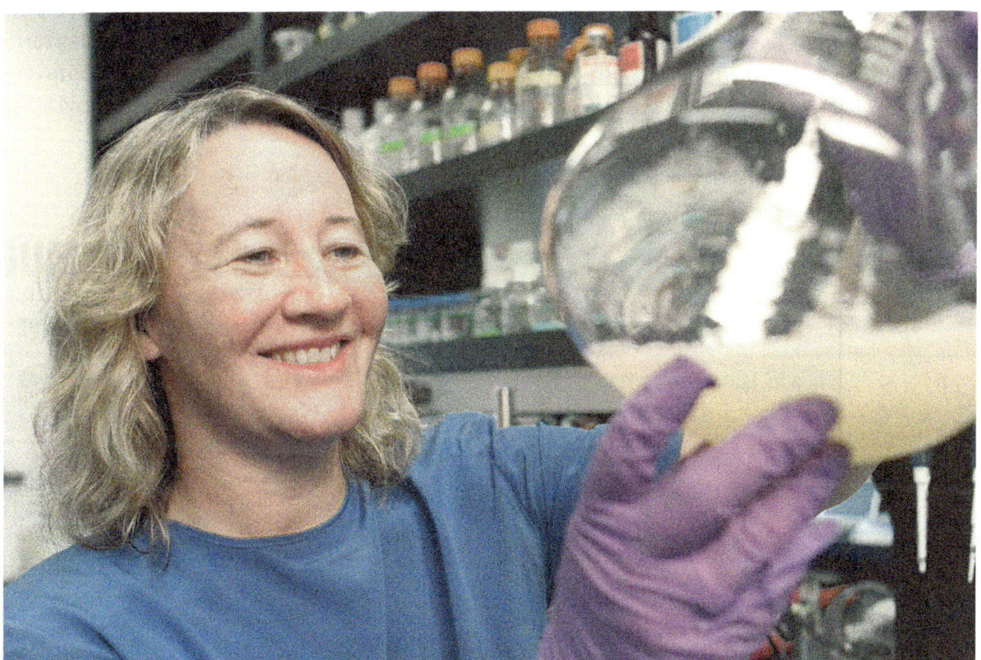

UPI/Newscom

Carol Greider, a Nobel Prize–winning professor of molecular biology and genetics, struggled with dyslexia from elementary school through graduate school. Although the condition was challenging, Greider states, "Perhaps my ability to pull more information out of context and to put together different ideas may have been affected by what I learned to do from dyslexia."

What Is Intelligence?

Intelligence is an individual's "ability to understand complex ideas, to adapt effectively to the environment, to learn from experience, to engage in various forms of reasoning, and to overcome obstacles" (Neisser et al., 1996, p. 77).

GL Archive/Alamy Stock Photo

Along with Théodore Simon, Alfred Binet devised a test aimed at identifying schoolchildren with intellectual disability. Binet and Simon's test laid the groundwork for today's intelligence testing.

Assessing Intelligence

The assessment, or testing, of intelligence represents an attempt to assign a number to an individual's abilities, allowing that person to be compared with others.

Formal intelligence testing began in 1904, when Alfred Binet was instructed by the French government to devise an objective assessment of schoolchildren. Binet and his colleague, Théodore Simon, assumed that relatively bright children behaved cognitively like older children, while less intelligent children behaved like younger children. They devised items that they believed would indicate children's mental age relative to their peers. In this system, children who successfully completed an item at an earlier age than most of their peers would have a higher mental age, while those who were not able to complete an item until they were older would have a lower mental age.

Stanford University professor Lewis Terman (1916) adapted Binet's test for use in the United States and named his revised version the Stanford–Binet Intelligence Scales. Terman began using the **intelligence quotient (IQ)**, which is computed by dividing children's mental age by their chronological age and, for convenience, multiplying by 100. For example, a bright child with a mental age of 15 and a chronological age of 12 would have an IQ score of 125 ($15/12 = 1.25$; $1.25 \times 100 = 125$).

The most frequently used intelligence tests today include the Stanford–Binet Intelligence Scales and the Wechsler Adult Intelligence Scale (WAIS). These tests no longer use the concept of mental age. Instead, contemporary tests place individual performance on a statistically normal curve, described in Chapter 2. Contemporary tests also incorporate new features designed to assess more accurately people of extremely low or high intellect, the elderly, and individuals with language difficulties.

As we discuss in Chapters 2 and 12, constructing a good test can be challenging. A good test must demonstrate both reliability and validity. In short, the test should provide consistent results (reliability) that correlate with other measures of the same construct (validity). Although no test is perfect, most IQ tests show excellent reliability (Kaufman, 2009). The validity of IQ tests is the subject of ongoing debate. If your goal is to predict school performance, their validity seems quite good. If your goal is to predict individual differences in the complex construct of intelligence described at the beginning of this section, the tests might not appear to be as successful. Consequently, it is not surprising to find that correlations between IQ score and performance in mathematics and verbal skills, which are essential for success in contemporary education, are relatively high but correlations between IQ score and performance in art and design are lower (Deary et al., 2007). Performance on the verbal components of many commonly used IQ tests are influenced by socioeconomic status, which further complicates the interpretations of the scores (Chapman et al., 2014). Improvements in scores over the last 60 years on tests that are supposedly culture fair suggest that it may be impossible to separate test performance from environmental factors (Fox & Mitchum, 2013; Flynn, 2016; see Figure 10.17).

intelligence The ability to understand complex ideas, adapt effectively to the environment, learn from experience, engage in reasoning, and overcome obstacles.

intelligence quotient (IQ) A measure of individual intelligence relative to a statistically normal curve.

general intelligence (g) A measure of an individual's overall intelligence as opposed to specific abilities.

General and Specific Abilities

In discussions of intelligence, some psychologists focus on an individual's overall abilities, while others focus on particular types of abilities.

Using the statistical technique of factor analysis, which he helped develop, Charles Spearman (1904, 1961) distinguished between a **general intelligence (g)** factor and specific factors that apply to single tasks. For example, Spearman argued that *g* was important for learning Latin but not for distinguishing between two musical tones.

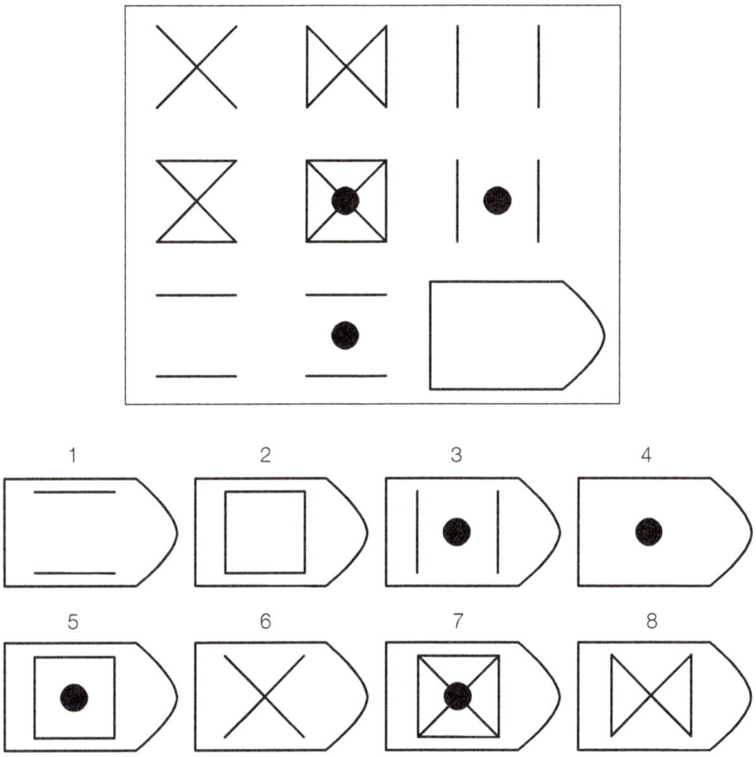

FIGURE **10.17**

Culture-Fair IQ Testing. Matrix reasoning tests are believed to be examples of culture-fair and nonverbal intelligence tests. This category of testing is showing the largest increases in performance worldwide, suggesting that our modern experience is making us better at extracting abstract concepts. Which of the items labeled 1 through 8 fits in the lower right corner of the matrix? The correct answer to this item is 4.

Source: M. C. Fox & A. L. Mitchum (2013). "A Knowledge-Based Theory of Rising Scores on Culture Free Tests," *Journal of Experimental Psychology: General, 142*(3), 979–1000. doi: 10.1037/a0030155

Raymond Cattell (1963) divided general intelligence into fluid intelligence and crystallized intelligence. **Fluid intelligence** refers to the ability to think logically without needing previously learned knowledge, such as seeing patterns in a visual stimulus, while **crystallized intelligence** requires specific, learned knowledge, such as vocabulary or the multiplication tables. A person needs pattern recognition, a type of fluid intelligence, to play chess or Sudoku well, but understanding the rules of the game requires crystallized intelligence. Fluid intelligence peaks in young adulthood and then declines, although it declines more slowly in individuals who continue to use fluid intelligence regularly, while crystallized intelligence remains more stable through adulthood (see Figure 10.18).

General intelligence theories do not provide explanations for splinter skills or islands of ability that occur against an overall background of lower functioning. Gloria Lenhoff, who has Williams syndrome and an IQ of about 55, cannot make change for a dollar or subtract 3 from 5, but she has performed as a lyric soprano with the San Diego Master Chorale and as an accordionist with Aerosmith (Maher, 2001). Leslie Lemke, who is both intellectually disabled and blind, listened one time to Pyotr Ilyich Tchaikovsky's Piano Concerto No. 1. Hours later, Lemke sat down at the piano, which he had never studied, and played the entire composition without error (Treffert & Wallace, 2002). Professional musicians are unlikely to be able to duplicate this feat.

The separability of "intelligences" in these exceptional cases suggests that intelligence is a combination of factors rather than a single thing, such as the processing speed of your computer. Howard Gardner (1983, 1999) interprets these and similar findings to mean that we have multiple, independent types of intelligence. Robert Sternberg proposed a triarchic theory of intelligence, in which a combination of analytical, creative, and practical abilities allows people to achieve success (Sternberg & Salter, 1982; Sternberg, 1985). He argues that it is possible to be gifted in one aspect without being gifted in others.

Both general and specific approaches to intelligence can be useful. We can assume that people have separate strengths and abilities, such as those outlined by Gardner and Sternberg. Among these diverse abilities, purely cognitive abilities, such as verbal, mathematical, spatial, and logical skills, show strong positive correlations with one another, supporting an argument for general intelligence, or *g*. At the same time, abilities involving sensory, motor,

fluid intelligence The ability to think logically without the need to use learned knowledge.

crystallized intelligence The ability to think logically using specific learned knowledge.

FIGURE **10.18**

Fluid and Crystallized Intelligence Across the Life Span. Fluid intelligence, like a reaction time measured with a stopwatch, includes abilities that do not require acquired knowledge. Fluid intelligence peaks in young adulthood and then gradually declines over the remaining life span. In contrast, crystallized intelligence, which does require acquired knowledge, remains fairly stable throughout adulthood. Composer John Williams has used his crystallized intelligence of music theory to contribute memorable soundtracks (for films including *Jaws*, *Star Wars*, and the Harry Potter series) in a career spanning more than six decades.

Source: Adapted from S. C. Li et al. (2004). "Transformations in the Couplings Among Intellectual Abilities and Constituent Cognitive Processes Across the Lifespan," *Psychological Science, 15*(3), 155–163. doi: 10.1111/j.0956-7976.2004.01503003.x

and personality factors are less likely to show strong correlations, supporting an argument for multiple intelligences in these domains (Visser et al., 2006).

Emotional and Social Intelligence

Traditional views of intelligence focused on education-related skills, but emotional and social skills are important to successful adaptation too. David Wechsler (1943), whose IQ tests remain widely used, suggested that IQ tests were not wrong, but merely incomplete. Pointing out that psychopaths, whose IQs tend to be modest, do a brilliant job of manipulating their environments, and that much more intelligent yet neurotic people often struggle to manage their lives, Wechsler recognized the gap between the academic focus of IQ testing and daily outcomes. He predicted that when tests were able to measure emotional and motivational factors as well as they do general abilities, "they will more nearly measure what in actual life corresponds to intelligent behavior" (p. 103). Lewis Terman, the controversial author of the Stanford-Binet intelligence test, argued that even his own test could "never serve as a detailed chart for the vocational guidance of children" (1916, p. 49).

DAVE YODER KRT/Newscom

Individuals with Williams syndrome provide examples of how general intellect can diverge from other abilities and talents. Gloria Lenhoff (right), has a tested IQ score of 55 but has performed as a lyric soprano and has played the accordion with Aerosmith.

Building on arguments in favor of multiple intelligences, and in recognition that previous work on intelligence seemed to neglect social skills, models of emotional and social intelligence were proposed (Mayer & Salovey, 1993; Goleman, 2006). Social and emotional intelligence allows people to manage emotions and reason about the mental states of others.

Clinical cases involving individuals with brain damage, psychological disorders, and intellectual disability provide evidence for social and emotional abilities that are separate from cognitive abilities. In Chapter 7, we discussed roles for the prefrontal cortex, amygdala, and insula in emotion. Patients with damage to connections between these structures performed very poorly on a standard measure of emotional and social intelligence, even though they have a normal IQ score and show no evidence of other psychological disorders (Bar-On et al., 2003). Individuals with autism spectrum disorder often display cognitive abilities that are superior to their social abilities. Individuals with Down syndrome, which produces moderate intellectual disability, display relatively strong social skills (Fidler et al., 2008).

Even if emotional and social intelligence can be separated from traditional measures of intelligence, these factors can still exert a strong influence on a person's academic and professional outcomes. In global assessments of math and science proficiency, students from East Asian countries (China, South Korea, and Japan) consistently outscore students from the United States and the European Union, who score around the mean (Guglielmi & Brekke, 2017). Further analysis suggests that the advantage shown by East Asian students is largely predicted by environmental factors, including parents' educational goals for their children and students' own educational goals, work ethic, and self-perception. Student self-perception includes a sense of academic efficacy (I can do this) and self-concept (I'm good at this). A not very intuitive finding is that self-concept related to math and science achievement is lowest in the very nations where performance is best! Overestimating one's abilities and achievements can result in poorer performance. As described in more detail in the Hub Science feature in this chapter, a student's mindset regarding improvement can also influence performance. The East Asian cultural norms of viewing the self as worthy of improvement increases students' willingness to accept negative feedback and make corrections (Guglielmi & Brekke, 2017).

RBlaser Photos/Alamy Stock Photo

Some psychologists view social and emotional intelligence as different from "school-based" intelligence and equally if not more important for success. In a classic study, children were given a single marshmallow with instructions to not eat it when an experimenter left the room. They were told that if they did not eat it, they would receive two marshmallows when the experimenter returned. When the children were tracked down 12 years later, the two-thirds who had been able to delay gratification (they didn't eat the marshmallow) were less stressed and more confident than the one-third who had not been able to delay gratification (Mischel et al., 1972). A later update attributed much of the differences observed by Mischel et al. to socioeconomic status rather than self-control (Watts et al., 2018). If you are poor, a "bird in the hand" approach is probably more adaptive than delayed gratification.

Biological Influences on Intelligence

Because the mind is the outcome of the brain, associations between its structure and activity and an individual's intelligence have been investigated. For the purposes of this type of research, standardized tests are used as the measure of intelligence.

Brain Structure, Brain Activity, and Intelligence Intelligence remains a very stable trait over the lifespan, which in turn implies that it is the outcome of relatively stable

In response to research showing that students from the poorest schools in Shanghai outscored the children of doctors and lawyers in the United Kingdom on math tests, the British government flew 60 English-speaking Chinese teachers to London to provide advice about how to improve British math achievement. Chinese teachers recommended teaching to the brightest students in the class, while also ensuring the children with moderate or lower abilities were also served. Chinese teachers and students commonly express a belief that hard work is more important than natural ability in math achievement.

Source: http://www.dailymail.co.uk/news/article-2578693/Chinese-teachers-improve-pupils-maths-Sixty-fly-Shanghai-promote-methods-bid-halt-slide-standards.html

Blue Jean Images/Alamy Stock Photo

PSYCHOLOGY AS A HUB SCIENCE

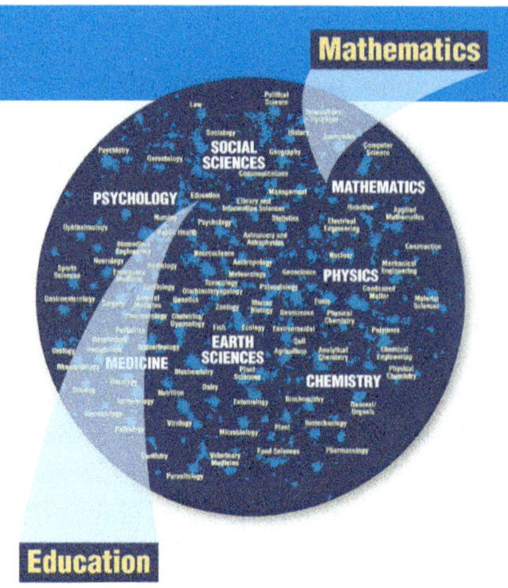

How Beliefs About Intelligence Impact Education

ACCORDING TO Carol Dweck (2000), people believe one of two theories about their own intelligence. Some people believe in an entity theory that states that people have a certain fixed, unmodifiable amount of intelligence. Others believe in an incremental theory that states that intelligence is something you can improve through learning. This second approach does not deny that learning is easier for some people than for others but simply suggests that everyone can improve through effort.

Students who believe in entity theory feel best when they complete easy, low-effort tasks and outperform other students. Challenges in the form of difficult tasks or higher performing peers threaten the self-esteem of the entity theorists. Dweck believes that the lavish praise heaped on today's students promotes belief in the entity theory, resulting in anxiety about looking smart, avoidance of challenges, and an inability to cope with the inevitable educational setbacks. In contrast, incremental theorists like to stretch their skills and put their knowledge to use. They view easy tasks as a waste of time. These students are not as affected by setbacks and worries about looking smart as their entity theorist peers.

Dweck's two theories about intelligence parallel cultural differences regarding proficiency in math. In the United States, we tend to hold an entity theory of math ability—you have it or you don't. People feel comfortable admitting that they are "bad at math" and view this as a good reason to stop taking math courses or working to improve. In East Asia, the incremental theory is dominant. Math is viewed as a difficult subject for most people that you must work to master. When Japanese and American students were randomly assigned to succeed or fail on a task by giving them either an easy or difficult task, the two groups responded very differently (Guglielmi & Brekke, 2017). The Americans who succeeded were more likely to persist on a follow-up task, view the tests as accurate, and rate the skills assessed by the task as important. This pattern was reversed for the Japanese students. The students who failed initially showed the same response as the Americans who had succeeded. As mentioned previously in this chapter, this difference in self-concept probably contributes to the superior achievement in math and science seen in East Asian students relative to their peers with different ethnicities.

According to Dweck, educators who view self-esteem (see Chapter 12) as something you "give" to a student through the application of easy tasks, lavish praise, and avoidance of failure are making a big mistake. Instead, self-esteem could be viewed as something students give themselves. Educators can better promote student self-esteem by teaching students to value learning over the appearance of being smart, promoting the love of challenge and effort, and helping students view mistakes as stepping stones to mastery. ■

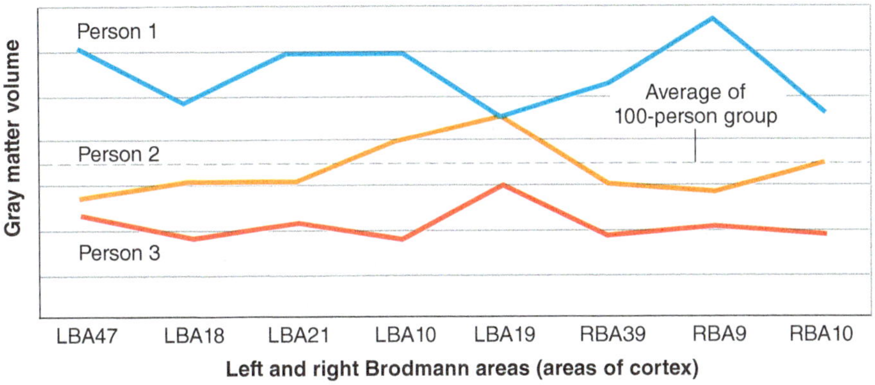

FIGURE **10.19**

Correlations Between Brain Structure and IQ Scores Show Multiple Patterns. The relationships between brain structure and IQ scores are complex. The individual depicted with the blue line had the highest IQ score out of 100 participants, and in each area of the brain believed to correlate with IQ results, he showed much higher than average gray matter volume. Person 2 and Person 3 had identical scores on an IQ test, but their patterns of gray matter volume were quite different from each other. Further research might help psychologists better understand the relationships between observed differences in brain structure and intelligence.

Source: Adapted from R. J. Haier (2009). "What Does a Smart Brain Look Like?" November/December 2009, *Scientific American Mind*, 26–33.

brain structure and function (Dubois et al., 2018). Because intelligence is such a broad concept, it is unlikely that we have "intelligence centers" in the brain. Dubois et al. (2018) liken the search for intelligence in the brain to a search for "physical fitness." Both intelligence and physical fitness do not represent a single thing, but rather the end results of multiple factors. Complicating the situation further is the fact that people with identical IQ scores do not have identical brain structure (see Figure 10.19).

Evidence for brain correlates for intelligence emerges from studies of individual differences in brain structure and networking efficiency. Brain imaging studies demonstrate that standard measures of intelligence positively correlate with overall brain volume (Deary et al., 2010; Nave et al., 2019). The frontal and parietal lobes and their connections are particularly implicated in individual differences in intelligence (Yoon et al., 2017).

Intelligent brains enjoy quick, efficient communication of information from one area to another along axon pathways (see Chapter 4). This is particularly true of people with high levels of verbal intelligence, which is more closely related to the crystallized intelligence discussed earlier (Khundrakpam et al., 2017). Studies of people with brain damage indicate that fluid intelligence, but not crystallized intelligence, is negatively affected by damage to the frontal lobes. These observations are consistent with studies showing high levels of frontal lobe activity during diverse tests believed to demonstrate fluid intelligence (Gray et al., 2003). Fluid intelligence abilities are highly correlated to working memory capacities (Khundrakpam et al., 2017).

Intelligence also seems to be related to the timing of brain development. As children approach puberty, the gray matter of the brain experiences a period of growth that slows down again later in adolescence. Children with average IQ scores showed a peak thickening of cortical gray matter around the age of 8, but children with superior IQ scores experienced a later peak, thickening around age 13 (Shaw et al., 2006).

Genetics and Intelligence As we observed in Chapter 3, simple either–or thinking about nature and nurture is rarely correct when considering human behavior, including intelligence. The influences of heredity (nature) interact intimately with experience and other environmental factors (nurture) to produce a result.

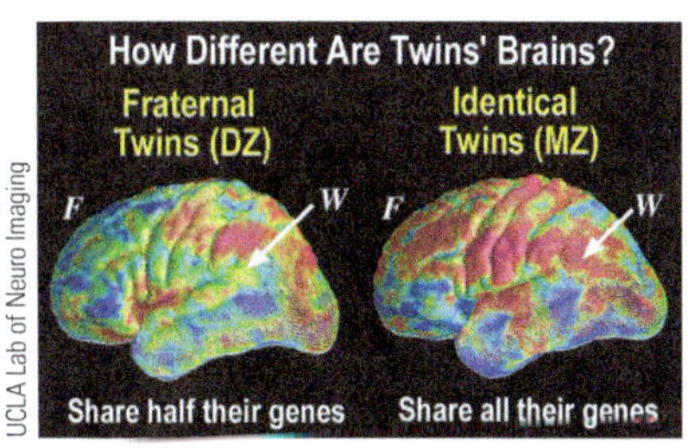

A comparison of the amount of gray matter in the brains of identical and fraternal twins showed that the identical twins were more like each other than were fraternal twins, as indicated by red and yellow coloring, especially in areas where gray matter volume is correlated with IQ test results. ("F" is for frontal lobe and "W" indicates Wernicke's area.)

Source: P. M. Thompson et al. (2001). "Genetic Influences on Brain Structure," *Nature Neuroscience*, 4(12), 1253–1258. doi: 10.1038/nn758

To recap the discussion in Chapter 3, heritability estimates how much of the variability in a characteristic observed in a population, such as variations in adult height, is because of genes. If genes play no role in this variation, such as the likelihood that people have tattoos, heritability is 0. When a condition is completely genetic, such as Huntington's disease, heritability is 1.0. The heritability of adult intelligence as measured by IQ tests is usually reported to be about .75 (Neisser et al., 1996). When we say that the heritability of intelligence is .75, we are saying that 75% of the variance in intelligence observed in the population can be attributed to genetics, not that 75% of an individual's intelligence is because of that person's genes.

As we observed in an earlier section, both overall brain size and proportion of gray matter are correlated with intelligence, and both are approximately 85% heritable, based on comparisons of identical and fraternal twins (Gray & Thompson, 2004). This high heritability does not mean that we have "a gene" for intelligence. As many as 1,041 different genes influence intelligence (Goriounova & Mansvelder, 2019). Each of these genes has a small impact, possibly at different times of development. Most of these seem especially important during prenatal brain development.

The fact that a trait demonstrates high heritability does not imply that change or improvement is impossible. A case in point is the highly heritable condition of phenylketonuria (PKU), in which a person cannot properly metabolize a particular amino acid found in many foods. Left unchecked, the condition leads to intellectual disability, discussed in a later section of this chapter. However, if a person with PKU is given an appropriate diet in which problem foods are avoided, intellectual development proceeds normally. The presence of data showing that IQ results are heritable does not mean we "give up" on anybody's intellectual development.

Worldwide increases in IQ scores of about 3 points per decade over the last 100 years illustrate the potential for change (Dickens & Flynn, 2001, 2006). This increase in IQ scores, known as the Flynn effect, has occurred far too quickly to represent genetic changes

CONNECTING TO RESEARCH

What Is Collective Intelligence?

WE HAVE BEEN DISCUSSING the concept of a general intelligence that characterizes an individual, but is it possible for the same sort of measure to describe the abilities of groups of people? Such a measure might be quite useful to organizations using teams.

The Question: Do groups of people have a "collective intelligence" that predicts their performance, and if so, what factors contribute to a group's collective intelligence?

METHODS

Nearly 700 people completed individual intelligence tests and then were randomly assigned to work groups of two to five individuals (Woolley et al., 2010). Each group was assigned several tasks to complete that varied in the amount of coordinated activity required for success, including solving visual puzzles, brainstorming, making collective moral judgments, and negotiating the allocation of limited resources. Some groups finished their session by playing checkers against a computerized opponent, while others completed an architectural design task. Additional measures were taken of factors believed to be related to group performance, including motivation, satisfaction, group cohesion, social sensitivity, and distribution of speaking turns.

ETHICS

This research does not pose any unusual ethical dilemmas. Routine protections of informed consent and confidentiality should be sufficient.

RESULTS

Evidence for a group or collective intelligence did emerge. For each group, performance across the different tasks was highly and positively correlated. Further statistical analyses ruled out the average individual intelligence of the group or the maximum individual intelligence of individuals in the group as significant predictors of group performance, leaving collective intelligence as a single, strong predictor of group performance (see ● Figure 10.21).

Surprisingly, typical group features such as motivation, satisfaction, or group cohesion failed to predict group performance. Individual features, such as the individual intelligence of the members, also failed to predict group performance. Instead, the (see Figure 10.20). Some researchers have argued that the increase has now slowed or even reversed, with IQ scores in some populations showing a drop in those born after 1975 (Bratsberg & Rogeberg, 2018). These data emphasize that environmental variables can have a substantial impact on intelligence scores.

Psychologists have produced long lists of environmental factors that influence intellectual development, including nutrition and exposure to mentally stimulating activities. Most of these environmental advantages are not cheap. Consequently, it is not surprising to find that socioeconomic status, a measure of family income, education, and other class factors, is positively correlated with IQ score (Turkheimer et al., 2003). This correlation does not tell us whether more intelligent people enjoy higher socioeconomic status, whether higher socioeconomic status provides means to optimize intelligence, whether some unknown third factor produces both high intelligence and high socioeconomic status, or whether some combination of these factors occurs. Nonetheless, poverty continues to be a significant risk for a low IQ score.

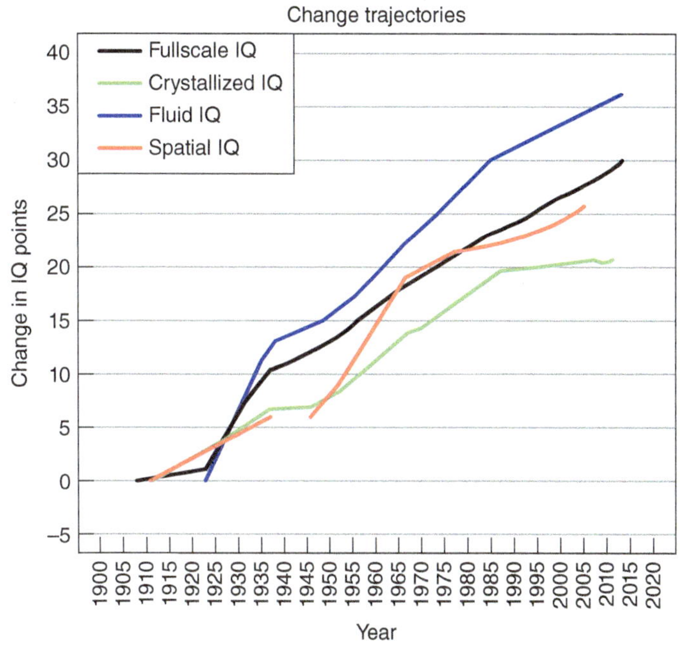

FIGURE **10.20**

The Flynn Effect. Data from a meta-analysis featuring nearly 4 million participants from 31 countries show that IQ test results have been gradually increasing worldwide over the past 100 years, although the exact causes for these changes are not completely understood.

Source: J. Pietschnig & M. Voracek (2015). "One Century of Global IQ Gains: A Formal Meta-analysis of the Flynn Effect (1909–2013)," *Perspectives on Psychological Science, 10*(3), 282–306. doi:10.1177/1745691615577701

Extremes of Intelligence

Assuming that IQ scores are normally distributed, with an average of 100 and a standard deviation of 15, about 68% of the population should fall within one standard deviation (85–115), and 95% of the population should fall within two standard deviations (70–130). The remaining 5% is divided between the two tails of the distribution, either above 130 or below 70 (see Figure 10.22).

members' scores on the social sensitivity instrument, called the Reading the Mind in the Eyes test, and how evenly speaking turns were distributed had a large impact on the group's collective intelligence.

CONCLUSIONS

You might have had opportunities to observe collective intelligence while working on group projects. This research shows that bringing together the most intelligent people might not guarantee the best results. Instead, groups of people who are more empathic and do not dominate the conversation might have the greatest success. ■

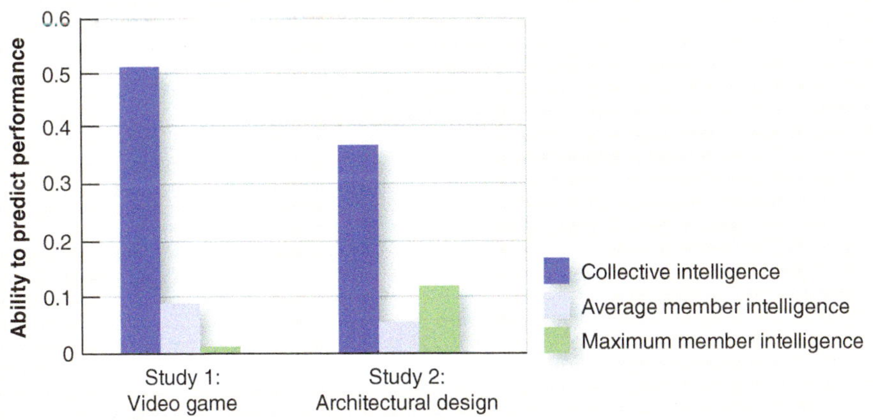

FIGURE **10.21**

Collective Intelligence. A group's performance on a variety of tasks, from playing video games to constructing a complex architectural design, was predicted better by the group's collective intelligence than by the average intelligence of the group's members or by the highest IQ score among the group's members.

Source: Adapted from A. W. Woolley et al. (2010). "Evidence for a Collective Intelligence Factor in the Performance of Human Groups," *Science, 330*, 686–688. doi: 10.1126/science.1193147

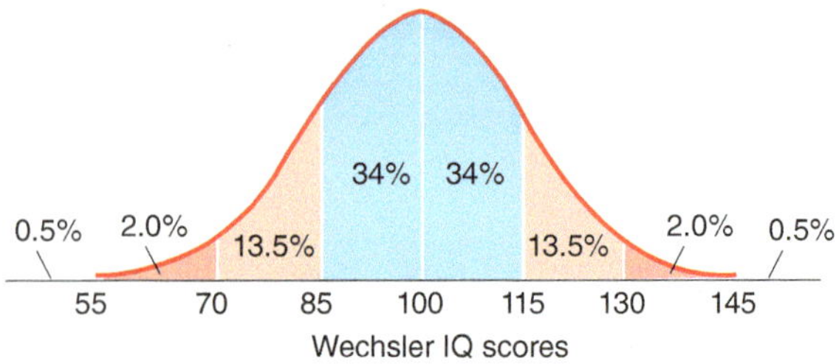

FIGURE **10.22**

IQ Distribution. IQ test results form an approximately normal distribution, which means that about 68% of the population falls between IQ scores of 85 and 115. Ninety-five percent of the population falls between IQ scores of 70 and 130, with the remaining 5% divided between the two tails.

intellectual disability A condition diagnosed in individuals demonstrating cognitive deficits apparent early in life and poor adaptive behaviors; also known as mental retardation.

Intellectual Disability According to the *Diagnostic and Statistical Manual of Mental Disorders* (*DSM-5*; APA, 2013; see Chapter 14), **intellectual disability** or intellectual developmental disorder is diagnosed in individuals who show deficits in intellectual functioning beginning early in childhood, accompanied by deficits in independent living skills. These behaviors might include the ability to balance a bank account, receive correct change from a cashier, read a bus schedule, buy groceries, maintain personal hygiene, and other skills required for independent living.

Intellectual disability is divided into categories of mild, moderate, severe, and profound based on the level of adaptive functioning (APA, 2013). Classification of the severity of intellectual disability is no longer based on IQ test scores. Individuals with mild intellectual disability make up 85 percent of the total population of people with intellectual disability. They can live independently with minimum levels of support. With proper intervention, individuals in this group are able to master a sixth-grade curriculum, although it will take them until age 18 to do so. Many work, marry, and have families.

Mild intellectual disability is typically not the result of genetic or medical problems (Zigler, 1967). As a result, mild intellectual disability is frequently called familial retardation, recognizing that it usually results from preventable, environmental causes. Poverty is an obvious risk factor for this condition because poor parents may be unable to obtain the health care, diet, and other environmental benefits needed to produce healthy children (see Figure 10.23).

Moderate intellectual disability usually requires some type of assisted living, such as living in a group home, although the type and extent of needed services vary widely among affected individuals. Unlike mild cases, moderate intellectual disability typically results from genetic or medical conditions rather than familial factors. Genetic conditions such as Down syndrome are likely to produce disability in this range. The academic attainment of most individuals in this category is limited to the second-grade curriculum, and again, most do not achieve this level until about the age of 18 years.

Individuals with severe intellectual disability require daily assistance with self-care activities and supervision to maintain safety. Individuals with profound intellectual disability require 24-hour care. Both severe and profound intellectual disabilities generally result from serious medical conditions and are identified at birth or early in infancy. Individuals with severe intellectual disability can learn a few high-priority words, such as "stop" or "hot." Individuals with profound intellectual disability can learn some basic self-care skills, such as feeding themselves or washing their hands.

FIGURE **10.23**

Poverty Is a Risk Factor for Intellectual Disability. Mild forms of intellectual disability, leading to IQ scores between 55 and 70, are also known as familial retardation because these cases are not due to medical or genetic problems. Poverty is a large risk factor for this level of intellectual disability. A little more than 5 in 1,000 children living above the poverty line have intellectual disability, but this number jumps to 9 in 1,000 among children living below the poverty line. Adapted from http://www.epa.gov/opeedweb/children/images/D7_2010hires.jpg

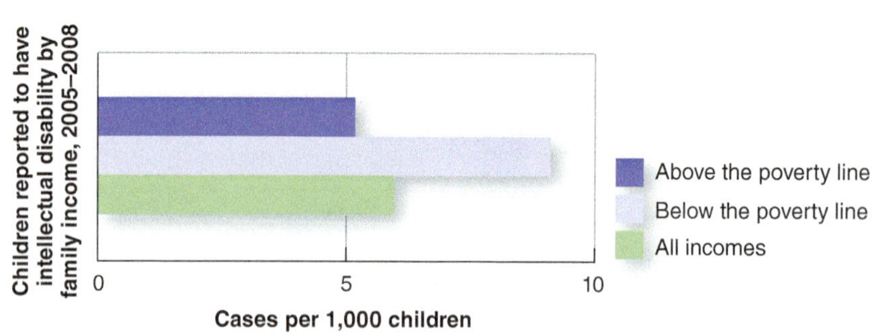

Individuals with intellectual disability face several common problems. Many children with intellectual disability form insecure attachments with their caregivers, described in detail in Chapter 11 (Vandesande et al., 2019). Ideally, children form a secure attachment characterized by demonstrating a clear preference for a caregiver over strangers, protesting when the caregiver leaves, and indicating a willingness to explore their environment (Ainsworth & Bowlby, 1965).

Language skills are affected depending on the severity of the intellectual disability (McDuffie et al., 2017). Children with intellectual disability have problems expressing themselves clearly, although they may understand a great deal that is said to them. In conjunction with typically poor social skills, these language deficits may result in peer rejection. Consequently, successful intervention programs address language and social skills, in addition to academic and life skill work.

Intellectual disability increases a person's risk for other emotional or behavioral disorders (Yoo et al., 2012). Anxiety, impulsiveness, and mood disorders are the most common disorders seen in this population. When intellectual disability is more severe, individuals may engage in pica, or the eating of nonedibles, or self-injurious behaviors, such as banging the head against the floor or wall.

Anton Oparin/Alamy Stock Photo

Australian model and fashion designer Madeline Stuart has Down syndrome.

Giftedness and Genius Individuals with intellectual **giftedness**, who make up approximately 1% to 3% of the population, score two or more standard deviations above the mean, or more than 130 on a standardized IQ test. There are no established criteria for defining "genius," but this term usually combines high intellect with remarkable creativity (Simonton, 2008).

giftedness An extreme of intelligence defined as having an IQ score of 130 or above.

Having a high IQ score provides advantages in many aspects of life. One of the longest running studies in psychology is a longitudinal examination of gifted children initiated in 1921 (Terman, 1925; Terman & Oden, 1959). The original participants were children selected because of their very high IQ scores, averaging 150. The gifted participants not only maintained their high IQ scores throughout their adult lives, but also enjoyed better physical health, emotional stability, occupational attainment, and social satisfaction.

High intellect, particularly as measured by an IQ score, does not capture completely what we mean by genius. Despite their successes, the gifted participants in the longitudinal study just cited did not produce genius work. Nor do all remarkable thinkers possess particularly high IQ scores. Nobel laureate Richard Feynman was disappointed to learn that his IQ score was "only" 124 (Gleick, 1992).

Like individuals on the lower extreme of IQ scores, children with high IQ scores benefit from educational opportunities tailored to their abilities. Unfortunately, the structure of public education in the United States, with its emphasis on grade levels based on age, rarely provides optimum learning for gifted children. A report by the U.S. Department of Education noted that children with IQ scores of 140 or above typically know at least half of a grade's curriculum before the school year even begins, and those with IQ scores of 170 or above know virtually all of it (U.S. Department of Education Office of Educational Research and Improvement, 1993). Their time in school is subsequently wasted, and the material is so easy that it encourages poor learning habits ill-suited to later educational challenges.

One solution to the educational needs of gifted youth has been academic acceleration, including skipping grades and taking advanced learning prior to graduation from high school (taking community college courses, etc.). Although this approach has been viewed negatively by some educators, a study of accelerated students over thirty-five years showed no negative impacts on social and emotional well-being (Bernstein et al., 2020).

NG Images/Alamy Stock Photo

These teens, standing with former astronaut and NASA administrator Charles Bolden, are not satisfied by finding the "right answer" to teachers' questions. Instead, they tackled tough problems to compete in the White House Science Fair.

THINKING SCIENTIFICALLY

Can Children's IQ Scores Be Increased with Special Baby Videos?

DESPITE ADVICE FROM the American Academy of Pediatrics telling parents that children under the age of 2 should have zero screen time (television, tablets, phones, or computers), the market for electronic media designed to make babies smarter is booming. Sporting names like *Baby Einstein, Brainy Baby,* and *Baby Genius,* these materials make their intent clear to consumers. The popularity of these programs indicates that today's parents take the need for nurture seriously.

WHAT AM I BEING ASKED TO BELIEVE OR ACCEPT?

We are being asked to accept that electronic media intended to make babies smarter actually work.

WHAT EVIDENCE SUPPORTS THIS POSITION?

Direct testing of infants exposed to *Baby Einstein* and infants with no media exposure showed no improvement in learning target words by the *Baby Einstein* group (Richert et al., 2010).

Watching baby videos actually seems to have a detrimental effect on young children's language acquisition. Infants younger than 16 months and exposed to the videos understood from six to eight fewer words for each hour of exposure compared to non-exposed infants (Zimmerman et al., 2007). This should not be surprising, given other research that emphasizes the social nature of language learning discussed in this chapter, such as the study showing that young children learn language from a speaker in the room, but not from the same speaker being televised.

ARE THERE OTHER WAYS THIS EVIDENCE COULD BE INTERPRETED?

Observations about screen time and language acquisition are usually correlational. It is possible that children who are least likely to develop language well are also those most likely to have higher screen time. When tested directly, however, no support was found for a causal role of language ability in determining the amount of screen time a child experiences (Madigan et al., 2019). One of the defenses posed by the producers of infant media products is that many infants are watching screens anyway, so they might as well be watching something geared to their developmental level.

WHAT OTHER EVIDENCE WOULD I NEED TO EVALUATE THESE ALTERNATIVES?

While we strive for objectivity in these features, it will be hard for us to view this as anything other than a fairly settled conclusion. These videos seem to have no appreciable benefits and instead raise the possibility of doing harm. There is a larger question here, too, that would benefit from further research—why do contemporary parents seek "expert" opinions on everyday behaviors like talking to their children? As this book goes to press, the creator of the original *Baby Einstein* videos has released an app called *ParentPal* that not only tracks daily routines of eating and sleeping but also recommends activities to "take the guesswork out of parenting" (prnewswire, 2020). Whether the app is more successful in meeting its lofty goals than the videos remains to be seen.

WHAT ARE THE MOST REASONABLE CONCLUSIONS?

Rather than investing in baby videos and apps, we hope that parents can sit back, relax, play with, and enjoy their children, who grow up all too quickly. We do encourage, however, regular reading of the psychological science of human development. ■

Vitalinka/Shutterstock.com

Despite advice from the American Academy of Pediatrics to avoid screen time for children under the age of 2 years, there is a booming market for apps and DVDs advertising their ability to make children smarter.

Interpersonal Relationships

The Cognitive Perspective

HOW DOES BEING A MAXIMIZER OR A SATISFICER AFFECT RELATIONSHIPS?

CLASSIC RESEARCH SUGGESTS that some people are "maximizers," who strive to reach the best outcome. "Satisficers" are more willing to choose outcomes that are merely acceptable (Simon, 1957). Maximizers are perfectionists who evaluate all choices before settling on one, so they do not make quick decisions. Because maximizers feel more regret when a decision doesn't work out well, they tend to avoid making decisions. Although they may experience better outcomes than satisficers on many occasions, maximizers might still feel worse. Satisficers are more likely to see their glass of life as half full, whereas maximizers are more likely to see their glass as half empty.

What does this distinction mean for interpersonal relationships? Finding a romantic partner and making a long-term commitment to that person involve some important decisions. Romance is consistently ranked among the top regrets in life for most people (Roese & Summerville, 2005). These facts suggest that maximizers might experience obstacles within the realm of relationships. Either they will let opportunities pass by because they are still looking for that perfect person, or they will avoid making a commitment for fear of regretting it later. Their perfectionist standards might make it impossible for them to appreciate a partner who is a good match, perhaps because that person does not look like a supermodel or squeezes the toothpaste tube the wrong way. Maximizers look at more profiles on online dating sites than satisficers do (Yang & Chiou, 2010). Even after a commitment is made, maximizers continue to rate their choice against all possible partners they continue to encounter, an obvious risk for infidelity (French & Meltzer, 2019).

iStock.com/adrian brockwell

Faced with a large array of choices, satisficers will pick one that works, but maximizers will evaluate all the options to find the perfect choice. We're guessing that most of these candies taste good.

Does this mean maximizers are doomed in relationships? Not at all. Recognizing that our automatic ways of behaving will not always lead us to our goals can help us identify areas where we need to take conscious, systematic control. Many maximizers blame their partners for a failed romance (the partner just didn't measure up) instead of taking a hard look at their own contributions to the relationship. If you know your maximizing tendencies are leading you in the wrong directions, you can use the steps to effective problem solving outlined earlier in this chapter to supply alternatives that might work better. ■

Psychology Takes On Real-World Problems

COVID-19 and the Availability Heuristic

As we have learned in this chapter, the availability heuristic suggests that topics that come easily to mind seem more likely. What makes something come "easily to mind"? Three factors stand out in particular: frequency, recency, and vividness of information.

As this textbook goes to press, news headlines continue to be dominated by the COVID-19 pandemic, and it is easy to find examples of the availability heuristic in action. In five countries, participants vastly overestimated both the percentage of cases and the resulting deaths (Kekst CNC, 2020, p. 365). In the United States, respondents believed that 20% of the population had contracted the virus at a time when the Centers for Disease Control and Prevention (CDC) reported that only 1% of the population had experienced a confirmed case. U.S. respondents also believed that 9% of the population had died from the virus, which would be an astonishing 29.5 million people, as opposed to the true 0.04% rate, or 131,280 national deaths reported at the time by the CDC.

In keeping with our emphasis in these sections on policy formation, we ask how policy makers might avoid this level of public misinformation. Although the scientific literature provides extensive insight into the availability bias itself, it provides relatively little advice about how to counter it. Education and information can be the answer if presented thoughtfully. Care must be taken to avoid stimulating fear and other strong emotions, which can lead to "probability neglect" (Sunstein, 2002). This phenomenon often leads the public to overestimate rare but heavily publicized events, such as air travel following the terrorist attacks of 9/11. An additional strategy, which we will discuss in more detail in Chapter 13, involves providing action steps following an emotional message. If people are experiencing strong negative emotions regarding COVID-19, reminding them of steps they can take to reduce their risk should alleviate some of the fear and hopefully reduce probability neglect at the same time.

Can you identify other heuristics and problem-solving issues relevant to COVID-19? Once again, psychological science can help us illuminate many otherwise puzzling human behaviors in the context of the big problems of the day. ■

Antonio Guillem Fernández/Alamy Stock Photo

Policy makers have the difficult task of providing information that stimulates appropriate responses to emergencies without overly frightening the public.

SUMMARY 10.3 Types of Intelligence

Type of intelligence	Description	Example
General intelligence (g) 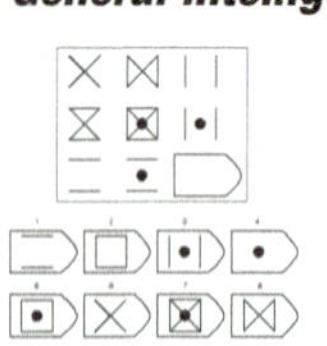	A single measure of an individual's intellectual ability that predicts most of that person's intellectual performance.	Verbal, mathematical, spatial, and logical skills showing high positive correlations within an individual.
Fluid intelligence 	A type of general intelligence that allows logical thinking without needing learned knowledge.	Recognizing relationships between geometric shapes.

Type of intelligence	Description	Example
Crystallized intelligence 	A type of general intelligence that requires learned knowledge.	Using your knowledge of the multiplication tables to figure out interest on a new car loan.
Multiple intelligences 	Single skills that tend to show relatively low correlations with one another and with general intelligence.	Strong musical abilities in people with Williams syndrome, which results in a lower than normal IQ score.
Emotional and social intelligence 	The ability to manage emotions and reason about other people's states of mind.	Managing anger appropriately and showing empathy for others.
Collective intelligence 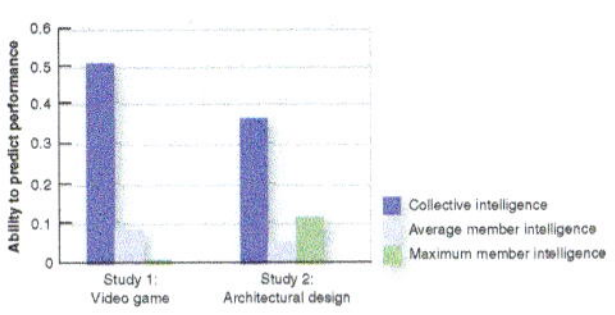	A quality of group process independent of individual group members' intelligence that predicts group performance.	A team featuring good social sensitivity and conversation sharing that completes a task successfully.

Credits: Second row—iStock.com/acilo; Third row—Carlo Allegri/Getty Images Entertainment/Getty Images; Fourth row—DAVE YODER KRT/Newscom; Fifth row—RBlaser Photos/Alamy Stock Photo.

KEY TERMS The Language of Psychological Science

Be sure that you can define these terms and use them correctly.

affect heuristic, p. 374
algorithm, p. 371
aphasia, p. 385
availability heuristic, p. 372
bilingual, p. 390
cognition, p. 362
concept, p. 363
crystallized intelligence, p. 393
exemplar, p. 365
fluid intelligence, p. 393
functional fixedness, p. 370
general intelligence (g), p. 392
giftedness, p. 401
heuristic, p. 371
intellectual disability, p. 400
intelligence, p. 392
intelligence quotient (IQ), p. 392
language, p. 382
morpheme, p. 384
phoneme, p. 384
problem, p. 368
problem solving, p. 369
prototype, p. 365
recognition heuristic, p. 371
representativeness heuristic, p. 373

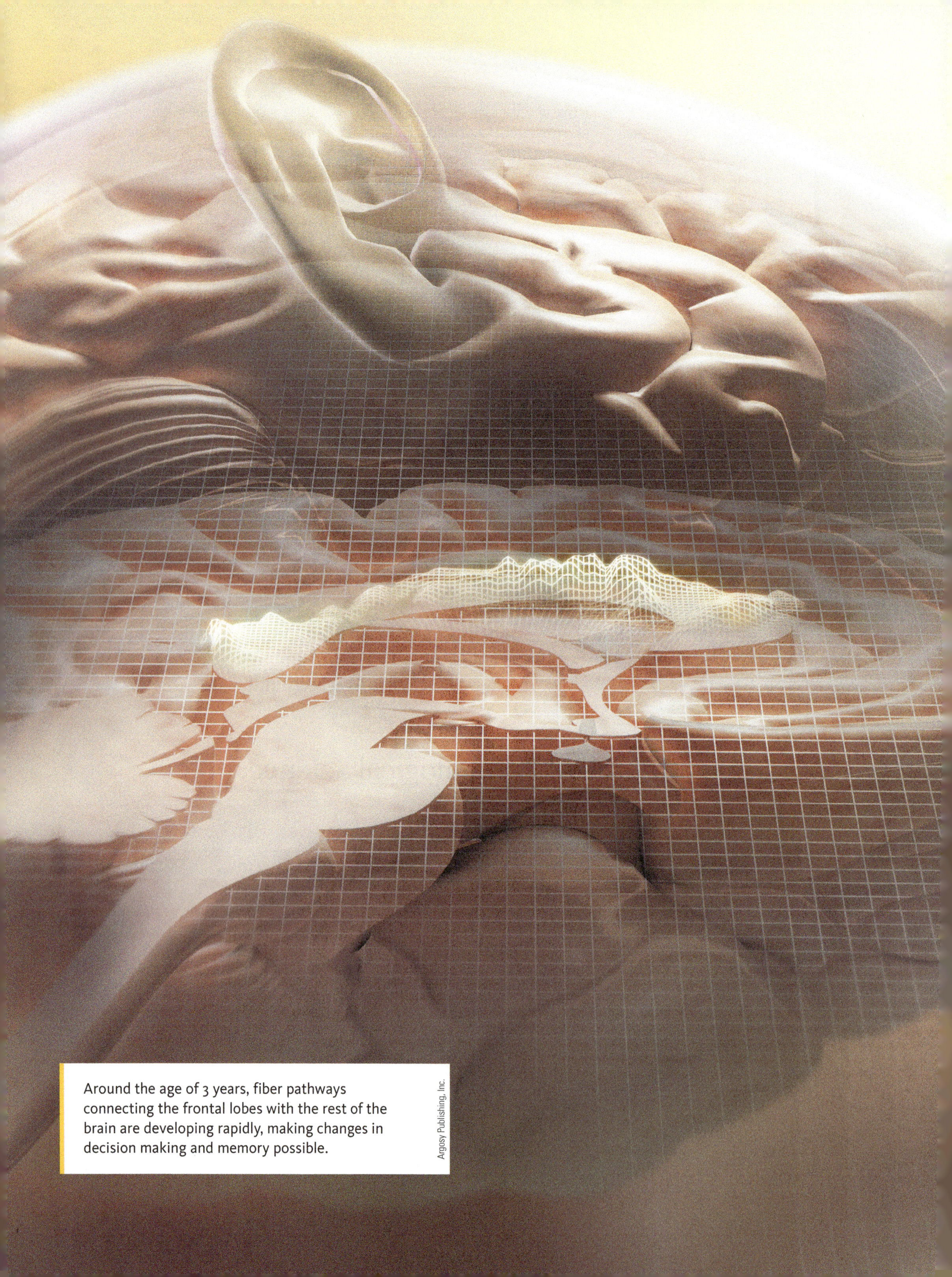

Around the age of 3 years, fiber pathways connecting the frontal lobes with the rest of the brain are developing rapidly, making changes in decision making and memory possible.

Argosy Publishing, Inc.

11

The Developing Mind

LIFE SPAN DEVELOPMENT

LEARNING OBJECTIVES

1. Evaluate the evidence for sensory capacities, preferences, and reflexes in newborn infants.
2. Identify major physical, cognitive, and social/emotional differences among the prenatal period, infancy, childhood, adolescence, and adulthood, and give examples of ways in which these three trajectories influence one another.
3. Differentiate Jean Piaget's four stages of cognitive development (sensorimotor, preoperational, concrete operational, and formal operational), and critique Piaget's theory, using research from alternate approaches.
4. Debate the adaptive function of infant attachment, and analyze the roles of temperament, culture, and parenting in driving individual attachment styles.
5. Identify epigenetic processes, critical or sensitive periods, and the impact of experience on biological development.
6. Debate the research evidence for continuity versus discontinuity in the trajectories of physical, cognitive, and social/emotional development.

WHAT IS YOUR EARLIEST MEMORY? A BIRTHDAY party? A new puppy? We are guessing that your earliest autobiographical memories, which we discussed in Chapter 9, probably date to when you were between 3 and 5 years old. Why this age period and not another?

Zooming in, we can see that one of the factors driving memory abilities is the development of the brain during childhood. As you will see in this chapter, changes taking place in the hippocampus and frontal lobes during the third year of life give children a boost in their abilities to form long-term memories, particularly about the sequences of events that make up our autobiographical memories. But there are other parts to this story.

iStock.com/Christopher Futcher

To form an autobiographical memory, children must have a sense of self. As we discussed in Chapter 6, babies as young as 18 months can recognize themselves in a mirror. In this chapter, you will learn about the further development of self-awareness as children gradually separate from their parents and family and move into adult roles in the community.

Zooming out still farther, we find that cultures influence the formation and timing of autobiographical memories. When white American adults are compared with Chinese adults, the white Americans access more autobiographical memories from earlier ages and provide

FIGURE **11.1**

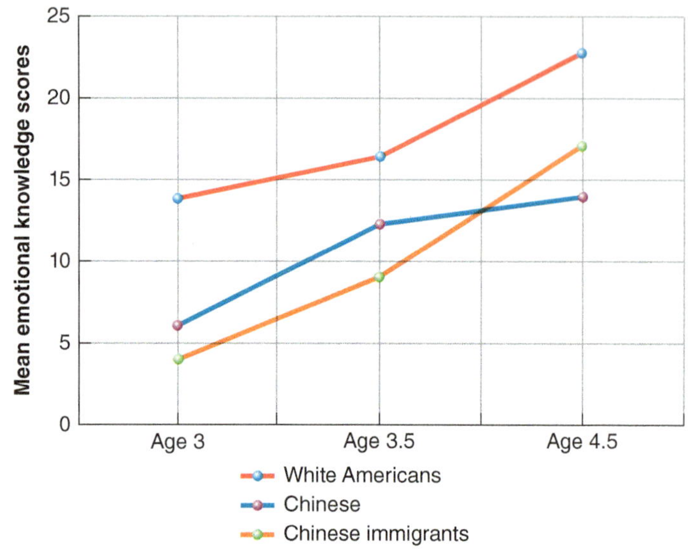

Cultural Influences on Emotion Knowledge. White American adults recall more childhood autobiographical memories in greater detail than do Chinese adults. These differences may have their roots in earlier cultural influences on emotional knowledge, or an understanding of how a situation can lead to emotions. When asked to describe situations that would make a person happy, sad, fearful, or angry, white American children provided more information than Chinese or Chinese immigrant children. Emotional knowledge increases when a person focuses on information relevant to the self rather than more general information.

Source: Adapted from Q. Wang (2008). "Emotion Knowledge and Autobiographical Memory Across the Preschool Years: A Cross-Cultural Longitudinal Investigation," *Cognition*, *108*(1), 117–135. doi: 10.1016/j.cognition.2008.02.002

trubach/Shutterstock.com

A major milestone in children's development of a sense of self is the ability to recognize themselves in a mirror by the age of 18 months.

more episodic details of these memories (Wang, 2008). Wang believes that this difference observed in adults originates earlier in childhood, when white American children show more "emotion knowledge," or an understanding of how situations can lead to emotions, than do Chinese children (see ● Figure 11.1). Emotion knowledge is assessed by asking children such questions as, "What makes people happy?" Cultures influence emotion knowledge development by focusing on information relevant to the self versus more general aspects of information.

To understand the development of autobiographical memory, psychologists must explore the biological, individual, developmental, social, and cultural contributions to this ability. At the same time, the development of an autobiographical memory capability forms reciprocal influences with these other aspects of the individual's behavior. In this chapter, we will explore many examples of how the normal changes that occur across the life span interact with our behavior and mental processing.

What Does It Mean to Develop?

In Chapter 8, we defined learning as a relatively permanent change in behavior due to experience. In this chapter, we will explore an additional force for changes in behavior—changes that unfold with the passage of time. The study of human development considers changes in behavior that correlate with growth or maturation.

As we explore the normal changes that occur at different stages of life, we will concentrate on three interwoven threads: physical development, cognitive development, and social/emotional development. Although we discuss each separately, they are constantly interacting. For example, moving independently by crawling or walking produces a more rapidly changing and interesting environment, which spurs an infant's cognitive growth. At the same time, a mobile infant is likely to elicit different reactions from parents or caretakers than one who is stationary, stimulating further social and emotional development.

In addition to documenting these three types of change over time, the study of development highlights several major questions that stretch across the entire life span. How does nature interact with nurture? Is development gradual and continuous or abrupt and discontinuous? How much of human development is universal across the human species or dependent upon a person's culture?

Kevin Dodge/Masterfile

Early developmental psychologists described normal age-related changes up through childhood to puberty but not beyond. Today, we know that the ages represented in these four generations bring their own set of characteristic behaviors.

Nature and Nurture Intertwined

Although we will be discussing the genetic heritage of individuals, as well as environmental influences on their development, we will be emphasizing the interactions between nature and nurture that predict developmental outcomes. Significant progress has been made in the understanding of how genes and the environment interact. As we discussed in Chapter 3, we now understand that the underlying deoxyribonucleic acid (DNA) that makes up our genes is turned on or off by the surrounding chemical tags (the epigenome) that accumulate through life. Among the external environmental factors that can chemically "tag" our DNA are diet, nurture, and stress.

Epigenetic influences accumulate over the life span. Because younger children have had less time for epigenetic interactions between their genes and their experience to take place, they have more in common with one another at any particular age than do older adults, whose decades of experience have caused their epigenetic paths to lead them in many different directions. A group of 8-year-olds is more consistent in its physical characteristics and behaviors than a group of 20-year-olds, who still have more in common with one another than any group of 65-year-olds. This contrast between children and adults might have led earlier psychologists to the mistaken belief that development "stopped" at some point in childhood or adolescence, when all they were seeing was a transition point where internal influences were becoming overshadowed by external ones.

Continuity or Discontinuity

Another major question asks whether development proceeds gradually and smoothly over time (continuity) or changes more abruptly from one stage to the next (discontinuity). The gradual approach might be visualized as a rainbow, with one color (stage) gradually merging into the next, with no bold line separating the two. In contrast, the discontinuity approach views development as a staircase to be climbed. The behavior on one step is qualitatively different from that on the step that preceded it, and the change from one step to the other is abrupt (see Figure 11.2).

Patrik Giardino/Stone/Getty Images

As children develop physically, they are able to move out into the world. Mobile children face new problems that stretch their cognitive abilities and new social and emotional challenges as they learn self-regulation and experience control from their parents.

FIGURE **11.2**

Continuity Versus Discontinuity in Development. Development can appear as a gradual, continuous process, such as the acorn growing into a mighty oak tree, or as a sudden, discontinuous process, such as the butterfly emerging from a chrysalis.

zygote The term used to describe a developing organism immediately following conception until the embryo stage, or the first 2 gestational weeks in humans.

embryo The term used to describe a developing organism between the zygote and the fetus stages, or between gestational weeks 3 and 8 weeks in humans.

fetus The term used to describe a developing organism between the embryo stage and birth, or between gestational weeks 8 and approximately 40 weeks in humans.

As in the case of nature and nurture, the continuity–discontinuity debate does not have a "right answer." Some features appear to be more continuous in their developmental course, such as the gradual development of infant temperament into later personality. Other features seem to develop more abruptly. Parents are often surprised when their child becomes suddenly more mobile, such as rolling across the bed or walking, although the underlying physical development is probably quite gradual.

Universal or Ecological Development

Psychologists taking the universal approach to development look for age-related behaviors that are found across the entire human species, whereas psychologists taking an ecological view ask questions about the impact of culture and environment on development.

Which approach is correct? Both universal and ecological approaches improve our understanding. Although we will see universals of development in this chapter, such as the age at which most children begin walking unassisted, we will also see that children growing up in cultures where early walking is encouraged walk at slightly younger ages than children growing up in cultures where restricting infant movement is the norm. Although a consideration of human universals is useful, most contemporary psychologists would be unwilling to consider many behaviors outside their context of social relationships and culture.

Epigenetic influences accumulate over the life span. Groups of 8-year-olds have more in common than groups of 20-year-olds, who have more in common than groups of older adults. The contrast between the degree of similarity seen in children and that seen in adults might have led early developmental psychologists to the mistaken conclusion that development stops.

Radius Images/Alamy Stock Photo

Image Source/Alamy Stock Photo

Phovoir/Shutterstock.com

How Do We Change Prenatally?

The 9 months between conception and birth are full of growth and activity. For the first 2 gestational weeks, the developing organism is known as a **zygote**. During the second gestational week, the zygote completes its journey through the mother's fallopian tube to the uterus, where it implants in the lining. During gestational weeks 3 through 8, we use the term **embryo**, and for the remainder of the pregnancy, we use the term **fetus**.

During the first gestational week, the zygote differentiates into three germ layers: ectoderm, mesoderm, and endoderm (see ● Figure 11.3). The ectoderm develops into nerve tissue and skin, while the mesoderm gives rise to muscle and bone. The endoderm is the source of the body's soft tissue, such as the organs of the digestive tract. By gestational week four, the central nervous system has differentiated into forebrain, midbrain, hindbrain, and spinal cord. By gestational week seven, cells that will form the cerebral cortex begin a carefully orchestrated journey from the lining of the neural tube (which will later mature into the ventricles of the brain) to their ultimate destinations.

Other systems, while perhaps not as dramatic as the nervous system, also begin to differentiate and develop during the embryonic stage. The heart, stomach, liver, and other organs are formed during this period. During the sixth gestational week, expression of a gene on the Y chromosome initiates the differentiation of the generic gonads into testes in males, while alternate genes guide the development of the gonads into ovaries in females.

The remainder of the pregnancy involves continued growth and maturation of the systems that are now in place (see ● Figure 11.4). During gestational month three, generic internal reproductive organs differentiate into the uterus, fallopian tubes, and upper portion of the vagina in females and into the seminal vesicles, vas deferens, and prostate in males. New neurons are born in large numbers and begin the process of forming connections with one another. Myelination of the nervous system begins at gestational month six (Rivkin et al., 1995). As you may recall from Chapter 4, myelin allows neurons to communicate faster and more efficiently. By gestational month seven, most of the neurons you will ever have are in place (Rakic, 2000) and brain waves can be recorded through the mother's abdomen.

AP Images/Mohamed Sheikh Nor

The universal approach sees development as common to all people, whereas the ecological approach emphasizes the influences of environment and culture on development. In the United States, we tend to look at child soldiers, some as young as 10 years old, as being a product of the poverty and lack of opportunity in their environments. However, some universal aspects of being a preteen or young teen, such as an immature sense of morality and greater obedience to adults, might apply equally to very young violent gang members in the United States.

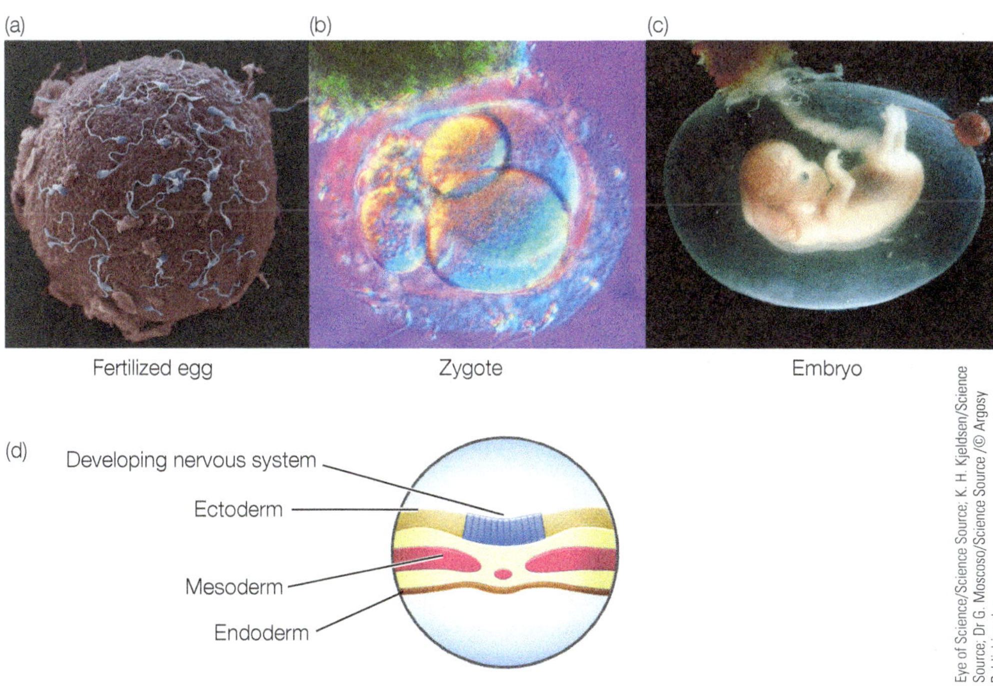

Eye of Science/Science Source; K. H. Kjeldsen/Science Source; Dr G. Moscoso/Science Source /© Argosy Publishing, Inc.

FIGURE **11.3**

Prenatal Development. (a) For the first 2 gestational weeks, the developing organism is known as a zygote. (b) Cell division continues at a rapid pace as the zygote travels down the mother's fallopian tube, reaching the uterus during its second week. (c) The embryo stage lasts from gestational week 3 through gestational week 8. (d) During the zygote stage, cells begin to differentiate into three types: the ectoderm, which is the source of cells making up the nervous system; the mesoderm, which develops into muscle and skeleton; and the endoderm, which will form internal organs.

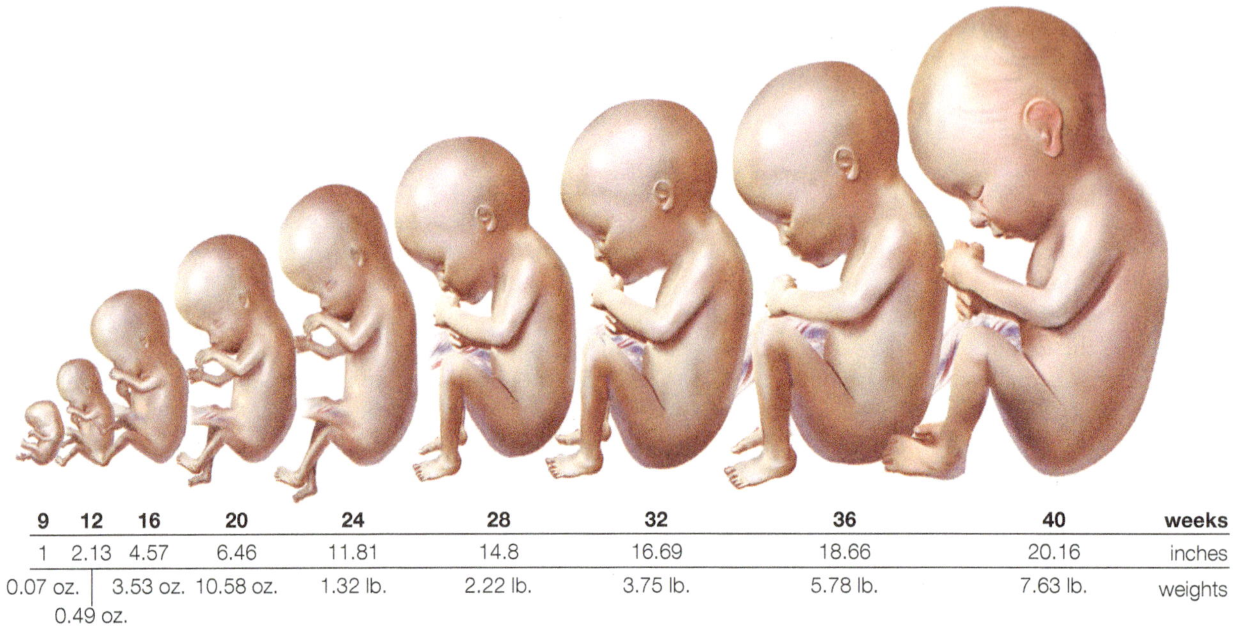

FIGURE **11.4**

Fetal Development. During the fetal stage, from gestational week 8 to approximately gestational week 40, considerable growth and maturation of organs and tissues prepare the fetus for birth.

You may be under the impression that the fetus resides in a rather isolated, self-contained environment in the womb, but this is not the case. The fetus's ability to hear develops by 28 gestational weeks (Das et al., 2020). Newborn babies show an immediate preference for their mother's voice (DeCasper & Fifer, 1980; Moon, 2017). When pregnant mothers read the Dr. Seuss classic *The Cat in the Hat* out loud twice a day, their infants later preferred to listen to tapes of their mothers, but not others, reading this story (DeCasper & Spence, 1986). This preference has obvious advantages in the attachment and bonding that occurs between mother and newborn.

Most pregnancies last about 40 weeks, and babies born between gestational weeks 37 and 42 are considered typical or term births. In the United States, about 10% of infants are born prior to 37 weeks of gestation (Chawanpaiboon et al., 2019). Premature infants are at greater risk than term infants for a number of conditions that can affect lifetime health and development, including disorders of the lungs, vision, and development of the brain (Cole et al., 2011).

In the United States, about 10% of babies are born at 37 or fewer weeks of gestation. The smallest surviving baby on record was born in December 2018, weighing only 8.6 oz with a length of 9 inches. Term newborns are usually about 20 inches long and weigh about 7 pounds. The earliest surviving baby was born at 21 weeks gestation in 1987, when neonatal care was much less advanced than today, but grew into a healthy adult.

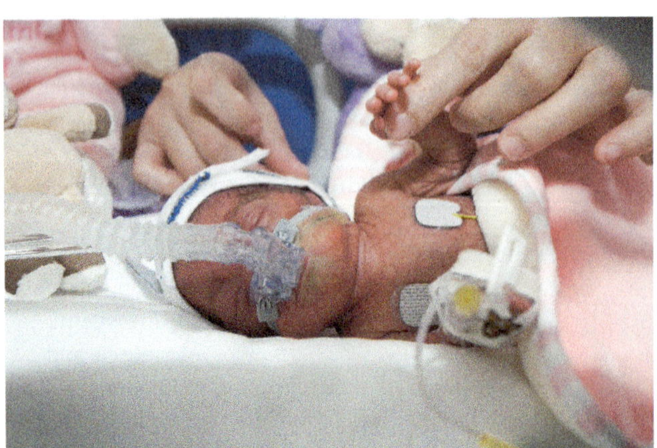

Genetic Risks to Development

In most cases, prenatal development proceeds according to plan. As we observed in Chapter 3, genetic abnormalities that have adverse effects are rarely passed along in large numbers.

The more common genetic abnormalities seen in children are those that become more likely when their parents are older, especially errors in the development of eggs and sperm. The final division of a woman's immature egg, formed during her own prenatal period, into a mature ovum does not occur until just before ovulation. Before they make this last crucial division, a 40-year-old woman's eggs have been exposed to 40 years of potentially harmful environmental influences that raise the probability that something will go wrong as they divide. In contrast, it takes a little over 2 months for a man to produce a sperm cell, which reduces the chances of the cell's exposure to harmful influences.

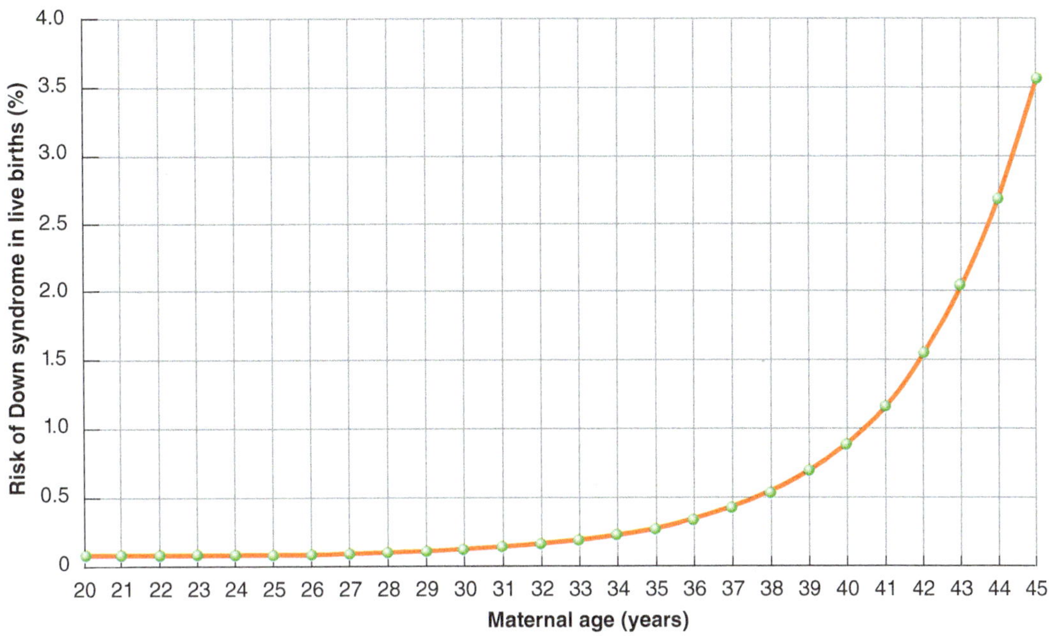

FIGURE **11.5**

Risk of Down Syndrome and Maternal Age. Many genetic disorders, such as Down syndrome, are more common as the age of the mother increases. Errors in the final cell division forming the mother's egg immediately before ovulation become more likely over time as a woman is exposed to more potentially harmful environmental influences, such as radiation.

Down syndrome, or trisomy 21, results when the child receives a third full or partial copy of the 21st chromosome along with the usual two, usually because of faulty cell division. Down syndrome results in intellectual disability (see Chapter 10), a pattern of mild physical abnormalities, and a probable life span of only 40 to 50 years. A woman's chances of giving birth to a child with Down syndrome are only about 1 in 2,000 at age 20 but rise to 1 in 30 at age 45 (see ● Figure 11.5).

Environmental Risks to Development

During pregnancy, the developing fetus is protected from exposure to toxins and disease-causing agents by the placenta, an organ attached to the wall of the mother's uterus that provides the fetus with nutrients and oxygen. This protection, however, is not perfect. In some cases, substances that are relatively safe for the mother can have devastating effects on the health and development of her fetus. Any agent that can produce harmful effects in the zygote, embryo, or fetus is known as a **teratogen** (see ● Figure 11.6). ● Table 11.1 lists some common teratogens and their effects.

teratogen A chemical agent that can harm the zygote, embryo, or fetus.

About 90% of pregnant women in the U.S. take at least one medication other than pregnancy-related vitamins (Centers for Disease Control, 2020). Both prescription and over-the-counter medications can produce adverse effects in the fetus. Exposure to commonly used antidepressant medications has been linked to higher rates of heart and other physical defects (Anderson et al., 2020). A link between antidepressants and autism spectrum disorder continues to be debated (Bölte et al., 2019; Vega et al., 2020; see Chapter 14). Use of acetaminophen (Tylenol and Anacin) during pregnancy is associated with higher risk for attention deficit hyperactivity disorder and autism spectrum disorder in children (Ji et al., 2020). Use of antifungal medications to treat common yeast infections reduces masculinization of male offspring (Mogensen et al., 2017). Because even the safest and most routine substances are capable of acting as teratogens, pregnant women are well advised to consult with health care providers before taking any type of prescription or over-the-counter medication.

According to one expert in medical ethics, today's technology makes it possible to screen embryos for every known disease-causing mutation in the human genome (Leroi, 2006). What would be the benefits and costs of this practice?

Recreational drugs consumed by the mother are the most common and preventable sources of adverse effects in the developing fetus. Infants born to women who use tobacco are at risk for premature birth and being underweight, circumstances that are major risk factors for numerous

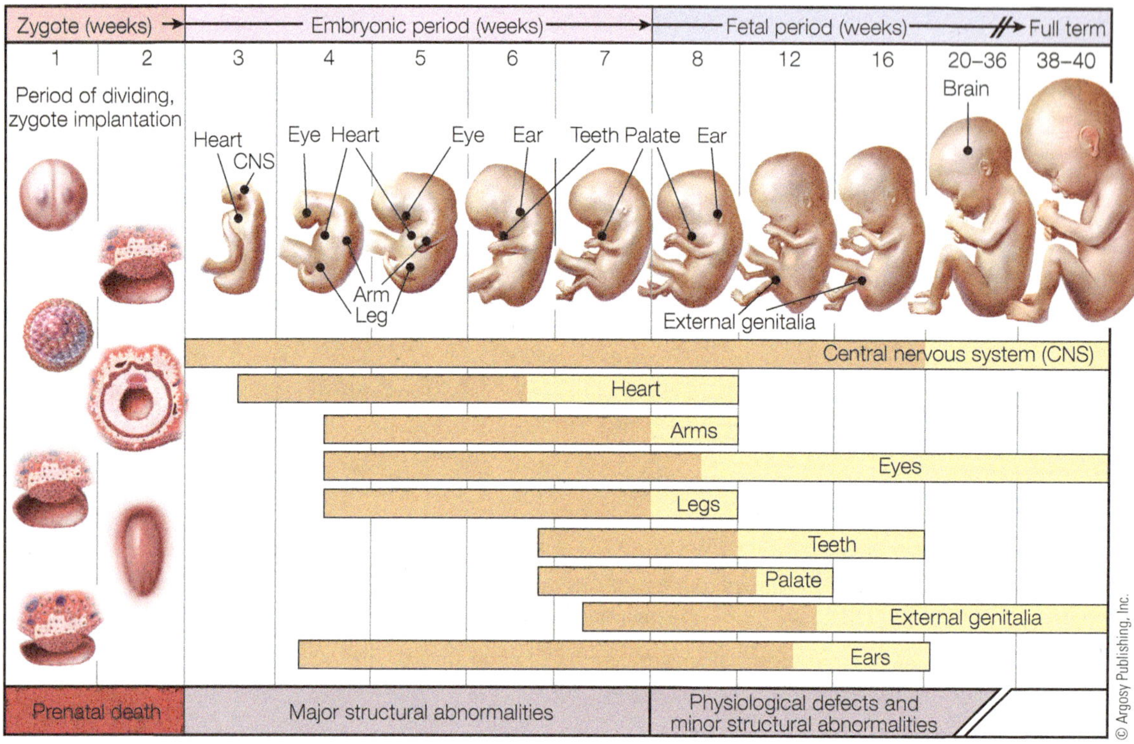

FIGURE **11.6**

Risks From Teratogens. The orange bars indicate times in which teratogens can cause major abnormalities and the yellow bars indicate times when teratogens will cause more minor abnormalities.

physical and psychological problems later on in the child's life (US Department of Health and Human Services, 2014). E-cigarettes do not reduce these risks, as it is the nicotine in the tobacco that causes most problems for the fetus, not the smoke itself (Hawkins et al., 2020).

Although the intricate programming of nervous system development in the fetus appears to be especially vulnerable to interruption by alcohol consumed by the mother during pregnancy, about 10% of pregnant women in the United States consume alcohol anyway (Dejong et al., 2019). Alcohol consumption by a pregnant woman can result in a condition known as **fetal alcohol syndrome (FAS)**. As shown in ● Figure 11.7, FAS produces a number of physical abnormalities, including growth retardation, skin folds at the corners of the eyes, nose, and mouth abnormalities, and a small head circumference, as well as cognitive and behavioral problems, including reduced IQ, attention problems, and poor impulse control (Dejong et al., 2019).

Prenatal exposure to opioids produces long-lasting cognitive and motor deficits (Yeoh et al., 2019). Cannabis use during pregnancy is associated with higher rates of autism spectrum disorder, intellectual disability, and learning disability (Corsi et al., 2020). A mother's use of alcohol, tobacco, marijuana, or cocaine during pregnancy significantly reduces the volume of gray matter of her child's brain, but combinations of two or more of these drugs produce even more dramatic reductions. As we mentioned in Chapter 4, gray matter refers to areas populated by neural cell bodies, and the thickness of cortical gray matter is correlated with measures of intelligence. These are not short-term effects because children exposed prenatally to multiple drugs show reduced gray matter thickness and head circumference at 10 to 13 years of age (Rivkin et al., 2008).

A pregnant woman can be exposed to viruses that can trigger conditions that occur immediately or later in the child's life (Lydholm et al., 2019). HIV can be passed from mother to child during pregnancy, birth, or breast-feeding. Prenatal exposure to the mosquito-borne Zika virus, first identified in Brazil in 2015, produces abnormally small brains (microcephaly) and other serious brain abnormalities in the fetus (Pomar et al., 2019). COVID-19 has been shown to produce more severe outcomes in pregnant women, and in very rare instances, it

fetal alcohol syndrome (FAS) A condition resulting from alcohol consumption by the mother during pregnancy that produces physical abnormalities and cognitive and behavioral problems in her child.

TABLE 11.1

Examples of Some Common Teratogens and Their Effects

Teratogen	Type	Possible effects on the child
Alcohol	Recreational drug	• Small stature • Facial abnormalities • Hyperactivity • Intellectual disability
Tobacco (Nicotine)	Recreational drug	• Low birth weight • Premature birth • Cleft lip and/or palate • Risk of SIDS • Lung and brain damage due to carbon monoxide in smoke • Possible link to ADHD
Cannabis	Recreational drug	• Autism spectrum disorder • Intellectual disability • Learning disability
Phenytoin (Dilantin)	Prescription medication for epilepsy	• Heart defects • Intellectual disability • Cleft palate • Slow growth
Selective serotonin reuptake inhibitors (Prozac, Zoloft, etc.)	Prescription antidepressants	• Premature birth • Heart and other physical defects • Possibly autism spectrum disorder
Varicella (chickenpox)	Viral infection	• Scars • Small head size • Blindness • Seizures • Malformed and paralyzed limbs
Zika	Viral infection	• Microencephaly
Aspirin	Over-the-counter pain medication	• Heart defects • Intellectual disability • Slow growth
Acetaminophen	Over-the-counter pain medication	• ADHD • Autism spectrum disorder

can be transmitted to the fetus (Vivanti et al., 2020). Previous pandemics with similar viruses have been linked to premature birth and fetal distress, but more data are needed to evaluate the potential risks of COVID-19 to the fetus. There is reason to believe that the effects will not be severe. COVID-19 differs from other viruses known to cause extensive birth defects, such as rubella and cytomegalovirus, in that it does not travel primarily through the blood, making intrusion through the placenta less likely. The types of cells that serve as entry points for the Zika virus are plentiful in the placenta, but the cells that serve as entry points for COVID-19 are not.

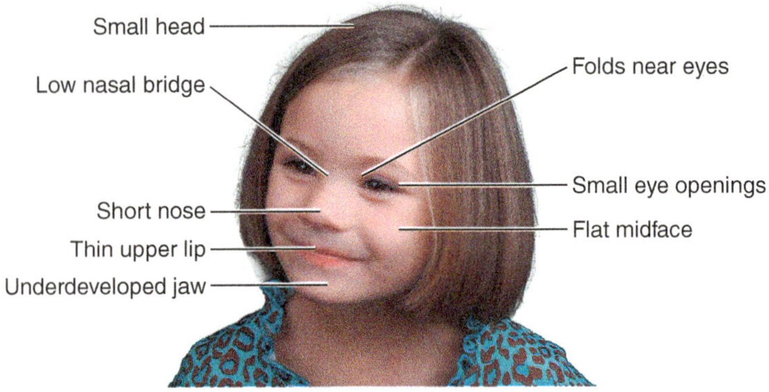

(a) Facial features of FAS

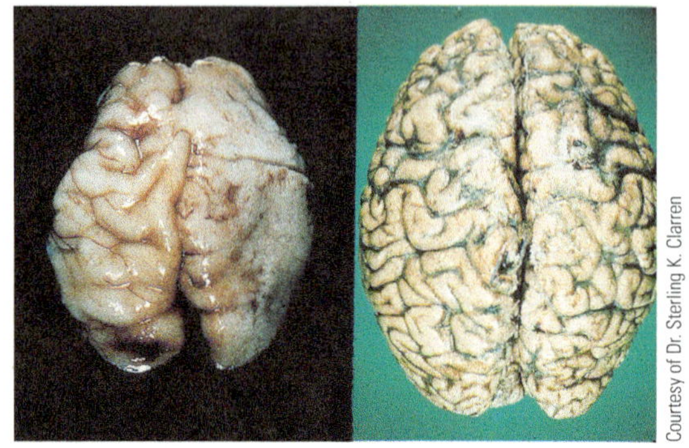

(b) Brain affected by FAS (left) compared to normal brain (right)

FIGURE **11.7**

Fetal Alcohol Syndrome (FAS). No known amount of alcohol consumption is considered safe during pregnancy, yet about 10% of pregnant women in the United States drink some alcohol (Dejong et al., 2019), and about 3.9% binge drink or have five or more drinks at one time (Denny et al., 2019). Drinking during pregnancy can result in FAS, which produces (a) characteristic facial features, (b) reduced brain volume compared to a typically developing fetus, and attentional and other behavioral problems in children.

Newborn babies grasp anything placed in their hand, including a parent's finger.

What Can Newborns Do?

Human development is characterized by a longer period of dependency than in other primates, including chimpanzees and gorillas. Physical abilities present at birth in other primates, such as independent movement, require about 1 year to develop in human infants (Walker, 1996). Human adults house, feed, clothe, protect, and educate their young for the better part of two decades, if not longer. However, even though human newborns are less mature than primate infants of other species, they come into the world with a number of useful capacities.

The Newborn's Reflexes

The newborn stage of life begins officially at birth and lasts 28 days. Newborns have a number of reflexive behaviors that begin to operate immediately (see ● Table 11.2). Babies immediately turn their head to the source of a touch, open their mouth, and search for the mother's nipple. This rooting reflex assists the newborn with the essential process of feeding. If an object is placed in the mouth, babies begin to suck reflexively, which also leads to effective feeding. Very young babies reflexively grasp any object placed in the hand, which leads to the later voluntary grasping of objects. If parents hold newborns upright with their feet touching a surface, babies show a stepping reflex, which possibly serves as a basis for later walking (Zelazo, 1998).

The Newborn's Activity

Newborns spend up to 16 to 18 hours per day sleeping. As we mentioned in Chapter 6, a large proportion of this time is spent in REM sleep, which might participate in the wiring of the newborn's brain.

During times of wakefulness, the baby alternates between periods of alert looking about and periods of physical movement of the arms and legs. Unfortunately for parents, most

TABLE 11.2

Newborn Reflexes

Reflex name	Action	Possible purpose
Babinski	Stroking the baby's foot causes toes to spread out.	Unknown; disappears as nervous system matures.
Blink	Eye closes in response to strong stimuli.	Protects eyes.
Moro	If the baby's head falls backward, the arms first spread out and then "hug."	A possible evolutionary remnant allowing primates to cling to an adult.
Palmar	Placing an object in the hand produces reflexive grasping.	A possible evolutionary remnant allowing primates to cling to an adult's fur.
Rooting	Stroking a baby's cheek results in the baby turning toward the touch and opening the mouth.	Helps the baby nurse.
Stepping	Placing the baby's feet on a flat surface initiates stepping.	Possible precursor to walking.
Sucking	The baby sucks anything that touches the roof of the mouth.	Helps the baby nurse.

newborns also spend about 2 to 3 hours per day either crying or being close to tears. As upsetting as this crying may be, it represents the infant's first efforts at communicating with the parents. Babies generally cry for a reason, such as hunger or pain, and most parents are stimulated by the crying to find ways to make their infant more comfortable.

© Retna/Photoshot

A child's sex chromosomes, XX or XY, typically begin a trajectory toward adult maleness and femaleness but not always. Intersex refers to the presence of male and female features in the same individual. Model Hanne Gaby Odiele recently disclosed that she has androgen insensitivity syndrome (AIS). People with AIS are genetic males (XY) who do not respond to circulating male hormones in utero. They are born with female-appearing external genitalia and typically maintain female gender identities. Because the female reproductive organs are suppressed during fetal development, these individuals are likely to be infertile.

The Newborn's Sex and Gender Development

We refer to physiological characteristics, such as having an XX or XY genotype, as "sex," while psychosocial aspects of the maleness–femaleness continuum are referred to as "gender." The sex chromosome genotype that a zygote receives at conception begins a cascade of hormonal, structural, and behavioral events that lead to mature sex and gender. An intersex outcome occurs when this cascade includes elements of both male and female development.

In the vast majority of cases, individuals have either an XX or XY genotype, but variations in sex chromosomes occur about once in every 426 births (Nielsen, 1991). These differences can take the form of having numbers of sex chromosomes other than two. For example, individuals with Turner syndrome have a single X chromosome and are phenotypically female. Individuals with Klinefelter syndrome have two X chromosomes and one Y chromosome, and are phenotypically male. In some cases, hormone therapy is used at puberty to suppress the development of female secondary sex characteristics, such as breast enlargement. Individuals with Jacob syndrome have one X chromosome and two Y chromosomes, and are phenotypically male. Cognitive and behavioral outcomes in these cases are quite variable, with many individuals experiencing normal development while others are at greater risk for psychological disorders. In particular, individuals with Jacob syndrome have high rates of autism spectrum disorder (van Rijn, 2019). One set of genetically identical twins having a very complicated genotype featured an individual who was phenotypically male and an individual who was phenotypically female (Maeda et al., 1991). These variations highlight the complicated nature of the contributions of genetic sex to adult phenotypes.

The appearance of the newborn's external genitalia remains an important marker of sex and gender. The appearance of the external genitalia is usually, but not always, consistent with genetic sex. In cases of androgen insensitivity syndrome (AIS), an individual with male genetic sex (XY) cannot respond to circulating male hormones, leading to female external appearance. A very rare condition known as 5-alpha-reductase syndrome results in ambiguous genitalia at birth with later masculinization at puberty. Congenital adrenal hyperplasia (CAH) exposes the fetus to excess male hormones, which has little effect on male sexual development but might masculinize the external genitalia and behavior of genetic females (Meyer-Bahlburg et al., 2004; Speiser et al., 2018).

The Newborn's Senses

Newborns have significant, although immature, sensory capacities. Because babies can't talk, researchers have had to be creative in assessing their sensory capacities (see Figure 11.8). Measures of heart rate, facial expression, and head movements correlate with distinctions among stimuli. Researchers also take advantage of habituation, the type of learning in which we reduce responding to repeated stimuli (see Chapter 8). Because of habituation, babies gaze longer at a new stimulus than at one they have seen previously. When babies spend equal time looking at two stimuli, we can assume they cannot tell the difference between them.

Newborns show considerable sensitivity to smells and respond differently to pleasant smells such as chocolate or honey than to unpleasant smells such as rotten eggs (Maurer & Maurer, 1988).

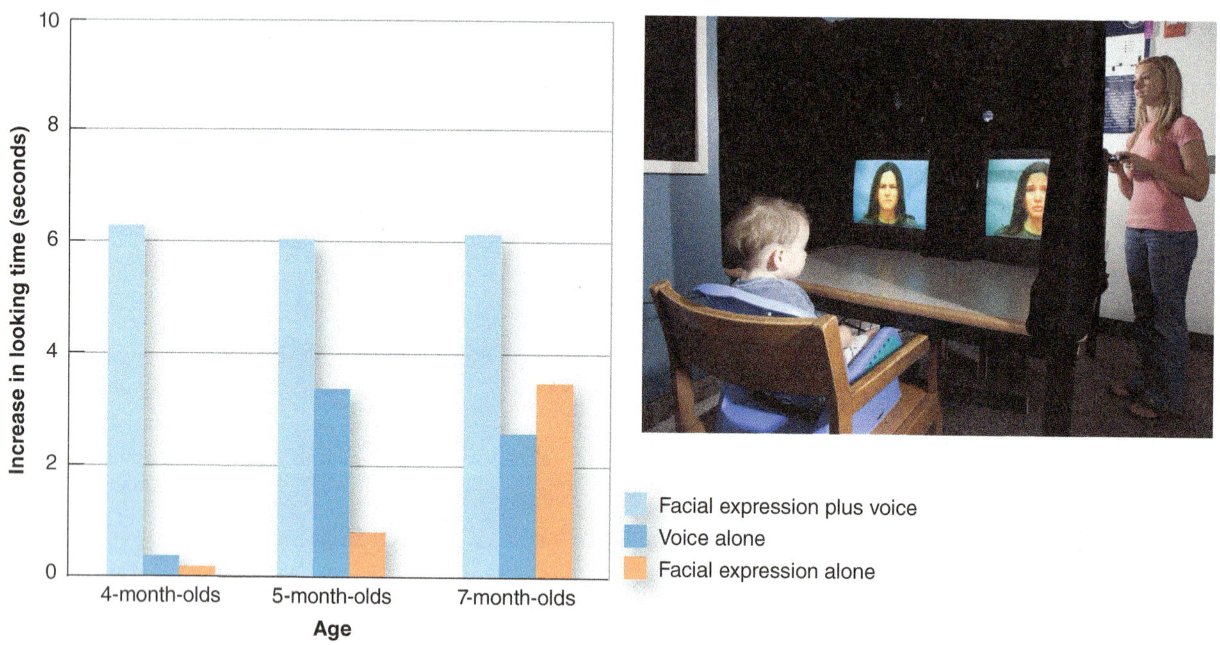

Mark Philbrick/Brigham Young University

FIGURE **11.8**

Studying Infants Requires Clever Experimental Methods. By studying the amount of time infants look at a new stimulus after habituation, such as the face of a person, Ross Flom and Lorraine Bahrick were able to demonstrate that infants as young as 4 months could correctly perceive emotional expression if they both saw and heard the same expression simultaneously. The ability to perceive emotion using voice alone appeared around the age of 5 months, and the ability to perceive emotion from facial expression alone appeared around 7 months.

Source: Adapted from R. Flom, & L. E. Bahrick, (2007). "The Development of Infant Discrimination of Affect in Multimodal and Unimodal Stimulation: The Role of Intersensory Redundancy," *Developmental Psychology*, *43*(1), 238–252. doi:10.1037/0012-1649.43.1.238

They are also capable of recognizing their mother by smell, which has obvious survival advantages. Babies even recognize their mother's favorite brand of perfume (Porter et al., 1991). Infants are quite sensitive to taste and can respond differentially to the major taste qualities of sweet, sour, bitter, and salty. They apparently have a sweet tooth and nurse longer when their breast-feeding mother has consumed sweet-tasting foods (Mennella & Beauchamp, 1996).

The fetus can hear quite well beginning in gestational month seven, but improvement in hearing continues after birth. We might tiptoe around a sleeping newborn, but older children and adults have superior hearing for very quiet sounds. The infant prefers sounds with higher frequencies (pitch) (Fernald & Kuhl, 1987). This might account for the spontaneous use of a higher voice, an aspect of "motherese," by most adults when speaking to children.

Infant vision can be tested by measuring the amount of time the child spends viewing a pattern rather than a uniform screen. Using this technique, we can demonstrate that young infants do not see detail at a distance as well as adults do. In addition, infants need more contrast than adults to see well. As we discussed in Chapter 5, contrast refers to differences in intensity between adjacent stimuli. The black letters on this white page are an example of high contrast, whereas dark gray letters on a black background would be an example of low contrast. These features of infant vision probably explain babies' preference for large, high-contrast, colorful objects.

Newborns demonstrate an innate preference for looking at faces (Otsuka, 2014) (see ● Figure 11.9). This capacity sets the stage for further social behavior and language learning. We know that infants who refuse to make eye contact often develop social and language impairments later (Knickmeyer et al., 2005). Other primates show similar preferences for faces, which may be related to the importance of social relationships in primate species, including our own (Thierry, 1994).

The emerging picture of the newborn infant is one of immature yet formidable capacities. The remainder of this chapter will explore the unfolding of these capabilities as the individual matures.

FIGURE **11.9**

Newborns Show a Preference for Facelike Stimuli. Newborns looked at the stimulus on the left for about 16 seconds longer than the less facelike stimulus on the right. Looking time has been used as one measure of preference for infants.

Source: Adapted from C. Turati et al. (2002). "Newborns' Preference for Faces: What Is Crucial?" *Developmental Psychology*, *38*(6), 875–882. doi: 10.1037/0012-1649.38.6.875

SUMMARY 11.1 Milestones of Prenatal and Newborn Development

Stage	Timing	Highlights
Zygote 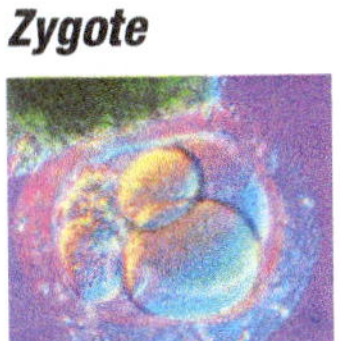	Gestational weeks 1–2	• Differentiation into germ layers
Embryo 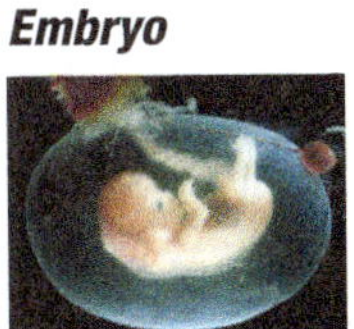	Gestational weeks 3–8	• Nervous system and organs form • Sex organs differentiate

Stage	Timing	Highlights
Fetus 	Gestational week 9 through remainder of pregnancy	• Growth and maturation of existing organs • REM sleep from seventh month of pregnancy • Good hearing from seventh month of pregnancy
Newborn 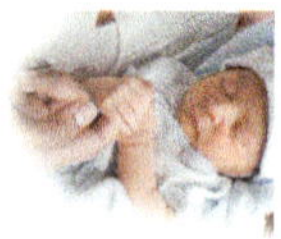	First 28 days of life	• Reflexive movement • Large amounts of sleep • Improving sensory capacities • Preference for faces

What Physical Changes Occur in Infancy and Childhood?

Physical development in infancy and childhood features rapid growth, particularly during the first year of life, when children triple their birth weight (see Figure 11.10).

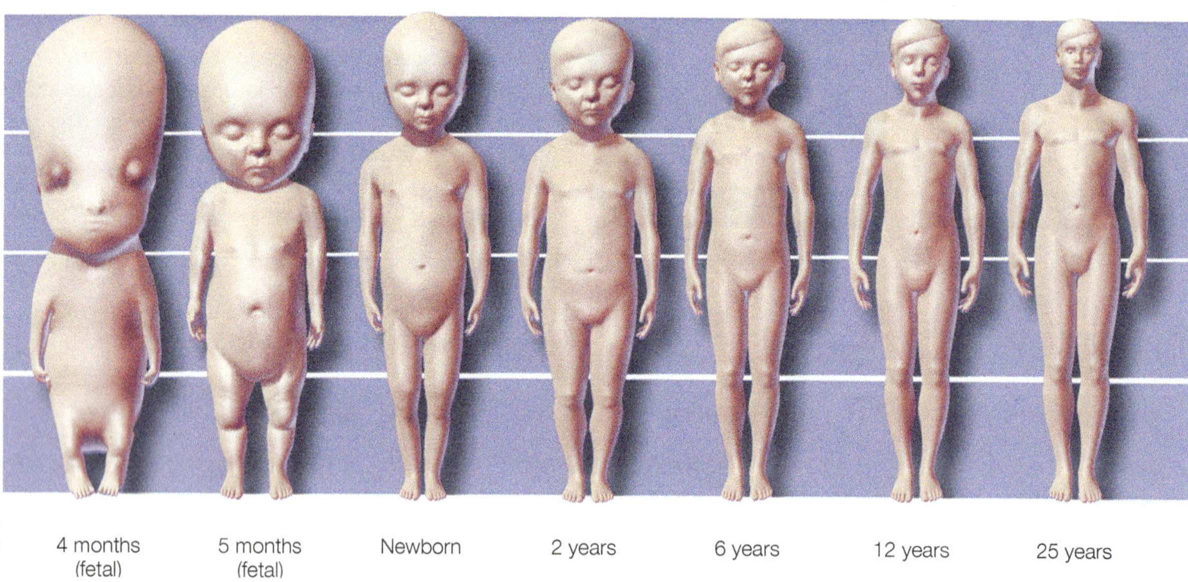

FIGURE **11.10**

Physical Growth Is Rapid in Childhood. Infants grow rapidly, tripling their birth weight during the first year alone. As they grow, their proportions also change significantly. The head takes up approximately one-quarter of a newborn's height, versus about one-seventh to one-eighth of an adult's height. In contrast, the ratio of the trunk to the overall height, about three-eighths, remains the same over the life span.

Source: Adapted from R. V. Kail & J. C. Cavanaugh (2010). *Human Development: A Life-Span View* (5th ed., p. 93). Belmont, CA: Wadsworth/Cengage Learning.

Nervous System Development

In the latter months of pregnancy and for the first 18 months of life, the human brain shows rapid growth in gray matter or collections of neural cell bodies, which we discussed in Chapter 4. Between birth and the end of the infant's third month, the brain grows 64% and goes from less than one quarter to about half the size of an adult brain (Holland et al., 2014). By the age of three years, the brain is about 80% of its eventual adult size.

The two- to three-year-old child has about twice as many synapses as an adult (Huttenlocher, 2009). Over time, cells and connections that are not useful are systematically deleted. In other words, we produce more neurons and synapses than we will eventually need and then keep only those that are working well for us (see Figure 11.11).

What does it mean to have neurons and synapses that are working well? The nervous system develops according to a "use it or lose it" principle, which emphasizes the important role of experience in wiring the brain. Children who are raised in a stimulating and enriched environment, with many things to explore, are likely to have the best outcomes. Children living in intellectually impoverished circumstances may retain too few connections, which may lead to mild forms of intellectual disability (see Chapter 10).

If a child's rate of growth during the first year of life continued, a 10-year-old would be about the size of a jumbo jet (McCall, 1979).

Myelination, the growth in white matter that begins around gestational month six, continues to develop throughout childhood and adolescence (see Figure 11.12) (Houston et al., 2013). Although myelination of the chimpanzee brain is complete by sexual maturity, myelination in the human brain extends into the early 20s (Miller et al., 2012).

Motor Development

As we mentioned earlier, newborn human infants are relatively helpless compared to their chimpanzee and gorilla counterparts. Newborn humans' mobility is handicapped by their

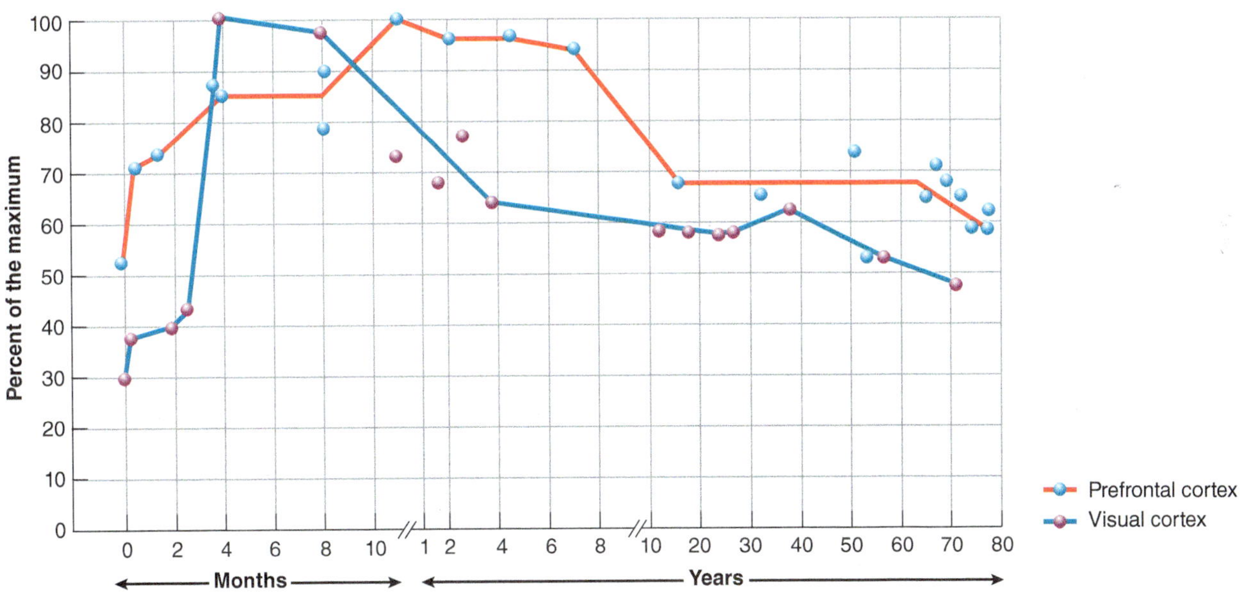

FIGURE **11.11**

Synaptic Connections Are Pruned in Response to Experience. During development, we produce more synapses than necessary. Synapses that are not useful are deleted in a process known as synaptic pruning. Pruning takes place at different rates in different systems, as illustrated by this comparison of pruning in the visual and prefrontal cortices. This process emphasizes the importance of experiencing enriched environments during development.

Source: P. R. Huttenlocher (1994). "Synaptogenesis, Synapse Elimination, and Neural Plasticity in Human Cerebral Cortex." In C. A. Nelson (Ed.), *Threats to Optimal Development: Integrating Biological, Psychological, and Social Risk Factors* (Vol. 27, pp. 35–54). Hillsdale, NJ: Erlbaum.

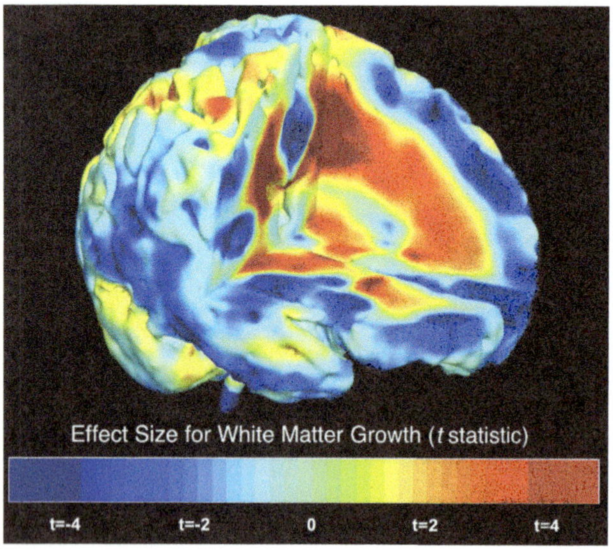

FIGURE **11.12**

Myelination Increases During Childhood. Imaging technologies have captured the progress of myelination (white matter growth) in childhood. Red and yellow areas show the largest changes. Myelinated systems are faster and more efficient than unmyelinated systems.

proportions. One quarter of their length is made up by newborns' heads. In contrast, adults' heads make up approximately one-seventh to one-eighth of their height.

Motor development, or change in our ability to move and perform physical skills, is largely driven by our human genetic blueprint. Identical twins typically reach motor milestones such as walking with more similar timing than that of fraternal twins or nontwin siblings (Fox et al., 1996). Because identical twins share more genes in common compared with fraternal twins, reaching milestones at the same time indicates an important role for genetics in early motor development. At the same time, children's motor development takes place within a complex context of opportunities to move and cultural child-rearing practices (Adolph & Hoch, 2019).

Motor development in childhood proceeds simultaneously in two directions. First, we see development in the head-to-toe direction. Controlling the muscles of the neck and shoulders allows 2-month-old infants to raise their head to look around. This achievement is followed by development of the muscles of the torso around 3 months of age, which are necessary for rolling and sitting. Between 6 and 9 months, babies begin to crawl, although some happily skip this stage. Finally, around the first birthday, the muscles of the legs are developed sufficiently to support the weight of a child when standing or walking. Well into middle childhood, children continue to improve their movement and coordination, demonstrated by the abilities to skip rope, hop on one foot, and combine movements, such as throwing a ball while running (see • Figure 11.13).

The second direction of motor development begins at the midline, an imaginary line dividing the human body in equal halves, and proceeds outward. Infants can bat at toys suspended above their cribs (3 months) before they are able to grasp objects (5 months). In other words, accurately directing the arms precedes the ability to direct the hands and fingers. Incidentally, infants learn to grasp objects before they learn to release them, a fact parents may wish to consider before wearing long hair or dangling earrings. Well into elementary school, children are continuing to master control over the fine muscle movements of the hands and fingers required for writing. Perhaps you recall the rather large-lined paper you used in first grade and the challenges of coloring "within the lines."

Parents in most cultures attempt to teach toileting practices when children are about 2 years old. Not coincidentally, the motor systems required to achieve sphincter control are generally myelinated somewhere around 21 months of age (Largo, Molinari, von Siebenthal, & Wolfensberger, 1996).

Although early motor milestones are driven largely by biology, they respond to experience. It is possible to slow down motor milestones by restricting movement. Some cultures, out of safety concerns, restrict the movement opportunities of young children, which slightly delays motor milestones such as walking alone (Kaplan & Dove, 1987; Karasik et al., 2018). In other cases, motor milestones may be reached slightly earlier

Kenyan parents often encourage early walking in their children. Compared to American children, whose average age of walking unassisted is about 1 year, Kenyan children observed by Super (1976) walked between the ages of 7 and 11 months. In contrast, infants in Tajikistan spend up to 20 hours bound in a special cradle called a gahvora (Karasik et al., 2018). The passing of these beautifully crafted cradles from generation to generation is marked by a huge celebration. While bound, the infant remains at the center of the family, surrounded by caregivers, siblings, and peers. Ongoing research is exploring the impact of restraint on infant motor and social skills.

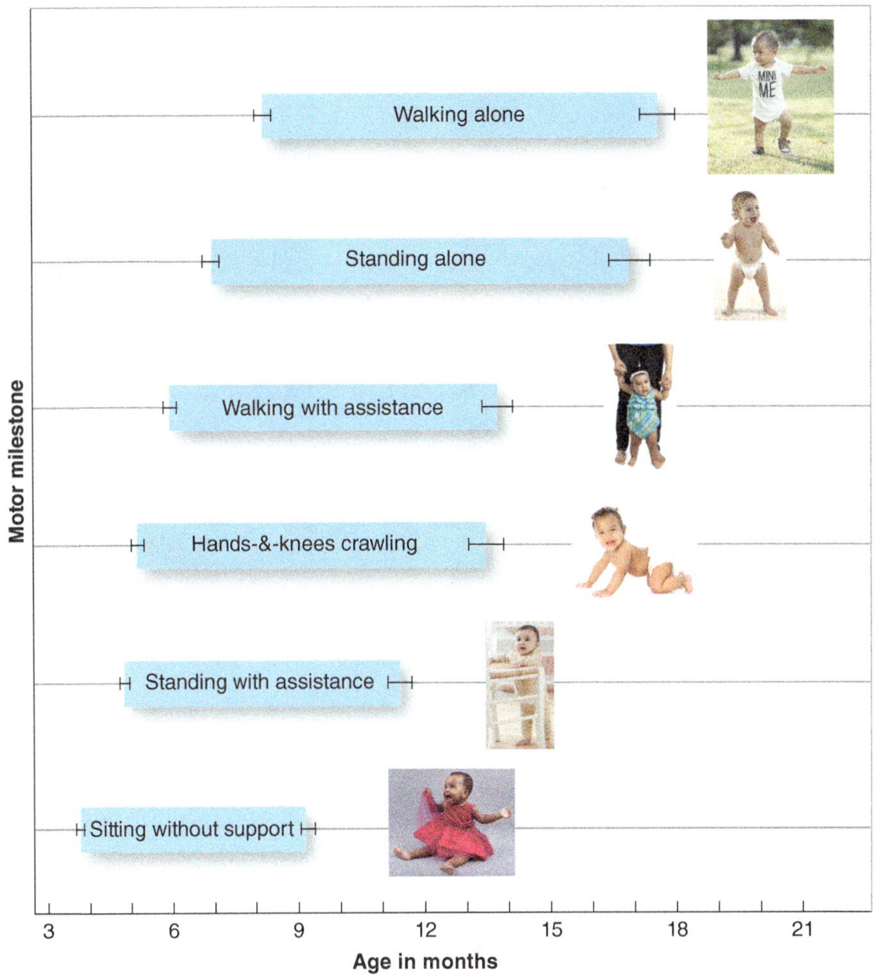

FIGURE **11.13**

Motor Milestones. These motor milestones emerge at predictable times over the course of childhood but can range significantly from child to child. This chart provides the typical windows of time at which children reach major motor milestones.

Credits Bottom to top: Samuel Borges Photography/Shutterstock.com, JGI/Jamie Grill/Tetra images/Getty Images, lostinbids/E+/Getty Images, aldomurillo/iStock/Getty Images, Golbay/Shutterstock.com, PIYAPHOTOGRAPHY/Shutterstock.com

by providing specific practice in sitting, standing, and walking (Super, 1976; Adolph & Hoch, 2019). These changes in the developmental timeline are usually slight, because myelination of motor nerves usually just precedes the achievement of a new skill. Once the relevant parts of the nervous system are sufficiently mature, new skills develop rapidly with little practice.

Gender Development in Childhood

Like most other types of human behavior, gender identity, or the sense of one's own place on a scale from maleness to femaleness, develops in response to both biological and environmental factors.

Children begin to prefer sex-typed toys between the ages of 12 and 18 months, although at this age, they are not yet able to match sex-typed toys (vehicles or dolls) with male or female faces and voices. This suggests that they have not yet been socialized to think of particular toys as "male" or "female" (Serbin et al., 2001). The fact that young vervet monkeys make similar sex-typed toy choices as young humans suggests that socialization has relatively little to do with these early differences in behavior (Alexander & Hines, 2002). Cases of girls

Very young vervet monkeys show the same toy preferences as young human children, suggesting that biology plays a role in the choice of sex-typical toys.

MCT/Tribune News Service/Getty Images

MCT/Tribune News Service/Getty Images

with CAH, who experience unusually high levels of prenatal exposure to male hormones, also provide insight into toy choice. In spite of the fact that girls with CAH receive more positive reinforcement from their parents for playing with "girl" toys than typically developing girls do, they nonetheless show much greater interest in masculine toys (see Figure 11.14) (Pasterski et al., 2005). This is not to say that parental and societal socialization has no impact

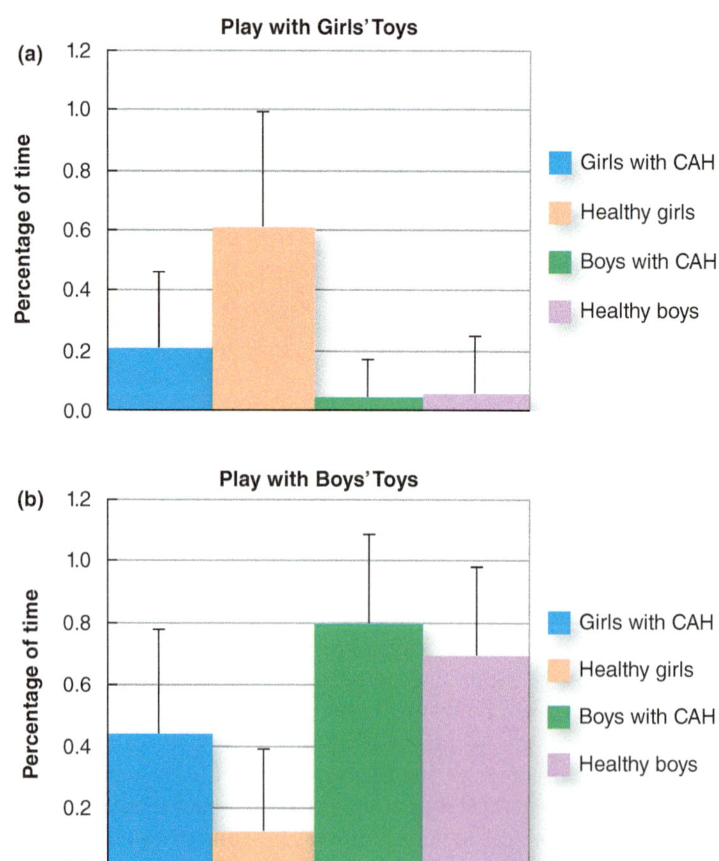

FIGURE **11.14**

Prenatal Hormones and Play Behavior. Congenital adrenal hyperplasia (CAH) results in higher prenatal exposure to male hormones in both females and males. Girls with CAH show less interest in girls' toys and more interest in boys' toys than is shown by healthy females. Boys with CAH show the same interest in both types of toys as do healthy boys.

Source: M. Hines (2010). "Sex-Related Variation in Human Behavior and the Brain," *Trends in Cognitive Sciences, 14*(10), 448–456. doi: 10.1016/j.tics.2010.07.005

Diverse Voices in Psychology

What Are the Implications of Gender Assignment?

The concept of gender has been transformed from a binary, categorical system (male or female) to a bimodal continuum (see Chapter 2). This transition is evident in the legal codes of many nations, where official government documents such as passports now provide options other than male or female, and in the social media giant Facebook's 58 choices for personal identifiers, plus unique identifiers that users choose for themselves.

Health care providers find no easy solutions within this environment when faced with cases of individuals with ambiguous physical features resulting from chromosome and hormonal influences. Gender assignment using the more traditional binary choices, in spite of passports and Facebook, remains a common goal within the medical community.

One of the most contentious areas of gender assignment involves individuals born with ovotesticular syndrome (Meyer-Bahlburg et al., 2016). These individuals used to be referred to as "true hermaphrodites," as they possess a gonad that contains both testicular tubular structures and ovarian follicles. Typically, about half of the newborns in this category are assigned to the female gender and the other half to the male gender, but clinicians do not necessarily agree on the criteria for making this judgment. Some are more influenced by the surgical challenges presented by an individual case while others consider fertility. As a result, many individuals with ovotesticular syndrome later develop gender dysphoria, a sense of mismatch between their assigned gender and their identities, and/or patient-initiated gender change.

Perhaps the fluidity of the concept of gender will make gender assignment decisions on the part of the medical community simply unnecessary. In the meantime, further research supporting evidence-based decisions (see Chapter 15) that include the goals of the patient would be very helpful (Lee et al., 2020). ■

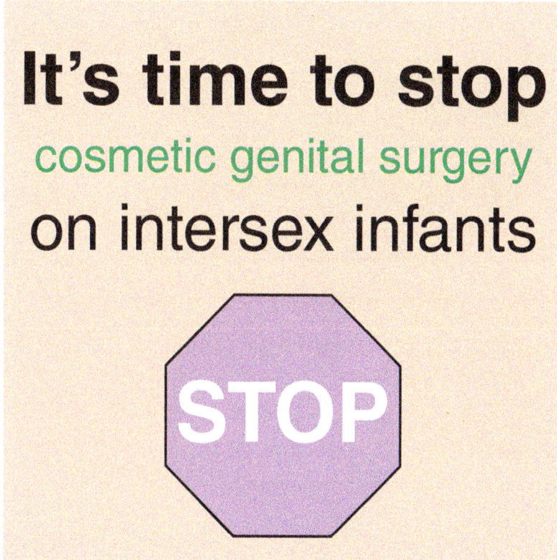

Advocates for individuals with intersex are encouraging medical professionals to postpone surgical and hormonal treatments until a child is old enough to participate in decisions about their sex and gender.

on gender identity, but rather to remind us that biology and experience interact to produce an outcome.

By the age of 3 years, children begin using gender labels consistently for themselves, although we don't know for certain whether this represents an awareness of their assigned gender or an identification with their assigned gender (Meyer-Bahlburg et al., 2016). A small number of children with unambiguous biological sex develop incongruent gender identity. Complex interactions among genetic, hormonal, cognitive, and psychosocial factors contribute to the development of a transgender identity. Young transgender children do not appear to be "confused," but rather show a strong preference for their expressed gender rather than their natal (at birth) sex (Olson et al., 2015).

How Does Cognition Change During Infancy and Childhood?

Interacting with brain development and the child's ability to move and explore the environment are changes in the way children process information and solve problems. Even when children are exposed to the same information as adults, their thinking often leads them to different conclusions. When asked why clouds move across the sky, a 4-year-old

ERIC PIERMONT/AFP/Getty Images

A preschool child might believe that airplanes pull clouds across the sky, but an adult is unlikely to come to the same conclusion, even though they are watching the same events.

might suggest that the clouds are pulled by airplanes, but an adult is unlikely to come to this conclusion. Both child and adult have observed clouds and airplanes moving across the sky, but viewing these occurrences as related is something that only a small child would do. To understand these differences, we need to examine how cognition changes as a function of age and experience.

One of the classic theories about the development of cognition was proposed by Swiss psychologist Jean Piaget (1896–1980). While working with Théodore Simon, who along with Alfred Binet developed some of the first intelligence tests (see Chapter 10), Piaget became more interested in the errors made by the children than in their correct responses. He believed that these errors were representative of growth in the child's ability to reason.

Like many early theorists in psychology, including Freud, Piaget has been criticized by more contemporary thinkers. After reviewing Piaget's theories, we will consider the points made by his critics along with more recent approaches to cognitive development.

Jean Piaget's Theory of Cognitive Development

According to Piaget's theory, cognitive abilities develop through regular stages, making Piaget's work a classic example of the discontinuity approach discussed earlier in this chapter. Cognition matures as the child increasingly uses concepts and organizing schemas to think. We discussed concepts and schemas in Chapters 9 and 10.

Two types of adjustments can be made to a schema, depending on the nature of discrepancies between the new information and the existing category. Assume that a child has a rather well-developed schema for birds, which includes features such as "has wings," "has feathers," and "can fly." If the child then learns about a new species of bird, such as a hawk, the child can assimilate the new information into the existing bird schema: Hawks have wings, feathers, and the ability to fly. In **assimilation**, no changes to the existing schema are required to add the new instance. However, let's now assume that the child meets a kiwi, a small, flightless bird from New Zealand. The kiwi doesn't fit neatly into the existing schema, which assumes that all birds can fly. The schema must be adapted to fit the new information, a

Bill Anderson/Science Source

Jean Piaget (1896–1980).

TABLE 11.3

Jean Piaget's Theory of Cognitive Development

Stage	Approximate age	Highlights
Sensorimotor stage	Birth to age 2	• Here and now rather than past and future • Exploration through moving and sensing • Object permanence
Preoperational stage	2–6 years	• Language acquisition • Egocentrism • Illogical reasoning
Concrete operational stage	6–12 years	• Logical reasoning • Mastery of conservation problems • Learning by doing
Formal operational stage	12 years and older	• Abstract reasoning • Idealism • Improved problem solving

process Piaget called **accommodation**. Through accommodation, the child now understands that although most birds can fly, some exceptions occur.

In addition to his interest in the development and refinement of schemas, Piaget made many other observations about cognition at different ages. We will now explore the particular characteristics found in each of Piaget's four stages (see ● Table 11.3).

Eric Isselee/Shutterstock.com

If children can learn about robins without making changes to their schema of "bird," assimilation will occur. In contrast, learning about flightless kiwis might require changes in the bird schema, and accommodation will occur.

The Sensorimotor Stage Piaget's first stage, the **sensorimotor stage**, begins at birth and lasts until the child's second birthday. The name of this stage reflects the infant's focus on the here and now rather than the past and the future. Sensations immediately evoke motor responses. As soon as they can crawl, infants work their way (usually quite rapidly) through the environment, exploring new objects by interacting with them physically, particularly by putting them in their mouths. Infants do not seem particularly deterred by features such as taste and are very likely to sample the drain cleaner under the sink unless parents take appropriate precautions to babyproof their home.

One of the major milestones that occur during the sensorimotor stage is the achievement of **object permanence**. Infants under the age of 8 months or so do not seem to be able to form clear memories or mental representations for objects once they are removed from the immediate present. If Piaget covered his gold pocket watch with his beret while an infant watched, the infant would not show signs of searching for the now missing watch. Around the age of 8 months or so, infants become more persistent. If he hid the pocket watch, 8-month-olds would look for it. Object permanence coincides with achieving sufficient growth in the prefrontal cortex in both human and non-human primate infants (Diamond & Goldman-Rakic, 1989).

During the sensorimotor period, the child's language abilities are developing rapidly. By the age of 18 months, children usually have a working vocabulary of 10 to 50 words, and by the age of 2 years, they are beginning to combine words into short but meaningful sentences, such as "Want cookie" or "Go bye-bye." These new ways of thinking symbolically lead the child into the subsequent preoperational stage.

The Preoperational Stage Piaget's **preoperational stage** lasts from approximately age 2 to age 6. The stage gets its name from the notion that children are still incapable of engaging in internal mental operations or manipulations, such as following the transformation of objects from one form to another.

assimilation The incorporation of new learning into an existing schema without the need to revise the schema.

accommodation The incorporation of new learning into an existing schema that requires revision of the schema.

sensorimotor stage Jean Piaget's stage of development beginning at birth and ending at the age of 2 years and characterized by active exploration of the environment.

object permanence The ability to form mental representations of objects that are no longer present.

preoperational stage Jean Piaget's stage of development beginning at the age of 2 years and ending at the age of 6 years and characterized by use of symbols, egocentrism, and limits on the ability to reason logically.

Lew Merrim/Science Source

Preoperational children are unlikely to recognize that pouring liquid from one glass to another of a different size and shape does not change the amount of liquid. They usually believe that the glass that is "higher" holds more. The abruptness with which children master conservation tasks led Jean Piaget to suggest that cognitive development proceeds in stages, but other psychologists believe changes occur more gradually.

Piaget used a variety of creative tasks to demonstrate the characteristics of the reasoning of the preoperational child. **Conservation** tasks require the child to recognize that changing the form or appearance of an object does not change its quantity. One of the observations that led Piaget to consider cognitive development as occurring in stages is the rather abrupt way in which conservation tasks are often solved. Children who could not solve the problem a few weeks earlier suddenly look at the adult experimenter with pity, as if to say, "This may be the world's stupidest grown-up."

In addition to difficulty with transitions, preoperational children have limited abilities to understand points of view other than their own, a characteristic described by Piaget as **egocentrism**. One kindergarten teacher asked his class where the sun went at night and received an enthusiastic response of "Yuba City" (which is located in northern California) from one of the students. As it turned out, the young student had moved recently from Yuba City to his current home in San Luis Obispo. Because these were the only two places on earth the child knew, if he was in one place and the sun wasn't there, there was only one other logical place for the sun to be. You guessed it—Yuba City.

Preoperational thinking is also limited by beliefs that appearances are real. While older children understand that movies feature real people dressed up and acting like superheroes, the younger child might believe that not only are superheroes real, but also that they can really fly.

The Concrete Operational Stage Piaget referred to the stage between the ages of 6 and 12 as the **concrete operational stage**. Rather suddenly, problems of conservation are easily solved, and thinking becomes more logical. The only remaining limitation is an inability to handle abstract concepts, which will not be resolved until the next and final stage.

Piaget used the term *concrete operations* for this stage because he observed that children reasoned best when allowed to engage in hands-on learning. This observation of Piaget's has had an enormous impact on the way early childhood education is conducted in many nations. Math instruction now features colorful boxes of manipulatives, which allow children to count and sort real things. Children's museums, petting zoos, interactive websites, and other opportunities for experiential learning have become commonplace.

The young child's inability to distinguish fantasy from reality has led to a lively debate about managing entertainment materials for children. Is it appropriate to let young children believe that fairy tales are real?

The Formal Operational Stage For Piaget, cognitive development matures in the **formal operational stage**, which begins around the age of 12. The final piece to be added to the child's cognitive skill set is the ability to handle abstract concepts. Abstract concepts usually involve "what if" types of questions and form the heart of scientific inquiry. If you were to ask a group of sixth graders what would happen if everyone on Earth became blind tomorrow, they would likely struggle to come up with a reasonable answer. A group of high school students, however, would readily reply that people who were already blind would become instant leaders because they would have existing skills for coping with blindness.

Accompanying the ability to think abstractly is a big improvement in problem solving. Younger children tend to approach problems by trying things out and seeing what happens, a rather inefficient trial-and-error approach. Teens are more likely to think through several alternatives more strategically. Abstract thinking ability also appears to stimulate a burst of idealism. What if we could solve world hunger? These are the types of questions teens begin to ask, and they are not always content with the more practical and less idealistic responses of older adults.

Criticisms of Jean Piaget's Theory Piaget's classic theory set the standard for his time, but more contemporary developmental psychologists argue that some aspects of his view of cognitive development need updating and revising. Piaget's methods do not always meet the standards we described in Chapter 2. One major part of his theories was based entirely on observations of his own three children.

conservation The ability to understand that changing the form or appearance of an object does not change its quantity.

egocentrism Limitations on the ability to understand the point of view of other people.

concrete operational stage Jean Piaget's stage of development beginning at the age of 6 years and ending at the age of 12 years and characterized by logical but not abstract reasoning.

formal operational stage Jean Piaget's stage of development beginning at age 12 and extending through adulthood and characterized by mature reasoning capabilities.

Piaget's strong interest in biology led him to look at human development from a species perspective, which in turn reduced his interest in individual differences. Other psychologists point out that individual cognitive development can be quite variable. Some adults fail to achieve the ability to reason abstractly or do so only on some problems and not on others. This variability makes cognitive development look more gradual and continuous than stagelike, as suggested by Piaget.

Piaget did not specify mechanisms responsible for moving from one stage to the next. Today, using brain imaging methods, we can explain some of these changes, such as the correlation between the achievement of object permanence and frontal lobe development. Other transitions, such as the relatively sudden mastery of conservation problems, are not so easily explained.

Many psychologists believe that Piaget underestimated the capabilities of young children. At the same time, he might have overestimated the cognitive abilities of adolescents. As we discussed in Chapter 4, the human brain is not fully mature until a person's early 20s, so we would not expect fully adult cognition in an adolescent.

Finally, Piaget has been criticized for viewing developing children in relative isolation from their family, community, and culture. These criticisms have formed the basis for extensions to Piaget's approach, described in the next section.

Lawrence Migdale/Science Source

One of Jean Piaget's legacies to early childhood education is his emphasis on hands-on learning. Colorful objects or manipulatives have replaced endless worksheets used to teach math concepts such as sorting to older generations of students.

Alternative Approaches to Cognitive Development

In the next sections, we will explore alternatives to Piaget's view of cognitive development.

Lev Vygotsky Soviet psychologist Lev Vygotsky (1896–1934) proposed an early alternative to Piaget's theories. Piaget and Vygotsky illustrate the theme of universal versus ecological development introduced at the beginning of the chapter. Unlike Piaget, whose interest viewed human development as universal across cultures, Vygotsky (1934/1962) stressed the role of culture and cultural differences in the development of the child. For Vygotsky, cultures teach children not only what to think but also how to think.

Piaget's developing individual learns to understand the world by actively exploring it, like a miniature scientist, whereas Vygotsky's individual gains knowledge of the world by interacting socially and collaboratively with parents, teachers, and other members of the community (see • Figure 11.15). Language was a particularly important aspect of cognitive development for Vygotsky. Children first use language to initiate social contact and opportunities to learn. Later, self-directed talk, such as "I need to finish my game before dinner," aids in problem solving and, in the older child, forms inner speech.

Information Processing Information processing models of cognitive development provide important extensions to Piaget's theory (Kail & Bisanz, 1991). These models describe specific changes in the child's ability to reason, such as the development of working memory.

Jemal Countess/UPI/Alamy Stock Photo

A burst of idealism, leading to a desire to make the world a better place, often accompanies the onset of formal operational thinking in adolescence. Swedish teen Greta Thunberg gained international recognition for her advocacy for mitigating climate change.

FIGURE **11.15**

Zone of Proximal Development. Unlike Jean Piaget, Lev Vygotsky viewed development as taking place within the social and cultural environments. His zone of proximal development included tasks that the child could learn to do with the assistance of parents, teachers, or other adults or peers. Vygotsky's advice is to provide children with activities that are within reach but neither too easy nor too hard.

The overall rate of processing information, analogous to your computer's CPU speed, increases during childhood (Cerella & Hale, 1994) and provides a foundation for many observed changes in reasoning ability (Kail et al., 2016). In tasks that require judgment, such as deciding which of two numbers is larger, adults are three times faster than 4- and 5-year-olds and twice as fast as 8- and 9-year-olds (Kail & Bisanz, 1992). Surprisingly, by the time children enter elementary school, their performance on tasks requiring focused attention and disregard of distracters reaches adult levels (McKay et al., 1994). In contrast, the ability to sustain attention over time remains limited until the age of 11 years. Around this age, attention span begins to lengthen significantly each year until adulthood.

Children's memory abilities change dramatically following their second year of life (Bauer & Lukowski, 2010; Bauer et al., 2011). These changes are probably due to maturation of brain structures related to memory. The amygdala and most of the hippocampus are relatively mature at a very early age, around 6 months, but changes in the frontal lobe and hippocampus during the third year of life allow children to form more long-term memories, particularly for sequences of events. Improved memory and a growing sense of self combine to produce some of the first autobiographical memories between the ages of 3 and 5 years (Wang, 2008).

Naïve Theories One of the ways in which Piaget possibly underestimated children was his suggestion that children's abilities to understand objects in their world develop slowly over time. Contemporary developmental psychologists believe that this assertion was wrong. Instead, very young children seem to understand a great deal about objects and how they work, even before they have had much experience interacting with them (Baillargeon et al., 2011). For example, infants as young as 2-½ months old looked longer at an impossible situation (a toy mouse that should have been seen moving between two blocks did not appear). Early reasoning extends from objects to the social environment. As shown in Figure 11.16, infants can distinguish between the different types of social power held by leaders and bullies (Margoni et al., 2018).

theory of mind (TOM) The understanding that others have thoughts that are different from one's own.

Theory of Mind Piaget used the concept of egocentrism to describe the young child's relative lack of awareness of the viewpoints of others. An elaboration of this concept, **theory of mind (TOM)**, has emerged as an important tool in tracking typical and abnormal

Intervention Event

FIGURE **11.16**

Children Possess Naïve Theories. Many contemporary psychologists believe that Jean Piaget underestimated the reasoning abilities of young children. Seventeen-month-old infants looked longer at a situation in which a "leader" (the bear in the middle) was expected to right a wrong (the bear on the right grabbed both toys) but failed to do so. The leader was established earlier in the experiment by having the other two bears follow instructions to face "front" or "back."

Source: Adapted from M. Stavans & R. Baillargeon (2019). "Infants Expect Leaders to Right Wrongs," *Proceedings of the National Academy of Sciences, 116*(33), 16292–16301. doi: 10.1073/pnas.1820091116

development. TOM occurs when people understand that others have beliefs, desires, and intentions that are different from their own (Premack & Woodruff, 1978). While Premack argued that TOM in humans was an extension of similar abilities in apes, others believed this was a uniquely human ability. Recent research making use of eye-tracking technology, however, has provided stronger evidence that Premack's observations about apes were correct (Krupenye et al., 2016).

The classic procedure for demonstrating TOM is the false belief task, often called the "Sally–Anne" task (Wimmer & Perner, 1983). Imagine that one doll, Sally, places her ball in a basket and then leaves the room. Another doll, Anne, enters the room, moves the ball from the basket to a box, and then leaves. If Sally comes back, where will she look for her ball? Children who have developed a TOM understand that their personal knowledge of where the ball is located is different from the knowledge of Sally, who was absent when the ball was moved. They will correctly decide that Sally will look in the basket (see Figure 11.17).

Developmental psychologists generally agree that TOM emerges in children around the age of 3 to 4 years, somewhat earlier than the end of Piaget's preoperational period. We can identify behaviors in younger children that seem to act as building blocks leading to the achievement of TOM. Joint attention, which includes behaviors such as following another person's gaze with one's own and using pointing to direct another person's attention to something in the environment, emerges in the first year of life (Barresi & Moore, 1996). The ability of young children to distinguish between living and nonliving objects is another important step in the development of TOM. Finally, young children appear to make distinctions between

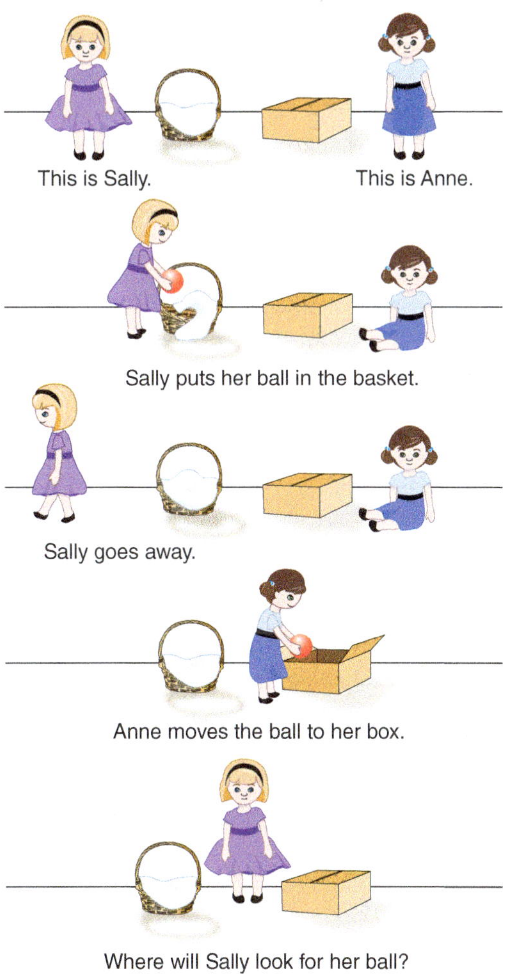

FIGURE **11.17**

Testing Theory of Mind (TOM). Children who have achieved TOM recognize that their personal knowledge of the whereabouts of Sally's ball is different from Sally's knowledge, and they will predict correctly that she will look in the basket.

intentional and unintentional behaviors, because 3-year-olds will imitate the former but not the latter (Williamson et al., 2010).

TOM appears critical to further social development, the topic of our next section. A failure to develop a typical TOM has been linked to the development of autism spectrum disorder, a condition characterized by extreme social difficulties that we discuss in more detail in Chapter 14 (Baron-Cohen, 2000; Rosenthal et al., 2019).

How Do Social and Emotional Behaviors Change During Infancy and Childhood?

The physical and cognitive development we have witnessed so far does not occur in a vacuum. Children mature within complex environments affected by their own intrinsic tendencies, the responses to those tendencies on the part of others, and the ways in which they are nurtured.

Temperament

Children's temperaments reflect their prevailing patterns of mood, activity, and emotional responsiveness. Differences along these initial dimensions predict adult personality. Mary Rothbart (2007) divided temperament into three categories: Surgency or extroversion (happy, active, vocal, and social), negative affect or mood (angry, fearful, shy, and frustrated), and effortful control (the ability to pay attention and inhibit behavior). The likelihood that individual differences in temperament have their roots in genetics is supported by the identification of similar differences among infant rhesus monkeys (Wood et al., 2020).

While temperament may predispose a child to interact with the environment in certain ways and affect the behavior elicited from caregivers and others, the environment in which children find themselves also has an impact. For example, fearful children with gentle parents develop a stronger internal sense of right and wrong than do fearful children with punitive parents (Rothbart, 2007). Similar interactions between temperament and parenting have also been reported in rhesus monkeys, emphasizing the possible biological and evolutionary contributions to these outcomes (Suomi, 2006). Rhesus infants with a particular genotype were more aggressive, but only if they were raised by their mothers rather than by peers (see Figure 11.18).

FIGURE **11.18**

Parenting and Temperament Interact. In rhesus monkeys, variations in a gene called monoamine oxidase A (MAOA) are related to aggressive behavior. Monkeys with the low-activity variant are typically more aggressive and attain higher rankings within the monkeys' dominance hierarchy than do monkeys with the high-activity variant of the gene. This relationship is seen when the monkeys are raised normally with their mothers. However, when monkeys are raised in peer groups without contact with their mothers, the relationship is reversed: The monkeys with the high-activity version are more aggressive. This research supports the goodness-of-fit interactions between child temperament and parenting style proposed by Alexander Thomas and Stella Chess (1977) and by Mary Rothbart (2007).

Source: Adapted from T. K. Newman, et al. (2005). "Monoamine Oxidase: A Gene Promoter Variation and Rearing Experience Influences Aggressive Behavior in Rhesus Monkeys," *Biological Psychiatry, 57*(2), 167–172. doi: 10.1016/j.biopsych.2004.10.012.

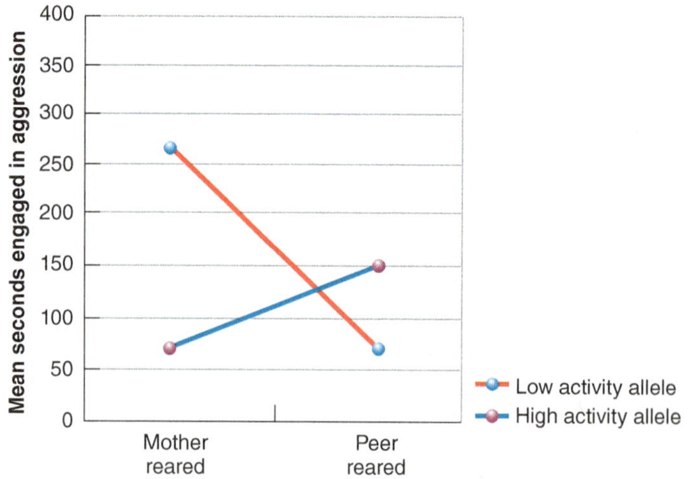

Temperament interacts not only with the socialization provided by parents but also with the larger-scale socialization provided by culture. In the United States, but not in China, children with higher effortful control showed lower levels of negative affect, such as anger. In China, but not in the United States, higher effortful control was correlated with less surgency or extroversion (Ahadi et al., 1993).

Attachment

Because of the physical dependency of the human infant on the adult caregiver, maintaining closeness is a high priority. Infants engage in a number of behaviors, such as smiling, cooing, and crying, that are effective in ensuring adult attention.

CONNECTING TO RESEARCH

The Evolution of Attachment Behavior

THERE IS A BIG DIFFERENCE between a newly hatched goose following its mother because of imprinting and the two-way interactions that promote attachment between human mothers and their newborns, including body contact, mutual gaze, and exaggerated facial expressions. Are these more sophisticated interactions exclusively human? Research evidence suggests that the answer to this question is "no." Rhesus monkeys also show complex mutual behaviors between mothers and their newborns (Ferrari et al., 2009).

The Question: Do rhesus monkeys have behaviors that are the equivalent of human mother–infant behaviors that promote bonding?

METHODS

Fourteen mother–infant rhesus monkey pairs were observed while they were living among social groups housed in indoor–outdoor enclosures. Six additional pairs were observed in a more naturalistic setting. For the first 2 months of the infants' lives, the researchers filmed and recorded the frequencies of mutual gaze (infants and mothers making eye contact) and lip smacking (an important rhesus social behavior).

ETHICS

All ethical principles regarding animal research outlined in Chapter 1 would apply here. The observational method used in this study poses little risk of violating these principles.

RESULTS

The rhesus infant–mother pairs engaged in frequent mutual gaze and lip-smacking behaviors. The infants spent more time gazing at their mothers than at other individuals, and this time increased with the age of the infant. Lip-smacking behavior was also a frequently observed method for mothers and infants to interact with each other. This behavior is never observed among adults, so it is exclusive to interactions with infants.

Mutual gaze and lip smacking both appear to be sensitive to the age of the infant. By the time the infant is in its second month of life, it is spending considerable time outside the mother's vicinity, much as a human child might do when it attends daycare or preschool. As the infant physically separates more frequently from the mother, the frequency of the mutual gaze and lip-smacking behaviors also decreases. The behaviors observed in the enclosed area were confirmed by observations in the more naturalistic setting.

CONCLUSIONS

Rhesus monkeys show some of the same types of mother–infant interactions, believed to enhance bonding, that have been observed in humans. This finding suggests that behaviors that set the stage for social interactions in humans are not unique to our species but rather have their roots in the evolutionary past. ■

Rhesus monkey mothers and infants show many of the same types of behavior that enhance bonding in human mothers and infants, including mutual gaze.
Source: Reprinted from P. F. Ferrari et al. (2009). "Reciprocal Face-to-Face Communication Between Rhesus Macaque Mothers and Their Newborn Infants," *Current Biology, 19*(20), 1768–1772. doi: 10.1016/j.cub.2009.08.055. Copyright © 2009, with permission from Elsevier.

Nina Leen/The LIFE Picture Collection/Getty Images

Harry Harlow (1905–1981) studied infant attachment by removing baby rhesus monkeys from their mothers at birth and providing them with a wire mother, such as the one shown here, and a similar mother covered with carpet. Regardless of which "mother" provided food, the infant monkeys spent more time cuddling with the cloth mother than the wire one. Harlow concluded that "contact comfort" provided by the mother was more important to attachment than the food she provided.

Attachment between child and parent is not unique to humans. To identify behaviors leading to attachment between infants and their mothers, Harry Harlow (1905–1981) investigated attachment in rhesus monkeys (1958). The Freudian theories still popular in Harlow's day suggested that the pleasure obtained through feeding formed the basis of infants' bond with their mothers. Behavioral approaches suggested that the infant was positively reinforced with food for staying near the mother. Harlow was not convinced by either of these arguments and set out to contrast the mother's ability to provide food with her ability to provide comfort, security, and safety.

In research heavily criticized on ethical grounds, Harlow removed newborn rhesus monkeys from their biological mothers. The infants were presented with two surrogate mothers, one made of wire and the other of cloth. Either surrogate could be rigged with a milk bottle, allowing Harlow to investigate all combinations of comfort and feeding. Regardless of which "mother" provided food, infant monkeys spent most of their time clinging to the cloth mother and ran to her immediately when threatened by a novel toy. The wire mothers were visited only if they provided food, and then for only as long as the infant was feeding. Based on his observations, Harlow concluded that the Freudian and behavioral emphasis on feeding was wrong. Instead, the mother's ability to provide contact comfort was critical in forming a strong attachment on the part of her infant.

Harlow's observations of the importance of contact comfort are consistent with more contemporary research demonstrating the importance of touch to infant development. Touch is one of the first senses to develop in the fetus. Touch enhances immune, endocrine, and nervous system development, as well as reducing stress and promoting infant social behavior toward caregivers (Simpson et al., 2019).

A key factor in predicting the timing of attachment appears to be mobility. Young birds that are mobile upon hatching need to form immediate attachments to a protective adult. Human infants, who are not particularly mobile until the second half of their first year of life, have more time to bond with a caregiver. About the same time infants begin to crawl, usually between 6 and 8 months, they also begin to show evidence of having bonded with particular people in the form of separation anxiety (Bowlby, 1969/1982, 1973/1999a, 1973/1999b). Before this stage, infants tolerate being handed around to admiring relatives and babysitters without much protest. Once children demonstrate stranger anxiety, however, they respond to unfamiliar people with crying and distress. Although stranger anxiety might be a nuisance for parents hiring a new sitter or an insult to visiting relatives, it is an important step forward in infants' social development. The children recognize who does and, more importantly, who does not belong in their social world.

UpperCut Images/Alamy Stock Photo

Secure attachment results from responsive parenting that teaches children that the parent is there for them. Unresponsive parenting teaches children that their needs may or may not be met, so their best strategy is to make regular, frequent, and persistent demands for the parent's attention.

Several patterns of attachment between infant and caregiver were demonstrated in classic research by Mary Ainsworth and her colleagues (1978). Young children in a laboratory playroom were observed through a two-way mirror as their mothers or a friendly stranger left or entered the room. Based on the children's reactions to these separations and reunions, their attachment to their mothers was classified as either secure or insecure. Children who demonstrated **secure attachment** played happily and interacted positively with the stranger as long as their mothers were present. However, when their mother left, the children responded by searching for her, crying, and showing other signs of distress. Efforts by a stranger to comfort the children were rejected. When their mother returned, she was greeted warmly, and the children returned to their play.

The remaining children demonstrated different patterns of **insecure attachment**. Two of these, avoidant and anxious–ambivalent attachment, were identified by Ainsworth, and a fourth, disorganized attachment, was identified by other researchers (Main & Solomon, 1986). Children with avoidant attachment did not react to their mother's leaving with distress and allowed themselves to be comforted by the stranger. When the mother returned, the child with an avoidant attachment did not immediately approach her. Children who showed anxious–ambivalent attachment never seemed comfortable, even when their mother was present. Her leaving was greeted with great distress, and the child was alternately clingy and rejecting when she returned. Children with disorganized attachment seemed confused and not well attached. Such children showed contradictory behavior, such as approaching the mother walking backward.

What types of parenting behavior might foster secure attachment? When you are in public places, such as parks and malls, take a minute to watch parents interact with their children. Some parents are sensitive and responsive to their children's needs (Cox et al., 1992). The responsive parents are teaching their children that the world is a predictable place in which their parents are there for them when needed. Consequently, these children feel free to explore their environment, knowing that if an emergency arises, they will be able to quickly and reliably obtain assistance from their parents. Small, securely attached children have a relatively short radius of exploration, which lengthens gradually as they get older.

In contrast, unresponsive or inconsistent parents are teaching their children that the world is an unpredictable place and that the parent may or may not be there for them when needed. In response to such insecure circumstances, children do not venture far from the parent. As suggested by the results of partial reinforcement experiments discussed in Chapter 8, children with unresponsive or inconsistent parents make regular, frequent, and persistent demands for attention because they know that only a small subset of these demands will be met. It might seem counterintuitive, but ignoring children results in clinginess and constant demands for attention, whereas meeting children's needs promptly and reliably fosters independence.

Cultural influences on parenting behaviors influence attachment. Although American psychologists view a secure attachment to be ideal, attachment might be better viewed with an ecological approach than with a universal approach. Secure attachment is a good model for relatively safe societies (Belsky, 1999). In a safe society, parents have the time and resources to be attentive to children, and exploration is unlikely to put the children in danger. In contrast, secure attachments in dangerous societies might be maladaptive. If the environment is dangerous, parents have less opportunity to be responsive to their children, and exploration might put the children in great danger. The message that "The world is an unpredictable place in which we may or may not be able to help you, so stay close" might be more realistic under these circumstances.

Childhood attachment styles continue to influence development later in life, affecting self-esteem and romantic relationships (Feeney & Noller, 1990). Secure attachment in childhood is associated with trusting, confident adult romantic relationships. Avoidant attachment in childhood predicts avoidance of intimacy in adult romantic relationships. The person often terminates a relationship that is getting "too close." Finally, anxious–ambivalent childhood attachment is correlated with a romantic style featuring dependency and possessiveness.

attachment Emotional bond linking an infant to a parent or caregiver.

secure attachment A pattern of infant–caregiver bonding in which children explore confidently and return to the parent or caregiver for reassurance.

insecure attachment A pattern of infant–caregiver bonding that can take several forms but is generally characterized as less desirable for the child's outcomes than secure attachment.

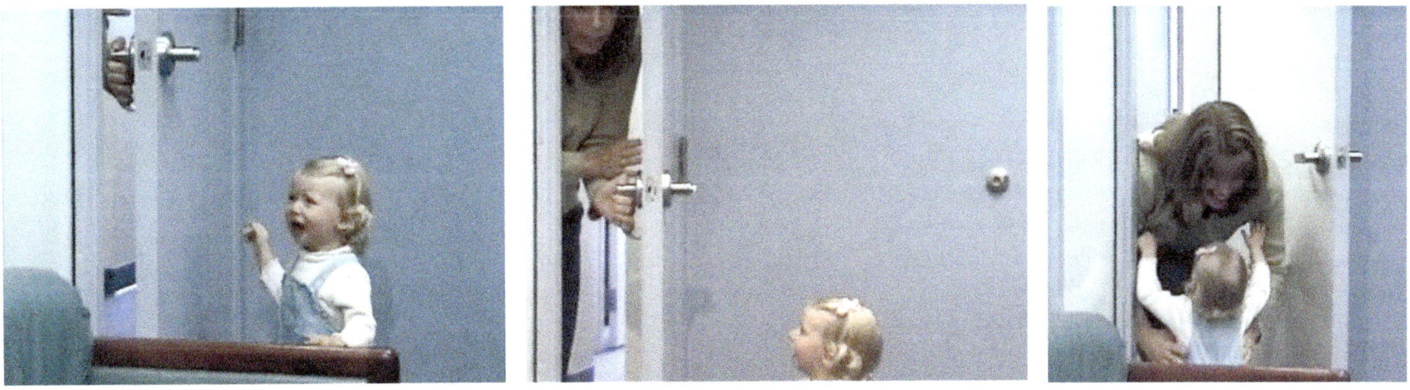

Mary Ainsworth used the "strange situation" to assess the quality of children's attachment to their mothers. While watched through a two-way mirror, the child's mother first leaves and then returns. Using a careful grading scale, researchers rate children as having a secure attachment or one of several variations of insecure attachments.

TABLE 11.4

Parenting Styles

	High parental support	Low parental support
High behavioral regulation	Authoritative	Authoritarian
Low behavioral regulation	Indulgent	Uninvolved

Although attachment styles are relatively stable across the lifespan, they can be modified by experience (Davila et al., 1997). A securely attached individual who experiences a series of negative relationships might become less secure, whereas an insecurely attached individual experiencing positive relationships might become more secure.

Parenting Styles

Not all parents approach parenting the same way. Parenting styles can be divided into four categories that vary along two dimensions: parental support and behavioral regulation (Baumrind, 1975; Maccoby & Martin, 1983). Parental support takes the form of empathy and recognition of the child's perspective. Behavioral regulation involves supervision of the child's behavior accompanied by consistent discipline and clear expectations (Luyckx et al., 2011).

If we look in the upper left-hand box of ● Table 11.4, we find the authoritative parenting style, a cross between high parental support and high behavioral regulation. This is the ideal style for parents, as evidenced by the superior outcomes among children raised by parents using this style (Milevsky et al., 2007; Simons & Conger, 2007). Limits are appropriate for the age and stage of the child's development, and consequences are educational, not punitive. Authoritative parents are consistent and firm but also warm and reasonable. They communicate their standards and invite feedback, but there is no question as to who is running the show.

harvardmagazine.com

In her 2011 book *Battle Hymn of the Tiger Mother,* Amy Chua described her initial efforts to raise her daughters in a "strict, Chinese" fashion instead of a Western style emphasizing self-esteem over achievement, followed by adjustments she made in response to her older daughter's rebelliousness at age 13. Contrary to fears expressed at the time the book was published, Chua's daughters seem to be doing just fine. Sophia graduated from Harvard and received her law degree from Yale. Lulu studied art history at Harvard and is pursuing a law degree from the same institution. How do Chua's experiences fit with our discussion of parenting styles?

The upper right-hand box contains the cross between low parental support and high behavioral regulation, or the authoritarian parenting style. The high behavioral regulation provided by these parents prepares children for the limits they inevitably meet in the community from other authority figures such as teachers and law enforcement personnel, but this is considered a less-than-ideal approach in most contemporary environments because of lower levels of warmth and support (Luyckx et al., 2011). Authoritarian parents have a greater tendency than authoritative parents to place a high value on obedience and to use harsh punishments, including physical punishment. Parents with low socioeconomic status are more likely to demonstrate authoritarian parenting (Friedson, 2016).

In the lower left-hand box, we find the indulgent parenting style, produced by crossing high parental support with low behavioral regulation. In addition to the classic characteristics of high support and low regulation, three dimensions of indulgence have been identified: material, relational, and behavioral (Cui et al., 2019). Material indulgence refers to the provision of excessive possessions. Relational indulgence occurs when parents are overly protective and do things their children should be doing for themselves. Finally, behavioral indulgence refers to parents' having low expectations for responsibility on the part of their children. Children of indulgent parents experience higher levels of depression and anxiety (Cui et al., 2019) and antisocial behavior (Luyckx et al., 2011).

The lower right-hand box represents the cross between low parental support and low behavioral regulation, or the uninvolved parenting style. This style generally does not occur unless there is something seriously wrong with the family situation. Illness, marital discord, psychopathology, or substance abuse can prevent parents from carrying out their duties in regards to their children. By the 12th grade, children of uninvolved parents drink and smoke nearly twice as much as children of authoritarian or authoritative parents, and sons of uninvolved parents are at a very high risk of antisocial behavior (Luyckx et al., 2011) (see Figure 11.19).

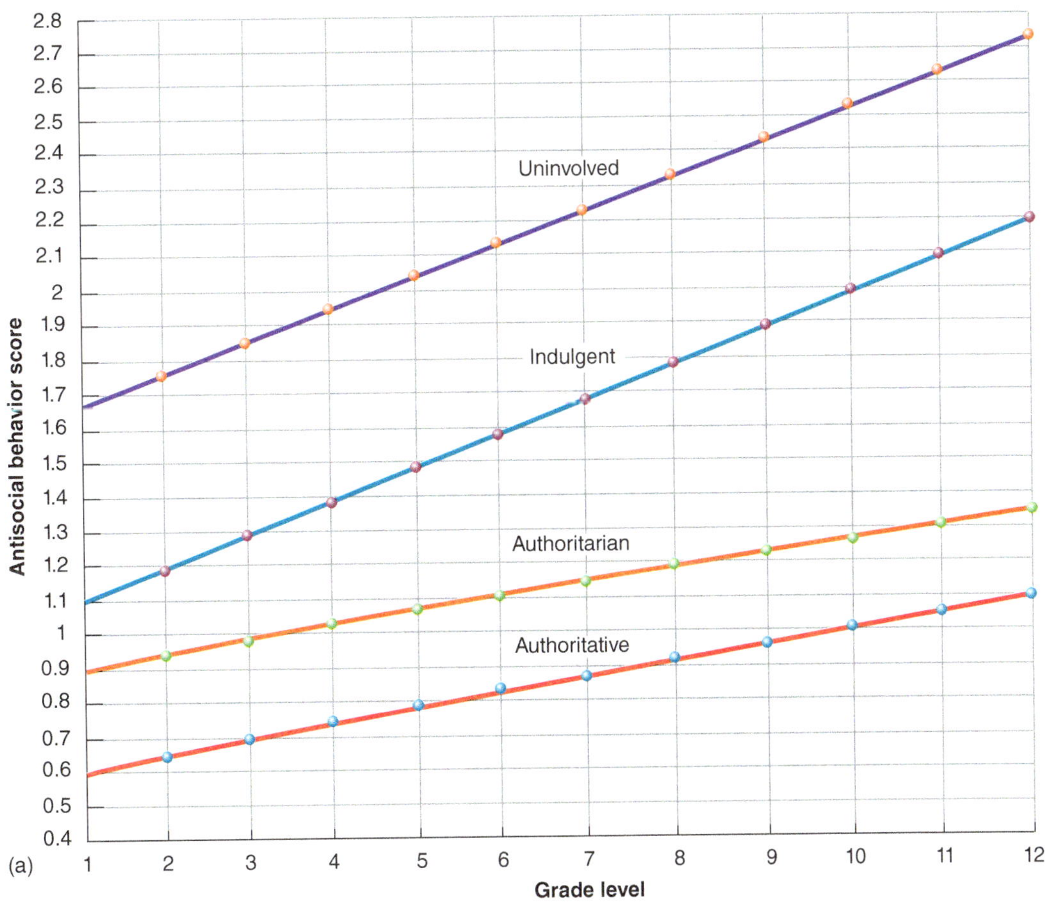

FIGURE **11.19**

Parenting Style and Child Outcomes. Authoritative and authoritarian parenting styles are associated with lower rates of antisocial behavior in children than the indulgent or uninvolved parenting styles. However, children with authoritarian parents experience more depression and withdrawal than do children of authoritative parents.

Source: Adapted from K. Luyckx et al. (2011). "Parenting and Trajectories of Children's Maladaptive Behaviors: A 12-Year Prospective Community Study," *Journal of Clinical Child and Adolescent Psychology, 40*(3), 468–478. doi: 10.1080/15374416.2011.563470

some aspects, this conclusion is correct. By the teens, areas of the brain that process language, spatial relations, hearing, and other sensory processes appear complete. However, much additional work remains to be done before we can consider the brain to be fully adult. Far from considering the brain complete at puberty, today's psychologists are viewing the early teen years as being a second critical period of brain growth, the first being prenatally up to age 18 months (Kuhn, 2008).

The onset of puberty is accompanied by substantial gray matter growth, which peaks between the ages of 11 and 12 years (Semple et al., 2013). Following this burst of growth, the gray matter of the frontal, parietal, and temporal cortex normally thins somewhat over the remainder of the teen years, a process that tapers off in the twenties (Tamnes et al., 2017; see ● Figure 11.21). Abnormalities in this process may be associated with the onset of schizophrenia, described in Chapter 14. Youth with early-onset forms of this disorder show four times more loss of gray matter in the frontal lobes than is usually seen in teens of the same age (Rapoport, 1999). White matter, or myelin, continues to mature gradually through the teen years and into young adulthood. Myelination of the frontal lobes is greater in adults 23 to 30 years old than in youth between the ages of 12 and 16. Unfortunately, an adolescent's white matter is more susceptible than an adult's to damage, such as that caused by binge drinking (McQueeny et al., 2009).

Structural differences between the brains of teens and those of adults affect their interpretations of the emotions of other people (Thomas et al., 2007; Yurgelun-Todd, 2007). Adults

EXPERIENCING PSYCHOLOGY

How Risky Are You?

IN THIS CHAPTER, we explore the impact of brain development on risk-taking. In general, we find that behaving in risky ways is more typical of teens, in spite of the fact that they perceive risk similarly to adults. How do psychologists know this? We can use instruments like the Domain-Specific Risk-Taking (DOSPERT) Scale (Blais & Weber, 2006). To complete this scale, rate each of the 30 items twice: Once for how likely you would be to do the behavior (your risk-taking score) and then for how risky you think the behavior is (your risk-perception score). Once you have your responses, use the codes at the end of the box to divide your scores into the five domains: ethical, financial, health/safety, recreational, and social. Add your scores for risk-taking and risk-perception for each domain. You might find that your behavior and perceptions are quite different from one domain to the next.

1. Admitting that your tastes are different from those of a friend.
2. Going camping in the wilderness.
3. Betting a day's income at the horse races.
4. Investing 10% of your annual income in a moderate growth mutual fund.
5. Drinking heavily at a social function.
6. Taking some questionable deductions on your income tax return.
7. Disagreeing with an authority figure on a major issue.
8. Betting a day's income at a high-stake poker game.
9. Having an affair with a married man/woman.
10. Passing off somebody else's work as your own.
11. Going down a ski run that is beyond your ability.
12. Investing 5% of your annual income in a very speculative stock.
13. Going whitewater rafting at high water in the spring.
14. Betting a day's income on the outcome of a sporting event
15. Engaging in unprotected sex.
16. Revealing a friend's secret to someone else.
17. Driving a car without wearing a seat belt.
18. Investing 10% of your annual income in a new business venture.

Risk-taking Scale:

1	2	3	4	5	6	7
Extremely Unlikely			Not Sure			Extremely Likely

Risk Perception Scale:

1	2	3	4	5	6	7
Not at all Risky						Extremely Risky

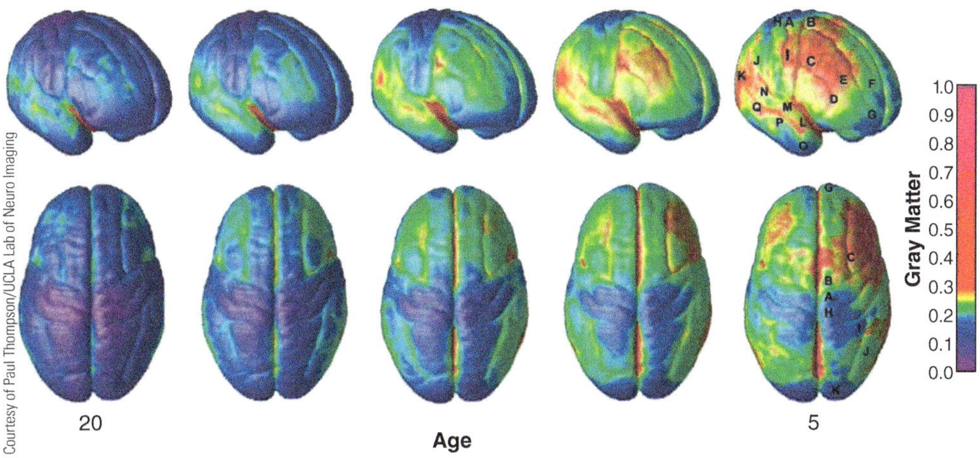

FIGURE **11.21**

Brain Growth in Adolescence. In contrast to early developmental theories such as Jean Piaget's theory that viewed the mind as mature at the outset of adolescence, gray matter growth continues into early adulthood, although the pace slows, and the cortex thins in some areas. Areas shown in red and yellow are experiencing the greatest rates of growth.

identify expressed emotions accurately, but teens frequently misunderstand the emotions being displayed. Brain imaging demonstrated that the amygdala, which provides a quick, subconscious assessment of emotion, showed the same pattern of activity in adults and teens. However, the adults showed more activity in the frontal lobes than the teens did, which might account for the adults' superior judgment of emotional expression.

19. Taking a skydiving class.
20. Riding a motorcycle without a helmet.
21. Choosing a career that you truly enjoy over a more secure one.
22. Speaking your mind about an unpopular issue in a meeting at work.
23. Sunbathing without sunscreen.
24. Bungee jumping off a tall bridge.
25. Piloting a small plane.
26. Walking home alone at night in an unsafe area of town.
27. Moving to a city far away from your extended family.
28. Starting a new career in your mid-30s.
29. Leaving your young children alone at home while running an errand.
30. Not returning a wallet you found that contains $200.

Ethical: 6, 9, 10, 16, 29, 30
Financial: 3, 4, 8, 12, 14, 18
Health/Safety: 5, 15, 17, 20, 23, 26
Recreational: 2, 11, 13, 19, 24, 25
Social: 1, 7, 21, 22, 27, 28

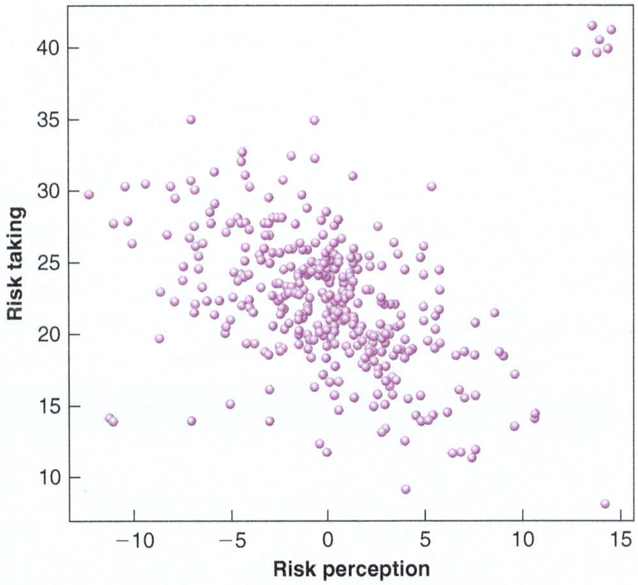

FIGURE **11.22**

Risk Taking and Risk Perception. Risk taking and risk perception are negatively correlated in individuals (see Chapter 2). As the perception of riskiness increases, people are less likely to take a risk.

Source: A.-R. Blais & E. U. Weber (2006). "A Domain Specific Risk-Taking (DOSPERT) Scale for Adult Populations," *Judgment and Decision Making*, 1(1) 33–47. doi: 10.1037/t13084-000.

ZUMA Press Inc/Alamy Stock Photo

During adolescence, youths apply their new executive strategies to problems and build their knowledge base for specific subjects. High school senior Ronit Abramson won an Intel International Science and Engineering Fair prize for her science project on marine biology.

A "mismatch model" has been proposed to account for the greater levels of risk-taking and sensation-seeking that characterizes adolescence as compared to childhood and adulthood (Dumontheil, 2016). The more emotional parts of the brain, including the amygdala and reward systems, mature earlier relative to the logical frontal lobes, possibly leading to reckless and drunk driving, driving without seatbelts, experimenting with drugs, and having unprotected sex. Risky behavior does not result from the teen's inability to judge what is risky or not (Fischhoff et al., 2010). Instead, teens typically believe that they are somehow immune from the consequences of risky behavior—for example, that drunk driving accidents happen to other people (Reyna & Farley, 2006). The teen brain also responds more vigorously to pleasure than does the adult brain, which means that the immediate pleasurable consequences of a risky behavior can overwhelm the teen's better judgment (Galvan et al., 2007).

Cognitive and Moral Development in Adolescence

The continuing maturity of the nervous system, interacting with the expanding physical and social environment of the adolescent, leads to more adult ways of thinking and reasoning.

Adolescent Cognition During adolescence, executive functions such as working memory reach adult levels (Murty et al., 2016). Adolescents begin to think more logically or analytically (Kokis et al., 2002). For example, children often use their personal experience as a heuristic (the teacher didn't catch my friend cheating on the test, so it's safe for me to cheat too) instead of the more logical, statistical reasoning of the teen (my friend might have had a lucky break, but this teacher is extra good at catching cheaters, so my odds of getting caught remain high despite my friend's experience).

Teens are hard at work acquiring data, and as they build up their knowledge bases, their ability to use executive processes such as strategies improves (Peverly et al., 2002). As we mentioned in Chapter 9, the more you know about a subject, the easier it becomes to learn new things about it. You acquire skills specific to a subject, such as how to solve statistics problems or prepare for a final covering thousands of pages of reading in your literature course.

Moral Reasoning Our human history and literature are filled with heroes and villains, and we are fascinated by their development. How does one child grow to be Mother Teresa and another to be Adolf Hitler?

Lawrence Kohlberg, a student of Piaget's, attempted to extend Piaget's theory of cognition to explain the development of moral reasoning (1981, 1984). To assess changes in moral reasoning, Kohlberg presented children, adolescents, and adults with a series of ethical dilemmas. He was not as interested in the choice participants would make in response to the dilemma as he was in the reasoning participants provided their choice.

Based on the participants' responses to his dilemmas, Kohlberg identified three major stages in moral reasoning, shown in ● Table 11.5. Children and young adolescents are typically in the **preconventional morality** stage. In this stage, children make moral choices based on

preconventional morality Lawrence Kohlberg's stage at which moral choices are made according to expectations of reward or punishment.

TABLE 11.5

Lawrence Kohlberg's Stages of Moral Development

Stage	Features
Preconventional	Uses probability of rewards and punishments to guide behavior.
Conventional	Maintains reputation and follows the law.
Postconventional	Follows self-chosen ethical principles.

their expectations of reward and punishment. Some individuals never progress beyond this stage, even in adulthood, and believe that stealing or cheating is okay as long as they don't get caught.

Kohlberg believed that during adolescence most of the population moves to the next stage, **conventional morality**, and stays there throughout adulthood. In this stage, rules are seen as governing moral behavior and are, therefore, to be followed. Conventionally moral people are also sensitive to public opinion. They want to do the right thing so that others will approve of their behavior. Although conventional morality adds to the stability of a society, it runs the risk of being arbitrary and rigid. In addition, history is full of situations in which local public opinion was supportive of morally abhorrent activities, such as genocide or slavery.

conventional morality Lawrence Kohlberg's stage of moral development in which moral choices are made according to law or public opinion.

postconventional morality Lawrence Kohlberg's stage at which moral choices are made according to personal standards and reason.

identity A consistent, unified sense of self.

The final step of moral development for Kohlberg was **postconventional morality**. Relatively few people, according to Kohlberg, attain this stage. In conjunction with the abstract reasoning of formal operations, the individual now recognizes that rules are made by humans and can, therefore, be flawed. Consequently, personal standards are used as reference points. If everybody used postconventional reasoning to select a driving speed on the highway, chaos would ensue. However, the postconventional thinker is likely to evaluate laws and rules critically before complying with them.

Kohlberg is not without his critics. Although Kohlberg's earlier stages appear to be universal across many cultures (Jia & Krettenauer, 2017), postconventional reasoning has been criticized as characteristic of males in Europe and the United States (Murphy et al., 1994). Children and adults living in the United States give responses to Kohlberg's dilemmas consistent with the culture's emphasis on personal justice and individual rights. Other cultures place a higher priority on interpersonal factors, such as duty and responsibility to others, and these values can lead to different responses to ethical dilemmas (Miller & Bersoff, 1992).

Kohlberg assumed that moral decisions were made through reasoning, but other psychologists view these as fairly automatic responses shaped by evolution. Jonathan Haidt (2007) identified five dimensions of morality: harm, fairness, ingroup, authority, and purity. Not only do cultures vary in their emphasis on these factors, but individuals endorsing liberal and conservative political ideologies do as well. In several countries, political liberals place more emphasis on harm and fairness than the other values, while conservatives weigh the five values more evenly (Graham et al., 2009).

Social and Emotional Development in Adolescence

As the teen prepares to transition to adulthood, questions emerge about what kind of adult to be. The focus of social activity begins to shift from the family to the peer group, which is where most adult interaction will be taking place.

Identity Formation in Adolescence We pick up social development in adolescence by introducing Erik Erikson, a student of Sigmund Freud who outlined stages of social development beginning in infancy, shown in ● Table 11.6. Erikson (1968) made significant contributions to our understanding of **identity**, or a unified, consistent sense of self. For Erikson, social development proceeds in stages, with each stage characterized by a fork in the road between a positive outcome and a less desirable outcome. Adolescence challenges teens to develop a sense of identity (the positive outcome). If they fail, the result is role confusion (obviously, the less desirable outcome).

Teens begin the process of identity formation by asking such questions as "Who am I?" and "What kind of person do I want to be?" These are profound questions, made possible by the newly developed abstract reasoning skills of the teen. The answers are not immediately apparent. Considerable exploration may be necessary before the teen discovers a direction. Many teens try on several identities, from jock to nerd to goth, before finding one that works.

SteveSimonsPhotography/Shutterstock.com

Many teens explore questions of identity by trying on different roles and affiliating with different groups.

TABLE 11.6

Erik Erikson's Psychosocial Stages

Stage	Challenge	Description
Birth to 18 months	Trust versus mistrust	Children view the world as a safe, dependable place.
18 months to 3 years	Autonomy versus shame and doubt	Children begin to explore.
3–6 years	Initiative versus guilt	Children begin to act on the world.
6–12 years	Industry versus inferiority	Children develop self-confidence.
Adolescence	Identity versus role confusion	Teens begin to form an identity by asking "Who am I?" Failure to achieve a stable identity leads to role confusion and problems with subsequent stages.
Young adulthood	Intimacy versus isolation	Young adults with clear identities form stable, intimate relationships, while others experience feelings of loneliness and isolation.
Midlife	Generativity versus stagnation	Midlife adults who find value in their lives, even if they have not met all their earlier goals, experience generativity. They are likely to "put back" energy into family, work, and community.
Late adulthood	Integrity versus despair	Toward the end of life, adults who feel that they have lived fully experience a sense of integrity and calm.

Because developing an identity can be somewhat unpleasant, teens may be tempted to short-circuit the process. One technique for prematurely adopting an identity is to assume the identity of a group (Erikson, 1968). By affiliating with a particular club, clique, or gang, teens take on a preformed identity and avoid the challenges of finding their individual identities. A second approach is the adoption of ready-made identities provided by parents or other mentors. Although parents may have valuable advice regarding choice of college major and career, these are highly individual choices with significant implications.

Erikson, like most classical theorists, is not without his critics. Erikson's approach to identity has been particularly influential compared to his other stages, but critics object to its focus on the Western male experience (Sorell & Montgomery, 2001).

The Benefits of Ethnic Identity For many adolescents, ethnic identity, or how an individual feels about being a member of a particular ethnic or racial group, is a major part of their overall identity (see Figure 11.23). Having an ethnic identity boosts the overall self-esteem of adolescents and young adults (Erol & Orth, 2011; Rivas-Drake et al., 2014). A growing number of individuals identify with more than one ethnic or racial group. In the United States, multiracial youth experience less racial identity affirmation than African-American youth, but both groups experience more affirmation than white youth (Fisher et al., 2014).

Family and Peer Influences Running parallel to the search for identity is a tendency on the part of teens to spend more time with peers and less with family. A healthy balance between family and peer influences appears to produce the best outcomes. Teens who continue to interact positively with their parents experience better outcomes (see Figure 11.24; Fulkerson et al., 2006). Eating dinner with family members is associated with better diet, fewer eating disorders, lower levels of substance abuse, and better academic performance (Walton et al., 2016).

The importance of the peer group to adolescents can be demonstrated by their heightened sensitivity to peer exclusion. Compared to adults over the age of 22, adolescents reported significantly worse mood following an experimental procedure designed to instill feelings of social exclusion (Blakemore & Mills, 2014). Teens are also more susceptible than adults to negative peer influence. Compared to young adults and older adults, adolescents made many more risky decisions when in the presence of peers than while alone (Chein et al., 2011; Simons-Morton et al., 2014).

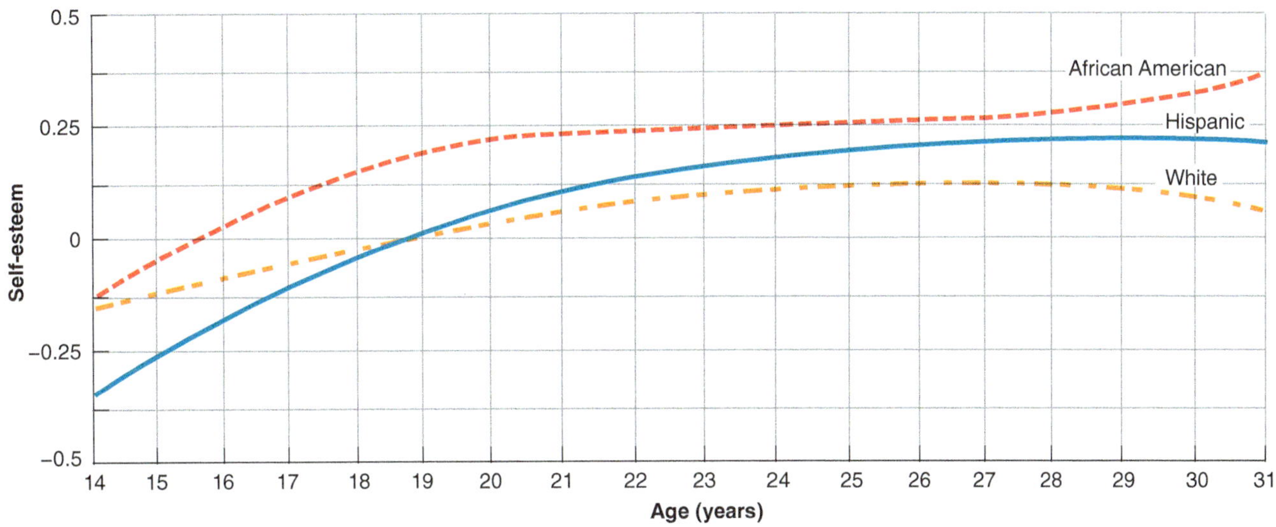

FIGURE **11.23**

Ethnic Identity May Lead to Higher Self-Esteem. Identifying with an ethnic group appears to boost the overall self-esteem of African American and Hispanic teens during adolescence and young adulthood. Psychologists have pointed out the need to obtain more data about Asian American ethnic identity and self-esteem.

Source: Adapted from R. Y. Erol & U. Orth (2011). "Self-esteem Development from Age 14 to 30 Years: A Longitudinal Study," *Journal of Personality and Social Psychology*, *101*(3), 607–619. doi:10.1037/a0024299

In contrast to popular press accounts of the "stormy" teen years, many teens (and their parents) navigate their passage to adulthood with no more than a few bumps and bruises (Steinberg & Levine, 1997). Compared to stages before and after adolescence; however, the negative emotionality, frequency of conflict with parents, and risk-taking behaviors that characterize adolescence can make this a more difficult time for many families (Arnett, 1999).

Sexuality looms large in the context of adolescent peer interactions. After all, the biological purpose of puberty is to prepare individuals for reproduction. The influence of high levels of sex hormones during adolescence makes sexuality highly salient. For both sexual-majority and sexual-minority youth, adolescence typically marks the start of exploration and sexual identity formation than extends into a person's late twenties (Kaestle, 2019).

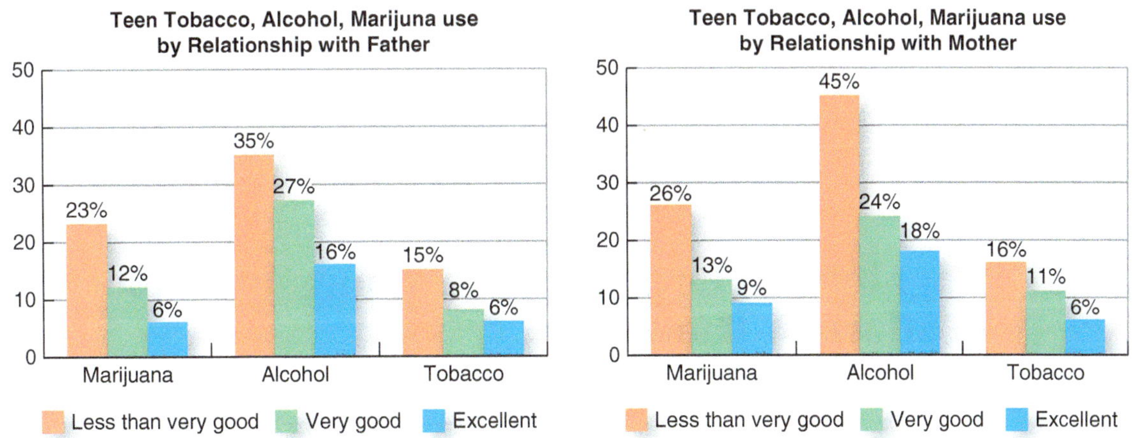

FIGURE **11.24**

Family Remains Important in Adolescence. Adolescence is a time characterized by increasing focus on relationships with peers, but strong relationships with family members remain important. Teens who report lower quality relationships with their parents are more likely to use marijuana, alcohol, and tobacco.

Source: http://www.centeronaddiction.org/addictionresearch/reports/importance-of -family-dinners-2012.

What Is It Like to Be an Emerging or Young Adult?

As we mentioned previously, defining the exact point when a person becomes an adult is not easy. Numerous roles are considered as marking this transition, including the completion of education, full-time employment, independent living, marriage, and parenthood. People do not usually assume all these roles simultaneously, leading to a gradual emergence of adulthood over a period of several years.

The experience of 18- to 25 year-olds in developed countries differs in several respects from the experience of young adulthood after the age of 25, leading to the identification of a stage of emerging adulthood (Arnett, 2014; see • Figure 11.25). Emerging adults continue the exploration of identity begun in adolescence. Their experience in love, work, and place of residence is relatively unstable. At no other time of life is self-focus stronger. Having moved away from the parental home and without having taken on marriage and parenting roles, the emerging adult has far fewer obligations to others than people at other stages of life. Emerging adults recognize a feeling of transition, being neither adolescents nor adults. They agree that at this stage of life, "it still seems like anything is possible."

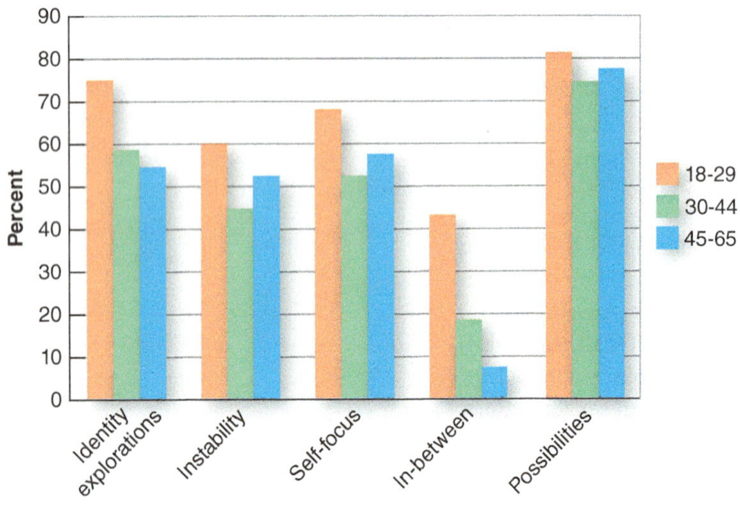

FIGURE **11.25**

Features of Emerging Adulthood. Jeffrey Arnett (2014) identified five factors that distinguish emerging adulthood from later stages of adulthood. Emerging adults are still more likely to be engaged in exploring identities. They are less stable in place of residence, romantic relationships, and work. They remain more focused on themselves and describe a feeling of being "in-between" adolescence and adulthood. They are slightly more likely than individuals in other age groups to believe many possibilities lie ahead of them.

Source: J. J. Arnett (2014). *Emerging adulthood: The winding road from the late teens through the twenties*. New York, NY: Oxford University Press.

Physical Status in Emerging and Young Adulthood

The young adult has reached the pinnacle of physical development. If you are in this age group, you are as tall, strong, and fit as you're ever likely to be. Your brain is mature by your early twenties, and your senses and reaction time are in excellent shape.

It is not too early for young adults to consider how to best maintain their physical health. Through childhood and adolescence, we have seen that physical development often follows a blueprint that is strongly genetic. In adulthood, however, lifestyle factors begin to play a greater role in a person's outcomes. Emerging adulthood represents a transition from the behavioral causes of death (unintentional accidents, suicide, and homicide) in adolescence and health-related causes of death in later life, such as diabetes and heart disease (Neinstein & Irwin, 2013). Continued risk-taking in emerging adulthood coupled with vocational instability leaves many emerging adults without appropriate health care.

Cognition in Emerging and Young Adulthood: Postformal Thought

In your college experience, you might have seen a professor become annoyed by a student's inquiry about "the right answer." The search for a single answer, however, is characteristic of formal operations as described by Piaget. At formal operations stage of cognitive development, the teen can follow a logical course of steps to solve a problem (Guignard & Lubart, 2006; Wu & Chiou, 2008). Lack of agreement with the solution is viewed by the formal operational thinker as a sign that the solution is incorrect.

Although many questions we face in college have right answers, such as an element's atomic weight or whether a hypothesis was shown to be incorrect, many more are open to debate. The professor's frustration with your fellow student's interest in only one right answer reflects a difference in adolescent versus adult thinking, or postformal thought. Postformal thought recognizes that the "right answer" is often "it depends" and that many important questions are complex and ambiguous (King & Kitchener, 2002). Adolescents are more likely to think in absolutes and defer to authorities, such as professors (Perry, 1970). Efforts to move adolescents toward independent, postformal thought are often described as critical thinking exercises, described in Chapter 2.

THINKING SCIENTIFICALLY

Are Younger Generations More Narcissistic Than Previous Generations?

Since the time of Aristotle, it has been almost a tradition to despair over the traits of young people. Younger generations are being accused of higher levels of narcissism (Twenge, 2013). In Chapter 14, we will explore narcissistic personality disorder, which is characterized by an inflated sense of importance, a high need for attention, troubled relationships, and reduced empathy. While the full disorder is rare, many people possess some of these characteristics, possibly in milder forms.

WHAT AM I BEING ASKED TO BELIEVE OR ACCEPT?

We are being asked to accept that younger generations are experiencing higher levels of narcissistic traits compared to older generations, possibly due to cultural changes such as parenting style and social media.

WHAT EVIDENCE SUPPORTS THIS POSITION?

Generational cohorts are shaped by their shared experiences, such as war, recession, and pandemics in ways that might shape narcissism (Vater et al., 2018). In 1963, only 12% of adolescents agreed with the statement "I am an important person," but levels of agreement went up to 77% to 80% by 1992 (Newsom et al., 2003). Twenge (2013) argues that the U.S. culture is becoming more individualistic and self-oriented. Television shows are more likely to focus on fame, books use more individualistic language than previously, and song lyrics are more narcissistic and antisocial. Scores on scales that measure narcissistic traits are increasing (see Figure 11.26). Simultaneously, scores on instruments measuring empathy declined (Konrath et al., 2011).

ARE THERE OTHER WAYS THIS EVIDENCE COULD BE INTERPRETED?

As we mentioned in Chapter 2, developmental research requires special methodologies. So it comes as no surprise that research showing an increase in narcissism across cohorts has been criticized on the basis of the methods and statistical analyses used (Wetzel et al., 2017).

WHAT OTHER EVIDENCE WOULD I NEED TO EVALUATE THESE ALTERNATIVES?

Most of the research in this area has been conducted with convenience samples of college students. Across decades, changing demographics, such as the proportion of racial and ethnic minorities attending college, might influence conclusions in significant ways. Comparisons of more representative samples would be useful. A better understanding of the trajectories of both narcissistic traits and empathy over the lifespan would provide a better foundation for evaluating cohort effects (Chopik & Grimm, 2019; Oh et al., 2020).

WHAT ARE THE MOST REASONABLE CONCLUSIONS?

We have conflicting reports, with the majority of researchers arguing that the observed changes in narcissism and empathy are real. Improved instruments and statistical analyses might eventually give us a clearer picture. Further research into the causes of narcissism and empathy would also be helpful. ■

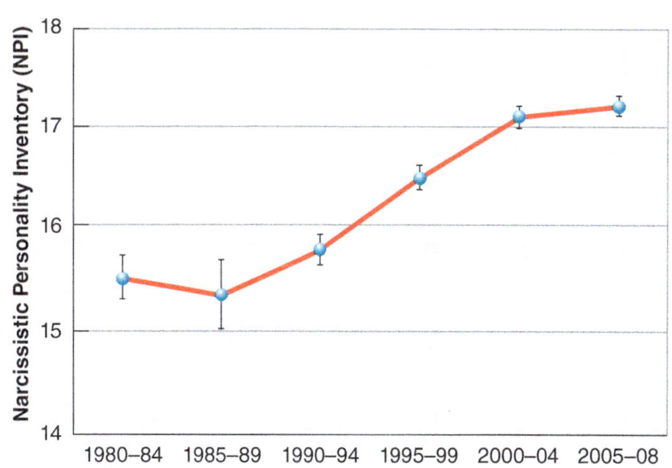

FIGURE **11.26**

Younger Generations and Narcissism. Scores on the Narcissistic Personality Inventory (NPI) have risen since 1990.

Source: J. M. Twenge (2013). "The Evidence for Generation Me and Against Generation We," *Emerging Adulthood, 1*(1), 11–16. doi: 10.1177/2167696812466548

Becoming a parent is no longer restricted to young adulthood. In 1970, the average age of first-time mothers was 21, and few women became mothers for the first time after the age of 35. Today, many women are postponing parenting until midlife.

Why is it important to embrace postformal ways of thinking? In Chapter 2, we discussed the importance of generating and testing new hypotheses to move science forward. Using formal operations, a student can evaluate a hypothesis and conclude whether it needs to be rejected. However, postformal thinking is an integral part of creativity, in science or in any other field (Guignard & Lubart, 2006). Scientists who are unable to look beyond the "right answers" already existing in their fields are unlikely to make creative contributions that stretch that knowledge.

Relationships in Emerging and Young Adulthood

As teens enter young adulthood, Erickson suggests that they confront a new challenge: Intimacy versus isolation. Those who fail to find the level of intimacy they seek might experience feelings of loneliness, which in turn can elicit behaviors that are more likely to alienate others instead of promoting intimacy (Cacioppo & Cacioppo, 2018). One key to successful intimacy, according to Erikson, is to have established a solid identity in adolescence. If you still don't know who you are, it is unlikely that you will make good judgments about the type of person who will make you happy. If the process of identity extends into emerging adulthood, as suggested by Arnett (2014), this will further delay relationship stability.

The general instability of emerging adulthood applies to relationships and sexuality (Arnett, 2014). For both sexual-majority and sexual-minority individuals, emerging adulthood can be a time of transition and exploration (Morgan, 2013). The major theme during this stage in life is diversity—no one pathway determines how people will develop sexual orientations and identities.

For those who choose to have children, the experience of being parents often dominates much of their adult lives. The relationship between the parenting role and happiness is complex and changing. Most parents experience an initial boost in happiness after the birth of a child followed by a gradual decline (Nelson-Coffey, 2018). Among the variables impacting the parenting experience are socioeconomic status and relationship quality. For example, couples' relationship quality acts as a significant buffer against depression in mothers of children with autism spectrum disorder (see Figure 11.27; Weitlauf et al., 2014).

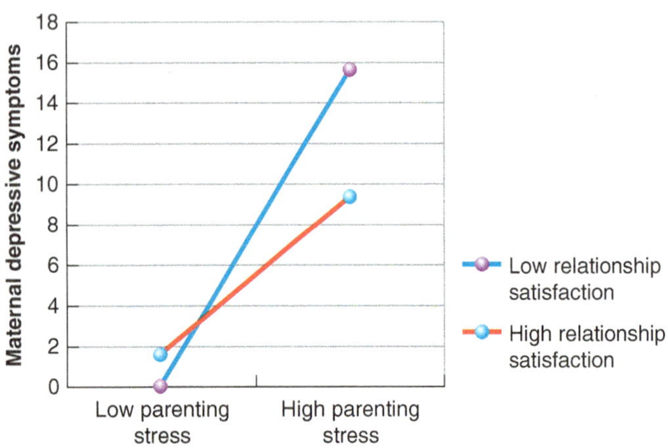

FIGURE 11.27

Marital Satisfaction Can Buffer Parenting Stress. Parenting is tough under any circumstances, but parenting children with special needs puts parents under considerable strain. Mothers of children with autism spectrum disorder are at higher risk for major depressive disorder, but less so when they have strong relationships with their partners. *Source:* A. S. Weitlauf et al. (2014). "Relationship Satisfaction, Parenting Stress, and Depression In Mothers of Children with Autism. *Autism, 18*(2), 194–198. doi: 10.1177/1362361312458039

What Happens During Midlife?

Just as our criteria for leaving adolescence for emerging and young adulthood were somewhat vague, we do not have a set of reliable characteristics that signal the transition between young and middle adulthood. Some people view a specific age, such as 40, as a starting point for midlife. Psychologists often point to physical changes, such as graying hair or menopause in women, as signposts for this new transition. Others suggest that a person's growing sense of mortality, possibly boosted by the death of a parent, leads to a feeling of being closer to death than to birth (Jaques, 1965).

Just as the "storm" of adolescence has been often exaggerated, you have probably heard popular accounts assuming that we all have some "midlife crisis" (Levinson et al., 1976). For most people, this is simply not true (Rosenberg, 1999). Middle adulthood is not without its challenges because many adults find themselves simultaneously caring for children and aging parents, working to meet their career and financial goals, and dealing with physical and possibly marital changes. However, there appears to be no evidence for a large-scale crisis associated with any one age.

Physical and Cognitive Aspects of Midlife

The major theme of physical and cognitive development in midlife is stability. Assuming that people maintain good health, changes in the physical and cognitive domains tend to be mild and gradual.

The most significant physical change in midlife for females is the end of their ability to reproduce. **Menopause** is the point where menstruation stops. For most females, menopause is complete in their early 50s, but loss of fertility is a gradual process beginning many years earlier. Menstrual cycles may become irregular in a female's 40s as her sex hormone levels that regulate the cycles begin to drop. During the period of transition between the start of irregular periods and the final disappearance of menstruation, females can experience a number of physical and psychological symptoms. Hot flashes, night sweats, headaches, joint pain, mood swings, and sleep disturbances are common complaints, and the severity of these issues can range from barely noticeable to nearly disabling. Hormone treatments to offset these symptoms are used quite cautiously because they can also increase a female's risk of stroke, heart attack, breast cancer, and later dementia (Banks & Canfell, 2009).

menopause The complete cessation of a woman's menstrual cycles.

Males experience more gradual changes in their reproductive status through the remainder of their lives. Sperm quantity may be reduced, but males in their 80s remain half as fertile as males who are 25. Most males experience little to no decrease in testosterone over the course of the midlife years, although other conditions, such as diabetes, can interfere with the maintenance of an active sex life. For both males and females in midlife, the availability of a partner is more predictive of sexual activity than any health issues (Karraker et al., 2011).

Social Changes in Midlife

In contrast to the relative stability in the physical and cognitive domains during midlife, this period of life is characterized by significant changes in social and work roles. Children grow up and move out. If you are the youngest child in your family, you may have noticed that your parents are beginning to feel somewhat more relaxed. For many parents, the "empty nest" period following their last child leaving home is accompanied by an improvement in marital satisfaction (Birchler, 1992). Your parents no doubt love you, but they're also relieved to leave many of the responsibilities of parenting behind them. However, as ● Figure 11.28 shows, the likelihood that negative emotions will accompany an empty nest varies from culture to culture (Mitchell & Lovegreen, 2009).

Blue Jean Images/Alamy Stock Photo

With increasing life expectancies on one side and later parenthood on the other, many contemporary midlife adults find themselves "sandwiched" or caring for their aging parents and growing children at the same time.

Adults in midlife continue to pursue their careers, becoming more expert, or they might initiate a new career that was not previously compatible with the financial and social responsibilities of raising a family. Recent economic and social changes have made midlife work less stable than it has been for previous generations. Today's midlife workers express intent to stay employed longer than previous cohorts (at least until age 65), but some find themselves taking jobs below their levels of skill and experience or withdrawing from employment (Elman, 2011).

During midlife, Erikson suggests that adults experience either generativity or stagnation. Many people, particularly during adolescence, set a number of goals for themselves. You may want to win a Nobel Prize or compete in the Olympics or simply help others have a better life. Whatever your goals, by the time you reach midlife, you will have a good idea about whether these goals will be met. In many cases, people find that progress has been made toward their goals, although they perhaps didn't meet them. Wherever an adult finds himself or herself at midlife, the question posed by Erikson is whether value exists.

FIGURE **11.28**

Responses to the Empty Nest Vary Across Cultures. Although most Americans report positive reactions to their last child leaving home, reactions vary across cultures. Among Canadians of different ethnic groups, being an empty-nest parent has different meanings. Parents from Chinese and Southern European cultures are less likely to report negative responses to their last child leaving home than are parents with a British background. Parents from India experienced the most negative response of all groups studied.

Source: Adapted from B. A. Mitchell & L. D. Lovegreen (2009). "The Empty Nest Syndrome in Midlife Families," *Journal of Family Issues, 30*(12), 1651–1670. doi:10.1177/0192513x09339020

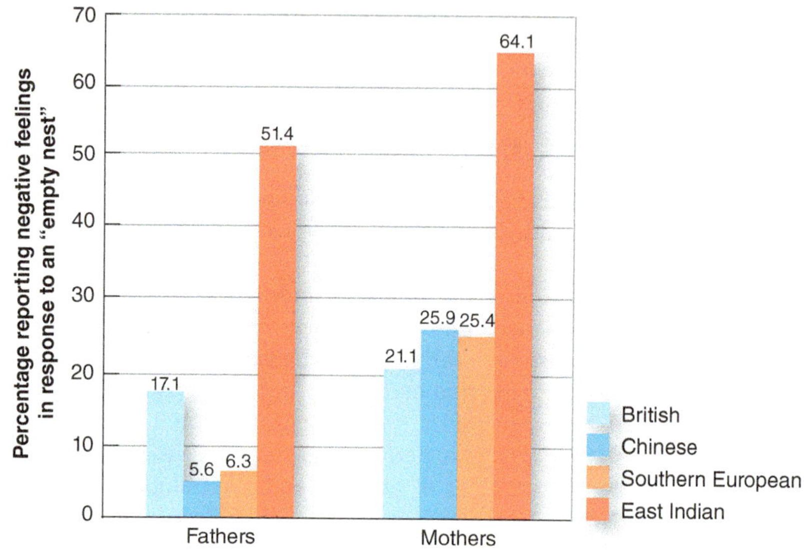

If people feel that their lives have had value, even if they fall short of their goals, they experience generativity. Adults experiencing stagnation, in contrast, have not found much satisfaction in their lives.

What Is Late Adulthood Like?

As we have seen in our discussion of previous stages of development, the starting point of late adulthood is vague. You might think of age 65, a common retirement age, as a starting point, but many of today's older adults are living and working longer than ever before and so are thinking about "old age" differently than in the past. For example, the baby boomers, or individuals born between 1945 and 1964, are more likely than other age groups to choose 72 as the start of old age (Cohn & Taylor, 2010). Current life expectancy at birth in the United States is 78.6 years (Centers for Disease Control, 2017).

Physical Changes in Late Adulthood

Assuming good health, the effects of aging on an adult's physical status are gradual and rather mild. Nonetheless, some physical change is inevitable, and understanding the nature of these changes provides guidance for coping with them.

The brain reaches maturity around age 25, and few further changes occur until about the age of 45. At that time, the weight of the brain begins to decrease, leading to about a 5% decrease by the age of 80 (Anderton, 1997). Decreases in volume are not even. Some structures, such as the hippocampus and the prefrontal white matter, are more impacted by age than other areas, such as the occipital lobe (Raz et al., 2005). Decreases also vary substantially from one individual to the next, possibly reflecting underlying lifestyle and health variables. As with other physical changes, age-related changes in sensory abilities are gradual, and their effects can be offset by the use of technologies, such as eyeglasses and hearing aids.

Cognition in Late Adulthood

The most notable cognitive changes in late adulthood involve memory. Episodic memory, or memory for personal experiences (see Chapter 9), begins to decline gradually from mid-life into late adulthood (Peters, 2006). Episodic memories are also the component of cognition

Fauja Singh, born in 1911, competed in marathons worldwide until his retirement in 2013 as part of the Sikhs in the City team, a group of four runners whose combined age is more than 330 years. Running marathons isn't necessary to prevent cognitive decline, but people who participate in 20 minutes or more per day of physical activity have the lowest rates of dementia.

most likely to be affected by Alzheimer's disease. In contrast, semantic memories, or memories for facts, increase gradually from mid-life until the early part of late adulthood, and then decrease in very late adulthood.

Intelligence remains relatively stable during adulthood, as long as general health is good. Although many people erroneously believe that aging is inevitably accompanied by loss of intellect, only about 8.8% of the population over the age of 65 experience dementia, such as Alzheimer's disease (Langa et al., 2017). Rates of dementia have been dropping over the last three decades (Satizabal et al., 2016) and nearly 25% between 2000 and 2012 alone (Langa et al., 2017). Improved control of cardiovascular disease and higher levels of education might account for some of these improvements.

Certain types of intelligence change more because of aging than others. As we discussed in Chapter 10, crystallized intelligence, or the use of accumulated knowledge, changes less than fluid intelligence, or a person's basic information processing skills (Horn & Hofer, 1992). Fluid intelligence correlates with speed of processing, whereas crystallized intelligence might be viewed as wisdom, or the ability to draw on past knowledge and experience to solve problems. The relatively gradual decrease in cognitive skills seen in older adults might represent the ability to use crystallized intelligence to compensate for decreasing fluid intelligence abilities, especially in domains that are familiar and well-practiced (Zaval et al., 2015). For example, many U.S. Supreme Court justices have served ably well into their 80s.

Creative output can also be tracked across the lifespan. Creative output usually peaks in a person's 30s to 40s then declines gradually (Simonton, 2017). Considerable individual variation occurs, however. The most creative people usually produce their first important work earlier, maintain a high level of output throughout their careers, and continue to produce later in life than less creative people.

Social and Emotional Aspects of Late Adulthood

In later adulthood, Erikson suggests that people experience either integrity or despair. Older people who are happy with their life's experiences generally experience integrity (Sneed et al., 2006; Vaillant & Koury, 1993). They met their goals for the most part and had a fun time doing so. In contrast, people who reach late adulthood feeling that life passed them by are likely to experience a sense of despair.

PSYCHOLOGY AS A HUB SCIENCE

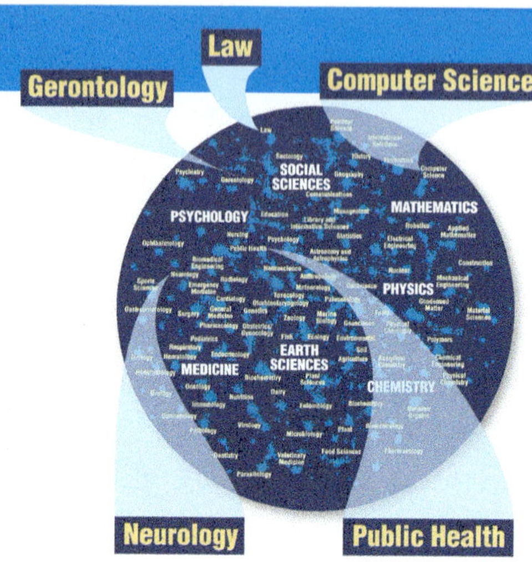

Psychology and the Well-being of Older Americans

PEOPLE TURNING 65 YEARS OF AGE in 1950 could expect to live about 13.8 more years, or until age 78.8, whereas people turning 65 in 2015 are likely to live 19.3 years longer, or until about age 84.3 (Gatz et al., 2016). Quantity, of course, does not guarantee quality, so psychologists have investigated ways to improve the well-being of older adults. These investigations have produced valuable results in five domains: knowledge about healthy cognitive aging, understanding decision-making, ways to encourage good health habits, understanding of stereotypes and bias, and improved adaptive technologies.

Not only has psychological research identified neural correlates of healthy and unhealthy cognitive aging, but psychologists have collaborated with legal experts regarding judgments of diminished capacity. As a result, older Americans with cognitive deficits enjoy better protection from abuse, neglect, and financial exploitation (Gatz et al., 2016). Psychology's contributions to improved understanding of decision-making, particularly the effects of aging on decision making, can assist older adults and those helping them make better decisions related to retirement and medical care.

In Chapter 8, we explored basic principles of behavior change related to classical and operant conditioning. Many habits, which respond to behavioral methods, have critical influence on healthy lifestyles, regardless of age. Developing healthy habits and reducing unhealthy behaviors can have significant effects on well-being. In an upcoming chapter, Chapter 13, you will learn more about how stereotyping and biases can have negative influences on the targets' outcomes. Psychology provides tools for tackling bias among health care providers, such as the willingness of physicians to rate suicidal ideation in 78-year-olds as normal and not needing treatment (Uncapher & Areán, 2000). New technologies, such as social media, have transformed the ability of all age groups to interact with others and seek information. Technologies have the potential to help older adults remain in their homes, but this will require access to digital devices and the knowledge of how to use them.

Monkey Business Images/Shutterstock.com

Overall, psychology has already made significant contributions to policy decisions and allocations of resources related to the aging population, and is likely to continue doing so in the future. ■

You might hold a common stereotype about older adults being sad and lonely. If so, you will probably be surprised to learn that psychological research has found that depression is higher in young people than in healthy, older adults (see ● Figure 11.29). Loneliness actually decreases with age into the 70s, when it begins to increase again (Hawkley et al., 2019). Given the frequent challenges of aging, including physical and cognitive changes, what could possibly account for this positive emotional well-being? Part of the explanation lies in the way people look at the time they have remaining in life (Carstensen et al., 2003, 2010). When people see a long stretch of time remaining in their lives, they pursue achievement, possibly at the expense of meeting their social and emotional needs. In contrast, when older adults are looking at a shorter period of remaining life, their goals are refocused toward seeking positive emotional experiences.

Grown children and grandchildren play an important part in the social life of many older adults. Unlike other primates, humans live long past their reproductive years, suggesting that grandparents may have historically contributed to the survival of their extended families.

One thing that doesn't change during our journey through the life span is the need for social connection. Older adults show significant benefits from their friendships, but they have fewer of them than younger adults and are less likely than younger adults to form new ones (Rawlins, 2004). Relationships with siblings can be especially meaningful for older adults (Gilligan et al., 2020).

Relationships with grown children and grandchildren also form a significant part of the social life of older adults. Historically, many parents entered the role of grandparent during midlife, but with more young adults postponing parenting, the grandparent role is occurring later as well. Humans are somewhat unusual among primates in their length of life span beyond their reproductive years, a phenomenon known as the "grandmother effect." A healthy woman might live 40 or 50 years past her age at menopause. It is possible that her contributions to the care of her grandchildren, freeing her children for other tasks, might have provided an adaptive advantage over the course of evolution (Herndon, 2010).

Marriage in late adulthood makes an important contribution to continued good health. In married older adults, interacting with the spouse contributes to happiness by buffering the individual from stress (Waldinger & Schulz, 2010). Seniors who have remained married to the same person for decades have seen many changes in their relationships over the years.

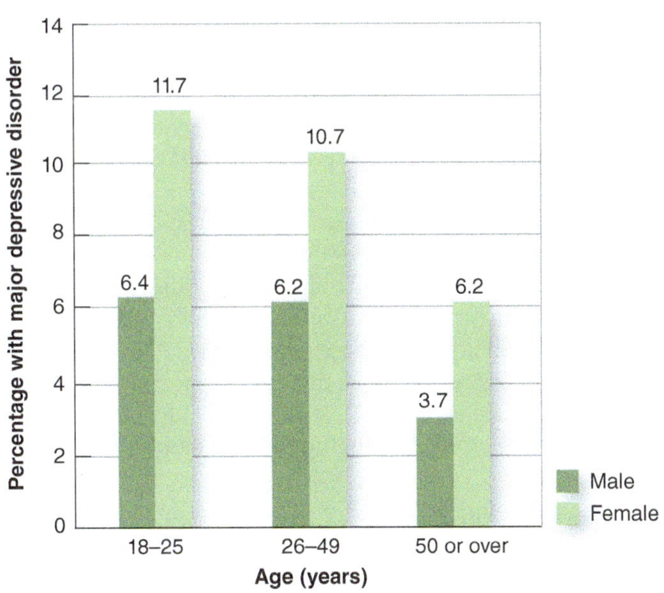

FIGURE **11.29**

Depression Rates Decrease Over the Life Span. In contrast to stereotypes about sad, older adults, depression rates are highest in late adolescence and young adulthood and decrease gradually over the life span.
Source: Adapted from R. C. Kessler et al. (2003). "The Epidemiology of Major Depressive Disorder: Results from the National Comorbidity Survey Replication (NCS-R)," *JAMA, 289*(23), 3095–3105. doi:10.1001/jama.289.23.3095

Relationships continue to play important roles in the social lives of older adults. Marriage is related to continued good health in older adults.

We observed earlier that parents of young children experience a drop in marital satisfaction, which improves as children leave the home as young adults. Long-term marriage partners show more similarities with each other because of a lifetime spent in each other's company, along with a characteristic lack of attention to past negative events and personality traits (O'Rourke & Cappeliez, 2005). In other words, they believe their relationship has been more positive than it was. These couples also show an interesting pattern of conflict avoidance, which contributes to higher levels of marital satisfaction.

Interpersonal Relationships
The Developmental Perspective

IS THERE A "PERFECT" TIME TO GET MARRIED?

One of your authors (LF) and her husband married, much to the horror of their respective families, at the age of 20. Gloom and doom predictions about the length of the marriage followed. But are there "good" and "bad" ages at which to get married?

What do you think is a good age for marriage? 25? 35? Never? Your answer might be based on a social clock, or the cultural norms for the timing of developmental milestones (Neugarten et al., 1965). You might find that you have many entries in your social clock—when to finish your education, when to be established in your career, when to marry, when to become a parent, when to retire—that are probably based on your cultural background and the observed experiences of your family and friends.

Did you choose a number in the late 20s as ideal for marriage? If so, you are probably reflecting the current median age at first marriage in the United States (27 for females, 29 for males; Bartle-Haring et al., 2018). The median age at first marriage reflects economic and social factors, dropping from 1900 (22 for females; 26 for males) to 1950 (20 for females; 23 for males) and then rising gradually to current levels.

The "right time" approach was supported initially by findings that satisfaction was highest for those who married in their early to mid-twenties (Glenn et al., 2010). Couples marrying earlier experienced more instability while those who married later tended to have stable, but less satisfying marriages. More recent research does not support this mid-20s "right time" hypothesis, however (Bartle-Haring et al., 2018). Instead, individual expectations and historical contexts interact with age at marriage in significant and complex ways to predict a couple's outcomes.

Were your author's detractors correct? No—she is still married decades later, and happily so. ■

Psychology Takes On Real-World Problems

Pandemic Anxiety Across the Lifespan

Do people of all ages respond the same way to the uncertainties and disruption of a major pandemic? Policy makers need to understand the extent of pandemic-related anxiety in the population. Anxiety can negatively impact the mental health of the public, but it can also serve as a motivator for positive behavioral changes.

Feelings of stress, worry, and anxiety are higher in younger individuals than in older individuals under the best of circumstances (Gould & Edelstein, 2010). COVID-19 has approximately doubled pre-pandemic rates of anxiety disorder (Kwong et al., 2020). Most respondents admit to moderate-to-high worry about COVID-19, but older adults, and particularly older males, were less worried than younger individuals and older females (Barber & Kim, 2020). This is not the result of unrealistic perceptions of risk. On the contrary, older adults accurately perceived their risk as being high. These findings are consistent with more general observations that younger adults experience more health anxiety than older adults (Gerolimatos & Edelstein, 2012).

COVID-19 is an unusual virus in that it is dramatically more dangerous for older adults, and older men in particular, compared to children and younger adults (Wortham, 2020). Does the reduced concern on the part of the most vulnerable individuals interfere with their taking necessary precautions? This appears to be the case. Older males are the least likely to engage in protective behaviors, such as wearing masks and social distancing (Barber & Kim, 2020).

Now that we have a better understanding of the problem, we can direct policy in effective ways. Younger adults need more interventions than older adults to bring anxiety under better control. Older adults, especially men, would benefit from targeted messaging that would encourage them to take more precautions. ■

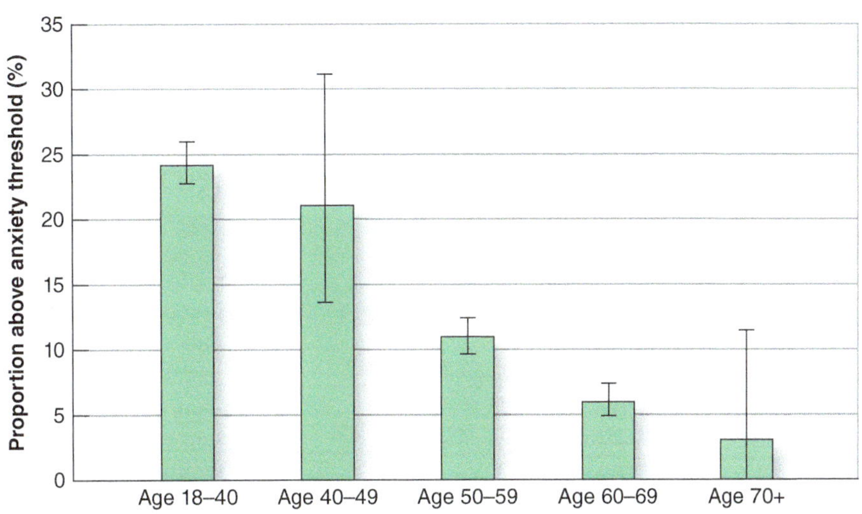

FIGURE **11.30**

Anxiety Rates Doubled During COVID-19. Rates of anxiety disorder during COVID-19 were twice as high as pre-pandemic levels measured in the same population (24% versus 13%). Anxiety was highest in younger age groups and declined gradually with age.

Source: A. S. F. Kwong, R. M. Pearson, M. J. Adams, K. Northstone, K. Tilling, D. Smith, D., . . . N. J. Timpson (2020). "Mental Health during the COVID-19 Pandemic in Two Longitudinal UK Population Cohorts," *The British Journal of Psychiatry*, 1–27. doi:10.1192/bjp.2020.242

SUMMARY 11.3 Highlights of Adolescent and Adult Development

Aspect of development	Highlights
Physical change 	• Adolescents mature sexually and reach adult height and weight. • The brain continues to grow through adolescence and into young adulthood. • Menopause is a major transition for women in midlife. • Among healthy older adults, physical changes are gradual.
Cognition 	• Working memory and reaction time reach adult levels during adolescence. • Thinking becomes more logical during adolescence and more independent in young adulthood. • Moral reasoning in adults is usually conventional or postconventional. • Intelligence remains relatively stable in healthy adults.
Social and emotional life 	• Adolescents seek to develop identity. • Relationships might lead to marriage and parenting in young adulthood. • Midlife adults may experience changes in family and work domains. • Older adults show significant benefits from social connections.

Credits: Top row—Universal Images Group North America LLC/Alamy Stock Photo; Second row—ZUMA Press Inc/Alamy Stock Photo; Bottom row—Blue Jean Images/Alamy Stock Photo.

KEY TERMS The Language of Psychological Science

Be sure that you can define these terms and use them correctly.

accommodation, p. 427
adolescence, p. 438
assimilation, p. 426
attachment, p. 434
concrete operational stage, p. 428
conservation, p. 428
conventional morality, p. 443
egocentrism, p. 428
embryo, p. 411
fetal alcohol syndrome (FAS), p. 414
fetus, p. 411
formal operational stage, p. 428
identity, p. 443
insecure attachment, p. 434
menopause, p. 449
object permanence, p. 427
postconventional morality, p. 443
preconventional morality, p. 442
preoperational stage, p. 427
puberty, p. 439
secondary sex characteristics, p. 439
secure attachment, p. 434
sensorimotor stage, p. 427
teratogen, p. 413
theory of mind (TOM), p. 430
zygote, p. 411

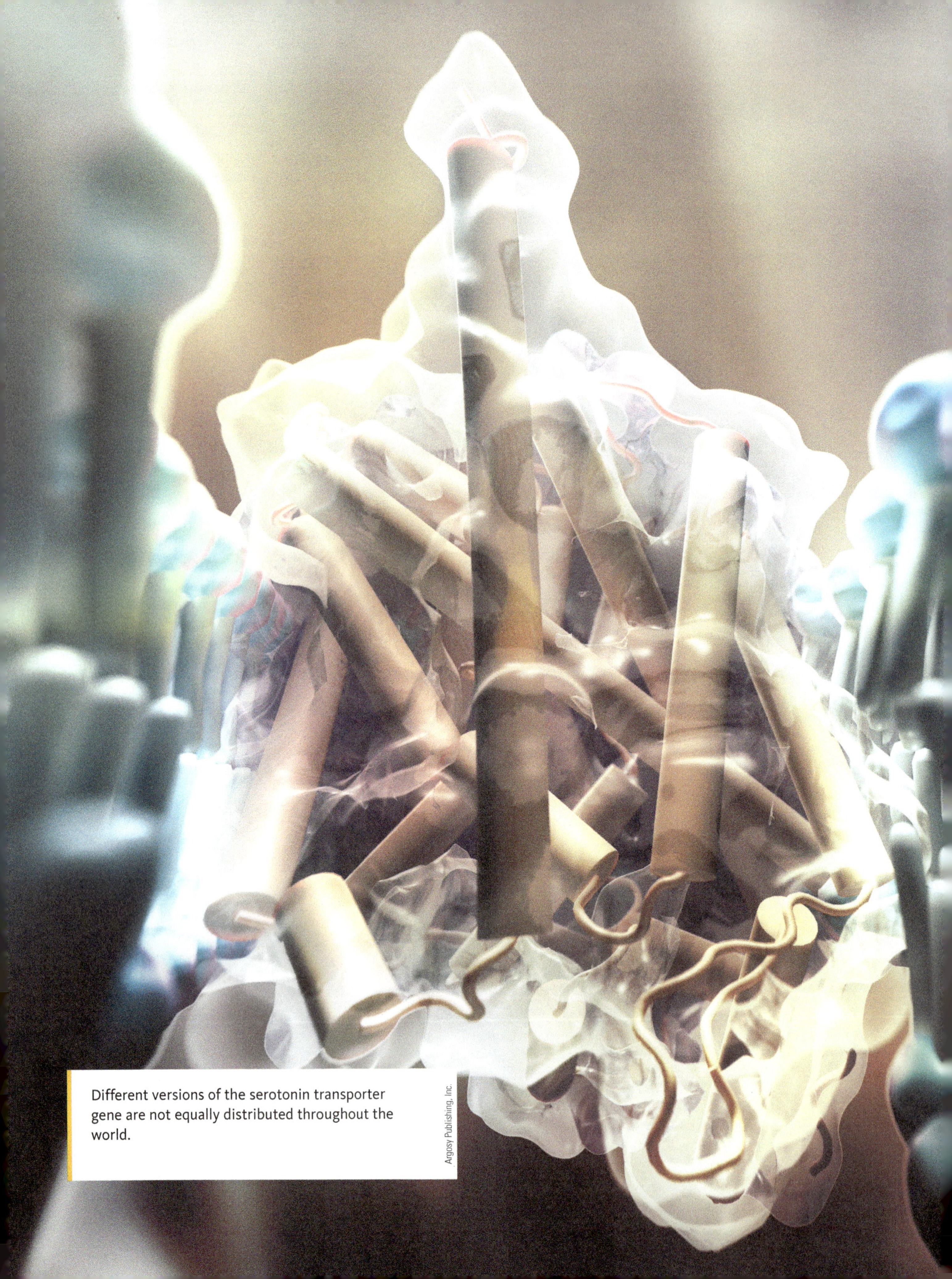

Different versions of the serotonin transporter gene are not equally distributed throughout the world.

Argosy Publishing, Inc.

12

The Individual Mind

PERSONALITY AND THE SELF

LEARNING OBJECTIVES

1. Compare and contrast the psychodynamic, humanistic, trait or Big Five, and social–cognitive theories of personality.
2. Debate the validity of self-report inventories versus projective tests as measures of personality.
3. Differentiate and illustrate several distinct aspects of self (self-concept, self-awareness, self-esteem, and self-regulation) in terms of their content, sources, and implications.
4. Analyze evidence for the biological bases of personality and the self.
5. Distinguish between the personal and interpersonal self, and relate these to cultural differences in individualistic versus collectivistic aspects of self-concept.

ALTHOUGH YOU MIGHT BE COMFORTABLE WITH THE IDEA THAT a trait like a moth's color can make it better adapted to one environment over another, how do you feel about your personality as an adaptation? Are there some types of personalities that thrive in some circumstances better than others? Can a culture shape personality? Can the personalities of a group of people shape their culture?

In Chapter 3, we introduced you to the serotonin transporter gene, which can come in two versions or alleles: Short (S) and long (L). Children with two short alleles (SS) were more likely than children with either a combination of alleles (SL) or two long alleles (LL) to react negatively to the experience of being bullied frequently (Sugden et al., 2010). Zooming out to the map of the world, you can see that these genotypes are not equally distributed worldwide. Yellow areas on the map have low frequencies of the S allele, and orange and red areas have higher frequencies. South Africa has a relatively small number of people with the S allele (28%) compared to the United States, Australia, and Great Britain (about 40% to 45%), which in turn have many fewer than China (about 80%).

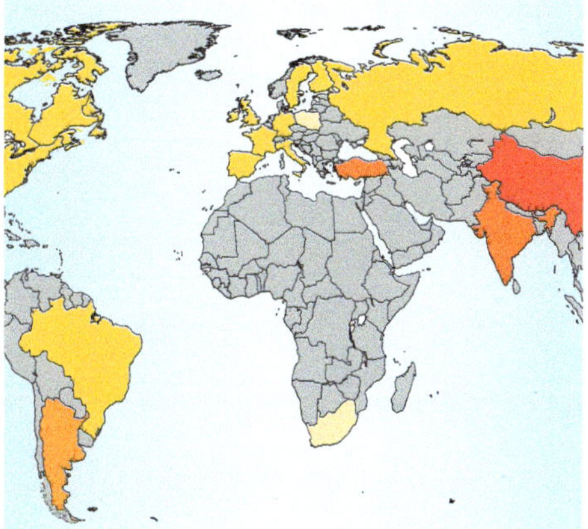

How can we explain these different distributions of the S allele? It is possible that unequal distributions of genes occur by chance, or genetic drift (see Chapter 3; Eisenberg & Hayes, 2011). However, cultural neuroscientists suggest an alternative explanation. It is possible that a particular environment shapes a population's genetics and culture, which in turn influence each other or coevolve (Mrazek et al., 2013; see ● Figure 12.1).

In this chapter, we will consider a number of variables that influence the individuals who develop and live within a culture, including dimensions of individualism and collectivism. Cultures can also be characterized by their strength of social norms and tolerance for deviant behavior, or

Glow Asia RF/Alamy Stock Photo

East Asians have a much higher probability of having the S allele of the serotonin transporter gene than do people living in many other parts of the world.

so-called tightness—looseness (Gelfand et al., 2011). Cultural tightness might have evolved in response to ecological threats, which can be biological, environmental, or human-made. Tight cultural norms, found in nations such as India, Singapore, Turkey, and Japan, encourage structured, coordinated responses to threat. In contrast, loose cultures, found in countries like Estonia, Hungary, Israel, and the Netherlands, face less frequent ecological threats requiring coordinated responses.

What role might genetics play in these cultural differences? Zooming in to the level of the individual, we find that people carrying the S allele are especially attentive to negative information, such as words and pictures that produce negative emotions (Beevers et al., 2007; Osinsky et al., 2008). This focus on negativity might help people detect and respond to risks in threatening environments. The L allele, in contrast, is associated with reduced responses to psychological and social sources of stress (Nardi et al., 2013; see Figure 12.2).

It is possible that dangerous environments favor those who are better at detecting threat, who in turn build tight cultures as a further mechanism for coping with anxiety and coordinating responses (Mrazek et al., 2013). At the same time, people with the S allele might be more successful in navigating the social structures that characterize tight cultures. As you will see in this chapter, individual differences are an important aspect of behavior and mental processing, but they are best understood when viewed within the larger contexts of the social and cultural environment.

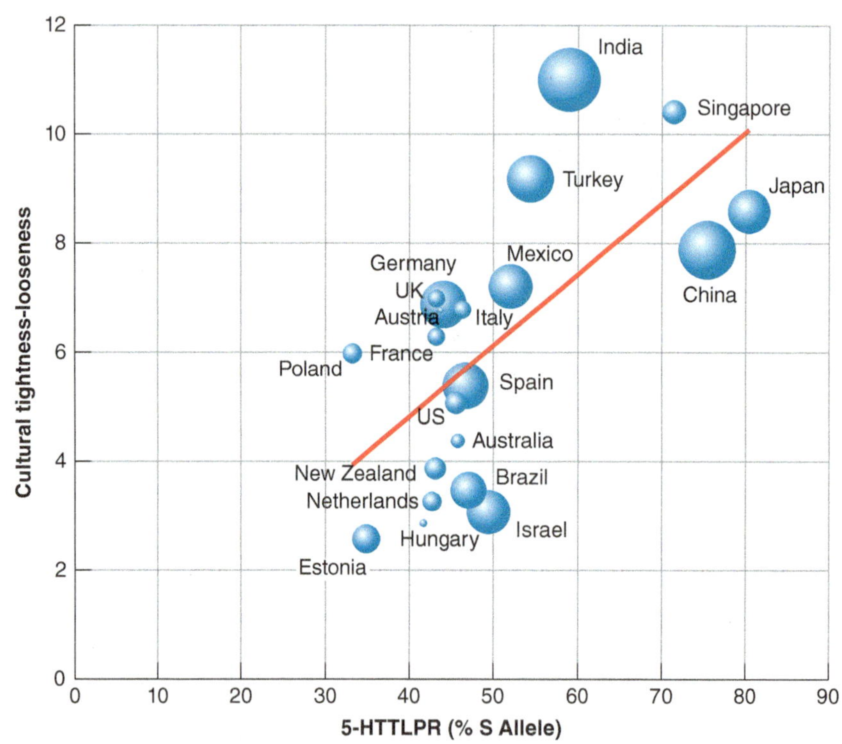

FIGURE **12.1**

The Distribution of the Short (S) Serotonin Transporter Allele as a Function of Culture Type. The percentage of people carrying the S allele of 5-HTTLPR, or the serotonin transporter gene, varies according to a culture's position on the continuum from tightness (highly structured with low tolerance of social deviance) to looseness (less structure and higher tolerance of social deviance). The size of the bubbles reflects a culture's level of ecological threat. Tight cultures are associated with greater ecological threat and higher proportions of the S allele within their populations.

Source: Adapted from A. J. Mrazek et al. (2013). "The Role of Culture-Gene Coevolution in Morality Judgment: Examining the Interplay between Tightness–Looseness and Allelic Variation of the Serotonin Transporter Gene," *Culture and Brain, 1,* 100–117. doi: 10.1007/s40167-013-0009-x

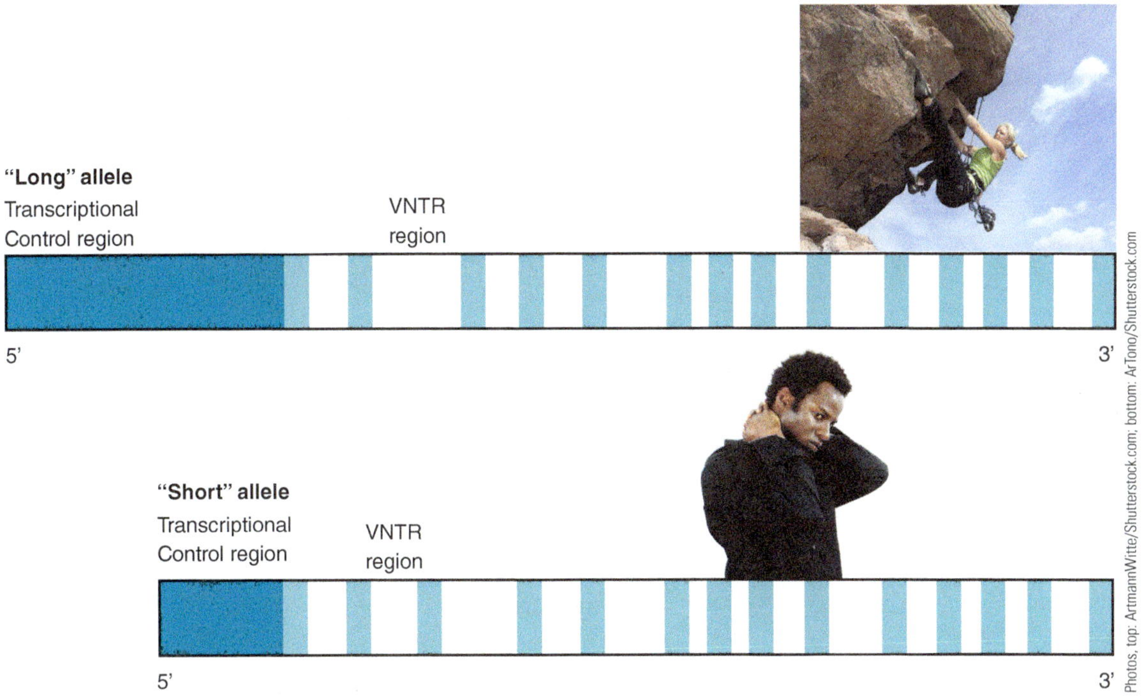

FIGURE **12.2**

The Serotonin Transporter Gene. The serotonin transporter gene comes in two versions or alleles. People with a copy of the short (S) allele tend to focus more on negative information, possibly leading to increased anxiety, whereas people with a copy of the long (L) allele are less influenced by psychological and physical sources of stress.

What Is Personality?

Suppose that you were given the following feedback about your personality (Forer, 1949, p. 120):

> You have a need for other people to like and admire you, and yet you tend to be critical of yourself. Although you have some weaknesses, you are generally able to compensate for them. You have considerable unused capacity that you have not turned to your advantage, however. Disciplined and self-controlled on the outside, you tend to be worrisome and insecure on the inside. At times, you have serious doubts as to whether you have made the right decision or done the right thing. You prefer a certain amount of change and variety and become dissatisfied when hemmed in by restrictions and limitations. You also pride yourself as an independent thinker and do not accept other's statements without satisfactory proof. But you have found it unwise to be too frank in revealing yourself to others.

How well does this description fit your beliefs about your personality? You might be impressed by how this paragraph presents such specific and personalized information about you. Ironically, you probably relate to this description because it applies to nearly everyone. So, the question is: If our personalities are so unique, how can we all be so easily described in a few brief sentences?

The science of personality explores characteristic patterns of thinking, feeling, and behaving. To what extent is a person's personality truly unique, and to what extent is personality based on general characteristics that describe nearly everyone? How consistent is our behavior across time and across situations? How much of a role does biology or experience play in developing our personalities? Is the basic nature of humans good or bad?

Personality is our characteristic way of thinking, feeling, and behaving. How unique are we? How much do our personalities overlap with the personalities of other people?

Rawpixel.com/Shutterstock.com

Personality theories represent far more than simple curiosity about human behavior. These theories are intimately bound to our views of normal and abnormal behavior, which we will discuss in Chapter 14. Many of the psychologists who proposed personality theories also contributed influential ideas to the treatment of psychological disorders.

Historical Approaches to Personality

The study of personality for the first half of the 20th century was dominated by the psychodynamic approaches of Sigmund Freud and his followers. Behaviorists such as B. F. Skinner attempted to apply principles of learning to personality. The humanistic psychologists, including Carl Rogers, actively rebelled against Freud's psychodynamic approach. While few contemporary psychologists adhere to these historical approaches to personality, these theories stimulated interest in individual differences.

How Do Psychodynamic Theories View Personality?

The term **psychodynamic** was first used by Ernst von Brücke in 1874 (Hall, 1954/2016). Von Brücke used the term as an extension of the first law of thermodynamics, which states that energy in a closed system can change from one form to another but cannot be created or destroyed. You may not have heard of von Brücke before, but you are likely to be familiar with one of his students, Freud, who made psychodynamics the foundation of his theory of personality.

As a young physician, Freud became famous for his success in treating patients with hysteria, a condition characterized by physical symptoms without medical cause that is known today as *somatic symptom disorder* (see Chapter 14). Freud sought to incorporate his observations of his patients into a new, unifying theory of psychology. His treatment approach, which we cover in Chapter 15, was known as **psychoanalysis**.

psychodynamic A theory put forward by Sigmund Freud in which psychic energy moves among the compartments of the personality: id, ego, and superego.

psychoanalysis Sigmund Freud's treatment approach based on his psychodynamic theory.

id The component of Sigmund Freud's personality theory containing primitive drives present at birth.

ego The component of Sigmund Freud's personality theory that is the self that others see.

The Id, Ego, and Superego

Personality was viewed by Freud as a closed energy system, in which "psychic" or instinctive energy moves among three compartments: id, ego, and superego (see ● Figure 12.3). Freud proposed that the **id**, which literally means "it" in Latin, is present at birth and contains the primitive drives that serve as a source of energy for the personality, such as hunger, thirst, and sex. Freud believed that the id operates according to the pleasure principle, seeking immediate gratification and relief. As a child begins to interact with parents and other social influences, the ego and the superego begin to control the id. The **ego** is the component of the personality that is readily seen by others, so it acts as the person's "self."

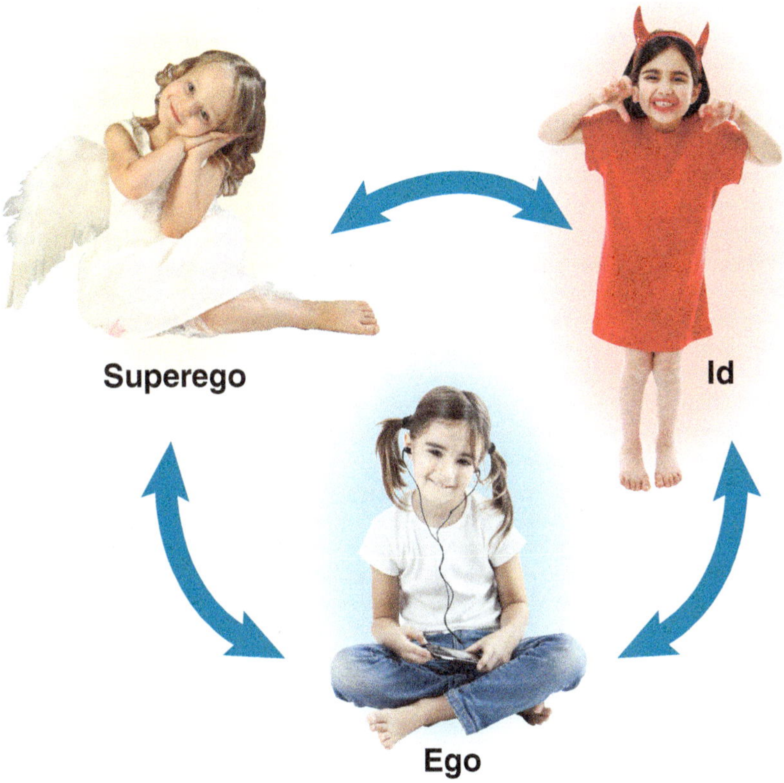

Photos, clockwise from top left: LukFu/Shutterstock.com; hartphotography/Shutterstock.com; iko/Shutterstock.com

FIGURE **12.3**

The Id, Ego, and Superego. Sigmund Freud viewed the mind as a closed system in which energy flows from one compartment to the next. It is the job of the ego, or self, to balance the pleasure-seeking impulses of the id with the morality imposed by the superego. Imbalances can be the source of unhealthy behavior. An overly dominant id can lead to antisocial behavior, and an overactive superego might produce too much guilt.

Its task is to coordinate the needs of the id with reality. The **superego** develops when a child begins to internalize society's rules for right and wrong, forming what we normally refer to as a conscience. As shown in ● Figure 12.4, we are not conscious of the operations of the id, although we might become consciously aware of the operations of the ego and superego.

Freudian Defense Mechanisms Threats to the balance of the id, ego, and superego can result in anxiety or the sense that danger is around the corner. When the ego is faced with anxiety, it engages in a variety of protective behaviors called **defense mechanisms**. According to Freud, each of these mechanisms helps us channel potentially self-destructive or painful psychic energy into more constructive or manageable behaviors. For example, when we use the defense mechanism of sublimation, we redirect negative energy. An aggressive teen might take up martial arts rather than starting fights at school. Freud noted, though, that each mechanism has its limits; if people continually use defense mechanisms, they risk doing damage to the ego or self as well.

Psychosexual Stages of Development For Freud, the development of the personality is critical to the remainder of his theories and to the therapeutic process of psychoanalysis. Freud assumed that the origins of his patients' problems could be found in their developmental past, not in their present circumstances. As the word *psychosexual* implies, Freud was interested in how the developing personality would deal with the sexual impulses of the id. Freud proposed five **psychosexual stages** of personality development: Oral, anal, phallic, latency, and genital. Personality, according to Freud, is the product of conflict occurring during these psychosexual stages. Personality characteristics emerge as the id, ego, and superego resolve their conflicts and struggle for balance. Should the conflict become so great as to produce a clash between ego and reality, psychosis (including abnormal behaviors characteristic of schizophrenia and other serious disorders) might occur (Freud, 1938).

superego The component of Sigmund Freud's personality theory that internalizes society's rules for right and wrong, or the conscience.

defense mechanism In Sigmund Freud's personality theory, a protective behavior that reduces anxiety.

psychosexual stage A stage in Sigmund Freud's theory of the developing personality.

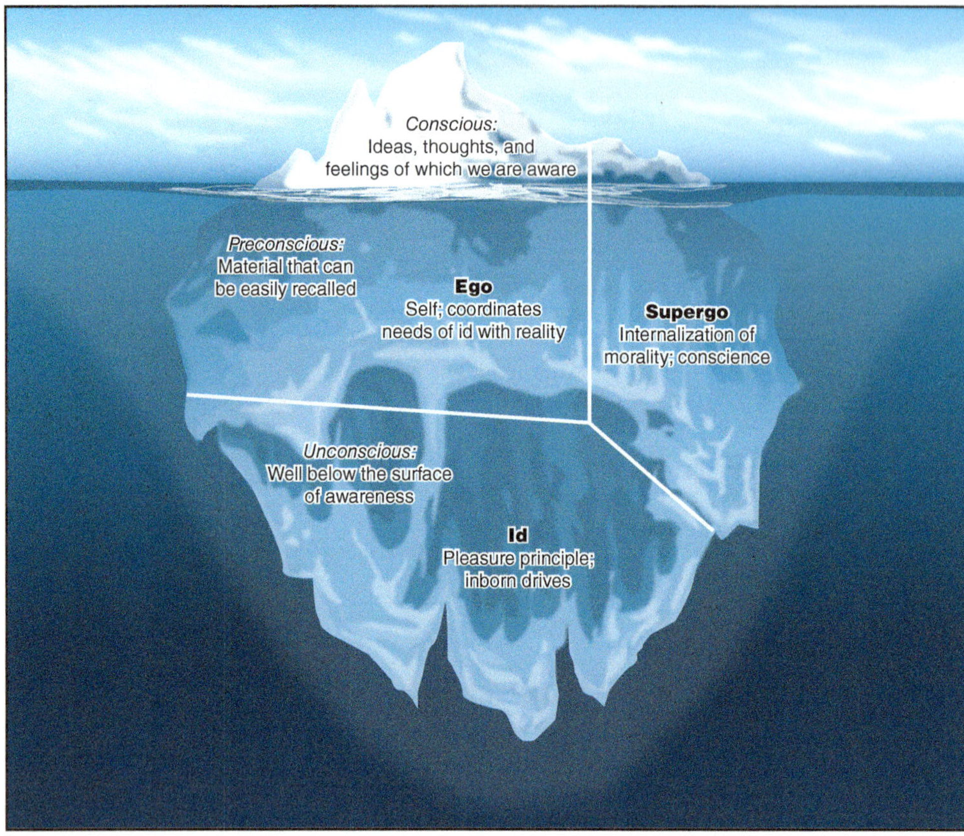

FIGURE **12.4**

Sigmund Freud's Levels of Conscious Awareness. According to Freud, we are consciously aware of only a small percentage of the mind's activities. Some information exists in the preconscious mind and can become conscious at any moment. Information in the unconscious mind can affect our behavior without our awareness.

Unemployed Philosophers Guild

Sigmund Freud has become a mainstay in popular culture.

Contemporary Assessments of Sigmund Freud's Approach Although there is no question regarding the tremendous influence Freud has had on modern thinking, his legacy today is considered mixed. Freud's approach to development contrasts sharply with the scientific theories of development we explored in Chapter 11, but his work remains important in that it had such a profound influence in psychology and popular culture.

A few Freudian constructs appear to be supported by scientific investigation, even though the theoretical mechanisms he proposed have been refuted. The notion of defense mechanisms, the distinction between conscious and unconscious processes, and the descriptions of some types of adult personalities remain topics of research in psychological science (Kline, 2013). However, contemporary scientists point out that Freud's ideas rarely lend themselves to scientific investigation. Some of his ideas, such as women's penis envy, are viewed today as remarkably sexist (Sprengnether, 1990). Additional criticisms center on the questionable effectiveness of psychoanalysis, which we discuss in more detail in Chapter 15.

The Neo-Freudians No theory as influential as Freud's is likely to be left alone without revision. Several of Freud's followers built on his approach to construct their own psychodynamic theories. We refer to these as "neo" or "new" Freudians. A common feature of the **neo-Freudian** theories was a substitution of social competence for sexuality and pleasure as the major motivation for human behavior. These theorists brought the psychodynamic approach closer to contemporary views of humans as social animals, a theme we discuss throughout this textbook. Unfortunately, neo-Freudian theories share one of Freud's greatest weaknesses—the proposal of constructs that do not lend themselves to scientific investigation. We will highlight a few of the notable contributions of this group.

Alfred Adler (1870–1937) contributed the notion of an inferiority complex to psychodynamic thought. According to Adler (1956), an inferiority complex or overwhelming feelings of inferiority can lead to overcompensation, usually in the form of seeking the appearance of superiority rather than the substance. For example, a person might overcompensate for feelings of inferiority by purchasing a fancy, expensive automobile. Adler was also one of the first psychologists to suggest that siblings, along with parents, influence development, leading to investigations of the effects of birth order. Contemporary research, however, casts serious doubt onto the existence of any birth order effects on personality or intelligence (Damian & Roberts, 2015).

AP Images/A yue gz/Imaginechina

Alfred Adler suggested that an inferiority complex can lead to overcompensation in the form of seeking the appearance of superiority. "Man heels" that add at least 2 inches of height have become increasingly popular and are worn frequently by Hollywood stars.

Carl Jung (1875–1961), a Swiss psychiatrist, divided the **unconscious mind** into two components. The personal unconscious remained the same as Freud's unconscious mind. Jung added a deeper level, the collective unconscious, composed of our common psychological predispositions as humans passed from generation to generation (Jung, 1928). After observing common themes in cultures around the world during his extensive travels, Jung argued that generations of experience with concepts such as darkness, power, death, and parents would lead to characteristic ways of unconsciously thinking about such topics. Jung's ideas are echoed in today's evolutionary approach to psychology, which views the mind as having adapted over the course of evolution (Walters, 1994).

In addition to his expansion of the concept of the unconscious, Jung deviated from Freud by providing more specific information about differences in individual personality. In particular, Jung's concepts of the personality characteristics of extroversion (outgoing) and introversion (relatively less outgoing) are still very much alive in current discussions of personality. Jung's personality characteristics form the basis for several popular personality tests, such as the Myers–Briggs Type Indicator (MBTI). Unfortunately, as we will see later, the MBTI does not hold up well to analyses of validity and reliability.

Sanjay Kanojia/AFP/Getty Images

This Tibetan mandala represents unity formed out of the four elements of earth, wind, water, and fire, a theme that Carl Jung believed was universal in the human collective unconscious.

Karen Horney (1885–1952) was one of the first female psychiatrists. Horney rejected many of Freud's ideas to concentrate on aspects of culture that contribute to women's feelings of inferiority. Simultaneously, while treating male patients, Horney became convinced that men envied women's ability to become pregnant and be mothers. Her emphasis on the impact of a male-dominated society on women helped set the stage for many subsequent feminist scholars (Horney, 1923–1937/1967, 1950).

Classic Behaviorist Approaches to Personality

Behaviorist approaches to personality emphasized learning as an important influence on personality development. Because learning is a lifetime process, behaviorists expected to see change in personalities over time.

According to B. F. Skinner, the principles of operant conditioning, discussed in Chapter 8, would lead to the development of stable "response tendencies" that might appear to others as

neo-Freudian A theorist who attempted to update and modify Sigmund Freud's original theory of personality.

unconscious mind The part of mental activity that cannot be voluntarily retrieved.

"traits." For example, if your parents were strict about enforcing rules at home, such as finishing chores, you might look like a conscientious person who always finishes assigned tasks on time.

Compared to stable personality traits, Skinner's response tendencies were more flexible and subject to change. If people experienced something new, their ways of responding would change to reflect that new interaction with the environment. If you move away from home to college, and you no longer have your parents to reward or punish you based on your completion of tasks, you may not be conscientious about finishing your homework on time. As we will see later in this chapter, many contemporary psychologists agree that an understanding of personality requires consideration of situations and environments.

Science Source

Karen Horney (1885–1952) was one of the first female psychiatrists, and although she is considered a neo-Freudian, she rejected many of Sigmund Freud's ideas to concentrate on the sources of women's feelings of inferiority.

How Do Humanistic Psychologists Approach Personality?

Until the 1960s, American psychology was dominated by two perspectives: behaviorism and the psychodynamic approach. At that time, some psychologists began to consider other ways of approaching psychology in general and in personality specifically. One alternative approach, initially called third-force psychology (behaviorism and psychodynamic theory were forces one and two), later became known as *humanistic psychology.*

Humanistic psychology differed from behaviorism and the psychodynamic approach in several ways. Humanistic psychologists were convinced that humans are unique, and they argued that the animal research favored by behaviorists was irrelevant. The humanistic psychologists' belief that human nature is basically good contrasts dramatically with the darker view of human nature put forward by Freud and other psychodynamic theorists. Humanistic psychologists believed that psychodynamic theories placed too much emphasis on abnormal behavior. Instead, they advocated studying exceptional people to see why they succeeded, a tactic continued by contemporary positive psychology approaches, discussed in Chapter 16.

One of the leading humanistic psychologists, Abraham Maslow, was interested in motivation, and we discussed his contributions to this area in Chapter 7. He did not attempt a full-fledged theory of personality, although he made some interesting conclusions about the characteristics of exceptional people. After reviewing biographies of people such as Albert Einstein, Jane Addams, William James, and Abraham Lincoln, Maslow (1950) observed that exceptional people shared a number of common traits. In addition to expected characteristics, such as creativity, realistic thinking, and concern for others, Maslow's exceptional people had some surprising qualities. They had few friends, well-developed senses of humor, and periodic mystic or peak experiences.

Courtesy of Ryan Whitlock

Early behaviorists like B. F. Skinner believed that personality traits represented response tendencies that were elicited consistently by different situations. Being at home and being at school might bring out different sets of behaviors for many people.

Carl Rogers (1951, 1980), another humanistic psychologist, put forward a theory of personality based on his experience as a therapist. We discuss Rogers's approach to therapy in Chapter 15. Rogers, like Maslow, believed that humans strive toward self-actualization or maximizing their individual potential. For Rogers, people who follow the path laid out by their feelings will lead productive, healthy lives. They will experience congruence, or similarity, between their real selves and their ideal selves. Congruence is most likely to occur in response to unconditional positive regard, or a nonjudgmental appreciation for a person's true nature. Being treated judgmentally makes people act in ways that are incongruent or inconsistent with their ideal selves, which might lead to disordered behaviors (see Figure 12.5).

As was also the case in psychodynamic theories, it is difficult to move from the humanistic psychologists' description of personality to our definition of personality as characteristic ways of thinking, feeling, and behaving. The humanistic psychologists are more interested in

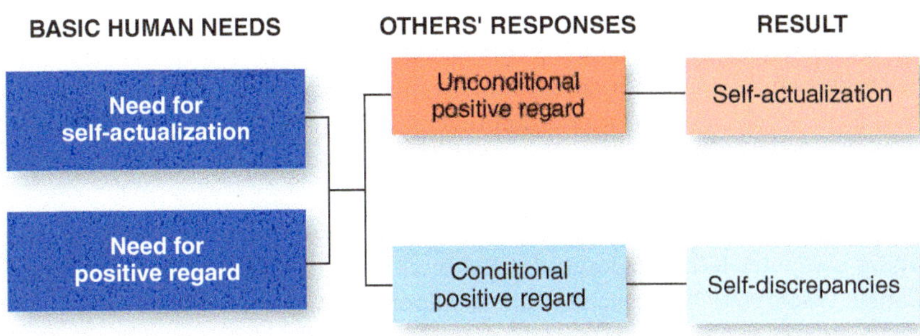

FIGURE 12.5

Carl Rogers's Humanistic Theory of Personality. Rogers, like other humanistic psychologists, believed that people strive for self-actualization or the ability to maximize their potential. Achieving that goal depended on the response of other people (family, friends, and society) to the self. If people receive unconditional positive regard or nonjudgmental acceptance, they can reach self-actualization. However, if their acceptance is conditional on whether they please others, the result is "self-discrepancies" that can lead to depression, anxiety, and other negative outcomes.

Source: Adapted from D. A. Bernstein (2011). *Essentials of Psychology*, 5th ed. Belmont, CA: Cengage.

the process by which personality develops than in the actual characteristics that emerge. Like the psychodynamic theories they rejected, the humanistic psychologists are subject to criticisms of being unscientific in their methods (Child, 1973).

How Do Trait Theories Explain Personality?

Following a discussion of psychodynamic, behaviorist, and humanistic approaches to personality, the trait approach seems relatively simple. A **trait** is a stable personality characteristic.

trait A stable personality characteristic.

Psychologists were hard at work testing personality traits long before they derived coherent theories to explain their findings. They realized intuitively that traits clustered together. An outgoing person might also be expected to be brave and cheerful. However, these approaches lacked the precision required by a true theory of personality. Statistical methods of correlation and factor analysis came to the rescue (see Figure 12.6). As we discussed in Chapter 2, correlations allow us to see whether two variables have some systematic relationship with each other, such as height and weight. Factor analysis allows a researcher to compare large numbers of correlations simultaneously, which makes the technique perfectly suited to the study of clustered personality traits (Spearman, 1904).

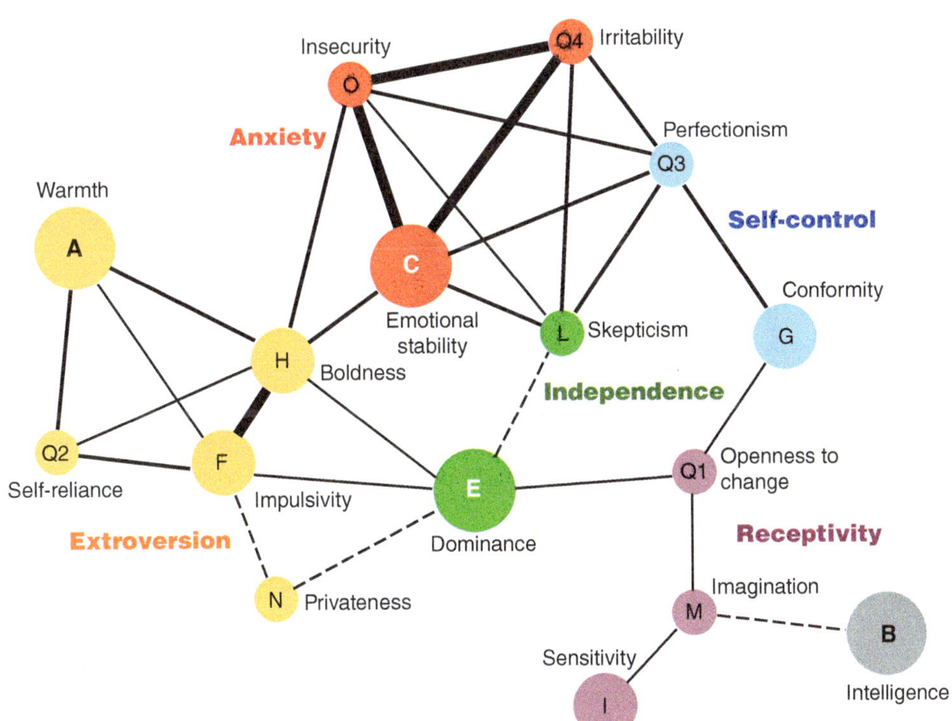

FIGURE 12.6

Factor Analysis Identifies Clusters of Personality Traits. The statistical technique of factor analysis allows psychologists to identify factors that positively correlate or cluster together, as well as the strengths of those relationships. Raymond Cattell identified 16 personality factors that formed five clusters (extroversion, anxiety, self-control, independence, and receptivity) that are similar to the factors in the Big Five theory later proposed by McCrae and Costa (1985). The darker lines represent stronger statistical relationships.

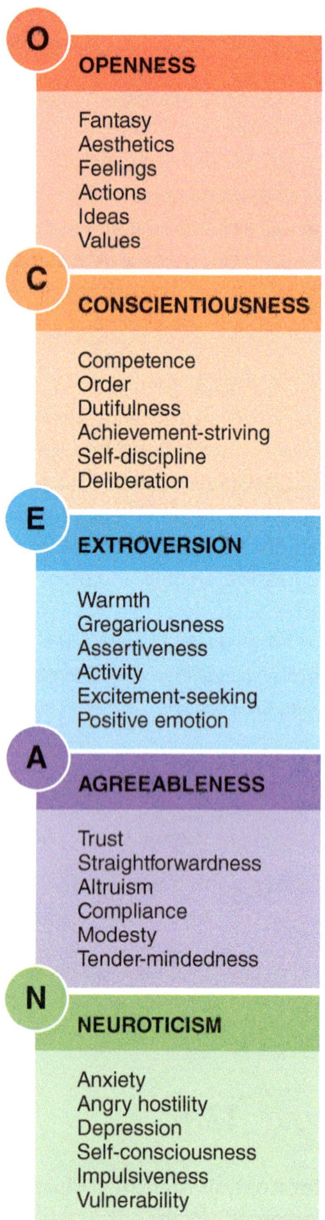

FIGURE **12.7**

The Big Five Theory of Personality.

Early Trait Theories

One of the earliest efforts to identify personality traits began with the selection of 4,500 words that described observable traits out of a dictionary (Allport & Odbert, 1936). Some of these terms were defined as central traits, or characteristics that most clearly define and differentiate a person (Allport, 1937). These are the terms you might use when trying to describe someone you know: smart, hardworking, and outgoing.

Emerging computer technologies in the 1940s allowed psychologists to refine lists of traits further (Cattell, 1946/1969). Using factor analysis, Allport and Odbert's original list of 4,500 words was reduced to 16 major personality traits. Each trait took the form of a continuum between opposites. For example, the trait of suspiciousness would range from "trusting" at one extreme to "suspicious" at the other. The basic methods and elements for trait theories were now in place.

The Big Five Theory

A common theme found in the work of early trait theorists is that relatively few traits are required to describe and predict an individual's behavior accurately. Based on this work, a **Big Five theory** identified five core traits: Openness to experience, conscientiousness, surgency (extroversion), agreeableness, and neuroticism (Norman, 1963; McCrae & Costa, 1985, 1987). To remember the Big Five traits, use the acronym OCEAN. The development of a personality test to measure the five traits has made it possible for many investigators to explore the Big Five theory scientifically (see ● Figure 12.7). The current version of the test is known as the NEO-PI-R Inventory (Costa & McCrae, 2011). You will have an opportunity to take a short version of this test in this chapter.

Each of the Big Five traits consists of a continuum from one extreme to the other. For example, the majority of people are "ambiverts," or somewhere in the middle of the extremes of introversion and extroversion (see ● Figure 12.8). We will discuss the five traits in order of the OCEAN acronym.

Openness to experience involves fantasy, aesthetics (an appreciation for the arts), feelings, actions, ideas, and values. People high on openness are curious, unconventional, and imaginative. They are interested in exploring aspects of life that are different from their own, whether this means trying new foods, traveling to exotic locations, or studying other religions. People low on openness are more practical, traditional, and conforming. They prefer the familiar over the new, choosing a chain restaurant in a new city rather than experimenting with the local cuisine.

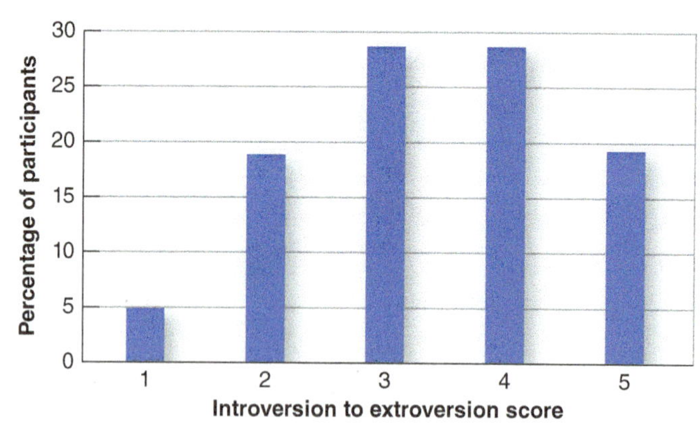

FIGURE **12.8**

Big Five Traits Are Not Either/Or. Data from nearly 300 students enrolled in a recent class taught by one of your authors show that most people are not extremely introverted or extroverted. Instead, the majority are ambiverts, or midway between the extremes of introversion and extroversion.
Source: L. Freberg

Big Five theory A trait theory that identifies five main characteristics that account for most individual differences in personality.

openness A Big Five personality trait characterized by an appreciation for fantasy, feelings, actions, ideas, values, and aesthetics.

Conscientiousness incorporates competence, order, dutifulness, achievement striving, self-discipline, and deliberation. People high on this trait are reliable, work hard, and complete tasks on time. People low on this trait are unreliable, somewhat lazy, and undependable. It is frustrating to work on group projects with people who are low in conscientiousness, but under some circumstances, they make valuable contributions. For example, they might identify unnecessary steps in a process, reducing the time pressure felt by a group, or promote some forms of "outside the box" thinking and problem solving.

Extroversion is characterized by warmth, gregariousness, assertiveness, activity, excitement seeking, and positive emotion, although extroverts also tend to be insensitive and overbearing. **Introversion** is characterized by coolness, reserve, passivity, and caution, although introverts also tend to be sensitive and reflective. Both introverts and extroverts enjoy social activity, but introverts tend to be more stimulated by it, which can be tiring (Grant, 2013).

Agreeableness includes trust, straightforwardness, altruism, compliance, modesty, and tender mindedness. People low in this trait are cynical, uncooperative, and rude. It is challenging to identify advantages for a trait like disagreeableness. In employment settings, however, disagreeable people are capable of making tough decisions, whereas their more agreeable colleagues find it difficult to supervise others (Rust, 1999). In one study, men who scored below the mean on measures of agreeableness earned 18% more than men who were more agreeable (Judge et al., 2012).

Finally, **neuroticism** combines anxiety, angry hostility, depression, self-consciousness, impulsivity, and vulnerability. The opposite trait could be described as emotional stability. Although scoring high on neuroticism sounds unpleasant, this trait has survival advantages (Zhang et al., 2005). In threatening and impoverished environments, high neuroticism increases a person's chances of surviving to reproduce. We observed a similar argument in Chapter 11, in which a child's insecure attachment to the parents had benefits for survival in a dangerous environment (Belsky, 1999). Whether considering a personality trait or attachment, the anxious, clinging child is more likely to stay near protection, enhancing survival in dangerous situations.

Big Five traits have provided a framework for investigating job performance (Barrick & Mount, 1991), parenting style (Prinzie et al., 2009), psychological disorders and substance abuse (Kotov et al., 2010), cognitive decline in older adulthood (Curtis et al., 2014), happiness (DeNeve & Cooper, 1998), academic performance (Komarraju et al., 2009), and many other specific

Mieke Dalle/Getty Images

People who score high on the trait of openness are curious, unconventional, and imaginative.

Across a range of professional, skilled, and unskilled job descriptions, the conscientiousness variable had the greatest positive correlation with work-related success (Barrick & Mount, 1991). Surprisingly, the same meta-analysis found little relationship between agreeableness and job performance.

wunkley/Alamy Stock Photo

Out of the Big Five characteristics, conscientiousness shows the highest positive correlation with work-related success, whether a person is employed in a professional, skilled, or unskilled job.

conscientiousness A Big Five personality trait characterized by competence, order, dutifulness, achievement striving, self-discipline, and deliberation.

extroversion One of the Big Five traits characterized by warmth, gregariousness, assertiveness, activity, excitement seeking, and positive emotion; opposite of introversion.

introversion One of the Big Five traits characterized by coolness, reserve, passivity, inactivity, caution, and negative emotion; opposite of extroversion.

agreeableness A Big Five personality trait characterized by trustworthiness, altruism, trust, compliance, modesty, and tender mindedness.

neuroticism A Big Five personality trait characterized by anxiety, angry hostility, depression, self-consciousness, impulsivity, and vulnerability.

outcomes. Evidence across diverse cultures, including the United States, Japan, South Korea, Germany, Portugal, Israel, and China, suggests that these personality traits represent universal human characteristics (McCrae & Costa, 1997).

How Do Situations Affect Personality?

Not all psychologists agree that personality originated in stable traits that produce consistent patterns of behavior across different situations. Research showing that situations could exert a stronger influence on people's behavior than any individual predispositions

EXPERIENCING PSYCHOLOGY

A Short Version of the Big Five Inventory

THE FULL VERSION of the Big Five Inventory (BFI) contains 44 items. The 10-item version in ● Table 12.1 has served as a reasonable substitute for the full test for research purposes when time is limited (Rammstedt & John, 2007). If reading about the different Big Five traits has left you wondering about your own personality, this is your chance to get an idea of where you stack up on each of these factors.

Circle the number that represents your best answer for each item. At the end, we'll tell you how to add up your scores. A self-report test like this is only as good as you make it by answering honestly. Wanting to appear socially desirable by downplaying your negative characteristics might make you feel better, but this approach reduces the validity of the test results. At the same time, no paper-and-pencil test is perfect, and if a result does not fit the way you honestly view your personality, feel free to disagree with the results. ■

TABLE 12.1

The BFI-10 Personality Test

1. I see myself as someone who is reserved.				
1	2	3	4	5
Disagree strongly	Disagree a little	Neither agree nor disagree	Agree a little	Agree strongly
2. I see myself as someone who is generally trusting.				
1	2	3	4	5
Disagree strongly	Disagree a little	Neither agree nor disagree	Agree a little	Agree strongly
3. I see myself as someone who tends to be lazy.				
1	2	3	4	5
Disagree strongly	Disagree a little	Neither agree nor disagree	Agree a little	Agree strongly
4. I see myself as someone who is relaxed, handles stress well.				
1	2	3	4	5
Disagree strongly	Disagree a little	Neither agree nor disagree	Agree a little	Agree strongly
5. I see myself as someone who has few artistic interests.				
1	2	3	4	5
Disagree strongly	Disagree a little	Neither agree nor disagree	Agree a little	Agree strongly
6. I see myself as someone who is outgoing, sociable.				
1	2	3	4	5
Disagree strongly	Disagree a little	Neither agree nor disagree	Agree a little	Agree strongly

highlighted limits to the general trait approach. We discuss several of these situations in Chapter 13. For example, studies of obedience or conformity might be better understood by evaluating the situations people encounter rather than the predispositions or traits they bring to the laboratory (Asch, 1951; Milgram, 1963). Kurt Lewin (1951) argued that a person's behavior is a function of the person and the person's environment. This led to a vigorous debate regarding which element, personality or the situation, produced the greatest influence on behavior.

Historically, many psychologists continued to focus on personality traits. More recent work has demonstrated an increasing respect for the influences of situational variables on behavior. Personality may predict typical behaviors performed by individuals, but situations often provide better insight into cases in which people behave in uncharacteristic ways (Sherman et al., 2015). As predicted by Lewin, personality and situations usually interact. For example, individual personality traits influence the types of situations we choose to encounter as well as the way we think about those situations, which in turn reinforces

7. I see myself as someone who tends to find fault with others.

1	2	3	4	5
Disagree strongly	Disagree a little	Neither agree nor disagree	Agree a little	Agree strongly

8. I see myself as someone who does a thorough job.

1	2	3	4	5
Disagree strongly	Disagree a little	Neither agree nor disagree	Agree a little	Agree strongly

9. I see myself as someone who gets nervous easily.

1	2	3	4	5
Disagree strongly	Disagree a little	Neither agree nor disagree	Agree a little	Agree strongly

10. I see myself as someone who has an active imagination.

1	2	3	4	5
Disagree strongly	Disagree a little	Neither agree nor disagree	Agree a little	Agree strongly

Here is how you should score your results. To ensure that you don't just pick the same number for each item, half of the questions "reverse" the scale. Follow the directions below carefully so that you obtain a correct score. Scores can range from 1 to 5 on each trait.

Extroversion: Q1R (Reverse) and Q6

Subtract your answer to Q1 from 6 and add to your answer to Q6. Divide by 2.

Scores of 1 or 2 are introverted, scores of 4 and 5 are extroverted, and a score of 3 is neutral.

Agreeableness: Q2 and Q7R (Reverse)

Add your response to Q2 to (6 minus your answer on Q7), and divide the sum by 2.

Scores of 1 or 2 are disagreeable, scores of 4 and 5 are agreeable, and a score of 3 is neutral.

Conscientiousness: Q3R (Reverse) and Q8

Add (6 minus your answer on Q3) to your answer on Q8, and divide the sum by 2.

Scores of 1 or 2 are low conscientiousness, scores of 4 and 5 are high conscientiousness, and a score of 3 is neutral.

Neuroticism: Q4R (Reverse) and Q9

Add (6 minus your answer on Q4) to your answer on Q9, and divide the sum by 2.

Scores of 1 or 2 are low neuroticism, scores of 4 and 5 are high neuroticism, and a score of 3 is neutral.

Openness: Q5R (Reverse) and Q10

Add (6 minus your answer on Q5) to your answer on Q10, and divide the sum by 2.

Scores of 1 or 2 are low openness, scores of 4 and 5 are high openness, and a score of 3 is neutral.

Vibe Images/Shutterstock.com

Is this man helping these women with their car troubles because of his individual personality traits? Or do situational variables do a better job than personality traits at predicting behavior?

the original personality traits (Rauthmann et al., 2015). In other cases, the power of situations can have large and lasting effects on personality. For example, the experience of unemployment produced long-term changes in individual levels of agreeableness, conscientiousness, and openness (Boyce et al., 2015).

Personality is usually studied, not surprisingly, in individuals, but one situation that might have a particularly strong influence on personality is being in a group. At least in the case of fish, individual personality is sometimes suppressed in groups in favor of the collective decisions of the school (McDonald et al., 2016). Fish, like humans, show individual differences in "boldness," or the willingness to choose reward over risk. The boldness of individual fish tested alone is quite consistent, but the behavior of the same fish within a school of fish is not. This suggests that at least in the area of risk-taking, testing individuals might give psychologists very different results than testing the same people in a group setting. Recognition of the importance of personality in social contexts led to a number of **social–cognitive learning theories** that are consistent with our observations that single perspectives in psychology do not always capture the whole story.

Locus of Control

One influential social–cognitive learning theory featured a concept known as **locus of control** (Rotter, 1966). If you have an external locus of control (*locus* means "place" in Latin), you expect that most of your outcomes occur because of chance, luck, opportunity, or other factors beyond your control. However, if you have an internal locus of control, you believe that most of your outcomes are due to your own talent and effort.

People with an internal locus of control manage stress more effectively, floss their teeth more regularly, are more likely to seek shelter in response to tornado warnings, use their seat belts more consistently while driving, and are more likely to practice effective birth control (Wallston, 2005). However, people with an internal locus of control tend to be less sympathetic with the plight of others, viewing their troubles as due to their choices and behavior as opposed to outside forces they can't control (Lane, 2001).

Reciprocal Determinism and Self-Efficacy

Albert Bandura, whom we met in Chapter 8, attempted to capture a balance between external, environmental factors and internal traits in his theory of **reciprocal determinism** (Bandura, 1990, 1993). Like other social–cognitive learning theorists, Bandura rejected the strict behaviorism of Skinner as applied to personality. He agreed with Skinner that the environment can determine behavior but thought that it does so reciprocally, as people influence the environment through both their internal cognitions and their behavior.

Bandura believed that observation of others' behavior played an important role in the development of personality. Although much of his work centered on aggression, Bandura believed that many other characteristics were learned in this same manner. He was particularly interested in self-efficacy (Bandura, 1990, 1993, 1995). This characteristic refers to confidence in your abilities to gain reinforcement. If self-efficacy is high, you have strong expectations that positive outcomes are within reach. If you study hard and get good grades, you expect to obtain a good job in your chosen career. However, if self-efficacy is low, you might doubt your abilities to reach your goals. Self-efficacy can be situation specific. You might be confident in your abilities in science but less so in your abilities in rock climbing. Self-efficacy influences a person's environment and experiences. A confident job candidate is probably more likely to be hired than an applicant who appears insecure.

social–cognitive learning theory A theory of personality that features cognition and learning, especially from the social environment, as important sources of individual differences in personality.

locus of control A cognitive expectancy featured in social–cognitive learning theories of personality about the source of individual outcomes; an external locus of control sees outcomes as resulting from luck or chance, while an internal locus of control sees outcomes as the result of individual effort.

reciprocal determinism A social–cognitive learning theory of personality that features the mutual influence of the person and that of the situation on each other.

If–Then Relationships

Walter Mischel argued that trait theories could not explain the variation in an individual's behavior across situations (Mischel, 1968). For example, when 51 boys at a summer camp were observed, their extroversion–introversion scores did not predict their extroverted or introverted behaviors across 21 situations (Newcombe, 1929). Instead of focusing on traits alone, Mischel argued that the stability we expect in a person's behavior arises from that individual's characteristic way of interpreting situations (Mischel, 2004).

To illustrate this process, consider two children who both score high on some measure of aggression. Trait theorists would expect the children to be consistently more aggressive than their low-scoring peers regardless of circumstances, yet these are precisely the results that Mischel found to be lacking in actual studies (Mischel, 1968). Instead, an individual child's behavior can be predicted by considering "if–then" relationships between situations and behavior (Mischel & Shoda, 1995). One child may be aggressive when approached by peers but respond passively to an adult's efforts to apply discipline, while another might show the opposite pattern. In other words, *if* the child experiences a particular situation (interacting with peers or adults), that child *then* responds with a unique, stable set of behaviors (aggressive or passive). These if–then patterns are characteristic of an individual, leading to the stable characteristics we think of as personality.

P.A. Lawrence, LLC./Alamy Stock Photo

People with an internal locus of control believe that most of our outcomes are due to our own efforts, while people with an external locus of control believe that our outcomes are more often due to factors beyond our control. Although people with an internal locus of control experience less stress, they tend to be less sympathetic with the plight of others. The person with an internal locus of control might believe this woman needs to try harder to escape homelessness, while the person with an external locus of control might believe this woman just needs help and better opportunities.

GABRIEL BOUYS/Getty Images

Self-efficacy is the belief that you can handle a challenging situation and obtain future rewards.

What Are the Biological Bases of Personality?

Biological theories of personality build bridges between observed traits and their underlying biological correlates. Among the biological variables connected to personality are temperament, genetic predispositions, and brain structure. These variables serve as behavioral phenotypes that can be used to compare and contrast underlying genetic profiles (Skuse, 2000).

Temperament and Personality

We introduced the concept of **temperament**, or a child's pattern of mood, activity, or emotional responsiveness, in Chapter 11. Contemporary psychologists believe that temperament is biological in origin (Rothbart, 2011) but quickly begins to interact with the social and physical environments. Not only does a bold, fearless child select different activities, but that child is treated differently than a quiet, cautious child by peers, parents, and teachers.

temperament A child's pattern of mood, activity, or emotional responsiveness linked to later personality.

FIGURE **12.11**

Comparisons Between Identical Twins Raised Together or Apart. Some characteristics, such as the number of ridges you have in your fingerprints, are more strongly influenced by genetics than other characteristics, such as your nonreligious social attitudes. Regardless of how much genetic influence a trait might have, identical twins show considerable similarity, whether they grow up in the same household or not.

Source: Adapted from T. Bouchard, Jr. et al. (1990). "Sources of Human Psychological Differences: The Minnesota Study of Twins Reared Apart," *Science, 250*, 223–228. doi: 10.1126/science.2218526

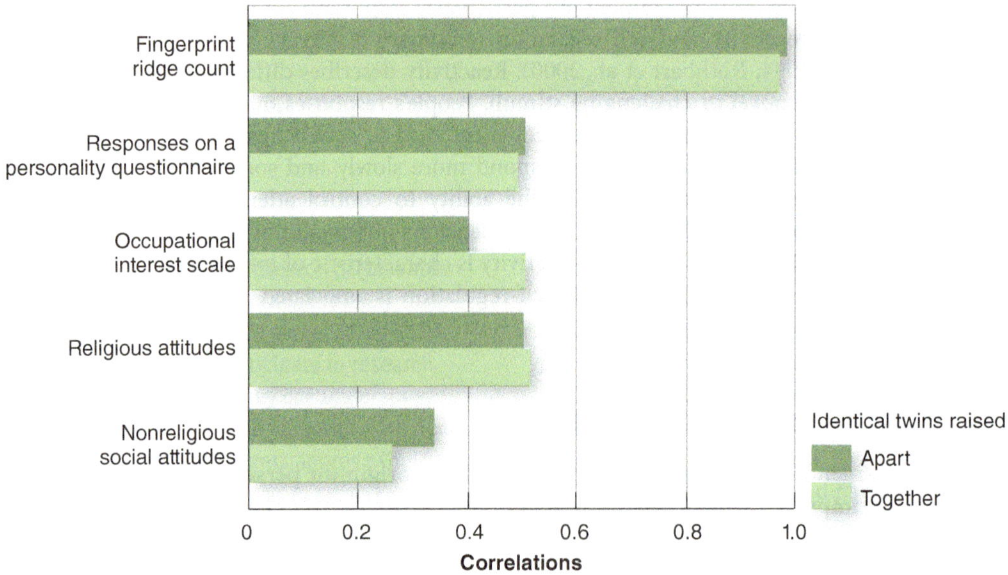

mean that 40% of a person's shyness is produced by genes and the other 60% is produced by the environment. Instead, a 0.40 heritability ratio suggests that across the human population, the variations we see in shyness from high to low are influenced moderately by both genetics and environmental factors.

Beth Eberth, St. Bonaventure University, St. Bonaventure, N.Y.

Adrian and Julian Riester were identical twin friars who died within hours of each other at the age of 92. Their shared experiences of more than 65 years as members of the Franciscan order probably accentuated their genetic similarities.

If genetics accounts for about half of the variability seen in the population's personality, what is the source of the other half? Environmental influences take the form of shared experiences, which affect all members of a family, and nonshared experiences, which affect an individual. For example, you and your siblings might attend the same elementary school and have Thanksgiving dinner with the extended family (shared experiences) while studying different musical instruments, having different friends, or playing different sports (nonshared experiences).

Knowing the heritability for a trait like extroversion does not tell us much about the development of an individual's personality. Heritability estimates are similar to knowing the overall average annual temperature in North America. Although this information could be useful for the study of global climate trends, it doesn't tell us whether California is likely to have more wildfires or whether the skiing industry in Colorado will have a good year. We know that the population heritability for positive emotionality is between .46 and .52, but this doesn't tell us how heritability interacts with shared and nonshared environments to produce particular outcomes (Krueger et al., 2008; Sanchez-Roige et al., 2018).

In spite of their heritability, personality traits are far from being set in stone. We observed earlier that confronting experiences such as unemployment can produce wide-ranging influences on personality. Researchers have even noted that if you want to change a personality trait (for example, by becoming more agreeable), that can actually be done (Hudson & Fraley, 2015). Not only can people change personality traits on purpose, but the change will be reflected in their relevant behaviors.

Personality, Brain Structure, and Brain Function

Genes produce proteins that build the nervous system, which in turn produces behavior, including personality differences. It follows, then, that personality traits might be reflected in the structures and activity of the nervous system. Early efforts to link personality and biology examined the correlations between extroversion and neuroticism traits and the activities of the autonomic nervous system and reticular formation, structures involved with arousal discussed in Chapter 4 (e.g., Eysenck, 1967).

Personality neuroscientists have investigated individual differences in neurochemical activity. We have already seen that variations in one gene related to serotonin function has implications for individual differences in personality. Dopamine and opioid activity appears to be related to extroversion (DeYoung & Allen, 2019). Variations in cortisol, a hormone released at times of stress, might be associated with different levels of neuroticism.

Early explorations suggested that brain structure differs across Big Five personality traits. However, more recent studies using larger numbers of participants, improved brain imaging technologies, and sophisticated statistical methods have failed to establish significant differences in cortical thickness, volume of structures, or white matter related to any of the Big Five traits (Avinun et al., 2020).

Courtesy of Jennifer Mather/University of Lethbridge and Roland Anderson/Seattle Aquarium

After noticing that staff at the Seattle Aquarium had been naming their octopuses based on their behavior (from shy Emily Dickinson to destructive Lucretia McEvil), Jennifer Mather tested 44 octopuses systematically for their responses to stimuli, such as being touched with a brush. The octopuses seemed to have unique and stable responses, similar to having a "personality."

Activity in brain networks, rather than structural differences, forms the basis of a personality model called reinforcement sensitivity theory (RST). Individual differences in approach, avoidance, and inhibition of behavior reflect the activity of three brain networks: the behavioral approach system (BAS), the fight–flight freeze system (FFFS), and the behavioral inhibition system (BIS) (Gray & McNaughton, 2003; Kennis et al., 2013). Using brain imaging, researchers have mapped the networks in which activity successfully predicts individual differences in these three dimensions of behavior (Kennis et al., 2013; Adrián-Ventura et al., 2019). Variations in BAS (approach) activity predict a person's response to reward, or impulsivity. The FFFS (flight–freeze) is active when an organism experiences unlearned punishment or lack of reward, while the BIS (inhibition) is active when an organism senses learned signals for punishment or lack of reward (Gray, 1970, 1987). Individual differences in FFFS (flight–freeze) activity correlate with reactivity, described earlier, while differences in BIS (inhibition) activity are associated with anxiety levels or neuroticism.

The Evolution of Personality

If we accept the idea that personality characteristics are influenced by genetic factors leading to individual differences in nervous system functioning, an interesting question arises: How might differences in personality have evolved? As we mentioned at the beginning of this chapter, cultures and genetic differences related to personality probably influenced each other over time. Variations exist across cultures, such as the proportions of highly neurotic individuals, but the Big Five traits in general are universal because they influence survival for the entire species (Buss, 1996, 1999).

Identifying "personality" in other species would support this evolutionary approach. Ivan Petrovich Pavlov, discussed in Chapter 8, noticed that individual dogs responded differently to frustration: Some responded "cheerfully," others responded with "anger," some went to sleep, and still others appeared to have a nervous breakdown (Pavlov, 1906). Using a modified human personality questionnaire to evaluate animals, extroversion and neuroticism have been identified in hyenas, octopuses, guppies, rats, pigs, dogs, cats, donkeys, monkeys, gorillas, and chimpanzees (Gosling et al., 2006). Humans and chimpanzees share variations in all of the Big Five traits, but over the course of evolution, humans lost a sixth trait related to dominance found in chimpanzees (King & Figueredo, 1997). These differences might have emerged from unique selection pressures experienced by the two species (Weiss, 2018).

Physical traits appear to change in predictable ways when animals are domesticated by breeding the most tame members of each generation to each other. The loss of fur color and the curliness of tails characterizing many domestic dogs also appeared when researchers attempted to breed tame foxes. These data suggest that evolution can act on personality and physical traits in interwoven and complex ways.

Source: L. Trut et al. (2009). "Animal Evolution During Domestication: The Domesticated Fox As a Model," *BioEssays*, *31*(3), 349-360. doi: 10.1002/bies.200800070

How Do We Assess Personality?

Personality is assessed or tested for a variety of reasons, including the refinement of personality theories, diagnosing psychological disorders, selecting employees, or making decisions in courts of law.

In everyday life, we assess other people's personalities by listening to them and watching their behavior. Observation remains one of the most reliable means of making personality judgments about others (Leichtman, 1995; Asendorpf et al., 2002). However, observation takes precious time and can be biased, as we will discuss in Chapter 13. In addition to observation, we rely on interviews. Although a skilled interviewer might obtain reliable information, it is also easy for the person being interviewed to conceal some aspects of personality.

To avoid the pitfalls of observation and interview, many psychologists turn to standardized tests of personality. In Chapter 2, we noted that good tests require validity and reliability. A valid test literally does the job it is advertised to do. For example, if you constructed a test of creativity, people with high scores on your test should demonstrate more creativity than do people with lower scores. A reliable test returns similar results when it is interpreted by different observers or is taken repeatedly.

The results of most standardized personality tests rely on self-report, which introduces errors. Self-reports can be influenced by a person's need to appear socially appropriate (Cyders & Coskunpinar, 2011). An individual applying for a job in sales is unlikely to admit to being shy. In Chapter 9, we distinguished between conscious or explicit and unconscious or implicit memories. Self-report measures do a good job of tapping into our explicit information about our personalities but may not capture implicit aspects of personality (Asendorpf et al., 2002). Furthermore, answers on a questionnaire may indicate a person's beliefs but have relatively less to say about how a person would behave. Claiming to be honest on a questionnaire says little about whether a cashier will steal money from the cash register, as we will explore in Chapter 13.

Analysis of data from cell phones and social media provides personality psychologists with ecologically valid snapshots of real behavior. Researchers constructed a computer algorithm that assesses a person's "likes" on Facebook (Youyou et al., 2015). The resulting assessment of a person's Big Five personality traits turned out to be more accurate than the assessments made by work colleagues, friends, roommates, and family members (see ● Figure 12.12). Only a person's spouse could rival the computer. As entertaining as these results might be, they do raise significant privacy concerns.

Personality Inventories

personality inventory An objective test, often using numbered scales or multiple choice, used to assess personality.

Personality inventories are objective tests, often using numbered scales or multiple choice, such as the short Big Five test that you took earlier in the chapter. These tests have

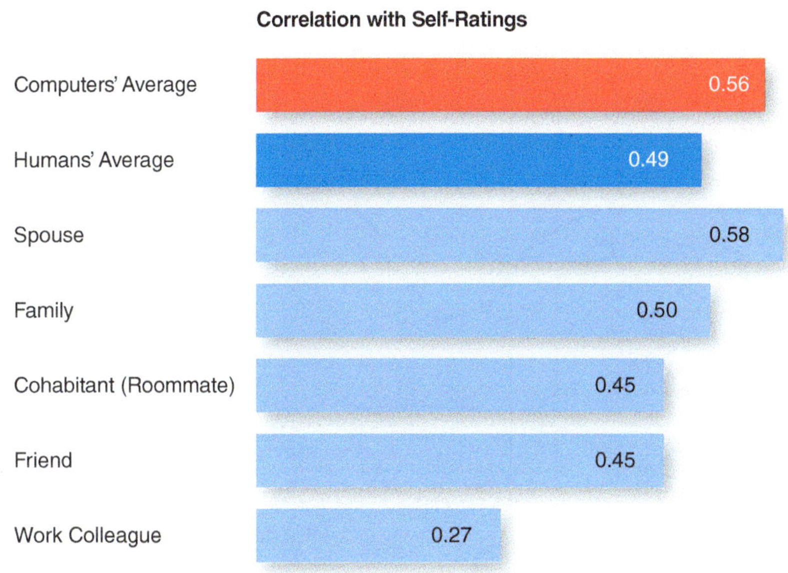

FIGURE **12.12**

Computers Can Judge Personality, Too. A computer analysis of the Facebook likes of 86,220 people provided a more accurate assessment of their personalities, as measured by responses to a 100-item online questionnaire, than judgments made by their human friends.

Source: Adapted from W. Youyou et al. (2015). "Computer-Based Personality Judgments Are More Accurate Than Those Made by Humans," *Proceedings of the National Academy of Sciences, 112*(4), 1036–1040. doi: 10.1073/pnas.1418680112

advantages over more subjective measures, such as interviews or observation. Large numbers of people can be assessed quickly and inexpensively. Many of the tests perform quite well in terms of reliability and validity (McCrae et al., 2011).

A frequently used personality inventory is the Minnesota Multiphasic Personality Inventory (MMPI), published in the early 1940s and most recently revised in 2020. The most recent version included new items to assess eating concerns, impulsivity, compulsivity, and self-importance and made a greater effort to include diverse participants in its development process. This test compares the responses to a number of true–false items made by typical people and those diagnosed with a psychological disorder (see ● Figure 12.13; Hathaway & McKinley, 1940, 1943). For example, responses to the statement "I usually feel that life is worthwhile and interesting" might differentiate between people who either are or are not depressed. People with schizophrenia, but not others, are likely to agree with the statement, "I seem to hear things that other people can't hear." Although the MMPI was designed to assist with clinical diagnosis, this is only one of its present-day uses. The publisher's website suggests that the test can also be used for medical, forensic, and public safety assessment (Pearson Assessments, 2020).

Olimpik/Shutterstock.com

We can learn quite a bit about "what kind of person" we have just met through an interview, but it is also relatively easy for people being interviewed to present an inaccurate view of their personality.

The MMPI has been joined by hundreds of additional objective tests featuring personality characteristics, including the NEO-PI-R, which assesses the Big Five traits. Most of these tests use response scales rather than the true–false options of the MMPI. These numbered scales are often called *Likert scales,* after Rensis Likert (1932). For example, you might be asked to select the number that best describes you:

Outgoing 7 6 5 4 3 2 1 Withdrawn

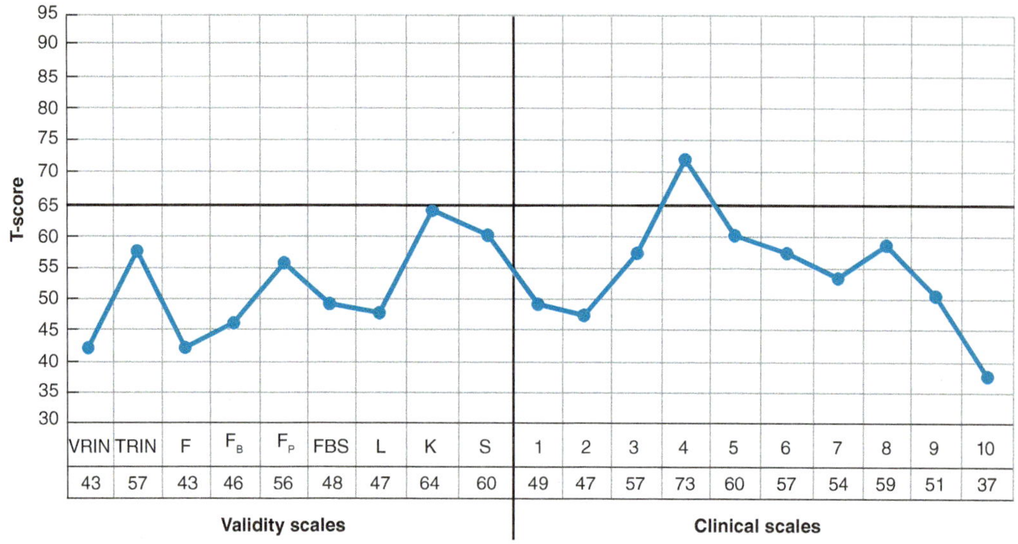

FIGURE **12.13**

The Minnesota Multiphasic Personality Inventory (MMPI). The MMPI compares a participant's responses along several dimensions to people with diagnosed psychological conditions. Scores above 65 are cause for concern. In this case, the individual scored normally with the exception of scale 4, which is the psychopathic deviate scale. This scale measures conflict, struggle, anger, and respect for society's rules. This person might be diagnosed with antisocial personality disorder, which we discuss in Chapter 14.

THINKING SCIENTIFICALLY

Evaluating the Validity and Reliability of Personality Tests

ONE OF THE most widely used personality tests is the Myers–Briggs Type Indicator (MBTI), which is based on the work of Carl Jung. More than 2 million Americans take the MBTI annually, and most of the top employers in the United States use it for employment purposes (Paul, 2010). After answering several forced-choice questions, the MBTI sorts you into 1 of 16 possible personality types combining four dimensions: Extroversion–introversion, sensing–intuition, thinking–feeling, and judging–perceiving. However, experts in psychological assessment have expressed serious reservations about the MBTI and many other popular personality tests.

WHAT AM I BEING ASKED TO BELIEVE OR ACCEPT?

We are being asked to believe that popular personality tests, such as the MBTI, might not meet our standards of a good test, including strong reliability and validity.

WHAT EVIDENCE SUPPORTS THIS POSITION?

One of the greatest weaknesses of the MBTI and other similar approaches is either/or thinking. As we have mentioned previously, traits such as introversion/extroversion are a continuum, with most individuals scoring as "ambiverts," or in the middle between the extremes (Grant, 2013).

In our discussion of personality testing, we noted that validity and reliability were essential features of any good test. How does the MBTI hold up on these criteria? Unfortunately, the answer is not well (Druckman & Bjork, 1991). Validity describes how well a test measures what it is supposed to measure. Two approaches to evaluating the validity of the MBTI are using factor analysis and assessing the predictive power of the MBTI (Pittenger, 1993).

Factor analysis allows researchers to explore correlations among items on a personality test such as the MBTI. If the MBTI is a valid model, the factor analysis should identify the four clusters, answers to the questions associated with each cluster should be highly correlated with each other, and the questions that fit in a cluster statistically should make sense. In other words, an item stating, "I like to be the life of the party" should be found in the extroversion–introversion cluster (Pittenger, 1993). Items in the MBTI do not meet these validity criteria well.

What about the predictive power of the MBTI? One of the major uses of the test is in career counseling and employment. Unfortunately, there is no evidence that certain MBTI types are more successful than others in an occupation, that certain types are more satisfied with their occupations, or that certain types remain in their occupation longer (Pittenger, 1993). The Myers & Briggs Foundation (2020) now states that the test is intended to be "descriptive" rather than "predictive" and that the test should not be used to screen applicants for employment.

What about the reliability of the MBTI? If your personality as measured by the MBTI is stable, we would expect little variation as you take the test multiple times. However, even with test–retest intervals as short as five weeks, as many as 50% of all test takers will be classified into different types on the second try (Pittenger, 1993). Pittenger's conclusions are disputed by the Myers & Briggs Foundation (2020), which claims four year re-test correlations of .57 to .81.

ARE THERE OTHER WAYS THAT THIS EVIDENCE COULD BE INTERPRETED?

These criticisms leave us wondering why tests that do not meet the standard criteria for validity and reliability are still used. Why is the Rorschach Inkblot Test still admissible to American courts of law? Why do employers invest in the MBTI for their

Projective Tests

projective test A test of personality based on Freudian theory that provides an ambiguous stimulus onto which test takers "project" their personality.

Projective tests are derived directly from projection, one of Freud's defense mechanisms. According to the psychodynamic approach, tests can access the unconscious mind by displaying an ambiguous stimulus, onto which the test participants "project" their personalities as they describe the object.

A famous projective test, the Rorschach Inkblot Test, contains 10 different inkblots, some in color and others in black and white (Rorschach, 1921). The job of the participants is to describe what each inkblot looks like to them. These responses are written down by the examiner and scored according to a manual. For example, the examiner might note that a participant talked about a portion of the inkblot instead

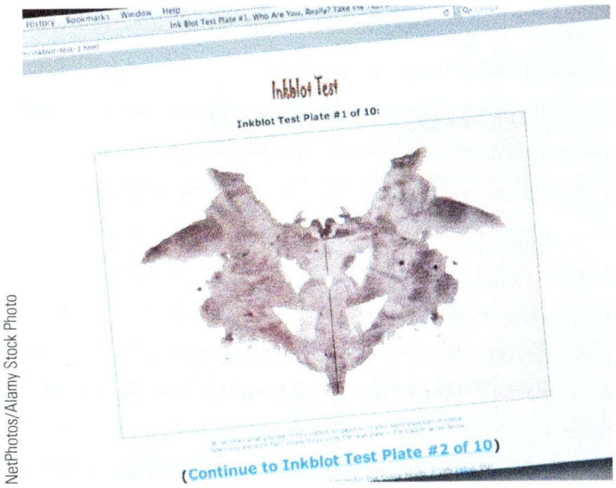

NetPhotos/Alamy Stock Photo

Swiss psychologist Hermann Rorschach (1884–1922), the son of an artist, was nicknamed "Klecks," or "inkblot," by his high school classmates because of his hobby of making inkblot pictures. After becoming a psychiatrist, he became curious about why people saw the inkblots differently, and he began analyzing their responses. Despite poor validity and reliability, the Rorschach Inkblot Test continues to be used widely.

employees? Why do so many top tech CEOs rely on enneagrams?

Academic experts in assessment frequently disagree about the usefulness of certain tools with practitioners, such as therapists, career advisors, and human relations practitioners, with practitioners much more influenced by brand name awareness (Furnham, 2018; Lake et al., 2019).

Another reason is our love of insight, which drives otherwise reasonable people to consult horoscopes, tarot cards, palm readers, and crystal balls. Upon receiving a description of their MBTI profile, many people have an "aha" moment, but the same could be said of horoscopes. In fairness, however, tests like the MBTI are so well marketed and used by so many reputable institutions that it is natural for the public to feel a level of trust (see ● Figure 12.14).

WHAT OTHER EVIDENCE WOULD I NEED TO EVALUATE THESE ALTERNATIVES?

In Chapter 10, we discussed how decision-making depended on a level of understanding of probability theory that might elude even college graduates, and a similar argument can be made about the evaluation of personality tests. Understanding their strengths and weaknesses requires a sophisticated mastery of statistics that most people simply do not possess.

WHAT ARE THE MOST REASONABLE CONCLUSIONS?

What we all can do is use our best critical thinking skills and ask meaningful questions about the validity and reliability of the tests rather than being influenced by brand loyalty or passively assuming the tests are what they're advertised to be. ■

Applied to a Target Customer

As a fun example of how this works, let's analyze Carrie—she's an ESFP and the target customer for the Ford Escape compact utility vehicle

Personal characteristics	Myers-Briggs preference	Favorite feature
Outgoing and social	**E**xtraversion	Spacious seating for five friends
She lives in the moment and travels to experience life	**S**ensing	Her powerful EcoBoost engine delivers the fuel efficiency to feed her curiosity
Stays true to her values, beliefs and ideals	**F**eeling	Intelligent 4WD system helps the vehicle stay grounded
"I know marriage and family is in my future. I crave change!"	**P**erceiving	Class-exclusive hands-free, foot-activated liftgate is perfect for her evolving lifestyle

Minerva Studio/Shutterstock.com

FIGURE **12.14**

What Not to Do With a Personality Test. Not only is the Myers–Briggs Type Indicator questionable in terms of validity and reliability, but this real-world application of the test to an automobile customer's choice for a "hands-free, foot-activated liftgate" in her car is not in the best scientific tradition.

of the entire image. This response would be scored as indicating the participant's concrete, rather than abstract, way of thinking. Despite serious questions about its reliability and validity (Wood et al., 2003; Wood et al., 2010), the Rorschach Inkblot Test remains more widely used than the MMPI. Out of a randomly selected group of 1,000 therapist members of the American Psychological Association, 82% reported using the Rorschach at least occasionally, and 43% use it frequently or always (Watkins et al., 1995).

The Ethics of Personality Testing

Personality tests are used by therapists, potential employers, judges, attorneys, educators, and others, raising important ethical concerns. Who gets to see these data? How are they stored? For what purposes may they be used? Is the examiner trained in the administration and evaluation of tests? In many cases, such as in the use of the MMPI, sensitive and private data are generated. In other cases, like the Rorschach Inkblot Test, the results are at best controversial. This widely used test has described normal children as having problems approaching psychosis (Hamel et al., 2000; Garb et al., 2005). Using invalid results to make important real-world decisions could be disastrous.

The American Psychological Association has wrestled with these questions, incorporating recommendations regarding the disclosure of test data into the organization's code of conduct (American Psychological Association, 2017). Should you be asked to take a personality test, it would be prudent to fully educate yourself regarding the test and make an informed decision about whether to proceed.

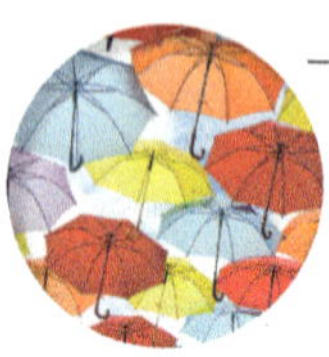

Diverse Voices in Psychology

Diversity and Personality Assessments

AT THE HEART OF RESEARCH related to diversity and personality is a dependence on the appropriate use of accurate assessments.

The practice of administering a personality test to people representing different groups and then concluding that any differences should be attributed to group membership is common but full of risks (Weiner & Greene, 2017). Many studies of this type fail to control for confounding variables such as socioeconomic status and education. The heterogeneity of large ethnic groups is often ignored. For example, the U.S. federal government recognizes over 500 distinct native entities, including Native American and Alaskan groups. Further difficulties arise when a person is asked to take an instrument in English when English is not the person's native language. We can easily imagine the potential for confusion for someone unfamiliar with English when responding to an MMPI item that states, "I am a good mixer." Even if we are familiar with English, we might assume the test is asking us if we are good bartenders or sound technicians rather than someone who is comfortable around new people.

Much work remains to be done to assess race, ethnicity, and other facets of diversity appropriately. Most standardized instruments have taken gender and age into consideration, although many approach gender in a binary manner. Challenges associated with the use of standardized instruments to assess personality as a function of sexual orientation (e.g., Bogaert et al., 2018) and disability status (e.g., Youngman, 2017) have only recently begun to be examined. ■

Cultura Creative (RF)/Alamy Stock Photo

Ethical uses of personality assessments take multiple types of diversity into account, including race, ethnicity, gender, age, sexual orientation, and disability.

SUMMARY 12.1 The Big Five Traits

Trait	Description
Openness to experience 	Artistic, curious, imaginative, insightful, original, wide interests, unusual thought processes, intellectual interests
Conscientiousness 	Efficient, organized, planful, reliable, thorough, dependable, ethical, productive
Extroversion 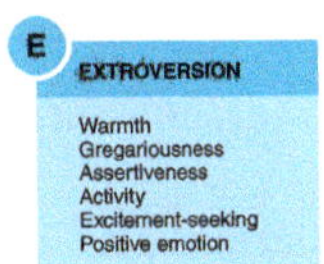	Active, assertive, energetic, outgoing, talkative, gesturally expressive, gregarious
Agreeableness 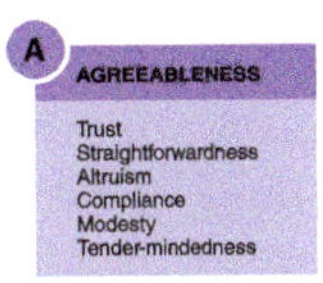	Appreciative, forgiving, generous, kind, trusting, noncritical, warm, compassionate, considerate, straightforward
Neuroticism 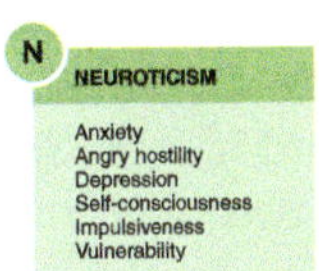	Anxious, self-pitying, tense, emotionally unstable, impulsive, vulnerable, touchy, prone to worry

Credits: Top row—Mieke Dalle/Getty Images; Second row—wunkley/Alamy Stock Photo.

What Does It Mean to Have a Self?

One of the most fundamental psychological distinctions we make is between our self and others. William James (1890, p. 330) argued in favor of "the belief in a distinct principle of selfhood" and believed that such a principle could be studied scientifically. Knowing something about the personalities of others makes it easier for us to anticipate what others will feel, think, or do and, therefore, to interact more effectively with them. But what about the patterns of thought, feelings, and actions we see in ourselves? When we think about this personal knowledge, we are thinking about the **self**.

A person's sense of self combines a number of separate factors (Kahn, 2013). Having a self means having a sense of unity, or of being a single human. The self incorporates a history or a sense of continuity. This aspect of self helps us organize our personal knowledge on a timeline, providing us with a past, present, and future. A sense of embodiment means that the self is embedded in the body (as opposed to the sensation of having an out-of-body experience, discussed in Chapter 6). A self has free will, or the feeling we can do whatever we want to do,

self Patterns of thought, feelings, and actions we perceive in our own minds.

and self-location, which means we understand our current location. The self uses a first-person perspective. Finally, the self is embedded in a social network and is influenced by the quality of those relationships.

Psychologists approach the study of the self by examining the ABCs: affect, behavior, and cognition. The affective or emotional components of the self include our evaluation of the self or level of self-esteem, discussed in greater detail later in this chapter. Behavior and self-concept form reciprocal relationships. We gain self-knowledge by observing our behavior, and our thoughts about the type of people we are influence our behavior. Cognitive processes help us organize information and think about the self.

Courtesy of John T. Cacioppo and Laura Freberg

Our self-concept captures the way we see ourselves, which we often portray through our choice of social networking profile pictures. Here are profile pictures on Facebook featuring your authors. What do your profile pictures say to others about you?

self-concept People's description of their own characteristics.

self-schema A cognitive organization that helps us think about the self and process self-relevant information.

Self-Concept

For the moment, set aside your reading and make a list of 10 things that complete the sentence "I am _____________."

If you are like most college students, this description of your **self-concept** includes references to demographic factors, such as age, sex, or student status (first year or psychology major); personality features (outgoing or shy); relationships with others (friend, lover, daughter, son, sister, or brother); physical attributes (pretty, tall, or brown eyed); and various other roles (athlete, club member, or Texan).

We use **self-schemas** to think about these many aspects of the self (Markus, 1977). As we discussed in Chapters 10 and 11, schemas provide cognitive structures for organizing information. The structure provided by a self-schema influences not only the way you view yourself but also how you view and interact with others.

A major implication of having a self-schema is that we process self-relevant information differently than information about others. For example, we might think about our own brown hair in different ways than we think about our neighbor's brown hair. This self-reference effect (SRE) was demonstrated when four groups of participants were given lists of adjectives to memorize with different instructions (Rogers et al., 1977). The first group judged the size of letters making up the word, the second group judged whether the word rhymed with another word, the third group judged whether the word had the same meaning as another word, and the last group judged whether the word described them. The fourth group's recall for the words was subsequently superior to recall by the other groups (see ● Figure 12.15). These results implied that the self provided "a superordinate schema" (Rogers et al., 1977, p. 685).

Questions remain, however, as to the true cause of the observed SRE. Is there something special about self-schemas, or is the SRE simply a result of general memory processes such as depth of processing or elaboration, which we discussed in Chapter 9? For example, memory

FIGURE **12.15**

Using a Self-Schema Improves Recall for Words. Participants in this experiment were asked whether a word was in larger font (structural), rhymed with another word (phonemic), meant the same thing as another word (semantic), or described the participant (self-reference). As you can see from these results, when participants used their self-schemas to consider a word, later recall for the word was better than when the word was considered structurally, phonemically, or semantically. These results suggest that your memory for material you are studying will be improved by thinking about how it relates to your own life.

Source: Adapted from T. B. Rogers et al. (1977). "Self-Reference and the Encoding of Personal Information," *Journal of Personality and Social Psychology, 35*(9), 677–688. doi:10.1037/0022-3514.35.9.677

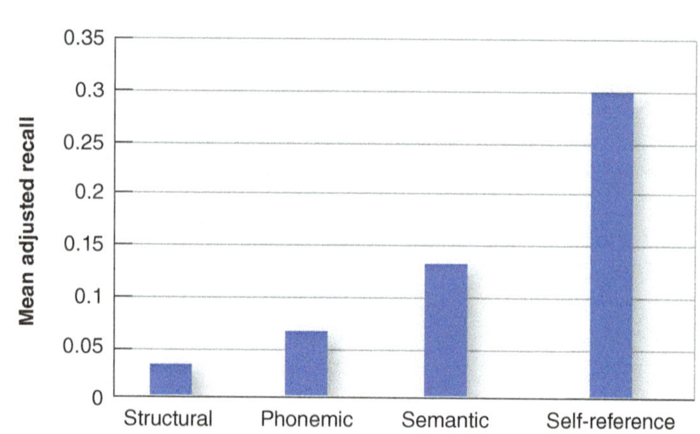

enhancement also occurred in a group that judged whether words described the study participants' mothers (Bower & Gilligan, 1979). We may remember self-relevant information simply because we know a lot about the subject—ourselves.

Self-Awareness

When answering the questions posed in the previous section, how do you know what to say? To know yourself requires you to make the self an object to be examined. Just as you try to figure out what kind of people your classmates and instructor are, you have the capacity to turn this analysis inward to the self. Self-awareness, or knowledge of your own internal traits, feelings, roles, and memories, is the result of this self-study. In addition, self-awareness allows us to establish boundaries between the self and other people. When we talk about ourselves, look at ourselves in a mirror, watch a video of ourselves, or stand out from the crowd in some way, we become more self-aware than usual. This state of heightened self-awareness can be quite unpleasant. Many people experience a negative mood when they look in a mirror (Fejfar & Hoyle, 2000).

Related to this negative self-awareness is the concept of self-consciousness, our awareness of our own characteristics and the way the self is perceived by others. In many cases, we overestimate how much attention others pay to our behavior, a phenomenon known as the spotlight effect. When student participants wearing an embarrassing T-shirt featuring 1970s pop singer Barry Manilow entered a room full of other students, they expected at least half of their fellow students to notice (Gilovich et al., 2000). In fact, only 23% of the students paid attention to the T-shirts. The particularly active spotlight effect that accompanies puberty is responsible for substantial pain during adolescence (Elkind, 1967; Elkind & Bowen, 1979). Teens are convinced that their every flaw and blemish is scrutinized by others. How reassuring it would be to understand that other teens are so worried about the imaginary audience's reactions to their own flaws that they scarcely have time to notice the flaws of others.

Self-consciousness might be unpleasant, but it makes people behave more ethically. When children were instructed by a sign to "take only one Halloween candy," they were more likely to comply when they could see their image in a mirror (Beaman et al., 1979). In a similar study, an honor-system coffee bar featured either a poster showing a pair of eyes or a poster showing a bouquet of flowers (Bateson et al., 2006). People were more likely to put money in the box to pay for their coffee when they saw the poster of the eyes (see Figure 12.16). Use of body cameras by police officers, raising their self-awareness of their actions, has decreased officers' use of force and number of complaints (Ariel et al., 2015).

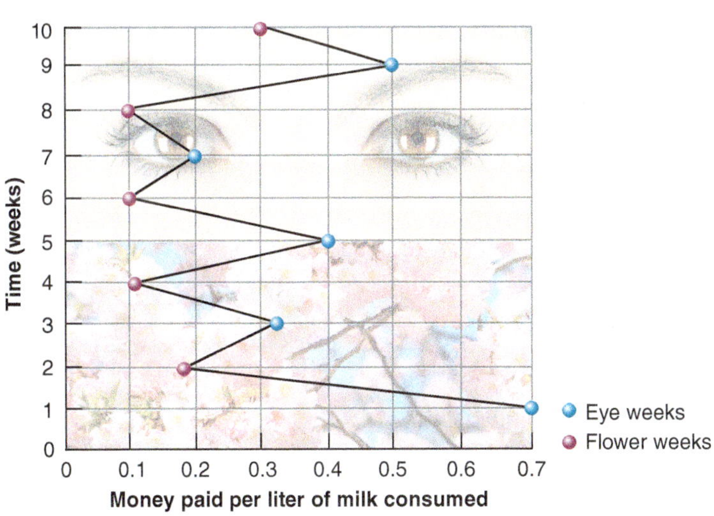

Photos: Blaj Gabriel/Shutterstock.com; Guzel Studio/Shutterstock.com

FIGURE 12.16

Self-Consciousness and Honesty. The amount of money collected in a college department honor-system coffee bar relative to consumption was measured by tracking milk consumption (this study was conducted in the United Kingdom, where coffee is rarely consumed black). Donations increased when a poster of eyes appeared above the bar and decreased when a poster of flowers appeared above the bar. Self-consciousness, perhaps from feeling "watched" by the photograph of eyes, typically results in more ethical behavior. Whether we are responding similarly to the large numbers of surveillance cameras in our environments remains to be demonstrated through future research.

Source: Adapted from M. Bateson et al. (2006). "Cues of Being Watched Enhance Cooperation in a Real-World Setting," *Biology Letters, 2*(3), 412–414. doi: 10.1098/rsbl.2006.0509

Barry Manilow might have sold millions of records in the 1970s, but students in 2000 thought wearing this shirt would be embarrassing. We tend to overestimate how much attention others pay to us, though, and only 23% of study participants noticed the T-shirt.

How do we obtain self-knowledge? An obvious source of self-awareness is the process of introspection, or the direct observation of one's own thoughts and feelings. After all, who is in a better position to know what goes on inside our heads than we are? Unfortunately, as we discussed in Chapter 1, introspection is not considered reliable.

Perhaps we could bypass mental states and focus instead on our observable behavior. People seem to use their behavior as a clue to their characteristics, just as any other observer does (Bem, 1972). If they see themselves behaving in a kindly way toward others, maybe they are kind people. In support of this approach, people who were gently encouraged to provide flattering descriptions of themselves scored higher on a subsequent test of self-esteem (Jones et al., 1981). In other words, if they observe themselves providing a positive self-analysis, it must be true.

The people around us also contribute to our self-knowledge. We use the reactions of other people like a mirror to "see" our own characteristics, developing a looking-glass self. We also incorporate the opinions of significant others into our self-concept. If our parents viewed us as brilliant, it is likely that we would view ourselves as brilliant too. Using the reactions of others works better when defining some characteristics than others. If our parents inaccurately view us as brilliant, we soon learn the truth at school. If they unfairly think we're lazy, though, it is more difficult to figure out they're wrong.

An obvious component of self-knowledge arises from autobiographical and episodic memories, described in Chapter 9. Who we are today is intimately linked with the self from the past that we remember. While offering valuable information about "who we are," episodic and autobiographical memories can provide a partial, incomplete, and occasionally inaccurate picture. As one psychologist noted, "The past is remembered as if it were a drama in which the self was the leading player" (Greenwald, 1980, p. 604).

Self-Esteem

Not only do we form a self-concept, but we also judge its value. This personal report card is known as **self-esteem**. Self-esteem may be global, based on our overall self-worth, or specific, relating to particular characteristics such as appearance or intelligence. Self-esteem introduces an emotional aspect to our self-concept. Not only do we judge ourselves, but we experience emotional responses to that judgment.

Judgments of the self are not necessarily accurate. Most people experience "positive illusions," which lead them to judge themselves more positively and less negatively than they judge others (Taylor & Brown, 1988). Despite inaccuracies, people who experience positive illusions enjoy a heightened sense of well-being.

People with high and low self-esteem respond differently to failure. The low self-esteem person overgeneralizes from failure (Brown & Mankowski, 1993). In other words, people with low self-esteem who fail one exam might assume that they are going to fail all their classes. This tendency to overgeneralize might explain why people with low self-esteem are more prone to depression (Sowislo & Orth, 2013), discussed further in Chapter 14. In contrast, people with high self-esteem respond to failure in one domain by exaggerating their abilities in other domains (Brown & Smart, 1991). If people with high self-esteem fail an exam, they are more likely to remind others about how great they are in sports, appearance, or dating.

Sources of Self-Esteem Because of the importance of self-esteem to psychological well-being, psychologists have looked at the origins of self-esteem carefully. Many psychologists believe that the process of developing self-esteem begins early in childhood (Cvencek et al., 2016). Across 48 nations, self-esteem is generally high during childhood, drops during adolescence, rises gradually in adulthood, then drops again slightly in old age (Bleidorn et al., 2016).

Self-esteem is influenced by social comparisons, or the judgments we make of our own worth relative to those around us (Festinger, 1954). The impact of social comparisons on self-esteem was demonstrated in an experiment in which researchers placed an advertisement for a research assistant (Morse & Gergen, 1970). Prospective employees found themselves in a waiting room with another candidate, who was actually an actor working for the

self-esteem A judgment of the value of the self.

Image Courtesy of The Advertising Archives

Dove, a division of Unilever that produces skin and hair care products, lists its social mission as building women's self-esteem. The company reports that only 4% of women worldwide consider themselves beautiful. To combat the influence of upward social comparisons, in which girls and women judge their attractiveness against the impossibly beautiful images of women in the media, Dove has committed to using diverse, natural looking models in their advertisements.

experimenters. The actor took the role of either Mr. Clean or Mr. Dirty. Participants waiting with Mr. Clean experienced drops in self-esteem, whereas the self-esteem of participants waiting with Mr. Dirty rose.

Psychologists have been curious about the effects of social media on social comparisons and self-esteem. Viewing selfies frequently on social media is negatively correlated with self-esteem (Wang et al., 2017). People with a high need for popularity responded more dramatically to viewing selfies. The same researchers reported that viewing groupies frequently was positively associated with self-esteem.

People with high self-esteem tend to make downward comparisons, in which they compare themselves to those they consider less worthy on a particular dimension. For example, a beautiful woman with high self-esteem is more likely to congratulate herself on how much better looking she is than her friends but is unlikely to compare herself with Hollywood beauties. In contrast, people with low self-esteem are likely to do the opposite. A beautiful woman with low self-esteem will engage in upward comparisons, chastising herself because she doesn't measure up to the most beautiful women in the world.

Regardless of self-esteem, we all seem to engage in a reassuring type of downward comparison when viewing our own pasts (Wilson & Ross, 2000). Most of us look back in time with a sense that we have improved. Our virtues are greater today than they used to be, and our faults are less.

Gender, Race, and Culture and Self-Esteem Given the influence of social comparisons on self-esteem, we might suspect that belonging to certain social groups would affect an individual's self-esteem. If you are a member of a privileged group in society, for example, shouldn't you have higher self-esteem than people who have experienced prejudice and discrimination?

Males appear to have a small to moderate advantage over females in self-esteem (Bleidorn et al., 2016). This finding is stable across 48 nations, suggesting the possibility of biological contributions to self-esteem. On the other hand, it is also possible that the male advantage emerges from social patterns that are universal across cultures. Further research is needed to clarify the sources of this gender difference.

The bask-in-reflected-glory (BIRG) effect predicts that sales of apparel featuring a winning team like the Ohio State Buckeyes are likely to be much higher than those for a losing team. Associating with those we admire can produce self-enhancement.

Meta-analyses of self-esteem demonstrated differences based on race and ethnicity in the United States (Twenge & Crocker, 2002; Erol & Orth, 2011). As we noted in Chapter 11, beginning in adolescence, African-Americans score higher than white Americans in measures of self-esteem. However, Americans identifying themselves as Asian or Native American scored below white Americans in measures of self-esteem. Hispanic adolescents had lower self-esteem than white teens but reported higher self-esteem at age 30 than white Americans (Erol & Orth, 2011).

Cultural differences among groups might account for some of these results. As we mentioned previously, people in more collectivistic cultures might avoid standing out from the group by giving themselves highly positive ratings (see ● Figure 12.17). Results from tests that tap into implicit attitudes by asking participants to associate themselves with either positive words (*glorious, happy, or laughter*) or negative words (*agony, horrible, or nasty*) suggest that Asian Americans have about the same level of self-esteem as white Americans, but cultural values of modesty usually override their outward expression of that self-esteem (Greenwald & Farnham, 2000).

Culture plays an additional role in self-esteem by setting the values by which people measure themselves. Adherence to cultural values, more so than to individual values, were shown to predict self-esteem across 20 different cultural settings (Becker et al., 2014). Although individual achievement is an important part of self-esteem, finding meaningfulness through belonging to multiple groups is also a predictor of a person's self-esteem (Jetten et al., 2015). The group membership effect on self-esteem is not simply a matter of having more friends but more likely from a sense of belonging to something larger than the self.

Using Self-Enhancement to Protect Self-Esteem The good news is that most of us feel rather positively about ourselves. The bad news is that we are a wee bit unrealistic. People who perform most poorly are the most likely to engage in self-enhancement by inflating their opinions of themselves. College students who performed in the bottom 12% on tests of logic, grammar, and humor guessed that they performed better than 62% of their peers (Kruger & Dunning, 1999). As student performance increased, the amount of inflation decreased.

Some people begin protecting their self-esteem long before a performance takes place. In self-handicapping, people begin to build an excuse in advance, just in case they fail (Berglas & Jones, 1978). Self-handicapping strategies take many forms, including taking drugs, failing to practice or do homework, commenting on poor health or stress, or sandbagging. Sandbagging occurs when you let everyone know how bad you are at something. By lowering expectations of your performance, nobody will notice much when you fail. Although self-handicapping may protect your self-esteem, it does not make you popular with others (Rhodewalt et al., 1995).

FIGURE **12.17**

Cultural Differences in Explicit and Implicit Measures of Self-Esteem. Apparent cultural differences in self-esteem must be evaluated carefully. Using explicit measures of self-esteem, it appears that white Americans have higher self-esteem than Asian Americans. However, when implicit measures of self-esteem are used, this difference disappears, suggesting that the observed difference is probably because of cultural norms related to modesty.

Source: Adapted from A. G. Greenwald & S. D. Farnham (2000). "Using the Implicit Association Test to Measure Self-Esteem and Self-Concept," *Journal of Personality and Social Psychology*, *79*, 1022–1038. doi: 10.1037/0022-3514.79.6.1022

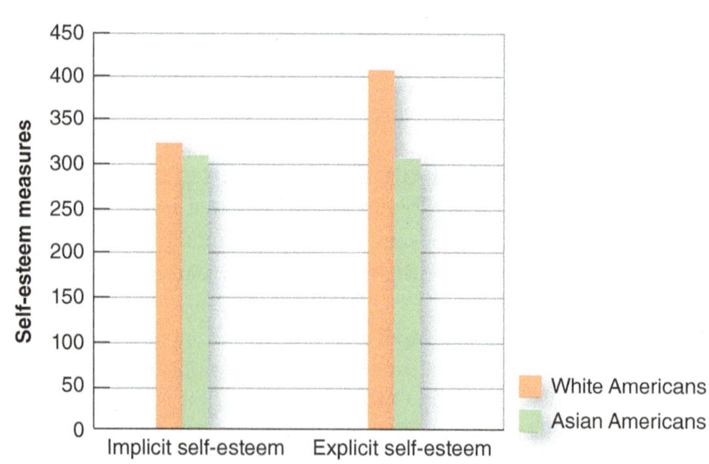

Another method of self-enhancement is to associate with others you admire. This approach has been labeled the bask-in-reflected-glory (BIRG) effect (Cialdini et al., 1976). On the Monday following a football game, university students are more likely to wear sweatshirts with their school's name if their team won than if it lost. We are equally quick to distance ourselves from failure. Many an athlete or performer has been surprised at how many friends they have during successful times and how quickly those friends disappear when times are tough.

Self-enhancement may serve to protect self-esteem, but it can have many unwanted effects. Primary among these negative side effects is being disliked by others. People who engage in self-enhancement typically make good first impressions, but these impressions do not last (Paulhus, 1998).

The Advantages of Self-Esteem Having high self-esteem provides several benefits both to the individual and to the groups to which the individual with high self-esteem belongs. Among the advantages of high self-esteem for individuals are happiness and persistence (Baumeister et al., 2003). These outcomes occur because high self-esteem acts as a buffer. When faced with bad news, people with high self-esteem are more likely to weather the storm than are people with low self-esteem. In addition, high self-esteem enhances social dominance within a peer group (Juvonen, 2005).

Self-esteem contributes to belongingness or the maintenance of good social relationships (Baumeister & Leary, 1995; Leary & Downs, 1995; Leary et al., 1995). Because social rejection could have such devastating effects on survival in our evolutionary past, self-esteem could have emerged as a way of estimating the likelihood of rejection. Self-esteem drops following the experience of social exclusion (Leary et al., 1995). A drop in self-esteem serves as an early warning signal that rejection by the group is imminent, and behavior designed to regain the favor of the group should be initiated.

A terror management theory suggests that self-esteem interacts with a cultural worldview to buffer our fear of death (Greenberg et al., 1986; Pyszczynski et al., 1991). Cultural worldviews can include shared beliefs that allow us to attain feelings of immortality, whether through producing children, writing books, or believing in an afterlife. By conforming to these cultural worldviews, people enjoy enhanced self-esteem that reduces their anxiety related to death.

Having members with high self-esteem is an advantage to groups in several respects. People with high self-esteem are more likely to speak critically when in groups (LePine & Van Dyne, 1998). Groups that do not have members who are willing to question group decisions might fall prey to poor decision-making, discussed further in Chapter 13. People with high self-esteem not only value themselves but also value the groups to which they belong (Aberson et al., 2000). People with low self-esteem do not show this favoritism. If a group is highly valued by its members, its overall success is likely to be enhanced, which in turn benefits its members.

© U. S. Department of Health and Human Services

Terror management theory suggests that self-esteem serves as a protection against our fear of death. When people are reminded of their own mortality, self-esteem can increase. Ironically, these labels proposed by the government for cigarette packages might have the unintended consequences of enhancing, rather than diminishing, favorable attitudes about smoking. Some smokers equate smoking with improving their image, which in turn improves their self-esteem (Hansen, Winzeler, & Topolinski, 2009).

PSYCHOLOGY AS A HUB SCIENCE

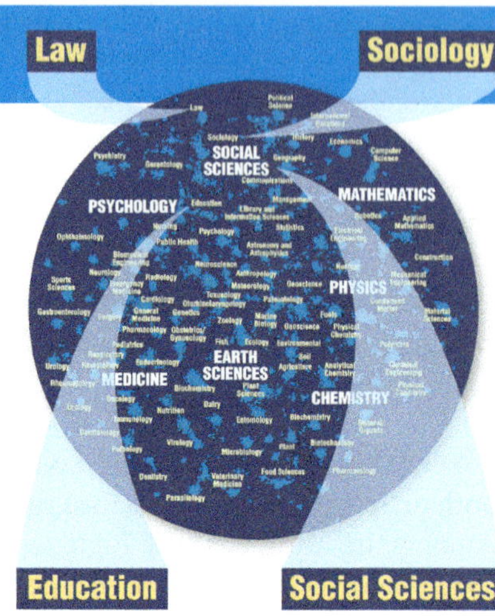

Self-Esteem, Academic Performance, and Aggression

Douglas Pulsipher/Alamy Stock Photo

Although many people believe that raising children's self-esteem is a good thing, research suggests that self-esteem is more likely to be the outcome rather than the cause of behavior. Providing feel-good messages that are not based in real achievement can backfire (Forsyth & Kerr, 1999).

IN 1989, THE CALIFORNIA TASK FORCE ON SELF-ESTEEM AND PERSONAL AND SOCIAL RESPONSIBILITY published a report that declared "many, if not most, of the major problems plaguing society have roots in the low self-esteem of many of the people who make up society" (Mecca et al., 1989, p. 1). Teachers, parents, and therapists express similar beliefs and actively work to increase the self-esteem of others. These approaches mirror a commonsense attitude toward self-esteem. High self-esteem seems more desirable than low self-esteem, and interventions designed to raise self-esteem appear on the surface to be a good thing. How accurate are these views of self-esteem?

Self-esteem and school grades are positively correlated, although the effects are surprisingly small (Baumeister et al., 2003). As with all correlations, we cannot reach conclusions about the cause of this relationship without further data. Explicit efforts to identify a causal relationship between self-esteem and school performance have failed to support the commonsense hypothesis that high self-esteem produces good performance. A sample of 1,600 young males in the 10th grade was followed for an additional 8 years (Bachman & O'Malley, 1977). No evidence for a causal role for self-esteem in school performance was discovered. Instead, third factors, including socioeconomic status, IQ, and early school performance, appeared responsible for the correlation between self-esteem and school performance. In fact, high self-esteem seems more likely to be a result of good grades, not vice versa (Rosenberg et al., 1989).

What do these findings mean for efforts such as the California Task Force, which sought to raise achievement by improving self-esteem? Unfortunately, interventions intended to boost self-esteem can backfire. When students receiving poor grades on a midterm were sent an e-mail message designed to boost their self-worth, they performed significantly worse on the next exams than did students in control groups (Forsyth & Kerr, 1999). This study provides an important lesson: Providing indiscriminate feel-good messages that are not anchored in achievement results in lower achievement.

If relationships between school achievement and self-esteem are weaker than many believe, what about the relationships between self-esteem and social problems such as aggression? Again, our commonsense hypotheses fail us. We have heard parents, teachers, and legislators lament that many social problems would dissipate if only we could raise self-esteem. This commonsense notion was challenged by Roy Baumeister and his colleagues, who discovered that aggressive people were more likely to have positive and frequently inflated views of their self-worth (Baumeister et al., 1999; Baumeister et al., 2003). ■

oliveromg/Shutterstock.com

Contrary to many stereotypes, bullies typically do not suffer from low self-esteem. They experience less depression, less anxiety, and less loneliness than prosocial youth and are likely to be considered by peers "the coolest kids in their classes." (Juvonen, 2005).

Self-Regulation

To meet the expectations we have for ourselves, we engage in self-regulation, also known as self-control or willpower. Self-regulation consists of conscious executive efforts to control our thoughts, motives, feelings, and behaviors (Carver & Scheier, 2000). Failures to regulate behavior frequently lead to some of the most perplexing problems facing society, including drug abuse, domestic violence, and binge eating. In addition, deficits in self-regulation characterize several psychological disorders we discuss in Chapter 14, including schizophrenia, attention deficit hyperactivity disorder (ADHD), and obsessive-compulsive disorder.

Individual differences in self-regulation, as we observed earlier in this chapter, are apparent at young ages. While a certain amount of self-regulation is related to training and supervision on the part of adults, individuals show different patterns of brain activation while facing temptation. Increased activity in the nucleus accumbens, which is implicated in processing reward and addiction, is associated with self-control failures, such as eating something we intended to pass by. Simultaneously, higher activity in the prefrontal cortex was associated with an individual's ability to withstand temptation (Lopez et al., 2014). In self-regulation, we make distinctions between what is good for the current self (eating a yummy treat) and what is good for the future self (having good health). We perceive the future self more like a different individual who stands in judgment of our current choices. Thus, activity in brain areas associated with self-centered (egocentric) thinking is associated with more impulsive and selfish decisions (Soutschek et al., 2016).

Self-regulation is made even more difficult because the harder we think about not doing something, the more likely we are to do it (Wegner, 1994). Try, for example, to avoid thinking about a white bear for the next 30 seconds. If you are like most people, your thoughts were suddenly dominated by images of white bears. We can explain this phenomenon as follows. When you try to control your behavior, you simultaneously activate a concern about failing. In an effort to avoid failure, you automatically pay more attention to the item or behavior to be avoided. "What exactly is this white bear thing I should avoid?" Because of this attention, we end up doing what we hoped to avoid doing.

Sometimes when we try to use our self-regulation abilities to not think of something ("Whatever you do, don't think about white bears"), we end up thinking quite a bit about the object we wish to avoid.

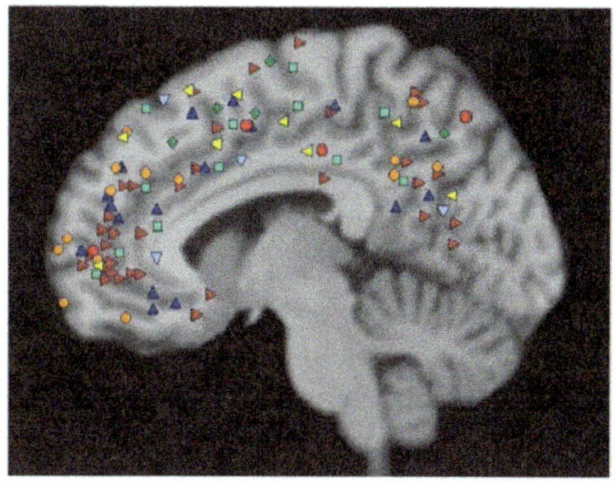

▲ Emotional domain: self > nonself
▽ Facial domain: self > nonself
□ Memory domain: self > nonself
◆ Motor domain: self > nonself
◁ Social domain: self ∩ other
● Social domain: self > other
✚ Spatial domain: self > nonself
▶ Verbal domain: self > nonself

A widely distributed network of brain structures participates in processing the different aspects of self. Self-referential processing, or the processing of information relevant to ourselves but not others, can occur in our emotional, facial, memory, motor, social, spatial, and verbal domains.

Source: G. Northoff et al. (2006). "Self-referential Processing In Our Brain—A Meta-analysis of Imaging Studies On the Self," *NeuroImage, 31*(1), 440–457. doi: 10.1016/j.neuroimage.2005.12.002

The Brain and the Self

If the mind is the product of the activity of the nervous system, is it possible to locate the self within these patterns of activity? This question suggests that information about the self is processed in unique and special ways by the nervous system (Gillihan & Farah, 2005). As we have seen so far in this chapter, the concept of self can mean many things. Brain correlates have been found for knowledge of our own bodies—their configuration, appearance, and location—as well as for memories of personal experiences, interpersonal connections, and use of a first-person perspective.

Given the large number of different aspects of the self, it should not be surprising that a widely distributed network of brain structures participates in the processing of the self (Cacioppo & Decety, 2011). Activity in the default mode network or DMN (see Chapter 6) is often associated with thinking about the self (Kahn, 2013). However, during thinking about the self, activity in the DMN is joined by activity in parts of the brain that process external sources of information, such as the awareness of other people and the environment. These observations remind us of our constant use of context when we think about ourselves.

An important aspect of the self is the recognition of our own faces. The right hemisphere plays a special role in distinguishing our own faces from those of other people. In one study, one hemisphere of each participant's brain was made inactive using an anesthetic. When study participants then viewed a photograph combining one half of their face with the half-face of a famous person, they recognized themselves when the left hemisphere was anesthetized but reported seeing the famous person when the right hemisphere was anesthetized (Keenan et al., 2001; see Figure 12.18).

In addition to playing an important role in recognizing our own faces, the right hemisphere is necessary for the construction of stable traits and attitudes. The location of brain damage (right hemisphere only, left hemisphere only, or both hemispheres) can be correlated with observed changes in personal characteristics that usually show little change over time, such as political views and religious beliefs (Miller et al., 2001). Only people with right hemisphere damage alone showed changes in these normally stable characteristics.

Schizophrenia, which we discuss in Chapter 14, produces distortions in a person's sense of self (Feinberg, 1978). One common symptom is a delusion of control, or the sense that some external agent is either monitoring or influencing a person's behavior. This delusion is highly relevant to our current discussion, because it represents confusion over the behavior produced

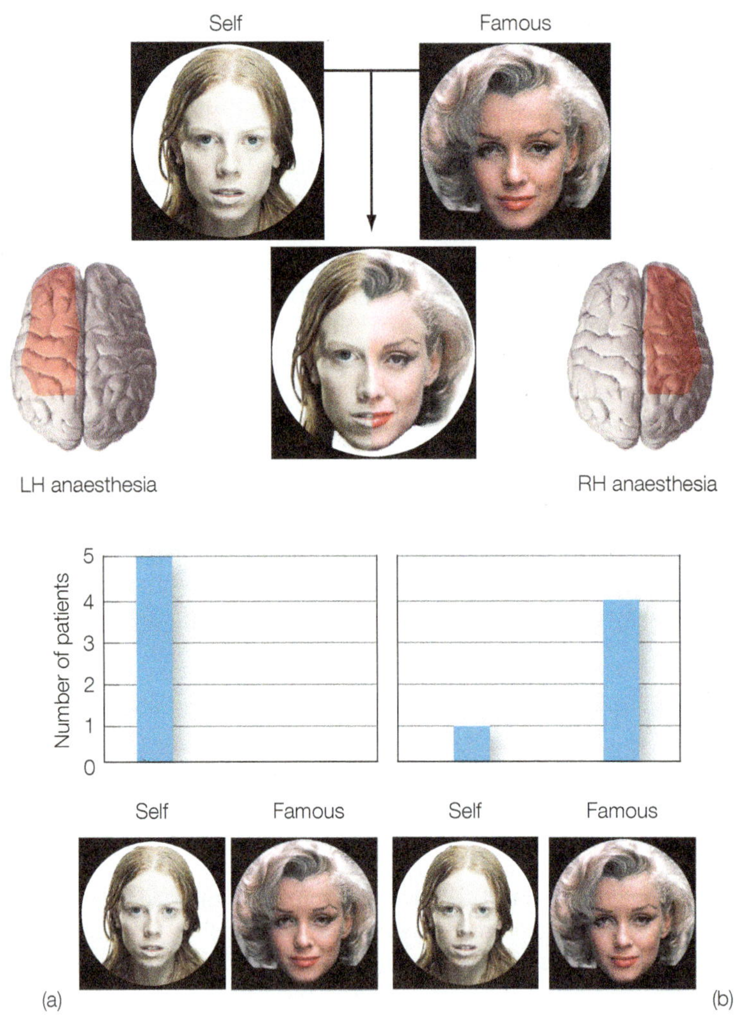

Illustration: Argosy Publishing, Inc.; photo (Marilyn): Image Source/Alamy Stock Photo; Alfred Eisenstaedt/Getty Images

FIGURE **12.18**

Recognizing Your Own Face. Participants in this experiment viewed blended faces made from one half of their own photograph and one half of a photograph of a famous person. When the participants' left hemispheres (LHs) were anesthetized, leaving the right hemisphere (RH) active, they believed the photo was their own **(a)**. When their right hemispheres were anesthetized, leaving the left hemisphere active, most believed the photo showed the famous person **(b)**. These results suggest that for many people, the right hemisphere plays a role in recognizing our own faces.
Source: Adapted from J. P. Keenan et al. (2001). "Self-Recognition and the Right Hemisphere," *Nature, 409*(6818), 305. doi: 10.1038/35053167

AISPIX/Shutterstock.com

mangostock/Shutterstock.com

When we interact with significant others, such as family members, we experience the relational self. When we interact with larger groups, for example, other fans supporting the same sports team, such as these Brazilian soccer fans, we experience the collective self.

by the self or by others. For example, people with this symptom might describe their behavior as controlled by others through implants in their brains. A comparison of brain activity during such delusions and after they recede indicated that the delusions of control were correlated with excess activity in the right hemisphere (Spence, 1997).

The Social Self

The self we have discussed so far represents the personal self or the attributes that differentiate an individual's self from all others (Brewer & Gardner, 1996). This self both shapes and is shaped by interactions with others. Just who those others are and how they interact with the self has been the subject of significant psychological inquiry.

The Interpersonal Self William James (1890) remarked that an individual has "as many different social selves as there are distinct groups of persons about whose opinion he cares" (p. 294). In other words, in addition to having a personal self, we experience an **interpersonal self**. In current psychological discussions of the self, influences on the interpersonal self fall into two categories: A person's significant others and the social groups to which the person belongs. Significant others include family members, friends, coworkers, and others with whom the self interacts or has interacted. As we interact with significant others, we experience the relational self (Brewer & Gardner, 1996; Chen et al., 2006). The influence of the larger groups to which we belong provides our collective self (Brewer & Gardner, 1996).

The concept of the interpersonal self implies that an individual's self is more flexible and complex than it would be based on a personal self alone. This flexibility is illustrated by the suggestion that we have a relational self when we are with a particular person, such as the "me when I'm with mom" (Chen et al., 2006, p. 153). It is likely that a great deal of overlap occurs among the many interpersonal selves we experience, but recognizing that we may not be consistent across all social situations is important. The differences we experience echo the discussion earlier in the chapter about personality traits and situations.

Cultural Influences on the Self Given the interpersonal dimensions of the self described in the previous section, it should come as no surprise that the concept of the self means different things in different cultures.

One aspect of cultural differences that is particularly relevant to the study of the self is the distinction between individualism and collectivism (see ● Figure 12.19). Individualism is characterized by an emphasis on independence and self-reliance. In contrast, core values of collectivism include interdependence, cooperation, and lack of conflict. As we discussed in the introduction to this chapter, these relative weightings of self and others tend to characterize entire nations. The United States, Australia, Great Britain, Canada, and the Netherlands appear to be the most individualistic, while Venezuela, Colombia, Pakistan, Peru, Taiwan, and China appear to be the most collectivistic (Hofstede, 1980). The individualistic–collectivistic nature of any particular culture is a moving target across time (Hamamura, 2012), and our characterization of particular social groups requires constant updating. The typical view of Japanese as collectivists and Americans as individualists was supported by only five out of

interpersonal self The self we are in the presence of other people.

FIGURE **12.19**

Individualism and Collectivism. Geert Hofstede compared cultures on five dimensions relevant to individualism and collectivism. Compared to the Chinese, Americans are less tolerant of unequal distributions of power (PDI), more likely to expect self-reliance (IDV), about equally assertive and competitive rather than modest and caring (MAS), more tolerant of ambiguity and lack of structure (UAI), and far less thrifty and persistent (LTO).
Source: Adapted from G. Hofstede (1980). *Culture's Consequences.* Beverly Hills, CA: Sage.

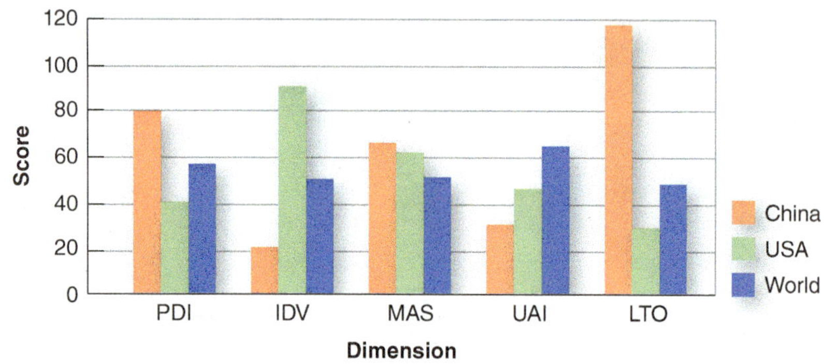

PDI: Less powerful accept and expect that power is distributed unequally.
IDV: Refers to individuals or groups, not the state, and their role in taking care of you.
MAS: Higher numbers indicate more assertive and competitive, rather than modest and caring.
UAI: Tolerance for ambiguity, unstructured situations.
LTO: Thrift, perseverance

30 reviewed studies (Takano & Osaka, 2018). Instead, 19 studies found no difference in collectivism and individualism between the cultures, and 11 studies reported that Japanese are more individualistic than Americans.

Two major differences occur between highly individualistic cultures and more collectivistic cultures (Markus & Kitayama, 1991). The first difference predicts a person's source of satisfaction. People in individualistic cultures feel best about themselves when they experience personal achievement, whereas people in collectivistic cultures feel good about belonging to a successful group. For example, a baseball player from an individualistic culture might take pride in having a terrific batting average even though his team is losing, whereas the player from a more collectivistic culture might feel better about being a member of the top team regardless of his personal performance.

The second difference predicts a person's sense of being similar to other group members. In individualistic cultures, people are more likely to see themselves as unique. In collectivistic cultures, conformity and appearing like others are more highly valued. White American and Korean study participants were offered the gift of a pen, which they were to choose from a group of three or four pens of the same color and one pen with a unique color. Whereas 74% of the white Americans chose the uniquely colored pen, 76% of the Koreans chose a pen with the more common color (Kim & Markus, 1999).

Interpersonal Relationships
The Personality Perspective

HOW DOES PERSONALITY AFFECT ATTRACTION?

PERSONALITY PROVIDES A PERFECT OPPORTUNITY to revisit the "birds of a feather flock together" theme that we discussed previously in this textbook. Is it true that people with similar personalities are attracted to each other?

People in long-term relationships who have similar personalities experienced different levels of satisfaction at different stages in their relationships (Shiota & Levenson, 2007). Early in a relationship, similarity was particularly important to promoting bonding and intimacy. But what happens when we take one more step backward in time to look at the effects of similarity when two people first meet each other?

In one study, pairs of heterosexual, opposite-sex college students were left in a waiting room while a researcher ran an errand (Cuperman & Ickes, 2009). Without their knowledge, the pairs' interactions were filmed. As predicted by "birds of a feather," pairs of introverts and pairs of extroverts reported having a better conversation and liking their partner more (see • Figure 12.20). However, similarity in agreeableness was not so important. Leaving two disagreeable people together did not result in a pleasant conversation. Surprisingly, though, having at least one agreeable person produced the same quality of interaction as having two agreeable people. Apparently, agreeable people know how to produce a good interaction whether or not their partner is equally capable.

You might be wondering how personality similarities compare to other factors when people first meet, and the answer is not well, at least in the context of a speed-dating session for college students (Luo & Zhang, 2009). Under these circumstances, the overwhelming determinant of attraction for both men and women was physical appearance. No similarity in attitudes and Big Five characteristics significantly predicted attraction. This outcome might be one of the reasons we are cautioned to "get to know each other better" before becoming involved in a serious relationship. If similarity plays an important role in long-term satisfaction, even with the bumps and bruises of middle age described by Shiota and Levenson (2007), it appears that we need more time than the speed-dating situation provides to make important relationship decisions. ■

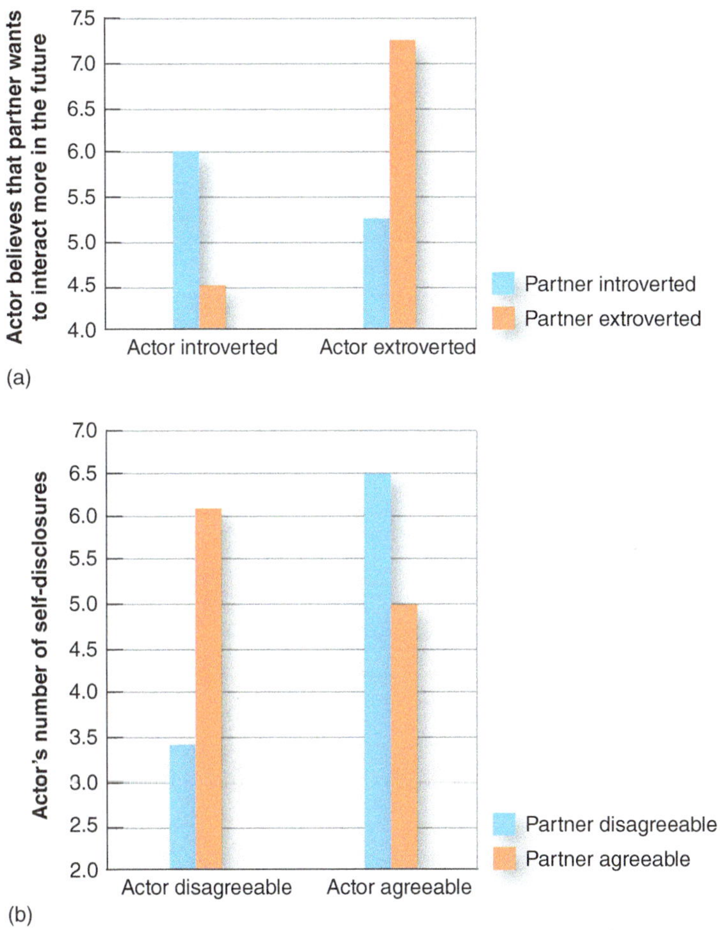

FIGURE **12.20**

Do Opposites Attract? Introverts conversing with other introverts and extroverts conversing with other extroverts were more likely to believe their partner would want to interact in the future than pairs in which one person was introverted and the other was extroverted. When agreeableness was investigated, one disagreeable person having a conversation with another disagreeable person was not very positive, but as long as one of the partners was agreeable, the conversation went well.

Source: Adapted from R. Cuperman & W. Ickes (2009). "Big Five Predictors of Behavior and Perceptions in Initial Dyadic Interactions: Personality Similarity Helps Extraverts and Introverts, but Hurts 'Disagreeables.'" *Journal of Personality and Social Psychology, 97*(4), 667–684. doi:10.1037/a0015741

Psychology Takes on Real-World Problems

Personality and Responses to a Pandemic

SEVERAL BIG FIVE PERSONALITY traits seem like they might predict individual responses to the COVID-19 pandemic, conscientiousness and neuroticism in particular. Is this commonsense hypothesis actually correct?

A recent study of U.S. adults compared results of a personality test administered in January and February of 2020, before public concerns about COVID-19 were prevalent, with questions about pandemic responses administered in late March of 2020 (Aschwanden et al., 2020). Personality factors were associated with both the precautions taken and estimates of the length of the pandemic.

As you have seen many times in this textbook, our commonsense notions of behavior are not always consistent with scientific data. Instead of predicting high levels of compliance with behaviors such as frequent hand washing and maintaining physical distance, neuroticism was actually negatively correlated with these behaviors (see ● Figure 12.21). In other words, the most neurotic people were the least likely to engage in pandemic precautions. It is possible that the real culprit in this case is depression (see Chapter 14), which is more common among people with high neuroticism. Depression can lead to more emotion-focused coping strategies rather than more problem-focused coping strategies (see Chapter 16). Less surprising is the finding that conscientious people were much more likely to engage in precautionary behaviors. Highly neurotic people were more pessimistic and highly extroverted people were more optimistic about the length of the pandemic.

In keeping with our belief in considering problems from multiple psychological perspectives, the influence of age appears to have been important in this study. Preparatory behaviors, such as stockpiling food and toilet paper, were higher in conscientious older adults, but not among middle or young adults. This might reflect a realistic assessment of their higher risk and the need to reduce trips to the store.

This section of each chapter focuses on the policy implications of relevant research results. In this case, we might argue that one-size-fits-all messaging from authorities might not be very effective. If there was a way to tailor messages to different personality types, these might be more persuasive. By understanding the interactions between personality and preparatory behaviors, authorities might do a better job of convincing the public to engage in healthy precautions and to stop stockpiling essential goods. ■

Precautions	Neuroticism	Conscientiousness
Wash hands 	–	+++
Hand sanitizer 	–	+
Avoid touching 	–	++
Physical distance 	–	++
Face mask 	0	–
Clean 	–	++

FIGURE **12.21**

Personality Predicts Pandemic Responses. Big Five characteristics of neuroticism and conscientiousness predicted participants' adherence to precautions related to a pandemic. Minus signs indicate negative correlations and plus signs indicate positive correlations. The 0 indicates no significant correlation. The number of plus signs indicates the strength of the correlations. Public health officials could modify messaging based on these different responses.

Source: Adapted from D. Aschwanden et al. (2020). "Psychological and Behavioural Responses to Coronavirus Disease 2019: The Role of Personality." *European Journal of Personality*. doi: 10.1002/per.2281

SUMMARY 12.2 Some Important *Self* Terms

Trait	Description
Self-concept 	Attributes assigned to the self, as in "I am a first-year botany major."
Self-schema 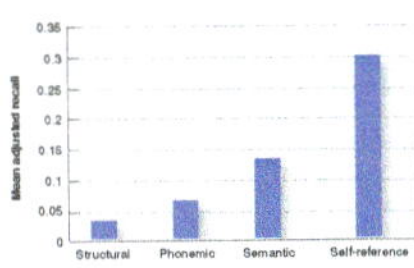	Collection of all self-concept attributes, used to organize thinking about the self.
Self-awareness 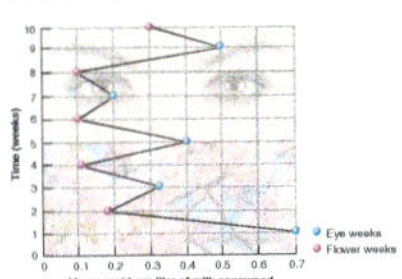	Knowledge of the self.
Self-esteem 	Judgments of the self's worth.
Self-regulation 	Self-control or conscious efforts to manage the self.

Credits: Top row—Courtesy of John T. Cacioppo and Laura Freberg; Third row—Photos: Blaj Gabriel/Shutterstock.com, Guzel Studio/Shutterstock.com; Fourth row—Image Courtesy of The Advertising Archives; Bottom row—Iakov Filimonov/Shutterstock.com.

KEY TERMS The Language of Psychological Science

Be sure you can define these terms and use them correctly.

agreeableness, p. 469
Big Five theory, p. 468
conscientiousness, p. 469
defense mechanism, p. 463
ego, p. 462
extroversion, p. 469
id, p. 462
interpersonal self, p. 493
introversion, p. 469
locus of control, p. 472
neo-Freudian, p. 465
neuroticism, p. 469
openness, p. 468
personality inventory, p. 478
projective test, p. 481
psychoanalysis, p. 462
psychodynamic, p. 462
psychosexual stage, p. 463
reciprocal determinism, p. 472
self, p. 483
self-concept, p. 484
self-esteem, p. 486
self-schema, p. 484
social–cognitive learning theory, p. 472
superego, p. 463
temperament, p. 473
trait, p. 467
unconscious mind, p. 465

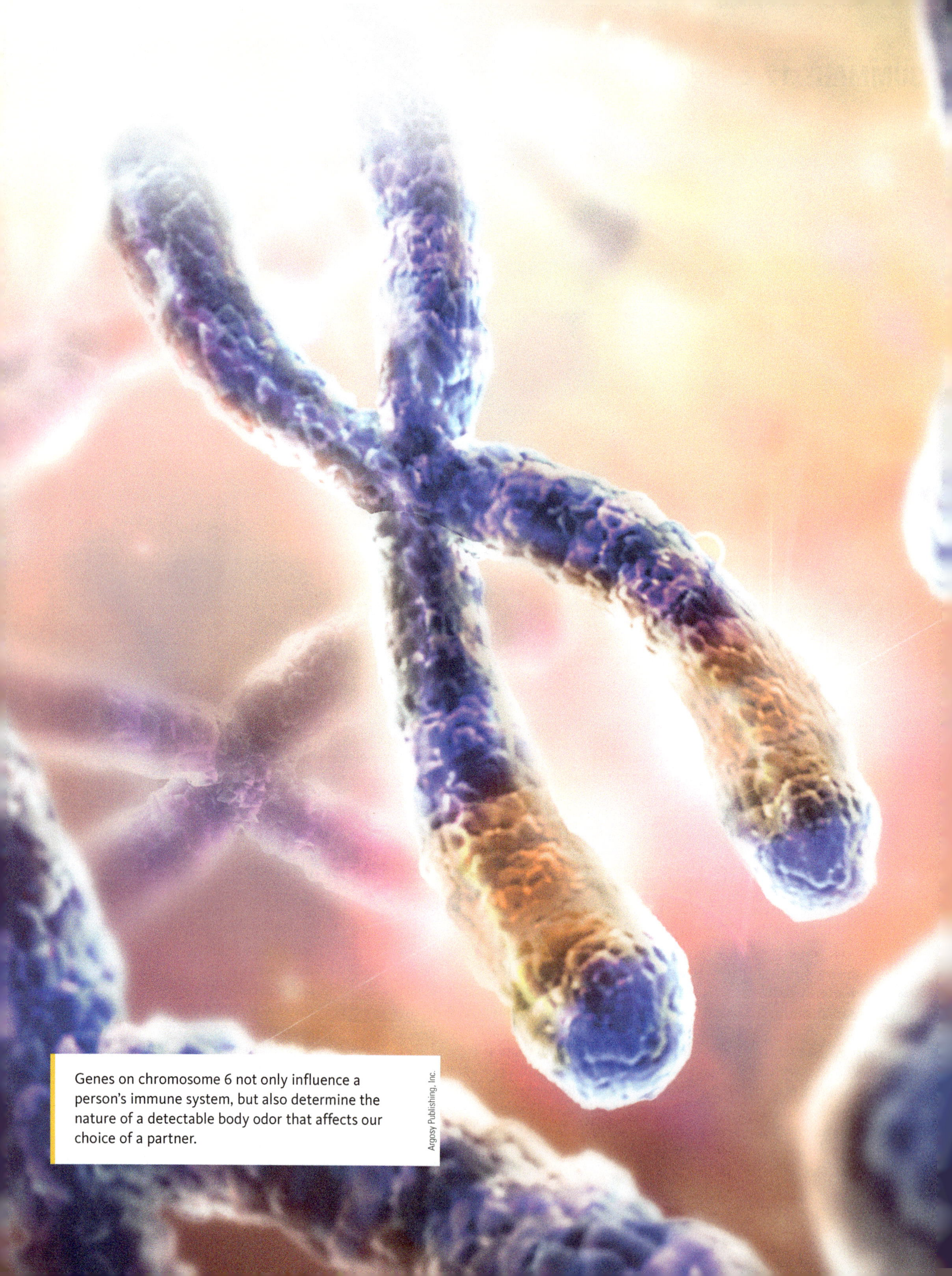

Genes on chromosome 6 not only influence a person's immune system, but also determine the nature of a detectable body odor that affects our choice of a partner.

Argosy Publishing, Inc.

13

The Connected Mind

SOCIAL PSYCHOLOGY

LEARNING OBJECTIVES

1. Discuss person perception, including first impressions, our use of dispositional and situational attributions, and the types of attributional biases that can occur.
2. Define attitude and discuss the origins of attitudes and their susceptibility to change.
3. Differentiate prejudice, stereotyping, and discrimination.
4. Evaluate social influence by distinguishing among conformity, compliance, and obedience.
5. Identify types of group influence, including social facilitation, social loafing, deindividuation, group polarization, and groupthink.
6. Summarize research on the mechanisms of attraction, cooperation and competition, and aggression.

MUCH OF OUR SUCCESS AS A SPECIES CAN BE attributed to our social nature. Our need to understand our complex social environment was one of the driving forces that shaped the development of our large human brains (Cacioppo & Cacioppo, 2020). But as we all know from personal experience, the social world can be challenging; consider, if you can, some truly embarrassing memories about social mistakes that you've made.

Among the social environments with the largest minefields is the connections that we make with others in intimate, romantic relationships. The two people in the photograph **at right** appear to find each other attractive, and they are engaged in behaviors—both variable and choreographed—designed to further their relationship. Looking at the developing relationship, psychologists can see a number of processes at work, such as first impressions and the effects of perceived similarities that are discussed in detail in this chapter.

Zooming in, however, we see a different set of processes at work. Although most of us believe that we choose romantic partners on the basis of perceived attractiveness and compatibility, there is some "chemistry" at work here too. Overall, humans share more genes in common with spouses (Domingue et al., 2014) and friends (Christakis & Fowler, 2014) than they do with strangers. In some cases, however, being genetically different from your partner is desirable. The highlighted genes in the larger image help determine a person's immune system response. Furthermore, variations of these genes, or alleles, are associated with different detectable body odors (Wedekind & Füri, 1997). As attractive and compatible as these individuals seem to each other, one might reject the other in response to this odor. Our evolutionary history has left us with the ability to detect a genetic compatibility in a partner, as well as more surface compatibilities.

Maridav/Shutterstock.com

Individual humans are not that impressive, but cooperating in groups makes our species more capable.

Hans Deryk/Reuters

Zooming out from our couple, we see that their romance takes place within a larger social context. What will their families and friends think of their relationship? How do cultural attitudes and biases shape the likelihood of their success? To what extent will they feel comfortable conforming to these cultural expectations or rejecting them? These external factors can help determine the course of their relationship.

Why Are Humans So Social?

Humans depend on each another. We sit in houses and offices built by contractors and laborers, work on computers designed and built by armies of engineers and technicians, eat food grown and transported by others, wear clothes made by people living halfway around the globe, and look forward to the next text message from a friend.

As far back as the historical record goes, we have evidence that humans lived in groups. What advantages might cooperative living have provided to our early ancestors? As predators or fighters, individual humans have rather modest equipment relative to other species. Our teeth and nails are not particularly frightening, and we are frequently outmatched in speed and strength. Instead, our strength lies not in our individual might, but in our ability to unite. What makes us a truly formidable species is our ability to collaborate, communicate, work together, and form alliances.

Early evolutionary pressures favored humans who chose to affiliate or associate with others, and by doing so, sculpted much of the social behavior that we observe today (Dunbar, 2011; Cacioppo et al., 2015). Social interaction is not just a helpful option but is also a basic human need, which can be more powerful than other basic needs such as hunger (Cacioppo et al., 2014). A mother's ability to comfort her infant through touch has a greater impact on the infant's attachment to her than her ability to provide food (Harlow & Harlow, 1973). Study participants expecting a painful electric shock prefer the company of strangers to facing their fears alone (Schachter, 1959). We depend on today's mobile technologies that allow us to carry our social networks wherever we go (Finkel et al., 2012; Przybylski & Weinstein, 2013).

We not only need social contact, but also react negatively when social support is withdrawn (see ● Figure 13.1). Perceived social isolation shares similar risks of death with obesity and a sedentary lifestyle and is positively correlated with risk of suicide (Cacioppo et al., 2015; Holt-Lunstad et al., 2015). Disruptions of social connections through divorce, bereavement, separation, or ridicule are known to be among the most stressful experiences people may face (Williams, 2007). Perceived isolation, or loneliness, can initiate a cascade of negative interactions that further separate individuals from the social contact they need and want,

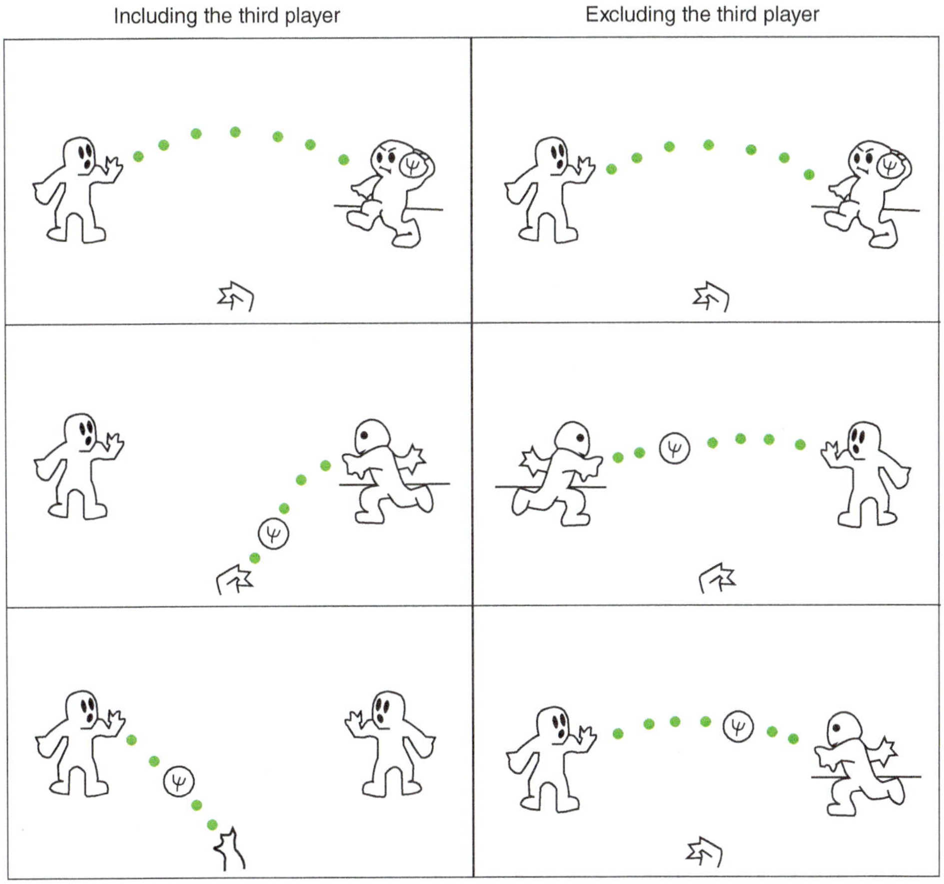

Courtesy of Kip Williams and David Yeager

FIGURE **13.1**

Eliciting Feelings of Exclusion. Psychologists have many ways to make study participants feel socially excluded for short periods so that they can evaluate the effects that social exclusion has on everything from brain activity to sharing cookies. Many experiments use this Cyberball game, developed by Kip Williams of Purdue University. The participant, represented by the little hand in the foreground, is initially included in the game of catch with the other two players, who are just part of a computer program. Midway through the game, the other players throw the ball between themselves, excluding the participant, whose little hand is left with nothing to do.

interfere with the quality of sleep, increase feelings of negative mood and hostility, and lead to a heightened sensitivity to threat and attack (Cacioppo et al., 2015; Cacioppo et al., 2010). The lonely person begins to behave in ways that are self-protective but that paradoxically push people away and promote further rejection and isolation. As a result, we are highly motivated to stay in the good graces of our social groups. In the remainder of this chapter, we will see how this need to maintain our social connectivity shapes many types of behavior, from the attitudes that we hold about brands of cereal to our responses as members of teams and committees.

How Accurate Are First Impressions?

Our success in the social world begins with our ability to perceive the characteristics and intentions of others. What was your immediate reaction to your psychology professor on your first day of class? If you're like most people, you came to some quick conclusions that are likely to last a long time. We form rapid and enduring first impressions of other people.

When we say first impressions are formed "rapidly," we are not talking about months, weeks, days, or hours, but in some cases, in as little as one-tenth of a second (Willis & Todorov, 2006). The responses to faces by infants are similar to those made by adults (Cogsdill et al., 2014), and strong cross-cultural agreement in perceptions of warmth and dominance has been observed (Zebrowitz et al., 2012). These observations suggest that forming first impressions is adaptive (Zebrowitz, 2017). We attend to cues about age, familiarity, fitness, and emotional

EXPERIENCING PSYCHOLOGY

The UCLA Loneliness Scale

IF YOU HAVE EXPERIENCED pangs of loneliness during your time at college, you are not alone. University students are especially susceptible to loneliness (Cutrona, 1982). Why do we feel loneliness? It might have evolved to provide our ancestors with an "early warning system" that their social connectivity needed repair (Cacioppo & Cacioppo, 2020).

The UCLA Loneliness Scale (Russell, 1996) is a standardized instrument that assesses a person's subjective self-report of loneliness. The scale, found in ● Table 13.1, includes 20 items; after you complete them, we will tell you how to score and interpret your results.

Adding up your scores: To obtain your final score, add up your responses to all the non-asterisked items. Then add up all the asterisked items and subtract this total from 45. You will notice that these items are "reversals," in which the "nonlonely" answers are the higher numbers. Questionnaires use this strategy to keep someone from just picking the same number all the way through an instrument. Add the two sums together to find your total score, which can range from 20 to 80.

Interpreting your score: Obviously, there are no right or wrong answers on an instrument like this, but higher numbers indicate higher levels of subjective loneliness. For comparison's sake, Russell (1996) administered this instrument to college students, nurses, public school teachers, and the elderly. The nurses had the highest scores (mean 40.14), followed by college students (40.08), older adults (31.51), and teachers (19.22). It might surprise you that the college students felt more loneliness than the older adults! This is probably because loneliness results from one's *perceived* disconnection, not absolute number of relationships. It is possible that college students have higher expectations for connectivity or that the elderly have had more time to establish meaningful relationships with others.

If your score seems on the high side, don't despair. Not only do psychological scientists understand quite a bit about loneliness, but they also have some empirically supported suggestions for alleviating it. One key to reducing feelings of loneliness is to understand how lonely people behave. Loneliness is associated with a number of maladaptive social cognitions, including increased sensitivity to social threats, better memory for negative social information, more negative social expectations, and behavior that confirms negative expectations. In other words, lonely people act in counterproductive ways that further drive them away from the social connectivity they seek (Cacioppo & Cacioppo, 2020). Interventions designed to reverse those maladaptive cognitions were found to reduce loneliness better than other strategies in a large meta-analysis (Masi et al., 2011). ■

TABLE 13.1

The UCLA Loneliness Scale

Item	Never	Rarely	Sometimes	Always
*1. How often do you feel that you are "in tune" with the people around you?	1	2	3	4
2. How often do you feel that you lack companionship?	1	2	3	4
3. How often do you feel that there is no one you can turn to?	1	2	3	4
4. How often do you feel alone?	1	2	3	4
*5. How often do you feel part of a group of friends?	1	2	3	4
*6. How often do you feel that you have a lot in common with the people around you?	1	2	3	4

7. How often do you feel that you are no longer close to anyone?

Never	Rarely	Sometimes	Always
1	2	3	4

8. How often do you feel that your interests and ideas are not shared by those around you?

Never	Rarely	Sometimes	Always
1	2	3	4

*9. How often do you feel outgoing and friendly?

Never	Rarely	Sometimes	Always
1	2	3	4

*10. How often do you feel close to people?

Never	Rarely	Sometimes	Always
1	2	3	4

11. How often do you feel left out?

Never	Rarely	Sometimes	Always
1	2	3	4

12. How often do you feel that your relationships with others are not meaningful?

Never	Rarely	Sometimes	Always
1	2	3	4

13. How often do you feel that no one really knows you well?

Never	Rarely	Sometimes	Always
1	2	3	4

14. How often do you feel isolated from others?

Never	Rarely	Sometimes	Always
1	2	3	4

*15. How often do you feel that you can find companionship when you want it?

Never	Rarely	Sometimes	Always
1	2	3	4

*16. How often do you feel that there are people who really understand you?

Never	Rarely	Sometimes	Always
1	2	3	4

17. How often do you feel shy?

Never	Rarely	Sometimes	Always
1	2	3	4

18. How often do you feel that people are around you, but not with you?

Never	Rarely	Sometimes	Always
1	2	3	4

*19. How often do you feel that there are people you can talk to?

Never	Rarely	Sometimes	Always
1	2	3	4

*20. How often do you feel that there are people you can turn to?

Never	Rarely	Sometimes	Always
1	2	3	4

Speed dating, in which people have a limited time to decide whether they would like further contact with another person, takes advantage of the rapid assessments of one another that we make. After only 30 seconds of contact, people make enduring evaluations of other people.

state that might have had significant consequences as hunter–gatherers interacted with one another.

We make quick assessments of others by focusing on a subset of traits and behaviors, rather than trying to sum up an entire person. In particular, people are likely to use faces to form impressions. Halo effects occur when one characteristic or a small number of characteristics have a large impact on overall perception. If people see characteristics that they value or dislike, they tend to make simple thumbs-up or thumbs-down assessments. One person might be attracted to blue eyes, and another might be turned on by tattoos. In one study, students hearing a professor described as "warm" instead of "cold" were willing to say after a brief encounter that he was a more effective teacher, less ruthless, and more humorous (Widmeyer & Loy, 1988).

First impressions are not only fast, but also persistent. Once we have reached a conclusion about a person, even after a brief social exchange in a speed-dating experiment, we tend to stick with that assessment for a long time. Most of us have formed a false first impression of others (either overly positive or overly negative) that breaks down only after extensive further exposure, if at all. However, in the face of certain types of new information, first impressions do change (Brannon & Gawronski, 2017; Mann & Ferguson, 2017). It would not be very adaptive to hold onto a false impression indefinitely, so it makes sense to think that we also have the ability to update our beliefs.

Although the tendency to make first impressions may be characteristic of all humans, our abilities to shape accurate judgments are also influenced by culture. As shown in ● Figure 13.2, Japanese and American participants successfully used their first impressions to predict which political candidates would win an upcoming election, but their predictions were more accurate for candidates from their own culture (Rule et al., 2010).

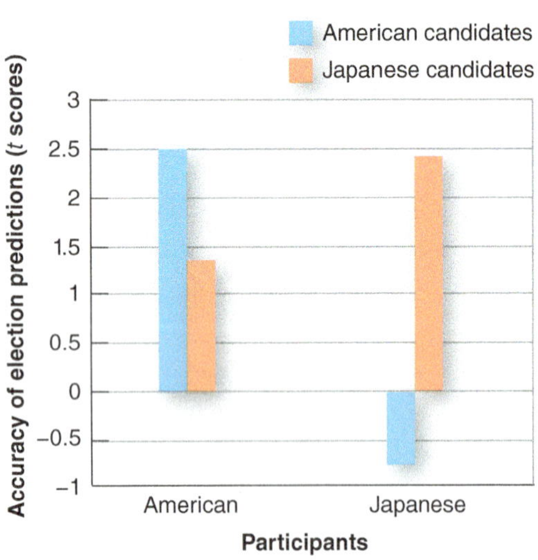

FIGURE 13.2

Judging Winners and Losers Across Cultures. Can you pick which of these candidates won or lost their elections?* Apparently, people can do this quite well, but they perform better within their own cultures. Based on viewing the photos of candidates' faces, without recognizing the candidate or even knowing that the person was running for office, Americans did a good job of predicting the outcome of an election for unfamiliar American candidates for the U.S. Senate but did not do as well when predicting the outcome for Japanese candidates for the *shugi-in* (the Japanese equivalent of the U.S. House of Representatives). Japanese participants predicted the success of Japanese candidates, but most of the American candidates who they expected to win ended up losing.

Source: Adapted from N. O. Rule et al. (2010). "Polling the Face: Prediction and Consensus Across Cultures," *Journal of Personality and Social Psychology*, *98*(1), 1–15. doi:10.1037/a0017673

*The two on the left won; the two on the right lost. (printed upside down)

Why Did That Just Happen?

We not only size up other people quickly in terms of their personal characteristics, but also ask why they behave the way they do. Being able to predict the behavior of others has significant survival value. Our answers to questions about why others behave in certain ways are **attributions**, or judgments about the causes of other people's behavior.

Behavior can be seen as resulting from some combination of **dispositional attribution** (internal) factors and **situational attribution** (external) factors (Heider, 1958). For example, if your friend just flunked an important exam, you could try to answer the question "Why?" by considering your friend's personal characteristics and circumstances. In considering your friend's disposition, you might recall that she is anxious (being anxious is dispositional), which might have interfered with her performance on a stressful test. In considering your friend's situation, you remember that she just broke up with her romantic partner of several years (breaking up is situational), which was depressing and distracting for her as she prepared for her test.

Thinking that disposition and situation act in an either/or fashion instead of interacting to produce an outcome is no more helpful to our understanding of behavior than using either/or thinking in considering nature and nurture (Funder, 2009; Johnson, 2009). However, as will be shown in the next section, the weight placed on dispositional and situational variables as explanations for behavior can vary dramatically from one case to the next. Although our attributions typically guide us in the right direction, we do make errors. We are not able to read minds, so we must make a logical leap from what we observe in a person's behavior to the internal state of mind that produced it. However, sometimes that leap takes us in the wrong direction. As we have seen in the case of visual illusions and heuristics, seeing the flaws in our mental processing can illuminate how systems usually work.

attribution A judgment about the cause of a person's behavior.

dispositional attribution A judgment assigning the cause of a person's behavior to personal qualities or characteristics.

situational attribution A judgment assigning the cause of a person's behavior to the environment.

correspondence bias The tendency to view behavior as the result of disposition, even when the behavior can be explained by the situation in which it occurs.

The Correspondence Bias and the Fundamental Attribution Error

When you hear about people flunking a test, you might start making conclusions about their dispositions ("she is a lazy student" or "he is not very smart"), even though you are quite aware that the professor giving the test has a reputation for writing brutal exams. This willingness to infer a person's disposition from observed behavior, even when strong situational factors are obvious, is known as the **correspondence bias** (Gilbert & Jones, 1986; Gilbert & Malone, 1995). In other words, we usually expect people's behavior to correspond to their dispositions, even when we know for sure that the situation is having a powerful effect.

Given the importance of making accurate attributions to our survival and social relationships, why would such a bias ever occur? Psychologists are still debating the reasons for this error. One possibility might be the genuine stability of personality traits (discussed in

AP Images/The Janesville Gazette/Dan Lassiter

Are the famous Wal-Mart greeters really friendly people? Or are they just doing their jobs? Because of the correspondence bias, we tend to view Wal-Mart greeters as friendly people, even though we fully understand that their jobs require them to act this way.

actor-observer bias Emphasizing dispositional attributions to explain the behavior of others while emphasizing situational attributions to explain our own behavior.

self-serving bias Attributing success to dispositional factors while attributing failure to situational factors.

Chapter 12). People often believe that the "You did it because that is the kind of person you are" explanation is accurate. There is some truth to these beliefs, which is why they persist. But at the same time, our discussion of personality showed that situations make important contributions to behavior. You might consider yourself to be a helpful person, but you might ignore someone with a flat tire when you're late for class or work.

Other factors that contribute to the correspondence bias include a lack of awareness of the power of the situation and unrealistic beliefs about how situations should affect people (Gilbert & Malone, 1995). In many everyday instances, we simply do not have enough information about somebody's circumstances to consider situational variables in our attributions. A grumpy, unenthusiastic professor might be having health or personal problems of which students in the classroom are unaware, but by default, the students believe that the professor is characteristically grumpy and unenthusiastic. In other cases, we seem to misjudge the likelihood that typical people will respond to a situation in a certain way. Later in this chapter, you will learn how a majority of individuals were willing to electrocute another participant simply because they were told to do so by an experimenter. You might think, "I would never respond to the situation like that," which might lead to your misjudging the power of the situation.

A concept closely related to the correspondence bias is known as the *fundamental attribution error* (*FAE*; Ross, 1977). According to this view, people do not just underestimate situational variables as proposed by correspondence bias, but instead completely fail to consider situational variables while making attributions. By default, this total neglect of situational influences leads to a reliance on dispositional contributions to explain the resulting observed behavior. Research evidence for a complete neglect of situational variables is lacking (Gawronski, 2004). For example, in the study mentioned earlier about administering shock, how do you think people view the minority of participants who did not comply and refused to shock another person? If we globally ignore situational variables, as required by the FAE, we should attribute the behavior of these individuals to their strong moral character (disposition), but this is not what usually happens (Gilbert & Malone, 1995). Instead, most people attribute the minority's behavior to simply responding to the situation "the way people ought to do." The situation still plays a significant role in people's interpretation of the observed behavior, which is inconsistent with the premises of the FAE. This leaves the correspondence bias as the superior explanation for how people balance their assessments of disposition and situation.

Defensive Attributions

EPA/FRANCK/Newscom

Olympic figure skater Rachael Flatt told a newspaper, "I was ultimately responsible for my work, no one else! No excuses! And, that is true in daily training. I am responsible for my own work, no one else." Elite athletes like Flatt rarely indulge in the self-serving bias, in which we attribute our successes to dispositional qualities (I'm a talented athlete) and our failures to situations (the judging wasn't fair or the ice wasn't prepared properly). By avoiding this bias, athletes can learn from their mistakes and continue to improve their performances.

The correspondence bias is not the only flaw in our judgment of behavior. When our personal needs and motives enter the picture, additional errors can occur. Classic studies suggested that an **actor–observer bias** occurs when we use situational variables to explain our own behavior while continuing to use dispositional variables to explain the behavior of others (Jones & Nisbett, 1972): If my friend and I both flunked a test, I flunked because I was sick, but my friend flunked because he's not a very hard worker. Although this suggestion has some intuitive appeal, a more recent meta-analysis suggested that people judge their own behavior similarly to the behavior of others (Malle, 2006).

Because of a **self-serving bias**, we view our successes differently than our failures (Miller & Ross, 1975). When we succeed, we are more likely to attribute our success to dispositional variables. For example, if you get an A in this course, you are likely to congratulate yourself for your brains and hard work.

CONNECTING TO RESEARCH

Farming, Collectivism, and Individualism

IT IS ERRONEOUS TO ASSUME that large populations, like the people of China, are all alike, yet many cross-cultural psychologists have assumed that Chinese culture is uniformly collectivist. Not only is this not the case, but researchers also have suggested some novel contributing factors to explain the variations in social structure that can be observed. For example, differences in the type of crops that you raise is probably not the first variable that comes to mind when we consider differences in individualism and collectivism, yet this variable seems to play a role (Talhelm et al., 2014).

The Question: Does the type of crop farmed predict the tendencies of a culture to be collectivist or individualist?

METHODS

More than 1,000 Han Chinese students in six areas of China (see Figure 13.3) completed measures of cultural thought, implicit individualism, and loyalty/nepotism. None of the measures were self-report because the researchers expressed concerns that the students would feel the need to answer in socially appropriate ways. For example, the cultural thought task asks the participants to decide which two items out of a group of three "go together." If we asked you to do this for "train, bus, tracks," what would you choose? People from individualistic cultures tend to make abstract pairings, such as *train* and *bus,* which belong to the same category. People from collectivistic cultures tend to make more holistic pairings, such as *train* and *tracks,* because they share a functional relationship. The responses of the students were analyzed in terms of their location in the wheat-growing north of China or the rice-growing south. Raising rice requires high levels of cooperation (a married couple cannot grow the rice needed to support a family by themselves), but growing wheat requires less, so the authors expected more collectivist responses from southern students than from northern students. The authors quoted a 17th-century Chinese farming guide that says, "If one is short of labor, it is best to grow wheat."

ETHICS

Chinese protections for research participants are similar to those in the United States, but there are some concerns about how these translate to a different culture. Participants who are expected to put the collective good ahead of their individual interests might participate when they otherwise would prefer not to.

RESULTS

The researchers tested their rice explanation against other potential explanations, such as the influence of pathogens or modernization. They found that the rice theory was the only one that consistently fit the cultural data. People from provinces that traditionally farmed rice performed more collectively and holistically, while people from provinces that traditionally farmed wheat performed more individualistically and analytically.

DISCUSSION

The participants were unlikely to have ever engaged in farming, but traditional farming practices had shaped their cultural values nonetheless. A history of having to cooperate to survive might have shaped the local culture for centuries.

These results also remind us that simple answers to psychological problems are usually not the best. Rather than thinking of East Asia as a consistent whole, it is more accurate and interesting to investigate the nuances of behavioral differences within cultures.

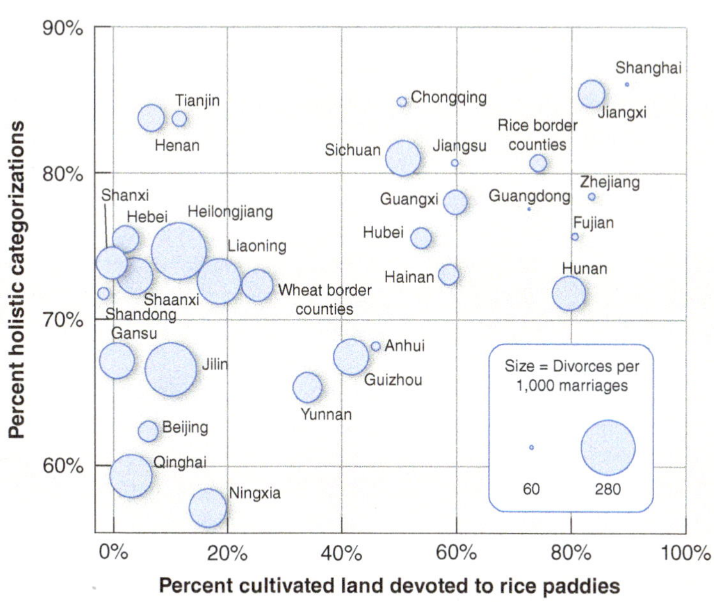

FIGURE **13.3**

Collectivism and Individualism Correlate with Regional Farming History. Han Chinese living in areas that have historically farmed rice scored higher on holistic thinking and were less likely to disrupt social organization through divorce than Han Chinese living in areas that have historically farmed wheat.

Source: Data from T. Talhelm et al. (2014). "Large-Scale Psychological Differences Within China Explained by Rice Versus Wheat Agriculture," *Science, 344*(6184), 603–608. doi: 10.1126/science.1246850

Marmaduke St. John/Alamy Stock Photo

A just-world belief leads people to expect good things to happen to good people and bad things to happen to bad people. A strong just-world belief might lead people to "blame-the-victim" thinking, making them less sympathetic to the poor and the sick.

In contrast, if you fail the course, it is because of situational factors, such as the professor's asking unfair questions on the final exam. The self-serving bias can make you feel better, but it also can make it harder to learn from experience. Elite athletes, for example, are less likely to use situational variables to excuse poor performance, such as blaming the weather when they lose a game (Roesch & Amirkhan, 1997). By considering their own contributions to failure, elite athletes can make the adjustments necessary for future success.

Similar attribution errors occur at the group level (Forsyth & Schlenker, 1977). In a group-serving bias, an organization tends to attribute success to its dispositional characteristics but blames failures on the situation. If a sports team wins, most members attribute the victory to team disposition, such as talent, good preparation, or sheer will. If the team loses, the members are unlikely to blame the loss on team dispositional factors (Sherman & Kim, 2005). By failing to consider dispositional factors that might be remedied in the future, a group might miss opportunities to correct its course of action.

In addition to self-serving bias, we frequently engage in other types of defensive reasoning. It is a short step from "Your behavior reflects your disposition" to causal judgments about the outcomes of behavior, such as "You get what you deserve." Through the **just-world belief**, people assume that good things happen to good people and bad things happen to bad people (Lerner & Miller, 1978). When you see something bad happen to a good person, you might reduce your anxiety by thinking that the person must have done something to deserve the bad outcome and that you can avoid that outcome by behaving differently. However, this reduction in personal anxiety can come at the expense of the victim, who is being blamed unfairly. Strong just-world beliefs have been positively correlated with negative attitudes toward the poor, people with HIV/AIDS, the elderly, and the unemployed (Sutton & Douglas, 2005).

Cultural Influences on Attribution

There are subtle differences in attribution between cultures that value individualism and cultures that value collectivism. Individualistic cultures, including the United States and many other Western nations, stress individual achievement and competition. Collectivistic cultures, including those in many East Asian nations, traditionally have valued cooperation as a means of attaining family and work group goals.

Members of collectivistic cultures tend to place more emphasis on situation than members of individualistic cultures do (Choi et al., 1999; Ho & Fung, 2011). As a result, members of individualistic cultures are more likely to demonstrate the correspondence bias (Dean & Koenig, 2019). For example, in the United States, murder is viewed as resulting from the disposition of the murderer, whereas in China, murder is often described in terms of the histories of the people involved and the situation in which the murder occurred (Morris & Peng, 1994).

These cultural differences in attribution may be rooted in the tendency for people in Eastern cultures to focus on context or situations and relationships, while people in Western cultures are more likely to focus on objects than on situations (Masuda & Nisbett, 2001). As mentioned earlier, we tend to attribute behavior to the factors that we perceive. If being raised in a particular culture leads you to focus on different features of the environment, the attributions that are made vary accordingly (see Figure 13.4).

Because of the importance placed on individual achievement in individualistic societies, members of these societies are more likely to use defensive attributions, such as self-serving bias (Leung et al., 2011). Members of more collectivistic cultures show an interesting group-serving bias, in which they attribute more success to the group than it deserves and less failure than it deserves (Leung et al., 2011). That is, if you were raised in a collectivistic culture, you

just-world belief The assumption that good things happen to good people and bad things happen to bad people.

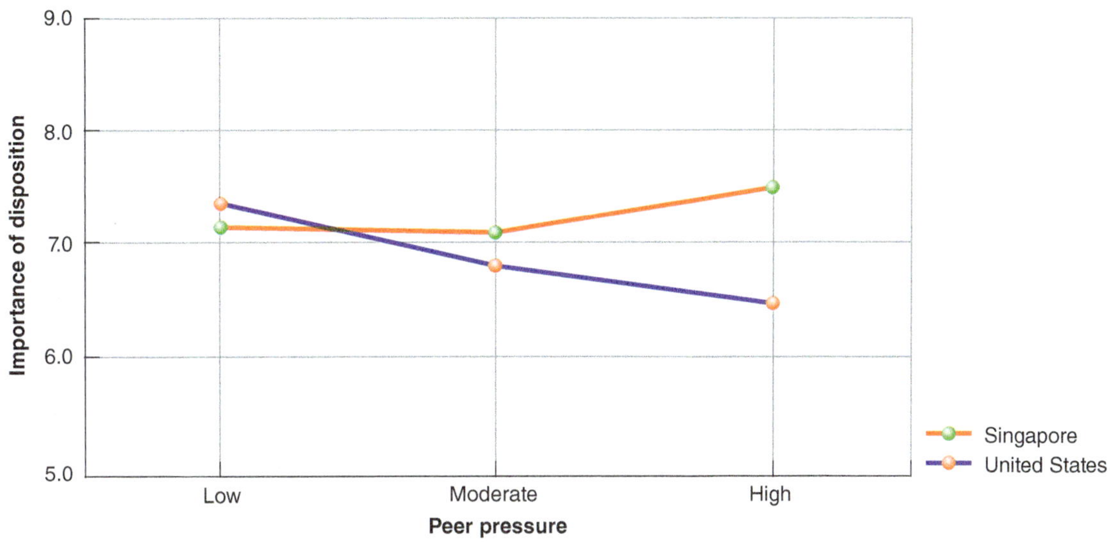

FIGURE **13.4**

Situational Attributions and Punishment Across Cultures. In the individualist U.S. culture, but not in collectivist Singapore, recognition of peer pressure leading to crime (a situational variable) reduces the attribution of the crime to a person's disposition. An American criminal who commits a crime because of peer pressure is not seen to be as bad as a person who acts without such pressure. As a result, extenuating circumstances usually lead to reduced sentences in the United States. Even though collectivist nations like Singapore place a higher emphasis on situational variables when making attributions overall, they do not view peer pressure as a reason to reduce punishment of an individual. If anything, the individual will be blamed for associating with the wrong peer group.

Source: Adapted from P. E. Tetlock et al. (2010). "The Punitiveness Paradox: When Is External Pressure Exculpatory—and When a Signal Just to Spread Blame?" *Journal of Experimental Social Psychology*, *46*(2), 388–395. doi:10.1016/j.jesp.2009.11.013

would show the same attributional biases about your in-group as individuals raised in an individualistic culture would show about themselves.

How Are Our Attitudes Influenced by Others?

To survive, all animals must make appropriate approach or avoidance responses to stimuli. The reflexes, fixed action patterns, and unconditioned responses discussed in Chapter 8 provide some guidance in simple situations, such as seeing a predator. To respond to more complex situations, humans form **attitudes**, or favorable or unfavorable evaluations that predispose behavior (Petty & Cacioppo, 1986).

Attitudes are pervasive. We form positive and negative attitudes about everything from world events to celebrities to brands of peanut butter, and attitudes provide an efficient means of communicating with others. If a friend asks you for a recommendation for a movie, restaurant, or class, a simple attitude statement ("I liked my psychology class!") can serve as a quick and efficient summary for a wide set of beliefs, behavioral experiences, and emotions. Decision making is simpler, faster, and less stressful when attitudes exist to serve as a guide. Attitudes can influence behavior, although their influence can vary in impact from weak to strong (Briñol et al., 2019). Many people hold attitudes related to controversial topics like abortion or gun control, but these positions do not always predict voting behavior.

attitude A positive or negative evaluation that predisposes behavior toward an object, person, or situation.

Because we depend on our attitudes to guide our behavior, we want to make sure that they are "correct" (Festinger, 1950). Imagine what would happen if you woke up one day

Jaguar PS/Shutterstock.com

Nippon News/Aflo Co. Ltd./Alamy Stock Photo

If you have any doubt whether people are emotional about their attitudes, just ask some friends whether they prefer an Apple (represented by the late Steve Jobs, left) or a PC (represented by Bill Gates, right). Be prepared to duck for cover.

to discover that your attitudes about people, objects, and issues were all wrong. Suddenly your closest friends would dislike you, your major would be a poor match for your interests and abilities, and your entire collection of music would sound dreadful. Occasional mistakes happen, but holding accurate attitudes makes it easier for us to maneuver through environments successfully.

Attitudes form networks comprised of three interacting elements: affect (i.e., emotion), behavior, and cognition (the ABCs; Dalege et al., 2016). For example, how might your attitudes about your college major be affected by hearing a negative news report about the job market for new college graduates in that field? The affective aspect of an attitude addresses emotional responses to the object. This information about your future job prospects could make you feel quite helpless, frightened, or angry. Behavior reflects the way that people respond to the object. After hearing the news, you might schedule an appointment with your adviser to discuss ways that you can pursue the subjects you love and still have a great career. The cognitive aspect of an attitude includes beliefs about the object. In response to this news, you might believe that you have chosen the wrong major or that the news report was inaccurate.

Attitude Formation

We form many attitudes on the basis of our personal experiences. You like a flavor of ice cream after sampling it, and you dislike the parking situation at your school because you can never find a spot near your classes. In other cases, we absorb attitudes from our contacts with peers, parents and other family members, religious leaders, teachers, and the media.

We often adopt the attitudes of those around us to strengthen our chances of being socially included. As a result, many people prefer to stay on the "winning side" by forming attitudes based on how frequently they hear an opinion expressed by others and in the media (Noelle-Neumann, 1984). Later in this chapter, we explore how fear of social rejection also can lead to conformity and strict adherence to social norms or values.

The learning principles explored in Chapter 8 play important roles in the development of attitudes. Operant conditioning suggests that approval or disapproval shapes a person's attitudes. An opinion expressed in class that is followed by nods and claps will be repeated in the future more than one that is met with horror and disgust. Because of classical conditioning, you are likely to form positive attitudes toward stimuli associated with positive outcomes. If a song is popular at a happy time of your life, it is likely that your subsequent attitude toward the song will be positive too. Observational learning also can be a powerful mechanism for learning attitudes. Children who are exposed to particular attitudes in their homes, communities, and media duplicate them, especially if they observe the person expressing the attitude being rewarded.

Some of our attitudes result from personal experience, but others are quickly absorbed from the world around us, especially through peers and the media.

WireStock/Alamy Stock Photo

Can attitudes be influenced by genetics? Identical twins who were adopted by different families at birth, making it unlikely that they were exposed to the same attitudes, still show a surprising amount of similarity in their attitudes as adults (Bouchard et al., 1990).

Cognitive Dissonance

Although our attitudes typically guide us well, attitude change is often desirable. After all, we are sometimes flat-out wrong. Addiction, for example, includes attitudes and preferences that are not in the best interests of anybody concerned. The addict by definition cannot easily change these attitudes and preferences, however. Similarly, people who are unable to change their attitudes in the face of new evidence can be quite handicapped. Understanding the circumstances in which attitude change takes place gives us additional insight into the formation of our attitudes and their role in guiding our behavior.

cognitive dissonance The uncomfortable state that occurs when behavior and attitudes do not match and that can be resolved through attitude change.

cognitive consistency A preference for holding congruent attitudes and beliefs.

Cognitive dissonance provides a powerful tool for producing attitude change (Festinger, 1957). Cognitive dissonance is an uncomfortable state that occurs when our outward behavior doesn't match our attitudes. For example, you might have been accepted by several colleges and universities, but you can choose to attend only one. Thinking about the positive features of the schools you reject causes dissonance (I like these schools, but I didn't choose them), which could be resolved either by becoming a "superfan" of your chosen school or by forming negative attitudes toward the schools that you reject. How could you even consider making another choice? Who would want to go to those other schools?

Cognitive dissonance helps explain why hazing, or requiring an unpleasant initiation to become a member of a group, increases the value of the group (Aronson & Mills, 1959). If you choose to endure so much to join, the group must be something special.

For attitude change to occur as result of cognitive dissonance, we must attribute our actions to our own voluntary, free will. In an early demonstration of cognitive dissonance (Festinger, & Carlsmith, 1959), students completed two boring tasks (putting empty spools on a tray, emptying the tray, then filling it again; turning square pegs one quarter-turn at a time). Afterward, they were asked to tell another person that the tasks were fun. This should produce some level of cognitive dissonance (I publicly said the tasks were fun, but I really think they're boring). The researchers offered to pay $1 (about $8.90 in 2020 dollars) or $20 (about $178.08 in 2020 dollars) to participants for saying that the tasks were fun. In contrast to students who were neither paid nor asked to say that the tasks were fun (the control group), the students paid $1 rated the tasks as much more fun. Rating of the tasks' enjoyability by the students paid $20, who could easily justify their behavior (I'm being paid well to do this), did not differ from the controls.

Neuroscience studies provide substantial support for cognitive dissonance. Making difficult choices, like choosing among the schools that accepted you, reliably produces cognitive dissonance. The dissonance is resolved after a decision is made by devaluing the option that was not chosen. EEG recordings in this type of situation were similar to recordings taken in many instances of performance monitoring, an executive process that helps us detect errors (Colosio et al., 2017).

Cognitive dissonance, which focuses on conflicts between attitudes and behaviors, is part of a broader phenomenon—our need for **cognitive consistency** (Gawronski & Brannon, 2016). We form many associations between ideas, which in turn lead to expectations. Discomfort caused by conflicts among these ideas might help us recognize errors in our belief systems. You might believe very strongly that being vegan will make people healthier, and your friend wants to be healthy, but she is not vegan. To resolve this inconsistency, one of these ideas needs to change. You might now believe that it's possible to be healthy without being vegan, your friend really doesn't want to be healthy, or your friend really is vegan and just doesn't want her

David Rafael Espejo Serrano/Alamy Stock Photo

Choosing to vape despite news reports of lung disease and greater risk in COVID-19 can produce cognitive dissonance. To reduce dissonance, this user might start to think that the warnings are not believable and that vaping isn't that bad for you.

persuasion A change in attitude in response to information provided by another person.

elaboration likelihood model (ELM) A model that predicts responses to persuasive messages by distinguishing between the central and the peripheral route to persuasion.

family to know. Aversive feelings that we experience when our ideas are inconsistent might motivate us to think more deeply about our beliefs.

Why Does Persuasion Happen?

Cognitive dissonance can produce attitude change, but it does not occur in response to a direct effort by another person. When we change our attitudes in response to information provided by others, **persuasion** occurs. Knowing how to persuade others and understanding the efforts of others to persuade you are important life skills.

The Elaboration Likelihood Model

The **elaboration likelihood model (ELM)** organizes and predicts our responses to persuasive messages by recognizing two major pathways leading to changes in attitudes (Petty & Cacioppo, 1981). The first, known as the *central route to persuasion*, occurs when a person considers persuasive arguments carefully and thoughtfully. The second, known as the *peripheral route to persuasion*, occurs when a person responds to peripheral cues, as described in the following section, without considering the quality of the argument carefully. Importantly, attitudes achieved through the central route are more enduring, more resistant to counter-persuasion, and more predictive of behavior than are attitudes achieved through the peripheral route (Petty & Cacioppo, 1986).

Why do we need two systems for responding to persuasive messages? Ideally, we would use the central route to consider all messages that we encounter. However, given our limited time, knowledge, and cognitive resources, a thorough evaluation of all the messages that we perceive is not practical. Using the peripheral route allows us to use heuristics, or rules of thumb (as described in Chapter 10), to react promptly to many situations. If you feel overwhelmed by the large number of candidates on your ballot, you might use the heuristic of voting along party lines or voting like your friends.

FREDERIC J. BROWN/AFP/Getty Images

Experts attending a technology trade show are likely to use the central route to persuasion while evaluating the speaker's message. They will concentrate on the logic of the message and will be relatively unimpressed by peripheral cues, such as the speaker's attractiveness or use of emotion.

Routes to Persuasion

What determines whether we use the central or peripheral route? According to the ELM, a person's motivation influences which route is used to evaluate a particular argument. When students are highly motivated to take time out of their busy schedules to attend a presentation by a guest speaker on campus because they know and care about the topic of the lecture, they are likely to use the central route and evaluate the speaker's points carefully.

People are also likely to use the central route to persuasion when they are well educated about a topic. However, even people who are knowledgeable occasionally take the peripheral rather than the central route. If you know about a topic but do not have the time to think about it or don't care about it, you might find the shortcuts provided by the peripheral route more useful. In addition, because using the central route requires so many cognitive resources, including attention, we are less likely to process persuasive messages this way when we are distracted by other information or activities. As you concentrate on driving down a busy highway, you do not have the cognitive resources to evaluate the messages on billboards carefully.

If a person is using the peripheral route to persuasion, what cues might influence the amount of attitude change that occurs? Peripheral cues usually apply to the persuasive message (e.g., the number of arguments), the manner in which the message is presented (e.g., speed of speech and accent), or the characteristics of the speaker (e.g., credibility or celebrity).

Emotional appeals can influence people using the peripheral route. Both positive and negative emotions can enhance persuasion. Students asked to read persuasive messages about topics such as curing cancer and the state of military forces were more likely to agree with the statement they read while happily snacking on Pepsi and peanuts (Dabbs & Janis, 1965). Efforts to persuade using negative emotions are especially common. We hear daily warnings about the dangers of drinking too much, not using our seatbelts, engaging in risky sex practices, riding a bicycle without a helmet, not maintaining social distance, and so on.

Robert Landau/Alamy Stock Photo

Driving down a busy street requires your full attention, making it unlikely that you will have the resources you need to evaluate persuasive messages using the central route. Instead, the advertisements that you pass on the road attempt to influence you in a few seconds to think better of the product that they are boosting or the message that they display.

Arousing negative emotions, such as fear, can be risky. If people are too frightened by a message, they go into a state of denial. "It's really not that bad," they will say, or "That can't happen here." Denial is most likely to occur if the audience is not given an action to do to reduce their anxiety. It is fine to scare smokers to death about the appearance of their lungs, so long as you include a message that tells them where to get help to quit smoking. Having a sense of control over their response will reduce the fear and make the message more persuasive (Ajzen, 1991).

A positive response to the speaker can enhance a message's persuasion. Despite the common-sense warning that "beauty is only skin deep," people have a deep-seated stereotype that what is beautiful is good (Dion et al., 1972). Student evaluations of a professor are heavily influenced by the perceived attractiveness of the professor (Hamermesh & Parker, 2003). People are more likely to be persuaded by people they like and with whom they share some similarity (Van Knippenberg & Wilke, 1992; Cialdini, 2001). Similarities need not be substantial to produce this effect; study participants who shared a first name or birthday with the supposed author of a persuasive essay were more likely to agree with the essay (Silvia, 2005).

The less a speaker stands to gain by persuading you, the more credibility the speaker appears to have. We understand that athletes and other celebrities are being paid large amounts of money to advertise particular products, so we tend to discount their opinions (Moore et al., 1994). A testimonial by someone who has nothing to gain by speaking in favor of a product or issue is more persuasive. As a result of these findings, bloggers must disclose whether they are being compensated for writing about a brand. Without this information, we might not evaluate their arguments correctly.

A credible speaker is usually more persuasive, especially when listeners are traveling the peripheral route. In turn, credibility is based on the speaker's perceived expertise and trustworthiness. Expertise is often established by a person's history and credentials. We suspect that your psychology professors would look different to you if they indicated that their degrees were in other subjects and that they really didn't know much about psychology.

Persuasion is also influenced by the medium used to communicate a message, from the face-to-face presentation of the door-to-door salesperson (a rarity these days) to print media, social media, the Internet, and movies and television. Typically, we find that the more a medium resembles a live interaction with another person, the more effective it is in transmitting a persuasive message. In general, face-to-face contact remains more effective than the use of other media (Bavelas et al., 1997). This arrangement is the most natural way for humans to communicate. Not only is face-to-face communication the first medium we learn in childhood, but various technologies allowing communication at a distance developed at much later points in human history.

Robert W. Ginn/AGE Fotostock

Children are more likely than adults to respond to persuasive messages emotionally rather than logically, making them more susceptible to persuasion. Threatened with lawsuits from public interest groups, several major U.S. food companies agreed to reduce their marketing to children and to make products that appeal to children healthier.

Finally, the age and intelligence of an audience can influence the effectiveness of a persuasive message. Young children are more likely to respond to persuasive arguments emotionally rather than logically, which might make them more susceptible to attitude change (and advertising) than adults. Intelligent, well-educated audiences are more difficult to persuade in most situations (Rhodes & Wood, 1992).

PSYCHOLOGY AS A HUB SCIENCE

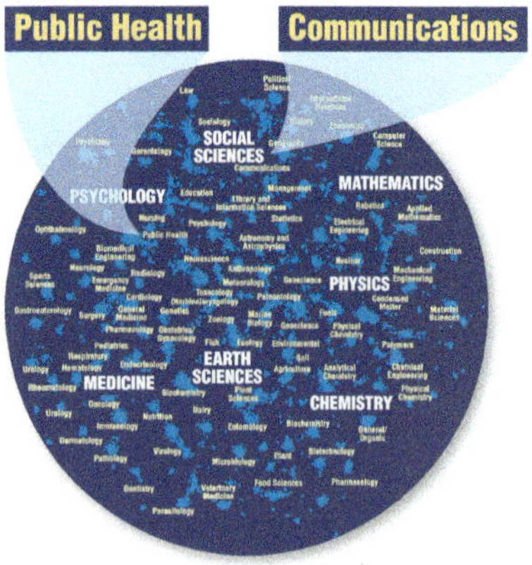

Social Media, Persuasion, and Fake News

THE INTERNET HAS PROVIDED NEW WAYS for people to communicate, from the use of webcams, video, and live chat to Twitter, Facebook, Instagram, Snapchat, TikTok, and blogs. Many of these new technologies have advantages in providing immediacy and collaboration. To the extent that they duplicate the advantages of face-to-face communication, we would expect them to provide effective means of persuading others.

The Internet not only provides a new medium for communicating persuasive messages, but also challenges the status of credible, expert sources. Trust in traditional news sources is very low, 42%, and dropping (Newman et al., 2019). Digital sources of news currently rank second only to television, and twice as many adults see news online compared to seeing news in print (Matsa & Lu, 2016). Historically, persuasive messages from traditional news outlets such as newspapers, magazines, radio, and television were more of a one-way street. However, in an environment in which everybody with a computer or phone can produce information, receivers of information can be influencers as well by sharing and commenting on messages in blogs and on social networking sites. Research in this area suggests that user-generated content in the form of blogs, uploaded videos, comments, and reviews is considered as credible and accurate as formal news reports prepared by professional journalists (Lee et al., 2010). In addition, knowing that content is "popular" with other users significantly raises a message's impact (Steyn et al., 2010).

As more people depend on online sources for their information, psychologists and other professionals have expressed concerns about the quality of that information (Lazer et al., 2018). So-called fake news is not a new concept, but the ability of the Internet to spread it brings a whole new dimension to its ability to persuade large numbers of people. At risk are people's collective memories, or our shared understanding of "what really happened." Fake news can occur in both traditional and online sources, and can range from clickbait to poorly researched information to maliciously constructed messages intended to do harm. Among the most widely spread fake news stories of 2016 included "Obama signs executive order banning the pledge of allegiance in schools nationwide" (with 2,177,000 Facebook shares, comments, and reactions) and "Pope Francis shocks world, endorses Donald Trump for President, releases statement" (with 961,000 Facebook shares, comments, and reactions). About 16% of Americans have admitted to having shared fake news by mistake (Barthel et al., 2016), and an alarming number seem to think satirical sites like The Onion and BabylonBee post real news stories.

In addition to the critical thinking steps outlined in Chapter 2, the following questions can help us avoid being fooled by fake news (Kiely & Robertson, 2016). Note that many of these steps are related to the peripheral cues for persuasion identified in this chapter, such as the credibility of a speaker, and thus require us to use the resource- and time-intensive central route instead. Because many people are unwilling to put in this work, fake news is likely to flourish.

1. Consider the source and evaluate the source's mission and purpose.
2. Read beyond the headline.
3. Check the authors for credibility.
4. Assess the supporting sources.
5. Check the date of publication.
6. Determine whether it is a joke or satire.
7. Reflect on your own biases related to the topic.
8. Ask experts.

Again, we see the power of the social group in shaping our ideas (see ● Figure 13.5). Emerging interactions between social media and credibility are likely to continue changing the landscape of persuasion. ■

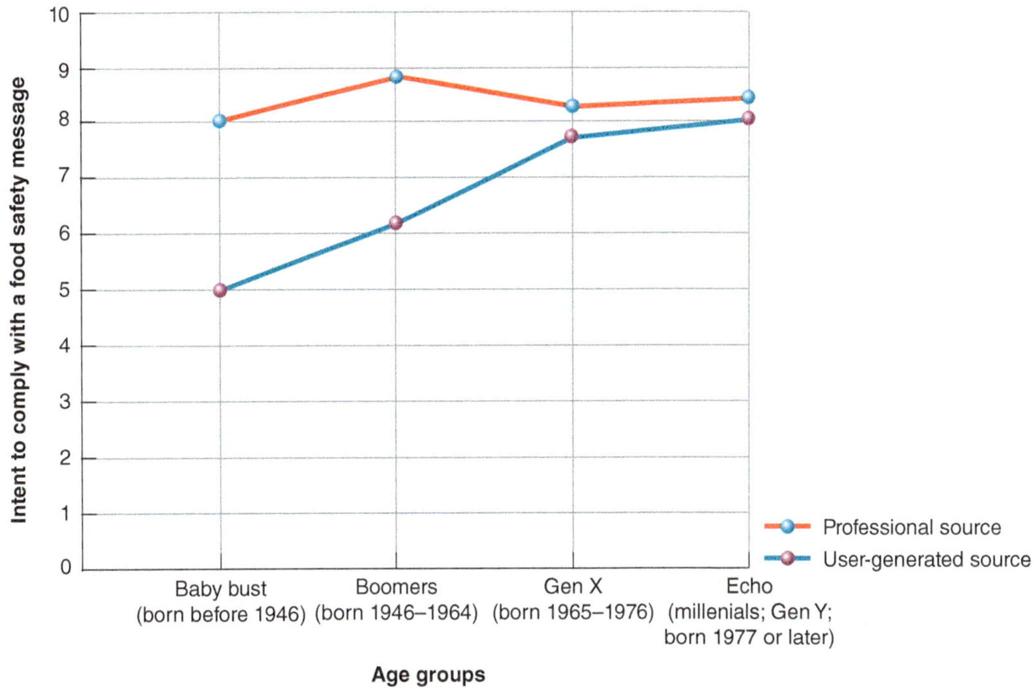

FIGURE **13.5**

Responses to User-Generated Messages by Age Group. Social media, with their ability to make users into spokespeople, raise new issues for our understanding of speaker credibility in persuasion. Different age groups have embraced user-generated content, such as blogs, tweets, and articles shared on Facebook, to different degrees. Younger age groups are as likely to say they would comply with a food recall message posted on their Facebook wall by a friend (user-generated message) as they are to an official notice from the Centers for Disease Control and Prevention (professional message), but older age groups are less likely to say that they would comply with the user-generated messages.

Source: Adapted from K. J. Freberg (2011). *Intention to Comply with Food Safety Messages in a Crisis as a Function of Message Source and Message Reliability* (doctoral dissertation), retrieved from http://trace.tennessee.edu/utk_graddiss/970/.

Again, the influence of cues related to the message, speaker, medium, or audience is greatest when people are using the peripheral route to persuasion. When people are using the central route, their focus remains on the quality of the arguments being presented.

The Neuroscience of Persuasion

Researchers are beginning to explore the underlying brain processes responsible for attitude changes in response to persuasion (Cacioppo et al., 2017). Examinations of neural correlates of source factors (such as expertise and celebrity) and message factors (such as positivity/negativity) identify areas of the prefrontal cortex as playing an important role, but many additional structures and networks also participate.

Some untapped possibilities for pursuing this research question involve studying the aging brain and manipulating brain activity through the use of magnetic stimulation (Cacioppo et al., 2018). The aging brain would enlighten this discussion because the prefrontal cortex undergoes more dramatic change during aging than many other areas of the brain. Older adults differ from younger adults in their susceptibility to deceptive advertising and their unwillingness to change their attitudes in the face of conflicting information. Assessing the differences in susceptibility to persuasion between younger and older participants could be very useful.

SUMMARY 13.1 Sources of Attribution Error

Type of Error	Definition	Example
Correspondence bias 	Overestimating the dispositional causes of a person's behavior	My friend flunked her exam because she's not very bright.
Self-serving bias 	Attributing personal success to dispositional causes, while attributing personal failure to situational causes	I got an A on one test because I'm smart, but I flunked the other test because it was unfair.
Group-serving bias	Attributing group success to dispositional causes, while attributing group failures to situational causes	Our team won its first game because we're talented and skilled but lost the second because the referees were biased.
Just-world belief 	Assuming that people get what they deserve	That homeless person doesn't try hard enough to get off the streets.

Credits: Top row—AP Images/The Janesville Gazette/Dan Lassiter; Second row—EPA/FRANCK/Newscom; Bottom row—Marmaduke St. John/Alamy Stock Photo.

prejudice A prejudgment, usually negative, of another person on the basis of membership in a group.

stereotype A simplified set of traits associated with membership in a group or category.

discrimination Unfair behavior based on stereotyping and prejudice.

Why Are We Prejudiced?

Among the most damaging perceptions that we form about other people are those based on their group memberships, which can include factors such as race, gender, age, socioeconomic status, height, weight, disabilities, attractiveness, sexual orientation, and religion. Psychologists use a group of related terms to discuss the assessment of others based on group membership. **Prejudice**, which literally means "to prejudge," is an attitude (usually negative) about others. Prejudice is supported by cognitions known as **stereotypes**, which are simplified sets of traits associated with group membership. A person might believe a stereotype that all blondes are dumb, which leads to negative attitudes (prejudice) about blondes. Behavior based on prejudice and stereotyping is **discrimination**. Hiring practices, housing, educational opportunities, and many other facets of modern living can be conducted in discriminatory ways.

Sources of Prejudice and Stereotyping

Without excusing prejudice and stereotyping and their negative social consequences, it helps to understand that some tendencies to develop prejudice and stereotypes are extensions of the typical ways that we process information. Chapter 10 noted that humans organize information and experience into schemas made up of categories or concepts, which is generally useful. Our concepts are associated with a variety of characteristics, such as "Birds have feathers." We frequently have exemplars, or best examples, of each category. If you think of the word *bird*, you are probably more likely to imagine a canary than an ostrich. Finally, we generalize from our known concepts when faced with new information. If we know that birds peck at objects placed before them, we are less likely to stick our fingers near the beak of a new type of bird. In other words, based on our past experience with or knowledge of birds, we are prejudging the behavior of an unfamiliar bird. This process of categorizing information enables us to make rapid decisions about new situations and objects, similar to the rules of thumb, or *heuristics*, discussed in Chapter 10.

Effective concepts are inclusive, recognizing a full range of associated characteristics. When our categories are oversimplified, we are left with stereotypes. Although it is true that most birds fly, it is inaccurate to oversimplify the matter by just saying "Birds fly," because ostriches do not. Stereotypes often contain an element of truth but become inaccurate because of the information that they exclude. Stereotypes form reciprocal relationships with prejudice, both feeding further prejudice and being shaped by prejudice (Phills et al., 2020). Associating negative qualities with a group enhances prejudice at the same time prejudice makes it more likely that you will form further negative associations. Perhaps most importantly, stereotypes conflict with our valid desire to be viewed and treated as individuals.

If stereotypes can lead us astray, why are they so pervasive and persistent? People tend to misjudge correlations between groups and their stereotypical behaviors. They might overestimate the percentage of Asian students who excel in math and science or underestimate the number of White athletes who play professional basketball. Attributions, discussed earlier, also contribute to continued stereotyping. If you see an exception to your stereotype (perhaps a female who is running faster than her male friend), you might view her success as the result of situational variables. Perhaps the man is letting her win to be nice. This type of thinking allows us to maintain a "women are weaker" stereotype.

You have probably noticed that people's prejudice toward a group often conflicts with their behaviors toward individual members of that group. Someone might express dramatically prejudiced opinions about a group and yet treat members of that group well. Individuals can be viewed as being different or exceptions, allowing people to retain their stereotypes in the face of conflicting observations. Instead of rethinking a stereotype about truck drivers and country music, you view your truck-driving friend who enjoys opera to be one of a kind.

As we observed in Chapters 11 and 12, maintaining a social identity can boost self-esteem, but this can also contribute to prejudice. A social identity refers to people's sense of who they are based on the groups to which they belong (Tajfel & Turner, 1979; Tajfel, 1982). In the process of developing social identities, people move from the categorization discussed earlier to adopting the identities of their groups. This can lead to both behavior (acting like a group member) and emotion (tying your own self-esteem to that of the group). Finally, social identity can lead to group comparisons. If the goal is to maintain our self-esteem, we might begin to think of our own group as superior to other groups. Expressing your school spirit at an athletic event featuring your chief rival builds in-group pride and cohesion, but it doesn't make you popular on the other side of the field. As Paolini et al. (2010) caution us, highlighting the differences that define our in-group status reminds others that they belong to an out-group.

Prejudice, like other types of attitudes, can result from direct experience (I had one boring history professor, so all history professors must be bad) or can be indirectly absorbed from the social world of peers, parents, the community, and the media. Human prejudice based on group membership, however, might have deeper roots in our evolutionary past. Recognizing and reacting to individuals based on group affiliation was probably an important skill for early hunter–gatherers, whose survival often depended on quickly identifying others as potential trading partners or foes. This pressure could have led to a tendency to distinguish between in-groups, or the group to which we belong, and out-groups, or everybody else (see ● Figure 13.6). This categorization is made primarily on the basis of physical appearance, and people still instantly (and often unconsciously) categorize others on the basis of physically observable features, including age, gender, and race (Fiske, 1998).

This type of categorization was demonstrated by recording brain activity as people viewed photographs of faces and made judgments about either race or gender (Ito & Urland, 2003). Study participants reacted quickly to both race and gender information, even when the information was irrelevant to their task. In other words, a participant who was asked to differentiate between male and female faces still showed evidence of having paid attention to the race of the faces, without being asked to do so.

People often have negative stereotypes about overweight people as a group. In one online survey, more than 75% of respondents believed that overweight people should either buy a second seat or pay a "fat tax" to travel on airplanes (Siegfried, 2010). Comedian Kevin Smith, ejected from a Southwest Airlines flight for "infringing on a portion of the next seat," tweeted that he "broke no regulation, offered no 'safety risk' (what, was I going to roll over on a fellow passenger?)."

s_bukley/Shutterstock.com

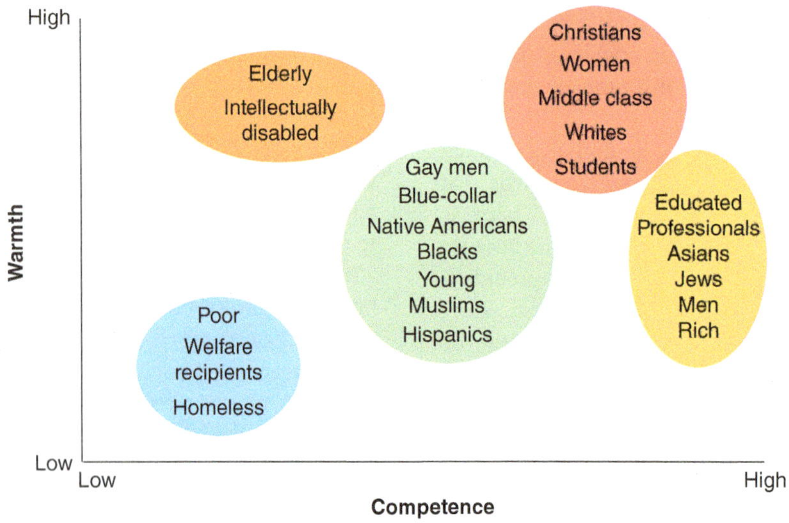

FIGURE **13.6**

American Perceptions of Out-Groups. Out-groups often elicit mixed reactions. Some out-groups (rich people) are respected for their perceived competence but disliked for their supposed lack of warmth. Elderly people and the disabled are viewed as low in competence, but they are viewed warmly because of the lack of threat that they pose. Groups such as the poor are viewed most harshly as a result of having both low status and representing a threat of exploiting the in-group.

Source: Adapted from S. T. Fiske et al. (2002). "A Model of (Often Mixed) Stereotype Content: Competence and Warmth Respectively Follow from Perceived Status and Competition," *Journal of Personality and Social Psychology, 82*(6), 878–902. doi:10.1037/0022-3514.82.6.878

Different emotional responses can accompany these instant categorizations. When study participants viewed faces from their own racial group, activity in the amygdala was lower than when they viewed faces from another racial group (Hart et al., 2000). As discussed in Chapter 4, activity in the amygdala is correlated with assessments of threat. Either realistic or imaginary threats from an out-group are viewed as a major source of prejudice (Stephan & Stephan, 2000). Furthermore, the intensity of the amygdala's response to race are correlated with several implicit measures of prejudice (Phelps et al., 2000). Implicit measures are designed to demonstrate subconscious associations between concepts (spiders and flowers, for example) and attitudes (good and bad) (e.g., Nosek, 2007). Psychologists continue to debate the extent to which implicit measures actually assess unconscious processing or predict actual prejudice (Brownstein et al., 2019).

Understanding that cognitive, biological, and evolutionary processes are involved with in-group/out-group differentiation does not make prejudice inevitable or acceptable. By understanding why we develop prejudice, we can better identify ways to reduce it. As we will see later in this section, prejudice can change.

Outcomes of Prejudice

Prejudice, whether subtle or overt, can lead to discriminatory behavior in a number of ways. Not only are African Americans convicted of murder more likely than Whites to be given the death penalty in the United States, but perceptions of "Blackness" are also predictive of a murderer being sentenced to death (Eberhardt et al., 2006). Researchers presented photographs of African American defendants to participants without telling them that the men depicted had been convicted of murder. The participants ranked the photographs on the basis of stereotypical Black features, such as broad nose, dark skin, and thick lips. The ratings were highly predictive of the men's sentences when the victim was White. Men who appeared more stereotypically African American were more than twice as likely to be given the death sentence as men whose physical appearance was less stereotypical. This difference disappeared, however, when the victim was also African American (see ● Figure 13.7).

Prejudice affects not only the way we view others, but also the way we view ourselves. Raising awareness of a negative stereotype about a group to which we belong has the ability to reduce our performance, a phenomenon known as *stereotype threat* (Steele & Aronson, 1995; Steele, 1997). Anxiety about confirming a negative stereotype attributed to your group can prevent you from doing your best work.

In a set of studies demonstrating this effect, researchers asked Stanford University undergraduate students to complete difficult items taken from the verbal portion of the Graduate Record Exam (GRE), used as part of the admissions process for some graduate programs (Steele & Aronson, 1995). One group of students, the stereotype threat group, was told that the test accurately assessed their cognitive abilities, a statement that was designed to stimulate thinking about possible racial stereotypes about intelligence. The other group was told that the test was a routine laboratory procedure. Subsequently, the performance of Black and White students on the test was compared. After controlling for the participants' previous Scholastic Aptitude Test (SAT) scores, the Black students in the stereotype threat group performed more poorly than did the White students. In contrast, in the nonthreatening condition, Blacks and

Oversimplified categories, such as "girl toys" or "boy toys," can lead to stereotypes.

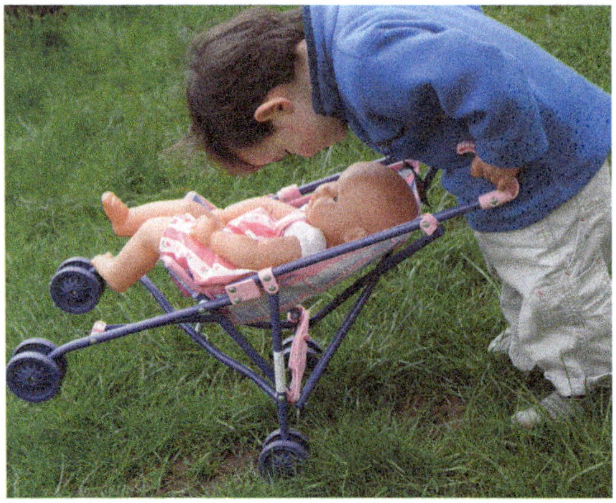

Jennie Hart/Alamy Stock Photo

Whites with equal SAT scores performed similarly on the GRE items, which is the result that we would expect because of the tests' reliability and validity, discussed in Chapter 2 (see ● Figure 13.8). However, it would be an inaccurate interpretation of Steele and Aronson's work to suggest that stereotype threat accounts for the bulk of group differences in performance (Stoet & Geary, 2012). Meta-analyses have supported the existence of the stereotype threat effect, but its contribution to overall performance appears to be small to moderate (Spencer et al., 2016). Nonetheless, any irrelevant influence on a person's performance is noteworthy, as these small individual effects can add up to larger influences at the level of entire populations.

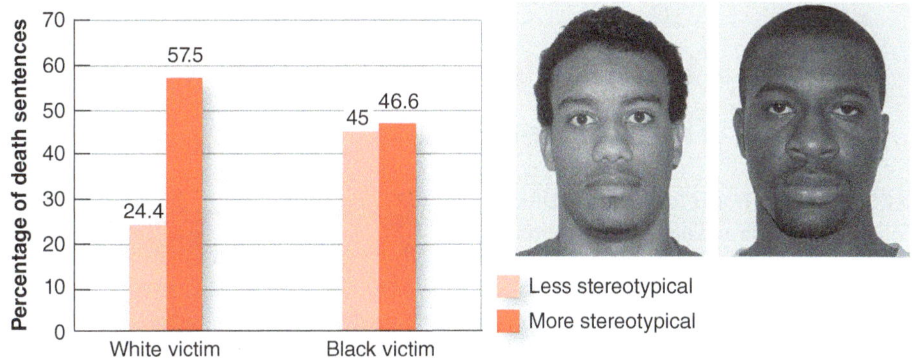

FIGURE **13.7**

Implications of Stereotyping. Study participants' ratings of stereotypical Black features predicted the men's likelihood of being sentenced for murder with the death penalty, but they did so only when the victim was described as White. The men in these photographs have no criminal records but are examples provided by the authors for individuals who were viewed as less stereotypical (left) and more stereotypical (right).

Source: J. L. Eberhardt et al. (2006). "Looking Deathworthy: Perceived Stereotypicality of Black Defendants Predicts Capital Sentencing Outcomes," *Psychological Science* 17(5), 383–386. doi: 10.1111/j.1467-9280.2006.01716.x Copyright © 2006 Association for Psychological Science. Reprinted by Permission of SAGE Publications

Reducing Prejudice

Although we would prefer a world in which prejudice never occurred, psychologists at least have gained insight into how prejudice can be reduced. Increased contact can reduce prejudice, as shown by dramatic changes in heterosexual attitudes toward sexual minorities (Herek & Glunt, 1993). Contact can be in person, over the Internet, or vicariously, as in the case of fictional role models

The Implicit Association Test (IAT) measures reaction time to assess people's unconscious attitudes. In this version of the test, either a face (African American or European American) or a word appears at the center of the screen. The participant pushes a specified key on a computer for the face (African American) and then again for the word (*joy* is Good). Later in the test, the combinations at the top of the screen are switched to African American or Bad and European American or Good. An implicit bias in favor of African Americans would be shown if reaction time in the first condition (African American or Good) is faster than in the second condition (African American or Bad).

Source: Project Implicit/Dr. Anthony Greenwald

Diverse Voices in Psychology

The Shooter Bias

RECENT NEWS STORIES HAVE FEATURED a number of tragic and often fatal shootings of unarmed African Americans by police. In many cases, the anger over these cases has boiled over to affect entire communities and the conscience of the nation. What does psychological science tell us about these situations?

Research demonstrates a consistent pattern. In computer simulations, White Americans, both real police officers and college undergraduates, are more likely to "shoot" unarmed African American than White suspects (Kenworthy et al., 2011). In many cases, the researchers explain their results in terms of cultural stereotypes. Stereotypical views of African American men as more dangerous might shape these quick decisions.

A video game including individuals holding guns or other objects has been used to examine the effect of race and ethnicity on decisions to "shoot." Civilians and police officers both make faster decisions to shoot an armed person if that person is African American and not to shoot an unarmed White target.

To directly assess the role of cultural stereotyping on the decision to shoot, researchers first gave participants a "personality" test that supposedly gave them a "red" or "green" personality (Miller et al., 2012). In actuality, participants were randomly assigned to red or green groups. In addition, participants completed a questionnaire assessing how dangerous they thought the world was. Next, the researchers presented faces of White males against a background of either red or green, which the participants were told reflected the personality of the individual. Results showed that no shooter bias occurred when participants were low to moderate in their beliefs about the danger of the world, but a bias did occur among those who saw the world as very dangerous. They were more likely to "shoot" the faces that were of the "other" personality color.

The researchers performed a second study using White, African American, and Asian faces. They assumed that there would be no cultural stereotype that Asian males are dangerous. All participants were still more likely to shoot the African American faces than the White or Asian faces, but participants with high scores on the "world is dangerous" scale were more likely to shoot Asian faces than White faces.

What have we learned from this research? Certainly, these studies confirm that cultural stereotyping is an important source of influence on quick, defensive decisions. In addition, a person's view of the world as a dangerous place is likely to accentuate a general defensiveness with regard to any out-group member. This research raises concerns about rhetoric among law enforcement personnel likening police work to combat and other factors that heighten a police officer's sense of being in mortal danger. Viewing our cities as war zones as opposed to communities is likely to produce more, not less, conflict. ■

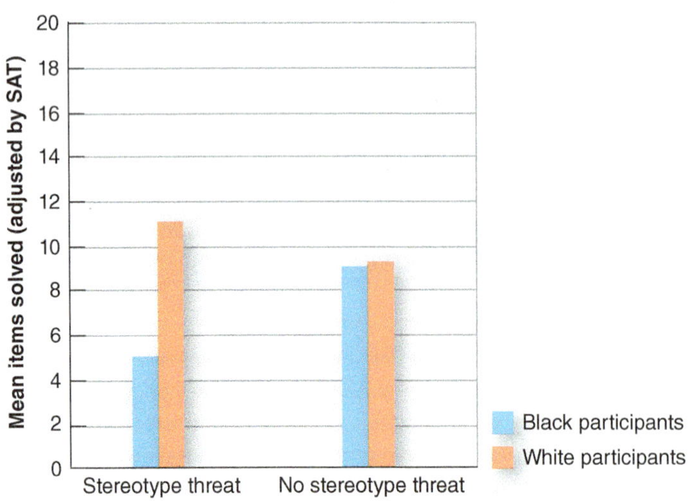

FIGURE 13.8

Stereotype Threat. Students at Stanford University were told that a verbal test measured their true abilities (stereotype threat). After controlling for prior performance on the SAT, the subsequent performance by African American participants was worse than when they were told that the test was being used to understand the "psychological factors involved in solving verbal problems" (no stereotype threat). The different instructions did not affect the performance of the White students.

Source: Adapted from C. M. Steele and J. Aronson (1995). "Stereotype Threat and the Intellectual Test Performance of African Americans," *Journal of Personality and Social Psychology, 69*, 797–811. doi: 10.1037/0022-3514.69.5.797

FIGURE **13.9**

The Reduction of In-Group and Out-Group Bias Through Cooperation. After arbitrarily dividing campers into two groups, the Rattlers and the Eagles, Sherif and his colleagues observed considerable in-group/out-group bias between the groups. During this phase, few of the campers reported having friends from the out-group. To resolve the resulting discord, the researchers set up false emergencies, such as a problem with the camp's water supply, which required the boys to cooperate. After cooperating, many of their previous biases were no longer present, and more boys reported having friends among the out-group.

Source: Adapted from M. Sherif et al. (1961). *The Robbers Cave Experiment: Intergroup Conflict and Cooperation*, Norman, OK: University of Oklahoma Institute of Intergroup Relations.

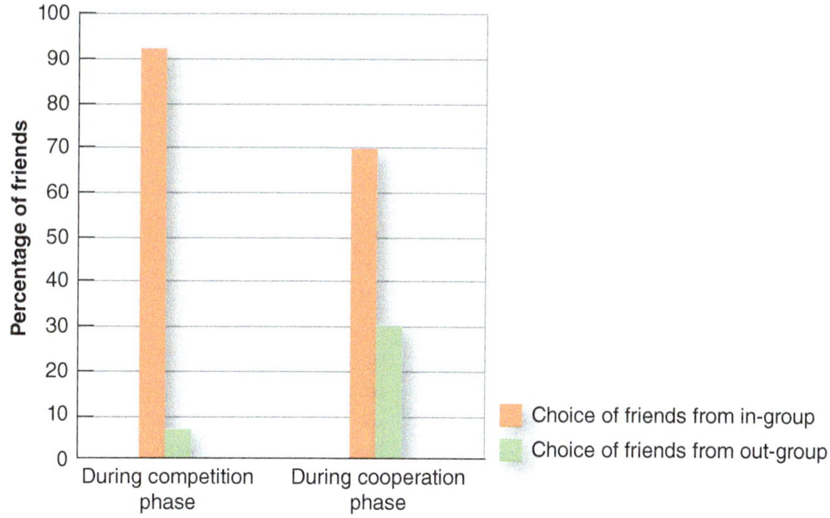

like Chadwick Boseman's *Black Panther.* However, not just any contact will have a positive effect. Allport (1954) suggested four criteria for positive contact: equal standing, common goals, cooperation, and support from authorities or customs.

Contact is particularly beneficial in reducing prejudice when groups participate in cooperative activities (see Figure 13.9). In a study using two groups of boys at a summer camp, negative feelings between the groups decreased after the boys cooperated to solve false emergencies, such as interruptions to the camp's water supply (Sherif et al., 1961). Another

Monkey Business Images/Shutterstock.com

Cooperative learning programs similar to Aronson's jigsaw classroom are used in most public schools in the United States today.

classic example of the effectiveness of cooperation in reducing prejudice is the jigsaw classroom, designed to reduce racial tensions in newly desegregated school districts in the 1970s (Aronson, 2011). Children in cooperative groups were assigned a part of the answer that their group needed to learn, leading to interdependence among the group members. White athletes showed less prejudice toward their African American teammates when competing in team sports requiring cooperation, like football, than in individual sports like tennis or swimming (Brown et al., 2003). Note that in addition to featuring cooperation, these circumstances also meet Allport's criteria of equal standing (e.g., among campers, school children, or sports team members), shared goals (solving problems or winning), and support from authorities or custom (adults in charge of camp or school, coaches and managers of teams).

Not all psychologists agree that contact, even under the ideal circumstances outlined by Allport, produces positive effects on prejudice. While contact can promote more positive intergroup attitudes, stereotypes are reduced only if the out-group member both contradicts stereotypes and is still perceived as "typical," a rather rarified set of circumstances (Park & Judd, 2005). It is even possible for contact to make prejudice worse. If a person has a bad experience with a member of another group, the typical response is to pay more rather than less attention to group membership (Paolini et al., 2010).

To the extent that prejudice originates in categorizing people and engaging in in-group/out-group thinking, another strategy for reducing prejudice is to expand the definition of the in-group. After 9/11, German Chancellor Gerhard Schröder described the terrorist attacks as "a declaration of war against the entire civilized world" (Schröder, 2001). Nations traditionally hostile to the United States, such as Cuba and North Korea, offered condolences and assistance. This expansion of the in-group obviously built a unity and resulted in kinder feelings toward the United States across many nations. However, establishing an in-group usually means there will be out-groups. In the case of 9/11, Muslims quickly became the new out-group and the target of increased prejudice.

Most of us have multiple social identities. You might think of yourself as a female Catholic student living in California. What happens when you focus on one of these identities in particular? Classic research in cross-categorization suggested that if a White female and an Asian female concentrate on the similarities that they share as women, they should experience fewer feelings of bias toward each other on the basis of race (Deschamps & Doise, 1978). Although this effect is not always seen in the laboratory (Vescio et al., 2004), when combined with real-world extended contact, the strategy seems to be promising (Eller et al., 2007). Unfortunately, cross-categorization in the real world becomes less likely when our multiple identities are not equally important to us (Brewer, 2000). Some single categories, such as race or religion, might become so dominant that areas of commonality are simply ignored and cannot be expected to reduce intergroup conflict.

We do not want to leave you with the idea that solving prejudice is hopeless. Many psychologists are working tirelessly to further our understanding of the causes of prejudice, which in turn should lead to more practical and effective ways to reduce it.

Why Do We Go Along with the Group?

When acceptance by a group is important to us, we are motivated to behave in ways that increase the likelihood of gaining the group's approval and avoiding rejection. Groups typically have rules for behavior, known as **social norms**. Social norms can be explicit, or conscious, like wearing a mask during the COVID-19 pandemic; they can also be implicit, or unconscious, like moving to the back of an elevator and turning to face the doors.

We often conform to social norms without being asked to do so. In contrast, compliance and obedience lead us to fulfill a request from another person. In compliance, the person making the request has no authority over us, but in obedience, the request is coming from an authority figure.

social norms Usually unwritten or unspoken rules for behavior in social settings.

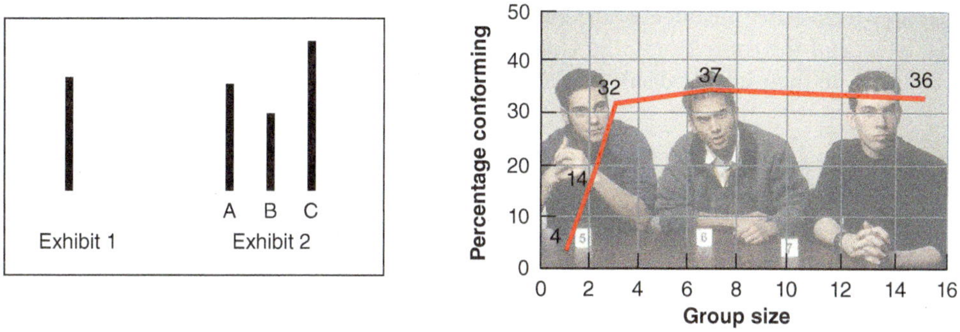

Joel Gordon

FIGURE **13.10**

Conformity. When a lone participant was asked to match the Exhibit 1 line to Line A, B, or C, the person chose the correct line, A. However, when placed in a group of confederates told to pick another line, people became more likely to go along. Conformity reached its peak in groups of three to four people and did not increase as the group became larger.

Source: Adapted from S. E. Asch (1951), "Effects of Group Pressure Upon the Modification and Distortion of Judgments." In H. Guetzkow (Ed.), *Groups, Leadership and Men: Research in Human Relations*, (pp. 177–190). Oxford, UK: Carnegie Press.

Conformity

Matching your behavior and appearance to the perceived social norms of a group constitutes **conformity**.

conformity Matching behavior and appearance to perceived social norms.

In a classic study of conformity by Solomon Asch (1951), participants were asked to match a reference line to one of three comparison lines. As you can see in Figure 13.10, the lines are sufficiently different that solving this task was not rocket science. In the conformity condition, one real participant was placed among a group of confederates (fake participants employed by the investigator). Before the real participant gave an answer, the confederates provided some wrong answers. Would the real participant tell the truth or conform to the answer given by the confederates? In about one-third of the trials, the real participants conformed by deliberately choosing a response that they knew was wrong. About three-quarters of the study participants conformed on at least one trial. In other words, the participants chose social cohesion over objective truth at least some of the time (Hodges & Geyer, 2006).

Conformity to expectations associated with roles was investigated in the Stanford Prison Study (Haney et al., 1973). In a short time, young men who had been randomly assigned to prisoner or guard roles quickly adopted behaviors consistent with those roles, leading to such inappropriate behavior (violence, etc.) that the study was stopped after only 6 days instead of the planned 14 days. The study has been criticized on the basis of methodological problems due to the active role taken by researcher Philip Zimbardo, who served as the warden in the study and thus influenced how the guards behaved. A similar prison experiment was conducted for BBC television, and this time, few of the guards acted inappropriately (Reicher & Haslam, 2006). In contrast to Zimbardo's active participation in his own study, the British prison experiment featured little direction from the investigators. However, the possibility that we unconsciously fulfill the roles expected of us by others remains an active area of scientific investigation.

Why do people conform? Conformity can be useful in ambiguous situations. If you are uncertain about what to do, such as how to dress at work, observing the behavior of others and conforming to it can be helpful. In a computer simulation comparing the effectiveness of social learning strategies, which includes imitation of others, to nonsocial learning strategies, such as trial and error, the social strategies proved far more successful (Rendell et al., 2010). The availability of others to copy might contribute to the overall success of group over independent living.

Conformity also reduces the risk of rejection by a social group, a situation that would have greatly threatened the survival of our human ancestors. Children as young as five years of age view conformity as a way to make friends (Cordonier et al., 2018). In a study demonstrating the rejection of nonconformists, participants were asked to debate the fate of an imaginary juvenile delinquent named Johnny Rocco (Schachter, 1951). Three members of the group were confederates. One was instructed to agree with the group consistently, another to disagree with the group consistently, and the third to switch positions from disagreeing to agreeing with the group. When the real participants rated how

From *The BBC Prison Study*. Copyright © BBC. Photograph courtesy of Alex Haslam, Ph.D.

In 2001, Stephen Reicher and Alexander Haslam re-created aspects of the classic Stanford Prison Study, which was conducted by Philip Zimbardo and his colleagues in the 1970s. Zimbardo argued that the roles of guard or prisoner overwhelmed individuality, but Reicher and Haslam believe that the study's participants were simply responding to Zimbardo's instructions. Scientists do not always agree with one another, and their debates bring us closer to realistic representations of our world.

compliance Agreement with a request from a person with no perceived authority.

door-in-the-face A persuasive technique in which compliance with a target request is preceded by a large, unreasonable request.

foot-in-the-door A persuasive technique in which compliance with a small request is followed by compliance with a larger request that might otherwise have been rejected.

low-balling Making further requests of a person who has already committed to a course of action.

obedience Compliance with a request from an authority figure.

well they liked other members of the group, members who agreed with the majority were all well liked, and the confederate who changed position was liked best. The participants were unanimous in their intense dislike of the confederate who disagreed with the group.

Compliance

Compliance occurs when we simply agree to do something because another person asks us to do it, even if that person has no authority over us. From messages in junk mail that tell us to "Open immediately. Do not discard" and advertising appeals to "Buy now" to medical instructions that we receive from our dentist or family physician, we are bombarded with requests for compliance.

Fulfilling requests from authority figures such as teachers or police officers can provide considerable advantages to society. It is more difficult, however, to explain why people would develop the tendency to comply with requests made by strangers who have no authority. It appears that our natural tendency to affiliate leads us to behave in ways that encourage the development of relationships, including being compliant.

Compliance is higher when factors that normally lead to the formation of relationships are present, such as perceived similarity and physical attraction. For example, we are more likely to comply with requests presented by physically attractive people (McCall, 1997; Lynn & Simons, 2000). This behavior provides yet another example of the "Beauty is good" stereotype that influences persuasion in general. People are more likely to comply with a request from a person who shares some similarity, even when the similarity is irrelevant, such as a shared birthday (Burger et al., 2004).

Many seemingly simple yet sophisticated sales techniques exploit our natural tendencies to comply in response to perceiving a social tie with another person (Cialdini & Goldstein, 2004). Once a sense of relationship is established, powerful norms of reciprocation are brought into play. *Reciprocation*, in which we feel obligated to give something back to people who have given something to us, is one of the most powerful tools of social influence (Gouldner, 1960). The importance of reciprocation to the cohesion of early human groups probably can't be overestimated. If somebody shared food with you, and you reciprocated by sharing yours, a powerful bond would be formed.

Reciprocation has been used to explain compliance in the **door-in-the-face** scenario, in which a large, unreasonable demand is followed by a smaller request, which is the one that the requester expects to work (Cialdini et al., 1975). For example, you might be asked to donate a large amount to an organization, followed by a request to "give what you can afford." By lowering the initial demand, the salesperson has made a concession. The rules of reciprocation now suggest that you have an obligation to that person and should respond to this concession with one of your own—sending a donation (see ● Figure 13.11).

In addition to reciprocity, the need to appear consistent may drive a considerable amount of compliance. The **foot-in-the-door** technique, in which a small request is followed up by a larger request, is especially effective in gaining compliance. "Liking" an organization on Facebook (a small request) can lead to more purchases and brand loyalty (larger requests). Another technique based on the need to appear consistent is the **low-balling strategy**, in which an initially favorable deal is revised upward once the buyer appears committed (Cialdini et al., 1978). Once you have made a commitment to buy a car, the salesperson leaves to "check" the deal with a supervisor and invariably returns with a few more charges to "make the deal work." The salesperson is counting on you to agree to the higher price because you have already made a public commitment to buy the car. If you stand up at this point and prepare to leave, it is likely that those extra charges will quickly disappear.

solomon7/Shutterstock.com

According to the foot-in-the-door technique, agreeing with a small request, such as clicking the "Like" button on Facebook, makes it more likely that you will agree with larger requests, such as buying products from a company.

Obedience

Obedience is defined as compliance with the request of an authority figure. When you take an exam from a professor or show your driver's license to a police officer, you are being obedient. The power of authorities to gain obedience is probably due to our perception of their legitimacy.

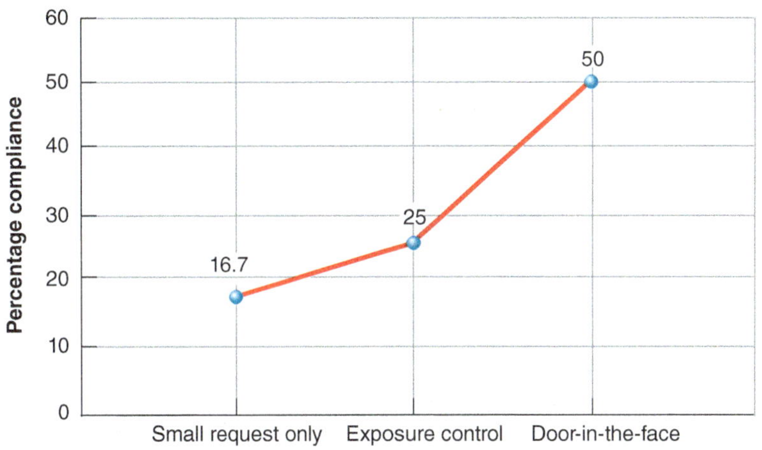

FIGURE **13.11**

Door in the Face. In a study by Cialdini et al. (1975), participants in the door-in-the-face condition were first asked to volunteer for 2 hours per week for 2 years as a "big brother" or "big sister" at a local juvenile detention center. None agreed. Subsequently, they were asked to spend 2 hours chaperoning a group of delinquents to a local zoo, and 50% agreed. In comparison, only 16.7% of the participants hearing only the zoo request agreed, and 25% of people asked whether they would choose one of the two activities agreed to the zoo request. It is possible that feeling guilty for turning down the first request makes people more likely to agree to a second, smaller request.

Source: Adapted from R. B. Cialdini et al. (1975). "Reciprocal Concessions Procedure for Inducing Compliance: The Door-in-the-Face Technique," *Journal of Personality and Social Psychology, 31,* 206–215. doi: 10.1037/h0076284

Men dressed in normal attire had less influence than men dressed as security guards when making simple requests of passersby, even though the requests ("Pick up that bag" or "Give that man a dime for the parking meter") had nothing to do with their perceived roles (Bickman, 1974).

In a series of classic experiments, Stanley Milgram attempted to demonstrate the power of authority over personal ethics (Milgram, 1974). Milgram's participants entered his laboratory at Yale University believing that they were to take part in a study of the effects of punishment on learning. The other "participant" present was a confederate, and the situation was rigged so that the real participant would take the role of teacher while the confederate took the role of learner. The punishment for failing to learn pairs of words was an electric shock, to be administered by the teacher to the learner using an intimidating piece of equipment. The learner or confederate received no actual shocks; his verbal responses to shocks were prerecorded.

The first challenge faced by Milgram's teacher occurred at 75 volts, at which time the learner's first recorded protest could be heard. When faced with this situation, many of Milgram's participants looked to the experimenter in the room for guidance. The experimenter assured the participant that "the experiment must continue" and "you have no choice." Although most participants showed signs of stress and verbally stated their concerns about the procedure, all of Milgram's original 40 participants went as far as 300 volts, and 26 out of the 40 (65%) fully complied by administering the maximum shock (450 volts). Milgram followed up his original scenario by modifying variables that might have influenced the large number of people willing to obey. No differences in outcome were observed when the experiment was conducted in an off-campus office or with participants of different ages and occupations.

Among the variables that did seem to influence Milgram's results was proximity, both between the teacher and the learner and between the teacher and the experimenter. The proximity between the teacher and the learner ranged from complete separation, in which the two people could neither see nor hear each other, to closeness, in which the teacher was instructed to physically hold the learner's hand on a shock grid. As proximity between the teacher and the learner increased, rates of obedience dropped to about 30% (see ● Figure 13.12).

The implications of this result for modern war technologies are clear. People are more likely to operate a drone that harms a person whom they can neither see nor hear than they are to harm a person whose pain is apparent. The proximity of the teacher and the experimenter also was quite influential. The experimenter communicated with the teacher while in the room, by telephone, or by tape recording. Obedience dropped dramatically as interaction with the experimenter, who represented authority, became more remote.

Obedience varies across cultures, but no one is immune. Milgram's data suggest that about 65% of the American population, with equal numbers of men and women, would fully comply in his basic experiment (Milgram, 1963). The highest rates of obedience are found in the general public of the Netherlands (92%; Meeus & Raaijmakers, 1995), Austria (80%; Schurz, 1985), and Germany (85%; Mantell, 1971). Australia reports some of the lowest levels

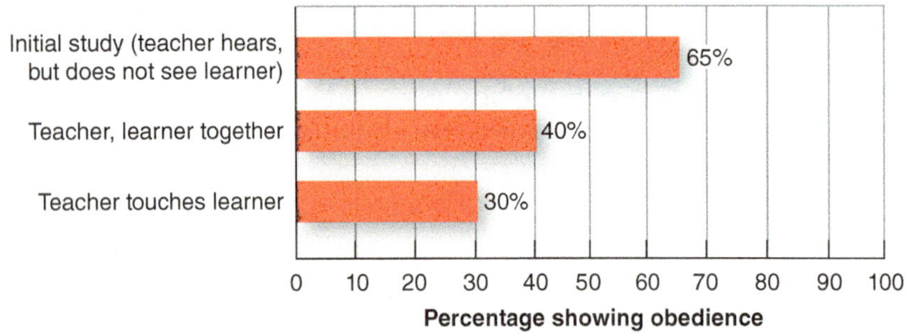

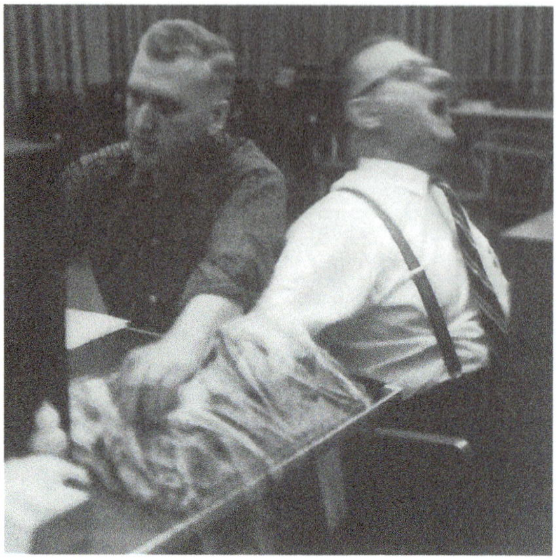

FIGURE **13.12**

Circumstances Affecting Obedience. After his initial study, in which the teacher could hear but not see the learner, Milgram varied the experimental circumstances to see what variables influenced the amount of obedience that his participants displayed. The "teacher, learner together" condition took place with both people in the same room. In the "teacher touches learner" condition, the teacher had to hold the learner's hand down on a shock device. As the teacher and learner came into more contact, obedience dropped, but it remained surprisingly high overall.

Source: From the film *Obedience 1968* by Stanley Milgram, © renewed 1993 by Alexandra Milgram, and distributed by Alexander Street Press. Permission granted by Alexandra Milgram.

of obedience, along with one of the few notable gender differences reported in the obedience literature—40% of Australian male students were fully obedient, but only 16% of Australian female students were fully obedient (Kilham & Mann, 1974).

Milgram's original goal was to illuminate some of the most troubling behavior of modern times, particularly the killing of millions of innocent people in the Holocaust, so it is no surprise that his results are among the most disturbing in modern psychology. Milgram clearly demonstrated that typical people are willing to harm others under the right sets of circumstances. But did he meet his goal of modeling Nazi obedience? He believed so. You may be more comfortable thinking that people who could carry out genocide are different from the students sitting next to you in class. But Milgram's findings suggest otherwise:

> Ordinary people, simply doing their jobs, and without any particular hostility on their part, can become agents in a terrible destructive process. Moreover, even when the destructive effects of their work become patently clear, and they are asked to carry out actions incompatible with fundamental standards of morality, relatively few people have the resources needed to resist authority. (Milgram, 1974, p. 6)

You might be thinking optimistically that people today are different from Milgram's participants in the 1960s. Between the 1920s and the 1980s, parents in the United States shifted their preferences for their children's outcomes from obedience to autonomy (Alwin, 1988). We can begin to evaluate the impact of this parenting change because Milgram's experiment has been partially replicated fairly recently by Burger (2009). By "partially replicated," we mean that Burger made procedural changes for the purposes of meeting ethical requirements, such as informing participants that they could leave if they felt uncomfortable. Despite these changes, Burger's results were similar to Milgram's (82.5% of Milgram's participants obeyed under the same circumstances in which 66.7% of Burger's male participants obeyed). Burger's participants were told explicitly that they could leave at any time, which raises questions about previous explanations of Milgram's results in terms of coercion (Griggs, 2017).

An alternative view of the reasons behind the behavior of Milgram's participants suggests that something called "engaged followership" is more important than coercion (Haslam et al., 2015). In engaged followership, people are willing to do unpleasant things, so long as they agree with the objectives. Leaders, like Milgram's experimenter, promote followers' identification with their objectives, which makes even the most unpleasant tasks seem virtuous. This in turn reduces the stress experienced by the followers. This model seems to present a clearer picture of

Milgram's participants, the Nazis that he wanted to understand, and fanatic followers of many types. It's sobering to realize that if people believe in a cause, there aren't too many things they wouldn't do to reach their goals, including harming others.

No society can exist without obedience. However, history is full of instances in which blindly following orders leads people into highly unethical behavior. Even in more commonplace situations, obedience to authority can overwhelm individual judgment. In one chilling obedience experiment, 22 nurses were telephoned by a doctor they didn't know and instructed to administer a drug not listed on a patient's chart in double its normal dose (Hofling et al., 1966). Astonishingly, 21 of the 22 nurses indicated that they would be willing to obey the order. We could argue that it is desirable for nurses to carry out the directions of physicians, but at what point do we want people to question authority?

AP Images/JEFF WIDENER

The anonymous Tank Man of the 1989 Tiananmen Square protests in Beijing, China, created a minutes-long standoff by maintaining his position in front of a column of tanks. Single individuals disagreeing with a majority with confidence and consistency can stimulate others to reconsider their positions. We do not know the fate of Tank Man today.

The Power of One

Our discussion of conformity, compliance, and obedience would be incomplete without considering the circumstances in which an individual or small group can influence a larger group. Asch provided a clue to the necessary conditions when he noted that conformity was greatest when a person faced a unanimous group. A single individual's willingness to take an opposing view may encourage others to also resist the pressure to conform to a misguided action, or at least to reconsider their original position.

To successfully influence the majority, a minority voice must display consistency and confidence. In a study designed to determine the factors that enabled a minority to influence a majority, people occasionally agreed with an individual who consistently stated that blue slides were green, but never agreed with an individual who judged blue to be green only part of the time (Moscovici et al., 1969). Individual voices that are raised confidently, as in the case of Mahatma Gandhi or Martin Luther King, Jr., are more likely to influence the majority than are more tentative efforts.

How Do Groups Work Together?

We have explored many instances in which situations seem to have a large impact on people's behavior. Given the sociability of our species, it should not be surprising to learn that one of the most powerful situational influences on our behavior is the presence of other people. How is our behavior different when we are with others compared to when we are alone?

social facilitation A situation in which the presence of other people changes performance.

Social Facilitation

Social facilitation occurs when the presence of other people changes individual performance. In 1898, Norman Triplett reported that cyclists riding in pairs rode faster than cyclists riding alone. Social facilitation is not limited to cycling. Children spinning fishing reels did so faster when in groups than when they were alone.

In contrast to Triplett's observations, we have all seen skilled performers "choke" in front of an important audience. Why does performance improve in front of audiences in some situations and become worse in others? Psychologists noticed that well-practiced skills, like riding a bicycle, improved with an audience, but that when people were still learning a new skill, they performed badly (Triplett, 1898; Zajonc, 1965; Zajonc & Sales, 1966). When we're performing a well-practiced skill, most of what we do is correct, but when we are learning something new, many of the things we do are wrong. The presence of the audience appears to enhance whichever patterns of behavior are dominant—the right moves in a well-practiced skill and the wrong moves in a new skill. The moral of this story is to make sure that you practice thoroughly before you perform in front of an audience.

Because of social facilitation, a well-practiced skill (like pedaling by these professional cyclists) is enhanced by the presence of others.

Gary Francis/ZUMA Press/Adelaide/South Australia/Australia/Newscom

Because of social loafing, we would expect the cheering by each of these fans in a nearly empty stadium to be louder than the cheering produced by individual fans in a packed stadium.

The complexity of a task also can interact with the presence of an audience to produce either improved or impaired performance (Bond & Titus, 1983). This result implies that one of the functions of the audience is to increase the performer's level of arousal. The Yerkes–Dodson law, discussed in Chapter 7, states that performance on simple tasks improves steadily with arousal, but that performance on complex tasks first improves and then becomes impaired as arousal continues to grow (Yerkes & Dodson, 1908). Improvements in performance due to arousal are more likely to occur when people are engaged in simple, well-practiced activities, such as riding a bicycle, as opposed to highly complex, novel activities, such as memorizing a difficult list of words.

Social Loafing

While working on group projects, you have probably had opportunities to observe **social loafing**, or the reduced motivation and effort shown by individuals working in a group as opposed to working alone. When engaged in a tug-of-war game at a picnic, members of a team exert less individual effort with each additional person added to their side (Kravitz & Martin, 1986). Individuals cheer less loudly in a large group than they do in a smaller group (Latané et al., 1979).

Individual, gender, cultural, and task variables interact to produce social loafing. Women are somewhat less likely to demonstrate social loafing than men, and people from Eastern cultures are less likely to loaf than those from the West (Karau & Williams, 1993). Simple physical tasks, such as screwing and unscrewing nuts and bolts, reliably produce social loafing in most people (Petty et al., 1988). Task complexity interacts with a need for cognition, or the motivation to engage in and enjoy effortful cognitive endeavors (Cacioppo et al., 1984). People with a low need for cognition showed social loafing during both a physical task and a brainstorming task in which they were asked to generate a list of possible uses for an object (Cacioppo et al., 1996). In contrast, individuals who demonstrate a high need for cognition take pleasure in difficult mental tasks, and although they showed social loafing on the simple physical task, they did not socially loaf during the more intellectually demanding brainstorming task. Individuals appear less likely to take the opportunity to socially loaf on tasks that they find intrinsically enjoyable to perform.

social loafing Reduced motivation and effort shown by individuals working in a group.

deindividuation Immersion of an individual within a group, leading to anonymity.

group polarization The intensifying of an attitude following discussion.

Deindividuation

Deindividuation refers to the immersion of the individual within a group, which makes the individual relatively anonymous. Deindividuation can lead normally law-abiding people to commit uncharacteristic atrocities, including riots and lynchings.

Why would people go along with the negative behavior of a surrounding group, especially if they are unlikely to behave this way on their own? One possibility is that anonymous people feel less accountable for their actions. In an experiment using a paradigm similar to Milgram's obedience experiments described earlier, participants dressed in hoods and oversized lab coats administered longer shocks than control participants who were dressed in normal clothing with name tags (Zimbardo, 1969). Other psychologists suggest that you do not necessarily "lose yourself" in a group, but that your attention shifts from a personal identity to the identity of the surrounding group (Lea & Spears, 1991). If the group with which you identify features antisocial group norms, you will now conform to those (Spears, 2017).

If you participate in online discussions, you might notice a difference in the way that people relate on platforms such as Facebook compared to the anonymous platforms in some message boards and chat rooms. Deindividuation predicts that anonymous message boards would feature less inhibition, such as less civil discussion, than would platforms where individual identity is obvious.

Group Polarization

Common sense suggests that discussion with others who express different opinions should produce more moderate attitudes for everyone in the group. Surprisingly, this is not always the case. In **group polarization**, a period of discussion pushes group members to take more extreme

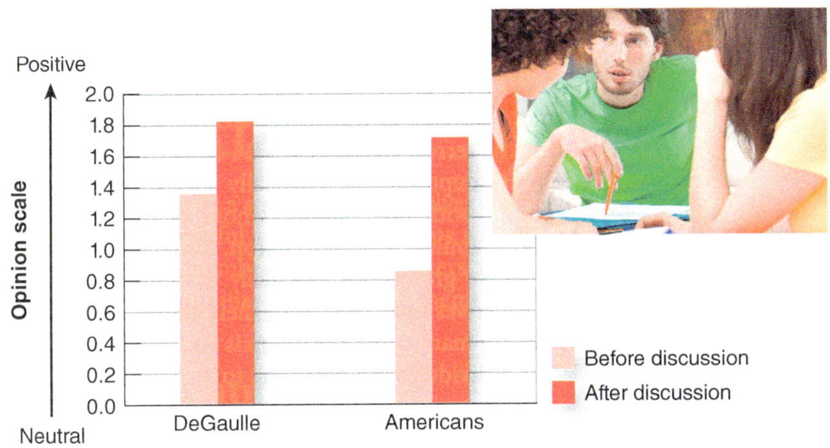

Photographee.eu/Shutterstock.com

FIGURE **13.13**

Group Polarization. We like to think that we can come together and talk out our differences, but that does not always happen. Discussion often moves individuals to take more extreme versions of their original positions. After individually rating French leader Charles de Gaulle and Americans in general (both of which were rated somewhat positively), groups of four French college students were asked to reach consensus on the ratings and then provide a second set of individual ratings. Following the group discussion leading to consensual ratings, the students' individual ratings were more extreme (more positive, in this example) than their first ratings had been.
Source: Adapted from S. Moscovici & M. Zavalloni (1969). "The Group as a Polarizer of Attitudes," *Journal of Personality and Social Psychology*, *12*, 125–135. doi:10.1037/h0027568

positions in the direction that they were already inclined to prefer (Moscovici & Zavalloni, 1969). Group polarization does not reverse the direction of attitudes, but rather accentuates the attitudes held at the outset (see ● Figure 13.13). If group members began mildly favoring gun control, their attitudes will be more favorable after discussion, whereas if group members began with a mildly unfavorable position on gun control, their attitudes will be more unfavorable after discussion.

Two pressures appear to push individuals to take more extreme positions following a group discussion. First, conformity and desire for affiliation contribute to group polarization. If the majority of a group is leaning in a particular direction, what could be a better way of fitting in than agreeing with that majority, and maybe even taking its argument one step farther? There is also a tendency for like-minded people to affiliate with one another, which can provide reinforcement for existing opinions, increase people's confidence in those opinions, lead to the discovery of new reasons for those opinions and counterarguments to opposing views, and reduce exposure to conflicting ideas. Second, exposure to discussion on a topic introduces new reasons for holding an attitude. If you are already opposed to gun control and you listen to additional arguments supporting your position, you might end up more opposed than you were originally.

Group polarization is frequently studied in the context of the behaviors of juries. Following deliberations, final sentencing decisions by mock juries are typically more severe or more lenient than the original opinions expressed by individual group members (Bray & Noble, 1978). Group polarization appears to be even more powerful in online discussions, where people are exposed to many more arguments on issues than they might generate on their own (Sia et al., 2002; Himelboim et al., 2013).

groupthink A type of flawed decision making in which a group does not question its decisions critically.

Groupthink

As we discovered in our discussion of conformity, the presence of others can influence the process of decision making. In Asch's experiments, individuals appeared to make a choice in favor of group harmony over accuracy. If group members suppress dissenting opinions in the interests of group cohesion, the group may fall into a state of **groupthink**.

This type of flawed decision making might account for a number of unfortunate group decisions throughout history (Janis, 1971). Among the examples most frequently described as results of groupthink are the Bay of Pigs invasion, the Korean and Vietnam Wars, and the Cuban missile crisis (Rose, 2011). These examples are notable because of their disastrous results, but they may not be representative

Deindividuation, or the loss of personal identity within a crowd, can lead people to do things that they would not do on their own, such as destroying this CVS Pharmacy during a protest following the death of George Floyd. Many psychologists believe that rather than "losing" oneself in a crowd, people instead adopt the norms of the crowd. If the crowd becomes violent, normally law-abiding people might follow along.

marchello74/Shutterstock.com

David M. Benett/Getty Images Entertainment/Getty Images; Ian West/PA Images/Alamy Stock Photo

Most long-term couples share an approximately equal level of attractiveness and may even have similar features or physique, as do Sophie Hunter and Benedict Cumberbatch.

to the students' attitudes, the students reported that the anonymous person was better liked, more intelligent, and better informed about current events. Apparently, assuming that we like ourselves, we find it easy to like people with whom we are similar. People tend to choose friends and romantic partners who hold similar deep values, such as honesty and loyalty, rather than on the basis of superficial traits like hair color (Cacioppo & Cacioppo, 2020). Consistent with these research findings, the number of interracial couples in the United States has grown dramatically since 1960 (Bryant & Duncan, 2019).

Although people may be initially attracted to those with whom they share similar characteristics, being attracted to another person also increases similarity, a process known as *attitude alignment*. Attitudes of dating partners grow closer together in a gradual process (Davis & Rusbult, 2001). At the same time, partners in stable relationships often overestimate the similarity of their attitudes (Murray et al., 2002).

Physical appearance is a dominant factor in romantic attraction. After completing questionnaires assessing personality and academic achievement, study participants were randomly paired for a "computer dance." Male participants were subsequently asked whether they would ask their partner for a second date. The only significant variable out of all the personality and other data collected that predicted the likelihood of a second date was the woman's physical attractiveness (Walster et al., 1966).

Cultures frequently have their own definitions of physical beauty, but we appear to have some underlying, biological preferences. Preferences for faces rated as beautiful by adults can be demonstrated in infants as young as 3 months of age (Langlois et al., 1990). Subjective judgments of beauty are heavily influenced by symmetry, or the degree of similarity between one half of the body or face and the other half. Symmetry appears to be particularly important in judging the physical attractiveness of potential romantic partners. Symmetry of faces was more important to heterosexual research participants in opposite-sex judgments of attractiveness than in same-sex judgments of attractiveness (Little et al., 2008).

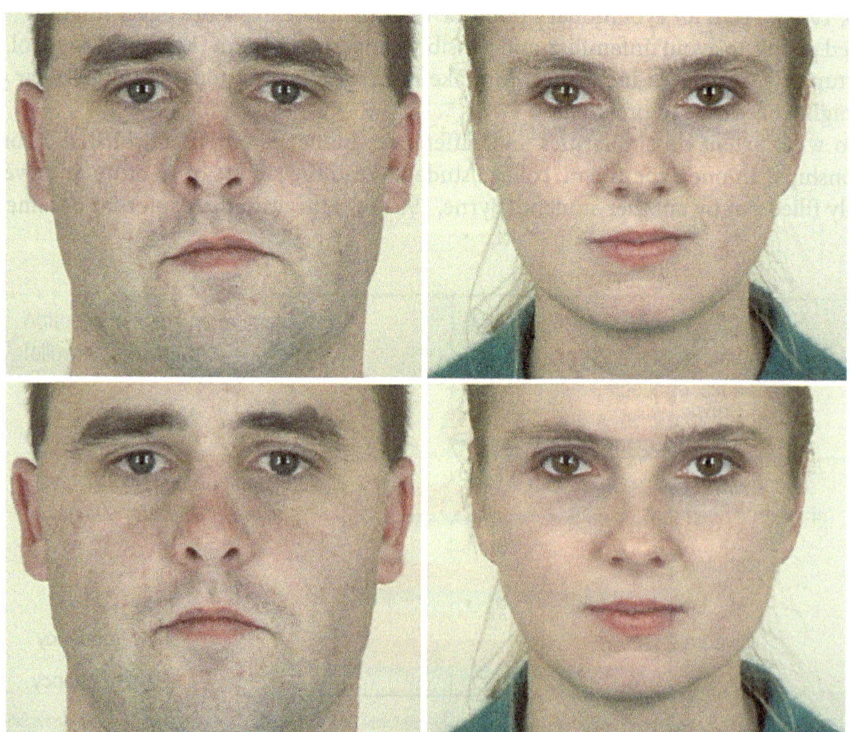

People show strong preferences for symmetrical faces (bottom row) compared to the less symmetrical versions of the same faces (top row). Symmetry may serve as an outward sign of genetic health.

Source: D. I. Perrett et al. (1999). "Symmetry and Human Facial Attractiveness." *Evolution and Human Behavior, 20*, 295–307. doi: 10.1093/beheco/arn049. Copyright © 2008 Oxford University Press.

Most romantic couples share a common level of physical attractiveness, a concept known as the *matching hypothesis*. Couples who were most similar in terms of physical attractiveness were more likely to be together 9 months later (White, 1980). However, when longer-lasting heterosexual relationships are examined, female partners tend to be rated as slightly more attractive than their male partners (McNulty et al., 2008).

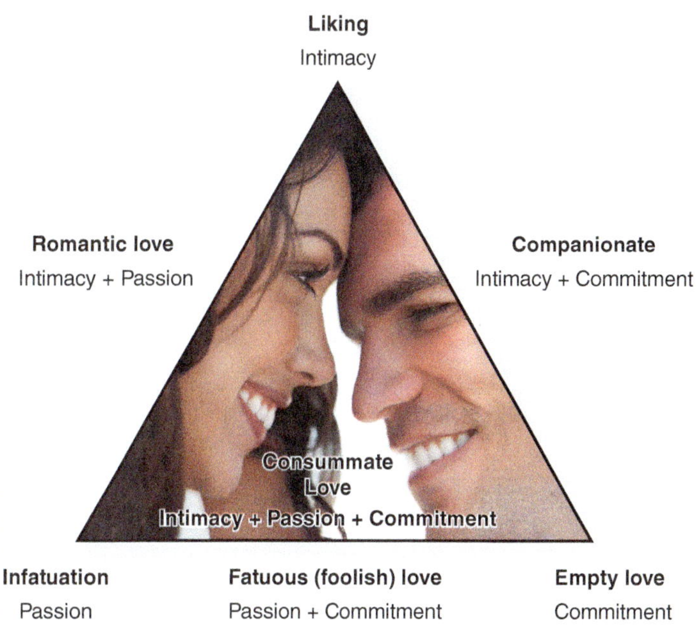

Yuri Arcurs/Shutterstock.com

FIGURE **13.15**

Robert Sternberg's Triangular Model of Love. According to Sternberg, close relationships vary along the dimensions of intimacy, passion, and commitment. Consummate love combines all three.

Building Relationships

Self-disclosure, or sharing personal information about yourself, follows a regular progression as people become more intimate with one another (Taylor & Altman, 1987). Acquaintances talk about general topics other than themselves. New friends might discuss their personal abilities and attitudes, whereas close friends move on to consider dreams and goals. Intimate friends might share fears and negative past behaviors.

Intimacy is highest when falling in love, but what does love look like under the microscope? Robert Sternberg's triangular model of love distinguishes the building of different types of relationships along dimensions of intimacy, passion, and commitment (Sternberg, 2004). Intimacy refers to the closeness or bonding that we experience with a significant other, passion includes arousal and romance, and commitment describes the promise you make to yourself to maintain that relationship over time. Intimacy without passion is characteristic of most friendships in which you share personal facts and intimate moments of your life. Passion by itself characterizes an infatuation directed toward a particular person. Commitment alone could describe the situation in which a person remains loyal to a partner whose health makes passion no longer possible, as in the case of a partner with dementia (see Figure 13.15).

Combinations of intimacy and passion define romantic love. Without the addition of commitment, this type of love can fade quickly. Intimacy and commitment occur together as companionate love. This love exists without passion in deep friendships or family relationships. A combination of passion and commitment can occur in an intense relationship, in which insufficient time has elapsed for the development of intimacy. Finally, people who are lucky enough to find all three components in the same relationship experience consummate, or so-called true love.

Maintaining Relationships

What factors keep people together? Some strategies seem particularly important to many types of relationships, including friendships, family relationships, and romantic relationships. People continue to use openness and self-disclosure as relationships mature, along with participation in joint activities, provision of reassurance, and communication (Berscheid, 1989; Canary et al., 1993).

Gottman and Gottman (2017) describe how turning toward a "bid" for attention offered by a partner rather than turning away or against is predictive of happier relationships. For example, one person might bid for a response from a partner by commenting on something of personal interest, such as "Look at that beautiful dog!" The partner can turn toward the bid ("Yes, I agree. That's a really pretty dog, but our dog is even prettier!"), away from the bid (ignoring it), or against the bid ("Don't bother me now. I'm reading!"). Responses to bids were observed in newlywed couples and marital status was assessed six years later. As newlyweds, now-divorced couples had a record of turning toward bids only 33% of the time compared to 86% of the time in couples still married.

gchutka/E+/Getty Images

In research by Gottman and Gottman (2017), successful couples are much more likely to "turn toward" a bid made by a partner, such as interest in the Super Bowl. Less successful couples are more likely to turn away from (don't bother me) or against (I hate football) a partner's bid.

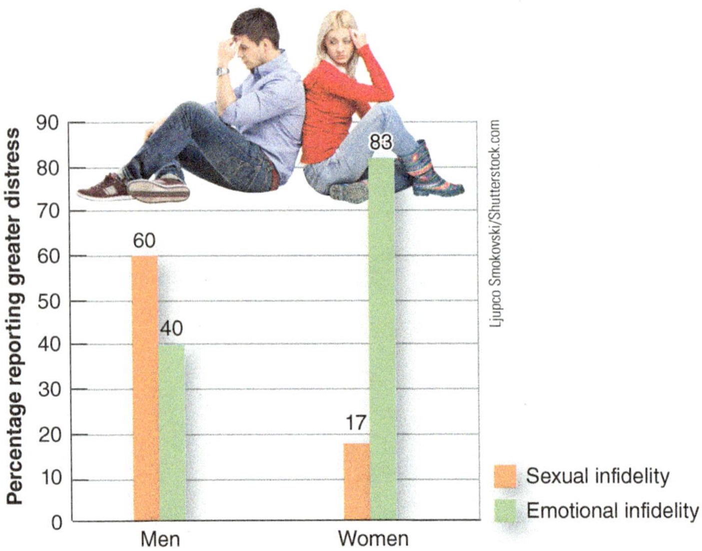

FIGURE 13.16

Gender Differences in Response to Partner Infidelity. When asked which would cause greater distress, your partner cheating on you sexually or becoming deeply emotionally involved with a rival, men reported greater distress from sexual infidelity, whereas women reported greater distress from emotional infidelity. *Source:* Adapted from D. M. Buss et al. (1992). "Sex Differences in Jealousy: Evolution, Physiology, and Psychology," *Psychological Science*, *3*, 251–255. doi: 10.1111/j.1467-9280.1992.tb00038.x

Maintaining a relationship may become easier over time. As couples spend more time together, they build a shared history, which provides them with a stronger basis for understanding each other. Couples who have been together for many years appear to have the ability to communicate a thought or emotion to each other with a single look (Schober & Carstensen, 2010). Long-term relationships can become boring, however. Couples who continue to engage in novel and exciting activities have higher relationship satisfaction (Aron et al., 2000).

Ending Relationships

As you are no doubt well aware, real life does not typically follow the scripts of fairy tales, in which the lovers ride off into the sunset to live happily ever after. Maintaining relationships takes time and effort, reciprocity, and cooperation. A sense of inequity or unfairness in a relationship may cause it to end. Equity in a relationship suggests that costs, such as curtailed freedom and less time to oneself, are offset by benefits, such as companionship and security. In general, more equitable romantic relationships are stable, enjoyable, and sexually intimate.

Most couples experience their share of ups and downs, but the relative number of their positive and negative experiences is related to the likelihood that the relationship will survive or end (Gottman et al., 2002). Couples appear to need about five positive interactions to offset one negative interaction. As the ratio of positive to negative interactions slips toward 1:1, the likelihood that the relationship will end increases. Couples with high levels of apparent conflict might still stay together, so long as they agree to disagree and their conflict is offset by a larger amount of positive times together.

Infidelity often contributes to the ending of a romantic relationship. Data describing how frequently romantic partners cheat on each other are difficult to obtain and show wide variations, as in the 33%–75% of men and 26%–70% of women reported to cheat on their partners in one review of the literature (Buss & Schmitt, 1993). Paternal discrepancy, or the identification of a child as biologically fathered by someone other than the male who believes himself to be the father, provides further insight into female infidelity. Estimates of paternal discrepancy range from 4% to 10% (Bellis et al., 2005). Males and females appear to respond to different aspects of cheating behavior (see Figure 13.16). Males become jealous of sexual infidelity, whereas females are more distressed by emotional infidelity (Buss et al., 1992).

SUMMARY 13.3 Sternberg's Three Types of Love

Type of Love	Combines	Excludes
Romantic love 	Intimacy + passion	Commitment
Companionate love	Intimacy + commitment	Passion
Consummate love	Intimacy + commitment + passion	Nothing

Credit: photo: Yuri Arcurs/Shutterstock.com.

Why Do We Cooperate in Some Situations and Compete in Others?

Our social interactions with one another can feature cooperation, or working together toward common goals, or competition, where we struggle with one another to obtain limited resources.

Both cooperation and competition have a long history in shaping our behavior. In Chapter 3, we described natural selection as an ongoing race among organisms competing for scarce resources and opportunities to reproduce (Darwin, 1859). The stakes in this race are high. Individuals with characteristics that give them an advantage over others are able to pass their genes along, while losers fail to reproduce and die. At the same time, because humans do not live alone, our survival depends on cooperation.

Competition and Cooperation in Animals

Individual animals frequently compete for food or opportunities to mate. Beginning with observations of "pecking order" among chickens (Schjedlderup-Ebbe, 1922), biologists have cataloged many species that use competition, usually in the form of fighting, to determine the allocation of mating opportunities, food, and other resources both within and between groups.

Too much competition among individual members hampers the cohesion of a group, breaking it into factions and possibly resulting in injuries among its members. Consequently, many animals minimize the extent of within-group conflict by displaying clear signals of dominance, or high status. The mandrill, a type of baboon, uses facial expressions and gestures to signify its position in a dominance hierarchy. The coloring of the mandrill's face, rump, and genitalia is also reflective of individual fighting abilities (Setchell & Wickings, 2005).

The advantages of cooperation can be illustrated by a real-life tale of two 1864 shipwrecks in the South Pacific. Members of one crew worked cooperatively with one another as equals, while members of the other maintained their formal command structure. After 1 year, the first crew managed to build a boat and get rescued, while the second was decimated by cold, hunger, and cannibalism (Druett, 2007).

Do humans have analogous signals of dominance? It appears that the male of the species does (Mazur & Mueller, 1996). Dominant human male faces are handsome and muscular, featuring strong chins, deep-set eyes, and prominent brows. In contrast, "baby-faced" males are rated by observers as being more submissive (McArthur & Berry, 1987). Humans have the advantage of augmenting their natural signals of status by purchasing and displaying expensive automobiles, homes, and jewelry.

Paul Wayne Wilson/PhotoStockFile/Alamy Stock Photo

Animals minimize the damage caused by competing for dominance by displaying clear signals of submission. The dog on its back is letting the other dog know that its dominance has been recognized.

Individual Differences in Cooperation and Competition

Individuals vary in their predisposition to cooperation or competition. In one experiment, groups of participants were given the opportunity to compete (by keeping tokens) or cooperate (by sharing tokens) while they observed the decisions made by their group members (Kurzban & Houser, 2005). Three types of dispositions emerged: 17% of the participants were "cooperators," who gave their tokens freely without paying much attention to the behavior of other group members; 20% were "free riders," who didn't give up any of their tokens; and 63% of the participants were "reciprocators," who cooperated only after seeing others do so. Even though cooperators are in the minority, their behavior is important to group survival. By contributing selflessly, they encourage the majority of the group to cooperate too.

The Influence of Culture on Competition and Cooperation

Members of successful groups are more likely to survive and reproduce than members of unsuccessful groups. Because it is in our best interest to belong to effective groups, we cooperate with other group members and are quick to conform to their norms and judgments. Cooperation becomes ingrained in the group's culture and is passed along to new members.

Why is cooperation so essential to successful group behavior? Without cooperation, there would be no basis for gathering diverse areas of individual expertise into a meaningful, useful whole. Under the influence of culture, humans have progressed from simple divisions of labor to highly specialized areas of expertise. Individuals might spend their entire academic careers exploring the structure of the frog retina or the surface characteristics of one of Saturn's moons. At the same time, no single person working alone would be able to put humans on the Moon or produce all the special effects expected by contemporary movie audiences. Few fans would pay to see an individual football player demonstrate his skills on an otherwise empty field on Sunday afternoon. Cooperation is the glue that holds productive groups together, from the operating room of a hospital to the baseball diamond.

The importance of group membership to survival is reflected in the remarkable loyalty that humans show to their culturally defined groups. Fans of a particular sports team may be every bit as loyal to their group (and as potentially violent toward others) as our early hunter–gatherer ancestors were to their tribe or clan. Unfortunately, the same loyalty and cultural distinctiveness that bind us to our groups may lead us into conflict with other groups, as discussed later in this chapter.

Cooperation is essential to successful group behavior.

Gonzalo Fuentes/Reuters

Choosing Between Cooperation and Competition

How do people decide when to compete and when to cooperate?

A classic model of competition and cooperation within groups is known as the prisoner's dilemma (Poundstone, 1992). Assume that you and another person have been arrested for a crime, but that the police have limited evidence against you. Without being able to communicate with your partner, you are given the choice to confess (defect from your partner) or to remain silent (cooperate with your partner). If you both remain silent, you will each be sentenced to 1 year. If you both confess, you will each receive 10 years. However, if one confesses and the other remains silent, the prisoner who confesses will be set free, and the silent prisoner will receive a 20-year sentence. The dilemma arises because the best individual strategy is to confess or defect from your partner, but if both of you figure this out and subsequently confess, your

Prisoner A	Prisoner B	
	Prisoner B stays silent.	Prisoner B confesses.
Prisoner A stays silent.	A and B both serve 1 year each.	A serves 20 years. B goes free.
Prisoner A confesses.	A goes free. B serves 20 years.	A and B both serve 10 years each.

FIGURE **13.17**

The Prisoner's Dilemma.

outcome is worse than if you both had remained silent (see Figure 13.17). In the prisoner's dilemma, cooperation is moderately rewarded (a 1-year sentence), while defection is punished (10 years). If only one of you confesses, however, the confessor is highly rewarded (freedom), while the other person is severely punished (20 years).

For real people, computers, and even animals, the most successful strategy in the prisoner's dilemma situation is the *tit-for-tat (TFT) strategy* (Axelrod & Hamilton, 1981). Using the TFT strategy, you make cooperation your first move and then repeat your partner's successive moves. The success of the TFT strategy has been attributed to three aspects: It is nice (you begin with cooperation), it is able to retaliate and punish uncooperative behavior (defection by your partner is followed by your own defection), and it is forgiving (you return immediately to cooperation following cooperation on the part of your partner; Brembs, 1996).

The research on individual differences in cooperation discussed earlier found that most human participants were reciprocators, whose behavior is most similar to the TFT strategy (Kurzban & Houser, 2005). The prevalence of this type might reflect its typical success. If most people are reciprocators, how can we explain the existence of the other types? Free riders clearly benefit from their selfish behavior, but what advantages might increase the chances of the cooperators' survival and reproductive success? It is easier to be generous when you are well off, so acting like a cooperator might make people believe that you have extensive resources, improving your chances of attracting a mate (Milinski et al., 2002). A person's reputation is also a powerful motivator for cooperation. In ongoing prisoner's dilemma games, participants use other people's record of cooperation (or lack thereof) to determine whether to cooperate with them (Milinski et al., 2002). In small hunter–gatherer bands or basketball teams, having a reputation for selfishness is not likely to make you successful.

Culture can shape a person's choice of competition and cooperation. When two people from different countries played the prisoner's dilemma game, less cooperation and more competition occurred than when two people from the same country participated together (Matsumoto & Hwang, 2011). Furthermore, the bigger the difference between the native countries of the participants along the dimension of individualism or collectivism, the less cooperation occurred. This finding reflects the in-group bias mentioned earlier in the chapter.

Contributing to our cooperative abilities is a deep-seated, possibly biological sense of fair play that is shared with other species in the animal kingdom. Capuchin monkeys will happily trade pebbles for slices of cucumber until they see another monkey receiving the more preferred grapes for its pebbles. After seeing the "unfairness" of their situation, they not only are no longer willing to work for cucumber slices, but they also respond by shaking their cages in anger (Brosnan & De Waal, 2003). When people playing a prisoner's dilemma game were observed with fMRI, viewing the faces of cooperators produced activation in brain areas normally linked to reward (Singer et al., 2004). In contrast, when people were treated unfairly, activation occurred in parts of the brain associated with anger, disgust, and pain (Sanfey et al., 2003).

A capuchin monkey refuses to exchange a pebble for a slice of cucumber after seeing another monkey receive a more highly valued grape for its pebble, suggesting that nonhuman primates have a sense of fairness.

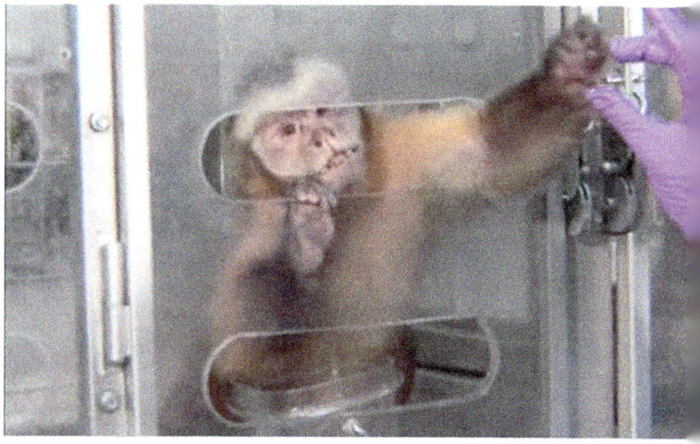

Science Nation, National Science Foundation

Altruism and Helping

We have all read stories about soldiers, firefighters, and others who have risked or even sacrificed their lives to save the lives of others. These instances are examples of altruism, a helping behavior that either fails to reward or actually harms the person who performs it, which was discussed in Chapter 3. Instances of altruism in which the helper is exposed to risk or experiences harm are often described as heroism (Franco et al., 2011).

The designation of *hero* is often given to people who are altruistic to the point of risking their lives to help others. In 2007, Wesley Autrey (shown here with his daughter) selflessly risked his life to save a young man who fell onto New York subway tracks after suffering a seizure.

Michael Loccisano/Getty Images

If behavior usually leads to improved survival and reproduction, how can we account for altruism? Charles Darwin suggested that "[a] tribe including many members who were always ready to give aid to each other and sacrifice themselves for the common good, would be victorious over most other tribes; and this would be natural selection" (Darwin, 1871, p. 166). Although this suggestion is attractive, it suffers from a major flaw in logic. The system suggested by Darwin would produce free riders who were not altruistic themselves, but who would benefit from the altruistic behaviors of the members of their group (Dawkins, 1976). These individuals, because they would undoubtedly live to reproduce (as opposed to the altruistic, who might not survive), should eventually swamp the group with "selfish" genes.

Several evolutionary mechanisms have been proposed that account for the continuation of cooperative, altruistic behavior (Nowak, 2006). Although altruistic behaviors may have costs for an individual, they may benefit the altruist's genetic relatives. Altruistic genes will survive in the population so long as the cost to an altruist is associated with a large-enough benefit to relatives (Hamilton, 1964). Japanese macaque monkeys are more likely to defend close relatives from attack than they are to defend unrelated monkeys (Kurland, 1977). People are more likely to help their relatives than they are strangers, such as in helping to raise their children. Altruism is also maintained by expectations that a favor might someday be returned by those you have helped, a process known as reciprocal altruism (Trivers, 1971). Vampire bats often regurgitate blood to share with bats who did not hunt successfully; bats are more likely to share with those who had shared with them recently (Wilkinson, 1984, 1990).

bystander intervention The study of situational variables related to helping a stranger, most notably the decreased likelihood of helping as the number of bystanders increases.

Selfishness might be limited by punishment administered by other group members. Study participants who had the opportunity to punish those who had not cooperated activated reward circuits in the brain, lending credence to the phrase "Revenge is sweet" (Fehr & Rockenbach, 2004). Unfortunately, the willingness to pay a big price to carry out revenge against those whose behavior seems unfair might also lead to irrational acts, such as suicide bombings.

However, other instances of altruism do not fit these models. People have been known to adopt unrelated children. Arland Williams, a passenger on an airplane that crashed into the freezing Potomac River in 1982, passed lifelines to other passengers before disappearing beneath the water. These altruistic acts represent psychological altruism, or conscious efforts to help. This type of altruism can be transmitted by a culture through learning (Dawkins, 1976). The role of learning in altruism is supported by observations that the tendency to feel pleasure when helping others is quite low in children and gradually increases into adulthood (Cialdini et al., 1981).

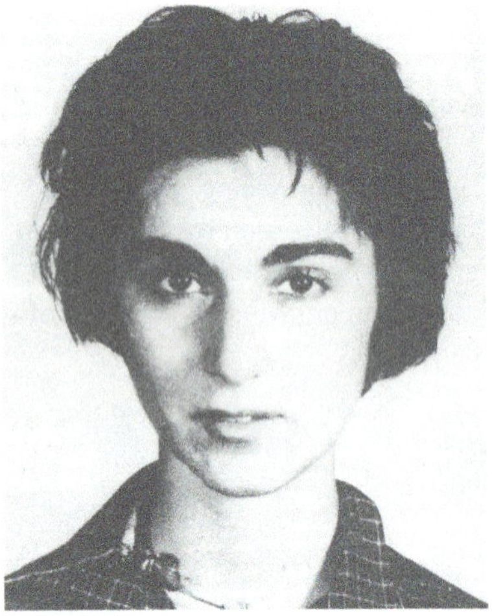

The New York Times Photo Archive/Redux Pictures

Sensational (though inaccurate) news accounts of the murder of Kitty Genovese stimulated research in bystander intervention, which asked questions about why people seem to help in some situations but not others.

If cooperation confers so many benefits to individuals and groups, how can we explain the failure of some individuals to provide help when it is desperately needed? In 1964, a young woman named Kitty Genovese was murdered on a New York City street near her home late at night. Sensational news reports at the time stated that 38 of her neighbors watched for more than half an hour while Kitty struggled with her attacker without intervening or calling the police. Although these reports were not confirmed by later court testimony in the case (one neighbor, Sophia Farrar, managed to reach Kitty before she died; Manning et al., 2007), the public outrage that they stimulated led to a series of experiments into **bystander intervention**. This research demonstrated that an individual's likelihood of helping drops as the number of other observers grows. In a typical experiment investigating this phenomenon, college students filled out a questionnaire as their room filled with smoke (Latané & Darley, 1968). The researchers were interested in how frequently and quickly the students reported the smoke. When the college students were alone, nearly 80% sought help within 6 minutes. When three study participants were tested together, however, only 40% reported the emergency within 6 minutes.

The effect of the number of observers on the likelihood of intervention is probably influenced by a sense of individual responsibility. When you are the only person available to help, your responsibility is clear. When a crowd of people is gathered around the scene of an accident, it is easier to assume that others have already called 911 or that a physician or nurse who is better qualified to help will be present. People also fail to act because of fears of appearing foolish as a result of misinterpreting a situation. Emergencies sometimes can be ambiguous. What sounds like a case of domestic violence next door might be a loud movie or video game or actors practicing a scene for a play. People who feel anonymous are less likely to help, which is consistent with our previous observations of how anonymity can lead to less socially desirable behavior. Finally, people are more likely to help when it is safe and convenient for them to do so. If you are heading for your car at the end of the day when you notice a classmate with a flat tire, you are likely to lend a hand. However, if you are late for work or a final exam, you may conveniently assume that someone else will take care of the situation as you continue on your way.

Why Are We Aggressive?

aggression The conscious intent to harm another.

Aggression is the conscious intent to harm others, and it can take several forms. Instrumental aggression is the intentional harm, usually physical, done to others to obtain a goal, such as attacking a person to steal a wallet or purse. Relational aggression harms another person's social standing through behaviors such as ignoring, excluding, and gossiping. Other types of aggression include defensive aggression, in which the person may do harm to others in self-defense; passive aggression, in which people who aren't comfortable being openly aggressive get what they want under the guise of still trying to please others; and maternal aggression, a rather common phenomenon in the animal world (and occasionally among humans) in which sickly or unwanted offspring are killed.

Like most of the behaviors discussed in this textbook, factors leading to human aggression form complex interactions. Efforts to find simple correlations between violence and single variables such as economic growth, population trends, illegal drug trade, availability of guns, and domestic violence versus stranger violence do not tell the whole story. We can capture the flavor of this complexity by examining homicide rates across cultures. The average homicide rate worldwide is about 0.7% of all deaths. Homicides account for less than 0.1% of deaths in Western Europe, 0.7% of deaths in the United States, but more than 9% of deaths in Honduras (Roser & Ritchie, 2019). Rates in large cities within the United States vary substantially. St. Louis, Missouri, is the 15th most dangerous city in the world, with a murder rate of 60.94 homicides per 100,000 residents (Statista Research Department, 2020). In comparison, there were 1.55 homicides per 100,000 in Virginia Beach, Virginia. Across all cultures, males are far more likely than females to be victims of homicide (81% to 19%), but 58% of females are killed by intimate partners or other family members (UNODC, 2019).

The Biological Psychology of Aggression

Is a capacity for aggression simply part of being human? Biological explanations of aggression point to several possible sources of human aggression: genetics, biochemistry, and nervous system structure and activity.

Aggression is clearly a disposition that can be selectively bred in animals, as evidenced by the development of the famous fighting bulls of Spain and hyperaggressive laboratory mice (Lagerspetz & Lagerspetz, 1983). Human twin and adoption studies imply that aggressive tendencies in humans are at least partly influenced by genetics (Rushton et al., 1986). As we

FIGURE **13.18**

Prenatal Exposure to Testosterone and Aggression. Both male and female preschoolers who had been exposed prenatally to higher than normal levels of testosterone were more physically aggressive than their same-sex siblings who experienced normal levels of prenatal testosterone.

Source: Adapted from J. M. Reinisch et al. (1991). "Hormonal Contributions to Sexually Dimorphic Behavioral Development in Humans," *Psychoneuroendocrinology, 16*, 213–278. doi: 10.1016/0306-4530(91)90080-D

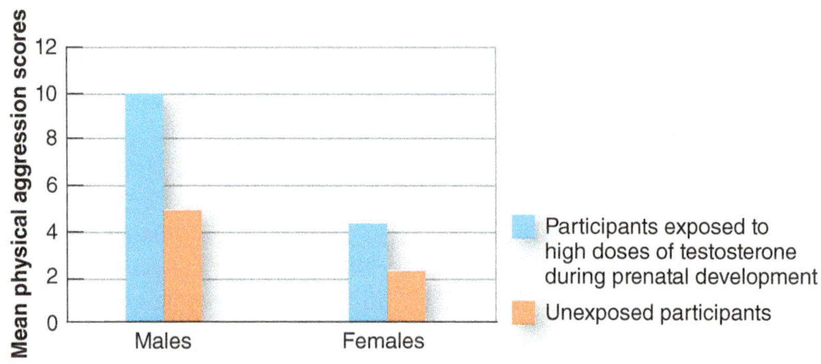

have seen so frequently in this textbook, genes associated with aggressive behavior interact with nurture or experience. Among children who were abused, those with one version of a gene linked to aggression in animals were likely to behave aggressively, while those with the other form rarely did so, even when the abuse experienced was severe (Craig, 2007; Fergusson et al., 2011).

Both naturally occurring chemicals and recreational drugs can influence aggression. Among the naturally occurring chemicals implicated in aggression are androgens, or male hormones such as testosterone (see • Figure 13.18). Prenatal exposure to high levels of androgens, which can occur naturally or because of medications occasionally given to pregnant women, increases the aggressive play of both male and female preschoolers (Reinisch et al., 1991). Adult men with higher levels of prenatal testosterone exposure score higher on standardized questionnaires of aggression (Bailey & Hurd, 2005; Burton et al., 2009). Testosterone levels on the high end of the typical range in teen and adult males are positively correlated with delinquency, drug abuse, and aggression (Dabbs & Morris, 1990). Testosterone levels for both male and female criminals correlate with the violent nature of the crimes for which they were sentenced, as well as the dominance and violence that they demonstrate while in prison (Dabbs et al., 1987; Dabbs & Hargrove, 1997). Testosterone appears to affect aggressive behavior by increasing the sensitivity of the amygdala to threatening stimuli, such as angry faces (Derntl et al., 2009). When feeling threatened, a person might engage in more aggressive behavior as a preemptive strike.

Serotonin levels are negatively correlated with aggressive behavior. Male vervet monkeys form precise social hierarchies, and higher rank is associated with higher levels of serotonin activity (Raleigh et al., 1992). Monkeys at the bottom of the hierarchy had lower serotonin levels and were much more aggressive than high-status monkeys. Serotonin might reduce aggression by enhancing empathy (Siegel & Crockett, 2013) or by promoting activity in frontal-lobe areas associated with inhibiting impulsive behavior (Heinz et al., 2011).

Many psychoactive substances affect the likelihood that a person will behave aggressively. For example, alcohol has been implicated in between 32% and 63% of violent crimes (Giancola, 2013). In addition, many suicides are committed under the influence of alcohol (Sher, 2006). The most likely mode of action for alcohol in stimulating aggression is its general disinhibiting effects on behavior. As discussed in Chapter 4, alcohol silences higher cortical areas responsible for impulse control, often leading to behavior that is normally actively suppressed, including aggression.

Keeping in mind the complexity of human aggression, we can point to variations in brain structure and function that are associated with senseless violence. Antisocial, violent behavior is correlated with some types of brain damage, although these findings interact with experience in ways similar to the genetics studies discussed earlier (Davidson et al., 2000). The diversity of patterns of brain activity leading to aggression was demonstrated in a study comparing brain activity in murderers who had experienced neglect, poverty, physical abuse, or sexual abuse and murderers who had experienced none of these social deficits (Raine et al., 1998). The brain activity of the neglected and abused murderers was quite similar to the nonviolent

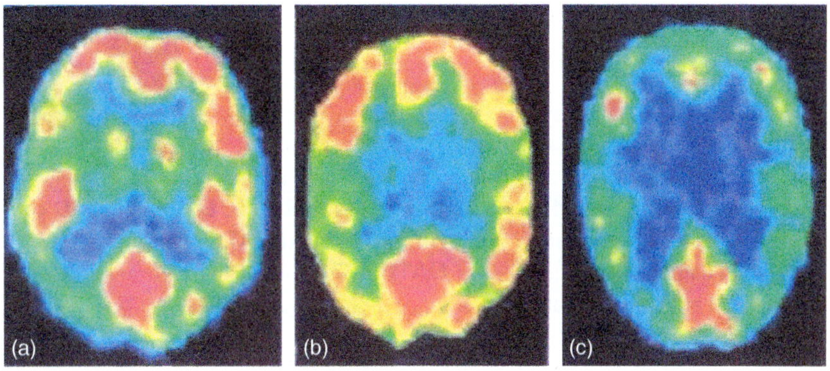

Courtesy of Dr. Adrian Raine, Departments of Criminology, Psychiatry, and Psychology, University of Pennsylvania

These brain images were taken from (a) a person with no history of criminal behavior, (b) a person who was convicted of murder and had a strong history of childhood abuse and neglect, and (c) a person who was convicted of murder but had no history of childhood abuse or neglect. The murderer who had been abused and neglected shows activity that is similar to that of the person without a criminal history. The murderer with no history of abuse or neglect shows little activity in the frontal lobes (toward the top of the image) or in the middle parts of the brain that usually respond to emotional stimuli.

control participants. In contrast, the brain activity of the non-abused murderers was quite different, suggesting that their violent behavior had different roots than in the murderers with a history of child abuse. The non-abused individuals showed an unusually reduced level of activity in the frontal lobes. Given the essential role of the frontal lobes in higher-order judgment and impulse control, this lower level of activity might help account for their inability to control their aggression.

Learning and Aggression

Although it is probably safe to say that our human heritage contains a capacity for aggression, the actual expression of aggression is elicited by environmental factors and modified by experience. As discussed in Chapter 8, Albert Bandura provided compelling evidence that children who observe aggression are likely to behave aggressively themselves (Bandura, 1973). In Bandura's classic demonstration of social learning, preschoolers who observed an adult attack an inflatable Bobo doll mimicked not just the violent actions, but also the yells of "Sock him in the nose," "Knock him down," and "Kick him."

Opportunities to observe violence are plentiful. Within the family, children who are disciplined with screaming, slapping, and beating are more likely to be physically aggressive with their peers at school (Grogan-Kaylor et al., 2018). Even when the parents are violent toward each other, without involving the child directly, the child's level of violent behavior may be affected. In studies of violent children and teens, recent exposure to violence in the home was a useful predictor for the child's violent behavior outside the home (Singer et al., 1998; Jouriles et al., 2018).

Additional opportunities to observe violence are provided by the media. By the age of 18, the average American has seen an estimated 200,000 acts of violence on television alone (Strasburger, 2007). Children and youth are exposed to increasingly violent and graphic images and ideas through films, video games, and music lyrics. As discussed in Chapter 2, however, care must be taken to avoid misinterpretation of the research results showing correlations between media exposure and aggression.

Preventing Aggression

The human species loses a smaller percentage of the population to war today than in the time of our hunter–gatherer ancestors (LeBlanc, 2003), but we still have a long way to go. As in the case of reducing prejudice, redefining the boundaries of the in-group might be contributing to this improvement. Instead of hunter–gatherer clans of 100 or so individuals fighting with neighboring clans, we have nations of millions that cooperate as units. Increasing economic dependencies among nations further reduces the advantages of between-group violence. Damage to one nation's critical infrastructure, such as its ability to produce or process oil, is likely to have adverse effects for all nations, including the attacker. Despite this progress, we remain plagued not only by continued war deaths, but also by homicides, domestic violence,

THINKING SCIENTIFICALLY

Brain Damage and Criminal Behavior

In fortunately rare cases, people who experience brain damage suddenly engage in uncharacteristic, criminal behavior. In 1966, Charles Whitman stabbed his mother and wife to death and then shot and killed 17 people the next day from the observation deck of the University of Texas, Austin tower. Whitman was killed by a police officer and was found to have a tumor pressing on his amygdala. Identifying common features of these cases might help us gain a better understanding of criminality.

WHAT AM I BEING ASKED TO BELIEVE OR ACCEPT?

We are being asked to accept that nervous system correlates of criminal behavior can be identified.

WHAT EVIDENCE SUPPORTS THIS POSITION?

A group of case studies were collected in which no record of criminal behavior occurred prior to brain damage, but did follow soon after the brain damage (Darby et al., 2018). The brain damage these individuals experienced affected different regions, but these regions were all part of the same network, which in turn is related to moral decision making. The circuit included parts of the prefrontal cortex, the orbitofrontal cortex, and the anterior temporal lobes, which contain the amygdala (see Chapter 4).

ARE THERE OTHER WAYS THAT THIS EVIDENCE COULD BE INTERPRETED?

The authors are careful to note that many factors contribute to criminal behavior, and that most patients with damage in the circuit identified in this study do not engage in criminal activity. Their sample was relatively small (17 individuals). They relied on published studies rather than having the opportunity to investigate each case themselves.

WHAT OTHER EVIDENCE WOULD I NEED TO EVALUATE THESE ALTERNATIVES?

The authors recommend following people with new lesions in the identified circuit to see how many engage in criminal activity.

WHAT ARE THE MOST REASONABLE CONCLUSIONS?

Lesions in the identified circuit might contribute to criminal behavior, but criminal behavior is not the inevitable result of this type of damage. In addition, brain damage should not be considered as the only reason these individuals engaged in criminal behavior. Further research is needed to understand the biological correlates of criminal behavior. ■

Bob Daemmrich/Alamy Stock Photo

Police officer Ramiro Martinez was recognized on the 50th anniversary of the first U.S. campus mass shooting event. In 1966, Charles Whitman, who was later discovered to have a rare tumor pressing on his amygdala, opened fire from the University of Texas clock tower, killing 17. Martinez shot and killed Whitman, ending the tragedy. Understanding the rare cases of brain damage that lead to violent behavior can give us a better idea of the brain circuits underlying other forms of violence.

rape, bullying, and other destructive aggressive behavior. Psychologists continue to search for effective ways to reduce aggression.

There are no simple solutions to the problem of aggression. You might think that we could take advantage of catharsis, or the reduction of an emotion through its expression, but the research results do not support this approach. Catharsis theories of aggression are common but suffer from the same weaknesses shown by catharsis explanations of emotion discussed in Chapter 7. Just as expressing an emotion typically heightens rather than decreases a feeling, people who engage in aggression experience an increase in aggression. In one typical experiment, participants first were angered by a person who criticized essays they had written (Bushman, 2002). Subsequently, the participants who were given opportunities to hit a punching bag while thinking about the critic specified a willingness to administer louder sound blasts to the critic when given the opportunity to retaliate than did participants in control groups. Despite the intuitive appeal of the notion of catharsis, when it comes to aggression, catharsis is generally ineffective.

Another frequent suggestion for reducing aggression that has failed to gain research support is an active teaching approach in which children are rewarded for sensitivity and cooperation. Cross-cultural data show that homicide rates are often high in cultures that feature a loving socialization of children and aversion to interpersonal conflict, such as the Inuit, !Kung Bushmen, and Gebusi of New Guinea, yet very low among cultures where children are explicitly taught to fight, like the Turkana of Kenya (Dyson-Hudson & Dyson-Hudson, 1995, 1999).

Much of the research discussed so far in this chapter focuses on individual variables, whether they are related to a person's genetic makeup or socialization. To truly understand aggression, we need to zoom out to see this behavior within the social context. For example, we know that if groups rarely interact, they are more likely to fight than to cooperate. In contrast, if groups interact regularly and anticipate future interactions, they may still compete, but they tend to do so in more prosocial ways.

The social environment also can determine whether aggressiveness escalates to actual violence. In a study using surveillance footage of public places, researchers observed actual fighting behavior (Levine et al., 2011). In many cases, one or more third parties (usually friends of the combatants) intervened to stop the fight. In an interesting contrast with the helping behavior observed in the bystander intervention literature discussed previously, third parties are more likely, not less likely, to intervene in a fight when the number of bystanders is larger. Perhaps the implications of the aggression spreading to include the whole group makes stopping the fight a very high priority for members of the group.

Image courtesy of Mark Levine, Department of Psychology, Exeter University

Research using surveillance camera footage shows that third parties often intervene in an effort to deescalate violence (Levine et al., 2011). Unlike most laboratory studies of bystander intervention, third parties in the filmed incidents were more, not less, likely to intervene as groups of onlookers became larger. Further research should help clarify the exact conditions leading to helping behavior.

Andrew Aitchison/Getty Images

Homicides among the Turkana of Kenya are quite rare, even though children are explicitly encouraged to be aggressive toward one another, under the watchful eyes of adults. However, the Turkana are exceedingly aggressive toward their neighbors. Over human history, the trait of aggression has probably been valued when turned against other groups, but not when it is turned inward.

Interpersonal Relationships

The Social Perspective

WHAT DO WE KNOW ABOUT MARRIAGES THAT BEGIN ONLINE?

THE ADVENT OF THE INTERNET is changing our social interactions right in front of our eyes. Classic research reviewed earlier in this chapter showed that Americans typically married someone who lived within five blocks of their home (Bossard, 1932). The Internet has changed all of that. Between 2005 and 2012, a surprising number of Americans, one out of three, met their spouses online (Cacioppo et al., 2013). Despite the comfort level of younger adults with the Internet, 30- to 39-year-olds were more likely to have met their spouse online than were those under 30. Those who met their spouse online were also more educated and had higher incomes, suggesting that the Internet has provided busy people opportunities to socialize.

Marriages begun online were slightly but significantly less likely to end in divorce or separation than marriages begun offline (see Figure 13.19). Online marriage partners rated their marriages as more satisfying. Even when factors such as age, education, and income were controlled, because these might account for higher satisfaction by themselves, the online marriages remained more successful.

What other factors might account for the success of the online marriages? People who seek a spouse online might differ from those who don't in important ways. Perhaps they are more motivated to maintain long-term relationships, or they might be more selective in their choices. Self-disclosure differs in the online and offline settings, leading to greater liking for people you meet in the online realm (Cacioppo et al., 2013). Finally, the matching algorithms used by online dating sites might result in people finding more compatible partners than they would through chance meetings in their face-to-face lives.

Further research is necessary to fully understand the impact of online meetings on relationship outcomes, but these initial results indicate that many Americans are using online dating with surprising success. ■

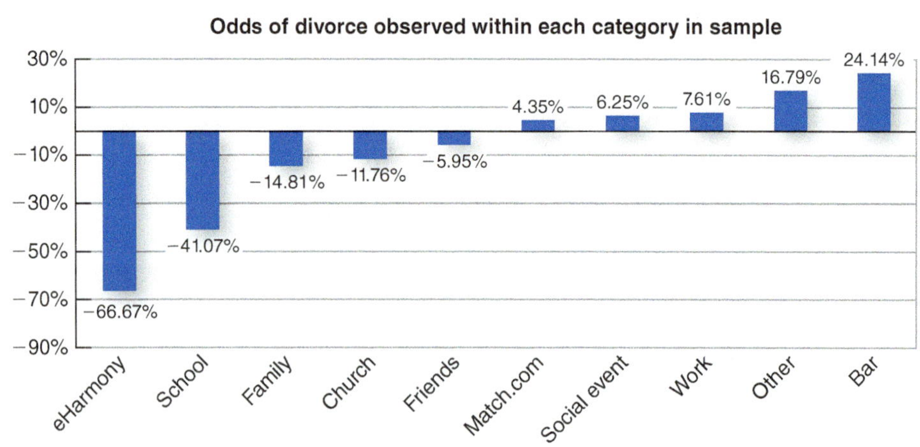

FIGURE **13.19**

Odds of Divorce Are Lower for Couples Meeting at eHarmony. Researchers at eHarmony reported that their now-married clients are much less likely to divorce than couples meeting in more traditional ways, such as through school, family, church, and work.

Source: http://www.eharmony.com/blog/how-you-meetyour-spouse-matters/#.WM2CafnsKUk

Psychology Takes On Real-World Problems

Persuasion During a Pandemic

It is difficult to choose among the many topics in this chapter to apply to the real-world problems raised by a pandemic. From compliance to social connectivity to cooperation to social norms, the social behaviors discussed in this chapter all have major impacts on how we respond to threats (Bavel et al., 2020). Of these many possibilities, we have chosen to focus on persuasion. While we would hope that most people would use the central route to persuasion to consider such an important issue as responses to a pandemic, we cannot assume that is the case. Regardless of how much attention each person is paying to the pandemic, what is the best way to persuade people to do what they need to do to keep themselves and their communities safe?

A first consideration is the credibility of the message source. Credibility results from being perceived as trustworthy and expert (Bavel et al., 2020). In the case of a pandemic, we would assume that medical experts would be likely choices as spokespersons. In today's social media world, these experts face a whole host of challenges, however (Smith & Wanless, 2020). Gone are the days when experts delivered information to a passive audience. Social media allows everyone to be a critic, and the critical voices can often outnumber or be louder than the expert voices. Scientists are trained to use evidence to support their recommendations, yet that evidence often takes time to acquire and interpret and might change as more research is conducted. For a public that is looking for black and white "truth," an expert's appropriate reluctance to say "we know without a doubt that masks prevent COVID-19" damages trust and credibility. Good science is objective, not political, but public health experts are inevitably drawn into the political sphere. Too much trust in them from the "wrong" side reduces their overall influence.

Assuming that experts can maintain some level of credibility, what types of messages should they deliver? A range of possibilities exists, including appealing to a desire to make yourself and others safer (wash your hands to save your grandparents), aligning with the public's moral values (it's a good thing to care for others), or reminding people about social norms and approval (people won't like you unless you practice good social distancing) (Bavel et al., 2020). As mentioned previously in this chapter, using emotions like fear to boost the impact of persuasive messages requires great caution. Unless the public sees a clear action step that will reduce their fear, they will tune out the messages. ■

David Kawai/Bloomberg/Getty Images

The task of providing appropriate guidance to the public regarding COVID-19 usually falls on medical experts, like Theresa Tam, Chief Public Health Officer in Canada. Psychological science related to persuasion can guide this process.

SUMMARY 13.4 Cooperation and Competition

	What Is It?	Influential Factors
Cooperation 	Working together to reach a goal	• Individual differences • TFT strategy • Culture • Innate sense of fair play
Competition 	A contest for resources	• Availability of resources • Signals for dominance and submission
Altruism 	Helping others without personal gain or with personal cost	• Number of potential helpers available • Relatedness to person needing help • Punishment for selfishness • Expectations for the future reciprocation • Conscious desire to help • Sense of personal responsibility to help
Aggression 	Conscious intent to harm another	• Interactions between genetics and child maltreatment • Use of alcohol and other drugs • Testosterone and serotonin levels • Brain structure and activity • Observational learning

Credits: Top row—Gonzalo Fuentes/Reuters/Corbis; Second row—Paul Wayne Wilson/PhotoStockFile/Alamy Stock Photo; Third row—Michael Loccisano/Getty Images; Bottom row—Andrew Aitchison/Getty Images.

KEY TERMS The Language of Psychological Science

Be sure you can define these terms and use them correctly.

actor–observer bias, p. 506
aggression, p. 539
attitude, p. 509
attribution, p. 505
bystander intervention, p. 538
cognitive consistency, p. 511
cognitive dissonance, p. 511
compliance, p. 524
conformity, p. 523
correspondence bias, p. 505
deindividuation, p. 528
discrimination, p. 516
dispositional attribution, p. 505
door-in-the-face, p. 524
elaboration likelihood model (ELM), p. 512
foot-in-the-door, p. 524
group polarization, p. 528
groupthink, p. 529
just-world belief, p. 508
low-balling, p. 524
mere exposure effect, p. 531
obedience, p. 524
persuasion, p. 512
prejudice, p. 516
self-serving bias, p. 506
situational attribution, p. 505
social facilitation, p. 527
social loafing, p. 528
social norms, p. 522
stereotype, p. 516

An interactome among genes implicated in autism spectrum disorder (ASD) with other cellular proteins confirmed links between ASD and several related conditions and identified new genes that warranted further study.

Argosy Publishing, Inc.

14

The Troubled Mind

PSYCHOLOGICAL DISORDERS

LEARNING OBJECTIVES

1. Analyze the general definition of psychological disorder and discuss its application in the *Diagnostic and Statistical Manual of Mental Disorders (DSM-5)*.
2. Debate the diagnostic criteria for autism spectrum disorder (ASD) and attention deficit hyperactivity disorder (ADHD), considering ways to distinguish symptoms of these disorders from normal childhood behavior.
3. Summarize the symptoms of schizophrenia and their biological and environmental correlates.
4. Discuss the role of bipolar disorder as a bridge between schizophrenia and major depressive disorder.
5. Identify common and differentiating symptoms of the anxiety disorders, obsessive-compulsive disorder, posttraumatic stress disorder, and dissociative and somatic symptom disorders.
6. Assess the psychological mechanisms that may support behavioral symptoms of antisocial, borderline, and narcissistic personality disorders.

OF ALL THE REASONS TO STUDY PSYCHOLOGY, FINDING ways to improve the lives of people with psychological disorders might be one of the most rewarding. This process begins with understanding the features and possible causes of a disorder.

Identifying the causes of psychological disorders requires us to pull together multiple threads leading from the genetic, biological, cognitive, developmental, and social aspects of being human. These causal factors interact with one another in complex ways, so the same disorder might look one way in one individual and quite different in another. We do not know what causes children to develop the symptoms of autism spectrum disorder (ASD), discussed in detail later in this chapter, but at least we know where to start looking.

We have cautioned you on several occasions in this textbook to avoid the idea that we have "genes for" this trait or the next because the reality is more complex. As we zoom in to analyze the genetic contributions to ASD, you will see that we have zoomed way past the traditional array of 46 human chromosomes featured in Chapter 3. Instead, we are looking at a visual representation of something that biologists call an *interactome*—a map of all interactions among proteins in a cell. In this particular case, the researchers were attempting to identify the relationships among the 539 proteins that formed interactions with proteins produced by 26 genes already implicated in ASD (Sakai et al., 2011). The resulting map not only confirmed links between ASD and several related conditions, but also identified genetic relationships that warranted further study. Further research indicated that individuals with ASD have many more mutations that affect the hubs in the interactome than their siblings who do not have ASD (Chen et al., 2018).

Laura Freberg

A self-portrait by one of the authors' (LF) daughters, who has ASD.

Laura Freberg

We refer to "people with autism spectrum disorder" instead of "autistic person" because people are so much more than their disorders. Many individuals with ASD, including author LF's daughter, enjoy varied interests, including art.

What does an interactome mean for a person with autism? Unfortunately, understanding more about the sources of ASD has not yet led to improved treatments. As mentioned in Chapters 8 and 15, the only effective treatment for ASD today is the use of behavioral therapies. Still, such discoveries have the potential to improve the lives of individuals with ASD down the road or to provide information that eventually will help us prevent further cases.

To fully understand the experience of individuals with ASD requires us to zoom out to consider overall development. Psychologists point out that we say "a person with autism spectrum disorder" instead of an "autistic person" for good reason. People are not their disorders, and much is happening in each individual's life that has nothing to do with ASD. We could consider the impact of parents, whose age might have been a risk factor for a child's ASD, or study their ability to manage their child's behavior. Zooming even further out, we can investigate the effects of the disorder on the social connectedness children with ASD experience as they venture out into the world.

In this chapter, you will discover a number of types of psychological disorders, each with a unique history and set of characteristics. The next chapter, Chapter 15, will explore the treatments and therapies that psychologists have developed to address the challenges to well-being posed by these disorders.

What Does It Mean to Have a Psychological Disorder?

Mental health experts define a psychological disorder as "a syndrome characterized by clinically significant disturbance in an individual's cognition, emotion regulation, or behavior that

	NORMAL	MILD
Emotions	Good alertness and positive emotional state.	Feeling sad or down temporarily, but not for lo
Cognitions	"I'm not getting the grades I want this semester, but I'll keep trying to do my best."	"I'm struggling at school this semester. I wish could study better, or I'll fail."
Behaviors	Going to classes and studying for the next round of tests. Talking to professors.	Going to classes with some trouble studying. Less contact with others.

reflects a dysfunction in the psychological, biological, or development processes underlying mental functioning" (American Psychiatric Association [APA], 2013, p. 20). But what does this definition actually mean?

Many behaviors considered abnormal are quite similar to normal behaviors. We all know what it feels like to be depressed at times, but how is that different from having major depressive disorder? This chapter will help you understand the distinctions, but because those distinctions can be subtle, we also caution you against "first-year medical student's disease," or the sense that you have all the disorders that you are studying.

The study of psychological disorders is called **abnormal psychology**. It is surprisingly difficult, but necessary, for psychologists to agree on the differences between typical and abnormal behaviors because deciding that an individual's behaviors and mental processes are abnormal is the first step toward labeling that person with a psychological disorder and providing treatment (see ● Figure 14.1).

We can start with the literal meaning of the word *abnormal*. In Latin, the prefix *ab* means "away from" and *norma* means "the rule." In other words, abnormal behavior is literally behavior that is not typical, usual, or regular. This meaning implies a statistical definition of abnormality. By this definition, behaviors that most people do are normal, whereas behaviors that characterize a minority of people are abnormal.

But is it true that only a minority of the population experiences psychological disorders? We actually don't know how many people have psychological disorders. A person can be diagnosed with **comorbid** disorders, which means more than one disorder occurs at the same time, so simply adding up the rates for each type of disorder is not a solution. Statistics can look different for different time frames. One estimate of the number of people who experience a psychological disorder during the previous year is around 26% (Kessler et al., 2005), but estimates of the number of people experiencing a disorder at least once during their lifetime can be much higher. In one longitudinal study of individuals from age 19–20 to age 50, the cumulative probability of experiencing at least one disorder was 73.9% (Angst et al., 2016). These numbers certainly challenge our conceptions of abnormal behavior as unusual.

The statistical approach does have the advantage of being clear (see ● Figure 14.2). For example, intellectual disability is one of the categories in the *Diagnostic and Statistical Manual of Mental Disorders*, a handbook for diagnosis that we discuss in more detail later in the chapter. The diagnosis of intellectual disability relies heavily on statistics. A score of 70 or below on a standard IQ test is the typical cutoff for identifying an individual with intellectual disability (APA, 2013). Even in this relatively clear situation, however, the statistical approach represents merely a starting point. A diagnosis of intellectual disability also requires an individual to demonstrate difficulties with adaptive skills, which include factors such as communication, self-care, safety, and use of community resources.

A purely statistical approach has several additional major drawbacks. First, it implies a cultural specificity that we would like to avoid. Because most members of one culture may behave in ways different from those of people in another, the purely statistical approach to abnormality might result in different definitions of psychological disorder from one culture to the next. Second, a statistical definition fails to capture the distress that often accompanies a

abnormal psychology The study of psychological disorders.

comorbid Two or more disorders in the same individual.

FIGURE **14.1**

A Continuum from Normal to Psychological Disorder. Psychological disorders can be understood both categorically, which means that each has its own set of distinct characteristics used for diagnosis, and as part of a continuum from normal behavior to severely disordered behavior. The diagnostic criteria discussed in this chapter guide psychologists in their identification of the types and severity of disorders their patients and clients might have.

Source: Adapted from C. A. Kearney, & T. J. Trull (2012). *Abnormal Psychology and Life: A Dimensional Approach*. Belmont, CA: Wadsworth/Cengage Learning.

MODERATE	PSYCHOLOGICAL DISORDER—LESS SEVERE	PSYCHOLOGICAL DISORDER—MORE SEVERE
Feeling sad, but a strong positive experience such as a good grade could lift mood.	Intense sadness most of the day with some trouble concentrating and some loss of appetite.	Extreme sadness all of the time with great trouble concentrating and complete loss of appetite.
"These bad grades really hurt. This may set me back for a while. I'm really worried."	"I'm so worried about these grades that my stomach hurts. I don't know what to do."	"These bad grades just show what a failure I am at everything. There's no hope; I'm not doing anything today."
Skipping a few classes and feeling somewhat unmotivated to study. Avoiding contact with professors and classmates.	Skipping most classes and unable to maintain eye contact with other people. Strong lack of motivation.	Unable to get out of bed, eat, or leave the house. Lack of energy and frequent crying.

FIGURE 14.2

Statistical Abnormality. The word *abnormal* literally means "away from the rule." Both intellectually gifted individuals, usually defined as having an IQ over 130, and individuals with intellectual disability, usually defined as having an IQ below 70, are equally "abnormal" in this statistical sense of the word. Academy Award–winning producer Quentin Tarantino (*Pulp Fiction, Kill Bill, Django Unchained, The Hateful Eight, Once Upon a Time in Hollywood*) has a reported IQ of 160. Although neither he nor his films are "typical," we are unlikely to refer to Tarantino as "abnormal." Statistics alone do not capture what we mean by abnormal behavior.

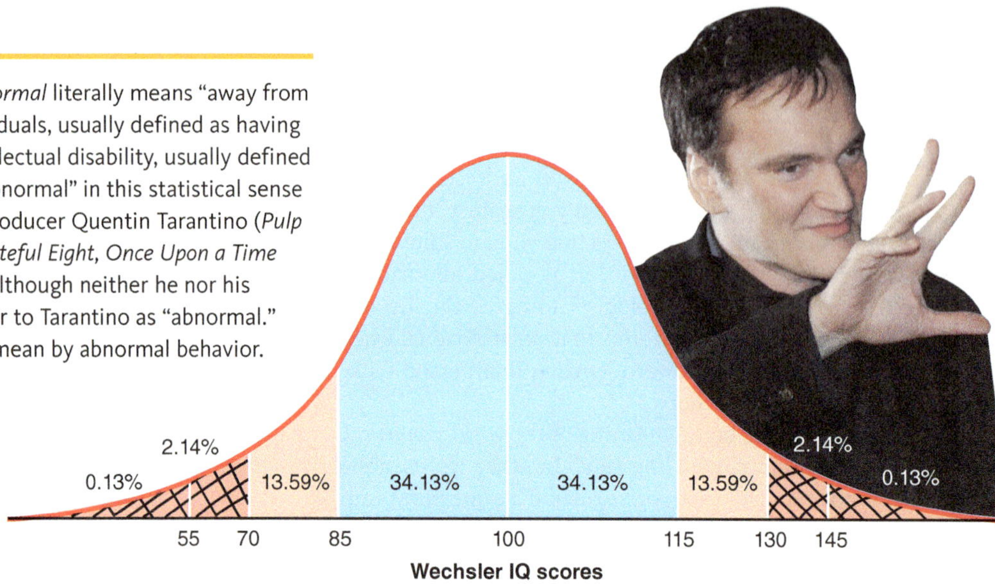

MARKA/Alamy Stock Photo

Our tolerance for people engaging in acts that are harmful to themselves is variable. For example, most states in the United States have prohibitions against committing suicide (the irony in prosecuting under such laws appears to have been lost on the legislators).

psychological disorder, both for the person experiencing the disorder and for those interacting with that person.

To address these concerns, we might suggest that abnormal behavior deviates from some ideal manner of behaving. This approach succeeds in capturing the general distress that most of us experience when observing or experiencing abnormal behavior. Unfortunately, this approach does nothing to avoid cross-cultural differences in defining disordered behavior. Different cultures are often characterized by diverse ideals. In Western nations, hearing voices that others cannot hear is generally considered abnormal. In other cultures, hearing voices may be viewed more positively, as a sign of religious giftedness (Al-Issa, 1977; Kurihara et al., 2000). More troublesome is the simple fact that it is difficult, if not impossible, to reach consensus regarding what constitutes ideal behavior. People, including experts in psychology, have deeply divided value judgments regarding sexual conduct, recreational drug use, and a host of other activities.

A simple modification of this "deviation from the ideal" approach can help us to achieve some consensus. Behaviors that cause harm to others are viewed as less than ideal. Unless the person is acting defensively, most of us would agree that such behavior is negative and undesirable. We are also sympathetic to those who have conditions that cause harm to themselves.

Peter Horree/Alamy Stock Photo

Defining abnormal behavior as a deviation from what is considered ideal immediately runs into problems of cultural specificity. Behaviors like hearing voices that others cannot hear might be considered less than ideal in Western cultures but a gift in others. The ability to hear voices was considered an advantage for shamans, like the one represented transforming into his jaguar spirit companion in this Costa Rican piece from 1000–1500 CE.

We can combine the best aspects of each of these approaches to construct a formal definition of abnormal behavior: Abnormal behavior is distressing and harmful to self or others.

Younger people seem especially vulnerable to psychological disorders. College students have the same rate of psychological disorders as their age peers who are not attending college, as shown in ● Figure 14.3. However, the rate of psychological disorders in young adults is higher than in the general population and appears to be increasing (Hunt & Eisenberg, 2010; Twenge et al., 2019). Serious psychological distress, major depression, suicidal thoughts, and suicide attempts have increased dramatically among adolescents and young adults, but not in other age cohorts, in the last 10 years (Twenge et al., 2019). Nearly half of the young adults under the age of 24 who were

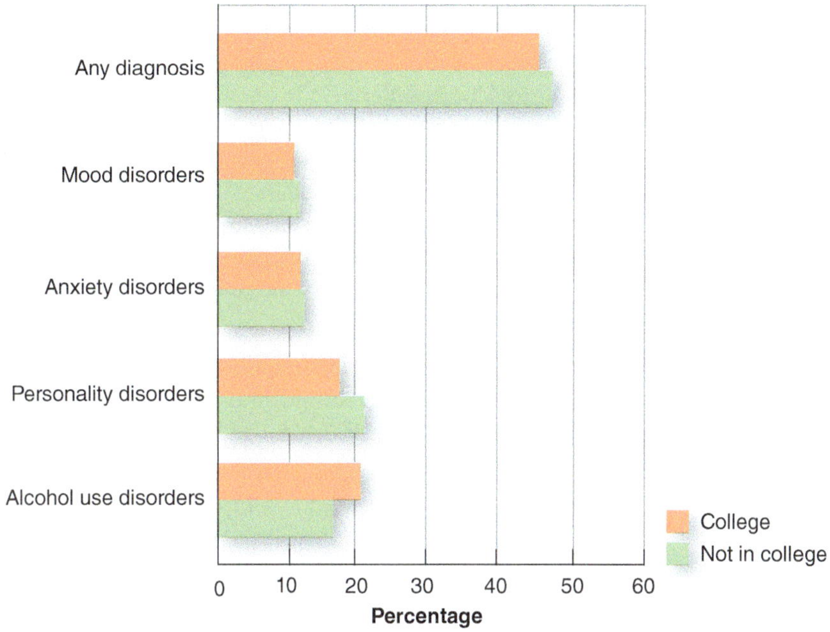

FIGURE **14.3**

Rates of Psychological Disorders in College Students. Based on face-to-face interviews, college students and their same-age peers who do not attend college have a high rate (nearly 50%) of meeting the criteria for at least one psychological disorder over the past 12 months. College students and age peers not in college did not differ significantly in their rates of psychological disorder, with the exception of alcohol-use disorders, which were higher among those attending college.
Source: Adapted from C. Blanco et al. (2008). "Mental Health of College Students and Their Non-College-Attending Peers: Results from the National Epidemiologic Study on Alcohol and Related Conditions," *Archives of General Psychiatry*, *65*(12), 1429–1437. doi:10.1001/archpsyc.65.12.1429

surveyed met criteria for at least one psychological disorder in the previous year, including 18% for a personality disorder, 12% for an anxiety disorder, and 11% for either major depressive disorder or bipolar disorder (Blanco et al., 2008). Each of these categories is discussed in more detail in this chapter.

How Are Psychological Disorders Diagnosed?

The first official effort in the United States to gather data on psychological disorders was the recording of a single category, "idiocy/insanity," in the 1840 census (APA, 2000).

When you visit your physician or student health center complaining of a sore throat, your health care provider notes your symptoms, compares them to known categories of illness, swabs your throat for a sample, and then determines your diagnosis: You have strep throat. Based on that diagnosis, you are given a prescription for an antibiotic. Unlike medical illnesses, however, psychological disorders are diagnosed purely on the basis of observable behaviors. There are no blood tests, brain scans, or other medical diagnostic procedures that can be used to determine whether a person has a psychological disorder.

To promote consistency in the diagnosis of psychological disorders, mental health professionals typically refer to the ***Diagnostic and Statistical Manual of Mental Disorders (DSM)***, first published by the American Psychiatric Association (APA) in 1952. The current, fifth edition is known as *DSM-5* (APA, 2013). A second classification system in wide use is the *International Statistical Classification of Diseases and Related Health Problems,* 11th edition *(ICD-11)*, which was published by the World Health Organization (WHO, 2018). Professionals responsible for the *DSM*

Diagnostic and Statistical Manual of Mental Disorders (DSM) A system for classification of psychological disorders published by the American Psychiatric Association.

Studio 101/Alamy Stock Photo

The *Diagnostic and Statistical Manual of Mental Disorders (DSM)* has undergone a number of revisions since its first edition in 1952. Over its history, the *DSM* has become less Freudian and more sensitive to cross-cultural issues. The *DSM* is published by the American Psychiatric Association.

Source: Reprinted with permission from the American Psychiatric Association (APA).

and *ICD-11* classification systems have coordinated their efforts to reduce the differences between the two systems (APA, 2013). However, some differences remain. The *ICD-11*, but not the *DSM-5*, has a category for gaming disorder. All categories of personality disorder found in *DSM-5* are grouped together as a single category of personality disorder in *ICD-11*.

The *DSM* is not without its critics. Beginning with *DSM-III* in 1980, some normal behaviors have been categorized as abnormal by the system. Allen Frances, the psychiatrist who chaired the task force in charge of writing the *DSM-IV* (published in 1994), expressed concern that the committee's well-meaning efforts had led to three "false epidemics"—attention deficit hyperactivity disorder (ADHD), autism, and childhood bipolar disorder—and that the *DSM-5* was even worse (Frances, 2010). For example, the *DSM-5* lists the following (very normal) behavior as a criterion for ADHD:

> often avoids, dislikes, or is reluctant to engage in tasks that require sustained mental effort (e.g. schoolwork or homework; for older adolescents and adults, preparing reports, completing forms, reviewing lengthy papers). (APA, 2013, p. 59)

It is unlikely that many of the readers of this textbook look forward to opportunities to fill out forms, but does this mean you have a psychological disorder? Additional criteria must be considered.

Despite its flaws, the *DSM* remains the most frequently used tool in the United States for the diagnosis of psychological disorders. Our discussion of types of psychological disorders, therefore, is grounded in the *DSM* system.

What Do the Psychological Perspectives Tell Us About Disorders?

We have seen many examples in this textbook of behaviors that are best understood when viewed from multiple perspectives. The study of psychological disorders provides yet another

Philippe Pinel (1745–1826) is often called "the father of modern psychiatry." After observing the more humane treatment of inmates by a former patient turned employee named Jean-Baptiste Pussin at Bicêtre Hospital outside Paris, Pinel followed Pussin's example by removing the patients' iron shackles. Instead of the usual "treatments" of the day—bleeding, purging, and blistering—Pinel made a practice of conversing with the patients regularly.

Philippe Pinel (1745–1826) releasing lunatics from their chains at the Salpetriere asylum in Paris in 1795 (colour litho)/Robert-Fleury, Tony (1837-1912) (after)/INDIVISION CHARMET/Bibliotheque des Arts Decoratifs, Paris, France/Bridgeman Images

Philippe Pinel (1745-1826) (oil on canvas)/Merimee

example of how an integration of multiple perspectives can be useful. This is particularly the case when considering the possible causes for abnormal behaviors.

What might an integrated approach to psychological disorder look like? First, we propose that the various perspectives discussed in this textbook (biological, clinical, developmental, cognitive, and social/personality) all have a great deal to say about disorders, but each has more to say about some disorders than about others. By considering the contributions of factors from multiple perspectives, we should have a greater appreciation of the complex interactions that occur among perspectives.

In addition, an integrated perspective helps us understand the reciprocal relationships among factors leading to psychological disorders. Just as a person who is diagnosed with depression might show low levels of serotonin activity in the brain, being in a leadership position boosts a person's serotonin levels. A simple biological explanation suggesting that chemical imbalances lead to depression, or a simple psychological explanation stating that people who feel powerless are more likely to be depressed, misses the nuances of these reciprocal relationships. The richer understanding of the causal factors leading to a psychological disorder pays off in the development of more effective treatments. Single-perspective thinking usually leads to single-perspective treatments. If you believe that depression is purely the result of chemical imbalances of the brain, then a simple prescription might do the trick. If you believe that hearing voices that others can't hear is the result of childhood communication patterns, you will miss the opportunity to provide medication that can effectively end these troubling symptoms. Inclusive models describing the entire range of causal factors are more likely to result in effective treatments tailored to the needs of individuals.

Which Disorders Emerge in Childhood?

Many disorders have their roots in childhood but are more typically diagnosed in adolescence and adulthood. The *DSM-5* uses the term *neurodevelopmental disorders* to refer to disorders that instead are diagnosed typically in childhood, yet often continue throughout the life span (APA, 2013). Two of these neurodevelopmental disorders are examined in this section: ASD and ADHD.

Autism Spectrum Disorder (ASD)

The word *autism* literally means "within oneself." In 1943, psychiatrist Leo Kanner worked with a group of children who shared problems in social communication and interaction along with restricted, repetitive patterns of behavior, interests, or activities. Kanner's observations form the basis of our current diagnostic criteria for **autism spectrum disorder** (**ASD**; APA, 2013), which combines previous categories of autism and Asperger's syndrome. ASD represents a spectrum because the severity of the observed deficits can vary widely from individual to individual. Adjustment can range from relatively normal, allowing independent living, to intellectual disability, requiring living with parents or in institutional settings.

Rates of ASD have been increasing rapidly over the last two decades (see ● Figure 14.4). Approximately 1 child out of every 54 has ASD, with boys diagnosed 4.3 times more frequently than girls (Maenner et al., 2020). Whether the rates are actually increasing or diagnostic criteria and awareness are changing remains unknown. In the United States, individuals can receive a medical diagnosis using the *DSM-5* or be educationally verified by teams of school personnel (Ramsey et al., 2016). These different methods of assessment produce different numbers, with higher rates of diagnosis in the educational than in the medical/psychological setting.

autism spectrum disorder (ASD) A disorder characterized by deficits in social relatedness and communication skills that are often accompanied by repetitive, ritualistic behavior.

Diagnosing ASD Problems with social relatedness are at the core of this disorder, regardless of the individual's level of intelligence and adjustment. Beginning in infancy, most children with ASD do not make eye contact or take pleasure in reciprocal games like peekaboo.

FIGURE **14.4**

The Prevalence of ASD Appears to Be Increasing. Rates of ASD continue to increase, but the reasons for this change remain a source of debate in the scientific community. It is possible that the rates are truly increasing, but greater awareness by parents and health care providers, relaxed applications of the diagnostic criteria, and improved availability of services might also be contributing to the observed change.

Source: M. J. Maenner et al. (2020). "Prevalence of Autism Spectrum Disorder among Children Aged 8 Years—Autism and Developmental Disabilities Monitoring Network, 11 Sites, United States, 2016," *MMWR Surveillance Summaries*, 69(4), 1.

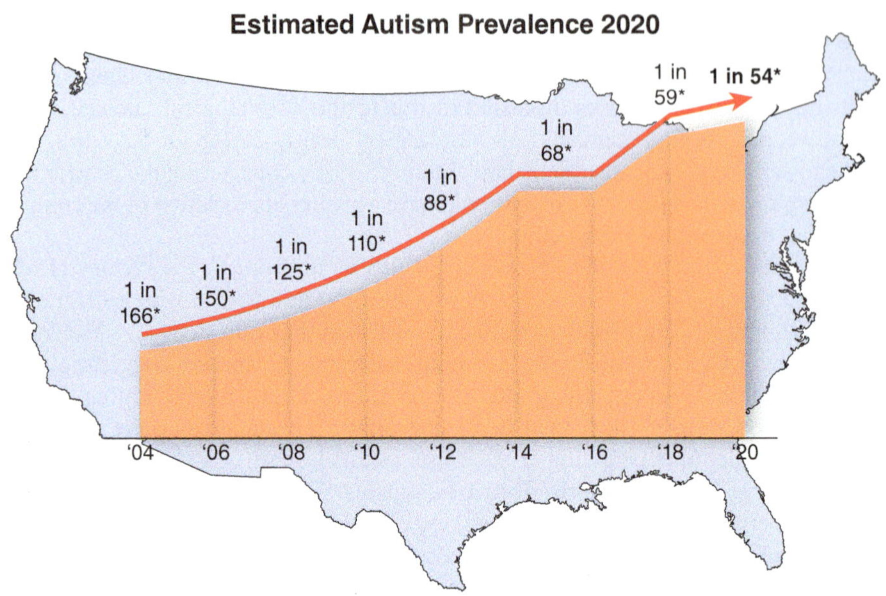

*Centers for Disease Control and Prevention (CDC) prevalence estimates are for 4 years prior to the report date (e.g., 2020 figures are from 2016)

Insight into the thoughts and points of view of others is particularly lacking. As discussed in Chapter 11, children develop a theory of mind by the time they are 3–4 years of age. A failure to develop a normal theory of mind might explain many of the social deficits observed in ASD (Baron-Cohen, 1991; Senju et al., 2009). However, adults with ASD show wide variations in their theory of mind abilities that are not related to the severity of their condition (Brewer et al., 2017). Language skills of individuals with ASD can also vary widely, from having no language abilities to delayed acquisition of language to normal skills (Ellis Weismer et al., 2010). Even when language skills are relatively normal, though, individuals with ASD usually experience difficulty maintaining conversations with others because of deficits in social skills.

Individuals with ASD often object strenuously to changes in their environments and show a high level of repetitive, routine behavior. Rituals may include repetitive movements, such as rocking, hand flapping, head banging, and twirling. Other individuals may engage in extremely limited preoccupations, such as learning all models of cars ever made by Ford. One possible source of this ritualistic behavior is a general dysfunction in sensory networks. Most individuals with ASD show unusually increased or decreased sensitivity to stimuli (Lane et al., 2010). Auditory processing is superior in people with ASD compared to typical controls (Remington & Fairnie, 2017). Absolute pitch, or the ability to name a musical note without a reference note, is rare in the general population but relatively common among people with ASD, and many musicians with absolute pitch have higher levels of autistic traits than those without absolute pitch (Wenhart et al., 2019). People with ASD may be relatively insensitive to pain or cold but distressed by normal sound levels (see ● Figure 14.5). Ritualistic behavior may control or override these troubling sensations.

Causes of ASD Although the causes of ASD remain somewhat mysterious and probably show variable patterns from case to case, scientists are making progress in their understanding. Family and twin studies provide strong evidence that ASD is influenced by genetics (Frazier et al., 2014). The concordance rate for ASD between identical twins may be 76% to 88%, and possibly more (Ronald & Hoekstra, 2011), which means that if one twin has ASD, the other twin has between a 76% and an 88% chance of also having ASD. Hundreds of genes are probably involved, and research attention is focusing on the expression of these genes during brain development (Sakai et al., 2011; Vorstman et al., 2017). Autopsies of the brains of people with ASD and people with no history of psychological disorder show dramatic differences (Voineagu et al., 2011). In the typical control brains, 174 genes were expressed differently in the frontal lobes than in the temporal lobes, but in the brains of people with ASD, no gene showed evidence of being expressed differently in these two areas.

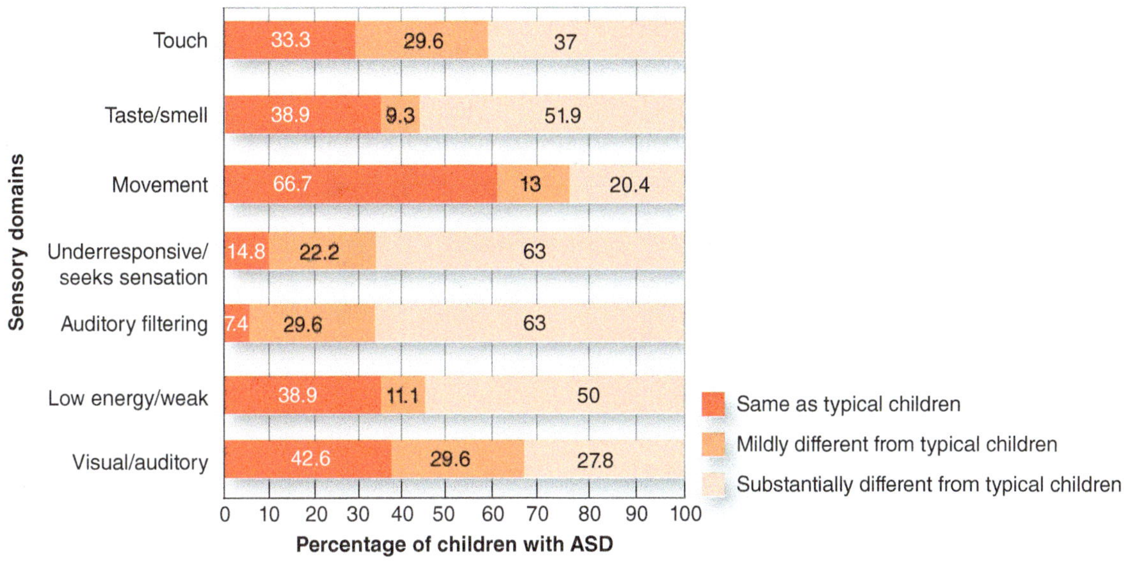

FIGURE **14.5**

Sensory Sensitivity Is Different in ASD. Children with ASD often show differences from typical children in their sensitivity to environmental stimuli. This graph shows the percentage of children with ASD whose scores on an instrument measuring sensitivity were the same as those of typical children, mildly different from those of typical children (between one and two standard deviations from the mean), and rare compared to those of typical children (more than two standard deviations from the mean). The domains measured included sensitivity to touch (tactile), sensitivity to taste and smell, sensitivity to movement (e.g., fear of falling), underresponsiveness (e.g., touches people), auditory filtering (e.g., fails to respond to name when called), low energy (e.g., tires easily), and visual or auditory (e.g., responds negatively to loud noises or bright lights).

Source: Adapted from A. Lane et al. (2010). "Sensory Processing Subtypes in Autism: Association with Adaptive Behavior," *Journal of Autism and Developmental Disorders*, *40*(1), 112–122. doi:10.1007/s10803-009-0840-2

Abnormalities in cortical development might lead to unusual minicolumns, vertical arrays of neurons perpendicular to the surface of the cerebral cortex that represent the smallest processing units of the brain. Individuals with ASD have narrower minicolumns containing normal numbers of cells, but spaced farther apart than those found in typical individuals. These structural differences are consistent with a pattern of connectivity that favors detailed focus, which could produce the unusual interests and hobbies of people with ASD, over more global processing, like understanding the social environment (Opris & Casanova, 2014).

Narrow minicolumns similar to those found in the brains of people with ASD were observed in the brains of three distinguished scientists, none of whom had ASD symptoms, who donated their brains for scientific study. These similarities suggest that the minicolumn structure might account for the extreme focus of interests typical in ASD (Casanova et al., 2007). Outstanding scientists, like people with autism, have been known to study minute details for long periods of time.

Additional structural abnormalities in cases of ASD have been observed in the amygdala, hippocampus, and cerebellum (Barnea-Goraly et al., 2014; Stoodley, 2014). A suggestion that ASD involved a "broken" mirror system has received little research support (Schulte-Rüther et al., 2017). As we mentioned in Chapter 8, mirror neurons respond to actions, regardless of who performs them, and are believed to support our ability to empathize with others.

Environmental factors interact with genetic factors associated with ASD during sensitive periods of brain development (Engel & Daniels, 2011; Piven et al., 2017). Parental age is a known risk factor, with older parents more likely than younger parents to give birth to a child with ASD. Prenatal exposure to infection, pesticides, nutritional factors, and drugs increase the risk for ASD. Cannabis use by the mother is associated with higher rates of ASD in offspring (Corsi et al., 2020). A number of meta-analyses have suggested that prenatal exposure to antidepressant medications raises the risk for ASD in offspring, but others dispute this finding (Vega et al., 2020). Prenatal antidepressant exposure in rodents leads to behavioral deficits similar to autism, even when maternal stress is controlled, suggesting caution in the use of antidepressants during pregnancy (Maloney et al., 2018). Markers for prenatal exposure

Minicolumns in the cerebral cortex function like the microprocessors in modern computers by serving as the basic unit that receives input, processes it, and responds. Individuals with ASD (lower image) have smaller minicolumns than do typical controls (top image). What does this difference mean for information processing? Smaller minicolumns favor the process of discrimination, described in Chapter 8 as distinguishing among stimuli, while larger minicolumns favor generalization, or applying a response to similar stimuli. Behavioral domains that are difficult for people with ASD, such as language, face recognition, and following another person's gaze, require more generalization than discrimination.

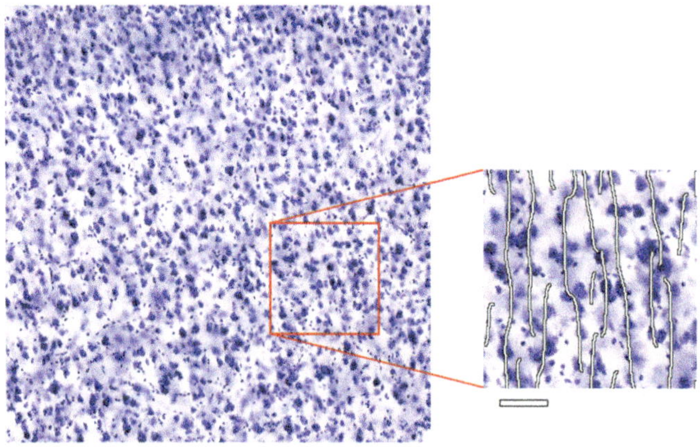

(a) Typical controls

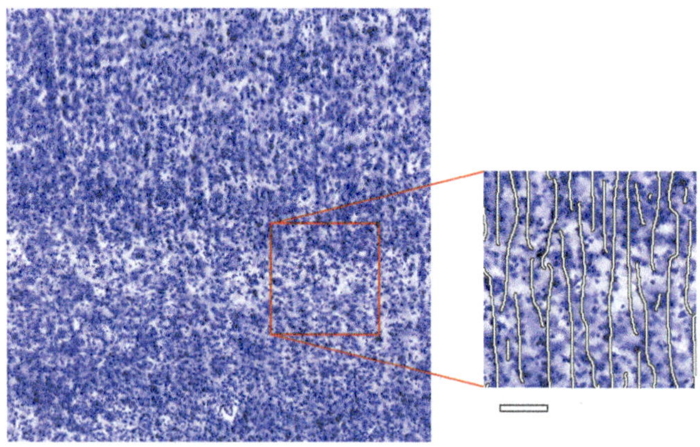

(b) Individuals with autism

Manuel F. Casanova, M.D., Department of Psychiatry and Behavioral Sciences, University of Louisville

to acetaminophen (e.g., Tylenol) in umbilical cord blood are associated with higher risk for diagnosis with autism (Ji et al., 2020).

One of the unfortunate consequences of the uncertainty surrounding the causes of ASD has been the vulnerability of concerned parents seeking answers. In a paper later retracted by the British medical journal *Lancet*, unsubstantiated claims that the routine measles, mumps, and rubella vaccination caused ASD were published. Similar controversies ensued in the United States about thimerosal, a mercury-containing preservative used in some vaccines.

In a meta-analysis involving over 1 million children, no relationship was found between ASD and vaccination in general, vaccination with the measles-mumps-rubella combination, or thimerosal (Taylor et al., 2014). Despite the clear data and reassurances from medical experts (see ● Figure 14.6), worried parents have withheld vaccinations from their children, leading to increasing numbers of cases of life-threatening, preventable diseases that had previously been believed to be under control. For example, in the first half of 2008, measles cases in the United States doubled compared to the rates observed between 2000 and 2007, and all cases involved unvaccinated school children (Centers for Disease Control [CDC], 2008).

Attention Deficit Hyperactivity Disorder (ADHD)

Attention deficit hyperactivity disorder (ADHD) is perhaps one of the most contentious categories described in the *DSM-5*. The criteria for the disorder are difficult to distinguish from the behaviors of many typical young children. Because many children diagnosed with ADHD are treated with medication, the stakes for accurately diagnosing the condition are high indeed.

attention deficit hyperactivity disorder (ADHD) A disorder characterized by either unusual inattentiveness, hyperactivity with impulsivity, or both.

Diagnosing ADHD ADHD involves inattention and hyperactivity. Some individuals show both inattention and hyperactivity, but others show inattention without hyperactivity or vice versa (APA, 2013). The core feature of inattention is the inability to maintain sustained

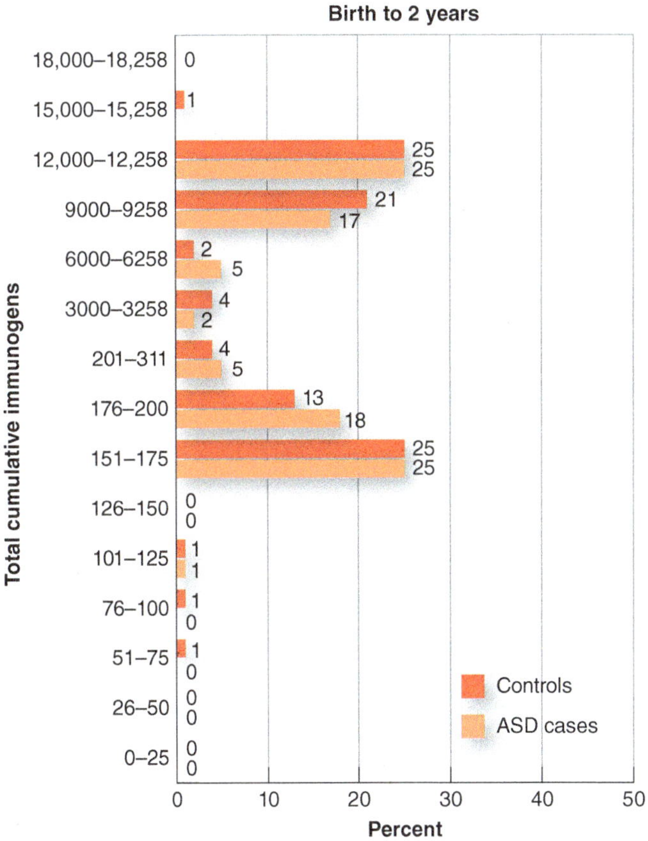

FIGURE **14.6**

Vaccines and Autism Spectrum Disorder (ASD) Are Not Linked. In spite of significant scientific evidence to the contrary, many people continue to believe that vaccination is responsible for recent increases in ASD diagnoses. There are a number of markers of vaccination influence that have been investigated, and none has shown evidence of vaccination effects on ASD. In this example using data from approximately 1,000 children, researchers traced rates of ASD as a function of total cumulative immunogens (molecules that can provoke an immune response) from vaccines given over the first two years of life. As you can see in this figure, children later diagnosed with ASD do not differ from typical control children.

Source: F. DeStefano et al. (2013). "Increasing Exposure to Antibody-Stimulating Proteins and Polysaccharides in Vaccines Is Not Associated with Risk of Autism," *The Journal of Pediatrics*, *163*(2), 561–567. doi: 10.1016/j.peds.2013.02.001

attention or on-task behavior for an age-appropriate length of time. This problem is evidenced in the diagnostic criteria for inattention, such as difficulties in following instructions, in organizing and completing work, and in avoiding careless mistakes. Children with hyperactivity express a high level of motor activity and struggle in structured activities, such as waiting in line or sitting quietly in class. These children are noisy, active, and boisterous, and they often appear to take action without thinking it through. Even as adults, individuals who were diagnosed with ADHD as children have more traffic accidents than do people without the disorder (Barkley & Cox, 2007).

One of the DSM-5 criteria for ADHD is "often fidgets with hands or feet or squirms in seat." If you have visited an elementary school classroom lately, you might have noticed that most children are active. At what point does squirming become a psychological disorder requiring medication?

Many of these behaviors are also seen in children who do not have psychological disorders. Although the *DSM-5* provides guidelines for distinguishing between normal and abnormal inattentiveness and hyperactivity, fewer than 40% of surveyed pediatricians reported using those criteria to evaluate cases of ADHD (Wasserman et al., 1999). More than half the children in a large sample who were receiving medication for ADHD did not meet even relaxed diagnostic criteria for the disorder, let alone the carefully constructed criteria spelled out in the *DSM-5* (Angold et al., 2000).

Suzanne Tucker/Shutterstock.com

All children can be active and noisy, but most usually learn quickly to restrict those behaviors to the right times and places. Children with ADHD often have trouble sitting quietly in class or waiting in line.

Using the *DSM* criteria, between 3% and 5% of children should be diagnosed with ADHD (Song et al., 2019). However,

FIGURE 14.7

Diagnoses of ADHD in the United States. Compared to the expected rate of 3% to 5% of children being diagnosed with ADHD, the actual number of children ever diagnosed with ADHD in a 2011 report from the Centers for Disease Control and Prevention (CDC) is much higher. Rate of diagnosis varied dramatically by region in the United States, from a low of less than 7% in Nevada to more than 13.1% in parts of the Midwest and Southeast. Reasons for these regional discrepancies are not clear, although low socioeconomic status is considered a risk factor for ADHD. The differences also might represent variations in how the diagnostic criteria are applied by local health care providers.

Source: CDC (2011). "State-Based Prevalence Data of Parent Reported ADHD Diagnosis by a Health Care Provider," https://www.cdc.gov/ncbddd/adhd/data/diagnosis-treatment-data.html

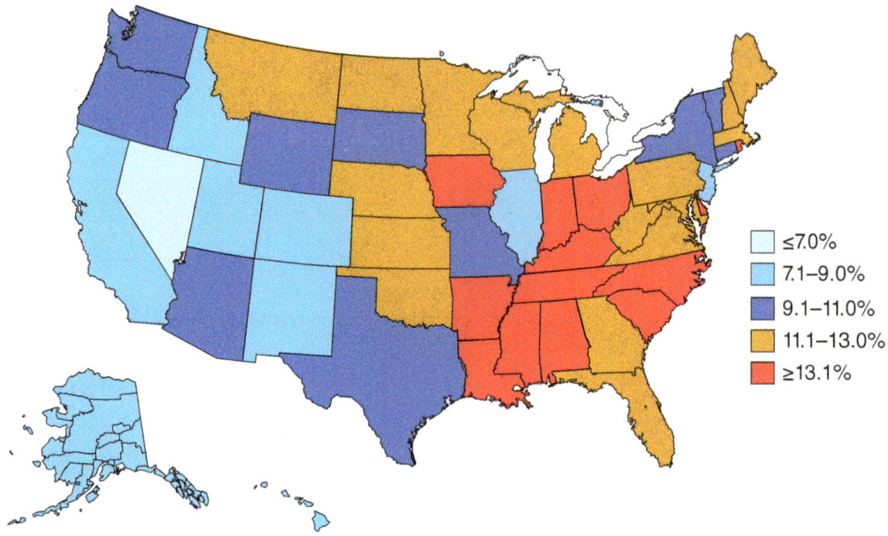

clinicians often use relaxed criteria in making diagnostic decisions, which leads to inflated numbers of cases. In 2011, 11% of children between the ages of 4 and 17 years had been diagnosed with ADHD in the United States, representing an increase of 42% over rates of ADHD since 2003 (Visser et al., 2014; see Figure 14.7). About 2.5% of adults over 17 meet criteria for ADHD. ADHD is diagnosed at least twice as frequently in males as in females, and females are more likely than males to be diagnosed with inattentiveness without hyperactivity (APA, 2013).

Causes of ADHD The National Institute of Mental Health (NIMH, 2009, p. 3) concluded that "scientists are not sure what causes ADHD." However, twin and adoption studies support a significant role for genetics in the development of ADHD. Heritability is reported to be 70% or more (Faraone & Larsson, 2019). Environmental factors might interact with genetic risk. Known environmental risks for ADHD are lead contamination, low birth weight, and prenatal exposure to tobacco, alcohol, and other drugs (Banerjee et al., 2007). We observed earlier that umbilical cord markers for prenatal exposure to acetaminophen were associated with increased risk of autism, and the same is true of ADHD (Ji et al., 2020).

ADHD is correlated with a number of structural and functional differences in the brain. The frontal lobes show structural abnormalities (Rubia et al., 2016) and may be underactive in cases of ADHD (Barkley, 1997). Because the frontal lobes inhibit unwanted behavior, lower activity in this part of the brain may lead to hyperactivity and impulsivity. In addition, smaller volume in the amygdala, basal ganglia, and hippocampus, and the brain as a whole was observed in ADHD (Hoogman et al., 2017). Disruption in the corpus callosum, a major white-matter pathway connecting the two cerebral hemispheres, was correlated with the severity of symptoms in ADHD (Ameis et al., 2016).

Different patterns of brain maturation have been observed in ADHD. The frontal lobes, and the prefrontal areas in particular, appear to mature more slowly in children with ADHD than in healthy controls (Shaw et al., 2007). Peak cortical thickness, a measure of brain maturity, occurred in healthy controls around the age of 7.5 years, but not until the age of 10.5 years in children with ADHD. Patterns of cortical thinning during adolescence predicted which individuals would continue to experience ADHD symptoms in adulthood and which would "outgrow" their symptoms (Shaw et al., 2013). White-matter circuits connecting the basal ganglia and the frontal lobes matured differently in people with and without ADHD (Helpern et al., 2011). A study of 1,713 individuals between the ages of 4 and 63 years with ADHD further supported the idea that ADHD involves delays in maturation (Hoogman et al., 2017).

The parts of the brain implicated in ADHD, such as the prefrontal cortex and the basal ganglia, feature large amounts of dopamine activity. As will be shown in Chapter 15, most of the medications used to treat ADHD, such as methylphenidate (Ritalin), dextroamphetamine (Dexedrine or Dextrostat), or amphetamine salts (Adderall), act by boosting the activity of dopamine, suggesting that dopamine activity might be lower than usual in cases of ADHD (Volkow et al., 2009).

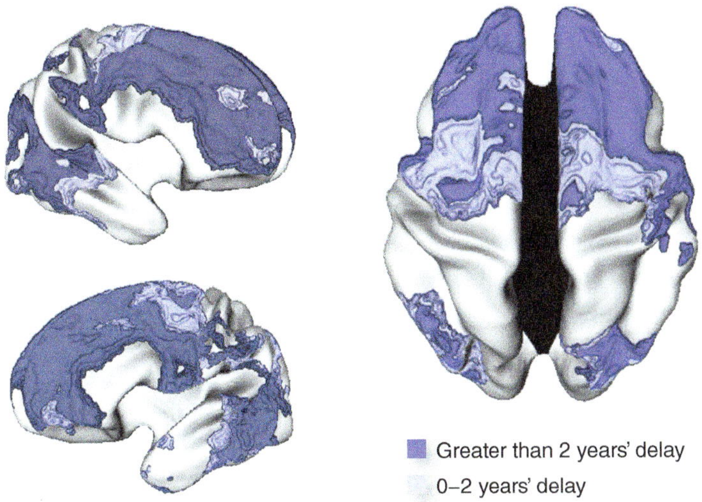

Among the many differences observed in the brains of children with ADHD compared to those of healthy controls is the rate of brain maturity, as measured by cortical thickening. These images demonstrate areas of the brain that developed later in children with ADHD than in healthy controls. Peak cortical thickness occurred around the age of 7.5 years in healthy children but was not seen in children with ADHD until an average age of 10.5 years. This finding implies that children with ADHD can be expected to lag their age peers in some tasks, but will eventually experience improvement.

Source: From P. Shaw et al. (2007). "Attention-Deficit/Hyperactivity Disorder Is Characterized by a Delay in Cortical Maturation," *Proceedings of the National Academy of Sciences of the United States of America*, *104*(49), 19649–19654. doi: 10.1073/pnas.0707741104. Copyright 2007 National Academy of Sciences. U.S.A.

As in ASD, myths about the causes of ADHD are common. Sugar is often blamed for hyperactive behavior, but evidence from carefully controlled studies does not support this belief (Milich, 1986; Wolraich, 1996). However, one well-controlled study suggested that combinations of common food additives made children who do not have ADHD demonstrate more hyperactivity (McCann et al., 2007). It is unlikely that "poor parenting" is responsible for ADHD symptoms (Schroeder & Kelley, 2009). Parents, however, can learn new behavioral management techniques that greatly improve their child's behavior.

SUMMARY 14.1 Neurodevelopmental Disorders

Disorder	Symptoms	Possible Causal Factors Under Investigation
Autism spectrum disorder (ASD) 	• Problems with social relatedness • Problems with communication • Ritualistic behavior	• Genetics • Parental age • Disruptions in brain development • Unknown environmental influences
Attention deficit hyperactivity disorder (ADHD) 	• Inattentiveness • Hyperactivity/Impulsivity	• Genetics • Brain development/exposure to toxins • Frontal lobe activity • Food additives

Credits: Top row—Laura Freberg; Bottom row—Suzanne Tucker/Shutterstock.com.

What Is Schizophrenia?

Schizophrenia is not the most common type of disorder, affecting approximately 1% of the human population worldwide (Kessler et al., 2007), but it is one of the most dramatic. This condition influences and distorts a range of behaviors, including perception, cognition, movement, and emotion.

schizophrenia A disorder characterized by hallucinations, delusions, disorganized thought and speech, disorders of movement, restricted affect, and avolition or asociality.

Ray Stubblebine/Reuters

Despite having been diagnosed with schizophrenia, John Nash shared the 1994 Nobel Prize in Economic Sciences. Nash was the subject of the 2001 film *A Beautiful Mind,* starring Russell Crowe. Sadly, both Nash and his wife were killed in a traffic accident in 2015.

Symptoms of Schizophrenia

The *DSM-5* places schizophrenia within a group of disorders called schizophrenia spectrum and other psychotic disorders (APA, 2013). Among the symptoms of schizophrenia are delusions, hallucinations, disorganized speech, and disorders of movement, which together indicate a state of psychosis. Schizophrenia also features negative symptoms (APA, 2013). Negative symptoms are behaviors that are seen in healthy people but not in patients. These symptoms include "diminished emotional expression and avolition" (APA, 2013, p. 88). A person with diminished emotional expression does not show typical outward signs of emotion, such as facial expressions and tone of voice, when an emotional response is expected. Avolition (the *a* means "lack of") refers to a patient's lack of "volition," or goal-oriented behavior.

Delusions are defined as unrealistic beliefs. These may take a number of forms, including delusions of persecution by others (paranoia), feelings of unrealistic power or importance (grandiosity), or beliefs that others are directing one's behavior (control).

Hallucinations are false perceptions. Although hallucinations may occur in several sensory modalities, 64% to 80% of hallucinations in schizophrenia are auditory (Tien, 1991; McCarthy-Jones et al., 2017). Patients often report hearing voices, which can be accusatory or otherwise unpleasant, contributing to the distress associated with the disorder. Auditory hallucinations are not imaginary; they are real sensations correlated with increased activity in the primary auditory cortex of the temporal lobe (Dierks et al., 1999; Jardri et al., 2013). Simply asking patients to remember or imagine sounds did not produce the type of activity in the auditory cortex seen during an auditory hallucination, indicating that the hallucination experience is different from simple memory or imagination.

A further symptom of schizophrenia involves disorganized patterns of speech. The patient jumps inexplicably from one topic to the next. People with schizophrenia appear to have difficulty inhibiting secondary meanings for some words (Titone et al., 2000). For example, the word *jam* can refer to either a fruit spread for toast or an impromptu musical session. Most people would use context (a conversation about food or music) to decide which meaning was appropriate. Patients with schizophrenia might not experience this filtering, leading their thoughts to jump from food to jazz and then on to other atypical connections.

This loosening of associations among ideas might occur because of the reduced latent inhibition in patients with schizophrenia, as discussed in Chapter 8. According to this argument, latent inhibition typically results in fewer associations being made to familiar stimuli. If you have had a lot of experience connecting jam and food, you are unlikely to consider other uses of the word *jam.* The person with schizophrenia, however, would be less inhibited in making connections among ideas, leading to trains of thought that seem bizarre to the rest of us.

Grunnitus Studio/Science Source

Some people with schizophrenia experience catatonia, which means that they maintain awkward or unusual body positions for hours at a time.

Schizophrenia also features "grossly disorganized or abnormal motor behavior" (APA, 2013, p. 88). Some people may be unusually active, while others may barely move throughout an entire day. Unusual behaviors can occur, including grimaces and gestures. The maintenance of awkward or unusual body positions for hours at a time is called catatonia. People experiencing catatonia appear aware of their surroundings, but they don't move. Most of us would find it difficult to sit for a few minutes, let alone hours, without shifting position.

Causes of Schizophrenia

Like many other types of psychological disorders, schizophrenia has multiple sources of causality. No one factor alone is sufficient to produce the disorder.

Biological Factors in Schizophrenia Significant evidence points to a genetic vulnerability for schizophrenia. People with close family members who have been diagnosed with schizophrenia are more likely to develop the disorder themselves (Gottesman, 1991). If one identical twin is diagnosed with the disorder, the other twin has nearly a 50% lifetime risk of developing the disorder (see • Figure 14.8). Comparisons of adopted children

delusion A false, illogical belief.
hallucination A false perception.

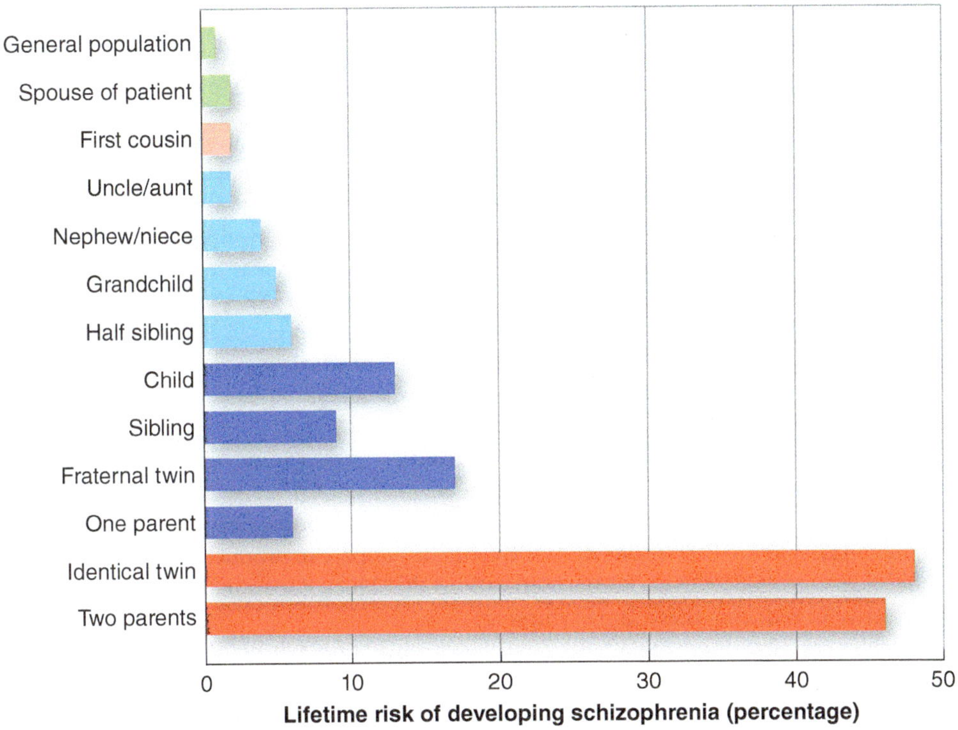

FIGURE **14.8**

Genetics and Schizophrenia. A person's lifetime risk of developing schizophrenia increases when closely related family members have been diagnosed with the disorder, suggesting that genes play a significant role. Having a spouse with schizophrenia doubles the risk (from 1% to 2%), which probably reflects the tendency for people to marry others with whom they share similarities.

Source: Adapted from I. I. Gottesman (1991). *Schizophrenia Genesis.* New York: W. H. Freeman & Co.

with their biological and adoptive parents also support a role for genetics (Kety et al., 1968). A large number of genes have been implicated in the development of schizophrenia and overlap with those involved with bipolar disorder (Cross-Disorder Group of the Psychiatric Genomics Consortium, 2013; Smeland et al., 2020). In one case of identical triplets, two of the triplets were diagnosed with schizophrenia and the third was diagnosed with bipolar disorder (McGuffin et al., 1982).

A possible genetic marker for schizophrenia is the occurrence of dysfunctional eye movements, first reported over 100 years ago (Diefendorf & Dodge, 1908). These dysfunctional eye movements represent difficulties in executive control and inhibition, and are also found in many healthy relatives of patients with schizophrenia (Radant et al., 2015). These types of behavioral differences between people with and without a disorder can guide further genetic research.

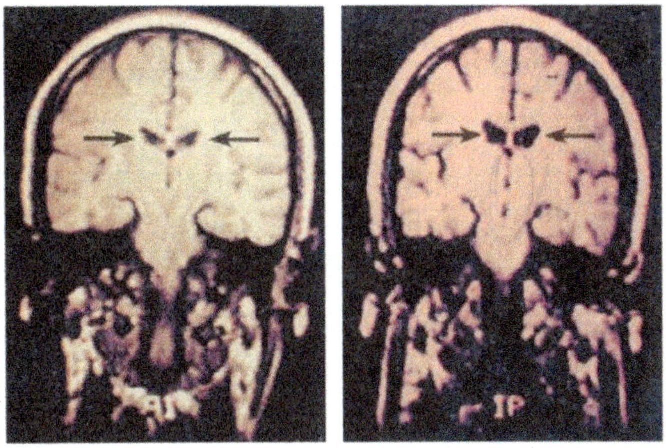

Courtesy D. R. Weinberger, NIMH, St. Elizabeth's Hospital

Magnetic resonance images of the brains of a pair of identical twins show the differences in the size of the lateral ventricles (arrows) found in healthy people (left) and in people with schizophrenia (right). The ventricles are fluid-filled spaces and enlarge whenever significant numbers of nearby neurons have died.

A number of structural and biochemical features accompany schizophrenia. One reliable correlate of schizophrenia is the presence of enlarged ventricles (Yotsutsuji et al., 2003). As discussed in Chapter 4, the ventricles are fluid-filled spaces in the brain that are not responsible for any particular behavior. The ventricles enlarge in response to any condition resulting in a loss of neural tissue in adjacent areas, so we can assume that schizophrenia is associated with neural degeneration.

Patients with schizophrenia demonstrate differences in brain activity compared with healthy people. For example, patients with schizophrenia often show a lower level of frontal lobe activity than that of healthy controls, both at rest and during effortful cognitive tasks (Berman et al., 1992). The importance of the frontal lobes to higher cognitive processes and attention suggests that this difference would have significant influences on behavior, and lower levels of activity might account for the emotional disturbances and social withdrawal seen in these patients (Andreasen et al., 1997). Pathways in the brain that manage olfaction, or the sense of smell, travel through the frontal lobe. Lower overall frontal lobe activity might account for some difficulties that patients with schizophrenia experience with their sense of smell. In addition, distortions in the brain's default

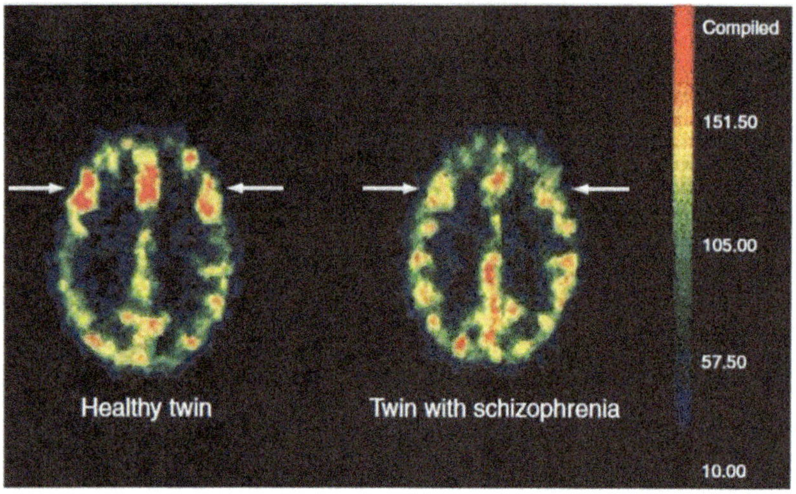

When the brain activity of these identical twins is observed through brain imaging, the frontal lobes (arrows) appear to be more active in the healthy twin (left) than in the twin with schizophrenia (right). Red and yellow areas indicate greater activity, while green and dark areas are relatively inactive.

Photo courtesy of Daniel R. Weinberger, M.D. E. Fuller Torrey, M.D. (formerly of NIMH) and Karen Berman, M.D. NIMH Clinical Brain Disorders Branch Division of Intramural Research Programs, NIMH 1990.

mode network (see Chapter 6) predict the severity of patients' psychotic symptoms (Garrity et al., 2007; Pomarol-Clotet et al., 2008).

Schizophrenia might involve abnormal brain development during adolescence. Teens typically experience a burst of cortical gray matter growth at puberty, followed by a wave of thinning of the gray matter extending into their early 20s. Healthy teens experience little loss of gray matter, whereas teens diagnosed with schizophrenia experience a loss that has been likened to a forest fire (Thompson et al., 2001). Cortical thinning is generally characteristic of patients with schizophrenia of all ages compared to healthy controls (Van Erp et al., 2018).

Abnormalities in dopamine activity might be the major biochemical culprit in schizophrenia (Howes et al., 2017). Drugs that boost dopamine activity, such as amphetamine and the Parkinson's disease treatment l-dopa, can produce hallucinations and paranoid delusions (Goetz et al., 2001). Medications that block dopamine activity are usually quite effective in reducing these same symptoms.

However, this dopamine hypothesis of schizophrenia is not perfect. About one-fourth of patients with schizophrenia do not respond favorably to drugs that reduce dopamine activity. In particular, the negative symptoms, such as diminished emotional expression, are not improved by these drugs (Kane & Freeman, 1994; Goff & Evins, 1998). In addition, medications that influence neurotransmitters other than dopamine are often effective (Syvalahti, 1994). Finally, phencyclidine (PCP, or angel dust) produces a syndrome that is quite similar to schizophrenia, although PCP acts on synapses using glutamate, not dopamine (Mössner et al., 2008). Because glutamate and dopamine are often important to the same brain circuits, it is possible that disturbances in one, the other, or both could lead to similar behavioral outcomes. Disturbances in the balance between brain excitation and inhibition, not related to any one neurochemical system, might also contribute to symptoms of schizophrenia (Jardri et al., 2016).

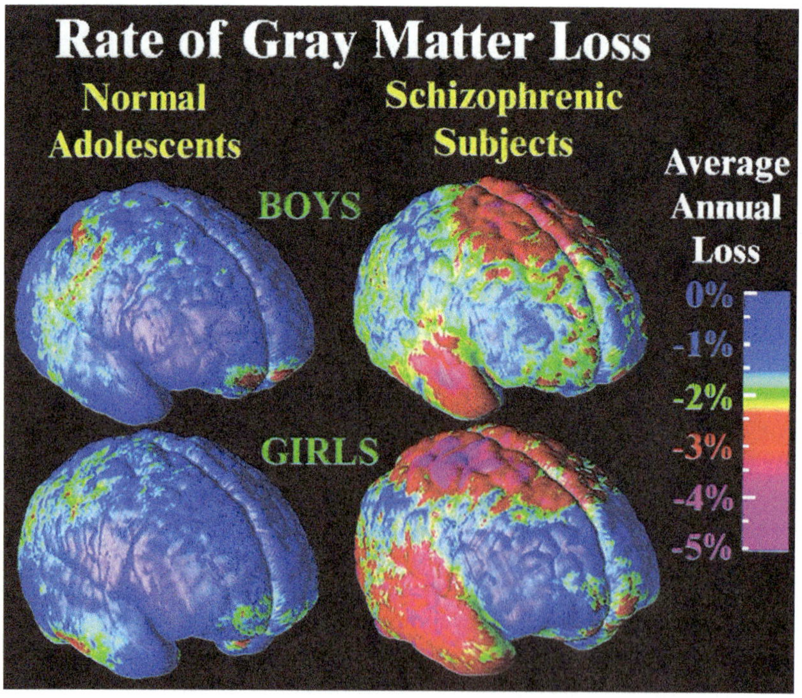

Teens typically experience a burst of gray matter growth at puberty, followed by a wave of gray matter thinning that extends into their early 20s. Compared with their healthy peers, teens diagnosed with schizophrenia experience much greater gray matter loss. Purple and red areas indicate the greatest amount of loss, followed by yellow and green areas. *Source:* From P. M. Thompson et al. (2001). "Mapping Adolescent Brain Changes Reveals Dynamic Wave of Accelerated Gray Matter Loss in Very Early-Onset Schizophrenia," *Proceedings of the National Academy of Sciences of the United States of America, 98*(20), 11650–11655. doi: 10.1073/pnas.201243998

Photo Courtesy of Paul Thompson/USC Institute for Neuroimaging and Informatics.

Environmental Factors in Schizophrenia The nearly 50% concordance rate for schizophrenia in identical twins indicates a role for genetics in the development of the disorder. However, 50% is not 100%, and we need to account for the remaining causal factors.

Extreme stress contributes to the appearance and severity of schizophrenia among genetically vulnerable people. Schizophrenia appears nearly five times more frequently in members of lower than in those of higher socioeconomic groups (Keith et al., 1991). The stress of living in poverty might trigger schizophrenia in vulnerable individuals. However, others argue that people who are susceptible to schizophrenia drift into lower-paying jobs. In other words, the disorder reduces the patients' socioeconomic status, accounting for the higher rates of the disorder among the poor. Other stresses might accompany a person's minority status in a community (Boydell & Murray, 2003). African immigrants living in London neighborhoods with the lowest proportions of African immigrants were twice as likely to be diagnosed with schizophrenia as African immigrants living in neighborhoods with the highest proportion of minorities (see ● Figure 14.9). The stress of social isolation because of minority status may have contributed to higher rates of schizophrenia.

When we talk about environmental influences, factors such as stress come to mind (see Chapter 16). However, environmental influences also include biological variables such as the prenatal environment, including the pregnant woman's exposure to viral illness. Another environmental variable that might trigger schizophrenia in genetically vulnerable individuals is marijuana use (Kelley et al., 2016; Marconi et al., 2016). A 25-year longitudinal study concluded that cannabis use nearly doubled the risk of schizophrenia (Fergusson et al., 2005). As mentioned in Chapter 11, adolescence is a time of brain growth, and heavy marijuana use during this period produces a reduction in white matter volume in the frontal lobes that might interact with a person's genetic vulnerabilities for schizophrenia (Ho et al., 2011).

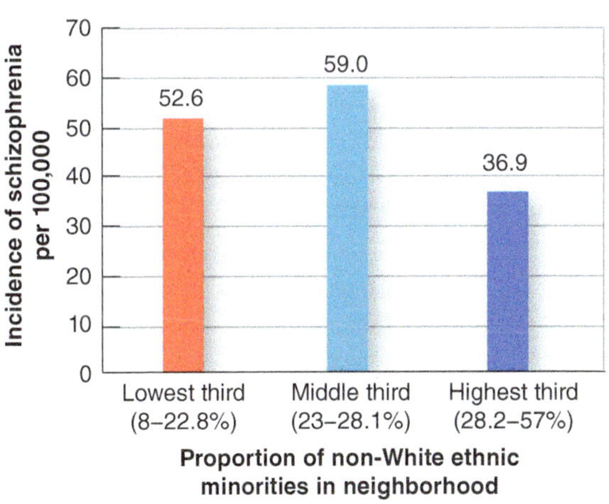

Janine Wiedel Photolibrary/Alamy Stock Photo

FIGURE **14.9**

Stress and Schizophrenia. African immigrants living in South London were more likely to be diagnosed with schizophrenia if they lived in a predominantly White neighborhood than if they lived in a primarily non-White neighborhood; that is, if you divide neighborhoods into thirds based on the percentage of non-Whites (high, medium, and low), schizophrenia was more common in the middle and lower groups. An explanation based on self-selection (people choosing to live in each type of neighborhood) is unlikely in this case because nearly all the study participants were assigned to public housing units rather than choosing where to live. These findings suggest that the stress of minority status might contribute to higher risk for schizophrenia.

Source: Adapted from J. Boydell et al. (2001). "Incidence of Schizophrenia in Ethnic Minorities in London: Ecological Study into Interactions with Environment," *British Medical Journal, 323*(7325), 1336–1338. doi: 10.1136/bmj.323.7325.1336

THINKING SCIENTIFICALLY

Does Cannabis Use Increase Risk of Schizophrenia?

As the United States continues a path of decriminalizing cannabis use, new questions related to public health emerge. As mentioned in this chapter, researchers have identified an association between cannabis use and schizophrenia. Can we conclude that this is a causal relationship? Due to ethical concerns, we are unlikely to randomly assign people to cannabis and no cannabis groups.

One research group attempted to answer this question by looking at the patterns of cannabis use and use of psychiatric services for a first psychotic episode across multiple centers in Europe (Di Forti et al., 2019). In a novel approach to the question, these researchers also considered whether high or low potency cannabis was the norm in each geographical area studied.

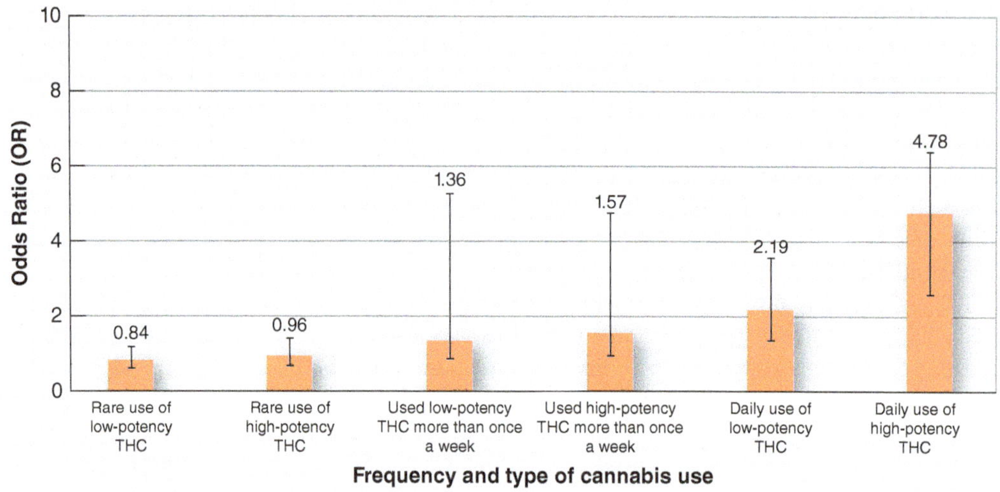

FIGURE **14.10**

Cannabis Use and Risk for Schizophrenia. Daily use of high-potency cannabis increased the odds of being diagnosed with schizophrenia nearly five times. It remains possible that people with a genetic predisposition to psychosis are also more likely to become heavy cannabis users.

Source: Adapted from M. DiFort et al. (2019). "The Contribution of Cannabis Use to Variation in the Incidence of Psychotic Disorder Across Europe (EU-GEI): A Multicentre Control Study," *The Lancet Psychiatry, 6*(5), 427–436. doi: 10.1016/S2215-0366(19)30048-3

WHAT AM I BEING ASKED TO BELIEVE OR ACCEPT?

We are being asked to believe that cannabis use contributes to the risk of developing schizophrenia.

WHAT EVIDENCE SUPPORTS THIS POSITION?

DiForti and her colleagues (2019) reported that daily cannabis use tripled the risk of psychosis compared to non-users. When only high-potency cannabis was available in an area, the risk of psychosis in daily users was five times higher than for non-users (see Figure 14.10). The researchers speculated that about 12% of psychosis cases over all 11 study sites could be prevented if high-potency cannabis was no longer available, with a 30% decrease in London and a 50% decrease in Amsterdam.

ARE THERE OTHER WAYS THIS EVIDENCE COULD BE INTERPRETED?

Genetic studies have suggested that there is an overlapping genetic risk for both cannabis use and psychosis (Verweij et al., 2017). In other words, the same underlying genetic profile might predispose a person to both heavy cannabis use and schizophrenia. Patients diagnosed with schizophrenia who have never used cannabis still show abnormalities in their natural, endogenous cannabinoids, suggesting that use of cannabis can distort existing problems in people already at risk for psychosis (Van Haren et al., 2013).

WHAT OTHER EVIDENCE WOULD I NEED TO EVALUATE THESE ALTERNATIVES?

Further research is needed to compare the effects of high-potency cannabis, which is becoming more common, and to identify the characteristics of individuals who seem to be at higher risk of adverse effects of cannabis use.

WHAT ARE THE MOST REASONABLE CONCLUSIONS?

Sufficient data is available to support public health messages warning individuals with a family history of psychosis that daily cannabis use, and use of high-potency cannabis in particular, is probably not a good idea. ■

What Is Bipolar Disorder?

Bipolar disorder serves as "a bridge between psychotic disorders, such as schizophrenia, and depressive disorders with respect to symptoms, family histories, and genetics" (APA, 2013, p. 123). Bipolar disorder features a period of **mania**, which may or may not be followed by a period of depression. The symptoms of depression that can accompany bipolar disorder are identical to those used to diagnose major depressive disorder, which is described in the next section of this chapter.

A manic phase consists of "a distinct period of abnormally and persistently elevated, expansive, or irritable mood, abnormally and persistently increased goal-directed activity or energy" (APA, 2013, p. 124). Patients may demonstrate grandiosity, in which they feel unrealistically special or important. The person's behavior, characterized by little need for sleep, rapid speech, difficulty concentrating, and rapidly shifting ideas, seems to be running at an abnormally high speed. Unlike many other disorders, however, mania increases productive, goal-directed behavior. However, because of the person's tendency to meet the *DSM-5* criterion for "excessive involvement in activities that have a high potential for painful consequences," hospitalization is often necessary for the patient's protection (APA, 2013, p. 124). Many variations occur in the timing and severity of the mania and depression observed in bipolar disorder.

Bipolar disorder affects approximately 2.6% of American adults each year (Kessler et al., 2005). Women are more likely to be diagnosed with bipolar disorder than men, by a ratio of approximately 3:2 (Holzman et al., 2016). The average age of onset for bipolar disorder is 25 years. Children and youth under the age of 18 years with symptoms of bipolar disorder are diagnosed instead with disruptive mood dysregulation disorder (APA, 2013).

Genetic predispositions play a significant role in bipolar disorder. Concordance rates between identical twins for bipolar disorder are commonly reported to be as high as 70% (Craddock & Sklar, 2013). Adoption studies also support a powerful role for genetics (Taylor et al., 2002). As mentioned previously, there is considerable overlap between the genes believed to play a role in bipolar disorder and those implicated in schizophrenia. Not surprisingly because of their genetic overlap, bipolar disorder shares some of the same abnormalities in brain structure and function as observed in schizophrenia (Ivleva et al., 2016).

Bipolar disorder is linked to oxidative stress and accelerated aging (Rizzo et al., 2014; Vasconcelos-Moreno et al., 2017). Similar changes in the brain are observed in patients with bipolar disorder as are seen in dementia. Fortunately, as we will see in Chapter 15, current treatments for bipolar disorder demonstrate antioxidant effects that offset these problems.

Among the many possible environmental factors that could interact with genes associated with bipolar disorder is diet. Omega-3 fatty acids, generally found in fish, may provide some protection from bipolar disorder (Noaghiul & Hibbeln, 2003). As shown in ● Figure 14.11, prevalence rates for bipolar disorder are highest in countries where fish is rarely consumed (such as Germany) and lowest in countries where fish is an important diet staple (such as Iceland). Patients with bipolar disorder have low levels of omega-3 fatty acids compared to healthy controls (McNamara & Weige, 2016). As you will see in Chapter 15, supplementation with omega-3 fatty acids is being explored as an aspect of treatment for bipolar disorder.

Many unanswered questions regarding the development of this condition remain. Bipolar disorder may be overrepresented in groups of people with artistic and creative talent (Jamison, 1993, 1995). Based on biographical accounts, the poet William Blake, the composers George Frideric Handel and Gustav Mahler, and visual artists Vincent van Gogh and Michelangelo might have had bipolar disorder. Many noted actors, including Carrie Fisher (*Star Wars*) and Vivien Leigh (*Gone with the Wind*), have been diagnosed with bipolar disorder. Comparisons between people with bipolar disorder and major depressive disorder and healthy people in creative and noncreative professions support this hypothesis. The patients with bipolar disorder scored similarly on tests of creativity to healthy people in creative occupations and higher than people with major depression and healthy people in noncreative occupations (Santosa et al., 2007). The parts of the brain that are affected in bipolar disorder are similar to those seen in cases of frontotemporal dementia. In both conditions, lower activity in these areas may reduce inhibition, which in turn leads to more creativity in some individuals (Seeley et al., 2008).

Cpuk/Alamy Stock Photo

Actors, poets, painters, and musicians seem to have a disproportionate risk for bipolar disorder compared to people in other occupations. The late Carrie Fisher, of *Star Wars* fame, was outspoken regarding her challenges with bipolar disorder. We do not know whether having bipolar disorder allows these creative people to express emotion more effectively in their art, the arts are simply more welcoming than the corporate boardroom to those who have psychological disorders, or some combination of the two is true.

bipolar disorder A mood disorder characterized by alternating periods of mania and depression.

mania A period of unrealistically elevated mood.

FIGURE **14.11**

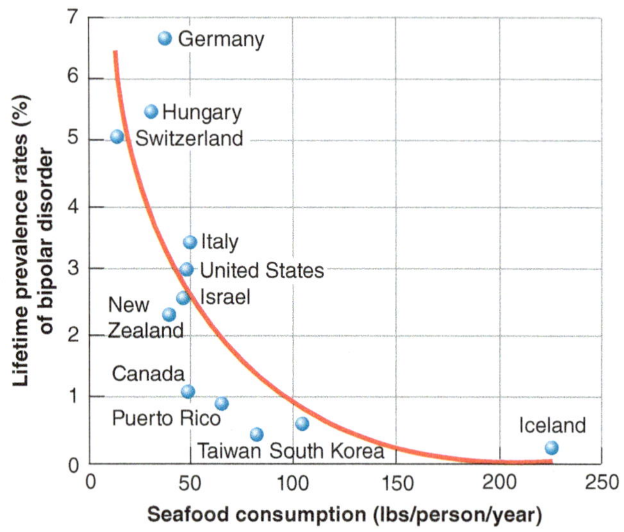

Bipolar Rates Are Lower in Nations with High Seafood Consumption. Rates of bipolar disorder are negatively correlated with a nation's consumption of seafood, suggesting that the omega-3 fatty acids contained in seafood might help prevent bipolar disorder.

Source: Adapted from S. Noaghiul & R. Hibbeln (2003). "Cross-National Comparisons of Seafood Consumption and Rates of Bipolar Disorders," *American Journal of Psychiatry*, *160*(12), 2222–2227. doi:10.1176/appi.ajp.160.12.2222

What Is Major Depressive Disorder (MDD)?

Although most of us experience the occasional "blues," these feelings are not as severe or chronic as the depressed feelings that characterize major depressive disorder. According to the *DSM-5*, **major depressive disorder (MDD)** is characterized by depressed mood most of the day, nearly every day, for a period of at least 2 weeks (APA, 2013). Patients with MDD complain about feeling sad and empty, and periods of tearfulness are common. The *DSM-5* also notes that MDD can produce anhedonia, or loss of pleasure. You are probably already familiar with the term *hedonist,* which refers to a person who is a pleasure seeker. *Anhedonia* refers to a person's disinterest in activities that previously provided pleasure, such as sex, eating, or social activities.

To be diagnosed with MDD, a person must show at least five symptoms, one of which must be either depressed mood or anhedonia. The remaining symptoms can be divided into physical and cognitive groups. The physical symptoms of MDD are related to disturbances in autonomic function typically found in the presence of high levels of stress, described in Chapter 16. Appetite and sleep may be disturbed. Some patients experience a loss of appetite, whereas others begin to eat too much. As observed in Chapter 6, many patients with depression experience frequent wakefulness, whereas others experience oversleeping (more than 9 hours per night). Fatigue or restlessness may occur. Among the cognitive symptoms of depression are difficulty concentrating, feelings of hopelessness and worthlessness, and in some cases, thoughts of suicide (APA, 2013).

Prevalence of MDD

MDD is one of the most frequently diagnosed psychological disorders, affecting approximately 7% of the adult population each year (APA, 2013). MDD decreases with age, and people between the ages of 18 and 29 years have rates that are three times as high as those for people over the age of 60 years.

major depressive disorder A disorder characterized by lengthy periods of depressed mood, loss of pleasure in normal activities, disturbances in sleep and appetite, difficulty concentrating, feelings of hopelessness, and possible thoughts of suicide.

Women experience MDD more frequently than men do (Nolen-Hoeksema, 1987; Nolen-Hoeksema et al.,1999). This discrepancy between rates of MDD in men and those in women has been observed to be independent of race, ethnicity, social class, and country of residence (Strickland, 1992; Üstün et al., 2004; see Figure 14.12). It is possible that female hormones participate in mood through some unknown mechanism. Mood disturbances can

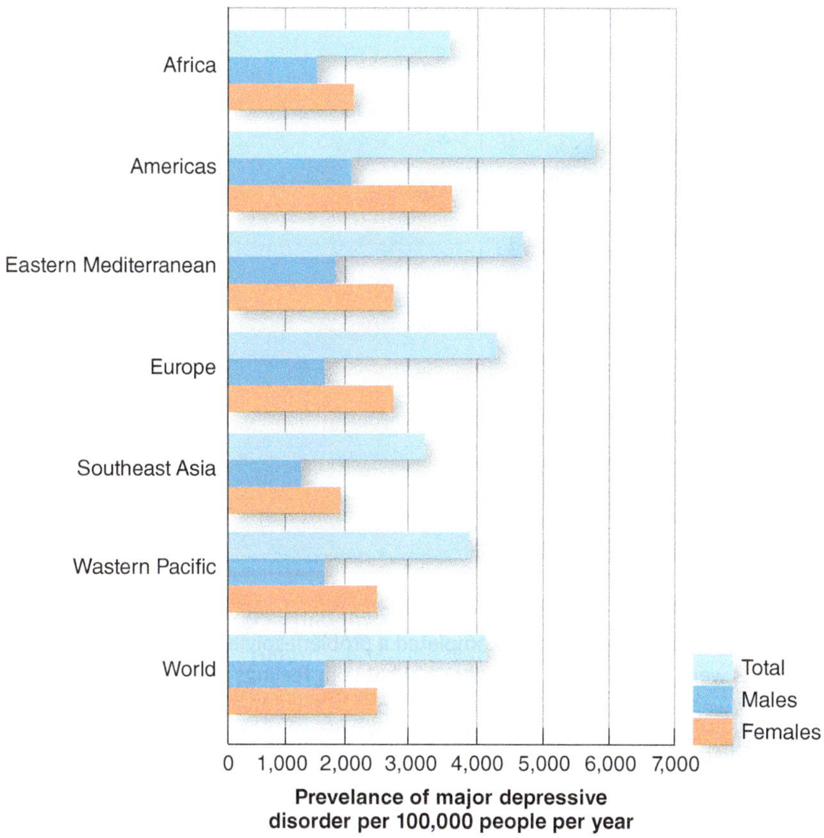

FIGURE **14.12**

Worldwide Gender Differences in Depression. Across many cultures, women are diagnosed with depression more frequently than men. *Source:* Adapted from T. B. Üstün et al. (2004). "Global Burden of Depressive Disorders in the Year 2000," *British Journal of Psychiatry*, *184*(5), 386–392. doi:10.1192/bjp.184.5.386

be associated with hormonal changes in women, including postpartum depression and mood changes accompanying menopause (Rapkin et al., 2002). However, it is also possible that women are more likely than men to admit feeling depressed to others and to seek help with depression. Men might mask or cover their depressed mood by engaging in activities such as drinking alcohol.

Causes of MDD

Theories attempting to explain MDD range from the learning, social, and cognitive to the strictly biological. It is likely that some combination of these approaches provides the greatest understanding of the sources of depression.

Learning Explanations for MDD According to learning theories, MDD occurs when a person experiences a reduction in positive reinforcement or an increase in negative outcomes. The loss of an important relationship can lead to MDD because it reduces a person's positive reinforcement.

A variation of the learning approach suggests that MDD results from **learned helplessness**, which is an application of operant conditioning. Classic research suggested that animals (and people) stop trying to escape when they learn that they cannot control an aversive situation. Contemporary research shows that this interpretation is incorrect (Maier & Seligman, 2016). The unwillingness to escape shock is not learned. Instead, inhibited escape is the default, unlearned response to the experience of lengthy aversive events. It is the ability to control aversive events that must be learned, which then leads to escape attempts. Maier and Seligman (2016) suggest that rather than demonstrating learned helplessness, these experiments represent learned hope that future aversive events can be controlled. This research provides interesting insight into the treatment of MDD, which we explore further in Chapter 15.

learned helplessness A state in which experiencing random or uncontrolled consequences leads to feelings of helplessness and possibly depression.

CONNECTING TO RESEARCH

Recognition of Facial Expression by People with Depression

HOW DOES THE WORLD LOOK to a person who is depressed? Does the experience of depression affect a person's attention to negative stimuli? As mentioned in Chapter 7, positive and negative emotions often serve as guides to approach and avoidance behaviors (Davidson & Irwin, 1999). Because it is usually more important to survival that we avoid predators and other dangers than that we miss approaching something positive, such as a tasty food, we have a bias toward noticing the negative. If we're experiencing an ongoing negative mood, does that have an effect on our sensitivities to positive and negative stimuli?

Among the important types of positive and negative stimuli that we need to process are facial expressions, because these are our clues to navigating the social environment successfully. Few of us would miss dramatic facial expressions, but the subtle ones require more attention (Gollan et al., 2010).

The Question: *How do people with MDD compare to control participants in their ability to detect subtle facial expressions of emotion?*

METHODS

In one study, 88 participants, half of whom had been diagnosed with major depressive disorder but were not treated with medication, observed photographs of facial expressions on a computer screen. The photographs depicted four basic emotions: happiness, surprise, sadness, and harsh (a category that combined photos showing disgust, fear, and anger). The photos were morphed to present intensities ranging from mostly neutral to very intense (see ● Figure 14.14). A total of 200 photos were presented for only 0.5 second each. The participants pushed one of six keys to identify the emotion being expressed.

ETHICS

It is unlikely that this procedure would produce distress in any of the participants. Because some of the participants are identified as having a psychological disorder, great care should be taken to protect their confidentiality.

RESULTS

The participants with MDD were more sensitive to sad faces than the control participants were. Specifically, all participants identified strong expressions of sadness, but participants with depression were more accurate in the identification of sadness when the emotion was expressed at a lower intensity. The groups were equally accurate in identifying the positive emotions (happiness and surprise) and the harsh emotions (fear, anger, and disgust). The severity of the participants' depression was positively correlated with their accuracy in recognizing sad faces, but not with their accuracy in recognizing other emotional expressions.

CONCLUSIONS

The participants with MDD were more sensitive to subtle expressions of sadness than the healthy control participants, and they were more likely to misidentify other emotional facial expressions as sad. In contrast, they were just as likely as control participants to misidentify happy, surprised, or harsh facial expressions. These findings indicate that people with depression not only are more likely to attend to sadder stimuli, but also might misinterpret neutral facial stimuli as sad. These tendencies might reinforce a person's depressive feelings. ■

A large body of research points to a role for serotonin in the regulation of mood. Genetic studies of MDD have focused on the serotonin transporter gene (Shadrina et al., 2018). Serotonin's role in brain systems responsible for mood, appetite, and sleep corresponds closely to the symptoms of MDD outlined in the *DSM-5*. Most effective medications for the treatment of depression boost the activity of serotonin at the synapse.

MDD might be part of a larger disturbance in daily, or circadian, rhythms (Soria et al., 2010). Recall that among the functions of serotonin is the regulation of sleep as well as mood (see Chapter 4). Among the genes suspected of being related to MDD are those involved with circadian rhythms (see Chapter 6; also see McClung, 2007; Buoli et al., 2018). The *DSM-5* criteria for MDD include sleeping either less than or more than a normal number of hours per night (7–9 hours) (APA, 2013). People with untreated MDD spend too much time in rapid eye movement (REM) sleep, and most medications that are used to treat MDD reduce REM sleep (Rijnbeek et al., 2003) (see ● Figure 14.16).

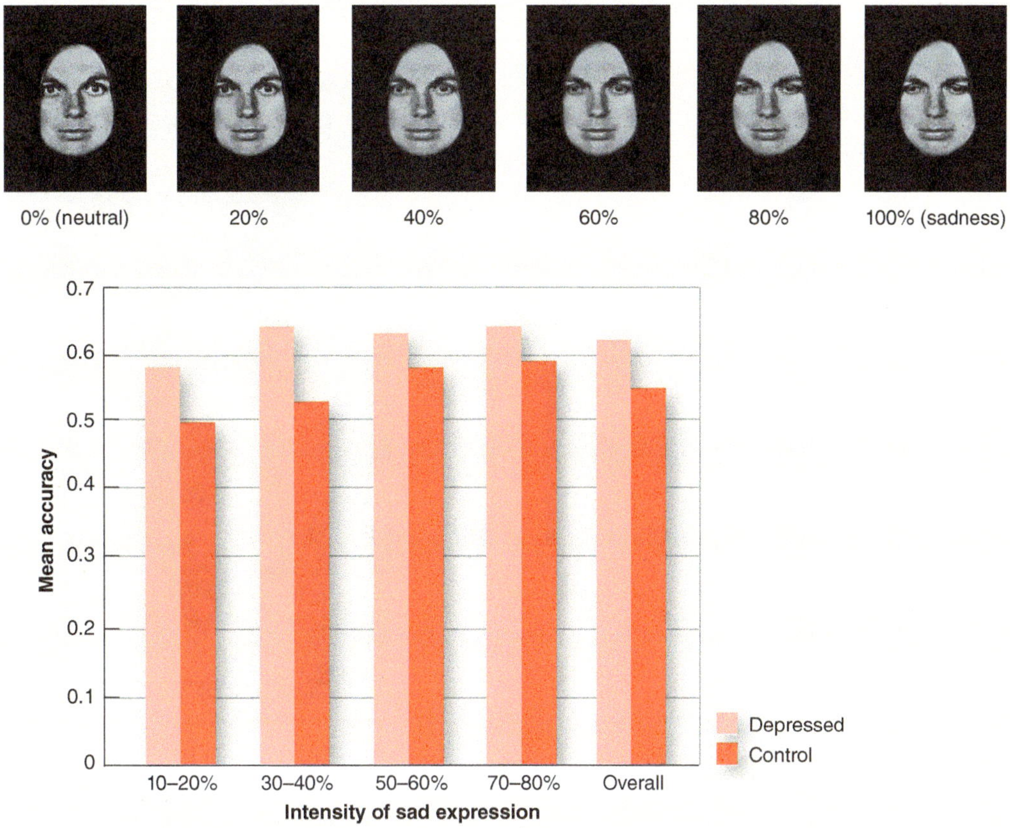

FIGURE **14.14**

Heightened Sensitivity to Sad Expressions in Depression. Study participants see one photo for only 0.5 second and must determine which of four emotions (happiness, surprise, sadness, harsh) is being displayed. Morphed images are made by combining neutral (0%) and high-intensity (100%) images. Each emotion is easier to identify as its intensity increases. Participants with MDD needed to see the same amount of intensity as healthy control participants before correctly identifying happy, surprised, or harsh facial expressions but needed to see less intensity than control participants before correctly identifying sad faces. This heightened sensitivity to the sad moods of others might reinforce the negative feelings of the person with depression.

Source: J. K. Gollan et al.(2010). "How Do Depressed and Healthy Adults Interpret Nuanced Facial Expressions?" *Journal of Abnormal Psychology, 119*(4), 804–810. https://doi.org/10.1037/a0020234

Stress and MDD The experience of severe stress, whether arising from the death of a loved one, illness, or frustration of major life goals, frequently occurs immediately before the onset of a depressive episode (Brown & Harris, 1989; Mazure, 1998). The physical and cognitive responses to high levels of stress, such as difficulty sleeping or concentrating, are quite similar to the symptoms of MDD. Researchers are beginning to discover biological bridges between stress and depression by studying a protein called p11 (Svenningsson et al., 2013; Seo et al., 2017). Both stressed mice and depressed humans have reduced levels of p11, which rebound when treated with antidepressants.

However, most people exposed to stressors do not respond by becoming depressed, reinforcing the complexity of the development of this disorder. Absolute levels of stress hormones, such as cortisol, fail to predict most cases of MDD (Nandam et al., 2020). Instead, MDD can be viewed within a **diathesis–stress model**. "Diathesis" means predisposition. It is likely that biological predispositions for MDD interact with a person's experience with stress (Zubin & Spring, 1977; Svenningsson et al., 2013; Seo et al., 2017).

diathesis–stress model A model that suggests that the experience of stress interacts with an individual's biological predisposition to produce a psychological disorder.

Diverse Voices in Psychology

Race, Ethnicity, Gender, Sexual Orientation, and Prevalence of Suicidality

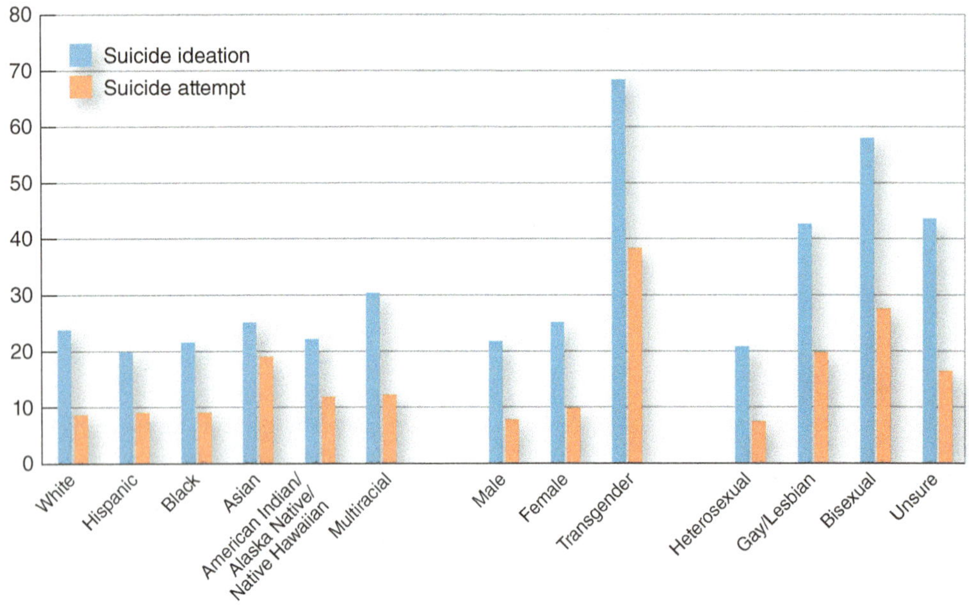

FIGURE **14.15**

Suicidal Ideation and Attempts in College Students. Rates of suicidal ideation (thinking about possibly attempting suicide) and suicide attempts varied among college students as a function of race and ethnicity, gender, and sexual orientation.

Source: C. H. Liu et al. (2019). "The Prevalence and Predictors of Mental Health Diagnoses and Suicide Among US College Students: Implications for Addressing Disparities in Service Use," *Depression and Anxiety, 36*(1), 8–17. doi: 10.1002/da.22830

Understanding that the combination of depression, impulsivity, alcohol or substance use, a history of suicide attempts, and a recent breakup or other traumatic event may increase the risk of suicide can help us offer support to a person who exhibits these characteristics.

As we have seen in this chapter, stress is a risk factor for a number of psychological disorders, including MDD. Depression in turn is a risk factor for suicidal ideation (thinking about suicide) and suicide attempts. Some groups of people seem to experience more stress than others, leading to differences in the rates of mental health problems and suicidal ideation and behavior. As university professors, we are saddened by data that show that depression, anxiety, and suicidality rates continue to increase among the students we teach (Liu et al., 2019).

Race and ethnicity form complicated relationships with mental health and suicidality (Liu et al., 2019). White college students have higher rates of depression and anxiety than students of other races and ethnicities, particularly African Americans, but suicidal ideation and attempts of White students are about the same or higher among students in racial and ethnic minority groups (see ● Figure 14.15).

In comparisons based on gender and sexual orientation, bisexual students are at greater risk of mental health problems and suicidality than are heterosexual or gay/lesbian students, with half engaging in suicidal ideation and over one quarter reporting a suicide attempt. Transgender students report significantly higher rates of mental health problems and suicidality than males or females.

It is important to note that Liu et al. (2019) looked at suicidal ideation and suicide attempts, but not rates of actual suicides. These numbers, too, show the influence of race, ethnicity, and gender. Among young adults aged 18 to 24, the Centers for Disease Control reports that young males were far more likely to commit suicide than females in all racial and ethnic categories (Jiang et al., 2015). Non-Hispanic Whites and American Indian or Alaska Native individuals had much higher rates of suicide than other races and ethnicities.

Awareness of the risks of mental health problems and suicidality among college students should stimulate the implementation of adequate mental health services and preventive strategies, with particular attention to groups who typically have lower rates of utilization of mental health services. We explore the intersection between diversity and treatment further in Chapter 15. ■

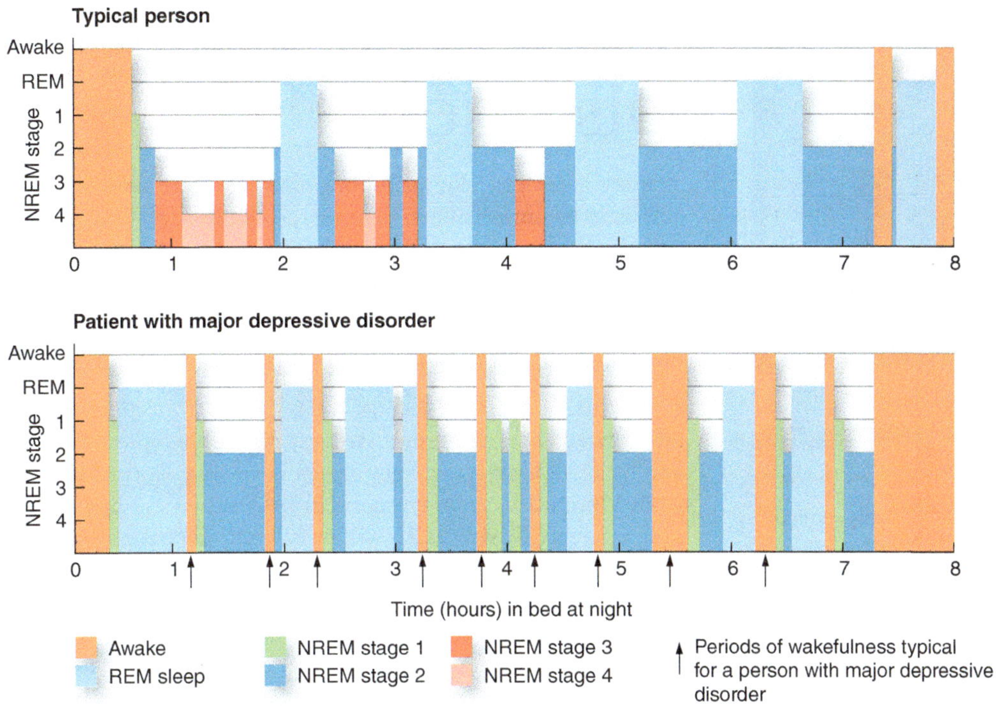

FIGURE **14.16**

Major Depressive Disorder Disrupts Sleep. These sleep records show the normal progression of non-REM and REM sleep (upper row) and the disrupted sleep of a person with major depressive disorder (bottom row). Note the lack of Stage 3 and 4 non-REM sleep and the frequent waking experienced by the person with depression (see Chapter 6 for more information).

Source: Adapted from J. C. Gillin and A. A. Borbély (1985). "Sleep: A Neurobiological Window on Affective Disorders," *Trends in Neurosciences*, *8*, 537–542. doi: 10.1016/0166-2236(85)90191-2

SUMMARY 14.2 Schizophrenia, Bipolar Disorder, and Major Depressive Disorder

Disorder	Symptoms	Possible Causal Factors Under Investigation
Schizophrenia 	• Delusions • Hallucinations • Disorganized thought and speech • Movement disorders • Restricted affect • Avolition or asociality	• Genetics • Reduced frontal lobe activity • Disruption of brain development • Dopamine and glutamate abnormalities • Stress • Prenatal environment • Marijuana use
Bipolar disorder 	• Elevated mood • Grandiosity • Little need for sleep • Rapid speech • Difficulty concentrating • Possible depression	• Genetics • Serotonin disturbances • Diet
Major depressive disorder 	• Chronic depressed mood • Lack of pleasure • Sleep disturbances • Appetite disturbances • Difficulty concentrating • Hopelessness • Possible suicidal thoughts	• Loss of positive reinforcement • Learned helplessness • Negative cognitions • Rumination • Depressive attributions • Stress • Genetics • Reduced serotonin activity • Patterns of brain activity • Circadian rhythms

Credits: Top row—Grunnitus Studio/Science Source; Second row—Cpuk/Alamy Stock Photo; Bottom row—Picture Partners/Alamy Stock Photo.

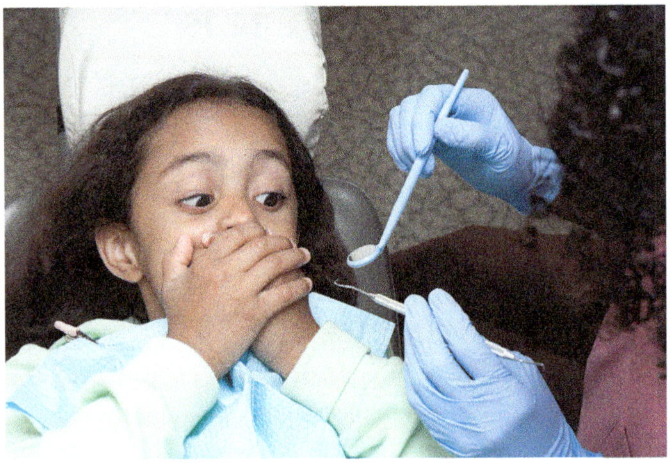

Anxiety is the anticipation of danger. Normal levels of anxiety remind us about the risks of engaging in dangerous activities, but disordered anxiety can prevent people from engaging in everyday activities.

What Is an Anxiety Disorder?

Anxiety disorders take many forms, but all share the core characteristic of unrealistic and counterproductive levels of anxiety. Anxiety has two major components: (1) strong negative emotions and (2) physical tension because of the anticipation of danger (Barlow, 1988). It is the anticipation of potential danger (whether real or not) that separates anxiety from the closely related emotion of fear. When we are afraid, usually something is happening in the present to produce that feeling, whereas anxiety occurs when we are worried about the future. **Anxiety disorders** represent an exaggeration of what is normally a useful response. Normal levels of anxiety protect us from engaging in risky activities, such as running up debts, driving recklessly, or failing to prepare for work or school, but excessive anxiety can cause a person to withdraw from positive life experiences and interpersonal relationships.

Approximately 30% of all Americans experience one or more anxiety disorders during their lifetime, although not all seek treatment (Kessler et al., 2005). People have genetic vulnerabilities for anxiety disorders in general, but not for specific types of anxiety disorders (DiLalla et al., 1994; Smoller, 2016). Families with members who are diagnosed with anxiety disorders are also likely to have members diagnosed with MDD because these types of problems appear to share an underlying genetic basis (Weissman et al., 1997; Micco et al., 2009). Anxiety disorders differ across gender and ethnicity for reasons that are not well understood. Women are more likely to be diagnosed with anxiety disorders than are men, and African Americans and Hispanics living in the United States are less likely to be diagnosed with anxiety disorders than are White Americans (Kessler et al., 2005).

Evidence of a predisposition to anxiety appears early in life (Biederman et al., 1990; Schwartz et al., 1999). As observed in Chapters 11 and 12, children's initial temperament and reactivity can predispose them to anxiety. In one study, young infants showed consistent levels of response to novel stimuli, such as the smell of cotton swabs dipped in alcohol (Kagan, 1997), and 20% of the infants were classified as "high reactives" to these stimuli because of their increased activity and distress when novel stimuli were presented. When the high-reactive children were placed in a novel laboratory environment at the ages of 4–5 years, they still showed heightened levels of anxiety compared to their peers.

Unlike most other types of psychological disorders, anxiety disorders do not impair a person's ability to think realistically. In most cases, adults with anxiety disorders recognize that their circumstances do not warrant their extremely anxious responses, but they feel unable to control them. A person looking out the window of a skyscraper is well aware that the likelihood of falling is quite low, but feelings of fear and anxiety persist. Young children with anxiety disorders are usually less aware than adults that their feelings are unrealistic.

Specific Phobias

Specific phobias are fears of objects or situations other than those associated with agoraphobia and social anxiety disorder (see • Figure 14.17). These fear stimuli may be animals, natural phenomena (water or earthquakes), blood and injury, or situations (flying, heights, bridges, and so on). People do not ordinarily form phobias about harmless objects such as coffee cups and keys (Mineka et al., 2006).

The evolutionary perspective suggests that phobias might be exaggerations of an otherwise useful sense of caution. The items that become fear stimuli have some realistic potential relationship to harm, such as snakes, spiders, and the sight of blood. As noted in Chapter 8, the connections formed in phobias can arise from classical conditioning. A stimulus (conditioned

anxiety disorder A disorder featuring anxiety that is not proportional to a person's circumstances.

specific phobia Fears of objects other than those associated with agoraphobia or social anxiety disorder.

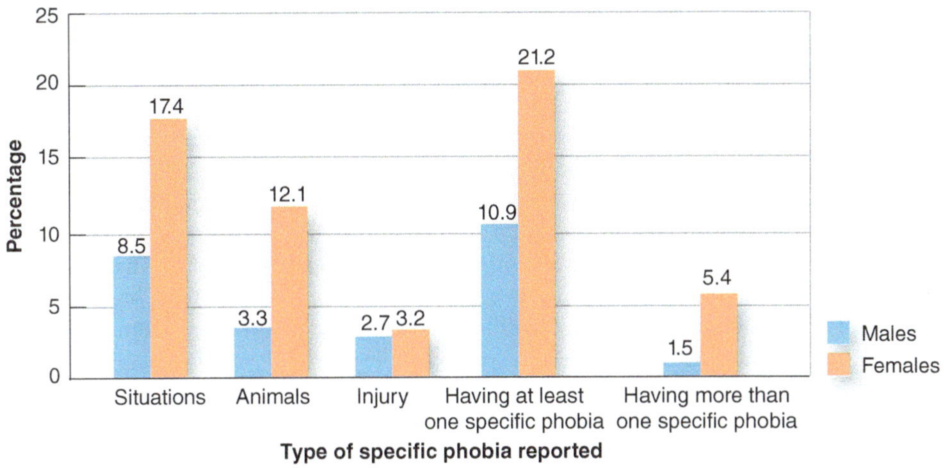

FIGURE **14.17**

Prevalence of Different Types of Specific Phobias. In a large random sample of adults, 21.2% of women and 10.9% of men reported having at least one specific phobia, as defined by the *DSM-5*. Gender differences were seen in the prevalence of situational phobias (lightning, enclosed spaces, darkness, flying, and heights) and animal phobias (primarily spiders and snakes). However, no gender differences occurred in injury phobias (injections, dentists, and injuries). More than one type of specific phobia was reported by 5.4% of the women and 1.5% of the men.

Source: Adapted from M. Fredrikson et al. (1996). "Gender and Age Differences in the Prevalence of Specific Fears and Phobias," *Behaviour Research and Therapy*, *34*(1), 33–39. doi:10.1016/0005-7967(95)00048-3

stimulus, or CS) becomes associated with a negative experience (unconditioned stimulus, or UCS) that results in fear (unconditioned response, or UCR), giving the CS the ability to elicit fear (conditioned response, or CR). We might be biologically prepared to form connections between certain stimuli and feelings of fear (Seligman, 1971). Learning also can influence the development of phobias through imitation and observation, such as when a child sees a parent scream when a spider creeps across the room.

Cognitions influence specific phobias. Even though a spider in your house or garden is simply minding its own business while doing spider things, people with spider phobias tend to believe that the spider is intending to attack them or move toward them (Riskind et al., 1995). People who have height phobias misjudge real physical heights, believing that they are higher than they really are (Stefanucci & Proffitt, 2009).

social anxiety disorder A disorder characterized by an unrealistic fear of being scrutinized and criticized by others.

Height phobia, or acrophobia, is somewhat unusual among the specific phobias due to its probable causality. Typically, individuals use a combination of vision, vestibular, and body position cues (see Chapter 5) to maintain balance. People with height phobias tend to rely more on vision (Hüweler et al., 2009), a preference that might in turn be influenced more by genetics than by experience. As height increases, visual cues for balance become less helpful, leading to discomfort and anxiety.

Social Anxiety Disorder

Social anxiety disorder is the fear of being scrutinized and criticized by others, particularly during public speaking and when meeting new people. Many of us are a little uneasy in these situations, but for people with social anxiety disorder, the fear and anxiety caused by these situations are out of proportion for the particular situation. In other words, the person with social

Shane Wilson Link/Shutterstock.com

People with spider phobias are often convinced that a spider is intent on harming them, when spiders are usually just being spiders.

In Japan, some people experience taijin kyofusho, which is a fear of offending or embarrassing other people with their odor, eye contact, or appearance (Tarumi et al., 2004). This condition is significantly different from the emphasis on a person's own embarrassment that is typical in social anxiety as experienced in Western cultures.

anxiety disorder feels crippling anxiety while doing things that most people take in stride, like introducing yourself to others at a party. In most cases, social anxiety disorder begins during adolescence. As discussed in Chapter 12, teens experience a spotlight effect, or a belief that others are scrutinizing them. For an anxious teen, this spotlight effect might be exaggerated, leading to social anxiety disorder.

Cultural variables influence the development of social anxiety. In the United States, White and Native American individuals were more likely to experience social anxiety than African American, Asian, or Hispanic individuals (Hasin & Grant, 2015). Prevalence is highest in high income countries, the Americas, and in the Western Pacific regions and lowest among low to lower-middle income countries and in the African and Eastern Mediterranean regions (Stein et al., 2017). Social anxiety is frequently less common in collectivistic cultures due to their greater emphasis on not offending others compared to embarrassing the self.

Morita Masatake (1874–1938) founded the Morita Therapy for the treatment of anxiety disorders, including the culture-bound syndrome *taijin kyofusho*, which affects 10% to 20% of the Japanese population. This condition, recognized in the *DSM*, is characterized by fear of offending others by blushing or by having an offensive appearance or body odor. Morita recommended treating anxiety by accepting your feelings, knowing your purpose, and doing what needs doing. His therapy continues to be used today.
Source: Reprinted by permission from *Morita Therapy and the True Nature of Anxiety-Based Disorders*, by S. Morita, the State University of New York Press 1998, State University of New York.

Panic Disorder

The *DSM-5* distinguishes between the experience of a single **panic attack**, characterized by intense fear and autonomic arousal, and the experience of **panic disorder**, which features repeated panic attacks and fear of future attacks (APA, 2013).

Having a panic attack does not mean that you should be diagnosed with panic disorder. It is not unusual for people to experience a few panic attacks in their lifetime. One quarter to one third of college students report having had at least one panic attack in the previous year (Asmundson & Norton, 1993). However, panic disorder is much less common, affecting 2.7% of the population in any given year (Kessler et al., 2005). Women are more likely to experience panic attacks and panic disorder than are men. More than half of people with panic disorder also have been diagnosed with MDD or another type of anxiety disorder (Kearney et al., 1997). Panic attacks begin to occur in adolescence and young adulthood (Robins & Regier, 1991).

By all reports, panic attacks are extremely unpleasant. Symptoms typically last about 10 minutes. Feelings of intense fear or discomfort are accompanied by both physical and cognitive symptoms. Strong arousal of the sympathetic nervous system leads to the experience of a pounding heart, sweating, trembling, shortness of breath, chest pain, nausea, and dizziness or faintness. Not too surprisingly, people experiencing such symptoms may believe they are dying or going crazy. For some individuals, panic attacks may be brought on by identifiable stimuli, such as being swept along in a crowd. For others, the attacks seem to come out of nowhere. In either case, many people experiencing repeated attacks may begin to fear leaving their homes, a condition known as agoraphobia, which will be discussed in a later section.

Biological Explanations for Panic Disorder A clue to the biological origin of panic attacks is that they can be produced artificially in people with panic disorder, but not in people without the disorder, by administering an injection of sodium lactate (Pitts & McClure, 1967; Papp et al., 1993). Sodium lactate interacts with orexins, chemical messengers that were discussed in Chapters 6 and 7. Orexins, which are released by cells in the hypothalamus, play important roles in wakefulness, vigilance, and appetite. People with panic disorder have larger quantities of orexins than do people without the disorder (Johnson et al., 2010). It is possible that disturbances involving the orexins might lead to panic attacks.

Cognitive Explanations for Panic Disorder Cognitive theories of panic attacks suggest that the interpretation of body symptoms, such as an increased heart rate, could lead to increasing anxiety and, ultimately, to panic (Clark, 1988; Bakker et al., 2002; Harvey et al., 2004). A person might interpret increased heart rate and rapid breathing as a heart attack instead of the result of having walked briskly from a parking lot. Concern about having a heart attack leads to further physiological arousal, which leads to more anxiety, and so on until a full state of panic is reached.

panic attack The experience of intense fear and autonomic arousal in the absence of real threat.

panic disorder A disorder characterized by repeated panic attacks and fear of future attacks.

INTERFOTO/AGE Fotostock

The Scream, a famous series of four paintings by Edvard Munch (1863–1944), was reportedly based on a panic attack that he suffered while out with two friends at sunset.

Social Explanations for Panic Disorder Social influences can be seen in the symptoms of panic disorder. Many people worry about appearing weird or crazy to other people, which can lead to increased anxiety and more panic attacks (Hicks et al., 2005). Culture plays an important role in how panic attacks are interpreted. Although the underlying physical characteristics remain similar from country to country, interesting variations have been observed. For example, dizziness is an important aspect of panic attacks in China, constipation and shortness of breath are common symptoms of panic in Rwanda, and gastrointestinal symptoms signal panic for patients in Thailand (Hinton & Good, 2009). Social factors also influence the development of panic disorder. Panic disorder is more common in children who have experienced parental loss or separation and in adults who have recently experienced significant, stressful life events (Klauke et al., 2010).

Integrating the Perspectives A combination of the factors just discussed is likely to provide the best explanation for the development and experience of panic disorder. A panic attack could occur as a result of a chain of events: (1) A person with a biological predisposition to panic, possibly involving the orexin systems of the brain, (2) is exposed to social stressors in the form of parental loss or separation or significant life stressors, (3) interprets physical symptoms of arousal as threatening or embarrassing, and finally (4) has cognitions leading to panic that are modulated by that individual's cultural expectations.

Agoraphobia

Agoraphobia is the fear of open spaces and is named after the ancient Greek *agora,* or "marketplace." As mentioned previously, agoraphobia is a common outcome of panic disorder. When people become afraid of the embarrassment of having panic attacks in public, they might opt to simply stay home. Fear can occur in a number of situations, including being outside the home alone, using public transportation, being in open spaces such as parking lots or in shops, or standing in line or in a crowd. Agoraphobia often prevents working or engaging in normal social activities (Kessler et al., 2005).

agoraphobia Unrealistic fear of open spaces, being outside the home alone, or being in a crowd.

Ryan McGinnis/Alamy Stock Photo

People with agoraphobia or fear of open places often dread being in crowds, like this one in Times Square in New York City.

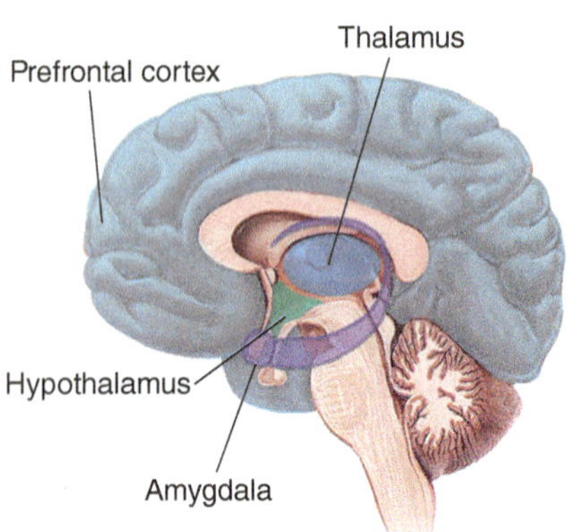

FIGURE **14.18**

Brain Circuits and GAD. People with GAD have higher levels of activity in the cortex, thalamus, amygdala, and hypothalamus (Wittchen & Hoyer, 2001). The prefrontal cortex was especially active when people with GAD saw angry faces, suggesting that this area had to "work harder" to control incoming danger signals from the amygdala (Monk et al., 2008).

Generalized Anxiety Disorder

Generalized anxiety disorder (GAD) is diagnosed when a person has experienced excessive anxiety and worry for 6 months that is not correlated with particular objects or situations (APA, 2013). In other words, the person experiences a great deal of worry, but the worry is focused on life in general, not upcoming midterms or spiders. GAD is associated with physical complaints, including headache, stomachache, and muscle tension. GAD is often comorbid, or coexisting, with other anxiety disorders, substance abuse, and MDD (APA, 2013).

Biological Explanations for GAD Like all anxiety disorders, GAD shows evidence of genetic predisposition (Kendler et al., 1995; Molina et al., 2011). A reasonable place to start looking for correlates of anxiety in brain structure and function is the fear circuit involving the amygdala, which was discussed in Chapters 4 and 7. The amygdala is particularly rich in receptors for GABA, a neurotransmitter that inhibits brain activity. As discussed in Chapter 6, drugs such as alcohol and the benzodiazepine tranquilizers (e.g., Valium) have their main anxiety-reducing effects at these GABA receptors. Not too surprisingly, then, people often self-medicate with alcohol and tranquilizers to reduce their anxiety level, leaving them vulnerable to substance abuse disorders.

The amygdala forms complex connections with the prefrontal areas of the frontal lobe (see ● Figure 14.18). As observed in the discussion of aggression in Chapter 13, the prefrontal cortex coordinates our decisions based on potential dangers identified by the amygdala. For example, if you see a driver's angry face in your rearview mirror, your amygdala alerts the prefrontal cortex about a potential threat or danger, and your prefrontal cortex uses memories of similar past experiences and reasoning to decide to pull over safely to the slower lane to let the angry driver go by. It is possible that this circuit is not responding typically in cases of GAD.

Cognitive Explanations for GAD Several cognitive models of GAD have been proposed (Beck, 1985). As discussed in Chapters 10 and 11, we often organize our thinking about the world into schemas, or systems of belief. If a high-reactive child develops a schema that says "The world is a dangerous place," even safe experiences begin to look dangerous through this filter. A different cognitive approach suggests that worrying can become a coping strategy for anxiety. By examining "what ifs," people might believe that they are coping, but so many situations are capable of triggering the coping response that the result is nearly constant worry (Wells, 2006). Bill Murray's character in the 1991 film *What About Bob?* expresses this type of worry when he asks his psychiatrist, "What if my bladder explodes?"

Social Explanations for GAD Individuals in lower socioeconomic classes in the United States are about twice as likely to be diagnosed with GAD as people in middle or upper socioeconomic classes (Kessler et al., 2005). Disruptions in social connectivity because of divorce, separation, death of a spouse, or loss of a job also are associated with higher rates of GAD (Wittchen & Hoyer, 2001).

Integrating the Perspectives Pulling these perspectives together into an integrated model, we might predict that GAD is most likely to occur in individuals with a high-reactive temperament, possibly because of their genetic background, who subsequently develop schemas and other cognitive patterns that maintain high levels of worry. When these individuals experience unusual amounts of stress because of socioeconomic factors and disruption of social networks, their risk for developing GAD is likely to be even higher.

generalized anxiety disorder (GAD) A disorder characterized by excessive anxiety and worry that is not correlated with particular objects or situations.

OCD and Related Disorders

The *DSM-5* groups obsessive-compulsive disorder (OCD), which was formerly an anxiety disorder, with body dysmorphic disorder, hoarding disorder, and other similar problems (APA, 2013).

Obsessive-Compulsive Disorder (OCD)

Individuals with **obsessive-compulsive disorder (OCD)** are haunted by distressing, intrusive thoughts (**obsessions**); the need to engage in repetitive, ritualistic behaviors (**compulsions**); or both. Between 2% and 3% of the U.S. population report experiencing OCD during their lifetime (Ruscio et al., 2010).

Obsessions are distinct from everyday worries, which usually focus on real-life problems. Common obsessions include concerns about contamination (catching diseases from shaking hands), repeated doubts (wondering whether you have hurt somebody), ordering (needing things arranged in a particular order or configuration), inappropriate impulses (hurting somebody else or shouting obscenities at a funeral), and sexual imagery (APA, 2013).

Compulsions appear to be efforts to ward off the anxiety produced by obsessions or some other feared event. For example, people troubled by obsessions about contamination may engage in compulsive hand washing hundreds of times per day. Other common compulsions include checking (for locked windows or faucets turned off), counting, ordering objects, and requesting or demanding assurances.

Randal Pfizenmaier/Alamy Stock Photo

Some people with obsessive-compulsive disorder must arrange their possessions in particular ways; otherwise, they will experience overwhelming anxiety.

Biological Explanations for OCD Twin studies suggest a strong genetic vulnerability for the disorder (Menzies et al., 2008; Pauls et al., 2014). It is probable that significant interactions between this genetic vulnerability and the environment occur.

Imaging studies provide insight into the patterns of brain activity that accompany obsessions and compulsions (see Figure 14.19). Frontal lobe areas, including the orbitofrontal and anterior cingulate cortices, form circuits with the thalamus and basal ganglia that influence the selection of voluntary behaviors. Abnormal patterns of activity in these circuits is strongly correlated with obsessions and compulsions (Pauls et al., 2014).

The childhood rhyme "Step on a crack, break your mother's back" captures the ineffectiveness of obsessive-compulsive thinking.

The evolutionary perspective suggests that OCD might have its roots in normal grooming and territoriality behaviors that somehow become overly exaggerated in some cases (Rapoport, 1989). Humans who anticipated threats like disease from dirty hands or threats from the perimeters of their territories probably benefited from proactive strategies like hand washing and checking their surroundings (Brune, 2006). Disordered behavior similar to OCD occurs elsewhere in the animal kingdom. Dogs may lick and chew their front paws to the point of causing extensive tissue damage, which can be prevented by giving the dogs the same medications used to treat humans with OCD (Seksel & Lindeman, 2001).

obsessive-compulsive disorder (OCD) A disorder associated with intrusive obsessions and compulsions.

obsession An intrusive, distressing thought.

compulsion Repetitive, ritualistic behavior associated with high anxiety.

Learning Explanations for OCD Learning explanations for OCD focus on the rewarding aspects of compulsions. As pointed out in the previous discussion of operant conditioning, any behavior that produces a positive outcome (reducing anxiety associated with an obsession) is likely

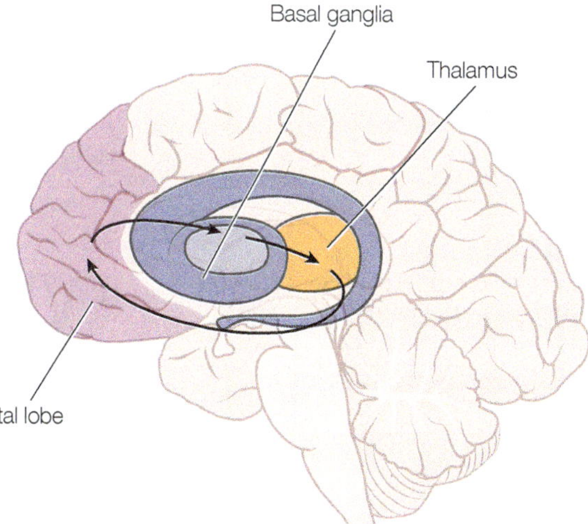

FIGURE **14.19**

Circuits Managing Voluntary Behavior Are Disrupted in Compulsions. An intention to behave is generated in the frontal lobe and passed to the basal ganglia for "approval." The basal ganglia either approves the proposed behavior, sending the message along to the thalamus, or stops the process. The thalamus sends messages back to the frontal lobe for implementation. Compulsive behaviors, like too frequent handwashing, might result from misfiring of these circuits.

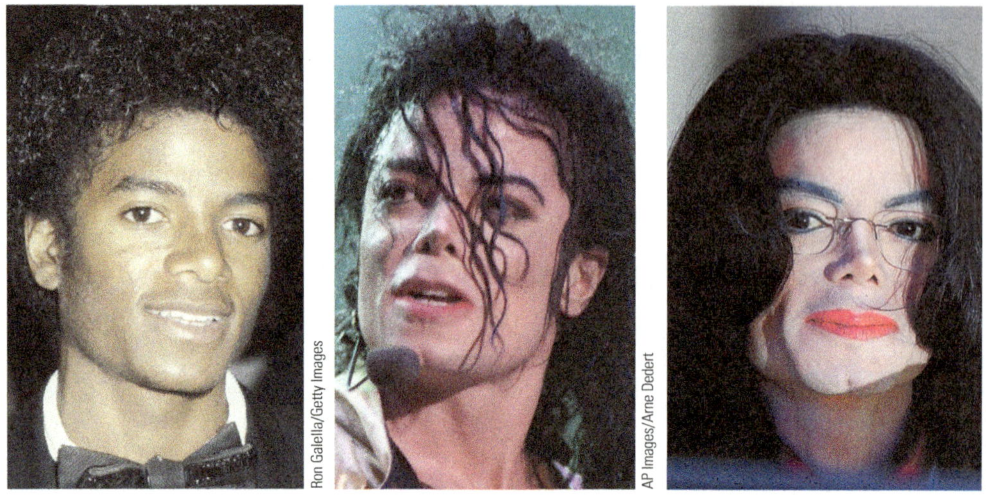

Ron Galella/Getty Images
AP Images/Arne Dedert
Carlo Allegri/Getty Images

Pop entertainer Michael Jackson was described by his mother as "addicted" to plastic surgery. She related that during adolescence, her son became obsessed with his perceived physical flaws. Although Jackson was never formally diagnosed with body dysmorphic disorder, many people with this disorder engage in similar types of body dissatisfaction and repeated requests for plastic surgery.

to be repeated in the future. For example, if hand washing reduced anxiety about germs and disease, hand washing might become progressively more frequent to the point where it would be considered abnormal. The *DSM-5* specifies that engaging in compulsive behavior for more than 1 hour per day is considered abnormal (APA, 2013).

Social Explanations for OCD Culture plays a role in how frequently OCD occurs and what obsessions and compulsions are more likely. Anthropologists have identified interesting parallels between cultural rituals and OCD. For example, many normal cultural rituals involve elements similar to OCD, including washing, special colors, stereotyped actions, and rigid rules (Dulaney & Fiske, 1994). Like the evolutionary perspective, this cultural view suggests that OCD might represent an exaggerated version of normal behaviors.

Body Dysmorphic Disorder

Body dysmorphic disorder (BDD) is characterized by the unrealistic perception of physical flaws. It affects as many as 2% of the population, with slightly more females than males experiencing the disorder (Bjornsson et al., 2010). Suicide rates for BDD are higher than for related conditions, including OCD and anorexia nervosa (Angelakis et al., 2016). Many people with this condition undergo numerous cosmetic surgeries. Others continually try to "perfect" their bodies through bodybuilding activities and other strategies.

Body dysmorphic disorder shows a significant influence of heredity (Feusner et al., 2010). In addition, people with this disorder might not be as out of touch with reality as you might think. Their visual perception of subtle facial distortions appears to be better than normal, so they may be noticing flaws that the rest of us cannot see (Reese et al., 2010).

body dysmorphic disorder (BDD) A disorder characterized by the unrealistic perception of physical flaws.

posttraumatic stress disorder (PTSD) A disorder caused by the experience of trauma, which leads to flashbacks, dreams, hypervigilance, and avoidance of stimuli associated with the traumatic event.

What Is Posttraumatic Stress Disorder?

Posttraumatic stress disorder (PTSD) is the current term used to describe a condition formerly known as *shell shock* or *battle fatigue*. PTSD is unique among disorders listed in the *DSM-5* because it is the only one with a specified cause: To be diagnosed with PTSD, you must have experienced trauma (APA, 2013). Although combat, especially hand-to-hand combat, is still recognized as one of the most likely experiences leading to PTSD, we now understand that other types of trauma may produce the same results (Insel, 2007). PTSD may follow the experience of automobile accidents, assaults, abuse, and natural disasters.

Getmilitaryphotos/Shutterstock.com

PTSD symptoms include hypervigilance, avoidance of stimuli associated with the trauma, emotional numbing, and reexperiencing in the form of repetitive, intrusive thoughts, flashbacks, and dreams about the traumatic event (APA, 2013). The last thing that a person in this situation wants to do is to relive the traumatic event, so these symptoms are upsetting. Children with PTSD often reenact the traumatic event in their play (Cohen et al., 2010). In other words, they may play "terrorist attack," "car crash," or "tsunami," possibly in an effort to reduce their fear. This reenactment play can have either positive or negative effects on the child. Children whose play included a reworking of the traumatic event (revenge or a happy ending) were less disturbed than children whose play was repetitive, without resolution.

PTSD affects between 3% and 4% of the adult population in the United States every year (Kessler et al., 2007). After large-scale traumatic events, health workers typically expect about 10% of the population to develop PTSD (Kessler et al., 1996; Shalev et al., 2019). For example, more than 12% of lower Manhattan residents developed PTSD following the terrorist attacks of 9/11 (DiGrande et al., 2008). Children are more vulnerable than adults, with 25% developing PTSD following automobile accidents in which they were injured, compared to 15% of their parents (de Vries et al., 1999). Between 8.5% and 14% of combat soldiers serving in Iraq and Afghanistan experienced severe impairment because of symptoms of PTSD after returning home, and up to 31% experienced some impairment (Thomas et al., 2010).

Biological Explanations for PTSD

Genetic studies in over 20,000 individuals suggests that PTSD is heritable and that its genetic profile overlaps significantly with schizophrenia (Duncan et al., 2018).

Brain imaging studies consistently show that PTSD is correlated with smaller hippocampal volume (Bremner et al., 2002; Bossini et al., 2008 see ● Figure 14.20). This leaves us with two competing hypotheses: Are people with a naturally smaller hippocampus more vulnerable to PTSD? Or is there something about the experience of trauma, such as the effect of stress hormones, that is toxic to the hippocampus? Both hypotheses seem reasonable. However, current data seem more consistent with the idea that smaller hippocampal volume is a risk factor for PTSD rather than an outcome of the disorder (Szeszko et al., 2018).

A disturbance in GABA activity (the major inhibitory neurochemical in the cortex; see Chapter 4) is associated with PTSD (Reuveni et al., 2018). Naturally occurring

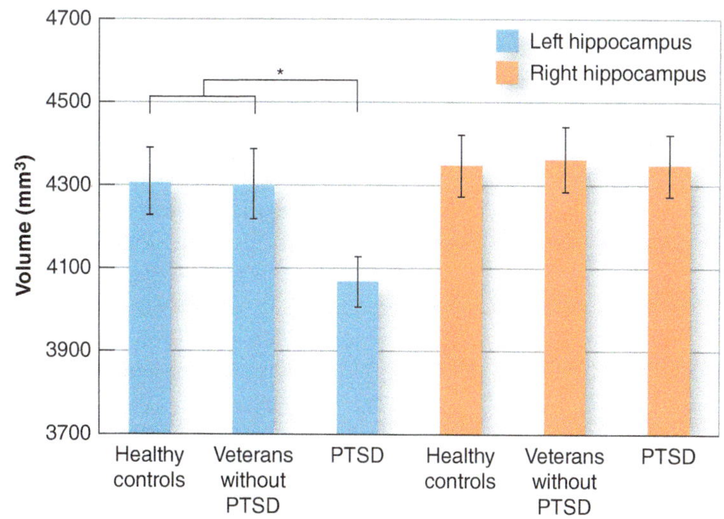

FIGURE **14.20**

Hippocampal Volume Is Reduced in PTSD. Volume in the left hippocampus is reduced in combat veterans with PTSD compared to healthy controls who have not experienced combat and combat-exposed veterans who do not have PTSD. Although it is possible that the stress related to PTSD might damage the hippocampus, it is more likely that smaller hippocampal volume is a risk factor for PTSD.

Source: Adapted from S. Van Rooij et al. (2015). "Smaller Hippocampal Volume As a Vulnerability Factor for the Persistence of Post-traumatic Stress Disorder," *Psychological Medicine, 45*(13), 2737–2746. doi: 10.1017/S0033291715000707

benzodiazepines and benzodiazepine medications (tranquilizers such as Valium) interact with GABA systems to reduce anxiety. Individuals with PTSD appear to have different responses to benzodiazepines than healthy controls do (Reuveni et al., 2018). Disturbed benzodiazepine systems might explain not only the heightened vigilance seen in PTSD but also the unfortunate tendency for people to self-medicate for PTSD with alcohol (Jakupcak et al., 2010). Alcohol reduces anxiety using biological mechanisms similar to those of the benzodiazepines.

Learning Explanations for PTSD

Learning, and classical conditioning in particular, contribute to the symptoms of PTSD. Individuals with PTSD show conditioned responses to stimuli associated with the traumatic event. Combat veterans with PTSD seem particularly sensitive to smells such as burning rubber and diesel (Rothbaum et al., 2010). Individuals with PTSD show increased generalization to conditioned fear stimuli, suggesting that over time, they will become responsive to more stimuli, not less (Kaczkurkin et al., 2016).

The effects of prior experience with trauma depend on the type of trauma involved. Risk of PTSD is higher as a result of the re-occurrence of physical violence, but actually reduced by the re-occurrence of sectarian violence and combat (Kessler et al., 2017).

Social and Cultural Explanations for PTSD

Social and cultural factors play significant roles in the development of PTSD. People reporting low social support in the 6 months before 9/11 were twice as likely to be diagnosed with PTSD as people who reported strong social support during this period (Galea et al., 2002). Cultural factors also influence the likelihood of PTSD. Following 9/11, PTSD was more common in New York City residents of some ethnicities than others, affecting 13.4% of Hispanics, 9.3% of African Americans, 6.5% of White Americans, and 3.2% of Asian Americans (Galea et al., 2002).

What Are Dissociative Disorders?

Dissociative disorders feature disruptions in a person's identity, memory, or consciousness (APA, 2013).

Dissociative disorders take several forms. Dissociative amnesia occurs when a person forgets important information about specific events, often following a frightening or traumatic event. In dissociative fugue, people become confused over their identity and often combine this loss of identity with sudden travel and the assumption of a new identity. These situations typically last a few hours or days, but not longer periods of time (Kopelman, 2002).

Depersonalization or derealization disorder occurs when a person experiences strong feelings of unreality about either the self or the surrounding environment (APA, 2013). People might feel as though they are watching their behavior from outside their bodies or that the world is dreamlike. However, they retain their ability to understand that their feelings are not realistic. In other words, they feel as if they're outside their bodies, but they don't believe that this is really happening.

Possibly the most controversial of the dissociative disorders is dissociative identity disorder, which was previously known as multiple personality disorder. According to the *DSM-5,* dissociative identity disorder is characterized by the experience of two distinct "personality states" (APA, 2013).

Dissociative identity disorder experienced a spike in popularity as a diagnosis in the mid-1990s but has since dropped in frequency. Media attention might have contributed to the frequency with which this disorder was diagnosed. Before the popularization of patients

dissociative disorder A disorder characterized by disruptions in a person's identity, memory, or consciousness.

Esther Lin/Zuffa LLC/Getty Images

Heisman Trophy winner, NFL star, and mixed martial arts fighter Herschel Walker has spoken about his experience with dissociative identity disorder to encourage military veterans to seek help for psychological disorders.

named Sybil and Eve in books and films, few cases of dissociative identity disorder had ever been described in the scientific literature. Following this media interest, thousands of cases were diagnosed, primarily in the United States and Canada. Responses to extreme stress frequently include detachment, numbness, or altered memory and cognition, but this is quite different from the development of additional identities. Well-meaning therapists can misinterpret these stress symptoms as dissociative identity disorder and, worse yet, suggest this possibility to their clients. People diagnosed with dissociative identity disorder, like those with other dissociative disorders, score very high on tests of suggestibility that predict a person's susceptibility to hypnosis, as well as in measures of being likely to fantasize (Giesbrecht et al., 2010). These findings imply that these people may have difficulty distinguishing between reality and fantasy and might accept a therapist's suggestion without considering it critically.

What Are Somatic Symptom Disorder and Related Disorders?

Somatic symptom disorder is diagnosed when people are unusually concerned and preoccupied with chronic somatic symptoms (APA, 2013). The *DSM-5* notes that these patients spend excessive amounts of time thinking about the seriousness of their symptoms, which is accompanied by a high level of anxiety. To the patient, the somatic symptoms appear quite serious and often disabling. Among the different symptoms are vague pain complaints, gastrointestinal upset, sexual problems, amnesia, breathing problems, or unexplained sensory or motor problems. People with somatic symptoms usually visit physicians frequently, report high numbers of physical complaints, and are at risk of becoming dependent on pain medication. They can become preoccupied with their health and often insist on unnecessary medical tests and procedures. At the same time, this category might raise the risk that people with genuine yet poorly understood medical conditions might be inappropriately diagnosed with a psychological disorder (Frances, 2013).

somatic symptom disorder A disorder characterized by having one or more chronic somatic symptoms about which a person is excessively concerned, preoccupied or fearful.

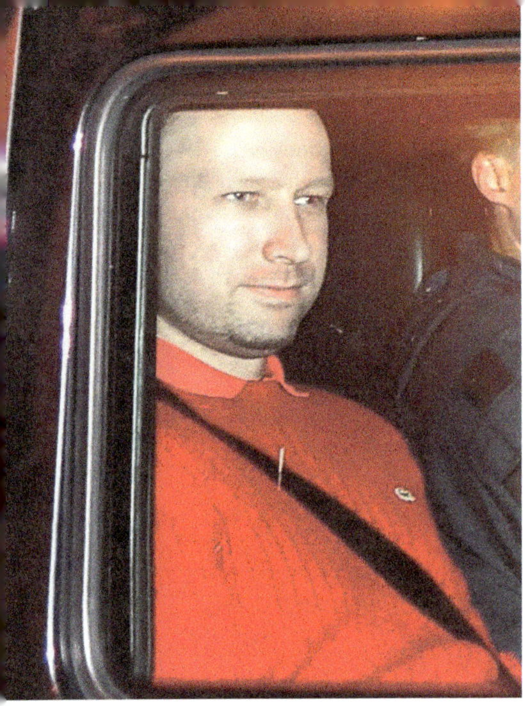

JON ARE BERG JACOBSEN/AFTENPOSTE/European Pressphoto Agency/OSLO/Norway/Newscom

Anders Behring Breivik killed 8 people with a bomb before shooting another 69 people at a nearby youth camp on July 22, 2011. Police told reporters that during a reenactment of the shootings, Breivik "didn't show any remorse." Although we don't know whether Breivik has been diagnosed with antisocial personality disorder, a callous lack of empathy and remorse is typical of people with this diagnosis.

What Are Personality Disorders?

A **personality disorder** is characterized by impairments in identity, in personality traits, and in establishment of empathy or intimacy. Personality disorders cannot be diagnosed in people under the age of 18. To illustrate this category of disorders, we will now look at three of the ten types of personality disorders in greater detail: antisocial personality disorder (ASPD), borderline personality disorder (BPD), and narcissistic personality disorder (NPD).

Antisocial Personality Disorder (ASPD)

Antisocial personality disorder (ASPD) is characterized by a "pervasive pattern of disregard for and violation of the rights of others" (APA, 2013, p. 659). Individuals with this disorder have little regard for normal social rules and conventions. Their behavior is frequently risky and irresponsible, and they form shallow, fleeting relationships with others.

ASPD is quite similar to the term psychopath, which has not been used by the *DSM* system since its third edition was published in 1980. Criteria for ASPD in the *DSM* system focuses on a person's behaviors, especially criminal behaviors, whereas the term psychopath implies flaws in the person's consistent traits or character (Hare, 2006). Between 0.2% and 3.3% of the population experiences ASPD in a given year (APA, 2013). Hare (2006) has estimated the number of psychopaths in the United States to be approximately 1%.

Most individuals with ASPD or psychopathy do not engage in outright criminal behavior, and not all criminals have ASPD or psychopathy. Noncriminal individuals with ASPD were easily recruited by placing a newspaper ad calling for "charming, aggressive, carefree people who are impulsively irresponsible but are good at handling people and at looking after number one" (Widom, 1978, p. 72).

Antisocial personality disorder has a heritability of approximately 50% (Ferguson, 2010). A genetic influence on a trait usually implies that the trait provides some advantage, but how can this be the case for a tendency toward antisocial behavior? One suggestion is that fearlessness characterizes both heroes and people with antisocial behavior (Lykken, 1982). Having heroic people in your population might offset the negative impact of having some antisocial people.

People with ASPD show reduced volume and activity in the prefrontal cortex (Glenn et al., 2013). Orbitofrontal abnormalities occur at higher rates among murderers and those diagnosed with ASPD (Davidson et al., 2000). As observed in Chapter 4, damage to the frontal areas of the cortex often leads to poor judgment and impulsivity. In one representative case, two adults who had been raised in stable, middle-class homes but who had experienced damage to the orbitofrontal cortex in infancy both showed a profound inability to understand the consequences of their negative behavior (Anderson et al., 1999). They engaged in stealing, lying, and aggressive behavior and were poor parents.

A relative lack of response to emotions, especially those of others, might also contribute to antisocial behavior disorder. While undergoing brain imaging, people with ASPD, unlike the control participants in a study, showed little activation of parts of the brain that are usually active during emotional processing when listening to words such as *torture, rape,* or *cancer* (Kiehl et al., 2001; Hare, 2006). Participants also were shown neutral scenes and rather gruesome images of murder scenes. Again, the people with ASPD showed different patterns of brain activation than did the typical control participants. In particular, the amygdalae of people with ASPD showed relatively little activity. As discussed in Chapters 4 and 7, the amygdala normally participates in the recognition of fear and other negative emotions in others. Other research indicates that children with antisocial tendencies are impaired in their ability to identify expressions of sadness and fear in others, a finding consistent with lower activity in the amygdala (Blair et al., 2001).

A genetic predisposition is likely to interact with child maltreatment, especially physical abuse, in cases of ASPD (DeLisi et al., 2019). As mentioned previously in this textbook, child maltreatment interacts with a genetic predisposition to violent antisocial behavior (Caspi et al., 2003).

personality disorder A disorder characterized by impairments in identity, in personality traits, and in establishment of empathy or intimacy.

antisocial personality disorder (ASPD) A disorder characterized by an unusual lack of remorse, empathy, or regard for normal social rules and conventions.

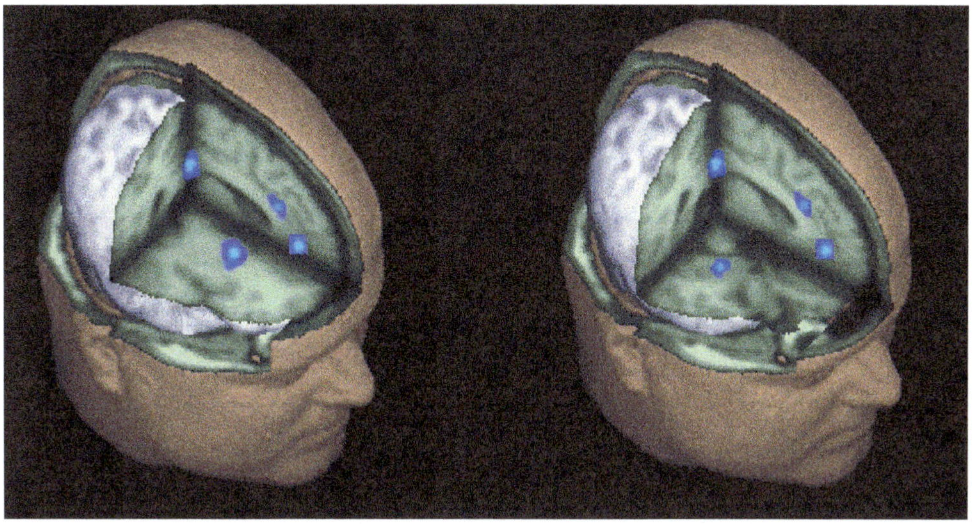
(a) (b)

The areas marked in blue showed less activity in criminal psychopaths than in noncriminal control participants in a study during the processing of negative emotional words like *rape* or *torture*. These areas are associated with emotional processing and include (a) the cingulate cortex and basal ganglia and (b) the hippocampus and amygdala. The failure of negative emotional stimuli to produce normal levels of arousal might allow the psychopath to engage in harmful behaviors without experiencing normal remorse or empathy.

Source: Reprinted from K. A. Kiehl et al. (2001). "Limbic Abnormalities in Affective Processing by Criminal Psychopaths as Revealed by Functional Magnetic Resonance Imaging," *Biological Psychiatry*, 50(9), 677–684. doi: 10.1016/s0006-3223(01)01222-7

Borderline Personality Disorder (BPD)

The term **borderline personality disorder (BPD)** originated from the idea that the characteristics of this disorder fell on the "border" between anxiety and psychosis.

According to the *DSM-5*, BPD is characterized by instability in interpersonal relationships, self-image, and emotion. Individuals with this disorder are extremely sensitive to perceived interpersonal slights, engage in frantic efforts to avoid abandonment, either real or imagined, and may behave in impulsive, self-destructive ways (see ● Figure 14.21). Suicide and self-mutilating behaviors, which were discussed in Chapter 8, are more common among people with this disorder. Relationships are often initially intense and idealized, but if the individual perceives any slight rejection, love can turn to anger quickly.

Borderline personality disorder affects about 2% of the population, with women outnumbering men by a factor of 3 to 1 (Skodol & Bender, 2003; Gunderson et al., 2018). People with BPD appear to be vulnerable to a number of additional disorders, including bipolar disorder, substance abuse, eating disorders, and other personality disorders.

Borderline personality disorder is five times more common among close relatives with the disorder than among the general population, suggesting a biological predisposition (APA, 2013). However, as many as 70% of individuals with this diagnosis have histories of abandonment, neglect, and physical or sexual abuse, or both types of abuse (Hunt, 2007). These findings suggest that traumatic experiences interact with a possible genetic predisposition to produce disordered behavior (Gunderson et al., 2018).

borderline personality disorder (BPD) A disorder characterized by instability in interpersonal relationships, self-image, and emotion.

narcissistic personality disorder (NPD) A disorder characterized by grandiosity, need for admiration, and low empathy.

Narcissistic Personality Disorder (NPD)

As defined by the *DSM-5*, **narcissistic personality disorder (NPD)** is characterized by grandiosity, need for admiration, and lack of empathy (APA, 2013). Renewed interest in NPD has

PSYCHOLOGY AS A HUB SCIENCE

The "Dark Side" of Leadership

AT A 2002 CONVENTION OF LAW ENFORCEMENT OFFICERS in Canada, psychologist Robert Hare (2002) made a startling suggestion. With slides in the background depicting convicted WorldCom chief executive officer Bernard Ebbers and Enron chief financial officer Andrew Fastow, Hare asked his audience why law enforcement personnel are screened for psychopathy, but not executives responsible for millions of dollars of people's savings and retirement funds.

When we hear the term *psychopath,* most of us think of characters like Hannibal Lecter from *The Silence of the Lambs.* However, Hare and other psychologists suggest that psychopaths are more likely to be the people next door, your coworkers, and maybe even your friends and relatives.

Psychopathy is one-third of a cluster of "Dark Triad" characteristics that can be found in people in important leadership positions, along with narcissism and Machiavellianism. The latter term refers to coldness, dishonesty, and calculated manipulation of others in order to meet one's goals (Paulhus & Williams, 2002). Narcissism and Machiavellianism are positively associated with objective career success, although psychopathy is not (Furtner et al., 2017).

Dark Triad leaders do not express the three traits evenly. Many leadership positions are occupied by primarily narcissistic leaders, as their narcissism drives them to find appreciation and acceptance (Maccoby, 2003). Narcissistic leaders are usually perceived to be charismatic. Both narcissistic and Machiavellian leaders embrace power and tend to act in authoritarian ways. Psychopathic leaders are unpredictable and impulsive, and typically have a negative impact on members of the organization and its efficacy (Boddy, 2017).

From an evolutionary perspective, we can see how the dominance exerted by Dark Triad personalities could lead to some success. A remaining question, however, is why we confuse these traits with "leadership" and select leaders personifying Dark Triad traits when they can be so destructive and counterproductive. ■

Stephen Chernin/Getty Images

Bernie Madoff built one of the most successful businesses on Wall Street and served as the nonexecutive chairman of the NASDAQ stock market before being convicted of perpetrating one of the largest financial frauds in U.S. history. Psychologists Paul Babiak and Robert Hare suggest that it might be difficult to distinguish between tough corporate leaders and those with antisocial tendencies.

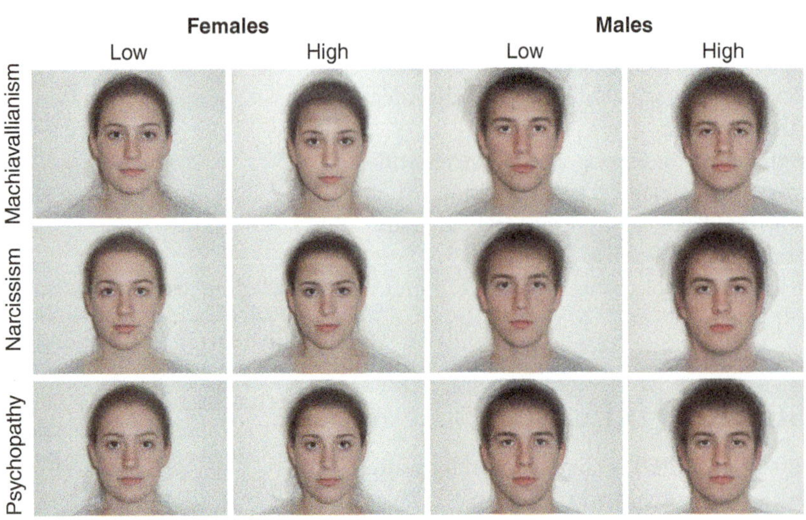

Elsevier

The "Dark Triad" characteristics of Machiavellianism, narcissism, and psychopathy commonly occur together. We apparently do a pretty good job of detecting Dark Triad traits in other people simply by viewing their appearance (Holtzman, 2011).

Source: From N. S. Holtzman (2011). "Facing a Psychopath: Detecting the Dark Triad from Emotionally Neutral Faces, Using Prototypes from the Personality Faceaurus," *Journal of Research in Personality, 45*(6), 648–654. doi: 19.1016/j.jrp.2011.09.002

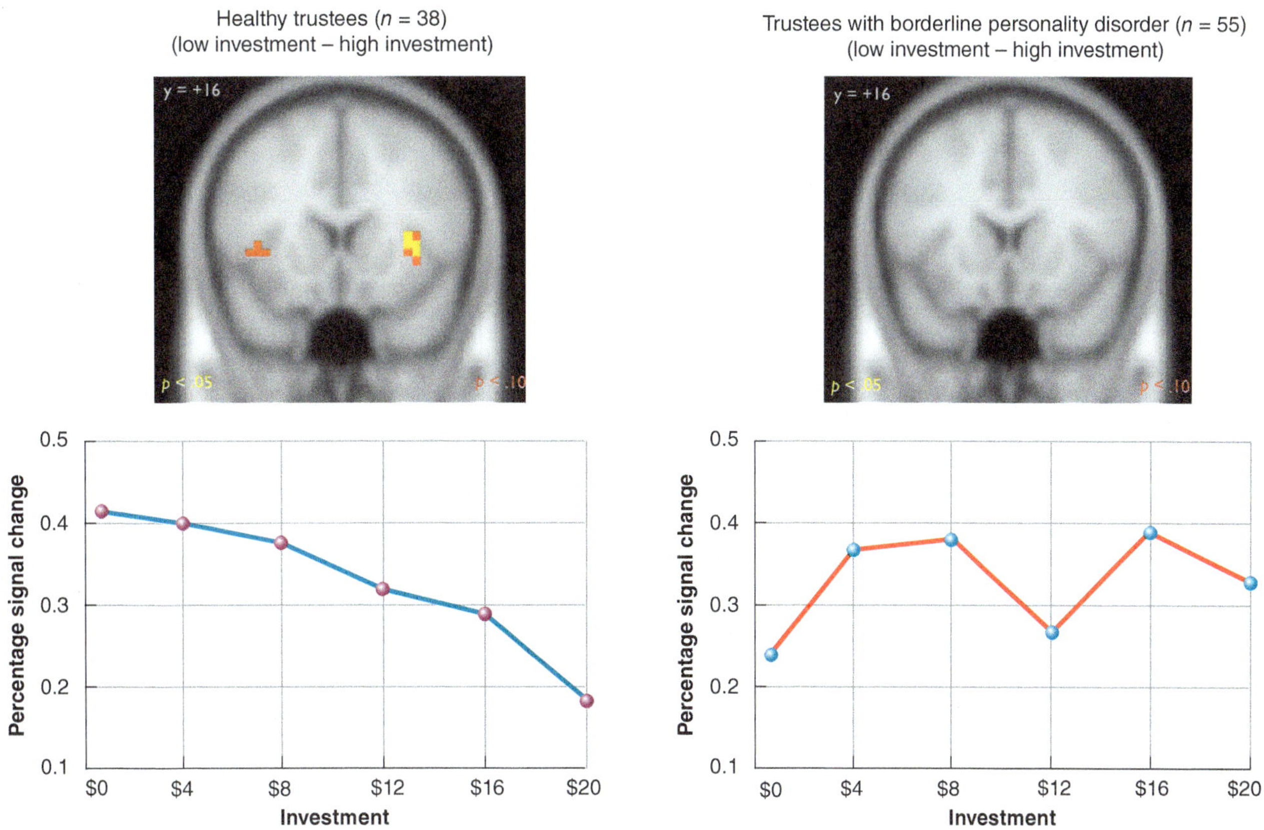

FIGURE **14.21**

Abnormal Responses to Trust in Borderline Personality Disorder. Not only do people with borderline personality disorder perform differently than healthy controls in experimental activities measuring trust, but their brain activity during a trust game is also different. In healthy study participants, activity in the anterior insula decreases when an offer is higher or fairer. In the participants with borderline personality disorder, insula activity did not correspond well with the offers that they received. This inability to respond to trust normally might explain some difficulties these people experience in building healthy relationships with others.

Source: From B. King-Casa et al. (2008). "The Rupture and Repair of Cooperation in Borderline Personality Disorder," *Science, 321*, 806–810. doi: 10.1126/science.1156902.

occurred in part due to questions about possible intersections between narcissism and social media use (McCain & Campbell, 2016). Other psychologists are tracking narcissistic traits as a function of age, with younger individuals showing more narcissism than older adults (Twenge & Campbell, 2009).

Although the *DSM-5* has only one category for NPD, psychologists continue to debate the relationship between two apparent subtypes—the grandiose narcissist and the vulnerable narcissist (Miller et al., 2011, 2017). The grandiose narcissist tends to show inflated views of self-worth, aggressiveness, and dominance, while the vulnerable narcissist combines inflated views of self-worth with insecurity, defensiveness, and negative emotions. According to Miller et al. (2011, 2017), the *DSM* emphasizes the grandiose version, which might result in clinicians being less aware of the vulnerable version among their clients. One possible solution is to use trait models like the Big Five traits, described in Chapter 12, to distinguish between the two patterns. For example, the grandiose narcissist is extroverted, while the vulnerable narcissist is shy and neurotic.

Narcissistic personality disorder combines grandiosity, need for attention, and low empathy. The social media phenomenon of the selfie is the perfect outlet for people with narcissistic tendencies (Weiser, 2015).

Chris Rout/Alamy Stock Photo

We are not certain how narcissistic behavior develops. The personality disorder itself is not to be diagnosed officially until adulthood, but the roots of narcissism might be found during childhood. Disturbances in attachment between parents and child are common in individuals with NPD (Yakeley, 2018). Narcissism might be the outgrowth of self-esteem strategies in the child (Thomaes et al., 2009). As such, narcissism might be simply an extreme version of the impression management and search for esteem that are considered normal in children and teens.

Narcissistic traits have been shown to be somewhat heritable, and they possibly have their beginnings in basic temperament (Thomaes et al., 2009). Chapter 12 discussed *reactivity,* or a child's tendency to either approach or avoid a stimulus. The pattern of behavior seen in the

EXPERIENCING PSYCHOLOGY

Assessing Narcissism

AS YOU HAVE READ IN THIS CHAPTER, narcissism is characterized by grandiosity, entitlement, and low empathy. While this doesn't sound very attractive, people who score high in narcissistic traits are also likely to score high on measures of creativity, happiness, and self-esteem, while scoring low on measures of anxiety and depression (Konrath et al., 2014).

Measuring narcissism is difficult because of the possible dual nature of this trait. In addition to the grandiose behaviors, many individuals show a vulnerable, hypersensitive quality, which makes them shy and fragile in the face of criticism. As a result, the many self-report scales for measuring narcissism do not always agree well with one another. What we present here are two short scales of narcissism, the Hypersensitive Narcissism Scale (Hendin & Cheek, 1997) and the Single-Item Narcissism Scale (Konrath et al., 2014). As you complete the scales, your results are more likely to be meaningful to you if you answer the items as honestly as possible (attempting to avoid social desirability effects). See if the two scales provide you with consistent results. Do you think these scales are valid?

Hypersensitive Narcissism Scale

Place a check in the appropriate box, and then add your scores for the 10 items.

	Very uncharacteristic or untrue; strongly disagree 1	2	3	4	Very characteristic or true; strongly agree 5
I can become entirely absorbed in thinking about my personal affairs, my health, my cares, or my relations to others.					
My feelings are easily hurt by ridicule or by the slighting remarks of others.					
When I enter a room, I often become self-conscious and feel that the eyes of others are upon me.					
I dislike sharing the credit of an achievement with others.					

grandiose narcissist is consistent with approach, while the vulnerable narcissist seems to show both approach and avoidant tendencies. As discussed in Chapter 12, temperament quickly interacts with environmental factors, particularly those in the surrounding social setting. Parents who overpraise their children might produce habituation to praise, leading a child to seek constantly higher levels of positive feedback. Cold parents with very high expectations for their children might also stimulate narcissistic behaviors as children attempt to protect themselves while craving positive feedback from others as compensation.

Understanding the roots of narcissistic behavior will help clinicians develop more effective interventions, which will be discussed in more detail in Chapter 15 on treatments. In the meantime, you have the opportunity to assess yourself for narcissism using several standardized instruments.

	Very uncharacteristic or untrue; strongly disagree 1	2	3	4	Very characteristic or true; strongly agree 5
I am appreciated by at least one of those present.					
I feel that I am temperamentally different from most people.					
I often interpret the remarks of others in a personal way.					
I easily become wrapped up in my own interests and forget the existence of others.					
I feel that I have enough on my hands without worrying about other people's troubles.					
I am secretly "put out" when other people come to me with their troubles, asking me for my time and sympathy.					

Add up all your scores. The totals can range from 5 to 50. There are no "right" or "wrong" answers on these types of scales, nor do we have a cutoff value that absolutely determines a person's status as a narcissist. The mean reported for college students is generally about 29.

The Single-Item Narcissism Scale

To what extent do you agree with this statement: "I am a narcissist." (Note: The word *narcissist* means an egotistical, self-focused, and vain person.) ■

1	2	3	4	5	6	7
Not very true of me						Very true of me

Interpersonal Relationships

The Clinical Perspective

Paul Burns/Getty Images

Both soldiers and their families are changed by war, and their reunions, while happy, are not always smooth. Strong social support is a critical variable in the development and course of PTSD resulting from combat.

HOW DOES PTSD AFFECT FAMILIES?

THERE ARE HIDDEN COSTS IN WAR. Soldiers, most of whom are about the same ages as those of you reading this textbook, are permanently changed by their experiences in ways that are often difficult for those of us who have not shared those experiences to understand. They have faced the fear of death and the realities of injury, held dying friends in their arms, and felt guilty that their lives were spared.

Some cope with these challenges better than others. As stated earlier in this chapter, between 8.5% and 14% of U.S. veterans serving in Iraq and Afghanistan experience severe PTSD, and up to 31% experience some impairment (Thomas et al., 2010). Veterans usually come home to their loved ones and families, who are also affected by the soldiers' combat experiences in what has been called secondary traumatization (Galovski & Lyons, 2004). Although not directly threatened, the soldiers' families have had challenges of their own as they cope with their helpless fear of loss. Understanding that bad news comes to the front door in the person of a military chaplain makes each FedEx delivery or visit by a neighbor a heart-pounding experience. The spouses who have learned over the course of a year to run households independently and balance the checkbook might not want to share some of these responsibilities with their returning partners.

Among the biggest challenges for veterans with PTSD and their families are the results of having symptoms of hyperarousal, emotional numbing, and stimulus avoidance (Monson et al., 2009). Although veterans without PTSD have the same rates of intimate aggression as the general population, the risk of intimate aggression is much higher in those with PTSD, and the severity of symptoms predicts the likelihood of aggression. Because of the emotional numbing and avoidance symptoms of PTSD, returning veterans do not engage in much self-disclosure, or discussion of their thoughts, feelings, and experiences. As discussed in Chapter 13, self-disclosure is an important component of intimacy.

A soldier's existing level of social support is one of the strongest protections against the initial development of PTSD (Brewin et al., 2000). After trauma, a person with PTSD recovers more quickly with strong social support. Unfortunately, with ongoing PTSD, that social support tends to diminish as the symptoms of PTSD take their toll on relationships (Kaniasty & Norris, 2008).

By recognizing the importance of the larger social network to PTSD, psychologists can begin to develop more effective preventions and interventions that take the entire social system into account, not just the individual with PTSD symptoms. ■

Psychology Takes on Real-World Problems

Is COVID-19 Making Cases of OCD Worse?

The most common form of obsessive-compulsive disorder (OCD) combines obsessions about contamination and compulsive hand washing. In addition, patients with this disorder often relapse at times of stress. How are these patients coping during the COVID-19 pandemic?

Many of the preventive measures recommended by public health officials might interact with OCD, leading to gradually worsening symptoms (Banerjee, 2020). Messages about hand washing can lead to increased frequency, while descriptions of "proper" washing technique can promote more ritualistic behavior. The patient might start justifying hand washing behavior as due to recommendations rather than due to the disorder. Media reports of the spread of the disease and concern from family and friends can lead to further fears of contamination. Stocking up on soaps and sanitizers could lead to the closely related hoarding disorder.

What policies might need to be adjusted in response to this issue? Banerjee (2020) recommends that health care providers be educated about the increased risk of OCD and how to recognize its symptoms. It might also be useful for the public to be made more aware of OCD and symptoms that indicate the need for counseling. ■

katunes pcnok/Shutterstock.com

Frequent reminders to engage in important preventive measures for coping with COVID-19, like handwashing, might contribute to the worsening of symptoms for some individuals with OCD.

SUMMARY 14.3 Anxiety Disorders, Obsessive-Compulsive Disorder (OCD), Body Dysmorphic Disorder, and Posttraumatic Stress Disorder (PTSD)

Disorder	Symptoms	Possible Causal Factors Under Investigation
Phobia 	• Excessive fear of an object or situation	• Exaggeration of normal caution • Classical conditioning • Cognitions about fear stimulus • Collectivist cultures emphasizing shame
Panic disorder 	• Repeated panic attacks, accompanied by excessive worry about having more panic attacks	• Possible abnormality in orexin function • Cognitions regarding symptoms • Expectations and embarrassment • Cultural influences
Generalized anxiety disorder (GAD) 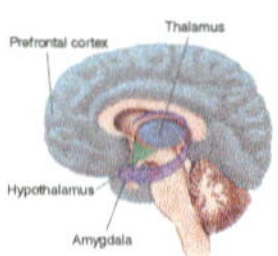	• Excessive anxiety for six months that is not correlated with specific objects or situations	• Genetic predisposition • Stress • Fearful schemas • Low socioeconomic status • Disruptions in social connectivity
Obsessive-compulsive disorder (OCD) 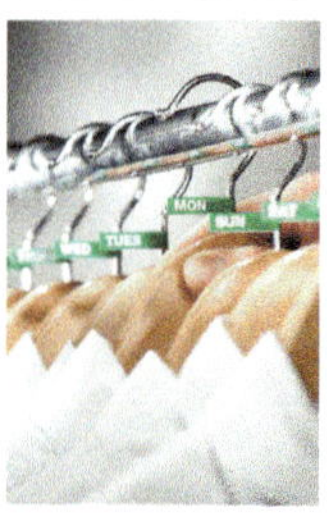	• Intrusive, repetitious, and anxiety-producing thoughts and behaviors	• Genetic predisposition • Low serotonin activity • Prefrontal and basal ganglia activity • Extension of grooming and territorial behaviors • Rewarding aspects of compulsions • Extension of cultural rituals
Body dysmorphic disorder 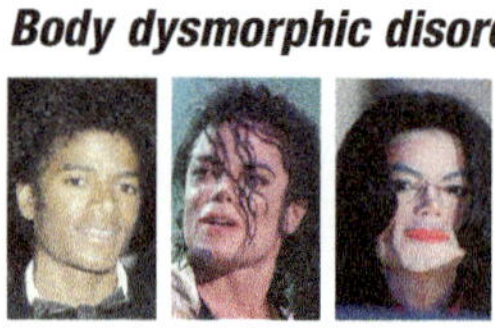	• Unrealistic perception of physical flaws	• Genetic predisposition • Superior perception of facial distortions
Posttraumatic stress disorder (PTSD) 	• Exposure to a traumatic event, followed by flashbacks, hypervigilance, and nightmares	• Hippocampus and prefrontal cortex • Benzodiazepine receptors • Classical conditioning • Social support

Credits: Top row—Shane Wilson Link/Shutterstock.com; Second row—Ryan McGinnis/Alamy Stock Photo; Fourth row—Randal Pfizenmaier/Alamy Stock Photo; Fifth row—Left to right: Ron Galella/Getty Images, AP Images/Arne Dedert, Carlo Allegri/Getty Images; Bottom row—Getmilitaryphotos/Shutterstock.com.

KEY TERMS The Language of Psychological Science

Be sure that you can define these terms and use them correctly.

abnormal psychology, p. 551
agoraphobia, p. 579
antisocial personality disorder (ASPD), p. 586
anxiety disorder, p. 576
attention deficit hyperactivity disorder (ADHD), p. 558
autism spectrum disorder (ASD), p. 555
bipolar disorder, p. 567
body dysmorphic disorder (BDD), p. 582
borderline personality disorder (BPD), p. 587
comorbid, p. 551
compulsion, p. 581
delusion, p. 562
Diagnostic and Statistical Manual of Mental Disorders (DSM), p. 553
diathesis–stress model, p. 573
dissociative disorder, p. 584
generalized anxiety disorder (GAD), p. 580
hallucination, p. 562
learned helplessness, p. 569
major depressive disorder (MDD), p. 568
mania, p. 567
narcissistic personality disorder (NPD), p. 587
obsession, p. 581
obsessive-compulsive disorder (OCD), p. 581
panic attack, p. 578
panic disorder, p. 578
personality disorder, p. 586
posttraumatic stress disorder (PTSD), p. 582
schizophrenia, p. 561
social anxiety disorder, p. 577
somatic symptom disorder, p. 585
specific phobia, p. 576

activity. The red and yellow areas are considerably more active than the green, blue, and dark areas. When people with OCD who have been treated with CBT are compared to people treated with medication, their PET scans show the same decrease in activity in the basal ganglia. Because medication can produce unwanted side effects and is not effective for all people, it is fortunate that alternate therapies are available.

This chapter will explore a number of approaches that have been used to improve the situations of people with psychological disorders. Some represent a variety of psychological treatments, like the behavioral approach to OCD discussed here, while others take the form of medication and other biological treatments. The effects of these treatments might have more in common than you think, as in the case of the changes in brain activity that result from the psychological and biological treatments of OCD. Just as we have argued for the advantages of integrating psychological perspectives to understand behavior and mental processes, the field of clinical psychology is recognizing the benefits of applying multiple perspectives to the treatment of psychological disorders.

How Do Psychologists Provide Therapy?

Chapter 14 explored a diverse range of problems that can contribute to personal and interpersonal distress. Once considered virtually untreatable, many of these disorders respond positively to the treatments available today. Unfortunately, many people with disorders still do not seek help, possibly because of stigma related to having a psychological problem or a lack of awareness that effective help is available (see Figure 15.1). Many people diagnosed with schizophrenia 60 years ago faced a discouraging future of institutionalization and little improvement (see Figure 15.2). About 30% of contemporary patients with schizophrenia do not seem to respond to available treatments, but the other 70% experience some relief from their troubling symptoms (Bobo & Meltzer, 2010).

At the same time, significant challenges remain. An analysis of data from Australia, Canada, the United Kingdom, and the United States between 1990 and 2015 showed that in spite of substantial increases in the provision of treatment, primarily in the form of antidepressant medication, rates of major depressive disorder (MDD) and anxiety disorders did not decrease (Jorm et al., 2017). This lack of progress might result from a failure to provide quality care to those in greatest need, as well as a lack of attention to preventive strategies. The researchers report no evidence suggesting an increase in risk factors or the effects of greater public awareness. Given the implications of psychological disorders in terms of lost functionality and quality of life, improving preventive and treatment strategies should be given high priority.

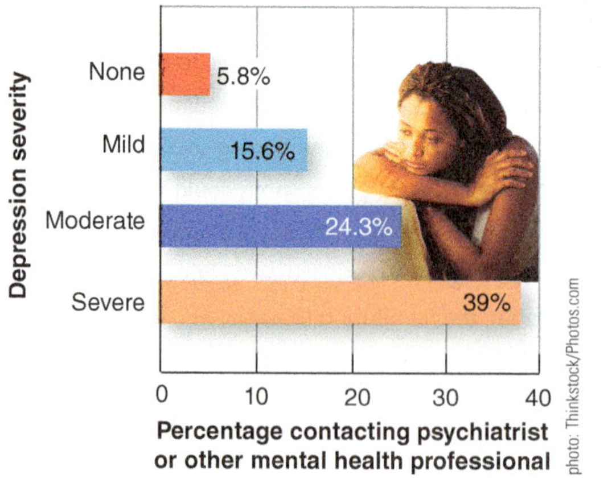

FIGURE **15.1**

Many People with Psychological Disorders Do Not Receive Care. As symptoms of depression become more severe, people become more likely to obtain treatment from a psychiatrist or mental health professional, which would include clinical psychologists. It is difficult to tell whether the remaining individuals receive no care or are seen by their family physicians or other health care providers.

Source: Adapted from L. A. Pratt & D. J. Brody (2008). "Depression in the United States Household Population, 2005–2006," *NCHS Data Brief No. 7*. Washington, DC: U.S. Department of Health and Human Services. Retrieved from http://www.cdc.gov /nchs/data/databriefs/db07 .pdf.

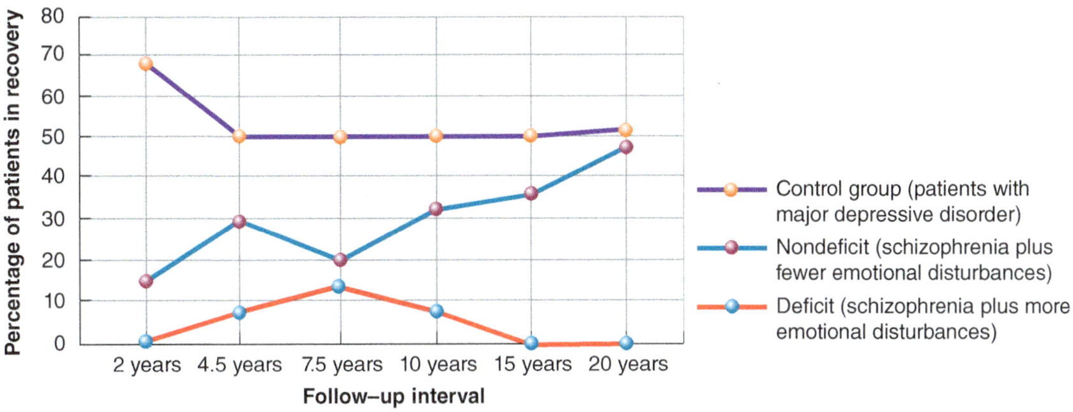

FIGURE **15.2**

Recovery in Schizophrenia. Scientists are making progress in identifying which patients with schizophrenia are more responsive to current treatments. A deficit group of patients differed from a nondeficit group primarily in having more emotional disturbances. *Recovery* was defined strictly in this study as no psychiatric hospitalizations, no major symptoms, and at least half-time work or the equivalent level of functioning. In a 20-year study of the patients' outcomes, using a group of patients diagnosed with depression as a comparison group, the nondeficit group made more progress than the deficit group. Identifying which patients respond to existing treatments will help researchers and health care providers develop more effective treatment plans for individuals.

Source: Adapted from G. P. Strauss et al. (2010). "Periods of Recovery in Deficit Syndrome Schizophrenia: A 20-Year Multi–Follow-up Longitudinal Study," *Schizophrenia Bulletin*, *36*(4), 788–799. doi:10.1093/schbul/sbn167

Approaches to Treatment

Psychological treatments, or **psychotherapies**, which generally involve a conversation between the professional providing the therapy and the person seeking help, are often combined with biological treatments, such as the medications described in detail in later sections of this chapter. For example, a person who is terrified of being part of a crowd might benefit from a combination of psychotherapy and medication for anxiety. As will be shown in this chapter, different combinations of methods can be tailored to different types of problems and to the individuals being treated.

Biological Approaches Biological approaches to treatment have their roots in our understanding of the biological factors that contribute to psychological disorders. Along with the overall burst of scientific and medical knowledge beginning in the 18th century, scientists began to learn more about psychological disorders and their causes. This knowledge in turn set the stage for the discovery of more effective biological treatments.

Improved medical knowledge made psychological disorders less mysterious. When untreated, syphilis (a common type of sexually transmitted disease caused by a bacterial infection) can produce a characteristic set of abnormal behaviors, including hallucinations, delusions, and changes in mood and personality. As noted in Chapter 14, these behaviors are characteristic of a number of psychological disorders, including schizophrenia. The discovery that behaviors like hallucinations could have a biological cause led to the recognition that abnormal behavior can result from infection or other medical conditions. In these cases, the abnormal behaviors should disappear when the underlying medical condition is treated.

The use of one biological approach to treatment, medication, revolutionized the care of people with many types of psychological disorder. In 1949, an Australian psychiatrist named John Cade discovered that lithium salts could produce remarkable improvements in the behavior of patients with bipolar disorder. Cade's discovery was followed quickly by breakthroughs in the use of medication to treat schizophrenia. Bolstered by these successes with some of the most troubling psychological conditions, the pharmaceutical industry quickly

psychotherapy A treatment designed to improve symptoms of psychological disorder through conversation between the therapist and the patient or client.

Australian psychiatrist John Cade searched for alternatives to the ECT, lobotomies, and psychoanalysis that were commonly used to treat psychological disorders in the 1940s. After observing that lithium salts had a sedating effect on guinea pigs, he tried lithium on himself to test for side effects. He then tried lithium on his patients and noticed that those with bipolar disorder appeared to respond favorably. Lithium is an element, so it could not be patented, providing little financial incentive for the pharmaceutical industry. However, lithium was approved for use in the United States in 1970. Lithium salts continue to be used extensively to treat bipolar disorder, although we now understand that this treatment has serious side effects.

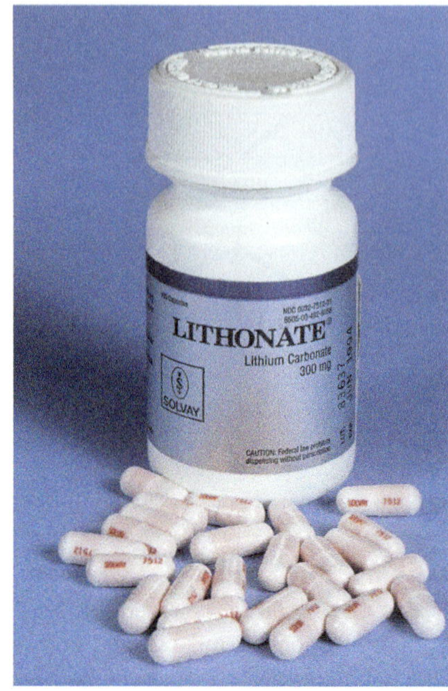

Phil Degginger/Science Source

Science Source

Franz Anton Mesmer (1734–1815), whose name gives us the term *mesmerized*, attempted to use hypnosis to treat people with hysteria, which would now fall into the somatic symptom disorders category. Mesmer's practices inspired Sigmund Freud to use hypnosis, although he eventually abandoned the technique in favor of other approaches.

introduced medications for depression and anxiety. These successes not only led to better outcomes for many patients, but also strengthened the credibility of using biological approaches to treat abnormal behaviors.

Psychological Approaches Running parallel to the successes of scientists engaged in biological approaches to disorders were significant contributions from those who focused on the psychological and emotional underpinnings of disorders.

During the 19th century, psychologists and psychiatrists were interested in hysteria, a condition that would be diagnosed today as somatic symptom disorder (see Chapter 14). Hysteria did not seem to have any biological basis and did not respond to the medical treatments of the day. Among the first efforts to treat hysteria through nonmedical means was the use of hypnosis by Franz Anton Mesmer (1734–1815), whose name gives us an alternative term for being hypnotized—*mesmerized*. Mesmer attempted to treat hysteria by inducing a hypnotic state, which was described in Chapter 6. In many cases, people with hysteria no longer experienced their symptoms under hypnosis and, following Mesmer's suggestions made during hypnosis, continued to be symptom free even after they left the hypnotic state.

Despite skepticism regarding Mesmer and his techniques, other scientists continued to explore hypnosis, suggestion, and hysteria. When positive outcomes were reported by the noted French neurologist Jean-Martin Charcot (1825–1893), hypnosis and suggestion took on a new legitimacy in the scientific community. Among the admirers of Charcot and his work were Josef Breuer (1842–1925) and his more famous colleague, Sigmund Freud (1856–1939). As will be discussed later in this chapter, Freud eventually abandoned his interest in hypnosis in favor of other approaches, which eventually gave rise to psychoanalysis. Instead of hypnotizing people, Freud encouraged them to speak freely about whatever came to mind.

Franz Anton Mesmer's methods for using hypnosis to treat hysteria were quite theatrical and were denounced as fraudulent by none other than Benjamin Franklin, who was serving as the U.S. ambassador to France at the time.

During the 20th century, psychological approaches to treatment reflected the rise of the behavioral and humanistic perspectives, described in Chapters 1, 8, and 12. The behaviorist perspective, unlike the biological and Freudian approaches, focused exclusively on observable behavior and approached the treatment of abnormal behavior using the principles of classical conditioning, operant conditioning, and observational learning, described in Chapter 8. The cognitive revolution of the second half of the 20th century added a recognition of the role of cognitions in abnormal behavior, leading to the development of cognitive behavioral therapy (CBT). Later in this chapter, the use of CBT for disorders such as phobias and depression will be explored.

The rise of humanistic psychology in the second half of the 20th century also led to new **humanistic therapies**. As discussed in Chapter 1, the humanistic psychologists specifically rebelled against psychodynamic thinking and the practice of psychoanalysis. Humanistic therapist Carl Rogers (1942) wished to separate his procedures, described in greater detail later in this chapter, from the more traditional Freudian psychotherapies of his time by referring to treatment as **counseling** rather than psychotherapy or psychoanalysis. Today's field of counseling psychology mirrors the more positive view of human nature held by the humanistic psychologists by focusing on personal strengths and development.

Michael Rougier/The LIFE Picture Collection/Getty Images

Carl Rogers and the humanistic psychologists rebelled against the practice of psychoanalysis and established new approaches of counseling psychology.

humanistic therapy A therapy approach patterned after the theories proposed by humanistic psychologists.

counseling A treatment originally proposed by humanistic therapists that includes a focus on personal strengths and development; the term is now used to refer to treatment for adjustment problems, as opposed to treatment for severe psychological disorders.

Evidence-Based Practice The beginning of the 21st century has featured greater demands to tie clinical practice to research on the outcomes of treatment. As shown in • Figure 15.3, evidence-based practice (EBP) combines research evidence, clinical expertise, and individual values to provide the best outcome for a patient or client (Straus et al., 2005; American Psychological Association Presidential Task Force on Evidence-based Practice, 2006). The movement toward EBP began in medicine, but it has since spread throughout the helping professions, including psychology.

EBP combines five steps (Thyer, 2004). The first is to construct an answerable question, such as "Which treatments produce the best outcomes in cases of PTSD?" Next, clinicians conduct a search for the most current scientific literature related to the question. In other words, doing something "because I've always done it this way in my practice" is no longer an option. Third, clinicians critically evaluate the relevant literature, using the standards for good science discussed in Chapter 2. This information is then integrated with data regarding particular cases, including the patients' values and circumstances. Finally, clinicians evaluate their performance based on the patients' outcomes and make any necessary adjustments.

If you think that these EBP steps sound like the problem-solving system introduced in Chapter 10, you're right. You might have assumed that your health care provider would take this approach automatically, but historically, many clinicians have been convinced that science can do little to assist them with an individual case and that clinical practice was more art than science. Large numbers of clinicians have traditionally valued their "clinical expertise" over the body of knowledge represented by science (Baker et al., 2008). Given the demanding financial realities of health care in the 21st century, however, a logical, scientific evidence–based approach to the delivery of health care services is not just the most effective approach, but also the necessary one.

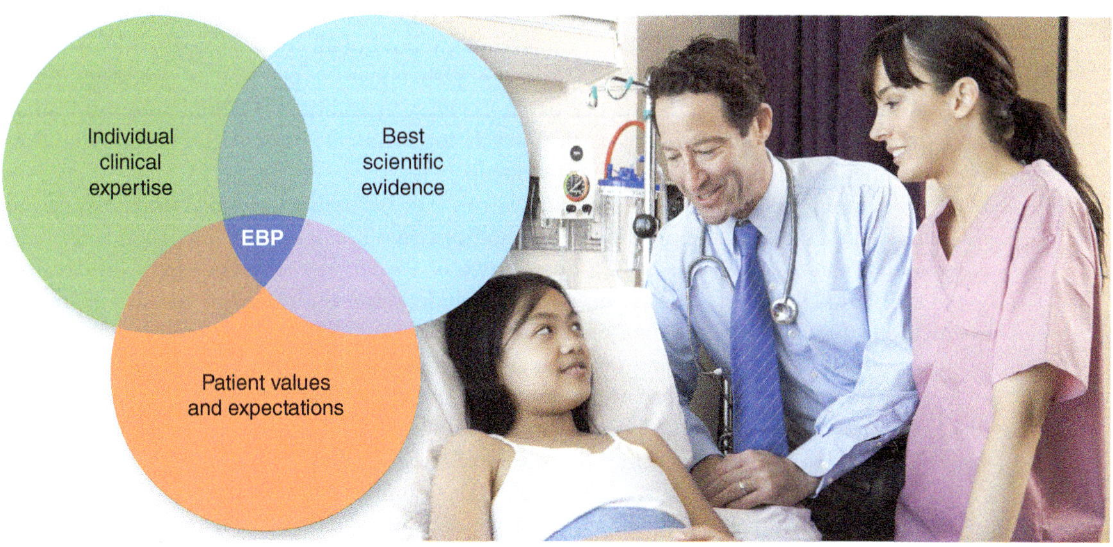

Monkey Business Images/Shutterstock.com

FIGURE **15.3**

EBP. Evidence-based practice (EBP) began in medicine and spread to psychotherapy and other helping professions. EBP combines the personal experience of the clinician, the best scientific evidence, and a consideration of patient values and expectations to tailor scientifically valid treatments to the individual.

Stock Montage/Getty Images

Everett Collection Inc/Alamy Stock Photo

Benjamin Rush (1749–1813), "the father of American psychiatry," believed that psychological disorders were caused by the "irritation" of the blood vessels in the brain. He invented the tranquilizer chair for patients and wrote a textbook published in 1812, *Medical Inquiries and Observations Upon Diseases of the Mind*, which was the standard in the field for the next 50 years.

Clinical Assessment Before therapists can provide any type of useful treatment, they need to understand the problems presented by the person to be treated. The choice of assessment methods is guided by the training and experience of the clinician, but it usually includes the methods described in Chapter 12: interviews, observations, and standardized tests (Groth-Marnat, 2009).

The Therapists

A range of professionals, including general medical practitioners, psychiatrists, psychologists, social workers, nurses, and religious leaders, provide counseling and psychotherapy. The licensing of these professionals to provide treatment for psychological disorders is administered by state governments in the United States and provincial governments in Canada. Requirements for licensing can vary widely from state to state and can result in a bewildering array of titles. For example, the simple term *therapist* is not regulated consistently across the United States. We will use the term **psychotherapist** to refer to any of the many types of licensed professionals described in this section who provide psychotherapy.

Psychiatrists first obtain a standard medical doctor (MD) degree and then spend an additional three to four years specializing in psychiatry. Because of their training and licensure as physicians, psychiatrists are allowed to perform the medical procedures reviewed later in this chapter, particularly the prescribing of medication. It is difficult to generalize across the entire profession, but psychiatrists are more likely to look for the causes of disorder in biological factors than in learned or environmental factors and to assume that a biological treatment such as medication will be most effective. In addition, the medical model does not see treatment as taking place within a relationship of equals. Instead, expertise is simply transmitted from the doctor to the patient, and little input is expected from the patient. We will see alternatives to this model in the procedures conducted by other types of therapists.

The word psychologist is used to describe professionals who have completed advanced degrees in psychology, including those who become psychotherapists. Most psychologists, including the professors teaching your introductory course, earn the traditional academic Doctor of Philosophy (PhD) degree in psychology, but not all choose career paths as licensed psychotherapists. Clinical psychology is the path taken by psychology graduate students who wish to study, teach, or practice psychotherapy. In addition to completing the academic requirements for a PhD degree, clinical psychology students must spend an additional year providing treatment in a supervised internship.

Beginning in the 1970s, an alternative route to becoming a clinical psychologist arose from suggestions that the practice of psychology could be modeled after dental and medical schools (Norcross & Castle, 2002). The Doctor of Psychology (PsyD) degree was developed to train students to provide services without undergoing the extensive training in research methods that characterizes the PhD degree.

Both PhD and PsyD programs can earn accreditation by the American Psychological Association (APA). PsyD programs are becoming increasingly popular with students (see Figure 15.4). However, the lack of emphasis on research that is characteristic of the PsyD degree has led to concerns about the ability of these graduates to think scientifically about their choice of methods (Baker et al., 2008). For example, without a solid background in science, objective evaluation of and adherence to the EBP model could be quite difficult. Of the faculty members in institutions granting the traditional PhD degree, 65% teach scientifically supported CBT techniques (Norcross & Castle, 2002). In contrast, only about 30% of faculty members in PsyD programs teach CBT techniques.

How do clinical psychologists and psychiatrists differ, other than that they earn different degrees? One of the traditional distinctions has been psychiatrists' ability to prescribe medication, but

psychotherapist A licensed professional who provides psychotherapy.

psychiatrist A medical doctor who specializes in psychiatry and can use medical procedures, such as the prescribing of medication, to treat psychological disorders.

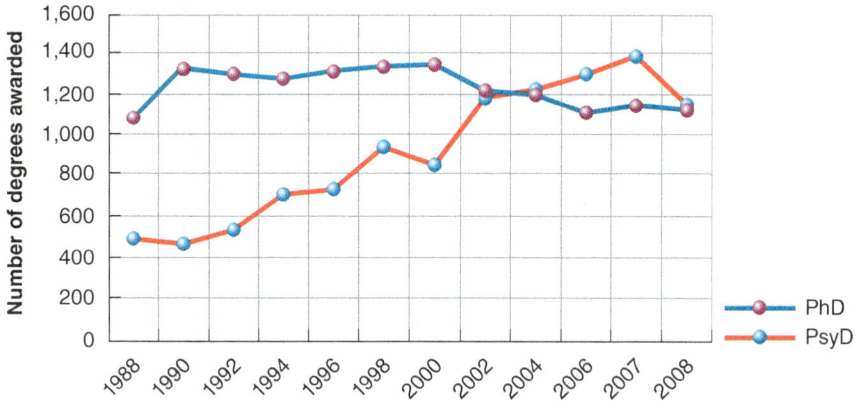

FIGURE **15.4**

PsyD Degrees Are Becoming More Common. While PhD degrees awarded in psychology have remained fairly constant, the number of PsyD degrees has grown dramatically since 1988. There are now approximately equal numbers of clinical PhD and PsyD degrees awarded each year.

Source: B. Hart & W. E. Pate (2011). *Salaries, Student Debt, and Employment Opportunities in Psychology.* Paper presented at the Midwestern Psychological Association Convention, Chicago, IL.

that difference is gradually disappearing. In 2002, New Mexico became the first state to allow select psychologists to prescribe medication, followed by Louisiana in 2004 (Daly, 2006), Illinois in 2014, Iowa in 2016, and Idaho in 2017 (American Psychological Association, 2017). The requirements for already-licensed clinical psychologists to gain prescription privileges are quite rigorous. Prescribing psychologists in these states must go through additional neuroscience coursework and many hours of clinical practicum and physician-supervised hours of care with patients.

In addition to treating people with diagnosed psychological disorders, clinical psychologists often provide marriage and family counseling, substance abuse counseling, vocational counseling, grief counseling, rehabilitation counseling, and prison counseling. However, these types of services are also provided by counselors, who typically do not provide services for psychological disorders such as schizophrenia. In other words, a couple experiencing marital conflict might seek either a counselor or a clinical psychologist, whereas a person experiencing hallucinations and delusions is more likely to be treated by a clinical psychologist or a psychiatrist. Counselors hold master's or doctoral degrees in psychology and related fields, such as education and social work.

Students pursuing undergraduate psychology degrees frequently ask what they can do in the mental health field without a graduate degree. About one-third of undergraduates in psychology obtain jobs that are closely related to the field (see ● Figure 15.5). Students completing an undergraduate degree in psychology often work in group homes and camps for troubled youth or in hospital or outpatient settings under supervision. Many others seek work in "people"-related professions, including human resources, sales, and teaching (see Chapter 1).

In recognition of the historical role of religious leaders in providing counseling to members of their congregations, most states allow religious leaders to provide this service without further licensure. The Master of Divinity (MDiv) degree typically includes human

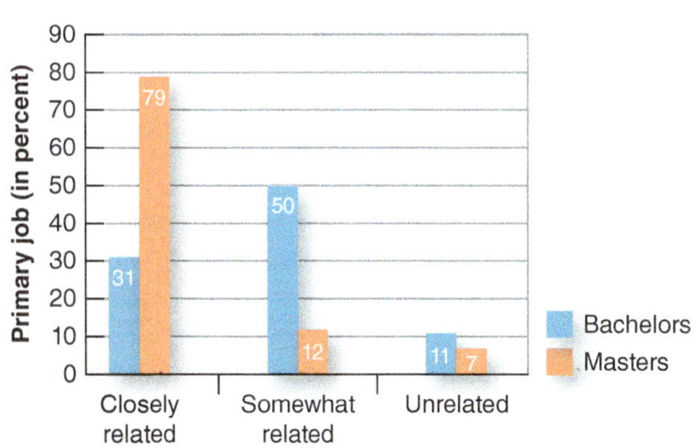

FIGURE **15.5**

Job Opportunities for Workers with Bachelor's or Master's Degrees in Psychology. More workers with master's degrees in psychology are employed in degree-relevant fields than are workers with bachelor's degrees. Closely related fields include professional services, teaching, and research. Somewhat related fields include management, sales, accounting, and employee relations.

Source: K. Stamm et al. (2016). "Datapoint: What Do People Do With Their Psychology Degrees?" *Monitor on Psychology*, 47(6), 12. http://apa.org/monitor/2016/06/datapoint

development and counseling courses taught at schools of divinity. Some universities offer MDiv degrees that prepare students to be either religious leaders or licensed counselors in the outside community.

Among the least frequently regulated practitioners in the United States are hypnotherapists, although nine states now regulate hypnotism in some manner (Hypnotherapists Union Local 472, 2019). The National Guild of Hypnotists cautions practitioners who are not also licensed health care professionals to use the title "Consulting Hypnotist" and to avoid using the terms *therapy, depression, anxiety, compulsive, phobia, psychological, medical, clinical,* and *counseling* (National Guild of Hypnotists, 2016). As mentioned in Chapter 6, there are many legitimate uses of hypnosis in therapy, and there are many legitimate therapists who use the technique. But that chapter also recounted the example of Zoe D. Katze, who is a hypnotherapist certified by the National Guild of Hypnotists, the American Board of Hypnotherapy, and the International Medical and Dental Hypnotherapy Association. She is a professional member of the American Association of Professional Hypnotherapists. As you may recall, Zoe also happens to be a cat, owned by a psychotherapist named Steve Eichel, who obtained the credentials for her to make a point about the weaknesses of accreditation in this area (Eichel, 2002).

Another unregulated area in the provision of psychological services is the field of life coaching, which requires no licensing. According to the International Coach Federation (ICF, n.d.), coaching is defined as "partnering with clients in a thought-provoking and creative process that inspires them to maximize their personal and professional potential." Substitute *psychotherapy* for *coaching* in this definition, and few would disagree with the resulting statement. Coaches seem to perform the same duties as psychotherapists and counselors. Some licensed psychotherapists have found that referring to themselves as coaches expands their practices, possibly because of the reduced stigma of seeing a coach rather than a therapist in the minds of some clients. Life coaching also provides the advantage of being more appealing to men, who generally seek more traditional psychotherapy in much smaller numbers than do women (Liddon et al., 2018). However, the lack of preparation required to refer to yourself as a life coach raises that specter that people with psychological disorders will trust their care to unqualified individuals, resulting in significant harm (Aboujaoude, 2020).

Matej Kastelic/Shutterstock.com

Although unlicensed, life coaches perform many of the same tasks as psychotherapists and counselors. Corporations are spending close to $12 billion per year for coaching services.

Few studies have attempted to evaluate the effectiveness of coaching, but those that have done so note a positive effect (Burt & Talati, 2017). Many studies appear in journals that are essentially trade publications, such as the *International Journal of Evidence-Based Coaching & Mentoring,* the *International Coaching Psychology Review,* and *Coaching: An International Journal.* Carefully controlled, objective research is badly needed.

In spite of the lack of regulation and licensure, life coaching is becoming a big part of the delivery of psychotherapeutic services, even within health care settings (Ammentorp et al., 2013). Corporations, including Google and many Fortune 500 firms, spend in the vicinity of $1.5 billion per year on workplace coaching services provided by the over 50,000 professional coaches who are active globally (ICF, 2016).

Although licensure provides significant protection for the public, any consumer of psychological services must thoroughly investigate prospective psychotherapists. Zoe D. Katze may be an extreme example, but we suspect that she is not unique. Credentials are not always what they seem. For example, the author of the 1992 bestseller *Men Are from Mars, Women Are from Venus* lists himself as "Dr. John Gray" ("John Gray's Professional Bio," 2017), but provides no information on his educational background or licensure. Gray spent nine years as a monk under the leadership of the Beatles' guru, Maharishi Mahesh Yogi. He earned bachelor's and master's degrees in the Science of Creative Intelligence from the unaccredited Maharishi European Research Institute in Switzerland, and a PhD degree from the now-defunct and unaccredited Columbia Pacific University in California, which was described by the state government as a "diploma mill." Because of his experience as a monk, the state of California recognizes him as a "spiritual counselor," which technically allows him to provide advice. More recently, Gray has been joined by his daughter Lauren, who also provides no educational or licensing material about herself on the website.

So far, we have focused our discussion on credentialing practices in the United States. Worldwide, an even greater variety of professionals perform psychotherapy and counseling under diverse licensure and oversight practices. The United Kingdom, Australia, and Canada provide systems that are similar to those in the United States for delivering psychotherapy (Priebe, 2006). In these countries, psychotherapy is conducted by a number of professionals, including physicians, psychologists, social workers, nurses, and others in similar professions. In each case, performing psychotherapy requires training beyond that needed to simply obtain the appropriate professional degree. Germany and Russia are particularly strict in their accreditation rules. Because of the prevalence of state-run health systems in Europe, assessments of treatment outcomes are regularly conducted (Priebe, 2006). In the United States, treatment outcomes are a question of interest to academic researchers but are rarely assessed as comprehensively as in many other nations, although that circumstance is likely to change with any further government involvement in health care.

Ned Redway/ZUMAPRESS/Newscom

Celebrity psychologists like "Dr. Phil" McGraw are often criticized by the profession for offering overly simple versions of psychological advice to the public.

Delivering Psychotherapy

Many people imagining a session of psychotherapy think of a stereotypical Freudian scenario. The patient reclines on a couch, while a bearded man sitting in a chair scribbles copious notes. Although some therapy continues to take place in such a setting (though perhaps the therapist isn't bearded—or a man), many more options are available.

brief therapy Psychotherapy provided over a short time frame, usually between three and five sessions.

group therapy Psychotherapy conducted with a group of people rather than individually.

Variations in Length of Treatment Most psychotherapy occurs in the form of individual therapy involving face-to-face, hourlong meetings between the therapist and the patient or client (as a subsequent section will demonstrate, terminology varies among practitioners). In traditional psychoanalysis, such meetings are quite frequent (four to five times per week) and take place over the course of years. In CBT, described in detail in a later section, sessions might occur once per week for about six weeks. Given rates of $150 or more per hour for individual therapy, insurance providers are pressuring psychotherapists to find faster, cheaper, and more efficient ways to provide treatment. Many insurance plans limit psychotherapy sessions to 10 per calendar year.

Brief therapy, another treatment regime, specifically avoids spending long periods searching for the historical basis of a person's problems. Instead, therapists using this approach focus on "solution-building rather than problem-solving" (Iveson, 2002, p. 149). Consequently, practitioners argue that only three to five sessions are necessary. Many brief therapy interventions involve only one session, and no cases require more than eight.

LightField Studios/Shutterstock.com

Many people thinking about psychotherapy imagine a bearded man scribbling notes next to a client reclining on a couch, but this stereotype is usually far from the truth.

Alternatives to Individual Therapy In addition to individual sessions, psychotherapy can take place with groups of patients or clients in **group therapy**. Group therapy does not imply a particular type of treatment approach. Although some treatment approaches seem better suited for group work than others, therapists of all persuasions are known to use groups in their work. The groups formed by the therapist can be homogeneous, in the sense that the group members share a common problem, or heterogeneous, in which the group members have diverse diagnoses. In most cases, groups are limited to between 6 and 12 individuals.

People participating in group therapy benefit from reduced feelings of isolation. Seeing the progress of others with the same condition raises hope and provides opportunities to model successful strategies.

iStock.com/Alina555

People with severe conditions, such as psychotic, suicidal, or antisocial tendencies, are usually excluded from groups until they progress sufficiently to behave as good group members.

Although many groups are organized and supervised by a licensed psychotherapist, leaderless self-help groups are also quite popular. Weight Watchers, Alcoholics Anonymous (AA), and other groups modeled after AA have become popular sources of support and self-improvement. These groups often operate with a member–leader who is not a psychotherapist, and they function outside the realm of government licensure and supervision.

In addition to the obvious cost-effectiveness of having a group split the therapist's fee, group therapy offers a number of other advantages (Yalom, 1995). For example, group therapy offers hope to the participants, who benefit from seeing others who have made more progress with their condition. Group members also benefit from knowing that others share their condition, decreasing their sense of isolation. Although practitioners generally believe that group therapy is effective, research on group therapy outcomes is difficult to conduct because of the large number of variables that must be considered. The need to control for such factors as different disorders and previous treatment history makes this area challenging for researchers.

family therapy A type of therapy in which family members participate individually and in combination with other family members.

couples therapy A type of family therapy that focuses on intimate relationships.

Family therapy, in which various family members participate in therapy individually and in combination with other family members, is another alternative to the purely individual provision of treatment. **Couples therapy** is a type of family therapy that focuses on intimate relationships. Family therapy is frequently used when a child or teen is experiencing problems, because these problems typically affect and are affected by the behavior of other family members. Family therapists face a number of significant challenges. In some cases, the member who seems to need treatment the most refuses to participate. In others, maintaining the confidentiality of all participants can be difficult. A teen might disclose information that will help the parents do their job better, but sharing this information with the parents could interrupt the trust that the therapist has built up with the teen.

Frank Pedrick/The Image Works

Family therapy combines individual sessions with sessions that include some combination of family members, like these parents and their young daughter.

Innovative Delivery Systems An emerging delivery system for psychotherapy is online therapy. When "online psychotherapy" is used as a Google search term, more than 66,100,000 results are returned. Although a necessity during the COVID-19 pandemic, online therapy has benefits that are likely to continue its popularity into the future.

The benefits of privacy, engaging in therapy from home, and the ability to choose a suitable therapist regardless of location provide significant advantages for some clients. In its early days, online therapy was conducted through e-mail or chat services. Because the written word conveys less information than a therapist obtains face to face, this method could be less desirable. However, many online therapists have taken advantage of Zoom, FaceTime, and other voice and video technologies. Online delivery of CBT has been shown to be as effective as face-to-face CBT for a number of psychological conditions, including major depressive disorder (Ahern et al., 2018).

Other technologies have influenced the delivery of psychotherapy. Therapists can buy products such as Wiley's TheraScribe, a computer program that includes more than 2,500 prewritten interventions, goals, objectives, and suggested diagnoses. The program generates reports catering to Medicare and other managed care organizations. The time savings provided by these technologies can be useful in controlling costs, but receiving a prewritten evaluation might seem somewhat impersonal to individuals seeking therapy. If you receive a treatment plan from your campus health center that is nearly identical to a friend's, you might not feel that the counselor cared about you as an individual.

Diverse Voices in Psychology

Psychotherapy with Native Americans

AMONG THE BARRIERS to obtaining counseling and psychotherapy services faced by racial and ethnic minority individuals in the United States are cultural distrust, racial and ethnic norms related to self-reliance and privacy, and concerns about culturally sensitive providers (Hayes et al., 2016).

Psychologists have begun to identify interventions that might address these barriers by offering greater cultural competency. Among the recommendations for more culturally competent therapy are using interventions that are consistent with the client's values, communicating in culturally sensitive ways (such as in the client's native language), expressing empathy and high regard, and avoiding equating cultural differences with deficits.

Compared to members of other races and ethnicities, Native Americans experience higher risk of medical disease and psychological disorders, including substance abuse disorders (Beitel et al., 2018). Compared to White clients, members of other ethnicities, including Native Americans, are more likely to quit psychotherapy after an initial session, raising the concern that the counseling process was unsatisfactory.

In a study of psychotherapy techniques in clinics serving Native Americans in Arizona, Minnesota, and Wisconsin, therapists were found to employ a wide range of methods tailored to the individual clients. The therapists emphasized a very warm, supportive environment, and more confrontational approaches to therapy were absent. In one example of an adaptation to cultural norms, the use of cognitive-behavioral therapy (CBT) was less common with older clients. In a culture where elders are treated with respect and deference, the "teaching/leading" role for the therapist in CBT might seem inappropriate.

Cultural adaptations in psychotherapy remain relatively under-studied, and much additional research is needed to support evidence-based practice in diverse communities. ■

gillmar/Shutterstock.com

Psychologists are recognizing the need to tailor methods to individuals in diverse communities for best results.

Agenturfotografin/Shutterstock.com

The benefits of privacy, engaging in therapy from home, frequent 24-7 coverage, video interactions using Zoom or similar technologies, and the ability to choose a suitable therapist regardless of location provide significant advantages for some clients. Online delivery of cognitive behavioral therapy has been shown to be as effective as face-to-face delivery (Ruwaard, Lange, Schrieken, Dolan, & Emmelkamp, 2012).

Contemporary Challenges in Treatment

Providing treatment for psychological disorders has changed dramatically since the days of Freud. Originally, therapy was provided by individual professionals in small private practices. However, this model became increasingly rare in the latter part of the 20th century, as psychological treatments became more likely to be managed by large organizations, including insurance companies. Many of the concerns about these new models of managed psychological treatment echo complaints from the medical community regarding contemporary medical treatment. Decisions formerly made by the therapist about the types of disorders that warranted treatment and the length, frequency, and type of treatment to be offered are now more likely to be made by insurance company personnel who lack medical or psychological training and focus more on costs (Baker et al., 2008).

In addition to the need to adapt to the managed care of psychological disorders, psychotherapy faces many of the same challenges as medicine in providing scientifically valid treatments. Just as we would expect a physician to provide a scientifically supported treatment for cancer, we should expect a psychotherapist to provide equally well-documented treatments for depression. In the earlier section on EBP, we joined most research clinical psychologists and psychiatrists in endorsing the use of science in selecting, implementing, and evaluating psychological treatments. However, as demonstrated in the discussion of the Rorschach Inkblot Test in Chapter 12, lack of scientific support does not always prevent an approach from being widely used.

Frustration over the lack of emphasis on science in psychotherapy has led to considerable debate. The American Psychological Association has the primary responsibility for accrediting programs that train clinical psychologists with either PhD or PsyD degrees in the United States. This system has been challenged by a new accreditation body, the Psychological Clinical Science Accreditation System (PCSAS, 2020), which specifically aims to increase the scientific basis of clinical treatment and research literacy among clinical psychologists. Since 2007, the PCSAS has accredited 43 programs, with several more under review (PCSAS, 2020). Time will tell whether PCSAS will be able to nudge the clinical psychology community into greater reliance on research-based methods.

SUMMARY 15.1 The Psychotherapists

Title	Degrees	Specialties
Psychiatrist 	Medical doctor (MD)	• Treats psychological disorders • Prescribes medication
Clinical psychologist 	Doctor of Philosophy (PhD) or Doctor of Psychology (PsyD)	• Treats psychological disorders and problems with adjustment • If specially licensed, prescribes medication
Counselor 	PhD, PsyD, Doctor of Education (EdD), or one of a number of master's degrees	• Specializes in problems with adjustment

Credits: Top row. Stock Montage/Getty Images. Second row. Frank Pedrick/The Image Works. Bottom row. Michael Rougier/The LIFE Picture Collection/Getty Images.

Historical Approaches to Psychotherapy

Because Freud is typically credited with being the first person to use "talk therapy" in his efforts to improve his patients' psychological symptoms, we begin our discussion of specific treatment approaches with **psychoanalysis**. A psychotherapist who uses psychoanalysis is typically known as a *psychoanalyst.*

Bjanka Kadic/Alamy Stock Photo

Freud's study featured not only the famous couch, but also Persian rugs and a sample of Freud's collection of antiquities.

Psychoanalysis

Freud's approach to psychotherapy reflected several key themes from his theory of personality (see Chapter 12). In particular, Freud emphasized the importance of conflict among the self (ego), the aggressive energy of the id, and the restrictions supplied by society (superego). Freud's view of the ability of the unconscious mind to affect behavior is also central to his therapeutic approach. Because of Freud's training as a physician, psychoanalysts take a directive role, which means that they are in charge of the session. Like your physician, the psychoanalyst does not expect contributions from you other than information about your symptoms.

Freud called his slips "faulty actions." For example, a man texting his partner "I wish you were her" instead of "I wish you were here" would have a great deal of explaining to do. Modern cognitive psychologists are more likely to blame slips on conflicts between grammar sequences than between the unconscious and the conscious minds.

Freud's psychoanalysis is a classic example of an **insight therapy**. Insight therapies assume that people will improve once they understand their problems. For Freud, many psychological disorders arose from problems that resided in the unconscious mind, unavailable to conscious awareness. Although the person might not be consciously aware of these continuing conflicts, the conflicts exert their influence on behavior and through dreams. For example, a patient might arrive at the therapist's office complaining about her inability to enjoy a satisfactory sex life with a beloved spouse. Although many factors could contribute to such problems, the psychoanalyst is likely to suspect the influence of some traumatic experience that is relatively unavailable to the patient's conscious thoughts. Perhaps the patient is the victim of childhood sexual abuse, or she might be experiencing a conflict between the ultrastrict morality that she learned from her parents and her current desire to have a fulfilling relationship with her partner. For the psychoanalyst, the "cure" lies in uncovering the unconscious contributions to the patient's problems. Once she understands the source of her problems (the insight), her situation should improve.

psychoanalysis The treatment approach developed by Freud and practiced by those who believe in psychodynamic theories.

insight therapy A therapy that improves symptoms of psychological disorder by building people's understanding of their situation.

free association The psychoanalytic technique of encouraging a patient to say whatever comes to mind, without attempting to censor the content.

How does one go about uncovering unconscious material? Although Freud experimented with the use of hypnosis to access the unconscious mind, he became dissatisfied with the results and abandoned the procedure. Instead, Freud decided to use the technique of **free association**. Free association occurs when a person says whatever comes to mind. As we mature, most of us become aware that we do not literally "speak our mind" out of consideration for our fellow humans. Although small children might tell a person, "You're fat," such comments, although they may be true, are not the type that most adults consider polite. We learn to think before we speak. To engage in free association, this self-censor must be turned off, allowing the patient to verbalize those thoughts that are typically withheld. Without the self-censor, the famous "Freudian slips" might occur and are assumed to reflect unconscious wishes.

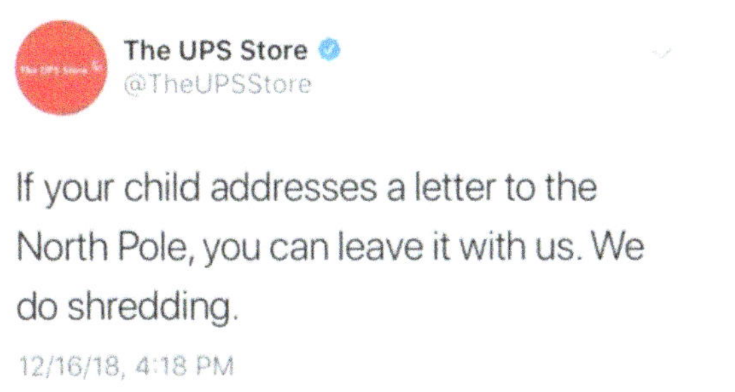

In free association, the patient says whatever comes to mind. Freud believed that we normally censor thoughts before speaking, but we wonder if he would think the same is true of conversations on social media. In response to some comments on social media, we shake our heads and ask, "what were they thinking?"
Source: The UPS Store

Not all psychoanalysts engage in dream analysis, but it is likely that therapists interested in dream analysis are psychoanalysts. For Freud, dreaming represented a reflection of unconscious wishes and, therefore, a potential source of useful insight into the unconscious mind. If patients are undergoing dream analysis, they are encouraged

Contemporary Approaches to Psychotherapy

Although a small minority of psychotherapists continue to use Freudian or humanistic approaches, most contemporary therapists use other methods.

Behavioral Therapies

Freud's psychodynamic theory, humanistic theory, and behaviorism were among the most dominant influences in psychology during the 20th century. We have seen how psychodynamic and humanistic theories were applied to psychotherapy in the form of psychoanalysis and Rogers's person-centered therapy, so it should come as no surprise to find that behaviorism has similar applications. Given our formal definition of learning as "a relatively permanent change in behavior or the capacity for behavior due to experience," it seems logical to use learning as a way to increase the frequency of desirable behaviors and decrease unwanted behaviors in the therapy setting.

Behavior therapies represent applications of classical and operant conditioning to problems of adjustment and psychological disorders. These techniques have proved helpful in both reducing unwanted behaviors and increasing the frequency of desirable behaviors over a range of psychological conditions, including autism spectrum disorder (ASD) and schizophrenia. The first book to use the term *behavior modification* in its title was Leonard Ullman and Leonard Krasner's *Case Studies in Behavior Modification,* published in 1965. The public initially distrusted behavioral treatment methods because they were based on animal research and assumed that human behavior was relatively simple. The mysticism of the psychoanalysts' unconscious drives and impulses seemed far more romantic. However, when behavior modification produced successful results in cases that were previously considered untreatable, such as in ASD, respect for the approach grew.

behavior therapy Applications of classical and operant conditioning principles to the treatment of symptoms of psychological disorder and adjustment problems.

Like behaviorism in general, behavior modification, now known as applied behavior analysis (ABA), focuses on what can be observed and makes few assumptions about such unseen factors as the unconscious mind. We can contrast the way that Freud and a therapist using ABA might approach Freud's case of Little Hans, a 5-year-old boy who had a phobia of horses (Freud, 1909/1976). For Freud, Hans's phobia resulted from the Oedipus complex issues that were supposedly at their height at his age. Horses, Freud argued, symbolized Hans's father. The boy had noted that he was especially frightened of horses with black bits in their mouths, which Freud suggested represented the father's mustache. Freud concluded that Hans's fear of horses resulted from his unconscious fear of retaliation by the father for sexual fantasies about his mother and would disappear with the resolution of Hans's Oedipus complex.

Bettmann/Getty Images

The subject of Freud's famous case study of "Little Hans" was actually named Herbert Graf. Graf grew up to be a successful opera producer at New York's Metropolitan Opera and the Salzburg Festival in Austria. He is shown here directing the great Marion Anderson as she rehearses for her operatic debut in Giuseppe Verdi's *Masked Ball* in 1954.

Now it is the behaviorist's turn. According to classical conditioning theory, phobias can result from conditioned fears. In Hans's day, horses were the most frequently used means of transportation, especially in large cities. Accidents involving horses were frequent and quite serious. Hans related that he was frightened of horses falling—and with good reason, because it is likely that viewing such accidents would be quite traumatic. Horses could become classically conditioned fear stimuli through their association with accidents and the resulting fear. To reduce the fear, Hans could be gradually exposed to horses in a safe environment (desensitization), rewarded for approaching horses (counterconditioning), or allowed to play with a group of children interacting with a horse (peer modeling). It is not necessary to know why Hans fears the horses to apply behavioral treatment successfully.

ABA has been used frequently to reduce unwanted habits. For example, let us suppose that Jennifer would like to stop smoking. The behavior therapist begins by evaluating Jennifer's current behavior by observing the circumstances in which she smokes. Based on these observations, the therapist might note that Jennifer rarely smokes alone. Instead, her smoking is quite social. If she is at a party or with friends who are smoking, she smokes. The therapist also takes notes of reinforcers or punishers that might be influencing the behavior. Perhaps Jennifer's friends praise her when she smokes, but her parents get angry when they notice evidence

Behavioral treatments for phobias have been improved with the development of virtual reality for exposing clients to fear-producing stimuli. Researchers at the University of Washington have developed SpiderWorld and successfully demonstrated that participants could reduce their fear of real spiders after undergoing three treatment sessions.

of her smoking. Jennifer's dentist also might warn her about the poor state of her oral hygiene, which smoking only worsens.

Based on these observations, the behavior therapist might attempt a number of techniques that will separate Jennifer from high-risk situations for smoking. She might be encouraged either to gain the support of her friends for her efforts to quit smoking or to spend more time with her nonsmoking friends. Jennifer's parents might be willing to provide some incentives for her to quit smoking. She could set aside the money that she normally spends on cigarettes for some special treat. Counterconditioning, in the form of asking Jennifer to smoke until she feels sick, is an unpleasant but effective strategy (Lichtenstein et al., 1973).

The effectiveness of behavior therapies is not restricted to changing negative habits such as tobacco use. As discussed in Chapter 8, token economies, in which reward tokens are later exchanged for preferred rewards, have been shown to increase the frequency of desirable behaviors across a variety of settings, including classrooms, prisons, and institutions (Hackenberg, 2018).

Cognitive Therapies

As the name implies, *cognitive therapies* are based on the notion that the way that we think about our circumstances is essential to our health and adjustment. According to this view, situations do not cause abnormal behavior, but the way that we think about situations might do so.

cognitive restructuring A technique used in cognitive therapies in which new, rational beliefs replace earlier, irrational beliefs held by the client.

One of the earliest versions of cognitive therapy was developed beginning in the 1940s by Aaron Beck (see ● Figure 15.6). According to Beck (1975), people run into psychological trouble when they adopt irrational, self-defeating ways of thinking. For example, it is unrealistic to think that other people will always treat you fairly and kindly, or that you must be perfect to be loved. An important aspect of the therapy process occurs when the therapist attempts to change the irrational beliefs of the client. For example, let's assume that a therapist is trying to help a group of students who suffer from test anxiety. Each student has an irrational belief that he or she is going to flunk out of school, despite having an adequate grade point average. To help the students realize that this belief is irrational, the therapist might ask each one to provide evidence of the likelihood of flunking out or to identify the worst possible outcome of giving up the belief. Faced with logic, each student begins to substitute a new, rational belief for the old, irrational belief. This substitution of rational for irrational beliefs is termed **cognitive restructuring**.

Behavior therapies have helped many people change negative habits.

A variation of cognitive therapy emerged from work by Albert Ellis, beginning in the 1950s. Ellis's version of cognitive therapy is known as rational emotive behavioral therapy

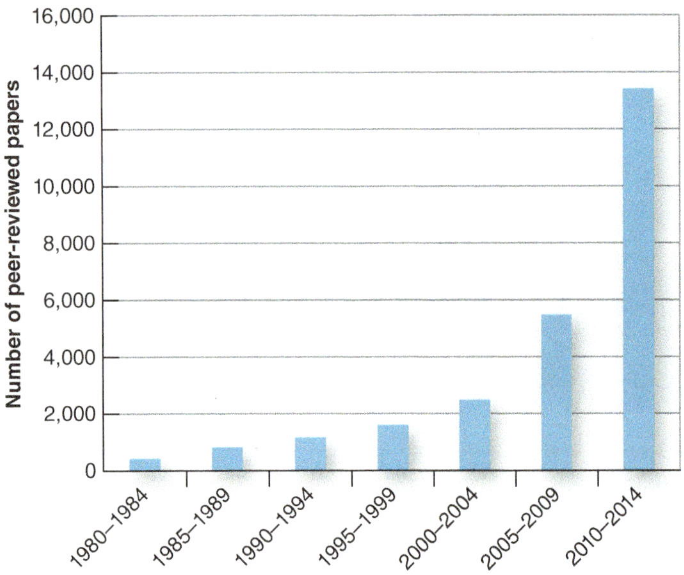

FIGURE **15.6**

CBT in the Scientific Literature. Increasing interest in CBT is reflected in the number of scholarly articles published on this topic, which has grown substantially over the past few decades. *Source:* D. Dobson, & K. S. Dobson (2016). *Evidence-Based Practice of Cognitive-Behavioral Therapy*. Guilford Publications.

Clem Murray/MCT/Newscom

Aaron Beck (1921–) developed one of the earliest types of cognitive therapies. Beck's approach featured cognitive restructuring, in which irrational beliefs, such as "Everyone must love me or I can't be happy," are replaced with more rational beliefs, such as "I can be happy because I have some people in my life who love me."

cognitive behavioral therapy (CBT) A combination of cognitive restructuring with behavioral treatments that has been shown to be effective in reducing symptoms of many psychological disorders.

biopsychosocial approach An integrated approach to therapy that combines treatments addressing the biological, personal, and social underpinnings of psychological disorders.

(REBT; Ellis, 1975). Compared to many other types of psychotherapy, REBT is somewhat confrontational because the therapist is more openly critical of a client's thinking. Ellis retained the need to produce cognitive restructuring but deemphasized the supportive role of the therapist.

As cognitive therapy expanded further, therapists began to use the term **cognitive behavioral therapy (CBT)**. In addition to promoting cognitive restructuring, therapists wanted to help clients initiate behavioral changes. For example, a person with major depressive disorder (MDD), as described in Chapter 14, can have irrational beliefs about hopelessness and worthlessness, coupled with behavior that is counterproductive to good mood, such as staying at home in bed watching television. Not only can the irrational beliefs be addressed by CBT, but behavioral methods can be used to encourage the client to take a brisk walk and to provide self-rewards for using more positive, rational patterns of thought.

CBT has an excellent record of success, particularly in the treatment of MDD (Dobson & Dobson, 2016). Because CBT typically requires fewer than 16 sessions and can be used for a variety of conditions, it is a favorite among insurance providers.

Biopsychosocial Approaches

Patient characteristics, the type of problems being addressed, and other variables influence the success of any particular treatment. Consequently, many therapists use the **biopsychosocial approach**, which combines elements of therapies designed to address the biological, psychological, and social underpinnings of an individual case. The therapist focuses on what works for an individual client, without adopting a single theoretical orientation (Lazarus, 2005). For example, a therapist might find that relaxation training seems to help one client, while role-playing is more effective with another.

What Are Biological Therapies?

The major types of biological treatments for psychological disorders include medication, electroconvulsive therapy (ECT), psychosurgery, brain stimulation, and neurofeedback.

Medication

Medication is the most commonly used of the medical therapies. Particularly in the last 60 years, the discovery of medications that effectively treated psychological disorders has dramatically shaped the outcomes of millions of patients. A comprehensive review of psychoactive medications is clearly beyond the scope of this text, but we will discuss the use of medication for some specific disorders later in this chapter.

The frequent use of medication is not consistent with patient preference. In a meta-analysis of patient treatment preferences for psychological disorders, 75% of the participants preferred psychological treatment to medication (McHugh et al., 2013). This preference was particularly strong in younger patients and in women.

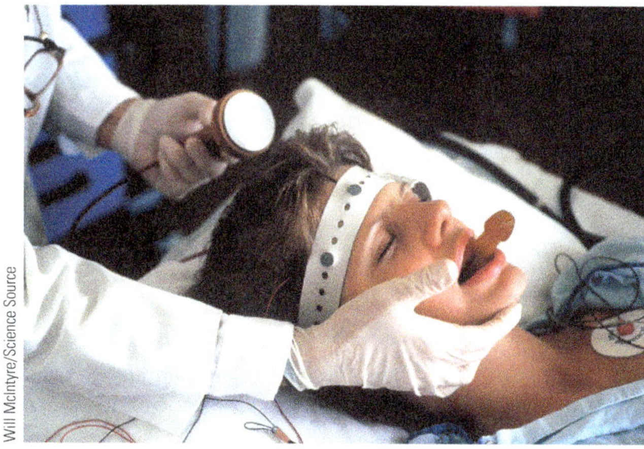

Will McIntyre/Science Source

A patient is shown being prepared for ECT for serious depression. The patient is anesthetized before electricity is applied through electrodes to the head, inducing seizures.

Electroconvulsive Therapy

Electroconvulsive therapy (ECT) is used in some severe cases of depression that do not respond to other treatments. In ECT, the patient is anesthetized and given a muscle relaxant before the induction of general seizures, which are produced by electricity applied through electrodes on the head. Between 6 and 12 treatments, at a rate of 3 treatments per week, are typically given. Over one million patients worldwide are treated with ECT each year (Leiknes et al., 2012).

Ladislas Meduna (1896–1964) recommended ECT for patients with schizophrenia after observing that people who had epilepsy had unusually high numbers of glia and people with schizophrenia had low numbers of glia (Kalinowsky, 1986). ECT was first used with patients with schizophrenia in the 1930s, with poor results. However, observations of improved mood in these patients following ECT led to further use with patients diagnosed with major depressive or bipolar disorder. This procedure is used primarily with patients who do not respond to conventional treatments with medication (Medda et al., 2009). Although the exact mode of action of ECT is unknown, some patients experience an increase in responsiveness to dopamine and norepinephrine, along with the desired reduction in subjective feelings of depression.

Although many people have a negative view of ECT (perhaps as a result of reading Ken Kesey's *One Flew Over the Cuckoo's Nest* or seeing the film or play of the same name), ECT is considered as safe as any minor surgery conducted under general anesthesia (Kellner et al., 2020). Critics continue to question the efficacy of ECT, citing the poor quality of research evaluating its outcomes (Read et al., 2020). Further concerns center on the side effects of the procedure. Approximately one-third of patients experience persistent memory loss following ECT (Rose et al., 2003). This memory loss specifically affects autobiographical memory, discussed in Chapter 9, which can be impaired for at least six months following treatment (Sackeim, 2014).

Trepanation has made a bizarre modern comeback in the form of an alternative medicine or elective procedure. People are doing this in their own homes, in a possible variation of the self-injurious behavior discussed in Chapter 8. They argue that the procedure improves brain circulation and metabolism, but research support for such claims is lacking (Moskalenko et al., 2008).

Psychosurgery

As observed in Chapter 1, the drilling of holes in the skull by ancient people might represent the first effort to use **psychosurgery**. Although particular functions might be localized to parts of the brain, it is a giant leap of faith from our current understanding of localization and brain networking to the idea that someone can use psychosurgery to treat psychological disorders.

Historically, one of the most frequent types of psychosurgery aimed at changing behavior was the frontal lobotomy, which was discussed in Chapter 4. After hearing about the calm that resulted following the procedure in chimpanzees, Egas Moniz encouraged his colleagues

electroconvulsive therapy (ECT) A biological treatment in which seizures are induced in an anesthetized patient; it is used primarily in the treatment of mood disorders that have not responded to medication or other treatments.

psychosurgery The attempt to improve symptoms of psychological disorders through operating on the brain.

AP Images/MW

Walter Freeman (1895–1972) performed more than 3,400 lobotomies at $25 per procedure, despite having no formal training in surgery. Although this procedure is considered barbaric today, Freeman enjoyed the respect of many of his colleagues, serving as cofounder and president of the American Board of Psychiatry and Neurology from 1946 to 1947. He nominated his mentor, Egas Moniz (1874–1955), for the Nobel Prize in Physiology and Medicine, which Moniz won in 1949.

to try the procedure on psychotic patients in the 1930s (Valenstein, 1986). Between 40,000 and 50,000 patients received the procedure between the 1930s and the 1950s, sometimes for vague problems such as mild depression in housewives or misbehavior in children (Sabatini, 1997). Walter Freeman popularized the procedure in the United States, traveling in a vehicle that he called his "lobotomobile." John Fulton, whose research with chimpanzees had formed the basis for Freeman's operation, was horrified. "What are these terrible things I hear about you doing lobotomies in your office with an ice pick?" he asked Freeman. "Why not use a shotgun?" (Kopell et al., 2005, p. 192).

As we have emphasized in several contexts in this textbook, the frontal lobes participate in some of the highest-order cognitive functions carried out by the human brain. Consequently, the deliberate damage to the frontal lobes and their connections to other parts of the brain involved with the lobotomy procedure has harmful effects on a person's judgment, personality, initiative, social behavior, and sense of self. Despite the outrage among many in the medical community, frontal lobotomies were performed well into the 1960s, until the use of medications for psychological disorders became an established practice (Sabatini, 1997). Today's psychosurgery is far removed from the lobotomy procedure. For example, high-intensity focused ultrasound has been used to reduce muscular tremor in patients with Parkinson's disease by causing precise damage to pathways connecting the cerebellum and thalamus (Mahoney & Green, 2020).

Brain Stimulation

Brain stimulation has a number of advantages over psychosurgery. Most importantly, the effects are usually reversible. In contrast, once the brain has been damaged by psychosurgery, there is no going back.

Following observations of mood changes in people undergoing **deep brain stimulation** through surgically implanted electrodes for the relief of Parkinson's disease, physicians attempted to use stimulation to address OCD and MDD. Microelectrodes are surgically inserted into specific parts of the brain, and in many cases, the patient controls the application of any current (Mayberg et al., 2005). A total of 50% of patients with severe depression who had not responded to more conventional treatments achieved improvements in mood following stimulation of the nucleus accumbens (Bewernick et al., 2010). In Chapter 4, we indicated that the nucleus accumbens was part of a circuit that processes feelings of reward. Stimulating this area improved patients' mood and led to their engagement in more pleasurable activities. Most studies of deep brain stimulation for psychological disorders involve very small numbers of patients, however, so firm conclusions about the overall effectiveness of this approach awaits further research (Mahoney & Green, 2020).

deep brain stimulation Electrical stimulation applied through surgically implanted electrodes that is used to treat some anxiety and mood disorders.

Deep brain stimulation requires surgery to implant the microelectrodes. Repeated transcranial magnetic stimulation (rTMS) provides an alternative way to stimulate the brain without surgery. When applied through a handheld device touching the scalp, low-frequency magnetic pulses change activity in underlying cortical regions. This technique has shown promise in treating MDD and mixed results in treating schizophrenia (Guo et al., 2017; also see ● Figure 15.7). Negative outcomes have been reported for the use of rTMS in cases of OCD (Slotema et al., 2010).

Electrical stimulation applied through surface electrodes (transcranial direct current stimulation or TDCS) has produced improvement in patients with auditory hallucinations, addictions, and MDD (Guo et al., 2017). Low cost and the ability of patients to administer treatment at home has made TDCS an attractive option.

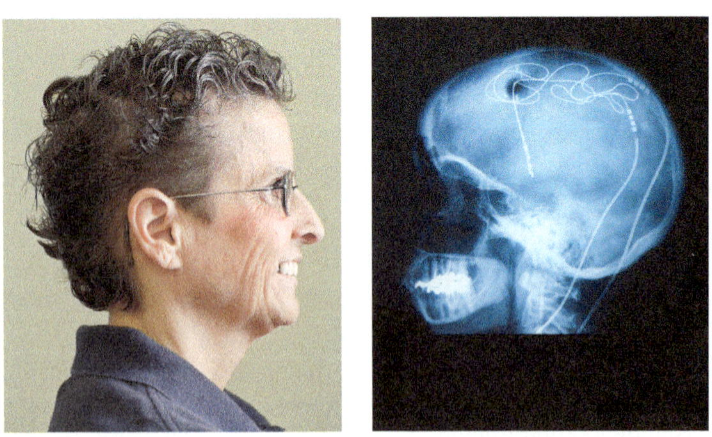

John B. Carnett/Bonnier Corp./Getty Images

After the successful use of deep brain stimulation for Parkinson's disease, the method was used to treat people with depression. The image on the right shows where an electrode was implanted in this woman's brain.

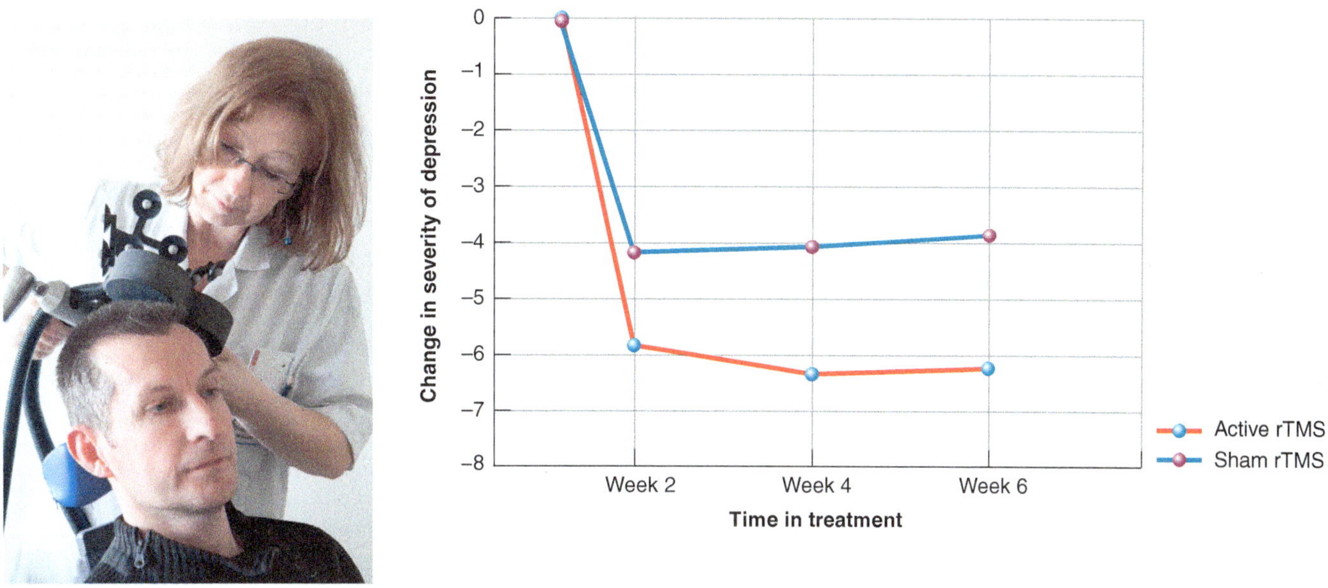

BSIP SA/Alamy Stock Photo

FIGURE **15.7**

Effects of rTMS on Depression. Compared to participants with depression undergoing a placebo version of rTMS (sham rTMS), participants receiving active rTMS showed significantly reduced scores on the standard Hamilton Depression Rating Scales. Participants showed rather strong placebo effects in the sham condition (note the drop in depression at week 2), which emphasizes the need for placebo-controlled studies in assessing the effectiveness of all types of treatment.

Source: Adapted from J. P. O'Reardon et al. (2007). "Efficacy and Safety of Transcranial Magnetic Stimulation in the Acute Treatment of Major Depression: A Multisite Randomized Controlled Trial," *Biological Psychiatry*, *62*(11), 1208–1216. doi:10.1016/j.biopsych.2007.01.018

neurofeedback A type of biofeedback used to treat attention deficit hyperactivity disorder (ADHD) and seizures by teaching the client to keep measures of brain activity within a certain range.

Neurofeedback

As mentioned in Chapter 4, biofeedback training allows participants to gain some conscious control over some otherwise unattended physical functions. For example, people can be taught to overcome "white coat hypertension," or the classically conditioned spike in blood pressure that occurs when a nurse or doctor (in a white lab coat) takes a measurement. By learning to relax instead of becoming tense in this situation, people can reduce their blood pressure, which is not a process that we typically try to control.

Neurofeedback is a type of biofeedback that concentrates on the activity of the brain. Recordings of brain activity, usually obtained from electroencephalography (EEG) but increasingly from functional magnetic resonance imaging (fMRI), are usually displayed for the participant, who is trained to keep readings in a desired range. In most cases, people are not consciously aware of what they are doing to comply. So far, however, rigorous studies have not provided strong support for the efficacy of EEG neurofeedback in the treatment of ADHD, ASD, OCD, generalized anxiety disorder (GAD), and MDD (Begemann et al., 2016; Riesco-Matías et al., 2019). Consequently, few insurance providers will cover this type of treatment.

Dr. Lise' DeLong/cognitive-connections.com

Neurofeedback, a type of biofeedback training that focuses on brain activity, has been used to treat ADHD in children.

SUMMARY 15.2 Approaches to Treating Psychological Disorders

Type of Therapy	Theoretical Perspective	Defining Features
Psychoanalysis 	• Psychodynamic theory	• Directive therapy • Free association • Dream analysis • Analysis of resistance • Analysis of transference
Humanistic therapy 	• Humanistic theory	• Nondirective therapy • Unconditional positive regard • Reflection • Empathy
Behavior therapy 	• Behaviorism	• Application of classical and operant learning principles in behavior modification • Therapy based only on observed behavior
Cognitive therapy 	• Cognition	• Cognitive restructuring • Combination of restructuring with applied behavior analysis in CBT
Biological treatments  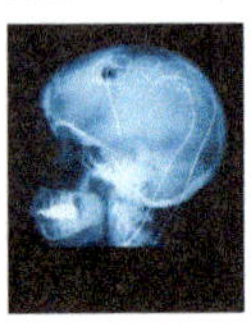	• Biology	• Medication • Electroconvulsive therapy • Psychosurgery • Brain stimulation • Neurofeedback

Credits: Top row—Bjanka Kadic/Alamy Stock Photo; Second row—Catchlight Visual Services/Alamy Stock Photo; Third row—Photo by Stephen Dagadakis, copyright Hunter Hoffman www.vrpain.com, World built by Firsthand Inc.; Fourth row—Clem Murray/MCT/Newscom; Bottom row—John B. Carnett/Bonnier Corp./Getty Images.

How Are Specific Disorders Treated?

As mentioned previously, approaches to treatment have differing success rates when applied to specific types of disorders. This section will outline the typical approaches to the psychological disorders discussed in Chapter 14.

Treating Neurodevelopmental Disorders

All therapy approaches discussed previously in this chapter have been applied to the treatment of children and adolescents. However, special care must be given to the use of biological therapies in childhood and adolescence because of the possible adverse effects of these treatments on the development of the nervous system.

Treating ASD Although ASD is accompanied by abnormalities in the neurotransmitters serotonin, GABA, and glutamate, no medications have proved effective in alleviating core symptoms of the disorder (DeFilippis & Wagner, 2016). This lack of a beneficial result

THINKING SCIENTIFICALLY

Should Autism Spectrum Disorder (ASD) Be Treated?

This might seem like a strange heading to find in a textbook on introductory psychology, especially given the fact that as we noted in Chapter 14, one of your authors is the parent of a daughter with autism spectrum disorder (ASD). We have learned in this chapter that applied behavior analysis (ABA) is the most effective treatment for ASD, so why wouldn't you take advantage of that? While many parents rely on ABA to help their children, others believe that ASD represents a type of neurodiversity rather than a problem to be fixed. They worry that the 40 hours or more per week that a child spends in ABA is actually cruel.

WHAT AM I BEING ASKED TO BELIEVE OR ACCEPT?

We are being asked to believe that ASD is more appropriately viewed as an example of neurodiversity, not in need of treatment or change, rather than a disability that requires treatment.

WHAT EVIDENCE SUPPORTS THIS POSITION?

Many of the dissenting voices regarding the treatment of ASD with ABA come from individuals with ASD who actually experienced ABA. However, these individuals have been joined by a number of leading researchers in ASD, who embrace the concept of neurodiversity (den Houting, 2019). A neurodiversity view advocates for interventions aimed at building strengths and addressing issues of importance to individuals with ASD as opposed to "normalizing" behavior.

ARE THERE OTHER WAYS THIS EVIDENCE COULD BE INTERPRETED?

Critics of the neurodiversity approach argue that for many individuals with ASD, the condition is definitely disabling. The neurodiversity approach might be appropriate for higher functioning individuals with ASD, but not necessarily for all. Critics express concern that viewing ASD as a "difference" will result in withdrawal of needed support, such as insurance coverage for ABA.

WHAT OTHER EVIDENCE WOULD I NEED TO EVALUATE THESE ALTERNATIVES?

As respected ASD researcher Simon Baron-Cohen states, "There is no single way for a brain to be normal" (Baron-Cohen, 2017, p. 746). He advocates for a thorough re-evaluation of the terms disorder, disability, difference, and disease, as these are used rather inconsistently across medicine and psychology. Research aimed at identifying interactions between client characteristics and treatment methods that produce the best outcomes would be helpful. This is unlikely to be a "one size fits all" approach.

WHAT ARE THE MOST REASONABLE CONCLUSIONS?

Our evidence-based practice model is useful here in the sense that messages are emerging

iadams/Shutterstock.com

Proponents of the concept of neurodiversity liken the experience of a person with autism spectrum disorder to being a "fish out of water." In other words, it is not the behavior itself that is the problem. Instead, the behavior is simply inappropriate for the circumstances surrounding the person.

from communities of individuals with ASD who want something different from traditional approaches to treatment. The desire for recognition of strengths as well as weaknesses is legitimate, as is the insistence that it is not just the personal characteristics of an individual with ASD that causes problems, but rather the existence of these characteristics within an environment to which they are not well-suited. As one individual with ASD stated, "We are fresh water fish in salt water" (Baron-Cohen, 2017, p. 746).

does not mean that medications are not prescribed in cases of ASD. Two antipsychotic medications have been approved by the U.S. Food and Drug Administration (FDA) for use in ASD and appear helpful in severe cases involving "irritability," which includes aggression, tantrums, and self-injury (Fung et al., 2016). Unfortunately, children treated with antipsychotic drugs experience the same side effects as adults, including weight gain, diabetes, motor dysfunction, and immune system problems. Antidepressants and several other types of drugs are commonly prescribed for children with ASD off-label, which means that the drugs have not been officially approved for this purpose on the basis of research demonstrating effectiveness (see Figure 15.8).

The most commonly used psychological treatment for ASD is applied behavior analysis (ABA), which builds on the principles of operant conditioning outlined in Chapter 8 (Smith & Lovaas, 1998). ABA focuses on observable, socially important behavior such as language

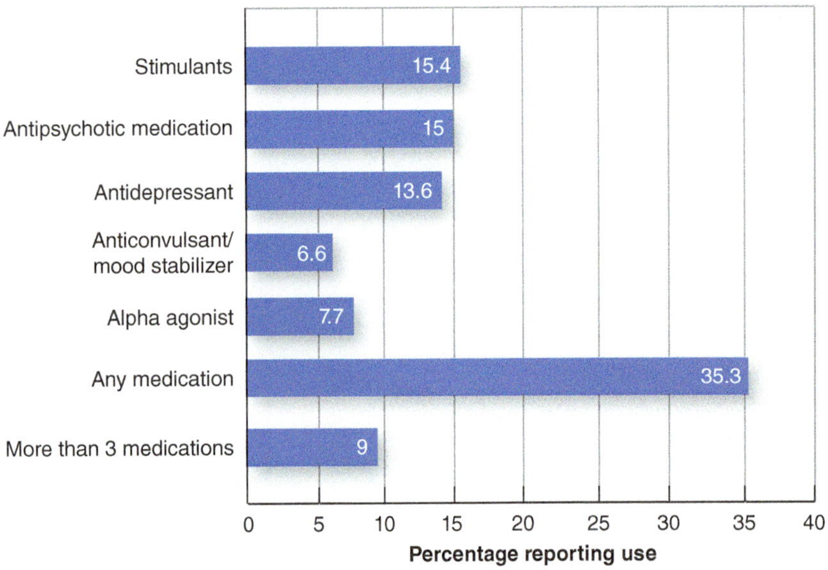

FIGURE **15.8**

Medications and ASD. Although only two medications (antipsychotic medications typically used to treat schizophrenia and bipolar disorder) have been approved by the FDA for use in treating ASD, large-scale studies show that many other medications are routinely prescribed by physicians for children with ASD. Alpha agonists are usually prescribed for high blood pressure and have a sedative effect. In this sample, 35.3% of the children had at least one prescription, and 9% had three or more drugs that they were taking simultaneously.

Source: Adapted from R. Rosenberg et al. (2010). "Psychotropic Medication Use Among Children with Autism Spectrum Disorders Enrolled in a National Registry, 2007–2008," *Journal of Autism and Developmental Disorders*, *40*(3), 342–351. doi:10.1007/s10803-009-0878-1

and should produce lasting improvements that generalize to settings outside the therapy setting (Baer et al., 1968). ABA in the treatment of ASD often involves therapy that takes up most of a child's waking hours, which is a large investment for families in terms of time and resources. Although studies are complicated by the child's initial level of functioning and many other variables, meta-analyses of the outcome of intensive, early-childhood behavioral interventions show positive effects of treatment on verbal IQ and language acquisition, but more moderate effects on social skills and daily functioning (see ● Figure 15.9; Makrygianni et al., 2010).

Because of the severity and lifelong nature of ASD, parents of children with this disorder are especially vulnerable to so-called cures that have little research support. Dietary interventions have become popular in recent years, but these appear to have few benefits. People with ASD show evidence of excess peptides from gluten (found in wheat) and casein (found in dairy products), but controlled studies do not demonstrate benefits from restricting these foods (Millward et al., 2008). "Chelation" treatments designed to remove heavy metals from the body are also popular but lack research support (Weber & Newmark, 2007). Even worse, at least one child died from this type of treatment because a physician substituted a toxic chemical for the correct one with a similar name (Sinha et al., 2006). Hyperbaric oxygen therapy, usually used to treat the bends in scuba divers, has not been shown to improve ASD symptoms in spite of Internet claims to the contrary (Granpeesheh et al., 2010; Xiong et al., 2016). Among treatments often advertised to parents are sensory integration treatment, massage, music, special diets, and animal-assisted therapies. While these latter approaches are unlikely to cause harm, with the possible exception of special diets, they are expensive and distract families from therapies with known efficacy, such as ABA.

Treating ADHD Many children with a diagnosis of ADHD are treated with medication, either alone or in combination with behavior therapy (Storebø et al., 2016). The use of medications for attention problems resulted from an accidental discovery. In 1937, Charles Bradley used a stimulant (benzedrine sulfate) to treat a group of children hospitalized for learning and behavior problems. He noted that during the week that the children used the drug, half demonstrated "a spectacular improvement in school performance" and became emotionally subdued (Bradley, 1937, p. 584).

The most commonly prescribed drugs for ADHD are the closely related stimulants methylphenidate (Ritalin), dextroamphetamine (Dexedrine or Dextrostat), and a combination of amphetamine salts (Adderall). These drugs increase the activity of dopamine

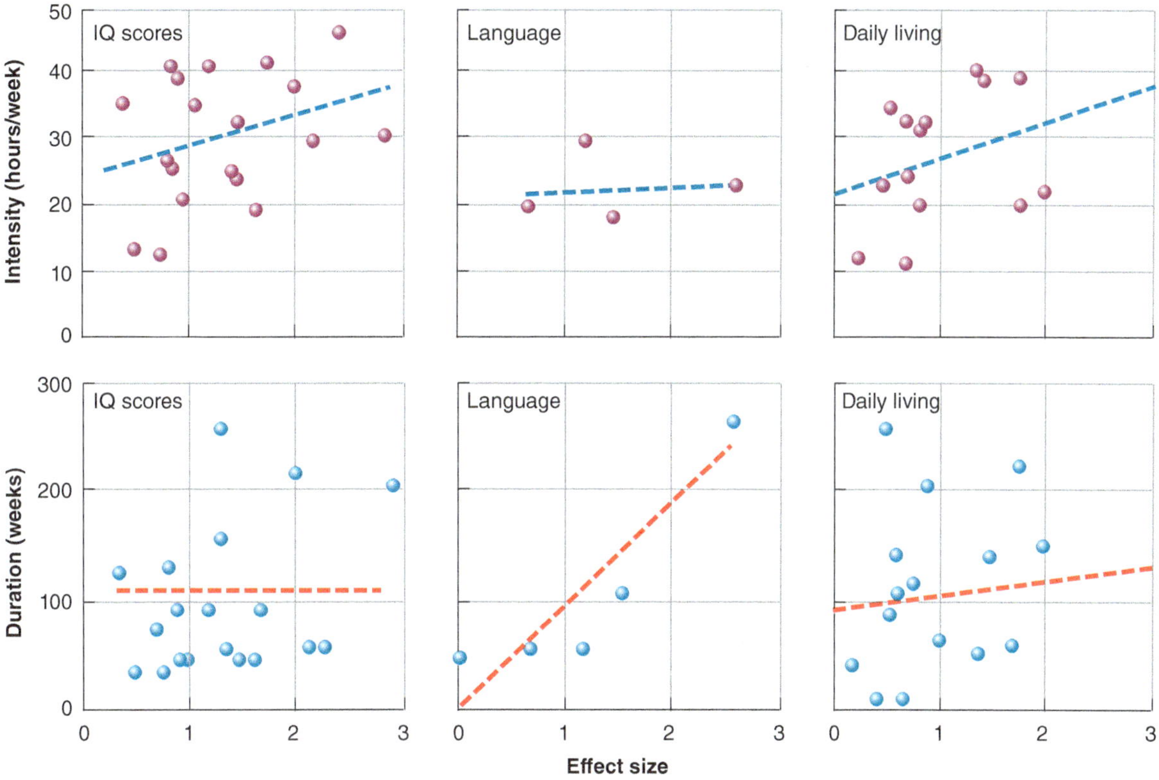

FIGURE **15.9**

Outcomes for Early Behavioral Intervention in ASD. A meta-analysis demonstrated that early behavioral intervention in ASD produced measurable improvements in IQ scores, language, and daily living. High-intensity treatment (measured by hours per week) seemed to have the greatest effects on IQ, but duration of treatment seemed to have the biggest impact on language. Most clinical psychologists suggest that an effect size of 1 for a treatment means that the treatment is very effective.

Source: Adapted from J. Virués-Ortega (2010). "Applied Behavior Analytic Intervention for Autism in Early Childhood: Meta-Analysis, Meta-Regression and Dose-Response Meta-Analysis of Multiple Outcomes," *Clinical Psychology Review*, *30*, 387–399. doi: 10.1016/j.cpr.2010.01.008

and norepinephrine. Most patients tolerate these medications well, but side effects of weight loss, sleep disturbance, and higher heart rate and blood pressure can occur. If children take the medications continuously for long periods, growth can also be suppressed. Methylphenidate does produce tolerance, and patients should stop the drug under medical supervision rather than on their own (Ross et al., 2002). Although it is chemically quite similar to amphetamine, methylphenidate is not considered an addictive drug, given its slower action on the brain (Volkow et al., 2005). Individuals who do not respond well to the stimulant drugs are often treated with nonstimulant drugs that increase norepinephrine activity (Prasad & Steer, 2008).

It might appear odd to treat a disorder that often features hyperactivity, or high

Courtesy of Bradley Hospital

Charles Bradley observed the behavior of 30 institutionalized children, who had a variety of problem behaviors, after they were administered a type of amphetamine used at the time for asthma and other breathing problems. Bradley's observations about the children's "spectacular improvement in school performance," as well as their becoming "emotionally subdued," led to the modern treatment of ADHD with stimulant medication, including other types of amphetamine.

FIGURE **15.10**

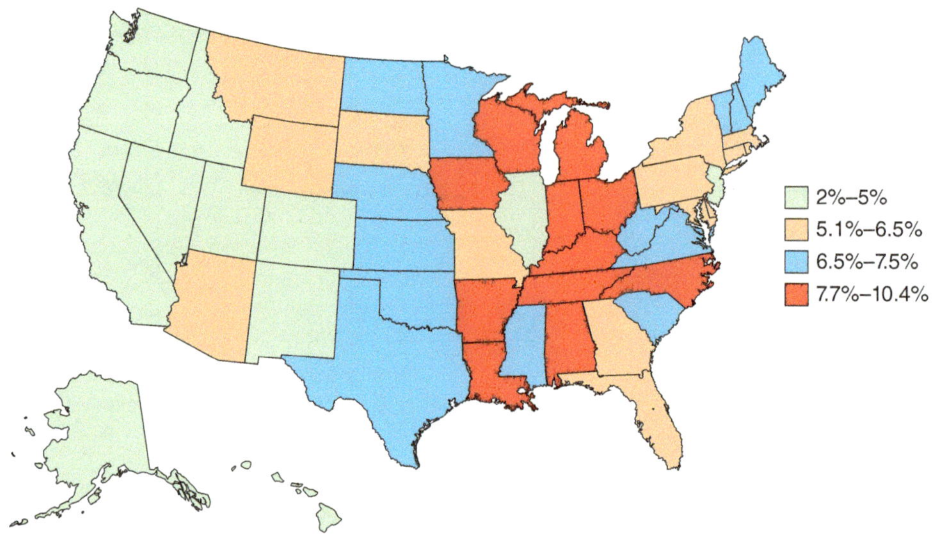

Use of Medication for Treating ADHD. This map of medication use for ADHD from the Centers for Disease Control and Prevention (CDC) shows the same regional variations that were observed in Chapter 14 for the prevalence of ADHD diagnoses. Together, these data suggest that about half of all children diagnosed with ADHD are prescribed medication. The use of medication produces short-term improvements in about 75%–80% of children with ADHD. However, children with ADHD who are treated with medication are no better off in adolescence or adulthood than children with ADHD who were not treated with medication.

Source: Adapted from CDC (2020). "State-Based Prevalence of ADHD Diagnosis and Treatment," retrieved from https://www.cdc.gov/ncbddd/adhd/data/diagnosis-treatment-data.html

levels of impulsive behavior, with a stimulant. Wouldn't it make more sense to try medications that have a calming effect? The rationale for stimulant treatment of ADHD suggests that impulsive hyperactivity occurs if the parts of the brain responsible for planned, thoughtful behavior, such as the basal ganglia and frontal lobes, are not active enough. Raising the activity in these areas theoretically should reduce impulsive behavior. One of the common myths about medications for ADHD, however, is that they have different effects on people who do and do not have the disorder. In other words, people mistakenly believe that the medications calm people with ADHD but stimulate those who do not have the disorder. This is not the case, as all individuals respond in similar ways with greater focus and alertness (Arnsten, 2006). Not surprisingly, then, medications prescribed for ADHD are commonly abused by those without the disorder.

The use of medication for ADHD in the United States is five times higher than in any other nation, leading to criticism of the practice (see ● Figure 15.10). An unusual percentage of published research reports on the efficacy of medication for ADHD has been sponsored directly by the pharmaceutical industry, leading to concerns about possible bias (Storebø et al., 2016). Using the "gold standard" of the double-blind, placebo-controlled design, approximately 75%–80% of children treated with medication alone experience significant short-term improvement on ratings of social compliance and sustained attention (Barkley, 1995). However, two large meta-analyses in the prestigious Cochrane Reviews found support for the use of stimulant drugs to be "inconclusive" (Storebà, 2019). In spite of the use of "double-blind" procedures, it is unlikely that children are truly "blind" to their treatment condition, as stimulant medications have immediate and obvious effects on heart rate. Research has not demonstrated long-term benefits of stimulant use on later outcomes in adolescence and adulthood (Loe & Feldman, 2007). In other words, children with ADHD treated with medication do not enjoy superior outcomes later in life compared to children with ADHD who do not receive medication.

College students are not the only ones using ADHD medications inappropriately. A survey in the prestigious scientific journal *Nature* found that 65% of the scientists who responded knew a colleague who used methylphenidate or similar drugs without a prescription for the purpose of improving focus and concentration (Maher, 2008).

Although two-thirds of children diagnosed with ADHD receive medication, fewer than half receive behavioral treatments (Danielson et al., 2018). Behavioral parent training, which builds the skills of parents of children with ADHD to use operant conditioning methods effectively, and behavioral classroom management, which applies learning principles in the school setting, are especially effective (Pelham & Fabiano, 2008). Unfortunately, it is often difficult to maintain the consistency needed for successful behavioral intervention without a great deal of cooperation among teachers, parents, and others working with the child.

Treating Schizophrenia

Before the 1950s, effective treatment for schizophrenia was virtually nonexistent. Patients were often subjected to odd "treatments" that had no basis in any scientific understanding of their condition and that were frankly dangerous in some cases. They were forcibly restrained in lukewarm baths with canvas covers that prevented their escape. Insulin shock therapy, in which injections of insulin were used to place patients in daily comas, enjoyed a brief fad status, as did the frontal lobotomy, discussed earlier in this chapter.

The discovery of effective medications for schizophrenia was accidental. A French surgeon, Henri Laborit, was impressed by the calming effects of the phenothiazines. He experimented with one of these drugs, chlorpromazine (Thorazine), to reduce stress and shock in his surgical patients. Based on his promising results, Laborit encouraged his psychiatric colleagues to try the drug on their psychotic patients, which they did with dramatic success. A new era of treatment began. Largely as a result of this new type of treatment, institutionalized populations dropped by about 50% in the United States between 1955 and 2000 (see ● Figure 15.11). People responding well to medication could now return to their communities instead of living in institutions.

Initially, nobody understood how phenothiazines reduced psychosis. One clue came from the fact that high doses of the drug produced symptoms similar to those of Parkinson's disease, such as muscular tremor. Parkinson's disease was known to result from the degeneration of motor neurons that used dopamine as their primary neurotransmitter. Further research indicated that phenothiazines acted as dopamine antagonists, blocking dopamine at the receptor site.

Phenothiazines are not without their share of problems, though. Nearly one-quarter of patients with schizophrenia do not respond to these drugs (Kane & Freeman, 1994). The drugs successfully reduce psychotic symptoms, such as hallucinations and delusions, but are often less effective in reducing negative symptoms, such as social withdrawal and emotional disturbance (Buchanan et al., 1995).

To address these deficits of phenothiazines, often called "typical" or "first-generation" antipsychotic medications, newer "atypical" or "second-generation" antipsychotic medications, such as clozapine (Clozaril), were introduced. Increasing numbers of patients with schizophrenia are prescribed the atypical antipsychotics (Meltzer et al., 2010). To reduce psychosis, a medication must influence dopamine activity. However, the newer drugs are often more effective than phenothiazines in treating the negative symptoms of schizophrenia because they affect a wide range of neurotransmitters in addition to dopamine, including serotonin.

All antipsychotic medications produce significant side effects. **Tardive dyskinesia**, (*tardive* means "slow" and *dyskinesia* means "difficulty moving") is a syndrome that results from the use of antipsychotic medications by some patients. The syndrome produces tremors and involuntary movements, especially of the face and tongue. These problems often continue even when medication stops. Although risk of tardive dyskinesia seems lower with the second-generation antipsychotics (Leucht et al., 2013), these drugs have their own set of side effects, including diabetes, weight gain, reductions in white blood cell count, aggravation of existing cancers, and seizure disorders.

tardive dyskinesia A movement syndrome that results from the use of medications used to treat symptoms of schizophrenia.

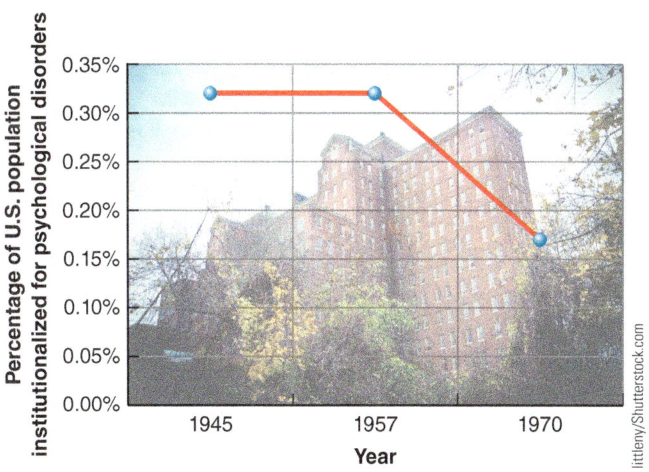

FIGURE **15.11**

The Discovery of Effective Medications for Schizophrenia Had Dramatic Effects. The percentage of the U.S. population that was institutionalized in asylums because of mental disorders was cut almost in half in the years following the discovery of antipsychotic medications.

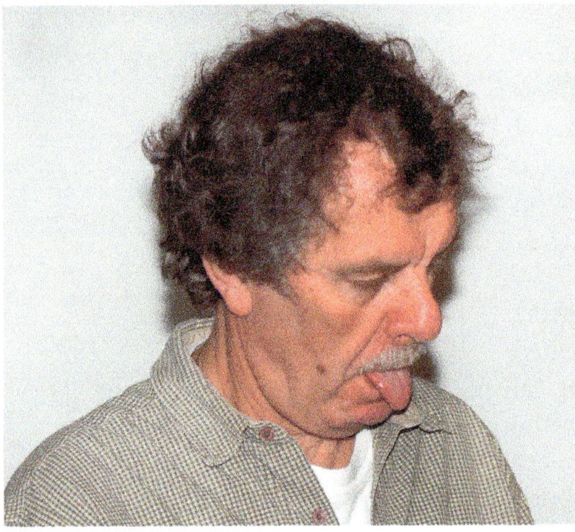

Art Directors & TRIP/Alamy Stock Photo

Medications used for schizophrenia often produce a movement disorder known as *tardive dyskinesia*. This patient is experiencing the intrusive, involuntary movements and tremors that characterize this condition, which is usually permanent. Newer medications for schizophrenia are somewhat less likely to produce tardive dyskinesia but have their own side effects, including diabetes, weight gain, reductions in immune system functioning, aggravation of existing cancers, and seizure disorders.

Most individuals with schizophrenia are treated with medication, but psychosocial treatments still have much to offer. The World Health Organization (WHO) noted that people with schizophrenia in developing countries, such as Nigeria, India, and Colombia, were recovering more frequently than patients in the United States and Europe (Hopper et al., 2007). Further research suggested that improved outcomes occur when patients remained in their homes and were given opportunities to do meaningful work. These observations led to the increased use of psychosocial rehabilitation for patients with schizophrenia (Bustillo et al., 2001). This approach emphasizes providing opportunities to do meaningful work, social skills training, education about schizophrenia and the importance of medication, affordable housing linked to services, and information about symptom management.

Treating Bipolar Disorder

The primary method of treating bipolar disorder is the use of medication. The most commonly prescribed medication is a simple salt, lithium carbonate. Not only does lithium prevent recurrences of mania, but it is uniquely preventive of suicidal behavior (Alda, 2015). Lithium's actions remain poorly understood. In general, lithium appears to protect individuals from further neurodegeneration (Alda, 2015), reverses and repairs oxidative stress, and resets circadian rhythms (Malhi & Outhred, 2016). Administration of lithium in patients with bipolar disorder results in increased gray matter relative to patients who are not treated with lithium (see ● Figure 15.12).

Unfortunately, lithium carbonate has a number of unpleasant and potentially dangerous side effects. Toxic levels of lithium produce nausea, vomiting, muscular tremor, coma, and seizures. Because of these risks, patients must have regular blood tests to monitor their lithium levels. The unpleasantness of these side effects also contributes to the poor compliance with their treatment plan that characterizes patients with bipolar disorder. These patients are less likely to follow treatment instructions than any other kind of patient on any other type of medication (Sajatovic et al., 2007). Other medications, including antipsychotics, are used in treating bipolar disorder but do not appear to be as effective as lithium in reducing hospital admissions (Joas et al., 2017).

Research demonstrating that bipolar disorder is more common in nations in which consumption of seafood is low, discussed in Chapter 14, has led to suggestions that omega-3 fatty acids in the diet might provide some protection from bipolar disorder (Noaghiul & Hibbeln, 2003). Lower levels of omega-3 fatty acids have been observed in patients with bipolar disorder, and levels following supplementation correlate with the severity of the patients' symptoms (Saunders et al., 2016). While not a substitute for treatment with lithium, the benefits of omega-3 fatty acids are obtained without side effects.

You have probably noticed that this discussion of treating bipolar disorder has not emphasized psychotherapy. Most individuals with bipolar disorder, like those with schizophrenia, appear to require medication for the alleviation of their symptoms, and psychotherapy alone is not typically considered an option. However, psychotherapy aimed at assisting individuals and their families with coping with bipolar disorder and adhering to treatment is often beneficial. Even in conditions like bipolar disorder that have strong bases in biology, integrating several perspectives when selecting treatment approaches can produce superior outcomes.

Sofiaworld/Shutterstock.com

Psychosocial rehabilitation for schizophrenia includes opportunities to do useful work. Socializing with peers, engaging in healthy outdoor physical activity, and earning a paycheck contribute to the clients' personal growth.

Treating Major Depressive Disorder (MDD)

Given the range of suspected causal factors in MDD, it should not surprise you that treatment approaches are diverse. Treatments range from medical, to cognitive, to behavioral, to simple aerobic exercise, and combinations of these approaches are common.

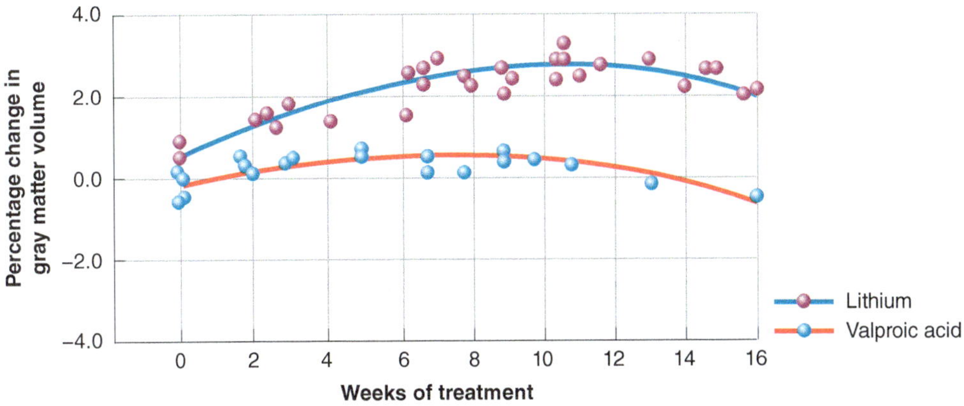

FIGURE **15.12**

Effects of Lithium Treatment on Gray Matter Volume. Newly diagnosed participants with bipolar disorder were randomly assigned to groups treated with lithium or valproic acid, which is also used to treat bipolar disorder. Over the next 16 weeks, these groups were compared to healthy controls using no medications. Gray matter volume increased in the group treated with lithium but did not change in the healthy controls or in the group treated with valproic acid. These results support the ability of lithium to increase neural growth, which might also explain its effectiveness in treating bipolar disorder.

Source: Adapted from I. K. Lyoo et al. (2010). "Lithium-Induced Gray Matter Volume Increase as a Neural Correlate of Treatment Response in Bipolar Disorder: A Longitudinal Brain Imaging Study," *Neuropsychopharmacology*, *35*(8), 1743–1750. doi: 10.1038/npp.2010.41

The most popular method for treating MDD today is the use of medication. **Antidepressant medications** are the third most common prescription drug taken by Americans (Pratt, Brody, & Gu, 2011). As shown in Figure 15.13, about 10% of Americans over the age of 12 years use antidepressants. Rates of antidepressant use in the United States increased nearly 400% between 1988 and 2008 (Pratt et al., 2011). Keep in mind that antidepressant medications are often prescribed for conditions other than MDD, such as anxiety disorders. This is still a remarkable number of prescriptions and raises the distinct possibility that, like barbiturates and benzodiazepines before them, antidepressants are being overprescribed. Controversy over the benefits of antidepressants over placebo as well as the relationship of benefits to side effects continues. A large meta-analysis of over 117,000 participants demonstrated modest, positive advantages of antidepressant medications over placebos in terms of effectiveness (Cipriani et al., 2018). However, the authors note that it was difficult to find studies that had not been funded by pharmaceutical organizations, suggesting the possibility of bias.

The most widely prescribed antidepressant medications are the selective serotonin reuptake inhibitors (SSRIs), which include popular brands like Prozac and Zoloft. As their name implies, these medications increase serotonin activity at the synapse by interfering with reuptake of the neurotransmitter, a process discussed in Chapter 4. As a result, more serotonin is available in the synapse (see Figure 15.14). The use of SSRIs is based on a belief that MDD results from unusually low serotonin activity and that therefore, boosting serotonin activity should improve mood.

In addition to inhibiting the reuptake of neurotransmitters at the synapse, antidepressants provide further benefit by increasing the number of neurons in the hippocampus (Anacker et al., 2011). Stress and depression both appear to reduce the number of neurons found in the hippocampus, and the administration of antidepressants may not only halt this loss, but also promote the birth of new neurons in this area (Micheli et al., 2018).

These medications have their share of risks and side effects too. Increases in thinking about suicide following use of SSRIs, especially in people under the age of 30, have prompted

antidepressant medication A medication designed to alleviate symptoms of depression, but often prescribed for other types of conditions.

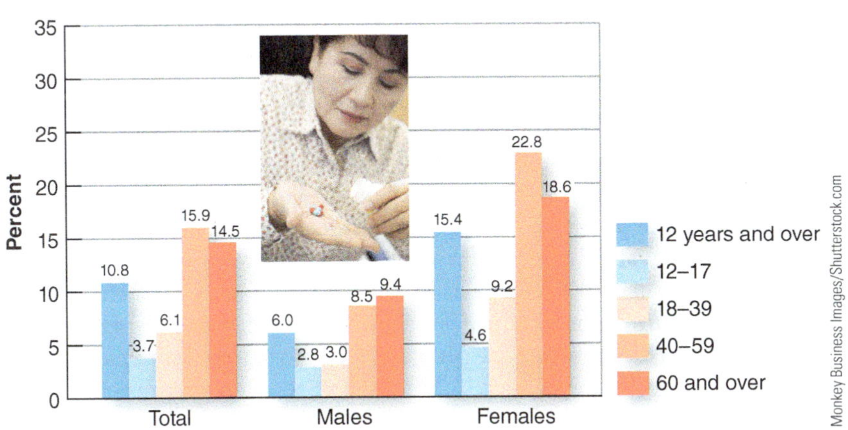

FIGURE **15.13**

Antidepressant Use in the United States. Use of antidepressant medication in the United States is high, with one in ten over the age of 12 years and more than one in five 40- to 59-year-old females using these medications.

Source: Adapted from Data Brief No. 76. *Antidepressant Use in Persons Aged 12 and Over: United States*, 2005–2008. Retrieved June 15, 2017, from http://www.cdc.gov/nchs/data/databriefs/db76_tables.pdf#1

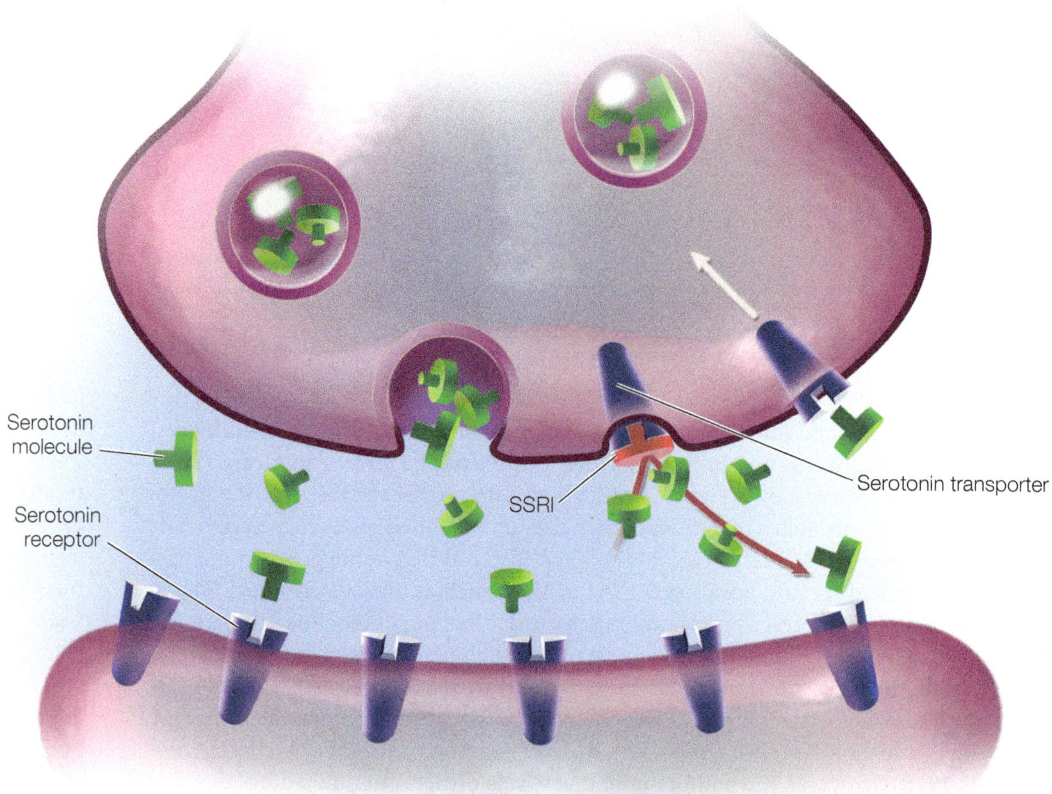

FIGURE **15.14**

SSRIs increase the amount of serotonin in the synaptic gap that is available to interact with serotonin receptors. These drugs achieve this effect by interacting with the serotonin transporters located in the membrane of the neuron releasing the serotonin. This interaction slows the rate of reuptake, or the process by which the neuron retrieves and repackages the molecules of serotonin that it has just released.

stronger warnings for close supervision by attending physicians (Courtet & Lopez-Castroman, 2017). Other side effects of SSRIs include nausea, reduction of rapid eye movement (REM) sleep, headache, weight gain, and sexual dysfunction. Antidepressants are responsible for problems with sexual activity in about 40% of the patients who are using them (Lorenz et al., 2016). When patients fail to respond to medication, other biological treatments might be used to treat MDD, such as ECT, deep brain stimulation, or rTMS.

In addition to biological treatment options, a number of psychotherapy alternatives are quite successful in alleviating depression and have the added benefit of producing no adverse side effects. One of the most popular approaches is the use of CBT. As described previously, this approach combines the restructuring of negative cognitions ("Nobody loves me" becomes "Not everybody loves me, but some people do") and behavioral techniques aimed at increasing the person's activity level and social skills (Beck et al., 1979). Between 40% and 60% of people with MDD treated with CBT not only experience relief from their symptoms, but also appear to be less susceptible to repeated bouts of depression than people who use medication alone (Hollon et al., 2002).

People who are depressed also benefit from adding aerobic exercise to their routine (see Figure 15.15; Morres et al., 2019). For cases of mild to moderate depression, exercise produces effects comparable to medication and psychotherapy, and it complements these treatments in cases of severe depression. Because people who are depressed face higher risks of cardiovascular disease and type 2 diabetes, exercise is a valuable addition in terms of patients' physical health as well.

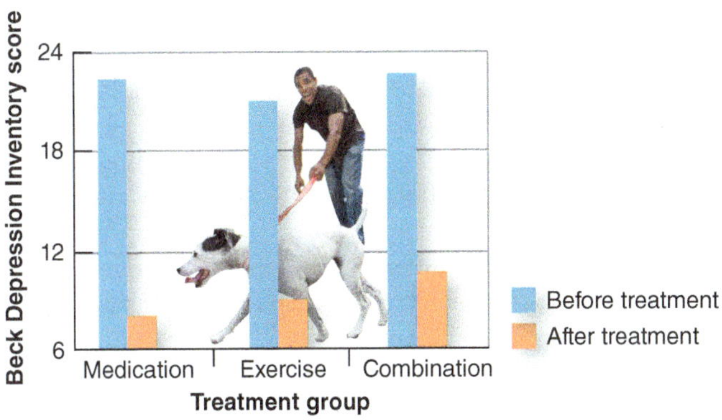

Jupiterimages/Photos.com

FIGURE **15.15**

Exercise and MDD. Participants with MDD who had not been previously treated were randomly assigned to medication alone, exercise alone, and medication plus exercise groups for a 12-week study. Because the participants were randomly assigned to groups, there were no statistically significant differences in the severity of their depression before treatment. All three treatment groups experienced improvement in their symptoms, as shown by their reduced scores on the Beck Depression Inventory. Although it appears that the medication group might have improved more than the exercise and combination groups, the differences between these three groups were not statistically significant. Therefore, we can conclude that exercise alone was equally effective in reducing symptoms of depression as medication alone or medication in combination with exercise.

Source: Adapted from J. A. Blumenthal et al. (1999). "Effects of Exercise Training on Older Patients with Major Depression," *Archives of Internal Medicine*, *159*(19), 2349–2356. doi: 10.1001/archinte.159.19.2349

CONNECTING TO RESEARCH

Mindfulness and the Prevention of Relapse in Major Depressive Disorder (MDD)

ALTHOUGH OUR METHODS FOR TREATING MDD are typically effective, there is a significant risk of recurrence. Some individuals experience low rates of recurrence when continuing to take antidepressant medications, even when their depressive symptoms are gone. However, these medications produce significant side effects, making this approach undesirable for many people. Continuation of CBT after recovery is typically more helpful than continuing to take medication, but many health plans pay for only limited numbers of sessions.

Recurrences of depression might occur because people who have experienced episodes of MDD think differently than people with no history of depression when a mildly negative mood state occurs (Teasdale et al., 2000). A technique known as *mindfulness-based cognitive therapy (MBCT)* combines aspects of CBT and mindfulness-based stress reduction. The idea of MBCT is to teach people to "detach" from depression-related thoughts and feelings by endorsing statements like "Thoughts are not facts" and "I am not my thoughts." How well does this approach work to prevent repeated episodes of MDD?

The Question: Does the addition of MBCT to MDD treatment produce better outcomes than treatment as usual alone?

METHODS

In one study, 145 patients in recovery from MDD were randomly assigned to continue with their treatments as usual or to receive additional MBCT training (Teasdale et al., 2000). Their progress at a 1-year follow-up was assessed.

Treatment as usual meant that the patients would seek help as they normally would, perhaps from a family doctor, if they experienced mood difficulties. Participants assigned to receive MBCT training attended eight weekly 2-hour group training sessions and completed daily homework exercises. Key themes included empowerment, freedom of choice, and awareness of experience in the moment.

ETHICS

Patients as participants require additional protections. Making treatment as usual available ensures that no participants are left untreated. Referrals to appropriate services should be provided to all participants, and confidentiality should be maintained with great care.

RESULTS

Among participants with three or more previous episodes of depression, who made up 77% of the sample, the addition of MBCT reduced recurrence rates by nearly 50% compared to treatment as usual alone.

CONCLUSIONS

This study indicated that MBCT provides a powerful tool for preventing further episodes of depression—a finding that has since been replicated and supported by a significant amount of research (Khoury et al., 2013; Warren et al., 2016; Tickell et al., 2020). The use of MBCT has been extended successfully from the treatment of MDD to the treatment of anxiety and stress (Khoury et al., 2013). ■

Treating Anxiety Disorders

Anxiety disorders, including GAD, phobias, and panic disorder, are typically treated by using medication, CBT, or a combination of the two (see ● Figure 15.16).

As discussed in Chapter 14, anxiety is associated with a heightened level of brain activity because of anticipated danger. Consequently, most efforts to medicate anxiety attempt to reduce brain activity, or produce a "tranquilizing" effect.

Because GABA is the major inhibitory neurotransmitter in the brain, a common method for slowing brain activity is to enhance its effects. As described in Chapter 6, many substances, including alcohol, barbiturates, and benzodiazepines, interact with the GABA receptor to produce stronger inhibition in the brain. Each of these types of substances produces a tranquilizing effect on the brain. Because these drugs have additive effects with one another and work at the same receptor site, taking combinations of these drugs is frequently fatal because of a life-threatening level of brain inhibition.

Barbiturates, developed in 1903, continue to be quite useful in the treatment of seizures, but their use as a treatment for anxiety is no longer considered desirable. They were one of the first of several medications used for psychological treatments to become vastly overprescribed. By the mid-1960s, enough barbiturates were being made to provide every American man, woman, and child with 40 to 50 doses per year (Regan, 2000). The addictive properties of barbiturates, as well as their frequent use in suicides, were definite drawbacks.

The discovery of benzodiazepines after World War II changed the treatment of anxiety dramatically, but like the

Knowing that one of the motivations for alcohol use might be to reduce the anxiety resulting from social events and other stressors can be helpful in avoiding problem drinking. If a person feels like she "can't face" a situation without being drunk, it would be more positive to seek professional help than to continue drinking.

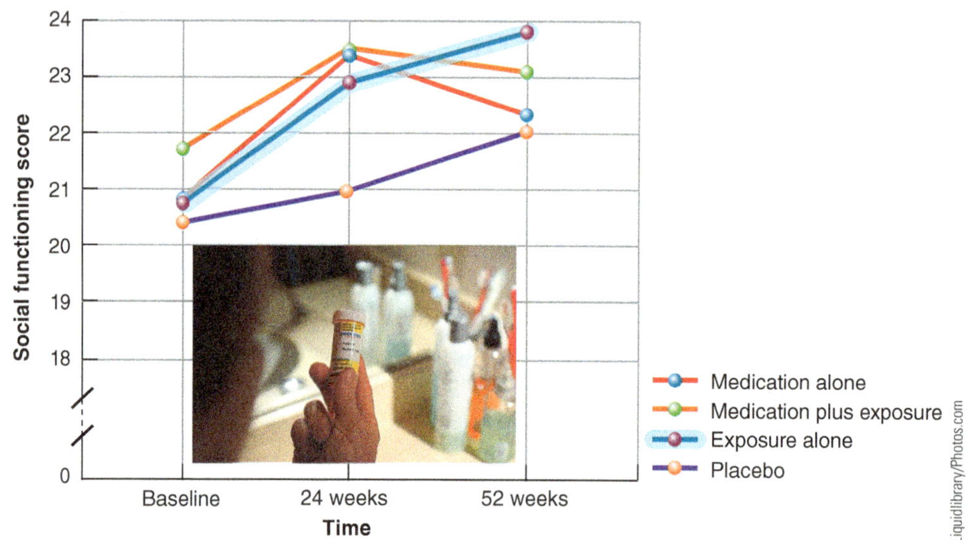

FIGURE **15.16**

Comparisons of Treatments in Social Anxiety Disorder. Medication, exposure therapy (in which the individual is gradually introduced to anxiety-producing situations), and combined medication and exposure therapy appear to produce approximately equal improvement in the functioning of people with social anxiety disorder. Scores of social functioning of people randomly assigned to these treatment conditions were significantly better than scores of the placebo group after 24 weeks of treatment. However, when treatment was discontinued after 24 weeks, the functioning of the groups that received medication and medication combined with exposure therapy deteriorated at the 1-year follow-up assessment, whereas the exposure-alone group continued to improve. These results suggest that patients choosing to use medication should continue treatment to maintain gains in functioning.

Source: Adapted from T. T. Haug et al. (2003). "Exposure Therapy and Sertraline in Social Phobia: 1-year Follow-up of a Randomised Controlled Trial," *British Journal of Psychiatry*, *182*, 312–318. doi: 10.1192/bjp.02.229

barbiturates, the benzodiazepines became overused. By the 1970s, chlordiazepoxide (Librium) and diazepam (Valium) were the most frequently prescribed drugs of their day. Alprazolam (Xanax) remains a widely used benzodiazepine, typically prescribed for panic disorder, GAD, and premenstrual syndrome. In some cases, alprazolam seems to be helpful in treating MDD, but its mechanism for doing so is not understood.

You might think that tranquilizers would be a logical medication for treating anxiety disorders. Although these drugs are used occasionally, the antidepressants discussed in a previous section of this chapter are typically more effective. This result might reflect a common underlying cause for both depression and anxiety.

Behavioral and cognitive behavioral techniques are commonly used to treat anxiety disorders and have the advantage over medication of having no side effects. Phobias, for instance, can be treated with exposure therapy, in which the person is gradually exposed to the fear stimulus or to other people interacting harmlessly with the fear stimulus while the person relaxes. Medication and psychological treatments produce similar levels of improvement for cases of anxiety (Baldwin et al., 2014).

Treating OCD

OCD can be treated with antidepressant medication, CBT, or a combination of both. CBT for OCD involves training the person to anticipate compulsive behavior and then to engage in a competing behavior. As mentioned earlier, a compulsive hand-washer could go outside, away from faucets and soap, to do some gardening. Meta-analyses show that CBT is a highly effective approach to treating OCD (Olatunji et al., 2013).

EXPERIENCING PSYCHOLOGY

Progressive Relaxation

AS YOU HAVE SEEN in this chapter, administering therapies for psychological disorders and problems with adjustment is typically the domain of highly trained professionals. However, there are a few activities that people can do safely on their own to reduce stress and change habits. Chapter 8 outlined a method that you could use to change unwanted habits based on behavioral therapies. This box reviews a progressive relaxation technique that you can use to reduce stress. These same techniques are often implemented to produce relaxation during exposure therapy.

To enhance your ability to relax, it is often beneficial to make an audio recording of the instructions. To begin, put on some loose, comfortable clothing and either lie down on your back or sit in a chair with your head supported. Breathe slowly and deeply. Each muscle group is tensed for 5 seconds (silently count "one–one thousand" at a normal speaking pace), followed by a pause of 20 seconds, during which you relax the muscle group and think of tension "draining" from that part of the body. The procedure can be repeated for more dramatic relaxation. With practice, you should be able to "will" yourself into a relaxed state rather easily. Here is the order of muscle groups to tense and relax:

1. Tense the muscles of your head and face.
2. Tense the muscles of your neck (gently).
3. Tense your elbows and biceps for 5 seconds, and then relax and straighten your arms.
4. Clench your fists tightly.
5. Tense the muscles of your chest.
6. Tense the muscles of your stomach.
7. Tense the muscles of your calves.
8. Tense the muscles of your feet and toes (gently, to avoid cramping).
9. If you are successful in achieving deep relaxation, someone should be able to pick up your arm or leg and it will be limp and unresisting. ■

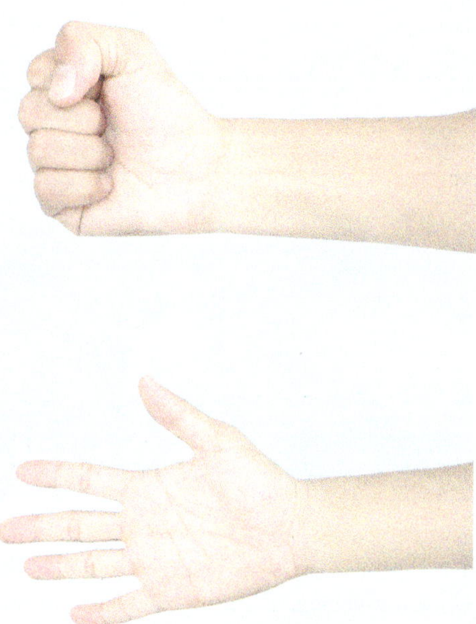
Anan Kaewkhammul/Shutterstock.com

Tensing and then relaxing each muscle group in the body leads to a deep state of relaxation.

Treating Body Dysmorphic Disorder

CBT is particularly helpful in cases of body dysmorphic disorder (Allen & Woolfolk, 2010). Cognitive restructuring can help the individual think more realistically about perceived physical flaws. Many individuals with this disorder, however, insist on continued treatment by cosmetic surgeons and resist suggestions that they should obtain psychotherapy.

Treating PTSD

The American Psychological Association and the U.S. Veteran's Administration strongly recommend three similar types of psychotherapy for PTSD: prolonged exposure therapy, cognitive processing therapy, and trauma-focused CBT (Watkins et al., 2018). Prolonged exposure

PSYCHOLOGY AS A HUB SCIENCE

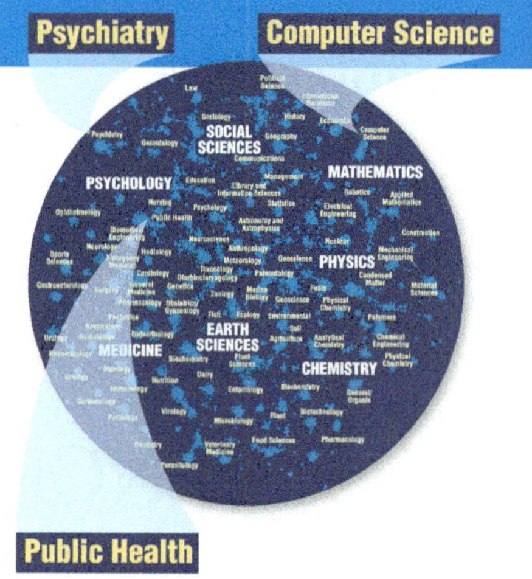

Using Virtual Reality (VR) to Treat Anxiety and PTSD

YOU MIGHT EXPECT virtual reality (VR), the presentation of realistic stimuli through a device worn on the head, to be more exciting to video gamers than to therapists. However, this new technology is showing remarkable promise for the treatment of phobias and PTSD.

As discussed in this chapter and in Chapter 8, one of the best ways to address these stress- and fear-related problems is to combine relaxation with a controlled exposure to the fear-producing stimuli. This application of classical conditioning was popularized by Joseph Wolpe in the 1950s (Wolpe, 1958). For example, people who are afraid of heights could imagine progressively more stressful situations (climbing a ladder or visiting the Empire State Building) while remaining relaxed. Eventually, the fear of heights should be reduced.

Defense Dept. photo by John J. Kruzel

The U.S. Army is testing "Virtual Iraq," a 360-degree, interactive, computer-generated environment, as a treatment for soldiers with PTSD. Soldiers are able to relate their traumatic experiences to the therapist, who can then program the environment to reproduce weather conditions, terrain, helicopter flyovers, types of attacks, and sound. Soldiers treated with VR are being compared with soldiers treated with other traditional psychotherapy approaches and a control group of soldiers on the waiting list for treatment.

Imagination is a wonderful capability of the mind, but it has its limitations. This is where VR comes in. Instead of asking a client to imagine a situation, the scenario can be presented in a realistic way through the use of VR technology. As our height-phobic client maneuvers through elevators, construction sites, and other high places, wind, vibration, and sound can be added to make the visual experience even more realistic. In addition to treating phobias, VR is being used to help combat veterans recover from PTSD (Spira et al., 2006). In these cases, odors from diesel fuel and gunpowder can be added to enhance the reality of the virtual experience.

Research comparing the effectiveness of VR therapies, alone or in conjunction with traditional CBT, suggests that VR therapy alone is about as effective as CBT alone in treating phobias, but the former might have an advantage in certain situations, such as fear of flying (Krijn et al., 2007). VR also performed well in comparisons with CBT in cases of PTSD (Baños et al., 2011). In particular, VR therapy appealed to people with PTSD who were unwilling to undergo more traditional treatments. People who grew up playing video games might find the VR approach more effective and comfortable. Technological advances allowing a shared VR experience for therapists and clients show further promise (Wiederhold & Riva, 2019). ■

therapy is based on the assumption that confronting the trauma rather than avoiding it can produce benefits. Cognitive processing therapy addresses inaccurate attributions and self-blame associated with the traumatic events. Trauma-focused CBT combines exposure and correction of guilt and other flawed cognitions.

Treating Dissociative Identity Disorder

The treatment of dissociative identity disorder can be quite controversial, as is the diagnosis of this condition, explained in Chapter 14. Some psychotherapists work on the assumption that dissociative identity disorder is a valid diagnostic category that often results from serious trauma (childhood sexual abuse in particular). Treatment is aimed toward integrating the various personalities by first identifying and "working through" the traumatic memories related to the disorder (International Society for the Study of Trauma and Dissociation, 2015). Hypnosis is commonly used by these therapists to assist in the recovery and resolution of traumatic memories, but this practice is not supported by scientific research. Under hypnosis, a suggestible person might be vulnerable to the manufacture of false memories, and individuals identified as having dissociative identity disorder appear to be more suggestible than the general public. In one notable case study, a woman sought therapy to cope with a traumatic event involving her daughter. Her psychiatrist employed hypnosis and convinced her that she had experienced horrific abuse as a child and now had more than 120 separate personalities (including one that was a duck), thereby illustrating the influence that therapists can have on the "memories" that they help recover (Loftus, 1997).

A particularly damaging finding regarding the state of treatment for dissociative identity disorder is the suggestion that individuals labeled with the disorder subsequently show even worse symptoms (Piper & Merskey, 2004). Treatments for dissociative identity disorders have been described as not "empirically supported" or supported by research results (Maxwell et al., 2018). Critics of the dissociative identity disorder classification suggest that psychotherapists should restrict their actions to resolving the stress, anxiety, and depression of the individual, without referring to dissociation.

Rex Features/Shutterstock.com

Kim Noble 2012

Kim Noble 2012

Kim Noble 2012

British painter Kim Noble has been diagnosed with dissociative identity disorder. This disorder is characterized by the experience of two or more "personality states." Noble paints quite differently when she feels that she is in a particular personality state as opposed to others and believes that she has improved her wellbeing by expressing her perceived personalities through her art.

Treating Somatic Symptom Disorders

Both biological and psychological treatments are commonly used to treat somatic symptom disorders, which involve unusual concerns about chronic somatic symptoms.

Among the biological treatments for somatic symptom disorders are medication with antidepressants and increased physical activity. Psychological treatments usually take the form of CBT (Allen & Woolfolk, 2010). Complicating the treatment of these disorders, most of these patients are seen by their primary physicians, and relatively few are willing to pursue psychotherapy. Between 50% and 80% of patients referred for psychological treatment by their physicians do not comply, possibly because of their continued belief that their problems are purely medical rather than psychological (Allen & Woolfolk, 2010).

Treating ASPD

Finding effective treatments for antisocial personality disorder (ASPD) has a high priority, given the extent of harm that individuals in this category can inflict on the rest of society. Unfortunately, effective treatments remain elusive (Bateman et al., 2015).

No known medications specifically reduce antisocial behavior, although many incarcerated individuals are treated with tranquilizing drugs, including antipsychotic and anticonvulsant medications (such as barbiturates), to make their aggressive, violent behavior more manageable. Even if effective medications are eventually discovered, individuals with ASPD tend to view themselves as "OK" and not in need of treatment. Compliance with effective treatments is likely to remain a problem.

Psychological treatments for ASPD include CBT and learning models that emphasize anger control, social skills, and moral reasoning (Frick et al., 2014). These treatments appear to be modestly effective in reducing antisocial behavior in children and youth, but they do not appear to have much benefit for individuals who show evidence of true psychopathy, or lack of guilt and empathy (Brazil et al., 2018). Despite the efforts of psychotherapists, many nations consider this condition untreatable and rely on incarceration of criminals with ASPD to protect the public.

Treating Borderline Personality Disorder

No medications are currently approved specifically for the treatment of borderline personality disorder, but medications are frequently prescribed. Among the commonly prescribed medications are antidepressants, antipsychotic medications, mood stabilizers (e.g., lithium), antianxiety medications (e.g., benzodiazepines), and anticonvulsants. Because of the potential for self-destructive behavior and serious depression, individuals with borderline personality disorder are occasionally hospitalized for a few days for their own safety.

Psychotherapy for borderline personality disorder often takes the form of CBT. In this case, the individual learns to manage stress, emotions, and relationships. In particular, psychotherapists emphasize skills aimed at reducing the individual's potential for suicidal thinking and behavior. An approach specifically designed for individuals with borderline personality disorder, dialectical behavior therapy (DBT), attempts to address symptoms in the order of their importance: reducing suicidal thoughts, reducing behaviors that interfere with therapy, and finally reducing behaviors that interfere with the quality of life (Linehan et al., 1991). Outcomes using DBT for borderline personality disorder appear superior to those produced by more conventional treatments with CBT (Linehan et al., 2006).

Treating NPD

Narcissistic personality disorder (NPD), while potentially disabling, is often accompanied by high overall levels of functioning (Ronningstam, 2014). In addition, many traits associated with this disorder (hypersensitivity, defensiveness, inability to see one's own role in problems) might reduce the likelihood that a person with it will seek treatment. Finally, lower-functioning individuals with NPD are likely to have other serious psychological problems that motivate them to seek treatment, such as depression, substance abuse, or suicidality, which take precedence over the narcissistic behaviors themselves. As a result, the scientific literature provides fewer details about treating NPD compared to some of the other personality disorders.

Therapists generally employ CBT with an emphasis on carefully building an alliance with the client (Kealy et al., 2017). Psychotherapy for NPD is likely to be most effective when the therapist is aware of the traits that might interfere with the process, such as defensiveness. Clarifying the difference between pathological and protective behaviors and reviewing situations and experiences that trigger narcissistic reactions can be particularly helpful (Ronningstam, 2014).

Integration of Specific Treatments

Perhaps after reading about the variations in both the biological and psychological treatments available for specific types of disorders, you will better appreciate why people who want to be therapists spend such a long time in school perfecting their skills and learning about their options.

Although some disorders seem to defy the available treatment methods, we do not want to leave you with the impression that therapy is somehow ineffective. Quite the contrary is true. Compared to the state of available therapies as recently as 60 years ago, psychologists and psychiatrists have made great strides in their ability to alleviate the distress of many millions of people. As we learn more about the causal factors underlying these disorders, as we surely will by pursuing integrative approaches, our abilities to help will expand. At the same time, we are making significant progress in our understanding about the prevention of many of these disorders, which we hope will make these problems a thing of the past.

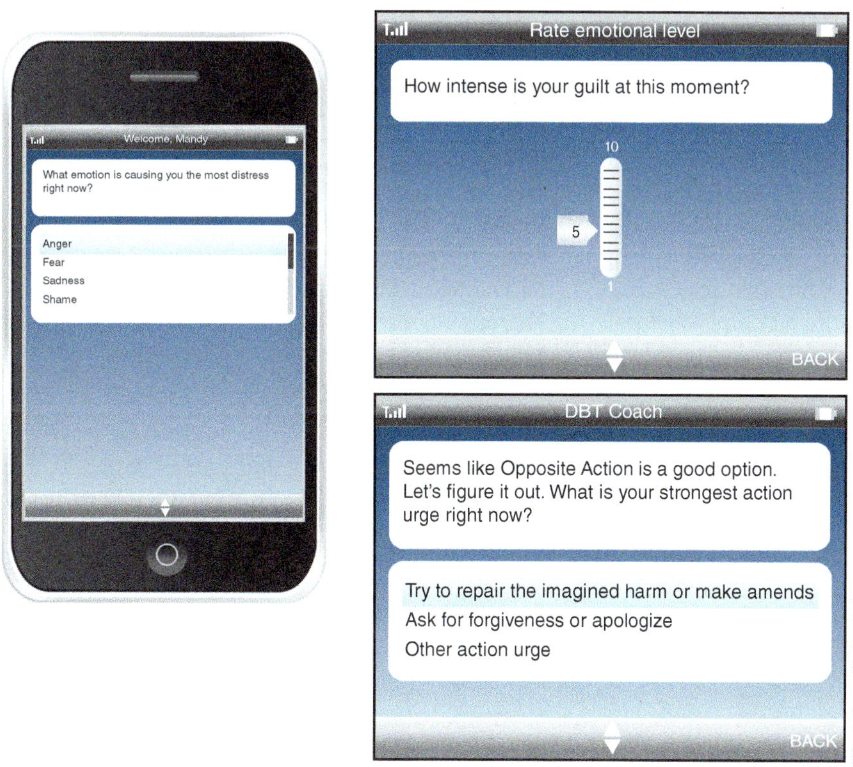

Viktoria Kurpas/Shutterstock.com

The use of DBT for borderline personality disorder has been simplified by the development of a smartphone app, which takes the place of keeping diary cards of emotions, events, and problem behaviors.

Source: Adapted from S. L. Rizvi et al. (2011). "A Pilot Study of the DBT Coach: An Interactive Mobile Phone Application for Individuals with Borderline Personality Disorder and Substance Use Disorder," *Behavior Therapy*, *42*, 589–600. doi: 10.1016/j.beth.2011.01.003 Copyright © 2011 Elsevier.

Interpersonal Relationships

The Treatment Perspective

TREATMENT BASED ON SOUND PSYCHOLOGICAL SCIENCE is the goal not only of those working with individuals who have diagnosed psychological disorders, but also counselors working with people who simply want to improve their relationships and well-being. Decades of careful research has informed the recommendations of John and Julie Gottman (2017). Their research method of assessing correlations between physiological arousal and behaviors as couples discuss areas of personal conflict now guides their approach to counseling (see ● Figure 15.17). These methods have predicted which couples will divorce within 5 years.

The Gottmans are fond of observing couples in states of conflict, which they consider to be normal regardless of the couples' reported happiness. Most couples get along during the good times—it's often the tough times that test the quality of the relationship. The Gottmans equip couples with simple measures of heart rate as they discuss areas of conflict. This approach is based on their observations that unhappy couples experience much higher levels of sympathetic arousal than happy couples do during conflict. If the measures get too high, the couple is instructed to take a break in the discussion. The general idea is that you can't solve problems if your levels of arousal are too high, and continuing conflict under these circumstances is destructive.

The first step asks the couple to postpone any efforts at persuasion until each person has clarified his or her position. The focus is on self-disclosure, not "attack–defend." A second step involves "reprocessing" past emotional injuries. Couples are guided through five steps with regard to processing past hurts: feelings they had, subjective realities, triggers, taking responsibility and apologizing, and constructive plans. Finally, in the Gottmans' lab work, they realized that couples raised the same conflicts at 3-year, 6-year, and 9-year intervals. To integrate this concept with their counseling, they worked with couples to accept each partner's personality (often the source of long-term conflict) and the ideal solutions imagined by each partner. While not removing the problem, the couples could learn to live with it.

The Gottmans' work in the lab has provided them with unique, scientific tools for helping people build more effective relationships with their partners, and even their children. Observations a few months after a wedding predicted the couple's happiness with their first-born. Data from the last trimester of pregnancy predicted the frequency of a baby's laughing, smiling, or crying. A 10-hour seminar over 2 days reversed relationship dissatisfaction in 77% of last-trimester couples, an effect replicated now in 24 countries. It is hard to imagine a better use of psychological science than to intervene positively in the happiness of these couples and their children. ■

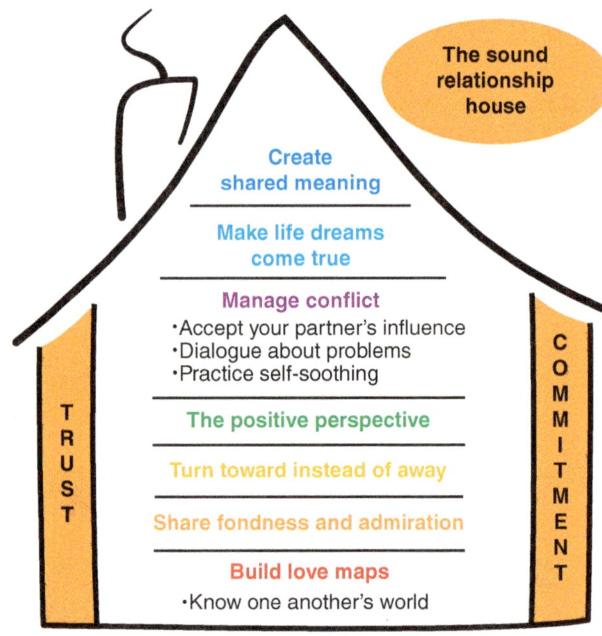

FIGURE **15.17**

Psychological Science Informs Marriage Therapy. Research by John and Julie Gottman has identified a number of principles that they believe should guide marriage counseling, which they incorporate into their "Sound Relationship House" model.

Psychology Takes On Real-World Problems

Online Therapy During the COVID-19 Pandemic

You might have heard your professors comment that doing online courses when you plan to do them is quite different from being forced to offer courses online due to COVID-19 social distancing. The reactions of psychotherapists to taking their practices online sounds quite similar.

Psychotherapists from North America and Europe were asked to evaluate their experience with online therapy during COVID-19 (Békés & Aafjes-van Doorn, 2020). About half of the psychotherapists in this sample had no previous experience with online therapy. Overall, however, the psychotherapists reported their experiences with online therapy as positive and many expressed interest in continuing to use online therapy in the future.

Like many of your professors, the psychotherapists experienced a variety of technical difficulties during sessions. As long as they perceived their clients as having a good experience, though, they were not concerned about these glitches.

The type of therapy provided by the psychotherapists had an impact on their attitudes toward online delivery. The most positive attitudes were held by psychotherapists who provided cognitive-behavioral therapy (CBT) and the least positive attitudes were held by psychoanalysts. This might reflect the dependence of the psychoanalyst on factors that are harder to perceive online, such as nonverbal communication.

It will be some time before we fully appreciate the impact that COVID-19 has had on the delivery of services, whether that is coursework or psychotherapy, via online technologies. It is possible that greater exposure to online delivery will increase its acceptance by both providers and consumers. ■

venimo/Shutterstock.com

SUMMARY 15.3 Common Treatments for Psychological Disorders

Disorder	Psychological Treatment	Biological Treatment
ASD 	• Applied behavior analysis	• Antipsychotic medications for self-injury
ADHD 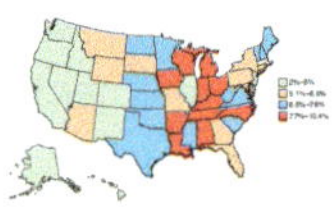	• Behavior therapy	• Stimulant medications
Schizophrenia 	• Psychosocial rehabilitation • Evaluation of expressed emotion	• Medication with antipsychotic drugs
Bipolar disorder 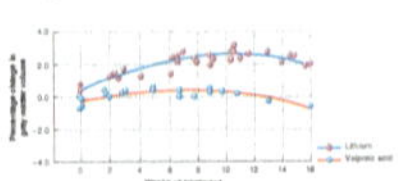	• Supportive CBT	• Medication with lithium carbonate • ECT for depression
MDD 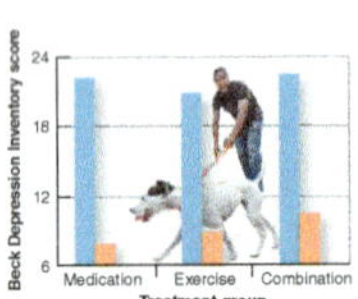	• CBT	• Medication with antidepressant drugs • ECT • Exercise
Anxiety, OCD, Body Dysmorphic Disorder, and PTSD 	• CBT	• Medication with antidepressant or antianxiety drugs
Personality disorders 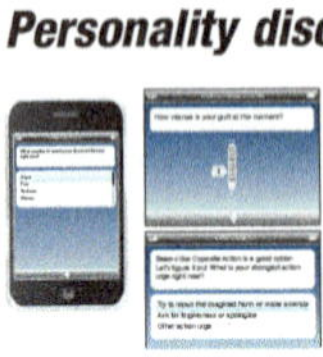	• Learning models for ASPD • DBT for borderline personality disorder • CBT for NPD	• No effective biological treatments, although medications are sometimes prescribed

Credits: Top row—iadams/Shutterstock.com; Third row—Sofiaworld/Shutterstock.com; Fourth row—Copyright © 2007 Society of Biological Psychiatry/Elsevier, Inc.; Fifth row—Jupiterimages/Photos.com; Sixth row—Defense Dept. photo by John J. Kruzel; Bottom row—Viktoria Kurpas/Shutterstock.com.

KEY TERMS The Language of Psychological Science

Be sure that you can define these terms and use them correctly.

antidepressant medication, p. 625
behavior therapy, p. 612
biopsychosocial approach, p. 614
brief therapy, p. 605
cognitive behavioral therapy (CBT), p. 614
cognitive restructuring, p. 613
counseling, p. 601
couples therapy, p. 606
deep brain stimulation, p. 616
electroconvulsive therapy (ECT), p. 615
family therapy, p. 606
free association, p. 609
group therapy, p. 605
humanistic therapy, p. 601
insight therapy, p. 609
neurofeedback, p. 617
person-centered therapy, p. 610
psychiatrist, p. 602
psychoanalysis, p. 609
psychosurgery, p. 615
psychotherapist, p. 602
psychotherapy, p. 599
resistance, p. 610
tardive dyskinesia, p. 623
transference, p. 610

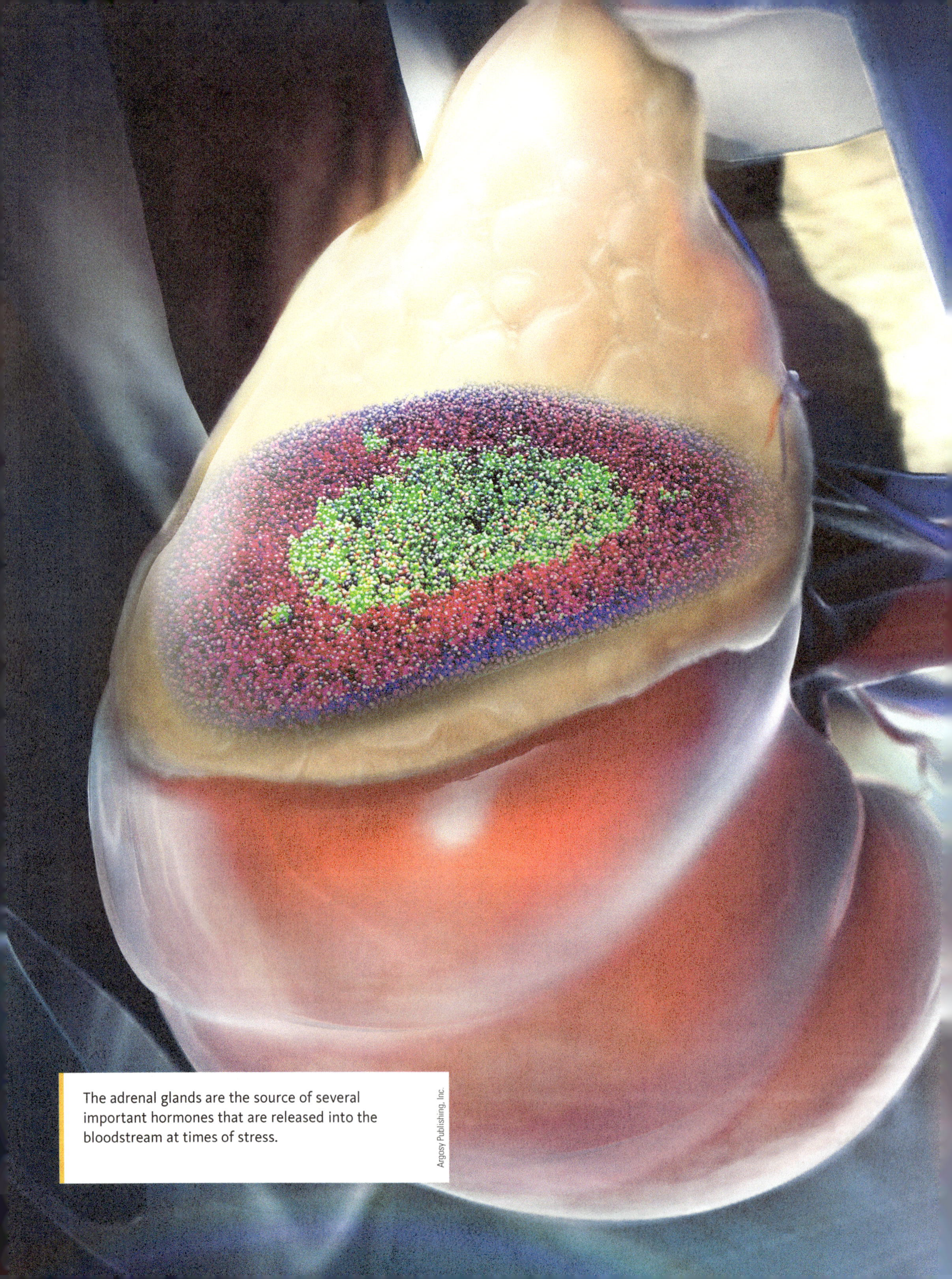

The adrenal glands are the source of several important hormones that are released into the bloodstream at times of stress.

16

The Healthy Mind

STRESS AND COPING, HEALTH PSYCHOLOGY, AND POSITIVE PSYCHOLOGY

LEARNING OBJECTIVES

1. Define stress, identifying key neural and hormonal aspects of Hans Selye's general adaptation syndrome (GAS).
2. Distinguish among adaptive elements of the short-term stress response and health problems linked to chronic stress.
3. Compare and contrast strategies for coping with stress, including problem-, emotion-, and relationship-focused strategies.
4. Summarize the psychosocial factors associated with smoking, nutrition, alcohol use, and lack of exercise, and propose behavioral interventions for these problems.
5. Differentiate the aims and principles of positive psychology from those of other major movements in psychology, as described in Chapter 1.
6. Distinguish among meanings of happiness (pleasant, good, and meaningful lives), and analyze the research evidence on what makes people happy.

WE HAVE ALL HAD DAYS LIKE THE WOMAN IN THIS PHOTO. Whether it comes in relatively minor forms (losing your keys, getting a traffic ticket, or doing poorly on an exam) or in large forms (death of a loved one or serious illness), stress is a fact of life.

We don't know what kind of stress is producing this woman's reactions, but we know a great deal about what is happening to her physically and psychologically in response to her stress. Zooming in, we look at one of her adrenal glands, shown in the larger image. Your adrenal glands are located on top of your kidneys in your lower back, and they are the source of hormones that are dumped into your bloodstream at times of stress. How does feeling stressed get translated into activity by a gland?

Cultura Creative (RF)/Alamy Stock Photo

Here is how the system works. First, the woman must identify something as a threat to her. Making that cognitive appraisal, or judgment, of her situation begins a cascade of processes designed to mobilize her to either run (flight) or fight. Messages from her amygdala to her hypothalamus result in the activation of hormones that tell the adrenal glands to release a hormone called cortisol. In Chapter 6, we noted that cortisol levels are naturally high in the morning. In other words, circulating cortisol wakes you up. In response to the cortisol released by the adrenal glands, the body is mobilized for action.

We also have had enough stress in our lives to understand that too much is not a good thing. Again, if we zoom in, we can understand that our bodies are usually protected from too much

REUTERS/Alamy Stock Photo

Professional athletes like Lydia Ko of New Zealand have learned to cope with stress to perform their best.

cortisol by a feedback loop that reduces cortisol release once circulating levels reach a certain point. It is likely that this feedback loop malfunctions in stress-related disorders, such as depression (see Chapter 14).

While still at the microscopic level, we might also see that one person's genetic makeup might predispose that individual to have a more or less dramatic response to perceived stressors. By now, you can probably anticipate that we have to zoom back out again to fully understand this situation. These genetic differences among individuals interact with developmental and social factors, such as the possibility that this woman was maltreated as a child or now enjoys a strong social network of family and friends.

We can't make your stress go away, and it is probably not in your best interests for us to do so. Some stress, such as the stress associated with exercise or even surviving a traumatic experience, actually can have quite beneficial effects on your overall health. Instead, we can acquaint you with research findings on coping and resilience that might help you deal with life's inevitable challenges.

What Is Stress?

College students rarely need much introduction to the concept of stress. They are no strangers to the stress that accompanies worrying about assignments and grades, money matters, world affairs, and relationships. **Stress** is an unpleasant emotional state that results from the perception of danger. The source of stress is called a **stressor**.

The key to our definition is the word *perception.* No one set of stressors reliably produces stress in everybody. People's stressors are highly individual and idiosyncratic. The object of one person's phobia may be another person's beloved (although scaly and slithery) pet. Regardless of the stressor responsible for feelings of stress, once people perceive that they are in some kind of danger, a common and predictable set of responses to the stressor is set in motion.

Stressors vary along a number of dimensions (Segerstrom & Miller, 2004). Brief stressors involve facing a short-term challenge, such as an exam, job interview, or close call on the highway. Chronic stressors are ongoing and long-lasting, and usually require us to rethink our identities and social roles. Chronic stressors are stable. We don't know if or when they will be gone. Stressors can arrive in sequence. For example, the loss of a loved one or a natural disaster leads to a train of related stressors.

Psychologists have identified positive outcomes of our responses to stress (Selye, 1975). Stress, by its nature, is a powerful adaptive response that mobilizes the body's resources to enhance survival in dangerous situations (Meaney, 2010). Although sometimes unpleasant, stress can motivate us to perform well and makes us healthier in the long run (Crum et al., 2013). The exercise we do at the gym is undeniably stressful, but it produces significant benefits down the road. Many of us do some of our best work under time pressure and are not too much the worse for the wear as a result.

Stress might have additional positive impacts on groups of people, not just individuals. People experiencing stress are actually more prosocial, at least with people they know well (Buchanan & Preston, 2014; Margittai et al., 2015). Stress increases our ability to empathize with others in pain (Tomova et al., 2016). While personally unpleasant, these advantages of stress for our social networks could produce enormous benefits.

However, in other cases, stress can be counterproductive and interfere with our performance and well-being. In extreme cases, as observed in Chapter 14, a diathesis–stress model predicts that stress can contribute to the development of major depressive disorder (MDD), schizophrenia, posttraumatic stress disorder (PTSD), and other serious conditions. These negative outcomes are more likely when we are unable to cope with or adapt to a stressor. We will be focusing most of our discussion on coping more effectively with these negative situations.

stress An unpleasant emotional state that results from the perception of danger.

stressor A stimulus that serves as a source of stress.

The Stress Response

Walter Cannon, whom we met in Chapter 7, demonstrated the ability of a number of stressors to activate the sympathetic division of the autonomic nervous system, described in Chapters 4 and 7. Cannon (1929) reported that extreme cold, lack of oxygen, and emotional experiences all had the capacity to initiate a fight-or-flight response. During such a response, heart rate, blood pressure, and respiration all increase, while nonessential functions, like digesting food, are inhibited. Stored energy is released, and blood is shunted from the surface of the body to the muscles needed for exertion. These physical responses reflect a process that has been finely tuned through evolution to maximize our survival in emergencies.

EXPERIENCING PSYCHOLOGY

What Is Your Stress Mindset?

USE THE SCALE in ● Table 16.1 to respond to the items listed. Select the number that best describes you in the space provided.

To obtain your overall mindset score, (1) add up your scores for items 1, 3, 5, and 7 and subtract this amount from 16, (2) add your scores for items 2, 4, 6, and 8, (3) add this total to the final number that you produced in step 1, and finally (4) divide the total by 8 to produce your mean Stress Mindset Measure (SMM) score. The higher the score, the more likely you are to believe that the effects of stress are enhancing. Among the college students participating in the study by Crum et al. (2013), the mean SMM was 1.6, or on the "Stress is debilitating" side of the scale. How does that mean compare with your score and your classmates' scores? What factors in your life do you think influence your score? ■

TABLE 16.1

The Stress Mindset Measure

The effects of stress are negative and should be avoided.				
0	1	2	3	4
Strongly Disagree	Disagree	Neither Agree nor Disagree	Agree	Strongly Agree
Experiencing stress facilitates my learning and growth.				
0	1	2	3	4
Strongly Disagree	Disagree	Neither Agree nor Disagree	Agree	Strongly Agree
Experiencing stress depletes my health and vitality.				
0	1	2	3	4
Strongly Disagree	Disagree	Neither Agree nor Disagree	Agree	Strongly Agree
Experiencing stress enhances my performance and productivity.				
0	1	2	3	4
Strongly Disagree	Disagree	Neither Agree nor Disagree	Agree	Strongly Agree
Experiencing stress inhibits my learning and growth.				
0	1	2	3	4
Strongly Disagree	Disagree	Neither Agree nor Disagree	Agree	Strongly Agree
Experiencing stress improves my health and vitality.				
0	1	2	3	4
Strongly Disagree	Disagree	Neither Agree nor Disagree	Agree	Strongly Agree
Experiencing stress debilitates my performance and productivity.				
0	1	2	3	4
Strongly Disagree	Disagree	Neither Agree nor Disagree	Agree	Strongly Agree
The effects of stress are positive and should be utilized.				
0	1	2	3	4
Strongly Disagree	Disagree	Neither Agree nor Disagree	Agree	Strongly Agree

Photocase Addicts GmbH/Alamy Stock Photo

maratr/Shutterstock.com

Older zoos featured cages that often contributed to stress and illness among the animals. Modern zoos go to great lengths to provide more natural, less stressful habitats for their animals, in recognition of the stress that often accompanies captivity.

stress in large numbers of people. In the three to five days following the 9/11 terrorist attacks, 90% of Americans reported feeling unusually stressed (Schuster et al., 2002). As this book goes to press, much work remains to be done to assess the impact of COVID-19 on stress, but early reports suggest that somewhere between one-quarter to one-third of the population is experiencing higher levels of stress than normal (Cooke et al., 2020; Salari et al., 2020).

Stress because of disasters can produce long-range and cross-generational effects. Researchers identified women who witnessed the 9/11 attacks in New York while pregnant and who subsequently developed PTSD (Yehuda et al., 2005). One year later, the women and their infants showed indications of long-term, chronic stress. As preschoolers, the children born to the women who were diagnosed with both PTSD and MDD following 9/11 showed evidence of higher reactivity to stimuli and more aggressive behavior than did children of terrorism-exposed mothers who did not develop these disorders (Chemtob et al., 2010). The ability of cortisol and other stress hormones to cross the placenta probably accounts for the effects of stress beginning in the prenatal environment (Weinstock, 2005; Galbally et al., 2019).

As mentioned in Chapter 14, children are especially susceptible to PTSD. Three weeks after a 2004 tsunami, prevalence of PTSD among children in areas of Sri Lanka ranged between 14% and 39% and could be predicted by variables such as family loss and severity of exposure (Neuner et al., 2006). To put these high numbers of cases into perspective, we would expect about 10% of the general population to experience PTSD after most large disasters (Kessler et al., 1996). Automobile accidents are a major source of PTSD in childhood, with as many as half of those injured in an accident going on to develop the disorder (de Vries et al., 1999; Pervanidou et al., 2007).

Although disasters are dramatic, they are not the only sources of stress that we face. Changes, including some changes for the better, can also trigger stress. Holmes and Rahe (1967) compiled a list of life events (good and bad) that they believed might be correlated with stress and then surveyed participants about the amount of adjustment that each event required. Subsequently, researchers used the Holmes and Rahe Social Readjustment Rating Scale (SRRS) to predict vulnerability to physical illness and psychological disorder because of different stressors (Derogatis & Coons, 1993; Scully et al., 2000). According to the scales, Christmas is more stressful than minor violations of the law. Getting married is more stressful than being fired from your job. Research results from studies using the SRRS suggest that we should consider spreading out controllable changes over time. In other words, it may not be the best strategy to graduate from college, get married, move to a new city, and start a new job all at the same time.

AP Images

This man is obviously stressed. Is somebody being injured? Is he in danger? No—he is witnessing a tense moment during a baseball game. Cognitive appraisal theories of stress suggest that different people are likely to respond to stimuli with varying levels of stress based on their individual appraisals of a situation.

Not all psychologists are convinced that so-called good life events are as stressful as bad ones, nor are they convinced that change per se is a reliable predictor of stress. Critics of the SRRS argue that most items are quite negative and that these negative items are responsible for more stress (McLean & Link, 1994). It is likely that stress associated with good changes occurs when the anticipated event does not live up to the person's expectations. Vacations and holidays may not be inherently stressful, but trying to fulfill unrealistic fantasies about what vacations and holidays should be like is probably stressful indeed.

Relatively insignificant sources of stress, often called hassles, also can contribute to a person's overall level of stress. Waiting in long lines, losing your keys, getting a parking ticket, and oversleeping on the day of an important exam are not life-threatening events. However, if enough of these hassles occur within a short period, people begin to react as if something larger had occurred. The number of hassles that people report experiencing predicts

goodluz/Shutterstock.com

Tetra Images/Aurora

According to Holmes and Rahe (1967), positive life events, such as weddings and holidays, can be equally or even more stressful than some negative events, such as flunking an important assignment.

psychological symptoms of stress, even when the impact of major life events is factored out (Kanner et al., 1981). You might hear advice to avoid "sweating the little stuff" because enough little stuff happening at the same time can still affect your well-being.

Some individuals, such as first responders and those serving in the military, deal with major stressors as part of their job. Concerns regarding stress and consequent mental health problems in the military have grown since the wars in Iraq and Afghanistan. Soldiers serving in these conflicts have experienced especially high rates of mental health disorders and suicide (Ramsawh et al., 2014). About 38% of living U.S. veterans have been exposed to combat (Thomas et al., 2017). Younger combat veterans had higher rates of lifetime (30.6%) and current (19.2%) PTSD and suicidal ideation (18.6%) than older combat veterans.

As in studies of civilians, research on military personnel suggests that feeling socially isolated (loneliness) may be an early warning sign of, if not a contributing factor to, these mental health disturbances (Solomon et al., 1986). Combat experiences do not lead directly to suicidal ideation and behaviors, but they might do so indirectly by producing symptoms of PTSD (see Chapter 14) and negative states including loneliness, sadness, anger, and frustration (Griffith, 2012, 2015). Leaving military service might disrupt the strong bonds that sustained veterans during combat, and many veterans feel alienated from others who cannot comprehend their experiences (Wilson et al., 2018). Soldiers who committed suicide had previously reported being lonelier and more depressed and tended to think in more catastrophic terms than soldiers who did not commit suicide (Lester et al., 2011; Cacioppo et al., 2015).

What Are the Biological and Social Correlates of Stress?

Regardless of the identity of a stressor, once you appraise a stimulus as a danger, you initiate Selye's GAS. The first stage, the alarm reaction, is accompanied by a coordinated reaction including physical, cognitive, and behavioral responses to perceived danger. Imagine for a moment that one of your ancient ancestors was out hunting and suddenly found himself face to face with a hungry lion. Physically, the autonomic nervous system prepared him for fight or flight. The brainstem, described in Chapter 4, initiated the release of the neurotransmitter norepinephrine, which increased vigilance and fear. Cognitively, your ancestor accessed his memory for information about lions, which he hoped would include ideas about how similar situations were handled in the past. Behaviorally, your ancestor carried out his plan for escape. We assume that given your presence today, your ancestor was successful.

oliveromg/Shutterstock.com

Feeling socially isolated makes us feel unsafe, which triggers stress responses. Loneliness makes people behave in ways that make them difficult to be around, such as displaying greater pessimism, anxiety, and hostility, beginning a loop of self-fulfilling prophesies and more loneliness.

Stress and the Amygdala

We can trace the neural pathways that coordinate these responses to potentially hazardous stimuli. Sensory pathways provide information to higher cognitive centers in the cerebral cortex, letting our hunter know that the object in front of him is a lion. Memories of lion behavior, including eating habits, contribute to accurately identifying the lion as a danger, and hence a stressor.

Simultaneously, sensory input travels from the thalamus to the amygdala, which plays an important role in the identification of dangerous stimuli, as discussed in Chapters 4 and 7. The amygdala participates in a "fear circuit" that provides a rapid assessment of a stimulus or situation as potentially dangerous (LeDoux, 2000, 2014). If the amygdala is lesioned, animals no longer respond with conditioned fear to previously learned classically conditioned associations between a stimulus (perhaps a tone or light) and an electric shock, an example of classical conditioning discussed in Chapter 8 (see ● Figure 16.3). Animals with lesions in the amygdala are also unable to learn to respond appropriately to unfamiliar dangerous stimuli (Wilensky et al., 2006).

Because sensory information can reach the amygdala along routes that are separate from the pathways for information going to the cortex, we might find ourselves frightened by stimuli that we don't immediately understand or consciously view as dangerous (Knight et al., 2003). As mentioned in Chapter 4, a man who was blind because of damage to his visual cortex still showed a normal response in his amygdala when shown faces expressing anger (Pegna et al., 2005). You might have found yourself feeling anxious while returning to your car after an evening class without knowing why you are reacting this way, but it is probably a good idea to listen to your amygdala until further information becomes available.

Once the amygdala has identified a stimulus as potentially dangerous, it communicates with the hypothalamus. As mentioned in Chapter 4, the hypothalamus most directly commands the autonomic nervous system, particularly the sympathetic division. This part of the autonomic nervous system is responsible for our fight-or-flight response to danger.

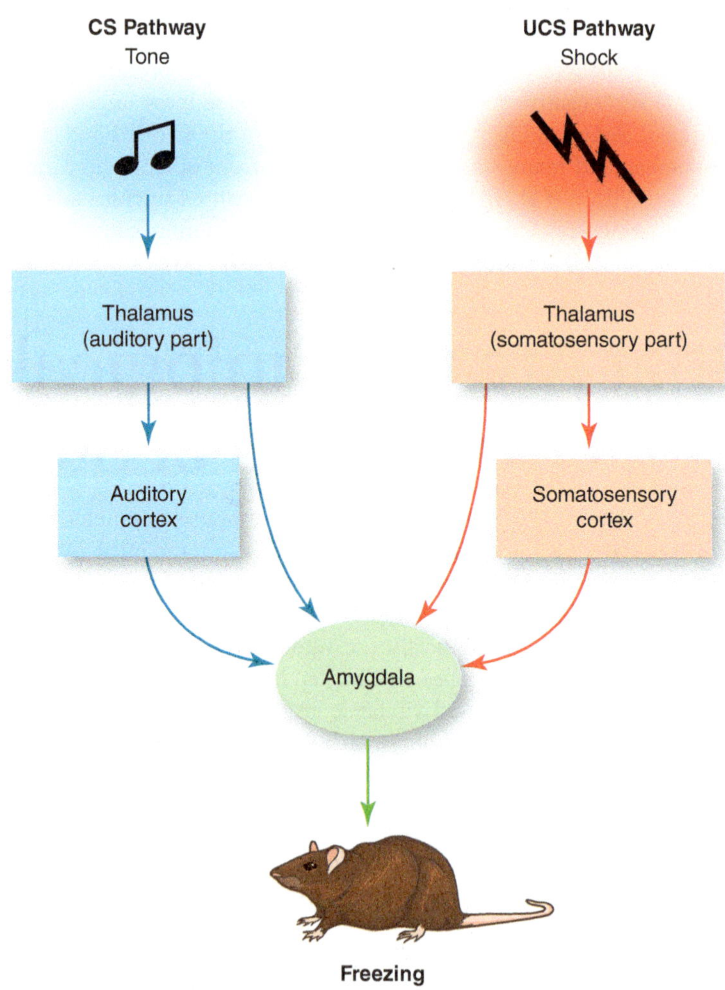

FIGURE **16.3**

The Amygdala and Fear. The amygdala participates in a "fear circuit" that provides a rapid response to a potentially dangerous stimulus. After rats learn a classically conditioned association of a tone (a conditioned stimulus, or CS) that signals the arrival of an electric shock (an unconditioned stimulus, or UCS), they freeze whenever they hear the tone. If the amygdala is lesioned, the rat no longer freezes when it hears the tone, and it is unable to learn about new signals for shocks.

Stress, the Sympathetic Adrenal–Medullary System, and the Hypothalamic–Pituitary–Adrenal Axis

Perceiving a potential source of danger mobilizes the body's resources using two systems—the **sympathetic adrenal–medullary (SAM) system** and the **hypothalamic–pituitary–adrenal (HPA) axis**. The SAM system initiates the release of adrenaline (also known as epinephrine) and norepinephrine into the bloodstream from the adrenal glands, located above the kidneys in your lower back. These chemical messengers circulate to many organs, including the brain, producing many of the immediate, short-lived, fight-or-flight responses to stress, such as a pounding heart and rapid breathing (see ● Figure 16.4).

Simultaneously, activation of the HPA axis sets an entirely different system in motion. Here's how the circuit works. The hypothalamus (H) communicates with the pituitary gland (P), located just above the roof of your mouth, which in turn tells the adrenal glands (A) to release a hormone known as **cortisol** into the bloodstream. Circulating cortisol boosts the energy available for dealing with a stressor. The HPA axis response to stress can continue longer than the SAM response, which explains many of the outcomes of chronic stress.

One of the possible outcomes of chronic stress is prolonged high levels of circulating cortisol. Long-term exposure to cortisol can produce a number of harmful effects, including the death of neurons. When rats received daily injections of the rat equivalent of cortisol, neural

sympathetic adrenal–medullary (SAM) system A circuit that responds to perceived stressors by initiating the release of epinephrine and norepinephrine into the bloodstream.

hypothalamic–pituitary–adrenal (HPA) axis A circuit that responds to perceived stressors by initiating the release of cortisol into the bloodstream.

cortisol A hormone released into the bloodstream from the adrenal glands.

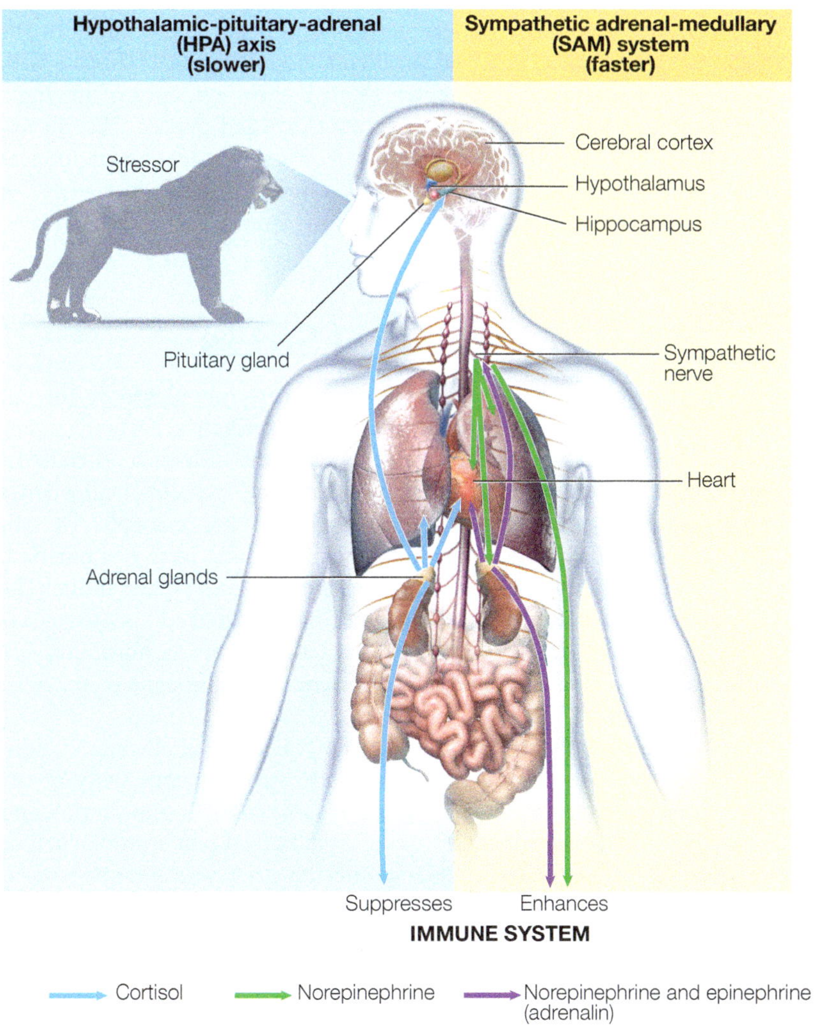

FIGURE **16.4**

Two Systems Respond to a Stressor. In response to the appraisal of a stimulus as a stressor, two systems mobilize the body's resources. The sympathetic adrenal–medullary (SAM) system responds quickly by initiating the release of epinephrine (adrenaline) and norepinephrine into the bloodstream by the adrenal glands. These chemical messengers initiate many immediate, short-lived responses, such as a pounding heart and rapid breathing. Simultaneously, activation of the hypothalamic–pituitary–adrenal (HPA) axis results in the release of cortisol into the bloodstream by the adrenal glands. Cortisol acts to boost the energy available for dealing with the stress. Cortisol receptors in the hippocampus serve as a feedback loop to keep the system from overreacting. The effects of HPA axis activity are slower to develop and last longer than those of the SAM response. HPA axis activity is associated with more of the effects of chronic stress, such as suppression of the immune system.

death began to occur in just a few weeks (Stein-Behrens et al., 1994). Identical amounts of neural death occurred if the rats were stressed daily instead of receiving the injections, suggesting that the action of cortisol is responsible for most of the neural damage observed to result from stress. Cushing's disease, a medical condition that causes unusually high cortisol levels, results in reduced hippocampus volume, memory problems, abnormal sleep patterns, and depression (Langenecker et al., 2012). Not only can high levels of cortisol damage neurons, but these same levels appear to inhibit neurogenesis, or the birth of neurons, which might help to offset the damage (Cowen, 2010; Borsini et al., 2020).

Normally, activity of the HPA axis is regulated by a feedback loop involving the hippocampus (Stokes, 1995). The hippocampus works like a rev limiter in an automobile engine that prevents the driver from going over a certain speed. The hippocampus contains large numbers of receptors for cortisol and other stress hormones. When the hippocampus detects high levels of these hormones, it signals the hypothalamus, which in turn tells the adrenal glands to reduce the release of cortisol, and arousal dissipates.

The role of the hippocampus as the rev limiter of the HPA axis might be the bridge between stress and MDD. As observed in Chapter 14, many cases of MDD are preceded by unusually stressful events. Consistently elevated levels of cortisol because of stress can overwhelm the hippocampus's feedback loop, leading instead to the continuous release of cortisol and constant arousal. Without the regulation of cortisol usually provided by the hippocampus acting as a rev limiter, a person can begin to experience depression (Stokes, 1995). People who are treated with cortisol and similar stress hormones for medical conditions such as rheumatoid arthritis are often troubled by deep depression, reinforcing the role of excess cortisol in depressed mood.

Not only can the hippocampus fail to regulate cortisol release under conditions of extreme stress, but continued stress can damage the hippocampus further. The stressed baboons mentioned earlier in this chapter experienced neural death, particularly in the hippocampus, in addition to their other medical problems (Sapolsky, 2001). People with PTSD, discussed in Chapter 14, also show evidence of having a smaller hippocampus than trauma-exposed people who do not develop PTSD (Logue et al., 2018). However, it remains unclear whether reduced hippocampal volume precedes the onset of PTSD (making it a risk factor), results from PTSD, or both (Hayes et al., 2017).

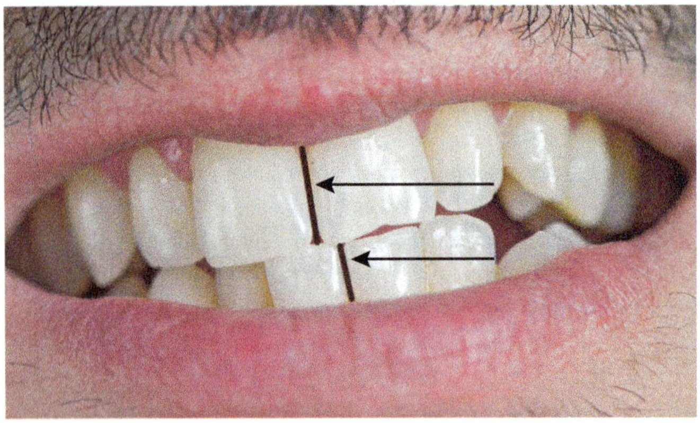
FCG/Shutterstock.com

The first 1,000 days after conception (until about age 2 years) strongly influences individual vulnerability to chronic disease and life expectancy. While low birth weight indicates stress during pregnancy, the 280 days or so between conception and birth are only a fraction of the first 1,000 days. Having an asymmetrical lower face, however, appears to be a reliable biomarker of stress during this early stage of childhood. The misalignment of this man's upper and lower front teeth illustrates this effect of prenatal stress.

The Epigenetics of Stress

In Chapter 3, we discussed the significant role played by the environment in determining whether and when a particular gene is expressed. We defined epigenetics as the influence on traits by factors that determine how genes perform. The field of epigenetics explores gene–environment interactions. For example, we observed how both rats and human children who were well nurtured by their mothers showed more resilience to stress later in life. The nurture received from the mother had influenced how the genes responsible for producing and reacting to stress hormones behaved during later stressful experiences (Champagne et al., 2003; Neigh et al., 2009).

Severe stress early in life produces lasting challenges, including increased HPA axis responses to stress, hyperactivity of the norepinephrine system, reduced volume in the hippocampus, and heightened responses by the amygdala to threat stimuli, such as negative facial expressions (Osório et al., 2016). Genes and life stress also interact to produce MDD. The rate of expression of genes linked to MDD interacts with an individual's quality of social experience, from adversity to support (Logue et al., 2018). These gene–stress interactions help explain why some people are more vulnerable to life stress, while others seem relatively well protected against it.

Gender Differences in the Stress Response

tend-and-befriend An alternative to fight-or-flight as a response to stressors, characterized by soothing and building social connections, which is possibly more characteristic of females.

Although psychologists typically discuss fight-or-flight as the common response to stressors, an alternative response has been suggested that might be more typical of female responses to stressors. Noting that from an evolutionary standpoint, a mother with small children is unlikely to find either fight or flight easy to do, Taylor (2006) suggested that women are more likely to **tend-and-befriend** in response to stressors. Soothing frightened children, hiding, and forming social alliances for further protection might be more effective strategies. Research support for tend-and-befriend includes a study showing that after being stressed, women, but not men, demonstrated an increase in caretaking motivation in response to videos showing crying infants (Probst et al., 2017). Instead of the traditional hormones associated with fight-or-flight, a tend-and-befriend response is more closely associated with the release of oxytocin, a hormone related to social bonding discussed in Chapters 4 and 7.

Sgt. Jessika Malott, 8th MP Bde. Public Affairs/photo courtesy of U.S. Army

As this family faces the stress of the father's overseas deployment, the mother responds with a tend-and-befriend approach by comforting her daughter.

Socioeconomic Status and Stress

Beginning with initial observations that death rates were negatively correlated with increases in occupational grades among British civil servants (Marmot et al., 1978; Marmot et al., 1984), scientists have become aware that health disparities exist worldwide as a function of wealth. People with lower socioeconomic status (SES) experience worse health. Absolute wealth is not the only factor here. People's subjective estimation of their own status in the community also predicts susceptibility to disease (Cohen et al., 2008).

What processes can explain SES effects on health disparities? The poor experience more noise, more toxins, more carcinogens, more violence, fewer resources, less health care, higher levels of drugs and alcohol abuse, less exercise, more anger, less control, and less trust (Adler, 2013). The items on this long list have something in common—all of these factors are associated with high stress. Residents of low-income neighborhoods reported higher rates of perceived stress, which in turn was related to more risky health-related behaviors, such as smoking and lower physical activity (Algren et al., 2018).

Visions of America, LLC/Alamy Stock Photo

Health disparities, or the differences between the health of wealthy and that of poor individuals, can result from the greater exposure of poor people to significant stressors.

How Does Stress Affect Our Health?

Our stress response was forged by the challenges that our hunter–gatherer ancestors were most likely to face. The result is a system that has beneficial effects in the short term but can lead to negative effects when stress becomes chronic (Cacioppo & Berntson, 2011). After all, it would not take your ancestors hours, days, months, or years to figure out what to do to escape a hungry lion. For better or for worse, the outcome would be decided quickly.

In contrast, many of the stressors that we face in modern living are not brief, and as a result, we are fairly constantly experiencing Selye's resistance phase, which combines stress and coping. You might be worried about finding a job after you graduate from college, which might be years away. Any long-term, chronic stress has the potential to affect health in negative ways. Not only does responding to stress require large amounts of energy, but while in the resistance stage, you do a less efficient job of storing nutrients and giving your body the rest and repair that it needs. Chronic stress accelerates the aging process, including the shortening of telomeres, the "caps" found at the end of chromosomes (Needham et al., 2013). Improved understanding of the relationships between modern stress and health can guide our quest for physical and psychological well-being.

Stress and the Immune System

immune system The body system that defends against infection and cancer.

Hans Selye believed that any stress produced a global reduction in immune response, but this turns out to be overly simplistic. Instead, short-term bursts of stress can have a beneficial effect on many biological systems, including the **immune system**, your body's frontline defense against infection and cancer (Segerstrom & Miller, 2004). After all, this is the type of stress that characterized the hunter–gatherer experience, so it is unlikely we would evolve a response to it that didn't work well. Participating in a stressful memory task was correlated with an improvement in the response of the immune system, as measured by markers of immune system activity in the saliva of volunteers (Bosch et al., 2001).

However, the immune system does not perform as well in the face of long-term, chronic sources of stress (see ● Figure 16.5). If stressors persist long enough, an overall reduction in immune response occurs. As a result, stress can lead to greater frequency and severity of viral illnesses, as you may have noticed immediately following final exam periods (Wadee et al., 2001). Numerous studies indicate that people experiencing chronic stress are more

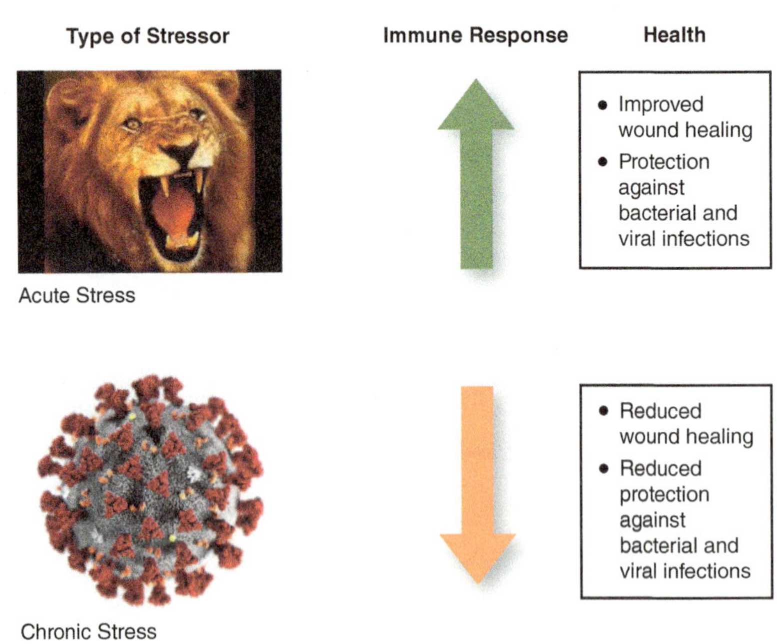

FIGURE **16.5**

Types of Stress Predict Immune Response. Acute, short-lived stress enhances our immune response in adaptive ways, promoting healing and resistance to infections. In contrast, chronic stressors reduce immune responses, delaying healing and inhibiting protection from infections like COVID-19.

Alex Dissanayake/Getty Images

Blend Images/Alamy Stock Photo

Many of the dangers faced by these San hunters in South Africa are likely to arise and resolve quickly. Our responses to stress are better suited for short-term stressors than for many of the ongoing, chronic sources of stress that we face.

vulnerable to infectious diseases, like colds and the flu (Cohen et al., 1991). White blood cells, or **lymphocytes**, protect us from invading organisms. Unfortunately, stress hormones directly suppress the activity of lymphocytes (Calcagni & Elenkov, 2006). Flare-ups of both oral and genital herpes are most likely to occur when a person is experiencing unusual stress (Cohen & Herbert, 1996). The progression of HIV infection to AIDS is influenced by the person's level of stress (Harper et al., 2006). Stressed students show greater vulnerability to the virus responsible for mononucleosis, which normally is kept in check by a robust immune system (Cacioppo & Berntson, 2011). Unfortunately, knowledge of these relationships can place an even greater burden on sick people, who may be led to believe that their illness wouldn't be so bad if they were somehow better at managing stress.

lymphocyte White blood cells that are products of the immune system.

Type A personality A competitive, workaholic, and in some cases hostile personality type.

Type B personality A mellow, laid-back personality type.

Stress related to our social relationships seems to be especially harmful to our ability to stay healthy. A meta-analysis of almost 300 studies and about 20,000 participants demonstrated that chronic stressors affecting people's social roles (e.g., death of a loved one or divorce) produce the greatest suppression of the immune system (Segerstrom & Miller, 2004). In particular, stressors that are outside a person's sense of control and lead to little hope for improvement have the most damaging effects. Those who are older and already ill are especially susceptible to adverse consequences of stress.

Stress and Heart Disease

Meyer Friedman and Ray Rosenman (1974) stimulated a large quantity of research by suggesting that highly competitive workaholics, whom they called **Type A personalities**, were more susceptible to heart disease than the mellower, laid-back people they called **Type B personalities**.

Further study, however, showed that simply being competitive had little to do with increased risk of heart disease. Instead, the Type As who did develop heart problems exhibited a pattern of interpersonal hostility. The Type As most at risk for heart disease were frequently suspicious, angry, and resentful of other people. It is possible that their own hostile behavior provoked more hostile situations and reactions from others, confirming their worldview and maintaining their negative behavior. In addition, hostile people are not likely to build up networks of friends and loved ones, who are often our best protectors from the untoward effects of stress (Jackson et al., 2007). In middle-aged adults, frequent conflict with members of a person's social network raised the risk of death 200% to 300% (Lund et al., 2014).

Stress puts the cardiovascular system at risk by affecting the ability of blood vessels to expand when necessary. People whose arteries are already stiff or clogged because of age, poor fitness, or disease often suffer from high blood pressure and might be especially susceptible to heart attacks following stress. In a heart attack, interruptions of blood flow to the heart trigger death of a part of the cardiac muscle. Flexible blood vessels maintain blood flow and blood pressure and lessen the chances of a heart attack. To test the effects of stress on blood flow, healthy participants were given a standardized mental stress task in which colored buttons were to be pushed as quickly as possible in response to flashing lights of the same color (Spieker, 2002). For the following 45 minutes, the ability of the participants' blood vessels to expand was reduced by a factor of 50%. A participant's change in blood pressure in response to a stressful situation was predictive of a later diagnosis with hypertension, or high blood pressure, which can lead to heart attacks or stroke (Spieker et al., 2002).

Ollyy/Shutterstock.com

Research shows that in middle-aged adults, frequent conflict with members of a person's social network increased the risk of death by 200% to 300%.

CONNECTING TO RESEARCH

Social Challenges Early in Life Affect the Developing Immune System

IN THIS TEXTBOOK, WE HAVE explored a number of examples of interactions between people's genetic makeup and their life experiences that predict psychological and physical health. We have also seen how some early life experiences, such as child maltreatment, seem to have especially pronounced effects on people's outcomes throughout the rest of their life. What is there about experiences early in life that is so important? How does the experience of stress early in life affect health later? To examine these questions, researchers evaluated the effects of early stress on genetic pathways that shape the immune system (Cole et al., 2012).

The Question: How does adverse early life experience affect later health?

METHODS

In Chapter 11, we reviewed work by Harry Harlow in which infant rhesus monkeys were raised by cloth and wire surrogate "mothers" to investigate questions about attachment. Steven Cole and his colleagues (2012) also exposed infant rhesus monkeys to surrogate mothers, other peers, or both instead of their real mothers. The researchers then conducted analyses of genetic changes in the infant monkeys' immune systems.

ETHICS

Some would object to the removal of an infant monkey from its parent because we know from other research that this can have long-term negative effects. The researchers would need to demonstrate "necessity," which means that they cannot answer their research question with other methods and that the importance of their research question justifies the harm being done to the animals.

RESULTS

When the monkeys were only 4 months old, the researchers identified changes in the expression of genes in the monkeys' developing immune systems. Genes that were related to inflammation and activation of the immune system were more active in monkeys raised by peers or by peers plus a surrogate mother than in monkeys raised by their biological mothers. Genes involved in basic defenses against bacteria and viruses were less active in these monkeys than in the monkeys raised by their biological mothers.

CONCLUSIONS

The researchers believed that sympathetic nervous system responses to the stress of being raised by peers or a surrogate mother and peers changed the basic way in which genes important to the immune system were expressed. Their results were similar to genetic studies of adults who had experienced adverse childhood events. These changes help to explain why people with early social challenges have a more difficult time responding to diseases caused by bacteria or viruses. ■

stevenku/Shutterstock.com

Rhesus infants raised by surrogate mothers or peers experienced changes in the expression of genes related to their immune systems. These results help explain the connection between adverse childhood experiences and poor adult health outcomes.

Stress, Mood, Sleep, and Obesity

As discussed in Chapters 4 and 14, mood, sleep, and appetite are closely intertwined. A change in one of these behaviors usually results in changes in the others. Long-term, chronic stress can begin a cascade of changes in mood, sleep, and appetite that compromise well-being. Disruptions of sleep because of stress are particularly hazardous to health because we need sleep to restore our bodies after the challenges of the day. Both sleep quantity and sleep quality are associated with both overall health and cognitive outcomes (Hawkley & Cacioppo, 2010).

Stress frequently serves as a trigger for a depressed mood. Self-reports of daily stressors, like having an argument with a friend, were correlated with the participants' mood (Stader & Hokanson, 1998). The ability of stress to alter levels of circulating cortisol, discussed earlier in this chapter, might form the basis for this connection between stress and depressed mood. As observed in Chapter 14, many people diagnosed with MDD show signs of abnormal cortisol function (Aihara et al., 2007).

Cortisol is not released just in response to perceived stressors. As observed in Chapter 6, it also plays a role in maintaining our natural cycles of sleep and waking. Cortisol is released in large quantities early in the morning, contributing to wakefulness. As the day progresses, cortisol levels drop off, reducing wakefulness and setting the stage for sleep. If you experience a big jolt of cortisol because of a stressor late in the evening, getting to sleep is going to be difficult, even when you're tired. Even when you do get to sleep, high levels of cortisol interfere with good sleep quality (Van Cauter et al., 2000). High levels of stress and MDD can both produce sleep disturbances, especially the experience of waking frequently throughout the night (Koenigsberg et al., 2004).

Mood and sleep can both affect appetite. Among the criteria for MDD are changes in appetite. Some people who are depressed lose weight without dieting, while others gain weight. By now, it shouldn't surprise you to learn that stress, along with depression, also can contribute to obesity. In response to stress-related hormones, fat cells behave differently, growing in both size and number (Kuo et al., 2009). Stressed mice gained more weight than mice that were not stressed, even when both were fed the same high-fat, high-sugar diet. In addition to this direct effect of stress on appetite, stress can produce indirect effects on obesity by interfering with sleep. Dieters who enjoyed a full night's sleep lost the same amount of weight as dieters who slept less, but there was a difference in the kind of weight that was lost (Nedeltcheva et al., 2010). Dieters who slept well lost a healthy amount of fat, while sleep-deprived dieters lost only half as much fat as the sleeping dieters, and three-quarters of their weight loss consisted of precious bone and muscle tissue instead of fat (see Figure 16.6).

Long before vaccinations and antibiotics were available, death rates because of infectious diseases began to drop in the United States. Improved wages and nutrition, coupled with more rest time away from work, allowed people to recover from their daily stresses (Cacioppo & Berntson, 2011).

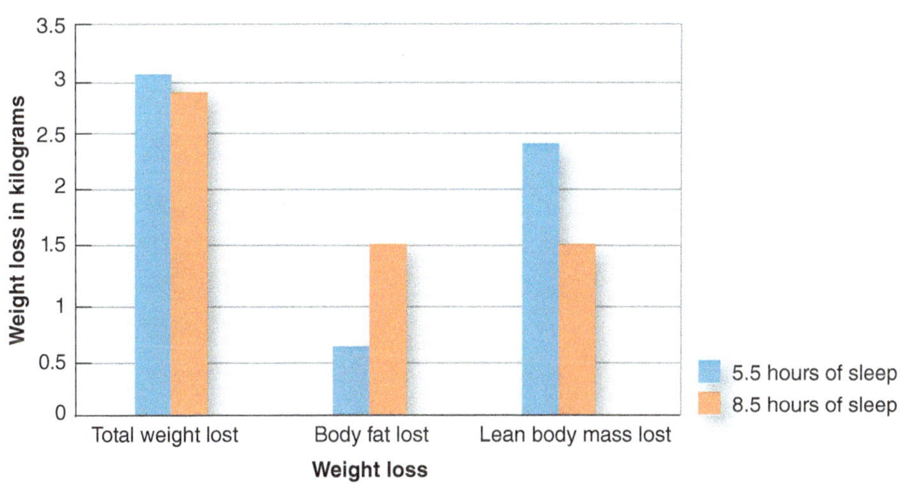

FIGURE **16.6**

Sleep and Diet Interact. Participants who slept 8.5 hours per night lost about the same amount of weight during a treatment program as participants who slept 5.5 hours per night, but the two groups differed in the amount of body fat and lean body mass that was lost. The group that slept 8.5 hours per night lost more body fat and less lean body mass, which is characteristic of desirable weight loss, than the group that slept 5.5 hours per night. These results remind us that many of our health habits are intimately interconnected, and that changing one can have a large effect on others.

Source: Adapted from A. V. Nedeltcheva et al. (2010). "Insufficient Sleep Undermines Dietary Efforts to Reduce Adiposity," *Annals of Internal Medicine*, *153*, 435–441. doi: 10.1059/0003-4819-153-7-201010050-00006

An Integrated View of Stress and Health

We have reviewed a number of studies in this section that demonstrate the adverse effects that chronic, prolonged stress can have on our health. Popular wisdom suggests that people with the highest levels of stress should therefore experience the worst health. However, we have already seen one example, the healthy Type As, in which this was not the case. In another study, 5,000 men reported their stress levels, which were then compared 20 years later to their medical records. Surprisingly, the men who had reported the highest levels of stress had experienced the least amount of heart disease (Macleod et al., 2002). How can we explain these apparently contradictory results?

One approach to reconciling the good health enjoyed by some stressed people with data demonstrating the harmful effects of stress in others is to step back and look at whole persons within their environments over the entire life span. Health can be described as not just the absence of disease, but also as the ability to respond to the challenges of being alive (Juster et al., 2010).

Personal factors, including your genes, interact with the parental care that you receive, as discussed previously in this chapter. Other protective factors, such as your social networks and sense of meaning or purpose in life, contribute to your resilience in the face of the negative and cumulative effects of a lifetime of responding to stressors (Cacioppo & Berntson, 2011). These protective factors occur at critical periods, such as the impact of parenting in early childhood, so a complete understanding of protective mechanisms should be examined within the context of life-span development. Once we fully understand these protective processes, psychologists should be in the exciting position of being able to design effective interventions for improving health and well-being (see ● Figure 16.7).

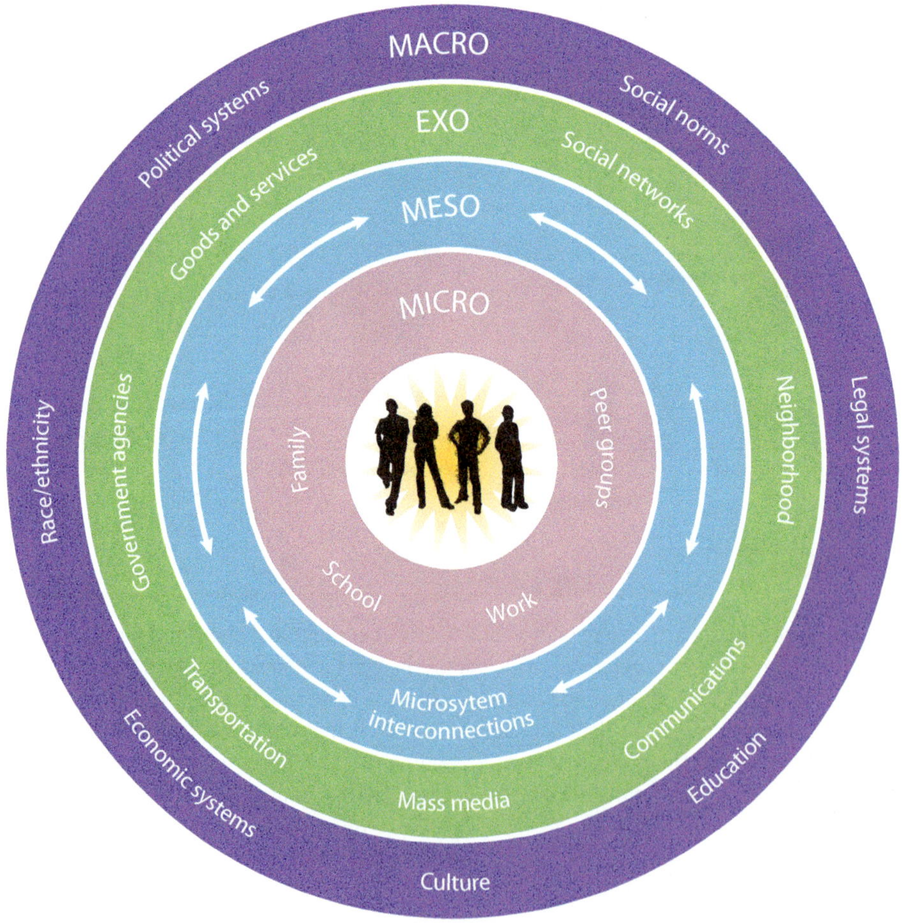

FIGURE 16.7

An Interactive View of Stress and Health. Individuals do not experience stress in a vacuum. Personal factors, like genes and everyday experiences, influence outcomes within an environment consisting of ever-larger circles of social connectivity. The relationships between social environment and personal factors are reciprocal. Individual actions influence the social environment, which in turn influences individual factors.

Source: Adapted from R.-P. Juster et al. (2010). "Allostatic Load Biomarkers of Chronic Stress and Impact on Health and Cognition," *Neuroscience and Biobehavioral Reviews, 35*(1), 2–16. doi:10.1016/j.neubiorev.2009.10.002

PSYCHOLOGY AS A HUB SCIENCE

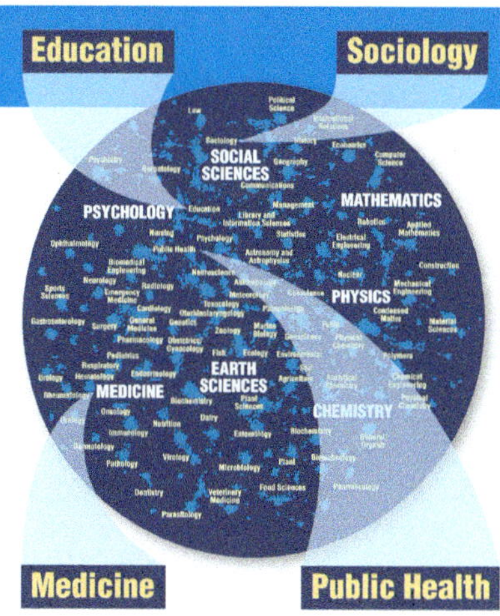

Belongingness, Stress, Achievement, and Health

WE DON'T NEED TO TELL YOU that being in college can be stressful. For many students, college can mean new environments, new rules and routines, new social interactions, less sleep, not-so-great eating habits, and more sitting than exercising. Can the application of psychological research make the transition into college easier and less stressful?

We can't make many of these stressors go away, but a simple, one-time intervention at the beginning of the first year of college made a large difference in the academic performance and health of a group of students in one study (Walton & Cohen, 2011). Incoming first-year students at Stanford University were randomly assigned to a control group or a social-belonging group. The social-belonging group read what they thought were the results of a survey of older students, who said that they had worried about fitting in during their first year but had grown more confident over time. Participants were asked to write an essay comparing their own first-year experiences with the survey results and then deliver a speech based on their essay to a video camera for use with future students. At no time were the participants aware that they were actually experiencing a "treatment" designed to make them see the social stressors of college life as typical of all students and of short duration.

Over the next three years, the participants' grade point averages (GPAs) and health were monitored. The "belongingness" intervention had little impact on the health and grades of White students, but it had significant and positive effects on African American students. Compared to African American students in the control group, the students who had received the one-time reassurance that their concerns about fitting in were normal and were not permanent had higher grades, fewer visits to the doctor, and higher subjective happiness (see Figure 16.8).

While further research is necessary to know how far these results can be generalized to other students, the results emphasize the importance to your overall performance, health, and well-being of how you interpret your situation and whether you feel like you belong. ■

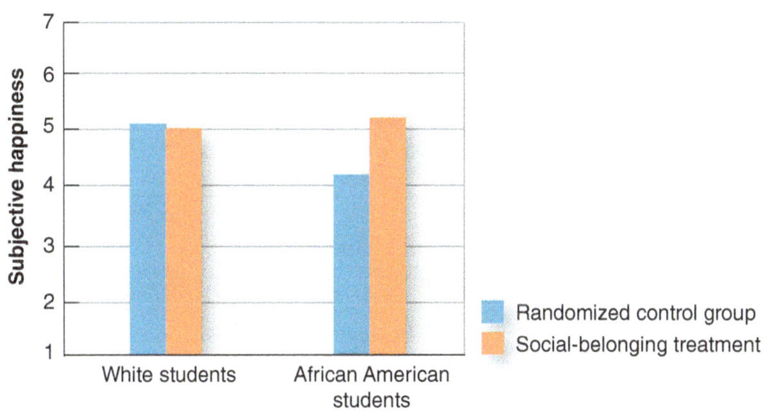

FIGURE **16.8**

A Belongingness Intervention Improved the Performance and Health of African American College Students. A one-time treatment aimed at framing the stress of fitting in to the college experience as common to most students and limited in duration significantly improved the grade point averages, happiness ratings, and health of African American students at Stanford University three years later. White students did not experience the same treatment-related differences, with both treated and nontreated White students experiencing the same health and subjective happiness as the treated African American students. This result suggests that "fitting in" was already framed by White students in positive ways.

Source: Adapted from G. M. Walton & G. L. Cohen (2011). "A Brief Social-Belonging Intervention Improves Academic and Health Outcomes of Minority Students," *Science*, *331*(6023), 1447–1451. doi:10.1126/science.1198364

Steven Errico/DigitalVision/Getty Images

The stress of middle school, such as attending school dances, is real to students at the time, but as we get older and more experienced, our capacity to manage stress improves. With age, people report feeling less stress, even though stressors tend to become more complicated and numerous at the same time.

How Can We Cope Effectively With Stress?

Stress is inevitable. That simple statement does not imply that there is nothing you can do about stress. Psychologists have identified a number of strategies that people can use to effectively reduce the negative impacts of stress on their happiness and health.

One of the most positive aspects of stress is that we adapt to it over time. Take a minute to jot down the things that you found most stressful five years ago and then make a list of the stressors that you face today. Would you trade today's list for the one from five years ago? Most people would do so in a heartbeat. Life gets more complicated and often more stressful, but our skills for coping improve at the same time. People tend to report less stress as they get older (Shields, 2004).

Earlier in this chapter, we described the role of cognitive appraisal in identifying a stimulus or event as a stressor. Appraisal plays an important role in coping with identified stressors as well. Once a stressor has been identified, a second set of appraisals occurs that guides our coping responses (Lazarus, 1966). What harm has already occurred? What threats remain? What resources do we need to overcome the challenge? Taking conscious control of our appraisals can contribute to our ability to cope.

Managing Stress

An obvious starting place for keeping your levels of stress low is to ask whether stressors can be eliminated. If you feel stressed about having too much to do and too little time to do it, it might be possible to reduce your workload or practice better time management skills. If money is tight, a visit to your campus's financial aid office might provide you with solutions that you had not considered. The worst possible approach is to withdraw and avoid stressors in the vain hope that they will go away. Your latest credit card statement is not going to get better magically if you ignore it. In fact, your emotional response to seeing the statement on your desk every day is likely to get a lot worse over time.

Even when a stressor takes us by surprise, we can regain a sense of control. Viktor Frankl (1959, p. 161), a Holocaust survivor, developed what he described as "tragic optimism" for coping with unforeseen disasters. Instead of asking why these disasters should happen to us, Frankl recommends that people exert a sense of control by asking, "How can I face this disaster with courage and responsibility?"

A major variable that predicts our response to stress is the sense of control. Feeling surprised by life or out of control can lead to significant stress. Some of the worst stressors are those that seem to strike randomly, such as being diagnosed with lung cancer when you never smoked (Pietrzak et al., 2011). These seemingly random events undercut our sense of control, countering the belief that "If I don't smoke, I am ensuring that my lungs will stay healthy."

Monkey Business Images/Shutterstock.com

Patients who educate themselves about their conditions and participate fully in treatment decisions experience less stress.

Many stressors are out of our control, however. We can't wish our cancer away or magically ensure that enough money appears in our bank accounts to pay this month's bills. However, we can respond to our stressors in ways that reduce our overall stress. This approach is consistent with the elements of positive psychology, which we review later in this chapter. Even if you are struggling with a life-threatening disease, stress can be reduced by educating yourself as much as possible about your condition and participating fully in decisions about your treatment. Residents of nursing homes who have more control over their choice of daily activities live longer than those who are not given such choices (Rodin, 1986). We observed in Chapter 12 that stressors have less effect on people who experience an internal locus of control, which means that they believe that most of their outcomes result from their personal efforts, as opposed to luck, chance, opportunities, or other external forces.

Because of the inevitability of stress, people cope best when they keep themselves as healthy as possible. If you follow good health habits, stress might still deplete your reserves and inhibit your immune system, but a healthy body can take more abuse than an unhealthy one. Students are more likely to get sick during final exams if they have neglected good eating, exercise, and sleeping habits all term long.

Alexander Raths/Photos.com

FIGURE 16.9

Exercise Reduces Mortality in Stressed Cardiac Patients. People with cardiovascular disease were assessed for psychosocial stress levels during a rehabilitation program that included exercise. A control group did not have a formal exercise program. Based on their improvement in physical measures following the exercise program, the study participants were divided into low and high exercise change groups. In a follow-up five years later, high levels of physical improvement because of exercise did not affect the mortality of the low psychosocial stress group but significantly reduced mortality in the high-stress group.

Source: Adapted from R. V. Milani & C. J. Lavie (2009). "Reducing Psychosocial Stress: A Novel Mechanism of Improving Survival from Exercise Training," *American Journal of Medicine, 122*(10), 931–938. doi:10.1016/ j.amjmed.2009.03.028

Regular aerobic exercise appears to be especially helpful. In one experiment, people with heart disease were observed as they engaged in exercise as part of their rehabilitation programs. The exercise reduced the overall stress levels of all participants (Milani & Lavie, 2009). Exercise seemed particularly beneficial for the participants who also scored high on psychosocial stress. None of the high-stress participants who showed the greatest physical benefits from exercise (such as increased oxygen uptake) died in the follow-up period, compared to 19% of the high-stress participants who showed relatively low physical benefits from exercise (see ● Figure 16.9). Students would be wise to engage in some level of activity to offset the effects of increased stress.

In Chapter 15, we discussed the use of mindfulness in the treatment of anxiety and MDD. Mindfulness, or the trained awareness of our current thoughts, emotions, and actions, has also been shown to be an effective method for reducing stress (Tang & Posner, 2009). In Chapter 6, we explored the effects of the altered state of consciousness produced through meditation. Although many people meditate within a religious context, a large meta-analysis indicated that meditation is an effective strategy for reducing psychological stress (Goyal et al., 2014).

One of the most powerful antidotes to unhealthy effects of stress is social connectedness and support. Social support from friends and family and belief systems that allow a person to make sense of the world provide powerful buffers against stress (Montpetit et al., 2010). As we have argued on many occasions in this textbook, people with good social relationships and support are far less vulnerable to adverse health and psychological conditions than are people who are lonely and isolated (Hostinar et al., 2013; Cacioppo et al., 2015). In times of distress, people frequently turn to others in an effort to cope. According to a study of responses to the terrorist attacks of 9/11, nearly 100% of the participants reported sharing their thoughts and feelings about the attacks with other people (Schuster et al., 2002). More than 90% reported either praying or engaging in spiritual contemplation appropriate to their faith. More than 60% engaged in relevant public activities. Nearly 40% focused on the needs of others by donating money or blood to relief efforts.

Understanding the importance of social support for coping helps to explain why people living in poor neighborhoods often experience more stress and have higher rates of MDD. Living in a neighborhood where few people know one another or help one another with tasks like child care increases the risk of developing MDD (Russell & Cutrona, 2010). These socially disconnected neighborhoods become more prevalent as the income of the residents decreases, making people living below the poverty line especially vulnerable to stress and depression.

Although it is ideal to receive your social support from other people, having a pet can also provide benefits to your health. Stockbrokers with high blood pressure who lived alone were selected to receive a cat or dog from a local shelter (Allen, 2003). When stressed, the pet owners experienced a much lower increase in blood pressure than their petless counterparts. The effect was most obvious among participants who listed few social connections with other people. Among individuals with Alzheimer's disease in residential care, the use of robotic pets was not only associated with reduced anxiety and stress, but also with reduced need for pain medication and psychoactive medications (Petersen et al., 2017).

Spc. Terence Ewings, 4th AAB PAO, 1st Cav. Div., USD-N/photo courtesy of U.S. Army

Specialist Lawrence Shipman and Sergeant First Class Jonathan Zeke, a combat stress–relief dog, received an award for their work in reducing the stress of soldiers deployed in Iraq. Shipman notes that Zeke acts as an icebreaker, encouraging soldiers to talk to the behavioral health counselors.

Fiona Hanson/PA Images/Alamy Stock Photo

Owning a pet confers many advantages, but individuals with dementia usually cannot care for a pet properly. The PARO robotic seal has produced such positive effects that many insurance companies are willing to pay the over $6,000 required to provide this "pet" to patients.

Many people find that having religious beliefs helps them cope with stress. People who report having religious beliefs appear to withstand the challenges of unemployment, low income, and widowhood better than people who report no religious beliefs (Diener & Seligman, 2004). In a sample of middle-aged and older adults with higher than average numbers of serious life stressors, religious service attendance was associated with lower levels of inflammation (Ironson et al., 2018). Across a number of nations practicing different forms of religion, a higher rate of belief in a god predicts higher ratings of life satisfaction and lower rates of suicide (Helliwell, 2003).

Three Types of Coping

Coping with a stressor can take three forms: problem-focused, emotion-focused, and relationship-focused (O'Brien & DeLongis, 1996). In each case, positive and negative versions of each style can be observed.

Problem-focused coping is designed to address an issue head-on. If you just flunked an important exam, positive problem-focused coping strategies might include making an appointment with your professor to discuss your options, hiring a tutor, taking a study skills seminar, or joining a study group formed by your classmates. Negative problem-focused coping can include escape and avoidance. Instead of confronting the problem, a student might stop going to class. Problem-focused coping is more frequently used for work-related stressors, which would include schoolwork, than for interpersonal stressors like the breakup of an important relationship (Terry, 1994).

Emotion-focused coping helps you deal with the negative emotions associated with a stressor. Flunking an exam might make you feel sad, discouraged, and depressed. Positive coping with these negative emotions might involve sharing your concerns with your friends or family, taking a break from your studies to enjoy a movie or go for a jog, or, when the negative emotions seem overwhelming, visiting your campus's counseling center for advice. Negative emotion-focused coping, such as eating food that you do not need or using alcohol to dull your stress, might simply add to your problems and increase your overall levels of stress.

Relationship-focused coping helps you maintain and protect social relationships in response to stress (O'Brien & DeLongis, 1996). This type of coping has both positive and negative aspects. For example, people caring for Alzheimer's patients, which can be stressful, exhibited both positive coping, including empathy, support, and compromise; and negative coping, including confronting, ignoring, blaming, and withdrawal (Kramer, 1993).

As we have seen so frequently in our discussions of human behavior, the choice of a coping approach results from interactions between people and the situation in question (Aldwin, 1994). For example, people who score high on the Big Five trait of neuroticism (discussed in Chapter 12) tend to experience more distress than people with low neuroticism scores (Bolger & Schilling, 1991). When responding to stressors in the work situation, people high in neuroticism are more likely to engage in negative problem-focused coping, such as escaping the situation (O'Brien & DeLongis, 1996). When dealing with interpersonal stress, however, people with high neuroticism use the negative relationship-focused coping strategy of confrontation.

problem-focused coping A response to stress designed to address specific problems by finding solutions.

emotion-focused coping A response to stress that targets the negative emotions arising from the situation.

relationship-focused coping A response to stress designed to maintain and protect social relationships.

(a)

Lucky Business/Shutterstock.com

(b)

Image navi - QxQ images/Alamy Stock Photo

(c)

suhendri/Shutterstock.com

At times of stress, we often engage in three types of coping. (a) Problem-focused coping is usually used to solve problems at work. (b) Emotion-focused coping helps us deal with the negative emotions of stress. The use of strategies like overeating, however, can lead to more problems. (c) Relationship-focused coping helps us maintain and strengthen social networks at times of stress.

People with high neuroticism also cope differently with stress involving close relationships (significant others, family members, and close friends) than with stress involving distant relationships (coworkers and neighbors). They are more likely to use a positive relationship-focused coping method, empathy, when dealing with distant relationships than when dealing with close relationships (O'Brien & DeLongis, 1996).

Resilience: Individual Differences in Response to Stress

Katharina Vesely/Imagno/Getty Images

Cover designed by Two Associates/Courtesy Rider Books/Ebury Publishing

Austrian psychiatrist Viktor Frankl (1905–1997) was sent to the dreaded Nazi concentration camp Auschwitz, where he lost his pregnant wife, parents, and brother. Frankl used his experiences in developing his theories of *logotherapy,* after *logos,* the Greek word for "meaning." The ability to find meaning even in the depths of despair by recalling pleasant memories or helping a suicidal inmate helped Frankl survive the stress and horror surrounding him.

You might have observed that under the same stressful circumstances, such as an upcoming exam, some students seem calm and others appear to be in a state of panic. What determines these individual differences in coping?

We have already seen how epigenetic interactions between genes and nurturing can influence later responses to stress. In addition, people differ in **resilience**, or the ability to adapt to life's challenges in positive ways. Early research in resilience focused on children's ability to thrive even in conditions of poverty, neglect, and abuse (Masten et al., 1999). Low resilient people have higher levels of perceived stress (García-León et al., 2019). Resilient people do not ignore feelings of sadness or stress, but like Holocaust survivor Viktor Frankl, they remain optimistic and confident about their abilities to cope with adversity. In contrast, when people lack resilience, they feel overwhelmed, helpless, and victimized. They become more vulnerable to the use of negative coping strategies, including alcoholism and drug abuse, to escape their problems.

The personality trait of hardiness contributes to resilience (Maddi, 2006). As mentioned in Chapter 12, a personality trait is likely to be stable and enduring over time. Compared to less hardy people, people with high hardiness experience less threat or disruption in response to the normal stressors of life. Hardiness combines commitment, control, and challenge (Bartone, 2000). People with high commitment see the world as interesting and seek involvement rather than withdrawal. *Control* refers to individuals' belief in their ability to influence events. *Challenge* is a state of mind that sees change and new experiences not as negative stressors, but as opportunities for learning and personal growth. Among college students, hardiness did not predict grades, but it was negatively correlated with health complaints and stress related to academic work (Hystad et al., 2009; also see Figure 16.10).

People who write "scripts" for how their life "should" happen, such as thinking that everyone should enjoy a set schedule of activities over a holiday, often experience high stress levels when events take an unexpected turn. Maintaining a flexible approach to meeting your life's goals is far less likely to create stress.

resilience The ability to adapt to life's challenges in positive ways.

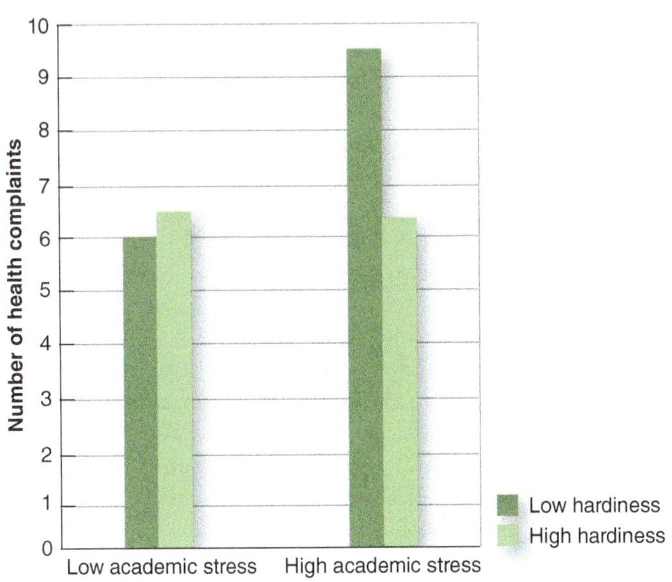

FIGURE **16.10**

Hardiness Protects Students From the Health Impacts of Stress. The personality trait of hardiness, which combines commitment, a sense of control, and the appraisal of stressors as challenges, seems to protect college students from the health consequences of high academic stress.

Source: Adapted from S. W. Hystad et al. (2009). "Academic Stress and Health: Exploring the Moderating Role of Personality Hardiness," *Scandinavian Journal of Educational Research, 53*(5), 421–429. doi:10.1080/00313830903180349

Other protective factors contributing to individual differences in resilience are cognitive skills, social skills, and flexibility in response to new situations (Garmezy, 1991). Individual differences in resilience might also have their roots in emotion. People who are generally more positive in mood tend to build the resources that they need, including strong social networks, to sustain them at difficult times (Cohn et al., 2009).

SUMMARY 16.1 Stages in Hans Selye's General Adaptation Syndrome

Stage	What's Happening?
Alarm 	Mobilization of resources for fight-or-flight
Resistance 	Continued coping with chronic stress
Exhaustion 	Systems begin to fail

Credits: Top row—AP Images; Second row—Sgt. Jessika Malott, 8th MP Bde. Public Affairs/photo courtesy of U.S. Army; Bottom row—oliveromg/Shutterstock.com

What Is the Relationship Between Psychology and Health?

health psychology A branch of psychology that investigates the relationships between psychological variables and health.

biopsychosocial model A model that sees health as the result of biological, psychological, and social factors.

You might be surprised to see a section about **health psychology** in your psychology textbook. Isn't health the exclusive domain of medical personnel rather than of psychologists? It all depends on how you define *health.* For most of its history, the field of medicine viewed health as a lack of disease (Juster et al., 2010). Treatments were designed to make sick people feel better. In more recent years, however, health has been more commonly defined as the attainment of a positive state of well-being rather than simply the absence of disease. Medicine today is more likely to use a **biopsychosocial model** of health, in which health is viewed as the sum of biological (such as genetics, infection, and injury), psychological (such as lifestyle, stress, and health beliefs), and social factors (such as culture, family, and social support; McEwen & Gianaros, 2011) (see ● Figure 16.11).

In 1948, the World Health Organization (WHO) proposed a definition that reflects this more contemporary model of health: "a state of complete physical, mental, and social well-being and not merely the absence of disease or infirmity" (World Health Organization [WHO], 2003, para. 1). In addition to making sick people feel better, which is an important

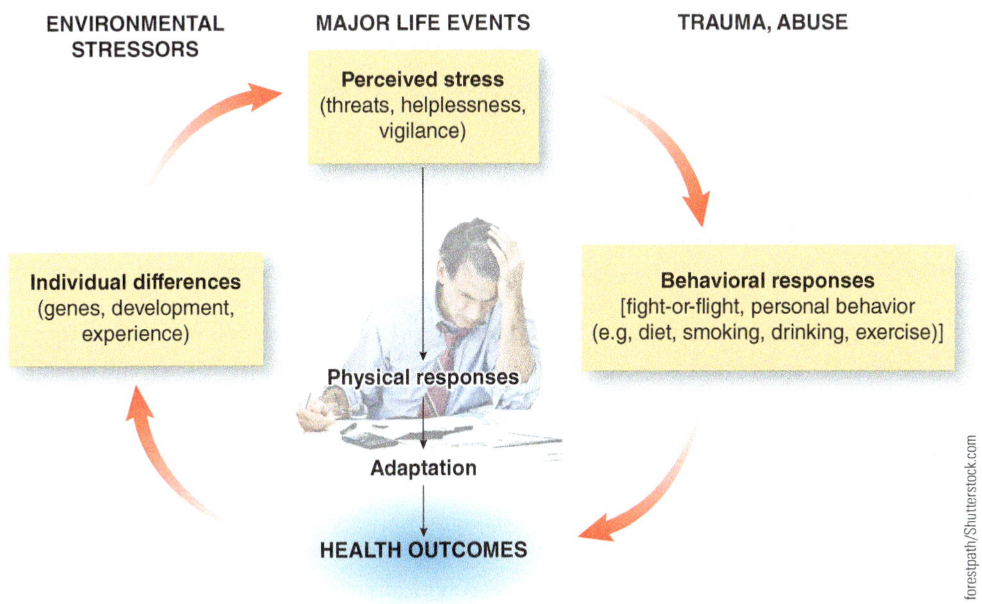

FIGURE 16.11

A Biopsychosocial Model of Health. Health today is viewed as the product of interactions among individual characteristics, life experiences, cognitions, and behavior.
Source: Adapted from R.-P. Juster et al. (2010). "Allostatic Load Biomarkers of Chronic Stress and Impact on Health and Cognition," *Neuroscience and Biobehavioral Reviews*, *35*(1), 2–16. doi:10.1016/j.neubiorev.2009.10.002

function of medicine, this new view of health seeks to improve the well-being of people who are not currently sick.

One reason for this transition from the biomedical model to the biopsychosocial model is the changing face of health and medicine over the last 100 years or so. Because of improved sanitation and vaccination, the threats to health faced today are quite different from those faced by earlier generations. In 1900, the leading causes of death in the United States were pneumonia, influenza, and tuberculosis, but by 2005, the leading causes of death were heart disease, cancer, lung disease, and stroke (see ● Figure 16.12). In other words, we have gone from facing major threats from infectious, short-duration conditions to noninfectious, long-term conditions. Perhaps this is one of the reasons why the threat of COVID-19 has been difficult to grasp—it is not typical of the health threats we normally face today. In the last few decades, considerable progress was made in the treatment of heart disease, cancer, and stroke. This improvement in turn has resulted in a larger number of Americans who are living long enough to be diagnosed with age-related conditions such as Alzheimer's disease and Parkinson's disease.

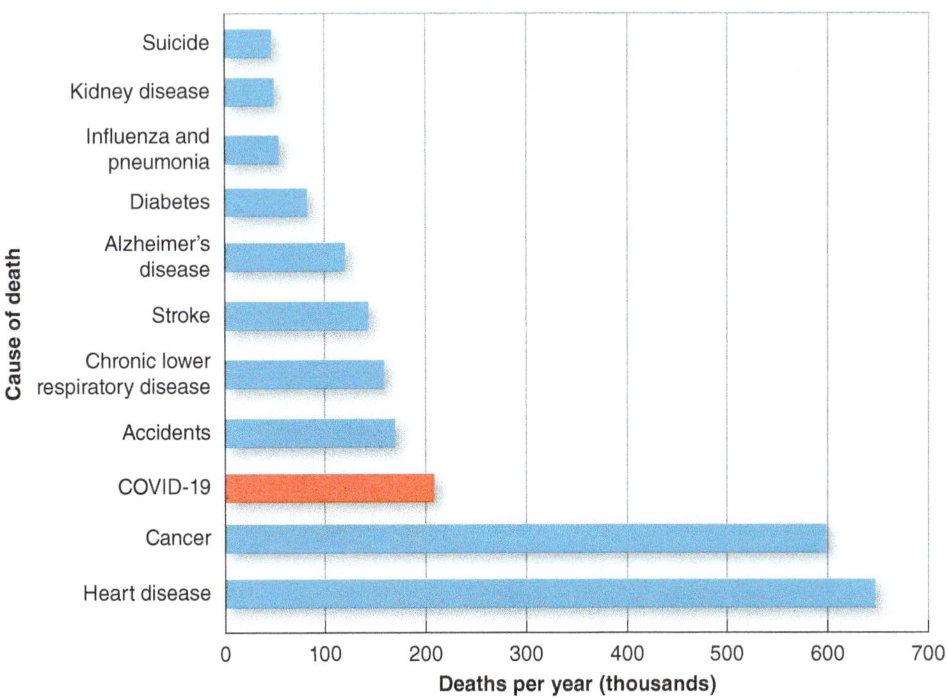

FIGURE 16.12

Leading Causes of Death in the United States. Over the last 100 years, infectious diseases had been replaced as the leading causes of death in the United States until the emergence of the COVID-19 pandemic.
Source: Adapted from the Centers for Disease Control and Prevention (CDC; 2020). "Leading Causes of Death." Retrieved from https://www.cdc.gov/nchs/fastats/leading-causes-of-death.htm

The contemporary leading causes of death just listed (heart disease, cancer, lung disease, and stroke) form significant interactions with behavior because their risk factors include obesity, smoking, lack of exercise, and alcohol consumption. Even when we consider infectious diseases, we see evidence of strong behavioral components, such as the amount of stress that you're experiencing (Cohen et al., 1991) or the likelihood that you practice prevention by social distancing, washing your hands, or wearing a mask. In addition, lifestyle factors and adherence to treatment plans can be extremely important to achieving and maintaining wellness. Health psychologists are interested in helping people to better prevent and recover from disease and to cope with the stress of chronic health problems and pain.

When we discuss the contributions of behavior to health, by no means do we want to "blame the victims" of poor health. People who have never smoked still get lung cancer, and thin, fit people get heart disease. The relationships between lifestyle factors and health are derived from the statistical analyses of large populations, not single individuals. At the same time, understanding that most people who engage in particular behaviors have certain health outcomes can provide us with clues for maintaining the healthiest lifestyles possible.

Behavior and Health

Consumer Reports conducted a survey of 1,000 Americans to see how many engaged in everyday prevention behaviors (Consumerreports.com, 2009). As shown in ● Table 16.2, the respondents did rather well in a number of categories (91% read the warnings that come with a prescription drug, and 87% report not drinking beer while using a power tool or mower) but neglected some obvious preventive steps (58% never wear a bike helmet, 24% report being in a car without using a seat belt, and 27% do not use sunscreen when outdoors for an extended period). We do worry about those 13% who are drinking beer while using power tools or mowing the lawn, but the point is that many of our choices contribute to the prevention of accidents and disease.

Behaviors that contribute to our major causes of death include smoking, poor nutrition, alcohol use, lack of exercise, and loneliness (see ● Figure 16.13), which are discussed in more detail in the following sections.

TABLE 16.2

Americans' Safety Practices

Behavior	Yes	No
Use cotton swabs to clean ears	73%	26%
Let your kids play on a trampoline	43%	56%
Eat raw dough when making cookies	39%	61%
Use the top step of a ladder	31%	69%
Fail to use the car's seat belt	24%	75%
Drink beer while using a power tool or mower	13%	87%
Have a rubber mat in the shower	39%	61%
Have a carbon-monoxide detector in home	51%	48%
Eat burgers only well done	67%	32%
Change batteries in the smoke alarm annually	79%	21%
Clean lint trap in the dryer after each use	81%	18%
Read warnings on prescription medicines	91%	9%
Wear a bike helmet	42%	58%
Wear sunscreen when outside for an extended time	73%	27%

Source: Adapted from ConsumerReports.com (2009). "Risky Business." Retrieved from http://www.consumerreports.org/cro/magazine-archive/march-2009/money/risk-taking/overview/risk-taking-ov.htm

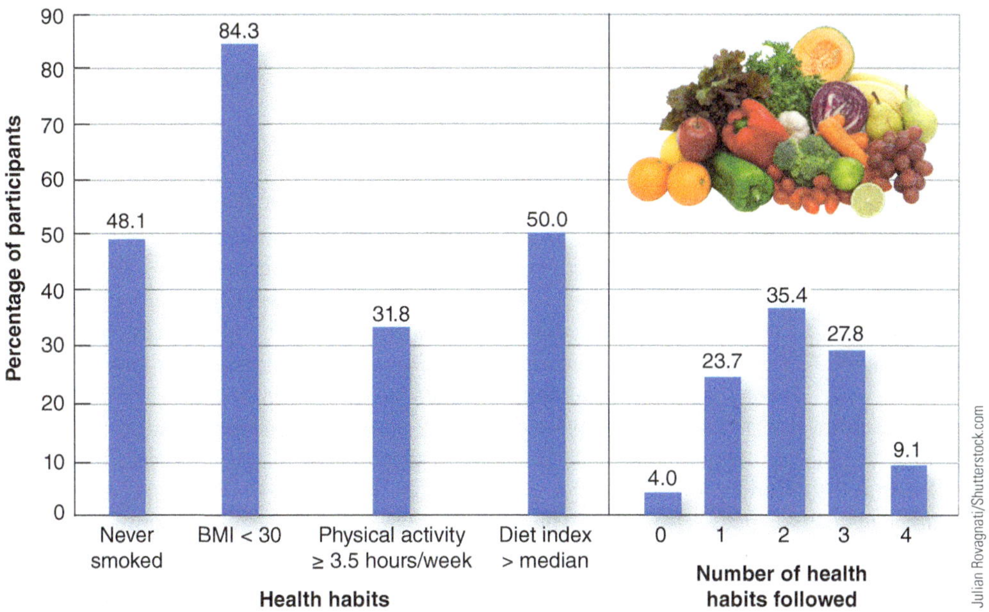

FIGURE **16.13**

Four Simple Habits Make Major Contributions to Health. Following four simple health habits—never smoking, exercising 30 minutes per day, maintaining a nonobese weight, and eating a healthy diet including fruits and vegetables—reduced overall risk of chronic disease by 78%. Unfortunately, only 9.1% of a sample of more than 20,000 adults between 35 and 65 years of age had all four habits. Most people reported following only one to three of the four health habits.

Source: Adapted from E. S. Ford et al. (2009). "Healthy Living Is the Best Revenge: Findings from the European Prospective Investigation into Cancer and Nutrition–Potsdam Study," *Archives of Internal Medicine, 169*(15), 1355–1362. doi:10.1001/archinternmed.2009.237

Tobacco Use Cigarette smoking is considered to be the leading preventable cause of death in the United States, with a direct responsibility in one of five deaths each year (Centers for Disease Control and Prevention [CDC], 2020c). Over 8 million people worldwide die due to tobacco each year (WHO, 2020b). On average, smokers die 13–14 years earlier than nonsmokers. Tobacco use can lead to additional health problems. Nicotine is a well-established gateway drug, capable of producing epigenetic changes that increase the likelihood of addiction to cocaine (Li et al., 2014). Tobacco's effects are not restricted to its users either. In the United States, exposure of nonsmokers to secondhand smoke causes 7,300 lung cancer deaths, 34,000 premature deaths from heart disease, 8,000 deaths in nonsmokers from stroke, higher rates of SIDS, and asthma attacks and ear infections in children (CDC, 2020b).

Cigarette smokers in the United States dropped from 21% of adults in 2005 to just 13.7% in 2018 (CDC, 2019; Jamal et al., 2016). Worldwide rates also continue to drop (see ● Figure 16.14; WHO, 2020b).

Gender, race, ethnicity, education, mental health, and income are strong determinants of the likelihood of smoking. In the United States, men are more likely to smoke than women (15.6%, as opposed to 12%). American Indians or Alaska Natives reported the highest incidence of smoking (22.6%), followed by non-Hispanic multirace individuals (19.1%), non-Hispanic Whites (15%), non-Hispanic Blacks (14.6%), Hispanics (9.8%), and Asians (7.1%). Lesbian/gay/bisexual individuals were more likely to smoke cigarettes (20.6%) than heterosexual individuals (13.5%). Smoking drops with increasing education, from 36% of individuals with a general equivalency diploma (GED) certificate to 3.7% of adults with a graduate degree. Poverty plays a strong role in smoking; 26.1% of adults living below the poverty line compared to 13.9% living at or above the poverty line report smoking.

You might be wondering how trends regarding e-cigarettes (i.e., vaping) might influence these numbers. It is unclear how much of the overall decline in cigarette use is related to e-cigarette use. In 2020, 3.2% of U.S. adults used e-cigarettes, and 58% of these were also current cigarette smokers (CDC, 2020a). However, among e-cigarette users aged 18–45, 40% have never used

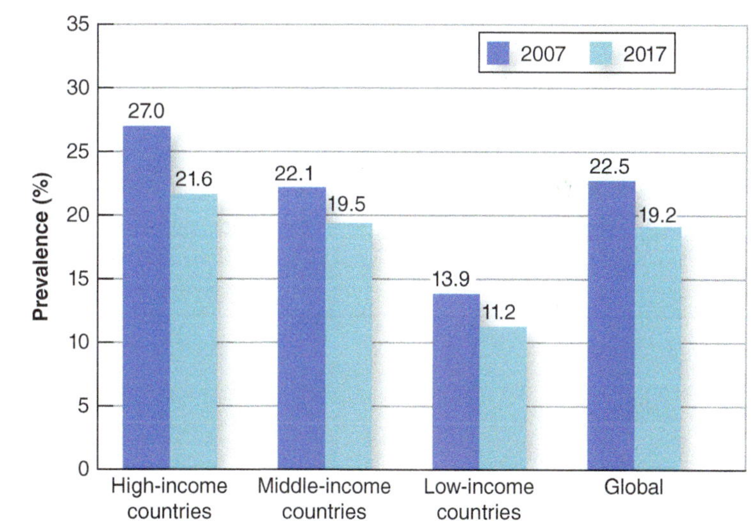

FIGURE **16.14**

Fewer People Are Smoking Cigarettes. Between 2007 and 2017, global rates of smoking among adults dropped from 22.5% to 19.2%. At the same time, however, use of e-cigarettes and heated tobacco increased. It is unclear how much of the drop in cigarette smoking is related to these alternate patterns of use.

Source: World Health Organization (WHO; 2019). *WHO report on the global tobacco epidemic, 2019.* Geneva: World Health Organization.

Carlos Barria/Reuters/Newscom

China is the world's largest consumer and producer of tobacco. Over 350 million Chinese smoke. Sixty percent of male Chinese physicians smoke, compared to 3.3% of physicians in the United States. The 2011 ban on smoking in bars, in restaurants, and on transportation does not apply to offices and factories. The ban was required when China signed the World Health Organization Framework Convention on Tobacco Control. Public health officials fear that the lack of an awareness program and penalties will encourage the population to ignore the ban.

regular cigarettes, suggesting that rates of e-cigarettes and cigarettes do not always overlap. Many people use e-cigarettes to consume cannabis alone or both cannabis and tobacco. Rates of use of e-cigarettes among middle (4.7%) and high school students (19.6%) are dropping. Serious lung injury attributed to e-cigarettes has resulted in legal restrictions on the sale of some items (Blagev et al., 2019).

Given the carnage produced by tobacco, why do people start smoking and then continue? An understanding of the initiation of tobacco use requires combining the perspectives discussed in this textbook—development, biological psychology, cognitive, clinical, and social/personality psychology.

Most tobacco users begin smoking in childhood or early adolescence, long before decision-making abilities are mature. Because of the addictive nature of nicotine, about half of those who experiment with tobacco continue to use it. In addition to its action on synapses where the neurotransmitter acetylcholine is released, as discussed in Chapter 6, nicotine has the ability to stimulate the dopamine reward circuits of the brain and to produce a particularly unpleasant set of withdrawal symptoms. As discussed in Chapter 11, adolescence is also a time when people try out new roles and learn important skills for getting along with peers, frequently making them susceptible to peer pressure. Teens often overestimate how many other people are using tobacco, so they might begin using it to avoid looking "different" (Institute of Medicine [IOM], 1994). Finally, most smokers have friends and parents who also smoke, suggesting a role for social learning (Biglan et al., 1995). It is also possible, however, that prenatal exposure to tobacco raises the likelihood that a child will smoke.

A troubling aspect of the initiation of smoking is the prevalence of tobacco use among people with diagnosed psychological disorders (see Figure 16.15). Of the approximately 20% of American adults diagnosed with any mental disorder (see Chapter 14), 40.6% were current smokers—a much higher rate than that found in the general population (Jamal et al., 2016). Adults diagnosed with mental disorders smoke 31.6% of all cigarettes consumed by adults in the United States (CDC, 2019). Tobacco use among people with schizophrenia and other severe mental illnesses is as high as 88%, many times higher than the approximately 14% of users in the general population as reported by the CDC (Lucatch et al., 2018).

In addition, the severity of smoking, which includes such factors as how many cigarettes are smoked per day, appears to be much higher among people with psychological disorders than in the general population. In a large-scale study of more than 50,000 adults who did not live in mental institutions, individuals with serious psychological distress (a global measure of psychological disorder) were more likely to smoke currently and heavily and were less likely to quit than individuals without serious psychological distress (Sung et al., 2011). Although

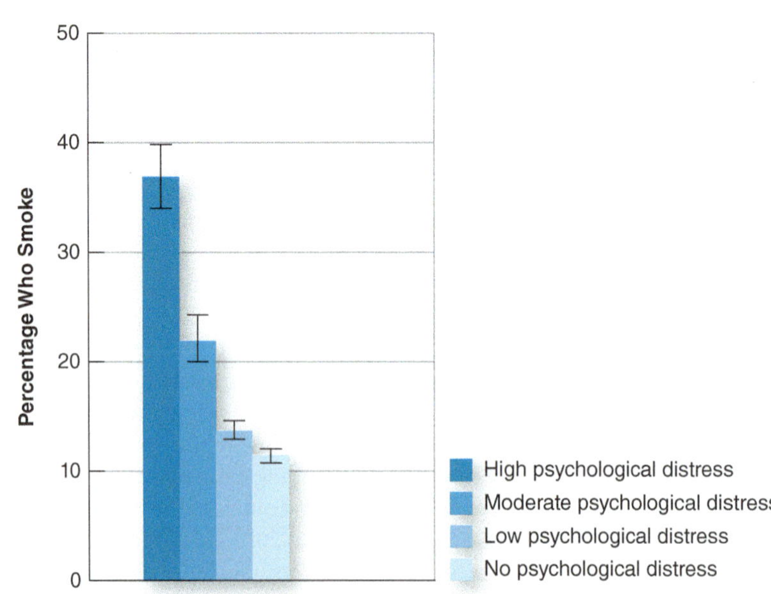

FIGURE **16.15**

Psychological Distress Is Related to Higher Rates of Smoking. Individuals identified as having high levels of psychological distress, including being diagnosed with severe psychological disorders such as schizophrenia, are more than three times as likely to smoke cigarettes as people with low or no psychological distress. This might represent efforts to self-medicate, but a causal role for tobacco in a number of psychological disorders has not been ruled out.

Source: Adapted from A. Jamal et al. (2016). "Current Cigarette Smoking Among Adults—United States, 2005–2015," *Morbidity and Mortality Weekly Report, 65*(44), 1205–1211. doi:10.15585/mmwr.mm6544a2

many smokers with psychological disorders report using cigarettes to feel better, most began smoking long before their symptoms emerged and they were diagnosed with a disorder (Sacco et al., 2005).

People do quit smoking, although many find it difficult. Again, the social nature of our species plays a role in this process. A person's chances of successfully quitting are reduced by 67% if a spouse smokes, 25% if a sibling smokes, 36% if a friend smokes, and 34% if a coworker smokes (Schroeder, 2008). We are not advocating that a prospective quitter abandon the essential social support needed at a difficult time; rather, we are suggesting that people trying to quit smoking might benefit from physically separating themselves when friends and family light up. As noted in Chapter 8, being exposed to conditioned stimuli, such as the smell of tobacco, can initiate a variety of conditioned behaviors that might make refusing a cigarette difficult for the person trying to quit.

NeydtStock/Shutterstock.com

In the United States, ex-smokers outnumber smokers (Chapman & MacKenzie, 2010). Smokers use a variety of techniques to quit, including simply stopping all use abruptly (cold turkey), gradually reducing intake, using nicotine patches and gum or other nicotine replacement tools, participating in counseling and support groups, or some combination of these.

Smoking cessation programs also can take advantage of the self-reference effect, discussed in Chapter 12. This effect explains the superior recall for information relevant to the self by suggesting that the self serves as an important schema for organizing information. Participants experiencing interventions for smoking that were tailored to their own lives, needs, interests, and obstacles not only were more successful at quitting smoking, but also showed brain activity in parts of the prefrontal cortex that are believed to participate in thinking about the self (Chua et al., 2011).

The benefits of quitting smoking appear within minutes to hours as the body begins to repair itself. After 5 years of abstention from smoking, risk of stroke is the same for ex-smokers and nonsmokers. After 10 years of abstention, the risk of lung cancer is cut in half. If the smoker quits before the age of 30 years, life expectancy remains the same as for someone who has never smoked (Doll et al., 2004).

Nutrition Nutrition plays a significant part in overall physical development, including brain development, and is believed to be responsible for many differences in psychological and health outcomes related to SES (Rosales et al., 2009). Prenatally, the maternal diet can have long-lasting epigenetic effects on a child's later risk for disease (Randunu & Bertolo, 2020). People need the right amount and quality of nutrients to support optimum health and brain functioning, and being either underweight or obese is associated with reduced health. Obesity increases the rates of many chronic conditions, including heart disease, stroke, diabetes, arthritis, and breast and colon cancers. As noted previously, maintaining a body mass index (BMI) below 30 (nonobese) was one of the four protective factors associated with much lower risk of disease. Returning the U.S. population to normal weight (a BMI of between 18.5 and 24.9) would produce about the same improvement in overall life expectancy as the elimination of smoking (Stewart et al., 2009).

As mentioned in Chapter 7, not only do we face problems in the form of eating disorders, such as anorexia nervosa and bulimia nervosa, but the world also has experienced an unprecedented obesity epidemic over the last 30 years (see ● Figure 16.16). In the United States, the percentage of obese adults rose from 12% in 1991 to 42% in 2018 (CDC, 2020). It is likely that multiple factors have contributed to this change, including our sedentary lifestyle, increases in caloric intake, changes in the types of food that we eat, changes in sleep patterns, and social factors. WHO (2020a) describes low- and middle-income countries as facing a "double burden" of disease because undernutrition and obesity occur at the same time, often in the same households. A combination of inadequate nutrition prenatally and in childhood, followed by exposure to high-calorie but nutrient-poor foods, sets the stage for a lifetime of poor health, possibly because of epigenetic factors (Haemer et al., 2009).

As was the case with smoking, we can see evidence of social factors that maintain our eating habits and weight. Our recent history of eating cheap, fatty, and sugary foods interacts with poverty. Nutritionists have raised the alarm that eating healthy foods is becoming more expensive than ever. Gender, ethnicity, and age also interact with obesity (Hales et al., 2020). Obesity is highest in non-Hispanic Black adults (49.6%), followed by Hispanic adults (44.8%) and non-Hispanic White adults (44.7%). Obesity is lowest among non-Hispanic Asian adults (17.4%).

Chuck Franklin/Alamy Stock Photo
iStock.com/Acilo
iStock.com/Arsgera; istock.com/assalve

One of the challenges that we face today is the high cost of eating a healthy diet. If you have $1.50 in your pocket, you can buy about 1,100 calories at McDonald's (breakfast of pancakes and sausage) or 250 calories of fresh apples. We can guess which choice financially struggling parents with hungry children are likely to make.

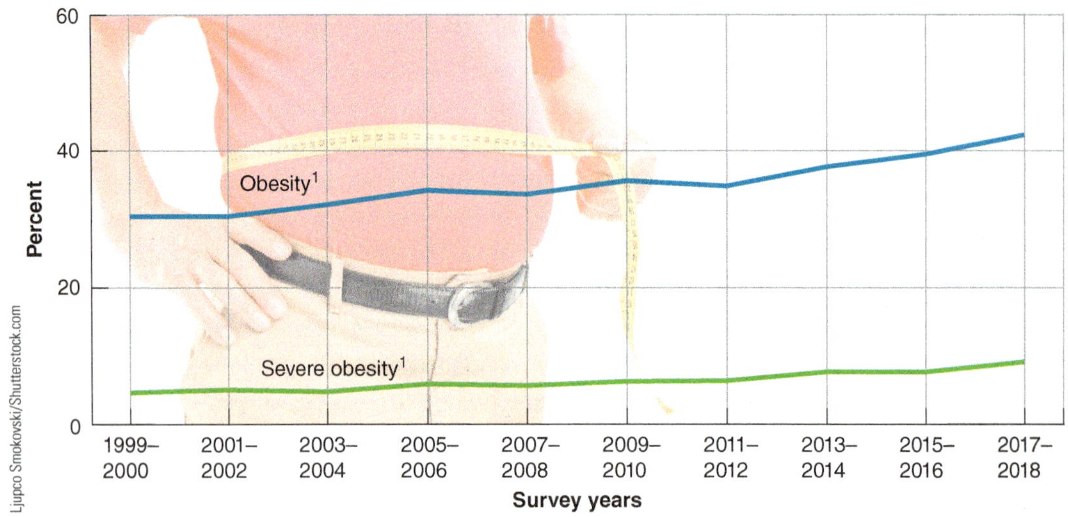

FIGURE **16.16**

The Obesity Epidemic. In 1960, fewer than 15% of American adults were obese (body mass index, or BMI, > 30), but today about 42% are obese. The number of people who are severely obese (BMI > 40) also has climbed during this period. The reasons for the obesity epidemic are not well understood and are likely to be complex.

Source: C. M. Hales et al. (2020). "Prevalence of Obesity and Severe Obesity Among Adults: United States, 2017–2018." *NCHS Data Brief No. 360.* Hyattsville, MD: National Center for Health Statistics. https://www.cdc.gov/nchs/products/databriefs/db360.htm

As observed in Chapter 7, there are no quick fixes for obesity and poor nutrition. Many of the same challenges face people who want to lose weight that we observed among people attempting to quit smoking. One advantage that would-be ex-smokers enjoy, however, is the option of complete abstinence. In contrast, we cannot abstain from eating; instead, we must choose to eat differently.

In addition to addressing concerns about obesity, current research in nutrition is focusing on the specific nutrients needed for healthy development and psychological well-being. As mentioned in Chapter 14, prevalence of bipolar disorder is much lower in countries consuming large amounts of seafood than in countries where seafood consumption is rare (Noaghiul & Hibbeln, 2003). Although much remains to be explored in this area, a further understanding of the consequences of changes in our modern diet should help us achieve a healthier lifestyle.

Alcohol Alcohol is widely used in the United States and in many other countries around the world. According to the National Institute on Alcohol Abuse and Alcoholism (NIAAA, 2020), 86.3% of American adults consumed alcohol at some point in their lifetime, 70% consumed alcohol in the past year, and 55.3% consumed alcohol in the past month. About 26% of the adult population engaged in binge drinking (five or more alcoholic beverages on the same occasion) during the past month, and 7% reported heavy drinking (five or more alcoholic beverages on one occasion on each of five or more days in the past month); 6% of adults and 1.6% of adolescents meet criteria for alcohol use disorder. Alcohol use is the third-leading preventable cause of death in the United States (number one is tobacco and number two is poor diet and inactivity).

Globally, alcohol contributes to 5.3% of deaths, but as shown in ● Figure 16.17, the contribution of alcohol to death varies by age (WHO, 2020). The largest threats to health from alcohol use are to the liver, which is responsible for clearing the body of toxins, but alcohol use also contributes to lower life spans because of stroke, high blood pressure, and some cancers (breast, digestive, and liver). In the United States alone, excessive alcohol consumption leads to approximately 88,000 deaths annually, at a cost of $249 billion (NIAAA, 2020). Alcohol-impaired driving accounts for 31% of all driving fatalities in the United States.

In addition, alcohol poses a risk of abuse and dependence for many people. Psychologists define alcohol abuse as repeated use despite adverse consequences and alcohol dependence

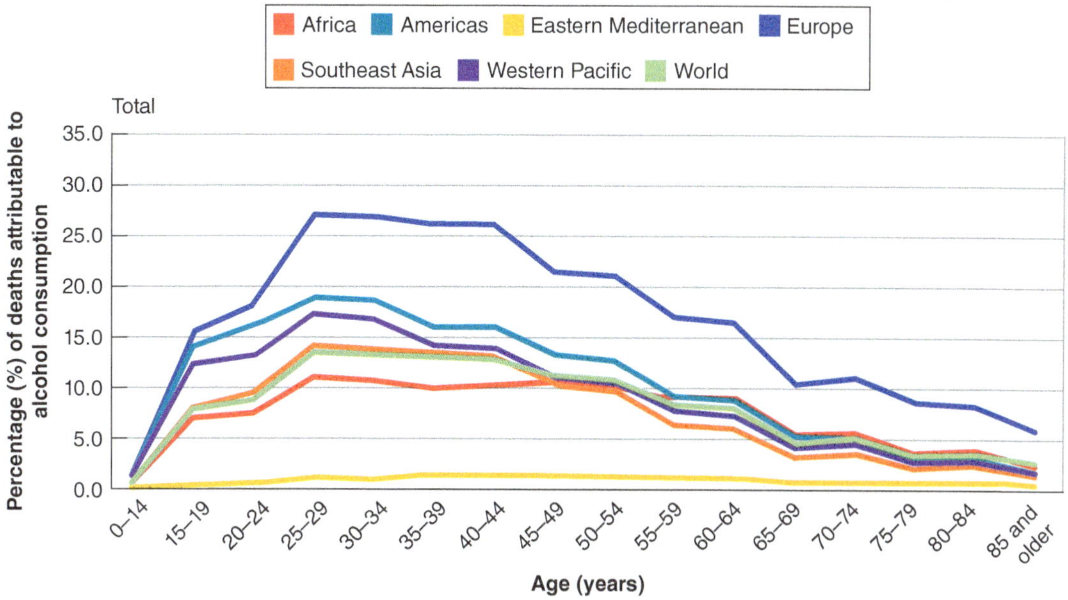

FIGURE **16.17**

Alcohol Contributes to Death and Disability. The World Health Organization (WHO) reports that worldwide, alcohol causes more deaths than tuberculosis, HIV/AIDS, and diabetes. In addition, alcohol is responsible for 5.1% of all disability-adjusted life years (DALYs). Alcohol accounts for more deaths of young and middle-aged adults compared to children, adolescents, and older adults.

Source: Adapted from World Health Organization (WHO; 2018). *Global Status Report on Alcohol and Health 2018.* Geneva, Switzerland: Author.

as alcohol abuse accompanied by tolerance, withdrawal, and a compulsive urge to drink more (APA, 2013). As observed in Chapter 4, tolerance is defined as the need to administer greater quantities of a drug to maintain the same subjective effect, and withdrawal refers to symptoms that occur when a habitually used drug is no longer used.

As we have seen in so many other domains of human behavior, complex interactions between biological and environmental factors lead to alcohol abuse and dependence. Genes related to the body's ability to break down alcohol in the liver are not evenly distributed across the world's populations. Certain types of genes found primarily in Asians are correlated with lower rates of alcohol dependence (Eng et al., 2007). As usual, genes are not the whole story. Consider the example of Native Americans. This ethnic group has much higher rates of alcohol dependence than do many others, despite a high prevalence of the supposedly "protective" genes (Ehlers, 2007). Among the environmental influences on problem drinking is the age of first intoxication (Newton-Howes et al., 2019). Age of first intoxication is more predictive of later drinking problems than the frequently used age at first drink measure.

Many of the same factors that encourage teens to begin smoking also encourage drinking. Peer pressure, the need to fit in or look cool, overestimates of "Everybody's doing it," modeling the behavior of parents and other family members, and the teen's characteristic sense of being immune to harm from risky behavior can contribute to decisions to begin drinking. Because alcohol reduces anxiety, socially anxious teens are especially at risk for problem drinking. If teens feel more socially competent while drinking, they are likely to continue this practice because of operant conditioning, as described in Chapter 8. Reduced feelings of anxiety are rewarding, so a person is likely to repeat the behavior (alcohol consumption, in this case) associated with this reward.

Treatment for very heavy drinkers often requires medical supervision because withdrawal from alcohol can produce life-threatening seizures. Recall from Chapter 4 that alcohol boosts the inhibition produced by GABA, leading to alcohol's classification as a central nervous system depressant. Because withdrawal symptoms are usually the opposite of drug effects, withdrawing from a depressant produces excitation, and too much excitation leads to seizures.

Diverse Images/Univer/AGE Fotostock

People who are exposed to alcohol at younger ages have the highest risk for alcohol abuse.

One of the remaining controversies in the treatment of alcohol dependence is whether a person can safely return to moderate drinking. Most psychologists do not believe that it is possible for recovered problem drinkers to resume alcohol consumption without relapse. In one 60-year longitudinal study of men with problem drinking, few returned to moderate drinking without experiencing a relapse (Vaillant, 2003). Other researchers suggest that relapsing individuals with occasional heavy drinking days show similar outcomes as those who completely abstain (Witkiewitz et al., 2020).

MBI/Alamy Stock Photo

In contrast to previous generations, who simply "played," it is not uncommon today to find children as young as 3 to 5 years of age involved with adult-organized formal sports. Further research is necessary to determine the long-term impacts of this social trend on adult patterns of play and exercising.

Exercise Exercise was not a choice for our hunter–gatherer ancestors, for whom physical work meant the difference between death and survival. In today's sedentary world, however, in which many workers spend hours commuting in cars to sit for more hours in front of computers, exercise becomes something that we must consciously remember to do. Children in previous generations would dash from school to play outdoors, but social changes, including lack of supervision at home and safety concerns, have led to much less spontaneous outdoor activity. Parents might prefer that their children stay indoors playing video games rather than ride their bicycles in the neighborhood. For many middle-aged and older adults, loneliness might lead to less physical activity (Hawkley et al., 2009; Hawkley & Cacioppo, 2010).

Lack of exercise and sitting are related but different issues. Children and adults in the United States spend an average of 55% of their day sitting while riding in cars, watching television, doing work or attending school, and playing video games or doing other computer work (Matthews et al., 2008). A person's amount of sitting time is correlated with risk of death (see Figure 16.18). However, high levels of moderately intense activity (60–75 minutes per day) seems to offset some of this risk (Ekelund et al., 2016). Although the highest risk of death occurs in obese individuals

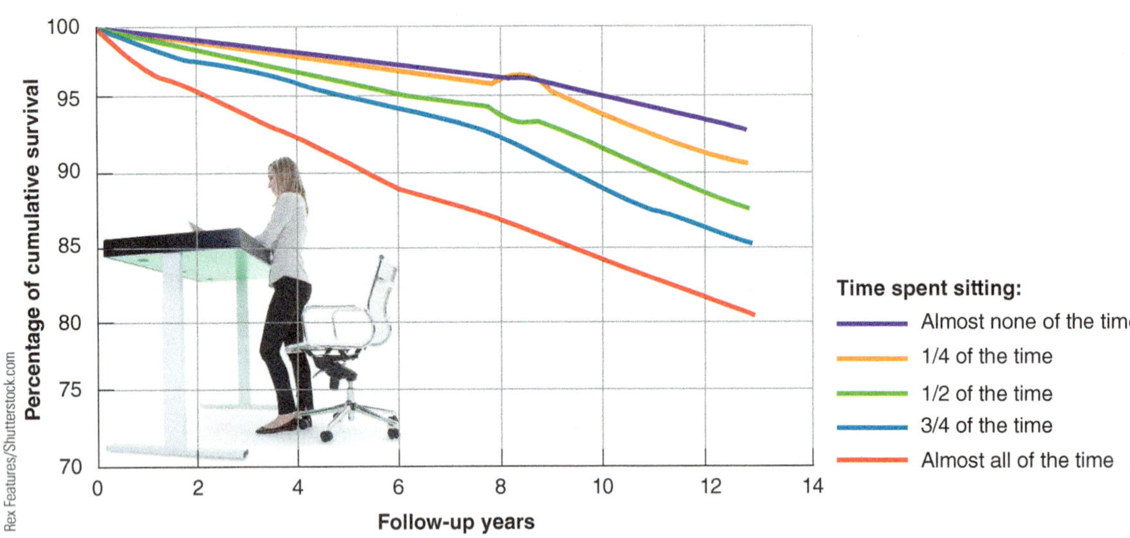

Rex Features/Shutterstock.com

FIGURE **16.18**

Time Spent Sitting and Mortality. Data showing decreased survival as a function of the amount of your day spent sitting have led to a market for "standing desks." If you find these desks comfortable, by all means use them, but recall that again, the sitting data are correlational, and we cannot conclude that sitting causes death. We are not randomly assigning people to sitting groups. People who sit all day are likely to be obese or have other health problems that contribute to their higher risk of mortality.

Source: Adapted from P. T. Katzmarzyk et al. (2009). "Sitting Time and Mortality from All Causes, Cardiovascular Disease, and Cancer," *Medicine and Science in Sports and Exercise, 41*(5), 998–1005. doi:10.1249/MSS.0b013e3181930355

who spend nearly all their time sitting, the amount of time spent sitting also predicts mortality within a group of active individuals (Katzmarzyk et al., 2009).

Exercise not only benefits our bodies by keeping our muscles and cardiovascular systems in good shape, but also benefits our psychological well-being. A brisk 30-minute walk has emerged as an effective way to treat MDD, as discussed in Chapter 15 (Blumenthal et al., 1999). In addition to improving mood, exercise increases cognitive performance (Hogan et al., 2013; Raichlen & Alexander, 2017). One mechanism for this improvement could be the increased delivery of oxygen to the brain resulting from a fit cardiovascular system. Other research suggests that exercise also has the capacity to boost neurogenesis, particularly in the hippocampus of the brain (Gibbons et al., 2014). As you learned in Chapter 4, the hippocampus plays important roles in learning and memory.

We mentioned in an earlier section that stress can be detrimental to the functioning of the immune system. Exercise can be stressful as well; so what effect could it have? Not too surprisingly, we find complex relationships between the amount and type of exercise that a person performs and the response of the immune system. Compared to sedentary people, those who engage in regular moderate exercise enjoy a lower rate of infection (Gleeson, 2007). However, too much of a good thing, in the form of continuous, prolonged, and high-intensity exercise such as preparation for and competition in marathons and triathlons, can produce a temporary decrease in immune system function for about a day. Elite athletes, because of their constant and intense training schedules, often experience more minor illnesses, such as sniffles and colds, but the long-term benefits of exercise far outweigh these small vulnerabilities.

Loneliness and Health Loneliness, or a perceived deficit in social connectivity, has long been understood as a risk factor for psychological disorders, but now it is understood to contribute to mortality in older adults as well (Cacioppo & Cacioppo, 2018). Even when other factors are controlled, loneliness produces a 26% increase in the odds of early death. Given the growing number of older adults and high prevalence of loneliness among them (20%–60% report being lonely some of the time, and 5%–10% feel lonely frequently or always), this presents a significant risk to health and well-being.

Loneliness produces risk for death along a number of pathways that are familiar to you by now: poor sleep quality, increased activity in the HPA axis, increased sympathetic activity relative to parasympathetic activity, altered gene expression in immune system cells, decreased immunity to viruses, increased inflammation, decreased impulse control, and increased symptoms of depression (Cacioppo & Cacioppo, 2018). While the amount of harm from changes in each of these pathways might be small, the combined and cumulative changes due to loneliness can produce significant damage to health and well-being (see ● Figure 16.19).

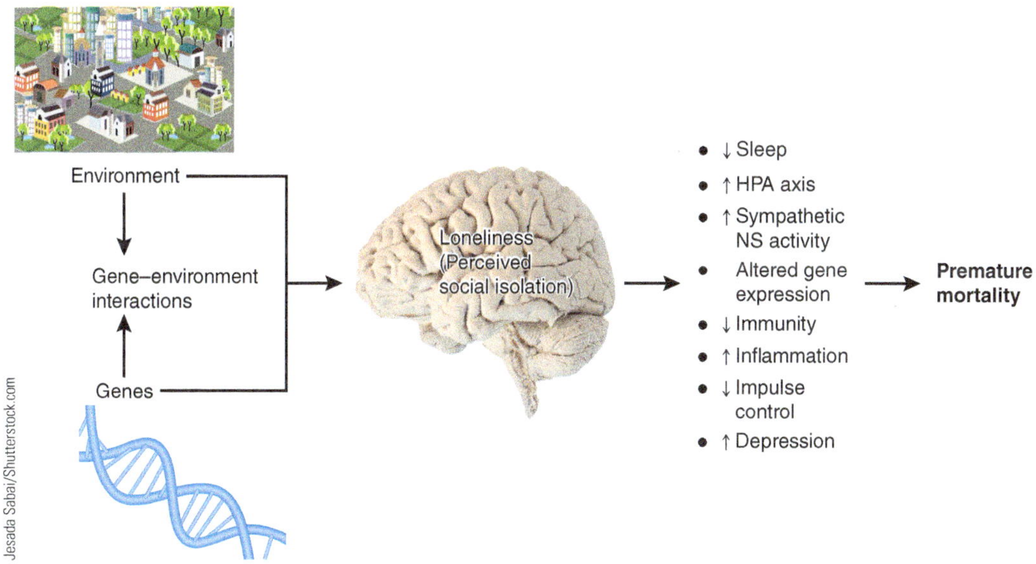

FIGURE **16.19**

Loneliness Is a Risk Factor for Mortality. Loneliness, or perceived social isolation, does not directly reduce life expectancy. Instead, loneliness exerts its influence on mortality through complex interactions between genetics and environment, which in turn affect important health factors like inflammation.
Source: Adapted from J. T. Cacioppo & S. Cacioppo (2018), "Loneliness in the Modern Age: An Evolutionary Theory of Loneliness (ETL)." *Advances in Experimental Social Psychology, 58*, 127–197. doi: 10.1016/bs.aesp.2018.03.003

Fortunately, loneliness can be reduced by several simple interventions. First, understanding loneliness can help people avoid the selfish, unattractive behaviors that can result from self-preservation (see Chapter 13). Although we often feel lonely in the absence of strong, significant relationships like having a romantic partner, daily small interactions, such as having a conversation with the barista making your coffee, can also do a good job of alleviating feelings of loneliness.

Culture and Health

Many health-related variables, including poverty, education, access to medical care, nutrition, and substance abuse, vary widely from country to country and within ethnic groups living in the United States. The United States, despite its high standard of living, ranks 36th among countries of the world in terms of life expectancy, suggesting that wealth alone is insufficient to guarantee good health (United Nations, 2020; also see ● Figure 16.20). However, within the United States, life expectancy increases continuously with income (Chetty et al., 2016). Life expectancy gaps between the highest and lowest 1% of income were 15 years for males and 10 years for females.

In the United States, death rates for all ethnic groups have declined over the last decade, but ethnic differences remain. Risk of death is lowest among Asians and Pacific Islanders and highest among the non-Hispanic Black population (Kochanek et al., 2017). Although life expectancy for White and Black Americans differs, the gap continues to narrow. In 2000, life expectancy for Whites was 5.5 years more than life expectancy for Blacks, but this gap was reduced to 3.8 years by 2010. Increases in life expectancy across all ethnic groups resulted from reductions in the rate of death from leading causes, including heart disease, cancer, chronic respiratory diseases, and stroke. However, COVID-19 has disproportionately impacted non-Hispanic Blacks, potentially widening the life expectancy gap back to previous levels.

In addition to ethnic and cultural differences in overall health and health habits, discrepancies occur in mental health. Minorities living in the United States have less access to mental health services, are less likely to receive needed services, receive a poorer quality of care, and are underrepresented in mental health research (U.S. Department of Health and Human

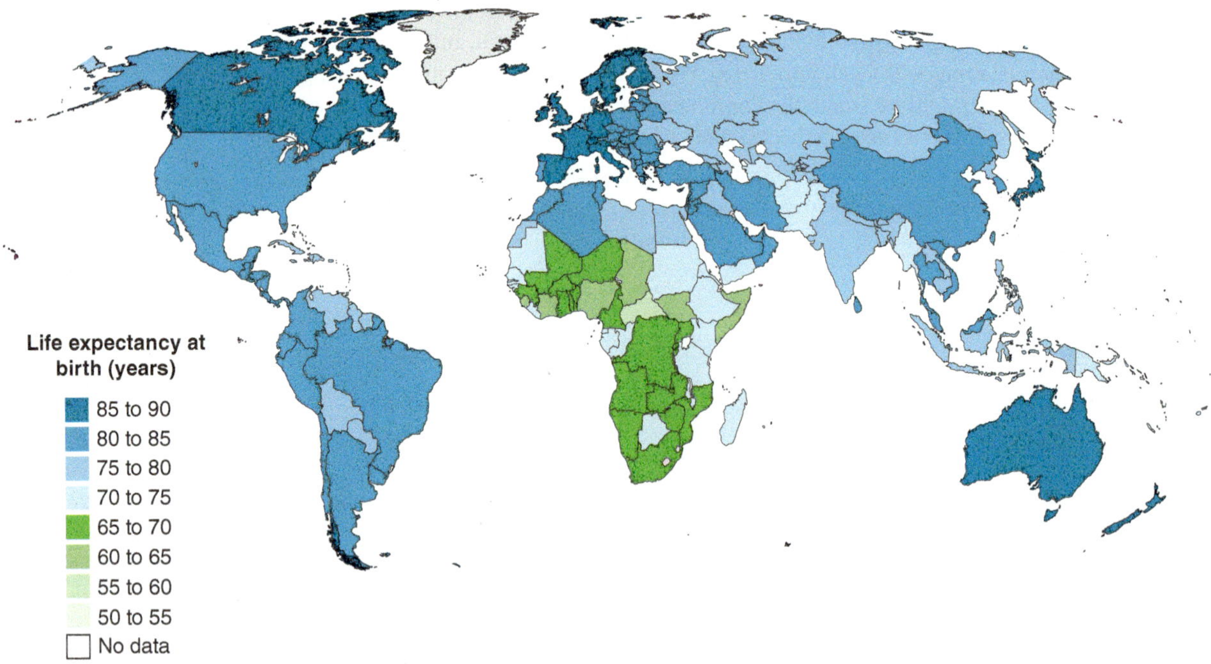

FIGURE 16.20

Culture and Health Interact to Predict Life Expectancy. Many health-related variables, including poverty, education, access to medical care, nutrition, and substance abuse, vary widely from country to country and interact to determine average life expectancy.
Source: Adapted from https://population.un.org/wpp/Maps/

Services; U.S. Public Health Service, 2007). Among possible variables accounting for increased mental health problems among minorities are poverty, discrimination, and violence. Poverty, in particular, is an important risk factor for psychological disorders, with people living at the lowest levels of the socioeconomic scale experiencing two to three times greater rates of psychological disorder (U.S. Department of Health and Human Services, U.S. Public Health Service, 2007). The exact prevalence remains unknown because many people living in poverty do not have access to care. Stress from poverty, discrimination, and violence might contribute to higher rates of stress-related health problems and disorders. Distrust of clinicians who might seem to be disrespectful or whose approach is culturally insensitive also might deter people from obtaining the treatment that they need.

Distinctive Images/Shutterstock.com

Poverty is a significant risk factor for many types of psychopathology.

An Integrated Understanding of Health Behaviors

If you haven't already noticed during our discussions of stress, sleep, nutrition, smoking, alcohol use, and exercise, let us highlight the fact that these variables interact. Stress can lead to poor sleep, additional consumption of calories, more smoking, more drinking, and less exercise. People who eat poorly are unlikely to sleep well or feel like going to the gym. Smoking reduces weight (naming a cigarette marketed to women "Virginia Slims" was no accident), but of course, it has negative effects on health that far outweigh that advantage. Problem drinkers either cut back on nutritious food or become obese (Breslow & Smothers, 2005). College students engage in drunkorexia, or the deliberate restriction of calories before planned alcohol consumption for the purpose of avoiding weight gain (Burke et al., 2010). Most of if not all these behaviors are affected by our social context. We eat, drink, and smoke but also exercise more in the company of our fellow humans.

These interactions in health behaviors remind us of the need to zoom out to look at the whole picture of individuals within their social contexts when we attempt to apply interventions leading to better health (see ● Figure 16.21). We have amassed a significant amount of data on why people engage in a particular problem behavior, whether that is smoking, drinking, or overeating, and we are now in a better position to identify the overlapping patterns of epigenesis, stress, child maltreatment, peer pressure, and motivation that underlie these behaviors.

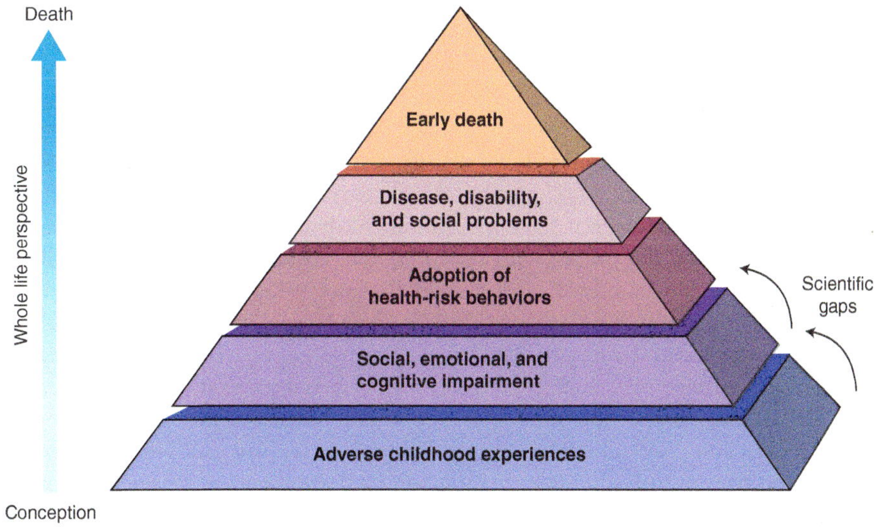

FIGURE **16.21**

The Adverse Childhood Experiences (ACE) Study: An Integrated Model of Health. An example of contemporary research that uses an integrated model of health is the ACE Study, being undertaken by researchers affiliated with the Centers for Disease Control and Prevention (CDC). The study plans to address identified gaps in our understanding about the relationships between adverse childhood experiences, such as abuse and neglect, and later social, emotional, and cognitive impairments, which in turn could influence the adoption of risky health behaviors. *Source:* Adapted from Centers for Disease Control and Prevention (CDC, 2010a). "Pyramid: Adverse Childhood Experiences (ACE) Study." http://www.cdc.gov/ace/pyramid.htm

SUMMARY 16.2 Five Domains of Health Behavior

Domain	Correlates
Tobacco Use 	• Smoking is the leading preventable cause of death in the United States.
Nutrition 	• Obesity increases rates of many chronic diseases, including heart disease, stroke, diabetes, arthritis, and some cancers. • Specific nutrients, not just calories, are necessary for optimum functioning.
Alcohol 	• Alcohol's main effect on life span is its contribution to accidents, but use is also correlated with liver disease, stroke, high blood pressure, and some cancers.
Exercise 	• Exercise improves overall health, mood, and cognition.
Loneliness 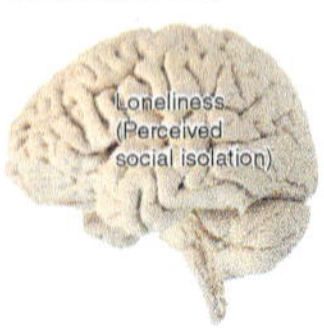	• Loneliness produces indirect effects on health by affecting sleep, immunity, HPA axis function, sympathetic nervous system function, gene expression, inflammation, impulse control, and depression.

Credits: Top row—Carlos Barria/Reuters/Newscom; Second row—iStock.com/Acilo, iStock.com/Arsgera, Chuck Franklin/Alamy Stock Photo, iStock.com/assalve; Third row—Diverse Images/Univer/AGE Fotostock; Fourth row—MBI/Alamy Stock Photo; Fifth row—Jesada Sabai/Shutterstock.com.

What Is Positive Psychology?

Although helping people with problems is an important part of psychology, some psychologists have pointed out that there are differences between making people less uncomfortable and helping them live happier, more fulfilling lives. The interventions explored in Chapter 15 are designed to alleviate psychological pain, but these treatments are not intended to make people who do not have psychological disorders happier. At the same time, we know a great deal about people with psychological problems, whom we described in Chapter 14 as representing a minority of the population. What about those who lead relatively untroubled, typical lives? As observed in Chapter 10, we quite possibly know the least about people with unusual strengths, such as talent and genius. The field of **positive psychology** focuses on these relatively neglected areas of behavior and mental processes by using scientific methods to understand positive human experiences and adjustment. A new set of interventions should emerge from this understanding that will guide individuals, families, and communities in their attempts to maximize their potential (Seligman & Csikszentmihalyi, 2000).

positive psychology An approach to psychology that emphasizes normal behavior and human strengths.

William James foreshadowed positive psychology in his 1902 book *The Varieties of Religious Experience.* In this book, James discussed people who achieve "healthy mindedness" as having an understanding of the "goodness of life" and a soul (a word often used by people in James's era as synonymous with *mind*) with "a sky-blue tint" (James, 1905, pp. 79–80). James goes further to speculate about the origins of healthy mindedness. For the lucky few, healthy mindedness occurs naturally and effortlessly. For others, it must be achieved through effort.

Despite James's efforts, psychology continued its fascination with the abnormal and the unhealthy into the 20th century and did not direct the same energy toward understanding the normal and healthy. Voices of dissent arose from among the humanistic psychologists, including Abraham Maslow, discussed in Chapters 7 and 12. Maslow argued that psychologists could learn more about human behavior by studying outstanding individuals than by studying people with severe problems. As part of Maslow's thinking about self-actualization, the pinnacle of social motivation in his theory, he took detailed notes on people he admired in a "GHB (Good Human Being) notebook" that he kept between 1945 and 1949 (Lowry, 1973). In addition to making observations of living people whom he admired, Maslow combed through biographies and autobiographies of famous people in search of common features of healthy mindedness.

Running parallel to the humanistic psychologists' rejection of a negative, sickness model of human behavior were innovations among cognitive and behavioral approaches. As mentioned in Chapter 15, Albert Ellis and Aaron Beck were achieving excellent results with cognitive restructuring around the same time that the humanistic psychologists began reconsidering Freud. Ellis and Beck were able to help their clients with MDD see a glass of water as half full as opposed to half empty, improving their mood and optimism in the process.

One of the most significant voices leading to contemporary positive psychology approaches is that of Martin Seligman (2019). (We discussed his concept of learned helplessness in Chapter 14.) If people's outcomes do not seem connected to their behaviors, the resulting feelings of helplessness and lack of control could result in depression. Based on his investigations of learned helplessness, Seligman proposed that **optimism**, or thinking positively about the future, can be learned, just as helplessness can (Seligman, 1990).

Positive psychology embraces humanistic emphases on human growth and fulfillment yet applies the scientific reasoning and research characteristic of cognitive and behavioral psychology. Positive psychology incorporates five elements of well-being into a PERMA model: positive emotion, engagement, relationships, meaning, and accomplishment (Seligman, 2012).

Mary Evans Picture Library/The Image Works

In his book *The Varieties of Religious Experience*, William James foreshadowed the development of positive psychology by considering what makes some people healthy minded and what gives others a "sick soul."

Positive Emotions

Positive emotions and the experiences that produce them, including happiness, love, gratitude, contentment, and hope, contribute to our well-being. For our social species, it is not an accident that many of the situations that produce these positive feelings, such as promotions at work, marriage, and other successes, involve people who are important to us.

optimism Thinking positively about the future.

Gaye Gerard/Getty Images

Martin Seligman (right) and the Dalai Lama (left), spiritual leader of Tibetan Buddhism, discussed the important role of positive emotions at a "Mind and Its Potential" conference in 2009.

What Is Happiness? We all know happiness when we experience it, and most people prefer the state of happiness to the alternatives of unhappiness and depression. Happiness is associated with a long list of positive outcomes, including longevity (Diener & Chan, 2011), advancement at work (De Neve et al., 2013), and staying married (Lyubomirsky et al., 2005).

Psychologists approach happiness from two different perspectives (Ryan & Deci, 2001). A hedonic approach focuses on obtaining pleasure and avoiding pain. A eudaimonic approach focuses on meaningfulness and self-realization.

Happiness often seems fleeting or transient. The primary reason for this elusiveness is that happiness is typically relative. We quickly adapt to our current circumstances, and it is only change in those circumstances that provokes feelings of happiness or unhappiness.

Research with identical twins suggests that we have a happiness "set point" that is largely influenced by genetics (Lykken & Tellegen, 1996). Changes in circumstances might raise or lower happiness from the set point, but the effect would be temporary. However, having a genetic predisposition to being happy or to being cranky does not mean that a person's behavior has no influence. Instead, people can do a great deal to improve their happiness. Rather than looking for external things to boost happiness, such as a new car or a new nose, looking within is more effective. Happiness can be improved by thinking carefully about what things interfere

Diverse Voices in Psychology

Optimism Across Race and Ethnicity

LIKE MOST OF AMERICAN PSYCHOLOGY, positive psychology has been criticized as being overly influenced by the values of the White majority. To what extent are concepts like happiness the same or different depending on race, ethnicity, or culture? To what extent are such values simply "human"?

Optimism, or a positive expectation for the future, is linked with both physical and psychological well-being (Carver et al., 2010). Previous studies have shown little variability in the level of optimism across cultures, although some differences seem to be associated with the individualistic–collectivistic dimension of cultures (Jeglic et al., 2016). While Asian and Asian American individuals report similar levels of optimism compared to White Americans, they report higher levels of pessimism at the same time (Chang, 1996; see Figure 16.22). Comparisons between American and Ghanaian college students found that the Ghanaian students demonstrated higher optimism and hope, while expressing less suicidal ideation (Eshun, 1999). While more research is needed regarding racial and ethnic differences in optimism within the United States, lack of hope was shown to be a risk factor for suicidal ideation for Hispanic and African American students, but not for White students (Davidson et al., 2010; Chang et al., 2013).

It is likely that concepts that are as value-oriented as those studied by positive psychologists will show nuanced variations across different groups, and our understanding of these concepts would be enriched by further investigation into these similarities and differences.

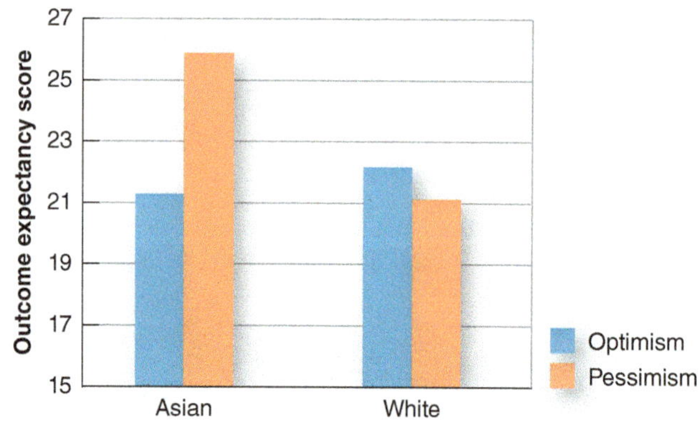

FIGURE **16.22**

Optimism and Pessimism Vary Across Cultures. White and Asian college students demonstrate similar levels of optimism, but the Asian students show much higher levels of pessimism. These perspectives appear to have different implications for White and Asian students, however. High levels of pessimism were associated with better problem-solving performance in Asian students, but worse performance in White students.

Source: E. C. Chang (1996). "Cultural Differences in Optimism, Pessimism, and Coping: Predictors of Subsequent Adjustment in Asian American and Caucasian American College Students," *Journal of Counseling Psychology, 43*(1), 113–123. doi: 10.1037/0022-0167.43.1.113

with our happiness, such as allowing ourselves to stay mad at a partner following an argument, and working to avoid these things.

One critical factor in people's happiness is the strength of their interpersonal relationships. When participants are asked, "What is necessary for your happiness?" or "Tell me what makes your life meaningful," nearly everybody talks about their close relationships first—family, friends, and romantic partners (Berscheid & Peplau, 1983). Happiness is also contagious, spreading out along networks of social contact (Fowler & Christakis, 2008). This finding is consistent with one of the ongoing themes of this text: our social environment plays a central role in human behavior.

Happiness and Marriage Among interpersonal relationships, the institution of marriage is particularly likely to contribute to happiness (see ● Figure 16.23). In a study of more than 42,000 Americans beginning in 1972, 40% of married adults, but only 22% of never-married adults, report that they are "very happy" (Davis et al., 2006). Also, 18% of divorced adults report being "very happy," and remarriage increases happiness only in a minority of cases. In a large-scale study that followed 13,000 adults for five years, people who remained married experienced higher well-being than those who separated or divorced (Waite et al., 2009; Waite & Gallagher, 2001). Among the benefits of marriage are reduced infidelity, longer-lasting relationships, and longer life (Waite & Gallagher, 2001).

People who are married and living with their spouse enjoy a significantly lower death rate than those who are unmarried. People who have never married, particularly males, experience an especially high risk for premature death (Kaplan & Kronick, 2006). Married individuals have lower cortisol levels compared to never married or previously married individuals (Chin et al., 2017). As we observed earlier, cortisol release is correlated with stress.

Why would marriage make people happy? One possibility is that the relationship between marriage and happiness is a false one because of the likelihood that happy people produce happy marriages instead of the other way around. However, careful research that controls for premarital happiness does not support this hypothesis (Horwitz et al., 1997; Grover & Helliwell, 2019). Regardless of how happy people are before marrying, on average being married makes them happier. The positive effects of marriage on happiness are about twice as large for couples who consider their spouse to be their best friend (Grover & Helliwell, 2019). If you're thinking of cases that you know in which married couples are miserable, time together seems to help. Among the unhappiest couples, only 12% report being unhappy five years later, and 70% of the formerly unhappy partners report being "very" or "quite" happy (Horwitz et al., 1997).

What is the source of this marital happiness? Traditionally, psychologists have suggested that marital happiness results from the perceptions that one partner has of the other. But more sophisticated analyses have shown that the factors associated with marital happiness are more complicated (Luo et al. 2010). While it's true that perceptions of your partner influence how satisfied you are in a relationship ("I'm with a great person"), it is also true that your overall satisfaction with the relationship affects how you see your partner ("I'm happy, so I must be with a great person"). Then, what is the source of that satisfaction? A major factor in satisfaction with a relationship is how you think your partner sees you ("My partner thinks I'm terrific, which makes me happy, and because I'm happy, I must be with a great person").

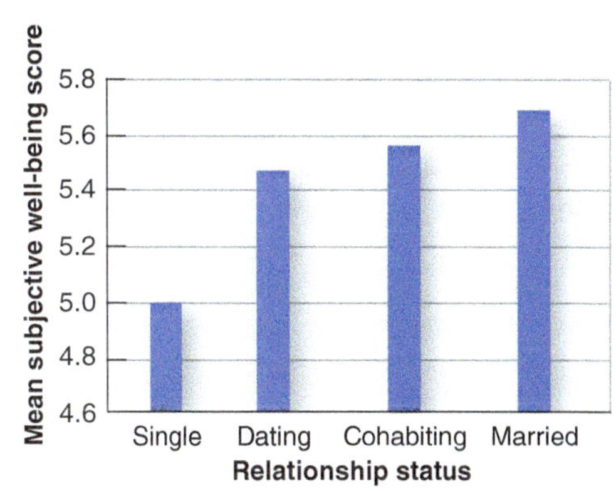

FIGURE **16.23**

Relationship Status and Happiness. Many studies have pointed to a strong relationship between being married and subjective well-being.

Source: Adapted from J. P. M. Soons et al. (2009). "The Long-Term Consequences of Relationship Formation for Subjective Well-Being," *Journal of Marriage and Family*, *71*(5), 1254–1270. doi:10.1111/j.1741-3737.2009.00667.x

Happiness and Wealth Another common-sense notion about happiness is that wealth can make you happy. After all, we see frequent images of ecstatic lottery winners and smiling sports superstars who have signed megabuck contracts. At both national and individual levels, being poor does appear to be correlated with being unhappy. However, once basic needs are met, additional money does not guarantee happiness (see ● Figure 16.24). Interviews with the 100 richest people in the United States indicated that they were only slightly happier than average (Diener et al., 1985). In addition, how people use their wealth can influence happiness. People who are less materialistic report being happier than people who are materialistic (Tsang et al., 2014). People who spend money on experiences rather than materialistic goods experience improved well-being (Howell & Hill, 2009).

FIGURE **16.24**

Wealth and Happiness. When adjusted for inflation, Americans' after-tax disposable income grew dramatically between 1946 and 1989, but measures of subjective well-being remained flat. Increases in income above a certain point where basic needs can be met tend to have mild, if any, long-term impact on happiness.
Source: Adapted from E. Diener et al. (1999). "Subjective Well-Being: Three Decades of Progress," *Psychological Bulletin, 125*(2), Figure 1. doi:10.1037/0033-2909.125.2.276

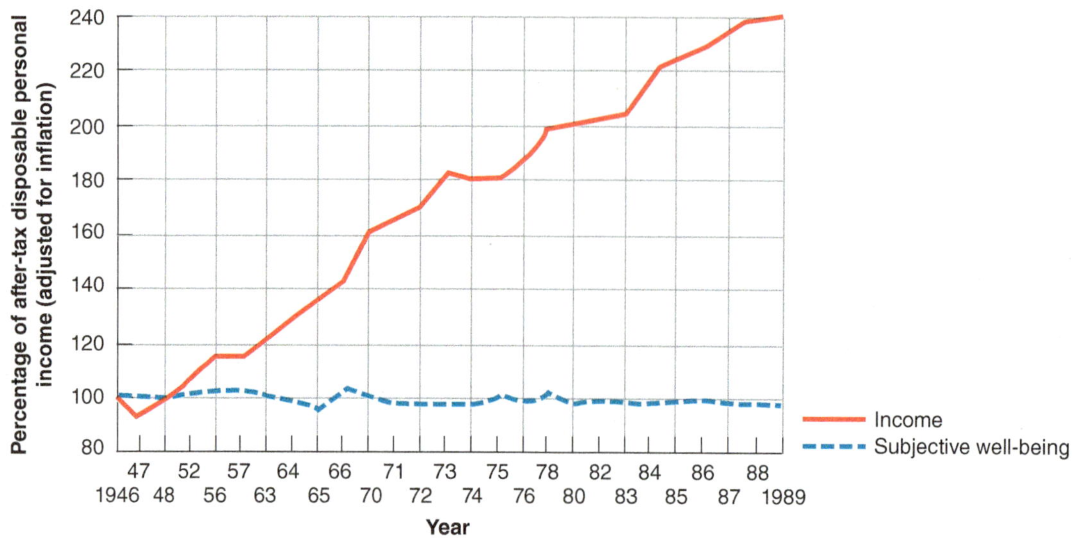

Now we return to the idea that happiness occurs because of changing circumstances. Perhaps the 100 richest Americans had simply adapted to their wealthy lifestyles. What about people who suddenly become wealthy? The Camelot Group, which manages the national lottery in the United Kingdom, reported that winning the lottery did have an impact on happiness (Camelot Group, 2004). According to these findings, 65% of winners reported that they

THINKING SCIENTIFICALLY

Does Parenting Increase Happiness?

IN CHAPTER 7, we noted that an update of Abraham Maslow's hierarchy of needs pyramid featured parenting at the top to represent this role's importance from an evolutionary perspective (Kenrick et al., 2010). If parenting is such an important motivation, do we feel happier when we fulfill it?

WHAT AM I BEING ASKED TO BELIEVE OR ACCEPT?

We are being asked to believe that being a parent makes people happier than they would be if they were not parents.

WHAT EVIDENCE SUPPORTS THIS POSITION?

Parenting in the 21st century probably shares little similarity with the way parenting was for our hunter–gatherer ancestors. The goal of contemporary marriages has less to do today with financial survival or raising families than it has with meeting partners' emotional needs (Dew & Wilcox, 2011). A major predictor of marital satisfaction is time spent with a partner, so where does that need fit with the challenges of meeting the demands of a family of young children?

Some research suggests that parenting results in reductions in marital satisfaction, which increase with the number of children (Twenge et al., 2003). This result is most pronounced among younger, higher-income mothers of infants. Even in the 21st century, the arrival of the first child has a tendency to "traditionalize" the gender roles of the new parents. Fathers begin to take on more of the income-earning responsibilities and mothers take on more of the childcare and housework. Her changing roles might make the new mother less happy with her circumstances (Dew & Wilcox, 2011).

Other researchers disagree. In another set of studies, parents evaluated their lives more positively than nonparents, felt better than nonparents from day to day, and found more satisfaction in caring for their children than in other daily activities (Nelson et al., 2013, 2014). Parenting contributed to more positive emotions on a daily basis and to the sense of having a meaningful life—concepts consistent with the approach to happiness held by some positive psychologists.

ARE THERE OTHER WAYS THIS EVIDENCE COULD BE INTERPRETED?

What might be the source of these conflicting findings? One possibility is were happier following the win because of financial security and increased freedom; 35% said that they were about as happy after winning as before; and none reported feeling less happy than before the win. Although the winners traded up in terms of lifestyle (most had bought new cars and new homes), 92% of those who were married when they won were still married to the same spouse.

The correlation between happiness and income has been assumed to reflect the effect of money on happiness. However, longitudinal research suggests that happiness may influence income (Cacioppo et al., 2008). As in prior studies, happiness and income in middle-age and older adults were correlated. However, happiness predicted bigger increases in income, whereas higher income did not predict increases in happiness. Happy people form better relationships, and these better relationships contribute to larger increases in income, perhaps because of improved job performance, better performance reviews and promotions, and better networking opportunities that lead in financially productive directions.

The World Happiness Report, now in its eighth edition, looks at measures of happiness in over 150 countries (Helliwell et al., 2020). The variables used to assess happiness did include financial measures, but also measures of positive and negative emotions, social support, freedom to make life choices, generosity, health, and perceptions of corruption. Based on these measures, Scandinavian countries appear to be very happy places, occupying the five top slots, including number 1 (Finland). The United States, ranked number 1 in the world in gross domestic product (GDP), is ranked number 18 in happiness. To be fair, the differences in happiness among the top 20 countries are quite slim. At the bottom of the list are Zimbabwe, South Sudan, and coming in last, Afghanistan (see ● Figure 16.25).

John Tlumacki/The Boston Globe/Getty Images

Lottery winners experience an increase in happiness, but they tend to be cautious about changing their lifestyles. Most continue working and attempt to maintain as normal a life as possible.

that parents as a group are highly diverse. Parenting under some circumstances can be more stressful than others. Young, unpartnered parents, not too surprisingly, reported less happiness and satisfaction than their nonparent age peers, yet they still indicated that they felt their lives were meaningful (Nelson et al., 2013). Parents may experience differing levels of support from governments, employers, communities, and families. Globally, institutional policies such as paid time off and child-care subsidies for parents are associated with less unhappiness on the part of parents (Glass et al., 2016).

WHAT OTHER EVIDENCE WOULD I NEED TO EVALUATE THESE ALTERNATIVES?

It is likely that we need further research outlining the characteristics, perhaps at the individual, family, and community levels, that predict happiness during parenting. This would also require some investigation of cohort effects (see Chapter 2).

WHAT ARE THE MOST REASONABLE CONCLUSIONS?

William James's concept of functionalism, described in Chapter 1, would predict that becoming a parent is likely to be highly motivating for many people. Nonetheless, insights from the different perspectives of psychology (biological, cognitive, developmental, social, and clinical) are needed to completely understand the circumstances leading to a happy parenting experience for any one individual. ■

Mint Images Limited/Alamy Stock Photo

Evolutionary theories view parenting as an important motivation for human behavior, yet contemporary psychologists debate whether parents are truly happier than nonparents.

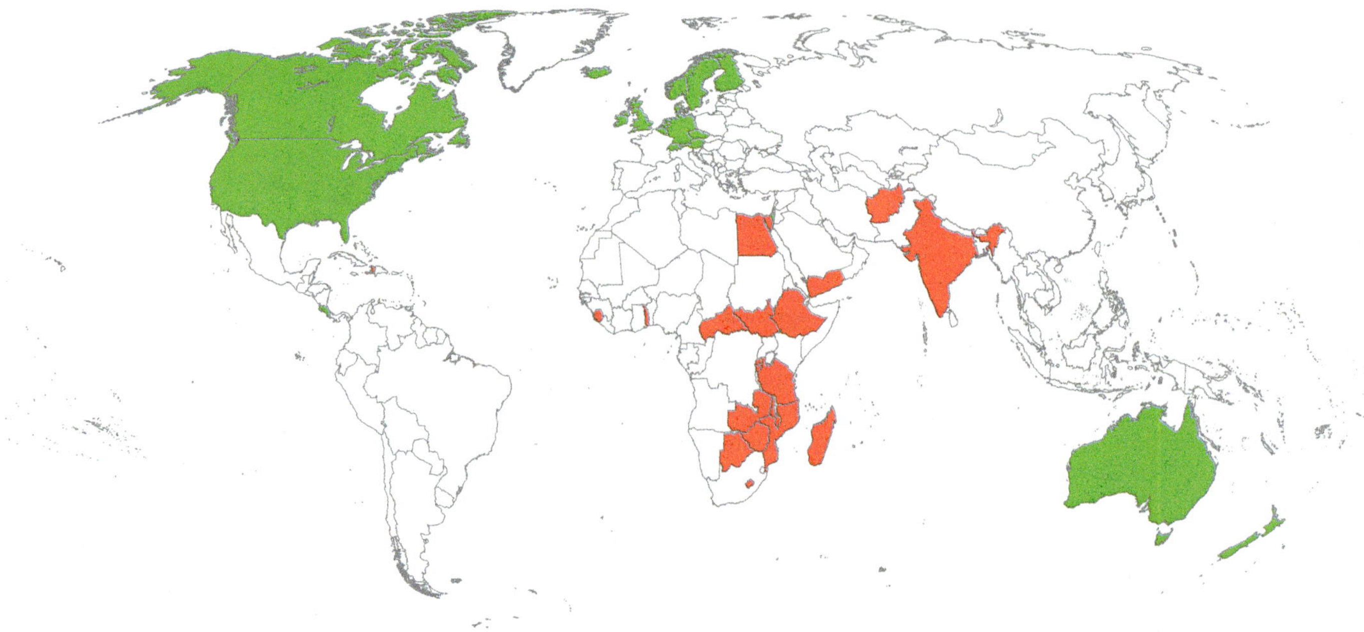

FIGURE **16.25**

Happiness Across the Globe. Happiness across the globe does reflect financial measures, but also varies according to positive and negative emotions, social support, freedom to make life choices, generosity, health, and perceptions of corruption. The 20 happiest countries appear in green and the 20 unhappiest countries appear in red.

Source: J. F. Helliwell et al. (2020). "Social Environments for World Happiness." In J. F. Helliwell, R. Layard, J. D. Sachs, & J.-E. De Neve (Eds.), *World happiness report* (pp. 13–46). New York: Sustainable Development Solutions Network.

Can We Increase Happiness? Some psychologists have moved past research identifying the causes and correlates of happiness to make recommendations for how to increase individual happiness. Among the steps recommended for improving happiness are practicing time management, exercising regularly, sleeping well, finding interesting work to do, nurturing close relationships, and following a chosen religious faith (Myers, 1993).

Methods for increasing happiness can be tailored to three types of happiness: the pleasant life (hedonics) and two sources of eudaimonic happiness—the good life and the meaningful life (Seligman & Csikszentmihalyi, 2000; Seligman, 2002). The pleasant life describes the pleasures that we enjoy from moment to moment. Enjoying a great meal or a beautiful sunset enhances our daily experiences. The good life occurs when we are maximizing our strengths in our work, hobbies, and other activities, making time subjectively slow down. The meaningful life describes our ability to focus away from the self to serve others or participate in something more permanent and larger than ourselves.

In general, people taking tests designed to assess their involvement with these three types of happiness are happiest overall if either their good life or their meaningful life score is high. If the score in one of these aspects is high, then a high score on the pleasant life can raise overall happiness, like having a cherry on top of an already-delicious ice cream sundae. Unfortunately, those who score highest on the pleasant life, without comparable scoring in either the good or the meaningful life category or both, tend to be less happy (Seligman, 2002).

Two reasons help explain why isolated pleasant life scores fail to greatly affect overall happiness. First, these scores tend to be highly heritable, which means that you can't do much to improve your sense of pleasure. Some people seem to respond more intensely than others to pleasurable experiences. Second, these feelings do not last long and habituate quickly. Think about the last time you had a delicious dessert. The first few bites are fantastic, but the last ones are usually less so. A short time later, you might have forgotten how delicious the dessert even was.

Even if heritability affects our ability to experience pleasure, positive psychology has some suggestions for enhancing our experiences. How often have you eaten your meals while watching television, reading, or working on your computer? If you try to multitask in this way, it is unlikely that you will derive much pleasure or satisfaction from your food, which can lead to overeating. Learning to "savor" pleasurable experiences by paying more attention to them can make them more memorable and enjoyable (Bryant & Veroff, 2007).

The good life is somewhat easier to modify than the pleasant life. To enhance your happiness from the good life, all you have to do is identify your strengths and find ways to use them in your important work and hobby activities. During activities that contribute to the good life, people experience **flow**, in which they are absorbed in their current activity, usually related to work, problem solving, or creativity (Csikszentmihalyi, 1990, 1996). The word *flow* was chosen to describe this experience on the basis of interviews in which people spontaneously used the metaphor to explain their own experiences. These experiences may qualify as altered states of consciousness and are usually perceived as highly positive. Time appears to stand still for people who are immersed in flow.

BlueOrange Studio/Shutterstock.com

Researchers studying happiness identify three types. The pleasant life consists of pleasures, like ice cream, that are enjoyed from moment to moment. The good life features "flow" and a sense that time is standing still. The meaningful life describes the positive emotions obtained by helping others.

flow A state characterized by complete absorption in a current activity, such as work, problem solving, or creativity.

People who do not play video games are often astonished by the nearly compulsive attractiveness of the activity for those who do play. However, video games meet many of the criteria for a flow experience (Csikszentmihalyi, 1990). The games have clear goals (reaching the next level or beating a dungeon boss), they provide the opportunity to focus, they encourage a merging of action and awareness (as opposed to self-consciousness), and players generally experience a distortion of subjective time. In addition, games provide instant and precise feedback (you succeed or not), a balance between ability and difficulty (gamers reject games that are either too easy or too challenging), and a sense of personal control (you're the one making the moves). Finally, gaming, like other flow activities, is intrinsically reinforcing. Many a parent has diabolically used access to gaming as a reinforcer for other desired behaviors, such as chores or homework. It is likely that video games, at least for some people, tap into a predisposition to find activities that meet these flow criteria to be highly reinforcing.

The meaningful life can take multiple forms and provides numerous opportunities to boost happiness. As we've already seen, many people find meaningfulness within religious practice, but that is not the only approach that works. People who perform acts of kindness toward others experience a boost in well-being (Layous et al., 2012). Volunteering for a cause that is close to your heart not only improves well-being but might also reduce feelings of depression (Jenkinson et al., 2013). Spending money on other people results in increased happiness (Dunn et al., 2014). Reminding us of the complexity of many psychological processes, we find that a strong personal identity, or the expression of an authentic self, gives people a sense of meaningfulness, but does not always correlate with happiness (Baumeister et al., 2013).

We are not suggesting that happiness can be found by spending all your time playing video games; instead, we recommend that you seek this type of flow in the work and hobbies that you enjoy.

aslysun/Shutterstock.com

According to Mihaly Csikszentmihalyi, video games can be compelling because they meet many of the criteria required of a flow-inducing experience, such as clear goals, the opportunity to focus, the merging of action and awareness, and the experience of distortion of time for the player. The popularity of team e-sports suggests that even watching others play can be reinforcing.

Positive Traits

In an effort to further understand the sources of well-being, positive psychologists have built upon the trait theories discussed in Chapter 12. Among the traits that contribute to well-being are hope, resilience, spirituality, and gratitude.

Hope refers to an expectation that your goals will be met in the future. You are probably hopeful that you will complete your college education and find a good job. The trait of hope is tightly linked to feelings of optimism. Hope in turn is determined by motivation and planning (Snyder, 1994). Your expectations for a college degree are based on beliefs that you can achieve a degree through hard work and that following your plans will give you the results that you desire. Being a hopeful person provides a number of benefits to well-being. Hopeful people can withstand more pain and stress because they believe that the future will be better (Snyder et al., 2005). Hopeful people are more capable problem solvers because they are likely to consider alternative pathways for meeting their goals instead of giving up at the first obstacle. Finally, hopeful people usually enjoy strong social networks because other people find hope attractive (Snyder et al., 2002).

We discussed resilience in an earlier section of this chapter. Resilience not only serves as a buffer for stress but can lead to growth following a traumatic experience (Davis & Nolen-Hoeksema, 2009). None of us likes being traumatized, but when we look back on difficult episodes of our lives, we often feel like a traumatic experience led to growth and improved strength. Among the positive changes associated with posttraumatic growth are perceptions of the self as a survivor rather than a victim, increased self-confidence and self-efficacy, and greater appreciation for the fragile nature of life. Many people respond to prior trauma with increased compassion for others, closer bonds with family and friends, and enhanced willingness to share emotions. Trauma also can lead people to reduce the value that they place on material aspects of life, such as money and possessions, while increasing their sense of what is truly meaningful about life. A resilience program developed by Martin Seligman and his colleagues for the U.S. Army resulted in lower rates among deployed soldiers of posttraumatic stress disorder, anxiety, and depression, and reduced the rate of substance abuse by half (Harms et al., 2013).

As we mentioned in a previous section, the experience of a meaningful life enhances well-being and happiness. Although finding meaning simply encompasses recognizing things that are bigger than one's personal existence, some people achieve meaningfulness through spirituality and religious practice (Myers, 1993). Religious beliefs and practice also have been associated with a long list of health benefits because most major world religions promote healthier lifestyles (Emmons et al., 2008). Many people find religious prohibitions to be a helpful tool for resisting the temptation to engage in risky, unhealthy behaviors. Although participation in religious or spiritual activities is a behavior, it is strongly predicted by a person's need for deeper meaning, or trait spirituality (Pargament & Krumrei, 2009).

Masterfile

Hopeful people are capable problem solvers who believe that their goals can be met in the future.

The idea of individual traits related to well-being has been extended to include shared social values and experiences, resulting in values or virtues. A value can be defined as "an enduring belief that a specific mode of conduct or end state of existence is personally or socially preferable to an opposite or converse mode of conduct or end state of existence" (Rokeach, 1968–1969, p. 5). The voluntary nature of values is stressed by many psychologists, including Gordon Allport, who defines a value as "a belief upon which a man acts by preference" (Allport, 1961, p. 454). One effort to identify values combined those listed by major world religions and such organizations as the Boy Scouts, Rotary International, and Alcoholics Anonymous with data from major personality tests (Franken, 2002). The resulting values are *social, cheerful, peaceful, tolerant, kind, generous, trusting, assertive, self-control, self-confidence, communication, leading,* and *autonomous.* Additional lists have added some interesting items, such as *awe* and *forgiving* (Peterson & Seligman, 2004).

One interesting difference between the positive psychologist's discussion of values and the personality psychologist's discussion of traits is the judgmental approach to values. In discussing personality traits, we don't want to think of traits as necessarily good or bad. A variety of personalities, such as the introverted computer programmer and the extroverted salesperson, helps meet the needs of society. In contrast, the values discussed by positive psychologists are good, and to be without them is not so good. This deviation from being nonjudgmental represents a significant departure by the positive psychologists from the humanistic psychologists, who argue strongly against any type of outward judgment of others.

Do values matter in everyday life? As we saw in Chapter 13, attitudes and behavior may or may not correlate. However, possessing certain values seems to correlate with a number of positive outcomes. Participants' self-ratings on the 13 values mentioned earlier are positively correlated with measures of self-esteem (Franken, 2002). In addition, explosiveness, or a propensity to violence, was negatively correlated with a person's values ratings. As ratings on the values increased, a person's potential for violent behavior decreased. People with high values scores were the least likely to experience alcohol or tobacco addictions or to experience anxiety and depression.

ZUMA Press Inc/Alamy Stock Photo

Nobody wants to experience trauma, but some survivors report experiencing posttraumatic growth. Mike Atherton lost both legs and his left arm in a boating accident, but he has returned to performing with the Tampa Bay Water Ski Show Team and reports feeling optimistic about his future.

Positive Institutions

Positive psychologists study the roles of institutions such as workplaces, schools, and families in promoting well-being in the community. What characteristics should we strive for in our institutions to raise the likelihood that members of the community will lead satisfying lives? Positive institutions share several features (Peterson, 2006). They share a purpose in the form of institutional goals. Their rules and consequences are fair. They feature a reciprocal caring by the institution for its members and by the members for the institution. A positive institution provides safety for its members and treats them with respect.

One of your goals in completing a college education is probably related to the type of work you'll be able to do as a result. Your future working conditions will have significant influence on your overall well-being. Positive psychologists have identified three ways that people feel about their work (Wrzesniewski et al., 1997). Some people just have jobs. A job is viewed as a way of supporting your family, and workers with jobs emphasize this role without asking more of their work life. A career not only pays the bills but also fulfills workers' needs for status and achievement. Finally, a calling satisfies both personal and cooperative goals. The worker pays the bills while gaining both personal achievement and a sense of contributing to the community. When workers view their employment as a calling, they are less concerned with work conditions, salary, benefits, and status. Positive workplaces facilitate the workers' abilities to meet their personal work-related goals.

Schools from kindergarten through college are particularly important to the health and future of a community. In a manner similar to psychology's emphasis on disorders, most of the research in education has focused on what goes wrong in schools rather than on what schools are doing well. Positive schools promote growth and produce a sense of satisfaction

Rotary International

SERVICE Above Self

Organizations such as Rotary International often reinforce the values of their members, such as "service above self."

Source: Service Above Self and the Service Above Self logo are trademarks of Rotary International and used herein with permission.

Forbes America's Best Employers

1. Trader Joe's	6. Google
2. Southwest Airlines	7. Stanford University
3. Lilly	8. SC Johnson
4. Costco Wholesale	9. Mayo Clinic
5. Garmin	10. Michelin Group

Forbes rankings of "best employers" for 2019 cover a wide variety of industries. Positive psychologists attempt to find common features of organizations that make them positive institutions.

in students. Although this area is sparsely studied, student satisfaction with schools predicts a number of positive outcomes, including higher grades and fewer problem behaviors, even as early as kindergarten (Ladd et al., 2000).

Significant challenges face today's families, and identifying what works could provide guidance for many. Family-centered positive psychology (FCPP) focuses on the characteristics of positive families (Sheridan & Burt, 2009). Consistent with the general approach of positive psychology, FCPP identifies the strengths of families rather than emphasizing their failures and weaknesses.

Positive Psychology and the Future

Positive psychology is not without its critics. Among the weaknesses seen in positive psychology are its unintended negative effects on people who face medical and psychological challenges (Held, 2004). Although research indicates that optimism and health are linked, this finding might give sick people the unfortunate impression that all they have to do to cure their illness is to maintain a positive attitude. A second criticism is related to the integration theme that we have featured in this textbook. Positive strengths are valuable, but they are best studied within the entire context of individuals interacting in environments. Positive and negative emotions can coexist, and we cannot fully understand one type of experience without considering the other (Cacioppo et al., 2011).

It is unlikely that psychology will ever abandon its goal of helping troubled people feel better, but positive psychology's emphasis on what goes right is also illuminating. We do not know at this time whether the label of positive psychology will drop out of favor, like Wilhelm Wundt's structuralism, or enjoy the fate of William James's functionalism by becoming so integrated into mainstream psychology that a label is no longer necessary. By applying the same evidence-based criteria that we have described for evaluating interventions for "negative" behaviors to interventions based on positive psychology, we will figure out the role that positive psychology should play in our continued search for understanding the human mind.

Interpersonal Relationships
The Health Psychology Perspective

HOW DO INVESTMENT AND EXPERIENCES OF GRATITUDE AFFECT RELATIONSHIPS?

WE HAVE STUDIED RELATIONSHIPS from the vantage points of 15 psychological perspectives so far in this textbook, and we end the journey with an analysis of the role of a positive emotion—gratitude—on relationship building.

Psychologists traditionally have focused on how an individual invests in relationships and report that individuals' perceptions of how much they have already invested (time, energy, and other resources) influence how committed they feel. However, researchers know relatively little about how our perceptions of our partner's investment in the relationship influence our commitment.

When a partner invests in a relationship, the typical response is the experience of the positive emotion of gratitude. Gratitude includes the feelings of thankfulness and appreciation felt for the partner, which in turn affects the perception of who the partner is as a person (Joel et al., 2013). When people experience gratitude for a partner, it stimulates further commitment. The amount of commitment that an individual experiences is linked to the perceived investment in the relationship on the part of the partner.

What types of investment promote more gratitude, and through those feelings, greater commitment? You might guess that financial investments would be important, but research has shown that intangible investments, like emotional involvement, have a greater impact on commitment (Goodfriend & Agnew, 2008). This is reminiscent of the finding discussed earlier that it is not wealth that makes us happy, but rather our social connectivity. ■

Matthias Tunger/Corbis

It's often the little things that people do for their partners that result in gratitude and a stronger commitment to the relationship.

Psychology Takes On Real-World Problems

Resilience in the Face of a Pandemic

Across the 15 previous chapters, we have explored ways that psychological science can help us understand the human elements involved with a pandemic. In this last entry, we will explore a concept central to positive psychology—resilience—and how we can maintain resilience in the face of high stress levels.

To recap, resilience refers to our ability to maintain coping in the face of strong stressors. Violent and life-threatening experiences are sadly not rare. As many as 70% of the population have one such experience during their lifetimes (Ozer et al., 2003). Some percentage of these individuals will go on to develop posttraumatic stress disorder (PTSD; see Chapter 14), but other patterns of response also occur. Following trauma, some individuals experience short term and less intense distress. Others recover quickly but then experience a decrease in their ability to cope. Finally, some people do not experience much disruption at all (see Figure 16.26; Bonanno, 2004). It is this latter group that displays resilience. Prior research shows that this is not a small group. Following most types of trauma, the resilient group makes up about two-thirds of those affected (Chen & Bonanno, 2020).

We are still too close to the ongoing COVID-19 pandemic to be able to make firm conclusions about how many people remain resilient, but we can use past pandemics to make some educated predictions. The 2003 severe acute respiratory syndrome (SARS) epidemic in Hong Kong can provide insight. SARS was more lethal than COVID-19, killing 14% to 15% of infected persons overall and more than 50% of those over the age of 64 years with infections. Nonetheless, at least half of the survivors demonstrated resilience (Chen & Bonnanno, 2020).

While resilience often occurs based on a variety of pre-existing factors, including personality and other individual differences, family context, and community characteristics, we can still take action to make ourselves more resilient. Chen and Bonano (2020) note the following ways that individuals can promote resilience:

- Nurture optimism
- Build social support and bonding
- Stay informed without over-indulging in media consumption
- Employ distraction strategies, including having fun and laughing
- Reduce isolation by using online communication technologies

This section of each chapter also focuses on policy development, and resilience can be promoted at both the family and community level through careful policies. Resilience at the family level has not been thoroughly investigated, but cohesion, adaptability, communication, and financial management appear to contribute to family-level resilience.

Resilient communities feature higher social cohesion, lower crime rates, and less disaster exposure. Socioeconomic status and access to health care are essential variables in community resilience. It is likely that individual, family, and community characteristics interact in important ways to influence resilience.

As we come to the end of our textbook and conclude this exploration of how psychological science can address some of the big problems of the day, our hope is that your increased understanding of human elements in the causes and solutions of problems is empowering. Just as our ancestors benefited from scientific explanations of lightning bolts, our contemporary understanding of psychology makes the world a less fearsome and more logical place. We see areas where our policies and interventions can make real differences in the lives of many. We can face the inevitable big problems around the corner with optimism, hope, and resilience. Thank you for accompanying us on this journey, and we hope you continue exploring the world of psychology. ■

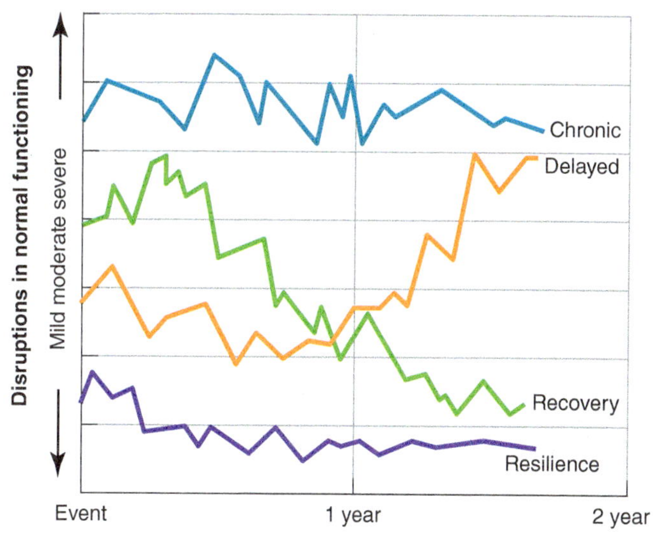

FIGURE 16.26

Posttraumatic Responses Are Diverse. Following a traumatic experience, people respond in one of four different ways. Some may experience chronic distress (blue line), potentially leading to a diagnosis of posttraumatic stress disorder (PTSD). A second group gradually recovers functioning over time (green line). A third responds well initially but experiences more disruption later on (orange line). Finally, resilience, which is the most frequent reaction, is characterized by relatively little disruption in ongoing functioning (purple line).

Source: G. A. Bonanno (2004). "Loss, Trauma, and Human Resilience: Have We Underestimated the Human Capacity to Thrive After Extremely Aversive Events?" *American Psychologist, 59*(1), 20–28. doi: 10.1037/0003-066X.59.1.20

SUMMARY 16.3 Types of Happiness

Source of Happiness	How to Get It	Examples
The pleasant life 	Savor your experience without trying to multitask.	Avoid distractions from technology (television, smartphone, etc.) when you're trying to enjoy a meal.
The good life 	Find ways to incorporate your key strengths into your activities.	Choose an occupation that you truly enjoy, not just one that pays the bills.
The meaningful life SERVICE Above Self	Focus on something bigger than yourself.	Volunteer for a cause that's important to you.

Credits: Top row—BlueOrange Studio/Shutterstock.com; Second row—aslysun/Shutterstock.com; Bottom row—Rotary International.

KEY TERMS The Language of Psychological Science

Be sure that you can define these terms and use them correctly.

alarm reaction, p. 642
biopsychosocial model, p. 660
cortisol, p. 647
emotion-focused coping, p. 658
exhaustion, p. 642
flow, p. 679
general adaptation syndrome (GAS), p. 642
health psychology, p. 660
hypothalamic–pituitary–adrenal (HPA) axis, p. 647
immune system, p. 650
lymphocyte, p. 651
optimism, p. 673
positive psychology, p. 672
problem-focused coping, p. 658
relationship-focused coping, p. 658
resilience, p. 659
resistance, p. 642
stress, p. 640
stressor, p. 640
sympathetic adrenal–medullary (SAM) system, p. 647
tend and befriend, p. 649
Type A personality, p. 651
Type B personality, p. 651

References

Abdo, H., Calvo-Enrique, L., Lopez, J. M., Song, J., Zhang, M.-D., Usoskin, D., El Manira, A., Adameyko, I., Hjerling-Leffler, J., & Ernfors, P. (2019). Specialized cutaneous Schwann cells initiate pain sensation. *Science, 365*(6454), 695–699. doi:10.1126/science.aax6452

Abdolmaleky, H. M., Zhou, J.-R., & Thiagalingam, S. (2015). An update on the epigenetics of psychotic diseases and autism. *Epigenomics, 7*(3), 427–449. doi:10.2217/epi.14.85

Aberson, C. L., Healy, M., & Robero, V. (2000). Ingroup bias and self-esteem: A meta-analysis. *Personality and Social Psychology Review, 4*, 157–173. doi:10.1207/S15327957PSPR0402_04

Aboujaoude, E. (2020). Where life coaching ends and therapy begins: Toward a less confusing treatment landscape. *Perspectives on Psychological Science, 15*(4), 973–977. doi:10.1177/1745691620904962

Abraham, G. E. (1974). Ovarian and adrenal contribution to peripheral androgens during the menstrual cycle. *The Journal of Clinical Endocrinology & Metabolism, 39*(2), 340–346. doi:10.1210/jcem-39-2-340

Abramson, L. Y., Seligman, M. E. P., & Teasdale, J. D. (1978). Learned helplessness in humans: Critique and reformulation. *Journal of Abnormal Psychology, 87*, 49–74. doi:10.1037/0021-843X.87.1.49

Abramzon, Y. A., Fratta, P., Traynor, B. J., & Chia, R. (2020). The overlapping genetics of amyotrophic lateral sclerosis and frontotemporal dementia. *Frontiers in Neuroscience, 14*(42). doi:10.3389/fnins.2020.00042

Adapted from A. Martin et al. (1996). "Neural Correlates of Category-specific Knowledge." *Nature, 379*, 649–652. doi:10.1038/379649a0

Adler, A. (1956). The individual psychology of Alfred Adler: A systematic presentation in selections from his writings. H. L. Ansbacher & R. R. Ansbacher (Eds.). New York: Harper Torchbooks.

Adler, N. E. (2013). Health disparities: Taking on the challenge. *Perspectives on Psychological Science, 8*(6), 679–681. doi:10.1177/1745691613506909

Adolph, K. E., & Hoch, J. E. (2019). Motor development: Embodied, embedded, enculturated, and enabling. *Annual Review of Psychology, 70*, 141–164. doi:10.1146/annurev-psych-010418-102836

Adolphs, R. (2007). Looking at other people: Mechanisms for social perception revealed in subjects with focal amygdala damage. *Novartis Foundation Symposia, 278*, 146–159; discussion 160–144, 216–121.

Adolphs, R. (2008). Fear, faces, and the human amygdala. *Current Opinion in Neurobiology, 18*(2), 166–172. doi:10.1016/j.conb.2008.06.006

Adolphs, R. (2016). How should neuroscience study emotions? By distinguishing emotion states, concepts, and experiences. *Social Cognitive and Affective Neuroscience, 12*(1), 24–31. doi:10.1093/scan/nsw153

Adolphs, R. (2018). Social cognition, the amygdala, and autism. In K. Shigemasu, S. Kuwano, T. Sato, & T. Matsuzawa (Eds.), *Diversity in Harmony – Insights from Psychology* (pp. 1–18). Hoboken, NJ: Wiley.

Adolphs, R., Gosselin, F., Buchanan, T. W., Tranel, D., Schyns, P., & Damasio, A. R. (2005). A mechanism for impaired fear recognition after amygdala damage. *Nature, 433*, 68–72. doi:10.1038/nature03086

Adolphs, R., Tranel, D., & Damasio, A. R. (1998). The human amygdala in social judgment. *Nature, 393*, 470–474. doi:10.1038/30982

Adolphs, R., Tranel, D., Damasio, H., & Damasio, A. (1994). Impaired recognition of emotion in facial expressions following bilateral damage to the human amygdala. *Nature, 372*, 669–672. doi:10.1038/372669a0

Adrián-Ventura, J., Costumero, V., Parcet, M. A., & Ávila, C. (2019). Linking personality and brain anatomy: A structural MRI approach to Reinforcement Sensitivity Theory. *Social Cognitive and Affective Neuroscience, 14*(3), 329–338. doi:10.1093/scan/nsz011

Agay, N., Yechiam, E., Carmel, Z., & Levkovitz, Y. (2010). Non-specific effects of methylphenidate (Ritalin) on cognitive ability and decision-making of ADHD and healthy adults. *Psychopharmacology, 210*(4), 511–519. doi:10.1007/s00213-010-1853-4

Ahadi, S. A., & Rothbart, M. K. (1994). Temperament, development, and the Big Five. In G. Kohnstamm, C. Halverson, & R. P. Martin (Eds.), *The developing structure of temperament and personality from infancy to adulthood* (pp. 189–207). Hillsdale, NJ: Lawrence Erlbaum Associates.

Aharoni, E., Vincent, G. M., Harenski, C. L., Calhoun, V. D., Sinnott-Armstrong, W., Gazzaniga, M. S., & Kiehl, K. A. (2013). Neuroprediction of future rearrest. *Proceedings of the National Academy of Sciences of the United States of America, 110*(15), 6223–6228. doi:10.1073/pnas.1219302110

Ahern, E., Kinsella, S., & Semkovska, M. (2018). Clinical efficacy and economic evaluation of online cognitive behavioral therapy for major depressive disorder: A systematic review and meta-analysis. *Expert Review of Pharmacoeconomics & Outcomes Research, 18*(1), 25–41. doi:10.1080/14737167.2018.1407245

Aihara, M., Ida, I., Yuuki, N., Oshima, A., Kumano, H., Takahashi, K., Fukuda, M., Oriuchi, N., Endo, K., Matsuda, H., & Mikuni, M. (2007). HPA axis dysfunction in unmedicated major depressive disorder and its normalization by pharmacotherapy correlates with alteration of neural activity in prefrontal cortex and limbic/paralimbic regions. *Psychiatry Research, 155*(3), 245–256. doi:10.1016/j.pscychresns.2006.11.002

Ainsworth, M., & Bowlby, J. (1965). *Child care and the growth of love*. London, UK: Penguin.

Ainswoth, M., Blehar, M. C., Waters, E., & Wall, S. (1978). *Patterns of attachment: A psychological study of the strange situation.* Potomac, MD: Erlbaum.

Ajzen, I. (1991). The theory of planned behavior. *Organizational Behavior and Human Decision Processes, 50*(2), 179–211. doi:10.1016/0749-5978(91)90020-t

Akane, A. (1998). Sex determination by PCR analysis of the X-Y amelogenin gene. In P. J. Lincoln & J. Thomson (Eds.), *Forensic DNA profiling protocols* (pp. 245–249). Totowa, NJ: Humana Press.

Akers, K. G., Chérasse, Y., Fujita, Y., Srinivasan, S., Sakurai, T., & Sakaguchi, M. (2018). Concise review: Regulatory influence of sleep and epigenetics on adult hippocampal neurogenesis and cognitive and emotional function. *Stem Cells, 36*(7), 969–976. doi:10.1002/stem.2815

Åkerstedt, T., & Fröberg, J. E. (1976). Interindividual differences in circadian patterns of catecholamine excretion, body temperature, performance, and subjective arousal. *Biological Psychology, 4*(4), 277–292. doi:10.1016/0301-0511(76)90019-3

Al-Issa, I. (1977). Social and cultural aspects of hallucinations. *Psychological Bulletin, 84*(3), 570–587. doi:10.1037/0033-2909.84.3.570

Alcock, J. (2011, 2011-01-06). *Back from the future: Parapsychology and the Bem affair. Skeptical Inquirer.* https://skepticalinquirer.org/exclusive/back_from_the_future/

Alda, M. (2015). Lithium in the treatment of bipolar disorder: Pharmacology and pharmacogenetics. *Molecular Psychiatry, 20*(6), 661–670. doi:10.1038/mp.2015.4

Aldwin, C. (1994). *Stress, coping, and development: An integrative perspective*. New York: Guilford.

Biological Psychology, 68, 215–222. doi:10.1016/j.biopsycho.2004.05.001
Bailey, C. H., & Chen, M. C. (1983). Morphological basis of long-term habituation and sensitization in Aplysia. *Science, 220*, 91–93. doi:10.1126/science.6828885
Bailey, J. M., Vasey, P. L., Diamond, L. M., Breedlove, S. M., Vilain, E., & Epprecht, M. (2016). Sexual orientation, controversy, and science. *Psychological Science in the Public Interest, 17*(2), 45–101. doi:10.1177/1529100616637616
Baillargeon, R., Li, J., Gertner, Y., & Wu, D. (2011). How do infants reason about physical events?. In U. Goswami (Ed.), *The Wiley-Blackwell handbook of childhood cognitive development* (pp. 11–48). Hoboken, NJ: Wiley-Blackwell.
Baker, T. B., McFall, R. M., & Shoham, V. (2008). Current status and future prospects of clinical psychology: Toward a scientifically principled approach to mental and behavioral health care. *Psychological Science in the Public Interest, 9*(2), 67–103. doi:10.1111/j.1539-6053.2009.01036.x
Bakker, A., Spinhoven, P., van Balkom, A. J. L. M., & van Dyck, R. (2002). Relevance of assessment of cognitions during panic attacks in the treatment of panic disorder. *Psychotherapy and Psychosomatics, 71*(3), 158–161. doi:10.1159/000056283
Baldwin, D. S., Anderson, I. M., Nutt, D. J., Allgulander, C., Bandelow, B., den Boer, J. A., Christmas, D. M., Davies, S., Fineberg, N., Lidbetter, N., Malizia, A., McCrone, P., Nabarro, D., O'Neill, C., Scott, J., van der Wee, N., & Wittchen, H.-U. (2014). Evidence-based pharmacological treatment of anxiety disorders, post-traumatic stress disorder and obsessive-compulsive disorder: A revision of the 2005 guidelines from the British Association for Psychopharmacology. *Journal of Psychopharmacology, 28*(5), 403–439. doi:10.1177/0269881114525674
Balschuna, D., Zuschrattera, W., & Wetzel, W. (2006). Allosteric enhancement of metabotropic glutamate receptor 5 function promotes spatial memory. *Neuroscience, 142*, 691–702. doi:10.1016/j.neuroscience.2006.06.043
Balthazart, J. (2011). Minireview: Hormones and human sexual orientation. *Endocrinology, 152*(8), 2937–2947. doi:10.1210/en.2011-0277
Bandura, A. (1965). Influence of models' reinforcement contingencies on the acquisition of imitative responses. *Journal of Personality and Social Psychology, 1*, 589–595. doi:10.1037/h0022070
Bandura, A. (1973). *Aggression: A social learning analysis*. Oxford, England: Prentice-Hall.
Bandura, A. (1990). Perceived self-efficacy in the exercise of personal agency. *Journal of Applied Sport Psychology, 2*, 128–163. doi:10.1080/10413209008406426
Bandura, A. (1993). Perceived self-efficacy in cognitive development and functioning. *Educational Psychologist, 28*, 117–148. doi:10.1207/s15326985ep2802_3
Bandura, A. (1995). Exercise of personal and collective efficacy in changing societies. In A. Bandura (Ed.), *Self-efficacy in changing societies* (pp. 1–45). New York: Cambridge University Press.
Bandura, A. (2001). Social cognitive theory: An agentic perspective. *Annual Review of Psychology, 52*(1), 1–26. doi:10.1146/annurev.psych.52.1.1
Bandura, A., Ross, D., & Ross, S. A. (1963). Imitation of film-mediated aggressive models. *The Journal of Abnormal and Social Psychology, 66*(1), 3–11. doi:10.1037/h0048687
Banerjee, D. (2020). The other side of COVID-19: Impact on obsessive compulsive disorder (OCD) and hoarding. *Psychiatry Research, 288*, 112966–112966. doi:10.1016/j.psychres.2020.112966
Banerjee, T. D., Middleton, F., & Faraone, S. V. (2007). Environmental risk factors for attention-deficit hyperactivity disorder. *Acta Paediatrica, 96*(9), 1269–1274. doi:10.1111/j.1651-2227.2007.00430.x
Banks, E., & Canfell, K. (2009). Invited commentary: Hormone therapy risks and benefits—The Women's Health Initiative findings and the postmenopausal estrogen timing hypothesis. *American Journal of Epidemiology, 170*(1), 24–28. doi:10.1093/aje/kwp113
Baños, R. M., Guillen, V., Quero, S., Garcia-Palacios, A., Alcaniz, M., & Botella, C. (2011). A virtual reality system for the treatment of stress-related disorders: A preliminary analysis of efficacy compared to a standard cognitive behavioral program. *International Journal of Human-Computer Studies, 69*(9), 602–613. doi:10.1016/j.ijhcs.2011.06.002
Bar-On, R., Tranel, D., Denburg, N. L., & Bechara, A. (2003). Exploring the neurological substrate of emotional and social intelligence. *Brain, 126*(8), 1790–1800. doi:10.1093/brain/awg177
Barber, S. J., & Kim, H. (2020). COVID-19 Worries and behavior changes in older and younger men and women. *The Journals of Gerontology: Series B*. doi:10.1093/geronb/gbaa068
Bard, P. (1934). Emotion: I. The neurohumoral basis of emotional reactions. In C. Murchison (Ed.), *Handbook of general experimental psychology* (pp. 264–311). Worcester, MA: Clark University Press.
Barkley, R. (1995). *Taking charge of ADHD: The complete, authoritative guide for parents.* New York: Guilford Press.
Barkley, R. (1997). *ADHD and the nature of self-control.* New York: Guilford Press.
Barkley, R. A., & Cox, D. (2007). A review of driving risks and impairments associated with attention-deficit/hyperactivity disorder and the effects of stimulant medication on driving performance. *Journal of Safety Research, 38*(1), 113–128. doi:10.1016/j.jsr.2006.09.004
Barlow, D. (1988). *Anxiety and its disorders: The nature and treatment of anxiety and panic.* New York: Guilford Press.
Barnea-Goraly, N., Frazier, T. W., Piacenza, L., Minshew, N. J., Keshavan, M. S., Reiss, A. L., & Hardan, A. Y. (2014). A preliminary longitudinal volumetric MRI study of amygdala and hippocampal volumes in autism. *Progress in Neuro-Psychopharmacology and Biological Psychiatry, 48*, 124–128. doi:10.1016/j.pnpbp.2013.09.010
Barnes, J., McRobbie, H., Dong, C. Y., Walker, N., & Hartmann-Boyce, J. (2019). Hypnotherapy for smoking cessation. *Cochrane Database of Systematic Reviews*(6). doi:10.1002/14651858.CD001008.pub3
Baron-Cohen, S. (1991). The development of a theory of mind in autism: Deviance and delay? *Psychiatric Clinics of North America, 14*, 33–51. doi:10.1177/1362361310366314
Baron-Cohen, S. (2000). Theory of mind and autism: A review. In L. M. Glidden (Ed.), *International review of research in mental retardation, 23*,169–184. doi:10.1016/S0074-7750(00)80010-5
Baron-Cohen, S. (2017). Editorial perspective: Neurodiversity – a revolutionary concept for autism and psychiatry. *Journal of Child Psychology and Psychiatry, 58*(6), 744–747. doi:10.1111/jcpp.12703
Baron-Cohen, S., Wheelwright, S., Hill, J., Raste, Y., & Plumb, I. (2001). The "Reading the Mind in the Eyes" Test Revised Version: A study with normal adults, and adults with Asperger syndrome or high-functioning autism. *The Journal of Child Psychology and Psychiatry and Allied Disciplines, 42*(2), |241–251. doi:10.1017/S0021963001006643
Baron, R. S. (2005). So right it's wrong: Groupthink and the ubiquitous nature of polarized group decision making. In M. P. Zanna (Ed.), *Advances in experimental social psychology* (Vol. 37, pp. 219–253). San Diego, CA: Elsevier Academic Press.
Barresi, J., & Moore, C. (1996). Intentional relations and social understanding. *Behavioral and Brain Sciences, 19*, 107–122. doi:10.1017/S0140525X00041790
Barrick, M. R., & Mount, M. K. (1991). The big five personality dimensions and job performance: A meta-analysis. *Personnel Psychology, 44*, 1–26. doi:10.1111/j.1744-6570.1991.tb00688.x
Bartels, A., & Zeki, S. (2000). The neural basis of romantic love. *NeuroReport, 11*(17), 3829–3834. doi:10.1097/00001756-200011270-00046
Bartels, A., & Zeki, S. (2004). The neural correlates of maternal and romantic love. *NeuroImage, 21*(3), 1155–1166. doi:10.1016/j.neuroimage.2003.11.003
Barthel, M., Mitchell, A., & Holcomb, J. (2016). *Many Americans believe fake news is sowing confusion.* http://www.journalism.org/2016/12/15/many-americans-believe-fake-news-is-sowing-confusion/

Bartle-Haring, S., Shannon, S., Holowacz, E., Patton, R., & Lotspeich-Younkin, F. (2018). Is there the "sweet spot" for age at marriage and positive marital outcomes? *Journal of Family Issues, 39*(4), 1085–1107. doi:10.1177/0192513x16686135

Bartlett, F. C. (1932/1967). *Remembering: A study in experimental and social psychology.* Cambridge: Cambridge University Press

Bartone, P. T. (2000). Hardiness as a resiliency factor for United States Forces in the Gulf War. In J. M. Violanti, D. Paton, & C. Dunning (Eds.), *Posttraumatic stress intervention: Challenges, issues, and perspectives.* (pp. 115–133). Springfield, IL: Charles C. Thomas.

Bartoshuk, L. M. (2000). Comparing sensory experiences across individuals: Recent psychophysical advances illuminate genetic variation in taste perception. *Chemical Senses, 25*, 447–460. doi:10.1093/chemse/25.4.447

Baruch, I., Hemsley, D. R., & Gray, J. A. (1988a). Differential performance of acute and chronic schizophrenics in a latent inhibition task. *Journal of Nervous and Mental Disease, 176*, 598–606. doi:10.1097/00005053-198810000-00004

Baruch, I., Hemsley, D. R., & Gray, J. A. (1988b). Latent inhibition and "psychotic proneness" in normal subjects. *Personality and Individual Differences, 9*, 777–783. doi:10.1016/0191-8869(88)90067-0

Bashore, T. R., Ridderinkhof, K. R., & W., van der Molen, M. (1997). The decline of cognitive processing speed in old age:. *Current Directions in Psychological Science, 6*(6), 163–169. doi:10.1111_1467-8721.ep10772944

Bateman, A. W., Gunderson, J., & Mulder, R. (2015). Treatment of personality disorder. *The Lancet, 385*(9969), 735–743. doi:10.1016/S0140-6736(14)61394-5

Bateson, M., Nettle, D., & Roberts, G. (2006). Cues of being watched enhance cooperation in a real-world setting. *Biology Letters, 2*(3), 412–414. doi:10.1098/rsbl.2006.0509

Bauer, P. J., & Lukowski, A. F. (2010). The memory is in the details: Relations between memory for the specific features of events and long-term recall during infancy. *Journal of Experimental Child Psychology, 107*(1), 1–14. doi:10.1016/j.jecp.2010.04.004

Bauer, P. J., Larkina, M., & Deocampo, J. (2011). Early memory development. In U. Goswami (Ed.), *The Wiley-Blackwell handbook of childhood cognitive development* (2nd ed., pp. 153–179). Hoboken, NJ: Wiley-Blackwell.

Bauer, R. M. (1984). Autonomic recognition of names and faces in prosopagnosia: A neuropsychological application of the guilty knowledge test. *Neuropsychologia, 22*(4), 457–469. doi:10.1016/0028-3932(84)90040-X

Baugh, J. (2017). Meaning-less differences: Exposing fallacies and flaws in "the word gap" hypothesis that conceal a dangerous "language trap" for low-income American families and their children. *International Multilingual Research Journal, 11*(1), 39–51. doi:10.1080/19313152.2016.1258189

Baumann, M. L., & Teasdale, B. (2018). Severe mental illness and firearm access: Is violence really the danger?. *International Journal of Law and Psychiatry, 56*, 44-49. doi:10.1016/j.ijlp.2017.11.003

Baumeister, R. F., & Leary, M. R. (1995). The need to belong: Desire for interpersonal attachments as a fundamental human motivation. *Psychological Bulletin, 117*(3), 497–529. doi:10.1037/0033-2909.117.3.497

Baumeister, R. F., Campbell, J. D., Krueger, J. I., & Vohs, K. D. (2003). Does high self-esteem cause better performance, interpersonal success, happiness, or healthier lifestyles? *Psychological Science in the Public Interest, 4*(1), 1–44. doi:10.1111/1529-1006.01431

Baumeister, R. F., Smart, L., & Boden, J. M. (1999). *Relation of threatened egotism to violence and aggression: the dark side of high self-esteem.* New York: Psychology Press.

Baumeister, R. F., Vohs, K. D., Aaker, J. L., & Garbinsky, E. N. (2013). Some key differences between a happy life and a meaningful life. *The Journal of Positive Psychology, 8*(6), 505–516. doi:10.1080/17439760.2013.830764

Baumrind, D. (1975). *Early socialization and the discipline controversy.* Morristown, NJ: General Learning Press.

Bavel, J. J. V., Baicker, K., Boggio, P. S., Capraro, V., Cichocka, A., Cikara, M., Crockett, M. J., Crum, A. J., Douglas, K. M., Druckman, J. N., Drury, J., Dube, O., Ellemers, N., Finkel, E. J., Fowler, J. H., Gelfand, M., Han, S.,Haslam, S. A., Jetten, J., . . . Willer, R. (2020). Using social and behavioural science to support COVID-19 pandemic response. *Nature Human Behaviour, 4*(5), 460–471. doi:10.1038/s41562-020-0884-z

Bavelas, J. B., Hutchinson, S., Kenwood, C., & Matheson, D. H. (1997). Using face-to-face dialogue as a standard for other communication systems. *Canadian Journal of Communication, 22*, 5–24. doi:10.22230/CJC.1997V22N1A973

Baxter, L. R., Schwartz, J. M., Bergman, K. S., Szuba, M. P., Guze, B. H., Mazziotta, J. C., Alazraki, A., Carl E. Selin, C. E., Huan-Kwang Ferng, H.-K., Munford, P., & Phelps, M. E. (1992). Caudate glucose metabolic rate changes with both drug and behavior therapy for obsessive-compulsive disorder. *Archives of General Psychiatry, 49*(9), 681–689. doi:10.1001/archpsyc.1992.01820090009002

Beaman, A. L., Klentz, B., Diener, E., & Svanum, S. (1979). Self-awareness and transgression in children: Two field studies. *Journal of Personality and Social Psychology, 37*, 1835–1846. doi:10.1037/0022-3514.37.10.1835

Beaton, A., Hudson, M., Milne, M., Port, R. V., Russell, K., Smith, B., Toki, V., Uerata, L., Wilcox P., Bartholomew, K., & Wihongi, H. (2016). Engaging Māori in biobanking and genomic research: a model for biobanks to guide culturally informed governance, operational, and community engagement activities. *Genetics In Medicine, 19*, 345. doi:10.1038/gim.2016.111

Bechara, A. (2005). Decision making, impulse control and loss of willpower to resist drugs: A neurocognitive perspective. *Nature Neuroscience, 8*(11), 1458–1463. doi:10.1038/nn1584

Bechara, A., Damasio, H., & Damasio, A. R. (2000). Emotion, decision-making, and the orbitofrontal cortex. *Cerebral Cortex, 10*, 295–307. doi:10.1093/cercor/10.3.295

Beck, A. T. (1975). *Cognitive therapy and the emotional disorders.* Madison, CT: International Universities Press.

Beck, A. T. (1985). Cognitive therapy, behavior therapy, psychoanalysis, and pharmacotherapy: A cognitive continuum. In M. Mahoney & A. Freeman (Eds.), *Cognition and psychotherapy* (pp. 197–220). New York: Plenum Press.

Beck, A. T., Rush, A., Shaw, B., & Emery, G. (1979). *Cognitive therapy of depression.* New York: Guilford Press.

Becker, A. E., Burwell, R. A., Herzog, D. B., Hamburg, P., & Gilman, S. E. (2002). Eating behaviours and attitudes following prolonged exposure to television among ethnic Fijian adolescent girls. *British Journal of Psychiatry, 180*, 509–514. doi:10.1192/bjp.180.6.509

Becker, M., Vignoles, V. L., Owe, E., Easterbrook, M. J., Brown, R., Smith, P. B., Bond, M. H., Regalia, C., Manzi, C., Brambilla, M., Aldhafri, S., González, R., Carrasco, D., Paz Cadena, M., Lay, S., Schweiger Gallo, I., Torres, A., Camino, L., Özgen, E., . . . Koller, S. H. (2014). Cultural bases for self-evaluation: Seeing oneself positively in different cultural contexts. *Personality and Social Psychology Bulletin, 40*(5), 657–675. doi:10.1177/0146167214522836

Beckerman, S., Erickson, P. I., Yost, J., Regalado, J., Jaramillo, L., Sparks, C., Iromenga, M., & Long, K. (2009). Life histories, blood revenge, and reproductive success among the Waorani of Ecuador. *Proceedings of the National Academy of Sciences of the United States of America, 106*(20), 8134–8139. doi:10.1073/pnas.0901431106

Beevers, C. G., Gibb, B. E., McGeary, J. E., & Miller, I. W. (2007). Serotonin transporter genetic variation and biased attention for emotional word stimuli among psychiatric inpatients. *Journal of Abnormal Psychology, 116*(1), 208–212. doi:10.1037/0021-843x.116.1.208

Begemann, M. J., Florisse, E. J., van Lutterveld, R., Kooyman, M., & Sommer, I. E. (2016). Efficacy of EEG neurofeedback in psychiatry: A comprehensive overview and meta-analysis. *Translational Brain Rhythmicity, 1*(1), 19–29. doi:10.15761/TBR.1000105

Beitel, M., Myhra, L. L., Gone, J. P., Barber, J. P., Miller, A., Rasband, A., Cutter, C. J., Schottenfeld, R. S., & Barry, D. T. (2018).

Psychotherapy with American Indians: An exploration of therapist-rated techniques in three urban clinics. *Psychotherapy, 55*(1), 45–51. doi:10.1037/pst0000156

Békés, V., & Aafjes-van Doorn, K. (2020). Psychotherapists' attitudes toward online therapy during the COVID-19 pandemic. *Journal of Psychotherapy Integration, 30*(2), 238–247. doi:10.1037/int0000214

Bellis, M. A., Hughes, K., Hughes, S., & Ashton, J. R. (2005). Measuring paternal discrepancy and its public health consequences. *Journal of Epidemiology and Community Health, 59*(9), 749–754. doi:10.1136/jech.2005.036517

Bellugi, U., Wang, P. O., & Jernigan, T. L. (1994). Williams syndrome: An unusual neuropsychological profile. In S. H. Broman & J. Grafman (Eds.), *Atypical cognitive deficits in developmental disorders: Implications for brain function* (pp. 23–56). Hillsdale, NJ: Erlbaum.

Belsky, J. (1999). Modern evolutionary theory and patterns of attachment. In J. Cassidy & P. R. Shaver (Eds.), *Handbook of attachment: Theory, research and clinical applications* (pp. 141–161). New York: Guilford Press.

Bem, D. J. (1972). Self-perception theory. In L. Berkowitz (Ed.), *Advances in experimental social psychology* (Vol. 6, pp. 1–62). New York: Academic Press.

Bem, D. J. (2001). Exotic becomes erotic: Integrating biological and experiential antecedents of sexual orientation. In A. R. D'Augelli & C. J. Patterson (Eds.), *Lesbian, gay, and bisexual identities and youth: Psychological perspectives.* (pp. 52–68). New York, NY US: Oxford University Press.

Bem, D. J. (2011). Feeling the future: Experimental evidence for anomalous retroactive influences on cognition and affect. *Journal of Personality and Social Psychology, 100*(3), 407–425. doi:10.1037/a0021524

Benedict, C., Vogel, H., Jonas, W., Woting, A., Blaut, M., Schürmann, A., & Cedernaes, J. (2016). Gut microbiota and glucometabolic alterations in response to recurrent partial sleep deprivation in normal-weight young individuals. *Molecular Metabolism, 5*(12), 1175–1186. doi:10.1016/j.molmet.2016.10.003

Benjamin, D. J., Berger, J. O., Johannesson, M., Nosek, B. A., Wagenmakers, E. J., Berk, R., Bolen, K. A., Brembs, B., Brown, L., Camerer, C., Cesarini, D., Chambers, C. D., Clyde, M., Cook, T. D., De Boeck, P., Dienes, Z., Dreber, A., Easwaran, K., Efferson, C., ... Johnson, V. E. (2018). Redefine statistical significance. *Nature Human Behaviour, 2*(1), 6–10. doi:10.1038/s41562-017-0189-z

Bennett, R. L., Batenhorst, R. L., Bivins, B. A., Bell, R. M., Graves, D. A., Foster, T. S., Wright, B. D., & Griffen, W. O. J. (1982). Patient-controlled analgesia: A new concept of postoperative pain relief. *Annals of Surgery, 195*(6), 700–705. doi:10.1097/00000658-198206000-00004.

Berglas, S., & Jones, E. E. (1978). Drug choice as a self-handicapping strategy in response to noncontingent success. *Journal of Personality and Social Psychology, 36*(4), 405–417. doi:10.1037/0022-3514.36.4.405

Berk, M., & Jacka, F. N. (2019). Diet and depression—From confirmation to implementation. *JAMA, 321*(9), 842–843. doi:10.1001/jama.2019.0273

Berkun, M. M., Bialek, H. M., Kern, R. P., & Yagi, K. (1962). Experimental studies of psychological stress in man. *Psychological Monographs: General and Applied, 76*(15), 1–39. doi:10.1037/h0093835

Berlim, M. T., Mattevi, B. S., Belmonte-de-Abreu, P., & Crow, T. J. (2003). The etiology of schizophrenia and the origin of language. Overview of a theory. *Comprehensive Psychiatry, 44*(1), 7–14. doi:10.1053/comp.2003.50003

Berman, K. F., Torrey, E. F., Daniel, D. G., & Weinberger, D. R. (1992). Regional cerebral blood flow in monozygotic twins discordant and concordant for schizophrenia. *Archives of General Psychiatry, 49*, 927–934. doi:10.1001/archpsyc.1992.01820120015004

Berman, M. G. (2009). In search of decay in verbal short term memory. *Journal of Experimental Psychology:Learning, Memory and Cognition, 35*(2), 317–333. doi:10.1037/a0014873

Bernhardt, P. C., Dabbs, J. M., Jr., Fielden, J. A., & Lutter, C. D. (1998). Testosterone changes during vicarious experiences of winning and losing among fans at sporting events. *Physiology and Behavior, 65*, 59–62. doi:10.1016/S0031-9384(98)00147-4

Bernstein, B. O., Lubinski, D., & Benbow, C. P. (2020). Academic acceleration in gifted youth and fruitless concerns regarding psychological well-being: A 35-year longitudinal study. *Journal of Educational Psychology*. doi:10.1037/edu0000500

Bernstein, D. (2011). *Essentials of psychology* (5 ed.). Belmont, CA: Cengage.

Berntson, G. G., Cacioppo, J. T., & Quigley, K. S. (1991). Autonomic determinism: The modes of autonomic control, the doctrine of autonomic space, and the laws of autonomic constraint. *Psychological Review, 98*, 459–487. doi:10.1037/0033-295X.98.4.459

Berscheid, E., & Peplau, L. A. (1983). The emerging science of relationships. In H. H. Kelley, E. Berscheid, A. Christensen, J. H. Harvey, T. L. Huston, G. Levinger, E. McClintock, L. A. Peplau, & D. R. Peterson (Eds.), *Close relationships* (pp. 1–19). New York: Freeman.

Berscheid, E., Snyder, M., & Omoto, A.M. (1989). The Relationship Closeness Inventory: Assessing the closeness of interpersonal relationships. *Journal of Personality and Social Psychology, 57*, 792–807. doi:10.1037/0022-3514.57.5.792

Bewernick, B. H., Hurlemann, R., Matusch, A., Kayser, S., Grubert, C., Hadrysiewicz, B., Axmacher, N., Lemke, M., Cooper-Mahkorn, D., Cohen, M. X., Brockmann, H., Lenartz, D., Sturm, V., & Schlaepfer, T. E. (2010). Nucleus accumbens deep brain stimulation decreases ratings of depression and anxiety in treatment-resistant depression. *Biological Psychiatry, 67*(2), 110–116. doi:10.1016/j.biopsych.2009.09.013

Bialystok, E., Craik, F. I., & Luk, G. (2012). Bilingualism: Consequences for mind and brain. *Trends in Cognitive Sciences, 16*(4), 240–250. doi:10.1016/j.tics.2012.03.001

Bickman, L. (1974). The social power of a uniform. *Journal of Applied Social Psychology, 4*(1), 47–61. doi:10.1111/j.1559-1816.1974.tb02599.x

Biederman, I. (1987). Recognition-by-components: A theory of human image understanding. *Psychological Review, 94*, 115–147. doi:10.1037/0033-295X.94.2.115

Biederman, J., Rosenbaum, J. F., Hirshfeld, D. R., Faraone, S. V., Bolduc, E. A., Gersten, M., Meminger, S. R., Kagan, J., Snidman, N., & Reznick, J. S. (1990). Psychiatric correlates of behavioral inhibition in young children of parents with and without psychiatric disorders. *Archives of General Psychiatry, 47*(1), 21–26. doi:10.1001/archpsyc.1990.01810130023004

Biezonski, D. K., & Meyer, J. S. (2011). The nature of 3, 4-Methylenedioxymethamphetamine (MDMA)-induced serotonergic dysfunction: Evidence for and against the neurodegeneration hypothesis. *Current Neuropharmacology, 9*(1), 84–90. doi:10.2174/157015911795017146

Biglan, A., Duncan, T. E., Ary, D. V., & Smolkowski, K. (1995). Peer and parental influences on adolescent tobacco use. *Journal of Behavioral Medicine, 18*(4), 315–330. doi:10.1007/bf01857657

Binder, J. R., Desai, R. H., Graves, W. W., & Conant, L. L. (2009). Where is the semantic system? A critical review and meta-analysis of 120 functional neuroimaging studies. *Cerebral Cortex, 19*(12), 2767–2796. doi:10.1093/cercor/bhp055

Birchler, G. R. (1992). Marriage. In V. B. V. Hasselt & M. Hersen (Eds.), *Handbook of social development: A lifespan perspective.* New York: Plenum.

Bisson, J. I., Roberts, N. P., Andrew, M., Cooper, R., & Lewis, C. (2013). Psychological therapies for chronic post-traumatic stress disorder (PTSD) in adults. *Cochrane Database of Systematic Reviews*, (12). doi:10.1002/14651858.CD003388.pub4

Bjornsson, A. S., Didie, E. R., & Phillips, K. A. (2010). Body dysmorphic disorder. *Dialogues in Clinical Neuroscience, 12*(2), 221–232. doi:10.31887/DCNS.2010.12.2/abjornsson

Blagev, D. P., Harris, D., Dunn, A. C., Guidry, D. W., Grissom, C. K., & Lanspa, M. J. (2019). Clinical presentation, treatment, and short-term outcomes of lung injury associated with e-cigarettes or vaping: a prospective observational cohort study. *The Lancet, 394*(10214), 2073–2083. doi:10.1016/S0140-6736(19)32679-0

Blair, R. J., Colledge, E., Murray, L., & Mitchell, D. G. (2001). A selective impairment in the processing of sad and fearful expressions in children with psychopathic tendencies.

Journal of Abnormal Child Psychology, 29, 491–498. doi:10.1023/A:1012225108281

Blais, A.-R., & Weber, E. U. (2006). A domain-specific risk-taking (DOSPERT) scale for adult populations. *Judgment and Decision making, 1*(1), 33–47.

Blake, R., & Sekuler, R. (2006). *Perception, 5th Ed.* New York: McGraw-Hill.

Blakemore, S.-J., & Mills, K. L. (2014). Is adolescence a sensitive period for sociocultural processing? *Annual Review of Psychology, 65*, 187–207. doi:10.1146/annurev-psych-010213-115202

Blakemore, S.-J., & Robbins, T. W. (2012). Decision-making in the adolescent brain. *Nature Neuroscience, 15*, 1184–1191. doi:10.1038/nn.3177

Blanchard, R. (1997). Birth order and sibling sex ratio in homosexual versus heterosexual males and females. *Annual Review of Sex Research, 8*, 27–67. doi:10.1080/10532528.1997.10559918

Blanco, C., Okuda, M., Wright, C., Hasin, D. S., Grant, B. F., Liu, S.-M., & Olfson, M. (2008). Mental health of college students and their non-college-attending peers: Results from the National Epidemiologic Study on Alcohol and Related Conditions. *Archives of General Psychiatry, 65*(12), 1429–1437. doi:10.1001/archpsyc.65.12.1429

Bledowski, C., Kaiser, J., & Rahm, B. (2010). Basic operations in working memory: Contributions from functional imaging studies. *Behavioural Brain Research, 214*(2), 172–179. doi:10.1016/j.bbr.2010.05.041

Bleidorn, W., Arslan, R. C., Denissen, J. J., Rentfrow, P. J., Gebauer, J. E., Potter, J., & Gosling, S. D. (2016). Age and gender differences in self-esteem—A cross-cultural window. *Journal of Personality and Social Psychology, 111*(3), 396–410. doi:10.1037/pspp0000078

Blevins, J. E., Morton, G. J., Williams, D. L., Caldwell, D. W., Bastian, L. S., Wisse, B. E., Schwartz, M. W., & Baskin, D. G. (2009). Forebrain melanocortin signaling enhances the hindbrain satiety response to CCK-8. *American Journal of Physiology-Regulatory, Integrative and Comparative Physiology, 296*(3), R476-R484. doi:10.1152/ajpregu.90544.2008

Bliss, T. V. P., & Lømo, T. (1973). Long-lasting potentiation of synaptic transmission in the dentate gyrus of the anesthetized rabbit following stimulation of the perforant path. *Journal of Physiology, 232*, 331–356. doi:10.1016/0006-8993(88)91499-0

Bloom, P. (2004). Can a dog learn a word? *Science, 304*(5677), 1605–1606. doi:10.1126/science.1099899

Blumenthal, J. A., Babyak, M. A., Moore, K. A., Craighead, W. E., Herman, S., Khatri, P., Waugh, R., Napolitano, M. A., Forman, L. M., Appelbaum, Murali Doraiswamy, P. M., & Krishnan, K. R. (1999). Effects of exercise training on older patients with major depression. *Archives of Internal Medicine, 159*(19), 2349–2356. doi:10.1001/archinte.159.19.2349

Boddy, C. R. (2017). Psychopathic leadership: A case study of a corporate psychopath CEO. *Journal of Business Ethics, 145*(1), 141–156. doi:10.1007/s10551-015-2908-6

Bogaert, A. F., Ashton, M. C., & Lee, K. (2018). Personality and sexual orientation: Extension to asexuality and the HEXACO model. *The Journal of Sex Research, 55*(8), 951–961. doi:10.1080/00224499.2017.1287844

Bogen, J. E. (1995). On the neurophysiology of consciousness: Part II. Constraining the semantic problem. *Consciousness and Cognition, 4*(2), 137–158. doi:10.1006/ccog.1995.1020

Bogen, J. E., Schultz, D. H., & Vogel, P. J. (1988). Completeness of callosotomy shown by magnetic resonance imaging in the long term. *Archives of Neurology, 45*, 1203–1205. doi:10.1001/archneur.1988.00520350041013

Bohart, A., O'Hara, M., & Leitner, L. (1998). Empirically violated treatments: Disenfranchisement of humanistic and other psychotherapies. *Psychotherapy Research, 8*(2), 141–157. doi:10.1093/ptr/8.2.141

Boksem, M. A. S., & Smidts, A. (2015). Brain responses to movie trailers predict individual preferences for movies and their population-wide commercial success. *Journal of Marketing Research, 52*(4), 482–492. doi:10.1509/jmr.13.0572

Bolger, N., & Schilling, E. A. (1991). Personality and the problems of everyday life: The role of neuroticism in exposure and reactivity to daily stressors. *Journal of Personality, 59*, 355–386. doi:10.1111/j.1467-6494.1991.tb00253.x

Bölte, S., Girdler, S., & Marschik, P. B. (2019). The contribution of environmental exposure to the etiology of autism spectrum disorder. *Cellular and Molecular Life Sciences, 76*(7), 1275–1297. doi:10.1007/s00018-018-2988-4

Bolz, L., Heigele, S., & Bischofberger, J. (2015). Running improves pattern separation during novel object recognition. *Brain Plasticity, 1*(1), 129–141. doi:10.3233/BPL-150010

Bomfim, I. L., Lamb, F., Fink, K., Szakács, A., Silveira, A., Franzén, L., Azhary, V., Maeurer, M., Feltelius, N., Darin, N., Hallböök T., Arnheim-Dahlström, L., Kockum, I., & Olsson, T. (2017). The immunogenetics of narcolepsy associated with A(H1N1)pdm09 vaccination (Pandemrix) supports a potent gene–environment interaction. *Genes & Immunity, 18*(2), 75–81. doi:10.1038/gene.2017.1

Bonanno, G. A. (2004). Loss, trauma, and human resilience: Have we underestimated the human capacity to thrive after extremely aversive events? *American Psychologist, 59*(1), 20–28. doi:10.1037/0003-066X.59.1.20

Bond, C. F., & Titus, L. J. (1983). Social facilitation: A meta-analysis of 241 studies. *Psychological Bulletin, 94*, 265–292. doi:10.1037/0033-2909.94.2.265

Boomsma, D. I. (2015). Loneliness across phylogeny and a call for comparative studies and animal models. *Perspectives on Psychological Science, 10*(2), 202–212. doi:10.1177/1745691614564876

Boomsma, D. I., Willemsen, G., Dolan, C. V., Hawkley, L. C., & Cacioppo, J. T. (2005). Genetic and environmental contributions to loneliness in adults: The Netherlands Twin Register Study. *Behavior Genetics, 35*(6), 745–752. doi:10.1007/s10519-005-6040-8

Booth, A., Shelley, G., Mazur, A., Tharp, G., & Kittok, R. (1989). Testosterone, and winning and losing in human competition. *Hormones and Behavior, 23*, 556–571. doi:10.1016/0018-506X(89)90042-1

Borjigin, J., Lee, U., Liu, T., Pal, D., Huff, S., Klarr, D., Sloboda, J., Hernandez, J., Wang, M. M., & Mashour, G. A. (2013). Surge of neurophysiological coherence and connectivity in the dying brain. *Proceedings of the National Academy of Sciences of the United States of America, 110*(35), 14432–14437. doi:10.1073/pnas.1308285110

Bornstein, M. H., Kessen, W., & Weiskopf, S. (1976). Color vision and hue categorization in young human infants. *Journal of Experimental Psychology: Human Perception and Performance, 2*, 115–119. doi:10.1037/0096-1523.2.1.115

Borsini, A., Stangl, D., Jeffries, A. R., Pariante, C. M., & Thuret, S. (2020). The role of omega-3 fatty acids in preventing glucocorticoid-induced reduction in human hippocampal neurogenesis and increase in apoptosis. *Translational Psychiatry, 10*(1), 219. doi:10.1038/s41398-020-00908-0

Borsook, D., Becerra, L., Fishman, S., Edwards, A., Jennings, C. L., Stojanovic, M., Papinicolas, L., Ramachandran, V. S., Gonzalez, R. G., & Breiter, H. (1998). Acute plasticity in the human somatosensory cortex following amputation. *NeuroReport, 9*, 1013–1017. doi:10.1097/00001756-199804200-00011

Bosch, J. A., De Geus, E. J. C., & Kelder, A. (2001). Differential effects of active versus passive coping on secretory immunity. *Psychophysiology, 38*, 836–846. doi:10.1017/S0048577201000488

Boss, L., Kang, D.-H., & Branson, S. (2015). Loneliness and cognitive function in the older adult: A systematic review. *International Psychogeriatrics, 27*(4), 541–553. doi:10.1017/S1041610214002749

Bossard, J. H. S. (1932). Residential propinquity in marriage selection. *American Journal of Sociology, 38*, 219–224. doi:10.1086/216031

Bossini, L., Tavanti, M., Calossi, S., Lombardelli, A., Polizzotto, N. R., Galli, R., Vatti, G., Pieraccini, F., & Castrogiovanni, P. (2008). Magnetic resonance imaging volumes of the hippocampus in drug-naïve patients with post-traumatic stress disorder without comorbidity conditions. *Journal of Psychiatric Research, 42*(9), 752–762. doi:10.1016/j.jpsychires.2007.08.004

Boston Globe. (2019, 2019-09-11). Single drivers are taking over Mass. carpool lanes. https://www.boston.com/cars/commute/2019/09/11/single-drivers-are-taking-over-mass-carpool-lanes

Bouchard, T., Jr. (1994). Genes, environment, and personality. *Science, 264*, 1700–1701. doi:10.1126/science.8209250

Bouchard, T., Jr., Lykken, D. T., McGue, M., Segal, N. L., & Tellegen, A. (1990). Sources of human psychological differences: The Minnesota Study of Twins Reared Apart. *Science, 250*, 223–228. doi:10.1126/science.2218526

Bower, G. H., & Gilligan, S. G. (1979). Remembering information related to one's self. *Journal of Research in Personality, 13*(4), 420–432. doi:10.1016/0092-6566(79)90005-9

Bowlby, J. (1969/1982). *Attachment and loss. Vol 1: Attachment*. New York: Basic Books.

Bowlby, J. (1973/1999a). *Attachment and loss. Vol 2: Separation: Anxiety and anger*. New York: Basic Books.

Bowlby, J. (1973/1999b). *Attachment and loss. Vol 3: Loss: Sadness and depression*. New York: Basic Books.

Boyce, C. J., Wood, A. M., Daly, M., & Sedikides, C. (2015). Personality change following unemployment. *Journal of Applied Psychology, 100*(4), 991–1011. doi:10.1037/a0038647

Boyce, R., Glasgow, S. D., Williams, S., & Adamantidis, A. (2016). Causal evidence for the role of REM sleep theta rhythm in contextual memory consolidation. *Science, 352*(6287), 812–816. doi:10.1126/science.aad5252

Boydell, J., & Murray, R. (2003). Urbanization, migration and risk of schizophrenia. In R. M. Murray, P. B. Jones, E. Susser, J. van Os, & M. Cannon (Eds.), *The epidemiology of schizophrenia* (pp. 49–67). Cambridge, UK: Cambridge University Press.

Bradley, C. (1937). The behavior of children receiving benzedrine. *American Journal of Psychiatry, 94*(3), 577–585. doi:10.1176/ajp.94.3.577

Brannon, S. M., & Gawronski, B. (2017). A second chance for first impressions? Exploring the context-(in) dependent updating of implicit evaluations. *Social Psychological and Personality Science, 8*(3), 275—283. doi:10.1177/1948550616673875.

Bransford, J. D., & Johnson, M. K. (1972). Contextual prerequisites for understanding: Some investigations of comprehension and recall. *Journal of Verbal Learning and Verbal Behavior, 11*, 717–726. doi:10.1016/S0022-5371(72)80006-9

Bratsberg, B., & Rogeberg, O. (2018). Flynn effect and its reversal are both environmentally caused. *Proceedings of the National Academy of Sciences of the United States of America, 115*(26), 6674–6678. doi:10.1073/pnas.1718793115

Bray, R. M., & Noble, A. M. (1978). Authoritarianism and decisions of mock juries: Evidence of jury bias and group polarization. *Journal of Personality and Social Psychology, 36*, 1424–1430. doi:10.1037/0022-3514.36.12.1424

Brazil, I. A., van Dongen, J. D. M., Maes, J. H. R., Mars, R. B., & Baskin-Sommers, A. R. (2018). Classification and treatment of antisocial individuals: From behavior to biocognition. *Neuroscience & Biobehavioral Reviews, 91*, 259–277. doi:10.1016/j.neubiorev.2016.10.010

Breit, S., Kupferberg, A., Rogler, G., & Hasler, G. (2018). Vagus nerve as modulator of the brain–gut axis in psychiatric and inflammatory disorders. *Frontiers in Psychiatry, 9*, 44. doi:10.3389/fpsyt.2018.00044

Breland, K., & Breland, M. (1961). The misbehavior of organisms. *American Psychologist, 16*, 681–684. doi:10.1037/h0040090

Brembs, B. (1996). Chaos, cheating and cooperation: Potential solutions to the Prisoner's Dilemma. *Oikos, 76*, 14–24. doi:10.2307/3545744

Bremner, J. D., Vythilingam, M., Vermetten, E., Nazeer, A., Adil, J., Khan, S., Staib, L. H., & Charney, D. S. (2002). Reduced volume of orbitofrontal cortex in major depression. *Biological Psychiatry, 51*(4), 273–279. doi:10.1016/S0006-3223(01)01336-1

Breslow, R. A., & Smothers, B. A. (2005). Drinking pattern and body mass index in never smokers: National Health Survey, 1997–2001. *American Journal of Epidemiology, 161*(4), 368–376. doi:10.1093/aje/kwi061

Brewer, J. A., Worhunsky, P. D., Gray, J. R., Tang, Y.-Y., Weber, J., & Kober, H. (2011). Meditation experience is associated with differences in default mode network activity and connectivity. *Proceedings of the National Academy of Sciences of the United States of America, 108*(50), 20254–20259.

Brewer, M. B. (2000). Reducing prejudice through cross-categorization: Effects of multiple social identities. In S. Oskamp (Ed.), *"The Claremont Symposium on Applied Social Psychology" Reducing prejudice and discrimination* (p. 165–183). Lawrence Erlbaum Associates Publishers.

Brewer, M. B., & Gardner, W. (1996). Who is this 'We'? Levels of collective identity and self representations. *Journal of Personality and Social Psychology, 71*(1), 83–93. doi:10.1037/0022-3514.71.1.83

Brewer, N., Keast, A., & Rishworth, A. (2002). The confidence-accuracy relationship in eyewitness identification: The effects of reflection and disconfirmation on correlation and calibration. *Journal of Experimental Psychology: Applied, 8*, 46–58. doi:10.1037/1076-898X.8.1.44

Brewer, N., Young, R. L., & Barnett, E. (2017). Measuring theory of mind in adults with autism spectrum disorder. *Journal of Autism and Developmental Disorders, 47*(7), 1927–1941. doi:10.1007/s10803-017-3080-x

Brewin, C. R., Andrews, B., & Valentine, J. D. (2000). Meta-analysis of risk factors for posttraumatic stress disorder in trauma-exposed adults. *Journal of Consulting and Clinical Psychology, 68*, 748–766. doi:10.1037/0022-006X.68.5.748

Bringsjord, S., Licato, J., Govindarajulu, N. S., Ghosh, R., & Sen, A. (2015). Real robots that pass human tests of self-consciousness. In *2015 24th IEEE International Symposium on Robot and Human Interactive Communication (RO-MAN)* (pp. 498-504). IEEE.

Briñol, P., Petty, R. E., & Stavraki, M. (2019). Structure and function of attitudes. In *Oxford Research Encyclopedia of Psychology*. doi:10.1093/acrefore/9780190236557.013.320

Brooks, L., Norman, G., & Allen, S. (1991). Role of specific similarity in a medical diagnostic task. *Journal of Experimental Psychology: General, 120*, 278-287. doi:10.1037/0096-3445.120.3.278

Brosnan, S. F. (2010). Behavioral development: Timing is everything. *Current Biology, 20*(3), R98-R100. doi:10.1016/j.cub.2009.12.009

Brosnan, S. F., & De Waal, F. B. (2003). Monkeys reject unequal pay. *Nature, 425*, 297–299. doi:10.1038/nature01963

Brown, G. W., & Harris, T. O. (1989). Depression.In G. W. Brown & T. O. Harris (Eds.), *Life events and illness* (pp. 49–93). New York: Guilford Press.

Brown, J. D., & Mankowski, T. A. (1993). Self-esteem, mood, and self-evaluation: Changes in mood and the way you see you. *Journal of Personality and Social Psychology, 64*(3), 421–430. doi:10.1037/0022-3514.64.3.421

Brown, J. D., & Smart, S. A. (1991). The self and social conduct: Linking self-representations to prosocial behavior. *Journal of Personality and Social Psychology, 60*(3), 368–375. doi:10.1037/0022-3514.60.3.368

Brown, K. T., Brown, T. N., Jackson, J. S., Sellers, R. M., & Manuel, W. J. (2003). Teammates on and off the field? Contact with black teammates and the racial attitudes of white student athletes. *Journal of Applied Social Psychology, 33*(7), 1379–1403. doi:10.1111/j.1559-1816.2003.tb01954.x

Brown, P., & Elliot, R. (1965). Control of aggression in a nursery school class. *Journal of Experimental Child Psychology, 2*, 103–109. doi:10.1016/0022-0965(65)90035-4

Brown, R. W., & McNeill, D. (1966). The "tip of the tongue" phenomenon. *Journal of Verbal Learning and Verbal Behavior, 5*, 325–337. doi:10.1016/S0022-5371(66)80040-3

Brownstein, M., Madva, A., & Gawronski, B. (2019). What do implicit measures measure? *Wiley Interdisciplinary Reviews: Cognitive Science, 10*(5), e1501. doi:10.1002/wcs.1501

Bruck, M., & Ceci, S. J. (2009). Reliability of child witnesses' reports. In J. L. Skeem, S. O. Lilienfeld, & K. S. Douglas (Eds.), *Psychological science in the courtroom: Consensus and controversy* (pp. 149–171). New York, NY US: Guilford Press.

Bruine de Bruin, W., Parker, A. M., & Fischhoff, B. (2007). Individual differences in adult decision-making competence. *Journal of*

Personality and Social Psychology, 92(5), 938–956. doi:10.1037/0022-3514.92.5.938
Brummelman, E., Thomaes, S., Orobio de Castro, B., Overbeek, G., & Bushman, B. J. (2014). "That's not just beautiful—That's incredibly beautiful!": The adverse impact of inflated praise on children with low self-esteem. *Psychological Science, 25*(3), 728–735. doi:10.1177/0956797613514251
Brummelman, E., Thomaes, S., Nelemans, S. A., Orobio de Castro, B., Overbeek, G., & Bushman, B. J. (2015). Origins of narcissism in children. *Proceedings of the National Academy of Sciences of the United States of America, 112*(12), 3659–3662. doi:10.1073/pnas.1420870112
Brune, M. (2006). The evolutionary psychology of obsessive-compulsive disorder: The role of cognitive metarepresentation. *Perspectives in Biology and Medicine, 49*(3), 317–329. doi:10.1353/pbm.2006.0037
Brunelli, M., Castellucci, V., & Kandel, E. R. (1976). Synaptic facilitation and behavioral sensitization in Aplysia: Possible role of serotonin and cyclic AMP. *Science, 194*(4270), 1178–1181. doi:10.1126/science.186870
Brunner, H., Nelen, M., Breakefield, X., Ropers, H., & van Oost, B. (1993). Abnormal behavior associated with a point mutation in the structural gene for monoamine oxidase A. *Science, 262*(5133), 578–580. doi:10.1126/science.8211186
Bryant, C. M., & Duncan, J. C. (2019). Interracial marriages: Historical and contemporary trends. In Nazarinia R. R. &, Rollins A. (eds) *Biracial families* (pp. 81-104): Cham, Switzerland: Springer. doi:10.1007/978-3-319-96160-6_5
Bryant, F. B., & Veroff, J. (2007). *Savoring: A new model of positive experience.* Mahwah, NJ: Lawrence Erlbaum Associates Publishers.
Brysbaert, M., Stevens, M., Mandera, P., & Keuleers, E. (2016). How many words do we know? Practical estimates of vocabulary size dependent on word definition, the degree of language input and the participant's age. *Frontiers in Psychology, 7*(1116). doi:10.3389/fpsyg.2016.01116
Buchanan, R. W., Breier, A., & Tamminga, C. A. (1995). Patient response and resource management: Another view of clozapine treatment of schizophrenia. *American Journal of Psychiatry, 152*(6), 827–832. doi:10.1176/ajp.152.6.827
Buchanan, T. W., & Preston, S. D. (2014). Stress leads to prosocial action in immediate need situations. *Frontiers in Behavioral Neuroscience, 8*, 5. doi:10.3389/fnbeh.2014.00005
Bulik, C. M., Kleiman, S. C., & Yilmaz, Z. (2016). Genetic epidemiology of eating disorders. *Current Opinion in Psychiatry, 29*(6), 383–388. doi:10.1097/YCO.0000000000000275
Buoli, M., Serati, M., Grassi, S., Pergoli, L., Cantone, L., Altamura, A. C., & Bollati, V. (2018). The role of clock genes in the etiology of major depressive disorder. *Journal of Affective Disorders, 234*, 351–357. doi:10.1016/j.jad.2017.11.015
Burch, M. R., & Bailey, J. S. (1999). *How dogs learn.* Hoboken, N.J.: Howell Book House.
Burger, J. M. (2009). Replicating Milgram: Would people still obey today? *American Psychologist, 64*(1), 1–11. doi:10.1037/a0010932
Burger, J. M., Messian, N., Patel, S., del Prado, A., & Anderson, C. (2004). What a coincidence! The effects of incidental similarity on compliance. *Personality and Social Psychology Bulletin, 30*, 35–43. doi:10.1177/0146167203258838
Burke, S. C., Cremeens, J., Vail-Smith, K., & Woolsey, C. (2010). Drunkorexia: Calorie restriction prior to alcohol consumption among college freshmen. *Journal of Alcohol and Drug Education, 54*(2), 17–34.
Burt, D., & Talati, Z. (2017). The unsolved value of executive coaching: A meta-analysis of outcomes using randomised control trial studies. *International Journal of Evidence Based Coaching and Mentoring, 15*(2), 17.
Burton, L. A., Henninger, D., Hafetz, J., & Cofer, J. (2009). Aggression, gender-typical childhood play, and a prenatal hormonal index. . *Social Behavior & Personality: An International Journal, 37*(1), 105–115. doi:10.2224/sbp.2009.37.1.105
Buscemi, N., Vandermeer, B., Friesen, C., Bialy, L., Tubman, M., Ospina, M., Klassen, T. P., & Witmans, M. (2007). The efficacy and safety of drug treatments for chronic insomnia in adults: A meta-analysis of RCTs. *Journal of General Internal Medicine, 22*(9), 1335–1350. doi:10.1007/s11606-007-0251-z
Bushdid, C., Magnasco, M. O., Vosshall, L. B., & Keller, A. (2014). Humans can discriminate more than 1 trillion olfactory stimuli. *Science, 343*(6177), 1370–1372. doi:10.1126/science.1249168
Bushman, B. J. (2002). Does venting anger feed or extinguish the flame? Catharsis, rumination, distraction, anger, and aggressive responding. *Personality and Social Psychology Bulletin, 28*, 724–731. doi:10.1177/0146167202289002
Bushnell, I. W. R. (2001). Mother's face recognition in newborn infants: Learning and memory. *Infant and Child Development, 10*, 67–74. doi:10.1002/icd.248
Buss, D. M. (1985). Human mate selection. *American Scientist, 73*, 47–51.
Buss, D. M. (1996). Evolutionary biology and personality psychology: Toward a conception of human nature and individual differences. In G.-H. Jennings (Ed.), *Passages beyond the gate: A Jungian approach to understanding the nature of American psychology at the dawn of the new millennium* (pp. 108–125). Needham Heights, MA: Simon & Schuster Custom Publishing.
Buss, D. M. (1999). Human nature and individual differences: The evolution of human personality. In L. A. Pervin & O. P. John (Eds.), *Handbook of personality: Theory and research* (2nd ed., pp. 31–56). New York: Guilford Press.
Buss, D. M., & Schmitt, D. P. (1993). Sexual Strategies Theory: An evolutionary perspective on human mating. *Psychological Review, 100*, 204–232. doi:10.1037/0033-295X.100.2.204
Buss, D. M., Larsen, R. J., & Westen, D. (1992). Sex differences in jealousy: Evolution, physiology, and psychology. *Psychological Science, 3*, 251–255. doi:10.1111/j.1467-9280.1992.tb00038.x
Bustillo, J. R., Lauriello, J., Horan, W. P., & Keith, S. J. (2001). The psychosocial treatment of schizophrenia: An update. *The American Journal of Psychiatry, 158*(2), 163–175. doi:10.1176/appi.ajp.158.2.163
Bynum, W. F., & Porter, R. (Eds.). (2005). *Oxford dictionary of scientific quotations.* Oxford, UK: Oxford University Press.
Byrne, D. (1961). Interpersonal attraction and attitude similarity. *Journal of Abnormal and Social Psychology, 62*, 713–715. doi:10.1037/h0044721
Cáceres, M., Lachuer, J., Zapala, M. A., Redmond, J. C., Kudo, L., Geschwind, D. H., Lockhart, D. J., Preuss, T. M., & Barlow, C. (2003). Elevated gene expression levels distinguish human from non-human primate brains. *Proceedings of the National Academy of Sciences of the United States of America, 100*(22), 13030–13035. doi:10.1073/pnas.2135499100
Cacioppo, J. T., Adler, A. B., Lester, P. B., McGurk, D., Thomas, J. L., Chen, H.-Y., & Cacioppo, S. (2015). Building social resilience in soldiers: A double dissociative randomized controlled study. *Journal of Personality and Social Psychology, 109*(1), 90–105. 10.1037/pspi0000022
Cacioppo, J. T., & Berntson, G. G. (2001). The affect system and racial prejudice. In J. Bargh & D. K. Apsley (Eds.), *Unraveling the complexities of social life: A festschrift in honor of Robert B. Zajonc* (pp. 95–110). Washington, D.C.: American Psychological Association.
Cacioppo, J. T., & Berntson, G. G. (2011). The brain, homeostasis, and health: Balancing demands of the internal and external milieu. In H. S. Friedman (Ed.), *The Oxford handbook of health psychology*. (pp. 121–137). New York: Oxford University Press.
Cacioppo, J. T., Berntson, G. G., Adolphs, R., Carter, C. S., Davidson, R. J., McClintock, M. K., & et al.. (2002). *Foundations in social neuroscience.* Cambridge, MA: MIT Press.
Cacioppo, J. T., Berntson, G. G., & Klein, D. J. (1992). What is an emotion? The role of somatovisceral afference, with special emphasis on somatovisceral "illusions." *Review of Personality and Social Psychology, 14*, 63–98.
Cacioppo, J. T., Berntson, G. G., Larsen, J. T., Poehlmann, K. M., & Ito, T. A. (2000). The psychophysiology of emotion. In M. Lewis

& J. M. Haviland-Jones (Eds.), *Handbook of emotions* (Vol. 2, pp. 173–191). New York: Guilford Press.
Cacioppo, J. T., Berntson, G. G., Norris, C. J., & Gollan, J. K. (2012). The evaluative space model. In *Handbook of theories of social psychology* (Vol. 1, pp. 50–72). Thousand Oaks, CA: Sage.
Cacioppo, J. T., & Cacioppo, S. (2014). Social relationships and health: The toxic effects of perceived social isolation. *Social and Personality Psychology Compass, 8*(2), 58–72. doi:10.1111/spc3.12087
Cacioppo, J. T., & Cacioppo, S. (2018a). Loneliness in the modern age: An Evolutionary Theory of Loneliness (ETL). In J. M. Olson (Ed.), *Advances in Experimental Social Psychology* (Vol. 58, pp. 127–197). New York, NY: Academic Press.
Cacioppo, J. T., & Cacioppo, S. (2018b). The growing problem of loneliness. *The Lancet, 391*(10119), 426. doi:10.1016/S0140-6736(18)30142-9
Cacioppo, J. T., Cacioppo, S., & Boomsma, D. (2014). Evolutionary mechanisms for loneliness. *Cognition and Emotion, 28*(1), 3–21. doi:10.1080/02699931.2013.837379
Cacioppo, J. T., Cacioppo, S., Capitanio, J. P., & Cole, W. W. (2015). The neuroendocrinology of social isolation. *Annual Review of Psychology, 66*, 733–767. doi:10/1146/annurev-psych-010814-015240
Cacioppo, J. T., Cacioppo, S., Cole, S. W., Capitanio, J. P., Goossens, L., & Boomsma, D. I. (2015). Loneliness across phylogeny and a call for comparative studies and animal models. *Perspectives on Psychological Science, 10*(2), 202–212. doi:10.1177/1745691614564876
Cacioppo, J. T., Cacioppo, S., Gonzaga, G. C., Ogburn, E. L., & VanderWeele, T. J. (2013). Marital satisfaction and break-ups differ across on-line and off-line meeting venues. *Proceedings of the National Academy of Sciences of the United States of America, 110*(25), 10135–10140. doi:10.1073/pnas.1222447110
Cacioppo, J. T., Chen, H. Y., & Cacioppo, S. (2017). Reciprocal influences between loneliness and self-centeredness: A cross-lagged panel analysis in a population-based sample of African American, Hispanic, and Caucasian adults. *Personality and Social Psychology Bulletin, 43*(8), 1125–1135. doi:10.1177/0146167217705120
Cacioppo, J. T., & Decety, J. (2011a). Social neuroscience: Challenges and opportunities in the study of complex behavior. *Annals of the New York Academy of Sciences, 1224*(1), 162–173. doi:10.1111/j.1749-6632.2010.05858.x
Cacioppo, J. T., & Decety, J. (2011b). An introduction to social neuroscience. In J. Decety & J. T. Cacioppo (Eds.), *The Oxford handbook of social neuroscience* (pp. 3–8). New York, NY: Oxford University Press.
Cacioppo, J. T., & Gardner, W. L. (1999). Emotion. *Annual Review of Psychology, 50*, 191–214. doi:10.1146/annurev.psych.50.1.191
Cacioppo, J. T., Hawkley, L. C., Berntson, G. G., Ernst, J. M., Gibbs, A. C., Stickgold, R., & Hobson, J. A. (2002). Do lonely days invade the nights? Potential social modulation of sleep efficiency. *Psychological Science, 13*, 384–387. doi:10.1111/1467-9280.00469
Cacioppo, J. T., Hawkley, L. C., Ernst, J. M., Burleson, M., Berntson, G. G., Nouriani, B., & Spiegel, D. (2006). Loneliness within a nomological net: An evolutionary perspective. *Journal of Research in Personality, 40*, 1054–1085. doi:10.1016/j.jrp.2005.11.007
Cacioppo, J. T., Hawkley, L. C., Kalil, A., Hughes, M. E., Waite, L., & Thisted, R. A. (2008). Happiness and the invisible threads of social connection: The Chicago Health, Aging, and Social Relations Study. In M. Eid & R. Larsen (Eds.), *The science of well-being* (pp. 195–219). New York: Guilford.
Cacioppo, J. T., Hawkley, L. C., & Thisted, R. A. (2010). Perceived social isolation makes me sad: 5-year cross-lagged analyses of loneliness and depressive symptomatology in the Chicago Health, Aging, and Social Relations Study. *Psychology and Aging, 25*(2), 453–463. doi:10.1037/a0017216
Cacioppo, J. T., Marshall-Goodell, B. S., Tassinary, L. G., & Petty, R. E. (1992). Rudimentary determinants of attitudes: Classical conditioning is more effective when prior knowledge about the attitude stimulus is low than high. *Journal of Experimental Social Psychology, 28*, 207–233. doi:10.1016/0022-1031(92)90053-M
Cacioppo, J. T., Norris, C. J., Decety, J., Monteleone, G., & Nusbaum, H. (2009). In the eye of the beholder: Individual differences in perceived social isolation predict regional brain activation to social stimuli. *Journal of Cognitive Neuroscience, 21*(1), 83–92. doi:10.1162/jocn.2009.21007
Cacioppo, J. T., & Patrick, W. (2008). *Loneliness: Human nature and the need for social connectedness*. New York: Norton.
Cacioppo, J. T., & Petty, R. E. (1981). Electromyograms as measures of extent and affectivity of information processing. *American Psychologist, 36*, 441–456. doi:10.1037/0003-066X.36.5.441
Cacioppo, J. T., Petty, R.E., Feinstein, J.A., & Jarvis, W.B.G. (1996). Dispositional differences in cognitive motivation: The life and times of individuals varying in need for cognition. *Psychological Bulletin, 119*, 197–253. doi:10.1037/0033-2909.119.2.1
Cacioppo, J. T., Petty, R.E., & Kao, C.F. (1984). The efficient assessment of need for cognition. *Journal of Personality Assessment, 48*, 306–307. doi:10.1037/0003-066X.36.5.441
Cacioppo, J. T., Semin, G. R., & Berntson, G. G. (2004). Realism, instrumentalism, and scientific symbiosis: Psychological theory as a search for truth and the discovery of solutions. *American Psychologist, 59*(4), 214–223. doi:10.1037/0003-066X.59.4.214
Cacioppo, S. (2016). Neural markers of interpersonal attraction: A possible new direction for couples therapy. *Emotion Researcher, ISRE's Sourcebook for Research on Emotion and Affect.* http://emotionresearcher.com/neural-markers-of-interpersonal-attraction-a-possible-new-direction-for-couples-therapy/
Cacioppo, S., Bangee, M., Balogh, S., Cardenas-Iniguez, C., Qualter, P., & Cacioppo, J. T. (2016). Loneliness and implicit attention to social threat: A high-performance electrical neuroimaging study. *Cognitive Neuroscience, 7*(1-4), 138–159. doi:10.1080/17588928.2015.1070136
Cacioppo, S., Bianchi-Demicheli, F., Hatfield, E., & Rapson, R. L. (2012). Social neuroscience of love. *Clinical Neuropsychiatry: Journal of Treatment Evaluation 9*, 3–13.
Cacioppo, S., & Cacioppo, J. T. (2013). Lust for life. *Scientific American Mind, 24*(5), 56–60.
Cacioppo, S., & Cacioppo, J. T. (2020). *Introduction to social neuroscience.* Princeton, NJ: Princeton University Press.
Cacioppo, S., Couto, B., Bolmont, M., Sedeno, L., Frum, C., Lewis, J. W., Manes, F., Ibanez, A., & Cacioppo, J. T. (2013). Selective decision-making deficit in love following damage to the anterior insula. *Current Trends in Neurology, 7*, 15–19.
Cai, X. J., Widdowson, P. S., Harrold, J., Wilson, S., Buckingham, R. E., Arch, J., Tadayyon, M., Clapham, J. C., Wilding, J., & Williams, G. (1999). Hypothalamic orexin expression: modulation by blood glucose and feeding. *Diabetes, 48*(11), 2132–2137. doi:10.2337/diabetes.48.11.2132
Cain, W. S., & Gent, J. F. (1991). Olfactory sensitivity: Reliability, generality, and association with aging. *Journal of Experimental Psychology: Human Perception and Performance, 17*, 382–391. doi:10.1037/0096-1523.17.2.382
Calcagni, E., & Elenkov, I. (2006). Stress system activity, innate and T helper cytokines, and susceptibility to immune-related diseases. *Annals of the New York Academy of Sciences, 1069*, 62–76. doi:10.1196/annals.1351.006
Caldwell, D. F., & Caldwell, M. C. (1976). Cetaceans. In T. A. Sebeok (Ed.), *How animals communicate* (pp. 794–808). Bloomington, IN: Indiana University.
Calkins, M. W. (1906). A reconciliation between structural and functional psychology, *Psychological Review*, 13, 61–81. doi:10.1037/h0071994
Calvin, W. H. (2004). *A brief history of the mind: From apes to intellect and beyond.* Oxford, UK: Oxford University Press.
Camelot Group. (2004). *Living the dream: Jackpot winners reveal their millionaire lifestyles.* http://www.camelotgroup.co.uk/Winnerfacts.pdf
Canary, D. J., Stafford, L., Hause, K. S., & Wallace, L. A. (1993). An inductive analysis of relational maintenance strategies: Comparisons among lovers, relatives, friends, and others. *Communication*

Research Reports, 10(1), 5–14. doi:10.1080/08824099309359913
Cannon, W. (1927). The James-Lange theory of emotions: A critical examination and an alternative theory. *American Journal of Psychology, 39*, 106–124. doi:10.2307/1415404
Cannon, W. (1932). *The wisdom of the body*. New York: W.W. Norton.
Cannon, W. B. (1929). *Bodily changes in pain, hunger, fear and rage* (2nd ed.). New York: Harper & Row.
Cannon, W., & Washburn, A. L. (1912). An explanation of hunger. *American Journal of Physiology, 29*, 441–454. doi:10.1152/ajplegacy.1912.29.5.441
Cantalupo, C., & Hopkins, W. D. (2001). Asymmetric Broca's area in great apes. *Nature, 414*(6863), 505–505. doi:10.1038/35107134
Capela, J. P., Fernandes, E., Remião, F., Bastos, M. L., Meisel, A., & Carvalho, F. (2007). Ecstasy induces apoptosis via 5-HT(2A)-receptor stimulation in cortical neurons. *Neurotoxicology, 28*(4), 868–875. doi:10.1016/j.neuro.2007.04.005
Cappelletti, M., & Wallen, K. (2016). Increasing women's sexual desire: The comparative effectiveness of estrogens and androgens. *Hormones and Behavior, 78*, 178–193. doi:10.1016/j.yhbeh.2015.11.003
Capshew, J. H. (1993). Engineering behavior: World War II, Project Pigeon, and the conditioning of B.F. Skinner. *Technology & Culture, 34*, 835–857. doi:10.2307/3106417
Cardin, V., Orfanidou, E., Kästner, L., Rönnberg, J., Woll, B., Capek, C. M., & Rudner, M. (2016). Monitoring different phonological parameters of sign language engages the same cortical language network but distinctive perceptual ones. *Journal of Cognitive Neuroscience, 28*(1), 20–40. doi:10.1162/jocn_a_00872 %M 26351993
Carew, T. J., & Kandel, E. R. (1973). Acquisition and retention of long-term habituation in *Aplysia*: Correlation of behavioral and cellular processes. *Science, 182*(4117), 1158–1160. doi:10.1126/science.182.4117.1158
Carhart-Harris, R. L., Muthukumaraswamy, S., Roseman, L., Kaelen, M., Droog, W., Murphy, K., Tagliazucchi, E., Schenberg, E. E., Nest, T., Orban, C., Leech, R., Williams, L. T., Williams, T. M., Bolstridge, M., Sessa, B., McGonigle, J., Sereno, M. I., Nichols, D., Hellyer, P. J., . . . Nutt, D. J. (2016). Neural correlates of the LSD experience revealed by multimodal neuroimaging. *Proceedings of the National Academy of Sciences of the United States of America, 113*(17), 4853–4858. doi:10.1073/pnas.1518377113
Carlsmith, J. M., & Anderson, C. A. (1979). Ambient temperature and the occurrence of collective violence: A new analysis. *Journal of Personality and Social Psychology, 37*(3), 337–344. doi:10.1037/0022-3514.37.3.337
Carney, D. R., Cuddy, A. J. C., & Yap, A. J. (2010). Power posing: Brief nonverbal displays affect neuroendocrine levels and risk tolerance. *Psychological Science, 21*(10), 1363–1368. doi:10.1177/0956797610383437
Carskadon, M. A., Wolfson, A. R., Acebo, C., Tzischinsky, O., & Seifer, R. (1998). Adolescent sleep patterns, circadian timing, and sleepiness at a transition to early school days. *Sleep, 21*, 871–881. doi:10.1093/sleep/21.8.871
Carstensen, L. L., Fung, H. H., & Charles, S. T. (2003). Socioemotional selectivity theory and the regulation of emotion in the second half of life. *Motivation and Emotion, 27*(2), 103–123. doi:10.1023/a:1024569803230
Carstensen, L. L., Turan, B., Scheibe, S., Ram, N., Ersner-Hershfield, H., Samanez-Larkin, G. R., Brooks, K. P, & Nesselroade, J. R. (2010). Emotional experience improves with age: Evidence based on over 10 years of experience sampling. *Psychology and Aging, 26*(1), 21–33. doi:10.1037/a0021285
Caruso, C. C. (2014). Negative impacts of shiftwork and long work hours. *Rehabilitation Nursing, 39*(1), 16–25. doi:10.1002/rnj.107
Carvalho, C., Caetano, J. M., Cunha, L., Rebouta, P., Kaptchuk, T. J., & Kirsch, I. (2016). Open-label placebo treatment in chronic low back pain: A randomized controlled trial. *Pain, 157*(12), 2766–2772. doi:10.1097/j.pain.0000000000000700
Carver, C. S., & Scheier, M. F. (2000). Origins and functions of positive and negative affect: A control-process view. In E. T. Higgins & A. W. Kruglanski (Eds.), *Motivational science: Social and personality perspectives* (pp. 256–272). New York: Psychology Press.
Carver, C. S., Scheier, M. F., & Segerstrom, S. C. (2010). Optimism. *Clinical Psychology Review, 30*(7), 879–889. doi:10.1016/j.cpr.2010.01.006
Casanova, M. F., Switala, A. E., Trippe, J., & Fitzgerald, M. (2007). Comparative minicolumnar morphometry of three distinguished scientists. *Autism, 11*(6), 557–569. doi:10.1177/1362361307083261
Cascio, C. J., Moore, D., & McGlone, F. (2019). Social touch and human development. *Developmental Cognitive Neuroscience, 35*, 5–11. doi:10.1016/j.dcn.2018.04.009
Caspi, A., McClay, J., Moffitt, T. E., Mill, J., Martin, J., Craig, I. W., . . . Poulton, R. (2002). Role of genotype in the cycle of violence in maltreated children. *Science, 297*(5582), 851–854. doi:10.1126/science.1072290
Caterina, M. J., Leffler, A., Malmberg, A. B., Martin, W. J., Trafton, J., Petersen-Zeitz, K. R., Koltzenburg, M., Basbaum, A. I., & Julius, D. (2000). Impaired nociception and pain sensation in mice lacking the capsaicin receptor. *Science, 220*, 306–313. doi:10.1126/science.288.5464.306
Caterina, M. J., Schumacher, M. A., Tominaga, M., Rosen, T. A., Levine, J. D., & Julius, D. (1997). The capsaicin receptor: A heat-activated ion channel in the pain pathway. *Nature, 389*, 816–824. doi:10.1038/39807
Cattell, R. B. (1946/1969). *Description and measurement of personality*. Yonkers, NY: World Book Company.
Cattell, R. B. (1963). Theory of fluid and crystallized intelligence: A critical experiment. *Journal of Educational Psychology, 54*(1), 1–22. doi:10.1037/h0046743
Centers for Disease Control and Prevention (CDC; 2017). *Life expectancy*. https://www.cdc.gov/nchs/fastats/life-expectancy.htm
Centers for Disease Control & Prevention. (2019) *Understanding the epidemic*. https://www.cdc.gov/drugoverdose/epidemic/index.html
Centers for Disease Control & Prevention (CDC; 2019). *Drug overdose deaths*. https://www.cdc.gov/drugoverdose/data/statedeaths.html
Centers for Disease Control and Prevention (CDC; 2019). *Current cigarette smoking among adults in the United States*. https://www.cdc.gov/tobacco/data_statistics/fact_sheets/adult_data/cig_smoking/index.htm
Centers for Disease Control and Prevention (CDC; 2020). *Adult obesity facts*. https://www.cdc.gov/obesity/data/adult.html
Centers for Disease Control and Prevention (CDC; 2020a). *About e-cigarettes*. https://www.cdc.gov/tobacco/basic_information/e-cigarettes/about-e-cigarettes.html
Centers for Disease Control and Prevention (CDC; 2020b). *Health effects of secondhand smoke*. https://www.cdc.gov/tobacco/data_statistics/fact_sheets/secondhand_smoke/health_effects/index.htm
Centers for Disease Control and Prevention (CDC; 2020c). *Smoking & tobacco use: Fast facts*. https://www.cdc.gov/tobacco/data_statistics/fact_sheets/fast_facts/index.htm#beginning
Centers for Disease Control and Prevention (CDC; 2020). *Research on medicines and pregnancy*. https://www.cdc.gov/pregnancy/meds/treatingfortwo/research.html
Cerella, J., & Hale, S. (1994). The rise and fall in information-processing rates over the life span. *Acta Psychologica, 86*, 109–197. doi:10.1016/0001-6918(94)90002-7
Chagnon, N. A. (1988). Life histories, blood revenge, and warfare in a tribal population. *Science, 239*, 985–992. doi:10.1126/science.239.4843.985
Champagne, F., Francis, D. D., Mar, A., & Meaney, M. J. (2003). Naturally-occurring variations in maternal care in the rat as a mediating influence for the effects of environment on the development of individual differences in stress reactivity. *Physiology & Behavior, 79*, 359–371. doi:10.1016/S0031-9384(03)00149-5
Chang, E. C. (1996). Cultural differences in optimism, pessimism, and coping: Predictors of subsequent adjustment in Asian American and Caucasian American college students. *Journal of Counseling Psychology, 43*(1), 113–123. doi:10.1037/0022-0167.43.1.113

Chang, E. C., Elizabeth, A. Y., Kahle, E. R., Jeglic, E. L., & Hirsch, J. K. (2013). Is doubling up on positive future cognitions associated with lower suicidal risk in Latinos?: A look at hope and positive problem orientation. *Cognitive Therapy and Research, 37*(6), 1285–1293. doi:10.1007/s10608-013-9572-x

Chang, Y. S., Wu, Y. H., Hsu, C. Y., Tang, S. H., Yang, L. L., & Su, S. F. (2011). Impairment of perceptual and motor abilities at the end of a night shift is greater in nurses working fast rotating shifts. *Sleep Medicine, 12*(9), 866–869. doi:https://doi.org/10.1016/j.sleep.2011.03.018

Chapman, B., Fiscella, K., Duberstein, P., Kawachi, I., & Muennig, P. (2014). Measurement confounding affects the extent to which verbal IQ explains social gradients in mortality. *Journal of Epidemiology and Community Health, 68*(8), 728–733. doi:10.1136/jech-2013-203741

Chapman, S., & MacKenzie, R. (2010). The global research neglect of unassisted smoking cessation: Causes and consequences. *PLoS Medicine, 7*(2), e1000216. doi:10.1371/journal.pmed.1000216

Chase, W. G., & Simon, H. A. (1973). Perception in chess. *Cognitive Psychology, 4*(1), 55–81. doi:10.1016/0010-0285(73)90004-2

Chatrian, G.-E. (1990). Coma, other states of altered responsiveness, and brain death. In D. D. Daly, & T. A. Pedley (Eds.), *Current practice of clinical electroencephalography* (pp. 425–487). New York: Raven Press.

Chaudhari, N., Landlin, A. M., & Roper, S. D. (2000). A metabotropic glutamate receptor variant functions as a taste receptor. *Nature Neuroscience, 3*, 113–119. doi:10.1038/72053

Chaudhri, N., Sahuque, L. L., & Janak, P. H. (2008). Context-induced relapse of conditioned behavioral responding to ethanol cues in rats. *Biological Psychiatry, 64*(3), 203–210. doi:10.1038/72053

Chawanpaiboon, S., Vogel, J. P., Moller, A.-B., Lumbiganon, P., Petzold, M., Hogan, D., . . . Gülmezoglu, A. M. (2019). Global, regional, and national estimates of levels of preterm birth in 2014: A systematic review and modelling analysis. *The Lancet Global Health, 7*(1), e37–e46. doi:10.1016/S2214-109X(18)30451-0

Chein, J., Albert, D., O'Brien, L., Uckert, K., & Steinberg, L. (2011). Peers increase adolescent risk taking by enhancing activity in the brain's reward circuitry. *Developmental Science, 14*(2), F1–F10. doi:10.1111/j.1467-7687.2010.01035.x

Chemtob, C. M., Nomura, Y., Rajendran, K., Yehuda, R., Schwartz, D., & Abramovitz, R. (2010). Impact of maternal posttraumatic stress sisorder and depression following exposure to the September 11 attacks on preschool children's behavior. *Child Development, 81*(4), 1129–1141. doi:10.1111/j.1467-8624.2010.01458.x

Chen, C., Nakagawa, S., An, Y., Ito, K., Kitaichi, Y., & Kusumi, I. (2017). The exercise-glucocorticoid paradox: How exercise is beneficial to cognition, mood, and the brain while increasing glucocorticoid levels. *Frontiers in Neuroendocrinology, 44*, 83–102. doi:https://doi.org/10.1016/j.yfrne.2016.12.001

Chen, S., & Bonanno, G. A. (2020). Psychologicaladjustment during the global outbreak of COVID-19: A resilience perspective. *Psychological Trauma: Theory, Research, Practice, and Policy, 12*(S1), S51–S54. doi:10.1037/tra0000685

Chen, S., Boucher, H. C., & Tapias, M. P. (2006). The relational self revealed: Integrative conceptualization and implications for interpersonal life. *Psychological Bulletin, 132*(2), 151–179. doi:10.1037/0033-2909.132.2.151

Chen, S., Fragoza, R., Klei, L., Liu, Y., Wang, J., Roeder, K., . . . Yu, H. (2018). An interactome perturbation framework prioritizes damaging missense mutations for developmental disorders. *Nature Genetics, 50*(7), 1032–1040. doi:10.1038/s41588-018-0130-z

Cherkas, L., Hochberg, F., MacGregor, A. J., Snieder, H., & Spector, T. D. (2000). Happy families: A twin study of humour. *Twin Research, 3*, 17–22. doi:10.1375/twin.3.1.17

Cherkassky, V. L., Kana, R. K., Keller, T. A., & Just, M. A. (2006). Functional connectivity in a baseline resting-state network in autism. *NeuroReport, 17*(16), 1687–1690. doi:10.1097/01.wnr.0000239956.45448.4c

Chertkow, H., Whitehead, V., Phillips, N., Wolfson, C., Atherton, J., & Bergman, H. (2010). Multilingualism (but not always bilingualism) delays the onset of Alzheimer disease: Evidence from a bilingual community. *Alzheimer Disease & Associated Disorders, 24*(2), 118–125. doi:10.1097/WAD.0b013e3181ca1221

Chetty, R., Stepner, M., Abraham, S., Lin, S., Scuderi, B., Turner, N., Bergeron, A., & Cutler, D. (2016). The association between income and life expectancy in the United States, 2001–2014. *JAMA, 315*(16), 1750–1766. doi:10.1001/jama.2016.4226

Chicago Social Brain Network. (2011). *Invisible forces and unseen powers: Gravity, gods, and minds.* Saddle River, NJ: Pearson.

Child, I. L. (1973). *Humanistic psychology and the research tradition: Their several virtues.* Oxford England: John Wiley & Sons.

Chin, B., Murphy, M. L., Janicki-Deverts, D., & Cohen, S. (2017). Marital status as a predictor of diurnal salivary cortisol levels and slopes in a community sample of healthy adults. *Psychoneuroendocrinology, 78*, 68–75. doi:10.1016/j.psyneuen.2017.01.016

Chiu, L.-H. (1972). A cross-cultural comparison of cognitive styles in Chinese and American children. *International Journal of Psychology, 7*(4), 235–242. doi:10.1080/00207597208246604

Cho, K., Ennaceur, A., Cole, J. C., & Suh, C. K. (2000). Chronic jet lag produces cognitive deficits. *Journal of Neuroscience, 20*(6), 1–5. doi:10.1523/JNEUROSCI.20-06-j0005.2000

Choi, I., Nisbett, R. E., & Norenzayan, A. (1999). Causal attribution across cultures: Variation and universality. *Psychological Bulletin, 125*(1), 47–63. doi:10.1037/0033-2909.125.1.47

Choi, J., Cutler, A., & Broersma, M. (2017). Early development of abstract language knowledge: Evidence from perception–production transfer of birth-language memory. *Royal Society Open Science, 4*(1), 160660. doi:10.1098/rsos.160660

Chomsky, N. (1957). *Syntactic structures.* The Hague, Netherlands: Mouton.

Chopik, W. J., & Grimm, K. J. (2019). Longitudinal changes and historic differences in narcissism from adolescence to older adulthood. *Psychology and Aging, 34*(8), 1109—1123. doi:10.1037/pag0000379

Chrea, C., Valentin, D., Sulmont-Rosse, C., Mai, H. L., Nguyen, D. H., & Abdi, H. (2004). Culture and odor categorization: Agreement between cultures depends upon the odors. *Food Quality and Preference, 15*, 669–679. doi:10.1016/j.foodqual.2003.10.005

Christakis, N. A., & Fowler, J. H. (2014). Friendship and natural selection. *Proceedings of the National Academy of Sciences of the United States of America, 111*(Supplement 3), 10796–10801. doi:10.1056/NEJMsa066082

Christakis, N., & Fowler, J. (2007). The spread of obesity in a large social network over 32 years. *New England Journal of Medicine, 357*, 370–379. doi:10.1056/NEJMsa066082

Christensen, A. C. (2000). Cats as an aid to teaching genetics. *Genetics, 155*(3), 999–1004.

Christoforou, C., Papadopoulos, T. C., Constantinidou, F., & Theodorou, M. (2017). Your brain on the movies: A computational approach for predicting box-office performance from viewer's brain responses to movie trailers. *Frontiers in Neuroinformatics, 11*(72). doi:10.3389/fninf.2017.00072

Chua, H. F., Ho, S. S., Jasinska, A. J., Polk, T. A., Welsh, R. C., Liberzon, I., & Strecher, V. J. (2011). Self-related neural response to tailored smoking-cessation messages predicts quitting. *Nature Neuroscience, 14*(4), 426–427. doi:10.1038/nn.2761

Cialdini, R. B. (2001). *Influence: Science and practice* (4th ed.). Boston: Allyn & Bacon.

Cialdini, R. B., Borden, R. J., Thorne, A., Walker, M. R., Freeman, S., & Sloan, L. R. (1976). Basking in reflected glory: Three (football) field studies. *Journal of Personality and Social Psychology, 34*(3), 366–375. doi:10.1037/0022-3514.34.3.366

Cialdini, R. B., Cacioppo, J., Bassett, R., & Miller, J. (1978). Low-ball procedure for producing compliance: Commitment then cost. *Journal of Personality and Social Psychology, 36*, 463–476. doi:10.1037/0022-3514.36.5.463

Cialdini, R. B., & Goldstein, N. J. (2004). Social influence: Compliance and conformity. *Annual Review of Psychology, 55*, 591–621. doi:10.1146/annurev.psych.55.090902.142015

Cialdini, R. B., Kenrick, D. T., & Baumann, D. J. (1981). Effects of mood on prosocial behavior in children and adults. In N. Eisenberg (Ed.), *The development of prosocial behavior* (pp. 339–359). New York: Academic Press.

Cialdini, R. B., Vincent, J., Lewis, S., Catalan, J., Wheeler, D., & Darby, B. L. (1975). Reciprocal concessions procedure for inducing compliance: The door-in-the-face technique. *Journal of Personality and Social Psychology, 31*, 206–215. doi:10.1037/h0076284

Cipolli, C., Ferrara, M., De Gennaro, L., & Plazzi, G. (2016). Beyond the neuropsychology of dreaming: Insights into the neural basis of dreaming with new techniques of sleep recording and analysis. *Sleep Medicine Reviews, 35*, 8—20. doi:10.1016/j.smrv.2016.07.005.

Cipolotti, L., Husain, M., Crinion, J., Bird, C. M., Khan, S. S., Losseff, N., Howard, R. S., & Leff, A. P. (2008). The role of the thalamus in amnesia: A tractography, high-resolution MRI and neuropsychological study. *Neuropsychologia, 46*(11), 2745–2758. doi:10.1016/j.neuropsychologia.2008.05.009

Cipriani, A., Furukawa, T. A., Salanti, G., Chaimani, A., Atkinson, L. Z., Ogawa, Y., Leucht, S., Ruhe, H. G., Turner, E. H., Higgins, J. P. T., Egger, M., Takeshima, N., Hayasaka, Y., Imai, H., Shinohara, K., Tajika, A., Ionnidis, J. P. A., & Geddes, J. R. (2018). Comparative efficacy and acceptability of 21 antidepressant drugs for the acute treatment of adults with major depressive disorder: A systematic review and network meta-analysis. *The Lancet, 391*(10128), 1357–1366. doi:10.1016/S0140-6736(17)32802-7

Clark, D. M. (1988). A cognitive model of panic attacks. In S. Rachman & D. Maser (Eds.), *Panic: Psychological perspectives* (pp. 71–89): Hillsdale, NJ: Lawrence Erlbaum Associates, Inc.

Clarke, A., & Butler, P. E. (2009). The psychological management of facial transplantation. *Expert Review of Neurotherapeutics, 9*(7), 1087–1100. doi:10.1586/ern.09.42

Coan, J. A., Schaefer, H. S., & Davidson, R. J. (2006). Lending a hand: Social regulation of the neural response to threat. *Psychological Science, 17*(12), 1032–1039. doi:10.1111/j.1467-9280.2006.01832.x

Coffey, S. F., Dansky, B. S., Carrigan, M. H., & Brady, K. T. (2000). Acute and protracted cocaine abstinence in an outpatient population: A prospective study of mood, sleep and withdrawal symptoms. *Drug and Alcohol Dependence, 59*(3), 277–286. doi:10.1016/S0376-8716(99)00126-X

Cogsdill, E. J., Todorov, A. T., Spelke, E. S., & Banaji, M. R. (2014). Inferring character from faces: A developmental study. *Psychological Science, 25*(5), 1132–1139. doi:10.1177/0956797614523297

Cohen, E., Chazan, S., Lerner, M., & Maimon, E. (2010). Posttraumatic play in young children exposed to terrorism: An empirical study. *Infant Mental Health Journal, 31*(2), 159–181. doi:10.1002/imhj.20250

Cohen, S., & Herbert, T.B. (1996). Health psychology: Psychological factors and physical disease from the perspective of human psychoneuroimmunology. *Annual Review of Psychology, 47*, 113–142. doi:10.1146/annurev.psych.47.1.113

Cohen, S., Alper, C., Adler, N., Treanor, J. J., & Turner, R. B. (2008). Objective and subjective socioeconomic status and susceptibility to the common cold. *Health Psychology, 27*(2), 268–274. doi:10.1037/0278-6133.27.2.268

Cohen, S., Tyrrell, D. A., & Smith, A. P. (1991). Psychological stress and susceptibility to the common cold. *New England Journal of Medicine, 325*(9), 606–612. doi:10.1056/NEJM199108293250903

Cohn, D., & Taylor, P. (2010). *Baby boomers approach age 65–glumly*. http://pewresearch.org/pubs/1834/baby-boomers-old-age-downbeat-pessimism

Cohn, M. A., Fredrickson, B. L., Brown, S. L., Mikels, J. A., & Conway, A. M. (2009). Happiness unpacked: Positive emotions increase life satisfaction by building resilience. *Emotion, 9*(3), 361–368. doi:10.1037/a0015952

Cokely, E. T., Feltz, A., Ghazal, S., Allan, J. N., Petrova, D., & Garcia-Retamero, R. (2018). Decision making skill: From intelligence to numeracy and expertise. In K. A. Ericsson, R. R. Hoffman, A. Kozbelt, & A. M. Williams (Eds.), *Cambridge handbook of expertise and expert performance* (2nd ed., pp. 476–505). New York, NY: Cambridge University Press.

Cole, F. S., Alleyne, C., Barks, J. D. E., Boyle, R. J., Carroll, J. L., Dokken, D., Edwards, W. H., Georgieff, M., Gregory, K., Johnston, M. V., Kramer, M., Mitchell, C., Neu, J., Pursley, D. M., Robinson, W. M., & Rowitch, D. H. (2011). NIH Consensus Development Conference Statement: Inhaled Nitric-Oxide Therapy for Premature Infants. *Pediatrics, 127*(2), 363-369. doi:10.1542/peds.2010-3507

Cole, J. (1955). Paw preference in cats related to hand preference in animals and man. *Journal of Comparative and Physiological Psychology, 48*, 137–140. doi:10.1037/h0040380

Cole, S. W., Capitanio, J. P., Chun, K., Arevalo, J. M., Ma, J., & Cacioppo, J. T. (2015). Myeloid differentiation architecture of leukocyte transcriptome dynamics in perceived social isolation. *Proceedings of the National Academy of Sciences of the United States of America, 112*(49), 15142–15147. doi:10.1073/pnas.1514249112

Cole, S. W., Conti, G., Arevalo, J. M. G., Ruggiero, A. M., Heckman, J. J., & Suomi, S. J. (2012). Transcriptional modulation of the developing immune system by early life social adversity. *Proceedings of the National Academy of Sciences of the United States of America, 109*(50), 20578–20583. doi:10.1073/pnas.1218253109

Collins, A. M., & Loftus, E. (1975). A spreading activation theory of semantic processing. *Psychological Review, 82*, 407–428. doi:10.1037/0033-295X.82.6.407

Colosio, M., Shestakova, A., Nikulin, V. V., Blagovechtchenski, E., & Klucharev, V. (2017). Neural mechanisms of cognitive dissonance (revised): An EEG study. *Journal of Neuroscience, 37*(20), 5074–5083. doi:10.1523/JNEUROSCI.3209-16.2017

Colwell, K., Hiscock-Anisman, C. K., Memon, A., Taylor, L., & Prewett, J. (2007). Assessment Criteria Indicative of Deception (ACID): An integrated system of investigative interviewing and detecting deception. *Journal of Investigative Psychology and Offender Profiling, 4*(3), 167–180. doi:10.1002/jip.73

Comings, D. E., & Blum, K. (2000). Reward deficiency syndrome: Genetic aspects of behavioral disorders. *Progress in Brain Research, 126*, 325–341. doi:10.1016/S0079-6123(00)26022-6

Connolly, T., & Zeelenberg, M. (2002). Regret in decision making. *Current Directions in Psychological Science, 11*(6), 212–216. doi:10.1111/1467-8721.00203

Consumerreports.com. (2009). *Risky business*. http://www.consumerreports.org/health/healthy-living/health-safety/risk-taking/overview/risk-taking-ov.htm

Conway, J. (2010). *A chronicle of the activities of the Canadian Psychological Association, 1938–2000*. https://cpa.ca/docs/File/A_Chronicle_of_the_Activities_of_CPA_1938_2000_Sept_13_10.pdf

Cooke, J. E., Eirich, R., Racine, N., & Madigan, S. (2020). Prevalence of posttraumatic and general psychological stress during COVID-19: A rapid review and meta-analysis. *Psychiatry Research, 292*, 113347. doi:10.1016/j.psychres.2020.113347

Cooper, S. J., & Dourish, C. T. (1990). Multiple cholecystokinin (CCK) receptors and CCK-monoamine interactions are instrumental in the control of feeding. *Physiology and Behavior, 48*, 849–857. doi:10.1016/0031-9384(90)90239-Z

Corballis, M. C. (2004). The origins of modernity: Was autonomous speech the critical factor? *Psychological Review, 111*(2), 543–552. doi:10.1037/0033-295X.111.2.543

Corballis, M. C. (2020). Crossing the Rubicon: Behaviorism, language, and evolutionary continuity. *Frontiers in Psychology, 11*, 653–653. doi:10.3389/fpsyg.2020.00653

Corbett, M. (1991). *American public opinion*. White Plains, NY: Longman.

Corder, G., Ahanonu, B., Grewe, B. F., Wang, D., Schnitzer, M. J., & Scherrer, G. (2019). An amygdalar neural ensemble that encodes the unpleasantness of pain. *Science, 363*(6424), 276–281. doi:10.1126/science.aap8586

Cordonier, L., Nettles, T., & Rochat, P. (2018). Strong and strategic conformity understanding by 3- and 5-year-old children. *British Journal of Developmental Psychology, 36*(3), 438–451. doi:10.1111/bjdp.12229

Coren, S. (1996). Daylight savings time and traffic accidents. *New England Journal of Medicine, 334*(14), 924–925. doi:10.1056/NEJM199604043341416

Coren, S. (2012). *Sleep thieves*: Simon and Schuster.

Corkin, S. (2002). What's new with the amnesic patient H.M.? *Nature Reviews Neuroscience, 3*(2), 153–160. doi:10.1038/nrn726

Cornford, F. M. (1957). *From religion to philosophy: A study in the origins of Western speculation*. New York: Harper Torchbooks.

Corsi, D. J., Donelle, J., Sucha, E., Hawken, S., Hsu, H., El-Chaâr, D., Bisnaire, L., Fell, D., Wen, S. W., & Walker, M. (2020). Maternal cannabis use in pregnancy and child neurodevelopmental outcomes. *Nature Medicine*. doi:10.1038/s41591-020-1002-5

Cosmides, L., & Tooby, J. (1997). *Evolutionary psychology: A primer*. http://www.psych.ucsb.edu/research/cep/primer.html

Costa, P. T., & McCrae, R. R. (2011). *NEO Personality Inventory-Revised (NEO PI-R)*. http://www4.parinc.com/Products/Product.aspx?ProductID=NEO-PI-R

Courchesne, E. (1997). Brainstem, cerebellar and limbic neuroanatomical abnormalities in autism. *Current Opinion in Neurobiology, 7*(2), 269–278. doi:10.1016/S0959-4388(97)80016-5

Courtet, P., & Lopez-Castroman, J. (2017). Antidepressants and suicide risk in depression. *World psychiatry: Official Journal of the World Psychiatric Association (WPA), 16*(3), 317–318. doi:10.1002/wps.20460

Cowan, N. (2000). The magical number 4 in short-term memory: A reconsideration of mental storage capacity. *Behavioral and Brain Sciences, 24*, 87–185. doi:10.1017/S0140525X01003922

Cowen, P. J. (2010). Not fade away: The HPA axis and depression. *Psychological Medicine, 40*(01), 1–4. doi:10.1017/S0033291709005558

Cox, M. J., Owen, M. T., Henderson, V. K., & Margand, N. A. (1992). Prediction of infant-father and infant-mother attachment. *Developmental Psychology, 28*(3), 474–483. doi:10.1037/0012-1649.28.3.474

Craddock, N., & Sklar, P. (2013). Genetics of bipolar disorder. *The Lancet, 381*(9878), 1654–1662. doi:10.1136/jmg.36.8.585

Craig, A., & Tran, Y. (2005). The epidemiology of stuttering: The need for reliable estimates of prevalence and anxiety levels over the lifespan. *Advances in Speech Language Pathology, 7*(1), 41–46. doi:10.1080/14417040500055060

Craig, I. W. (2007). The importance of stress and genetic variation in human aggression. *Bioessays, 29*(3), 227–236. doi:10.1002/bies.20538

Craik, F. I. M., & Lockhart, R. S. (1972). Levels of processing: A framework for memory research. *Journal of Verbal Learning and Verbal Behavior, 11*, 671–684. doi:10.1016/S0022-5371(72)80001-X

Craik, F. I., & Tulving, E. (1975). Depth of processing and the retention of words in episodic memory. *Journal of Experimental Psychology: General, 104*(3), 268–294. doi:10.1037/0096-3445.104.3.268

Crick, F., & Koch, C. (2003). A framework for consciousness. *Nature Neuroscience, 6*(2), 119–126. doi:10.1038/nn0203-119

Cross-Disorder Group of the Psychiatric Genomics Consortium. (2013). Genetic relationship between five psychiatric disorders estimated from genome-wide SNPs. *Nature Genetics, 45*(9), 984–994. doi:10.1038/ng.2711

Crum, A. J., Corbin, W. R., Brownell, K. D., & Salovey, P. (2011). Mind over milkshakes: Mindsets, not just nutrients, determine ghrelin response. *Health Psychology, 30*(4), 424–429. doi:10.1037/a0023467

Crum, A. J., Salovey, P., & Achor, S. (2013). Rethinking stress: The role of mindsets in determining the stress response. *Journal of Personality and Social Psychology, 104*(4), 716–733. doi:10.1037/a0031201

Csikszentmihalyi, M. (1990). *Flow: The psychology of optimal experience*. New York: Harper and Row.

Csikszentmihalyi, M. (1996). *Creativity: Flow and the psychology of discovery and invention*. New York: Harper Collins.

Cuddy, A. J. C., Schultz, S. J., & Fosse, N. E. (2018). P-curving a more comprehensive body of research on postural feedback reveals clear evidential value for power-posing effects: Reply to Simmons and Simonsohn (2017). *Psychological Science, 29*(4), 656–666. doi:10.1177/0956797617746749

Cui, M., Darling, C. A., Coccia, C., Fincham, F. D., & May, R. W. (2019). Indulgent parenting, helicopter parenting, and well-being of parents and emerging adults. *Journal of Child and Family Studies, 28*(3), 860–871. doi:10.1007/s10826-018-01314-3

Cui, M., Graber, J. A., Metz, A., & Darling, C. A. (2019). Parental indulgence, self-regulation, and young adults' behavioral and emotional problems. *Journal of Family Studies, 25*(3), 233–249. doi:10.1080/13229400.2016.1237884

Cumming, G. (2013). The New Statistics: Why and how. *Psychological Science, 25*(1), 7–29. doi:10.1177/0956797613504966

Cuperman, R., & Ickes, W. (2009). Big Five predictors of behavior and perceptions in initial dyadic interactions: Personality similarity helps extraverts and introverts, but hurts "disagreeables". *Journal of Personality and Social Psychology, 97*(4), 667–684. doi:10.1037/a0015741

Curtis, R. G., Windsor, T. D., & Soubelet, A. (2014). The relationship between Big-5 personality traits and cognitive ability in older adults–A review. *Aging, Neuropsychology, and Cognition, 22*(1), 42–71. doi:10.1080/13825585.2014.888392.

Cutrona, C. E. (1982). Transition to college: Loneliness and the process of social adjustment. In L. A. Peplau & D. Perlman (Eds.), *Loneliness: A sourcebook of current theory, research, and therapy* (pp. 291–309). New York, NY: Wiley.

Cvencek, D., Greenwald, A. G., & Meltzoff, A. N. (2016). Implicit measures for preschool children confirm self-esteem's role in maintaining a balanced identity. *Journal of Experimental Social Psychology, 62*, 50–57. doi:10.1016/j.jesp.2015.09.015

Cyders, M. A., & Coskunpinar, A. (2011). Measurement of constructs using self-report and behavioral lab tasks: Is there overlap in nomothetic span and construct representation for impulsivity? *Clinical Psychology Review, 31*(6), 965–982. doi:http://dx.doi.org/10.1016/j.cpr.2011.06.001

D'Mello, A. M., & Gabrieli, J. D. (2018). Cognitive neuroscience of dyslexia. *Language, Speech, and Hearing Services in Schools, 49*(4), 798–809. doi:10.1044/2018_LSHSS-DYSLC-18-0020

Dabbs, J. M., & Janis, I. L. (1965). Why does eating while reading facilitate opinion change? An experimental inquiry. *Journal of Experimental Social Psychology, 1*, 133–144. doi:10.1016/0022-1031(65)90041-7

Dabbs, J. M., Jr., & Hargrove, M. F. (1997). Age, testosterone, and behavior among female prison inmates. *Psychosomatic Medicine, 59*, 477–480. doi:10.1097/00006842-199709000-00003

Dabbs, J. M., Jr., & Morris, R. (1990). Testosterone, social class, and antisocial behavior in a sample of 4,462 men. *Psychological Science, 1*, 209–211. doi:10.1111/j.1467-9280.1990.tb00200.x

Dabbs, J. M., Jr., Frady, R. L., Carr, T. S., & Besch, N. F. (1987). Saliva testosterone and criminal violence in young adult prison inmates. *Psychosomatic Medicine, 49*, 174–182. doi:10.1097/00006842-198703000-00007

Dahl, R. E., Holttum, J., & Trubnick, L. (1994). A clinical picture of child and adolescent narcolepsy. *Journal of the American Academy of Child & Adolescent Psychiatry, 33*(6), 834–841. doi:10.1097/00004583-199407000-00009

Dalege, J., Borsboom, D., van Harreveld, F., van den Berg, H., Conner, M., & van der Maas, H. L. (2016). Toward a formalized account of attitudes: The Causal Attitude Network (CAN) model. *Psychological Review, 123*(1), 2–22. doi:10.1037/a0039802

Daly, R. (2006). Psychiatrists proactive in scope-of-practice battles. *Psychiatric News, 41*(5), 17–34.

Damasio, A. R. (1994). *Descartes' error: Emotion, reason, and the human brain*. New York: G.P. Putnam's Sons.

Damasio, A. (2003). Feelings of emotion and the self. *Annals of the New York Academy of Sciences, 1001*(1), 253–261. doi:10.1196/annals.1279.014

Damasio, A., Bellugi, U., Damasio, H., Poizner, H., & Van Gilder, J. (1986). Sign language aphasia during left-hemisphere Amytal injection. *Nature, 322*(6077), 363–365. doi:10.1038/322363a0

Damasio, A. R., Grabowski, T. J., Bechara, A., Damasio, H., Ponto, L. L., Parvizi, J., & Hichwa, R. D. (2000). Subcortical and cortical brain activity during the feeling of self-generated emotions. *Nature Neuroscience, 3,* 1049–1056. doi:10.1038/79871

Damasio, H., Grabowski, T., Frank, R., Galaburda, A. M., & Damasio, A. R. (1994). The return of Phineas Gage: Clues about the brain from the skull of a famous patient. *Science, 264* 1102–1105. doi:10.1126/science.8178168

Damian, R. I., & Roberts, B. W. (2015). The associations of birth order with personality and intelligence in a representative sample of US high school students. *Journal of Research in Personality, 58,* 96–105. doi:10.1016/j.jrp.2015.05.005

Dani, J. A., & Harris, R. A. (2005). Nicotine addiction and comorbidity with alcohol abuse and mental illness. *Nature Neuroscience, 8*(11), 1465–1470. doi:10.1038/nn1580

Danielson, M. L., Bitsko, R. H., Ghandour, R. M., Holbrook, J. R., Kogan, M. D., & Blumberg, S. J. (2018). Prevalence of parent-reported ADHD diagnosis and associated treatment among US children and adolescents, 2016. *Journal of Clinical Child & Adolescent Psychology, 47*(2), 199–212. doi:10.1080/15374416.2017.1417860

Danziger, K., & Ballantyne, P. F. (1997). Psychological experiments. In W. G. Bringmann, H. E. Luck, R. Miller, & C. E. Early (Eds.), *Pictorial history of psychology* (pp. 233-239). New York: Oxford University Press.

Darby, R. R., Horn, A., Cushman, F., & Fox, M. D. (2018). Lesion network localization of criminal behavior. *Proceedings of the National Academy of Sciences of the United States of America, 115*(3), 601–606. doi:10.1073/pnas.1706587115

Darby, R. R., Laganiere, S., Pascual-Leone, A., Prasad, S., & Fox, M. D. (2016). Finding the imposter: Brain connectivity of lesions causing delusional misidentifications. *Brain, 140*(2), 497–507. doi:10.1093/brain/aww288

Darwin, C. (1859). *On the origin of the species by means of natural selection, or the preservation of favoured races in the struggle for life.* London: John Murray.

Darwin, C. (1871). *The descent of man and selection in relation to sex.* London: John Murray.

Darwin, C. (1872). *The expression of emotions in man and animals.* London: Murray.

Das, R., Jana, N., Arora, N., & Sengupta, S. (2020). Ultrasound assessment of fetal hearing response to vibroacoustic stimulation. *The Journal of Maternal-Fetal & Neonatal Medicine, 33*(14), 2326–2332. doi:10.1080/14767058.2018.1548600

Data Source: T. S. Critchfield et al. (2003). A half century of scalloping in the work habits of the United States Congress. *Journal of Applied Behavior Analysis, 36*(4), 465–486. doi:10.1901/jaba.2003.36-465

Dator, J. (2015). *James Harrison took away his kids' trophies.* https://www.sbnation.com/lookit/2015/8/15/9160799/james-harrison-kids-participation-trophies-facebook-steelers-nfl

Dauvilliers, Y., Montplaisir, J., Cochen, V., Desautels, A., Einen, M., Lin, L., Kawashima, M., Bayard, S., Monaca, C., Tiberge, M., Filipini, D., Tripathy, A.,, Nguyen, B. H., Kotagal, S., & Mignot, E. (2010). Post-H1N1 narcolepsy-cataplexy. *Sleep, 33*(11), 1428–1430. doi:10.1093/sleep/33.11.1428

Dauvilliers, Y., Arnulf, I., Lecendreux, M., Charley, C. M., Franco, P., Drouot, X.,d'Ortho, M.-P., Lanois, S., Lingot, S., Bourgin, P., Nogues, B., Rey, M., Bayard, S., Scholz, S., Lavault, S., Tubert-Bitter, P., Saussier, C., Pariente, A., & NarcofluVF Study Group (2013). Increased risk of narcolepsy in children and adults after pandemic H1N1 vaccination in France. *Brain, 136*(8), 2486-2496. doi:10.1093/brain/awt187

Davidson, C. L., Wingate, L. R., Slish, M. L., & Rasmus, K. A. (2010). The great black hope: Hope and its relation to suicide risk among African Americans. *Suicide and Life-Threatening Behavior, 40*(2), 170–180. doi:10.1521/suli.2010.40.2.170

Davidson, R. J., Putnam, K. M., & Larson, C. L. (2000). Dysfunction in the neural circuitry of emotion regulation—A possible prelude to violence. *Science, 289,* 591–594. doi:10.1126/science.289.5479.591

Davila, J., Burge, D., & Hammen, C. (1997). Why does attachment style change? *Journal of Personality and Social Psychology, 73*(4), 826–838. doi:10.1037/0022-3514.73.4.826

Davis, C. G., & Nolen-Hoeksema, S. (2009). Making sense of loss, perceiving benefits, and posttraumatic growth. In S. J. Lopez & C. R. Snyder (Eds.), *Oxford handbook of positive psychology* (4th ed., pp. 641–649). New York, NY: Oxford University Press.

Davis, J. A., Smith, T.W., & Marsden, P.V. (2006). *General Social Survey (GSS).* http://www.norc.uchicago.edu/projects/gensoc.asp

Davis, J. L., & Rusbult, C. E. (2001). Attitude alignment in close relationships. *Journal of Personality and Social Psychology, 81,* 65–84. doi:10.1037/0022-3514.81.1.65

Davis, M. (2007). *An introduction to sine-wave speech.* http://www.mrc-cbu.cam.ac.uk/people/matt.davis/sine-wave-speech/

Dawkins, R. (1976). *The selfish gene.* Oxford, U. K.: Oxford University Press.

de Gelder, B., Snyder, J., Greve, D., Gerard, G., & Hadjikhani, N. (2004). Fear fosters flight: A mechanism for fear contagion when perceiving emotion expressed by a whole body. *Proceedings of the National Academy of Sciences of the United States of America, 101,* 16701–16706. doi:10.1073/pnas.0407042101

de Lecea, L., Kilduff, T. S., Peyron, C., Gao, X. B., Foye, P. E., Danielson, P. E., Fukuhara, C., Battenberg, E. L. F., Gautvik, V. T., Bartlett II, F. S., Frankel, W. N., van den Pol, A. N., Bloom, F. E., Gautvik, K. M., & Sutcliffe, J. G. (1998). The hypocretins: Hypothalamus-specific peptides with neuroexcitatory activity. *Proceedings of the National Academy of Sciences of the United States of America, 95*(1), 322–327. doi:10.1073/pnas.95.1.322

De Neve, J. E., Diener, E., Tay, L., & Xuereb, C. (2013). The objective benefits of subjective well-being. *World happiness report.* New York, NY: Sustainable Development Solutions Network.

De Valois, R. L., & De Valois, K.K., & (1980). Spatial vision. *Annual Review of Psychology, 31,* 309–341. doi:10.1146/annurev.ps.31.020180.001521

de Voogd, L. D., Kanen, J. W., Neville, D. A., Roelofs, K., Fernandez, G., & Hermans, E. J. (2018). Eye-movement intervention enhances extinction via amygdala deactivation. *bioRxiv,* 282467. doi:10.1101/282467

de Vries, A. P., Kassam-Adams, N., Cnaan, A., Sherman-Slate, E., Gallagher, P. R., & Winston, F. K. (1999). Looking beyond the physical injury: Posttraumatic stress disorder in children and parents after pediatric traffic injury. *Pediatrics, 104,* 1293–1299. doi:10.1542/peds.104.6.1293

Dean, K. K., & Koenig, A. M. (2019). Cross-cultural differences and similarities in attribution. In K. D. Keith (Ed.), *Cross-Cultural Psychology: Contemporary Themes and Perspectives,* (pp. 575–597). Hoboken, NJ: John Wiley.

Dear Abby. (January 14, 2006). *Man ready to scrap marriage after wife wrecks his car.* http://www.uexpress.com/dearabby/?uc_full_date=20060114

Deary, I. J., Penke, L., & Johnson, W. (2010). The neuroscience of human intelligence differences. *Nature Reviews Neuroscience, 11*(3), 201–211. doi:10.1038/nrn2793

Deary, I. J., Strand, S., Smith, P., & Fernandes, C. (2007). Intelligence and educational achievement. *Intelligence, 35*(1), 13–21. doi:10.1016/j.intell.2006.02.001

Deater-Deckard, K., & Dodge, K. A. (1997). Externalizing behavior problems and discipline revisited: Nonlinear effects and variation by culture, context, and gender. *Psychological Inquiry, 8*(3), 161–175. doi:10.1207/s15327965pli0803_1

DeCasper, A. J., & Fifer, W. P. (1980). Of human bonding: Newborns prefer their mothers' voices. *Science, 208,* 1174–1176. doi:10.1126/science.7375928

DeCasper, A. J., & Spence, M. J. (1986). Prenatal maternal speech influences newborns' perception of speech sounds. *Infant Behavior and Development, 9,* 133–150. doi:10.1016/0163-6383(86)90025-1

DeCharms, R. (1968). *Personal causation.* New York: Academic.

Deci, E. L., & Ryan, R. M. (2000). The "what" and "why" of goal pursuits: Human needs and the self-determination of behavior. *Psychological Inquiry, 11,* 227–268. doi:10.1207/S15327965PLI1104_01

Deese, J. (1959). Influence of inter-item associative strength upon immediate free recall.

Psychological Reports, 5, 305–312. doi:10.2466/PR0.5.3.305-312
DeFilippis, M., & Wagner, K. D. (2016). Treatment of autism spectrum disorder in children and adolescents. *Psychopharmacology Bulletin, 46*(2), 18–41.
Dejong, K., Olyaei, A., & Lo, J. O. (2019). Alcohol use in pregnancy. *Clinical Obstetrics and Gynecology, 62*(1), 142–155. doi:10.1097/GRF.0000000000000414
Del Maschio, N., & Abutalebi, J. (2020). Language organization in the bilingual and multilingual brain. In J. W. Schwieter & M Paradis (Eds.), *The handbook of the euroscience of multilingualism.* doi:10.1002/9781119387725.ch9
DeLisi, M., Drury, A. J., & Elbert, M. J. (2019). The etiology of antisocial personality disorder: The differential roles of adverse childhood experiences and childhood psychopathology. *Comprehensive Psychiatry, 92*, 1–6. doi:10.1016/j.comppsych.2019.04.001
Della Rosa, P. A., Videsott, G., Borsa, V. M., Canini, M., Weekes, B. S., Franceschini, R., & Abutalebi, J. (2013). A neural interactive location for multilingual talent. *Cortex, 49*(2), 605–608. doi:10.1016/j.cortex.2012.12.001
Dement, W. (1960). The effect of dream deprivation. *Science, 131*(3415), 1705–1707. doi:10.1126/science.131.3415.1705.
Dement, W., & Kleitman, N. (1957). The relation of eye movements during sleep to dream activity: An objective method for the study of dreaming. *Journal of Experimental Psychology, 53*, 339–346. doi:10.1037/h0048189
den Houting, J. (2019). Neurodiversity: An insider's perspective. *Autism, 23*(2), 271–273. doi:10.1177/1362361318820762
DeNeve, K. M., & Cooper, H. (1998). The happy personality: A meta-analysis of 137 personality traits and subjective well-being. *Psychological Bulletin, 124*(2), 197–229. doi:10.1037/0033-2909.124.2.197
Denny, C. H., Acero, C. S., Naimi, T. S., & Kim, S. Y. (2019). Consumption of alcoholic beverages and binge drinking among pregnant women aged 18—44 years—United States, 2015–2017. *MMWR Morbidity and Mortality Weekly Report, 68*, 365–368. doi:10.15585/mmwr.mm6816a1
Derntl, B., Windischberger, C., Robinson, S., Kryspin-Exner, I., Gur, R. C., Moser, E., & Habel, U. (2009). Amygdala activity to fear and anger in healthy young males is associated with testosterone. *Psychoneuroendocrinology, 34*(5), 687–693. doi:10.1016/j.psyneuen.2008.11.007
Derogatis, L. R., & Coons, H. L. (1993). Self-report measures of stress. In L. Goldberger & S. Breznitz (Eds.), *Handbook of stress: Theoretical and clinical aspects* (2nd ed., pp. 200–233). New York: Free Press.
Deschamps, J. C., & Doise, W. (1978). Crossed category membership in intergroup relations. In H. Tajfe (Ed.), *Differentiation between social groups* (pp. 141–158). London: Academic Press.
Deschrijver, E., Wiersema, J. R., & Brass, M. (2017). Disentangling neural sources of the motor interference effect in high functioning autism: An EEG-study. *Journal of Autism and Developmental Disorders, 47*(3), 690–700. doi:10.1007/s10803-016-2991-2
Dew, J., & Wilcox, W. B. (2011). If Momma ain't happy: Explaining declines in marital satisfaction among new mothers. *Journal of Marriage and Family, 73*(1), 1–12. doi:10.1111/j.1741-3737.2010.00782.x
DeYoung, C. G., & Allen, T. A. (2019). Personality neuroscience: A developmental perspective. In D. P. McAdams, R. L. Shiner, & J. L. Tackett (Eds.), *Handbook of personality development.* (pp. 79–105). New York, NY: The Guilford Press.
Di Forti, M., Quattrone, D., Freeman, T. P., Tripoli, G., Gayer-Anderson, C., Quigley, H., Rodriguez, V., Jongsma, H. E., Ferraro, L., La Cascia, C., La Barbera, D., Tarricone, I., Berardi, D., Szöke, A., Arango, C., Tortelli, A., Velthorst, E., Bernardo, M., Del-Ben, C. M., . . . the EU-GEI WP2 Group (2019). The contribution of cannabis use to variation in the incidence of psychotic disorder across Europe (EU-GEI): a multicentre case-control study. *The Lancet Psychiatry, 6*(5), 427–436. doi:10.1016/S2215-0366(19)30048-3
Di Noto, P. M., Newman, L., Wall, S., & Einstein, G. (2012). The hermunculus: What is known about the representation of the female body in the brain? *Cerebral Cortex, 23*(5), 1005–1013. doi:10.1093/cercor/bhs005
Di Noto, P. M., Newman, L., Wall, S., & Einstein, G. (2012). The hermunculus: What Is known about the representation of the female body in the brain? *Cerebral Cortex, 23*(5), 1005–1013. doi:10.1093/cercor/bhs005
di Pellegrino, G., Fadiga, L., Fogassi, L., Gallese, V., & Rizzolatti, G. (1992). Understanding motor events: A neurophysiological study. *Experimental Brain Research, 91*(1), 176–180. doi:10.1007/bf00230027
Diamond, A., & Goldman-Rakic, P. S. (1989). Comparison of human infants and rhesus monkeys on Piaget's AB task: Evidence for dependence on dorsolateral prefrontal cortex. *Experimental Brain Research, 74*(1), 24–40. doi:10.1007/BF00248277
Diamond, D. M., Campbell, A. M., Park, C. R., Halonen, J., & Zoladz, P. R. (2007). The temporal dynamics model of emotional memory processing: A synthesis on the neurobiological basis of stress-induced amnesia, flashbulb and traumatic memories, and the Yerkes-Dodson Law. *Neural Plasticity*, 60803. doi:10.1155/2007/60803
Diamond, L. M. (2004). Emerging perspectives on distinctions between romantic love and sexual desire. *Current Directions in Psychological Science, 13*(3), 116–119. doi:10.1111/j.0963-7214.2004.00287.x
Diamond, L. M. (2012). The desire disorder in research on sexual orientation in women: Contributions of dynamical systems theory. *Archives of Sexual Behavior, 41*(1), 73–83. doi:10.1007/s10508-012-9909-7
Dias, B. G., & Ressler, K. J. (2013). Parental olfactory experience influences behavior and neural structure in subsequent generations. *Nature Neuroscience, 17*(1), 89–96. doi:10.1038/nn.3594
Dick, A. S., Garcia, N. L., Pruden, S. M., Thompson, W. K., Hawes, S. W., Sutherland, M. T., Riedel, M. C., Laird, A. R., & Gonzalez, R. (2019). No evidence for a bilingual executive function advantage in the ABCD study. *Nature Human Behaviour, 3*(7), 692–701. doi:10.1038/s41562-019-0609-3
Dickens, W. T., & Flynn, J. R. (2001). Heritability estimates versus large environmental effects: the IQ paradox resolved. *Psychological Review, 108*(2), 346. doi:10.1037/0033-295X.108.2.346
Dickens, W. T., & Flynn, J. R. (2006). Black Americans reduce the racial IQ gap: Evidence from standardization samples. *Psychological Science, 17*(10), 913–920. doi:10.1111/j.1467-9280.2006.01802.x
Dickhaus, J., Brown, K. A., Ferrucci, P., & Anderson, M. L. (2019). And the award goes to: Examining the effects of the "trophy culture" on millenials. *Journal of Contemporary Athletics, 13*(1), 39–51.
Diefendorf, A. R., & Dodge, R. (1908). An experimental study of the ocular reactions of the insane from photographic records. *Brain, 31*(3), 451–489. doi:10.1093/brain/31.3.451
Diekelmann, S., & Born, J. (2010). The memory function of sleep. *Nature Reviews Neuroscience, 11*(2), 114–126. doi:10.1038/nrn2762
Diener, E., & Chan, M. Y. (2011). Happy people live longer: Subjective well-being contributes to health and longevity. *Applied Psychology: Health and Well-Being, 3*(1), 1–43. doi:10.1111/j.1758-0854.2010.01045.x
Diener, E., & Seligman, M. E. P. (2004). Beyond money: Toward an economy of well-being. *Psychological Science in the Public Interest, 5*, 1–31. doi:10.1111/j.0963-7214.2004.00501001.x
Diener, E., Horwitz, J., & Emmons, R. A. (1985). Happiness of the very wealthy. *Social Indicators, 16*, 263–274. doi:10.1007/BF00415126
Dierks, T., Linden, D. E., Jandl, M., Formisano, E., Goebel, R., Lanfermann, H., & Singer, W. (1999). Activation of Heschl's gyrus during auditory hallucinations. *Neuron, 22*, 615–621. doi:10.1016/S0896-6273(00)80715-1
Dietrich, A., & Al-Shawaf, L. (2018). The transient hypofrontality theory of altered states of consciousness. *Journal of Consciousness Studies, 25*(11–12), 226–247.
DiGrande, L., Perrin, M. A., Thorpe, L. E., Thalji, L., Murphy, J., Wu, D., Farfel, M., & Brackbill, R. M. (2008). Posttraumatic stress

symptoms, PTSD, and risk factors among lower Manhattan residents 2–3 years after the September 11, 2001 terrorist attacks. *Journal of Traumatic Stress, 21*(3), 264–273. doi:10.1002/jts.20345

DiLalla, L. F., Kagan, J., & Reznick, J. S. (1994). Genetic etiology of behavioral inhibition among 2-year-old children. *Infant Behavior and Development, 17*, 405–412. doi:10.1016/0163-6383(94)90032-9

Dion, K., Berscheid, E., & Walster, E. (1972). What is beautiful is good. *Journal of Personality and Social Psychology, 24*, 285–290. doi:10.1037/h0033731

Dobson, D., & Dobson, K. S. (2016). *Evidence-based practice of cognitive-behavioral therapy*. New York, NY: Guilford Publications.

Doctors warn of the dangers of trepanning (2000). *BMJ: British Medical Journal, 320*(7235), 602. doi:10.1136/bmj.320.7235.602/c

Dodet, P., Chavez, M., Leu-Semenescu, S., Golmard, J.-L., & Arnulf, I. (2015). Lucid dreaming in narcolepsy. *Sleep, 38*(3), 487–497. doi:10.5665/sleep.4516

Dold, M., Aigner, M., Klabunde, M., Treasure, J., & Kasper, S. (2015). Second-generation antipsychotic drugs in anorexia nervosa: A meta-analysis of randomized controlled trials. *Psychotherapy and Psychosomatics, 84*(2), 110–116. doi:10.1159/000369978

Dolinoy, D. C., Huang, D., & Jirtle, R. L. (2007). Maternal nutrient supplementation counteracts bisphenol A-induced DNA hypomethylation in early development. *Proceedings of the National Academy of Sciences of the United States of America, 104*, 13056–13061. doi:10.1073/pnas.0703739104

Doll, R., Peto, R., Boreham, J., & Sutherland, I. (2004). Mortality in relation to smoking: 50 years' observations on male British doctors. *British Medical Journal, 328*(7455), 1519. doi:10.1136/bmj.38142.554479.AE

Domanski, C. W. (2013). Mysterious "Monsieur Leborgne": The mystery of the famous patient in the history of neuropsychology is explained. *Journal of the History of the Neurosciences, 22*(1), 47–52. doi:10.1080/0964704X.2012.667528

Domingue, B. W., Fletcher, J., Conley, D., & Boardman, J. D. (2014). Genetic and educational assortative mating among US adults. *Proceedings of the National Academy of Sciences of the United States of America, 111*(22), 7996–8000. doi:10.1073/pnas/1321426111

Domínguez-Clavé, E., Soler, J., Elices, M., Pascual, J. C., Álvarez, E., de la Fuente Revenga, M., Friedlander, P., Feilding, A., & Riba, J. (2016). Ayahuasca: Pharmacology, neuroscience and therapeutic potential. *Brain Research Bulletin, 126, Part 1*, 89–101. doi:10.1016/j.brainresbull.2016.03.002

Doty, R. L., Shaman, P., & Dann, M. (1984). Development of the University of Pennsylvania Smell Identification Test: A standardized microencapsulated test of olfactory function. *Physiology & Behavior, 32*(3), 489–502. doi:10.1016/0031-9384(84)90269-5

Dresler, M., Eibl, L., Fischer, C. F., Wehrle, R., Spoormaker, V. I., Steiger, A., Czisch, M., & Pawlowski, M. (2013). Volitional components of consciousness vary across wakefulness, dreaming and lucid dreaming. *Frontiers in Psychology, 4*, 987. doi:10.3389/fpsyg.2013.00987.

Dronkers, N. F., Ivanova, M. V., & Baldo, J. V. (2017). What do language disorders reveal about brain-language relationships? From classic models to network approaches. *Journal of the International Neuropsychology Society, 23*(9–10), 741–754. doi:10.1017/S1355617717001126

Dronkers, N. F., Pinker, S., & Damasio, A. (2000). Language and the aphasias. In E. R. Kandel, J. H. Schwartz, & T. M. Jessell (Eds.), *Principles of neural science* (Vol. 4, pp. 1169–1187). New York: McGraw-Hill.

Druckman, D. E., & Bjork, R. A. (1991). *In the mind's eye: Enhancing human performance*. Washington, DC: National Academy Press.

Dubernard, J.-M., Owen, E. R., Lanzetta, M., & Hakim, N. (2001). What is happening with hand transplants? *The Lancet, 357*, 1711–1712. doi:10.1016/S0140-6736(00)04846-7

Dubois, J., Galdi, P., Paul, L. K., & Adolphs, R. (2018). A distributed brain network predicts general intelligence from resting-state human neuroimaging data. *Philosophical Transactions of the Royal Society B: Biological Sciences, 373*(1756), 20170284. doi:10.1098/rstb.2017.0284

Dudai, Y. (2004). The neurobiology of consolidations, or, how stable is the engram? *Annual Review of Psychology, 55*, 51–86. doi:10.1146/annurev.psych.55.090902.142050

Dulaney, S., & Fiske, A. P. (1994). Cultural rituals and obsessive-compulsive disorder: Is there a common psychological mechanism? *Ethos, 22*(3), 243–283. doi:10.1525/eth.1994.22.3.02a00010

Dumontheil, I. (2016). Adolescent brain development. *Current Opinion in Behavioral Sciences, 10*, 39–44. doi:10.1016/j.cobeha.2016.04.012

Dunbar, R. I. (2011). Evolutionary basis of the social brain. In J. Decety & J. T. Cacioppo (Eds.), *Oxford handbook of social neuroscience* (pp. 28–38). New York: Oxford University Press.

Dunbar, R. I. M., & Schultz, S. (2007). Evolution in the social brain. *Science, 317*, 1344–1347. doi:10.1126/science.1145463

Duncan, L. E., Ratanatharathorn, A., Aiello, A. E., Almli, L. M., Amstadter, A. B., Ashley-Koch, A. E., Baker, D. G., Beckham, J. Bierut, L. J., Bisson, J., Bradley, B., Chen, C.-Y., Dalvie, S., Farrer, L. A., Galea, S., Garrett, M. E., Gelernter, J. E., Guffanti, G., Hauser, M. A., . . . Koenen, K. C. (2018). Largest GWAS of PTSD (N=20 070) yields genetic overlap with schizophrenia and sex differences in heritability. *Molecular Psychiatry, 23*(3), 666–673. doi:10.1038/mp.2017.77

Dunn, E. W., Aknin, L. B., & Norton, M. I. (2014). Prosocial spending and happiness: Using money to benefit others pays off. *Current Directions in Psychological Science, 23*(1), 41–47. doi:10.1177/0963721413512503

Dutton, D. G., & Aron, A. P. (1974). Some evidence for heightened sexual attraction under conditions of high anxiety. *Journal of Personality and Social Psychology, 30*, 510–517. doi:10.1037/h0037031

Dweck, C. (2012). *Mindset: How you can fulfil your potential*. London: Hachette UK.

Dweck, C. S. (2000). *Self-theories: Their role in motivation, personality, and development*. New York, NY: Psychology Press.

Dyson-Hudson, N., & Dyson-Hudson, R. (1999). The social organization of resource exploitation in South Turkana. In M. A. Little & P. W. Leslie (Eds.), *Turkana herders of the dry savanna: Ecology and biobeahvioral response of nomads to an uncertain environment* (pp. 68–86). Oxford: Oxford University Press.

Dyson-Hudson, R., & Dyson-Hudson, N. (1995). *South Turkana homicide: A proximate view*. Paper presented at the Human Behavior and Evolution Conference, Santa Barbara, CA. http://www.hbes.com/HBES/abst95.htm#South_Turkana

Eberhardt, J. L., Davies, P. G., Purdie-Vaughns, V. J., & Johnson, S. L. (2006). Looking deathworthy: Perceived stereotypicality of Black defendants predicts capital-sentencing outcomes. *Psychological Science, 17*, 383–386. doi:10.1111/j.1467-9280.2006.01716.x

Ehlers, C. L. (2007). Variations in ADH and ALDH in Southwest California Indians. *Alcohol Research and Health, 30*(1), 14–17.

Eichel, S. K. D. (2002). *Credentialing: It may not be the cat's meow*. http://users.snip.net/~drsteve/Articles/Dr_Zoe.htm.

Einstein, A. (1945). A testimonial from Professor Einstein (Appendix II). In J. Hadamard (Ed.), *An essay on the psychology of invention in the mathematical field* (pp. 142–143). Princeton, NJ: Princeton University Press.

Eisenberg, D. T. A., & Hayes, M. G. (2011). Testing the null hypothesis: Comments on 'Culture-gene coevolution of individualism-collectivism and the serotonin transporter gene'. *Proceedings. Biological Sciences, 278*(1704), 329–332. doi:10.1098/rspb.2010.0714

Ekelund, U., Steene-Johannessen, J., Brown, W. J., Fagerland, M. W., Owen, N., Powell, K. E., Bauman, A., Lee, I.-M., & the Lancet Sedentary Behaviour Working Group. (2016). Does physical activity attenuate, or even eliminate, the detrimental association of sitting time with mortality? A harmonised meta-analysis of data from more than 1 million men and women. *The Lancet, 388*(10051), 1302–1310. doi:10.1016/S0140-6736(16)30370-1

Ekirch, A. R. (2001). Sleep we have lost: Pre-industrial slumber in the British Isles. *The American Historical Review, 106*(2), 343–386. doi:10.2307/2651611

Ekman, P. (1996). Why don't we catch liars? *Social Research, 63*, 801–817. https://www.jstor.org/stable/40972316

Ekman, P., & O'Sullivan, M. (1991). Who can catch a liar? *American Psychologist, 46*(9), 913–920. doi:10.1037/0003-066X.46.9.913

Ekman, P., Davidson, R. J., & Friesen, W. V. (1990). The Duchenne smile: Emotional expression and brain physiology: II. *Journal of Personality and Social Psychology, 58*(2), 342. doi:10.1037/0022-3514.58.2.342

Ekman, P., Friesen, W. V., & Ellsworth, P. (1972). *Emotion in the human face: Guidelines for research and an integration of findings.* London: Pergamon Press.

Elbert, T., Pantev, C., Weinbruch, C., Rockstroh, B., & Taub, E. (1995). Increased cortical representation of the fingers of the left hand in string players. *Science, 270*, 305–307. doi:10.1126/science.270.5234.305

Elkind, D. (1967). Egocentrism in adolescence. *Child Development, 38*, 1025–1034. doi:10.2307/1127100

Elkind, D., & Bowen, R. (1979). Imaginary audience behavior in children and adolescents. *Developmental Psychology, 15*, 38–44. doi:10.1037/0012-1649.15.1.38

Elkins, G. R., Barabasz, A. F., Council, J. R., & Spiegel, D. (2015). Advancing research and practice: The revised APA Division 30 definition of hypnosis. *American Journal of Clinical Hypnosis, 57*(4), 378–385. doi:10.1080/00207144.2014.961870

Eller, A., Abrams, D., Viki, G. T., & Imara, D. A. (2007). When my friend's friend is a police officer: Extended contact, cross-categorisation, and public-police relations of black and white people. *South African Journal of Psychology, 37*(4), 783–802.

Ellinghaus, D., Degenhardt, F., Bujanda, L., Buti, M., Albillos, A., Invernizzi, P., Fernández, J., Prati, D., Baselli, G., Asselta, R., Grimsrud, M.M., Milani, C., Aziz, F., Kässens, J., May, S., Wendorff, M., Wienbrandt, Uellendahl-Werth, L. F., Zheng, T., . . . Karlsen, T. H. (2020). Genomewide association study of severe Covid-19 with respiratory failure. *New England Journal of Medicine.* doi:10.1056/NEJMoa2020283

Elliot, A. J. (1999). Approach and avoidance motivation and achievement goals. *Educational Psychologist, 34*(3), 169–189. doi:10.1207/s15326985ep3403_3

Elliot, A. J., & Murayama, K. (2008). On the measurement of achievement goals: Critique, illustration, and application. *Journal of Educational Psychology, 100*(3), 613–628. doi:10.1037/0022-0663.100.3.613

Ellis Weismer, S., Lord, C., & Esler, A. (2010). Early language patterns of toddlers on the autism spectrum compared to toddlers with developmental delay. *Journal of Autism and Developmental Disorders, 40*(10), 1259-1273. doi:10.1007/s10803-010-0983-1
Ellis Weismer, S., Lord, C., & Esler, A. (2010). Early language patterns of toddlers on the autism spectrum compared to toddlers with developmental delay. *Journal of Autism and Developmental Disorders, 40*(10), 1259–1273. doi:10.1007/s10803-010-0983-1
Ellis, A. (1975). *A new guide to rational living.* Upper Saddle River, NJ: Prentice Hall.

Ellis, H. C., & Hunt, R. R. (1983). *Fundamentals of human memory and cognition.* Dubuque, IA: William C. Brown.

Ellsworth, P. C. (1994). *Sense, culture, and sensibility.* In S. Kitayama & H. R. Markus (Eds.), *Emotion and culture: Empirical studies of mutual influence* (pp. 23–50). Washington, DC: American Psychological Association. doi:10.1037/10152-001

Elman, C. (2011). The midlife years: Human capital and job mobility. In J. L. Angel, J. R. A. Settersten, & R. Settersten (Eds.), *Handbook of sociology of aging* (pp. 245–261). New York: Springer.

EMDR Institute. (2019). *What is EMDR?* https://www.emdr.com/what-is-emdr/

Emery, N. J., Capitanio, J. P., Mason, W. A., Machado, C. J., Mendoza, S. P., & Amaral, D. G. (2001). The effects of bilateral lesions of the amygdala on dyadic social interactions in rhesus monkeys *(Macaca mulatta). Behavioral Neuroscience, 115*, 515–544. doi:10.1037/0735-7044.115.3.515

Emlen, S. T., & Oring, L. W. (1977). Ecology, sexual selection, and the evolution of mating systems. *Science, 197*, 215–223. doi:10.1126/science.327542

Emmons, R. A., Barrett, J. L., & Schnitker, S. A.(2008). Personality and the capacity for religious and spiritual experience. In O. P. John, R. W. Robins, & L. A. Pervin (Eds.), *Handbook of personality psychology: Theory and research* (3rd ed., pp. 634–653). New York, NY: Guilford Press.

Eng, M. Y., Luczak, S. E., & Wall, T. L. (2007). ALDH2, ADH1B, and ADH1C genotypes in Asians: A literature review. *Alcohol Research and Health, 30*(1), 22–27.

Engel, S. M., & Daniels, J. L. (2011). On the complex relationship between genes and environment in the etiology of autism. *Epidemiology, 22*(4), 486–488. doi:10.1097/EDE.1090b1013e31821daf31821c.

English, T., & John, O. P. (2013). Understanding the social effects of emotion regulation: The mediating role of authenticity for individual differences in suppression. *Emotion, 13*(2), 314–329. doi:10.1037/a0029847

Entertainment Software Rating Board (ESRB). (2019). *Rating process from ESRB.* https://www.esrb.org/ratings/ratings_process.aspx

Erikson, E. H. (1968). *Identity: Youth and crisis.* Oxford, England: Norton & Co.

Erol, R. Y., & Orth, U. (2011). Self-esteem development from age 14 to 30 years: A longitudinal study. *Journal of Personality and Social Psychology, 101*(3), 607–619. doi:10.1037/a0024299

Eshun, S. (1999). Cultural variations in hopelessness, optimism, and suicidal ideation: A study of Ghana and US college samples. *Cross-Cultural Research, 33*(3), 227–238. doi:10.1177/106939719903300301

Eskelinen, M. H., & Kivipelto, M. (2010). Caffeine as a protective factor in dementia and Alzheimer's disease. *Journal of Alzheimer's Disease, 20*(Suppl. 1), S167–S174. doi:10.3233/JAD-2010-1404

Eslinger, P. J., & Damasio, A. R. (1985). Severe disturbance of higher cognition after bilateral frontal lobe ablation: Patient EVR. *Neurology, 35*, 1731–1741. doi:10.1212/WNL.35.12.1731

Espitia-Bautista, E., Velasco-Ramos, M., Osnaya-Ramírez, I., Ángeles-Castellanos, M., Buijs, R. M., & Escobar, C. (2017). Social jet-lag potentiates obesity and metabolic syndrome when combined with cafeteria diet in rats. *Metabolism, 72*, 83–93. doi:10.1016/j.metabol.2017.04.006

Evans, P. D., Anderson, J. R., Vallender, E. J., Gilbert, S. L., Malcom, C. M., Dorus, S., & Lahn, B. T. (2004). Adaptive evolution of ASPM, a major determinant of cerebral cortical size in humans. *Human Molecular Genetics, 13*, 489–494. doi:10.1093/hmg/ddh055

Evans, P. D., Gilbert, S. L., Mekel-Bobrov, N., Vallender, E. J., Anderson, J. R., Vaez-Azizi, L. M., & al., e. (2005). Microcephalin, a gene regulating brain size, continues to evolve adaptively in humans. *Science, 309*, 1717–1720. doi:10.1126/science.1113722

Eysenck, H. J. (1967). *The biological basis of personality*. Springfield, IL: Thomas.

Falcone, G., & Jerram, M. (2018). Brain activity in mindfulness depends on experience: A meta-analysis of fMRI studies. *Mindfulness, 9*(5), 1319–1329. doi:10.1007/s12671-018-0884-5

Faraone, S. V., & Larsson, H. (2019). Genetics of attention deficit hyperactivity disorder. *Molecular Psychiatry, 24*(4), 562–575. doi:10.1038/s41380-018-0070-0

Farrell, M. S., Werge, T., Sklar, P., Owen, M. J., Ophoff, R. A., O'Donovan, M. C., Corvin, A., Cichon, S., & Sullivan, P. F. (2015). Evaluating historical candidate genes for schizophrenia. *Molecular Psychiatry, 20*, 555. doi:10.1038/mp.2015.16

Farstad, S. M., McGeown, L. M., & von Ranson, K. M. (2016). Eating disorders and personality, 2004–2016: A systematic review and meta-analysis. *Clinical Psychology Review, 46*, 91–105. doi:http://dx.doi.org/10.1016/j.cpr.2016.04.005

Fatemi, S. H., Aldinger, K. A., Ashwood, P., Bauman, M. L., Blaha, C. D., Blatt, G. J., Chauhan, A., Chauhan, V., Dager, S. R., Dickson, P. E., Estes, A. M., Goldowitz, D., Heck, D. H., Kemper, T. L., King, B. H., Martin, L. A., Millen, K. J., Mittleman, G., . . . Welsh, J. P. (2012). Consensus paper: Pathological role of the cerebellum in autism. *The Cerebellum, 11*(3), 777–807. doi:10.1007/s12311-012-0355-9

Feeney, J. A., & Noller, P. (1990). Attachment style as a predictor of adult romantic relationships. *Journal of Personality and Social Psychology, 58*(2), 281–291. doi:10.1037/0022-3514.58.2.281

Fehr, E., & Rockenbach, B. (2004). Human altruism: Economic, neural, and evolutionary perspectives. *Current Opinion in Neurobiology, 14*, 784–790. doi:10.1016/j.conb.2004.10.007

Feinberg, I. (1978). Efference copy and corollary discharge: Implications for thinking and its disorders. *Schizophrenia Bulletin, 4*, 636–640. doi:10.1093/schbul/4.4.636

Feinstein, J. S., Adolphs, R., Damasio, A., & Tranel, D. (2011). The human amygdala and the induction and experience of fear. *Current Biology 21*(1), 34–38. doi:10.1016/j.cub.2010.11.042

Fejfar, M. C., & Hoyle, R. H. (2000). Effect of private self-awareness on negative affect and self-referent attribution: A quantitative review. *Personality and Social Psychology Review, 4*(2), 132–142. doi:10.1207/S15327957PSPR0402_02

Fenton, N., & Neil, M. (2012). *Risk assessment and decision analysis with Bayesian networks.* London, UK: CRC Press.

Ferdenzi, C., Joussain, P., Digard, B., Luneau, L., Djordjevic, J., & Bensafi, M. (2016). Individual differences in verbal and non-verbal affective responses to smells: Influence of odor label across cultures. *Chemical Senses, 42*(1), 37–46. doi:10.1093/chemse/bjw098

Ferguson, C. J. (2010). Genetic contributions to antisocial personality and behavior: A meta-analytic review from an evolutionary perspective. *The Journal of Social Psychology, 150*(2), 160–180. doi:10.1080/00224540903366503

Fergusson, D. M., Boden, J. M., & Horwood, L. J. (2015). Psychosocial sequelae of cannabis use and implications for policy: Findings from the Christchurch Health and Development Study. *Social Psychiatry and Psychiatric Epidemiology, 50*(9), 1317–1326. doi:10.1007/s00127-015-1070-x

Fergusson, D. M., Boden, J. M., Horwood, L. J., Miller, A. L., & Kennedy, M. A. (2011). MAOA, abuse exposure and antisocial behaviour: 30-year longitudinal study. *The British Journal of Psychiatry, 198*(6), 457–463. doi:10.1192/bjp.bp.110.086991

Fergusson, D. M., Horwood, L. J., & Ridder, E. M. (2005). Tests of causal linkages between cannabis use and psychotic symptoms. *Addiction, 100*, 354–366. doi:10.1111/j.1360-0443.2005.01001.x

Fernald, A., & Kuhl, P. (1987). Acoustic determinants of infant preference for motherese speech. *Infant Behavior and Development, 10*(3), 279–293. doi:10.1016/0163-6383(87)90017-8

Fernald, A., & Weisleder, A. (2015). Twenty years after "meaningful differences," it's time to reframe the "deficit" debate about the importance of children's early language experience. *Human Development, 58*(1), 1–4. doi:10.1159/000375515

Ferrari, P. F., Paukner, A., Ionica, C., & Suomi, S. J. (2009). Reciprocal face-to-face communication between rhesus macaque mothers and their newborn infants. *Current Biology, 19*(20), 1768–1772. doi:10.1016/j.cub.2009.08.055

Festinger, L. (1950). Informal social communication. *Psychological Review, 57*, 271–282. doi:10.1037/h0056932

Festinger, L. (1954). A theory of social comparison processes. *Human Relations, 7*, 117–140. doi:10.1177/001872675400700202

Festinger, L. (1957). *A theory of cognitive dissonance.* Stanford, CA: Stanford University Press.

Festinger, L., & Carlsmith, J.M. (1959). Cognitive consequences of forced compliance. *Journal of Abnormal and Social Psychology, 58*, 203–210. doi:10.1037/h0041593

Feusner, J. D., Neziroglu, F., Wilhelm, S., Mancusi, L., & Bohon, C. (2010). What causes BDD? *Psychiatric Annals, 40*(7), 349–355. doi:10.3928/00485713-20100701-08

Fidler, D. J., Most, D. E., Booth-LaForce, C., & Kelly, J. F. (2008). Emerging social strengths in young children with Down syndrome. *Infants & Young Children, 21*(3), 207–220. doi:10.1097/01.IYC.0000324550.39446.1f

Field, Y., Boyle, E. A., Telis, N., Gao, Z., Gaulton, K. J., Golan, D., Yengo, L., Rocheleau, G., Froguel, P., McCarthy, M. I., & Pritchard, J. K. (2016). Detection of human adaptation during the past 2000 years. *Science, 354*(6313), 760–764. doi:10.1101/052084

Fisher, P. A., Van Ryzin, M. J., & Gunnar, M. R. (2011). Mitigating HPA axis dysregulation associated with placement changes in foster care. *Psychoneuroendocrinology, 36*(4), 531–539. doi:10.1016/j.psyneuen.2010.08.007

Fink, G. R., Markowitsch, H. J., Reinkemeier, M., Bruckbauer, T., Kessler, J., & Heiss, W.-D. (1996). Cerebral representation of one"s own past: Neural networks involved in autobiographical memory. *Journal of Neuroscience, 16*(13), 4275–4282. doi:10.1523/JNEUROSCI.16-13-04275.1996

Finkel, E. J., Eastwick, P. W., Karney, B. R., Reis, H. T., & Sprecher, S. (2012). Dating in a digital world. *Scientific American Mind, 23*(4), 26–33.

Fischhoff, B., de Bruin, W. B., Parker, A. M., Millstein, S. G., & Halpern-Felsher, B. L. (2010). Adolescents' perceived risk of dying. *Journal of Adolescent Health, 46*(3), 265–269. doi:10.1016/j.jadohealth.2009.06.026

Fisher, M. L., Worth, K., Garcia, J. R., & Meredith, T. (2012). Feelings of regret following uncommitted sexual encounters in Canadian university students. *Culture, Health & Sexuality, 14*(1), 45–57. doi:10.1080/13691058.2011.619579

Fisher, P. A., Van Ryzin, M. J., & Gunnar, M. R. (2011). Mitigating HPA axis dysregulation associated with placement changes in foster care. *Psychoneuroendocrinology, 36*(4), 531–539. doi:10.1016/j.psyneuen.2010.08.007

Fisher, P. A., Van Ryzin, M. J., & Gunnar, M. R. (2011). Mitigating HPA axis dysregulation associated with placement changes in foster care. *Psychoneuroendocrinology*, 36(4), 531

Fisher, R. P., & Geiselman, R. E. (2010). The cognitive interview method of conducting police interviews: Eliciting extensive information and promoting therapeutic jurisprudence. *International Journal of Law and Psychiatry, 33*(5–6), 321–328. doi:10.1016/j.ijlp.2010.09.004

Fisher, S., Reynolds, J. L., Hsu, W.-W., Barnes, J., & Tyler, K. (2014). Examining multiracial youth in context: Ethnic identity development and mental health outcomes. *Journal of Youth and Adolescence, 43*(10), 1688–1699. doi:10.1007/s10964-014-0163-2

Fiske, S. T. (1998). Stereotyping, prejudice, and discrimination. In D. T. Gilbert, S. T. Fiske, & G. Lindzey (Eds.), *The handbook of social psychology* (4th ed., Vol. 2, pp. 357–411). New York: McGraw-Hill.

Fleischman, J. (2002). *Phineas Gage: A gruesome but true story about brain science.* Boston: Houghton Mifflin.

Flexser, A. J., & Tulving, E. (1978). Retrieval independence in recall and recognition. *Psychological Review, 85*, 153–171. doi:10.1037/0033-295X.85.3.153

Flick, C. (2015). Informed consent and the Facebook emotional manipulation study. *Research Ethics, 12*(1), 14–28. doi:10.1177/1747016115599568

Flynn, J. R. (1999). Searching for justice: The discovery of IQ gains over time. *American Psychologist, 54*, 5–20. doi:10.1037/0003-066X.54.1.5

Flynn, J. R. (2016). No population is frozen in time: The sociology of intelligence. *Psychological Inquiry, 27*(3), 205–209. doi:10.1080/1047840X.2016.1181518

Forer, B. R. (1949). The fallacy of personal validation: A classroom demonstration of gullibility. *The Journal of Abnormal and Social Psychology, 44*(1), 118–123. doi:10.1037/h0059240

Forrest, A. D., Coto, C. A., & Siegel, S. J. (2014). Animal models of psychosis: Current state and future directions. *Current Behavioral Neuroscience Reports, 1*(2), 100–116. doi:10.1007/s40473-014-0013-2

Forsyth, D. R., & Kerr, N. A. (1999). Are adaptive illusions adaptive? Poster presented at the Annual Meeting of the American Psychological Association, Boston, MA.

Forsyth, D. R., & Schlenker, B. R. (1977). Attributing the causes of group performance: Effects of performance quality, task importance, and future testing. *Journal of Personality, 45*(2), 220–236. doi:10.1111/j.1467-6494.1977.tb00148.x

Foulkes, D. (1999). *Children's dreaming and the development of consciousness.* Cambridge, MA: Harvard University Press.

Foutz, A., Mitler, M., Cavalli-Sforza, L., & Dement, W. (1978). Genetic factors in canine narcolepsy. *Sleep, 1*(4), 413–421. doi:10.1093/sleep/1.4.413

Fowler, J. H., & Christakis, N. A. (2008). Dynamic spread of happiness in a large social network: Longitudinal analysis over 20 years in the Framingham Heart Study. *British Medical Journal, 337*, a2338. doi:10.1136/bmj.a2338

Fox, K. C., Nijeboer, S., Solomonova, E., Domhoff, G. W., & Christoff, K. (2013). Dreaming as mind wandering: Evidence from functional neuroimaging and first-person content reports. *Frontiers in Human Neuroscience, 7*, 412. doi:10.3389/fnhum.2013.00412

Fox, K. C. R., Nijeboer, S., Dixon, M. L., Floman, J. L., Ellamil, M., Rumak, S. P., Sedlmeier, P., & Christoff, K. (2014). Is meditation associated with altered brain structure? A systematic review and meta-analysis of morphometric neuroimaging in meditation practitioners. *Neuroscience & Biobehavioral Reviews, 43*, 48–73. doi:10.1016/j.neubiorev.2014.03.016

Fox, M. C., & Mitchum, A. L. (2013). A knowledge-based theory of rising scores on "culture-free" tests. *Journal of Experimental Psychology: General, 142*(3), 979–1000. doi:10.1037/a0030155

Fox, P. W., Hershberger, S. L., & Bouchard, T. J., Jr. (1996). Genetic and environmental contributions to the acquisition of a motor skill. *Nature, 384*(6607), 356–358. doi:10.1038/384356a0

Fraga, M. F., Ballestar, E., Paz, M. F., Ropero, S., Setien, F., Ballestar, M. L., et al. (2005). Epigenetic differences arise during the lifetime of monozygotic twins. *Proceedings of the National Academy of Sciences of the United States of America, 102*, 10604–10609.

Frances, A. (2010). It's not too late to save 'normal': Psychiatry's latest manual goes too far in creating disorders. *Los Angeles Times*. http://articles.latimes.com/2010/mar/01/opinion/la-oe-frances1-2010mar01

Frances, A. (2013). The new somatic symptom disorder in DSM-5 risks mislabeling many people as mentally ill. *BMJ : British Medical Journal, 346*, f1580. doi:10.1136/bmj.f1580

Franco, Z. E., Blau, K., & Zimbardo, P. G. (2011). Heroism: A conceptual analysis and differentiation between heroic action and altruism. *Review of General Psychology, 15*(2), 99–113. doi:10.1037/a0022672

Frank, M. G., & Ekman, P. (1993). Not all smiles are created equal: The differences between enjoyment and nonenjoyment smiles. *Humor-International Journal of Humor Research, 6*(1), 9–26. doi:10.1515/humr.1993.6.1.9

Franken, D. (2002). *Personal strengths, positive psychology, optimum psycho-social lifeskills*. Holland, MI: Wellness Publications.

Frazier, T. W., Thompson, L., Youngstrom, E. A., Law, P., Hardan, A. Y., Eng, C., & Morris, N. (2014). A twin study of heritable and shared environmental contributions to autism. *Journal of Autism and Developmental Disorders*, 1–13. doi:10.1007/s10803-014-2081-2

Freedman, D. G. (1964). Smiling in blind infants and the issue of innate vs. acquired. *Journal of Child Psychology and Psychiatry, 5*(3–4), 171–184. doi:10.1111/j.1469-7610.1964.tb02139.x

French, J. E., & Meltzer, A. L. (2019). Maximizing tendencies in marriage: Accentuating the implications of readily observable partner characteristics for intimates' satisfaction. *Personality and Social Psychology Bulletin, 45*(10), 1468–1481. doi:10.1177/0146167219832337

Freud, S. (1900/1953). Interpretation of dreams. In J. Strachey (Ed.), *The standard edition of the complete psychological works of Sigmund Freud (Vols. 4 and 5)*. London: Hogarth Press.

Freud, S. (1909/1976). Analysis of a phobia of a five year old boy. In *The Pelican Freud library: Case Histories I* (Vol. 8, pp. 169–306). Harmondsworth, England: Penguin Books.

Frick, P. J., Ray, J. V., Thornton, L. C., & Kahn, R. E. (2014). Can callous-unemotional traits enhance the understanding, diagnosis, and treatment of serious conduct problems in children and adolescents? A comprehensive review. *Psychological Bulletin, 140*(1), 1–57. doi:10.1037/a0033076

Friedman, J. M., & Halaas, J. L. (1998). Leptin and the regulation of body weight in mammals. *Nature, 395*(6704), 673–770. doi:10.1038/27376

Friedman, M., & Rosenman, R. H. (1974). *Type A behavior and your heart*. New York: Knopf.

Friedson, M. (2016). Authoritarian parenting attitudes and social origin: The multigenerational relationship of socioeconomic position to childrearing values. *Child Abuse & Neglect, 51*, 263–275. doi:10.1016/j.chiabu.2015.10.001

Frisch, R. E. (1983). Fatness, menarche, and fertility. In S. Golub (Ed.), *Menarche: The transition from girl to woman* (pp. 5–20). Lexington, MA: Lexington Books.

Frost, P. (2006). European hair and eye color. *Evolution and Human Behavior, 27*, 85–103. doi:10.1016/j.evolhumbehav.2005.07.002

Fulkerson, J. A., Story, M., Mellin, A., Leffert, N., Neumark-Sztainer, D., & French, S. A. (2006). Family dinner meal frequency and adolescent development: Relationships with developmental assets and high-risk behaviors. *Journal of Adolescent Health, 39*(3), 337–345. doi:10.1016/j.jadohealth.2005.12.026

Funder, D. C. (2009). Persons, behaviors and situations: An agenda for personality psychology in the postwar era. *Journal of Research in Personality, 43*(2), 120–126. doi:10.1016/j.jrp.2008.12.041

Fung, L. K., Mahajan, R., Nozzolillo, A., Bernal, P., Krasner, A., Jo, B., Coury, D., Whitaker, A., Veenstra-Vanderweele, J., & Hardan, A. Y. (2016). Pharmacologic treatment of severe irritability and problem behaviors in autism: A systematic review and meta-analysis. *Pediatrics, 137*(Supplement 2), S124-S135. doi:10.1542/peds.2015-2851K

Furnham, A. (2018). The great divide: Academic versus practitioner criteria for psychometric test choice. *Journal of Personality Assessment, 100*(5), 498–506. doi:10.1080/00223891.2018.1488134

Furtner, M. R., Maran, T., & Rauthmann, J. F. (2017). Dark leadership: The role of leaders' dark triad personality traits. In M. G. Clark & C. W. Gruber (Eds.), *Leader development deconstructed* (pp. 75–99). New York: Springer International Publishing.

Gabriel, P. O., Halbert, P., & Golightly, R. T. (2014). *Steller's jay aversion treatment in the Santa Cruz Mountains in 2013*. https://www.researchgate.net/publication/272790325_Steller's_Jay_Conditioned_Aversion_Treatment_in_the_Santa_Cruz_Mountains_in_2013/citation/download

Gainotti, G. (2019). The role of the right hemisphere in emotional and behavioral disorders of patients with frontotemporal lobar degeneration: An updated review. *Frontiers in Aging Neuroscience, 11*(55). doi:10.3389/fnagi.2019.00055

Galbally, M., van Rossum, E. F., Watson, S. J., de Kloet, E. R., & Lewis, A. J. (2019). Trans-generational stress regulation: Mother-infant cortisol and maternal mental health across the perinatal period. *Psychoneuroendocrinology, 109*, 104–374. doi:10.1016/j.psyneuen.2019.104–374.

Galea, S., Ahern, J., Resnick, H., Kilpatrick, D., Bucuvalas, M., Gold, J., & Vlahov, D. (2002). Psychological sequelae of the September 11 terrorist attacks in New York City. *The New England Journal of Medicine, 346*(13), 982–987. doi:10.1056/NEJMsa013404

Gallup Poll News Service. (2005). *Three in four Americans believe in paranormal*. http://home.sandiego.edu/~baber/logic/gallup.html

Gallup, G. G. (1970). Chimpanzees: Self-recognition. *Science, 167*, 86–87. doi:10.1126/science.167.3914.86

Gallup, G. G., & Suarez, S. D. (1986). Self-awareness and the emergence of mind in humans and other primate. In J. Suls & A. Greenwald (Eds.), *Psychological perspectives on the self (Vol. 3)* (pp. 3–26). Hillsdale, NJ: Erlbaum.

Galovski, T., & Lyons, J. A. (2004). Psychological sequelae of combat violence: A review of the impact of PTSD on the veteran's family and possible interventions. *Aggression and Violent Behavior, 9*(5), 477–501. doi:10.1016/s1359-1789(03)00045-4

Galvan, A., Hare, T., Voss, H., Glover, G., & Casey, B. J. (2007). Risk-taking and the adolescent brain: Who is at risk? *Developmental Science, 10*(2), F8–F14. doi:10.1111/j.1467-7687.2006.00579.x

Ganna, A., Verweij, K. J. H., Nivard, M. G., Maier, R., Wedow, R., Busch, A. S., Abdelaoui, A., Guo, S., Sathirapongsasuti, J. F., 23andMe Research Team, Lichtenstein, P., Lundström, S., Långström, N., Auton, A., Harris, K. M., Beecham, G. W., Martin, E. R., Sanders, A. R., Perry, J. R. B., . . . Zietsch, B.

P. (2019). Large-scale GWAS reveals insights into the genetic architecture of same-sex sexual behavior. *Science, 365*(6456), eaat7693. doi:10.1126/science.aat7693

Gantt, W. H. (1928). Ivan P. Pavlov: A biographical sketch. In I. P. Pavlov (Ed.), *Lectures on conditioned reflexes (W. H. Gantt, Trans.)* (pp. 11–34). New York: International Universities Press.

Garb, H. N., Wood, J. M., Lilienfeld, S. O., & Nezworski, M. T. (2005). Roots of the Rorschach controversy. *Clinical Psychology Review, 25*, 97–118. doi:10.1016/j.cpr.2004.09.002

García-León, M. Á., Pérez-Mármol, J. M., Gonzalez-Pérez, R., García-Ríos, M. d. C., & Peralta-Ramírez, M. I. (2019). Relationship between resilience and stress: Perceived stress, stressful life events, HPA axis response during a stressful task and hair cortisol. *Physiology & Behavior, 202*, 87–93. doi:10.1016/j.physbeh.2019.02.001

Garcia, J., & Koelling, K. W. (1966). Relation of cue to consequence in avoidance learning. *Psychonomic Science, 4*, 123–124. doi:10.3758/BF03342209

Gardner, H. (1976). *The shattered mind: The person after brain damage.* New York, NY: Knopf.

Gardner, H. (1983). *Frames of mind: The theory of multiple intelligences.* New York: Basic Books.

Gardner, H. (1999). *Intelligence reframed: Multiple intelligences for the 21st century.* New York: Basic Books.

Gardner, R. A., & Gardner, B. T. (1969). Teaching sign language to a chimpanzee. *Science, 165*(3894), 664–672. doi:10.1126/science.165.3894.664

Garmezy, N. (1991). Resilience and vulnerability to adverse developmental outcomes associated with poverty. *American Behavioral Scientist, 34*(4), 416–430. doi:10.1177/0002764291034004003

Garrity, A., Pearlson, G., McKiernan, K., Lloyd, D., Kiehl, K., & Calhoun, V. (2007). Aberrant "default mode" functional connectivity in schizophrenia. *American Journal of Psychiatry, 164*(3), 450–457. doi:10.1176/appi.ajp.164.3.450

Garver-Apgar, C. E., Gangestad, S. W., Thornhill, R., Miller, R. D., & Olp, J. J. (2006). Major histocompatibility complex alleles, sexual responsivity, and unfaithfulness in romantic couples. *Psychological Science, 17*(10), 830–835. doi:10.1111/j.1467-9280.2006.01789.x

Gasquoine, P. G. (2014). Contributions of the insula to cognition and emotion. *Neuropsychology review, 24*(2), 77–87. doi:10.1007/s11065-014-9246-9

Gatz, M., Smyer, M. A., & DiGilio, D. A. (2016). Psychology's contribution to the well-being of older Americans. *American Psychologist, 71*(4), 257–267. doi:10.1037/a0040251.

Gautam, P., Warner, T. D., Kan, E. C., & Sowell, E. R. (2015). Executive function and cortical thickness in youths prenatally exposed to cocaine, alcohol and tobacco. *Developmental Cognitive Neuroscience, 16*, 155–165. doi:10.1016/j.dcn.2015.01.010

Gawronski, B. (2004). Theory-based bias correction in dispositional inference: The fundamental attribution error is dead, long live the correspondence bias. *European Review of Social Psychology, 15*, 183–217. doi:10.1080/10463280440000026

Gawronski, B., & Brannon, S. M. (2019). What is cognitive consistency, and why does it matter? In E. Harmon-Jones (Ed.), *Cognitive dissonance: Reexamining a pivotal theory in psychology* (p. 91–116). Washington, DC: American Psychological Association. doi:10.1037/0000135-005

Gazzaniga, M. S. (1967). The split brain in man. *Scientific American, 217*, 24–29. doi:10.1038/scientificamerican0867-24

Gazzaniga, M. S. (2011). *Who's in charge? Free will and the science of the brain.* New York, NY: HarperCollins.

Geiser, S., & Studley, R. (2002). UC and the SAT: Predictive validity and differential impact of the SAT I and SAT II at the University of California. *Educational Assessment, 8*(1), 1–26. doi:10.1207/S15326977EA0801_01

Gelfand, M. J., Raver, J. L., Nishii, L., Leslie, L. M., Lun, J., Lim, B. C., Duan, L., Almaliach, A., Ang, S., Arnadottir, J., Aycan Z., Boehnke, K., Boski, P., Cabecinhas, Chan, R. D., Chhokar, J., D'Amato, A., Ferrer, M., Fischlmayr, I. C., Fischer, R., . . . Yamaguchi, S. (2011). Differences between tight and loose cultures: A 33-nation study. *Science, 332*(6033), 1100–1104. doi:10.1126/science.1197754

Gendron, M., Roberson, D., van der Vyver, J. M., & Barrett, L. F. (2014). Perceptions of emotion from facial expressions are not culturally universal: Evidence from a remote culture. *Emotion, 14*(2), 251–262. doi:10.1037/a0036052

Genzel, L., Kroes, M. C., Dresler, M., & Battaglia, F. P. (2014). Light sleep versus slow wave sleep in memory consolidation: A question of global versus local processes? *Trends in Neurosciences, 37*(1), 10–19. doi:10.1016/j.tins.2013.10.002

Gerolimatos, L. A., & Edelstein, B. A. (2012). Predictors of health anxiety among older and young adults. *International Psychogeriatrics, 24*(12), 1998–2008. doi:10.1017/S1041610212001329

Gershoff, E. T., Lansford, J. E., Sexton, H. R., Davis-Kean, P., & Sameroff, A. J. (2012). Longitudinal links between spanking and children's externalizing behaviors in a national sample of White, Black, Hispanic, and Asian American families. *Child Development, 83*(3), 838–843. doi:10.1111/j.1467-8624.2011.01732.x

Gershoff, E. T., Sattler, K. M. P., & Ansari, A. (2017). Strengthening causal estimates for links between spanking and children's externalizing behavior problems. *Psychological Science, 29*(1), 110–120. doi:10.1177/0956797617729816

Gettler, L. T., McDade, T. W., Feranil, A. B., & Kuzawa, C. W. (2011). Longitudinal evidence that fatherhood decreases testosterone in human males. *Proceedings of the National Academy of Sciences of the United States of America.* doi:10.1073/pnas.1105403108

Ghosh, A. (2017). Linking elementary properties of the human brain to the behaviour captured on touchscreen smartphones. In C. Montag & M. Reuter (Eds.), *Internet addiction: Neuroscientific approaches and therapeutical implications including smartphone addiction* (pp. 373–381). New York, NY: Springer International Publishing.

Gialluisi, A., Andlauer, T. F., Mirza-Schreiber, N., Moll, K., Becker, J., Hoffmann, P., Ludwig, K. U., Czamara, D., St. Pourcain, B., Brandler, W., Honbolygó, F., Tóth, D., Csépe, V., Huguet, G., Morris, A. P., Hulslander, J., Willcutt, E. G., DeFries, J. C., Olson, R. K., . . . Schulte-Körne, G. (2019). Genome-wide association scan identifies new variants associated with a cognitive predictor of dyslexia. *Translational Psychiatry, 9*(1), 1–15. doi:10.1038/s41398-019-0402-0

Giancola, P. R. (2013). *Alcohol and aggression: Theories and mechanisms*: Wiley-Blackwell: Chichester, UK.

Gibbons, T., Pence, B., Bhattacharya, T., Mach, H., Ossyra, J., McCusker, R., Kelley, K., Rhodes, J., Johnson, R., & Woods, J. (2014). Diet, exercise, neurogenesis and cognition. *The FASEB Journal, 28*(1 Supplement), 1025.4.

Gibson, M. A. (2008). Does investment in the sexes differ when fathers are absent? Sex-biased infant survival and child growth in rural Ethiopia. *Human Nature, 19*(3), 263–276. doi:10.1007/s12110-008-9044-2

Giedd, J. N., Raznahan, A., Alexander-Bloch, A., Schmitt, E., Gogtay, N., & Rapoport, J. L. (2015). Child Psychiatry Branch of the National Institute of Mental Health Longitudinal Structural Magnetic Resonance Imaging Study of Human Brain Development. *Neuropsychopharmacology, 40*(1), 43–49. doi:10.1038/npp.2014.236

Giesbrecht, T., Lynn, S. J., Lilienfeld, S. O., & Merckelbach, H. (2010). Cognitive processes, trauma, and dissociation—Misconceptions and misrepresentations: Reply to Bremner (2010). *Psychological Bulletin, 136*(1), 7–11. doi:10.1037/a0018068

Gigerenzer, G. (2008). Why heuristics work. *Perspectives on Psychological Science, 3*(1), 20–29. doi:10.1111/j.1745-6916.2008.00058.x

Gilbert, D. T., & Jones, E. E. (1986). Perceiver-induced constraint: Interpretations of self-generated reality. *Journal of Personality and Social Psychology, 50*(2), 269–280. doi:10.1037/0022-3514.50.2.269.

Gilbert, D. T., & Malone, P. S. (1995). The correspondence bias. *Psychological Bulletin, 117*(1), 21–38. doi:10.1037/0033-2909.117.1.21

Haidt, J. (2007). The new synthesis in moral psychology. *Science, 316*(5827), 998–1002. doi:10.1126/science/1137651

Halaas, J. L., Gajiwala, K. S., Maffei, M., Cohen, S. L., Chait, B. T., Rabinowitz, D., Lallone, R. L., Burley, S. K., & Friedman, J. M. (1995). Weight-reducing effects of the plasma protein encoded by the obese gene. *Science, 269*, 543–546. doi:10.1126/science.7624777

Hales, C. M., Carroll, M. D., Fryar, C. D., & Ogden, C. L. (2020). *Prevalence of obesity and severe obesity among adults: United States, 2017–2018.* https://www.cdc.gov/nchs/products/databriefs/db360.htm

Hall, C. S. (1954/2016). *A primer of Freudian psychology* New York, NY: Pickle Partners Publishing.

Halmi, K. A., Casper, R. C., Eckert, E. D., Goldberg, S. C., & Davis, J. M. (1979). Unique features associated with age of onset of anorexia nervosa. *Psychiatry Research, 1*(2), 209–215. doi:10.1016/0165-1781(79)90063-5

Halpern, D. F., Benbow, C. P., Geary, D. C., Gur, R. C., Hyde, J. S., & Gernsbacher, M. A. (2007). The science of sex differences in science and mathematics. *Psychological Science in the Public Interest, 8*(1), 1–51. doi:10.1111/j.1529-1006.2007.00032.x

Halpern, J. H., & Pope, H. G., Jr. (2003). Hallucinogen persisting perception disorder: What do we know after 50 years? *Drug and Alcohol Dependence, 69*(2), 109–119. doi:10.1016/s0376-8716(02)00306-x

Halverson, M. S., & Bolnick, D. A. (2008). An ancient DNA test of a founder effect in Native American ABO blood group frequencies. *American Journal of Physical Anthropology, 137*(3), 342–347. doi:10.1002/ajpa.20887

Hamamura, T. (2012). Are cultures becoming individualistic? A cross-temporal comparison of individualism–collectivism in the United States and Japan. *Personality and Social Psychology Review, 16*(1), 3–24. doi:10.1177/1088868311411587

Hamel, M., Shaffer, T. W., & Erdberg, P. (2000). A study of nonpatient preadolescent Rorschach protocols. *Journal of Personality Assessment, 75*(2), 280–294. doi:10.1207/s15327752jpa7502_8

Hamermesh, D. S., & Parker, A. M. (2003). Beauty in the classroom: Professors' pulchritude and putative pedagogical productivity. *Economics of Education Review, 24*(4), 369–376. doi:10.1016/j.econedurev.2004.07.013

Hamilton, W. D. (1964). The genetical evolution of social behaviour: I and II. *Journal of Theoretical Biology, 7*, 1–16 and 17–52. doi:10.1016/0022-5193(64)90038-4

Han, S., & Ma, Y. (2015). A culture–behavior–brain loop model of human development. *Trends in Cognitive Sciences, 19*(11), 666–676. doi:10.1016/j.tics.2015.08.010

Han, T.-U., Root, J., Reyes, L. D., Huchinson, E. B., du Hoffmann, J., Lee, W.-S., Barnes, T. D., & Drayna, D. (2019). Human GNPTAB stuttering mutations engineered into mice cause vocalization deficits and astrocyte pathology in the corpus callosum. *Proceedings of the National Academy of Sciences of the United States of America, 116*(35), 17515–17524. doi:10.1073/pnas.1901480116

Haney, C., Banks, C., & Zimbardo, P. (1973). Interpersonal dynamics in a simulated prison. *International Journal of Criminology and Penology, 1*, 69–97.

Hare, R. D. (2002). *The predators among us.* Paper presented at the Canadian Police Association Annual General Meeting, St. John's, Newfoundland and Labrador.

Hare, R. D. (2006). Psychopathy: A clinical and forensic overview. *Psychiatric Clinics of North America, 29*(3), 709–724. doi:10.1016/j.psc.2006.04.007

Harlow, H. (1958). The nature of love. *American Psychologist, 13*, 573–685. doi:10.1037/h0047884

Harlow, H. F., & Harlow, M. K. (1973). Social deprivation in monkeys. In W. T. Greenough (Ed.), *The nature and nurture of behavior: Readings from the Scientific American* (pp. 108—116). San Francisco, CA: Freeman.

Harms, P. D., Herian, M., Krasikova, D. V., Vanhove, A. J., & Lester, P. B. (2013). *The Comprehensive Soldier and Family Fitness Program Evaluation. Report # 4: Evaluation of resilience training and mental and behavioral health outcomes.* https://digitalcommons.unl.edu/pdharms/10/

Harper, F. K., Schmidt, J. E., Beacham, A. O., Salsman, J. M., Averill, A. J., Graves, K. D., & Andrykowski, M. A. (2006). The role of social cognitive processing theory and optimism in positive psychosocial and physical behavior change after cancer diagnosis and treatment. *Psychooncology, 16*, 79–91. doi:10.1002/pon.1068

Hart, A. J., Whalen, P. J., Shin, L. M., McInerney, S. C., Fischer, H., & Rauch, S. L. (2000). Differential response in the human amygdala to racial outgroup vs ingroup face stimuli. *Neuroreport, 11*, 2351–2355. doi:10.1097/00001756-200008030-00004

Hart, B., & Risley, T. R. (1995). *Meaningful differences in the everyday experience of young American children*: Baltimore, MD: Paul H Brookes Publishing.

Hart, W., & Albarracin, D. (2009). The effects of chronic achievement motivation and achievement primes on the activation of achievement and fun goals. *Journal of Personality and Social Psychology, 97*(6), 1129–1141. doi:10.1037/a0017146

Harvey, A., Watkins, E., Mansell, W., & Shafran, R. (2004). *Cognitive behavioural processes across psychological disorders.* New York: Oxford University Press.

Haselton, M. G., Bryant, G. A., Wilke, A., Frederick, D. A., Galperin, A., Frankenhuis, W. E., & Moore, T. (2009). Adaptive rationality: An evolutionary perspective on cognitive bias. *Social Cognition, 27*(5), 733–763. doi:10.1521/soco.2009.27.5.733

Hashmi, A., Nere, A., & Tononi, G. (2013). Sleep-dependent synaptic down-selection (II): Single-neuron level benefits for matching, selectivity, and specificity. *Frontiers in Neurology, 4*(148). doi:10.3389/fneur.2013.00148

Hasin, D. S., & Grant, B. F. (2015). The National Epidemiologic Survey on Alcohol and Related Conditions (NESARC) Waves 1 and 2: Review and summary of findings. *Social Psychiatry and Psychiatric Epidemiology, 50*(11), 1609–1640. doi:10.1007/s00127-015-1088-0

Haslam, S. A., Reicher, S. D., Millard, K., & McDonald, R. (2015). 'Happy to have been of service': The Yale archive as a window into the engaged followership of participants in Milgram's 'obedience' experiments. *British Journal of Social Psychology, 54*(1), 55–83. doi:10.1111/bjso.12074

Hathaway, S. R., & McKinley, J. C. (1940). A multiphasic personality schedule (Minnesota): I. Construction of the schedule. *Journal of Psychology, 10*, 249–254. doi:10.1080/00223980.1940.9917000

Hathaway, S. R., & McKinley, J. C. (1943). *The Minnesota Multiphasic Personality Inventory manual.* New York: Psychological Corporation.

Haubrich, J., & Nader, K. (2016). Memory reconsolidation. *Current Topics in Behavioral Neuroscience, 37*, 151–176. doi:10.1007/7854_2016_463

Havekes, R., Park, A. J., Tudor, J. C., Luczak, V. G., Hansen, R. T., Ferri, S. L., . . . Abel, T. (2016). Sleep deprivation causes memory deficits by negatively impacting neuronal connectivity in hippocampal area CA1. *eLife, 5*, e13424. doi:10.7554/eLife.13424

Hawkins, S. S., Wylie, B. J., & Hacker, M. R. (2020). Use of ENDS and cigarettes during pregnancy. *American Journal of Preventive Medicine, 58*(1), 122–128. doi:10.1016/j.amepre.2019.08.031

Hawkley, L. C., & Cacioppo, J. T. (2010). Loneliness matters: A theoretical and empirical review of consequences and mechanisms. *Annals of Behavioral Medicine, 40*(2), 218–227. doi:10.1007/s12160-010-9210-8

Hawkley, L. C., Thisted, R. A., & Cacioppo, J. T. (2009). Loneliness predicts reduced physical activity: Cross-sectional & longitudinal analyses. *Health Psychology, 28*(3), 354–363. doi:10.1037/a0014400

Hawkley, L. C., Wroblewski, K., Kaiser, T., Luhmann, M., & Schumm, L. P. (2019). Are US older adults getting lonelier? Age, period, and cohort differences. *Psychology and Aging, 34*(8), 1144–1157. doi:10.1037/pag0000365

Hayes, J. A., McAleavey, A. A., Castonguay, L. G., & Locke, B. D. (2016). Psychotherapists' outcomes with White and racial/ethnic minority clients: First, the good news. *Journal of Counseling Psychology, 63*(3), 261–268. doi:10.1037/cou0000098

Hayes, J. P., Logue, M. W., Reagan, A., Salat, D., Wolf, E. J., Sadeh, N., Spielberg, J. M., Sperbeck, E., Hayes, S. M., McGlinchey, R. E., Millberg, W. P., Verfaille, M., Stone, A., Schichman, S. A., & Miller, M. W. (2017). COMT Val158Met polymorphism

moderates the association between PTSD symptom severity and hippocampal volume. *Journal of Psychiatry & Neuroscience, 42*(2), 95–102. doi:10.1503/jpn.150339
Hecht, S., Shlaer, S., & Pirenne, M. H. (1942). Energy, quanta, and vision. *Journal of General Physiology, 25*, 819–840. doi:10.1085/jgp.25.6.819
Heider, F. (1958). *The psychology of interpersonal relations*. New York: Wiley.
Heinz, A. J., Beck, A., Meyer-Lindenberg, A., Sterzer, P., & Heinz, A. (2011). Cognitive and neurobiological mechanisms of alcohol-related aggression. *Nature Reviews Neuroscience, 12*(7), 400–413. doi:10.1038/nrn3042
Held, B. S. (2004). The negative side ofpositive psychology. *Journal of HumanisticPsychology, 44*(1), 9–46. doi:10.1177/0022167803259645
Helliwell, J. F. (2003). How's life? Combining individual and national variables to explain subjective well-being. *Economic Modeling, 20*, 331–360. doi:10.1016/S0264-9993(02)00057-3
Helliwell, J. F., Huang, H., Wang, S., & Norton, M. (2020). Social environments for world happiness. In J. F. Helliwell, R. Layard, J. D. Sachs, & J.-E. De Neve (Eds.), *World happiness report* (pp. 13–46). New York, NY: Sustainable Development Solutions Network.
Helpern, J. A., Adisetiyo, V., Falangola, M. F., Hu, C., Di Martino, A., Williams, K., Castellanos, F. X., & Jensen, J. H. (2011). Preliminary evidence of altered gray and white matter microstructural development in the frontal lobe of adolescents with attention-deficit hyperactivity disorder: A diffusional kurtosis imaging study. *Journal of Magnetic Resonance Imaging, 33*(1), 17–23. doi:10.1002/jmri.22397
Hendin, H. M., & Cheek, J. M. (1997). Assessing hypersensitive narcissism: A reexamination of Murray's Narcism Scale. *Journal of Research in Personality, 31*(4), 588–599. doi:10.1006/jrpe.1997.2204
Henkel, L. A., & Mather, M. (2007). Memory attributions for choices: How beliefs shape our memories. *Journal of Memory and Language, 57*(2), 163–176. doi:10.1016/j.jml.2006.08.012
Hennenlotter, A., Schroeder, U., Erhard, P., Haslinger, B., Stahl, R., Weindl, A., von Einseidel, H. G., Lange, K. W., & Ceballos-Baumann, A. (2004). Neural correlates associated with impaired disgust processing in pre-symptomatic Huntington's disease. *Brain, 127*(6), 1446–1453. doi:10.1093/brain/awh165
Herek, G. M., & Glunt, E. K. (1993). Interpersonal contact and heterosexuals' attitudes toward gay men: Results from a national survey. *The Journal of Sex Research, 30*(3), 239–244. doi:10.1080/00224499309551707
Hernandez, T. L., Kittelson, J. M., Law, C. K., Ketch, L. L., Stob, N. R., Lindstrom, R. C., Scherzinger, A., Stamm, E. R., & Eckel, R. H. (2011). Fat redistribution following suction lipectomy: Defense of body fat and patterns of restoration. *Obesity, 19*(7), 1388–1395. doi:10.1038/oby.2011.64
Herndon, J. G. (2010). The grandmother effect: Implications for studies on aging and cognition. *Gerontology, 56*(1), 73–79. doi:10.1159/000236045
Herpertz, S. C., Werth, U., Lukas, G., Qunaibi, M., Schuerkens, A., Kunert, H. J., Freese, R., Flesch, M., Mueller-Isberner, R., Osterheider, M., & Sass, H. (2001). Emotion in criminal offenders with psychopathy and borderline personality disorder. *Archives of General Psychiatry, 58*, 737–745. doi:10.1001/archpsyc.58.8.737
Herrnstein, R. J. (1979). Acquisition, generalization, and discrimination reversal of a natural concept. *Journal of Experimental Psychology: Animal Behavior Processes, 5*(2), 116–129. doi:10.1037/0097-7403.5.2.116
Herrnstein, R. J., & Boring, E. G. (1965). *A source book in the history of psychology*. Cambridge, MA: Harvard University Press.
Herrnstein, R. J., & de Villiers, P. A. (1980). Fish as a natural category for people and pigeons. In G. H. Bower (Ed.), *The psychology of learning and motivation* (Vol. 14, pp. 59–95). New York, NY: Academic Press.
Herrnstein, R. J., & Heyman, G. M. (1979). Is matching compatible with reinforcement maximization on concurrent variable-interval, variable ratio? *Journal of the Experimental Analysis of Behavior, 31*, 209–223. doi:10.1901/jeab.1979.31-209
Herxheimer, A., & Waterhouse, J. (2003). The prevention and treatment of jet lag. *British Medical Journal*, 326(7384), 296–297. doi:10.1136/bmj.326.7384.296
Herz, D. M., Tan, H., Brittain, J.-S., Fischer, P., Cheeran, B., Green, A. L., FitzGerald, J., Aziz, T. Z., Ashkan, K., Little, S., Foltynie, T., Limousin, P., Zrinzo, L., Bogacz, R., & Brown, P. (2017). Distinct mechanisms mediate speed-accuracy adjustments in cortico-subthalamic networks. *eLife, 6*, e21481. doi:10.7554/eLife.21481
Herz, R. (2003). The effect of verbal context on olfactory perception. *Journal of Experimental Psychology: General, 132*, 595–606. doi:10.1037/0096-3445.132.4.595
Hicks, T. V., Leitenberg, H., Barlow, D. H., Gorman, J. M., Shear, M. K., & Woods, S. W. (2005). Physical, mental, and social catastrophic cognitions as prognostic factors in cognitive-behavioral and pharmacological treatments for panic disorder. *Journal of Consulting and Clinical Psychology, 73*(3), 506–514. doi:10.1037/0022-006x.73.3.506
Himelboim, I., McCreery, S., & Smith, M. (2013). Birds of a feather tweet together: Integrating network and content analyses to examine cross-ideology exposure on Twitter. *Journal of Computer-Mediated Communication, 18*(2), 40–60. doi:10.1111/jcc4.12001
Hinton, D. E., & Good, B. (Eds.). (2009). *Culture and panic disorder*. Stanford, CA: Stanford University Press.
Hirshkowitz, M., & Moore, C. A. (1996). Sleep-related erectile activity. *Neurologic Clinics, 14*(4), 721–737. doi:10.1016/s0733-8619(05)70282-6
Ho, B.-C., Wassink, T. H., Ziebell, S., & Andreasen, N. C. (2011). Cannabinoid receptor 1 gene polymorphisms and marijuana misuse interactions on white matter and cognitive deficits in schizophrenia. *Schizophrenia Research, 128*(1–3), 66–75. doi:10.1016/j.schres.2011.02.021
Ho, M. Y., & Fung, H. H. (2011). A dynamic process model of forgiveness: A cross-cultural perspective. *Review of General Psychology, 15*(1), 77–84. doi:10.1037/a0022605
Hobson, J., & McCarley, R. W. (1977). The brain as a dream state generator: An activation-synthesis hypothesis of the dream process. *American Journal of Psychiatry, 134*, 1335–1348. doi:10.1176/ajp.134.12.1335
Hodges, B. H., & Geyer, A. L. (2006). A nonconformist account of the Asch experiments: Values, pragmatics, and moral dilemmas. *Personality and Social Psychology Review, 10*(1), 2–19. doi:10.1207/s15327957pspr1001_1
Hodgkin, A. L., & Huxley, A. F. (1952). A quantitative description of membrane current and its application to conduction and excitation in nerve. *Journal of Physiology, 117*, 500–544. doi:10.1113/jphysiol.1952.sp004764
Hoebel, B. G., & Teitelbaum, P. (1966). Effects of forcefeeding and starvation on food intake and body weight in a rat with ventromedial hypothalamic lesions. *Journal of Comparative and Physiological Psychology, 61*, 189–193. doi:10.1037/h0023126
Hoeft, F., McCandliss, B. D., Black, J. M., Gantman, A., Zakerani, N. Hulme, C., Lyytinen, H., Whitfield-Gabrieli, S., Glover, G. H., Reiss, A. L., & Gabrieli, J. D. E. (2011). Neural systems predicting long-term outcome in dyslexia, *Proceedings of the National Academy of Sciences of the United States of America, 108*(1), 361–366. doi:10.1073/pnas.1008950108
Hoff, T. L. (1992). Psychology in Canada one hundred years ago: James Mark Baldwin at the University of Toronto. *Canadian Psychology, 33*, 683–694. doi:10.1037/h0078745
Hofling, C. K., Brotzman, E., Dalrymple, S., Graves, N., & Pierce, C. M. (1966). An experimental study in nurse-physician relationships. *Journal of Nervous and Mental Disease, 143*, 171–180. doi:10.1097/00005053-196608000-00008
Hofstede, G. (1980). *Culture's consequences*. Beverly Hills, CA: Sage.
Hofstede, G. (1984). The cultural relativity of the quality of life concept. *The Academy of Management Review, 9*(3), 389–398. doi:10.5465/AMR.1984.4279653

Hogan, C. L., Mata, J., & Carstensen, L. L. (2013). Exercise holds immediate benefits for affect and cognition in younger and older adults. *Psychology and Aging, 28*(2), 587–594. doi:10.1037/a0032634

Holder, M. K. (1999). *Influences and constraints on manual asymmetry in wild African primates: Reassessing implications for the evolution of human handedness and brain lateralization*. Ph.D. dissertation. Rutgers University. New Brunswick, New Jersey, USA.

Holingue, C., Newill, C., Lee, L.-C., Pasricha, P. J., & Daniele Fallin, M. (2018). Gastrointestinal symptoms in autism spectrum disorder: A review of the literature on ascertainment and prevalence. *Autism Research, 11*(1), 24–36. doi:10.1002/aur.1854

Holland, D., Chang, L., Ernst, T. M., Curran, M., Buchthal, S. D., Alicata, D., Skranes, J., Johansen, H., Hernandez, A., Yamakawa, R., Kuperman, J. M., & Dale, A. M. (2014). Structural growth trajectories and rates of change in the first 3 months of infant brain development. *JAMA Neurology, 71*(10), 1266–1274. doi:10.1001/jamaneurol.2014.1638

Hollon, S. D., Thase, M. E., & Markowitz, J. C. (2002). Treatment and prevention of depression. *Psychological Science in the Public Interest, 3*(2), 39–77. doi:10.1111/1529-1006.00008

Holmes, T. H., & Rahe, R. H. (1967). The social readjustment rating scale. *Journal of Psychosomatic Research, 11*, 213–218. doi:10.1016/0022-3999(67)90010-4

Holt-Lunstad, J., Smith, T. B., Baker, M., Harris, T., & Stephenson, D. (2015). Loneliness and social isolation as risk factors for mortality: A meta-analytic review. *Perspectives on Psychological Science, 10*(2), 227–237. doi:10.1177/1745691614568352

Holt, L. H., Lotto, A. J., & Kleuender, K. R. (1998). Incorporating principles of general learning in theories of language acquisition. In M. Gruber, C. D. Higgins, K. S. Olson, & T. Wysocki (Eds.), *Chicago Linguistic Society: Vol. 34: The panels* (pp. 253–268). Chicago, IL: Chicago Linguistic Society.

Holtmann, O., Bruchmann, M., Mönig, C., Schwindt, W., Melzer, N., Miltner, W. H. R., & Straube, T. (2020). Lateralized deficits of disgust processing after insula-basal ganglia damage. *Frontiers in Psychology, 11*(1429). doi:10.3389/fpsyg.2020.01429

Holtzman, J. N., Miller, S., Hooshmand, F., Wang, P. W., Chang, K. D., Goffin, K. C., Hill, S. J., Ketter, T. A., & Rasgon, N. L. (2016). Gender by onset age interaction may characterize distinct phenotypic subgroups in bipolar patients. *Journal of Psychiatric Research, 76*, 128–135. doi:10.1016/j.jpsychires.2016.02.009

Hölzel, B. K., Lazar, S. W., Gard, T., Schuman-Olivier, Z., Vago, D. R., & Ott, U. (2011). How does mindfulness meditation work? Proposing mechanisms of action from a conceptual and neural perspective. *Perspectives on Psychological Science, 6*(6), 537–559. doi:10.1177/1745691611419671

Holzgrabe, U., Kapkova, P., Alptuzun, V., Scheiber, J., & Kugelmann, E. (2007). Targeting acetylcholinesterase to treat neurodegeneration. *Expert Opinion on Therapeutic Targets 11*(2), 161–179. doi:10.1517/14728222.11.2.161

Hoogman, M., Bralten, J., Hibar, D. P., Mennes, M., Zwiers, M. P., Schweren, L. S., van Hulzen K. J. E., Medland, S. E., Shumskaya, E., Jahanshad, N., de Zeeuw, P., Szekely, E., Sudre, G., Wolfers, T., Onnink, A. M. H., Dammers, J. T., Mostert, J. C., Vives-Gilabert, Y., Kohls, G., . . . Franke, B. (2017). Subcortical brain volume differences in participants with attention deficit hyperactivity disorder in children and adults: A cross-sectional mega-analysis. *The Lancet Psychiatry, 4*(4), 310–319. doi:10.1016/S2215-0366(17)30049-4

Hopkins, W. D. (2006). Comparative and familial analysis of handedness in great apes. *Psychological Bulletin, 132*(4), 538–559. doi:10.1037/0033-2909.132.4.538

Hopper, K., Harrison, G., Janca, A., & Sartorius, N. (2007). *Recovery from schizophrenia: An international perspective: A report from the WHO Collaborative Project, the international study of schizophrenia*. New York, NY US: Oxford University Press.

Horn, J. L., & Hofer, S. M. (1992). Major abilities and development in the adult period. In R. J. Sternberg & C. A. Berg (Eds.), *Intellectual development* (pp. 44–99). Cambridge, U.K.: Cambridge University Press.

Horney, K. (1923-1937/1967). *Feminine psychology*. New York: Norton.

Horney, K. (1950). *The collected works of Karen Horney*. New York: Norton.

Horwitz, A. V., White, H. R., & Howell-White, S. (1997). Becoming married and mental health: A longitudinal study of a cohort of young adults. *Journal of Marriage and the Family, 58*, 895–907. doi:10.2307/353978

Hosobuchi, Y., Adams, J., & Linchitz, R. (1977). Pain relief by electrical stimulation of the central gray matter in humans and its reversal by naloxone. *Science, 197*(4299), 183–186. doi:10.1126/science.301658

Hostinar, C. E., Sullivan, R. M., & Gunnar, M. R. (2013). Psychobiological mechanisms underlying the social buffering of the hypothalamic–pituitary–adrenocortical axis: A review of animal models and human studies across development. *Psychological Bulletin, 140*(1), 256–282. doi:10.1037/a0032671

Hou, Y., Song, B., Hu, Y., Pan, Y., & Hu, Y. (2020). The averaged inter-brain coherence between the audience and a violinist predicts the popularity of violin performance. *NeuroImage, 211*, 116655. doi:10.1016/j.neuroimage.2020.116655

House, J. S., Landis, K. R., & Umberson, D. (1988). Social relationships and health. *Science, 241*, 540–545. doi:10.1126/science.3399889

Houston, S. M., Herting, M. M., & Sowell, E. R. (2013). The neurobiology of childhood structural brain development: Conception through adulthood. *Current Topics in Behavioral Neuroscience, 16*, 3–17. doi:10.1007/7854_2013_265

Hove, M. J., & Stelzer, J. (2018). Biological foundations and beneficial effects of trance. *Behavioral and Brain Sciences, 41*, e76. doi:10.1017/S0140525X17002072

Howard, A. D., Feighner, S. D., Cully, D. F., Arena, J. P., Liberator, P. A., Rosenblum, C. I., Hamelin, M. Hreniuk, D. L., Palyha, O. C., Anderson, J., Paress, P. S., Diaz, C., Chou, M., Liu, K. K., McKee, K. K., Pong, S-S., Chaung, L-Y., Elbrecht, A., Dashkevicz, M., . . . Van der Ploeg, L. H. T. (1996). A receptor in pituitary and hypothalamus that functions in growth hormone release. *Science, 273*(5277), 974–977. doi:10.1126/science.273.5277.974

Howell, R. T., & Hill, G. (2009). The mediators of experiential purchases: Determining the impact of psychological needs satisfaction and social comparison. *The Journal of Positive Psychology, 4*(6), 511–522. doi:10.1080/17439760903270993

Howes, O. D., McCutcheon, R., Owen, M. J., & Murray, R. M. (2017). The role of genes, stress, and dopamine in the development of schizophrenia. *Biological Psychiatry, 81*(1), 9–20. doi:10.1016/j.biopsych.2016.07.014

H. P. Nair & L. J. Young (2006). Vasopressin and pair-bond formation: Genes to brain to behavior. *Journal of Physiology, 21*(2), 146–152. doi:10.1152/physiol.00049.2005

Hrdy, S. B. (2005). Comes the child before the man: How cooperative breeding and prolonged postweaning dependence shaped human potential. In B. S. Hewlett & S. E. Lamb (Eds.), *Hunter-gatherer childhoods: Evolutionary, developmental and cultural perspectives* (pp. 65–91). New Brunswick, NJ: Transaction publishers.

Hübel, C., Leppä, V., Breen, G., & Bulik, C. M. (2018). Rigor and reproducibility in genetic research on eating disorders. *International Journal of Eating Disorders, 51*(7), 593–607. doi:10.1002/eat.22896

Hubel, D. H., & Livingstone, M. S. (1987). Segregation of form, color, and stereopsis in primate area 18. *Journal of Neuroscience, 7*, 3378–3415. doi:10.1523/JNEUROSCI.07-11-03378.1987

Hubel, D. H., & Wiesel, T. N. (1959). Receptive fields of single neurons in the cat's striate cortex. *Journal of Physiology, 148*, 574–591. doi:10.1113/jphysiol.1959.sp006308

Hudson, J. I., Hiripi, E., Pope, H. G., & Kessler, R. C. (2007). The prevalence and correlates of eating disorders in the National Comorbidity Survey Replication. *Biological Psychiatry, 61*(3), 348–358. doi:10.1016/j.biopsych.2006.03.040

Hudson, N. W., & Fraley, R. C. (2015). Volitional personality trait change: Can people choose to change their personality traits? *Journal of Personality and Social Psychology, 109*(3), 490–507. doi:10.1037/pspp0000021

Hudspeth, A. (1983). The hair cells of the inner ear. *Scientific American, 248*, 54–64. doi:10.1038/scientificamerican0183-54

Hugenberg, K., Young, S. G., Bernstein, M. J., & Sacco, D. F. (2010). The categorization-individuation model: An integrative account of the other-race recognition deficit. *Psychological Review, 117*(4), 1168–1187. doi:10.1037/a0020463

Hull, C. L. (1943). *Principles of Behaviour*. New York: Appleton-Century-Crofts.

Hunt, H. T. (1989). *The multiplicity of dreams*. New Haven, CT: Yale University Press.

Hunt, J., & Eisenberg, D. (2010). Mental health problems and help-seeking behavior among college students. *Journal of Adolescent Health, 46*(1), 3–10. doi:10.1016/j.jadohealth.2009.08.008

Hupka, R. B., Lenton, A. P., & Hutchison, K. A. (1999). Universal development of emotion categories in natural language. *Journal of Personality and Social Psychology, 77*, 247–278. doi:10.1037/0022-3514.77.2.247

Huttenlocher, P. R. (2009). *Neural plasticity*. Cambridge, MA: Harvard University Press.

Hüweler, R., Kandil, F. I., Alpers, G. W., & Gerlach, A. L. (2009). The impact of visual flow stimulation on anxiety, dizziness, and body sway in individuals with and without fear of heights. *Behaviour Research and Therapy, 47*(4), 345–352. doi:10.1016/j.brat.2009.01.011

Hypnotherapists Union Local 472. (2019). Summary of state laws regarding hypnosis. https://hypnotherapistsunion.wildapricot.org/statelaws

Hystad, S. W., Eid, J., Laberg, J. C., Johnsen, B. H., & Bartone, P. T. (2009). Academic stress and health: Exploring the moderating role of personality hardiness. *Scandinavian Journal of Educational Research, 53*(5), 421–429. doi:10.1080/00313830903180349

Igielnik, R. (2020). *Most Americans say they regularly wore a mask in stores in the past month; Fewer see others doing it*. Pew Research Center. https://www.pewresearch.org/fact-tank/2020/06/23/most-americans-say-they-regularly-wore-a-mask-in-stores-in-the-past-month-fewer-see-others-doing-it/

Inman, C. S., Manns, J. R., Bijanki, K. R., Bass, D. I., Hamann, S., Drane, D. L., Fasano, R. E., Kovach, C. K., Gross, R. E., & Willie, J. T. (2018). Direct electrical stimulation of the amygdala enhances declarative memory in humans. *Proceedings of the National Academy of Sciences of the United States of America, 115*(1), 98–103. doi:10.1073/pnas.1714058114

Insel, T. R. (2007). *Post-traumatic stress disorder research at the National Institute of Mental Health*. http://www.hhs.gov/asl/testify/2007/05/t20070524a.html

Instant Chemistry. (2019). *Instant Chemistry uses biological and psychological factors to determine relationship compatibility*. https://instantchemistry.com/pages/relationship-compatibility

Institute of Medicine (IOM). (1994). *Growing up tobacco free: Preventing nicotine addiction in children and youths*. Washington, DC: National Academy Press.

International Coach Federation (ICF). (2016). *2016 ICF Global Coaching Study*. https://coachfederation.org/app/uploads/2017/12/2016ICFGlobalCoachingStudy_ExecutiveSummary-2.pdf

International Coach Federation (ICF). (n.d.). *FAQs*. http://coachfederation.org/faqs

International Society for the Study of Trauma and Dissociation. (2015). *Guidelines for treating dissociative identity disorder in adults*. http://www.isst-d.org/default.asp?contentID=49

Ioannou, C. C., Guttal, V., & Couzin, I. D. (2012). Predatory fish select for coordinated collective motion in virtual prey. *Science, 337*(6099), 1212–1215. doi:10.1126/science.1218919

Ironson, G., Lucette, A., Hylton, E., Pargament, K. I., & Krause, N. (2018). The relationship between religious and psychospiritual measures and an inflammation marker (CRP) in older adults experiencing life event stress. *Journal of Religion and Health, 57*(4), 1554–1566. doi:10.1007/s10943-018-0600-8

Ishunina, T. A., & Swaab, D. F. (1999). Vasopressin and oxytocin neurons of the human supraoptic and paraventricular nucleus; Size changes in relation to age and sex. *Journal of Clinical Endocrinology & Metabolism, 84*(12), 4637–4644. doi:10.1210/jc.84.12.4637

Ito, T. A., & Urland, G. R. (2003). The influence of processing objectives on the perception of faces: An ERP study of race and gender perception. *Cognitive, Affective, and Behavioral Neuroscience, 5*, 21–36. doi:10.3758/CABN.5.1.21

Ittleson, W. H. (1952). *The Ames demonstrations in perception*. Princeton, NJ: Princeton University Press.

Iveson, C. (2002). Solution-focused brief therapy. *Advances in Psychiatric Treatment, 8*, 149–156. doi:10.1192/apt.8.2.149

Ivleva, E. I., Clementz, B. A., Dutcher, A. M., Arnold, S. J., Jeon-Slaughter, H., Aslan, S., et al. (2016). Brain structure biomarkers in the psychosis biotypes: Findings from the bipolar-schizophrenia network for intermediate phenotypes. *Biological Psychiatry, 82*(1) 26–39. doi:10.1016/j.biopsych.2016.08.030

Jackson, B., Kubzansky, L. D., Cohen, S., Jacobs, D. R., Jr., & Wright, R. J. (2007). Does harboring hostility hurt? Associations between hostility and pulmonary function in the Coronary Artery Risk Development in (Young) Adults (CARDIA) study. *Health Psychology, 26*(3), 333–340. doi:10.1037/0278-6133.26.3.333

Jackson, J. H. (1884). The Croonian lectures of evolution and dissolution of the nervous system. Lecture 1. *British Medical Journal, 1*, 591–593. doi:10.1136/bmj.1.1214.660

Jakupcak, M., Tull, M. T., McDermott, M. J., Kaysen, D., Hunt, S., & Simpson, T. (2010). PTSD symptom clusters in relationship to alcohol misuse among Iraq and Afghanistan war veterans seeking post-deployment VA health care. *Addictive Behaviors, 35*(9), 840–843. doi:10.1016/j.addbeh.2010.03.023

Jamal, A., King, B. A., Neff, L. J., Whitmill, J., Babb, S. D., & Graffunder, C. M. (2016). Current cigarette smoking among adults — United States, 2005–2015. *Morbidity and Mortality Weekly Report 65* (44), 1205–1211. doi:10.15585/mmwr.mm6544a2

James, W. (1884/1969). What is an emotion? In *William James: Collected essays and reviews* (pp. 244–280). New York: Russell and Russell.

James, W. (1887). What is an instinct? *Scribner's Magazine, 1*, 355–365.

James, W. (1890). *Principles of psychology*. New York: Henry Holt.

James, W. (1899). *Talks to teachers on psychology: And to students on some of life's ideals*. New York, NY: Holt.

James, W. (1905). *The varieties of religious experience: A study in human nature*. New York: Longmans, Green, and Company.

Jamison, K. (1993). *Touched with fire: Manic-depressive illness and the artistic temperament*. New York: Free Press.

Jamison, K. R. (1995). Manic-depressive illness and creativity. *Scientific American, 272*, 62–67. doi:10.1038/scientificamerican0295-62

Jancke, L., & Kaufmann, N. (1994). Facial EMG responses to odors in solitude and with an audience. *Chemical Senses, 19*, 99–111. doi:10.1093/chemse/19.2.99

Jang, K. L., Livesley, W. J., & Vernon, P. A. (1996). Heritability of the big five personality dimensions and their facets: A twin study. *Journal of Personality, 64*, 575–592. doi:10.1111/j.1467-6494.1996.tb00522.x

Janik, V. M., Sayigh, L. S., & Wells, R. S. (2006). Signature whistle shape conveys identity information to bottlenose dolphins. *Proceedings of the National Academy of Sciences of the United States of America, 103*, 8293–8297. doi:10.1073/pnas.0509918103

Janis, I. (1971). Groupthink. *Psychology Today, 5*, 43–46; 74–76.

Janusonis, S. (2008). Origin of the blood hyperserotonemia of autism. *Theoretical Biology & Medical Modelling, 5*, 10. doi:10.1186/1742-4682-5-10

Jaques, E. (1965). Death and the midlife crisis. *International Journal of Psycho-analysis, 46*, 502–514.

Jardri, R., Hugdahl, K., Hughes, M., Brunelin, J., Waters, F., Alderson-Day, B., Smailes, D., Sterzer, P., Corlett, P. R., Leptourgos, P., Debbané, M., Cachia, A., & Denève, S. (2016). Are hallucinations due to an imbalance between excitatory and inhibitory influences on the brain? *Schizophrenia Bulletin, 42*(5), 1124–1134. doi:10.1093/schbul/sbw075

Jardri, R., Thomas, P., Delmaire, C., Delion, P., & Pins, D. (2013). The neurodynamic organization of modality-dependent hallucinations. *Cerebral Cortex, 23*(5), 1108–1117. doi:10.1093/cercor/bhs082

Jeglic, E., Miranda, R., Polanco-Roman, L., Chang, E., Downey, C., Hirsch, J., & Lin, N. (2016). Positive psychology in the context of race and ethnicity. In E. Chang, C.

A. Downey, J. K. Hirsch, & N. Lin (Eds.), *Positive Psychology in Racial and Ethnic Groups* (pp.13–33). Washington, DC: American Psychological Association.

Jegou, A., Schabus, M., Gosseries, O., Dahmen, B., Albouy, G., Desseilles, M., Sterpenich, V., Phillips, C., Maquet, P., Grova, C., & Dang-Vu, T. T. (2019). Cortical reactivations during sleep spindles following declarative learning. *NeuroImage, 195*, 104–112. doi:10.1016/j.neuroimage.2019.03.051

Jenkinson, C. E., Dickens, A. P., Jones, K., Thompson-Coon, J., Taylor, R. S., Rogers, M., Bambra, C. L., Lang, I., & Richards, S. H. (2013). Is volunteering a public health intervention? A systematic review and meta-analysis of the health and survival of volunteers. *BMC Public Health, 13*(1), 773. doi:10.1186/1471-2458-13-773

Jensen, R., & Burgess, H. (1997). Mythmaking: How introductory psychology texts present B. F. Skinner's analysis of cognition. *Psychological Record, 47*(2), 221–232. doi:10.1007/BF03395221

Jepson, T. L., Ernst, M. E., & Kelly, M. W. (1998). Current perspectives on the management of seasonal affective disorder. *Journal of the American Pharmaceutical Association, 39*(6), 822–829.

Jerabeck, J. M., & Ferguson, C. J. (2013). The influence of solitary and cooperative violent video game play on aggressive and prosocial behavior. *Computers in Human Behavior, 29*(6), 2573–2578. doi:10.1016/j.chb.2013.06.034

Jetten, J., Branscombe, N. R., Haslam, S. A., Haslam, C., Cruwys, T., Jones, J. M., Cui, L., Dingle, G., Liu, J., Murphy, S., Thai, A., Walter, Z., & Zhang, A. (2015). Having a lot of a good thing: Multiple important group memberships as a source of self-esteem. *PloS one, 10*(5), e0124609. doi:10.1371/journal.pone.0124609

Ji, Y., Azuine, R. E., Zhang, Y., Hou, W., Hong, X., Wang, G., Riley, A., Pearson, C., Zuckerman, B., & Wang, X. (2020). Association of cord plasma biomarkers of in utero acetaminophen exposure with risk of attention-deficit/hyperactivity disorder and autism spectrum disorder in childhood. *JAMA Psychiatry, 77*(2), 180–189. doi:10.1001/jamapsychiatry.2019.3259
Ji, Y., Azuine, R. E., Zhang, Y., Hou, W., Hong, X., Wang, G., Riley, A., Pearson, C., Zuckerman, B., & Wang, X. (2020). Association of cord plasma biomarkers of in utero acetaminophen exposure with risk of attention-deficit/hyperactivity disorder and autism spectrum disorder in childhood. *JAMA Psychiatry, 77*(2), 180–189. doi:10.1001/jamapsychiatry.2019.3259
Jia, F., & Krettenauer, T. (2017). Recognizing moral identity as a cultural construct. *Frontiers in Psychology, 8*(412). doi:10.3389/fpsyg.2017.00412

Jiang, C., Mitran, A., Minino, A., & Ni, H. (2015). Racial and gender disparities in suicide among young adults aged 18–24: United States, 2009–2013. https://www.cdc.gov/nchs/data/hestat/suicide/racial_and_gender_2009_2013.htm

Joas, E., Karanti, A., Song, J., Goodwin, G. M., Lichtenstein, P., & Landén, M. (2017). Pharmacological treatment and risk of psychiatric hospital admission in bipolar disorder. *The British Journal of Psychiatry, 210*(3), 197–202. doi:10.1192/bjp.bp.116.187989

Joel, S., Gordon, A. M., Impett, E. A., MacDonald, G., & Keltner, D. (2013). The things you do for me: Perceptions of a romantic partner's investments promote gratitude and commitment. *Personality and Social Psychology Bulletin, 39*(10), 1333–1345. doi:10.1177/0146167213497801

Joëls, M. (2006). Corticosteroid effects in the brain: U-shape it. *Trends in Pharmacological Sciences, 27*(5), 244–250. doi:10.1016/j.tips.2006.03.007

Johns, M. W. (1991). A new method for measuring daytime sleepiness: The Epworth sleepiness scale. *Sleep, 14*(6), 540–545. doi: 10.1093/sleep/14.6.540

Johnson, J. A. (2009). Wrong and right questions about persons and situations. *Journal of Research in Personality, 43*(2), 251–252. doi:10.1016/j.jrp.2008.12.022

Johnson, P. L., Truitt, W., Fitz, S. D., Minick, P. E., Dietrich, A., Sanghani, S., Träskman-Bendz, L., Goddard, A. W., Brundin, L., & Shekhar, A. (2010). A key role for orexin in panic anxiety. *Nature Medicine, 16*(1), 111–115. doi:10.1038/nm.2075

Johnson, S. P., & Aslin, R. N. (1995). Perception of object unity in 2-month-old infants. *Developmental Psychology, 31*, 739–745. doi:10.1037/0012-1649.31.5.739

Jones, B. C., Hahn, A. C., Fisher, C. I., Wang, H., Kandrik, M., & DeBruine, L. M. (2018). General sexual desire, but not desire for uncommitted sexual relationships, tracks changes in women's hormonal status. *Psychoneuroendocrinology, 88*, 153–157. doi:https://doi.org/10.1016/j.psyneuen.2017.12.015

Jones, E. E., & Nisbett, R. E. (1972). The actor and the observer: Divergent perceptions of the causes of the behavior. In E. E. Jones, D. E. Kanouse, H. H. Kelley, R. E. Nisbett, S. Valins, & B. Weiner (Eds.), *Attribution: Perceiving the causes of behavior* (pp. 79–94). Morristown, NJ: General Learning Press.

Jones, E. E., Rhodewalt, F., Berglas, S., & Skelton, J. A. (1981). Effects of strategic self-presentation on subsequent self-esteem. *Journal of Personality and Social Psychology, 41*, 407–421. doi:10.1037/0022-3514.41.3.407

Jones, M. C. (1924). The elimination of children's fears. *Journal of Experimental Psychology, 7*, 382–390. doi:10.1037/h0072283

Jones, M. E., Schoemaker, M. J., McFadden, E. C., Wright, L. B., Johns, L. E., & Swerdlow, A. J. (2019). Night shift work and risk of breast cancer in women: The Generations Study cohort. *British Journal of Cancer, 121*(2), 172–179. doi:10.1038/s41416-019-0485-7

Jorm, A. F., Patten, S. B., Brugha, T. S., & Mojtabai, R. (2017). Has increased provision of treatment reduced the prevalence of common mental disorders? Review of the evidence from four countries. *World Psychiatry, 16*(1), 90–99. doi:10.1002/wps.20388

Jouriles, E. N., Rosenfield, D., McDonald, R., Vu, N. L., Rancher, C., & Mueller, V. (2018). Children exposed to intimate partner violence: Conduct problems, interventions, and partner contact with the child. *Journal of Clinical Child & Adolescent Psychology, 47*(3), 397–409. doi:10.1080/15374416.2016.1163706

Judge, T. A., Livingston, B. A., & Hurst, C. (2012). Do nice guys—and gals—really finish last? The joint effects of sex and agreeableness on income. *Journal of Personality and Social Psychology, 102*(2), 390–407. doi:10.1037/a0026021

Jung, C. G. (1928). *Contributions to analytical psychology*. New York: Harcourt Brace Jovanovich.

Juster, R.-P., McEwen, B. S., & Lupien, S. J. (2010). Allostatic load biomarkers of chronic stress and impact on health and cognition. *Neuroscience & Biobehavioral Reviews, 35*(1), 2–16. doi:10.1016/j.neubiorev.2009.10.002

Juvonen, J. (2005). Myths and facts about bullying in schools. *Behavioral Health Management, 25*, 36–40.

Kaczkurkin, A. N., Burton, P. C., Chazin, S. M., Manbeck, A. B., Espensen-Sturges, T., Cooper, S. E., Sponheim, S. R., & Lissek, S. (2016). Neural substrates of overgeneralized conditioned fear in PTSD. *American Journal of Psychiatry, 174*(2), 125–135. doi:10.1176/appi. ajp.2016.15121549

Kaestle, C. E. (2019). Sexual orientation trajectories based on sexual attractions, partners, and identity: A longitudinal investigation from adolescence through young adulthood using a US representative sample. *The Journal of Sex Research, 56*(7), 811–826. doi:10.1080/00224499.2019.1577351

Kagan, J. (1997). Temperament and the reactions to unfamiliarity. *Child Development, 68*, 139–143. doi:10.2307/1131931

Kagan, J., Kearsley, R. B., & Zelazo, P. R. (1978). *Infancy: Its place in human development*. Cambridge, MA: Harvard University Press.

Kahn, D. (2013). Brain basis of self: Self-organization and lessons from dreaming. *Frontiers in Psychology, 4*, 408. doi:10.3389/fpsyg.2013.00408.

Kail, R. V., Lervåg, A., & Hulme, C. (2016). Longitudinal evidence linking processing speed to the development of reasoning. *Developmental Science, 19*(6), 1067–1074. doi:10.1111/desc.12352

Kail, R., & Bisanz, J. (1991). Developmental change in speed of processing during childhood and adolescence. *Psychological Bulletin, 109*, 490–501. doi:10.1037/0033-2909.109.3.490

Kail, R., & Bisanz, J. (1992). The information-processing perspective on cognitive development in childhood and adolescence. In R. J. Sternberg & C. A. Berg (Eds.), *Intellectual development* (pp. 229–260). New York: Cambridge University Press.

Kalinowsky, L. B. (1986). History of convulsive therapy. *Annals of the New York Academy of Sciences, 462*(1), 1–4. doi:10.1111/j.1749-6632.1986.tb51233.x

Kalisch, R., & Gerlicher, A. M. V. (2014). Making a mountain out of a molehill: On the role of the rostral dorsal anterior cingulate and dorsomedial prefrontal cortex in conscious threat appraisal, catastrophizing, and worrying. *Neuroscience & Biobehavioral Reviews, 42*(0), 1–8. doi:10.1016/j.neubiorev.2014.02.002

Kamin, L. J. (1959). The delay-of-punishment gradient. *Journal of Comparative and Physiological Psychology, 52*(4), 434–437. doi:10.1037/h0045089

Kamin, L. J. (1968). "Attention-like" processes in classical conditioning. In M. R. Jones (Ed.), *Miami symposium on the prediction of behavior: Aversive stimulation* (pp. 9–31). Miami, FL: University of Miami Press.

Kamin, L. J. (1969). Predictability, surprise, attention, and conditioning. In B. A. Campbell & R. M. Church (Eds.), *Punishment and aversive behavior* (pp. 279–296). New York: Appleton-Century-Crofts.

Kandel, D. B. (1978). Similarity in real-life adolescent friendship pairs. *Journal of Personality and Social Psychology, 36*, 306–312. doi:10.1037/0022-3514.36.3.306

Kandel, E. R., & Wurtz, R. H. (2000). Constructing the visual image. In E. R. Kandel, J. H. Schwartz, & T. M. Jessell (Eds.), *Principles of Neural Science* (4th ed., pp. 492–506). New York: McGraw-Hll.

Kane, J. M., & Freeman, H. L. (1994). Towards more effective antipsychotic treatment. *The British Journal of Psychiatry, 165*(Suppl. 25), 22–31. doi:10.1192/S0007125000293173

Kang, C., Riazuddin, S., Mundorff, J., Krasnewich, D., Friedman, P., Mullikin, J. C., & Drayna, D. (2010). Mutations in the lysosomal enzyme–targeting pathway and persistent atuttering. *New England Journal of Medicine, 362*(8), 677–685. doi:10.1056/NEJMoa0902630

Kaniasty, K., & Norris, F. H. (2008). Longitudinal linkages between perceived social support and posttraumatic stress symptoms: Sequential roles of social causation and social selection. *Journal of Traumatic Stress, 21*, 274–281. doi:10.1002/jts.20334

Kanner, A. D., Coyne, J. C., Schaefer, C., & Lazarus, R. S. (1981). Comparison of two modes of stress measurement: Daily hassles and uplifts versus major life events. *Journal of Behavioral Medicine, 4*, 1–39. doi:10.1007/BF00844845

Kanner, L. (1943). Autistic disturbances of affective contact. *Nervous Child, 2*, 217–250.

Kant, I. (1798/1978). *Anthropology from a pragmatic point of view* (V. L. Dodwell, Trans.). Carbondale, IL: Southern Illinois University Press.

Kaplan, H., & Dove, H. (1987). Infant development among the Ache of Eastern Paraguay. *Developmental Psychology, 23*, 190–198. doi:10.1037/0012-1649.23.2.190

Kaplan, R. M., & Kronick, R. G. (2006). Marital status and longevity in the United States population. *Journal of Epidemiology & Community Health, 60*(9), 760–765. doi:10.1136/jech.2005.037606

Karasik, L. B., Tamis-LeMonda, C. S., Ossmy, O., & Adolph, K. E. (2018). The ties that bind: Cradling in Tajikistan. *PloS One, 13*(10), e0204428. doi:10.1371/journal.pone.0204428

Karau, S. J., & Williams, K. D. (1993). Social loafing: A meta-analytic review and theoretical integration. *Journal of Personality and Social Psychology, 65*, 681–706. doi:10.1037/0022-3514.65.4.681

Karraker, A., DeLamater, J., & Schwartz, C. R. (2011). Sexual frequency decline from midlife to later life. *The Journals of Gerontology Series B: Psychological Sciences and Social Sciences, 66B*(4), 502–512. doi:10.1093/geronb/gbr058

Kass, A. E., Kolko, R. P., & Wilfley, D. E. (2013). Psychological treatments for eating disorders. *Current Opinion in Psychiatry, 26*(6), 549–555. doi:510.1097/YCO.1090b1013e328365a328330e.

Katzenberg, D., Young, T., Finn, L., Lin, L., King, D. P., Takahashi, J. S., & Mignot, E. (1998). A CLOCK polymorphism associated with human diurnal preference. *Sleep, 21*, 569–578. doi:10.1093/sleep/21.6.569

Katzmarzyk, P. T., Church, T. S., Craig, C. L., & Bouchard, C. (2009). Sitting time and mortality from all causes, cardiovascular disease, and cancer. *Medicine & Science in Sports & Exercise, 41*(5), 998–1005. doi:10.1249/MSS.0b013e3181930355

Kaufman, A. S. (2009). *IQ testing 101*: Springer Publishing Company.

Kealy, D., Goodman, G., Rasmussen, B., Weideman, R., & Ogrodniczuk, J. S. (2017). Therapists' perspectives on optimal treatment for pathological narcissism. *Personality Disorders: Theory, Research, and Treatment, 8*(1), 35–45. doi:10.1037/per0000164

Kearney, C. A., Albano, A. M., Eisen, A. R., Allan, W. D., & Barlow, D. H. (1997). The phenomenology of panic disorder in youngsters: An empirical study of a clinical sample. *Journal of Anxiety Disorders, 11*, 49–62. doi:10.1016/S0887-6185(96)00034-5

Kearns, D. N., Weiss, S. J., Schindler, C. W., & Panlilio, L. V. (2005). Conditioned inhibition of cocaine seeking in rats. *Journal of Experimental Psychology: Animal Behavior Processes, 31*, 247–253. doi:10.1037/0097-7403.31.2.247

Kecklund, G., & Axelsson, J. (2016). Health consequences of shift work and insufficient sleep. *BMJ, 355*, i5210. doi:10.1136/bmj.i5210

Keenan, J. P., Nelson, A., O'Connor, M., & Pascual-Leone, A. (2001). Self-recognition and the right hemisphere. *Nature, 409*(6818), 305. doi:10.1038/35053167

Keith, S. J., Regier, D. A., & Rae, D. S. (1991). Schizophrenic disorders. In L. N. Robins & D. A. Regier (Eds.), *Psychiatric disorders in America* (pp. 33–52). New York: Free Press.

Kekst CNC. (2020). *COVID-19 Opinion Tracker*. https://www.kekstcnc.com/media/2793/kekstcnc_research_covid-19_opinion_tracker_wave-4.pdf?fbclid=IwAR3L3ODW0-8C4TgfBNyjrSpCKAMzShQNMi8KA-CY0sOo-gek6qNpxd90LaZE

Keller, H. (1933). *Helen Keller in Scotland: A personal record by herself* (J. K. Love, Ed.). London, UK: Methuen and Co.

Kelley, M. E., Wan, C. R., Broussard, B., Crisafio, A., Cristofaro, S., Johnson, S., Reed, T. A., Amar, P., Kaslow, N. J., Walker, E. F., & Compton, M. T. (2016). Marijuana use in the immediate 5-year premorbid period is associated with increased risk of onset of schizophrenia and related psychotic disorders. *Schizophrenia Research, 171*(1), 62–67. doi:10.1016/j.schres.2016.01.015

Kellner, C. H., Obbels, J., & Sienaert, P. (2020). When to consider electroconvulsive therapy (ECT). *Acta Psychiatrica Scandinavica, 141*(4), 304–315. doi:10.1111/acps.13134

Kellogg, W. N., & Kellogg, L. A. (1933). *The ape and the child*. New York: McGraw-Hill.

Kelly, D., Miellet, S., & Caldara, R. (2010). Culture shapes eye movements for visually homogeneous objects. *Frontiers in Psychology, 1*(6). doi:10.3389/fpsyg.2010.00006

Kelly, T. L., Neri, D. F., Grill, J. T., Ryman, D., Hunt, P. D., Dijk, D.-J., Shanahan, T. L., & Czeisler, C. A. (1999). Nonentrained circadian rhythms of melatonin in submariners scheduled to an 18-hour day. *Journal of Biological Rhythms, 14*(3), 190–196. doi:10.1177/074873099129000597

Keltner, D., & Ekman, P. (2000). Facial expression of emotion. In M. Lewis & J. M. Haviland-Jones (Eds.), *Handbook of emotions* (2nd ed., pp. 236–250). New York: Guilford Press.

Kendler, K. S., Walters, E. E., Neale, M. C., Kessler, R. C., Heath, A. C., & Eaves, L. J. (1995). The structure of the genetic and environmental risk factors for six major psychiatric disorders in women: Phobia, generalized anxiety disorder, panic disorder, bulimia, major depression, and alcoholism. *Archives of General Psychiatry, 52*(5), 374–383. doi:10.1001/archpsyc.1995.03950170048007

Kendzerska, T., Gershon, A. S., Hawker, G., Leung, R. S., & Tomlinson, G. (2014). Obstructive sleep apnea and risk of cardiovascular events and all-cause mortality: A decade-long historical cohort study. *PLOS*

Medicine, 11(2), e1001599. doi:10.1371/journal.pmed.1001599
Kennedy, G. C. (1953). The role of depot fat in the hypothalamic control of food intake in the rat. *Proceedings of the Royal Society of London B, 140*, 578–592. doi:10.1098/rspb.1953.0009
Kennis, M., Rademaker, A. R., & Geuze, E. (2013). Neural correlates of personality: An integrative review. *Neuroscience & Biobehavioral Reviews, 37*(1), 73–95. doi:10.1016/j.neubiorev.2012.10.012
Kenrick, D. T., Griskevicius, V., Neuberg, S. L., & Schaller, M. (2010). Renovating the pyramid of needs: Contemporary extensions built upon ancient foundations. *Perspectives on Psychological Science, 5*(3), 292–314. doi:10.1177/1745691610369469
Kenworthy, J. B., Barden, M. A., Diamond, S., & del Carmen, A. (2011). Ingroup identification as a moderator of racial bias in a shoot–no shoot decision task. *Group Processes & Intergroup Relations, 14*(3), 311–318. doi:10.1177/1368430210392932
Kessler, R. C., Aguilar-Gaxiola, S., Alonso, J., Benjet, C., Bromet, E. J., Cardoso, G., Degenhardt, L., de Girolamo, G., Dinolova, R. V., Ferry, F., Florescu, S., Gureje, O., Haro, J. M., Huang, Y., Karam, E. G., Kawakami, N., Lee, S., Lepine, J.-P., Levinson, D., . . . Koenen, K. C. (2017). Trauma and PTSD in the WHO World Mental Health Surveys. *European Journal of Psychotraumatology, 8*(sup5), 1353383. doi:10.1080/20008198.2017.1353383
Kessler, R. C., Angermeyer, M., Anthony, J. C., De Graaf, R., Demyttenaere, K., Gasquet, I., de Girolamo, G., Gluzman, S., Gureje, O., Haro, J. M., Kawakami, N., Karam, A., Levinson, D., Mora, M. E. M., Browne, M. A. O., Posada-Villa, J., Stein, D. J., Tsang, C. H. A., Aguilar-Gaxiola, S., . . . Ustün, T. B. (2007). Lifetime prevalence and age-of-onset distributions of mental disorders in the World Health Organization's World Mental Health Survey Initiative. *World Psychiatry, 6*(3), 168–176.
Kessler, R. C., Chiu, W. T., Demler, O., & Walters, E. E. (2005). Prevalence, severity, and comorbidity of twelve-month DSM-IVdisorders in the National Comorbidity Survey Replication (NCS-R). *Archives of General Psychiatry, 62*, 617–627. doi:10.1001/archpsyc.62.6.617
Kessler, R. C., Sonnega, A., Bromet, E., Hughes, M., & Nelson, C. B. (1996). Posttraumatic stress disorder in the National Comorbidity Survey. *Archives of General Psychiatry, 52*, 1048–1060. doi:10.1001/archpsyc.1995.03950240066012
Kety, S. S., Rosenthal, D., Wender, P. H., & Schulsinger, F. (1968). The types and prevalence of mental illness in the biological and adoptive families of adopted schizophrenics. In D. Rosenthal & S. S. Kety (Eds.), *The transmission of schizophrenia* (pp. 345–362). Oxford, UK: Pergamon Press.
Keys, A., Brozek, J., Henschel, A., Mickelsen, O., & Taylor, H. L. (1950). *The biology of human starvation*. Minneapolis, MN: University of Minnesota Press.
Khoury, B., Lecomte, T., Fortin, G., Masse, M., Therien, P., Bouchard, V., Chapleau, M.-A., Paquin, K., & Hofmann, S. G. (2013). Mindfulness-based therapy: A comprehensive meta-analysis. *Clinical Psychology Review, 33*(6), 763–771. doi:10.1016/j.cpr.2013.05.005
Khundrakpam, B. S., Lewis, J. D., Reid, A., Karama, S., Zhao, L., Chouinard-Decorte, F., Evans, A. C., & Brain Development Cooperative Group (2017). Imaging structural covariance in the development of intelligence. *NeuroImage, 144*, 227–240. doi:10.1016/j.neuroimage.2016.08.041
Kiehl, K. A., Anderson, N. E., Aharoni, E., Maurer, J. M., Harenski, K. A., Rao, V., Claus, E. D., Harenski, C., Koenigs, M., Decety, J., Kosson, D., Wager, T. D., Calhoun, V. D., & Steele, V. R. (2018). Age of gray matters: Neuroprediction of recidivism. *NeuroImage: Clinical, 19*, 813–823. doi:10.1016/j.nicl.2018.05.036
Kiehl, K. A., Smith, A. M., Hare, R. D., Mendrek, A., Forster, B. B., Brink, J., & Liddle, P. F. (2001). Limbic abnormalities in affective processing by criminal psychopaths as revealed by functional magnetic resonance imaging. *Biological Psychiatry, 50*(9), 677–684. doi:10.1016/S0006-3223(01)01222-7
Kiely, E., & Robertson, L. (2016). *How to spot fake news*. https://www.factcheck.org/2016/11/how-to-spot-fake-news/
Kikkert, M. A., Ribbers, G. M., & Koudstaal, P. J. (2006). Alien hand syndrome in stroke: A report of 2 cases and review of the literature. *Archives of Physical Medicine and Rehabilitation, 87*(5), 728–732. doi:10.1016/j.apmr.2006.02.002
Kilham, W., & Mann, L. (1974). Level of destructive obedience as a function of transmitter and executant roles in the Milgram obedience paradigm. *Journal of Personality and Social Psychology, 29*, 696–702. doi:10.1037/h0036636
Kim, H., & Markus, H. R. (1999). Deviance or uniqueness, harmony or conformity? A cultural analysis. *Journal of Personality and Social Psychology, 77*, 785–800. doi:10.1037/0022-3514.77.4.785
King, J. E., & Figueredo, A. J. (1997). The five-factor model plus dominance in chimpanzee personality. *Journal of Research in Personality, 31*(2), 257–271. doi:10.1006/jrpe.1997.2179
King, P. M., & Kitchener, K. S. (2002). The Reflective Judgment Model: Twenty years of research on epistemic cognition. In B. K. Hofer & P. R. Pintrich (Eds.), *Personal epistemology: The psychology of beliefs about knowledge and knowing*. (pp. 37–61). Mahwah, NJ: Lawrence Erlbaum Associates Publishers.
Kirk, K., Bailey, J., & Martin, N. (2000). Etiology of male sexual orientation in an Australian twin sample. *Psychology, Evolution & Gender, 2*(3), 301–311. doi:10.1080/14616660010024418
Klauke, B., Deckert, J., Reif, A., Pauli, P., & Domschke, K. (2010). Life events in panic disorder—An update on "candidate stressors." *Depression and Anxiety, 27*(8), 716–730. doi:10.1002/da.20667
Klein, R. A., Ratliff, K. A., Vianello, M., Jr., R. B. A., Bahník, Š., Bernstein, M. J., Bocian, K., Brandt, M. J., Brooks, B., Brumbaugh, C. C., Cimalcilar, Z., Chandler, J., Cheong, W., Davis, W. E., Devos, T., Eisner, M., Frankowska, N., Furrow, D., Galliani, E. M., . . . Nosek, B. A. (2014). Investigating variation in replicability. *Social Psychology, 45*(3), 142–152. doi:10.1027/1864-9335/a000178
Klein, R. M., Christie, J., & Parkvall, M. (2016). Does multilingualism affect the incidence of Alzheimer's disease?: A worldwide analysis by country. *SSM-Population Health, 2*, 463–467. doi:10.1016/j.ssmph.2016.06.002
Klein, S. B., Cosmides, L., & Tooby, J. (2002). Decisions and the evolution of memory: Multiple systems, multiple functions. *Psychological Review, 109*, 306–329. doi:10.1037/0033-295X.109.2.306
Kleinmuntz, B., & Szucko, J. J. (1984). A field study of the fallibility of polygraph lie detection. *Nature, 308*, 449–450. doi:10.1038/308449a0
Klima, E. S., & Bellugi, U. (1979). *The signs of language*. Cambridge, MA: Harvard.
Kline, P. (2013). *Fact and fantasy in Freudian theory*. Philadephia, PA:Routledge.
Klüver, H., & Bucy, P. (1939). Preliminary analysis of functions of the temporal lobe in monkeys. *Archives of Neurology and Psychiatry, 42*, 979–1000. doi:10.1001/archneurpsyc.1939.02270240017001
Kneer, J., Jacobs, R., & Ferguson, C. (2018). You could have just asked: The perception of motivations to play violent video games. *Studies in Media and Communication, 6*(2), 1–11. doi:10.11114/smc.v6i2.3389
Knickmeyer, R., Baron-Cohen, S., Raggatt, P., & Taylor, K. (2005). Foetal testosterone, social relationships, and restricted interests in children. *Journal of Child Psychology and Psychiatry, and Allied Disciplines, 46*(2), 198–210. doi:10.1111/j.1469-7610.2004.00349.x
Knight, D. C., Nguyen, H. T., & Bandettini, P. A. (2003). Expression of conditional fear with and without awareness. *Proceedings of the National Academy of Sciences of the United States of America, 100*(25), 15280–15283. doi:10.1073/pnas.2535780100
Knowlton, B. J., Squire, L. R., Paulsen, J. S., Swerdlow, N. R., Swenson, M., & Butters, N. (1996). Dissociations within nondeclarative memory in Huntington's Disease. *Neuropsychology, 10*(4), 538–548. doi:10.1037/0894-4105.10.4.538
Knyazev, G. G., Slobodskoj-Plusnin, J. Y., Bocharov, A. V., & Pylkova, L. V. (2011). The default mode network and EEG alpha

oscillations: An independent component analysis. *Brain Research, 1402*, 67–79. doi:10.1016/j.brainres.2011.05.052

Kobayakawa, T., Wakita, M., Saito, S., Gotow, N., Sakai, N., & Ogawa, H. (2005). Location of the primary gustatory area in humans and its properties, studied by magnetoencephalography. *Chemical Senses, 30*(suppl_1), i226-i227. doi:10.1093/chemse/bjh196

Kochanek, K. D., Murphy, S. L., Xu, J., & Tejada-Vera, B. (2017). Deaths: Final data for 2014. *National Vital Statistics Report, 65*(4), 1–122.

Koeda, T., Seki, A., Uchiyama, H., & Sadato, N. (2011). Dyslexia: Advances in clinical and imaging studies. *Brain and Development, 33*(3), 268–275. doi:10.1016/j.braindev.2010.11.006

Koenigsberg, H. W., Teicher, M. H., Mitropoulou, V., Navalta, C., New, A. S., Trestman, R., & Siever, L. J. (2004). 24-h Monitoring of plasma norepinephrine, MHPG, cortisol, growth hormone and prolactin in depression. *Journal of Psychiatric Research, 38*(5), 503–511. doi:10.1016/j.jpsychires.2004.03.006

Koffka, K. (1935). *Principles of Gestalt psychology*. London: Lund Humphries.

Kohlberg, L. (1981). *The philosophy of moral development: Essays on moral development* (Vol. 1). San Francisco: Harper & Row.

Kohlberg, L. (1984). *Essays on moral development: The psychology of moral development* (Vol. 2). San Francisco: Harper & Row.

Kohler, C. G., Walker, J. B., Martin, E. A., Healey, K. M., & Moberg, P. J. (2009). Facial emotion perception in schizophrenia: A meta-analytic review. *Schizophrenia Bulletin, 36*(5), 1009–1019 doi:10.1093/schbul/sbn192.

Kohn, G., Apodaca, J., Munoz, M., Strebe, S., White, S., & Wright, T. (2019). FoxP2 expression and vocal learning abilities in the budgerigar (Melopsittacus undulatus). *Integrative and Comparative Biology, 59*, E127.

Kokis, J. V., Macpherson, R., Toplak, M. E., West, R. F., & Stanovich, K. E. (2002). Heuristic and analytic processing: Age trends and associations with cognitive ability and cognitive styles. *Journal of Experimental Child Psychology, 83*(1), 26–52. doi:10.1016/S0022-0965(02)00121-2

Komarraju, M., Karau, S. J., & Schmeck, R. R. (2009). Role of the Big Five personality traits in predicting college students' academic motivation and achievement. *Learning and Individual Differences, 19*(1), 47–52. doi:10.1016/j.lindif.2008.07.001

Konopka, G., Bomar, J. M., Winden, K., Coppola, G., Jonsson, Z. O., Gao, F., Peng, S., Preuss, T. M., Wohlschlegel, J. A., & Geschwind, D. H. (2009). Human-specific transcriptional regulation of CNS development genes by FOXP2. *Nature, 462*, 213–217. doi:10.1038/nature08549

Konrath, S. H., O'Brien, E. H., & Hsing, C. (2011). Changes in dispositional empathy in American college students over time: A meta-analysis. *Personality and Social Psychology Review, 15*(2), 180–198. doi:10.1371/journal.pone.0103469

Konrath, S., Meier, B. P., & Bushman, B. J. (2014). Development and validation of the single item narcissism scale (SINS). *PLOS One, 9*(8), e103469. doi:10.1371/journal.pone.0103469

Kopell, B. H., Machado, A. G., & Rezai, A. R. (2005). Not your father's lobotomy: Psychiatric surgery revisited. *Clinical Neurosurgery, 52*, 315–330.

Kopelman, M. D. (2002). Disorders of memory. *Brain: A Journal of Neurology, 125*(10), 2152–2190. doi:10.1093/brain/awf229

Kosslyn, S. M. (1978). Measuring the visual angle of the mind's eye. *Cognitive Psychology, 10*, 356–389. doi:10.1016/0010-0285(78)90004-X

Kosslyn, S. M. (1980). *Image and mind.* Cambridge, MA: Harvard University Press.

Kotov, R., Gamez, W., Schmidt, F., & Watson, D. (2010). Linking "big" personality traits to anxiety, depressive, and substance use disorders: A meta-analysis. *Psychological Bulletin, 136*(5), 768–821. doi:10.1037/a0020327

Kramer, A. D. I., Guillory, J. E., & Hancock, J. T. (2014). Experimental evidence of massive-scale emotional contagion through social networks. *Proceedings of the National Academy of Sciences of the United States of America, 111*(24), 8788–8790. doi:10.1073/pnas.1320040111

Kramer, B. J. (1993). Expanding the conceptualization of caregiver coping: The importance of relationship-focused coping strategies. *Family Relations, 42*(4), 383–391. doi:10.2307/585338

Kravitz, D. A., & Martin, B. (1986). Ringelmann rediscovered: The original article. *Journal of Personality and Social Psychology, 50*, 936–941. doi:10.1037/0022-3514.50.5.936

Krebs, H., Hogan, N., Hening, W., Adamovich, S., & Poizner, H. (2001). Procedural motor learning in Parkinson's disease. *Experimental Brain Research, 141*, 425–437. doi:10.1007/s002210100871

Krijn, M., Emmelkamp, P. M. G., Ólafsson, R. P., Bouwman, M., van Gerwen, L. J., Spinhoven, P., Schuemie, M. J., & van der Mast, C. A. P. G. (2007). Fear of flying treatment methods: Virtual reality exposure vs. cognitive behavioral therapy. *Aviation, Space, and Environmental Medicine, 78*(2), 121–128.

Kross, E., Gard, D., Deldin, P., Clifton, J., & Ayduk, O. (2012). "Asking why" from a distance: Its cognitive and emotional consequences for people with major depressive disorder. *Journal of Abnormal Psychology, 121*(3), 559–569. doi:10.1037/a0028808

Krous, H. (2014). Sudden infant death syndrome (SIDS), sudden unexpected death in infancy (SUDI), and sudden unexplained death in childhood (SUDC). In K. A. Collins, & R. W. Byard (Eds.), *Forensic pathology of infancy and childhood* (pp. 193–206). New York: Springer. doi:10.1007/987-1-61779-403-2_32

Krueger, R. F., South, S., Johnson, W., & Iacono, W. (2008). The heritability of personality is not always 50%: Gene-environment interactions and correlations between personality and parenting. *Journal of Personality, 76*(6), 1485–1522. doi:10.1111/j.1467-6494.2008.00529.x

Kruger, J., & Dunning, D. (1999). Unskilled and unaware of it: How difficulties in recognizing one's own incompetence lead to inflated self-assessments. *Journal of Personality and Social Psychology, 77*, 1121–1134. doi:10.1037/0022-3514.77.6.1121

Krupenye, C., Kano, F., Hirata, S., Call, J., & Tomasello, M. (2016). Great apes anticipate that other individuals will act according to false beliefs. *Science, 354*(6308), 110–114. doi:10.1126/science.aaf8110

Kuhl, B. A., Dudukovic, N. M., Kahn, I., & Wagner, A. D. (2007). Decreased demands on cognitive control reveal the neural processing benefits of forgetting. *Nature Neuroscience, 10*(7), 908—914. doi:10.1038/nn1918

Kuhl, P. K. (2007). Is speech learning 'gated' by the social brain? *Developmental Science, 10*(1), 110–120. doi:10.1111/j.1467-7687.2007.00572.x

Kuhl, P. K. (2011). Early language learning and literacy: Neuroscience implications for education. *Mind, Brain, and Education, 5*(3), 128–142. doi:10.1111/j.1751-228X.2011.01121.x

Kuhl, P. K., & Meltzoff, A. N. (1982). The bimodal perception of speech in infancy. *Science, 218*(4577), 1138–1141. doi:10.1126/science.7146899

Kuhl, U., Neef, N. E., Kraft, I., Schaadt, G., Dörr, L., Brauer, J., Czepezauer, I., Müller, B., Wilcke, A., Kirsten, H., Emmrich, F., Boltze, J., Friedericia, A. D., & Skeide, M. A. (2020). The emergence of dyslexia in the developing brain. *NeuroImage, 211*, 116633. doi:10.1016/j.neuroimage.2020.116633

Kuhn, D. (2008). Formal operations from a twenty-first century perspective. *Human Development, 51*(1), 48–55. doi:10.1159/000113155

Kulik, J. A., Mahler, H. I., & Moore, P. J. (1996). Social comparison and affiliation under threat: Effects on recovery from major surgery. *Journal of Personality and Social Psychology, 71*(5), 967–979. doi:10.1037/0022-3514.71.5.967

Kuo, L. E., Czarnecka, M., Kitlinska, J. B., Tilan, J. U., Kvetňanský, R., & Zukowska, Z. (2009). Chronic stress, combined with a high-fat/high-sugar diet, shifts sympathetic signaling toward neuropeptide Y and leads to obesity and the metabolic syndrome. In R. Kvetňanský, G. Aguilera, D. Goldstein, D. Jezova, O. Krizanova, E. L. Sabban, & K. Pacak (Eds.), *Stress, neurotransmitters, and hormones: Neuroendocrine and genetic mechanisms.* (pp. 232–237). New York, NY: Wiley-Blackwell.

Kurihara, T., Kato, M., Sakamoto, S., Reverger, R., & Kitamura, T. (2000). Public attitudes towards the mentally ill: A cross-cultural study between Bali and Tokyo. *Psychiatry and Clinical Neurosciences, 54*, 547–552. doi:10.1046/j.1440-1819.2000.00751.x

Kurland, J. A. (1977). Kin selection in the Japanese monkey. *Contributions to Primatology, 12*, 1–145. doi:10.1525/aa.1980.82.1.02a00600

Kurzban, R., & Houser, D. (2005). Experiments investigating cooperative types in humans: A complement to evolutionary theory and simulations. *Proceedings of the National Academy of Sciences of the United States of America, 102*, 1803–1807. doi:10.1073/pnas.0408759102

Kuster, J. M. (2015). *Folk myths about stuttering.* http://www.mnsu.edu/comdis/kuster/Infostuttering/folkmyths.html

Kwong, A. S. F., Pearson, R. M., Adams, M. J., Northstone, K., Tilling, K., Smith, D., Fawns-Ritchie, C., Bould, H., Warne, N., Zammit, S., Gunnell, D., Moran, P., Micali, N., Reichenberg, A., Hickman, M., Rai, D., Haworth, S., Campbell, A., Altschul, D., . . . Timpson, N. J. (2020). Mental health during the COVID-19 pandemic in two longitudinal UK population cohorts. *The British Journal of Psychiatry, 1-27*. doi:10.1192/bjp.2020.242

La Tona, G., Terranova, M. C., Vernuccio, F., Lo Re, G., Salerno, S., Zerbo, S., & Argo, A. (2020). Lie detection: fMRI. In G. Lo Re, A. Argo, M. Midiri, & C. Cattaneo (Eds.), *Radiology in forensic medicine: From identification to post-mortem imaging* (pp. 197–202).New York, NY: Springer International Publishing.

Ladd, G. W., Buhs, E. S., & Seid, M. (2000). Children's initial sentiments about kindergarten: Is school liking an antecedent of early classroom participation and achievement? *Merrill-Palmer Quarterly: Journal of Developmental Psychology, 46*(2), 255–279. https://www.jstor.org/stable/23093716

Lafer-Sousa, R., Hermann, K. L., & Conway, B. R. (2015). Striking individual differences in color perception uncovered by 'the dress' photograph. *Current Biology, 25*(13), R545-546. doi:10.1016/j.cub.2015.04.053

Lagerspetz, K. M. J., & Lagerspetz, K. Y. H. (1983). Genes and aggression. In E. C. Simmel, M. E. Hahn, & J. K. Walters (Eds.), *Aggressive behavior: Genetic and neural approaches* (pp. 89–102). Hillsdale, NJ: Erlbaum.

Lahey, B. B. (1995). *Psychology: An Introduction* (5th ed.). Dubuque, IA: WCB Brown & Benchmark.

Lahham, D. & Green, C. D. (2013). John Wallace Baird: The first Canadian president of the American Psychological Association. *Canadian Psychology, 54*, 124–132. doi:10.1037/a0026286

Lai, C. S., Fisher, S. E., Hurst, J. A., Vargha-Khadem, F., & Monaco, A. P. (2001). A fork-head-domain gene is mutated in a severe speech and language disorder. *Nature, 413*(6855), 519–523. doi:10.1038/35097076

Lake, C. J., Carlson, J., Rose, A., & Chlevin-Thiele, C. (2019). Trust in name brand assessments: The case of the Myers-Briggs Type Indicator. *The Psychologist-Manager Journal, 22*(2), 91–107. doi:10.1037/mgr0000086

Lakin, J. L., Chartrand, T. L., & Arkin, R. M. (2008). I am too just like you: Nonconscious mimicry as an automatic behavioral response to social exclusion. *Psychological Science.19*(8), 816–822. doi:10.1111/j.1467-9280.2008.02162.x

Lane, A., Young, R., Baker, A., & Angley, M. (2010). Sensory processing subtypes in autism: Association with adaptive behavior. *Journal of Autism and Developmental Disorders, 40*(1), 112–122. doi:10.1007/s10803-009-0840-2

Lane, R. E. (2001). Self-reliance and empathy: The enemies of poverty–and of the poor. *Political Psychology, 22*(3), 473–492. doi:10.1111/0162-895X.00250

Langa, K. M., Larson, E. B., Crimmins, E. M., Faul, J. D., Levine, D. A., Kabeto, M. U., & Weir, D. R. (2017). A comparison of the prevalence of dementia in the United States in 2000 and 2012. *JAMA Internal Medicine, 177*(1), 51–58. doi:10.1001/jamainternmed.2016.6807

Lange, C. G. (1885/1912). The mechanisms of the emotions. In B. Rand (Ed.), *The classical psychologists* (pp. 672–284). Boston: Houghton Mifflin.

Langenecker, S. A., Weisenbach, S. L., Giordani, B., Briceño, E. M., Guidotti Breting, L. M., Schallmo, M.-P., Leon, H. M., Noll, D. C., Zubieta, J.-K., Schteingart, D. E., & Starkman, M. N. (2012). Impact of chronic hypercortisolemia on affective processing. *Neuropharmacology*, 61(2), 217–225. doi:10.1016/j.neuropharm.2011.07.006

Langleben, D., Hakun, J., Seelig, D., Wang, A., Ruparel, K., Bilker, W., & Gur, R. (2016). Polygraphy and functional magnetic resonance imaging in lie detection: A controlled blind comparison using the concealed information test. *Journal of Clinical Psychiatry, 77*(10),1372–1830. doi:10.4088/JCP.15m09785

Langleben, D. D., & Moriarty, J. C. (2013). Using brain imaging for lie detection: Where science, law, and policy collide. *Psychology, Public Policy, and Law, 19*(2), 222–234. doi:10.1037/a0028841

Langley, J. (1921). *The autonomic nervous system*. Cambridge, UK: Heffer & Sons.

Langlois, J. H., Roggman, L. A., & Rieser-Danner, L. A. (1990). Infants' differential social responses to attractive and unattractive faces. *Developmental Psychology, 26*(1), 153–159. doi:10.1037/0012-1649.26.1.153

Långström, N., Rahman, Q., Carlström, E., & Lichtenstein, P. (2010). Genetic and environmental effects on same-sex sexual behavior: A population study of twins in Sweden. *Archives of Sexual Behavior, 39*(1), 75–80. doi:10.1007/s10508-008-9386-1

Largo, R. H., Molinari, L., von Siebenthal, K., & Wolfensberger, U. (1996). Does a profound change in toilet-training affect development of bowel and bladder control? *Developmental Medicine and Child Neurology, 38*, 1106–1116. doi:10.1111/j.1469-8749.1996.tb15074.x

Larner, A. J. (2014). Effect size (Cohen's d) of cognitive screening instruments examined in pragmatic diagnostic accuracy studies. *Dementia and Geriatric Cognitive Disorders Extra, 4*(2), 236–241. doi:10.1159/000363735

Lassek, W. D., & Gaulin, S. J. C. (2009). Costs and benefits of fat-free muscle mass in men: Relationship to mating success, dietary requirements, and native immunity. *Evolution and Human Behavior, 30*(5), 322–328. doi:10.1016/j.evolhumbehav.2009.04.002

Latané, B., & Darley, J. M. (1968). Group inhibition of bystander intervention in emergencies. *Journal of Personality and Social Psychology, 10*, 215–221. doi:10.1037/h0026570

Latané, B., Williams, K., & Harkins, S. (1979). Many hands make light the work: The causes and consequences of social loafing. *Journal of Personality and Social Psychology, 37*, 822–832. doi:10.1037/0022-3514.37.6.822

Lau, J. (2019). *Improve our thinking skills.* https://philosophy.hku.hk/think/critical/improve.php

Laumann, E. O., Paik, A., Glasser, D. B., Kang, J.-H., Wang, T., Levinson, B., Moreira, Jr, E. D., Nicolosi, A., & Gingell, C. (2006). A cross-national study of subjective sexual well-being among older women and men: Findings from the global study of sexual attitudes and behaviors. *Archives of Sexual Behavior, 35*(2), 145–159. doi:10.1007/s10508-005-9005-3

Law, M., & Tang, J. (1995). An analysis of the effectiveness of interventions intended to help people stop smoking. *Archives of Internal Medicine, 155*(18), 1933–1941. doi:10.1001/archinte.1995.00430180025004

Layous, K., Nelson, S. K., Oberle, E., Schonert-Reichl, K. A., & Lyubomirsky, S. (2012). Kindness counts: Prompting prosocial behavior in preadolescents boosts peer acceptance and well-being. *PLoS One, 7*(12), e51380. doi:10.1371/journal.pone.0051380

Lazar, S. W., Bush, G., Gollub, R. L., Fricchione, G. L., Khalsa, G., & Benson, H. (2000). Functional brain mapping of the relaxation response and meditation. *NeuroReport, 11*(7), 1581–1585.

Lazar, S. W., Kerr, C. E., Wasserman, R. H., Gray, J. R., Greve, D. N., Treadway, M. T., McGarvey, M., Quinn, B. T., Dusek, J. A., Benson, H., Rauch, S. L., Moore, C. I., & Fischl, B. (2005). Meditation experience is associated with increased cortical thickness. *NeuroReport, 16*(17), 1893.

Lazarus, A. A. (2005). Multimodal therapy. In J. C. Norcross & M. R. Goldfried (Eds.), *Handbook of psychotherapy integration* (pp. 105–120). New York: Oxford.

Lazarus, R. S. (1966). *Psychological stress and the coping process*. New York: McGraw-Hill.

Lazer, D. M., Baum, M. A., Benkler, Y., Berinsky, A. J., Greenhill, K. M., Menczer, F., Metzger,

M. J., Nyhan, B., Pennycook, G., Rothschild, D., Schudson M., Sloman, S. A., Sunstein, C. R., Thorson, E. A., Watts, D. J., & Zittrain, J. L. (2018). The science of fake news. *Science, 359*(6380), 1094–1096. doi:10.1126/science.aao2998

Le, N., Loll, F., & Pinkwart, N. (2013). Operationalizing the continuum between well-defined and ill-defined problems for educational technology. *IEEE Transactions on Learning Technologies, 6*(3), 258–270. doi:10.1109/TLT.2013.16

Lea, M., & Spears, R. (1991). Computer-mediated communication, de-individuation and group decision-making. *International Journal of Man Machine Studies, 34*, 283–301. doi:10.1016/0020-7373(91)90045-9

Leary, M. R., & Downs, D. L. (1995). Interpersonal functions of the self-esteem motive: The self-esteem system as a sociometer. In M. H. Kernis (Ed.), *Efficacy, agency, and self-esteem* (pp. 123–144). NewYork: Plenum.

Leary, M. R., Tambor, E. S., Terdal, S. K., & Downs, D. L. (1995). Self-esteem as an interpersonal monitor: The sociometer hypothesis. *Journal of Personality and Social Psychology, 68*, 518–530. doi:10.1037/0022-3514.68.3.518

LeBlanc, S. A. (2003). *Constant battles: The myth of the peaceful, noble savage.* New York: St. Martin's Press.

Lecomte, T., Dumais, A., Dugré, J. R., & Potvin, S. (2018). The prevalence of substance-induced psychotic disorder in methamphetamine misusers: A meta-analysis. *Psychiatry Research, 268*, 189–192. doi:10.1016/j.psychres.2018.05.033

LeDoux, J. E. (2000). Emotion circuits in the brain. *Annual Review of Neuroscience, 23*, 155–184. doi:10.1146/annurev.neuro.23.1.155

LeDoux, J. E. (2014). Coming to terms with fear. *Proceedings of the National Academy of Sciences of the United States of America, 111*(8), 2871–2878. doi:10.1073/pnas.1400335111

LeDoux, J. E., Cicchetti, P., Xagoraris, A., & Romanski, L. M. (1990). The lateral amygdaloid nucleus: Sensory interface of the amygdala in fear conditioning. *Journal of Neuroscience, 10*, 1062–1069. doi:10.1523/JNEUROSCI.10-04-01062.1990

Lee, H., Park, S.-A., Lee, Y.-A., & Cameron, G. T. (2010). Assessment of motion media on believability and credibility: An exploratory study. *Public Relations Review, 36*, 310–312. doi:10.1016/j.pubrev.2010.04.003

Lee, J.-Y., Bachrach, D. G., & Lewis, K. (2014). Social network ties, transactive memory, and performance in groups. *Organization Science, 25*(3), 951–967. doi:10.1287/orsc.2013.0884

Lee, P. A., Fuqua, J. S., Houk, C. P., Kogan, B. A., Mazur, T., & Caldamone, A. (2020). Individualized care for patients with intersex (disorders/differences of sex development): part I. *Journal of Pediatric Urology, 16*(2), 230—237. doi:10.1016/j.jpurol.2020.02.013

Leichsenring, F., & Rabung, S. (2008). Effectiveness of long-term psychodynamic psychotherapy: A meta-analysis. *JAMA, 300*(13), 1551–1565. doi:10.1001/jama.300.13.1551

Leichtman, M. (1995). Behavioral observations. In J. N. Butcher (Ed.), *Clinical personality assessment: Practical approaches* (pp. 251–266). New York: Oxford University Press.

Leiknes, K. A., Jarosh-von Schweder, L., & Høie, B. (2012). Contemporary use and practice of electroconvulsive therapy worldwide. *Brain and Behavior, 2*(3), 283–344. doi:10.1002/brb3.37

LePine, J. A., & Van Dyne, L. (1998). Predicting voice behavior in work groups. *Journal of Applied Psychology, 83*, 853–868. doi:10.1037/0021-9010.83.6.853

LePort, A. K. R., Mattfeld, A. T., Dickinson-Anson, H., Fallon, J. H., Stark, C. E. L., Kruggel, F., Cahill, L., & McGaugh, J. L. (2012). Behavioral and neuroanatomical investigation of Highly Superior Autobiographical Memory (HSAM). *Neurobiology of Learning and Memory, 98*(1), 78–92. doi:10.1016/j.nlm.2012.05.002

Lerner, M. J., & Miller, D. T. (1978). Just world research and the attribution process: Looking back and ahead. *Psychological Bulletin, 85*, 1030–1051. doi:10.1037/0033-2909.85.5.1030

Leroi, A. M. (2006). The future of neo-eugenics. *EMBO Reports, 7*(12), 1184-1187. doi:10.1038/sj.embor.7400860

Leslie, M., Turton, R., Burgess, E., Nazar, B. P., & Treasure, J. (2018). Testing the addictive appetite model of binge eating: The importance of craving, coping, and reward enhancement. *European Eating Disorders Review, 26*(6), 541–550. doi:10.1002/erv.2621

Lester, P. B., Harms, P. D., Bulling, D. J., Herian, M. N., & Spain, S. M. (2011). *Evaluation of relationships between reported resilience and soldier outcomes. Report 1: Negative outcomes (suicide, drug use, and violent crimes)*: DTIC Document. http://www.dtic.mil/docs/citations/ADA538618

Leucht, S., Cipriani, A., Spineli, L., Mavridis, D., Örey, D., Richter, F., Samara, M., Barbui, C., Engel, R. R., Geddes, J. R., Kissling, W., Stapf, M. P., Lässig, B., Salanti, G., & Davis, J. M. (2013). Comparative efficacy and tolerability of 15 antipsychotic drugs in schizophrenia: A multiple-treatments meta-analysis. *The Lancet, 382*(9896), 951–962. doi:10.1016/S0140-6736(13)60733-3

Leung, A. K.-y., Kim, Y.-H., Zhang, Z.-X., Tam, K.-P., & Chiu, C.-y. (2011). Cultural construction of success and epistemic motives moderate American-Chinese differences in reward allocation biases. *Journal of Cross-Cultural Psychology, 43*(1), 46–52. doi:10.1177/0022022111405660

LeVay, S. (1991). A difference in hypothalamic structure between heterosexual and homosexual men. *Science, 253*, 1034–1037. doi:10.1126/science.1887219

Levenson, R. W., Ekman, P., & Friesen, W. V. (1990). Voluntary facial action generates emotion-specific autonomic nervous system activity. *Psychophysiology, 27*, 363–384. doi:10.1111/j.1469-8986.1990.tb02330.x

Levine, M., Taylor, P. J., & Best, R. (2011). Third parties, violence, and conflict resolution. *Psychological Science, 22*(3), 406–412. doi:10.1177/0956797611398495

Levinson, D., Darrow, C. M., Klein, E. B., Levinson, M. H., & McKee, B. (1976). Periods in the adult development of men: Ages 18–14. *The Counseling Psychologist, 6*(1), 21–25. doi:10.1177/001100007600600105

Lewin, K. (1951). *Field theory in social science: Selected theoretical papers* (D. Cartwright, Ed.). New York: Harper.

Lewis, M., & Brooks-Gunn, J. (1979). *Social cognition and the acquisition of self.* New York: Plenum Press.

Li, H., Bu, Q., Chen, B., Shao, X., Hu, Z., Deng, P., Zhu, R., Li, Y., Zhang, B., Hou, J., Du, C., Zhao, Q., Fu, D., Zhao, Y., & Cen, X. (2014). Mechanisms of metabonomic for a gateway drug: Nicotine priming enhances behavioral response to cocaine with modification in energy metabolism and neurotransmitter level. *PLoS One, 9*(1), e87040. doi:10.1371/journal.pone.0087040

Li, S.-C., Lindenberger, U., Hommel, B., Aschersleben, G., Prinz, W., & Baltes, P. B. (2004). Transformations in the couplings among intellectual abilities and constituent cognitive processes across the life span. *Psychological Science, 15*(3), 155–163. doi:10.1111/j.0956-7976.2004.01503003.x

Li, W., Ma, L., Yang, G., & Gan, W.-B. (2017). REM sleep selectively prunes and maintains new synapses in development and learning. *Nature Neuroscience, 20*, 427–437. doi:10.1038/nn.4479

Libet, B., Gleason, C. A., Wright, E. W., & Pearl, D. K. (1993). Time of conscious intention to act in relation to onset of cerebral activity (readiness-potential). In B. Libet (Ed.), *Neurophysiology of consciousness* (pp. 249–268). Boston, MA: Birkhäuser Boston.

Libon, D. J., McMillan, C., Avants, B., Boller, A., Morgan, B., Burkholder, L., Chandrasekaran, K., Elman, L., McCluskey, L., & Grossman, M. (2012). Deficits in concept formation in amyotrophic lateral sclerosis. *Neuropsychology, 26*(4), 422–429. doi:10.1037/a0028668

Lichtenberg, J. D., Lachmann, F. M., & Fosshage, J. L. (2013). *The clinical exchange: Techniques derived from self and motivational systems* (Vol. 16): Routledge.

Lichtenstein, E., Harris, D. E., Birchler, G. R., Wahl, J. M., & Schmahl, D. P. (1973). Comparison of rapid smoking, warm, smoky air, and attention placebo in the modification of smoking behavior. *Journal of Consulting and Clinical Psychology, 40*, 92–98. doi:10.1037/h0034039

of Fluency Disorders, 25(1), 47–57. doi:10.1016/S0094-730X(99)00023-6

Mantell, D. M. (1971). The potential for violence in Germany. *Journal of Social Issues, 27*, 101–112. doi:10.1111/j.1540-4560.1971.tb00680.x

Mäntylä, T., & Nilsson, L.-G. (1988). Cue distinctiveness and forgetting: Effectiveness of self-generated retrieval cues in delayed recall. *Journal of Experimental Psychology: Learning, Memory, and Cognition, 14*(3), 502–509. doi:10.1037/0278-7393.14.3.502

Marconi, A., Di Forti, M., Lewis, C. M., Murray, R. M., & Vassos, E. (2016). Meta-analysis of the association between the level of cannabis use and risk of psychosis. *Schizophrenia Bulletin, 42*(5), 1262–1269. doi:10.1093/schbul/sbw003

Margittai, Z., Strombach, T., van Wingerden, M., Joels, M., Schwabe, L., & Kalenscher, T. (2015). A friend in need: Time-dependent effects of stress on social discounting in men. *Hormones and Behavior, 73*, 75–82. doi:10.1016/j.yhbeh.2015.05.019

Margoni, F., Baillargeon, R., & Surian, L. (2018). Infants distinguish between leaders and bullies. *Proceedings of the National Academy of Sciences of the United States of America, 115*(38), E8835-E8843. doi:10.1073/pnas.1801677115

Mark, K. P., Garcia, J. R., & Fisher, H. E. (2015). Perceived emotional and sexual satisfaction across sexual relationship contexts: Gender and sexual orientation differences and similarities. *The Canadian Journal of Human Sexuality, 24*(2), 120–130. doi:10.3138/cjhs.242-A8

Mark, K. P., Vowels, L. M., & Murray, S. H. (2018). The impact of attachment style on sexual satisfaction and sexual desire in a sexually diverse sample. *Journal of Sex & Marital Therapy, 44*(5), 450–458. doi:10.1080/0092623X.2017.1405310

Marks, G. A., Shaffery, J. P., Oksenberg, A., Speciale, S. G., & Roffwarg, H. P. (1995). A functional role for REM sleep in brain maturation. *Behavioural Brain Research, 69*(1), 1–11. doi:10.1016/0166-4328(95)00018-O

Markus, H. (1977). Self-schemata and processing information about the self. *Journal of Personality and Social Psychology, 35*(2), 63–78. doi:10.1037/0022-3514.35.2.63

Markus, H. R., & Kitayama, S. (1991). Culture and the self: Implications for cognition, emotion, and motivation. *Psychological Review, 98*, 223–253. doi:10.1037/0033-295X.98.2.224

Marmot, M. G., Rose, G., Shipley, M., & Hamilton, P. J. (1978). Employment grade and coronary heart disease in British civil servants. *Journal of Epidemiology and Community Health, 32*(4), 244–249. doi:10.1136/jech.32.4.244

Marmot, M. G., Shipley, M. J., & Rose, G. (1984). Inequalities in death—specific explanations of a general pattern? *The Lancet, 323*(8384), 1003–1006. doi:10.1016/S0140-6736(84)92337-7

Marner, L., Nyengaard, J. R., Tang, Y., & Pakkenberg, B. (2003). Marked loss of myelinated nerve fibers in the human brain with age. *Journal of Comparative Neurology, 462*(2), 144–152. doi:10.1002/cne.10714

Marsh, A. A., & Blair, R. J. R. (2008). Deficits in facial affect recognition among antisocial populations: A meta-analysis. *Neuroscience & Biobehavioral Reviews, 32*(3), 454–465. doi:10.1016/j.neubiorev.2007.08.003

Marsh, B. U., Pezdek, K., & Ozery, D. H. (2016). The cross-race effect in face recognition memory by bicultural individuals. *Acta Psychologica, 169*, 38–44. doi:10.1016/j.actpsy.2016.05.003

Marsh, E. J., Cantor, A. D., & M. Brashier, N. (2016). Believing that humans swallow spiders in their sleep: False beliefs as side effects of the processes that support accurate knowledge. In B. H. Ross (Ed.), *Psychology of learning and motivation* (Vol. 64, pp. 93–132). Cambridge, MA: Academic Press.

Marshall, G. D., & Zimbardo, P. G. (1979). Affective consequences of inadequately explained physiological arousal. *Journal of Personality and Social Psychology, 37*(6), 970–988. doi:10.1037/0022-3514.37.6.970

Marsvenus.com (n.d.). *Bio*. https://www.marsvenus.com/john-gray/

Martial, C., Cassol, H., Charland-Verville, V., Pallavicini, C., Sanz, C., Zamberlan, F., Vivot, R. M., Erowid, F., Erowid, E., Laureys, S., Greyson, B., & Tagliazucchi, E. (2019). Neurochemical models of near-death experiences: A large-scale study based on the semantic similarity of written reports. *Consciousness and Cognition, 69*, 52–69. doi:10.1016/j.concog.2019.01.011

Martin, A., Wiggs, C. L., Ungerleider, L. G., & Haxby, J. V. (1996). Neural correlates of category-specific knowledge. *Nature, 379*, 649–652. doi:10.1038/379649a0

Martin, G. N. (2019). (Why) do you like scary movies? A review of the empirical research on psychological responses to horror films. *Frontiers in Psychology, 10*, 2298. doi:10.3389/fpsyg.2019.02298

Masi, C. M., Chen, H.-Y., Hawkley, L. C., & Cacioppo, J. T. (2011). A meta-analysis of interventions to reduce loneliness. *Personality and Social Psychology Review, 15*(3), 219–266. doi:10.1177/1088868310377394

Maslow, A. H. (1943). A theory of human motivation. *Psychological Review, 50*, 370–396. doi:10.1037/h0054346

Maslow, A. H. (1950). *Self-actualizing people: A study of psychological health*. New York: Grune and Stratton.

Mason, M. F., Norton, M. I., Van Horn, J. D., Wegner, D. M., Grafton, S. T., & Macrae, C. N. (2007). Wandering minds: The default network and stimulus-independent thought. *Science, 315*(5810), 393–395. doi:10.1126/science.1131295

Mason, W. A., Capitanio, J. P., Machado, C. J., Mendoza, S. P., & Amaral, D. G. (2006). Amygdalectomy and responsiveness to novelty in rhesus monkeys (*Macaca mulatta*): Generality and individual consistency of effects. *Emotion, 6*, 73–81. doi:10.1037/1528-3542.6.1.73

Masten, A. S., Hubbard, J. J., Gest, S. D., Tellegen, A., Garmezy, N., & Ramirez, M. (1999). Competence in the context of adversity: Pathways to resilience and maladaptation from childhood to late adolescence. *Development and Psychopathology, 11*(1), 143–169. doi:10.1017/s0954579499001996

Masuda, T., & Nisbett, R. E. (2001). Attending holistically versus analytically: Comparing the context sensitivity of Japanese and Americans. *Journal of Personality and Social Psychology, 81*(5), 922–934. doi:10.1037/0022-3514.81.5.922

Matsa, K. E., & Lu, K. (2016). 10 facts about the changing digital news landscape. Retrieved from http://www.pewresearch.org/fact-tank/2016/09/14/facts-about-the-changing-digital-news-landscape/

Matsumoto, D., & Hwang, H. S. (2011). Cooperation and competition in intercultural interactions. *International Journal of Intercultural Relations, 35*(5), 677–685.doi:10.1016/j.ijintrel.2011.02.017

Matsumoto, D., & Willingham, B. (2009). Spontaneous facial expressions of emotion of congenitally and noncongenitally blind individuals. *Journal of Personality and Social Psychology*, 96(1), 1–10. doi:10.1037/a0014037

Matthews-Ewald, M. R., Zullig, K. J., & Ward, R. M. (2014). Sexual orientation and disordered eating behaviors among self-identified male and female college students. *Eating Behaviors, 15*(3), 441–444. doi:http://dx.doi.org/10.1016/j.eatbeh.2014.05.002

Matthews, C. E., Chen, K. Y., Freedson, P. S., & al., e. (2008). Amount of time spent in sedentary behaviors in the United States, 2003–2004. *American Journal of Epidemiology, 167*, 875–881. doi:10.1093/aje/kwm390

Maurer, D., & Maurer, C. (1988). *The world of the newborn*. New York: Basic Books.

Maxwell, R., Merckelbach, H., Lilienfeld, S. O., & Lynn, S. J. (2018). The treatment of dissociation: An evaluation of effectiveness and potential mechanisms. In D. David, S. J. Lynn, & G. H. Montgomery (Eds.), *Evidence-based psychotherapy: The state of the science and practice* (pp. 329–361). Wiley-Blackwell.

Mayberg, H. S., Lozano, A. M., Voon, V., McNeely, H. E., Seminowicz, D., Hamani, C., . . . Kennedy, S. H. (2005). Deep brain stimulation for treatment-resistant depression. *Neuron, 45*(5), 651–660. doi:10.1016/j.neuron.2005.02.014

Mayer, D., & Salovey, P. (1993). The intelligence of emotional ntelligence. *Intelligence, 17*, 433–442. doi:10.1016/0160-2896(93)90010-3

Mayer, J. (1955). Regulation of energy intake and the body weight: The glucostatic theory and the lipostatic hypothesis. *Annals of the New York Academy of Sciences, 63*, 15–43. doi:10.1111/j.1749-6632.1955.tb36543.x

Mazur, A., & Booth, A. (1998). Testosterone and dominance in men. *Behavioral and Brain Sciences, 21*, 353–363. doi:10.1017/S0140525X98001228

Mazur, A., & Michalek, J. (1998). Marriage, divorce and male testosterone. *Social Forces, 77*, 315–331. doi:10.1093/sf/77.1.315
Mazur, A., & Mueller, E. (1996). Facial dominance. In A. Somit & S. Peterson (Eds.), *Research in biopolitics* (Vol. 4, pp. 99–111). London: JAI Press.
Mazure, C. M. (1998). Life stressors as risk factors in depression. *Clinical Psychology: Science and Practice, 5*, 291–313. doi:10.1111/j.1468-2850.1998.tb00151.x
Mazza, S., Gerbier, E., Gustin, M.-P., Kasikci, Z., Koenig, O., Toppino, T. C., & Magnin, M. (2016). Relearn faster and retain longer: Along With practice, sleep makes perfect. *Psychological Science, 27*(10), 1321–1330. doi:10.1177/0956797616659930
McArthur, L. Z., & Berry, D. S. (1987). Cross-cultural agreement in perceptions of babyfaced adults. *Journal of Cross-Cultural Psychology, 18*(2), 165–192. doi:10.1177/0022002187018002003
McCain, J. L., & Campbell, W. K. (2016). Narcissism and social media use: A meta-analytic review. *Psychology of Popular Media Culture, 7*(3), 308–327. doi:10.1037/ppm0000137
McCall, M. (1997). The effects of physical attractiveness on gaining access to alcohol: When social policy meets social decision making. *Addiction, 92*, 597–600. doi:10.1111/j.1360-0443.1997.tb02916.x
McCann, D., Barrett, A., Cooper, A., Crumpler, D., Dalen, L., Grimshaw, K., Kitchin, E., Lok, K., Porteous, L., Prince, E., Sonuga-Barke, E., Warner, J. O., & Stevenson, J. (2007). Food additives and hyperactive behaviour in 3-year-old and 8/9-year-old children in the community: A randomised, double-blinded, placebo-controlled trial. *The Lancet, 370*(9598), 1560–1567. doi:10.1016/s0140-6736(07)61306-3
McCarley, R. W. (2007). Neurobiology of REM and NREM sleep. *Sleep Medicine, 8*(4), 302–330. doi:10.1016/j.sleep.2007.03.005
McCarthy-Jones, S., Smailes, D., Corvin, A., Gill, M., Morris, D. W., Dinan, T. G., Murphy, K. C., O'Neill, F. A., Waddington, J. L., Australian Schizophrenia Research Bank, Donohoe, G., & Dudley, R. (2017). Occurrence and co-occurrence of hallucinations by modality in schizophrenia-spectrum disorders. *Psychiatry Research, 252*, 154–160. doi:10.1016/j.psychres.2017.01.102
McClelland, D. C. (1985). *Human motivation*. Glenview, IL: Scott, Foresman.
McClung, C. A. (2007). Circadian genes, rhythms and the biology of mood disorders. *Pharmacology and Therapeutics, 114*(2), 222–232. doi:10.1016/j.pharmthera.2007.02.003
McClure, S. M., Li, J., Tomlin, D., Cypert, K. S., Montague, L. M., & Montague, P. R. (2004). Neural correlates of behavioral preference for culturally familiar drinks. *Neuron, 44*(2), 379–387. doi:10.1016/j.neuron.2004.09.019
McComb, K., Baker, L., & Moss, C. (2006). African elephants show high levels of interest in the skulls and ivory of their own species. *Biology Letters, 2*(1), 26–28. doi:10.1098/rsbl.2005.0400
McConnell, R. A., & Clark, T. K. (1991). National Academy of Sciences' opinion on parapsychology. *Journal of the American Society for Psychical Research, 71*, 261–271.
McCrae, R. R., & Costa, P. T., Jr. (1997). Personality trait structure as a human universal. *American Psychologist, 52*(5), 509–516. doi:10.1037/0003-066x.52.5.509
McCrae, R. R., & Costa, P. T. (1985). Updating Norman's 'adequacy taxonomy': Intelligence and personality dimensions in natural language and in questionnaires. *Journal of Personality and Social Psychology, 49*, 710–721. doi:10.1037/0022-3514.49.3.710
McCrae, R. R., & Costa, P. T. (1987). Validation of the five-factor model of personality across instruments and observers. *Journal of Personality and Social Psychology, 52*, 81–90. doi:10.1037/0022-3514.52.1.81
McCrae, R. R., Kurtz, J. E., Yamagata, S., & Terracciano, A. (2011). Internal consistency, retest reliability, and their implications for personality scale validity. *Personality and Social Psychology Review, 15*(1), 28–50. doi:10.1177/1088868310366253
McDonald, N. D., Rands, S. A., Hill, F., Elder, C., & Ioannou, C. C. (2016). Consensus and experience trump leadership, suppressing individual personality during social foraging. *Science Advances, 2*(9), e1600892. doi:10.1126/sciadv.1600892
McDuffie, A., Thurman, A. J., Channell, M. M., & Abbeduto, L. (2017). Language disorders in children with intellectual disability of genetic origin. In R. G. Schwarz (Ed.), *Handbook of child language disorders* (2nd ed., pp. 52–81). Milton Park, UK: Taylor and Francis.
McEwen, B. S., & Gianaros, P. J. (2011). Stress- and allostasis-induced brain plasticity. *Annual Review of Medicine, 62*(1), 431–445. doi:10.1146/annurev-med-052209-100430
McGann, J. P. (2017). Poor human olfaction is a 19th-century myth. *Science, 356*(6338), eaam7263. doi:10.1126/science.aam7263
McGraw, A. P., Mellers, B. A., & Tetlock, P. E. (2005). Expectations and emotions of Olympic athletes. *Journal of Experimental Social Psychology, 41*(4), 438–446. doi:10.1016/j.jesp.2004.09.001
McGuffin, P., Reveley, A., & Holland, A. (1982). Identical triplets: non-identical psychosis? *British Journal of Psychiatry, 140*, 1–6. doi:10.1192/bjp.140.1.1
McHugh, R. K., Whitton, S. W., Peckham, A. D., Welge, J. A., & Otto, M. W. (2013). Patient preference for psychological vs. pharmacological treatment of psychiatric disorders: A meta-analytic review. *The Journal of Clinical Psychiatry, 74*(6), 595–602. doi:10.4088/JCP.12r07757
McKay, D. (2011). Methods and mechanisms in the efficacy of psychodynamic psychotherapy. *American Psychologist, 66*(2), 147–148. doi:10.1037/a0021195
McKay, K. E., Halperin, J. M., Schwartz, S. T., & Sharma, V. (1994). Developmental analysis of three aspects of information processing: Sustained attention, selective attention, and response organization. *Developmental Neuropsychology, 10*(2), 121–132. doi:10.1080/87565649409540572
McLean, D. E., & Link, B. G. (1994). Unraveling complexity: Strategies to refine concepts, measures, and research designs in the study of life events and mental health. In W. R. Avison & I. H. Gotlib (Eds.), *Stress and mental health: Contemporary issues and prospects for the future* (pp. 15–42). New York: Plenum Press.
McNamara, R. K., & Welge, J. A. (2016). Meta-analysis of erythrocyte polyunsaturated fatty acid biostatus in bipolar disorder. *Bipolar Disorders, 18*(3), 300–306. doi:10.1111/bdi.12386
McNulty, J. K., Neff, L. A., & Karney, B. R. (2008). Beyond initial attraction: Physical attractiveness in newlywed marriage. *Journal of Family Psychology, 22*(1), 135–143. doi:10.1037/0893-3200.22.1.135
McPherson, M., Smith-Lovin, L., & Brashears, M. E. (2006). Social isolation in America: Changes in core discussion networks over two decades. *American Sociological Review, 71*(3), 353–375. doi:10.1177/000312240607100301
McQueeny, T., Schweinsburg, B. C., Schweinsburg, A. D., Jacobus, J., Bava, S., Frank, L. R., & Tapert, S. F. (2009). Altered white matter integrity in adolescent binge drinkers. *Alcoholism: Clinical and Experimental Research, 33*(7), 1278–1285. doi:10.1111/j.1530-0277.2009.00953.x
Meaney, M. J. (2010). Epigenetics and the biological definition of gene x environment interactions. *Child Development, 81*(1), 41–79. doi:10.1111/j.1467-8624.2009.01381.x
Mecca, A. M., Smelser, N. J., & Vasconcellos, J. (Eds.). (1989). *The social importance of self-esteem*. Berkeley, CA: University of California Press.
Medda, P., Perugi, G., Zanello, S., Ciuffa, M., & Cassano, G. (2009). Response to ECT in bipolar I, bipolar II and unipolar depression. *Journal of Affective Disorders, 118*(1), 55–59. doi:10.1016/j.jad.2009.01.014
Meddis, R., Pearson, A., & Langford, G. (1973). An extreme case of healthy insomnia. *Electroencephalography and Clinical Neurophysiology, 35*(2), 213–214. doi:10.1016/0013-4694(73)90180-6
Medvec, V. H., Madey, S. F., & Gilovich, T. (1995). When less is more: Counterfactual thinking and satisfaction among Olympic medalists. *Journal of Personality and Social Psychology, 69*(4), 603–610. doi:10.1037/0022-3514.69.4.603
Meeus, W. H. J., & Raaijmakers, Q. A. W. (1995). Obedience in modern society: The Utrecht

studies. *Journal of Social Issues, 51*, 155–175. doi:10.1111/j.1540-4560.1995.tb01339.x
Meissner, C. A., & Brigham, J. C. (2001). Thirty years of investigating the own-race bias in memory for faces: A meta-analytic review. *Psychology, Public Policy, and Law, 7*(1), 3–35. doi:10.1037/1076-8971.7.1.3
Meltzer, H. Y., Bobo, W. V., Lee, M. A., Cola, P., & Jayathilake, K. (2010). A randomized trial comparing clozapine and typical neuroleptic drugs in non-treatment-resistant schizophrenia. *Psychiatry Research, 177*(3), 286–293. doi:10.1016/j.psychres.2010.02.018
Meltzoff, A. N., Kuhl, P. K., Movellan, J., & Sejnowski, T. J. (2009). Foundations for a new science of learning. *Science, 325*(5938), 284–288. doi:10.1126/science.1175626
Melzack, R., & Wall, P. D. (1965). Pain mechanisms: A new history. *Science, 150*, 971–979. doi:10.1126/science.150.3699.971
Melzack, R., & Wall, P. D. (1983). *The challenge of pain*. New York: Basic Books.
Mendel, G. (1866). *Experiments in plant hybridization* (W. Bateson & R. Blumberg, Trans.). http://www.esp.org/foundations/genetics/classical/gm-65-f.pdf
Mennella, J. A., & Beauchamp, G. K. (1996). The human infant's response to vanilla flavors in mother's milk and formula. *Infant Behavior and Development, 19*, 13–19. doi:10.1016/S0163-6383(96)90040-5
Mennella, J. A., Jagnow, C. P., & Beauchamp, G. K. (2001). Prenatal and postnatal flavor learning by human infants. *Pediatrics, 107*, E88. doi:10.1542/peds.107.6.e88
Mental Health Foundation. (2020). *Loneliness during coronavirus*. https://www.mentalhealth.org.uk/coronavirus/coping-with-loneliness
Menzel, E. W. (1978). Cognitive mapping in chimpanzees. In S. H. Hulse, H. Fowler, & W. K. Honig (Eds.), *Cognitive processes in animal behavior* (pp. 375–422). Hillsdale, N. J.: Erlbaum.
Menzies, L., Chamberlain, S. R., Laird, A. R., Thelen, S. M., Sahakian, B. J., & Bullmore, E. T. (2008). Integrating evidence from neuroimaging and neuropsychological studies of obsessive-compulsive disorder: The orbitofronto-striatal model revisited. *Neuroscience and Biobehavioral Reviews, 32*(3), 525–549. doi:10.1016/j.neubiorev.2007.09.005
Mery, F., & Kawecki, T. J. (2005). A cost of long-term memory in Drosophila. *Science, 308*, 1148. doi:10.1126/science.1111331
Merzenich, M. M., & Jenkins, W. M. (1993). Reorganization of cortical representations of the hand following alterations of skin inputs induced by nerve injury, skin island transfers, and experience. *Journal of Hand Therapy, 6*, 89–104. doi:10.1016/S0894-1130(12)80290-0
Mestre-Bach, G., Jiménez-Murcia, S., Fernández-Aranda, F., & Potenza, M. N. (2019). Addressing controversies surrounding food addiction. In P. Cottone, V. Sabino, C. F. Moore, & G. F. Koob (Eds.), *Compulsive eating behavior and food addiction* (pp. 419–448). Cambridge, MA: Academic Press.
Meyer-Bahlburg, H. F., Dalke, K. B., Berenbaum, S. A., Cohen-Kettenis, P. T., Hines, M., & Schober, J. M. (2016). Gender assignment, reassignment and outcome in disorders of sex development: Update of the 2005 Consensus Conference. *Hormone Research in Paediatrics, 85*(2), 112–118. doi:10.1159/000442386
Meyer-Bahlburg, H. F., Dolezal, C., Baker, S. W., & New, M. I. (2008). Sexual orientation in women with classical or non-classical congenital adrenal hyperplasia as a function of degree of prenatal androgen excess. *Archives of Sexual Behavior, 37*(1), 85–99. doi:10.1007/s10508-007-9265-1
Meyer-Bahlburg, H. F., Dolezal, C., Baker, S. W., Carlson, A. D., Obeid, J. S., & New, M. I. (2004). Prenatal androgenization affects gender-related behavior but not gender identity in 5–12-year-old girls with congenital adrenal hyperplasia. *Archives of Sexual Behavior, 33*(2), 97–104. doi:10.1023/b:aseb.0000014324.25718.51
Meyer-Lindenberg, A., Domes, G., Kirsch, P., & Heinrichs, M. (2011). Oxytocin and vasopressin in the human brain: Social neuropeptides for translational medicine. *Nature Reviews Neuroscience, 12*(9), 524–538. doi:10.1038/nrn3044
Meyer, D. E., & Schvanevelt, R. W. (1971). Facilitation in recognizing pairs of words: Evidence of a dependence between retrieval operations. *Journal of Experimental Psychology, 90*, 227–234. doi:10.1037/h0031564
Micco, J. A., Henin, A., Mick, E., Kim, S., Hopkins, C. A., Biederman, J., & Hirshfeld-Becker, D. R. (2009). Anxiety and depressive disorders in offspring at high risk for anxiety: A meta-analysis. *Journal of Anxiety Disorders, 23*(8), 1158–1164. doi:10.1016/j.janxdis.2009.07.021
Micheau, J., & Marighetto, A. (2011). Acetylcholine and memory: A long, complex and chaotic but still living relationship. *Behavioural Brain Research, 221*(2), 424–429. doi:10.1016/j.bbr.2010.11.052
Micheli, L., Ceccarelli, M., D'Andrea, G., & Tirone, F. (2018). Depression and adult neurogenesis: Positive effects of the antidepressant fluoxetine and of physical exercise. *Brain Research Bulletin, 143*, 181–193. doi:10.1016/j.brainresbull.2018.09.002
Mieda, M., Williams, S. C., Richardson, J. A., Tanaka, K., & Yanagisawa, M. (2006). The dorsomedial hypothalamic nucleus as a putative food-entrainable circadian pacemaker. *Proceedings of the National Academy of Sciences of the United States of America, 103*(32), 12150–12155. doi:10.1073/pnas.0604189103
Milani, R. V., & Lavie, C. J. (2009). Reducing psychosocial stress: A novel mechanism of improving survival from exercise training. *The American Journal of Medicine, 122*(10), 931–938. doi:10.1016/j.amjmed.2009.03.028
Milevsky, A., Schlechter, M., Netter, S., & Keehn, D. (2007). Maternal and paternal parenting styles in adolescents: Associations with self-esteem, depression and life-satisfaction. *Journal of Child and Family Studies, 16*(1), 39–47. doi:10.1007/s10826-006-9066-5
Milgram, S. (1963). Behavioral study of obedience. *Journal of Abnormal and Social Psychology, 67*, 371–378. doi:10.1037/h0040525
Milgram, S. (1974). *Obedience to authority*. New York: Harper & Row.
Milich, R., & Pelham, W. E. (1986). Effects of sugar ingestion on the classroom and playground behavior of attention deficit disordered boys. *Journal of Consulting and Clinical Psychology, 54*, 714–718. doi:10.1037/0022-006X.54.5.714
Milinski, M., Semmann, D., & Jrambeck, H.-J. (2002). Reputation helps solve the 'tragedy of the commons'. *Nature, 415*, 424–426. doi:10.1038/415424a
Miller, B. L., Seeley, W. W., Mychack, P., Rosen, H. J., Mena, I., & Boone, K. (2001). Neuroanatomy of the self: Evidence from patients with frontotemporal dementia. *Neurology, 57*(5), 817–821. doi:10.1212/WNL.57.5.817
Miller, D. J., Duka, T., Stimpson, C. D., Schapiro, S. J., Baze, W. B., McArthur, M. J., Fobbs, A. J., Sousa, A. M. M., Šestan, N., Wildman, D. E., Lipovitch, L., Kuzawa, C. W., Hof, P. R., & Sherwood, C. C. (2012). Prolonged myelination in human neocortical evolution. *Proceedings of the National Academy of Sciences of the United States of America, 109*(41), 16480–16485. doi:10.1073/pnas.1117943109
Miller, D. T., & Ross, M. (1975). Self-serving biases in the attribution of causality: Fact or fiction? *Psychological Bulletin, 82*, 213–225 doi:10.1037/h0076486.
Miller, G. A. (1956). The magical number seven, plus or minus two: Some limits on our capacity for processing information. *Psychological Review, 63*, 81–97. doi:10.1037/h0043158
Miller, J. D., Hoffman, B. J., Gaughan, E. T., Gentile, B., Maples, J., & Keith Campbell, W. (2011). Grandiose and vulnerable narcissism: A nomological network analysis. *Journal of Personality, 79*(5), 1013–1042. doi:10.1111/j.1467-6494.2010.00711.x
Miller, J. D., Lynam, D. R., Hyatt, C. S., & Campbell, W. K. (2017). Controversies in narcissism. *Annual Review of Clinical Psychology, 13*(1), 291–315. doi:10.1146/annurevclinpsy-032816-045244
Miller, J. G., & Bersoff, D. M. (1992). Culture and moral judgment: How are conflicts between justice and interpersonal responsibilities resolved? *Journal of Personality & Social Psychology, 62*(4), 541–554. doi:10.1037/0022-3514.62.4.541
Miller, K. D., Choi, S., & Pentland, B. T. (2014). The role of transactive memory in the formation of organizational routines. *Strategic Organization, 12*(2), 109–133. doi:10.1177/1476127014521609
Miller, N. E. (1944). Experimental studies in conflict. In J. M. Hunt (Ed.), *Personality and*

the behavior disorders. New York: Ronald Press.
Miller, R. (2007). Theory of the normal waking EEG: From single neurones to waveforms in the alpha, beta and gamma frequency ranges. *International Journal of Psychophysiology, 64*(1), 18–23. doi:10.1016/j.ijpsycho.2006.07.009
Miller, S. L., Zielaskowski, K., & Plant, E. A. (2012). The basis of shooter biases: Beyond cultural stereotypes. *Personality and Social Psychology Bulletin, 38*(10), 1358–1366. doi:10.1037/h0076486
Million, M., Angelakis, E., Maraninchi, M., Henry, M., Giorgi, R., Valero, R., Vialettes, B., & Raoult, D. (2013). Correlation between body mass index and gut concentrations of *Lactobacillus reuteri, Bifidobacterium animalis, Methanobrevibacter smithii* and *Escherichia coli*. *International Journal of Obesity, 37*(11), 1460–1466. doi:10.1038/ijo.2013.20
Millward, C., Ferriter, M., Calver, S., & Connell-Jones, G. (2008). Gluten- and casein-free diets for autistic spectrum disorder. *Cochrane Database of Systematic Reviews, 2,* CD003498. doi:10.1002/14651858.CD003498.pub3
Milner, B. (1966). Amnesia following operation on the temporal lobe. In C. W. M. Whitty & O. L. Zangwill (Eds.), *Amnesia* (pp. 109–133). London: Butterworth.
Milner, B. (2005). The medial temporal-lobe amnesic syndrome. *The Psychiatric Clinics of North America, 28,* 599–611. doi:10.1016/j.psc.2005.06.002
Mindess, A. (2006). *Reading between the signs* (2nd ed.). Boston, MA: Intercultural Press.
Mineka, S., Sutton, J., Craske, M. G., Hermans, D., & Vansteenwegen, D. (2006). Contemporary learning theory perspectives on the etiology of fears and phobias. In M. G. Craske, D. Hermans, & D. Vansteenwegen (Eds.), *Fear and learning: From basic processes to clinical implications.* (pp. 75–97). Washington, DC: American Psychological Association.
Mischel, W. (1968). *Personality and assessment*. New York: Wiley.
Mischel, W. (2004). Toward an integrative science of the person. *Annual Review of Psychology, 55,* 1–22. doi:10.1146/annurev.psych.55.042902.130709
Mischel, W., & Shoda, Y. (1995). A cognitive-affective system theory of personality: Reconceptualizing situations, dispositions, dynamics, and invariance in personality structure. *Psychological Review, 102*(2), 246–268. doi:10.1037/0033-295X.102.2.246
Mitchell, B. A., & Lovegreen, L. D. (2009). The empty nest syndrome in midlife families. *Journal of Family Issues, 30*(12), 1651–1670. doi:10.1177/0192513x09339020
Mitchell, K. R., Mercer, C. H., Prah, P., Clifton, S., Tanton, C., Wellings, K., & Copas, A. (2019). Why do men report more opposite-sex sexual partners than women? Analysis of the gender discrepancy in a British National Probability Survey. *The Journal of Sex Research, 56*(1), 1–8. doi:10.1080/00224499.2018.1481193
Mogensen, D. M., Pihl, M. B., Skakkebæk, N. E., Andersen, H. R., Juul, A., Kyhl, H. B., Swan, S., Kristensen, D. M., Andersen, M. S., Lind, D. V., & Jensen, T. K. (2017). Prenatal exposure to antifungal medication may change anogenital distance in male offspring: A preliminary study. *Environmental Health, 16*(1), 68. doi:10.1186/s12940-017-0263-z
Moldofsky, H., & Scarisbrick, P. (1976). Induction of neurasthenic musculoskeletal pain syndrome by selective sleep stage deprivation. *Psychosomatic Medicine, 38*(1), 35–44 doi:10.1097/00006842-197601000-00006.
Molendijk, M., Molero, P., Ortuño Sánchez-Pedreño, F., Van der Does, W., & Angel Martínez-González, M. (2018). Diet quality and depression risk: A systematic review and dose-response meta-analysis of prospective studies. *Journal of Affective Disorders, 226,* 346–354. doi:10.1016/j.jad.2017.09.022
Molina, E., Cervilla, J., Rivera, M., Torres, F., Bellón, J. Á., Moreno, B., King, M., Nazareth, I., & Gutiérrez, B. (2011). Polymorphic variation at the serotonin 1-A receptor gene is associated with comorbid depression and generalized anxiety. *Psychiatric Genetics, 21*(4), 195–201. doi:10.1097/YPG.0b013e3283457a48
Monson, C. M., Taft, C. T., & Fredman, S. J. (2009). Military-related PTSD and intimate relationships: From description to theory-driven research and intervention development. *Clinical Psychology Review, 29*(8), 707–714. doi:10.1016/j.cpr.2009.09.002
Montpetit, M. A., Bergeman, C. S., Deboeck, P. R., Tiberio, S. S., & Boker, S. M. (2010). Resilience-as-process: Negative affect, stress, and coupled dynamical systems. *Psychology and Aging, 25*(3), 631–640. doi:10.1037/a0019268
Moon, C. (2017). Prenatal experience with the maternal voice. In M. Filippa, P. Kuhn, & B. Westrup (Eds.), *Early vocal contact and preterm infant brain development: Bridging the gaps between research and practice* (pp. 25–37). New York, NY: Springer International Publishing.
Moon, C., Cooper, R. P., & Fifer, W. P. (1993). Two-day-olds prefer their native language. *Infant Behavior and Development, 16,* 495–500. doi:10.1016/0163-6383(93)80007-U
Moon, H. Y., Becke, A., Berron, D., Becker, B., Sah, N., Benoni, G., Janke, E., Lubejko, S. T., Greig, N. H., Mattison, J. A., Duzel, E., & van Praag, H. (2016). Running-induced systemic cathepsin B secretion is associated with memory function. *Cell Metabolism, 24*(2), 332–340. doi:10.1016/j.cmet.2016.05.025
Moon, R. Y., & Task Force on Sudden Infant Death Syndrome. (2016). SIDS and other sleep-related infant deaths: Evidence base for 2016 updated recommendations for a safe infant sleeping environment. *Pediatrics,* e20162940. doi:10.1542/peds.2016-2940
Moore, D. J., Mowen, J. C., & Reardon, R. (1994). Multiple sources in advertising appeals: When product endorsers are paid by the advertising sponsor. *Journal of the Academy of Marketing Science, 22*(3), 234–243. doi:10.1177/0092070394223004
Moors, A., Ellsworth, P. C., Scherer, K. R., & Frijda, N. H. (2013). Appraisal theories of emotion: State of the art and future development. *Emotion Review, 5*(2), 119–124. doi:10.1177/1754073912468165
Morgan, E. M. (2013). Contemporary issues in sexual orientation and identity development in emerging adulthood. *Emerging Adulthood, 1*(1), 52–66. doi:10.1177/2167696812469187
Morin, C. M., & Carrier, J. (2020). The acute effects of the COVID-19 pandemic on insomnia and psychological symptoms. *Sleep Medicine,* S1389-9457(20)30261-6. doi:10.1016/j.sleep.2020.06.005
Morres, I. D., Hatzigeorgiadis, A., Stathi, A., Comoutos, N., Arpin-Cribbie, C., Krommidas, C., & Theodorakis, Y. (2019). Aerobic exercise for adult patients with major depressive disorder in mental health services: A systematic review and meta-analysis. *Depression and Anxiety, 36*(1), 39–53. doi:10.1002/da.22842
Morris, M. W., & Peng, K. (1994). Culture and cause: American and Chinese attributions for social and physical events. *Journal of Personality and Social Psychology, 67,* 949–971. doi:10.1037/0022-3514.67.6.949
Morse, S., & Gergen, K. J. (1970). Social comparison, self-consistency, and the concept of self. *Journal of Personality and Social Psychology, 16,* 148–156. doi:10.1037/h0029862
Moscovici, S., & Zavalloni, M. (1969). The group as a polarizer of attitudes. *Journal of Personality and Social Psychology, 12,* 125–135. doi:10.1037/h0027568
Moscovici, S., Lage, S., & Naffrechoux, M. (1969). Influence of a consistent minority on the responses of a majority in a color perception task. *Sociometry, 32,* 365–380. doi:10.2307/2786541
Moscovitch, M., Nadel, L., Winocur, G., Gilboa, A., & Rosenbaum, R. S. (2006). The cognitive neuroscience of remote episodic, semantic and spatial memory. *Current Opinion in Neurobiology, 16*(2), 179–190. doi:10.1016/j.conb.2006.03.013
Moskalenko, Y., Mozhaev, S., Weinstein, G., Kravenchko, T., Riabchikova, N., Feilding, A., Halvorson, P., Semernia, V., Panov, A., & Medvedev, S. (2008). Effects of cranial trepanation on the functioning of cerebrovascular and cerebrospinal fluid systems. *International Journal of Psychophysiology, 69*(3), 302–303. doi:10.1016/j.ijpsycho.2008.05.301
Mössner, R., Schuhmacher, A., Schulze-Rauschenbach, S., Kühn, K.-U., Rujescu, D., Rietschel, M., Zobel, A., Franke, P., Wölwer, W., Gaebel, W., Häfner, H., Wagner, M., & Maier, W. (2008). Further evidence for a

functional role of the glutamate receptor gene GRM3 in schizophrenia. *European Neuropsychopharmacology, 18*(10), 768–772. doi:10.1016/j.euroneuro.2008.05.007
Mota-Rolim, S. A., & Araujo, J. F. (2013). Neurobiology and clinical implications of lucid dreaming. *Medical Hypotheses, 81*(5), 751–756. doi:10.1016/j.mehy.2013.04.049
Mrazek, A. J., Chiao, J. Y., Blizinsky, K. D., Lun, J., & Gelfand, M. J. (2013). The role of culture–gene coevolution in morality judgment: examining the interplay between tightness–looseness and allelic variation of the serotonin transporter gene. *Culture and Brain, 1*(2), 100–117. doi:10.1007/s40167-013-0009-x
Muehlenbein, M. P., & Bribiescas, R. G. (2005). Testosterone-mediated immune functions and male life histories. *American Journal of Human Biology, 17*(5), 527–558. doi:10.1002/ajhb.20419
Mueller, P. A., & Oppenheimer, D. M. (2014). The pen is mightier than the keyboard: Advantages of longhand over laptop note taking. *Psychological Science, 25*(6), 1159–1168. doi:10.1177/0956797614524581
Mundorf, N., Weaver, J., & Zillmann, D. (1989). Effects of gender roles and self perceptions on affective reactions to horror films. *Sex Roles, 20*(11), 655–673. doi:10.1007/BF00288078
Murdoch, B. B., Jr. (1962). The serial position effect in free recall. *Journal of Experimental Psychology, 64*, 482–488. doi:10.1037/h0045106
Murphy, J. M., Gilligan, C., & Puka, B. (1994). *Moral development in late adolescence and adulthood: A critique and reconstruction of Kohlberg's theory*. New York, NY Garland Publishing.
Murphy, K. D., Rose, M. W., Chinkes, D. L., Meyer III, W. J., Herndon, D. N., Hawkins, H. K., & Sanford, A. P. (2007). The effects of gammahydroxybutyrate on hypermetabolism and wound healing in a rat model of large thermal injury. *Journal of Trauma and Acute Care Surgery, 63*(5), 1099–1107. doi:10.1097/TA.0b013e318157d9d0
Murray, H. A. (1938). *Explorations in personality*. New York: Oxford University Press.
Murray, S. L., Holmes, J. G., Gellavia, G., Griffin, D. W., & Dolderman, D. (2002). Kindred spirits? The benefits of egocentrism in close relationships. *Journal of Personality and Social Psychology, 82*, 563–581. doi:10.1037/0022-3514.82.4.563
Murty, V. P., Calabro, F., & Luna, B. (2016). The role of experience in adolescent cognitive development: Integration of executive, memory, and mesolimbic systems. *Neuroscience & Biobehavioral Reviews, 70*, 46–58. doi:10.1016/j.neubiorev.2016.07.034
Myers & Briggs Foundation (2020). *Misconceptions about the MBTI Assessment*. https://www.myersbriggs.org/more-about-personality-type/misconceptions-about-the-MBTI-assessment/.
Myers, C. R. (1982). Psychology at Toronto. In M. J. Wright & C. R. Myers (Eds.) *A History of Academic Psychology in Canada* (pp. 68–99) Toronto: C. F. Hogrefe.
Myers, D. G. (1993). *The pursuit of happiness*. New York: Avon.
Nadig, A. S., Ozonoff, S., Young, G. S., Rozga, A., Sigman, M., & Rogers, S. J. (2007). A prospective study of response to name in infants at risk for autism. *JAMA Pediatrics, 161*(4), 378–383. doi:10.1001/archpedi.161.4.378
Nandam, L. S., Brazel, M., Zhou, M., & Jhaveri, D. J. (2020). Cortisol and major depressive disorder-translating findings from humans to animal models and back. *Frontiers in Psychiatry, 10*, 974–974. doi:10.3389/fpsyt.2019.00974
Nardi, B., Marini, A., Turchi, C., Arimatea, E., Tagliabracci, A., & Bellantuono, C. (2013). Role of 5-HTTLPR polymorphism in the development of the inward/outward personality organization: A genetic association study. *PloS One, 8*(12), e82192. doi:10.1371/journal.pone.0082192
National Guild of Hypnotists. (2016). 2016 *NGH state law guide*. https://ngh.net/wp-content/uploads/2010/11/StateLawGuide.pdf
National Institute of Child Health and Human Development (NICHHD). (2003). *SIDS: Back to sleep campaign*. http://www.nichd.nih.gov/sids/
National Institute of Mental Health (NIMH). (2009). *What causes ADHD?* http://www.nimh.nih.gov/health/publications/attention-deficit-hyperactivity-disorder/what-causes-adhd.shtml
National Institute on Alcohol Abuse and Alcoholism (NIAAA). (2020). *Alcohol facts and statistics*. https://www.niaaa.nih.gov/publications/brochures-and-fact-sheets/alcohol-facts-and-statistics
National Institute on Alcohol Abuse & Alcoholism. (2018). *Alcohol facts and statistics | National Institute on Alcohol Abuse and Alcoholism (NIAAA)*. https://www.niaaa.nih.gov/alcohol-health/overview-alcohol-consumption/alcohol-facts-and-statistics
National Sleep Foundation. (2009). *Restless leg syndrome (RLS) and sleep*. http://www.sleepfoundation.org/article/sleep-related-problems/restless-legs-syndrome-rls-and-sleep
Nave, G., Jung, W. H., Karlsson Linnér, R., Kable, J. W., & Koellinger, P. D. (2019). Are bigger brains smarter? Evidence from a large-scale preregistered study. *Psychological Science, 30*(1), 43–54. doi:10.1177/0956797618808470
Neal, D. T., & Chartrand, T. L. (2011). Embodied emotion perception: Amplifying and dampening facial feedback modulates emotion perception accuracy. *Social Psychological and Personality Science, 2*(6), 673–678. doi:10.1177/1948550611406138
Nedeltcheva, A. V., Kilkus, J. M., Imperial, J., Schoeller, D. A., & Penev, P. D. (2010). Insufficient sleep undermines dietary efforts to reduce adiposity. *Annals of Internal Medicine, 153*, 435–441. doi:10.7326/0003-4819-153-7-201010050-00006
Nee, D. E., Brown, J. W., Askren, M. K., Berman, M. G., Demiralp, E., Krawitz, A., & Jonides, J. (2013). A meta-analysis of executive components of working memory. *Cerebral Cortex, 23*(2), 264–282. doi:10.1093/cercor/bhs007
Needham, B. L., Adler, N., Gregorich, S., Rehkopf, D., Lin, J., Blackburn, E. H., & Epel, E. S. (2013). Socioeconomic status, health behavior, and leukocyte telomere length in the National Health and Nutrition Examination Survey, 1999–2002. *Social Science & Medicine, 85*, 1–8. doi:10.1016/j.socscimed.2013.02.023
Neigh, G. N., Gillespie, C. F., & Nemeroff, C. B. (2009). The neurobiological toll of child abuse and neglect. *Trauma, Violence, & Abuse, 10*(4), 389–410. doi:10.1177/1524838009339758
Neinstein, L. S., & Irwin, C. E. (2013). Young adults remain worse off than adolescents. *Journal of Adolescent Health, 53*(5), 559—561. doi:10.1016/j.jadohealth.2013.08.014
Neisser, U., Boodoo, G., Bouchard Jr, T. J., Boykin, A. W., Brody, N., Ceci, S. J., . . . Sternberg, R. J. (1996). Intelligence: knowns and unknowns. *American Psychologist, 51*(2), 77–101. doi:10.1037/0003-066X.51.2.77
Nelson-Coffey, S. (2018). Married . . . with children: The science of well-being in marriage and family life. In E. Diener, S. Oishi, & L. Tay (Eds.), *Handbook of well-being*. Salt Lake City, UT: Noba Scholar.
Nelson, S. K., Kushlev, K., Dunn, E. W., & Lyubomirsky, S. (2014). Parents are slightly happier than nonparents, but causality still cannot be inferred: A reply to Bhargava, Kassam, and Loewenstein (2014). *Psychological Science, 25*(1), 303–304. doi:10.1177/0956797613508561
Nelson, S. K., Kushlev, K., English, T., Dunn, E. W., & Lyubomirsky, S. (2013). In defense of parenthood: Children are associated with more joy than misery. *Psychological Science, 24*(1), 3–10. doi:10.1177/0956797612447798
Neugarten, B. L., Moore, J. W., & Lowe, J. C. (1965). Age norms, age constraints, and adult socialization. *American Journal of Sociology, 70*(6), 710–717. doi:10.1086/223965
Neuner, F., Schauer, E., Catani, C., Ruf, M., & Elbert, T. (2006). Post-tsunami stress: A study of posttraumatic stress disorder in children living in three severely affected regions in Sri Lanka. *Journal of Traumatic Stress, 19*, 339–347. doi:10.1002/jts.20121
Neville, H. J., Bavelier, D., Corina, D., Rauschecker, J., Karni, A., Lalwani, A., Braun, A., Clark, V., Jezzard, P., & Turner, R. (1998). Cerebral organization for language in deaf and hearing subjects: Biological constraints and effects of experience. *Proceedings of the National Academy*

of Sciences of the United States of America, 95(3), 922–929. doi:10.1073/pnas.95.3.922
Newcombe, T. M. (1929). *Consistency of certain extrovert-introvert behavior patterns in 51 problem boys*. New York: Columbia University Teachers College Press.
Newell, A., & Simon, H. (1972). *Human problem solving*. Englewood Cliffs, NJ: Prentice-Hall.
Newman, N., Fletcher, R., Kalogeropoulos, A., & Nielsen, R. (2019). *Reuters Institute Digital News Report 2019*. http://www.digitalnewsreport.org/
Newsom, C. R., Archer, R. P., Trumbetta, S., & Gottesman, I. I. (2003). Changes in adolescent response patterns on the MMPI/MMPI-A across four decades. *Journal of Personality Assessment, 81*(1), 74–84. doi:10.1207/S15327752JPA8101_07
Newton-Howes, G., Cook, S., Martin, G., Foulds, J. A., & Boden, J. M. (2019). Comparison of age of first drink and age of first intoxication as predictors of substance use and mental health problems in adulthood. *Drug and Alcohol Dependence, 194*, 238–243. doi:10.1016/j.drugalcdep.2018.10.012
Nguyen, D. (2016). Brain death and true patient care. *The Linacre Quarterly, 83*(3), 258–282. doi:10.1080/00243639.2016.1188472
Nielsen Neuroscience. (2017). *Case study: The brains behind better ads–optimizing the cute and cuddly*. https://www.nielsen.com/us/en/insights/case-study/2014/the-brains-behind-better-ads-optimizing-the-cute-and-cuddly-2/#
Nielsen, J., & Wohlert, M. (1991). Sex chromosome abnormalities among 34,910 newborn children: Results from a 13-year incidence study in Århus, Denmark. *Birth Defects: Original Article Series, 26*, 209–223. doi:10.1007/BF01213097
Nielsen, T. A., Zadra, A. L., Simard, V., Saucier, S., Stenstrom, P., Smith, C., & Kuiken, D. (2003). The typical dreams of Canadian university students. *Dreaming, 13*(4), 211–235. doi:10.1023/B:DREM.0000003144.40929.0b
Nilsson, K. W., Åslund, C., Comasco, E., & Oreland, L. (2018). Gene–environment interaction of monoamine oxidase A in relation to antisocial behaviour: Current and future directions. *Journal of Neural Transmission, 125*(11), 1601–1626. doi:10.1007/s00702-018-1892-2
Nielsen, T. A., Zadra, A. L., Simard, V., Saucier, S., Stenstrom, P., Smith, C., & Kuiken, D. (2003). The typical dreams of Canadian university students. *Dreaming, 13*(4), 211–235. doi:10.1023/B:DREM.0000003144.40929.0b
Noaghiul, S., & Hibbeln, J. R. (2003). Cross-national comparisons of seafood consumption and rates of bipolar disorders. *American Journal of Psychiatry, 160*(12), 2222–2227. doi:10.1176/appi.ajp.160.12.2222
Noah, T., Schul, Y., & Mayo, R. (2018). When both the original study and its failed replication are correct: Feeling observed eliminates the facial-feedback effect. *Journal of Personality and Social Psychology, 114*(5), 657–664. doi:10.1037/pspa0000121
Noël, X., Brevers, D., & Bechara, A. (2013). A neurocognitive approach to understanding the neurobiology of addiction. *Current Opinion in Neurobiology, 23*(4), 632–638. doi:10.1016/j.conb.2013.01.018
Noelle-Neumann, E. (1984). *The spiral of silence: Public opinion–Our social skin*. Chicago: University of Chicago Press.
Nolen-Hoeksema, S. (1987). Sex differences in unipolar depression: Evidence and theory. *Psychological Bulletin, 101*(2), 259. doi:10.1037/0033-2909.101.2.259
Nolen-Hoeksema, S. (1991). Responses to depression and their effects on the duration of depressive episodes. *Journal of Abnormal Psychology, 100*, 569–582. doi:10.1037/0021-843X.100.4.569
Nolen-Hoeksema, S. (2003). *Women who think too much: How to break free of overthinking and reclaim your life*. New York: Henry Holt and Company.
Nolen-Hoeksema, S., & Girgus, J. S. (1994). The emergence of gender differences in depression during adolescence. *Psychological Bulletin, 115*, 424–443. doi:10.1037/0033-2909.115.3.424
Nolen-Hoeksema, S., & Morrow, J. (1993). Effects of rumination and distraction on naturally occurring depressed mood. *Cognition & Emotion, 7*(6), 561–570. doi:10.1080/02699939308409206
Nolen-Hoeksema, S., Larson, J., & Grayson, C. (1999). Explaining the gender difference in depressive symptoms. *Journal of Personality and Social Psychology, 77*, 1061–1072. doi:10.1037/0022-3514.77.5.1061
Norcross, J. C., & Castle, P. H. (2002). Appreciating the Psy.D.: The facts. *Eye on Psi Chi, 7*, 22–26.
Nordenbæk, C., Jørgensen, M., Kyvik, K. O., & Bilenberg, N. (2014). A Danish population-based twin study on autism spectrum disorders. *European Child & Adolescent Psychiatry, 23*(1), 35–43. doi:10.1007/s00787-013-0419-5
Norman, G. J., Berntson, G. G., & Cacioppo, J. T. (2014). Emotion, somatovisceral afference, and autonomic regulation. *Emotion Review, 6*(2), 113–123. doi:10.1177/1754073913512006
Norman, W. T. (1963). Toward an adequate taxonomy of personality attributes: Replicated factor structure in peer nomination personality ratings. *Journal of Abnormal & Social Psychology, 66*, 574–583. doi:10.1037/h0040291
Nosek, B. A. (2007). Understanding the individual implicitly and explicitly. *International Journal of Psychology, 42*(3), 184–188. doi:10.1080/00207590601068159
Nosek, B. A., Aarts, A. A., Alexander, A., Anderson, C. J., Anderson, J. E., Kappes, H. B., et al.,. (2015). Estimating the reproducibility of psychological science. *Science, 349*(6251), aac4716. doi:10.1126/science.aac4716
Nowak, M. A. (2006). Five rules for the evolution of cooperation. *Science, 314*, 1560–1563. doi:10.1126/science.1133755
O'Brien, T. B., & DeLongis, A. (1996). The interactional context of problem-, emotion-, and relationship-focused coping: The role of the Big Five personality factors. *Journal of Personality, 64*(4), 775–813. doi:10.1111/j.1467-6494.1996.tb00944.x
O'Donnell, S., Webb, J. K., & Shine, R. (2010). Conditioned taste aversion enhances the survival of an endangered predator imperilled by a toxic invader. *Journal of Applied Ecology, 47*(3), 558–565. doi:10.1111/j.1365-2664.2010.01802.x
O'Keefe, J., & Nadel, L. (1978). *The hippocampus as a cognitive map*. Oxford, U.K.: Oxford University Press.
O'Rourke, N., & Cappeliez, P. (2005). Marital satisfaction and self-deception: Reconstruction of relationship histories among older adults. *Social Behavior and Personality, 33*(3), 273–282. doi:10.2224/sbp.2005.33.3.273
Office of Juvenile Justice and Deliquency Prevention (OJJDP; 2016). *Child victims of stereotypical kidnappings known to law enforcement*. https://ojjdp.ojp.gov/sites/g/files/xyckuh176/files/pubs/249249.pdf
Ogden, C. L., Carroll, M. D., Fryar, C. D., & Flegal, K. M. (2015). Prevalence of obesity among adults and youth: United States, 2011–2014. *NCHS Data Brief, 219*(219), 1–8.
Oh, J., Chopik, W. J., Konrath, S., & Grimm, K. J. (2020). Longitudinal changes in empathy across the life span in six samples of human development. *Social Psychological and Personality Science, 11*(2), 244–253. doi:10.1177/1948550619849429
Okely, J. A., & Deary, I. J. (2018). Longitudinal associations between loneliness and cognitive ability in the Lothian Birth Cohort 1936. *The Journals of Gerontology: Series B, 74*(8), 1376–1386. doi:10.1093/geronb/gby086
Olatunji, B. O., Davis, M. L., Powers, M. B., & Smits, J. A. (2013). Cognitive-behavioral therapy for obsessive-compulsive disorder: A meta-analysis of treatment outcome and moderators. *Journal of Psychiatric Research, 47*(1), 33–41. doi:10.1016/j.jpsychires.2012.08.020
Olsho, L. W., Koch, E. G., Halpin, C. F., & Carter, E. A. (1987). An observer-based psychoacoustic procedure for use with young infants. *Developmental Psychology, 23*, 627–640. doi:10.1037/0012-1649.23.5.627
Olson, K. R., Key, A. C., & Eaton, N. R. (2015). Gender cognition in transgender children. *Psychological Science, 26*(4), 467–474. doi:10.1177/0956797614568156
Opris, I., & Casanova, M. F. (2014). Prefrontal cortical minicolumn: From executive control to disrupted cognitive processing. *Brain, 137*(7), 1863–1875. doi:10.1093/brain/awt359
Ormel, J., Hartman, C. A., & Snieder, H. (2019). The genetics of depression: Successful genome-wide association studies introduce

new challenges. *Translational Psychiatry, 9*(1), 114. doi:10.1038/s41398-019-0450-5

Orne, M. T., & Evans, F. J. (1965). Social control in the psychological experiment: Antisocial behavior and hypnosis. *Journal of Personality and Social Psychology, 1*(3), 189–200. doi:10.1037/h0021933

Orr, A. G., Hsiao, E. C., Wang, M. M., Ho, K., Kim, D. H., Wang, X., Guo, W., Kang, J., Yu, G.-Q., Adame, A., Devidze, N., Dubal, D. B., Maslieh, E., Conklin, B. R., & Mucke, L. (2015). Astrocytic adenosine receptor A2A and Gs-coupled signaling regulate memory. *Nature Neuroscience, 18*(3), 423–434. doi:10.1038/nn.3930

Ortigue, S., Sinigaglia, C., Rizzolatti, G., & Grafton, S. T. (2010). Understanding actions of others: The electrodynamics of the left and right hemispheres. A high-density EEG neuroimaging study. *PLoS ONE, 5*(8), e12160. doi:10.1371/journal.pone.0012160

Osinsky, R., Reuter, M., Küpper, Y., Schmitz, A., Kozyra, E., Alexander, N., & Hennig, J. (2008). Variation in the serotonin transporter gene modulates selective attention to threat. *Emotion, 8*(4), 584–588. doi:10.1037/a0012826

Osório, C., Probert, T., Jones, E., Young, A. H., & Robbins, I. (2016). Adapting to stress: Understanding the neurobiology of resilience. *Behavioral Medicine*, 1–16. doi:10.1080/08964289.2016.1170661

Otsuka, Y. (2014). Face recognition in infants: A review of behavioral and near-infrared spectroscopic studies. *Japanese Psychological Research, 56*(1), 76–90. doi:10.1111/jpr.12024

Owen, A. M. (2019). The search for consciousness. *Neuron, 102*(3), 526–528. doi:10.1016/j.neuron.2019.03.024

Ozer, E. J., Best, S. R., Lipsey, T. L., & Weiss, D. S. (2003). Predictors of posttraumatic stress disorder and symptoms in adults: A meta-analysis. *Psychological Bulletin, 129*(1), 52–73. doi:10.1037/0033-2909.129.1.52

Pace, G. T., Lee, S. J., & Grogan-Kaylor, A. (2019). Spanking and young children's socioemotional development in low-and middle-income countries. *Child Abuse & Neglect, 88*, 84–95. doi:10.1016/j.chiabu.2018.11.003

Paolini, S., Harwood, J., & Rubin, M. (2010). Negative intergroup contact makes group memberships salient: Explaining why intergroup conflict endures. *Personality and Social Psychology Bulletin, 36*(12), 1723–1738. doi:10.1177/0146167210388667

Papagno, C., Pisoni, A., Mattavelli, G., Casarotti, A., Comi, A., Fumagalli, F., Vernice, M., Fava, E., Riva, M., & Bello, L. (2016). Specific disgust processing in the left insula: New evidence from direct electrical stimulation. *Neuropsychologia, 84*, 29–35. doi:10.1016/j.neuropsychologia.2016.01.036

Papp, L. A., Klein, D. F., Martinez, J., Schneier, F., Cole, R., Liebowitz, M. R., Hollander, E., Fryer, A. J., Jordan, F., & Gorman, J. M. (1993). Diagnostic and substance specificity of carbon-dioxide-induced panic. *American Journal of Psychiatry, 150*, 250–257. doi:10.1176/ajp.150.2.250

Paquet, A., Golse, B., Girard, M., Olliac, B., & Vaivre-Douret, L. (2017). Laterality and lateralization in autism spectrum disorder, Using a standardized neuro-psychomotor assessment. *Developmental Neuropsychology, 42*(1), 39–54. doi:10.1080/87565641.2016.1274317

Paracchini, S., Diaz, R., & Stein, J. (2016). Advances in dyslexia genetics—New insights into the role of brain asymmetries. In T. Friedmann, J. C. Dunlap, & S. F. Goodwin (Eds.), *Advances in genetics* (Vol. 96, pp. 53–97). Cambridge, MA: Academic Press.

Paradiso, S., Ostedgaard, K., Vaidya, J., Ponto, L. B., & Robinson, R. (2013). Emotional blunting following left basal ganglia stroke: The role of depression and fronto-limbic functional alterations. *Psychiatry Research: Neuroimaging, 211*(2), 148–159. doi:10.1016/j.pscychresns.2012.05.008

Pargament, K. I., & Krumrei, E. J. (2009). Clinical assessment of clients' spirituality. In J. D. Aten & M. M. Leach (Eds.), *Spirituality and the therapeutic process: A comprehensive resource from intake to termination.* (pp. 93–120). Washington, DC: American Psychological Association.

Paris, J. (2017). Is psychoanalysis still relevant to psychiatry? *The Canadian Journal of Psychiatry, 62*(5), 308–312. doi:10.1177/0706743717692306

Park, B., & Judd, C. M. (2005). Rethinking the link between categorization and prejudice within the social cognition perspective. *Personality and Social Psychology Review, 9*(2), 108–130. doi:10.1207/s15327957pspr0902_2

Park, G., Schwartz, H. A., Eichstaedt, J. C., Kern, M. L., Kosinski, M., Stillwell, D. J., Ungar, L. H., & Seligman, M. E. (2015). Automatic personality assessment through social media language. *Journal of Personality and Social Psychology, 108*(6), 934–952. doi:10.1037/pspp0000020

Parker, E. S., Cahill, L., & McGaugh, J. L. (2006). A case of unusual autobiographical remembering. *Neurocase, 12*(1), 35–49. doi:10.1080/13554790500473680

Parner, E. T., Baron-Cohen, S., Lauritsen, M. B., Jørgensen, M., Schieve, L. A., Yeargin-Allsopp, M., & Obel, C. (2012). Parental age and autism spectrum disorders. *Annals of Epidemiology, 22*(3), 143–150. doi:10.1016/j.annepidem.2011.12.006

Pascual-Leone, A., & Torres, F. (1993). Plasticity of sensorimotor cortex representation of the reading finger in Braille readers. *Brain, 116*, 39–52. doi:10.1093/brain/116.1.39

Pasterski, V. L., Geffner, M. E., Brain, C., Hindmarsh, P., Brook, C., & Hines, M. (2005). Prenatal hormones and postnatal socialization by parents as determinants of male-typical toy play in girls with congenital adrenal hyperplasia. *Child Development, 76*(1), 264–278. doi:10.1111/j.1467-8624.2005.00843.x

Patterson, F. (1978, October). Conversations with a gorilla. *National Geographic,* 438–465.

Patterson, F. (1984). Self-recognition by gorilla (Gorilla gorilla). *Gorilla, 7*, 2–3.

Patterson, F. G. P., & Cohn, R. H. (1994). Self-recognition and self-awareness in lowland gorillas. In S. T. Parker, R. W. Mitchell, & M. L. Boccia (Eds.), *Self-awareness in animals and humans: Developmental perspectives* (pp. 273–290). New York: Cambridge University Press.

Patterson, K. D., & Pyle, G. F. (1991). The geography and mortality of the 1918 influenza pandemic. *Bulletin of the History of Medicine, 65*(1), 4–21. doi:10.1086/651472

Pauker, K., Weisbuch, M., Ambady, N., Sommers, S. R., Adams, R. B., & Ivcevic, Z. (2009). Not so black and white: Memory for ambiguous group members. *Journal of Personality and Social Psychology, 96*(4), 795–810. doi:10.1037/a0013265

Paul, A. M. (2010). *The cult of personality testing: How personality tests are leading us to miseducate our children, mismanage our companies, and misunderstand ourselves.* New York, NY: Simon and Schuster.

Paulhus, D. I. (1998). Interpersonal and intrapsychic adaptiveness of trait self-enhancement. A mixed blessing? *Journal of Personality and Social Psychology, 74*, 1197–1208. doi:10.1037/0022-3514.74.5.1197

Paulhus, D. L., & Williams, K. M. (2002). The dark triad of personality: Narcissism, Machiavellianism, and psychopathy. *Journal of Research in Personality, 36*, 556–563. doi:10.1037/0022-3514.74.5.1197

Pauls, D. L., Abramovitch, A., Rauch, S. L., & Geller, D. A. (2014). Obsessive–compulsive disorder: An integrative genetic and neurobiological perspective. *Nature Reviews Neuroscience, 15*(6), 410–424. doi:10.1038/nrn3746

Pavlov, I. P. (1906). The scientific investigation of the psychical faculties or processes in the higher animals. *Science, 24*, 613–619. doi:10.1126/science.24.620.613

Pavlov, I. P. (1927). *Conditioned reflexes.* Oxford, U.K.: Oxford University Press.

Pearce, M. T., Ruiz, M. H., Kapasi, S., Wiggins, G., & Bhattacharya, J. (2010). Unsupervised statistical learning underpins computational, behavioural, and neural manifestations of musical expectation. *NeuroImage.* doi:10.1016/j.neuroimage.2009.12.019

Pearson Assessments. (2020). *MMPI-3.* https://www.pearsonassessments.com/store/usassessments/en/Store/Professional-Assessments/Personality-%26-Biopsychosocial/Minnesota-Multiphasic-Personality-Inventory-3/p/P100000004.html?tab=product-details

Pedersen, C. B., Mors, O., Bertelsen, A., Waltoft, B. L., Agerbo, E., McGrath, J. J., Mortensen, P. B., & Eaton, W. W. (2014). A comprehensive nationwide study of the incidence rate and lifetime risk for treated mental disorders. *JAMA Psychiatry, 71*(5), 573–581. doi:10.1001/jamapsychiatry.2014.16

Pegna, A. J., Khateb, A., Lazeyras, F., & Seghier, M. L. (2005). Discriminating emotional faces without primary visual cortices involves the right amygdala. *Nature Neuroscience, 8*(1), 24–25. doi:10.1038/nn1364

Pelham Jr, W. E., & Fabiano, G. A. (2008). Evidence-based psychosocial treatments for attention-deficit/hyperactivity disorder. *Journal of Clinical Child & Adolescent Psychology, 37*(1), 184–214. doi:10.1080/15374410701818681

Pelios, L. V., MacDuff, G. S., & Axelrod, S. (2003). The effects of a treatment package in establishing independent academic work skills in children with autism. *Education and Treatment of Children, 26*, 1–21. https://www.jstor.org/stable/42900533

Peltokorpi, V. (2008). Transactive memory systems. *Review of General Psychology, 12*(4), 378–394. doi:10.1037/1089-2680.12.4.378

Peltokorpi, V., & Hood, A. C. (2019). Communication in theory and research on transactive memory systems: A literature review. *Topics in Cognitive Science, 11*(4), 644–667. doi:10.1111/tops.12359

Penfield, W., & Boldrey, E. (1937). Somatic motor and sensory representation in the cerebral cortex of man as studied by electrical stimulation. *Brain, 60*(4), 389–443. doi:10.1093/brain/60.4.389

Pepperberg, I. M. (2014). Interspecies communication with Grey parrots: A tool for examining cognitive processing. In G. Witzany (Ed.), Biocommunication of animals (pp.213–232). Dordrecht, Netherlands: Springer. doi:10.1007/978-94-007-7414-8_12

Perez, M. F., & Lehner, B. (2019). Intergenerationaland transgenerational epigenetic inheritance in animals. *Nature Cell Biology, 21*(2), 143–151. doi:10.1038/s41556-018-0242-9

Perfect, T. J., & Askew, C. (1994). Print adverts: Not remembered but memorable. *Applied Cognitive Psychology, 8*(7), 693–703. doi:10.1002/acp.2350080707

Perikleous, E. P., Steiropoulos, P., Paraskakis, E., Constantinidis, T. C., & Nena, E. (2018). E-Cigarette use among adolescents: An overview of the literature and future perspectives. *Frontiers in Public Health, 6*(86). doi:10.3389/fpubh.2018.00086

Perry, R. J., Watson, P., & Hodges, J. R. (2000). The nature and staging of attention dysfunction in early (minimal and mild) Alzheimer's disease: Relationship to episodic and semantic memory impairment. *Neuropsychologia, 38*(3), 252–271. doi:10.1016/S0028-3932(99)00079-2

Perry, W. I. (1970). *Forms of intellectual and ethical development in the college years.* New York: Holt, Rinehart & Winston.

Pervanidou, P., Kolaitis, G., Charitaki, S., Lazaropoulou, C., Papassotiriou, I., Hindmarsh, P., Bakoula, C., Tsiantis, J., & Chrousos, G. P. (2007). The natural history of neuroendocrine changes in pediatric posttraumatic stress disorder (PTSD) after motor vehicle accidents: Progressive divergence of noradrenaline and cortisol concentrations over time. *Biological Psychiatry, 62*(10), 1095–1102. doi:10.1016/j.biopsych.2007.02.008

Peters, R. (2006). Ageing and the brain. *Postgraduate Medical Journal, 82*(964), 84–88. doi:10.1136/pgmj.2005.036665

Petersen, S., Houston, S., Qin, H., Tague, C., & Studley, J. (2017). The utilization of robotic pets in dementia care. *Journal of Alzheimer's Disease, 55*, 569–574. doi:10.3233/JAD-160703

Peterson, C. (2006). *A primer in positive psychology*. New York, NY US: Oxford University Press.

Peterson, C., & Seligman, M. E. P. (2004). *Character strengths and virtues: A handbook and classification*. Washington, D.C.: APA Press and Oxford University Press.

Peterson, C., & Whalen, N. (2001). Five years later: Children's memory for medical emergencies. *Applied Cognitive Psychology, 15*(7), S7-S24. doi:10.1002/acp.832

Peterson, L. R., & Peterson, M. J. (1959). Short-term retention of individual verbal items. *Journal of Experimental Psychology, 58*, 193–198. doi:10.1037/h0049234

Petty, R. E., & Cacioppo, J. T. (1981). *Attitudes and persuasion: Classic and contemporary approaches*. Dubuque, Iowa: Wm. C. Brown.

Petty, R. E., & Cacioppo, J. T. (1986). The elaboration likelihood model of persuasion. *Advances in Experimental Social Psychology, 19*, 123–205. doi:10.1016/S0065-2601(08)60214-2

Petty, R. E., Cacioppo, J. T., & Kasmer, J. (1988). The role of affect in the elaboration likelihood model of persuasion. In L. Donohew, H. Sypher, & E. T. Higgins (Eds.), *Communication, social cognition, and affect* (pp. 117–146). Hillsdale, N J: Erlbaum.

Peverly, S. T., Brobst, K. E., & Morris, K. S. (2002). The contribution of reading comprehension ability and meta-cognitive control to the development of studying in adolescence. *Journal of Research in Reading, 25*(2), 203–216. doi:10.1111/1467-9817.00169

Phan, K. L., Wager, T., Taylor, S. F., & Liberzon, I. (2002). Functional neuroanatomy of emotion: A meta-analysis of emotion activation studies in PET and fMRI. *NeuroImage, 16*, 331–348. doi:10.1006/nimg.2002.1087

Phelps, E. A., O'Connor, K. J., Cunningham, W. A., Funayama, E. S., Gatenby, J. C., Gore, J. C., & Banaji, M. R. (2000). Performance on indirect measures of race evaluation predicts amygdala activation. *Journal of Cognitive Neuroscience, 12*, 729–738. doi:10.1162/089892900562552

Phills, C. E., Hahn, A., & Gawronski, B. (2020). The bidirectional causal relation between implicit stereotypes and implicit prejudice. *Personality and Social Psychology Bulletin*, doi:10.1177/0146167219899234.

Pietrzak, R. H., Goldstein, R. B., Southwick, S. M., & Grant, B. F. (2011). Prevalence and Axis I comorbidity of full and partial posttraumatic stress disorder in the United States: Results from Wave 2 of the National Epidemiologic Survey on Alcohol and Related Conditions. *Journal of Anxiety Disorders, 25*(3), 456–465. doi:10.1016/j.janxdis.2010.11.010

Pietschnig, J., & Voracek, M. (2015). One century of global IQ gains: A formal meta-analysis of the Flynn Effect (1909–2013). *Perspectives on Psychological Science, 10*(3), 282–306. doi:10.1177/1745691615577701

Pilgrim, J. L., Gerostamoulos, D., & Drummer, O. H. (2011). Deaths involving MDMA and the concomitant use of pharmaceutical drugs. *Journal of Analytical Toxicology, 35*(4), 219–226. doi:10.1093/anatox/35.4.219

Pinker, S. (1994). *The language instinct: The new science of language and mind*. London, UK: Penguin.

Pittenger, D. J. (1993). Measuring the MBTI . . . and coming up short. *Journal of Career Planning and Employment, 54*(1), 48–52.

Pitts, F. N., & McClure, J. N. (1967). Lactate metabolism in anxiety neurosis. *New England Journal of Medicine, 277*, 1329–1336. doi:10.1056/NEJM196712212772502

Piven, J., Elison, J. T., & Zylka, M. J. (2017). Toward a conceptual framework for early brain and behavior development in autism. *Molecular Psychiatry, 22*(10), 1385–1394. doi:10.1038/mp.2017.131

Plomin, R., & Spinath, F. M. (2004). Intelligence: Genetics, genes, and genomics. *Journal of Personality and Social Psychology, 86*, 112–129. doi:10.1037/0022-3514.86.1.112

Plotnik, J. M., de Waal, F. B. M., & Reiss, D. (2006). Self-recognition in an Asian elephant. *Proceedings of the National Academy of Sciences of the United States of America, 103*(45), 17053–17057. doi:10.1073/pnas.0608062103

Plous, S. (1993). *The psychology of judgment and decision making*. New York, NY: McGraw-Hill.

Pohl, R. F., Michalkiewicz, M., Erdfelder, E., & Hilbig, B. E. (2017). Use of the recognition heuristic depends on the domain's recognition validity, not on the recognition validity of selected sets of objects. *Memory & Cognition, 45*(5), 776–791. doi:10.3758/s13421-017-0689-0

Polya, G. (1957). *How to solve it*. Garden City, NY: Doubleday and Co.

Pomar, L., Musso, D., Malinger, G., Vouga, M., Panchaud, A., & Baud, D. (2019). Zika virus during pregnancy: From maternal exposure to congenital Zika virus syndrome. *Prenatal Diagnosis, 39*(6), 420–430. doi:10.1002/pd.5446

Pomarol-Clotet, E., Salvador, R., Sarro, S., Gomar, J., Vila, F., Martinez, A., Guerrero, A., Ortiz-Gil, J., Sans-Sansa, B., Capdevila, A., Cebamanos, J. M., & McKenna, P. J. (2008). Failure to deactivate in the prefrontal cortex in schizophrenia: Dysfunction of the default mode network? *Psychological*

Medicine, 38(8), 1185–1194. doi:10.1017/S0033291708003565
Porter, R. H., Makin, J. W., Davis, L. B., & Christensen, K. M. (1991). An assessment of the salient olfactory environment of formula-fed infants. *Physiology and Behavior, 50*, 907–911. doi:10.1016/0031-9384(91)90413-I
Posner, M. I. (2018). Rehabilitating the brain through meditation and electrical stimulation. *Cortex*. doi:10.1016/j.cortex.2018.07.022
Posner, M. I., & Keele, S. W. (1970). Retention of abstract ideas. *Journal of Experimental Psychology, 83*(2, Pt.1), 304–308. doi:10.1037/h0028558
Poundstone, W. (1992). *Prisoner's dilemma*. New York: Doubleday.
Povinelli, D. J. (1993). Reconstructing the evolution of mind. *American Psychologist, 48*, 493–509. doi:10.1037/0003-066X.48.5.493
Prasad, S., & Steer, C. (2008). Switching from neurostimulant therapy to atomoxetine in children and adolescents with attention-deficit hyperactivity disorder. *Pediatric Drugs, 10*(1), 39–47. doi:10.2165/00148581-200810010-00005
Prata, D. P., Costa-Neves, B., Cosme, G., & Vassos, E. (2019). Unravelling the genetic basis of schizophrenia and bipolar disorder with GWAS: A systematic review. *Journal of Psychiatric Research, 114*, 178–207. doi:10.1016/j.jpsychires.2019.04.007
Pratt, L. A., Brody, D. J., & Gu, Q. (2011). Antidepressant use in persons aged 12 and over: United States, 2005–2008. *NCHS Data Brief, 76*, 1—8.
Premack, D. (1965). Reinforcement theory. In D. Levine (Ed.), *Nebraska Symposium on Motivation* (Vol. 13, pp. 3–41). Lincoln, NE: University of Nebraska Press.
Premack, D. G., & Woodruff, G. (1978). Does the chimpanzee have a theory of mind? *Behavioral and Brain Sciences, 1*, 515–526. doi:10.1017/S0140525X00076512
Priebe, S. (2006). *The provision of psychotherapy: An international comparison*. http://cep.lse.ac.uk/textonly/research/mentalhealth/StefanPriebe_provision-of-incapacity-benefit.pdf
Prinzie, P., Stams, G. J. J. M., Deković, M., Reijntjes, A. H. A., & Belsky, J. (2009). The relations between parents' Big Five personality factors and parenting: A meta-analytic review. *Journal of Personality and Social Psychology, 97*(2), 351–362. doi:10.1037/a0015823
Prior, H., Schwarz, A., & Güntürkün, O. (2008). Mirror-induced behavior in the magpie (*Pica pica*): Evidence of self-recognition. *PLoS Biology, 6*(8), e202. doi:10.1371/journal.pbio.0060202
prnewswire. (2020). *New parent coaching app helps parents with young children at home during COVID manage daily routines and engage in activities that support child development and well-being*. https://www.prnewswire.com/news-releases/new-parent-coaching-app-helps-parents-with-young-children-at-home-during-covid-manage-daily-routines-and-engage-in-activities-that-support-child-development-and-well-being-301040190.html
Probst, F., Meng-Hentschel, J., Golle, J., Stucki, S., Akyildiz-Kunz, C., & Lobmaier, J. S. (2017). Do women tend while men fight or flee? Differential emotive reactions of stressed men and women while viewing newborn infants. *Psychoneuroendocrinology, 75*, 213–221. doi:10.1016/j.psyneuen.2016.11.005
Przybylski, A. K., & Weinstein, N. (2013). Can you connect with me now? How the presence of mobile communication technology influences face-to-face conversation quality. *Journal of Social and Personal Relationships, 30*(3), 237–246. doi:10.1177/0265407512453827
Psychological Clinical Science Accreditation System (PCSAS). (2020). *Accredited programs*. http://www.pcsas.org/accredited-programs
Public Broadcasting Service (PBS). (2005). *The story of . . . smallpox–and other deadly Eurasian germs*. http://www.pbs.org/gunsgermssteel/variables/smallpox.html
Puts, D. A., Pope, L. E., Hill, A. K., Cárdenas, R. A., Welling, L. L. M., Wheatley, J. R., & Marc Breedlove, S. (2015). Fulfilling desire: Evidence for negative feedback between men's testosterone, sociosexual psychology, and sexual partner number. *Hormones and Behavior, 70*, 14–21. doi:10.1016/j.yhbeh.2015.01.006
Pyszczynski, T., Greenberg, J., & Solomon, S. (1991). A terror management analysis of self-awareness and anxiety: The hierarchy of terror. In R. Schwarzer & R. A. Wicklund (Eds.), *Anxiety and self-focused attention* (pp. 67–85). Amsterdam, Netherlands: Harwood Academic Publishers.
Qiu, D.-l., & Knopfel, T. (2007). An NMDA receptor/nitric oxide cascade in presynaptic parallel fiber-Purkinje neuron long-term potentiation. *The Journal of Neuroscience, 27*(13), 3408–3415. doi:10.1523/jneurosci.4831-06.2007
Radant, A. D., Millard, S. P., Braff, D. L., Calkins, M. E., Dobie, D. J., Freedman, R., Green, M. F., Greenwood, T. A., Gur, R. E., Gur, R. C., Lazzeroni, L., Light, G. A., Meichle, S., Nuechterlein, K. H., Olincy, A., Seidman, L. J., Siever, L., Silverman, J., Stone, W. S., . . . Tsuang, D. W. (2015). Robust differences in antisaccade performance exist between COGS schizophrenia cases and controls regardless of recruitment strategies. *Schizophrenia Research, 163*(1), 47–52. doi:10.1016/j.schres.2014.12.016
Raichle, M. E. (2015). The brain's default mode network. *Annual Review of Neuroscience, 38*, 433–447. doi:10.1146/annurev-neuro-071013-014030
Raichle, M. E., & Gusnard, D. A. (2002). Appraising the brain's energy budget. *Proceedings of the National Academy of Sciences of the United States of America, 99*(16), 10237–10239. doi:10.1073/pnas.172399499
Raichle, M. E., & Snyder, A. Z. (2011). Intrinsic brain activity and consciousness. In S. Laureys & G. Tononi (Eds.), *The neurology of consciousness: Cognitive neuroscience and neuropathology* (pp. 81–88). Oxford, UK: Elsevier Academic Press.
Raichlen, D. A., & Alexander, G. E. (2017). Adaptive capacity: An evolutionary neuroscience model linking exercise, cognition, and brain health. *Trends in Neurosciences, 40*(7), 408–421. doi:10.1016/j.tins.2017.05.001
Raine, A. (2019). The neuromoral theory of antisocial, violent, and psychopathic behavior. *Psychiatry Research, 277*, 64–69. doi:10.1016/j.psychres.2018.11.025
Raine, A., Lencz, T., Bihrle, S., LaCasse, L., & Colletti, P. (2000). Reduced prefrontal gray matter volume and reduced autonomic activity in antisocial personality disorder. *Archives of General Psychiatry, 57*, 119–127. doi:10.1001/archpsyc.57.2.119
Raine, A., Stoddard, J., Bihrle, S., & Buchsbaum, M. (1998). Prefrontal glucose deficits in murderers lacking psychosocial deprivation. *Neuropsychiatry, Neuropsychology, & Behavioral Neurology, 11*(1), 1–7.
Rakic, P. (2000). Molecular and cellular mechanisms of neuronal migration: Relevance to cortical epilepsies. *Advances in Neurology, 84*, 1–14.
Raleigh, M. J., Brammer, G. L., McGuire, M. T., Pollack, D. B., & Yuwiler, A. (1992). Individual differences in basal cisternal cerebrospinal fluid F0HIAA and HVA in monkeys: The effects of gender, age, physical characteristics, and matrilineal influences. *Neuropsychopharmacology, 7*, 295–304. doi:10.1016/0006-8993(91)90001-C
Ramachandran, V. S., & Rogers-Ramachandran, D. (2000). Phantom limbs and neural plasticity. *Archives of Neurology, 57*, 317–320. doi:10.1001/archneur.57.3.317
Ramírez-Esparza, N., García-Sierra, A., & Kuhl, P. K. (2014). Look who's talking: Speech style and social context in language input to infants are linked to concurrent and future speech development. *Developmental Science, 17*(6), 880–891. doi:10.1111/desc.12172
Rammstedt, B., & John, O. P. (2007). Measuring personality in one minute or less: A 10-item short version of the Big Five Inventory in English and German. *Journal of Research in Personality, 41*(1), 203–212. doi:10.1016/j.jrp.2006.02.001
Ramo, S. (2005). *Conquering complexity*. London, UK: University College London.
Ramos, R. L., Fokas, G. J., Bhambri, A., Smith, P. T., Hallas, B. H., & Brumberg, J. C. (2011). Undergraduate neuroscience education in the U.S.: An analysis using data from the National Center for Education Statistics. *Journal of Undergraduate Neuroscience Education, 9*(2), A66–A70.
Ramsawh, H. J., Fullerton, C. S., Mash, H. B. H., Ng, T. H. H., Kessler, R. C., Stein, M. B., & Ursano, R. J. (2014). Risk for suicidal

behaviors associated with PTSD, depression, and their comorbidity in the US Army. *Journal of Affective Disorders, 161*, 116–122. doi:10.1016/j.jad.2014.03.016

Ramsey, E., Kelly-Vance, L., Allen, J. A., Rosol, O., & Yoerger, M. (2016). Autism spectrum disorder prevalence rates in the United States: Methodologies, challenges, and implications for individual states. *Journal of Developmental and Physical Disabilities, 28*(6), 803–820. doi:10.1007/s1088

Randall, K. (2011). *Rise of neurocinema: How Hollywood studios harness your brainwaves to win Oscars*. https://www.fastcompany.com/1731055/rise-neurocinema-how-hollywood-studios-harness-your-brainwaves-win-oscars

Randunu, R. S., & Bertolo, R. F. (2020). The effects of maternal and postnatal dietary methyl nutrients on epigenetic changes that lead to non-communicable diseases in adulthood. *International Journal of Molecular Sciences, 21*(9), 3290. doi:10.3390/ijms21093290

Ranehill, E., Dreber, A., Johannesson, M., Leiberg, S., Sul, S., & Weber, R. A. (2015). Assessing the robustness of power posing: No effect on hormones and risk tolerance in a large sample of men and women. *Psychological Science, 26*(5), 653–656. doi:10.1177/0956797614553946

Rapkin, A. J., Mikacich, J. A., Moatakef-Imani, B., & Rasgon, N. (2002). The clinical nature and formal diagnosis of premenstrual, postpartum, and perimenopausal affective disorders. *Current Psychiatry Reports, 4*, 419–428. doi:10.1007/s11920-002-0069-7

Rapoport, J. (1989). *The boy who couldn't stop washing: The experience and treatment of obsessive-compulsive disorder.* New York: Dutton.

Rapoport, J. L., Giedd, J.N., Blumenthal, J., Hamburger, S., Jeffries, N., Fernandez, T., Nicolson, R., Bedwell, J., Lenane, M., Zijdenbos, A., Paus, T., & Evans, A. (1999). Progressive cortical change during adolescence in childhood-onset schizophrenia. A longitudinal magnetic resonance imaging study. *Archives of General Psychiatry, 56*, 649–654. doi:10.1001/archpsyc.56.7.649

Rasch, B., & Born, J. (2013). About sleep's role in memory. *Physiological Reviews, 93*(2), 681–766. doi:10.1152/physrev.00032.2012

Raschle, N. M., Chang, M., & Gaab, N. (2011). Structural brain alterations associated with dyslexia predate reading onset. *NeuroImage, 57*(3), 742–749. doi:10.1016/j.neuroimage.2010.09.055

Rasmussen, T., & Milner, B. (1977). The role of early left-brain injury in determining lateralization of cerebral speech functions. *Annals of the New York Academy of Sciences, 299*, 355–369. doi:10.1111/j.1749-6632.1977.tb41921.x

Rauthmann, J. F., Sherman, R. A., Nave, C. S., & Funder, D. C. (2015). Personality-driven situation experience, contact, and construal: How people's personality traits predict characteristics of their situations in daily life. *Journal of Research in Personality, 55*, 98–111. doi:10.1016/j.jrp.2015.02.003

Rawlins, W. K. (2004). Friendships in later life. In J. F. Nussbaum & J. Coupland (Eds.), *Handbook of communication and aging research (2nd ed.).* (pp. 273–299). Mahwah, NJ: Lawrence Erlbaum Associates Publishers.

Raz, A., Kirsch, I., Pollard, J., & Nitkin-Kaner, Y. (2006). Suggestion reduces the Stroop effect. *Psychological Science, 17*(2), 91–95. doi:10.1111/j.1467-9280.2006.01669.x

Raz, N., Lindenberger, U., Rodrigue, K. M., Kennedy, K. M., Head, D., Williamson, A., Dahle, C., Gerstorf, D., & Acker, J. D. (2005). Regional brain changes in aging healthy adults: General trends, individual differences and modifiers. *Cerebral Cortex, 15*(11), 1676–1689. doi:10.1093/cercor/bhi044

Raza, M. H., Mattera, R., Morell, R., Sainz, E., Rahn, R., Gutierrez, J., Paris, E., Root, J., Solomon, B., Brewer, C., Basra, M. A. R., Khan, S., Riazzudin, S., Braun, A., Bonifacino, J. S., & Drayna, D. (2015). Association between rare variants in AP4E1, a component of intracellular trafficking, and persistent stuttering. *The American Journal of Human Genetics, 97*(5), 715–725. doi:10.1016/j.ajhg.2015.10.007

Read, J., Kirsch, I., & McGrath, L. (2020). Electroconvulsive therapy for depression: A review of the quality of ECT versus sham ECT trials and meta-analyses. *Ethical Human Psychology and Psychiatry.* doi:10.1891/EHPP-D-19-00014

Redfield, A., & Thouin-Savard, M. I. (2017). Electronic dance music events as modern-day ritual. *The International Journal of Transpersonal Studies, 36*, (1), 52–66. doi:10.24972/ijts.2017.36.1.52.

Reese, H. E., McNally, R. J., & Wilhelm, S. (2010). Facial asymmetry detection in patients with body dysmorphic disorder. *Behaviour Research and Therapy, 48*(9), 936–940. doi:10.1016/j.brat.2010.05.021

Regan, C. (2000). *Intoxicating minds.* London: Weidenfeld & Nicolson.

Register, P. A., & Kihlstrom, J. F. (1987). Hypnotic effects on hypermnesia. *International Journal of Clinical and Experimental Hypnosis, 35*(3), 155–170. doi:10.1080/00207148708416051

Reicher, S., & Haslam, S. A. (2006). Rethinking the psychology of tyranny: The BBC prison study. *British Journal of Social Psychology, 45*(1), 1–40. doi:10.1348/014466605X48998

Reinisch, J. M., Ziemba-Davis, M., & Sanders, S. A. (1991). Hormonal contributions to sexually dimorphic behavioral development in humans. *Psychoneuroendocrinology, 16*, 213–278. doi:10.1016/0306-4530(91)90080-D

Reisenzein, R. (1983). The Schachter theory of emotion: Two decades later. *Psychological Bulletin, 94*, 239–264. doi:10.1037/0033-2909.94.2.239

Remez, R. E., Rubin, P. E., Pisoni, D. B., & Carell, T. D. (1981). Speech perception without traditional speech cues. *Science, 212*, 947–950. doi:10.1126/science.7233191

Remington, A., & Fairnie, J. (2017). A sound advantage: Increased auditory capacity in autism. *Cognition, 166*, 459–465. doi:10.1016/j.cognition.2017.04.002

Rendell, L., Boyd, R., Cownden, D., Enquist, M., Eriksson, K., Feldman, M. W., Fogarty, L., Ghirlanda, S., Lillicrap, T., & Laland, K. N. (2010). Why copy others? Insights from the social learning strategies tournament. *Science, 328*, 208–213. doi:10.1126/science.1184719

Rescorla, R. A. (1968). Probability of shock in the presence and absence of CS in fear conditioning. *Journal of Comparative and Physiological Psychology, 66*, 1–5. doi:10.1037/h0025984

Rescorla, R. A., & Wagner, A. R. (1972). A theory of Pavlovian conditioning: Variations in the effectiveness of reinforcement and nonreinforcement. In A. H. Black & W. F. Prokasy (Eds.), *Classical conditioning, Vol. II: Current theory and research* (pp. 64–99). New York: Appleton-Century-Crofts.

Reuveni, I., Nugent, A. C., Gill, J., Vythilingam, M., Carlson, P. J., Lerner, A., Neumeister, A., Charney, D. S., Drevets, W. C., & Bonne, O. (2018). Altered cerebral benzodiazepine receptor binding in post-traumatic stress disorder. *Translational Psychiatry, 8*(1), 206. doi:10.1038/s41398-018-0257-9

Reyna, V. F. (2008). A theory of medical decision making and health: Fuzzy Trace Theory. *Medical Decision Making, 28*(6), 850–865. doi:10.1177/0272989x08327066

Reyna, V. F., & Farley, F. (2006). Risk and rationality in adolescent decision making: Implications for theory, practice, and public policy. *Psychological Science in the Public Interest, 7*(1), 1–44. doi:10.1111/j.1529-1006.2006.00026.x

Rhodes, N., & Wood, W. (1992). Self-esteem and intelligence affect influenceability: The mediating role of message reception. *Psychological Bulletin, 111*, 156–171. doi:10.1037/0033-2909.111.1.156

Rhodewalt, F., Sandonmatsu, D. M., Tschanz, B., Feick, D. L., & Waller, A. (1995). Self-handicapping and interpersonal trade-offs: The effects of claimed self-handicaps on observers' performance evaluations and feedback. *Personality and Social Psychology Bulletin, 21*, 1042–1050. doi:10.1177/01461672952110005

Richert, R. A., Robb, M. B., Fender, J. G., & Wartella, E. (2010). Word learning from baby videos. *Archives of Pediatrics & Adolescent Medicine, 164*(5), 432–437. doi:10.1001/archpediatrics.2010.24

Riesco-Matías, P., Yela-Bernabé, J. R., Crego, A., & Sánchez-Zaballos, E. (2019). What do meta-analyses have to say about the efficacy of neurofeedback applied to children with ADHD? Review of previous meta-analyses and a new meta-analysis. *Journal of Attention Disorders*, doi:10.1177/1087054718821731

Rijnbeek, B., de Visser, S. J., Franson, K. L., Cohen, A. F., & van Gerven, J. M. A. (2003). REM sleep effects as a biomarker for the effects of antidepressants in healthy volunteers. *Journal of Psychopharmacology, 17*(2), 196–203. doi:10.1177/0269881103017002008

Rilling, J. K., & Sanfey, A. G. (2011). The neuroscience of social decision-making. *Annual Review of Psychology, 62*(1), 23–48. doi:10.1146/annurev.psych.121208.131647

Rips, L. J. (1975). Inductive judgments about natural categories. *Journal of Verbal Learning and Verbal Behavior, 14*(6), 665–681. doi:10.1016/S0022-5371(75)80055-7

Rips, L. J., & Collins, A. (1993). Categories and resemblance. *Journal of Experimental Psychology: General, 122*(4), 468–486. doi:10.1037/0096-3445.122.4.468

Riskind, J. H., Moore, R., & Bowley, L. (1995). The looming of spiders: The fearful perceptual distortion of movement and menace. *Behaviour Research and Therapy, 33*(2), 171–178. doi:10.1016/0005-7967(94)e0023-c

Rivas-Drake, D., Seaton, E. K., Markstrom, C., Quintana, S., Syed, M., Lee, R. M., Schwartz, S. J., Umaña-Taylor, A. J., French, S., Yip, T., & Racial Identity in the 21st Century Study Group. (2014). Ethnic and racial identity in adolescence: Implications for psychosocial, academic, and health outcomes. *Child Development, 85*(1), 40–57. doi:10.1111/cdev.12200

Rivkin, M. J., Davis, P. E., Lemaster, J. L., Cabral, H. J., Warfield, S. K., Mulkern, R. V., Robson, C. D., Rose-Jacobs, R., & Frank, D. A. (2008). Volumetric MRI study of brain in children with intrauterine exposure to cocaine, alcohol, tobacco, and marijuana. *Pediatrics, 121*(4), 741–750. doi:10.1542/peds.2007-1399

Rivkin, M. J., Flax, J., Mozell, R., Osathanondh, R., Volpe, J. J., & Villa-Komaroff, L. (1995). Oligodendroglial development in human fetal cerebrum. *Annals of Neurology, 38*(1), 92–101. doi:10.1002/ana/410380116

Rizzo, L. B., Costa, L. G., Mansur, R. B., Swardfager, W., Belangero, S. I., Grassi-Oliveira, R., . . . Brietzke, E. (2014). The theory of bipolar disorder as an illness of accelerated aging: Implications for clinical care and research. *Neuroscience and Biobehavioral Reviews, 42*, 157-169. doi:10.1016/j.neubiorev.2014.02.004

Rizzolatti, G., & Craighero, L. (2004). The mirror-neuron system. *Annual Review of Neuroscience, 27*(1), 169–192. doi:10.1146/annurev.neuro.27.070203.144230

Rizzolatti, G., & Sinigaglia, C. (2016). The mirror mechanism: A basic principle of brain function. *Nature Reviews Neuroscience, 17*, 757. doi:10.1038/nrn.2016.135

Robins, L. N., & Regier, D. A. (Eds.). (1991). *Psychiatric disorders in America: The Epidemiologic Catchment Area Study*. New York: The Free Press.

Robinson, A., Bonnette, A., Howard, K., Ceballos, N., Dailey, S., Lu, Y., & Grimes, T. (2019). Social comparisons, social media addiction, and social interaction: An examination of specific social media behaviors related to major depressive disorder in a millennial population. *Journal of Applied Biobehavioral Research, 24*(1), e12158. doi:10.1111/jabr.12158

Roche, G. (2020), Abandoning endangered languages: Ethical loneliness, language oppression, and social justice. *American Anthropologist, 122*, 164–169. doi:10.1111/aman.13372

Rodin, J. (1986). Aging and health: Effects of the sense of control. *Science, 233*, 1271–1276. doi:10.1126/science.3749877

Roediger III, H. L., & Butler, A. C. (2011). The critical role of retrieval practice in long-term retention. *Trends in Cognitive Sciences, 15*(1), 20–27. doi:10.1016/j.tics.2010.09.003

Roenneberg, T., Kuehnle, T., Pramstaller, P. P., Ricken, J., Havel, M., Guth, A., & Merrow, M. (2004). A marker for the end of adolescence. *Current Biology, 14*(24), R1038–R1039. doi:10.1016/j.cub.2004.11.039

Roesch, S. C., & Amirkhan, J. H. (1997). Boundary conditions for self-serving attributions: Another look at the sports pages. *Journal of Applied Social Psychology, 27*, 245–261. doi:10.1111/j.1559-1816.1997.tb00631.x

Roese, N. J., & Summerville, A. (2005). What we regret most . . . and why. *Personality and Social Psychology Bulletin, 31*(9), 1273–1285. doi:10.1177/0146167205274693

Rogers, C. (1951). *Client-centered therapy: Its current practice, implications and theory*. London: Constable.

Rogers, C. A. (1980). *A way of being*. Boston: Houghton Mifflin.

Rogers, C. R. (1942). *Counseling and psychotherapy: New concepts in practice*. Boston: Houghton Mifflin.

Rogers, L. J. (2000). Evolution of hemispheric specialization: Advantages and disadvantages. *Brain and Language, 73*, 236–253. doi:10.1006/brln.2000.2305

Rogers, T. B., Kuiper, N. A., & Kirker, W. S. (1977). Self-reference and the encoding of personal information. *Journal of Personality and Social Psychology, 35*, 677–688. doi:10.1037/0022-3514.35.9.677

Rogers, T. B., Kuiper, N. A., & Kirker, W. S. (1977). Self-reference and the encoding of personal information. *Journal of Personality and Social Psychology, 35*(9), 677–688. doi:10.1037/0022-3514.35.9.677

Rohrer, D., & Pashler, H. (2010). Recent research on human learning challenges conventional instructional strategies. *Educational Researcher, 39*(5), 406–412. doi:10.3102/0013189x10374770

Rokeach, M. (1968-1969). The role of values in public opinion research. *Public Opinion Quarterly, 32*, 547–559. doi:10.1086/267645

Rolls, E. T. (2000). The orbitofrontal cortex and reward. *Cerebral Cortex, 10*, 284–294. doi:10.1093/cercor/10.3.284

Rolls, E. T. (2015). Limbic systems for emotion and for memory, but no single limbic system. *Cortex, 62*, 119–157. doi:10.1016/j.cortex.2013.12.005

Ronald, A., & Hoekstra, R. A. (2011). Autism spectrum disorders and autistic traits: A decade of new twin studies. *American Journal of Medical Genetics Part B: Neuropsychiatric Genetics, 156*(3), 255–274. doi:10.1002/ajmg.b.31159

Roney, J. R., Hanson, K. N., Durante, K. M., & Maestripieri, D. (2006). Reading men's faces: Women's mate attractiveness judgments track men's testosterone and interest in infants. *Proceedings of the Royal Society of London, Series B: Biological Sciences, 273*, 2169–2175. doi:10.1098/rspb.2006.3569

Ronningstam, E. (2014). Beyond the diagnostic traits: A collaborative exploratory diagnostic process for dimensions and underpinnings of narcissistic personality disorder. *Personality Disorders: Theory, Research, and Treatment, 5*(4), 434–438. doi:10.1037/per0000034

Roozendaal, B., McEwen, B. S., & Chattarji, S. (2009). Stress, memory and the amygdala. *Nature Reviews Neuroscience, 10*(6), 423–433. doi:10.1038/nrn2651

Rorschach, H. (1921). Psychodiagnostik: Methodik und Ergebnisse eines wahrnehmungsdiagnostischen Experiments; (Deutenlassen von Zufallsformen). (Psychodiagnostics: Methodology and results of a diagnostic perception experiment suggesting random forms).In *Arbeiten zur angewandten Psychiatrie* (Vol. 2). Bern: Bircher.

Rosales, F., Reznick, J. S., & Zeisel, S. (2009). Understanding the role of nutrition in the brain and behavioral development of toddlers and preschool children: Identifying and addressing methodological barriers. *Nutritional Neuroscience, 12*(5), 190–202. doi:10.1179/147683009x423454

Rosch, E. (1983). Prototype classification and logical classification: The two systems. In E. Scholnick (Ed.), *New trends in cognitive representation: Challenges to Piaget's theory* (pp. 73–86). Hillsdale, NJ: Erlbaum.

Rosch, E. H. (1973). Natural categories. *Cognitive Psychology, 4*(3), 328–350. doi:10.1016/0010-0285(73)90017-0

Rose, D., Fleischmann, P., Wykes, T., Leese, M., & Bindman, J. (2003). Patients' perspectives on electroconvulsive therapy: Systematic review. *BMJ, 326*(7403), 1363. doi:10.1136/bmj.326.7403.1363

Rose, J. (2011). Diverse perspectives on the Groupthink theory–a literary review. *Emerging Leadership Journeys, 4*(1), 37–57.

Rose, J. E., Behm, F. M., Murugesan, T., & McClernon, F. J. (2010). Silver acetate interactions with nicotine and non-nicotine smoke components. *Experimental and Clinical Psychopharmacology, 18*(6), 462–469. doi:10.1037/a0021966

Roselli, C. E., Larkin, K., Resko, J. A., Stellflug, J. N., & Stormshak, F. (2004). The volume of a sexually dimorphic nucleus in the ovine medial preoptic area/anterior hypothalamus varies

with sexual partner preference. *Endocrinology, 145*, 478–483. doi:10.1210/en.2003-1098
Rosenberg, J., & Tunney, R. J. (2008). Human vocabulary use as display. *Evolutionary Psychology, 6*, 538–549. doi:10.1177/147470490800600318
Rosenberg, M., Schooler, C., & Schoenbach, C. (1989). Self-esteem and adolescent problems: Modeling reciprocal effects. *American Sociological Review, 54*, 1004–1018. doi:10.2307/2095720
Rosenberg, S. D., Rosenberg, H. J., & Farrell, M. P. (1999). The midlife crisis revisited. In S. L. Willis & J. D. Reid (Eds.), *Life in the middle* (pp. 47–73). San Diego, CA: Academic Press.
Rosenstein, D., & Oster, H. (1988). Differential facial responses to four basic tastes in newborns. *Child Development, 59*, 1555–1568. doi:10.2307/1130670
Rosenthal, I. A., Hutcherson, C. A., Adolphs, R., & Stanley, D. A. (2019). Deconstructing theory-of-mind impairment in high-functioning adults with autism. *Current Biology, 29*(3), 513–519. e516. doi:10.1016/j.cub.2018.12.039
Roser, M., & Ritchie, H. (2019). *Homicides*. https://ourworldindata.org/homicides
Ross, D. C., Fischhoff, J., & Davenport, B. (2002). Treatment of ADHD when tolerance to methylphenidate develops. *Psychiatric Services, 53*(1), 102–102. doi:10.1176/appi.ps.53.1.102
Ross, G. W., & Petrovitch, H. (2001). Current evidence for neuroprotective effects of nicotine and caffeine against Parkinson's disease. *Drugs and Aging, 18*(11), 797–806. doi:10.2165/00002512-200118110-00001
Ross, L. (1977). The intuitive psychologist and his shortcomings: Distortions in the attribution process. In L. Berkowitz (Ed.), *Advances in experimental social psychology* (Vol. 10, pp. 174–221). New York: Academic Press.
Rossion, B., & Michel, C. (2011). An experience-based holistic account of the other-race face effect. In G. Rhodes, A. Calder, M. Johnson, & J. V. Haxby (Eds.), *Oxford handbook of face perception* (pp. 215–244). New York: Oxford University Press.doi:10.1093/oxfordbh/9780199559053.013.0012
Roth, G., & Dicke, U. (2005). Evolution of the brain and intelligence. *Trends in Cognitive Sciences, 9*(5), 250–257. doi:10.1016/j.tics.2005.03.005
Rothbart, M. K. (2007). Temperament, development, and personality. *Current Directions in Psychological Science, 16*(4), 207–212. doi:10.1111/j.1467-8721.2007.00505.x
Rothbart, M. K. (2011). *Becoming who we are: Temperament and personality in development*. New York: The Guilford Press.
Rothbart, M. K., & Derryberry, D. (1981). Development of individual differences in temperament. In M. E. Lamb & A. L. Brown (Eds.), *Advances in developmental psychology* (Vol. 1, pp. 37–86). Hillsdale, NJ: Erlbaum.
Rothbart, M. K., Ahadi, S. A., & Evans, D. E. (2000). Temperament and personality: Origins and outcomes. *Journal of Personality and Social Psychology, 78*(1), 122–135. doi:10.1037/0022-3514.78.1.122
Rothbart, M. K., Sheese, B. E., Rueda, M. R., & Posner, M. I. (2011). Developing mechanisms of self-regulation in early life. *Emotion Review, 3*(2), 207–213. doi:10.1177/1754073910387943
Rothbaum, B. O., Rizzo, A. S., & Difede, J. (2010). Virtual reality exposure therapy for combat-related posttraumatic stress disorder. *Annals of the New York Academy of Sciences, 1208*(1), 126–132. doi:10.1111/j.1749-6632.2010.05691.x
Rotter, J. B. (1966). Generalized expectancies for internal versus external control of reinforcement. *Psychological Monographs, 80*, 1–27. doi:10.1037/h0092976
Rowland, L. W. (1939). Will hypnotized persons try to harm themselves or others? *The Journal of Abnormal and Social Psychology, 34*(1), 114–117. doi:10.1037/h0055818
Rubia, K., Norman, L., Lukito, S., Carlisi, C., Mataix-Cols, D., & Radua, J. (2016). Top-down control in ADHD: Disorder-specificity relative to CD, autism and OCD. *European Neuropsychopharmacology, 2*(26), S149-S150. doi:10.1016/S0924-977X(16)30960-9
Rule, N. O., Ambady, N., Adams, R. B., Jr., Ozono, H., Nakashima, S., Yoshikawa, S., & Watabe, M. (2010). Polling the face: Prediction and consensus across cultures. *Journal of Personality and Social Psychology, 98*(1), 1–15. doi:10.1037/a0017673
Ruscio, A., Stein, D., Chiu, W., & Kessler, R. (2010). The epidemiology of obsessive-compulsive disorder in the National Comorbidity Survey Replication. *Molecular Psychiatry, 15*(1), 53–63. doi:10.1038/mp.2008.94
Rushton, D. H., Dover, R., Sainsbury, A. W., Norris, M. J., Gilkes, J. J., & Ramsey, I. D. (2001). Why should women have lower reference limits for haemoglobin and ferritin concentrations than men? *British Medical Journal, 322*, 1355–1357. doi:10.1136/bmj.322.7298.1355
Rushton, J. P., Fulker, D. W., Neale, M. C., Nias, D. K. B., & Eysenck, H. J. (1986). Altruism and aggression: The heritability of individual differences. *Journal of Personality and Social Psychology, 50*, 1192–1198. doi:10.1037/0022-3514.50.6.1192
Russell, D. W. (1996). UCLA Loneliness Scale (Version 3): Reliability, validity, and factor structure. *Journal of Personality Assessment, 66*(1), 20–40. doi:10.1207/s15327752jpa6601_2
Russell, D., & Cutrona, C. (2010). *Stressful effects of where you live: Studying the influence of neighborhood context over time*. Paper presented at the World Conference on Stress and Anxiety Research, Galway, Ireland.
Russell, D., Peplau, L. A., & Cutrona, C. E. (1980). The revised UCLA Loneliness Scale: Concurrent and discriminant validity evidence. *Journal of Personality and Social Psychology, 39*(3), 472–480. doi:10.1037/0022-3514.39.3.472
Russell, J. A. (1980). A circumplex model of affect. *Journal of Personality and Social Psychology, 39*, 1161–1178. doi:10.1037/h0077714
Russell, J. A., & Mehrabian, A. (1978). Approach-avoidance and affiliation as functions of the emotion-eliciting quality of an environment. *Environment and Behavior, 10*(3), 355–387. doi:10.1177/0013916578103005
Russell, J. A., Epstein, L. G., Greer, D. M., Kirschen, M., Rubin, M. A., & Lewis, A. (2019). Brain death, the determination of brain death, and member guidance for brain death accommodation requests. *AAN Position Statement, 92*(5), 228–232. doi:10.1212/wnl.0000000000006750
Russell, W. M. S., & Burch, R. L. (1959). *The principles of humane experimental technique*. London, UK: Methuen.
Russo, R., & Mammarella, N. (2002). Spacing effects in recognition memory: When meaning matters. *European Journal of Cognitive Psychology, 14*, 49–59. doi:10.1080/09541440042000133
Rust, J. (1999). Discriminant validity of the 'big five' personality traits in employment settings. *Social Behavior and Personality, 27*(1), 99–108. doi:10.2224/sbp.1999.27.1.99
Ruwaard, J., Lange, A., Schrieken, B., Dolan, C. V., & Emmelkamp, P. (2012). The effectiveness of online cognitive behavioral treatment in routine clinical practice. *PLoS One, 7*(7), e40089. doi:10.1371/journal.pone.0040089
Ryan, R. M., & Deci, E. L. (2001). On happiness and human potentials: A review of research on hedonic and eudaimonic well-being. *Annual Review of Psychology, 52*(1), 141–166. doi:10.1146/annurev.psych.52.1.141
Rychlowska, M., Miyamoto, Y., Matsumoto, D., Hess, U., Gilboa-Schechtman, E., Kamble, S., Muluk, H., Masuda, T., & Niedenthal, P. M. (2015). Heterogeneity of long-history migration explains cultural differences in reports of emotional expressivity and the functions of smiles. *Proceedings of the National Academy of Sciences of the United States of America, 112*(19), E2429–E2436. doi:10.1073/pnas.1413661112
S. Laureys & G. Tononi (Eds.), *The neurology of consciousness: Cognitive neuroscience and neuropathology* (pp. 81–88). Oxford, UK: Elsevier Academic Press.
Saarimäki, H., Gotsopoulos, A., Jääskeläinen, I. P., Lampinen, J., Vuilleumier, P., Hari, R., . . .Nummenmaa, L. (2015). Discrete neural signatures of basic emotions. *Cerebral Cortex, 26*(6), 2563–2573. doi:10.1093/cercor/bhv086
Sabatini, R. M. E. (1997). *The history of lobotomy*. http://www.cerebromente.org.br/n02/historia/lobotomy.htm

Sacco, K. A., Termine, A., & Seyal, A. (2005). Effects of cigarette smoking on spatial working memory and attentional deficits in schizophrenia: Involvement of nicotinic receptor mechanisms *Archives of General Psychiatry, 62*(6), 649–659. doi:10.1001/archpsyc.62.6.649

Sackeim, H. A. (2014). Autobiographical memory and ECT: Don't throw out the baby. *The Journal of ECT, 30*(3), 177–186. doi:10.1097/YCT.0000000000000117

Sackett, G. P. (1966). Monkeys reared in isolation with pictures as visual input: Evidence for an innate releasing mechanism. *Science, 154*, 1468–1473. doi:10.1126/science.154.3755.1468

Sajatovic, M., Valenstein, M., Blow, F., Ganoczy, D., & Ignacio, R. (2007). Treatment adherence with lithium and anticonvulsant medications among patients with bipolar disorder. *Psychiatric Services, 58*(6), 855–863. doi:10.1176/appi.ps.58.6.855

Sakai, Y., Shaw, C. A., Dawson, B. C., Dugas, D. V., Al-Mohtaseb, Z., Hill, D. E., & Zoghbi, H. Y. (2011). Protein interactome reveals converging molecular pathways among autism disorders. *Science Translational Medicine, 3*(86), 86ra49. doi:10.1126/scitranslmed.3002166

Sakurai, T., Amemiya, A., Ishii, M., Matsuzaki, I., Chemelli, R. M., Tanaka, H., Williams, S. C., Richardson, J. A., Kozlowski, G. P., Wilson, S., Arch, J. R., Buckingham, R. E., Haynes, A. C., Carr, S. A., Annan, R. S., McNulty, D. E., Liu, W. S., Terret. J. A., Elshourbagy, N. A., . . . Yanagisawa, M. (1998). Orexins and orexin receptors: a family of hypothalamic neuropeptides and G proteincoupled receptors that regulate feeding behavior. *Cell, 92*(5), 573–585. doi:10.1016/S0092-8674(00)80949-6

Salari, N., Hosseinian-Far, A., Jalali, R., Vaisi-Raygani, A., Rasoulpoor, S., Mohammadi, M., Rasoulpoor, S., & Khaledi-Paveh, B. (2020). Prevalence of stress, anxiety, depression among the general population during the COVID-19 pandemic: A systematic review and meta-analysis. *Globalization and Health, 16*(1), 57. doi:10.1186/s12992-020-00589-w

Salgado, S., & Kaplitt, M. G. (2015). The nucleus accumbens: A comprehensive review. *Stereotactic and Functional Neurosurgery, 93*(2), 75–93. doi:10.1159/000368279

Salovey, P., & Mayer, J. D. (1990). Emotional intelligence. *Imagination, Cognition and Personality, 9*(3), 185–211. doi:10.2190/DUGG-P24E-52WK-6CDG

Sanchez-Roige, S., Gray, J. C., MacKillop, J., Chen, C.-H., & Palmer, A. A. (2018). The genetics of human personality. *Genes, Brain and Behavior, 17*(3), e12439. doi:10.1111/gbb.12439

Sandstrom, G. M., & Dunn, E. W. (2014). Social interactions and well-being: The surprising power of weak ties. *Personality and Social Psychology Bulletin, 40*(7), 910–922. doi:10.1177/0146167214529799

Sanfey, A. G., Rilling, J. K., Aronson, J. A., Nystrom, L. E., & Cohen, J. D. (2003). The neural basis of economic decision-making in the Ultimatum Game. *Science, 300*, 1755–1758. doi:10.1126/science.1082976

Santosa, C. M., Strong, C. M., Nowakowska, C., Wang, P. W., Rennicke, C. M., & Ketter, T. A. (2007). Enhanced creativity in bipolar disorder patients: A controlled study. *Journal of Affective Disorders, 100*(1–3), 31–39. doi:10.1016/j.jad.2006.10.013

Sapolsky, R. (2001). *A primate's memoir.* New York: Scribner.

Sarnoff, I., & Zimbardo, P. G. (1961). Anxiety, fear, and social isolation. *The Journal of Abnormal and Social Psychology, 62*(2), 356–363. doi:10.1037/h0046506

Satizabal, C. L., Beiser, A. S., Chouraki, V., Chêne, G., Dufouil, C., & Seshadri, S. (2016). Incidence of dementia over three decades in the Framingham Heart Study. *New England Journal of Medicine, 374*(6), 523–532. doi:10.1056/NEJMoa1504327

Saunders, D. T., Roe, C. A., Smith, G., & Clegg, H. (2016). Lucid dreaming incidence: A quality effects meta-analysis of 50 years of research. *Consciousness and Cognition, 43*, 197–215. doi:10.1016/j.concog.2016.06.002

Saunders, E. F., Ramsden, C. E., Sherazy, M. S., Gelenberg, A. J., Davis, J. M., & Rapoport, S. I. (2016). Omega-3 and omega-6 polyunsaturated fatty acids in bipolar disorder: A review of biomarker and treatment studies. *The Journal of Clinical Psychiatry, 77*(10), 1301–1308. doi:10.4088/JCP.15r09925

Savage-Rumbaugh, S., Shanker, S. G., & Taylor, T. J. (1998). *Apes, language, and the human mind.* New York, NY: Oxford University Press.

Savin-Williams, R. C., & Vrangalova, Z. (2013). Mostly heterosexual as a distinct sexual orientation group: A systematic review of the empirical evidence. *Developmental Review, 33*(1), 58–88. doi:10.1016/j.dr.2013.01.001

Savine, R., & Sönksen, P. (2000). Growth hormone–hormone replacement for the somatopause? *Hormone Research in Paediatrics, 53*(Suppl. 3), 37–41. doi:10.1159/000023531

Schachter, S. (1951). Deviation, rejection, and communication. *Journal of Abnormal Psychology, 46*, 190–207. doi:10.1037/h0062326

Schachter, S. (1959). *The psychology of affiliation: Experimental studies of the sources of gregariousness* (Vol. 1). Stanford, CA: Stanford University Press.

Schachter, S., & Singer, J. (1962). Cognitive, social and physiological determinants of emotional state. *Psychological Review, 69*, 379–399. doi:10.1037/h0046234

Schartner, M. M., Carhart-Harris, R. L., Barrett, A. B., Seth, A. K., & Muthukumaraswamy, S. D. (2017). Increased spontaneous MEG signal diversity for psychoactive doses of ketamine, LSD and psilocybin. *Scientific Reports, 7*, 46421–46421. doi:10.1038/srep46421

Scheepens, D. S., van Waarde, J. A., Lok, A., de Vries, G., Denys, D. A. J. P., & van Wingen, G. A. (2020). The link between structural and functional brain abnormalities in depression: A systematic review of multimodal neuroimaging studies. *Frontiers in Psychiatry, 11*(485). doi:10.3389/fpsyt.2020.00485

Schenck, C. H., Bundlie, S. R., Ettinger, M. G., & Mohowald, M. (2002). Chronic behavioral disorders of human REM sleep: A new category of parasomnia. *Sleep, 25*(2), 119–119. doi:10.1093/sleep/9.2.293

Schifani, C., Pruessner, J., Tseng, H.-H., Rao, N., Tagore, A., Wilson, A. A., Houle, S., Rusjan, P. M., & Mizrahi, R. (2019). Stress-induced cortical dopamine response is altered in subjects at clinical high risk for psychosis using cannabis. *Addiction Biology, 25*, e12812. doi:10.1111/adb.12812

Schimmelmann, B. G., Friedel, S., Nguyen, T. T., Sauer, S., Vogel, C. I. G., Konrad, K., Wilhelm, C., Sinzig, J., Renner, T. J., Romanos, M., Palmason, H., Dempfle, A., Walitza, S., Freitag, C., Meyer, J., Linder, M., Schäfer, H., Warnke, A., Lesch, K. P., Herpertz-Dalman, P., & Hebebrand, J. (2009). Exploring the genetic link between RLS and ADHD. *Journal of Psychiatric Research, 43*(10), 941–945. doi:10.1016/j.jpsychires.2009.01.003

Schjedlderup-Ebbe, T. (1922). Beiträge zur Sozialpsychologie des Haushuhns (Contributions to the social psychology of the house chicken). *Zeitschrift für Psychologie, 88*, 225–252.

Schlaug, G., Forgeard, M., Zhu, L., Norton, A., Norton, A., & Winner, E. (2009). Training-induced neuroplasticity in young children. *Annals of the New York Academy of Science, 1169*, 205–208. doi:10.1111/j.1749-6632.2009.04842.x

Schlaug, G., Jancke, L., Huang, Y., & Steinmetz, H. (1995). In vivo evidence of structural brain asymmetry in musicians. *Science, 267*, 699–701. doi:10.1126/science.7839149

Schober, M. F., & Carstensen, L. L. (2010). Does being together for years help comprehension? In E. Morsella (Ed.), *Expressing oneself/expressing one's self: Communication, cognition, language, and identity.* (pp. 107–124). Hove, U.K.: Psychology Press/Taylor& Francis.

Schön, D., Gordon, R., Campagne, A., Magne, C., Astésano, C., Anton, J.-L., & Besson, M. (2010). Similar cerebral networks in language, music and song perception. *NeuroImage, 51*(1), 450–461. doi:10.1016/j.neuroimage.2010.02.023

Schroeder, S. (2008). Stranded in the periphery—The increasing marginalization of smokers. *New England Journal of Medicine, 358*(21), 2284–2286. doi:10.1056/NEJMe0802708

Schroeder, V., & Kelley, M. (2009). Associations between family environment, parenting practices, and executive functioning of children with and without ADHD. *Journal of Child and Family Studies, 18*(2), 227–235. doi:10.1007/s10826-008-9223-0

Schroder, G. (2001). *Full solidarity with the United States.* http://ghdi.ghi-dc.org/sub_document.cfm?document_id=3724

Schulte-Rüther, M., Otte, E., Adigüzel, K., Firk, C., Herpertz-Dahlmann, B., Koch, I., & Konrad, K. (2017). Intact mirror mechanisms for automatic facial emotions in children and adolescents with autism spectrum disorder. *Autism Research, 10*(2), 298–310. doi:10.1002/aur.1654

Schurz, G. (1985). Experimentelle Überprüfung des Zusammenhangs zwischen Persönlichkeitsmerkmalen und der Bereitschaft zum destruktiven Gehorsam gegenüber Autoritäten [Experimental examination of the relationship between personality characteristics and the readiness to destructive obedience to authorities]. *Zeitschrift für experimentelle und angewandte Psychologie, 32*, 160–177.

Schuster, M. A., Stein, L. H., Jaycox, R. L., Marshall, G. N., Elliott, M. N., & Zhou, J. e. a. (2002). *After 9/11: Stress and coping across America*. http://www.rand.org/pubs/testimonies/2005/CT198.pdf

Schwartz, B. (1984). *Psychology of learning and behavior* (2nd ed.). New York: Norton.

Schwartz, C. E., Snidman, N., & Kagan, J. (1999). Adolescent social anxiety as an outcome of inhibited temperament in childhood. *Journal of the American Academy of Child and Adolescent Psychiatry, 38*(8), 1008–1015. doi:10.1097/00004583-199908000-00017

Schwarz, M., & Susswein, A. J. (1992). Presence of conspecifics facilitates learning that food is inedible in Aplysia fasciata. *Behavioral Neuroscience, 106*(2), 250–261. doi:10.1037/0735-7044.106.2.250

Scott, J. G., Matuschka, L., Niemelä, S., Miettunen, J., Emmerson, B., & Mustonen, A. (2018). Evidence of a causal relationship between smoking tobacco and schizophrenia spectrum disorders. *Frontiers in Psychiatry, 9*(607). doi:10.3389/fpsyt.2018.00607

Scott, S. G., & Bruce, R. A. (1995). Decision-making style: The development and assessment of a new measure. *Educational and Psychological Measurement, 55*(5), 818–831. doi:10.1177/0013164495055005017

Scott, V., & Gijsbers, K. (1981). Pain perception in competitive swimmers. *British Medical Journal, 283*, 91–93. doi:10.1136/bmj.283.6284.91

Scully, J. A., Tosi, H., & Banning, K. (2000). Life event checklists: Revisiting the Social Readjustment Rating Scale after 30 years. *Educational and Psychological Measurement, 60*, 864–876. doi:10.1177/00131640021970952

Sczesny, S., Formanowicz, M., & Moser, F. (2016). Can gender-fair language reduce gender stereotyping and discrimination? *Frontiers in Psychology, 7*(25). doi:10.3389/fpsyg.2016.00025

Seeley, W. W., Matthews, B. R., Crawford, R. K., Gorno-Tempini, M. L., Foti, D., Mackenzie, I. R., & Miller, B. L. (2008). Unravelling Boléro: Progressive aphasia, transmodal creativity and the right posterior neocortex. *Brain, 131*(1), 39–49. doi:10.1093/brain/awm270

Segerstrom, S. C., & Miller, G. E. (2004). Psychological stress and the human immune system: A meta-analytic study of 30 years of inquiry. *Psychological Bulletin, 130*(4), 601–630. doi:10.1037/0033-2909.130.4.601

Seksel, K., & Lindeman, M. J. (2001). Use of clomipramine in treatment of obsessive-compulsive disorder, separation anxiety and noise phobia in dogs: A preliminary, clinical study. *Australian Veterinary Journal, 79*, 252–256. doi:10.1111/j.1751-0813.2001.tb11976.x

Seligman, M. E. (1971). Phobias and preparedness. *Behavior Therapy, 2*(3), 307–320. doi:10.1016/s0005-7894(71)80064-3

Seligman, M. E. (2012). *Flourish: A visionary new understanding of happiness and well-being.* New York, NY: Simon and Schuster.

Seligman, M. E. (2019). Positive psychology: A personal history. *Annual Review of Clinical Psychology, 15*, 1–23. doi:10.1146/annurev-clinpsy-050718-095653

Seligman, M. E. P. (1987). *Predicting depression, poor health, and presidential elections.* Paper presented at the Science and Public Policy Seminar sponsored by the Federation of Behavioral, Psychological and Cognitive Sciences, Washington, D.C.

Seligman, M. E. P. (1990). *Learned optimism.* New York: Simon & Schuster.

Seligman, M. E. P. (2002). *Authentic happiness: Using the new positive psychology to realize your potential for lasting fulfillment.* New York, NY: Simon and Schuster.

Seligman, M. E. P., & Csikszentmihalyi, M. (2000). Positive psychology: An introduction. *American Psychologist, 55*(1), 5–14. doi:10.1037/0003-066x.55.1.5

Selye, H. (1975). Confusion and controversy in the stress field. *Journal of Human Stress, 1*(2), 37–44. doi:10.1080/0097840X.1975.9940406

Semple, B. D., Blomgren, K., Gimlin, K., Ferriero, D. M., & Noble-Haeusslein, L. J. (2013). Brain development in rodents and humans: Identifying benchmarks of maturation and vulnerability to injury across species. *Progress in Neurobiology, 106–107*, 1–16. doi:10.1016/j.pneurobio.2013.04.001

Senju, A., Southgate, V., White, S., & Frith, U. (2009). Mindblind eyes: An absence of spontaneous theory of mind in Asperger syndrome. *Science, 325*(5942), 883–885. doi:10.1126/science.1176170

Seo, J. S., Wei, J., Qin, L., Kim, Y., Yan, Z., & Greengard, P. (2017). Cellular and molecular basis for stress-induced depression. *Molecular Psychiatry, 22*(10), 1440–1447. doi:10.1038/mp.2016.118

Serbin, L. A., Poulin-Dubois, D., Colburne, K. A., Sen, M. G., & Eichstedt, J. A. (2001). Gender stereotyping in infancy: Visual preferences for and knowledge of gender-stereotyped toys in the second year. *International Journal of Behavioral Development, 25*(1), 7–15. doi:10.1080/01650250042000078

Sereno, M. I., & Tootell, R. B. H. (2005). From monkeys to humans: What do we now know about brain homologies? *Current Opinion in Neurobiology, 15*, 135–144. doi:10.1016/j.conb.2005.03.014

Sessa, B., & Johnson, M. W. (2015). Can psychedelic compounds play a part in drug dependence therapy? *The British Journal of Psychiatry, 206*(1), 1–3. doi:10.1192/bjp.bp.114.148031

Sessa, B., Higbed, L., & Nutt, D. (2019). A review of 3,4-methylenedioxymethamphetamine (MDMA)-assisted psychotherapy. *Frontiers in Psychiatry, 10*(138). doi:10.3389/fpsyt.2019.00138

Setchell, J. M., & Wickings, E. J. (2005). Dominance, status signals and coloration in male mandrills (Mandrillus sphinx). *Ethology, 111*, 25–50. doi:10.1111/j.1439-0310.2004.01054.x

Shadrina, M., Bondarenko, E. A., & Slominsky, P. A. (2018). Genetics factors in major depressive disease. *Frontiers in Psychiatry, 9*(334). doi:10.3389/fpsyt.2018.00334

Shalev, A. Y., Gevonden, M., Ratanatharathorn, A., Laska, E., van der Mei, W. F., Qi, W., Lowe, S., Lai, B. S., Bryant, R. A., Delahanty, D., Matsuoka, Y. J., Olff, M., Schnyder, U., Seedat, S., deRoon-Cassini, T. A., Kessler, R. C., Koenen, K. C., & International Consortium to Predict PTSD. (2019). Estimating the risk of PTSD in recent trauma survivors: Results of the International Consortium to Predict PTSD (ICPP). *World Psychiatry, 18*(1), 77–87. doi:10.1002/wps.20608

Shallice, T., & Warrington, E. K. (1970). Independent functioning of verbal memory stores: A neuropsychological study. *Quarterly Journal of Experimental Psychology, 22*, 261–273. doi:10.1080/00335557043000203

Shaw, P. J., Cirelli, C., Greenspan, R. J., & Tononi, G. (2000). Correlates of sleep and waking in Drosophila melanogaster. *Science, 287*(5459), 1834–1837. doi:10.1126/science.287.5459.1834

Shaw, P., Eckstrand, K., Sharp, W., Blumenthal, J., Lerch, J. P., Greenstein, D., Clasen, L., Evans, A., Giedd, J., & Rapoport, J. L. (2007). Attention-deficit/hyperactivity disorder is characterized by a delay in cortical maturation. *Proceedings of the National Academy of Sciences of the United States of America, 104*(49), 19649–19654. doi:10.1073/pnas.0707741104

Shaw, P., Greenstein, D., Lerch, J., Clasen, L., Lenroot, R., Gogtay, N., Evans, A., Rapoport, J., & Giedd, J. (2006). Intellectual ability and cortical development in children and adolescents. *Nature, 440*(7084), 676–679. doi:10.1038/nature04513

Shaw, P., Malek, M., Watson, B., Greenstein, D., de Rossi, P., & Sharp, W. (2013). Trajectories of cerebral cortical development in childhood and adolescence and adult attention-deficit/hyperactivity disorder. *Biological Psychiatry, 74*(8), 599–606. doi:10.1016/j.biopsych.2013.04.007

Shaywitz, S. E. (1996). Dyslexia. *Scientific American, 275,* 98–105.
Shaywitz, S. E., & Shaywitz, B. A. (2005). Dyslexia (Specific Reading Disability). *Biological Psychiatry, 57*(11), 1301–1309. doi:10.1016/j.biopsych.2005.01.043
Shaywitz, S. E., Shaywitz, B. A., Pugh, K. R., Fulbright, R. K., Constable, R. T., Mencl, W. E., Shankweiler, D. P., Liberman, A. M., Skudlarski, P., Fletcher, J. M., Katz, L., Marchione, K. E., Lacadie, C., Gatenby, C., & Gore, J. (1998). Functional disruption in the organization of the brain for reading in dyslexia. *Proceedings of the National Academy of Sciences of the United States of America, 95*(5), 2636–2641. doi:10.1073/pnas.95.5.2636
Shechter, A., Kim, E. W., St-Onge, M.-P., & Westwood, A. J. (2018). Blocking nocturnal blue light for insomnia: A randomized controlled trial. *Journal of Psychiatric Research, 96,* 196–202. doi:10.1016/j.jpsychires.2017.10.015
Shedler, J. (2012). The efficacy of psychodynamic psychotherapy. *American Psychologist,* 65(2), 98–109. doi:10.1037/a0018378
Sheldon, S., Farb, N., Palombo, D. J., & Levine, B. (2016). Intrinsic medial temporal lobe connectivity relates to individual differences in episodic autobiographical remembering. *Cortex, 74,* 206–216. doi:10.1016/j.cortex.2015.11.005
Shepard, R. N. (1990). *Mind Sights: Original visual illusions, ambiguities, and other anomalies with a commentary on the play of mind in perception and art.* New York: W.H. Freeman.
Sher, L. (2006). Alcohol consumption and suicide. *QJM: Monthly Journal of the Association of Physicians, 99*(1), 57–61. doi:10.1093/qjmed/hci146
Sheridan, S. M., & Burt, J. D. (2009). Family-centered positive psychology. In S. J. Lopez & C. R. Snyder (Eds.), *Oxford handbook of positive psychology (2nd ed.).* (pp. 551–559). New York, NY: Oxford University Press.
Sherif, M., Harvey, L. J., White, B. J., Hood, W. R., & Sherif, C. (1961). *The Robbers Cave experiment: Intergroup conflict and cooperation.* Norman, OK: University of Oklahoma Institute of Intergroup Relations.
Sherman, D. K., & Kim, H. S. (2005). Is there an "I" in "team"? The role of the self in group-serving judgments. *Journal of Personality and Social Psychology, 88*(1), 108–120. doi:10.1037/0022-3514.88.1.108
Sherman, R. A., Rauthmann, J. F., Brown, N. A., Serfass, D. G., & Jones, A. B. (2015). The independent effects of personality and situations on real-time expressions of behavior and emotion. *Journal of Personality and Social Psychology, 109*(5), 872–888. doi:10.1037/pspp0000036
Shi, J., Potash, J., Knowles, J., Weissman, M., Coryell, W., Scheftner, W., Lawson, W. B., DePaulo Jr., D. P., Gejman, P. V., Sanders, A. R., Johnson, J. K., Adams, P., Chaudhury, S., Jancic, D., Evgrafov, O., Zvinyatskovskiy, A., Ertman, N., Gladis, M., Neimanis, K., . . . Levinson, D. F. (2011). Genome-wide association study of recurrent early-onset major depressive disorder. *Molecular Psychiatry, 16*(2), 193–201. doi:10.1038/mp.2009.124
Shields, M. (2004). Stress, health, and the benefit of social support. *Health Reports (Statistics Canada, Catalogue 82–003), 15,* 9–38.
Shiota, M. N., & Levenson, R. W. (2007). Birds of a feather don't always fly farthest: Similarity in Big Five personality predicts more negative marital satisfaction trajectories in long-term marriages. *Psychology and Aging, 22*(4), 666–675. doi:10.1037/0882-7974.22.4.666
Shu, L. L., Gino, F., & Bazerman, M. H. (2011). Dishonest deed, clear conscience: When cheating leads to moral disengagement and motivated forgetting. *Personality and Social Psychology Bulletin, 37*(3), 330–349. doi:10.1177/0146167211398138
Sia, C.-L., Tan, B. C. Y., & Wei, K.-K. (2002). Group polarization and computer-mediated communication: Effects of communication cues, social presence, and anonymity. *Information Systems Research, 13*(1), 70–90. doi:10.1287/isre.13.1.70.92
Siegel, J. M. (2001). The REM sleep-memory consolidation hypothesis. *Science, 294*(5544), 1058–1063. doi:10.1126/science.1063049
Siegel, J. Z., & Crockett, M. J. (2013). How serotonin shapes moral judgment and behavior. *Annals of the New York Academy of Sciences, 1299*(1), 42–51. doi:10.1111/nyas.12229
Siegel, S. (2016). The heroin overdose mystery. *Current Directions in Psychological Science, 25*(6), 375–379. doi:10.1177/0963721416664404
Siegel, S., Hinson, R., Krank, M., & McCully, J. (1982). Heroin "overdose" death: Contribution of drug-associated environmental cues. *Science, 216*(4544), 436–437. doi:10.1126/science.7200260
Siegfried, J. (2010). Airlines might charge fat people higher fares. http://www.examiner.com/airlines-airport-in-national/airlines-might-charge-fat-peoplehigher-fares
Siegle, G., Sagratti, S., & Crawford, C. (1999). *Effects of rumination and initial severity on response to cognitive therapy for depression.* Paper presented at the Meeting of the Association for the Advancement of Behavior Therapy, Toronto, ON.
Siever, L. J. (2008). Neurobiology of aggression and violence. *The American Journal of Psychiatry, 165*(4), 429–442. doi:10.1176/appi.ajp.2008.07111774
Silva, B. A., Mattucci, C., Krzywkowski, P., Cuozzo, R., Carbonari, L., & Gross, C. T. (2016). The ventromedial hypothalamus mediates predator fear memory. *The European Journal of Neuroscience, 43*(11), 1431–1439. doi:10.1111/ejn.13239
Silva, B. A., Mattucci, C., Krzywkowski, P., Murana, E., Illarionova, A., Grinevich, V., Canteras, N. S., Ragozzino, D., & Gross, C. T. (2013). Independent hypothalamic circuits for social and predator fear. *Nature Neuroscience, 16*(12), 1731–1733. doi:10.1038/nn.3573
Silver, D., Huang, A., Maddison, C. J., Guez, A., Sifre, L., van den Driessche, G., Schrittwieser, J., Antonoglu, I., Panneershelvam, V., Lanctot, M., Dieleman, S., Grewe, D., Nham, J., Kalchbrenner, N., Sutskever, I., Lillicrap, T., Leach, M., Kavukcuoglu, K., Graepel, T., & Hassabis, D. Hassabis, D. (2016). Mastering the game of Go with deep neural networks and tree search. *Nature, 529*(7587), 484–489. doi:10.1038/nature16961
Silvia, P. J. (2005). Deflecting reactance: The role of similarity in increasing compliance and reducing resistance. *Basic and Applied Social Psychology, 27,* 277–284. doi:10.1207/s15324834basp2703_9
Simon, H. A. (1957). *Models of man: Social and rational; Mathematical essays on rational human behavior in society setting*: New York, NY: Wiley.
Simons-Morton, B. G., Bingham, C. R., Falk, E. B., Li, K., Pradhan, A. K., Ouimet, M. C., Almani, F., Shope, J. T. (2014). Experimental effects of injunctive norms on simulated risky driving among teenage males. *Health Psychology 33*(7), 616–627. doi:10.1037/a0034837
Simons, D. J. (2014). The value of direct replication. *Perspectives on Psychological Science, 9*(1), 76–80. doi:10.1177/1745691613514755
Simons, L. G., & Conger, R. D. (2007). Linking mother-father differences in parenting to a typology of family parenting styles and adolescent outcomes. *Journal of Family Issues, 28*(2), 212–241. doi:10.1177/0192513X06294593
Simonton, D. K. (2008). Creativity and genius. In O. P. John, R. W. Robins, & L. A. Pervin (Eds.), *Handbook of personality: Theory and research* (pp. 679–698). New York, NY: The Guilford Press.
Simonton, D. K. (2017). Creative productivity across the life span. In J. A. Plucker (Ed.), *Creativity and innovation: Theory, research, and practice* (pp. 119–132). Waco, TX: Prufrock Press.
Simpson, D. (2005). Phrenology and the neurosciences: Contributions of F. J. Gall and J. G. Spurzheim. *ANZ Journal of Surgery, 75*(6), 475. doi:10.1111/j.1445-2197.2005.03426.x
Simpson, E. A., Maylott, S. E., Lazo, R. J., Leonard, K. A., Kaburu, S. S. K., Suomi, S. J., Paukner, A., & Ferrari, P. F. (2019). Social touch alters newborn monkey behavior. *Infant Behavior and Development, 57,* 101368. doi:10.1016/j.infbeh.2019.101368
Singer, M. I., Miller, D. B., Guo, S., Slovak, K., & Frierson, T. (1998). *The mental health consequences of children's exposure to violence.* Cleveland, OH: Cayahoga County Community Mental Health Research Institute, Mandel School of Applied Social Sciences, Case Western Reserve University.
Singer, T., Kiebel, S. J., Winston, J. S., Dolan, R. J., & Frith, C. D. (2004). Brain responses

to the acquired moral status of faces. *Neuron, 41*, 653–662. doi:10.1016/S0896-6273(04)00014-5
Sinha, Y., Silove, N., & Williams, K. (2006). Chelation therapy and autism. *BMJ: British Medical Journal, 333*(7571), 756. doi:10.1136/bmj.333.7571.756
Skene, D. J., Lockley, S. W., & Arendt, J. (1999). Use of melatonin in the treatment of phase shift and sleep disorders. In G. Huether, W. Kochen, T. J. Simat, & H. Steinhart (Eds.), *Tryptophan, serotonin, and melatonin* (pp. 79–84). New York, NY: Springer.
Skinner, B. F. (1953). Some contributions of an experimental analysis of behavior to psychology as a whole. *American Psychologist, 8*, 69–78. doi:10.1037/h0054118
Skinner, B. F. (1960). Pigeons in a pelican. *American Psychologist, 15*, 28–37. doi:10.1037/h0045345
Skinner, B. F. (1971). *Beyond freedom and dignity*. New York: Knopf.
Skodol, A. E., & Bender, D. S. (2003). Why are women diagnosed borderline more than men? *Psychiatric Quarterly, 74*(4), 349–360. doi:10.1023/A:1026087410516
Skuse, D. H. (2000). Behavioural phenotypes: What do they teach us? *Archives of Disease in Childhood, 82*(3), 222–225. doi:10.1136/adc.82.3.222
Slattery, J., MacFabe, D., Kahler, S., & Frye, R. (2016). Enteric ecosystem disruption in autism spectrum disorder: Can the microbiota and macrobiota be restored? *Current Pharmaceutical Design, 22*(40), 6107–6121. doi:10.2174/1381612822666160905123953
Slobodchikoff, C. N., Perla, B. S., & Verdoli, J. L. (2009). *Communication and community in an animal society*. Cambridge, MA: Harvard University Press.
Slomski, A. (2019). Hypnotherapy provides IBS relief: Clinical trials update. *JAMA, 321*(4), 335–335. doi:10.1001/jama.2018.22028
Slotema, C. W., Dirk Blom, J., Hoek, H. W., & Sommer, I. E. (2010). Should we expand the toolbox of psychiatric treatment methods to include repetitive transcranial magnetic stimulation (rTMS)? A meta-analysis of the efficacy of rTMS in psychiatric disorders. *Journal of Clinical Psychiatry, 71*(7), 873–884. doi:10.4088/JCP.08m04872gre
Slovic, P., Peters, E., Finucane, M. L., & MacGregor, D. G. (2005). Affect, risk, and decision making. *Health Psychology, 24*(4, Suppl), S35-S40. doi:10.1037/0278-6133.24.4.S35
Smeland, O. B., Bahrami, S., Frei, O., Shadrin, A., O'Connell, K., Savage, J., Watanabe, K., Krull, F., Bettella, F., Steen, N. E., Ueland, T., Posthuma, D., Djurovic, S., Dale, A. M., & Andreassen, O. A. (2020). Genome-wide analysis reveals extensive genetic overlap between schizophrenia, bipolar disorder, and intelligence. *Molecular Psychiatry, 25*(4), 844–853. doi:10.1038/s41380-018-0332-x
Smith, A. M., Floerke, V. A., & Thomas, A. K. (2016). Retrieval practice protects memory against acute stress. *Science, 354*(6315), 1046–1048. doi:10.1126/science.aah5067
Smith, E. E., & Grossman, M. (2008). Multiple systems of category learning. *Neuroscience and Biobehavioral Reviews, 32*(2), 249–264. doi:10.1016/j.neubiorev.2007.07.009
Smith, E. E., Shoben, E. J., & Rips, L. J. (1974). Structure and process in semantic memory: A featural model for semantic decisions. *Psychological Review, 81*(3), 214–241. doi:10.1037/h0036351
Smith, S., Ferguson, C., & Beaver, K. (2018). A longitudinal analysis of shooter games and their relationship with conduct disorder and self-reported delinquency. *International Journal of Law and Psychiatry, 58*, 48–53. doi:10.1016/j.ijlp.2018.02.008
Smith, T., & Lovaas, I. (1998). Intensive early behavioral intervention with autism: The UCLA Young Autism Project. *Infants and Young Children, 10*, 67–78. doi:10.1007/s10803-008-0596-0
Smith, V., & Wanless, A. (2020). *Unmasking the truth: Public health experts, the coronavirus, and the raucous marketplace of ideas*. https://carnegieendowment.org/2020/07/16/unmasking-truth-public-health-experts-coronavirus-and-raucous-marketplace-of-ideas-pub-82314
Smoller, J. W. (2016). The genetics of stress-related disorders: PTSD, depression, and anxiety disorders. *Neuropsychopharmacology, 41*(1), 297–319. doi:10.1038/npp.2015.266
Sneed, J. R., Whitbourne, S. K., & Culang, M. E. (2006). Trust, identity, and ego integrity: Modeling Erikson's core stages over 34 years. *Journal of Adult Development, 13* (3–4), 148–157. doi:10.1007/s10804-007-9026-3
Snyder, C. R. (1994). *The psychology of hope: You can get there from here*. New York, NY: Free Press.
Snyder, C. R., Berg, C., Woodward, J. T., Gum, A., Rand, K. L., Wrobleski, K. K., Brown, J. Hackman, A. (2005). Hope against the cold: Individual differences in trait hope and acute pain tolerance on the cold pressor task. *Journal of Personality, 73*(2), 287–312. doi:10.1111/j.1467-6494.2005.00318.x
Snyder, C. R., Rand, K. L., & Sigmon, D. R. (2002). Hope theory: A member of the positive psychology family. In C. R. Snyder & S. J. Lopez (Eds.), *Handbook of positive psychology* (pp. 257–276). New York, NY US: Oxford University Press.
Society for Neuroscience. (2019). *For press*. http://www.sfn.org:443/For Press
Solomon, Z., Mikulincer, M., & Hobfoll, S. E. (1986). Effects of social support and battle intensity on loneliness and breakdown during combat. *Journal of Personality and Social Psychology, 51*(6), 1269–1276. doi:10.1037/0022-3514.51.6.1269
Son, J. Y. (2018, February 6). Influential living psychologists: Women + POC. https://jaeyoungson.com/psychblog-jelly/2018/1/30/influential-living-psychologists-women-poc
Song, M., Dieckmann, N. F., & Nigg, J. T. (2019). Addressing discrepancies between ADHD prevalence and case identification estimates among U.S. children utilizing NSCH 2007–2012. *Journal of Attention Disorders, 23*(14), 1691–1702. doi:10.1177/1087054718799930
Soon, C. S., Brass, M., Heinze, H.-J., & Haynes, J.-D. (2008). Unconscious determinants of free decisions in the human brain. *Nature Neuroscience, 11*(5), 543–545. doi:10.1038/nn.2112
Sorell, G. T., & Montgomery, M. J. (2001). Feminist perspectives on Erikson's theory: Their relevance for contemporary identity development research. *Identity: An International Journal of Theory and Research, 1*(2), 97–128. doi:10.1207/S1532706XID0102_01
Soria, V., Martinez-Amoros, E., Escaramis, G., Valero, J., Perez-Egea, R., Garcia, C., Gutiérrez-Zotes, A.,Puigdemont, D., Bayés, M., Crespo, J. M., Martorell, L., EVilella, E., Labad, A., Vallejo, J. Pérez, V., Menchón, J. M., Estivill, X., Gratacòs, M., & Urretavizcaya, M. (2010). Differential association of circadian genes with mood disorders: CRY1 and NPAS2 are associated with unipolar major depression and CLOCK and VIP with bipolar disorder. *Neuropsychopharmacology, 35*(6), 1279-1289. doi:10.1038/npp.2009.230
Soutschek, A., Ruff, C. C., Strombach, T., Kalenscher, T., & Tobler, P. N. (2016). Brain stimulation reveals crucial role of overcoming self-centeredness in self-control. *Science Advances, 2*(10), e1600992. doi:10.1126/sciadv.1600992
Sowislo, J. F., & Orth, U. (2013). Does low self-esteem predict depression and anxiety? A meta-analysis of longitudinal studies. *Psychological Bulletin, 139*(1), 213–240. doi:10.1037/a0028931
Spearman, C. (1904). General intelligence objectively determined and measured. *American Journal of Psychology, 15*, 107–197. doi:10.2307/1412107
Spearman, C. E. (1904). 'General intelligence' objectively determined and measured. *American Journal of Psychology, 5*, 201–293. doi:10.2307/1412107
Spears, R. (2017). Deindividuation. In S. G. Harkins, K. D. Williams, & J. M. Burger (Eds.), *Oxford library of psychology. The Oxford handbook of social influence* (pp. 279–297). New York, NY: Oxford University Press.
Speiser, P. W., Arlt, W., Auchus, R. J., Baskin, L. S., Conway, G. S., Merke, D. P., Meyer-Bahlburg, H. F. L., Miller, W. L., Murad, M. H., Oberfield, S. E., & White, P. C. (2018). Congenital adrenal hyperplasia due to steroid 21-hydroxylase deficiency: An Endocrine Society Clinical Practice Guideline. *The Journal of Clinical Endocrinology & Metabolism, 103*(11), 4043–4088. doi:10.1210/jc.2018-01865
Spence, S. A., Brooks, D. J., Hirsch, S. R., Liddle, P. F. Meehan, J., & Grasby, P. M. (1997). A PET study of voluntary movement in

schizophrenic patients experiencing passivity phenomena (delusions of alien control). *Brain Research: Brain Research Reviews, 120*, 1997–2011. doi:10.1093/brain/120.11.1997

Spencer, S. J., Logel, C., & Davies, P. G. (2016). Stereotype threat. *Annual Review of Psychology, 67*, 415–437. doi:10.1146/annurev-psych-073115-103235

Sperling, G. (1960). The information available in brief visual presentations. *Psychological Monographs, 74* (whole no. 11), 1–29. doi:10.1037/h0093759

Sperry, R. W. (1982). Some effects of disconnecting the cerebral hemispheres. *Science, 217*, 1223–1226. doi:10.1007/BF01115112

Spieker, L. E., Sudano, I., Hürlimann, D., Lerch, P. G., Lang, M. G., Binggeli, C., Corti, R., Ruschitzka, F., Lüscher, T. F., & Noll, G. (2002). High-density lipoprotein restores endothelial function in hypercholesterolemic men. *Circulation, 105*, 1399–1402. doi:10.1161/01.CIR.0000013424.28206.8F

Spira, J. L., Pyne, J. M., Wiederhold, B., Wiederhold, M., Graap, K., & Rizzo, A. (2006). Virtual reality and other experiential therapies for combat-related posttraumatic stress disorder. *Primary Psychiatry, 13*(3), 58–64.

Sprengnether, M. (1990). The spectral mother: Freud, feminism and psychoanalysis. Ithaca, NY: Cornell University Press.

Springer, S. P., & Deutsch, G. (1998). *Left brain, right brain* (5th ed.). New York: Freeman.

Squire, L. R. (1987). *Memory and the brain.* New York: Oxford University Press.

Stader, S. R., & Hokanson, J. E. (1998). Psychosocial antecedents of depressive symptoms: An evaluation using daily experiences methodology. *Journal of Abnormal Psychology, 107*(1), 17–26. doi:10.1037/0021-843x.107.1.17

Stanley, S. A., Connan, F., Small, C. J., Murphy, K. G., Todd, J. F., Ghatei, M., & al., e. (2003). Elevated circulating levels of cocaine- and amphetamine-regulated transcript (CART) in anorexia nervosa. *Endocrine Abstracts, 5*, OC30.

Stanton, C. A., Keith, D. R., Gaalema, D. E., Bunn, J. Y., Doogan, N. J., Redner, R., Kurti, A. N., Roberts, M. E., & Higgins, S. T. (2016). Trends in tobacco use among US adults with chronic health conditions: National Survey on Drug Use and Health 2005–2013. *Preventive Medicine, 92*, 160–168. doi:10.1016/j.ypmed.2016.04.008

Statista Research Department. (2020). *Murder rate in U.S. cities with 250k or more residents in 2018.* https://www.statista.com/statistics/718903/murder-rate-in-us-cities-in-2015/

Steblay, N. M., Dysart, J., Fulero, S., & Lindsay, R. C. L. (2001). Eyewitness accuracy rates in sequential and simultaneous lineup presentations: A meta-analytic comparison. *Law and Human Behavior, 25*, 459–474. doi:10.1023/A:1012888715007

Steele, C. M. (1997). A threat in the air: How stereotypes shape intellectual identity and performance. *American Psychologist, 52*, 613–629. doi:10.1037/0003-066X.52.6.613

Steele, C. M., & Aronson, J. (1995). Stereotype threat and the intellectual test performance of African Americans. *Journal of Personality and Social Psychology, 69*, 797–811. doi:10.1037/0022-3514.69.5.797

Stefanucci, J. K., & Proffitt, D. R. (2009). The roles of altitude and fear in the perception of height. *Journal of Experimental Psychology: Human Perception and Performance, 35*(2), 424–438. doi:10.1037/a0013894

Steiger, B. (2000). *American Indian medicine dream book.* Atglen, PA: Whitford Press.

Steigerwald, S., Wong, P. O., Cohen, B. E., Ishida, J. H., Vali, M., Madden, E., & Keyhani, S. (2018). Smoking, vaping, and use of edibles and other forms of marijuana among U.S. adults. *Annals of Internal Medicine, 169*(12), 890–892. doi:10.7326/m18-1681

Stein-Behrens, B., Mattson, M. P., Chang, I., Yeh, M., & Sapolsky, R. (1994). Stress exacerbates neuron loss and cytoskeletal pathology in the hippocampus. *Journal of Neuroscience, 14*, 5373–5380. doi:10.1523/JNEUROSCI.14-09-05373

Stein, D. J., Lim, C. C. W., Roest, A. M., de Jonge, P., Aguilar-Gaxiola, S., Al-Hamzawi, A., Alonso, J., Benjet, C., Bromet, E. J., Bruffaerts, R., de Girolamo, D., Florescu, S., Gureje, O., Haro, J. M., Harris, M. G., He, Y., Hinkov, H., Horiguchi, I., Hu, C., . . . WHO World Mental Health Survey Collaborators (2017). The cross-national epidemiology of social anxiety disorder: Data from the World Mental Health Survey Initiative. *BMC medicine, 15*(1), 143–143. doi:10.1186/s12916-017-0889-2

Steinberg, L., & Levine, A. (1997). *You and your adolescent: A parents' guide for ages 10 to 20.* New York, NY: Harper Perennial.

Stephan, W. S., & Stephan, C. W. (2000). An integrated threat theory of prejudice. In S. Oskamp (Ed.), *Reducing prejudice and discrimination* (pp. 23–46). New York, NY: Psychology Press.

Sternberg, R. J. (1985). *Beyond IQ: A triarchic theory of human intelligence*. New York, NY: Cambridge University Press.

Sternberg, R. J. (2004). A triangular theory of love. In H. T. Reis & C. D. Rusbult (Eds.), *Close relationships: Key readings* (pp. 213–227). Philadelphia, PA: Taylor & Francis.

Sternberg, R. J., & Salter, W. (1982). Conceptions of intelligence. In R. J. Sternberg (Ed.), *Handbook of human intelligence* (pp. 3–28). New York, NY: Cambridge University Press.

Sternberg, S. (1966). High speed scanning in human memory. *Science, 153*, 652–654. doi:10.1126/science.153.3736.652

Sternberg, S. (1967). Retrieval of contextual information from memory. *Psychonomic Science, 8*, 55–56. doi:10.3758/BF03330664

Sternberg, S. (1969). Memory scanning: Mental processes revealed by reaction-time experiments. *American Scientist, 57*, 421–457. https://www.jstor.org/stable/27828738

Sternglanz, R. W., Morris, W. L., Morrow, M., & Braverman, J. (2019). A review of meta-analyses about deception detection. In T. Docan-Morgan (Ed.), *The Palgrave handbook of deceptive communication* (pp. 303–326). Cham, Switzerland: Springer International Publishing.

Stevens, M. C., Levy, H. C., Hallion, L. S., Wootton, B. M., & Tolin, D. F. (2020). Functional neuroimaging test of an emerging neurobiological model of hoarding disorder. *Biological Psychiatry: Cognitive Neuroscience and Neuroimaging, 5*(1), 68–75. doi:10.1016/j.bpsc.2019.08.010

Stevens, S. S. (1960). Psychophysics of sensory function. *American Scientist, 48*, 226-252. https://www.jstor.org/stable/27827540

Stewart, S. T., Cutler, D. M., & Rosen, A. B. (2009). Forecasting the effects of obesity and smoking on U.S. life expectancy. *New England Journal of Medicine, 361*(23), 2252–2260. doi:10.1056/NEJMsa0900459

Stewart, W. K., & Fleming, L. W. (1973). Features of a successful therapeutic fast of 382 days' duration. *Postgraduate Medical Journal, 49*, 203–209. doi:10.1136/pgmj.49.569.203

Steyn, P., Wallstrom, A., & Pitt, L. (2010). Consumer-generated content and source effects in financial services advertising: An experimental study. *Journal of Financial Services Marketing, 15*(1), 49–61. doi:10.1057/fsm.2010.3

Stickgold, R., & Walker, M. P. (2007). Sleep-dependent memory consolidation and reconsolidation. *Sleep Medicine, 8*(4), 331–343. doi:10.1016/j.sleep.2007.03.011

Stickgold, R., James, L., & Hobson, J. A. (2000). Visual discrimination learning requires sleep after training. *Nature Neuroscience, 3*, 1237–1238. doi:10.1038/81756

Stoet, G., & Geary, D. C. (2012). Can stereotype threat explain the gender gap in mathematics performance and achievement? *Review of General Psychology, 16*(1),93–102. doi:10.1037/a0026617

Stokes, P. E. (1995). The potential role of excessive cortisol induced by HPA hyperfunction in the pathogenesis of depression. *European Neuropsychopharmacology, 5*, 77–82. doi:10.1016/0924-977x(95)00039-r

Stoller, R. J., & Herdt, G. H. (1985). Theories of origins of male homosexuality. A cross-cultural look. *Archives of General Psychiatry, 42*, 399–404. doi:10.1001/archpsyc.1985.01790270089010

Stomp, W., ten Duis, H.-J., & Nijsten, M. W. N. (2010). The impact of the lunar cycle on the incidence of trauma. *Trauma, 13*(2), 121–124.doi:10.1177/1460408610384655

Stoodley, C. (2014). Distinct regions of the cerebellum show grey matter decreases in autism, ADHD and developmental dyslexia. *Frontiers in Systems Neuroscience, 8*, 92. doi:10.3389/fnsys.2014.00092

Storebà, O. J. (2019). Methylphenidate benefits and harms in children and adolescents with attention deficit/hyperactivity disorder: Two Cochrane systematic reviews. *Movement and Nutrition in Health and Disease, 3*, 21–25. doi:10.5283/mnhd.15

Storebø, O. J., Pedersen, N., Ramstad, E., Krogh, H. B., Moreira-Maia, C. R., Magnusson, F. L., Holmskov, M., Gerner, T., Skoog, M., Rosendal, S., Groth, C., Gillies, D., Rasmussen, K. B., Gauci, D., Zwi, M., Kirubakaran, R., Håkonsen, S. J., . . . Gluud, C. (2016). Methylphenidate for attention deficit hyperactivity disorder (ADHD) in children and adolescents-Assessment of harmful effects in non-randomised studies. *Cochrane Database of Systematic Reviews, 2*, CD012069. doi:10.1002/14651858.CD012069.

Strack, F., Martin, L. L., & Stepper, S. (1988). Inhibiting and facilitating conditions of the human smile: A nonobtrusive test of the facial feedback hypothesis. *Journal of Personality and Social Psychology, 54*(5), 768–777. doi:10.1037/0022-3514.54.5.768

Strait, D. L., Kraus, N., Parbery-Clark, A., & Ashley, R. (2010). Musical experience shapes top-down auditory mechanisms: Evidence from masking and auditory attention performance. *Hearing Research, 261*(1-2), 22–29. doi:10.1016/j.heares.2009.12.021

Strasburger, V. C. (2007). First do no harm: Why have parents and pediatricians missed the boat on children and media? *The Journal of Pediatrics, 151*(4), 334–336. doi:10.1016/j.jpeds.2007.05.040

Straus, S. E., Richardson, W. S., Glasziou, P., & Haynes, R. B. (2005). *Evidence-based medicine: how to practice and teach EBM. (4th ed.).* Edinburgh, UK: Churchill Livingstone.

Strickland, B. R. (1992). Women and depression. *Current Directions in Psychological Science, 1*, 132–135. doi:10.1111/1467-8721.ep10769766

Stroop, J. R. (1935). Studies of interference in serial verbal reactions. *Journal of Experimental Psychology, 18*(6), 643–662. doi:10.1037/h0054651.

Stuss, D. T. (2011). Traumatic brain injury: Relation to executive dysfunction and the frontal lobes. *Current Opinion in Neurology, 24*(6), 584–589. doi:10.1017/S1355617711000695

Sugden, K., Arseneault, L., Harrington, H., Moffitt, T. E., Williams, B., & Caspi, A. (2010). Serotonin transporter gene moderates the development of emotional problems among children following bullying victimization. *Journal of the American Academy of Child & Adolescent Psychiatry, 49*(8), 830–840. doi:10.1016/j.jaac.2010.01.024

Sung, H.-Y., Prochaska, J. J., Ong, M. K., Shi, Y., & Max, W. (2011). Cigarette smoking and serious psychological distress: A population-based study of California adults. *Nicotine & Tobacco Research, 13*(12), 1183–1192. doi:10.1093/ntr/ntr148

Sunstein, C. R. (2002). Probability neglect: Emotions, worst cases, and law. *The Yale Law Journal, 112*(1), 61–107.

Suomi, S. J. (2006). Risk, Resilience, and gene × environment interactions in rhesus monkeys. *Annals of the New York Academy of Sciences, 1094*(1), 52–62. doi:10.1196/annals.1376.006

Super, C. M. (1976). Environmental effects on motor development: A case of African infant precocity. *Developmental Medicine and Child Neurology, 18*, 561–567. doi:10.1111/j.1469-8749.1976.tb04202.x

Susswein, A. J., Schwarz, M., & Feldman, E. (1986). Learned changes of feeding behavior in Aplysia in response to edible and inedible foods. *Journal of Neuroscience, 6*, 1513–1527. doi:10.1523/JNEUROSCI.06-05-01513

Sutton, R. M., & Douglas, K. M. (2005). Justice for all, or just me? More evidence of the importance of the self-other distinction in just world beliefs. *Personality and Individual Differences, 39*, 637–645. doi:10.1016/j.paid.2005.02.010

Svenningsson, P., Kim, Y., Warner-Schmidt, J., Oh, Y.-S., & Greengard, P. (2013). p11 and its role in depression and therapeutic responses to antidepressants. *Nature Reviews. Neuroscience, 14*(10), 673–680. doi:10.1038/nrn3564

Swaminathan, R., Burrows, G., & McMurray, J. (1982). Energy cost of sodium pump activity in man: An in vivo study of metabolic rate in human subjects given digoxin. *IRCS Medical Science, 10*, 949.

Swap, W. C. (1977). Interpersonal attraction and repeated exposure to rewarders and punishers. *Personality and Social Psychology Bulletin, 3*, 248–251. doi:10.1177/014616727700300219

Syvalahti, E. K. G. (1994). I. The theory of schizophrenia: Biological factors in schizophrenia. *British Journal of Psychiatry, 164*, 9–14.

Szalavitz, M. (2016). The genes for pot addiction have been identified. *Time*. https://time.com/4275880/the-genes-for-pot-addiction-have-been-identified/

Szeszko, P. R., Lehrner, A., & Yehuda, R. (2018). Glucocorticoids and hippocampal structure and function in PTSD. *Harvard Review of Psychiatry, 26*(3)142-157. doi:10.1097/HRP.0000000000000188

Taheri, S., & Mignot, E. (2002). The genetics of sleep disorders. *The Lancet Neurology, 1*(4), 242–250. doi:10.1016/S1474-4422(02)00103-5

Tajfel, H. (1982). Social psychology of intergroup relations. *Annual Review of Psychology, 33*(1), 1–39. doi:10.1146/annurev.ps.33.020182.000245

Tajfel, H., & Turner, J. (1979). An integrative theory of intergroup conflict. In W. G. Austin & S. Worchel (Eds.), *The social psychology of intergroup relations* (pp. 33–47). Monterey, CA: Brooks/Cole.

Takano, Y., & Osaka, E. (2018). Comparing Japan and the United States on individualism/collectivism: A follow-up review. *Asian Journal of Social Psychology, 21*(4), 301–316. doi:10.1111/ajsp.12322

Takooshian, H., Plous, S., Gielen, U. P., Rich, G. J., & Velayo, R. S. (2016). Internationalizing undergraduate psychology education: Trends, techniques, and technologies. *American Psychologist, 71*(2), 136–147. doi:10.1037/a0039977

Talhelm, T., Zhang, X., Oishi, S., Shimin, C., Duan, D., Lan, X., & Kitayama, S. (2014). Large-scale psychological differences within China explained by rice versus wheat agriculture. *Science, 344*(6184), 603–608. doi:10.1126/science.1246850

Tallal, P., Ross, R., & Curtiss, S. (1989). Familial aggregation in specific language impairment. *Journal of Speech and Hearing Disorders, 54*(2), 167–173. doi:10.1044/jshd.5402.167

Tamnes, C. K., Herting, M. M., Goddings, A. L., Meuwese, R., Blakemore, S. J., Dahl, R. E., Güroğlu, B., Raznahan, A., Sowell, E. R., Crone, E. A., & Mills, K. L. (2017). Development of the cerebral cortex across adolescence: A multisample study of inter-related longitudinal changes in cortical volume, surface area, and thickness. *Journal of Neuroscience, 37*(12), 3402–3412. doi:10.1523/jneurosci.3302-16.2017

Tang, Y.-Y., & Posner, M. I. (2009). Attention training and attention state training. *Trends in Cognitive Sciences, 13*(5), 223–227. doi:10.1016/j.tics.2009.01.009

Tarumi, S., Ichimiya, A., Yamada, S., Umesue, M., & Kuroki, T. (2004). Taijin kyofusho in university students: Patterns of fear and predispositions to the offensive variant. *Transcultural Psychiatry, 41*(4):533–546. doi:10.1177/1363461504047933

Taylor, D. A., & Altman, I. (1987). Communication in interpersonal relationships: Social penetration processes. In M. E. Roloff & G. R. Miller (Eds.), *Interpersonal processes: New directions in communication research* (pp. 257–277). Thousand Oaks, CA: Sage.

Taylor, D. A., & Genkov, K. A. (2019). Hypnotherapy for the treatment of persistent pain: A literature review. *Journal of the American Psychiatric Nurses Association, 26(2):157–161.*, 1078390319835604. doi:10.1177/1078390319835604

Taylor, L. E., Swerdfeger, A. L., & Eslick, G. D. (2014). Vaccines are not associated with autism: An evidence-based meta-analysis of case-control and cohort studies. *Vaccine, 32*(29), 3623–3629. doi:10.1016/j.vaccine.2014.04.085

Taylor, L., Faraone, S. V., & Tsuang, M. T. (2002). Family, twin, and adoption studies of bipolar disease. *Current Psychiatry Reports, 4*, 130–133. doi:10.1007/s11920-002-0046-1

Taylor, S. E. (2006). Tend and befriend: Biobehavioral bases of affiliation under stress. *Current Directions in Psychological Science, 15*(6), 273–277. doi:10.1111/j.1467-8721.2006.00451.x

Taylor, S. E., & Brown, J. D. (1988). Illusion and well-being: A social psychological perspective on mental health. *Psychological Bulletin, 103*, 193–210. doi:10.1037/0033-2909.103.2.193

Teasdale, J. D., Segal, Z. V., Williams, J. M. G., Ridgeway, V. A., Soulsby, J. M., & Lau, M. A. (2000). Prevention of relapse/recurrence in major depression by mindfulness-based cognitive therapy. *Journal of Consulting and Clinical Psychology, 68*(4), 615–623. doi:10.1037/0022-006X.68.4.615

Temple, J. L., Bernard, C., Lipshultz, S. E., Czachor, J. D., Westphal, J. A., & Mestre, M. A. (2017). The safety of ingested caffeine: A comprehensive review. *Frontiers in Psychiatry, 8*(80). doi:10.3389/fpsyt.2017.00080

Terman, L. (1916). *The measurement of intelligence*. Boston, MA: Houghton Mifflin.

Terman, L. (1925). *Genetic studies of genius: Vol. 1. Mental and physical traits of a thousand gifted children*. Stanford, CA: Stanford University Press.

Terman, L., & Oden, M. H. (1959). *Genetic studies of genius: Vol. 5. The gifted group at midlife*. Stanford, CA: Stanford University Press.

Terrace, H. S. (1979). How Nim Chimpsky changed my mind. *Psychology Today, 13*(6), 65–76.

Terry, D. J. (1994). Determinants of coping: The role of stable and situational factors. *Journal of Personality and Social Psychology, 66*(5), 895–910. doi:10.1037/0022-3514.66.5.895

Thannickal, T. C., Moore, R. Y., Nienhuis, R., Ramanathan, L., Gulyani, S., Aldrich, M., Cornford, M., & Siegel, J. M. (2000). Reduced number of hypocretin neurons in human narcolepsy. *Neuron, 27*(3), 469–474. doi:10.1016/S0896-6273(00)00058-1

The Premier's Highly Skilled Workforce Panel (2016). Building the workforce of tomorrow. https://www.ontario.ca/page/building-workforce-tomorrow-shared-responsibility

The World Bank. (2017). Fertility rate, total (births per woman) | Data. https://data.worldbank.org/indicator/SP.DYN.TFRT.IN?end=2017&start=1960&view=chart

Theusch, E., Basu, A., & Gitschier, J. (2009). Genome-wide study of families with absolute pitch reveals linkage to 8q24.21 and locus heterogeneity. *American Journal of Human Genetics, 85*(1), 112–119. doi:10.1016/j.ajhg.2009.06.010

Thierry, B. (1994). Emergence of social organizations in non-human primates. *Revue Internationale de Syste mique, 8*, 65–77.

Thomaes, S., Bushman, B. J., De Castro, B. O., & Stegge, H. (2009). What makes narcissists bloom? A framework for research on the etiology and development of narcissism. *Development and Psychopathology, 21*(04), 1233–1247. doi:10.1017/S0954579409990137

Thomas, A., & Chess, S. (1977). *Temperament and development*. New York, NY: Brunner/Mazel.

Thomas, J. L., Wilk, J. E., Riviere, L. A., McGurk, D., Castro, C. A., & Hoge, C. W. (2010). Prevalence of mental health problems and functional impairment among Active Component and National Guard soldiers 3 and 12 months following combat in Iraq. *Archives of General Psychiatry, 67*(6), 614–623. doi:10.1001/archgenpsychiatry.2010.54

Thomas, L. A., De Bellis, M. D., Graham, R., & LaBar, K. S. (2007). Development of emotional facial recognition in late childhood and adolescence. *Developmental Science, 10*(5), 547–558. doi:10.1111/j.1467-7687.2007.00614.x

Thomas, M. M., Harpaz-Rotem, I., Tsai, J., Southwick, S. M., & Pietrzak, R. H. (2017). Mental and physical health conditions in US combat veterans: Results from the National Health and Resilience in Veterans Study. *The Primary Care Companion for CNS Disorders, 19*(3),17m02118. doi:10.4088/PCC.17m02118

Thompson, M. A., Callaghan, P. D., Hunt, G. E., Cornish, J. L., & McGregor, I. S. (2007). A role for oxytocin and 5-HT(1A) receptors in the prosocial effects of 3,4 methylenedioxymethamphetamine ("ecstasy"). *Neuroscience, 146*(2), 509–514. doi:10.1016/j.neuroscience.2007.02.032

Thompson, P. M., Vidal, C., Giedd, J. N., Gochman, P., Blumenthal, J., Nicolson, R., Toga, A. W., & Rapoport, J. L. (2001). Mapping adolescent brain change reveals dynamic wave of accelerated gray matter loss in very early-onset schizophrenia. *Proceedings of the National Academy of Sciences of the United States of America, 98*, 11650–11655. doi:10.1073/pnas.201243998

Thorndike, E. L. (1913). *Educational psychology: Briefer course*. New York, NY: Teachers College, Columbia University.

Thornhill, R., & Gangestad, S. W. (1994). Fluctuating asymmetry correlates with lifetime sex partner numbers and age at first sex in *Homo sapiens*. *Psychological Science, 5*, 297–303. doi:10.1111/j.1467-9280.1994.tb00629.x

Thorpe, W. H. (1963). *Learning and instinct in animals* (2nd ed.). Cambridge, MA: Harvard University Press.

Thyer, B. A. (2004). What is evidence-based practice? *Brief Treatment and Crisis Intervention, 4*(2), 167—176. doi:10.1093/brief-treatment/mhh013

Tickell, A., Ball, S., Bernard, P., Kuyken, W., Marx, R., Pack, S., Strauss, C., Sweeney, T., & Crane, C. (2020). The effectiveness of mindfulness-based cognitive therapy (MBCT) in real-world healthcare services. *Mindfulness, 11*(2), 279–290. doi:10.1007/s12671-018-1087-9

Tien, A. Y. (1991). Distribution of hallucinations in the population. *Social Psychiatry and Psychiatric Epidemiology, 26*(6), 287–292. doi:10.1007/bf00789221

Tinbergen, N. (1951). *The study of instinct*. New York: Oxford University Press.

Titone, D., Levy, D. L., & Holzman, P. S. (2000). Contextual insensitivity in schizophrenic language processing: Evidence from lexical ambiguity. *Journal of Abnormal Psychology, 109*, 761–767. doi:10.1037/0021-843X.109.4.761

Todorova, R., & Zugaro, M. (2019). Isolated cortical computations during delta waves support memory consolidation. *Science, 366*(6463), 377–381. doi:10.1126/science.aay0616

Tolman, E. C. (1948). Cognitive maps in rats and men. *Psychological Review, 55*, 189–208. doi:10.1037/h0061626

Tolman, E. C. (1959). Principles of purposive behavior. In S. Koch (Ed.), *Psychology: A study of a science* (Vol. 2, pp. 92–157). New York, NY: McGraw-Hill.

Tolman, E. C., Richie, B. F., & Kalish, D. (1946). Studies in spatial learning: II. Place learning vs. response learning. *Journal of Experimental Psychology, 36*, 221–229. doi:10.1037/h0060262

Tomova, L., Majdandžić, J., Hummer, A., Windischberger, C., Heinrichs, M., & Lamm, C. (2016). Increased neural responses to empathy for pain might explain how acute stress increases prosociality. *Social Cognitive and Affective Neuroscience, 12*(3), 401–408. doi:10.1093/scan/nsw146

Toro, J. M. (2016). Something old, something new: Combining mechanisms during language acquisition. *Current Directions in Psychological Science, 25*(2), 130–134. doi:10.1177/0963721416629645

Touitou, Y., Reinberg, A., & Touitou, D. (2017). Association between light at night, melatonin secretion, sleep deprivation, and the internal clock: Health impacts and mechanisms of circadian disruption. *Life Sciences, 173*, 94–106. doi:10.1016/j.lfs.2017.02.008

Travis, F. (2001). Autonomic and EEG patterns distinguish transcending from other experiences during Transcendental Meditation practice. *International Journal of Psychophysiology, 42*(1), 1–9. doi:10.1016/S0167-8760(01)pp143-X

Travis, F. (2020). Temporal and spatial characteristics of meditation EEG. *Psychological Trauma: Theory, Research, Practice, and Policy , 12*(2), 111–115. doi:10.1037/tra0000488

Treffert, D. A., & Wallace, G. L. (2002). Islands of genius. *Scientific American, 286*(6), 76–85.

Treynor, W., Gonzalez, R., & Nolen-Hoeksema, S. (2003). Rumination reconsidered: A psychometric analysis. *Cognitive Therapy and Research, 27*(3), 247–259. doi:10.1023/A:1023910315561

Trimble, J. E., Stevenson, M. R., & Worrell, J. P. (2003). *Toward an inclusive psychology:*

Infusing the introductory psychology textbook with diversity content. Washington, D.C.: American Psychological Association.
Triplett, N. (1898). The dynamogenic factors in pacemaking and competition. *American Journal of Psychology, 9*, 507–533. doi:10.2307/1412188
Trivers, R. L. (1971). The evolution of reciprocal altruism. *The Quarterly Review of Biology, 46*(1), 35–57. doi:10.2307/2822435
Trivers, R., & Burt, A. (1999). Kinship and genomic imprinting. *Results and Problems in Cell Differentiation, 25*, 1–21. doi:10.1007/978-3-540-69111-2_1
Trockel, M. T., Barnes, M. D., & Egget, D. L. (2000). Health-related variables and academic performance among first-year college students: Implications for sleep and other behaviors. *Journal of American College Health, 49*(3), 125–131. doi:10.1080/07448480009596294
Tsang, J.-A., Carpenter, T. P., Roberts, J. A., Frisch, M. B., & Carlisle, R. D. (2014). Why are materialists less happy? The role of gratitude and need satisfaction in the relationship between materialism and life satisfaction. *Personality and Individual Differences, 64*, 62–66. doi:10.1016/j.paid.2014.02.009
Tulving, E. (1972). Episodic and semantic memory. In E. Tulving & W. Donaldson (Eds.), *Organization and memory* (pp. 381–403). New York, NY: Academic Press.
Tulving, E. (1983). *Elements of episodic memory.* Oxford, England: Clarendon Press/Oxford University Press.
Tulving, E. (1985). How many memory systems are there? *American Psychologist, 40*, 385–398. doi:10.1037/0003-066X.40.4.385
Tulving, E. (1989). Memory: Performance, knowledge, and experience. *European Journal of Cognitive Psychology, 1*, 3–26. doi:10.1080/09541448908403069
Tulving, E. (1995). Organization of memory. In M. S. Gazzaniga (Ed.), *The cognitive neurosciences* (pp. 839–853). Cambridge, MA: The MIT Press.
Tulving, E., & Psotka, J. (1971). Retroactive inhibition in free recall: Inaccessibility of information available in the memory store. *Journal of Experimental Psychology, 87*, 1–8. doi:10.1037/h0030185
Tulving, E., & Thomson, D.M. (1973). Encoding specificity and retrieval processes in episodic memory. *Psychological Review, 80*, 352–373. doi:10.1037/h0020071
Turkheimer, E., Haley, A., Waldron, M., d'Onofrio, B., & Gottesman, I. I. (2003). Socioeconomic status modifies heritability of IQ in young children. *Psychological Science, 14*(6), 623–628. doi:10.1046/j.0956-7976.2003.psci_1475.x
Turnbaugh, P. J., Ley, R. E., Mahowald, M. A., Magrini, V., Mardis, E. R., & Gordon, J. I. (2006). An obesity-associated gut microbiome with increased capacity for energy harvest. *Nature, 444*(7122), 1027–1131. doi:10.1038/nature05414
Turnbull, H. W. (1959). *The correspondence of Isaac Newton* (Vol. 1). Cambridge, UK: Cambridge University Press for the Royal Society.
Turner, C. E., Byblow, W. D., Stinear, C. M., & Gant, N. (2014). Carbohydrate in the mouth enhances activation of brain circuitry involved in motor performance and sensory perception. *Appetite, 80*(0), 212–219. doi:10.1016/j.appet.2014.05.020
Tversky, A., & Kahneman, D. (1973). Availability: A heuristic for judging frequency and probability. *Cognitive Psychology, 5*(2), 207–232. doi:10.1016/0010-0285(73)90033-9
Tversky, A., & Kahneman, D. (1974). Judgment under uncertainty: Heuristics and biases. *Science, 185*(4157), 1124–1131. doi:10.1126/science.185.4157.1124
Tversky, A., & Kahneman, D. (1987). Rational choice and the framing of decisions. In R. M. Hogarth & M. W. Reder (Eds.), *Rational choice: The contrast between economics and psychology* (pp. 67–94). Chicago: University of Chicago Press.
Twenge, J. M. (2013). The evidence for Generation Me and against Generation We. *Emerging Adulthood, 1*(1), 11–16. doi:10.1177/2167696812466548
Twenge, J. M. (2014). *Generation me: Why today's young Americans are more confident, assertive, entitled-and more miserable than ever before.* New York, NY: Simon & Schuster.
Twenge, J. M., & Campbell, W. K. (2009). *The narcissism epidemic: Living in the age of entitlement* . New York, NY: Simon and Schuster.
Twenge, J. M., & Crocker, J. (2002). Race and self-esteem: Meta-analyses comparing Whites, Blacks, Hispanics, Asians, and American Indians. *Psychological Bulletin, 128*, 371–408. doi:10.1037/0033-2909.128.3.371
Twenge, J. M., Baumeister, R. F., Tice, D. M., & Stucke, T. S. (2001). If you can't join them, beat them: Effects of social exclusion on aggressive behavior. *Journal of Personality and Social Psychology, 81*(6), 1058–1969. doi:10.1037/0022-3514.81.6.1058
Twenge, J. M., Campbell, W. K., & Foster, C. A. (2003). Parenthood and marital satisfaction: A meta-analytic review. *Journal of Marriage and Family, 65*(3), 574–583. doi:10.1111/j.1741-3737.2003.00574.x
Twenge, J. M., Cooper, A. B., Joiner, T. E., Duffy, M. E., & Binau, S. G. (2019). Age, period, and cohort trends in mood disorder indicators and suicide-related outcomes in a nationally representative dataset, 2005–2017. *Journal of Abnormal Psychology, 128*(3), 185–199. doi:10.1037/abn0000410
Ueda, Y., Chen, L., Kopecky, J., Cramer, E. S., Rensink, R. A., Meyer, D. E., Kitayama, S., & Saiki, J. (2018). Cultural differences in visual search for geometric figures. *Cognitive Science, 42*(1), 286–310. doi:10.1111/cogs.12490
Ullman, L. P., & Krasner, L. (1965). *Case studies in behavior modification.* New York, NY: Holt. Rinehart and Winston.
Uncapher, H., & Areán, P. A. (2000). Physicians are less willing to treat suicidal ideation in older patients. *Journal of the American Geriatrics Society, 48*(2), 188–192. doi:10.1111/j.1532-5415.2000.tb03910.x
Underwood, B. J. (1957). Interference and forgetting. *Psychological Review, 64*, 49–60. doi:10.1037/h0044616
United Nations. (2020). World population prospects: The 2019 revision. https://population.un.org/wpp/Maps/
UNODC. (2019). *Global study on homicide.* Vienna, Austria: United Nations.
U. S. Department of Education Office of Educational Research and Improvement. (1993). *National excellence: A case for developing America's talent.* Washington, DC: U.S. Government Printing Office.
US Department of Health and Human Services. (2014). The health consequences of smoking—50 years of progress: A report of the Surgeon General. Atlanta, GA: US Department of Health and Human Services, Centers for Disease Control and Prevention, National Center for Chronic Disease Presention and Health Promotion, Office on Smoking and Health.
U.S. Fish and Wildlife Service. (2014). *Mexican Wolf Recovery Program: Progress report #17.* https://www.fws.gov/southwest/es/mexicanwolf/pdf/2014_MW_Progress_Report.pdf
Üstün, T. B., Ayuso-Mateos, J. L., Chatterji, S., Mathers, C., & Murray, C. J. L. (2004). Global burden of depressive disorders in the year 2000. *The British Journal of Psychiatry, 184*(5), 386–392. doi:10.1192/bjp.184.5.386
Vaillant, G. E. (2003). A 60-year follow-up of alcoholic men. *Addiction, 98*(8), 1043–1051. doi:10.1046/j.1360-0443.2003.00422.x
Vaillant, G. E., & Koury, S. H. (1993). Late midlife development. In G. H. Pollock & S. I. Greenspan (Eds.), *The course of life, Vol. 6: Late adulthood (rev. and exp. ed.).* (pp. 1–22). Madison, CT US: International Universities Press, Inc.
Vaitl, D., Birbaumer, N., Gruzelier, J., Jamieson, G. A., Kotchoubey, B., Kübler, A., Lehmann, D., Miltner, W. H. R., Ott, U., Pütz, P., Sammer, G., Strauch, I., Strehl, U., Wackermann, J., & Weiss, T. (2005). Psychobiology of altered states of consciousness. *Psychological Bulletin, 131*(1), 98–127. doi:10.1037/0033-2909.131.1.98
Valenstein, E. S. (1986). *Great and desperate cures.* New York, NY: Basic Books.
Van Cauter, E., Leproult, R., & Plat, L. (2000). Age-related changes in slow wave sleep and REM sleep and relationship with growth hormone and cortisol levels in healthy men. *JAMA, 284*(7), 861–868. doi:10.1001/jama.284.7.861
Van Erp, T. G., Walton, E., Hibar, D. P., Schmaal, L., Jiang, W., Glahn, D. C., Pearlson, G.

D., Yao, N., Fukunaga, M., Hashimoto, R., Okada, N., Yamamori, H., Bustillo, J. R., Clark, V. P., Agartz, I., Mueller, B. A., Cahn, W., de Zwarte, S. M. C., . . . Turner, J. A. (2018). Cortical brain abnormalities in 4474 individuals with schizophrenia and 5098 control subjects via the Enhancing Neuro Imaging Genetics Through Meta Analysis (ENIGMA) Consortium. *Biological Psychiatry, 84*(9), 644–654. doi:10.1016/j.biopsych.2018.04.023

Van Haren, N., Cahn, W., Hulshoff Pol, H., & Kahn, R. (2013). Confounders of excessive brain volume loss in schizophrenia. *Neuroscience & Biobehavioral Reviews, 37*(10), 2418–2423. doi:10.1016/j.neubiorev.2012.09.006

Van Haren, N. E., Cahn, W., Hulshoff Pol, H. E., & Kahn, R. S. (2013). Confounders of excessive brain volume loss in schizophrenia. *Neuroscience & Biobehavioral Reviews, 37*(10, Part 1), 2418–2423. doi:10.1016/j.neubiorev.2012.09.006

Van Horn, J. D., Irimia, A., Torgerson, C. M., Chambers, M. C., Kikinis, R., & Toga, A. W. (2012). Mapping connectivity damage in the case of Phineas Gage. *PLoS ONE, 7*(5), e37454. doi:10.1371/journal.pone.0037454

Van Knippenberg, D., & Wilke, H. (1992). Prototypicality of arguments and conformity to ingroup norms. *European Journal of Social Psychology, 22*, 141–155. doi:10.1002/ejsp.2420220204

van Londen, L., Goekoop, J. G., van Kempen, G. M. J., Frankhuijzen-Sierevogel, A. C., Wiegant, V. M., van der Velde, E. A., & De Wied, D. (1997). Plasma levels of arginine vasopressin elevated in patients with major depression. *Neuropsychopharmacology, 17*, 284–292. doi:10.1016/S0893-133X(97)00054-7

van Rijn, S. (2019). A review of neurocognitive functioning and risk for psychopathology in sex chromosome trisomy (47, XXY, 47, XXX, 47, XYY). *Current Opinion in Psychiatry, 32*(2), 79–84. doi:10.1097/YCO.0000000000000471

Vandesande, S., Bosmans, G., Schuengel, C., & Maes, B. (2019). Young children with significant developmental delay differentiate home observed attachment behaviour towards their parents. *Journal of Applied Research in Intellectual Disabilities, 32*(1), 106–120. doi:10.1111/jar.12513

VanRullen, R., & Reddy, L. (2019). Reconstructing faces from fMRI patterns using deep generative neural networks. *Communications Biology, 2*(1), 193. doi:10.1038/s42003-019-0438-y

Vasconcelos-Moreno, M. P., Fries, G. R., Gubert, C., Dos Santos, B., Fijtman, A., Sartori, J., . . . Guma, F. (2017). Telomere length, oxidative stress, inflammation and BDNF levels in siblings of patients with bipolar disorder: Implications for accelerated cellular aging. *The International Journal of Neuropsychopharmacology. 20*(6):445-454. doi:10.1093/ijnp/pyx001

Vater, A., Moritz, S., & Roepke, S. (2018). Does a narcissism epidemic exist in modern western societies? Comparing narcissism and self-esteem in East and West Germany. *PloS One, 13*(1), e0188287. doi:10.1371/journal.pone.0188287

Vega, M. L., Newport, G. C., Bozhdaraj, D., Saltz, S. B., Nemeroff, C. B., & Newport, D. J. (2020). Implementation of advanced methods for reproductive pharmacovigilance in autism: A meta-analysis of the effects of prenatal antidepressant exposure. *American Journal of Psychiatry, 177*(6), 506–517. doi:10.1176/appi.ajp.2020.18070766

Velickovic, K., Wayne, D., Leija, H. A. L., Bloor, I., Morris, D. E., Law, J., Budge, H., Sacks, H., Symonds, M. E., & Sottile, V. (2019). Caffeine exposure induces browning features in adipose tissue in vitro and in vivo. *Scientific Reports, 9*(1), 9104. doi:10.1038/s41598-019-45540-1

Verdejo-Garcia, A., Clark, L., & Dunn, B. D. (2012). The role of interoception in addiction: A critical review. *Neuroscience & Biobehavioral Reviews, 36*(8), 1857–1869. doi:10.1016/j.neubiorev.2012.05.007

Vermetten, E., Schmahl, C., Southwick, S. M., & Bremner, J. D. (2007). Positron tomographic emission study of olfactory induced emotional recall in veterans with and without combat-related posttraumatic stress disorder. *Psychopharmacology Bulletin, 40*(1), 8–30.

Verweij, K. J., Abdellaoui, A., Nivard, M. G., Cort, A. S., Ligthart, L., Draisma, H. H., Minică, C. C., International Cannabis Consortium, Gillespie, N. A., Willemsen, G., Hottenga, J.-J., Boomsma, D. I., & Vink, J. M. (2017). Genetic association between schizophrenia and cannabis use. *Drug and Alcohol Dependence, 171*, 117–121. doi:10.1016/j.drugalcdep.2016.09.022

Vescio, T. K., Judd, C. M., & Kwan, V. S. Y. (2004). The crossed-categorization hypothesis: Evidence of reductions in the strength of categorization, but not intergroup bias. *Journal of Experimental Social Psychology, 40*(4), 478–496. doi:10.1016/j.jesp.2003.09.005

Vestergaard-Poulsen, P., van Beek, M., Skewes, J., Bjarkam, C. R., Stubberup, M., Bertelsen, J., & Roepstorff, A. (2009). Long-term meditation is associated with increased gray matter density in the brain stem. *NeuroReport, 20*(2), 170–174. doi:10.1097/WNR.0b013e328320012a

Vijayan, S., Lepage, K. Q., Kopell, N. J., & Cash, S. S. (2017). Frontal beta-theta network during REM sleep. *eLife, 6*, e18894. doi:10.7554/eLife.18894

Virués-Ortega, J. (2010). Applied behavior analytic intervention for autism in early childhood: Meta-analysis, meta-regression and dose–response meta-analysis of multiple outcomes. *Clinical Psychology Review, 30*(4), 387–399. doi:10.1016/j.cpr.2010.01.008

Visser, B. A., Ashton, M. C., & Vernon, P. A. (2006). Beyond g: Putting multiple intelligences theory to the test. *Intelligence, 34*(5), 507–510. doi:10.1016/j.intell.2006.02.004

Visser, S. N., Danielson, M. L., Bitsko, R. H., Holbrook, J. R., Kogan, M. D., Ghandour, R. M., Perou, R., & Blumberg, S. J. (2014). Trends in the parent-report of health care provider-diagnosed and medicated attention-deficit/hyperactivity disorder: United States, 2003–2011. *Journal of the American Academy of Child & Adolescent Psychiatry, 53*(1), 34–46. doi:10.1016/j.jaac.2013.09.001

Vivanti, A. J., Vauloup-Fellous, C., Prevot, S., Zupan, V., Suffee, C., Do Cao, J., Benachi, A., & De Luca, D. (2020). Transplacental transmission of SARS-CoV-2 infection. *Nature Communications, 11*(1), 3572. doi:10.1038/s41467-020-17436-6

Voineagu, I., Wang, X., Johnston, P., Lowe, J. K., Tian, Y., Horvath, S., Mill, J., Cantor, R. M., Blencowe, B. J., & Geschwind, D. H. (2011). Transcriptomic analysis of autistic brain reveals convergent molecular pathology. *Nature, 474*(7351), 380–384. doi:10.1038/nature10110

Volk, D. W., & Lewis, D. A. (2016). The role of endocannabinoid signaling in cortical inhibitory neuron dysfunction in schizophrenia. *Biological Psychiatry, 79*(7), 595–603. doi10.1016/j.biopsych.2015.06.015

Volkow, N. D., Swanson, J. M., Evins, A. E., DeLisi, L. E., Meier, M. H., Gonzalez, R., Bloomfield, M. A. P., Curran, H. V., & Baler, R. (2016). Effects of cannabis use on human behavior, including cognition, motivation, and psychosis: A review. *JAMA Psychiatry, 73*(3), 292–297. doi:10.1001/jamapsychiatry.2015.3278

Volkow, N. D., Wang, G.-J., Fowler, J. S., & Ding, Y.-S. (2005). Imaging the effects of methylphenidate on brain dopamine: New model on its therapeutic actions for attention-deficit/hyperactivity disorder. *Biological Psychiatry, 57*(11), 1410–1415. doi:10.1016/j.biopsych.2004.11.006

Volkow, N. D., Wang, G.-J., Kollins, S. H., Wigal, T. L., Newcorn, J. H., Telang, F., Fowler, J. S., Zhu, W., Logan, J., Ma, Y., Pradhan, K., Wong, C., & Swanson, J. M. (2009). Evaluating dopamine reward pathway in ADHD: Clinical implications. *JAMA, 302*(10), 1084–1091. doi:10.1001/jama.2009.1308

Vorstman, J. A., Parr, J. R., Moreno-De-Luca, D., Anney, R. J., Nurnberger Jr, J. I., & Hallmayer, J. F. (2017). Autism genetics: Opportunities and challenges for clinical translation. *Nature Reviews Genetics, 18*, 362–376. doi:10.1038/nrg.2017.4

Vries, S. K., & Meule, A. (2016). Food addiction and bulimia nervosa: New data based on the Yale Food Addiction Scale 2.0. *European Eating Disorders Review, 24*(6), 518–522. doi:10.1002/erv.2470

Vrij, A. (2015). A cognitive approach to lie detection. In P. Granhag, V. A., & B. Verschuere (Eds.), *Deception detection:*

Current challenges and new approaches (pp. 205–229). Malden, MA: Wiley-Blackwell.

Wade, M., Fox., N. A., Zeanah, C. H., & Nelson, C. A. (2018). Effect of foster care intervention on trajectories of general and specific psychopathology among children with histories of institutional rearing: A randomized clinical trial. *JAMA Psychiatry, 75,* 1137–1145.doi:10.1001/jamapsychiatry.2018.2556

Wadee, A. A., Kuschke, R. H., Kometz, S., & Berk, M. (2001). Personality factors, stress and immunity. Stress and Health. *Journal of the International Society for the Investigation of Stress, 17*(1), 25–40. doi:10.1002/1532-2998(200101)17:1<25::AIDSMI873>3.0.CO;2-N

Wagenmakers, E.-J., Beek, T., Dijkhoff, L., Gronau, Q. F., Acosta, A., Adams, Jr., R. B., Alborn, D. N., Allard, E. S., Benning, S. D., Blouin-Hudon, E.-M., Bulnes, L. C., Caldwell, T. L., Calin-Jageman, R. J., Capaldi, C. A., Carfagno, N. S., Chasten, K. T., Cleeremans, A., Connell, L., DeCicco, J. M., Dijkstra, K., ... Zwaan, R. A. (2016). Registered replication report: Strack, Martin, & Stepper (1988). *Perspectives on Psychological Science, 11*(6), 917–928. doi:10.1177/1745691616674458

Wager, T. D., & Barrett, L. F. (2017). From affect to control: Functional specialization of the insula in motivation and regulation. *bioRxiv*, 102368. doi:10.1101/102368

Wagner, D. R. (1996). Disorders of the circadian sleep–wake cycle. *Neurologic Clinics, 14*(3), 651–670. doi:10.1016/S0733-8619(05)70278-4

Wainer, H., & Steinberg, L. (1992). Sex differences in performance on the mathematics section of the Scholastic Aptitude Test: A bidirectional validity study. *Harvard Educational Review, 62*(3), 323–337. doi:10.17763/haer.62.3.1p1555011301r133

Waite, L. J., Luo, Y., & Lewin, A. C. (2009). Marital happiness and marital stability: Consequences for psychological well-being. *Social Science Research, 38*(1), 201–212. doi:10.1016/j.ssresearch.2008.07.001

Waite, L., & Gallagher, M. (2001). *The case for marriage: Why married people are happier, healthier, and better off financially.* New York, NY: Random House.

Waldinger, R. J., & Schulz, M. S. (2010). What's love got to do with it? Social functioning, perceived health, and daily happiness in married octogenarians. *Psychology and Aging, 25*(2), 422–431. doi:10.1037/a0019087

Walker, A., & Shipman, P. (1996). *The wisdom of the bones: In search of human origins.* New York, NY: Alfred A. Knopf, Inc.

Walker, J. (2001). *Control and the psychology of health: Theory, measurement and applications.* Philadelphia, PA: Open University Press

Walster, E., Aronson, V., & Abrahams, D. (1966). Importance of physical attractiveness in dating behavior. *Journal of Personality and Social Psychology, 4,* 508–516. doi:10.1037/h0021188

Walters, S. (1994). Algorithms and archetypes: Evolutionary psychology and Carl Jung's theory of the collective unconscious. *Journal of Social and Evolutionary Systems, 17*(3), 287–306. doi:10.1016/1061-7361(94)90013-2

Walton, G. M., & Cohen, G. L. (2011). A brief social-belonging intervention improves academic and health outcomes of minority students. *Science, 331*(6023), 1447–1451. doi:10.1126/science.1198364

Walton, K., Kleinman, K. P., Rifas-Shiman, S. L., Horton, N. J., Gillman, M. W., Field, A. E., Austin, S. B., Neumark-Sztainer, D., & Haines, J. (2016). Secular trends in family dinner frequency among adolescents. *BMC Research Notes, 9*(1), 35. doi:10.1186/s13104-016-1856-2

Wang, C. X., Hilburn, I. A., Wu, D.-A., Mizuhara, Y., Cousté, C. P., Abrahams, J. N. H., Bernstein, S. E., Matani, A., Shimojo, S., & Kirschvink, J. L. (2019). Transduction of the geomagnetic field as evidenced from alpha-band activity in the human brain. *eneuro, 6*(2), ENEURO.0483-0418.2019. doi:10.1523/eneuro.0483-18.2019

Wang, Q. (2008). Emotion knowledge and autobiographical memory across the preschool years: A cross-cultural longitudinal investigation. *Cognition, 108*(1), 117–135. doi:10.1016/j.cognition.2008.02.002

Wang, R., Yang, F., & Haigh, M. M. (2017). Let me take a selfie: Exploring the psychological effects of posting and viewing selfies and groupies on social media. *Telematics and Informatics, 34*(4), 274–283. doi:10.1016/j.tele.2016.07.004

Ward, A. F., Duke, K., Gneezy, A., & Bos, M. W.(2017). Brain drain: The mere presence of one's own smartphone reduces available cognitive capacity. *Journal of the Association for Consumer Research, 2,* 140–154. doi/10.1086/691462

Ward, B. W., Dahlhamer, J. M., Galinsky, A. M., & Joestl, S. S. (2014). Sexual orientation and health among US adults: National Health Interview Survey, 2013. *National Health Statistics Report, 77*(77), 1–10.

Ward, D. (2013). Risk factors and stuttering: Evaluating the evidence for clinicians. *Journal of Fluency Disorders, 38*(2), 134–140. doi:10.1016/j.jfludis.2013.02.007

Warren, F., Kuyken, W., Taylor, R. S., Whalley, B., Crane, C., Bondolfi, G., Hayes, R., Huijbers, M., Ma, H., Schweizer, S., Segal, Z., Speckens, A., Teasdale, J. D., van Heeringen, K., Williams, M., Byford, S., Byng, R., & Dalgheish, T. (2016). Efficacy and moderators of mindfulness-based cognitive therapy in prevention of depressive relapse: an individual patient data meta-analysis from randomized trials. *JAMA Psychiatry, 73*(6), 565–574. doi:10.1001/jamapsychiatry.2016.0076

Wasserman, R. C., Kelleher, K. J., Bocian, A., Baker, A., Childs, G. E., Indacochea, F., Stulp, C., & Gardner, W. P. (1999). Identification of attentional and hyperactivity problems in primary care: A report from pediatric research in office settings and the ambulatory sentinel practice network. *Pediatrics, 103,* E 38. doi:10.1542/peds.103.3.e38

Watkins, C. E., Campbell, V. L., & Nieberding, R. (1995). Contemporary practice of psychological assessment by clinical psychologists. *Professional Psychology: Research and Practice, 26,* 54–60. doi:10.1037/0735-7028.26.1.54

Watkins, E., & Brown, R. G. (2002). Rumination and executive function in depression: An experimental study. *Journal of Neurology, Neurosurgery, and Psychiatry, 72,* 400–402. doi:10.1136/jnnp.72.3.400

Watkins, L. E., Sprang, K. R., & Rothbaum, B. O. (2018). Treating PTSD: A review of evidence-based psychotherapy interventions. *Frontiers in Behavioral Neuroscience, 12*(258). doi:10.3389/fnbeh.2018.00258

Watson, J. B., & Rayner, R. (1920). Conditioned emotional reactions. *Journal of Experimental Psychology, 3,* 1–14. doi:10.1037/h0069608

Watts, T. W., Duncan, G. J., & Quan, H. (2018). Revisiting the marshmallow test: A conceptual replication investigating links between early delay of gratification and later outcomes. *Psychological Science, 29*(7), 1159–1177. doi:10.1177/0956797618761661

Waxenberg, S. E., Drellich, M. G., & Sutherland, A. M. (1959). The role of hormones in human behavior. I. Changes in female sexuality after adrenalectomy. *The Journal of Clinical Endocrinology & Metabolism, 19*(2), 193–202. doi:10.1210/jcem-19-2-193

Weber, W., & Newmark, S. (2007). Complementary and alternative medical therapies for attention deficit/hyperactivity disorder and autism. *Pediatric Clinics of North America, 54*(6), 983–1006. doi:10.1016/j.pcl.2007.09.006

Wechsler, D. (1943). Non-intellective factors in general intelligence. *The Journal of Abnormal and Social Psychology, 38*(1), 101–103. doi:10.1037/h0060613

Wedekind, C., & Füri, S. (1997). Body odour preferences in men and women: Do they aim for specific MHC combinations or simple heterogeneity? *Proceedings of the Royal Society of London, Series B, 264,* 1471–1479. doi:10.1098/rspb.1997.0204

Wegner, D. M. (1986). Transactive memory: A contemporary analysis of the group mind. In B. Mullen & G. R. Goethals (Eds.), *Theories of group behavior* (pp. 185–208). New York, NY: Springer-Verlag.

Wegner, D. M. (1994). Ironic processes of mental control. *Psychological Review, 101,* 34–52. doi:10.1037/0033-295X.101.1.34

Wegner, D. M., Erber, R., & Raymond, P. (1991). Transactive memory in close relationships. *Journal of Personality and Social Psychology, 61*(6), 923–929. doi:10.1037/0022-3514.61.6.923

Wegner, D. M., Giuliano, T., & Hertel, P. (1985). Cognitive interdependence in close relationships. In W. J. Ickes (Ed.), *Compatible and*

incompatible relationships (pp. 253–276). New York, NY: Springer-Verlag.
Weiner, I. B., & Greene, R. L. (2017). *Handbook of personality assessment*. New York, NY: John Wiley & Sons, Incorporated.
Weingartner, H., Miller, H., & Murphy, D. L. (1977). Mood-state-dependent retrieval of verbal associations. *Journal of Abnormal Psychology, 86*, 276–284. doi:10.1037/0021-843X.86.3.276
Weinstein, A. M., & Gorelick, D. A. (2011). Pharmacological treatment of cannabis dependence. *Current Pharmaceutical Design, 17*(14), 1351–1358. doi:10.2174/138161211796150846
Weinstock, M. (2005). The potential influence of maternal stress hormones on development and mental health of the offspring. *Brain, Behavior, and Immunity, 19*(4), 296–308. doi:10.1016/j.bbi.2004.09.006
Weisberg, P., & Waldrop, P. B. (1972). Fixed-interval work habits of Congress. *Journal of Applied Behavior Analysis, 5*, 93–97. doi:10.1901/jaba.1972.5-93
Weiser, E. B. (2015). # Me: Narcissism and its facets as predictors of selfie-posting frequency. *Personality and Individual Differences, 86*, 477–481. doi:10.1016/j.paid.2015.07.007
Weiss, A. (2018). Personality traits: A view from the animal kingdom. *Journal of Personality, 86*(1), 12–22. doi:10.1111/jopy.12310
Weiss, S. R. B., Blanco, C., & Wargo, E. M. (2017). Clarifying the link between cannabis use and risk for psychosis. *Acta Psychiatrica Scandinavica, 136*(1), 3–4. doi:10.1111/acps.12764
Weissman, M. M., Warner, V., Wickramaratne, P., Moreau, D., & Olfson, M. (1997). Offspring of depressed parents: 10 years later. *Journal of Affective Disorders, 15*, 269–277. doi:10.1001/archpsyc.1997.01830220054009
Weitlauf, A. S., Vehorn, A. C., Taylor, J. L., & Warren, Z. E. (2014). Relationship satisfaction, parenting stress, and depression in mothers of children with autism. *Autism, 18*(2), 194–198. doi:10.1177/1362361312458039
Wells, A. (2006). Metacognitive therapy for worry and generalised anxiety disorder. In G. C. L. Davey & A. Wells (Eds.), *Worry and its psychological disorders: Theory, assessment and treatment.* (pp. 259–272). Hoboken, NJ: Wiley Publishing.
Wells, G. L., Memon, A., & Penrod, S. D. (2006). Eyewitness evidence: Improving its probative value. *Psychological Science in the Public Interest, 7*(2), 45–75. doi:10.1111/j.1529-1006.2006.00027.x
Wenhart, T., Bethlehem, R. A. I., Baron-Cohen, S., & Altenmüller, E. (2019). Autistic traits, resting-state connectivity, and absolute pitch in professional musicians: shared and distinct neural features. *Molecular Autism, 10*(1), 20. doi:10.1186/s13229-019-0272-6
Wernicke, C. (1874). *Der aphasische symptomenkomplex: Eine psychologische Studie auf anatomischer Basis [Aphasias: A psychological study of their anatomical basis]*. Breslau, Poland: Cohn & Weigart.
Wetzel, E., Brown, A., Hill, P. L., Chung, J. M., Robins, R. W., & Roberts, B. W. (2017). The narcissism epidemic is dead; Long live the narcissism epidemic. *Psychological Science, 28*(12), 1833–1847. doi:10.1177/0956797617724208
White, G. L. (1980). Physical attractiveness and courtship progress. *Journal of Personality and Social Psychology, 39*, 660–668. doi:10.1037/0022-3514.39.4.660
Whorf, B. L. (1956). Science and linguistics. InJ. B. Carroll (Ed.), *Language, thought, and reality: Selected writings of Benjamin Lee Whorf* (pp. 207–219). Cambridge, MA: MIT Press.
Widmeyer, W. N., & Loy, J. W. (1988). When you're hot, you're hot: Warm-cold effects in first impressions of persons and teaching effectiveness. *Journal of Educational Psychology, 80*(1), 118–121. doi:10.1037/0022-0663.80.1.118
Widom, C. (1978). A methodology for studying non-institutionalized psychopaths. In R. D. Hare & D. Schalling (Eds.), *Psychopathic behaviour: Approaches to research* (pp. 71–84). Chichester, UK: Wiley.
Wiech, K. (2016). Deconstructing the sensation of pain: The influence of cognitive processes on pain perception. *Science, 354*(6312), 584–587. doi:10.1126/science.aaf8934
Wiederhold, B. K., & Riva, G. (2019). Virtual reality therapy: Emerging topics and future challenges. *Cyberpsychology, Behavior, and Social Networking, 22*(1), 3–6. doi:10.1089/cyber.2018.29136.bkw
Wielgosz, J., Goldberg, S. B., Kral, T. R. A., Dunne, J. D., & Davidson, R. J. (2019). Mindfulness meditation and psychopathology. *Annual Review of Clinical Psychology, 15*(1), 285–316. doi:10.1146/annurev-clinpsy-021815-093423
Wigfield, A., Eccles, J. S., Fredricks, J. A., Simpkins, S., Roeser, R. W., & Schiefele, U. (2015). Development of achievement motivation and engagement. In M. E. Lamb & R. M. Lerner (Eds.), *Handbook of child psychology and developmental science: Socioemotional processes* (p. 657–700). Hoboken, NJ: John Wiley & Sons Inc.
Wilbanks, C. A. (2014). Alternative methods of predator control. http://agrilife.org/texnatwildlife/coyotes/table-of-contents/alternative-methods-of-predator-control/
Wilensky, A. E., Schafe, G. E., Kristensen, M. P., & LeDoux, J. E. (2006). Rethinking the fear circuit: The central nucleus of the amygdala is required for the acquisition, consolidation, and expression of Pavlovian fear conditioning. *Journal of Neuroscience, 26*(48), 12387–12396. doi:10.1523/JNEUROSCI.4316-06.2006
Wilent, W. B., Oh, M. Y., Buetefisch, C. M., Bailes, J. E., Cantella, D., Angle, C., & Whiting, D. M. (2010). Induction of panic attack by stimulation of the ventromedial hypothalamus. *112*(6), 1295–1298. doi:10.3171/2009.9.Jns09577
Wilke, A., Hutchinson, J. M. C., Todd, P. M., & Kruger, D. J. (2006). Is risk taking used as a cue in mate choice? *Evolutionary Psychology, 4*, 367–393. doi:10.1177/147470490600400130
Wilkinson, G. S. (1984). Reciprocal food sharing in the vampire bat. *Nature, 308*, 181–184.doi:10.1038/308181a0
Wilkinson, G. S. (1990). Food sharing in vampire bats. *Scientific American, 62*, 76–82.
Williams, H., Conway, M. A., & Cohen, G. (2008). Memory in the real world. In G. Cohen & M. A. Conway (Eds.), *Memory in the real world* (pp. 21–90). New York: Psychology Press.
Williams, K. D. (2007). Ostracism. *Annual Review of Psychology, 58*, 425–452. doi:10.1146/annurev.psych.58.110405.085641
Williamson, A. M., & Feyer, A.-M. (2000). Moderate sleep deprivation produces impairments in cognitive and motor performance equivalent to legally prescribed levels of alcohol intoxication. *Occupational and Environmental Medicine, 57*(10), 649–655. doi:10.1136/oem.57.10.649
Williamson, R. A., Jaswal, V. K., & Meltzoff, A. N. (2010). Learning the rules: Observation and imitation of a sorting strategy by 36-month-old children. *Developmental Psychology, 46*(1), 57–65. doi:10.1037/a0017473
Willis, J., & Todorov, A. (2006). First impressions: Making up your mind after a 100-ms exposure to a face. *Psychological Science, 17*(7), 592–598. doi:10.1111/j.1467-9280.2006.01750.x
Wilson, A. E., & Ross, M. (2000). The frequency of temporal and social comparisons in people's personal appraisals. *Journal of Personality and Social Psychology, 78*, 928–942. doi:10.1037/0022-3514.78.5.928
Wilson, E. O. (1975). *Sociobiology: The new synthesis*. Cambridge, MA: Belknap Press of Harvard University Press.
Wilson, G., Hill, M., & Kiernan, M. (2018). Loneliness and social isolation of military veterans: Systematic narrative review. *Occupational Medicine, 68*(9), 600–609. doi:10.1093/occmed/kqy160
Wimmer, H., & Perner, J. (1983). Beliefs about beliefs: Representation and constraining function of wrong beliefs in young children's understanding of deception. *Cognition, 13*, 103–128. doi:10.1016/0010-0277(83)90004-5
Wimmer, R. D., Schmitt, L. I., Davidson, T. J., Nakajima, M., Deisseroth, K., & Halassa, M. M. (2015). Thalamic control of sensory selection in divided attention. *Nature, 526*(7575), 705–709. doi:10.1038/nature15398
Winkelman, M. (2003). Complementary therapy for addiction: "Drumming out drugs." *American Journal of Public Health, 93*(4), 647–651. doi:10.2105/ajph.93.4.647

Winkler, A. D., Spillmann, L., Werner, J. S., & Webster, M. A. (2015). Asymmetries in blue-yellow color perception and in the color of 'the dress'. *Current Biology, 25*(13), R547–548. doi:10.1016/j.cub.2015.05.004

Wirz-Justice, A. (2018). Seasonality in affective disorders. *General and Comparative Endocrinology, 258*, 244–249. doi:10.1016/j.ygcen.2017.07.010

Witkiewitz, K., Pearson, M. R., Wilson, A. D., Stein, E. R., Votaw, V. R., Hallgren, K. A., Maisto, S. A., Swan, J. E., Schwebel, F. J., Aldridge, A., Zarkin, G. A., & Tucker, J. A. (2020). Can alcohol use disorder recovery include some heavy drinking? A replication and extension up to 9 years following treatment. *Alcoholism: Clinical and Experimental Research, 44*(9), 1862–1874. doi:10.1111/acer.14413

Wittchen, H.-U., & Hoyer, J. (2001). Generalized anxiety disorder: Nature and course. *Journal of Clinical Psychiatry, 62*(Suppl.11), 15–19.

Wittgenstein, L. (1953). *Philosophical investigations* (G. E. M. Anscombe, Trans.). Oxford, UK: Blackwell.

Wixted, J. T., Mickes, L., Clark, S. E., Gronlund, S. D., & Roediger III, H. L. (2015). Initial eyewitness confidence reliably predicts eyewitness identification accuracy. *American Psychologist, 70*(6), 515–526. doi:10.1037/a0039510

Wobber, V., Wrangham, R., & Hare, B. (2010). Bonobos exhibit delayed development of social behavior and cognition relative to chimpanzees. *Current Biology, 20*(3), 226–230. doi:10.1016/j.cub.2009.11.070

Wolpe, J. (1958). *Psychotherapy by reciprocal inhibition.* Palo Alto, CA: Stanford University Press.

Wolraich, M. L., Wilson, D.B., & White, J.W. (1996). The effect of sugar on behavior or cognition in children. A meta-analysis. *Journal of the American Medical Association, 274*, 1617–1621. doi:10.1001/jama.1995.03530200053037

Wood, E. K., Higley, J. D., Champoux, M., Marsiske, M., Olsen, J. A., Suomi, S. J., & Kay, D. B. (2020). Multi-group multi-time point confirmatory factor analysis of the triadic structure of temperament: A non-human primate model. *Developmental Psychobiology*. doi:10.1002/dev.21985

Wood, J. M., Lilienfeld, S. O., Nezworski, M. T., Garb, H. N., Allen, K. H., & Wildermuth, J. L. (2010). Validity of Rorschach Inkblot scores for discriminating psychopaths from nonpsychopaths in forensic populations: A meta-analysis. *Psychological Assessment, 22*(2), 336–349. doi:10.1037/a0018998

Wood, J. M., Nezworski, M. T., & Lilienfeld, S. O. (2003). *What's wrong with the Rorschach?: Science confronts the controversial inkblot test.* San Francisco, CA: Jossey-Bass.

Woolley, A. W., Chabris, C. F., Pentland, A., Hashmi, N., & Malone, T. W. (2010). Evidence for a collective intelligence factor in the performance of human groups. *Science, 330*(6004), 686–688. doi:10.1126/science.1193147

World Health Organization (WHO). (2003). WHO definition of health. http://www.who.int/about/definition/en/print.html

World Health Organization (WHO). (2018). International classivication of diseases for mortality and morbidity statistics (11th Revision). https://icd.who.int/browse11/l-m/en

World Health Organization (WHO). (2020a). Obesity and overweight. https://www.who.int/en/news-room/fact-sheets/detail/obesity-and-overweight

World Health Organization (WHO). (2020b). Tobacco. https://www.who.int/news-room/fact-sheets/detail/tobacco

Wortham, J. M. (2020). Characteristics of persons who died with COVID-19—United States, February 12–May 18, 2020. *MMWR. Morbidity and Mortality Weekly Report, 69.*

Wright, G. A., Baker, D. D., Palmer, M. J., Stabler, D., Mustard, J. A., Power, E. F., Borland, A. M., & Stevenson, P. C. (2013). Caffeine in floral nectar enhances a pollinator's memory of reward. *Science, 339*(6124), 1202–1204. doi:10.1126/science.1228806

Wrzesniewski, A., McCauley, C., Rozin, P., & Schwartz, B. (1997). Jobs, careers, and callings: People's relations to their work. *Journal of Research in Personality, 31*(1), 21–33. doi:10.1006/jrpe.1997.2162

Wu, P.-L., & Chiou, W.-B. (2008). Postformal thinking and creativity among late adolescents: A post-Piagetian approach. *Adolescence, 43*(170), 237–251.

Xie, W., Campbell, S., & Zhang, W. (2020). Working memory capacity predicts individual differences in social-distancing compliance during the COVID-19 pandemic in the United States. *Proceedings of the National Academy of Sciences of the United States of America,* 202008868. doi:10.1073/pnas.2008868117

Xiong, T., Chen, H., Luo, R., & Mu, D. (2016). Hyperbaric oxygen therapy for people with autism spectrum disorder (ASD). *Cochrane Database of Systematic Reviews, 10*,CD010922. doi:10.1002/14651858.CD010922.pub2.0

Yakeley, J. (2018). Current understanding of narcissism and narcissistic personality disorder. *BJPsych Advances, 24*(5), 305–315. doi:10.1192/bja.2018.20

Yalom, I. D. (1995). *The theory and practice of group psychotherapy* (4th ed.). New York, NY: Basic Books.

Yamakawa, M., Tsujimura, S.-i., & Okajima, K. (2019). A quantitative analysis of the contribution of melanopsin to brightness perception. *Scientific Reports, 9*(1), 7568. doi:10.1038/s41598-019-44035-3

Yanagisawa, M. (1998). Orexins and orexin receptors: a family of hypothalamic neuropeptides and G protein-coupled receptors that regulate feeding behavior. *Cell, 92*(5), 573–585. doi:10.1016/S0092-8674(00)80949-6

Yang, B.-Z., Zhang, H., Ge, W., Weder, N., Douglas-Palumberi, H., Perepletchikova, F., Gelernter, J., & Kaufman, J. (2013). Child abuse and epigenetic mechanisms of disease risk. *American Journal of Preventive Medicine, 44*(2), 101–107. doi:10.1016/j.amepre.2012.10.012

Yang, M.-L., & Chiou, W.-B. (2010). Looking online for the best romantic partner reduces decision quality: The moderating role of choice-making strategies. *Cyberpsychology, Behavior, and Social Networking, 13*(2), 207–210. doi:10.1089/cyber.2009.0208

Yee, N. (2006). The demographics, motivations and derived experiences of users of massively-multiuser online graphical environments. *Presence: Teleoperators and Virtual Environments, 15*, 309–329. doi:10.1162/pres.15.3.309

Yehuda, R., Engel, S. M., Brand, S. R., Seckl, J., Marcus, S. M., & Berkowitz, G. S. (2005). Transgenerational effects of posttraumatic stress disorder in babies of mothers exposed to the World Trade Center attacks during pregnancy. *The Journal of Clinical Endocrinology & Metabolism, 90*(7), 4115–4118. doi:10.1210/jc.2005-0550

Yeoh, S. L., Eastwood, J., Wright, I. M., Morton, R., Melhuish, E., Ward, M., & Oei, J. L. (2019). Cognitive and motor outcomes of children with prenatal opioid exposure: a systematic review and meta-analysis. *JAMA Network Open, 2*(7), e197025–e197025. doi:10.1001/jamanetworkopen.2019.7025

Yerkes, R. M., & Dodson, J. D. (1908). The relation of strength of stimulus to rapidity of habit-formation. *Journal of Comparative and Physiological Psychology, 18*, 459–482. doi:10.1002/cne.920180503

Yoo, J. H., Valdovinos, M. G., & Schroeder, S. R. (2012). The epidemiology of psychopathology in people with intellectual disability: A forty-year review. *International Review of Research in Developmental Disabilities, 42*, 31–56. doi:10.1016/B978-0-12-394284-5.00002-4

Yoon, J. H., Grandelis, A., & Maddock, R. J. (2016). Dorsolateral prefrontal cortex GABA concentration in humans predicts working memory load processing capacity. *The Journal of Neuroscience, 36*(46), 11788–11794. doi:10.1523/jneurosci.1970-16.2016

Yoon, Y. B., Shin, W.-G., Lee, T. Y., Hur, J.-W., Cho, K. I. K., Sohn, W. S., Kim, S.-G., Lee, K.-H., & Kwon, J. S. (2017). Brain structural networks associated with intelligence and visuomotor ability. *Scientific Reports, 7*(1), 2177. doi:10.1038/s41598-017-02304-z

Yotsutsuji, T., Saitoh, O., Suzuki, M., Hagino, H., Mori, K., Takahashi, T., Kurokawa, K., Matsui, M., Seto, H., & Kurachi, M. (2003). Quantification of lateral ventricular subdivisions in schizophrenia by high-resolution three-dimensional magnetic resonance imaging. *Psychiatry Research, 122*, 1–12. doi:10.1016/S0925-4927(02)00105-1

Young, P. C. (1952). Antisocial uses of hypnosis. In L. M. LeCron (Ed.), *Experimental hypnosis* (pp. 376–409). New York, NY: Macmillan

Young, S. G., & Claypool, H. M. (2010). Mere exposure has differential effects on attention allocation to threatening and neutral stimuli. *Journal of Experimental Social Psychology, 46*(2), 424–427. doi:10.1016/j.jesp.2009.10.015

Youngman, J. F. (2017). The use and abuse of pre-employment personality tests. *Business Horizons, 60*(3), 261–269. doi:10.1016/j.bushor.2016.11.010

Youyou, W., Kosinski, M., & Stillwell, D. (2015). Computer-based personality judgments are more accurate than those made by humans. *Proceedings of the National Academy of Sciences of the United States of America, 112*(4), 1036–1040. doi:10.1073/pnas.1418680112

Yudell, M., Roberts, D., DeSalle, R., & Tishkoff, S. (2016). Taking race out of human genetics. *Science, 351*(6273), 564–565. doi:10.1126/science.aac4951

Yurgelun-Todd, D. (2007). Emotional and cognitive changes during adolescence. *Current Opinion in Neurobiology, 17*(2), 251–257. doi:10.1016/j.conb.2007.03.009

Zager, A., Andersen, M. L., Ruiz, F. S., Antunes, I. B., & Tufik, S. (2007). Effects of acute and chronic sleep loss on immune modulation of rats. *American Journal of Physiology. Regulatory, Integrative and Comparative Physiology, 293*(1), R504–509. doi:10.1152/ajpregu.00105.2007

Zajonc, R. B. (1965). Social facilitation. *Science, 149*, 269–274. doi:10.1126/science.149.3681.269

Zajonc, R. B. (1968). Attitudinal effects of mere exposure. *Journal of Personality and Social Psychology Monograph Supplement, 9*, 1–27. doi:10.1037/h0025848

Zajonc, R. B., & Sales, S. M. (1966). Social facilitation of dominant and subordinate responses. *Journal of Experimental Social Psychology, 2*(2), 160–168. doi:10.1016/0022-1031(66)90077-1

Zaval, L., Li, Y., Johnson, E., & Weber, E. (2015). Complementary contributions of fluid and crystallized intelligence to decision making across the life span. In T. H. Hess, J. Strough, & C. E. Lockenhoff (Eds.), *Aging and decision making: Empirial and applied perspectives* (pp. 149–168). Boston, MA: Elsevier.

Zebrowitz, L. A. (2017). First impressions from faces. *Current Directions in Psychological Science, 26*(3), 237–242. doi:10.1177/0963721416683996

Zebrowitz, L. A., Wang, R., Bronstad, P. M., Eisenberg, D., Undurraga, E., Reyes-García, V., & Godoy, R. (2012). First impressions from faces among US and culturally isolated Tsimane'people in the Bolivian rainforest. *Journal of Cross-Cultural Psychology, 43*(1), 119–134. doi:10.1177/0022022111411386

Zelazo, P. R. (1998). McGraw and the development of unaided walking. *Developmental Review, 18*(4), 449–471. doi:10.1006/drev.1997.0460

Zerjal, T., Xue, Y., Bertorelle, G., Wells, S., Bao, W., Suling, Z., Qamar, R., Ayub, Q., Mohyuddin, A., Fu, S., Li, P., Yuldasheva, N., Ruzibakiev, R., Xu, J., Shu, Q., Du, R., Yang, H., Hurles, M. E., Robinson, E., ... Tyler-Smith, C. (2003). The genetic legacy of the Mongols. *American Journal of Human Genetics, 72*, 717-721. doi:10.1086/367774

Zhang, T. Y., Chrétien, P., Meaney, M. J., & Gratton, A. (2005). Influence of naturally occurring variations in maternal care on prepulse inhibition of acoustic startle and the medial prefrontal cortical dopamine response to stress in adult rats. *The Journal of Neuroscience, 25*, 1493–1502. doi:10.1523/JNEUROSCI.3293-04.2005

Zhang, Y., Proenca, R., Maffei, M., Barone, M., Leopold, L., & Friedman, J. M. (1994). Positional cloning of the mouse obese gene and its human homologue. *Nature, 372*, 425–432. doi:10.1038/372425a0

Zigler, E. (1967). Familial mental retardation: A continuing dilemma. *Science, 155*(3760), 292–298. doi:10.1126/science.155.3760.292

Zimbardo, P. G. (1969). The human choice: Individuation, reason, and order vs. deindividuation, impulse and chaos. In W. J. Arnold & D. Levine (Eds.), *Nebraska symposium on motivation* (pp. 237–307). Lincoln, NE: University of Nebraska Press.

Zimmer, C. (2009). On the origin of tomorrow. *Science, 326*, 1334–1336. doi:10.1126/science.326.5958.1334

Zimmerman, F. J., Christakis, D. A., & Meltzoff, A. N. (2007). Associations between media viewing and language development in children under age 2 years. *The Journal of Pediatrics, 151*(4), 364–368. doi:10.1016/j.jpeds.2007/04.071

Zimmerman, F. J., Gilkerson, J., Richards, J. A., Christakis, D. A., Xu, D., Gray, S., & Yapanel, U. (2009). Teaching by listening: The importance of adult-child conversations to language development. *Pediatrics, 124*(1), 342–349. doi:10.1542/peds.2008-2267.

Zubin, J., & Spring, B. (1977). Vulnerability: A new view of schizophrenia. *Journal of Abnormal Psychology, 86*, 103–126. doi:10.1037/0021-843X.86.2.103

Zuscho, H. (1983). Posttraumatic anosmia. *Archives of Otolaryngology—Head and Neck Surgery, 4*, 252–256. doi:10.1001/archotol.1982.00790500026006

Name Index

Page numbers followed by f and t indicate figure and table

A

Aafjes-van Doorn, K., 634
Aaker, J. L., 679
Abbeduto, L., 401
Abdellaoui, A., 566
Abdi, H., 181, 187
Abdolmaleky, H. M., 86
Aberson, C. L., 489
Aboujaoude, E., 604
Abraham, G. E., 256
Abraham, S., 670, 675
Abrahams, D., 532
Abrahamsm J. N. H., 178
Abramovitch, A., 581
Abramovitz, R., 644
Abramson, L. Y., 571
Abramson, R., 442
Abramzon, Y. A., 367
Abutalebi, J., 390, 391
Accero, C. S., 416f
Acebo, C., 202
Achor, S., 640, 641
Acker, J. D., 450
Adamantidis, A., 354
Adamovich, S., 349
Adams, J., 182, 466
Adams, M. J., 455, 455f
Adams, R. B., Jr., 504, 504f
Adiguzel, K., 557
Adil, J., 583
Adisetiyo, V., 560
Adler, A. B., 267, 500, 645, 657
Adler, N. E., 649
Adolph, K. E., 422, 423
Adolphs, R., 93, 117, 118, 118f, 239, 240, 242, 243f, 397, 432
Adrian-Ventura, J., 476
Agay, N., 222
Agerbo, E., 260
Agnew, C. R., 682
Aguilar-Gaxiola, S., 578, 584
Ahadi, S. A., 433, 475
Ahanonu, B., 182
Ahern, E., 607
Ahern, J., 584
Ahorani, E., 123
Aiello, A. E., 583
Aigner, M., 261
Aihara, M., 653
Ainsworth, M., 401, 434
Ajzen, I., 513
Akane, A., 77
Akers, K. G., 206
Akerstedt, T., 202
Akula, S., 557
Akyildiz-Kunz, C., 649
Al-Hamzawi, A., 578
Al-Issa, I., 552
Al-Shawaf, I., 225
Albano, A. M., 578
Albarracin, D., 269
Albert, D., 444
Albillos, A., 83
Albouy, B., 204
Alcaniz, M., 630, 630
Austin Alchon, S., 105
Alcock, J., 61
Alda, M., 624
Alderson-Day, B., 564
Aldinger, K. A., 115
Aldrich, M., 209
Aldwin, C., 658
Alexander-Bloch, A., 136
Alexander, G. M., 423
Alexander, N., 460
Alexander, R. D., 96
Algren, M. H., 649
Allan, J. N., 374
Allen, J. A., 555
Allen, K., 657
Allen, L. A., 630, 632
Allen, L. S., 266
Allen, M. S., 620
Allen, N. B.
Allen, T. A., 476
Allen, W. D., 578
Allgulander, C., 629
Allison, T., 195
Allmon, D., 632
Alloway, R. G., 355
Alloway, T. P., 355
Allport, G. W., 21, 36, 37, 468, 521, 680
Ally, B. A., 330
Almli, L. M., 583
Alonso, J., 584
Alper, C., 649
Alpers, G. W., 577
Alptuzun, V., 349
Altamura, A. C., 572
Altenmuller, E., 177, 556
Altman, I., 533
Altman, J. D., 270
Alvarez, E., 219
Alwin, D. F., 526
Amaral, D. G., 242, 243
Ambady, N., 504, 504f
Ambeskovic, M., 83
Ameis, S. H., 560
Amemiya, A., 256
American Academy of Pediatrics (AAP), 210
Ames, A., 164
Ames, E., 8
Amico, J. A., 263
Amirkhan, J. H., 508
Ammentorp, J., 604
Ammon, K., 193
Amstadter, A. B., 583
An, Y., 354
Anacker, C., 625
Anand, B., 256
Anddreassen, O. A., 563
Andersen, H. R., 413
Andersen, M. L., 206
Andersen, P. T., 649
Anderson, C., 524
Anderson, C. A., 53
Anderson, I. M., 629
Anderson, J. A., 413
Anderson, J. R., 93
Anderson, K. N., 391
Anderson, M. C., 320, 324
Anderson, M. L., 270
Anderson, N. E., 123
Anderson, S. W., 122, 586
Anderton, B. H., 450
Andlauer, T. F., 390
Andreasen, N. C., 563
Andrew, M., 119
Andrews, B., 592
Andrews, J. A., 436, 437, 437f
Andrykowski, M. A., 651
Angel Martinez-Gonzalez, M., 86
Angel, F., 604
Angelakis, E., 259
Angelakis, I., 582
Angeles-Castellanos, M., 200
Angermeyer, M., 561, 578, 583
Angle, C., 242
Angley, M., 556, 557f
Angold, A., 559
Annas, P., 577f
Annese, J., 45
Anney, R. J., 556
Annunziato, A., 85
Anokhin, A. P., 248
Ansaro, A., 299
Anthony, J. C., 561, 583
Anton, J.-L., 240
Antonova, I., 346
Antunes, I. B., 206
Apodaca, J., 388
Araujo, J. F., 208
Arbib, M. A., 124
Arch, J., 256
Archer, R. P., 447
Arean, P. A., 452
Arena, J. P., 256
Arendt, J., 200
Arevalo, J. M. G., 106, 652
Argo, A., 250
Argote, L., 354
Ariel, B., 485
Arimatea, E., 460
Aristotle, 8, 108
Aritake-Okada, S., 206
Armstrong, H. E., 632
Armstrong, L., 259
Arnett, J. J., 438, 445, 446, 448
Arnett, K. H., 336
Arnold, S. J., 567
Arnsten, A. F., 621
Arnulf, I., 208
Aron, A., 235, 475, 534
Aron, E. N., 475, 534
Aronson, E., 522
Aronson, J., 518, 520f
Aronson, J. A., 537
Aronson, V., 532
Arora, N., 412
Arora, R., 678
Arpin-Cribbie, C., 626
Arseneault, L., 75, 459
Arslan, R. C., 486, 487
Ary, D. V., 664, 664
Asch, S. E., 471, 523, 523f
Aschwanden, D., 496, 496f
Asendorpf, J. B., 477
Aserinsky, E., 208
Ashley-Koch, A. E., 583
Ashley, R., 176
Ashton, J. R., 534
Ashton, M. C., 482
Ashwood, P., 115
Askren, M. K., 347
Aslan, S., 567
Aslin, R. N., 167
Astesano, C., 240
Atherton, J., 390
Atkinson, L. Z., 625
Atkinson, Q. D., 383, 384f
Atkinson, R. C., 319, 321f
Atri, A., 349
Avants, B., 367
Averbach, E., 321
Averill, A. J., 651
Avila, C., 476
Avinun, R., 476
Axelrod, R., 537
Axelsson, J., 200
Ayduk, O., 370
Ayres, M. M.

Caramazza, A., 367, 368f
Cardenas-Inguez, C., 189
Cardenas, R. A., 262
Cardin, V., 391
Cardoso, G., 584
Carell, T. D., 177
Carew, T. J., 286, 346
Carhart-Harris, R. L., 218
Carlisle, R. D., 675
Carlsen, E. B., 604
Carlsmith, J. M., 53, 511
Carlson, A. D., 425
Carlson, J., 481
Carlson, P. J., 583, 584
Carlstrom, E., 266
Carneal, M., 45
Carney, D. R., 235
Carpenter, T. P., 675
Carr, T. S., 540
Carrier, C. M.., 228
Carrier, J., 228
Carrigan, M. H., 215
Carroll, D., 654
Carroll, M. D., 257, 665, 665, 666f, 666f
Carskadon, M. A., 202
Carson, W. E., 650
Carstensen, L. L., 452, 534, 669
Carter, C. S., 93
Carter, E. A., 177
Caruso, C. C., 200
Carvalho, C., 182
Carvalho, F., 222
Carvalho, L. A., 625
Carver, C. S., 491, 674
Casanova, M. F., 557
Cascio, C. J., 179
Casey, B. J., 442
Cash, S. S., 205
Casper, R. C., 59
Caspi, A., 28, 75, 84, 459, 586
Cassano, G. B., 614, 615
Cassol, H., 213
Castellucci, V., 346
Castle, P. H., 602
Castleberry, E. H., 336
Castonguay, L. G., 607
Castro, C. A., 583, 592, 645
Castrogiovanni, P., 583
Catalan, J., 524, 525f
Catani, C., 644
Caterina, M. J., 181, 184
Cattaneo, A., 625
Cattell, J. K., 20
Cattell, R. B., 468
Cavalli-Sforza, L., 209
Cavanaugh, J. C., 420f
Ceballos-Baumann, A., 244
Ceballos, N., 38
Ceccarelli, M., 625
Ceci, S. J., 341, 398
Centers for Disease Control & Prevention (CDC), 223, 258, 404, 556, 558, 560, 598, 622, 625, 661, 663, 664, 665, 666, 671
Cerella, J., 430
Cervilla, J., 580
Chaar, D., 557
Chabris, C. F., 398, 399f
Chagnon, N. A., 99
Chaimani, A., 625
Chait, B. T., 257
Chamberlain, S. R., 581
Chambers, M. C., 122
Champagne, F., 85, 648
Champoux, M., 432
Chan, M. Y., 674
Chandler, K., 557
Chang, E., 674
Chang, I., 647, 675
Chang, K. D., 567
Chang, M., 390
Chang, Y. S., 200
Channell, M. M., 401
Chaplin, J. P., 13
Chapman, B., 392
Charcot, M., 600
Charitaki, S., 644
Charland-Verville, V., 213
Charles, S. T., 452
Charman, T., 168
Charney, D. S., 583
Chartrand, T. L., 236, 237
Chase, W. G., 325
Chatrian, G., 212
Chattarji, S., 341
Chaudhari, N., 184, 290
Chavez, M., 208
Chawabpaiboon, S., 412
Chazan, S., 583
Chazin, S. M., 584
Cheek, J. M., 590
Cheeran, B., 378
Chein, J., 444
Chemelli, R. M., 256
Chemtob, C. M., 644
Chen, B., 663
Chen, C., 354
Chen, C., -H., 475, 476
Chen, H., 620
Chen, H.-Y., 189, 267, 500, 502, 515, 645, 657
Chen, J. A., 574
Chen, K. Y., 668
Chen, L., 169
Chen, M. C., 346, 346f
Chen, R., 228
Chen, S., 493, 549, 683
Chen, T. J., 626
Chene, G., 451
Cherasse, Y., 206
Cherkas, L., 99
Cherkassky, V. I., 198
Chertkow, H., 390
Chess, S., 432f
Chetty, R., 670
Chia, R., 367
Chiao, J. Y., 107, 459, 460, 460f
Child, I. L., 466
Childs, G. E., 559
Chin, B., 675
Chinkes, D. L., 206
Chiou, W.-B., 403, 446
Chiu, C.-Y., 508
Chiu, L.-H, 169
Chiu, W., 581
Chiu, W. T., 551, 567, 576, 578, 579, 580
Chlevin-Thiele, C., 481
Cho, K., 200
Cho, K. I. K., 397
Choi, I., 508
Choi, J., 387
Choi, S., 354
Chomsky, N., 21, 388
Chopik, W. J., 447
Chouinard-Decorte, F., 397
Chouraki, V., 451
Chrea, C., 187
Chretien, P., 469
Christakis, D. A., 387
Christakis, N. A., 259, 474, 499, 675
Christensen, A. C., 75
Christensen, K. M., 419
Christensen, U., 651, 651
Christidis, P., 28, 29, 603f
Christie, J., 391
Christoff, K., 208
Christoforou, C., 361
Chrousos, G. P., 644
Chua, A., 436
Chua, H. F., 665
Chudler, E., 14
Chun, K., 106
Chung, J. M., 447
Church, C. L., 668f, 669
Church, T. S., 661f, 669
Cialdini, R. B., 489, 513, 524, 525f, 538
Cichetti, D. V., 195
Cichocka, A., 545
Cikara, M., 545
Cipolli, C., 208
Cipriani, A., 623, 625
Cirelli, C., 195
Clark, D. M., 578
Clark, K., 27
Clark, L., 215
Clark, M., 27
Clark, R., 664
Clark, S. E., 341
Clark, T. K., 61
Clarke, A., 137
Clasen, L., 397
Claypool, H. M., 531
Clegg, H., 624
Clementz, B. A., 567
Clifton, J., 370
Clifton, S., 58
Cnaan, A., 583, 644
Coan, J. A., 188
Cobb, ly, 128
Coccia, C., 437
Cofer, J., 540
Coffey, S., 215
Cogsdill, E. J., 501
Cohen, A. F., 572
Cohen, B. E., 217
Cohen, E., 583
Cohen, G., 329, 330
Cohen, G. L., 444, 655, 655f
Cohen, J. D., 537
Cohen, M. X., 616
Cohen, S., 649, 651, 662, 676
Cohen, S. L., 257
Cohn, D., 450
Cohn, M. A., 660
Cohn, R. H., 196
Cokely, E. T., 374
Cola, P., 623
Colburne, K. A., 423
Cole, F. S., 412
Cole, J., 126
Cole, J. C., 200
Cole, R., 578
Cole, S. W., 106, 500, 501, 652, 652, 657
Coleman, R. M., 206*f*
Colledge, E., 118f, 586
Colletti, P., 122
Collins, A., 333, 333f, 365, 538
Colosio, M., 511
Colwell, K., 251
Comings, D. E., 118
Comoutos, N., 626
Conant, L. L., 347
Conger, R. D., 436
Conley, D., 499
Connan, F., 261
Connell-Jones, G., 620
Conner, M., 510
Connolly, T., 375
Constable, R. T., 389, 390
Constantinidis, T. C., 220
Constantinidou, F., 361
Conti, G., 652
Conway, A. M., 660
Conway, B. R., 149
Conway, M. A., 329, 330
Cook, S., 667
Cooke, J. E., 644
Coons, H. L., 644
Cooper, A., 561
Cooper, A. B., 552
Cooper, C. M., 339f
Cooper, H., 469, 674
Cooper, R., 119
Cooper, R. P., 177
Cooper, S. E., 584
Cooper, S. J., 257
Copas, A., 58
Coppola, G., 77
Corballis, M. C., 383, 388
Corbett, A., 557
Corbett, M., 47
Corbin, W. R., 108
Corder, G., 182
Cordone, S., 204
Cordonier, L., 523
Coren, S., 127t, 201, 206
Corina, D., 391
Corkin, S., 45, 317, 318

Cornford, F. M., 36
Cornish, J. L., 222, 564
Correa, J. B., 664
Corsi, D. J., 414, 557
Cort, A. S., 566
Corti, R., 651
Corvin, A., 562
Coryell, W., 571
Coskunpinar, A., 477
Cosme, G., 83
Cosmides, L., 95, 319
Costa-Neves, B., 83
Costa, P. T., Jr., 467f, 468, 475
Costello, E. J., 559
Costumero, V., 476
Coto, C. A., 217
Cotting, D. I., 645
Council, J. R., 224, 522
Courchesne, E., 115
Courtet, P., 626
Couste, C. P., 178
Couto, B., 264, 544
Cowan, N., 322
Cowen, P. J., 648
Cownden, D., 523
Cox, D., 559
Cox, M. J., 435
Coyne, J. C., 645
Craddock, N., 567
Craig, A., 35
Craig, C. L., 668f, 669
Craig, I. W., 28, 84, 540, 571, 583, 586
Craighead, W. E., 669
Craighero, L., 124
Craik, F. I., 325, 326, 326f, 391
Cramer, E. S., 169
Crane, C., 627
Craske, M. G., 576
Crawford, C., 570
Crawford, R. K., 567
Crego, A., 617
Cremeens, J., 671
Crespin, T.R., 650
Crick, F., 197
Crimmins, E. M., 451
Crisafio, A., 565
Cristofaro, S., 565
Crockett, M. J., 540
Crow, T. J., 126
Crum, A. J., 108, 640, 641
Crumpler, D., 561
Cruwys,T., 488
Csikszentmihalyi, M., 672, 679, 680
Cuddy, A. J. C., 235
Cuddy, P., 518f
Cui, M., 437
Culang, M. E., 451
Cully, D. F., 256
Cumming, G., 63
Cunha, L., 182
Cunitz, A. R., 327–328
Cunningham, W. A., 518
Cuperman, R., 494, 495f
Curtin, L. R., 671
Curtiss, S., 389
Cutler, A., 387
Cutler, D., 670, 675
Cutler, J., 66
Cutrona, C., 502, 657
Cvencek, D., 486
Cyders, M. A., 477
Czachor, J. D., 218, 220
Czarnecka, M., 653, 653
Czeisler, C. A., 200

D

d eVries, A. P., 583, 644
D'Andrea, G., 625
d'Haenens, L., 683
D'Mello, A.M., 390
D'Onofrio, B., 399
Dabbs, J. M., Jr., 262, 513, 518, 540
Dahl, R. E., 209, 440
Dahlhamer, J. M., 264, 265
Dahmen, B., 204
Dailey, S., 38
Dalege, J., 510
Dalen, L., 561
Dalrymple, S., 527
Daly, M., 472
Daly, R., 603
Damasio, A. R., 122, 241, 242, 243, 243f, 245, 386, 391, 586
Damasio, H., 122, 242, 244, 245, 391, 586
Damian, R. I., 465
Dang-Vu, T. T., 204
Dani, J. A., 220
Daniel, D. G., 563
Daniele Fallin, M., 130
Daniels, J. L., 557
Daniels, S. R., 665
Danielson, M. L., 622
Danielson, P. E., 256
Dann, M., 186
Dansky, B. S., 215
Danziger, K., 11
Darby, B. L., 524, 525f
Darby, R. R., 212, 542
Darley, J. M., 539
Darling, C. A., 437
Darrow, C. M., 448
Darwin, C., 12, 14, 89, 95, 97, 98, 239, 240, 245, 535, 538
Das, R., 412
Dator, J., 270
Dauvilliers, Y., 210
Davenport, B., 621
Davey Smith, G., 654
Davidson, C. L., 674
Davidson, R. J., 93, 188, 225, 540, 572, 586
Davies, P. G., 518, 519
Davila, J., 436
Davis, C. G., 680
Davis, J. A., 675
Davis, J. L., 532
Davis, J. M., 59, 208
Davis, L. B., 419
Davis, M., 177
Davis, P. E., 414
Davis, S. L., 648
Dawkins, R., 21, 313, 538
Dawson, B. C., 549, 556
De Bellis, M. D., 440
de Bruin, W. B., 442
De Castro, B. O., 590
de Gelder, B., 240
De Gennaro, L., 204
De Geus, E. J. C., 650, 650
De Graaf, R., 561, 583
de Jonge, P., 578
de Kloet, E. R., 644
de la Fuente Revenga, M., 219
de Lecea, L., 256
De Luca, D., 415
De Rossi, P., 560
De Valois, K. K., 162
De Valois, R. L., 162
de Villiers, P. A., 363
de Visser, S. J., 572
de Voogd, L. D., 119
de Vries, A. P., 644
de Vries, G., 571
De Waal, F. B., 196, 537
De Wied, C., 263
Dean, K. K., 508
Deary, I. J., 392, 397
Deater-Deckard, K., 300
Deboeck, P. R., 657
DeBruine, L. M., 262, 532
DeCasper, A. J., 412
Decety, J., 93, 491
DeCharms, R., 253
Deci, E. L., 253, 267, 674
Deckert, J., 579
Deese, J., 345
DeFilippis, M., 618
Degenhardt, E., 83
Dejong, K., 414, 416f
Del Maschio, N., 391
del Prado, A., 524
DeLamater, J., 449
Deldin, P., 370
Delion, P., 562
DeLisi, L. E., 217
DeLisi, M., 586
Della Rosa, P., 390
Delmaire, C., 562
DeLongis, A., 658, 659
Dement, W., 207, 207f, 208. 209
Demiralp, E., 347
Demler, O., 551, 567, 575, 576, 578, 579, 580
Demyttenaere, K., 561, 583
den Boer, J. A., 629
den Houting, J., 619
Denburg, N. L., 395
DeNeve, K. M., 469, 674
Deng, P., 663
Denissen, J. J., 486, 487
Dennett, D., 197
Dennis, E. L., 648
Denny, C. H., 416f
Denys, D. A. J. P., 571
Deocampo, J., 430
Derntl, B., 540
Derogatis, L. R., 644
Derryberry, D., 475
Desai, R. H., 347
DeSalle, R., 80
Descartes, R., 106
Deschamps, J. C., 522
Deschrijver, E., 181
Desseilles, M., 204
DeStefano, F., 559f
Deutsch, G., 126
Dew, J., 676
DeYoung, C. G., 474, 476
Di Forti, M., 566, 566f
Di Martino, A., 560
Di Noto, P. M., 181
Di Pellegrino, G., 124
Diamond, A., 427
Diamond, D. M., 340
Diamond, L. M., 263, 265, 265f
Dias, B. G., 87
Diaz, R., 390
Dick, A. S., 391
Dicke, U., 93
Dickens, A. P., 679
Dickens, W. T., 398
Dickhaus, J., 270
Dickinson-Anson, H., 330
Dickinson, J., 635
DiClemente, C., 664
Didie, E. R., 582
Dieckmann, N. F., 559
Diefendorf, A. R., 563
Diekelmann, S., 349
Diener, E., 485, 658, 674, 675, 676f
Dierks, T., 562
Dietrich, A., 225, 578
Difede, J., 584
DiGilio, D. A., 452
diGrande, L., 583
Dijk, D.-J., 200
DiLalla, L. F., 576
Dill, K. E., 53
Dinan, T. G., 562
Dincan, L. E., 583
Ding, Y.-S., 560, 621
Dion, K., 513
Dirk Blom, J., 616
Dixon, D. R., 620
Dixon, L., 664
Do Cao, J., 415
Dobie, D. J., 563
Dobson, D., 614
Dobson, K. S., 614
Dodet, P., 208
Dodge, K. A., 300
Dodge, R., 563
Dodson, J. D., 240, 528
Doise, W., 522
Dolan, C. B., 268
Dolan, C. V., 101
Dolan, R. J., 537
Dold, M., 261

Dolderman, D., 532
Dolezal, C., 245
Dolinoy, D. C., 72, 259
Doll, R., 665
Domanski, C. W., 385
Domes, G., 133
Domhoff, G. W., 208
Domingue, B. W., 499
Dominguez-Clave, E., 219
Domschke, K., 579
Donahue, M. J., 330
Donders, F. C., 11
Donelle, J., 414, 557
Dong, C. Y., 224
Donlea, J., 194
Donohoe, G., 562
Doogan, N. J., 220
Dorr, L., 390
Dorus, S., 93
Doty, R. I., 186
Dougherty, J. D., 557
Douglas, K. M., 508
Dourish, C. T., 257
Dove, H., 422
Dover, R., 262
Downey, C., 674
Downs, D. L., 489
Draisma, H. H., 566
Drane, D. L., 340
Drayna, D., 35
Dresler, M., 208, 354
Dronkers, N. F., 386
Droog, W., 218
Druckman, D. E., 480
Druett, J., 535
Drummer, O. H., 222
Drury, A. J., 586
du Hoffmann, J., 35
Duan, D., 507, 507f
Dubernard, J.-M., 137
Duberstein, P., 392
Dubois, J., 397
Dudai, Y., 344
Dudukovic, N. M., 343
Duffy, M. E., 552
Dufouil, C., 451
Dugas, D. V, 549, 556
Dugre, J. R., 221
Duka, T., 421
Dulaney, S., 582
Dumais, A., 221
Dumontheil, I., 442
Dunbar, R. I. M., 93, 500
Duncan, G. J., 395
Duncan, T. E., 664, 664
Dunn, A., 664
Dunn, B. D., 215
Dunn, E. W., 314, 676, 677
Dunne, J. D., 225
Dunning, D., 488
Durante, K. M., 98
Durbin, C. E., 474f
Duriez, B., 436, 437, 437f
Dutcher, A. M., 567
Dutton, D. G., 235
Dweck, C. S., 269, 396
Dysart, J., 341
Dyson-Hudson, N., 543
Dyson-Hudson, R., 543

E

Easterbrook, M. J., 488
Eastwick, P. W., 500
Eastwood, J., 414
Eaves, L. J., 577
Eberhardt, J. L., 518, 519f
Eberhart, C. G., 618
Eccles, J. S., 268, 269
Eckel, R. H., 259
Eckert, E. D., 59
Edelstein, B. A., 455
Edwards, A., 180
Edwards, E. M., 668
Egger, H. L., 559
Egget, D. L., 48
Ehlers, C. L., 667
Ehrensvard, M., 604
Eibl, L., 208
Eichel, S. K. D., 604
Eichstedt, J. A., 423
Eid, J., 659, 659f
Einstein, A., 363, 466
Eirich, R., 644
Eisen, A. R., 578
Eisenberg, D., 552
Eisenberg, D., 459, 501
Ekelund, U., 668
Ekholm, O., 649
Ekirch, A. R., 200
Ekman, P., 234, 245, 248, 250
El-Chaar, D., 414
Elbert, M. J., 586
Elbert, T., 181, 644
Elder, C., 472
Elenkov, I., 651
Elices, M., 219, 220
Elion, J., 29
Elison, J. T., 557
Elizabeth, A. Y., 674
Elkind, D., 485
Elkins, G. R., 224
Ellamil, M., 225
Eller, A., 522, 522
Ellinghaus, D., 83
Elliot, A. J., 269, 270
Elliot, R., 300
Elliott, M. N., 644, 657
Ellis Weismer, S., 554, 556
Ellis, A., 613, 614, 673
Ellis, H. C., 321
Ellis, M. S., 224
Ellsworth, P. C., 239, 247, 248
Elman, C., 449
Emery, G., 626
Emery, N. J., 116, 242
Emery, S. L., 218
Emlen, S. T., 98
Emmelkamp, P. M. G., 630
Emmerson, B., 221
Emmons, R. A., 675, 680
Eng, C., 556
Eng, M. Y., 667
Engel, S. M., 557, 644
English, T., 246, 676, 677
Ennaceur, A., 200, 200
Enoch, M. A., 668
Enquist, M., 523, 523
Enseleit, F., 651
Eppig, C., 398
Epprecht, M., 265, 265f, 266
Epstein, L. G., 212
Erber, R., 356
Erdberg, P., 482
Erdfelder, E., 372
Erhard, P., 244
Erickson, C. A., 618
Erickson, P. I., 99
Erikson, E. H., 443, 444, 449, 451, 485
Eriksson, K., 523, 523
Erkanli, A., 559
Ernst, M. E., 90, 201
Erol, R. Y., 444, 445f, 488
Ersboll, A. K., 649
Escobar, C., 200
Eshun, S., 675
Eskelinen, M. H., 220
Esler, A., 55
Eslick, G. D., 558, 567
Eslinger, P. J., 122
Espensen-Sturges, T., 584
Espitia-Bautista, E., 200
Esposito, L., 211
Ettinger, M. G., 205
Evans, A. C., 420
Evans, D. E., 475
Evans, F. J., 224
Evans, P. D., 93
Evans, S. W., 621
Evins, A. E., 217, 564
Eyal, N., 390
Eysenck, H. J., 476, 539
Eysenck, M. W., 320, 324

F

Fabiano, G. A., 622
Fadiga, G., 124
Fadiga, L., 124
Fagerland, M. W., 668
Fairnie, J., 556
Falangola, M. F., 560
Falcone, G., 225
Falk, E. B., 444
Fallon, J. H., 330
Fan, J., 107f
Fan. C., -C., 475, 475f
Farah, M. J., 491
Faraone, S. V., 560, 576
Farb, N., 348
Farley, F., 442
Farnham, S. D., 488, 488f
Farrar, S., 538
Farrar, W. A., 485
Farrell, M. S., 83
Farstad, S. M., 262
Fastow, A., 588
Fatemi, S. H., 115
Faubion, S., 626
Faul, J. D., 451
Faulkerson, J. A., 444
Fechner, G. T., 9, 153
Feeney, J. A., 435
Fehr, E., 538
Feick, D. L., 488
Feighner, S. D., 256
Feinberg, D. R., 532
Feinberg, I., 492
Feinstein, J. A., 528
Fejfar, M. C., 485
Feldman, E., 278
Feldman, H., 621, 622
Feldman, M. W., 523
Feltz, A., 374
Fender, J. G., 402
Fenton, N., 371
Feranil, A. B., 262
Ferguson, C., 47, 48
Ferguson, C. J., 54, 586
Fergusson, D. M., 28, 84, 217, 217f, 540, 565
Fernald, A., 388, 419
Fernandes, E., 222, 392
Fernandez-Aranda, F., 261
Fernandez, G., 119
Ferrara, M., 208
Ferrari, P. F., 312, 433, 434
Ferriero, D. M., 440
Ferriter, M., 620
Ferrucci, P., 270
Festinger, L., 486, 509, 511
Feyer, A.-M., 206
Fidler, D. J., 395
Field, A. E., 444
Field, Y., 90
Fielden, J.A., 262, 518
Fifer, W. P., 177, 412
Figueredo, A. J., 476
Fincham, F. D., 437
Fink, G. R., 348
Fink, K., 209
Finkel, E. J., 500
Finn, L., 202
Finucane, M., 375
Firk, C., 557
Fiscella, K., 392
Fischer, C. F., 208
Fischer, H., 518, 577f
Fischer, P., 378
Fischhoff, B., 374, 442
Fischhoff, J., 621
Fisher, C. I., 262
Fisher, H. E., 264
Fisher, M. L., 264
Fisher, P. A., 86
Fisher, R. P., 251
Fisher, S. E., 388
Fishman, S., 180
Fiske, A. P., 582
Fiske, S. T., 517, 518f
Fitz, S. D., 578
Flaum, M., 563
Flax, J., 411

Flegal, K. M., 257
Fleischman, J., 121
Fleischmann, P., 615
Fleming, L. W.
Fletcher, J., 499
Fletcher, J. M., 389, 390
Fletcher, R., 514
Flexser, A. J., 337
Flick, C., 65
Floerke, V. A., 353, 353f
Flom, R., 418f
Florisse, E. J., 617
Flynn, J. R., 54, 93, 392, 398
Fogassi, I., 124
Fokas, G. J., 109
Forbach, G. B., 270
Formanowics, M., 382
Formisano, E., 562
Forrest, A. D., 217
Forsyth, D. R., 490, 508
Fortin, G., 627
Fosse, N. E., 235
Fosshage, J. L., 610
Foster, B. B., 586
Foster, C.A., 676
Foster, T. S., 183
Foti, D., 567
Foulds, J. A., 667
Foulkes, D., 208
Foutz, A., 209
Fowler, J. H., 259, 474, 499, 675
Fowler, J. S., 560, 621
Fox, K. C., 208
Fox, M. C., 392, 393f
Fox, M. D., 212, 542
Fox, P. W., 422
Foye, P. E., 256
Frady, R. L., 540
Fraga, M. F., 83
Fragoza, R., 549
Fraley, R. C., 476
Frances, A., 554, 585
Franceschini, R., 390
Francis, D. D., 85, 648
Franco, Z. E., 537
Frank, D. A., 414
Frank, L. R., 440
Frank, M. G., 248
Frank, R., 122
Franken, D., 680, 681
Frankenhuis, W. E., 371
Frankhuijzen-Sierevogel, A. C., 263
Frankl, V. E., 656, 659
Franks, N. R., 196
Franson, K. L., 572
Franz, C., 475, 475f
Franzen, L., 209
Fratta, P., 367
Frazier, T. W., 556, 557
Frederick, D. A., 371
Fredman, S. J., 592
Fredricks, J. A., 268, 269
Fredrickson, B. L., 660
Freedman, D. G., 245
Freedman, R., 563
Freedson, P. S., 668
Freeman, H. L., 564, 623
Freeman, S., 489
Freeman, T. P., 566, 566f
Frei, O., 563
French, J. E., 403
French, S. A., 444
Freud, S., 13–14, 16, 195, 208, 443, 463, 600, 612
Fricchione, G. L., 225
Frick, P. J., 632
Friedel, S., 210
Friedman, J. M., 256, 257
Friedrikson, M., 577f
Friedson, M., 437
Frierson, T., 541
Friesen, C., 209
Friesen, W. V., 234, 248
Frijda, N. H., 239
Frisch, M. B., 675
Frisch, R. E., 439
Frith, C. D., 537
Frith, U., 556
Froberg, J. E., 202
Frost, P., 90
Frum, C., 41, 263f, 264, 544
Fryar, C. D., 257, 665, 666f
Frye, R., 130, 386
Fryer, R., 254
Fujita, Y., 206
Fulbright, R. K., 389, 390
Fulero, S., 341
Fulker, D. W., 539
Fullerton, C. S., 645
Funayama, E. S., 518
Funder, D. C., 472, 505
Fung, H. H., 452, 508, 565
Fung, L. K., 619
Furi, S., 101, 499
Furnham, A., 481
Furtner, M. R., 588
Furukawa, T. A., 625

G

Gaab, N., 390
Gaalema, D. E., 220
Gabriel, P. O., 293
Gabrieli, J. D., 390
Gabrieli, J. D. E., 475
Gaceres, M., 77
Gainotti, G., 125
Gajiwala, K. S., 257
Galaburda, A. M., 122
Galanis, P., 620
Galbally, M., 644
Galdi, P., 397
Galea, S., 584
Galinsky, A. M., 264, 265
Gallagher, M., 675
Gallagher, P. R., 583, 644
Gallese, V., 124
Galli, R., 583
Gallup, G. G., 196
Galovski, T., 592
Galperin, A., 371
Galton, F., 73
Galvan, A., 442
Gamez, W., 469
Gan, W., -B., 207
Gandevia, S. C., 193
Ganguly-Fitzgerald, I., 194
Ganna, A., 265
Ganoczy, D., 624
Gant, N., 185
Gantt, W. H., 293
Gao, F., 77
Gao, X., 256
Gao, Z., 90
Garabedian, M. J., 625
Garb, H. N., 482
Garbinsky, E. N., 679
Garcia-Leon, M. A., 659
Garcia-Palacios, A., 630
Garcia-Retamero, R., 374
Garcia-Rios, M. d. C., 659
Garcia-Sierra, A., 388
Garcia, J., 288, 293
Garcia, J. R., 264
Garcia, N. L., 391
Gard, D., 370
Gard, T., 225
Gardner, A., 385
Gardner, B., 386
Gardner, H., 393
Gardner, W. L., 184, 493
Gardner, W. P., 559
Garmezy, N., 659, 660
Gasquet, I., 561, 583
Gasquoine, P. G., 243
Gatenby, J. C., 518
Gates, B., 196
Gatz, M., 452
Gaughan, E. T., 589
Gaulin, S. J. C., 91
Gaulton, K. J., 90
Gautam, P., 50
Gawronski, B., 504, 506, 511, 517, 518
Gayer-Anderson, C., 566, 566f
Gazzaniga, M. S., 123, 125, 194, 195
Geary, D. C., 63, 519
Gebauer, J. E., 486, 487
Geddes, J. R., 623, 625
Geiselman, R. E., 251
Geiser, S., 57
Gelenberg, A. J., 208
Gelfand, M. J., 460, 460f
Gellavia, G., 532
Geller, D. A., 581
Gena, A., 620
Gendron, M., 245
Genkov, K. A., 224
Gennaro, L., 208
Genovese, K., 538
Gent, J. F., 186
Gentile, B., 589
Genzel, L., 354
George, T. P., 664
Gerbier, E., 207
Gergen, K. J., 486
Gerlach, A. L., 577
Gerlicher, A. M. V., 244
Gernsbacher, M. A., 63
Gerolimatos, L. A., 455
Gerostamoulos, D., 222
Gershoff, E. T., 299, 300
Gershon, A. S., 209
Gersten, M., 576
Geschwind, D. H., 77, 556
Gest, S. D., 659
Gettler, L. T., 262
Geuze, E., 476
Gevonden, M., 583
Gewirtz, J. C., 291
Geyer, 523
Ghandour, R. M., 622
Ghatei, M., 261
Ghazal, S., 374
Gherig, Lou, 128
Ghosh, A., 181
Gialluisi, A., 390
Gianaros, P. J., 660
Giancola, P. R., 540
Gibb, B. E., 460
Gibbons, T., 669
Gibson, M. A., 98
Giedd, J. N., 136, 564f
Gieddd, J., 397
Giesbrecht, T., 585
Gigerenzer, G., 371, 372
Gijsbers, K., 183
Gilbert, D. T., 43, 505, 506
Gilbert, L. R., 447
Gilbert, S. L., 93
Gilboa-Schechtman, E., 249, 249f, 348
Gilboa, A., 347
Gilkerson, J., 387
Gilkes, J. J., 262
Gill, J., 583, 584
Gill, M., 562
Gillespie, C. F., 86, 648
Gilligan, M., 453
Gilligan, S. G., 485
Gillihan, S. J., 491
Gillin, J. C., 575, 575f
Gillman, M. W., 444
Gilman, S. E., 261
Gilovich, T., 231, 485
Gimlin, K., 440
Gino, F., 345
Giordani, B., 648
Giorgi, R., 259
Girard, M., 126
Girdler, S., 413
Girgus, J. S., 570
Gitschier, J., 177
Giuliano, T., 354
Glahn, D. C., 564
Glanzer, M., 327–328
Glascher, J., 118f
Glasgow, S. D., 354
Glasziou, P., 601
Gleason, C. A., 193
Gleeson, M., 669
Gleick, J., 401

Glenn, A. L., 586
Glenn, N. D., 454
Glick, P., 518f
Gliga, T., 168
Glover, G., 442
Glunt, E. K., 519
Gochman, P., 564f
Godden, D. R., 337, 337f
Goddings, A. L., 440
Godoy, R., 501
Goebel, R., 562
Goekoop, J. G., 263
Goetz, C. G., 564
Goff, D. C., 564
Goffin, K. C., 567
Gogtay, N., 136, 397
Golan, D., 90
Gold, J., 584
Goldberg, S. B., 225
Goldberg, S. C., 59
Goldman-Rakic, P. S., 427
Goldstein, D. G., 372
Goldstein, E. B., 185
Goldstein, N. J., 524
Goldstein, R. B., 643f, 656
Goleman, D., 395
Golgi, C., 109
Golightly, R. T., 293
Gollan, J. K., 116, 572, 650
Golle, J., 649
Gollub, R. L., 225
Golmard, J., -L., 208
Golosheykin, S., 248
Golse, B., 126
Gone, J. P., 607
Gonzalez-Perez, R., 659
Gonzalez-Tapia, M. L., 84
Gonzalez, R., 217, 370, 391
Good, B., 579
Goodall, J., 46
Goodfriend, W., 682, 683
Gooding, P. A., 582
Goodman, G., 633
Goodwin, G. M., 624
Goossens, L., 500, 501
Goostman, E., 197
Gordon, A. M., 682
Gordon, J. I., 259
Gordon, N., 36
Gordon, R., 240
Gore, J. C., 518
Gorelick, D. A., 218
Gorgoni, M., 204
Goriounova, N. A., 398
Gornik, A. E., 474f
Gorno-Tempini, M. L., 567
Gorski, R. A., 266
Goschke, T., 378
Gosling, S. D., 476, 486, 487
Gosselin, F., 243f
Gosseries, O., 204
Gotow, N., 185
Gotsopoulos, A., 245
Gottesman, I. I., 208, 399, 447, 562, 563f
Gottman, J., 273, 533, 534, 634
Gould, C. E., 455
Gouldner, A., 524
Goyal, M., 657
Graap, K., 630
Grabowski, T. J., 122, 245
Graff, J., 338
Graffunder, C. M., 653, 664f
Grafton, S. T., 124, 203
Graham-Bermann, S. A., 541
Graham, J., 443
Graham, R., 440, 441
Grandelis, A., 350
Grandin, T., 363
Granpeesheh, D., 620
Granrud, C. E., 167
Grant, A. M.., 469, 480
Grant, B. F., 553, 553f, 577, 643f, 656
Grass, J. A., 290
Grassi, S., 572
Gratton, A., 469
Graves, D. A., 183
Graves, K. D., 651
Graves, N., 527
Graves, W. W., 347
Gray, J., 604
Gray, J. A., 291, 476
Gray, J. C., 475, 476
Gray, J. R., 225, 398, 476
Gray, P. B., 262
Gray, S., 387
Green, A. L., 378, 616
Greenberg, J., 53, 489
Greene, R. L., 482
Greengard, P., 573
Greenhill, K. M., 514
Greenspan, R. J., 195
Greenspoon, J., 337
Greenstein, D., 397, 560
Greenwald, A. G., 486, 488, 488f
Greer, D. M., 212, 213
Greicius, M. D., 198, 348, 349
Greider, C., 389
Grewe, B. F., 182
Grewen, K. M., 263
Griffin, D. W., 532
Griffith, J., 645
Grigg-Damberger, M. M., 207
Griggs, R. A., 526
Grill, J. T., 200
Grimes, T., 38
Grimm, K. J., 447
Grimshaw, K., 561
Grinevich, V., 242
Griskevicius, V., 271f, 273, 274, 676
Grissom, C. K., 664
Grizzard, M., 280
Grogan-Kaylor, A., 300, 541
Gronli, J., 209
Gronlund, S. D., 341
Gross, C. T., 242
Gross, J. J., 246, 247, 248
Grossman, M., 54, 330, 367
Groth-Marnat, G., 602
Group, B. D. C., 397
Group, L. S. B. W., 668
Grover, S., 675
Grubert, C., 616
Grundy, J. G, 413
Gruzelier, J., 203, 226, 227
Gu, Q., 625
Guenther, C. A., 90
Guez, L., 378f
Guglielmi, R. S., 395, 396
Guidotti Breting, L. M., 648
Guidry, D. W., 664
Guignard, J.-H., 446, 448
Guillen, V., 630
Guillory, J. E., 63, 64
Gulmezoglu, A. M., 412
Gulyani, S., 209
Gum, A., 680
Gunderson, J., 632
Gunderson, J. G., 587
Gunnar, M.R., 657
Gunturkun, O., 196, 469
Guo, Q., 354, 616
Guo, S., 541
Gur, R., 250
Gur, R. C., 63, 540
Gurung, R., 6, 23, 24, 27
Gusnard, D. A., 93
Gustavson, C. R., 293
Gustin, M.-P., 207
Guth, A., 202
Gutierrez, B., 580
Gutterrrez, J., 35
Guynn, M. J., 336
Guze, B. H., 597

H

Haake, J. J., 167
Habel, U., 540
Haber, R. B., 363
Haber, R. N., 363
Hackenberg, T. D., 613
Hacker, M. R., 414
Hackman, A., 680
Hadrysiewicz, B., 616
Haemer, M. A., 665
Hafetz, J., 540
Hagino, H., 563
Hahn, A., 517
Hahn, A. C., 262
Hahn, L., 280
Haidt, J., 443
Haier, R. J., 397f
Haigh, M. M., 487
Haines, J., 444
Hakim, N., 137
Hakun, J., 250
Halaas, J. L., 257
Halbert, P., 293
Hale, S., 430
Hales, C. M., 665, 666f
Haley, A., 399
Hall, C. S., 462
Hall, G., 198
Hall, G. S., 20
Hallas, B. H., 109
Hallgren, K. A., 668
Hallion, L. S., 378
Hallmayer, J. F., 556
Halmi, K. A., 59
Halonen, J., 340
Halperin, J. M., 430
Halpern-Felsher, B. L., 442
Halpern, D. F., 63
Halpin, C. F., 177
Halverson, M. S., 89
Hamamura, T., 493
Hamani, C., 616
Hamann, S., 340
Hamburg, P., 261
Hamel, M., 482
Hamermesh, D. S., 513
Hamilton, P. J., 649
Hamilton, W. D., 537, 538
Hammen, C., 436
Hampson, S. E., 436, 437, 437f
Hamre, B., 209
Han, S., 107f
Han, T. -U., 35
Hancock. J. T., 63, 64
Handel, G. F., 567
Haney, 523
Hansen, J., 489f
Hanson, K. N., 98
Hardan, A. Y., 556, 557, 619
Hardison, P., 137
Hare, B., 183
Hare, R., 588
Hare, R. D., 586
Hare, T., 442
Harenski, C. L., 123
Hargrove, M. F., 540
Hari, R., 245
Hariri, A. R., 476
Harkins, S., 528
Harlow, H., 434, 500
Harlow, M. K., 500
Harms, P. D., 645, 680
Harpaz,-Rotem, I., 645
Harper, F. K., 651
Harrington, H., 75, 459
Harris, D., 664
Harris, D. E., 613
Harris, R. A., 220
Harris, T., 500
Harris, T. O., 573
Harrison, G., 624
Harrison, J., 270
Harrold, J., 256
Hart, A. J., 518
Hart, B., 388, 603f
Hart, W., 269
Hartman, C. A., 571
Hartmann-Boyce, J., 224
Harvey, A., 578
Harvey, L. J., 521, 521f
Harwood, J., 517, 522
Haselton, M. G., 371
Hashimoto, R., 564
Hashmi, A., 207
Hashmi, N., 398, 399f

Hashtroudi, S., 340
Hasiao, E. C., 349
Hasin, D.S., 553, 553f, 578
Haslam, A., 523
Haslam, C., 488
Haslam, S. A., 488, 526
Haslinger, B., 244
Hatfield, E., 144
Hatzigeorgiadis, A., 626
Haubrich, 338
Haug, T. T., 628f
Hause, K. S., 533
Havel, M., 202
Hawes, S. W., 391
Hawken, S., 414, 557
Hawker, G., 209
Hawking, S., 196
Hawkins, H. K., 206
Hawkins, R. D., 346
Hawkins, S. S., 414
Hawkley, L. C., 30, 268, 452, 501, 502, 571, 652, 668, 677
Hawrylewics, K., 413
Haxby, J. V., 347, 367
Hayes, J. A., 607
Hayes, J. P., 648
Hayes, M. G., 459
Haynes, J.-D., 193
Haynes, R. B., 601
Haythorn, W., 336
Head, D., 450
Healey, K. M., 250
Healy, M., 489
Heard, H. L., 632
Heath, A., 248
Heatherton, T. F., 491
Hecht, S., 158
Heckman, J. J., 652
Hedden, T., 475
Heider, F., 505
Heigele, S., 354
Heinrichs, M., 133, 640
Heinz, A., 540
Heinz, A. J., 540
Heinze, H.-J., 193
Heiss, W.D., 348
Held, B. S., 682
Helliwell, J. F., 658, 675, 677, 678f
Helpern, J. A., 560
Hemsley, D. R., 291
Henderson, G. V., 213
Henderson, V. K., 435
Hendin, H. M., 590
Henin, A., 576
Hening, W., 349
Henkel, L. A., 345
Henley, T., 11, 15
Hennenlotter, A., 244
Hennig, C., 93
Hennig, J., 460
Henninger, D., 540
Henry, M., 259
Henschel, A., 272
Herbert, T. B., 651
Herdt, G. H., 265
Herek, G. M., 519
Hergenhahn, B., 11, 15
Herian, M., 680
Herian, M. N., 645
Herman, S., 669
Hermann, K. L., 149
Hermans, D., 576
Hermans, E. J., 119
Hernandez, T. L., 259
Herndon, D. N., 206
Herndon, J. G., 453
Herpertz-Dahlmann, B., 557
Herpertz, S. C., 246, 587
Herrnstein, R. J., 304, 363, 385
Hershberger, S. L., 422
Herskovits, M. J.
Hertel, P., 354
Herting, M. M., 421, 440
Herxheimer, A., 200
Herz, D. M., 378
Herz, R., 185
Herzog, D. B., 261
Heslop, P., 654
Hess, U., 249, 249f
Hevevrabd, J., 210
Heyman, G. M., 304
Heyman, R. E., 534
Hibar, D. P., 560, 564
Hibbeln, J. R., 567, 568f, 624, 666
Hibi, M., 206
Hichwa, R. D., 245, 563
Higbed, L., 222
Higgins, S. T., 220
Higley, J. D., 432
Hilbig, B. E., 372
Hilburn, I. A., 178
Hill, A. K., 262
Hill, D. E., 549, 556
Hill, F., 472
Hill, P. L., 447
Himelboim, I., 529
Hindmarsh, P., 644
Hinds, D. A., 475, 475f
Hines, M., 266, 423, 424f
Hinney, A., 262
Hinson, R., 292
Hinton, D. E., 579
Hirata, S., 431
Hiripi, E., 260
Hirsch, J., 674
Hirsch, J. K., 674
Hirsch, N., 212
Hirshfeld-Becker, D. R., 576
Hirshfeld, D. R., 576
Hirshkowitz, M., 205
Hiscock-Anisman, C., 251
Hitch, G. J., 323, 324, 324f
Ho, K., 349
Ho, M. Y., 508, 565
Ho, S. S., 665
Hobfoll, S. E., 645
Hobson, J., 208, 354
Hoch, J. E., 422, 423
Hochberg, F., 99
Hodges, 523
Hodges, J. R., 347
Hodgkin, A. L., 138
Hoebel, B. G., 257
Hoeft, F., 390
Hoek, H. W., 616
Hoekstra, R. A., 556
Hofer, S. M., 451
Hoffman, B. J., 589
Hoffmann, P., 390
Hofling, C. K., 527
Hofmann, S. G., 627
Hofmann, W., 491
Hofstede, G., 273, 493, 494f
Hogan, C. L., 669
Hogan, D., 412
Hogan, N., 349
Hoge, C. W., 583
Hokanson, J. E., 652
Holbrook, J. R., 622
Holcomb, J., 514
Holder, M. K., 126
Holguin, Roberto., 123
Holingue, C., 130
Hollon, S. D., 626
Holmes, J. G., 532
Holowacz, E., 454
Holt-Lunstad, J., 500
Holt, L. H., 384
Holtmann, O., 244
Holttum, J., 209
Holtzman, N. S., 588
Holzel, B. K., 225
Holzgrabe, U., 349
Holzman, P. S., 562, 566
Home, J., 204*f*
Hong, X., 413, 558
Hood, A. C., 354
Hood, W.R., 521, 521f
Hoogman, M., 560
Hooshmand, F., 567
Hopkins, C. A., 576
Hopkins, W. D., 386
Hopper, K., 624
Horan, W. P., 624
Horn, J. L., 451
Horne, J., 204
Horney, K., 465
Horton, N. J., 444
Horvath, S., 556
Horwitz, A. V., 675
Horwitz, J., 675
Horwood, L. J., 28, 84, 217, 217f, 540, 565
Hosobuchi, Y., 182
Hosseinian-Far, A., 644
Hostinar, C. E., 657
Hottenga, J. -J., 566
Hou, W., 413, 558, 560
Hou, Y., 241
House, J. S., 267
Houser, D., 536, 537
Houston, S., 657
Houston, S. M., 421
Hove, M. J., 227
Howard, A. D., 256
Howard, K., 38
Howell-White, S., 675
Howell, R. T., 675
Howes, O. D., 564
Hoyer, J., 580
Hoyle, R. H., 485
Hrdy, S. B., 93
Hsing, C., 447
Hsu, C. Y., 200
Hsu, H., 414, 557
Hu, C., 560
Hu, Y., 241
Hu, Z., 663
Huang, C. J., 378f
Huang, D., 72, 259
Huang, H., 677, 678f
Huang, T. T., 665
Hubbard, J. J., 659
Hubel, D. H., 159
Huchinson, E. B., 35
Hudson, J. I., 260
Hudson, M., 80
Hudson, N. W., 476
Hudspeth, A., 174
Huff, S., 213
Hugdahl, K., 564
Hugenberg, K., 336
Hughes, J. R., 290
Hughes, K., 534
Hughes, M., 564, 583, 644
Hughes, M. E., 677
Hughes, S., 534
Hull, C. L., 253
Hulme, C., 430
Hummer, A., 640
Hunt, G. E., 222, 321, 564
Hunt, H. T., 208
Hunt, J., 552
Hunt, M., 587
Hunt, P. D., 200
Hupka, R. B., 246
Hur, J., -W., 397
Hurd, P. L., 540
Hurlemann, R., 616
Hurlimann, D., 651
Hurst, C., 469
Hurst, J. A., 388
Hussey, E. P., 330
Hutcherson, C. A., 432
Hutchinson, J. M. C., 99
Hutchinson, S., 513
Hutchison, K.A., 246
Huttenlocher, P. R., 421f
Huttunen, M., 397
Huweler, R., 577
Huxley, A. F., 138
Hwang, H. S., 537
Hyatt, C. S., 589
Hyde, J. S., 63
Hylton, E., 658
Hystad, S. W., 659, 659f

I

Iacono, W., 476
Ida, I., 653
Idzik, P., 280
Igielnik, R., 68

Lauriello, J., 624
Lauritsen, M. B., 48
Lavie, C. J., 657, 657f
Law, C. K., 259
Law, J., 42
Law, M., 309
Law, P., 556
Layous, K., 679
Lazar, S. W., 225
Lazaropoulou, C., 644
Lazarus, A. A., 614
Lazarus, R. S., 643, 645, 656
Lazer, D. M., 514
Lazeyras, F., 646
Lazo, R. J., 434
Le, N., 369
Lea, M., 528
Leary, M. R., 267, 489
LeBlanc, S. A., 541
Leborgne, L., 385
Lecomte, T., 221, 627
LeDoux, J. E., 646
Lee, H., 514
Lee, J. H., 496, 496f
Lee, J. M., 354
Lee, J., -Y., 354
Lee, K., 482
Lee, L. C., 130
Lee, M. A., 623
Lee, S. J., 300
Lee, T. Y., 397
Lee, U., 213
Lee, W., 560
Lee, W. -S., 35
Lee, Y.-A., 514
Leese, M., 615
Leffert, N., 444
Leffler, A., 184
Lehner, B., 87
Lehrner, A., 583
Leichsenring, F., 610
Leichtman, M., 477
Leija, H. A. L., 42
Leitner, L., 611
Lemaster, J. L., 414
Lencz, T., 122
Lenroot, R., 397
Lenton, A. P., 246
Leonard, K. A., 434
Leopold, L., 256
Lepage, K. Q., 205
LePine, J. A., 489
LePort, A. K., 330
Leppa, V., 262
Leproult, R., 206, 653
Leptourgos, P., 564
Lerch, J., 397, 560
Lerch, P. G., 651
Lerner, A., 583, 584
Lerner, M., 583
Lerner, M. J., 508
Leroi, A. M., 413
Lervag, A., 430
Leslie, L. M., 460
Leslie, M., 261
Lester, P. B., 267, 500, 645, 657, 680
Leu-Semenescu, S., 208
Leucht, S., 623
Leung, A. K.-Y., 508
Leung, R. S., 209
Leurgans, S., 564
LeVay, S., 266f, 267
Levenson, R. W., 234, 494, 495
Levine, A., 445
Levine, B., 348
Levine, D. A., 451
Levine, J. D., 181, 184
Levine, M., 538, 543
Levinson, D., 448
Levinson, M. H., 448
Levy, D. L., 562
Levy, H. C., 378
Lewin, A. C., 675
Lewin, K., 471
Lewis, A., 212
Lewis, A. J., 644
Lewis, C. M., 565
Lewis, D. A., 217
Lewis, J. D., 397
Lewis, J. W., 41, 263f, 264, 544
Lewis, K., 354
Lewis, M., 195
Lewis, S., 524, 525f
Ley, R. E., 259
Li, C., 354
Li, H., 663
Li, K., 444
Li, S.-C., 394f
Li, W., 207
Li, Y., 451, 663
Liang, F.-X., 228
Liberator, P. A., 256
Liberzon, I., 244, 665
Libet, B., 193
Libon, D. J., 367
Lichtenberg, J. D., 610
Lichtenstein, E., 613
Lichtenstein, P., 266, 624
Lidbetter, N., 629
Liddle, P. E., 586
Liddon, L., 604
Lieberman, J. D., 53
Liebowitz, M. R., 578
Light, K. C., 263
Ligthart, L., 566
Liguori, A., 290
Likert, R., 479
Lilienfeld, S. O., 482, 585, 631
Lim, B. C., 460
Lim, C. C. W., 578
Lin, L., 28, 29, 202, 603f
Lin, L. -y., 228
Lin, N., 674
Lin, S., 670, 675
Linchitz, R., 182
Lind, J. N., 391, 413
Lindeman, M. J., 581
Linden, D. E., 562
Lindenberger, U., 450
Lindsay, D. S., 340
Lindsay, R. C. L., 341
Lindstrom, R. C., 259
Linehan, M. M., 632
Link, B. G., 644
Lipshultz, S. E., 218, 220
Lissek, S., 584
Little, A. C., 532
Liu, C. H., 574, 574f
Liu, S.-M., 553, 553f
Liu, T., 213
Liu, Y., 549
Liversedge, T., 212
Livesley, W. J., 475
Livingston, B. A., 469
Livingston, E. H., 260
Livingstone, M. S., 159
Livshits, G., 259
Ljung, R., 202
Lo Re, G., 250
Lo, J. O., 414, 416f
Lo, M.-T., 475, 475f
Lo, S. L., 474f
Lobmaier, J. S., 649
Locke, B. D., 607
Locke, J., 8
Lockhart, R. S., 325
Lockley, S. W., 200
Loe, I., 622
Loehlin, J. C., 475
Loftus, E., 333, 333f, 338, 339f, 341, 345, 631
Logel, C., 519
Logie, R. H., 322
Logue, M. W., 648
Lok, A., 571
Loll, F., 369
Lombardelli, A., 583
Lomo, T., 346
Long, K., 99
Lopez-Castroman, J., 626
Lopez, J. M., 181
Lopez, R. B., 491
Lopez, S. R., 27
Lorenz, T., 626
Lotspeich-Younkin, F., 454
Lotto, A., 384
Lovaas, O. I., 309, 619
Love, R. W., Jr., 454
Lovegreen, L. D., 449, 450f
Lovett, M. C., 369, 370
Lovie, A. D., 64
Lovie, P., 64
Lowe, D. J. E., 664
Lowe, J. C., 454
Lowe, J. K., 556
Lowry, R., 673
Loy, J. W., 504
Lozano, A. M., 616
Lu, K., 514
Lu, Y., 38
Lubart, T., 446, 448
Lubinski, D., 401
Lubow, R. E., 286, 291
Lucas, R. E., 676f
Lucatch, A. M., 664
Lucette, A., 658
Luchetti, M., 496, 496f
Luczak, S. E., 667
Luhmann, M., 452
Luk, G., 391
Lukas, G., 246
Lukowski, A. F., 430
Lumbiganon, P., 412
Lun, J., 459, 460, 460f
Lund, R., 651
Luo, L., 90
Luo, R., 620
Luo, S., 494, 495, 675
Luo, Y., 675
Lupien, S. J., 654, 654f, 660, 661f
Lutter, C. D., 262, 518
Luyckx, K., 77t, 436, 437, 437f
Lydholm, C. N., 414
Lykken, D. T., 81, 475, 476f, 510, 586, 674
Lynam, D. R., 589
Lynn, M., 524
Lynn, S. J., 585, 631
Lyons, J. A., 592
Lyoo, I. K, 625f
Lyu, W., 68
Lyubomirsky, S., 674, 676, 677, 679

M

Ma, J., 106, 541
Ma, L., 207
Ma, Y., 107
Maccoby, E. E., 436
Maccoby, M., 588
MacDonald, A., 213f
MacDonald, G., 682
MacFabe, D., 130
MacGregor, A. J., 99
MacGregor, D. G., 375
Mach, H., 669
Machado, A. G., 616
Machado, C. J., 242
MacKenzie, I. R., 567
MacKillop, J., 475, 476
Macleod, J., 654
Macpherson, R., 442
MacQueen, G., 198
Macrae, C. N., 203
Madden, E., 217
Maddi, S., 659
Maddison, A., 378f
Maddock, R. J., 350
Madey, S. F., 231
Madigan, S., 402, 644
Madva, A., 518
Maeda, T., 418
Maenner, M. J., 555, 556f
Maes, B., 401
Maes, J. H. R., 632
Maestripieri, D., 98
Maffei, M., 256, 257
Maggard, M. A., 260
Maglione, M., 260
Magnasco, M. O., 185
Magne, C., 240
Magnin, M., 207
Magnusson, F. L., 620, 622

Magrini, V., 259
Mahajan, R., 619
Maher, B., 393, 622
Mahler, G., 567
Mahler, H. I. M., 268
Mahon, B. Z., 367, 368f
Mahoney, D. E., 616
Mahowald, M. W., 259
Mai, H. L., 187
Maier, R., 265
Maier, S. F., 569
Maier, W., 564
Maimon, E., 583
Majdandžic, J., 640
Mak, L. E., 198
Makin, J. W., 419
Makrygianni, M. K., 620
Malcom, C. M., 93
Malek, M., 560
Malhi, G. S., 624
Malinger, G., 414
Malle, B. F., 506
Malmberg, A. B., 184
Malmberg, K. J., 319
Malone, P. S., 505, 506
Malone, T. W., 398, 399f
Maloney, S. E., 557
Malt, B. C., 365
Mammarella, N., 352
Manbeck, A. B., 584
Mandera, P., 384, 385f
Maner, J., 47
Mankowski, T. A., 486
Mann, L., 526
Manning, R., 538
Mannix, R., 112
Manns, J. R., 340
Mansell, W., 578
Mansson, H., 35
Mansvelder, H. D., 398
Mantell, D. M., 525
Mantyla, T., 336
Manuel, W. J., 522
Maples, J., 589
Mar, A., 85, 648
Maran, T., 588
Maraninchi, M., 259
Marc Breedlove, S., 262
Marconi, A., 565
Marcus, S. M., 644
Mardis, E. R., 259
Margand, N. A., 435
Margittai, Z., 640
Margoni, F., 430
Marighetto, A., 349
Marini, A., 460
Mariske, M., 432
Mark, K. P., 262, 264
Markowitsch, H. J., 348
Markowitz, J. C., 626
Marks, G. A., 207
Markus, H., 484
Markus, H. R., 494
Marmot, M. G., 649
Marner, L., 118
Mars, R. B., 632
Marschik, P. B., 413
Marsden, P. V., 675
Marsh, A. A., 118, 250
Marsh, B.U., 40
Marsh, E. J., 336
Marshall-Goodell, B. S., 291
Marshall, G. D., 237
Marshall, G. N., 644, 657
Martial, C., 213
Martin, A., 348, 367
Martin, B., 528
Martin, E. A., 250
Martin, G., 667
Martin, J., 28, 84, 586
Martin, J. A., 436
Martin, W. J., 184
Martinez, J., 578
Martinez, R., 542
Marx, R., 627
Mash, H. B. H., 645
Mashour, G. A., 213
Masi, C. M., 502
Maslow, A. H., 14, 22, 271, 272, 466, 676
Mason, M. F., 203
Mason, W. A., 242
Masse, M., 627
Masten, A. S., 659
Masuda, T., 508
Mata, J., 669
Mather, M., 345
Mathers, C., 568, 569f
Matheson, D. H., 513
Matsa, K. E., 514
Matsumoto, D., 246, 247f, 249, 249f, 537
Matsuzaki, I., 256
Mattera, R., 35
Mattevi, B. S., 124
Mattfeld, A. T., 330
Matthews-Ewald, M. R., 260
Matthews, B. R., 567
Matthews, C. E., 668
Mattucci, C., 242
Matusch, A., 616
Matuschka, L., 221
Maurer, C., 418
Maurer, D., 418
Maurer, J. M., 123
Mavridis, D., 623
Max, W., 664
Maxwell, R., 631
May, R. W., 437
Mayberg, H. S., 616
Mayer, D., 395
Mayer, J., 248, 256
Maylott, S. E., 434
Mazur, A., 262, 535
Mazure, C. M., 573
Mazza, S., 207
Mazziotta, J. C., 597
McAleavey, A. A., 607
McArthur, L. Z., 535
McArthur, M. J., 421
McCain, J. L., 589
McCall, M., 524
McCann, D., 561
McCarley, R. W., 207, 208
McCarthy-Jones, S., 562
McCarthy, M. I., 90
McCauley, C., 681
McClay, I., 28
McClay, J., 84, 586
McClelland, D. C., 268, 269
McClernon, F. J., 290
McClintock, M. K., 93
McClung, C. A., 572
McClure, J. N., 578
McComb, K., 196
McConnell, R.A., 61
McCrae, R. R., 467f, 468, 475, 479
McCullough, K. B., 557
McCully, J., 292
McCusker, R., 669
McCutcheon, R., 564
McDade, T. W., 262
McDaniel, M. A., 336
McDonald, N. D., 472
McDonald, R., 526, 541
McDuffie, A., 401
McEwen, B. S., 54f, 341, 660, 661f, 6546
McFall, R. M., 601, 602, 608
McGann, J. P., 183
McGaugh, J. L., 330
McGeary, J. E., 460
McGeown, L. M., 262
McGlone, F., 179
McGrath, J. J., 260
McGrath, L., 615
McGraw, A. P., 231
McGreery, S., 529
McGregor, H. A., 53
McGregor, I. S., 222, 564
McGue, M., 81, 475, 476f, 510
McGuire, M. T., 540
McGurk, D., 267, 500, 583, 592, 657
McHugh, R. K., 615
McInerney, S. C., 518
McKay, D., 610
McKay, K. E., 430
McKee, B., 448
McKenna, C., 534
McLean, D. E., 644
McMillan, C., 367
McMurray, J., 140
McNally, R. J., 582
McNamara, R. K., 567
McNaughton, N., 476
McNeely, H. E., 616
McNeill, D., 338
McNulty, J. K., 533
McQueeny, T., 440
McRobbie, H., 224
Meaney, M. J., 469, 640, 648
Mecca, A. M., 490
Medda, P., 615
Meddis, R., 209
Meduna, L., 615
Medvec, V. H., 231, 485
Meehan, W. P. III., 112
Meeus, W. H. J., 525
Mehrabian, A., 240
Meier, B. P., 590
Meier, M. H., 217
Meisel, A., 222
Meissner, C. A., 336
Mekel-Bobrov, N., 93
Melhuish, E., 414
Mellers, B. A., 231
Mellin, A., 444
Meltzer, A. L., 403
Meltzer, H. Y., 598, 623
Meltzoff, A. N., 307, 388, 432, 486
Melzack, R., 182
Melzer, N., 244
Memon, A., 251, 341
Mena, I., 492
Mencl, W. E., 389, 390
Menczer, F., 514
Mendel, G., 89
Mendoza, S. P., 242
Mendrek, A., 586
Meng-Hentschel, J., 649
Mennella, J. A., 188, 419
Mennes, M., 560
Menon, V., 198, 348
Menzel, E. W., 306
Menzies, L., 581
Mercer, C. H., 58
Merckelbach, H., 585, 631
Meredith, T., 264
Merrow, M., 202
Merskey, H., 631
Mery, F., 319
Merzenich, M. M., 180
Mesmer, F. A., 600
Messer, S. C.
Messian, N., 524
Mestre-Bach, G., 261
Mestre, M. A., 218, 220
Metcalfe, C., 654
Metz, G. A. S., 83
Meule, A., 261
Meuwese, R., 440
Meyer-Bahlburg, H. F., 266, 425
Meyer-Lindenberg, A., 133, 540
Meyer, D. E., 169, 331, 331f
Meyer, J. S., 222
Meyer, W. J., III., 206
Mezzofanti, G. C., 390
Miao, Q., 228
Micco, J. A., 576
Michalek, J., 262
Michalkewicz, M., 372
Micheau, J., 349
Michel, C., 336
Micheli, L., 625
Mick, E., 576
Mickelsen, O., 272
Mickes, L., 341
Middleton, F., 560
Mieda, M., 200
Miettunen, J., 221
Mignot, E., 202, 209, 210
Mikacich, J. A., 569

Mikels, J. A., 660
Mikulincer, M., 645
Mikuni, M., 653
Milani, I., 419f
Milani, R. V., 657, 657f
Milev, R., 198
Milevsky, A., 436, 438
Milgram, S., 471, 525, 526f
Milich, R., 561
Milinski, M., 537
Mill, J., 28, 84, 586
Millard, K., 526
Millard, S. P., 563
Miller, A., 607
Miller, A. L., 28, 84, 540
Miller, B. L., 492, 567
Miller, D. B., 541
Miller, D. J., 421
Miller, D. T., 506, 508
Miller, G., 21
Miller, G. A., 322, 323
Miller, G. E., 640, 650, 651
Miller, H., 337
Miller, I. W., 460
Miller, J., 524
Miller, J. D., 589
Miller, J. G., 443
Miller, K. D., 354
Miller, M. W., 648
Miller, N. E., 272
Miller, R., 203
Miller, S., 567
Miller, S. L., 520
Million, M., 259
Mills, K. L., 440, 444
Millstein, S. G., 442
Millward, C., 620
Milne, M., 80
Milner, B., 125, 127, 317, 347, 348f
Miltner, W. H. R., 244
Mindess, A., 178
Mineka, S., 576
Minick, P. E., 578
Minshew, N. J., 557
Minuzzi, L., 198
Miranda, R., 674
Mirza-Schreiber, N., 390
Mischel, W., 473
Mitchell, A., 514
Mitchell, A. A., 391, 413
Mitchell, B. A., 449, 450f
Mitchell, D. G., 118, 586
Mitchell, K. R., 58
Mitchum, A. L., 392, 393f
Mitler, M. N., 209
Mitropoulou, V., 653
Miyamoto, Y., 249, 249f
Mizrahi, R., 217
Mizuhara, Y., 178
Moatakef-Imani, B., 569
Moberg, P. J., 250
Mochizuiki, Y., 206
Moffitt, T. E., 75, 84, 459, 586
Mogensen, D. M., 413
Mohammadi, M., 644
Mohowald, M., 205
Mohtaseb, Z., 549, 556
Mojtabai, R., 598
Molaison, H., 45, 317, 328, 347, 348f, 349
Moldofsky, H., 206
Molendijk, M., 86
Molero, P., 86
Molina, E., 580
Moll, K., 390
Mollaghan, D. M., 476
Moller, A., -B., 412
Monaco, A. P., 388
Monig, C., 244
Monpetit, M. A., 657
Monson, C. M., 592
Montgomery, M. J., 444
Monti, M. M., 213f
Moon, C., 177, 412
Moon, H. Y., 354
Moon, R. Y. & Task Force on Sudden Infant Death Syndrome, 210
Moore, A. U., 286
Moore, C., 431
Moore, C. A., 205
Moore, D., 179
Moore, J. W., 454
Moore, K. A., 669
Moore, P. J., 268
Moore, R., 577
Moore, R. Y., 209, 210
Moore, T., 371
Moors, A., 239
Moreau, D., 576
Moreira-Maia, C. R., 620, 622
Morell, R., 35
Moreno-De-Luca, D., 556
Moreno, B., 580
Morey, R. A., 648
Morgan, B., 367
Morgan, E. M., 448
Mori, C., 402, 418
Mori, K., 563
Moriarty, D., 293
Moriarty, J. C., 250
Morin, C. M. 228
Moritz, S., 447
Morres, I. D., 626
Morris, D. E., 42
Morris, D. W., 562
Morris, K. S., 442
Morris, M. W., 508
Morris, N., 556
Morris, R., 540
Morris, W. L., 250
Morrow, J., 370
Morrow, M., 250
Mors, O., 260
Morse, S., 486
Mortensen, P.B., 414
Morton, G. J., 257
Morton, R., 414
Moscovici, S., 529, 529f
Moscovitch, M., 347
Moser, F., 382, 540
Moskalenko, Y., 615
Moss, C., 196
Mossner, R., 564
Most, D. E., 395
Mota-Rolim, S. A., 208
Mount, M. K., 469
Movellan, J., 307
Mozell, R., 411
Mrazek, A. J., 459, 460, 460f
Mu, D., 620
Mucke, D., 477
Mucke, L., 349
Muehlenbein, M. P., 91
Mueller, E., 535
Mueller, P. A., 351, 351f
Mueller, V., 541
Muennig, P., 392
Mulder, R., 632
Mulkern, R. V., 414
Munch, Edvard, 579
Mundorf, N., 362
Mundorff, J., 35
Munford, P., 597
Munoz, M., 388
Murana, E., 242
Murayama, K., 269
Murdoch, B. B., Jr., 327
Murphy, D. L., 337
Murphy, J., 583
Murphy, K., 218
Murphy, K. D., 206
Murphy, K. G., 261
Murphy, S., 488
Murphy, S. L., 670
Murray, C. J. L., 565, 568, 569f
Murray, H. A., 267, 268
Murray, I., 586
Murray, L., 118
Murray, R. M., 564, 565
Murray, S. H., 262, 264
Murray, S. L., 532
Murugesan, T., 290
Musial, Stan, 128
Musk, Elon, 196
Musso, D., 414
Mustonen, A., 221
Muthukumaraswamy, S. D., 218
Mychack, P., 492
Myers, D. G., 678
Myhra, L. L., 607

N

Nadam, L. S., 573
Nadel, L., 306, 347
Nader, K., 338
Nadig, A. S., 177
Naimi, T. S., 416f
Nakagawa, S., 247f, 354
Nakashima, S., 504, 504f
Nardi, B., 460
Narr, K. L, 397
National Institute of Child Health and Human Development (NICHHD), 210
National Sleep Foundation, 210
Navalta, C., 653
Nave, C. S., 472
Nave, G., 397
Nazar, B. P., 261
Nazeer, A., 583
Neal, D. T., 236, 237
Neal, J. W., 474f
Neale, M. C., 539, 580
Nedeltcheva, A. V., 653, 653f
Nee, D. E., 347
Neef, N. E., 390
Neff, L. A., 533
Neff, L. J., 663, 664, 664f
Neigh, G. N., 86, 648
Neil, M., 371
Neinstein, L. S., 446
Neisser, U., 18, 19, 22, 398
Nelen, M., 84
Nelsen, 417
Nelson-Coffey, S., 448
Nelson, A., 492, 492f
Nelson, C. B., 583, 644
Nelson, S. K., 676, 677, 679
Nemeroff, C. B., 86, 413, 557, 648
Nena, E., 220
Nere, A., 207
Neri, D. F., 200
Netter, S., 436, 438
Nettle, D., 485f
Nettles, T., 524
Neuberg, S. L., 271f, 273, 274, 676
Neugarten, B. L., 454
Neumark-Sztainer, D., 444
Neuner, F., 644
Neville, D. A., 119
Neville, H. J., 391
New, A. S., 653
New, M. I., 425
Newcombe, T. M., 473
Newell, A., 19
Newill, C., 130
Newman, N., 514
Newman, T. K., 432f
Newmark, S., 620
Newport, D. J., 413, 557
Newport, G. C., 413, 557
Newsom, C. R., 447
Newton-Howes, G., 667
Nezworski, M. T., 482
Ng, T. H. H., 645
Nguyen, D. H., 187
Nguyen, H. T., 646
Nguyen, T. T., 210, 213
Nias, D. K. B., 539
Nicolas, M. M., 349
Nicolaus, L., 293
Nicolson, R., 564f
Nieberding, R., 482
Niedenthal, P. M., 249
Nielsen, J., 417
Nielsen, L., 649
Nielsen, R., 514
Nielsen, T. A. 7
Niemela, S., 221

Nienhuis, R., 209
Nigg, J. T., 559
Nijeboer, S., 208
Nijsten, M. W., 48
Nikulin, V. V., 511
Nilssson, C. J., 651
Nilsson, K. W., 28
Nilsson, L.-G., 336
Nimmo-Smith, I., 322
Nisbett, R. E., 506, 508
Nishii, L., 460
Nitkin-Kaner, Y., 224
Nivard, M. G., 265, 566
Noaghiul, S., 567, 568f, 624, 666
Noah, T., 43
Noble-Haeusslein, L. J., 440
Noble, A. M., 529
Nodtvedt, O, 209
Noel, X., 215
Noelle-Neumann, E., 510
Nolen-Hoeksema, S., 370, 568, 570
Noller, P., 435
Nomura, Y., 644
Nopoulos, P., 563
Norcross, J. C., 602
Nordahl, C. W., 243
Nordenbak, C., 81
Nordentoft, M., 414
Norenzayan, A., 508
Norman, C. C., 534
Norman, G. J., 241
Norman, K. A., 349
Norman, W. T., 468
Norris, C. J., 116, 650
Norris, M. J., 262
Northoff, G., 491
Northstone, K., 455, 455f
Norton, M., 677, 678f
Norton, M. I., 203
Nosek, B. A., 42, 43, 443
Nowak, M. A., 538
Nowakowska, C., 567
Nozzolillo, A., 619
Nugent, A. C., 583, 584
Nummenmaa, L., 245
Nurnberger, J. I., Jr., 556
Nutt, D., 222
Nutt, D. J., 218, 629
Nyengaard, J. R., 118
Nystrom, L. E., 537

O

O'Brien, E. H., 447
O'Brien, L., 444
O'Brien, T. B., 658, 659
O'Connell, K., 563
O'Connor, K. J., 518
O'Connor, M., 492, 492f
O'Donnell, S., 293
O'Donovan, M. C., 83
O'Hara, M., 611
O'Keefe, J., 306
O'Leary, D. S., 563
O'Malley, G., 123
O'Malley, P. M., 490
O'Reardon, J. P., 617f
O'Sullivan, M., 248, 250
Obbels, J., 615
Obeid, J. S., 425
Obel, C., 48
Oberle, E., 679
Obsuth, I., 84
Ochiai, R., 206
Odbert, H. S., 468
Odegard, T. N., 339f
Oden, M. H., 401
Oei, J. L., 414
Ogawa, H., 185
Ogawa, W., 625
Ogden, C. L., 257, 665, 666f
Ogrodniczuk, J. S., 633
Oh, J., 447
Oh, M. Y., 242
Oh, Y. -S., 573
Oishi, S., 507, 507f
Oksenberg, A., 207
Okuda, M., 553, 553f
Olafsson, R. P., 630
Olatunji, B. O., 629
Olfson, M., 553, 553f, 576
Olliac, B., 126
Olsen, J. A., 432
Olsho, L. W., 177
Olsson, T., 209
Olyaei, A., 414, 416f
Ong, M. K., 664
Ophoff, R. A., 83
Oppenheimer, D. M., 351, 351f
Opris, I., 557
Orey, D., 623
Orfanidou, E., 391
Oring, L. W., 98
Ormel, J., 571
Orne, M. T., 224
Orobio de Castro, B., 297
Orr, M. T., 349
Orth, U., 444, 445f, 486, 488
Ortigue, S., 124
Ortuno Sanchez-Pedreno, F., 86
Osaka, E., 494
Osathanondh, R., 411
Oshima, A., 653
Osinsky, R., 460
Oskina, I., 477f
Osnaya-Ramirez, I., 200
Osorio, C., 648
Ospina, M., 209
Ossmy, O., 422
Ossyra, J., 669
Ostedgaard, K., 244
Oster, H., 186
Otsuka, Y., 419
Ott, U., 225
Otte, E., 557
Otto, M. W., 615
Ou-yang, X., -y., 228
Ouimet, M. C., 444
Outhred, T., 624
Overbeek, G., 297
Owe, E., 488
Owen, A. M., 212
Owen, E. R., 137
Owen, M. J., 83, 564
Owen, M. T., 435
Owen, N., 668
Ozery, D. H., 40
Ozono, H., 504, 504f
Ozonoff, S., 177

P

Pace, G. T., 300
Pack, S., 627
Pakkenberg, B., 118
Pal, D., 213
Pallavicini, C., 213
Pallesen, S., 209
Palmer, A. A., 475, 476
Palmer, J. C., 338, 339f, 341
Palombo, D. J., 348
Pan, Y., 241
Panaioti, M., 582
Panchaud, A., 414
Panlilio, L. V., 285
Pantev, C., 181
Paolini, S., 517, 522
Papadopoulos, T. C., 361
Papagno, C., 243
Papassotiriou, I., 644
Papp, L. A., 578
Pappert, E., J., 564
Paquet, A., 126
Paracchini, S., 390
Paradiso, S., 244
Paraskakis, E., 220
Parbery-Clark, A., 176
Parcet, M. A., 476
Pargament, K. I., 658
Pargament, K., I., 680
Pariante, C. M., 625, 648
Paris, J., 610
Park, B., 522
Park, C. R., 340
Park, G., 25
Park, S.-A., 514
Parker, A. M., 442
Parker, A., M., 374, 513
Parkvall, M., 391
Parner, E. T., 48
Parr, J. R., 556
Parvizi, J., 245
Pascual-Leone, A., 112, 181, 212, 492, 492f, 542
Pascual, J. C., 219
Pashler, H., 352, 354
Pasricha, P. J., 130
Pate, W. E., 603f
Patel, S., 524
Patrick, W., 116, 267
Patten, S. B., 598
Patterson, F., 386
Patterson, F. G. P., 196
Patterson, K. D., 105
Patton, R., 454
Paukmer. A., 433
Paukner, A., 312
Paul, A. M., 480
Paul, L. K., 397
Paulhus, D. I., 489, 588
Pauli, P., 579
Pauls, D. L., 581
Paulsen, J. S., 349
Pavlov, I. P., 16–17, 20, 22, 38, 41, 281, 285, 476
Pawlowski, M., 208
Pearce, M. T., 176
Pearl, D. K., 193
Pearson, A., 209, 490
Pearson, M. R., 668
Pearson, R. M., 455, 455f
Peckham, A. D., 615
Pedersen, C. B., 260
Pedersen, N., 620, 622
Pegna, A. J., 645
Pelham, W. E., 622
Pelios, L. V., 305
Peltokorpi, V., 354
Pence, B., 669
Penev, P. D., 653, 653f
Penfield, W., 180, 181
Peng, K., 508
Penke, L., 397
Penrod, S. D., 341
Pentland, A., 398, 399f
Pentland, B. T., 354
Peplau, L. A., 675
Pepperberg, I. M., 387
Peralta-Ramirez, M. I., 659
Perez-Marmol, J. M., 659
Perez, M. F., 87
Perfoli, L., 572
Perikleous, E. P., 220
Permack, D. G., 431
Perner, J., 431
Perrin, M. A., 583
Perry, R. J., 347
Perry, W. I., 447
Perugi, G., 615
Pervanidou, P., 644
Peters, E., 375
Peters, R., 450
Petersen, L., 414
Petersen, S., 657
Peterson-Zeitz, K. R., 184
Peterson, C., 341, 680, 681
Peterson, L. R., 321, 323f
Peterson, M., 436, 437, 437f
Peterson, M. J., 321, 323f
Peto, R., 665
Petrova, D., 374
Petrovitch, H., 220
Pettigrew, S., 43
Petty, R. E., 291, 326, 509, 512, 528
Petzold, M., 412
Peverly, S. T., 442
Peyron, C., 256
Pfaus, J. G., 41, 263f, 264
Pfeifer, M. A., 255f
Phan, K. L., 244
Phelps, E. A., 518

Phillips, K. A., 582
Phillips, N., 390
Phills, C. E., 517
Piacenza, L., 557
Piaget, J., 21, 426
Pierce, C. M., 527
Pietrzak, R. H., 643f, 645, 656
Pietschnig, J., 399f
Pihl, M. B., 413
Pilgrim, J. L., 222
Pinel, P., 554f
Pinker, S., 386, 388
Pinkwart, N., 369
Pins, D., 562
Piper, A., 631
Pipitone, J., 560
Pirenne, M. H., 158
Pisoni, D. B., 177
Pitt, L., 514
Pittenger, D. J., 480
Pitts, F. N., 578
Piven, J., 557
Plant, E. A., 520
Plat, L., 206, 653
Plazzi, G., 208
Plomin, R., 82
Plous, S., 373f
Poehlmann, K. M., 242
Pohl, R. F., 372
Poizner, H., 349, 391
Pol, H. H., 217
Polanco-Roman, L., 674
Polizzotto, N. R., 583
Polk, T. A., 665
Pollack, D. B., 540
Pollard, J., 224
Polya, G., 369
Pomar, L., 414
Ponto, L. B., 244, 245
Ponto, L. L. B., 563
Pope, H. G., Jr., 260
Pope, L. E., 262
Port, R. V., 80
Porter, R., 76
Porter, R. H., 419
Posner, M. I., 365, 475, 657
Postman, L. J., 36, 37
Potash, J., 571
Potenza, M. N., 261
Potter, J., 486, 487
Potvin, S., 221
Poulin-Dubois, D., 423
Poulton, R., 28, 84
Poundstone, W., 536
Povinelli, D. J., 196
Powell, K. E., 668
Prabhu, S., 280
Pradham, A. K., 444
Prah, P., 58
Pramstaller, P. P., 202
Prasad, S., 212, 542, 621
Prata, D. P., 83
Pratt, C., 304
Pratt, L. A., 598f, 625
Premack, D., 296
Preston, S. D., 640
Preussner, J., 217
Prevot, S., 415
Prewett, J., 251
Price, C. S., 559f
Priebe, S., 605
Prinzie, P., 469
Prior, H., 196
Prittie, B. A., 270
Prnewswire, 402
Probert, T., 648
Probst, F., 649
Prochaska, J. J., 664
Proenca, R., 256
Proffitt, D. R., 577
Pruden, S. M., 391
Przybylski, A. K., 500
Psotka, J., 344
Pugh, K. R., 389, 390
Purdie-Vaughns, V. J., 518
Putnam, K. M., 540, 586
Puts, D. A., 262
Putz, P., 203, 226
Pyle, G. F., 105
Pyle, N., 335
Pylkova, L. V., 203
Pyne, J. M., 630
Pyszczynski, T., 489

Q

Qi, W., 583
Qin, H., 657
Qin, L., 573
Qiu, D.-L., 349
Qualter, P., 189
Quan, H., 395
Quattrone, D., 566, 566f
Quero, S., 630
Quigley, H., 566, 566f
Quigley, K.S., 130
Qunaibi, M., 246

R

Raaijmakers, J. G. W., 319
Raaijmakers, Q. A. W., 525
Rabinowitz, D., 257
Rabung, S., 610
Racine, N., 402, 418, 644
Radant, A. D., 563
Rademaker, A. R., 476
Rae, D. S., 565
Raggatt, P., 419
Rahm, B., 348
Rahman, Q., 266
Rahn, R., 35
Raichle, M. E., 93, 198
Raine, A., 122, 586
Rajendran, K., 644
Rakic, P., 411
Raleigh, M. J., 540
Ramachandran, V. S., 180
Raman, R., 564
Ramanathan, L., 209
Ramiao, F., 222
Ramirez-Esparza, N., 388
Ramirez, J. M., 336
Ramirez, M., 659
Rammstedt, B., 470
Ramon y Cajal, S., 109
Ramos, R. L., 109
Ramsawh, H. J., 645
Ramsden, C. E., 208
Ramsey, E., 555
Ramsey, I. D., 262
Ramstad, E., 620, 622
Rancher, C., 541
Rand, K. L., 680
Randall, K., 361
Rands, S. A., 472
Randunu, R. S., 665
Ranyard, R., 337
Rao, N., 217
Rao, V., 123
Raoult, D., 259
Rapkin, A. J., 569
Rapoport, J., 581
Rapoport, J. L., 136, 440, 564f
Rapoport, S. I., 208
Rapson, R. L., 144
Rasband, A., 607
Rasch, B., 206
Raschle, N. M., 390
Rasgon, N., 569
Rasmussen, B., 633
Rasmussen, T., 125
Rasoulpoor, S., 644
Ratanatharathorn, A., 583
Ratliff, K. A., 42
Rauch, S. L., 518, 581
Rauschecker, J., 391
Rauthmann, J. F., 471, 472, 588
Raver, J. L., 460
Rawlins, W. K., 453
Ray, J. V., 632
Raymond, P., 356
Raynor, R., 289
Raz, A., 224
Raz, N., 450
Raza, M. H., 35
Raznahan, A., 136
Read, J., 615
Reagan, A., 648
Rebouta, P., 182
Reddy, L., 109
Redfield, A., 227
Redmond, J. C., 77
Redner, R., 220
Reefhuis, J., 391, 413
Reese, H. F., 582
Regalado, J., 99
Regan, C., 628
Regier, D. A., 565, 578
Register, P. A., 224
Reicher, S., 523
Reicher, S. D., 526
Reid, A., 397
Reif, A., 579
Reinberg, A., 200
Reinisch, J. M., 540f
Reinkemeier,M., 348
Reis, H. T., 500
Reisenzein, R., 238
Reiss, A. L., 198, 348, 557
Reiss, D., 196
Remez, R. E., 177
Remington, A., 556
Rendell, L., 523
Rennicke, C. M., 567
Rensink, R. A., 169
Rentfrow, P. J., 486, 487
Rescorla, R., 284, 287
Resko, J. A., 267
Resnick, H., 584
Ressler, K. J., 87
Restak, R., 7
Reuter, M., 460
Reuveni, I., 583, 584
Reverby, S., 66
Reverger, R., 552
Reyes-Garcia, V., 501
Reyes, L. D., 35
Reyna, V. F., 339, 339f, 442
Rezai, A. R., 616
Reznick, J. S., 576
Rhodes, N., 513
Rhodewalt, F., 486, 488
Riazuddin, S., 35
Riba, J., 219
Ribbers, G. M., 121
Richards, S. H., 679
Richardson, J. A., 200, 387
Richardson, W. S., 601
Richert, R. A., 402
Richie, B. F., 305
Richter, F., 623
Ricken, J., 202
Ridder, E.M., 565
Rieger, M. A., 557
Riehle-Colarusso, T., 391, 413
Riesco-Matias, P., 617
Rieser-Danner, L. A., 532
Rietschel, M., 564
Rifas-Shiman, S. L., 444
Rijnbeek, B., 572
Rilling, J. K., 378, 537
Rips, L., 364, 365, 367
Rishworth, A., 341
Riskind, J. H., 577
Risley, T. R., 388, 620
Ritchie, H., 539
Riva, G., 630
Rivas-Drake, 444
Rivera, M., 580
Rivi, S. L., 633f
Riviere, L. A., 583, 592
Rivkin, M. J., 411, 414
Rizzo, A., 630
Rizzo, A. S., 584
Rizzo, L. B., 567
Rizzolatti, G., 124
Robb, M. B., 402
Robbins, I., 648
Robbins, T. W., 379
Robero, V., 489
Roberson, D., 245
Roberts, B. W., 447, 465

Roberts, D., 80
Roberts, G., 485f
Roberts, J. A., 675
Roberts, M., 161
Roberts, N. P., 119
Robertson, L., 514
Robins, L. N., 578
Robins, R. W., 447
Robinson, A., 38
Robinson, J. D., 213
Robinson, R., 244
Robinson, S., 540
Rochat, P., 524
Roche, G., 383
Rockstroh, B., 181
Rod, N. H., 651
Rodin, J., 656
Rodrigue, K. M., 450
Roe, C. A., 624
Roeder, K., 549
Roediger Lii, H. L., 341, 352
Roelofs, K., 119
Roenneberg, T., 202
Roepke, S., 447
Roepstorff, A., 225
Roesch, S. C., 508
Roese, N. J., 403
Roeser, R. W., 268, 269
Roest, A. M., 578
Roffwarg, H. P., 207f
Rogeberg, O., 93
Rogers-Ramachandran, D., 180
Rogers, C. R., 15, 16, 21, 466, 601, 610
Rogers, M., 679
Rogers, S. J., 177
Rogers, T. B., 354, 484, 484f
Roggman, L. A., 532
Rohrer, D., 352
Rokeach, M., 680
Rolls, E. T., 116, 185
Romanski, L. M.
Ronald, A., 556
Ronnberg, J., 391
Ronningstam, E., 632
Roosevelt, E., 272
Root, J., 35
Roozendaal, B., 341
Roper, S. D., 184
Ropers, H., 84
Rorschach, H., 481
Rose Markus, H., 475
Rose, A., 481
Rose, D., 615
Rose, G., 649
Rose, J., 529, 530
Rose, J. E., 290
Rose, M. W., 206
Roselli, C. E., 267
Roseman, L., 218
Rosen, H. J., 492
Rosen, T. A., 181, 184
Rosenbaum, J. F., 576
Rosenbaum, R. S., 347
Rosenberg, H. J., 448
Rosenberg, J., 99
Rosenberg, R., 620f
Rosenblum, C. I., 256
Rosendal, S., 620, 622
Rosenfield, D., 541
Rosenstein, D., 186
Rosenthal, D., 563
Rosenthal, I. A., 432
Rosenthal, R., 248
Roser, M., 539
Rosol, O., 555
Ross, D., 310, 311
Ross, D. C., 621
Ross, G. W., 220
Ross, L, 506
Ross, M., 487
Ross, R., 389
Ross, S. A., 310, 311
Rossion, B., 336
Roth, G., 93
Rothbart, M. K., 432, 433, 473, 475
Rothbaum, B. O., 584, 630
Rothschild, D., 514
Rotter, J. B., 472
Rousseau, J.-J., 14
Rovee-Collier, C., 24
Rowland, L. W., 224
Rozga, A., 177
Rozhdaraj, D., 557
Rozin, P., 257f, 681
Rubin, M., 517, 522
Rubin, M. A., 212
Rubin, P. E., 177
Rudner, M., 391
Rueda, M. R., 475
Ruf, M., 644
Ruff, C. C., 491
Ruggiero, A., 312
Ruggiero, A. M., 652
Ruiz, F. S., 206
Ruiz, M. H., 176
Rujescu, D., 564
Rule, N. O., 504, 504f
Rullo, J., 626
Ruparel, K., 250
Rusbult, C. E., 532
Ruscio, A., 581
Rush, A., 626
Rush, B., 602
Rushton, D. H., 262
Rushton, J. P., 539
Russell, D. W., 232, 502, 657
Russell, J. A., 212, 240
Russell, K., 80
Russo, R., 352
Ruth,Babe, 128
Ryan, R. M., 253, 267, 674
Rychlowska, M., 249, 249f
Ryman, D., 200

S

Saarimaki, H., 245
Sabatini, R. M. E., 616
Sacco, D. F., 336
Sacco, K. A., 665
Sackeim, H. A., 615
Sackett, G. P., 246
Sadato, N., 323
Sadeh, N., 648
Sagratti, S., 570
Sahakian, B. J., 581
Sahuque, L. L., 290
Saiki, J., 169
Sainsbury, A. W., 262
Sainz, E., 35
Saito, S., 185
Saitoh, O., 563
Sajatovic, M., 624
Sakaguchi, M., 206
Sakai, N., 185
Sakai, Y., 549, 556
Sakamoto, S., 552
Sakurai, T., 206, 256
Salanti, G., 625
Salari, N., 644
Salat, D., 648
Salerno, S., 250
Sales, S. M., 527
Salgado, S., 244
Salovey, P., 108, 248, 395, 640, 641
Salsman, J. M., 651
Salstein-Orda, N., 291
Salter, W., 393
Saltz, S. B., 413, 557
Sanchez-Roige, S., 475, 476
Sanchez-Zaballos, E., 617
Sanders, A., 571
Sanders, S. A., 540f
Sandonmatsu, D. M., 488
Sandstrom, G., 314
Sanfey, A. G., 378, 537
Sanford, A. P., 206
Sanghani, S., 578
Santosa, C. M., 567
Sanz, C., 213
Sapolsky, R., 643, 648
Sarasso, S., 204
Sarnoff, I., 268
Sartorius, N., 624
Satisabal, C. L., 451
Sattler, K. M., 299
Sauer, S., 210
Saunders, D. T., 624
Saunders, E. F., 208
Savage-Rumbaugh, S., 386
Savage, J., 563
Savin-Williams, R. C., 265
Savine, R., 206
Savitsky, K., 485
Sayigh, L. S., 196, 386
Scarisbrick, P., 206
Scaroekku, S., 204
Schaadt, G., 390
Schabus, M., 204
Schachter, S., 236, 237, 238, 268, 500, 523
Schaefer, C., 645
Schaefer, H. S., 188
Schafe, G. E., 646
Schaller, M., 271f, 273, 274, 676
Schallmo, M.-P., 648
Schapiro, S. J., 421
Schartner, M. M., 218
Schauer, E., 644
Scheepens, D. S., 571
Scheftner, W., 571
Scheiber, J., 349
Scheier, M. F., 491, 674
Schenck, C. H., 205
Scherer, K. R., 239
Scherrer, G., 182
Schiefele, U., 268, 269
Schieve, L. A., 48
Schifani, C., 217
Schilling, E. A., 658
Schimmelmann, B. G., 210
Schindler, C. W., 285
Schlechter, M., 436, 438
Schlenker, B. R., 508
Schmaal, L., 564
Schmahl, C., 187
Schmahl, D. P., 613
Schmeck, R. R., 469
Schmidt, F., 469
Schmidt, J. E., 651
Schmitt, D. P., 534
Schmitt, E., 136
Schmitz, A., 460
Schneier, F., 578
Schnitker, S.A., 680
Schnitzer, M. J., 182
Schober, J. M., 424
Schober, M. F., 534
Schoeller, D. A., 653, 653f
Schon, D., 240
Schonert-Reichl, K. A., 679
Schooler, C., 522
Schroeder, S., 665
Schroeder, S. R., 401
Schroeder, U., 244
Schroeder, V., 561
Schuengel, C., 401
Schuerkens, A., 246
Schuhmacher, A., 564
Schuhmacher, M. A., 184
Schulsinger, F., 563
Schulte-Ruther, M., 557
Schultz, D. H., 93, 125
Schultz, S. J., 235
Schulz, M. S., 453
Schulze-Rauschenbach, S., 564
Schumacher, M. A., 181
Schuman-Olivier, Z., 225
Schumann, C. M., 243
Schumm, L. P., 452
Schurz, G., 525
Schuster, M. A., 644, 657
Schvanevelt, R. W., 331, 331f
Schwabe, L., 640
Schwartz, B., 299, 681
Schwartz, C. E., 576
Schwartz, C. R., 449
Schwartz, D., 644
Schwartz, J. M., 597
Schwartz, S. T., 430
Schwarz, A., 196

Tobler, P. N., 491
Todd, J. F., 261
Todd, P. M., 99
Todorov, 501
Todorov, A. T., 501
Todorova, R., 354
Toga, A. W., 122
Tolman, E. C., 305
Tomasello, M., 431
Tominaga, M., 181, 184
Tomlinson, G., 209
Tomova, L., 640
Tonomi, G., 207
Tononi, G., 195
Tooby, J., 95, 319
Tootell, R. B. H., 156
Toplak, M. E., 442
Topolinski, S., 489f
Toppino, T. C., 207
Torgersem. S., 587
Torgerson, C. M., 122
Toro, J. M., 386
Torres, F., 181, 580
Torrey, E. F., 563
Tosi, H., 644
Tough, S., 402, 418
Touitou, D., 200
Touitou, Y., 200
Trafton, J., 184
Tran, Y., 35
Tranel, D., 242, 243f, 395, 586
Travis, F. T., 225
Traynor, B. J., 367
Treanor, J. J., 649
Treasure, J., 261
Treffert, D. A., 393
Trestman, R., 653
Treynor, W., 370
Trimble, J. E., 27
Triplett, N., 307, 527
Tripoli, G., 566, 566f
Trivers, R., 97, 538
Trockel, M. T., 48
Trubnick, L., 209
Truglia, I., 204
Truitt, W., 578
Trumbetta, S., 447
Trut, L., 477f
Tsang, J.-A., 675
Tschanz, B., 488
Tseng, H., -H., 217
Tsujimura, S, -i., 159
Tubman, H., 210
Tubman, M., 209
Tucker, J. A., 668
Tufik, S., 206
Tulving, E., 325, 326, 326f, 329, 337, 344, 348
Tung, J. Y., 475, 475f
Tunney, R. J., 99
Turati, C., 419f
Turchi, C., 460
Turing, A., 197
Turkheimer, E., 399
Turnbaugh, P. J., 259
Turnbull, H. W., 41
Turner, C. E., 184
Turner, J., 517
Turner, N., 670, 675
Turner, R. B., 649
Turton, R., 261, 391
Tversky, A., 372, 373, 376, 376f
Twenge, J. M., 267, 270, 447, 447f, 552, 589, 676
Tyler, V., 49
Tyrrell, D. A., 651
Tyszka, J. M., 118f
Tzischinsky, O., 202

U

Uchida, S., 206
Uchiyama, H., 323
Uckert, K., 444
Uecker, J. E., 454
Ueda, Y., 169
Uhrenfeldt, L., 604
Ullman, L., 612
Umberson, D., 267
Umilta, C., 419f
Uncapher, H., 452
Underwood, B. J., 344
Undurraga, E., 501
Ungerleider, L. G., 347, 367
Urland, G. R., 517
Ursano, R. J., 645
Ustun, T. B., 561, 568, 583

V

V. P. Poutanen, M., 397
Vaez-Azizi, L. M., 93
Vago, D. R., 225
Vaidya, J., 244
Vail-Smith, K., 671
Vaillant, G. E., 451, 668
Vaisi-Raygani, A., 644
Vaitl, D., 203, 226, 227
Vaivre-Douret, L., 126
Valdovinos, M. G., 401
Valenstein, E. S., 616
Valenstein, M., 624
Valentin, D., 187
Valentine, J. D., 592
Valero, R., 259
Vali, M., 217
Vallender, E. J., 93
van Balkom, A. J., 578
Van Beek, M., 225
Van Cauter, E., 206, 653
van den Berg, H., 510
Van Den Driessche, G., 378f
Van der Does, W., 86
van der Maas, H. L., 510
van der Mei, W. F., 583
Van der Ploeg, L. H. T., 256
van der Velde, E. A., 263
van der Vyver, J. M., 245
van Dongen, J. D. M., 632
van Dyck, R., 578
Van Dyne, L., 489
Van Erp, T. G., 564
van Gerven, J. M. A., 572
van Gerwen, L. J., 630
Van Gilder, J., 391
Van Haren et al, 566
Van Haren, N. E., 217, 566
van Harreveld, F., 510
Van Horn, J. D., 122, 203
Van Kempen, G. M. J., 263
Van Knippenberg, D., 513
Van Lange, P. A. M., 476
van Londen, L., 263
van Lutterveld, R., 617
van Oost, b., 84
van Rijn, S., 418
Van Rooji, S. J. H., 583, 583f, 648
van Rossum, E. F., 644
van Waarde, J. A., 571
van Wingen, G. A., 571
van Wingerden, M., 640
Vandermeer, B., 209
Vandesande, 401
Vanhove, A. J., 680
VanRullen, R., 109
Vansteenwegen, D., 576
Varelas, P. N., 213
Vargha-Khadem, F., 388
Vasconcelos-Moreno, M. P., 567
Vasey, P. L., 265, 265f, 266
Vassos, E., 83, 565
Vater, A., 447
Vauloup-Fellous, C., 415
Vega, M. L., 413, 557
Vehorn, A. C., 448
Velasco-Ramos, M., 200
Velickovic, K., 42
Verdejo-Garcia, A., 215
Vermetten, E., 187, 583
Vernon, P. A., 475
Vernuccio, F., 250
Veroff, J., 679
Verweij, K. J., 265, 566
Vescio, T. K., 522
Vestergaard-Poulsen, P., 225
Vianello, M., 42
Vidal, C., 564f
Videsott, G., 390
Vignoles, V. L., 488
Vijayan, S., 205
Vilain, E., 265, 265f, 266
Villa-Komaroff, L., 411
Vincent, G. M., 123
Vincent, J., 524, 525f
Virues-Ortega, J., 621f
Visalberghi, E., 312
Vivanti, A.J., 415
Viviano, J. D., 560
Vlahov, D., 584
Vogel, C. I. G., 210
Vogel, J. P., 412
Vogel, P. J., 125
Vohs, K. D., 490, 679
Voineagu, I., 556
Volckmar, A.-L., 262
Volk, D. W., 217
Volkow, N. D., 217, 560, 621
Volpe, J. J., 411
von Helmholtz, H., 8–9, 10, 11, 14
von Ranson, K. M., 262
Voon, V., 616
Voracek, M., 399f
Vorstman, J. A., 556
Voss, H., 442
Vosshall, L. B., 185
Votaw, V. R., 668
Vouga, M., 414
Vowels, L. M., 262, 264
Vrangalova, Z., 265
Vries, S. K., 261
Vrij, A., 251
Vu, N. L., 541
Vuilleumier, P., 245
Vygotsky, L. S., 429
Vythilingam, M., 583, 584

W

Wadee, A. A., 650
Wagenmakers, E.-J., 43
Wager, T., 243, 244
Wagner, A. D.
Wagner, A. R., 287
Wagner, D. D., 491
Wagner, D. R., 200
Wagner, K. D., 618
Wahl, J. M., 613
Wainer, H., 63
Waite, L., 677
Waite, L. J., 675
Wakita, M., 185
Waldinger, R. J., 453
Waldron, M., 399
Waldrop, P. B., 302
Walker, A., 416
Walker, E. F., 565
Walker, J. B., 250
Walker, M., 414, 557
Walker, M. P., 206
Walker, M. R., 489
Walker, N., 224
Wall, P. D., 182
Wall, S., 434
Wall, T. L., 667
Wallace, G. L., 393
Wallen, K., 144, 262
Waller, A., 488
Wallston, K., 472
Wallstrom, A., 514
Walster, E., 513, 532
Walters, E. E., 551, 567, 576, 578, 579, 580
Walters, S., 465
Waltoft, B. L., 260
Walton, E., 564
Walton, G. M., 655, 655f
Wan, C. R., 565
Wang, A., 250
Wang, C. X., 178
Wang, G., 413, 558, 560
Wang, G.-J., 560, 621
Wang, H., 262
Wang, H. H., 213

Wang, J., 228, 354, 549, 616
Wang, M. M., 349
Wang, P. W., 567
Wang, P.O.., 389
Wang, Q., 408
Wang, R., 487, 501
Wang, S., 677, 678f
Wang, T., 227
Wang, X., 349, 413, 556, 558, 560
Wang, Y., 475, 475f
Wanless, A., 545
Ward, B. W., 260, 264, 265
Ward, D., 36
Ward, M., 414
Warfield, S. K., 414
Wargo, E. M., 217
Warner-Schmidt, J., 573
Warner, T. D., 50
Warner, V., 576
Warren, Z. E., 448
Warrington, E. K., 328
Wartella, E., 402
Washburn, A. L., 254, 255
Wasserman, R. C., 559
Watable, M., 504
Waterhouse, J., 200
Waters, E., 434
Waters, F., 564
Watkins, C. E., 482
Watkins, E., 570, 570f, 578
Watkins, G. L., 563
Watkins, L. E., 630
Watson, B., 560
Watson, D., 469, 675
Watson, J. B., 16–17, 20, 289
Watson, P., 347
Watson, S. J., 644
Watts, T. W., 395
Wayne, D., 42
Weaver, J., 225, 362
Webb, J. K., 293
Weber, E., 451
Weber, E. U., 440, 441f
Weber, R., 280
Weber, W., 620
Webster, M. A., 149
Wechsler, D., 394
Wedekind, C., 101, 499
Wedrow, R., 265
Weekes, B. S., 390
Wegner, D. M., 203, 356, 491
Wehby, G. L., 68
Wehrle, R., 208
Wei, J., 573
Wei, K. -K., 529
Weideman, R., 633
Weige, J. A., 567
Weinberger, D. R., 563
Weinbruch, C., 181
Weindl, A., 244
Weiner, I. B., 482
Weingartner, H., 337
Weinstein, A. M., 218
Weinstein, N., 500
Weinstock, M., 644
Weintraub, E. S., 559f
Weir, D. R., 451
Weisberg, P., 302
Weisenbach, S. L., 648
Weiser, E. B., 589
Weisleder, A., 388
Weiss, A., 476
Weiss, S. J., 285
Weiss, S. R. B., 217
Weissman, M., 571, 576
Weisz, R., 236
Weitlauf, A. S., 448
Welge, J. A., 615
Welling, L. L. M., 262
Wellings, K., 58
Wells, A., 580
Wells, G. L., 341
Wells, R. S., 196, 386
Welsh, J. P., 115
Welsh, R. C., 665
Wender, P. H., 563
Wenhart, T., 177, 556
Werge, T., 83
Werner, J. S., 149
Wernicke, C., 385
Werth, U., 246
Wertheimer, M., 12, 20
West, R. F., 442
Westen, D., 534
Westphal, J. A., 218, 220
Westwood, A. J., 209
Wetzel, E., 447
Wetzel, W., 349
Whalen, N., 341
Whalen, P. J., 518
Wheatley, J. R., 262
Wheeler, D., 525f
Whitbourne, S. K., 451
White, B. J., 521, 521f
White, G. L., 533
White, H. R., 675
White, S., 556
White, W., 521f
Whitehead, V., 390
Whiting, D. M., 242
Whitman, C., 542
Whitmill, J., 663, 664, 664f
Whitton, S. W., 615
Whorf, B. L., 382, 383
Wickings, E. J., 535
Wickramaratne, P., 576
Widdowson, P. S., 256
Widmeyer, W. N., 504
Widom, C, 586
Wiech, K., 182
Wiederhold, B., 630
Wiederhold, M., 630
Wiegant, V. M., 263
Wielgosz, J., 225
Wiersema, J. R., 181
Wiesel, T. N., 159
Wigfield, A., 268, 269
Wiggins, G., 176
Wiggs, C. L., 347, 367
Wijdicks, E. E. M., 213
Wik, G., 577f
Wilbanks, C. A., 293
Wilcox, W. B., 676
Wilensky, A. E., 646
Wilent, W. B., 242
Wilfley, D. E., 261
Wilhelm, S., 582
Wilk, J. E., 583, 592
Wilke, A., 99, 371
Wilke, A. E., 620
Wilke, H., 513
Wilkinson, G. S., 538
Willemsen, G., 101, 268
Willer, R., 545
Williams, A., 538
Williams, B., 75, 459
Williams, D. L., 257
Williams, G., 256
Williams, H., 329, 330
Williams, J. M., 627
Williams, K., 560, 620
Williams, K. D., 500, 528
Williams, K. M., 588
Williams, S., 298, 312, 354
Williams, S. C., 200
Williams, Ted, 128
Williamson, A., 450
Williamson, A. M., 206
Williamson, R. A., 432
Willie, J. T., 340
Willingham, B., 246
Willis, J. 501
Wilson, A. A., 217
Wilson, A. D., 668
Wilson, A. E., 487
Wilson, S., 256
Wilson, S. G., 259
Wilson, T. D., 43
Wimmer, H., 431
Winden, K., 77
Windischberger, C., 540, 640
Wingate, L. R., 674
Winkelman, M., 227
Winkler, A. D., 149
Winocur, G., 347
Winston, F. K., 583, 644
Winston, J. S., 537
Winzeler, S., 489f
Wirz-Justice, A., 201
Wisse, B. E., 257
Witkiewitz, K., 668
Witmans, M., 209
Wittchen, H.-U., 580
Wittgenstein, L., 364
Wixted, J. T., 341
Wobber, V., 183
Wohlert, M., 417
Wolf, E. J., 648
Wolf, M. M., 620
Wolfson, A. R., 202
Wolfson, C., 390
Woll, B., 391
Wolpe, J., 290, 630
Wolraich, M. L., 561
Wong, P. O., 217
Wong, S. H., 574
Wood, A. M., 472
Wood, E. K., 432
Wood, J. M., 482
Wood, W., 513
Woodruff, G., 431
Woods,J., 669
Woodward, J. T., 680
Wooleey, C., 671
Woolfolk, R. L., 630, 632
Woolley, A. W., 398, 399f
Wootton, B. M., 378
Worhunsky, P. D., 225
Worth, K., 264
Wortham, J. M., 455
Wrangham, R., 183
Wright, C., 553, 553f
Wright, E. W., 193
Wright, G. A., 350
Wright, I. M., 414
Wright, R. J., 651
Wright, T., 388
Wrobleski, K., 452
Wrobleski, K. K., 680
Wrzesniewski, A., 681
Wu, D., 583
Wu, D. A., 178
Wu, P.-L., 446
Wu, Y. H., 200
Wundt, W., 10–11, 12, 14, 15, 20, 163
Wurtman, R. J.
Wurtz, R. H., 156
Wyatt, G., 27
Wykes, T., 615
Wylie, B. J., 414

X

Xie, W., 355
Xiong, T., 620
Xu, D., 387
Xu, J., 518f, 670

Y

Yagi, K., 53
Yakeley, J., 590
Yalom, I. D., 606
Yamagata, S., 479
Yamaguchi, S., 460
Yamakawa, M., 159
Yan, Z., 573
Yanagisawa, M., 200
Yang, F., 487
Yang, G., 207
Yang, L. L., 200
Yang, M. -L., 403
Yap, A. J., 235
Yasui, M., 574
Yeargin-Allsopp, M., 48
Yee, N., 304
Yehuda, R., 583, 644
Yela-Bernabe, J. R., 617
Yeoh, S. L., 414
Yerkes, R. M., 240, 528
Yoerger, M., 554
Yolken, R. H., 414
Yonas, A., 167

Yoo, J. H., 401
Yoo, S. H., 247f, 350
Yoon, Y. B., 397
Yoshikawa, S., 504
Yost, J., 99
Yotsutsuji, T., 563
Young, A. H., 648
Young, G. S., 177
Young, P. C., 224
Young, R., 556, 557f
Young, R. L., 556
Young, S. G., 336, 531
Young, T., 202
Youngman, J. E., 482
Youngstrom, E. A., 556
Youyou, W., 478
Yu, H., 549
Yudell, M., 80
Yurgelun-Todd, D., 440
Yuuki, N., 653
Yuwiler, A., 540

Z

Zager, A., 206
Zajonc, R. B., 307, 527, 531, 531f
Zamberlan, F., 213
Zanarini, M. C., 587
Zanello, S., 615
Zapala, M. A., 77
Zaval, L., 451
Zavalloni, M., 529, 529f
Zebrowitz, L. A., 501
Zeelenberg, M., 375
Zeki, S., 67, 116
Zelazo, P. R., 245, 416
Zerbo, S., 250
ZerJal et al, 98
Zerjal, T., 98
Zhang, G., 494, 495, 675
Zhang, J., 107f
Zhang, M, -D., 181
Zhang, T. Y., 469
Zhang, W., 355
Zhang, X., 507, 507f
Zhang, Y., 256, 558
Zhang, Z.-X., 508
Zhao, L., 397
Zhou, J., 644, 657
Zhou, J.-R., 86
Zhou, M., 573
Zhu, Y., 107f
Ziebell, S.
Zielaskowski, K., 520
Ziemba-Davis, M., 540, 540f
Zietsch, B. P., 265
Zigler, E., 400
Zillmann, D., 362
Zimbardo, P., 523
Zimbardo, P. G., 237, 268, 528, 537
Zimmer, C., 89
Zimmerman, F. J., 387
Zoghbi, H. Y., 549, 556
Zoladz, P. R., 340
Zubin, J., 573
Zugaro, M., 354
Zukowska, Z., 653
Zullig, K. J., 260
Zunszain, P. A., 625
Zupan, V., 415
Zuscho, H., 183
Zuschrattera, W., 349
Zwiers, M. P., 560
Zylka, M. J., 557

Subject Index/Glossary

Note: Page numbers with *f* and *t* indicate figures and tables, respectively. Page numbers following **bold** terms indicate definitions.

A

ABA. *See also* applied behavior analysis (ABA); also known as behavior modification.
Abnormal psychology, 551. The study of psychological disorders.
Absence seizures, 214
Absolute threshold, 153. The smallest amount of stimulus that can be detected.
  measuring perception and, 153, 154*f*
Accommodation, 427. The incorporation of new learning into an existing schema that requires revision of the schema.
Acetylcholine (ACh), 143, 349, 350*f*
Achievement motivation, 268. A desire to excel or outperform others, 269–270
Acoustic codes, 320
Acquisition, 283. The development of a learned response, 283–284, 283*f*
Action potential, 137. The electrical signal arising in a neuron's axon, 137, 139, 139*f*
Activation-synthesis theory, 208–209
Actor-observer bias, 506. Emphasizing dispositional attributions to explain the behavior of others while emphasizing situational attributions to explain our own behavior, 508
Adaptation, 91. A change because of natural selection, 91–92, 94
Adderall, 222. *See also* amphetamine salts.
Addiction, 215. Brain networks for, 216*f*
  conditioning and, 290–291
  consequences of, 215
  decision-making and, 378–379
  tolerance and, 215
  withdrawal and, 215
ADHD. *See* Attention deficit hyperactivity disorder (ADHD)
Adolescence, 438. A period of development beginning at puberty and ending at young adulthood.
  decision-making and, 379, 379*f*
  eating disorders and, 261
  physical development in, 439–440
  self-injury, 296
Adolescents
  alcohol consumption, 666
  cognitive development, 442–443
  highlight of, 456
  identity formation, 443–444
    ethnic, 444–445, 445*f*
    family and, 444–445, 445*f*
    influences on, 445
    peer groups and, 444–445
    psychosocial stages, 443, 444, 444*t*
  moral reasoning, 442–443
  physical development in, 439–442
    brain growth, 439–441, 441*f*
    puberty and, 439, 439*f*
    sex and gender development, 439
  risk-taking, 440*f*–441*f*
  schizophrenia and, 564
  smoking and, 664
  social and emotional development, 443–445
Adoption studies, 81
Adrenal glands, 132
Adulthood. *See* Late adulthood; Midlife; Young adulthood
Adverse Childhood Experiences (ACE) survey, 671*f*
Affect heuristic, 374. A rule of thumb in which we choose between alternatives based on emotional or "gut" reactions to stimuli.
Affiliation, 267. Being associated with other people.
  motivation and, 267–268
  stress and, 268
Aggression, 539. The conscious intent to harm another.
  biological psychology of, 539–541
  catharsis theories of, 543
  defensive, 539
  imitation and, 311–312
  instrumental, 539
  learning and, 541
  maternal, 539
  media and, 541
  observational learning and, 311–312
  passive, 539
  prenatal exposure to testosterone and, 540, 540*f*
  preventing, 541, 543
  relational, 539
Agoraphobia, 579. Unrealistic fear of open spaces, being outside the home alone, or being in a crowd.
Agouti gene, 72, 83, 86
Agreeableness, 469. A Big Five personality trait characterized by trustworthiness, altruism, trust, compliance, modesty, and tender mindedness, 467, 468, 472, 495
Alarm reaction, 643. The first stage of the general adaptation syndrome (GAS), characterized by sympathetic arousal and mental clarity, 642
Alcohol, 222–223
Alcohol consumption
  abuse of, 666–667
  adolescent, 666
  aggression and, 540
  dependence on, 666–667
  health and, 666–668, 667*f*
  pregnancy and, 414, 415*t*, 416*f*
  social factors in, 667
  suicide and, 540
  treatment for, 668
Algorithm, 371. A precise, step-by-step set of rules that will reliably generate a solution to a problem.
Alien hand syndrome, 121
Allele, 74. One of several versions of a gene, as in having an A, B, or O blood type allele, 73*f*
  for blond hair, 89–90, 90*f*
  bullying and, 75, 76*f*, 459
  dominant, 74, 74*f*, 76*f*
  eye color and, 82, 82*f*
  in genetics, 74–76
  hemophilia, 77, 77*f*
  heterozygous, 74, 74*f*
  homozygous, 74, 74*f*
  long (L) SERT, 459–460
  recessive, 74, 74*f*, 77
  short (S) SERT, 459–460
Allport, Gordon, 21*f*
Alpha coma, 212
Alpha waves, 202. A waveform of 9 to 12 cycles per second recorded by electroencephalogram that usually indicates relaxed waking, 202–203
AlphaGo program, 377, 378*f*
Altered consciousness
  dancing and, 227
  drumming and, 227
  environmental conditions and, 225–226
  hallucinogens and, 219
  hypnosis and, 224–225
  meditation and, 225, 226*f*
  psychoactive drugs and, 216–218, 219*f*, 220–223
  raves and, 227
  spinning and, 225–226
  trance states and, 226
  vision quests and, 225
Altruism, 96. Behavior on behalf of another that fails to benefit or harms the individual performing it, 96–97
  helping and, 537–539
  heroism and, 537–538
  psychological, 538
  reciprocal, 97, 538
Alzheimer's disease
  Acetylcholine (ACh) and, 143, 349
  bilingualism and, 390–391
  caffeine and, 220
American Psychological Association (APA), 5
American Sign Language (ASL), 178, 391
Ames room, 164, 165*f*
Amphetamine salts (Adderall), 222, 560, 620
Amphetamines, 221–222
Amygdala, 117. A subcortical structure located in the temporal lobe believed to participate in emotional processing.
  damage to, 117–118, 118*f*
  damage to, results of, 242–243, 242*f*
  emotions and, 242–243
  fear and, 646*f*
  fear and aggression, 118
  insula and, 242
  stress and, 645–646
Amyotrophic lateral sclerosis (ALS), 367
Anandamide, 218
Androgen insensitivity syndrome (AIS), 417
Animal research
  attachment and, 434
  Bisphenol A (BPA) study, 72
  care and, 63
  ethics and, 65–66
  purpose and, 66
  self-awareness and, 195–196

Animals
collective intelligence, 196
imitation and, 312
instincts and, 279
language ability of, 386–387
reflexes and, 278
response to environment, 278–279
vision and, 151*f*, 163*f*
Anorexia nervosa, 260. An eating disorder characterized by the maintenance of unusually low body weight and a distorted body image.
Anterior cingulate cortex (ACC), 117, 123, 581
Antidepressant medication, 625. A medication designed to alleviate symptoms of depression, but often prescribed for other types of conditions, 625*f*
Antisocial personality disorder (ASPD), 583. A disorder characterized by an unusual lack of remorse, empathy, or regard for normal social rules and conventions.
causes of, 586
diagnosis of, 586
emotions and, 586
orbitofrontal cortex and, 586
prefrontal cortex and, 122
treatment for, 632
Anxiety disorder, 576. A disorder featuring anxiety that is not proportional to a person's circumstances.
agoraphobia, 576, 578, 579
GABA and, 628
generalized, 580
genetics and, 576
panic disorder, 578, 579
race and ethnicity and, 574, 574*f*
social anxiety disorder, 577–578
specific phobias and, 576–577, 577*f*
treatment for, 578, 628–629, 628*f*, 636
Anxiety, during pandemic, 228
Anxious-ambivalent attachment, 434
Aphasia, 385. The loss of the ability to speak or understand language, 391
Aplysia californica sea slug, 286
Applied behavior analysis (ABA); also known as behavior modification, 612–613
Appraisal, 239. The detection and assessment of stimuli that are relevant to personal well-being.
Approach and avoidance, 271
Aristotle, 8, 9
Arousal, 240*f*
Artificial consciousness, 196–197
Artificial intelligence, 196–197
Artificial lighting, 200
Artificial selection, 89
Artificiality in research, 52, 56
ASD. *See* Autism spectrum disorder (ASD)
ASPD. *See* Antisocial personality disorder (ASPD)
Assimilation, 427. The incorporation of new learning into an existing schema without the need to revise the schema.
Association cortex, 120
Associative learning, 280. The formation of associations, or connections, among stimuli and behaviors.
classical conditioning, 280
operant conditioning, 280
Astigmatism, 168, 168*f*
Atkinson-Shiffrin Model of Memory, 321*f*
Attachment, 435. Emotional bond linking an infant to a parent or caregiver, 434–436
anxious-ambivalent, 434–435
avoidant, 434–435
behavior, evolution of, 433
child development and, 433–436
disorganized, 434–435
ecological approaches to, 435
evolution of, 433
insecure, 434
parenting and, 434
rhesus monkeys and, 433
secure, 434
universal approaches to, 435
Attention deficit hyperactivity disorder (ADHD), 558. A disorder characterized by either unusual inattentiveness, hyperactivity with impulsivity, or both, 558–561, 560*f*
basal ganglia and, 116
brain and, 560
causes of, 560–561
diagnosis of, 558–560, 560*f*
divided attention and, 152
food additives and, 561
medications for, 222, 560, 620–622, 622*f*
restless legs syndrome (RLS), 210
symptoms of, 560–561
treatment for, 620–622, 636
Attitude, 509. A positive or negative evaluation that predisposes behavior toward an object, person, or situation, 509–510
cognitive consistency and, 511–512
cognitive dissonance and, 510–512
conditioning and, 290–291
elements of, 510
formation of, 510
Attitude alignment, 532
Attraction and liking, 531–533, 531*f*
Attribution, 505. A judgment about the cause of a person's behavior.
correspondence bias and, 505–506
cultural influences on, 508–509
defensive, 506, 508
depression and, 571
dispositional, 505
fundamental attribution error, 505–506
just-world belief, 508
situational, 505
Attribution error, 516
Audition, 172. The sense of hearing.
biology of, 172–175
auditory canal, 172
auditory cortex, 175*f*
auditory nerve, 174
basilar membrane, 174
cochlea, 174
organ of Corti, 174
oval window, 173
parts of the ear, 173*f*
pinna, 172
thalamus, 174
tympanic membrane, 173*f*, 174, 174*f*
developmental and individual differences in, 177
Auditory cortex, 119, 121*f*, 123, 174–175, 175*f*
Auditory nerve, 174. The nerve carrying sound information from the cochlea to the brain.
Authoritarian parenting, 436–437
Authoritative parenting, 436–437
Autism spectrum disorder (ASD), 555. A disorder characterized by deficits in social relatedness and communication skills that are often accompanied by repetitive, ritualistic behavior, 555–558
amygdala and, 243
brain and, 556–557
causes of, 556–558
diagnosis of, 555–559
early behavioral intervention outcomes, 621*f*
environmental factors and, 557–558
facial expressions and, 250
genetics and, 556
increase in, 555, 556*f*
interactomes and, 549–550
medications for, 620*f*
response to stimuli, 168
sensory sensitivity in, 557*f*
serotonin and, 130
superior visual search in, 168*f*
symptoms of, 558–559
touch and, 181
treatment for, 618–620, 620*f*, 636
vaccinations and, 558, 559*f*
Autobiographical memory, 330. Semantic or episodic memories that reference the self.
Autonomic nervous system, 129–130. The division of the peripheral nervous system that directs the activity of glands, organs, and smooth muscles. 131*f*.
emotions and, 241–242
enteric nervous system, 130, 131*f*
parasympathetic nervous system, 130, 131*f*
sympathetic nervous system, 129
Autonomy, 526
Availability heuristic, 372. A rule of thumb in which the frequency of an event's occurrence is predicted by the ease with which the event is brought to mind, 373*f*
COVID-19 and, 404
Aversion therapy, 290. An application of counterconditioning in which a conditioned stimulus (CS) formerly paired with a pleasurable unconditioned stimulus (UCS) is instead paired with an unpleasant UCS.
Avoidance, approach and, 271
Avoidant attachment, 434
Axon, 134. The branch of a neuron that is usually responsible for transmitting information to other neurons.
action potential and, 137–138
auditory nerve and, 174
myelinated, 136, 139–140
squid, 138
synapses and, 143
unmyelinated, 136, 139–140
white matter and, 134
Axon terminal
action potential and, 141
synaptic vesicles in, 134
Ayahuasca, 219

B

Basal ganglia, 116. A collection of subcortical structures that participate in the control of movement, 116*f*
cingulate cortex and, 243–244, 244*f*
procedural memory and, 348–349
Basilar membrane, 174. Membrane in the cochlea on which the organ of Corti is located.
Bask-in-reflected glory (BIRG) effect, 489
Battle fatigue. *See* Posttraumatic stress disorder (PTSD)
Behavior
bad habits and, 309
brain and, 109

building blocks of, 73–75
evolution and, 95, 103
health and (*see* Health psychology)
influencing others to behave toward us, 313
social (*see* Social behavior)
unconscious, 227
Behavior modification; also known as applied behavior analysis (ABA), 612–613
Behavior therapy, 612. Applications of classical and operant conditioning principles to the treatment of symptoms of psychological disorder and adjustment problems, 612–613
Behavioral approach system (BAS), 477
Behavioral genetics, 78. The scientific field that attempts to identify and understand links between genetics and behavior.
concordance rates and, 81–82
heritability and, 78–79
twin studies in, 81
Behavioral inhibition system (BIS), 477
Behavioral neuroscience, 19*f*, 23, 107
Behaviorism, 15. An approach that features the study and careful measurement of observable behaviors, 15–19
behavioral neuroscience and, 19*f*
personality and, 465–466
Behaviorists, 15–18
"black box" model and, *19f*
Pavlov, 16–17
Simon, 19
Thorndike, 17, 18*f*, 20*f*
Watson, 16–17, 17*f*
Berger, Hans, 21*f*
Beta waves, 202. A waveform of 15 to 30 cycles per second recorded by electroencephalogram that usually indicates alert waking, 202–203
Bias
actor-observer, 506, 508
correspondence, 505–506
self-serving, 506–507
shooter, 520
Big Five theory, 468. A trait theory that identifies five main characteristics that account for most individual differences in personality, 468*f*, 470*t*–471*t*, 475–476
Big Five traits, 483
Bilingual, 390. Proficient in two languages.
Binet, Alfred, 20*f*
Binge-eating disorder, 261. An eating disorder characterized by eating abnormally large amounts of food at one sitting and feeling that eating is out of control, without compensatory behaviors such as induced vomiting or the use of laxatives.
Binocular cues, 165. A depth cue that requires the use of both eyes, 164, 166
Binocular disparity, 167
Biological clock, 199. An internal mechanism that provides an approximate schedule for various physical processes, 200
Biological psychology, 22. The psychological perspective that focuses on the relationships between mind and behavior, as well as their underlying biological processes, including genetics, biochemistry, anatomy, and physiology; also known as behavioral neuroscience, 23, 23*f*
contemporary approaches in, 109
criminal justice and, 123
decision-making and, 377–379
early attempts to understand, 108
influence of, 106–108
research methods in, 110*t*
Biological therapies
brain stimulation, 616
electroconvulsive therapy (ECT), 615
medication and, 615
neurofeedback, 617
psychosurgery, 615–616
Biopsychosocial approach, 614. An integrated approach to therapy that combines treatments addressing the biological, personal, and social underpinnings of psychological disorders.
Biopsychosocial model, 660. A model that sees health as the result of biological, psychological, and social factors, 661*f*
Bipolar disorder, 567. A mood disorder characterized by alternating periods of mania and depression.
causes of, 567
creativity and, 567
diet and, 567
genetics and, 567
mania and, 567
medications for, 624
norepinephrine activity and, 143
rates of, 567, 567*f*
symptoms of, 575
treatment for, 567, 636
Birth rate, 98*f*
Bisphenol A (BPA), 72
Black box model, 19*f*
Blind spots, 158
Blocking, 352
Blond allele, 90, 90*f*
Blood-brain barrier, 135, 136*f*
Body dysmorphic disorder, 582. A disorder characterized by the unrealistic perception of physical flaws, 580
symptoms of, 594
treatment for, 630, 636
Body language, 240–241, 241*f*
Body mass index (BMI), 257. A height-to-weight ratio used to identify healthy weight, underweight, overweight, and obesity, 258*f*, 261, 665
Borderline personality disorder (BPD), 586. A disorder characterized by instability in interpersonal relationships, self-image, and emotion, 589*f*
treatment for, 632
Botox, 143, 236*f*, 237, 237*f*
Bottom-up processing, 152. Perception based on building simple input into more complex perceptions, 153
Brain. *See also specific parts*
adolescent, 439–441, 441*f*
anxiety disorders and, 580*f*
appearance of, 106, 111–112
associated with sexual desire and romantic love, 144, 144*f*
behavior and, 109
cannabinoid receptors in, 216*f*
concepts and, 367
consciousness and, 197, 198, 198*f*, 199
culture and, 107, 107*f*
decision-making and, 377–379
default mode network in, 198, 198*f*, 199, 225, 226*f*
endorphins and, 144
evolution of, 92–93, 92*f*
fusiform face area, 212
hemisphere dominance, 126
human, contemporary, 93
human, evolution of, 92–93, 92*f*
insula, 144
intelligence and, 93, 395, 397*f*
lateralization, 124–126
law, responsibility and, 123
left, 124–126
lonely, 145
long-term memory and, 347–349
meditation and, 225, 226*f*
perception and, 151–152
personality and, 476–477
right, 124–126
right-left brain myths, 126
self and, 491–493
semantic memories and, 349*f*
sexual orientation and, 266, 266*f*
social cognition in, 145
spinal cord, 111–112
split-brain operation, 124*f*
study of, 5
subcortical structures, 116–118
top-down processing and, 152
ventricles of, 112, 112*f*, 113
working memory and, 347
Brain damage
brain death and, 212–213
Capgras syndrome, 211–212
coma, 212
consciousness and, 211–214
face recognition and, 211
intelligence and, 395
language deficits, 385–386, 388
memory and, 347
near-death experiences and, 213, 214
prosopagnosia, 212
seizures and, 213–214
semantic information and, *368f*
vegetative state and, 213, 213*f*
Brain death, 213, 213*f*
Brain imaging
aggression and, 540–541
intelligence and, 397
meditation and, 225
REM sleep and, 209
research in, 144
Brain stimulation, 616–617
Brain-imaging technologies, 35–36, 124. *See also* Electroencephalogram (EEG); Functional magnetic resonance imaging (fMRI)
Brainstem, 114. The part of the brain containing the midbrain, pons, and medulla.
cerebellum, 113–114, 115
medulla, 115, 174
midbrain, 115–116
pons, 115
reticular formation, 116
structure of, 115*f*
Brief therapy, 605. Psychotherapy provided over a short time frame, usually between three and five sessions.
British empiricists, 10.
Broca's aphasia, 385, 391
Broca's area, 121*f*, 121, 123, 385–386
Bulimia nervosa, 260. An eating disorder characterized by bingeing, purging, and having feelings of depression, disgust, and lost control.
Bullying, 75, 76*f*
Bystander intervention, 538. The study of situational variables related to helping a stranger, most notably the decreased likelihood of helping as the number of bystanders increases, 539, 543

C

Caffeine, 218, 220
sources of, 219*f*
Calkins, Mary Whiton, 12*f*, 20*f*
Candidate gene, 82. A gene that has a greater impact on a trait of interest than other genes, 83

Cross-sectional study, 54. An experimental design for assessing age-related changes in which data are obtained simultaneously from people of differing ages.
Crystallized intelligence, 393. The ability to think logically using specific learned knowledge, 394*f*
Cues, 337. A stimulus that aids retrieval, 336–337
encoding, 337
encoding specificity and, 337
role in memory retrieval, 336
Cultural diversity, 24, 25. Variations in the practices, values, and goals shared by groups of people
Cultural neuroscience, 107, 107*f*
Culture
adaptations in therapy, 607
alleles and, 459–460, 460*f*
brain and, 107, 107*f*
collectivist, 459–460, 493–494, 494*f*, 508, 509*f*
emotional expressivity and, 249*f*
emotional knowledge and, 408*f*
entheogens and, 219
eye contact in, 251
genetics and evolution, 99–100
health and, 670–671
holistic reasoning and, 169
individualistic, 459–460, 493–494, 494*f*, 508–509
intelligence and, 392*f*
interdependence *vs.* independence in, 493–494
life expectancy, 670*f*
optimism and, 674, 674*f*
parenting and, 434
pessimism and, 674*f*
physical punishment and, 300
Cyberball game, 501*f*

D

Dancing, 227
Dark Triad personality traits, 588
Darwin, Charles, 12, 14, 95, 97
Data, 56–63
central tendency and, 58
descriptive statistics and, 57–60
inferential statistics and, 62–63
reliability in, 57
validity of, 57
Daydreaming, 203, 208
Daylight savings time, 201, 202*f*
DBT. *See* Dialectical behavior therapy (DBT)
Death, causes of, 661*f*
Decay, 343. A reduction in ability to retrieve rarely used information over time.
Decibels (dB), 172, 172*f*
Decision-making. *See also* Problem solving
adolescents and, 379*f*
biological psychology of, 377–379
computer models and, 377
framing in, 376
groupthink and, 529–530
probability and, 376
signal detection and, 154
styles of, 380*t*–381*t*
utility theory and, 375–376
Declarative memory, 328. A consciously retrieved memory that is easy to verbalize, including semantic, episodic, and autobiographical information; also known as explicit memory, 328–329
autobiographical, 330
cerebral cortex and, 347–348
episodic, 329
hippocampus and, 347
vs. nondeclarative, 348*f*
semantic, 329
Deep brain stimulation, 616. Electrical stimulation applied through surgically implanted electrodes that is used to treat some anxiety and mood disorders.
Deese-Roediger-McDermott (DRM) paradigm, 359
Default mode network (DMN), 198, 198*f*, 199, 225, 226*f*
Defense mechanism, 463. In Sigmund Freud's personality theory, a protective behavior that reduces anxiety.
Defensive aggression, 539
Defensive attributions, 506, 508
Deindividuation, 528. Immersion of an individual within a group, leading to anonymity
Déjà vu, 214
Delta waves, 204. A waveform of 1 to 4 cycles per second recorded by electroencephalogram that usually indicates deep non-rapid eye movement sleep.
Delusions, 562. A false, illogical belief.
Dendrite, 134. A branch from the neural cell body that usually receives input from other neurons.
Deoxyribonucleic acid (DNA), 341
environment and, 71–72
epigenome and, 409
fingerprint, reading, *82t*
identical twins and, 71, 72*t*
variations in, 82
Dependent variable, 51. A measure that demonstrates the effects of an independent variable; the "result" part of a hypothesis, 51*f*, 52, 53, 54, 63
Depersonalization disorder, 584
Depression. *See also* Major depressive disorder (MDD)
facial expressions and, 572, 573*f*
gender and, 568, 569*f*
rates of, 453*f*
rTMS and, 617*f*
self-esteem and, 486
suicide and, 574, 574*f*
Depth perception, 165. The ability to use the two-dimensional image projected on the retina to perceive three dimensions, 164–165
Ames room and, 165*f*
Muller-Lyer illusion, 165, 166*f*
Ponzo illusion, 165, 166*f*
Depth, recognizing
binocular cues, 164, 166
depth perception, 164
monocular cues, 164–165
retinal disparity and, 166
Derealization disorder, 584
Descent of Man, The (Darwin), 12
Descriptive methods, 44. Research methods designed for making careful, systematic observations.
case study in, 44–45
naturalistic observation, 46
survey, 46–47, 48*f*
Descriptive statistics, 57. Statistical methods that organize data into meaningful patterns and summaries, such as finding the average value.
central tendency and, 58
data and, 57–62
frequency distributions and, 58, 58*f*
mean and, 58
median and, 58, 59*f*
mode and, 58
normal distribution in, 59–60, 59*f*
scatterplots, 60, 62*f*
standard deviation and, 59, 59*f*, 60
two variables and, 60
variance and, 59, 59*f*
Development, 408–450. *See also individual stages*
adolescent, 438–445
childhood, 420–438
continuity and discontinuity, 409–410, 410*f*
ecological approaches to, 410
infant, 420–423
midlife, 448–450
nature and nurture in, 409
newborn, 412, 417–418
prenatal, 411–412, 411*f*
psychosexual stages of, 463
universal approaches to, 410
young adulthood, 446–448
Developmental psychology, 25. A psychological perspective that examines the normal changes in behavior that occur across the life span, 23*f*, 24
Dextroamphetamine (Dexedrine/Dextrostat), 560
Diabetes
insulin and, 255*f*
Type 2, 255*f*
***Diagnostic and Statistical Manual of Mental Disorders (DSM)*, 553.** A system for classification of psychological disorders published by the American Psychiatric Association, 553–554
Dialectical behavior therapy (DBT), 632
Diathesis-stress model, 573. A model that suggests that the experience of stress interacts with an individual's biological predisposition to produce a psychological disorder.
Difference threshold, 153. The smallest detectable difference between two stimuli.
measuring perception and, 153
Discontinuity, *vs.* continuity in development, 409–410, 410*f*
Discrimination, 285, 516. (a) A learned ability to distinguish between stimuli. (b) Unfair behavior based on stereotyping and prejudice, 286*f*
Disorganized attachment, 434
Display rule, 247. A cultural norm that specifies when, where, and how a person should express an emotion.
Dispositional attribution, 505. A judgment assigning the cause of a person's behavior to personal qualities or characteristics.
Dissociative amnesia, 584
Dissociative disorder, 584. A disorder characterized by disruptions in a person's identity, memory, or consciousness, 584–585
treatment for, 631
Dissociative fugue, 584
Dissociative identity disorder, 584
Distributed practice, 350, 352
Diversity, personality assessments and, 482
Divided attention, 152
Divorce, 544*f*
DNA. *See* Deoxyribonucleic acid (DNA)
DNA methylation, 85, 85*f*, 86, 87
Doctor of philosophy (PhD) degree, 602
Doctor of psychology (PSyD) degree, 602
Domain-Specific Risk-Taking (DOSPERT) Scale, 440
Dominant, 74. A feature of an allele that determines a phenotype in either the homozygous or the heterozygous condition

Door-in-the-face, 524. A persuasive technique in which compliance with a target request is preceded by a large, unreasonable request.
Dopamine, 143, 221–222, 223, 560, 564
Down syndrome, 389, 395, 413, 413*f*
Dreaming, 208. A mental state that usually occurs during sleep that features visual imagery.
activation-synthesis theory of, 208
default mode network in, 208
EEG recordings and, 208
lucid, 208
themes of, 7*f*
Drive, 253. A state of tension and arousal triggered by cues important for survival.
Drive reduction, 253. The state of relief and reward produced by removing the tension and arousal of the drive state.
DRM paradigm. *See* Deese-Roediger-McDermott (DRM) paradigm
Drumming, 227
Drunkorexia, 671
DSM. *See Diagnostic and Statistical Manual of Mental Disorders (DSM)*
Dyslexia, 389–390

E

Eating. *See* Hunger; Obesity
Eating disorders, 260–261
anorexia nervosa, 260, 261
binge-eating disorder, 261
bulimia nervosa, 260, 261
culture and, 260–261
environmental factors and, 261
genetic influences on, 261
male/female rates of, 260–261
Echoic memories, 320
Ecological development, 410
Ecstasy, 222
Education
giftedness and, 402
intelligence and, 396
positive schools and, 682
self-esteem and, 490
Ego, 462. The component of Sigmund Freud's personality theory that is the self that others see, 462–463, 463*f*
Egocentrism, 428. Limitations on the ability to understand the point of view of other people.
Elaboration likelihood model (ELM), 512. A model that predicts responses to persuasive messages by distinguishing between the central and the peripheral route to persuasion.
Electrical signaling, 137–139
Electrical stimulation, 110*t*
Electroconvulsive therapy (ECT), 615. A biological treatment in which seizures are induced in an anesthetized patient; it is used primarily in the treatment of mood disorders that have not responded to medication or other treatments, 343
Electroencephalogram (EEG), 110*t*, 202–203, 204*f*, 208, 212*f*, 617
Electromagnetic energy, 151*f*
Element of surprise, in learning, 287
Embryo, 410. The term used to describe a developing organism between the zygote and the fetus stages, or between 3 and 8 weeks following conception in humans, 411
Emotion, 232. A combination of arousal, physical sensations, and subjective feelings that occurs spontaneously in response to environmental stimuli.
approaches to, 238–239
arousal and, 240, 240*f*
arts and, 240–241
biology of, 241–245
adolescent, 442
amygdala and, 242–243
autonomic nervous system and, 241–242
basal ganglia and, 244, 244*f*
cerebral cortex and, 244–245
cingulate cortex and, 243–244, 244*f*
hypothalamus and, 242
insula and, 243
body language and, 240–241, 241*f*
continuous *vs.* discrete view of, 232*f*
evolution of, 239–241
expressing, 245–248
culture and, 249, 249*f*
development of, 245–246
display rules and, 247–248
evolution and, 245–246
eye contact, 251
facial expressions and, 245
lying, 250–251
regulation of, 246–247, 247*f*, 248
smiling and, 249
words for, 246
interpersonal relationships and, 273
interpreting, 248–251, 441
accuracy in, 250
culture and, 249
individual differences in, 248
smiling and, 249–250
memory and, 340–341
mood and, 233
vs. motivation, 233
negative, 513
sexual satisfaction and, 264
theories of, 233–239, 252
appraisals in, 239
Cannon-Bard theory, 233*f*, 235–236
contemporary approaches in, 238–239
James-Lange theory, 233–235, 233*f*
Schachter-Singer two-factor theory, 233*f*, 236–237
somatovisceral afference model of emotion (SAME), 238
Yerkes-Dodson law and, 240–241
Emotion-focused coping, 658. A response to stress that targets the negative emotions arising from the situation.
Emotional intelligence, 248, 395
Emotional knowledge, 408, 408*f*
Emotional regulation, 248
Empathy, 117
Empiricism, 7
Empty nest, 450*f*
Encoding, 318. The transformation of information from one form to another.
Encoding cues, 337
Encoding specificity, 337. A process in which memories incorporate unique combinations of information when encoded.
Endocrine system, 132–133. A system responsible for the release of hormones into the bloodstream.
glands of, 132–133, 132*f*
adrenal glands, 132–133
islets of Langerhans, 132, 132*f*, 133
ovaries, 132
pineal gland, 132*f*, 133
pituitary gland, 132, 132*f*, 133
testes, 132, 132*f*, 133
thyroid gland, 131, 132*f*, 133
peripheral nervous system and, 133
Endorphin receptors, 223
Endorphins, 144, 146
Engaged followership, 526–527
Enteric nervous system, 130. A division of the autonomic nervous system consisting of nerve cells embedded in the lining of the gastrointestinal system, 131*f*
function of, 130
Entheogens, 219
Entitlement, participation trophies and, 270
Epigenetics, 83. The study of gene-environment interactions in the production of phenotypes.
gene expression and, 83
lifespan, 409
mechanisms of change in, 85*f*
nutrition and, 83
psychological disorders and, 86
stress and, 648
transgenerational change and, 87, 87*f*
Epilepsy, 213
Episodic buffer, 324
Episodic memory, 329. A memory for personal experience, 329–330
cerebral cortex and, 347–348
Epworth sleepiness scale, 204
Ethical research. *See* Research ethics
Ethics, of personality testing, 482
Ethnic identity, 444, 445*f*
Eudaimonic approach, 674
Event-related potential (ERP), 110*t*
Evidence-based practice, 601, 601*f*
Evolution, 89. Descent with modification from a common ancestor.
behavior, influence on, 95–102
of emotions, 239–241
of the human brain, 92–93, 92*f*
mechanisms of, 89–90
adaptation, 91–02
genetic drift, 89–90
migration, 89–90
mutation, 89–90
natural selection, 89
of personality, 477
principles of, 94
Evolutionary psychology, 22. A psychological perspective that investigates how physical structure and behavior have been shaped by their contributions to survival and reproduction, 23, 23*f*, 24, 32
Excitatory messages, 141, 141*f*
Exemplar, 365. A specific member of a category used to represent the category, 365–367
Exercise
cardiac patients and, 657*f*
depression and, 626, 627*f*
health and, 668–669
memory and, 354
play and, 668
sitting and, 668–669
stress and, 657–658, 657*f*
well-being and, 669
Exhaustion, 643. The third and last stage of the general adaptation syndrome (GAS), characterized by depletion of physical and psychological resources, 642–643
Experiment, 51. A research method that tests hypotheses and allows researchers to make conclusions about causality.
artificiality in, 53
confounding variables in, 51

Experiment (*continued*)
control group in, 51, 51*f*, 52*f*
dependent variable in, 51, 51*f*, 52*f*
design of, 51*f*
experimental group in, 51, 51*f*
hypothesis in, 51
independent variable in, 51, 51*f*, 52*f*
limitations of, 53
meta-analyses and, 53–54
multiple perspectives, benefits of, 54
operationalization and, 53
random assignment in, 51, 51*f*
unethical, 50, 50*f*, 65, 65–66, 66
video game use, 53
Experimental group, 51. A group of participants who are exposed to the independent variable.
Exposure therapy, 289–290
Extinction, 284. The reduction of a learned response. In classical conditioning, extinction occurs when the unconditioned stimulus (UCS) no longer follows the conditioned stimulus (CS). In operant conditioning, extinction occurs when the consequence no longer follows the learned behavior, 285*f*, 300, 303
Extrasensory perception (ESP), 58–59
Extraversion, 475*f*, 481*f*
Extrinsic reward, 253
A reward from an outside source.
Extroversion, 469. One of the Big Five traits characterized by warmth, gregariousness, assertiveness, activity, excitement seeking, and positive emotion; opposite of introversion, 465, 468, 476
Eye, 157*f*
Eye contact, 250, 251
Eye movement desensitization and reprocessing (EMDR), 119
Eye movements, emotions and, 119*f*
Eyewitnesses, reliability of, 341

F

Face recognition
brain and, 492*f*
brain damage and, 211
own-race bias in, 336
Facial expressions
Botox and, 236*f*, 237*f*
depression and, 572, 573*f*
emotions and, 239–240, 245
evolution of, 239–240
interpreting, 250
Factor analysis, 64, 467*f*
Faith, 36
Fake news, 514
False memories, 334, 339, 340, 345
Family therapy, 606. A type of therapy in which family members participate individually and in combination with other family members.
Family-centered positive psychology (FCPP), 682
Family, defining, 447, 447*f*
Fear
amygdala and, 646*f*
overcoming, 289–290
Fechner, Gustav, 9
Fetal alcohol syndrome (FAS), 414. A condition resulting from alcohol consumption by the mother during pregnancy that produces physical abnormalities and cognitive and behavioral problems in her child, 416*f*
Fetus, 410. The term used to describe a developing organism between the embryo stage and birth, or between 8 and approximately 40 weeks following conception in humans, 91*f*, 411, 412*f*
Fight-flight freeze system (FFFS), 477
First impressions, 501, 504, 504*f*
Fitness, 90. The ability of one genotype to reproduce more successfully relative to other genotypes.
Fixed action patterns, 279
Fixed interval (FI) schedule, 302. A schedule of reinforcement in which the first response following a specified interval is reinforced, 303*f*
Fixed ratio (FR) schedule, 301. A schedule of reinforcement in which reinforcement occurs following a set number of behaviors, 301–302
Flashbulb memory, 340. An especially vivid and detailed memory of an emotional event, 340–341
Flooding, 289
Flow, 679. A state characterized by complete absorption in a current activity, such as work, problem solving, or creativity
Fluid intelligence, 393. The ability to think logically without the need to use learned knowledge, 394*f*
Flynn effect, 398–399, 399*f*
Food additives, attention deficit hyperactivity and, 561
Foot-in-the-door, 524. A persuasive technique in which compliance with a small request is followed by compliance with a larger request that might otherwise have been rejected.
Forensic psychologists, 28*f*
Forgetting, 342. A decrease in the ability to remember a previously formed memory, 342–343
decay and, 343
interference and, 343–344
motivated, 344–345
types of, 358
Formal operational stage, 428. Jean Piaget's stage of development beginning at age 12 and extending through adulthood and characterized by mature reasoning capabilities
Fovea, 158. An area of the retina that is specialized for highly detailed vision. 157*f*
FOXP-2 gene, 383, 388
Framing effects, 376, 376*f*
Free association, 609. The psychoanalytic technique of encouraging a patient to say whatever comes to mind, without attempting to censor the content.
Frequency distributions, 58, 58*f*
Freud, Sigmund, 13–14, 13*f*
Frontal lobe, 118. The most forward of the four lobes of the cerebral cortex; location of the primary motor cortex and areas responsible for some of the most complex cognitive processes.
Broca's area, 121, 121*f*, 123
cognitive functions of, 121
damage to, 244
Frontal lobotomy, 122, 616
orbitofrontal cortex and, 122
Phineas Gage accident and, 122
prefrontal cortex and, 121, 121*f*
Fryer, Roland, 254*f*
Functional fixedness, 370. A possible barrier to successful problem solving in which a concept is considered only in its most typical form.
Functional magnetic resonance imaging (fMRI), 110*t*
behavior and, 477
brain and, 109
finger-tapping, 109
honesty and, 250, 251*f*
hunger and, 4
love and, 67
meditation and, 225
memory suppression and, 345
mirror systems, 123
neurofeedback and, 617
tennis serves and, 123
vegetative state and, 213*f*
Functionalism, 11
An approach that saw behavior as purposeful and contributing to survival
James and, 12
Fundamental attribution error, 505–506
Fusiform face area (FFA), 212

G

Gamma waves, 202. A waveform of more than 30 cycles per second recorded by electroencephalogram that indicates attention to sensory input, 202–203
GAS. *See* General adaptation syndrome (GAS)
Gate theory, 182. The theory that suggests that input from touch fibers competes with input from pain receptors, possibly preventing pain messages from reaching the brain.
Gen Y, 446*f*
Gender
concept of, 425
depression and, 568, 569*f*, 570
development of, 417–418, 423–425
intersex, 417, 425
response to infidelity, 534*f*
self-esteem and, 487–488
stress responses, 649
transgender, 425
Gender assignment, 425
Gender dysphoria, 425
Gender identity, 423, 425
Gene, 72. A small segment of DNA located in a particular place on a chromosome that produces a protein, 73
alleles for, 74, 76*f*
bullying and, 75, 76*f*
chromosomes, 73, 75, 76–77, 83, 84
environment and, 71–72, 73, 81, 83, 91, 91*f*
eye color and, 82
hemophilia and, 77, 78*f*
interpersonal relationships and, 101
serotonin transporter (SERT), 75, 76*f*
shared with other species, 79*f*
variation in, 76
Gene expression, 74. The process in which genetic instructions are converted into a feature of a living well, 83, 85
General adaptation syndrome (GAS), 642. Hans Selye's three-stage model for an organism's response to stressors, 642*f*, 643, 660
General intelligence (g), 392. A measure of an individual's overall intelligence as opposed to specific abilities.

Generalization, 285. The tendency to respond to stimuli that are similar to an original conditioned stimulus (CS), 286*f*
Generalize, 62. To extend conclusions to larger populations outside your research sample.
Generalized anxiety disorder (GAD), 580. A disorder characterized by excessive anxiety and worry that is not correlated with particular objects or situations.
biological explanations for, 580
brain circuits and, 580, 580*f*
cognitive explanations for, 580
integrating perspectives on, 580
social explanations for, 580
symptoms of, 594
Generalized seizures, 214, 214*f*
Genetic drift, 89. Change in a population's genes from one generation to the next because of chance or accident, 89–90
Genetic research, social prejudice in, 80–83
Genetic variation, 76
Genetics
behavioral, 78–80
of cats, 75
development risks and, 412–413
intelligence and, 397–398
major concepts in, 73–77, 88
allele, 73–74
dominant, 74
gene, 73–74
gene expression, 74
genetic variation, 76
genotype, 73–74
heterozygous, 74
homozygous, 74
recessive, 74
relatedness, 76, 77*f*
sex chromosomes, 76–77
personality and, 475–476
psychology and field of, 77–88
to select a mate, 101
subfields of, 79*t*
Genius, 401
Genomewide association study (GWAS), 83. A scan of complete sets of DNA from many participants, which is performed to look for variations associated with a particular phenotype, condition, or disease.
Genotype, 72. An individual's profile of alleles, 73, 74*f*, 475*f*
Gestalt psychologists
Koffka, 12
Köhler, 12
Wertheimer, 12
Gestalt psychology, 11
An approach that saw experience as being different from the sum of its elements.
closure in, 164, 165*f*
continuity and, 163–164, 165*f*
organization and, 163
proximity and, 164, 164*f*
recognizing objects and, 163–164
similarity and, 164, 164*f*
simplicity and, 164
Giftedness, 401. An extreme of intelligence defined as having an IQ score of 130 or above.
Gist, 339
Glia, 134
axons and, 135
blood-brain barrier and, 136*f*
function of, 135
Global happiness, 678*f*
myelin and, 135–136, 136*f*
Glucose, 255. A type of sugar that plays an important role in hunger levels.
Glutamate, 349
Golden rectangles, 153*f*
Goose bumps, 278–279
Grafton, Scott, 23*f*
Gratings, 163, 163*f*
Gratitude, 683
Gray matter, 134, 625*f*
Group polarization, 528. The intensifying of an attitude following discussion, 528–529, 529*f*
Group therapy, 605. Psychotherapy conducted with a group of people rather than individually, 605–606
Grouping, 176
Groupthink, 529. A type of flawed decision making in which a group does not question its decisions critically, 529–530
Growth hormone, 132
Growth mindsets, 269
Gustation, 183. *See also* Chemical senses
The sense of taste.
biology of
papillae, 185
taste buds, 185, 186
taste receptors, 185, 185*f*
supertasters, 186
thalamus and, 185

H

Habituation, 280. A simple form of learning in which reactions to repeated stimuli that are unchanging and harmless decrease
Haka, 234
Hall, G. Stanley, 20*f*
Hallucinations, 562. A false perception.
Hallucinogen, 216. A drug that stimulates the experience of false perceptions, 218–219, 222
Halo effects, 504
Handedness, 127
Happiness
defining, 674
eudaimonic approach to, 674
flow and, 679
genetics and, 674
global, 678*f*
hedonic approach to, 674
increasing, 678–679
interpersonal relationships and, 675 , 675*f*
marriage and, 448, 448*f*, 675
parenting and, 448, 676
types of, 684
wealth and, 675–677, 676*f*
Haptic codes, 320
Hardiness, 659, 659*f*
Hassles, 644–645
Health
biopsychosocial model of, 660–661, 661*f*
exercise and, 657*f*
heart disease and, 651
immune system and, 650–651
mood and, 652–653
obesity and, 652–653
sleep and, 652–653
socioeconomic status and, 649
stress and, 640–654, 654*f*
Health psychology, 660. A branch of psychology that investigates the relationships between psychological variables and health.
alcohol consumption, 666–668, 667*f*
behavior and, 662–672
biopsychosocial model of, 660–661, 661*f*
causes of death, 661*f*, 662
culture and, 670–671
exercise and, 668–669
habits for, 663*f*
interpersonal relationships and, 683
life expectancy, 670*f*
loneliness and, 669–670
nutrition and, 665–666
safety practices, 662*t*
sitting and, 668–669, 668*f*
tobacco use, 663–665, 663*f*, 664*f*
Hearing loss, 177
Heart disease, 651
Hedonic approach, 674
Hemispatial neglect, 124*f*
Hemophilia, 75, 77, 77*f*, 78*f*
Heritability, 78. The statistical likelihood that variations observed in a population are because of genetics.
behavioral genetics and, 78–79
environment and, 79, 80*f*
of human conditions, 81*f*
misunderstanding of, 82
perceived loneliness and, 102*f*
Heroin, 223, 223*f*
Heroism, 537–538
Heterozygous, 74. Having two different alleles for a gene.
Heuristic, 371. A shortcut to problem solving; also known as a rule of thumb.
affect, 374
availability, 372–373, 373*f*
recognition, 371–372, 372*f*
representativeness, 373–374
types of, 382
Hierarchy of needs, Maslow's, 271–272, 271*f*, 676
Higher-order conditioning, 286. Learning in which stimuli associated with a conditioned stimulus (CS) also elicit conditioned responses (CRs).
Highly superior autobiographical memory (HSAM), 330
Hippocampus, 117. A subcortical structure that participates in memory.
declarative memories and, 347
long-term memory and, 117
memory and, 316–317
Histology, 110*t*
Histone modification, 85, 85*f*, 86
Hoarding behavior, 378
Holistic reasoning, 169
Holmes and Rahe scales, 644
Homeostasis, 253. A steady internal balance, or equilibrium.
Hominins, 92–93
Homo erectus, 92
Homo sapiens, 93
Homozygous, 74. Having two of the same alleles for a gene.
Honesty, 485*f*
Hormones, prenatal development and, 424*f*
Hot nose sign, 213*f*
Human behavior, myths about, 7*t*
Human eye, 157*f*
Human growth hormone, 206*f*
Human participants, 65–66, *69*
Humanistic psychologists, 13–15
Maslow, 15
Rogers, 15
Humanistic psychology, 14. An approach that saw people as inherently good and motivated to learn and improve.
motivation and, 14, 466
personality and, 466–467
self-actualization and, 466, 467*f*
therapy and, 14
Humanistic therapy, 601. A therapy approach patterned after the theories proposed by humanistic psychologists, 610–611
Hunger
autonomic nervous system, 257, 257*f*
fat stores and, 256, 257*f*
glucose and, 255–256
insulin and, 255, 255*f*
leptin and, 256, 257*f*
metabolism and, 256, 257*f*
motivation and, 253

Hunger (*continued*)
satiety and, 256–257
sensation of, 254
stomach contractions and, 255, 255*f*
Hunter-gatherer societies, 96
Huntington's disease, 94, 349
Hydrocephalus, 112
Hyperpolarization, 138, 141
Hypnosis, 224. An altered state of consciousness characterized by relaxation and increased suggestibility
in psychotherapy, 600, 604
Stroop Test and, 225, 225*f*
Hypnotherapists, 604
Hypothalamic-pituitary-adrenal (HPA) axis, 647. A circuit that responds to perceived stressors by initiating the release of cortisol into the bloodstream.
Hypothalamus, 117. "4F" A subcortical structure that participates in the regulation of thirst, temperature, hunger, sexual behavior, and aggression.
behaviors, 117
emotions and, 242
homeostasis and, 117
lateral, 256
motivation and, 117
satiety and, 257*f*
stress and, 646
ventromedial, 256–257, 257*f*
Hypothesis, 41. A proposed explanation for a situation, usually taking the form "If A happens, then B will be the result," 41–42
developing and testing, 51*f*
evaluating, 42
in experiments, 51–53
generating, 41–42
null, 62
Hysteria. *See* Somatic symptom disorder

I

Iconic memories, 320–321
Id, 462. The component of Sigmund Freud's personality theory containing primitive drives present at birth, 463*f*
Identity, 443. A consistent, unified sense of self.
If-then relationships, 473
Imitation, 311. Copying behavior that is unlikely to occur naturally and spontaneously, 316
Immigration, emotional expressivity and, 249, 249*f*
Immune system, 650. The body system that defends against infection and cancer, 650–651, 650*f*
Implicit Association Test (IAT), 519
Imprinting, 279
In-groups, 521*f*
Incentive, 253. A reward that pulls an organism's behavior in a particular direction, 254*f*
Independence *vs.* interdependence, 493–494
Independent variable, 51. An experimental variable controlled and manipulated by the experimenter; the "if A happens" part of a hypothesis, 51*f*, 52, 54, 63
Individualistic culture, 459–460, 493–494, 494*f*, 508
Indulgent parenting, 436*t*, 437
Infants. *See also* Childhood development
audition and, 177
computational language learning, 387, 387*f*, 388
emotional expressivity and, 418*f*
emotions and, 245
ethical research with, 65
faces and, 418, 418*f*
facial expressions and, 240
gender development, 423, 425
language acquisition stages, 388
motor development, 421–423, 423*f*
nervous system development, 421
physical development, 420, 420*f*
REM sleep and, 207
separation protests, 246*f*
sudden infant death syndrome, 210
touch and, 180
vision and, 166–167
Inferential statistics, 62. Statistical methods that allow experimenters to extend conclusions from samples to larger populations, 63*f*
data and, 62–63
generalizations and, 62
null hypothesis in, 62
statistical significance in, 62
Infidelity, 534, 534*f*
Information processing, 318. A continuum including attention, sensation, perception, learning, memory, and cognition, 319*f*, 429–431
Informed consent, 65. Permission obtained from a research participant after the risks and benefits of an experimental procedure have been thoroughly explained, 63
Inhibition, 285. A feature of classical conditioning in which a conditioned stimulus (CS) predicts the nonoccurrence of an unconditioned stimulus (UCS)
Inhibitory messages, 141, 142*f*
Insecure attachment, 435. A pattern of infant-caregiver bonding that can take several forms but is generally characterized as less desirable for the child's outcomes than secure attachment, 434–435
Insight therapy, 609. A therapy that improves symptoms of psychological disorder by building people's understanding of their situation.
Insomnia, 209. A sleep disorder characterized by an inability to either initiate or maintain normal sleep, 228
Instinct, 278. An inborn pattern of behavior elicited by environmental stimuli; also known as a fixed action pattern, 279
Instinctive drift, 307
Institutional animal care and use committees (IACUCs), 64
Institutional review boards (IRBs), 64
Instrumental aggression, 539
Instrumental conditioning, 295
Insula, 243*f*. Regions of cortex located at the junction of the frontal and temporal lobes.
anterior insula, 144
emotions and, 243
Insulin, 255, 255*f*
Intellectual disability, 400. A condition diagnosed in individuals with IQ scores below 70 and poor adaptive behaviors; also known as mental retardation, 400–401, 401*f*
categories of, 400
diagnosis of, 551
Down syndrome, 389, 395, 413, 413*f*
IQ and, 552*f*
language and, 389, 401
poverty and, 400*f*
skills and abilities, 393, 395
Williams syndrome, 389, 393, 395
Intelligence, 392. The ability to understand complex ideas, adapt effectively to the environment, learn from experience, engage in reasoning, and overcome obstacles.
abilities, general and specific, 392–394
assessing, 392
biological influences on, 395–399
brain development and, 397
brain structures and, 395, 397*f*
genetics and, 397–398
collective, 196, 398–399
crystallized, 393, 394*f*
cultural differences and, 396
education and, 396
emotional, 394–395
emotional and social, 394–395
extremes of, 399–402
fluid, 393–394, 394*f*
general, 392–394
genius and, 401
giftedness and, 401
intellectual disabilities and, 400–401
multiple, 394, 395
self-concept and, 395
types of, 404
Intelligence quotient (IQ), 392. A measure of individual intelligence relative to a statistically normal curve.
brain structures and, 397*f*
culture-free testing of, 393*f*, 398
distribution of, 400*f*
giftedness and, 401
human brain and, 93
increase in, 398
increasing, 402
intellectual disabilities and, 400
socioeconomic status and, 398–399
Interactome, 549–550
Interdependence *vs.* independence, 493–494
Interference, 343–344. Competition between newer and older information in memory, 344*f*
Interleaving, 352
International Statistical Classification of Diseases and Related Health Problems (ICD), 553
Internet memes, 313
Interneurons, 114
Interpersonal relationships, sexual and emotional
biological perspective, 144
consciousness and, 227
emotions and, 273
genetics and, 101
gratitude and, 683
happiness and, 675, 675*f*
health psychology and, 683
marital satisfaction and, 454
maximizers and satisficers, 403
methodological perspective, 67
methodological perspective, like *vs.* love, 67
online relationships and, 544
operant conditioning and, 313–314
opposites and attraction, 495*f*
pain and, 188
personality and, 494–495
psychological perspectives and, 30
PTSD and, 592
satisfaction and, 264, 264*f*
sexual orientation and, 264–267
transactive memory and, 356
treatment and, 634
using relationships to illustrate psychological perspectives, 30

Interpersonal self, 493. The self we are in the presence of other people
Intersex, 417, 425
Intersexual selection, 99, 101
Intimacy, 533
Intrasexual selection, 99
Intrinsic reward, 253. A reward that arises internally.
Introspection, 5. A personal observation of your own thoughts, feelings, and behavior, 4
Introversion, 469. One of the Big Five traits characterized by coolness, reserve, passivity, inactivity, caution, and negative emotion; opposite of extroversion, 465, 468
IQ. *See* Intelligence quotient (IQ)
Iris, 157. The brightly colored circular muscle surrounding the pupil of the eye.
Ishihara Color Test, 161*f*
Islets of Langerhans, 131, 131*f*

J

Jamais vu, 214
James-Lange theory, 233. A theory of emotion that proposes that physical sensations lead to subjective feelings.
- catharsis and, 234
- physical responses and subjective feelings of, 233–235, 233*f*

James, William, 20*f*
- functionalism and, 12, 12*f*

Jet lag, 200–201, 201*f*
Just-world belief, 508. The assumption that good things happen to good people and bad things happen to bad people.

K

Kanzi, 386
Kavadis, 183
K complexes, 204, 204f
KE family, 388
Kenyan children, 422
Ketamine, 213, 217, 218
KITLG gene, 89
Kiwi, 426
Klinefelter syndrome, 417
Knee-jerk reflex, 114, 114f
Knee tapping, 278
Knowledge, 363
- emotion, 408
- learned, 393
- philosophical debate about source of, 8
- psychological science study and, 6
- scientific, 8, 36, 37, 42
- self-knowledge, 486
- semantic, 328, 348

Koko, 386

L

L SERT allele, 459–460, 460*f*
Language
- handedness and, 127*t*
- lateralization of, 125, 126*f*

Language, 382. A system for communicating thoughts and feelings using arbitrary signals.
- biological psychology of, 384–387
- building blocks of, 384
- disorders, 385–387
  - Broca's aphasia, 385
  - Wernicke's aphasia, 385–386
- *FOXP-2* gene and, 383, 388
- gap in acquisition of, 388
- gender-neutral, 382–383
- intellectual disabilities and, 389, 401, 402
- learning, 387–389
- morphemes and, 384
- nonhuman animals and ability, 386–387
- origins of, 383
- phonemes and, 384, 384*f*
- processing variations, 389–391
  - American Sign Language (ASL), 391
  - bilingualism, 390
  - dyslexia, 389–390
  - multilingualism, 390–391, 390*f*
- vocabulary and, 382–383, 385*f*

Late adulthood, 450–453
- cognition in, 450–451
- physical changes in, 450
- social and emotional aspects of, 451–454
  - depression and, 452
  - marriage and, 453–454
  - relationships and, 453–454
- well-being and, 452

Latent inhibition, 286. The slower learning that occurs when a conditioned stimulus (CS) is already familiar compared to when the CS is unfamiliar, 287, 291
Latent learning, 305. Learning that occurs in the absence of reinforcement, 305–306
Lateral hypothalamus (LH), 256
Lateral preference inventory, 127*t*
Lateralization
- defined, 124–125
- emotional behavior and, 125
- function of, 125
- handedness and, 127, 127*t*
- of language, 125, 125*f*
- right/left brain myths, 126
- split-brain operation, 124, 124*f*

Law of effect (Thorndike), 17, 18*f*, 295
Law, lie detection and, 250
Leadership, 588
Learned helplessness, 569. A state in which experiencing random or uncontrolled consequences leads to feelings of helplessness and possibly depression.
Learning, 278. A relatively permanent change in behavior or the capacity for behavior due to experience, 279
- aggression and, 541
- associative, 280
  - classical conditioning, 280, 282–283, 284–294
  - operant conditioning, 280, 295–309
- cultural transmission of, 312–313
- imprinting and, 279
- instincts and, 279
- latent, 305–306
- modeling and, 280
- nonassociative, 280
- observational, 280, 310–314
- reflexes and, 278–279
- social, 280
- synapses and, 345–347
- types of, 280, 281

Learning disabilities, 389
Left cerebral hemisphere, localization of functions in, 124–125
Lens, 157. The clear structure behind the pupil that bends light toward the retina.
Leptin, 256. A hormone secreted by fat cells that helps the body maintain an appropriate level of stored fat.
Lesions, 110*t*
Levels of processing theory, 325. The depths (shallow to deep) of processing applied to information that predict its ease of retrieval, 325–326, 326*f*
Lickert scales, 479
Lie detection, 250–251
Life coaches, 604
Light spectrum, 156*f*
Linear perspective, 164
Lithium chloride (LiCl), 288, 293
Lithium treatment, 599–600, 624, 625*f*
Lobes, 118, 119–123
- frontal, 121–122
- occipital, 122
- parietal, 123, 124*f*
- temporal, 121*f*, 122–123

Localization, language, hardedness and, 127*t*
Loci, Method of, 355
Locke, John, 8
Locus of control, 472. A cognitive expectancy featured in social-cognitive learning theories of personality about the source of individual outcomes; an external locus of control sees outcomes as resulting from luck or chance, while an internal locus of control sees outcomes as the result of individual effort.
Logotherapy, 659
Loneliness
- exercise and, 668
- health and, 669–670
- instruments for, 502
- learning to become less lonely, 314
- mortality and, 669*f*
- motivation and, 268

Loneliness, pandemic during, 145
Long-term memory, 325. The final stage of the Atkinson-Shiffrin model that is the location of permanent memories, 325–326
- declarative, 329–330
- hippocampus and, 117
- levels of processing theory, 325–326
- moving information into, 325–326
- nondeclarative, 330–331
- organization of, 333–335
  - connectionist theories, 333–334
  - inferences using schemas, 334–335
  - spreading activation model, 333–334, 333*f*
- retrieval, 336–341, 344
  - emotional events, 340–341
  - flashbulb memories, 340–341
  - reconstruction and, 338–340
  - tip of the tongue, 337–338
- role of cues, 336–337
- serial position effect and, 326–327
- types of, 328–332, 328*f*
- *vs.* working memory, 326–328

Long-term potentiation (LTP), 346. The enhancement of communication between two neurons resulting from their synchronous activation, 346*f*
Longhand notes *vs.* typing notes, 351*f*
Longitudinal study, 54. An experimental design for assessing age-related changes in which data are obtained from the same individuals at intervals over a long period of time.
Loudness, 175–176, 175*f*
Love
- brain imaging of, 67*f*, 144*f*
- companionate, 533, 533*f*
- consummate, 533, 533*f*
- oxytocin and, 144
- romantic, 533–534
- triangle model of, 533, 533*f*
- types of, 534

Low-balling, 524. Making further requests of a person who has already committed to a course of action.
LSD (lysergic acid diethylamide), 218
Lucid dreaming, 208. A conscious awareness of dreaming accompanied by the ability to control the content of the dream, 209
Lying, 250–251
Lymphocyte, 651. White blood cells that are products of the immune system.

Occlusion, 167
Olfaction, 183–184. *See also* Chemical senses
The sense of smell.
biology of, 183–184
olfactory pathways and, 183–184
olfactory receptors and, 184*f*
sociocultural influences on, 187–188
thalamus and, 184
Olfactory bulb, 183. One of two structures below the frontal lobes of the brain that receive input from the olfactory receptors in the nose.
Olfactory nerve, 183. A nerve carrying olfactory information from the olfactory receptors to the olfactory bulbs.
Olfactory receptors, 184*f*
Omega-3 fatty acids, 567
Online therapy, 606–607
Onset insomnia, 209
Openness, 468. A Big Five personality trait characterized by an appreciation for fantasy, feelings, actions, ideas, values, and aesthetics.
Operant conditioning, 280. A type of learning in which associations are formed between behaviors and their outcomes.
applying, 307–308
behavior therapies, 308–309
token economies, 308
biological influences on, 306–307
cognitive influences on, 305–306
consequences, 296, 296*t*
interpersonal relationships and, 313–314
method of successive approximations/shaping and, 305–306
negative reinforcement, 298
personality and, 465–466
positive reinforcement, 296–298
punishment and, 299
schedules of reinforcement, 300–304
social influences on, 307
Operationalization, 53. Defining variables in ways that allow them to be measured.
Opiates, 223
Opioid overdose, 292, 292*f*
Opioids, 144, 223
Opponent process theory, 160. A theory of color vision that suggests we have a red-green color channel and a blue-yellow color channel in which activation of one color in each pair inhibits the other color, 160–161
Optic disk, 157*f*, 158
Optic nerve, 159. The nerve exiting the retina of the eye.
Optic tracts, 159. Nerve pathways traveling from the optic chiasm to the thalamus, hypothalamus, and midbrain.
Optimism, 673. Thinking positively about the future, 674, 674*f*
Optogenetics, 110*t*
Orbitofrontal cortex, 122. A part of the prefrontal cortex located right behind the eyes that participates in impulse control.
antisocial personality disorder and, 586
damage to, 122, 122*f*
obsessive-compulsive disorder and, 581
Orexins, 256
Organ of Corti, 174. A structure located on the basilar membrane that contains auditory receptors.
Organization, in Gestalt psychology, 163–164
Origin of Species (Darwin), 12, 89
Out-groups, 518*f*, 521*f*
Ovaries, 132–133
Ovotesticular syndrome, 425
Own-race bias (ORB), 336
Oxytocin, 133, 144, 222, 263, 263*f*

P

Pain, 181–182. *See also* Somatosensation
expectation and, 182
gate theory of, 182, 182*f*
pain messages and, 181–182
pain receptors and, 181
perception of, 182
placebo effects on, 182
relationships and, 188
thalamus and, 181–182
tolerance of, 183
Pandemic. *See* COVID-19 Pandemic
Panic attack, 578. The experience of intense fear and autonomic arousal in the absence of real threat, 578–579
Panic disorder, 578. A disorder characterized by repeated panic attacks and fear of future attacks.
biological explanations for, 578
cognitive explanations for, 578
culture and, 579
integrating perspectives on, 579
panic attacks and, 578
social explanations for, 579
symptoms of, 594
Papillae, 185. Small bumps on the tongue that contain taste buds.
Paradoxical sleep, 205
Parallelogram illusion, 170
Parasympathetic nervous system, 130. The part of the autonomic nervous system associated with rest, repair, and energy storage.
function of, 130
Parental investment, 98
Parenting styles
attachment and, 434–436
authoritarian, 436*f*, 436*t*
authoritative, 436, 436*f*, 436*t*, 437
autonomy in, 526
behavioral regulation, 436, 436*t*
child outcomes and, 437*f*
cultural influences on, 435
indulgent, 436*f*, 436*t*
obedience and, 526
parental support, 436–437, 436*t*
responsive, 434
temperament and, 432*f*
uninvolved, 436–437, 436*f*, 436*t*
Parents
happiness and, 448, 676
marital satisfaction, 448*f*
Parietal lobe, 118. The lobe of the cerebral cortex that lies at the top of the head between the frontal and the occipital lobes; location of the primary somatosensory cortex.
damage to, 124*f*
somatosensory cortex, 121*f*, 123
Parkinson's disease, 116
caffeine and, 220
dopamine and, 143
facial expressions and, 245
medications for, 623
procedural memory and, 349
Partial reinforcement, 301. The reinforcement of a desired behavior on some occasions, but not others.
Partial reinforcement effect in extinction, 303. The more rapid extinction observed following continuous reinforcement compared to that following partial reinforcement
Partial seizures, 214, 214*f*
Participation trophies, entitlement, competitiveness, and, 270
Passive aggression, 539
Pavlov, Ivan Petrovich, 16, 20*f*, 22*f*, 281
Peer groups, 444–445
Peer review, 42. The process of having other experts examine research prior to its publication
Perception, 150. The process of interpreting sensory information.
assessing, 156
auditory, 175–178
autistic children and, 168
bottom-up processing and, 152–153, 162
color vision and, 160*f*
measurement of
absolute threshold and, 153
difference threshold and, 153
psychophysics and, 153
sensation and, 150
sensory adaptation and, 151–152
signal detection and, 153–154
top-down processing and, 152–153
visual illusions and, 165*f*–166*f*, 170, 170*f*
Performance, arousal and, 240*f*
Peripheral nervous system (PNS), 111. The nerves exiting the central nervous system that carry sensory and motor information to and from the rest of the body, 133
autonomic nervous system, 129–130, 131*f*
endocrine system and, 132–133
somatic nervous system, 129
Person-centered therapy, 610. A humanistic therapy approach developed by Carl Rogers to help clients achieve congruence, or an alignment of the real and ideal selves.
Personality, 25. An individual's characteristic way of thinking, feeling, and behaving, 23*f*, 26*f*
assessing (*see* Personality assessment)
biological bases of, 473–477
brain function and, 475–476
brain structures and, 475–476
evolution of, 477
genetics and, 475–476
temperament, 473–475, 474*f*
classic behaviorist approaches, 465–466
Dark Triad traits, 99
humanistic approach to, 466–467, 467*f*
interpersonal relationships and, 494–495
marital satisfaction and, 454
neo-Freudians, 464–465
psychodynamic theories of, 462–465
responses to pandemic and, 496, 496*f*
situations affecting, 470–473
social media and, 25*f*
social-cognitive learning theories, 472
test, 481*f*
theories of, 461–462
trait theories of, 467–470
big five theory, 468–470, 468*f*
early, 468
factor analysis, 467*f*
twin studies in, 475, 476*f*
unconscious mind and, 465
Personality assessment
computers and, 479*f*
diversity and, 482
ethics of, 482

personality inventories, 478–479, 480*f*
projective tests, 481–482
reasons for, 478
self-reports, 478
social media and, 478
standardized tests for, 478
validity of, 481*f*
Personality disorders, 586. A disorder characterized by impairments in identity in personality traits, and in establishment of empathy or intimacy.
antisocial personality disorder (ASPD), 58
borderline personality disorder (BPD), 587, 589*f*
narcissistic personality disorder (NPD), 587, 589–590
treatment for, 636
Personality inventory, 478. An objective test, often using numbered scales or multiple choice, used to assess personality, 478–479
Persuasion, 512. A change in attitude in response to information provided by another person, 512–513, 515
audience age and intelligence, 514, 515*f*
elaboration likelihood model and, 512
fake news and, 514
medium used and, 513
negative emotions and, 513
neuroscience of, 515
routes to, 512–515
central, 512–515
peripheral, 512–515
similarity and, 513
social media and, 514, 515*f*
Pessimism, 674*f*
Phantom limbs, 180
Phenothiazines, 623
Phenotype, 72. An observable characteristic, 73, 74*f*
Philosophy, 7
The discipline that systematically examines basic concepts, including the source of knowledge.
Phobia, symptoms of, 594
Phonemes, 384. A speech sound, 384*f*
Phrenology, 109
Physical punishment, 300
Piaget, Jean, 21*f*
Piloerection, 278–279
Pineal gland, 132*f*
Pitch, 174*f*, 175
Pituitary gland, 132–133
Plan in problem solving
carrying out, 376–377
computer models and, 377
evaluating, 377
making, 370–376
solutions in
affect heuristic, 375
algorithms, 371
availability heuristic, 372
deciding on, 374–376
framing effects, 375–376, 376*f*
heuristics, 371–374
recognition heuristic, 372–373
representativeness heuristic, 373–374
Pons, 115. A part of the brainstem located between the medulla and the midbrain.
Population, 46. The entire group from which a sample is taken., 46–47
Positive emotions, 673–679. *See also* Happiness
Positive institutions, 681–682
Positive psychology, 672. An approach to psychology that emphasizes normal behavior and human strengths, 672–673
future and, 682
happiness and, 674–679
healthy mindedness and, 672–673
optimism and, 673
positive emotions and, 673–679
positive institutions, 681–682
positive traits, 680–681
Positive punishment, 299. A consequence that eliminates or reduces the frequency of a behavior by applying an aversive stimulus, 299
Positive reinforcement, 296–298
Positive traits, 680–681
Positron emission tomography (PET), 109, 110*t*, 597–598
Postconventional morality, 443. Lawrence Kohlberg's stage at which moral choices are made according to personal standards and reason
Posterior cingulate cortex (PCC), 117
Postformal thought, 446–447
Posttraumatic stress disorder (PTSD), 582. A disorder caused by the experience of trauma, which leads to flashbacks, dreams, hypervigilance, and avoidance of stimuli associated with the traumatic event.
biological explanations for, 583–584
children and, 583, 644
flashbulb memories, 340–341
interpersonal relationships and, 592
learning explanations for, 584
MDMA (Ecstasy) and, 222
norepinephrine activity and, 143
prevalence of, 583
social and cultural explanations for, 584
symptoms, 583, 594
trauma and, 643*f*
treatment for, 630–631, 636
virtual reality (VR) and, 630
Poverty
health and, 671
intellectual disabilities and, 400*f*
psychopathology and, 671
Power of one, 527
Preconventional morality, 442. Lawrence Kohlberg's stage at which moral choices are made according to expectations of reward or punishment.
Prediction, 41
Prefrontal cortex, 121. The most forward part of the frontal lobe of the cerebral cortex.
antisocial behavior and, 122
damage to, 122
decision-making and, 378
dyslexia and, 389–390
myelin and, 135–137
orbitofrontal cortex and, 121–122
Pregnancy
alcohol consumption, 414, 415*t*
duration of, 412
premature birth and, 412
recreational drugs, 413–414
teratogens and, 413–416, 415*t*
viruses and, 414–415, 415*t*
Prejudice, 516. A prejudgment, usually negative, of another person on the basis of membership in a group.
categorization and, 517, 522
conditioning and, 290–291
latent inhibition and, 291
out-groups and, 517*f*
outcomes of, 518–519
reducing, 519, 521–522
sources of, 516–518
Premack principle, 296
Premature birth, 412
Prenatal development
Down syndrome and maternal age, 413*f*
duration of pregnancy, 412
embryonic stage, 411
environmental risks and, 413–416
alcohol consumption, 414, 416*f*
recreational drugs, 413–414
teratogens and, 413–414, 414*f*, 415*t*
viruses and, 414–415, 415*t*
fetus and, 411–412, 412*f*
genetic risks to, 412–413, 413*f*
hormones and, 424*f*
milestones in, 420
premature birth and, 412
testosterone and aggression in, 540, 540*f*
zygote, 411
Preoperational stage, 427. Jean Piaget's stage of development beginning at the age of 2 years and ending at the age of 6 years and characterized by use of symbols, egocentrism, and limits on the ability to reason logically.
Primary auditory cortex, 174–175
Primary reinforcers, 297
Primary sensory cortex, 180
Primary visual cortex, 159, 159*f*
Priming, 330. A change in a response to a stimulus as a result of exposure to a previous stimulus, 331, 331*f*
Principles of Psychology (James), 12
Prisoner's dilemma, 536–537, 537*f*
Privacy, 65
Proactive interference, 344, 344*f*
Problem, 368. A situation in which a current state is separated from an ideal state by obstacles.
Problem solving, 369. *See also* Decision-making
The use of information to meet a specific goal.
flow chart, 369*f*
functional fixedness and, 370
personal biases and, 369
plan in (*see* Plan in problem solving)
process of, 369
rumination and, 570, 570*f*
systems engineering process of, 369*f*
understanding the problem, 370
Problem-focused coping, 658. A response to stress designed to address specific problems by finding solutions.
Procedural memory, 330. A nondeclarative or implicit memory for how to carry out skilled movement, 330–331
basal ganglia and, 348–349
Product placement, 291
Progressive relaxation, 629
Project Pigeon, 307, 308
Projective tests, 481. A test of personality based on Freudian theory that provides an ambiguous stimulus onto which test takers "project" their personality, 481–482
Prosopagnosia, 211–212
Prototype, 365. A representation of a category formed by averaging all members of the category.
Proximity, in Gestalt psychology, 164, 164*f*
Psychiatrist, 602. A medical doctor who specializes in psychiatry and can use medical procedures, such as the prescribing of medication, to treat psychological disorders, 602–603

Psychoactive drugs, 215. Any drug with the capability of altering a person's state of consciousness.
addiction to, 215, 216*f*
blood supply and concentrations, 220*f*
commonly used, 216–218, 219*f*, 220–223, 228–229
culture and, 219
tolerance of, 215
withdrawal from, 215
Psychoanalysis, 609. Sigmund Freud's treatment approach based on his psychodynamic theory, 462, 601, 605, 609–610
Psychodynamic, 462. A theory put forward by Sigmund Freud in which psychic energy moves among the compartments of the personality: Id, ego, and superego.
Freud's theories, 462–463
conscious awareness, 464*f*
contemporary assessment of, 464
defense mechanisms, 463
id, ego, and superego, 462–463, 463*f*
psychosexual stages, 463
somatic symptom disorder, 462
Psychological altruism, 538
Psychological disorders
anxiety disorders, *580*, 594
biological treatments for, 614–617
brain stimulation, 616
electroconvulsive therapy (ECT), 615
medication and, 615
neurofeedback, 617
psychosurgery, 615–616
bipolar disorder, 567–568
body dysmorphic disorder, 582, 594
continuum of, 550–551*f*
defining, 550–551
diagnosis of, 553–554
dissociative disorders, 584–585
emerging in childhood, 555–561
epigenetics and, 83
genotypes and, 475*f*
interpersonal relationships and, 634
major depressive disorder (MDD), 568–575
obsessive-compulsive disorder (OCD), 581–582, 594
personality and, 475*f*
personality disorders, 586–590
posttraumatic stress disorder, 582–584, 594
psychological perspectives on, 554–555
rates of, 553, 553*f*
schizophrenia, 561–565
somatic symptom disorder, 585
stress and, 640
treatment for, 608, 618–636
treatment integrations, 633
Psychological perspectives, 22–26, 26*f*
biological psychology, 22, 23, 23*f*
clinical psychology, 26
cognitive psychology, 23*f*, 24, 24*f*
cultural diversity, 24, 25
developmental psychology, 23*f*, 24, 24*f*, 25
evolutionary psychology, 22, 23, 24*f*, 95
five main perspectives, 23*f*, 32*f*
integrating, 26, 26*f*
interpersonal relationships and, 30
multiple perspectives, benefits of, 26*f*, 54
personality, 23*f*, 24, 25
psychological disorders and, 554–555
social psychology, 23*f*, 24, 24*f*, 25
Psychologists, 28–30
bachelor degrees, 28, 29*f*
clinical, 29
counseling, 29
doctoral degrees, 29, 29*f*
employment for, 28, 29*f*
forensic, 28
master's degrees, 28–29, 29*f*
medical doctor, 30
school, 29
specialties of, 29
sports, 29
Psychology, 5. The scientific study of behavior, mental processes, and brain functions, 4
culture and diversity, 27
experiencing, 14–22
milestones in the history of, 20*f*
origin of, 7–9
pioneering approaches to, 10–22, 20–22*f*
behaviorism, 18–19, 19*f*
cognitive revolution, 15–22
first experiments in, 11
functionalism, 11
Gestalt psychology, 11, 12
humanism, 13–14
milestones in, 19*f*
structuralism and Wihelm Wundt, 10, 10*f*, 12
real-world problems and, 228
reason for studying, 6
roots of, 8–10
ancient Greek philosophers, 8, 10
ancient physicians, 8, 10
British empiricists, 7, 10
clinical, 13–15
Fechner, 9
philosophical, 7, 8
scientific, 8–9
von Helmholtz, 8–9, 10
studying science of, 3–5
tracking the problem of pandemic, 31
Psychopaths
antisocial personality disorder and, 586
corporate, 588
emotions and, 586
prevalence of, 588
Psychophysics, 153. The study of relationships between the physical qualities of stimuli and the subjective responses they produce.
measuring perception and, 153
Psychosexual stage, 463. A stage in Sigmund Freud's theory of the developing personality.
Psychosis
amphetamines and, 221–222
cannabis and, 217
Psychosocial stages, 444*t*
Psychosurgery, 615. The attempt to improve symptoms of psychological disorders through operating on the brain, 615–616
Psychotherapists, 602. A licensed professional who provides psychotherapy.
clinical psychologists, 602–603, 608
counselors, 603–604
credentialing practices, 605
degree, 602, 603*f*
doctor of philosophy (PhD), 602
doctor of psychology (PsyD), 602
hypnotherapists, 604
job opportunities for, 603, 603*f*
life coaches, 604
master of divinity (MDiv) degree, 603–604
psychiatrists, 602–603, 608
psychologists, 602, 608
Psychotherapy, 599. A treatment designed to improve symptoms of psychological disorder through conversation between the therapist and the patient or client.
approaches to, 599–602
biological, 599–600
clinical assessment, 602
evidence-based practice, 601
psychological, 600–601
brief therapy and, 605
contemporary approaches to, 612–613
behavioral therapies, 612–613
biopsychosocial approaches, 614
cognitive therapies, 613–614
couples therapy and, 606
delivering, 605–607
family therapy and, 606
group therapy and, 605–606
historical approaches to, 609–611
humanistic therapies, 610–611
psychoanalysis, 609–610
hypnosis and, 600, 604
innovative systems for, 606–607
with Native Americans, 607
online, 606–607
self-help groups and, 606
treatment challenges, 608
PTSD. *See* Posttraumatic stress disorder (PTSD)
Puberty, 439. A period of physical changes leading to sexual maturity, 439*f*
Publication bias, 54
Punishment, 299. A consequence that eliminates or reduces the frequency of a behavior
Pupil, 157. An opening formed by the iris.

R

Race
anxiety disorders and, 574, 574*f*
genetic research and, 80
optimism and, 674
prejudice and, 517–518
self-esteem and, 487–488
shooter bias and, 520
stereotypes and, 517–518
Random assignment, 51. The procedure in which each participant has an equal chance of being placed in any group in an experiment, 52*f*
Rapid eye movement (REM) sleep, 203. The component of sleep characterized by waveforms resembling waking, as measured by electroencephalogram, accompanied by rapid motion of the eyes, muscular paralysis, and sympathetic nervous system activation.
benefits of, 206–208
body paralysis in, 205
EEG recordings and, 204*f*, 205
infants and, 207
lifespan, 207*f*
lucid dreaming and, 208
mood and, 207–208
paradoxical sleep and, 205
pattern of, 205*f*, 206
REM rebound and, 207
stages of, 205–206
Raves, 227
Reaction time, testing, 14–15
Reactivity, 475
Recency effect, 327, 327*f*
Receptor, 141. A special channel in the membrane of a neuron that interacts with neurotransmitters released by other neurons.
Recessive, 74. A feature of an allele that produces only a phenotype in the homozygous condition, 74*f*
Reciprocal altruism, 97. Help that you provide for another person when you expect the person to return the favor in the future, 538
Reciprocal determinism, 472. A social-cognitive learning

theory of personality that features the mutual influence of the person and that of the situation on each other.
Reciprocation, 524
Recite, 354
Recognition heuristic, 371. A rule of thumb in which a higher value is placed on the more easily recognized alternative, 372*f*
Reconstruction, 338. Rebuilding a memory out of stored elements, 338–340
Recreational drugs, 413–414
Reflection techniques, 611
Reflex, 278. An inevitable, involuntary response to stimuli, 279
  of newborns, 416, 417*t*
Rehearsal, 322. Repetition of information.
Reinforcement sensitivity theory (RST), 477
Relatedness, 76. The probability that two people share the same allele from a common ancestor, 77*f*
Relational aggression, 539
Relationship-focused coping, 658. A response to stress designed to maintain and protect social relationships.
Reliability, 54. The consistency of a measure, including test-retest, interrater, intermethod, and internal consistency.
REM rebound, 207
Repeated transcranial magnetic stimulation (rTMS), 616, 617*f*
Replication, 42. Repeating an experiment and producing the same results.in science, 42–43, 61
Representativeness heuristic, 373. A rule of thumb in which stimuli similar to a prototype are believed to be more likely than stimuli that are dissimilar to a prototype.
Repression of memories, 345
Rescorla-Wagner Model, 287, 288*f*
Research ethics, 64–68
  animal subjects, 66
  confidentiality and, 66
  correlational methods, 48–49, 49*f*
  experimental methods, 51–54
  genetic research and, 80
  human participants, 65–66
  informed consent and, 65–66
  principles of, 69
  privacy and, 66
Research methods
  in biological psychology, 110*t*
  correlational methods, 48–49
  dependent variable in, 51, 51*f*
  descriptive method, 44–47
  diversity in, 47
  experimental methods, 51–54
  independent variable in, 51, 51*f*
  interpersonal relationships and, 67
  principles of, 55
  time, assessing effects of, 54–55
  unethical experiments and, 49, 49*f*, 52
Research participants, recruiting diverse, 47–48
Resilience
  in the face of COVID-19 Pandemic, 683
Resilience, 659. The ability to adapt to life's challenges in positive ways.
  challenge and, 659
  control and, 659
  hardiness and, 659
  stress and, 659–660
Resistance, 610. (a) A psychoanalytic technique in which the patient's reluctance to accept the interpretations of the therapist indicate that the interpretations are correct. (b) The second stage of the general adaptation syndrome (GAS), characterized by coping with ongoing stress, 608, 642, 643
Resting potential, 138. The measure of the electrical charge across a neural membrane when the neuron is not processing information.
Restless legs syndrome (RLS), 210. A disorder characterized by the involuntary movement of an extremity, usually one leg
Reticular formation, 116. A collection of structures located along the midline of the brainstem that participate in mood, arousal, and sleep.
Retina, 157. Layers of visual processing cells in the back of the eye, 158*f*
Retinal disparity, 166. The difference between the images projected onto each eye, 167*f*
Retrieval, 319. The recovery of stored information.
  from long-term memory, 336–341
    emotional events, 340–341
    reconstruction and, 338–340
    role of cues, 336–337
    tip of the tongue, 337–338
  from short-term memory, 335
Retroactive interference, 344, 344*f*
Reuptake, 141. A process in which molecules of neurotransmitter in the synaptic gap are returned to the axon terminal from which they were released
Ribonucleic acid (RNA), 85
Right cerebral hemisphere, localization of functions in, 124–125
Risk perception, 440–441, 441*f*
Risk-taking, 440–441
Ritalin, 222
Rods, 158. A photoreceptor specialized to detect dim light, 158*f*, 159
Rogers, Carl, 15, 16*f*, 21*f*
Romantic love, 533–534
Rorschach Inkblot Test, 480, 481
Rouge test, 195
rTMS. *See* Repeated transcranial magnetic stimulation (rTMS)
Rumination, 570–571, 570*f*
Runner's high, 144

S

S SERT allele, 459–460, 460*f*
SAME. *See* Somatovisceral afference model of emotion (SAME)
Sample, 46. A subset of a population being studied.
Sandbagging, 488
SAT data, 56, 57, 60, 61*f*, 63, 63*f*
Satiety, 256. A sense of feeling full and not requiring further food, 257
Satisficers, 403
Scatterplot, 60, 62*f*
Schachter-Singer two-factor theory, 236. A theory of emotion in which general arousal leads to assessment, which in turn leads to subjective feelings.
  physical responses and subjective feelings of, 233*f*, 236–238
Schedules of reinforcement, 301*f*, 310
  comparing, 303–304
  fixed interval schedules, 302, 303*f*
  fixed ratio schedules, 301–302
  partial reinforcement, 301–302
  partial reinforcement effect in extinction, 303
  variable interval schedules, 302
  variable ratio schedules, 302
Schema, 334. A set of expectations about objects and situations.
  concepts and, 367
  false memories and, 334
  memory and, 334–335
Schizophrenia, 561. A disorder characterized by hallucinations, delusions, disorganized thought and speech, disorders of movement, restricted affect, and avolition or asociality, 561–566
  biological factors in, 561–565
  cannabis and, 566, 566*f*
  causes of, 562–565
  dopamine and, 564
  environmental factors and, 565, 565*f*
  genetics and, 563, 563*f*
  latent inhibition and, 291
  medications for, 623–624, 623*f*
  nicotine and, 221
  psychosocial rehabilitation of, 624
  recovery in, 599*f*
  self and, 492–493
  stress and, 565, 565*f*
  symptoms of, 562, 575
  treatment for, 623–624, 636
School psychologists, 29
Science, 36. A method for learning about reality through systematic observation and experimentation, 35–44
  communicating, 42
  critical thinking in, 38, 38*f*, 51
  hypothesis in, 41–42
  objectivity in, 36
  peer review in, 42, 54
  replication in, 42
  systematic observations in, 38*f*, 51
  theories in, 40–41, 41*f*
Scientific enterprise, 40–43
Scientific mindset, developing, 36–37
Secondary reinforcers, 297
Secondary sex characteristics, 439. Physical changes occurring at puberty associated with sexual maturity.
Secure attachment, 434. A pattern of infant-caregiver bonding in which children explore confidently and return to the parent or caregiver for reassurance, 435
Seizures, 214. An abnormal level of brain activation with a sudden onset, 213–214
  absence, 214
  coma and, 214
  GABA and, 213
  generalized, 214, 214*f*
  partial, 214, 214*f*
  tonic-clonic, 214
Selective serotonin reuptake inhibitor (SSRI), 143, 261, 625–626, 626*f*
Self, 483. Patterns of thought, feelings, and actions that we perceive in our own minds, 483–484
  brain and, 491–493
  culture and, 493–494
  self-awareness and, 485–486, 497
  self-concept and, 484–485, 497
  self-esteem and, 486–490, 497
  self-regulation and, 491
  self-schemas and, 484, 484*f*, 497
  social, 493–495

Self-actualization, 271. A state of having fulfilled your potential, 273
Self-awareness, 194–197. The special understanding of the self as distinct from other stimuli, 497
consciousness as, 195–197
honesty and, 485*f*
rouge test and, 195
self-consciousness and, 485
self-knowledge and, 486
Self-concept, 484. People's description of their own characteristics, 484–485, 497
Self-consciousness, 485
Self-control, 491
Self-efficacy, 472
Self-enhancement, 488–489
Self-esteem, 486. A judgment of the value of the self, 497
academic performance and, 490
advantages of, 489
culture and, 487–488, 488*f*
gender and, 487–488
high/low, 486
intelligence and, 396
race and, 487–488
self-enhancement to protect, 488–489
social comparisons and, 486–487
sources of, 486–487
terror management theory and, 489
Self-handicapping, 488
Self-help groups, 606
Self-injury, 296
Self-knowledge, 486
Self-reference effect (SRE), 484, 665
Self-regulation, 475, 491, 497
Self-schema, 484. A cognitive organization that helps us think about the self and process self-relevant information, 484–485, 497
Self-serving bias, 506. Attributing success to dispositional factors while attributing failure to situational factors, 508
Selfishness, 538
Semantic memory, 329. A general knowledge memory, 329–330
brain and, 349*f*, 368*f*
Sensation, 150. The process of detecting environmental stimuli or stimuli arising from the body.
autistic children and, 168
perception and, 150
transduction and, 151
Senses of newborns, 418–419
Sensitization, 280. An increased reaction to many stimuli following exposure to one strong stimulus.
Sensorimotor stage, 427. Jean Piaget's stage of development beginning at birth and ending at the age of 2 years and characterized by active exploration of the environment.
Sensory adaptation, 152. The tendency to pay less attention to a nonchanging source of stimulation.
Sensory *homunculus*, 180
Sensory memory, 320. The first stage of the Atkinson-Shiffrin model that holds large amounts of incoming data for brief amounts of time, 320–321
acoustic codes and, 320
haptic codes and, 320
iconic memories and, 320–321
short-term memory and, 321
Sperling's demonstration of, 322*f*
visual codes and, 320
Serial position effect, 326–327, 327*f*
Serotonin
aggression and, 540
depression and, 143, 572
enteric nervous system and, 130
hallucinogens and, 219
LSD and, 218
MDMA (Ecstasy) and, 222
midbrain and, 116
REM sleep and, 208
Serotonin activity, 143
Serotonin transporter gene (SERT), 75, 76*f*, 88, 459, 460*f*
Set point, 253. A value that is defended to maintain homeostasis.
Sex chromosomes, 78–79, 417
Sex hormones, 133
Sex-linked characteristics, 77
Sexual maturation, 439
Sexual motivation, 262–267
biology of, 262–264
hormones and, 262, 263
ovulation and menstrual cycles, 262–263
oxytocin and, 263, 263*f*
testosterone and, 262–263, 263*f*
vasopressin and, 263, 263*f*
cross-cultural comparison of, 264*f*
culture and, 264
desire and, 262–263
emotional satisfaction and, 264–267, 264*f*
romantic love and, 264
satisfaction and, 264
sexual orientation and, 264–267
Sexual orientation, 264. A stable pattern of attraction to members of a particular sex.
birth order and, 266
brain structures and, 266, 266*f*
culture and, 265–266
genetic influences on, 266
identification and, 265
prenatal hormones and, 266
sexual satisfaction and, 264
Sexual preference, 267
Sexual selection, 98. The development of traits that help an individual compete for mates.
behavior and, 98
genes and, 98
parental investment and, 98
traits influenced by, 99
Shaping, 304–305
Shell shock. *See* Posttraumatic stress disorder (PTSD)
Shepard, Roger, 170
Shooter bias, 520
Short-term memory (STM), 320. The second stage of the Atkinson-Shiffrin model that holds a small amount of information for a limited time, 321–325
chunking in, 323
duration of, 321–322, 323*f*
rehearsal in, 322
retrieval, 335
working memory, 323–324
Signal detection, 154. The analysis of sensory and decision-making processes in the detection of faint, uncertain stimuli.
decision-making and, 154
perception and, 153
possible outcomes in, 155*t*
Similarity, in Gestalt psychology, 164, 164*f*
Simon, Herbert, 19
Simplicity, in Gestalt psychology, 164
Sine waves, 177, 178, 178*f*
Single cell recording, 110*t*
Situational attribution, 505. A judgment assigning the cause of a person's behavior to the environment.
Skin conductance response, 110*t*
Skinner boxes, 18, 295*f*, 299, 301, 302, 303, 304
Skinner, B. F., 18, 21*f*
Sleep, 199. *See also* Non-rapid eye movement (N-REM) sleep; Rapid eye movement (REM) sleep
A normal state of consciousness characterized by reduced awareness of external stimuli.
American worker and, 200*f*
benefits of, 206–208
circadian rhythms and, 199–202
consciousness and, 199
depression and, 575*f*
diet and, 653*f*
dreaming and, 208–209
Epworth sleepiness scale and, 204
features of, 211
human growth hormone and, 206*f*
memory and, 206–207, 354
mood and, 207–208
nightly patterns of, 205*f*
during pandemic, 228
stages of, 203–206
stress and, 652–653
Sleep apnea, 209. A sleep disorder in which the person stops breathing while asleep, 210
Sleep deprivation, 200*f*, 202*f*, 206
Sleep disorders
cataplexy, 209
insomnia, 209
narcolepsy, 208–209
nightmares, 208–209
restless legs syndrome (RLS), 210
sleep apnea, 209
sleep talking, 205
sleep terrors, 208–209
sleepwalking, 205
sudden infant death syndrome, 210
Sleep talking, 205
Sleep terror, 209. A sleep disorder occurring in non-rapid eye movement sleep in which the sleeper wakes suddenly in great distress but without experiencing the imagery of a nightmare, 208–209
Sleepwalking, 205
Smiling, 249–250
Smoking, 663–665, 663*f*, 664*f*
Smoking cessation programs, 665
Sobriety tests, 115
Social anxiety disorder, 577. A disorder characterized by an unrealistic fear of being scrutinized and criticized by others, 577–578, 628*f*
Social behavior
altruism and, 97
cooperation and, 96–97
culture and, 99–100
origins of, 95–97
self-awareness and, 195–196
sexual selection and, 98–99
social interactions and, 96*t*
Social belonging, 655, 655*f*
Social distancing
pandemic during, 145
working memory and compliance with, 357
Social diversity, 23*f*
Social exclusion, 268*f*, 501*f*
Social facilitation, 527. A situation in which the presence of other people changes performance, 307, 527–528
Social intelligence, 394–395
Social interactions, 96*t*, 99
as a human need, 500
memory and, 318
Social isolation, 268, 500–501, 645
learning to become less lonely, 314
Social learning, 280. *See also*: Observational learning
Social loafing, 528. Reduced motivation and effort shown by individuals working in a group.

Social media
fake news and, 514
narcissistic personality disorder and, 587
personality and, 25*f*, 478
persuasion and, 514
Social norms, 522. Usually unwritten or unspoken rules for behavior in social settings.
compliance, 524
conformity, 523–524, 523*f*
door-in-the-face, 524, 525*f*
foot-in-the-door, 524
obedience, 524–527, 526*f*
power of one, 527
Social prejudice, 80–82
Social psychology, 24
A psychological perspective that examines the effects of the social environment on the behavior of individuals, 23*f*, 25
aggression and, 539–543
attitudes and, 509–512
attributions and, 505–506, 508–509
cooperation and competition, 535–539, 546
first impressions and, 501, 504, 504*f*
group processes, 530
deindividuation, 528
group polarization, 528–529, 529*f*
groupthink and, 529–530
social facilitation and, 527–528
social loafing, 528
persuasion and, 512–515
prejudice and, 516–522
social interactions and, 500–501
social norms and, 522–527
social relationships and, 531–534
Social relationships, 531–534
attitude alignment, 532
attraction and liking, 531–533
building, 533
ending, 534
infidelity in, 534*f*
maintaining, 533–534
matching hypothesis, 533
mere exposure effect, 531–533
stress and, 651
Social self, 493–496
cultural influences on, 493–494
interpersonal relationships and, 494–495
interpersonal self and, 493
Social-cognitive learning theory, 472. A theory of personality that features cognition and learning, especially from the social environment, as important sources of individual differences in personality.
if-then relationships, 473
locus of control and, 472
reciprocal determinism and, 472
self-efficacy and, 472
Socialization, 433
Socioeconomic status (SES)
health and, 649
IQ and, 398–399
stress and, 649
Somatic nervous system, 129. The part of the peripheral nervous system that brings sensory information to the central nervous system and transmits commands to the muscles.
cranial nerves and, 129, 129*f*
spinal nerves and, 129
Somatic symptom disorder, 585. A disorder that is diagnosed when people are unusually concerned and preoccupied with chronic somatic symptoms, 462, 600
treatment for, 632
Somatosensation, 178. The body senses, including body position, touch, skin temperature, and pain.
biology of
body position, 179
pain, 181–182
touch, 179–180
vestibular system, 179
somatosensory stimuli, 178–179
Somatosensory cortex, 119, 121*f*, 123, 124, 180–181
Somatovisceral afference model of emotion (SAME), 238. A model of emotion in which a range of physical sensations from precise to general requires varying degrees of cognitive processing prior to subjective feelings, 238*f*
Sound
localization of, 176, 177, 177*f*
Sound waves, 172, 172*f*
Specific phobia, 576. Fears of objects other than those associated with agoraphobia or social anxiety disorder, 575–576, 577*f*
Sperling's demonstration of sensory memory, 322*f*
Spinal cord, 111. A long cylinder of neural tissue extending from the medulla of the brain down to the middle of the back; part of the central nervous system, 113*f*–114*f*
Spinal nerves, 113, 113*f*, 129
Spinal reflexes, 113*f*, 114
Spinning, 225–226
Split-brain operation, 124*f*
Spontaneous recovery, 284. During extinction training, the reappearance of conditioned responses (CRs) after periods of rest, 285*f*
Sports psychologists, 29
Spreading activation model, 333. A connectionist theory proposing that people organize general knowledge based on their individual experiences, 333–334, 333*f*
Squid axons, 138
Standard deviation, 59. A measure of how tightly clustered around the mean a group of scores is, 59*f*
Standing desks, 668*f*
Stanford Prison Study, 523
Stanford-Binet Intelligence Scales, 392
Statistical abnormality, 551–552
Statistical significance, 62. A standard for deciding whether an observed result is because of chance.
Stereotype, 516. A simplified set of traits associated with membership in a group or category, 516–518, 519*f*
Stereotype threat, 520–522, 520*f*
Stimulants, 219. Any drug that increases the activity of the nervous system.
Storage, 318. The retention of information, 318–319
Stranger anxiety, 434
Stream of consciousness, 194–195
Stress, 640. An unpleasant emotional state that results from the perception of danger.
affiliation and, 268
belongingness and, 655, 655*f*
biological correlates of, 645–649
amygdala and, 645–646
epigenetics of, 648
gender differences in, 649
hypothalamic-pituitary adrenal axis, 647, 647*f*, 648
hypothalamus and, 646
socioeconomic status and, 649
sympathetic adrenal medullary system, 647, 647*f*, 648
coping with, 658–659
emotion-focused, 658
problem-focused, 658
relationship-focused, 658
resilience and, 659–660
cortisol and, 639–640, 647, 653
depression and, 571
general adaptation syndrome and, 642–643
hassles and, 644–645
health effects of, 650–654, 654*f*
identifying, 639
immune system and, 650–651, 650*f*
managing, 656–658
exercise and, 657–658, 657*f*
mindfulness and, 657
pets and, 657
religious beliefs and, 658
sense of control and, 656
social support and, 657
tragic optimism and, 656
memory and, 353, 353*f*
mindset for, 641*t*
during pandemic, 228
posttraumatic stress disorder and, 643*f*, 644
psychological disorders and, 640
resistance and, 642
response to, 640–642, 642–643, 649
schizophrenia and, 565 , 565*f*
social isolation and, 645
social relationships and, 651
sources of, 643–645
Stressor, 640. A stimulus that serves as a source of stress.
Stroop Test, 224, 225, 225*f*
Structuralism, 10. An approach in which the mind is broken into the smallest elements of mental experience, 11
Gestalt psychologists challenged, 12–13
Structuralists
Titchener, 12
Wundt, 10, 12
Stuttering, 35
Subcortical structures
amygdala, 117–118, 118*f*
basal ganglia, 116
cerebral cortex, 117*f*
cingulate cortex, 117
hippocampus, 117
hypothalamus, 117
nucleus accumbens, 118
thalamus, 116
Subjectivity, 36
Sudden infant death syndrome (SIDS), 210. A sleep disorder in which an otherwise healthy infant dies while asleep
Sufis, 226
Suicide
alcohol consumption and, 540
antidepressant medicines and, 625–626
depression and, 574, 574*f*
law and, 552
social isolation and, 500
Summer, Francis Cecil, 14*f*, 21*f*
Superego, 463. The component of Sigmund Freud's personality theory that internalizes society's rules for right and wrong, or the conscience, 463*f*
Supertasters, 186
Suppression of emotion, 246–247, 247*f*
Suppression of memories, 344
Surprise, element of, in learning, 287
Survey, 46. A descriptive method in which participants are asked the same questions, 47, 48*f*
samples used in, 44
video game use, 44, 48*f*

Sympathetic adrenal-medullary (SAM) system, 647. A circuit that responds to perceived stressors by initiating the release of epinephrine and norepinephrine into the bloodstream.
Sympathetic nervous system, 129. The division of the autonomic nervous system that coordinates arousal.
function of, 129
Synapse, 140. A point of communication between two neurons, 141, 143, 345–347, 421*f*
Synaptic pruning, 421*f*
Synaptic vesicles, 134
Systematic desensitization, 290. A type of counterconditioning in which people relax while being exposed to stimuli that elicit fear.
Systematic observation, 36, 38*f*, 51
Systems engineering process, 369*f*

T

Tardive dyskinesia, 623. A movement syndrome that results from the use of medications used to treat symptoms of schizophrenia, 624
Taste. *See also* Gustation
categories of, 184–185
sensitivity to, 3–4, 24
Taste aversion, 288–289, 293
Taste buds, 185. A structure found in papillae that contains taste receptor cells.
Taste receptors, 185, 185*f*
Temperament, 473. A child's pattern of mood, activity, or emotional responsiveness linked to later personality, 473–475
child development and, 431–432, 432*f*, 474*f*
personality and, 474*f*, 477–475
Temporal lobe, 119. The lobe of the cerebral cortex that curves around the side of each hemisphere; location of the primary auditory cortex.
auditory cortex, 122–123
visual cortex and, 123
Wernicke's area, 123
Tennis serves, 125
Teratogen, 413. A chemical agent that can harm the zygote, embryo, or fetus, 413, 414*f*, 415*t*
Terror management theory, 489
Testes, 132–133
Testosterone, 262. A male hormone.
aggression and, 540
disease and, 91
facial features and, 98
levels of, 262
prenatal exposure to, 540, 540*f*
reproductive advantage of, 91
sexual motivation and, 262
Tetanus, 141, 142*f*
Tetrahydrocannabinol (THC), 216
Thalamus, 159*f*
Thalamus, 116. A subcortical structure involved with the processing of sensory information, states of arousal, and learning and memory, 116*f*
audition and, 174
consciousness and, 197
gustation and, 185
olfactory pathways and, 185
somatosensory pathways and, 182
vision and, 159, 159*f*
Theodore, Simon, 20*f*
Theory, 38. A set of facts and relationships between facts that can explain and predict related phenomena.
concepts as, 366–367
developing and testing, 39*f*
scientific, 13–14, 51
Theory of mind (TOM), 430. The understanding that others have thoughts that are different from one's own, 430–433, 430*f*
Therapy
behavior, 612–613
brief, 605
couples, 606
cultural adaptations in, 607
family, 606
group, 605
insight, 609
online, 606–607
person-centered, 610–611
psychologists providing, 600–601
psychotherapies, 598–602
virtual reality (VR) and, 630
Theta wave, 203. A waveform of four to seven cycles per second recorded by electroencephalogram (EEG) that is characteristic of lighter stages of non-rapid eye movement (N-REM) sleep.
Third variable, 46. A variable that is responsible for a correlation observed between two other variables of interest.
correlation and, 50, 50*f*
Thorndike, Edward, 17*f*, 20*f*
Thoughts
as concepts, 363–365
as images, 363
Thyroid gland, 132
Time, assessing effects of
cross-sectional studies, 54
longitudinal studies, 54–55
mixed longitudinal design, 55
Tip-of-the-tongue (TOT) phenomenon, 337–338
Tit-for-tat (TFT) strategy, 537
Tobacco use, 663–665, 663*f*
Token economy, 308. An application of operant conditioning in which tokens that can be exchanged for other reinforcers are used to increase the frequency of desirable behaviors.
Tolerance, 215. The need to administer greater quantities of a drug to achieve the same subjective effect
Tolman's maze, 306*f*
Tonic-clonic seizures, 214
Top-down processing, 152. A perceptual process in which memory and other cognitive processes are required for interpreting incoming sensory information, 153
Touch, 179–181. *See also* Somatosensation
infants and, 179
primary sensory cortex and, 180
sensory *homunculus* and, 180
social communication and, 179
somatosensory cortex and, 180–181
touch receptors and, 180*f*
Touch receptors, 180*f*
Tragic optimism, 656
Trait, 467. A stable personality characteristic.
sexual selection and, 99
Trait theories of personality
Big Five, 468–470
factor analysis, 467*f*
Trance states, 226
Transactive memory, 356
Transcranial magnetic stimulation (TMS), 110*t*, 193
Transduction, 151. The translation of incoming sensory information into neural signals.
Transference, 610. A psychoanalytic technique in which the therapist uses the responses of the patient to the therapist to understand the patient's approach to authority figures in general.
Transgender identity, 425
Trauma, 643*f*
Trepanation, 615
Triangle model of love, 533, 533*f*
Trichromatic theory, 160. A theory of color vision based on the existence of different types of cones for the detection of short, medium, and long wavelengths, 161
Tritanopes, 150
Turing test, 197
Turning the Tables illusion, 170
Tuskegee syphilis experiment, 65
Twins
chromosomes, 83
concordance rates, 81
correlational methods, 81*f*
differences in, 72, 81
DNA and, 71–72
epigenetics and, 83
fraternal, 80*f*, 81
intelligence and, 397
personality and, 475, 476*f*
phenotypes of, 80
schizophrenia and, 564
Type 2 diabetes, 255*f*
Type A personality, 651
A competitive, workaholic, and in some cases hostile personality type.
Type B personality, 651
A mellow, laid-back personality type.

U

UCLA loneliness scale, 502*t*–503*t*
Ultrasound, 172, 173*f*
Unconditioned response (UCR), 283. A response to an unconditioned stimulus that requires no previous experience, 283, 283*f*
Unconditioned stimulus (UCS), 283. A stimulus that elicits a response without prior experience, 283, 283*f*
Unconscious behaviors, 227
Unconscious mind, 465. The part of mental activity that cannot be voluntarily retrieved.
Uninvolved parenting, 436–437, 436*t*
Universal development, 410
Utility theory, 375

V

Vaccinations, 558, 559*f*
Validity, 57. A quality of a measure that leads to correct conclusions (i.e., the measure evaluates the concept that it was designed to do).
Values, 680–681
Variable, 48. A factor that has a range of values.
confounding, 51
dependent, 51
descriptive statistics and, 57–60
independent, 51
measurement of, 48–50
third variable, 50
Variable interval (VI) schedule, 302. A schedule of reinforcement in which the first response following a varying period is reinforced.

Variable ratio (VR) schedule, 302. A schedule of reinforcement in which reinforcement occurs following some variable number of behaviors.
Variance, 59
Vasopressin, 133, 263, 263*f*
Vegetative state (VS), 212. An abnormal state following brain injury featuring wakefulness without consciousness.
characteristics of, 212
coma and, 212
Ventricles, 112, 112*f*, 113
Ventromedial hypothalamus (VMH), 256–257, 257*f*
Vestibular receptors, 179
Vestibular system, 179. The system in the inner ear that provides information about body position and movement.
Video game use
aggression and, 46–48, 49, 51–54
cooperative, 54
experiments on, 51–53
naturalistic observation, 46–47
survey on, 46–47, 48*f*
Virtual reality (VR), 630
Vision, 156. The sense that allows us to process reflected light.
biology of, 157–159, 171
blind spots, 158
cornea, 157
fovea, 158
human eye, 157*f*
iris, 157
lens, 157
pupil, 157
retina, 157–158, 158*f*
rods and cones, 158, 158*f*, 159
thalamus, 159
color vision and, 151*f*, 160
developmental and individual differences in, 166–168
recognizing depth and, 164–166
recognizing objects and, 162–166
visual pathways, 159, 159*f*
visual stimulus and, 156
Vision quests, 225
Visual codes, 320
Visual cortex, 121*f*, 122, 124, 159
Visual imagery, 363
Visual pathways
optic nerve, 159*f*
optic tracts, 159
primary visual cortex and, 159
Visual stimulus, 156
von Helmholtz, Hermann, 8, 9, 10

W

Waking, 199. A normal state of consciousness characterized by alertness and awareness of external stimuli.
beta, alpha, gamma waves and, 202–203
circadian rhythms and, 199–202
consciousness and, 199
daydreaming and, 203
EEG recordings and, 202–203
features of, 212
Waorani, 99–100, 107
Warrior gene" concept of, 84–85
Watson, John B., 16–17, 17*f*, 21*f*
Wealth, happiness and, 675–678, 676*f*
Web design
accessibility of, 162*f*
color vision and, 161–162
Wechsler Adult Intelligence Scale (WAIS), 392, 400*f*, 552*f*
Weight loss, 259–260, 653*f*
Wernicke's aphasia, 385–386, 391
Wernicke's area, 123, 385–386
Wertheimer, Max, 12*f*, 20*f*
White matter, 134
Whole-genome sequencing (WGS), 83
Wildlife conservation, 293
Williams syndrome, 389, 393, 395
Willpower, 491
Withdrawal, 215. Physical responses to the removal of some habitually administered drugs, 216, 220
Working memory, 323. An extension of the concept of short-term memory that includes the active manipulation of multiple types of information simultaneously, 323–324, 324*f*, 326–328
brain and, 347
Wundt, Wilhelm, 10, 11*f*, 20*f*

X

X chromosome, 75

Y

Y chromosome, 77
Yagua, 143
Yanomamö, 99, 107
Yawning, contagious, 279
Yerkes-Dodson law, 240. A description of the relationships among task complexity, arousal, and performance, 240*f*
Young adulthood, 446–448
cognitive development, 446–447
physical status in, 446
relationships and, 448
Younger generations
narcissism and, 447*f*

Z

Zeitgebers, 200
Zone of proximal development, 430*f*
Zygote, 410. The term used to describe a developing organism immediately following conception until the embryo stage, or the first 2 weeks following conception in humans, 411

EY TERMS The Language of Psychological Science

e sure you can define these terms and use them correctly.

bsolute threshold, p. 153
udition, p. 172
uditory nerve, p. 174
asilar membrane, p. 174
inocular cue, p. 164
ottom-up processing, p. 152
ochlea, p. 174
one, p. 158
ornea, p. 157
epth perception, p. 164
ifference threshold, p. 153
ovea, p. 158
ate theory, p. 182
ustation, p. 183
iris, p. 157
lens, p. 157
monocular cue, p. 164
olfaction, p. 183
olfactory bulb, p. 183
olfactory nerve, p. 183
opponent process theory, p. 161
optic nerve, p. 159
optic tracts, p. 159
organ of Corti, p. 174
papillae, p. 185
perception, p. 150
psychophysics, p. 153
pupil, p. 157
retina, p. 157
retinal disparity, p. 166
rod, p. 158
sensation, p. 150
sensory adaptation, p. 152
signal detection, p. 154
somatosensation, p. 178
taste bud, p. 185
top-down processing, p. 152
transduction, p. 151
trichromatic theory, p. 160
vestibular system, p. 179
vision, p. 156

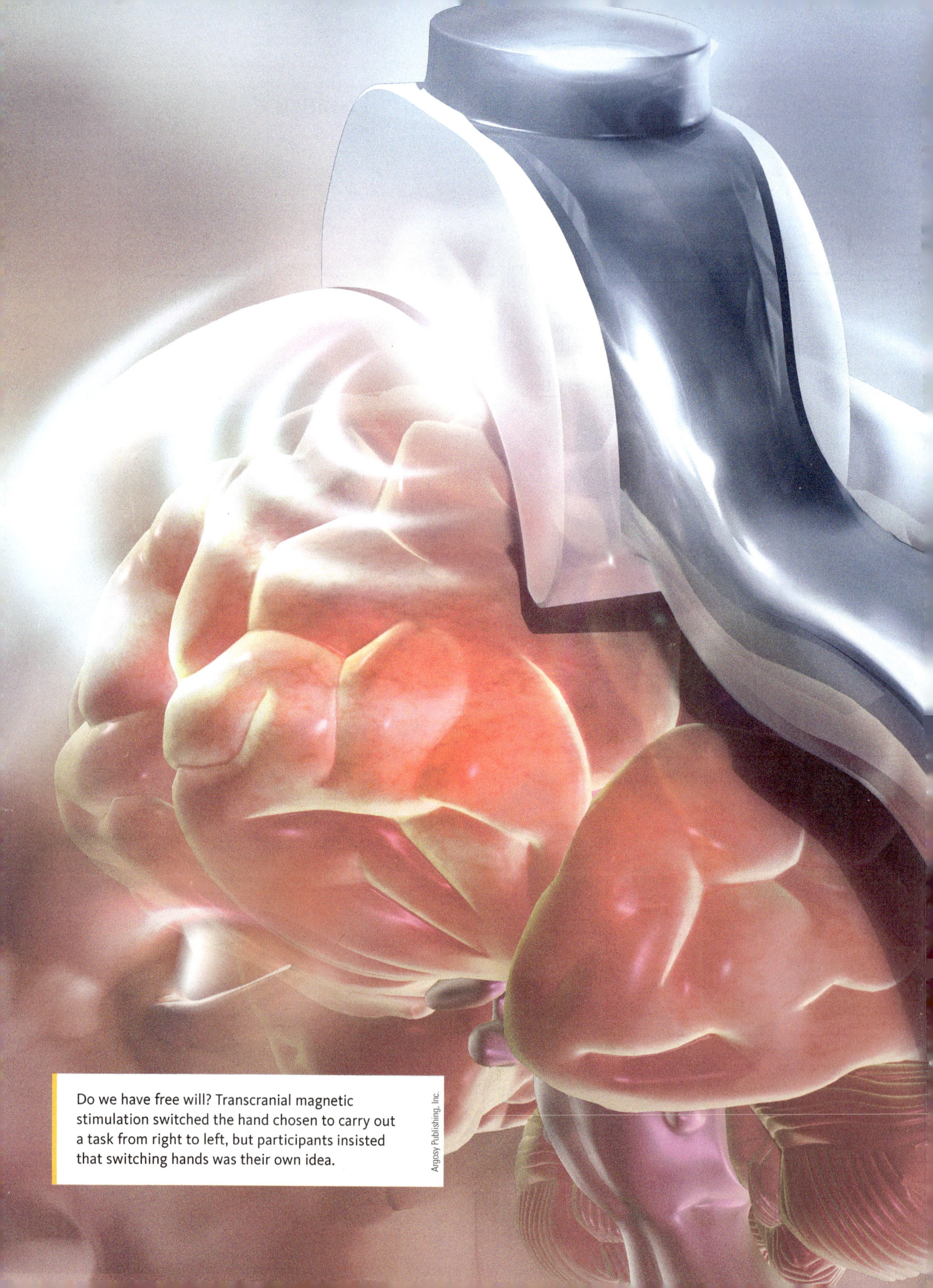

Do we have free will? Transcranial magnetic stimulation switched the hand chosen to carry out a task from right to left, but participants insisted that switching hands was their own idea.

Argosy Publishing, Inc.